1982 SONG WRITER'S MARKET™

WHERE TO SELL YOUR SONGS

Edited by Barbara Norton Kuroff

Writer's Digest Books

Cincinnati, Ohio

Acknowledgments

The gold record on the cover is ''Who Will Answer,'' written by Sheila Davis and recorded by Ed Ames. A special thanks to Frankie MacCormick, manager / archivist of New York City's Song-writers' Hall of Fame Museum where the record is displayed, and most especially to Sheila, owner of the record, for allowing us to photograph it.

—*The Editor*

International Standard Serial Number 0161-5971
International Standard Book Number 0-89879-055-7/6x9

Contents

The Profession

The Markets

Services & Opportunities

Appendix

Glossary

Index

The Profession

Introduction

This book is your direct link to hundreds of offices of music executives across the United States and Canada. We've done all the research and footwork for you by phone, by mail, and through correspondents in the music centers of Los Angeles, New York and Nashville.

This year we focus on the demo—the one area where a songwriter cannot afford to make a mistake. Our upfront article on demo-making will give you tips on how to make your demo the best possible representative of your work—whether for the popular song market, the theater, advertising agencies or audiovisual firms.

In addition, you will get firsthand advice from interviews (Close-ups) with music executives and successful songwriters. Among those to comment on the demo, the business, and their careers are Barry Manilow; Jeff Barry; Randy Cate (Snuff Garrett Music Enterprises); John Cougar; Michael Gore ("Fame"); Carol Hall ("Best Little Whorehouse in Texas"); Rupert Holmes; and Amanda McBroom ("The Rose").

The Appendix in the back of this book gives more information on the business of songwriting: how to submit, contracts, copyright, the structure of the music business, who to submit to first, where your payment comes from, performance rights organizations, and more.

All listings have been updated and this edition includes over 600 new listings.

Each market section has an introduction. Reading these will give you added insight into that specific market area with comments on trends and advice on how to deal with that particular market category.

This book is a valuable tool, compiled to give you the competitive edge when marketing your songs. Read it thoroughly to approach the music business with the right tools, the right attitude and the right information.

Barbara Norton Kuroff

Using Your Songwriter's Market

Following the directions in this book can make your dreams of songwriting success come true by getting your songs through the doors and onto the desks of hundreds of music executives who want to hear them.

This is not just another directory of names and addresses, however. After reading the articles in the front and in the Appendix, go to the "Markets" section for a wealth of detailed information about submitting to specific music publishers; record companies; record producers; play producers; advertising agencies; audiovisual firms; and personal managers. Included in each listing is information on whom to contact, how to submit and what to submit.

As you read the listings, keep these facts in mind:

- The information you are reading came directly from representatives of the companies listed. It is reported exactly as they gave it to us.
- Listings in this book are reviewed, researched and updated annually.
- All correspondence and submissions should be addressed to the contact person named in the listing.
- All mail should contain a stamped, self-addressed envelope (SASE).
- "Does not accept unsolicited material" means you should never submit anything before you query *and* receive permission to submit.
- "Query" means to contact the company by phone or mail *before* submitting anything.
- The types of music, the number of songs you may include in the submission, and the way you should submit your songs are stated in each listing. Your close attention to the exact specifications of a particular listing will help assure your success.
- The Glossary in the back of this book will explain unfamiliar terms you might encounter while reading the listing.
- The year the company was established will be given only for companies established in 1979 and after. The risk is sometimes greater when dealing with new companies. So far as we know, all are reputable but some are unable to compete with larger, older companies. Many do survive, however, and become very successful. And most all new companies are wide open to material from new songwriters.
- Figures given (e.g., number of songs published, released or produced per year or number of new songwriters published per year) are approximations to help you determine a market's activity and its openness to material from new songwriters.
- The length of time companies say they need to report back to songwriters on submissions is also approximate. Publishers especially go through periods of unbelievably heavy loads of submissions. If a market doesn't respond within several weeks after the time frame given in its listing, follow up with a brief, friendly letter giving detailed information about your submission: Include your name, address and phone number; titles of songs submitted; type of demo submitted; and date of submission.
- Listings are based on editorial interviews and questionnaires. They are *not* advertisements, nor are markets reported here necessarily endorsed by the editor.

Looking for a particular market? Check the Index. If you don't find it there, it is because 1) It's not interested in receiving material at this time. 2) It's no longer in business or has merged with another company. 3) It charges (counter to our criteria for inclusion) for services a songwriter should receive free. 4) It has failed to verify or update its listing annually. 5) It has requested that it not be listed. 6) We have received reports from songwriters about unresolved problems they've had with the company.

The "Services and Opportunities" section contains listings of special interest to songwriters: contests and awards, professional organizations and clubs, publications of interest and workshops.

Don't limit your attention and marketing efforts to one section of this book. There are many diverse opportunities to earn rewards for your songwriting skills. It's our hope your wise use of the information presented here will get your songs to the people in music who can make them hits.

How to Make a Demo

BY JAMES RIORDAN

The demo is the key to it all. The difference between a good demo and a poor one is the difference between success and failure. One of the secrets to making a good demo is to remember what it is, i.e., a *demonstration*. It is also important to remember *what* you are demonstrating. People often get confused about this point. We are talking about songs here and a song demo is just that. You are displaying your songs—not your voice, guitar, piano, producing capabilities, arrangements, pet dog, or Little League batting average. What is important here is melody and lyric and very little else. You must make sure that the melody and lyric are properly displayed however, and that's where you get into quality, performance, and production.

Songwriters should also be aware of the market for ad jingles, audiovisual music, and plays. We will cover these accordingly, but first let's deal with the bulk of the market—the popular song.

Songs can be sold to artists, managers, agents, publishers, producers, and record companies and there are subtle differences in each presentation. Realistically, however, one demo will have to suffice for all these areas, so the idea is to make one that covers all the bases.

Choosing the Songs

The music industry is in agreement that only a few songs should be displayed on a demo. As Teal Markley, of the Jerry Heller Agency (L.A.) says, "I think the industry as a whole prefers less songs on a demo than they used to. At one time it was somewhat acceptable to send an entire album-worth of material, but you can tell after the first two songs if you're going to like it or not."

More than a couple of songs won't get listened to anyway, so it's important to hit them with your best shot first. Fred Bourgoise of Bug Music, a Los Angeles publishing firm, elaborates: "I'd rather see a writer go for the swan song plus one. Every writer knows the one song that is his best and I feel he should go for broke with it, but in any case I wouldn't want more than a couple of songs at the maximum." The only point in favor of including additional songs is showing diversity as New York producer Ric Browde of Next City Corporation points out. "It can be good to vary the material. If I have a stack of twenty demos to listen to and I don't like the first song, I'll fast forward it to see if the next song is different. If it's radically different and I like it, I'll keep listening."

The songs you put on a demo should be ones you feel are your absolute best—not ones you've chosen because you heard the person you're submitting to likes songs about trains or mother, or songs with *love* in the title.

A look at the listings in this book will show that today's music markets are open to a variety of styles. And a song that tops the pop chart, for instance, may also do very well on the country, R&B or adult contemporary charts. In general, the *kind*, or style, of material is nowhere as important as the quality.

The Production

Now that you have your three or four best songs picked out, how should you record them? Well, first you put in a call to the London Philharmonic and see when

James Riordan *is a writer who has been in the music business for fifteen years as a songwriter, producer, and manager. He is a contributing editor for many music publications; writes a nationally syndicated music column called* Rock-Pop; *and also finds time to write for screen and television. He co-authored* The Platinum Rainbow (How to Succeed in the Music Business Without Selling Your Soul)—*listed in the Publications of Interest section of this book—with Grammy Award-winning record producer Bob Monaco.*

they are available to record . . . wrong! Keep it simple. In most cases the more production you slap on the demo the more your song will disappear into the mesh. A good song doesn't need a lot of production. "Production does not matter to me," says Rick Bloom of the Rick Bloom Agency in Los Angeles. "A well thought out, great song will shine through any kind of production."

True, but unfortunately there are other elements to consider. Gary Gersh of EMI Records (L.A.) points out one of the most important. "A good production on a demo can make a difference because some people don't have enough imagination to recognize a good song without it. Also, some songs are built around a particular production and therefore should be done that way."

You have still another choice to make. Does your song require a particular production? *Require* is the key word here because you are taking some risks when you get into anything but the most basic production. When you make a song sound country in your production you are reducing the possibility of it being recorded by a pop or R&B artist, for instance. In effect, you are limiting your song and that's the last thing you want to do. Another important point concerning production is expressed by Tom Trumbo of Chrysalis Records in Los Angeles. "Don't try to influence the listener as to who should record the song. We had hundreds of songs submitted for Pat Benatar and most of them sounded like copies of things she had already done. If a writer tries to produce a song to sound like a particular artist it might only hurt the song. Leave production up to the listener."

The goal, as Bearsville Records' (N.Y.) Don Schmitzerle puts it, is to "use the production to make sure the personality of the song comes through." That's all you need.

Make sure that the people who play on your demo are competent. A piano and voice demo is fine, but not if the piano player is playing an entirely different song than what's being sung. In some cases a backbeat may be important. "An up tempo song should have some sort of backbeat," says Fred Bourgoise, "but you can use a rhythm machine and it would still be fine."

Recording

The quality of recording should be very good. You should use the best tape and equipment available to you. This does not have to be expensive, as noted by Ann Sumner-Davis of the Pasha Music Organization (L.A.). "A four track, eight track, sixteen, or more can be used, but if you have good enough mikes and a decent machine you can record it on a home cassette player."

The level of production and quality of recording necessary also depend on how the demo is being presented. If you're submitting the tape unsolicited to be listened to with a hundred others, the quality had better be good or the reject button will be pushed. It isn't easy to listen to a hundred tapes and ears become sensitive to static very quickly. If you're taking the tape in for your third best buddy and longtime publisher to hear, it can be recorded on a cheap cassette player with a broken condenser microphone and still do the job. Your case probably falls somewhere in between these two situations so judge accordingly—make decisions, don't avoid them.

There is little question that the industry as a whole prefers to hear demos on cassettes. Dan Howell of Rubicon Music in Los Angeles sums it up. "While cassettes may be less quality than reel to reel, most people want cassettes because they can listen to them anywhere. A lot of people listen to demos in their cars or at home—having it on a cassette means having a better chance of getting it heard."

It is important to enclose your name, address, and phone number, and a self-addressed stamped envelope if you want the tape returned. A typed lyric sheet for each song is very important. Lead sheets are usually not required, but Chrysalis' Tom Trumbo offers an interesting idea in this area. "It might be good to send just the lyric sheet and not a lead sheet. If a person wants the lead sheet it creates the opportunity for him to call you back on it and further stimulate his interest in the material."

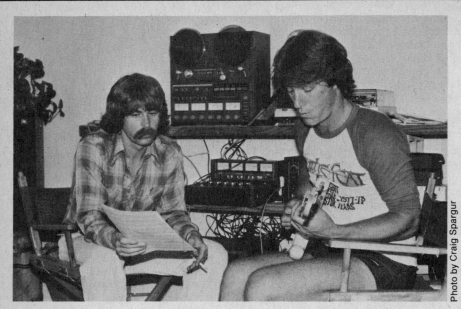

Photo by Craig Spargur

In this photo author James Riordan (left) and songwriter/guitarist Shane Mathe are working at home on a song demo. Songwriters today have the option to invest in professional-quality recording equipment like that pictured here for use when making demos.

Submitting to the Artist and/or His Producer

The most difficult way to market a song is to approach the artists themselves. This is rare for an unknown songwriter but if you are able to get a tape to a well-known recording artist then, of course, play your songs for him. But be forewarned that he will undoubtedly first check it out with his producer. Demo your song, then, keeping in mind the artist's style, but realizing that the producer—who will probably make the final choice of material—needs room in which to add his own style. Producer Ric Browde talks about doing a demo for a record producer. ''Obviously, if you're trying to sell a song to a producer you don't need much production because he can 'hear' and he would prefer it simple. If you're submitting to a record company, however, you probably need more production because they don't want to have to 'imagine' it at this stage.''

Submitting to Record Companies

Record companies are an obvious market for songs—after all, it's in the recording studio that a songwriter's work comes to life. When submitting to a record company, however, you are competing with publishers for the label's listening time. With that availability of material from publishers, many record companies choose not to accept unsolicited submissions from individual songwriters.

Many record companies *do* accept material and listen to it, especially if they have their own publishing branch. Don Schmitzerle of Bearsville Records says, ''If a record company has a publishing company, they are more likely to listen to songs for their artists from unknown writers, but it all depends on the agressiveness of their A&R department. When an artist needs material for an album, the producer usually goes to his publishing and writing friends. I would say the best shot is to send songs to the publishing companies or to the producers.

Submitting to Publishing Companies

Publishing companies receive a deluge of material and the name of the game is to make contact in advance so that when your tape arrives it gets special attention (like being heard). One method is a query letter explaining the type of material you have and asking about the publisher's needs and current submission policies. Buzz Cason of Southern Writers Group is one of many who recommends contacting the publisher first with a query letter or telephone call. "It's best to find out if there is someone there who does listen to outside material. That way, you can direct it to his attention and gear it to what he wants." To increase chances of getting your tape listened to, carefully read the *How to Contact* information contained in the listings in this book—before submitting material.

Dan Howell elaborates on the approach one should take when calling publishers. "There is a fine line between being aggressive and obnoxious, but sometimes you can come across in a one minute phone conversation in a way which a letter can't convey. And, of course, the letter might never get opened. I think you should call publishers *even though* I know that publishers don't want a lot of people calling them. Even if you talk to the secretary and mention that in your letter it can serve as some reinforcement when the tape comes in."

Howell also offers a unique idea for presenting the songs. "If I want someone to know that I have a whole package I may segue the songs up front. I'll put twenty or thirty seconds of each song at the beginning of the tape. I do just enough to give the meat of the song and then have the entire pieces on the tape as well. If a guy can listen to ninety seconds and think he may have just heard three hit singles you've got his full attention."

The Music Centers

The prime music markets are in Los Angeles, New York, and Nashville, but there are many other cities with a thriving music business as well. Most of the policies are the same no matter in what city the firm is located, but there are some people in the business who feel there is a different attitude among the three major centers of activity. Dan Howell philosophizes: "L.A. is a very laid back situation. People want you to come in and throw a hit across the desk but you have to hit them in the face with it. In New York people lean over the desk and demand one. If you don't have a hit they want you out of there and on the elevator. Nashville is a Southern laid back. They are very, very nice and they don't want to discourage you in any way, but as a result it is harder to determine who is really interested in you."

Of course there is no substitute for personal contact and a good way to promote your songs is to spend some time in one of the three music centers. Being in the area means you can meet people who can help your career. Actually, moving to one of these cities may not be possible for you right now or ever and that's why you should work your hardest at making real contact with the people to whom you're submitting demos. Follow up with more material and try to develop a relationship. Ask for their advice and show them you are really interested in succeeding as a songwriter.

Ad Agencies

A good but often overlooked market for songwriters is advertising agencies. But there are differences in making a demo for an ad agency and making one for a music publisher or record company. For one thing ad agencies rarely use the material that is sent to them. The purpose of the demo submitted to an ad agency is to display what type of music the writer is *capable* of so they can assign him something if they choose. The types of assignments a songwriter can expect will vary. The agency might write the lyric and assign the writer the job of composing the music. In some cases music alone is all that is required; in others, the agency will ask for music and/or lyrics from the same writer.

Breaking into the advertising market is not easy. Many agencies don't listen to unsolicited material either because they do not have the time and staff required to screen submissions or because of legal complications that can arise. Gene Toshoff of Grey, Conahay, & Lyon Inc. in New York elaborates. "We don't want any unsolicited speculative songs because there's always the chance that someone will bring in an idea for an account which is turned down and then sue us a year later because they say we used the same four chords."

When submitting to a particular agency in this book, be sure you read the company's listing carefully and submit exactly as they ask. Advertising agencies deal with specific clients and usually know well what sort of material they need to satisfy their clients' needs.

Agencies often work with established writers who have proven they can do the job rather than chance a new writer. They also purchase a lot of material from music production houses. Toshoff continues: "The music houses come around with a reel of material that has been done either speculatively or as a finished piece for other accounts. We listen for their ability to create a song around a concept or to score and arrange. A good thing for a songwriter to do is go to the music production houses that use freelancers and employ staff writers to do their advertising agency work. That way the writer can later get in on the strength of what he has done with the music house and his individual lack of experience may not ever have to be communicated to the agency."

Some agencies do accept material from unknown writers if the demo is impressive. One of the common mistakes made in agency demos is trying to gear the production to the specific clients the agency handles. Just as in song demos the best thing is to display your best and not try to color it to make it more appealing. Bruce Levitt of J. Walter Thompson in Atlanta comments, "The only thing that matters is that the tape is good. If I like what I hear I will go with it no matter where it came from. If a writer has a particular specialty he should show that and if he is versatile he should show that as well."

Agencies seem to be in agreement that a full production is one of the signs of a professional in the field as Robert Fienberg of Bozell & Jacobs in Los Angeles explains. "If you send just a piano track you're implying that you don't have any experience or credentials. Advertising people don't want to deal with somebody who is not a proven quantity. You won't find any philanthropists in this business." Bruce Levitt agrees. "I think it should be full production. You shouldn't send things that are not finished. Reel-to-reel is more standard for ad agencies and ten selections are plenty. It should be a good demo with simplified orchestration."

After an assignment is made by an agency the writer puts together a working demo. He may receive money upfront for the project or may, just to be part of the competition, work on speculation. The demo here can be anything from a guitar or piano to a full-blown production. The agency then approves or disapproves the work done up to that point.

More and more pop songs are becoming part of commercials and Gene Toshoff comments on the reasons: "A commercial is intruding on a listener's time and you try to make it less of an intrusion by making it entertaining. Pop songs do this very well because the listening audience is younger now and more people grew up on pop/rock music. Of course it all depends on the product."

Audiovisual

The audiovisual market is similar to the advertising market in many ways. The music here is almost always instrumental and again the demos are a basis for future assignments rather than actual submissions to be used. Tom Carr of TCA Films (L.A.) describes the demo for an audiovisual firm. "It should be three to five pieces of different styles so that I can get a basic idea of what the writer does. I want a good cross-section. It should be on cassette and the production doesn't have to be elaborate at all. The kind of things we want usually require four or five musicians."

Audiovisual companies tend to work with writers who have done a job for them in

Photo by Art Rex

The advantages of using a professional recording studio when you demo your songs are obvious in this photo taken at Creative Space, a composer's pre-production workshop in Los Angeles. Each of eight songwriting suites is equipped with simple, step-by-step instructions, piano, 4-track recorder, drum computor, reverb, amplifier, mixdown cassette recorder, microphones, head-phones and speakers.

the past, but there is room for a new writer if his demo is in line with their specifications and musical tastes. Once again it is very important to inquire and *make contact* before you send material.

Musicals

In many ways the market for plays is another business entirely, but musicals have produced some of our greatest songs. It is a very difficult business to break into and the actual staging of the musical is more important than a demo. Larry Harbison of Samuel French in New York describes what it takes to have a musical published. "Get it produced in a two million dollar Broadway production. Seriously, however, if an author is interested in writing musicals and he doesn't have a big name in the field he should write an easy-to-stage musical that can be done very inexpensively. He tries to get that staged so he can get a reputation which will hopefully lead him to a bigger production on Broadway or off-Broadway."

Presenting a musical to a play publisher or producer requires both a demo tape and a book of the play. The production on the demo can be simple with piano and voice sufficing, but it is important to list the orchestration. Kaleta Brown of the Cypress College Theater Arts Department in Cypress, California, elaborates. "The writer should be careful to list the orchestration if he is not sending the scoring. Some directors prefer seeing the scores because they want to look at the orchestration. It is to the writer's advantage to have the musical scored because there are not many musical directors who will take the time to score a musical."

Summary

In summation, making a demo requires you, as a songwriter, to make some objective decisions. What is your best material? Whom should you send it to or are you prepared to present it in person? Does your song *require* any more production than one instrument and vocals? If it does, make sure you get competent players to help you, good recording equipment, and a qualified person to operate it. If you do it at home make sure it's under optimum conditions (no barking dogs or screaming babies in the background) and use top quality recording tape. In most cases you want cassette copies and it's better to send a letter of inquiry or call first to insure that your tape will be received. Include a self-addressed stamped envelope if you want the tape returned (no, this doesn't hurt your chances) and send several out at a time. Really listen to your demos before you send them out and after you get them back. How can you make them better? Work at it.

Most importantly, *don't get discouraged* by rejections. People in this business sometimes reject tapes for *no* reason. Songwriting is not an exact science. This is a business of taste and it's important to remember that plenty of people passed on artists as great as Bob Dylan and The Beatles. Learn from your rejections if possible, but don't analyze yourself into anxiety. The important thing is to *keep at it*. Often the difference between those who are successful and those who are not is basic—those who failed simply gave up first; those who succeeded didn't. It's all up to you.

What Is a Hit?

BY MICHAEL J. KOSSER

Are you ready to write hit songs? The answer to that relates largely to self appraisal versus wishful thinking. If you're still falling in love with each song you've just finished writing, then you probably need to write some more until you can listen to a line you've written and *know* that you ought to rewrite it, make it better, if it's to be a hit song.

If you were to isolate the elements of a song, you might come up with terms like lyric, melody, rhythm, rhyme, phrasing and hook.

Lyrics of course, are the words in a song. Just a note if you are a lyric writer in search of a composer. Nowadays most songwriters, even those who collaborate, write both melody and lyrics. Don't run off to Nashville or Los Angeles with a notebook full of lyrics, hoping to find a distinguished composer willing to set your words to immortal melody. Few beginning lyricists write lyrics so compelling that they come to life on a printed page. Instead, learn to compose (and it *can* be done) or seek out a budding composer in your home vicinity and learn the art of collaboration.

Melody is the tune, the succession of tones, rests, holds and slurs to which the song owes much of its musical uniqueness. *Rhythm* is the pattern of recurring accents in a musical piece.

Rhyme is the use of words in which the corresponding syllables of several sound alike, or almost alike. Although these words usually occur at the ends of lines, songs frequently use rhyming words within a line to accent the rhythm. Rhyme is intimately related to rhythm; the more you learn about their relationship, the better will be the songs you write.

Phrasing is the way the lyric line is related to the melody and rhythm. It is most important that the song sing naturally—that the accents of the words match the accents of the music, that the proper syllables are slurred, and that the melody be used to enhance the meaning of the lyric.

The **hook** is the part of the song the listener should focus on; usually that part of the lyric or melody that the listener is most likely to walk away from the radio singing. The hook is often, but not always, the title. Sometimes it is a line, sometimes it's a complete chorus, but almost always it's repeated more often than any other part of the song.

Put these elements together, add a little production (the magic of studio or home arrangement) and you get *feel*, that indefinable sound that gives the song its own special quality. Never mind that the lyric is a little muddy here, or the melody a little trite there, or the rhythm is repetitive ad nauseum everywhere. If it feels good to enough people it's going to be a hit, no matter what its flaws.

That doesn't mean you should take your lyric and melody lightly and just hope that lightning will strike and grant you a song that feels good. The reason great songwriters like Paul Simon, Michael MacDonald, Carol King and Kris Kristofferson have written so many hit songs is that they are constantly aware of what makes a song feel good.

To gain that awareness you must learn the rules, so you know when to keep them and when to break them. There are books and classes that can teach you those rules, but the best way I know is to listen to a lot of music, write a lot of songs, play them for

Mike Kosser *is a songwriter, journalist and lecturer, a staff writer for Tree International in Nashville and currently secretary of the Nashville Songwriters Association. His credits include songs for the Kendalls, Bill Anderson, Barbara Mandrell, George Jones, Tammy Wynette, Charlie Rich and Joe Sun. He also authored the book,* Bringing It to Nashville.

people whose opinions you respect, then listen and write some more. Hopefully you will begin to develop the writer's most important skill: the ability to critique his own work and rewrite accordingly.

Beginning songwriters frequently ask questions like, "Do you start a song with the melody, or the story idea, or what?" Or they'll ask, "How many songs a year do you write?" or "Do you use a guitar or piano when you write?" Writers with these questions seem to believe that if they do it the same way as successful writers do then they must be on the right track. This is incorrect thinking. Every writer has his or her own way. And because every writer has his or her own way I'll say only one more thing about the actual writing of a song. *Learn what feel is, and write feel.* The old pop writers like Irving Berlin, Hoagy Carmichael, George Gershwin and Jerome Kern knew, or know, what feel is. You can almost *taste* the music in songs like "Blue Skies," "Stardust" or "Old Man River." That doesn't mean you should try to write carbon copies of "Stardust." But learn to sense the differences in the sounds of words and how they relate to the feel of the song (for example, choppy syllables seldom belong in gentle love songs). Learn the subtle variations in chord changes and experiment with intervals between notes. Don't just take the first comfortable melody that comes to mind. And for goodness sake learn about rhythm. The slightest change in rhythm or tempo can sometimes change the entire feel of the song. I'm repeating myself, but finally, learn when and how to violate the rules. It's those violations that sometimes give birth to the hits.

The title of this piece is "What Is a Hit?" Don't let anybody fool you with any subjective definitions. A hit is a song that has been accepted by a public which judged it a hit by buying the record or sheet music, requesting it on the radio, singing it in the streets and causing it to make a lot of money for the people who created it. A hit is *commercial*, and I use the word commercial with pride. Commercial is not "shoddy" or "trite" as some outsiders would have you believe. Commercial simply means something that many people like or accept—enough people, in the case of the recording industry, to bring a record company profit on the product it releases.

Even the most successful people in the music business do not have the infallible ability to know a hit when they hear it, but they must be right often enough not to overlook the rare gems that enter their offices once in a blue moon, or to invest too heavily, or too often, in wrong guesses.

A Hit Is What's Happening

As a commercial songwriter, you must be aware of how public taste changes from time to time. Basic emotions, the stuff of which hit songs are often made, do not change, but the way to communicate these emotions to the public does. "Me and My Shadow," and "Help Me Make it Through the Night" are both songs about loneliness, but they are also songs of their times, so their styles are very different.

Those of you who would like to make a living writing songs are well advised to listen to pop, country and black contemporary radio stations as well as to read record industry trade magazines such as *Billboard*, *Record World* or *Cashbox* to get a good idea of what's happening in music today. In 1965, you might have written a song about surfing and made a fortune, but today your chances of having a surfing hit would be slim. Of course, next year they might be surfin' in the grooves once again.

A great song about how much you love your woman (or man) is *always* welcome, but a song about how much you love your goldfish might be limited to fish fanciers. Listen, listen, and don't think that just because country songs emphasize simple down-to-earth ideas, and rhythm and blues often features repetitious hooks, that they're easy to write. It takes understanding of the music and its audience to achieve success in any musical field.

Markets

Music Publishers

Music publishers depend on talented songwriters for fresh, creative material. Songwriters, likewise, count on publishers to get their songs recorded and to take care of the business end of publishing: copyrights, demo-making, lead sheet preparation and royalty payments.

Publishers are looking for quality material with strong lyrics and well-constructed melodies—songs that sound as good with just a voice and guitar as they would with a symphonic background. Individual listings give specifics for submitting—tape size and number of songs per tape, as well as the type of material they have published and are currently seeking.

If there is a trend in what publishers want today it would be songs that appeal to many different tastes. Big on publishers' lists are songs with "crossover" potential—ones that are not readily classified as rock or country or R&B, for instance. Such songs are not only easier for a publisher to place, but, when they are recorded, generate greater income to both publisher and songwriter through increased air-play, more live performances and a higher number of record sales.

"Standards," songs that have become classics, are a publisher's dream. Songs like Eddie Miller's "Release Me" or Irving Berlin's chain of hits that include standards like "Blue Skies," "God Bless America," and "White Christmas" are ageless and will be recorded time and time again by a variety of artists. Their beauty in dollars and cents is that, with the new Copyright Law, a writer and his heirs are entitled to royalties for life plus fifty years.

Many publishers are opening their doors to specialized trends in music such as Spanish, reggae, punk rock and new wave. Gospel music, especially contemporary gospel with special appeal to teenagers and young adults, is also becoming increasingly popular with publishers.

While most publishers will consider many or at least several types of music, some are looking for songs in markets as specialized as polkas, waltzes, "old-time country," novelty songs and more. Even disco, which has been declared dead by some authorities, is still in demand by certain companies.

With so many options, your only problem will be which publishers to contact. To keep up week-by-week on which companies are publishing the hits, check charts in *Billboard*, *Record World* and *Cashbox*.

If you plan a trip to Los Angeles, New York or Nashville, check the geographic list of publishers directly after this section. It will refer you quickly to publishers located in each of those cities.

Some companies we contacted did not give us the information needed for a listing. The names of those companies appear at the very end of this section along with a synopsis of their reasons for not listing and a note on how to contact them.

Additional names and addresses of publishers can be found in the *Billboard International Buyer's Guide*, though it contains no submission information.

ABLE MUSIC, INC., Box 306, Vansant VA 24631. (703)498-4556. Affiliates: Modoc Music (SESAC) and ASAI Records (ASCAP). Vice President: T. Day. Music publisher. BMI. Publishes 200 songs/year; publishes 50 new songwriters/year. Pays standard royalty. Pays staff writers $100/week plus royalties to develop new material.
How to Contact: Submit demo tape and lyric sheet. Prefers 7½ ips reel-to-reel or cassette with 3-6 songs on demo. SASE. Reports in 2 weeks.
Music: Bluegrass; blues; church/religious; C&W; disco; easy listening; folk; gospel; jazz; MOR; progressive; R&B; rock (hard); soul; and top 40/pop. Recently published "Angel in Disguise" and "Your Song," recorded by Roy John Fuller (C&W); and "The Biggest Lie," recorded by Ken Jordan (C&W).

ACCRETIVE COPYRIGHT (ASCAP)/ACCUMULATED COPYRIGHTS (BMI), Doug Moody Productions, 6277 Selma Ave., Hollywood CA 90028. (213)464-9667. President: Doug Moody. Coordinator: Nancy Faith. Music publisher, record company and production company. Publishes 100 songs/year. Pays standard royalty. "We charge only if they wish to produce masters or demos not to be published by us."
How to Contact: Submit demo tape or submit demo tape and lead sheet. Prefers 7½ ips quarter-track, 15 ips half-track, or cassette. SASE. Reports in 1 month. "Submit c/o Mystic Sound Recording Studios."
Music: Blues; church/religious; C&W; easy listening; gospel (modern rock/pop); MOR; jazz (instrumental; R&B); rockabilly; soul; top 40/pop; and spoken word plays (up to 1 hour in length). "We produce and orginate TV and film themes. We need instrumental music: country and pop." Recently published "Hang Gliding," recorded by Gary Joe Wade/Mystic Records (rockabilly); "Van Nuys Boulevard," recorded by Dennis and the Angels/Mystic Records (pop); *LBS On Tour*, recorded by the Long Beach Southernairs/Hooks Records (gospel LP); and "Hey Taxi," by Debbie Stewart/Mystic Records.

ACOUSTIC MUSIC, INC., Box 1546, Nashville TN 37202. (615)242-9198. Affiliates: Lawday Music Corp. (BMI), Daydan Music Corp. (ASCAP), and Allmusic Inc. (ASCAP). Administrator: Nancy Dunne. Music publisher. BMI. Publishes 35-50 songs/year. Pays standard royalties.
How to Contact: Submit demo tape and lyric sheet. Prefers 7½ ips reel-to-reel with 2-3 songs on demo. SASE. Reports in 1 month.
Music: C&W; folk; MOR and gospel. Recently published "Ready to Take My Chances" (by Dewayne Orender and Helen Cornelius), recorded by Oak Ridge Boys/MCA Records; "You've Got a Friend in Me" (by Lamar Morris and D. Orender), recorded by Faron Young/MCA Records; and "Holidays" (by D. Orender), recorded by Patti Page.

ADAMS-ETHRIDGE PUBLISHING, Box 434, 5028 Avenue N., Galveston TX 77550. (713)763-8344. Affiliate: Isle City (ASCAP). Professional Manager: Leon Ethridge. Music publisher, record producer and record company. BMI. Pays standard royalty.
How to Contact: Submit demo tape and lyric sheet. Prefers 7½ ips reel-to-reel or cassette with 1-4 songs on demo. SASE. Reports in 2 weeks.
Music: Blues; C&W; easy listening; folk; MOR; R&B; rock; soul; and top 40/pop.

ADONIKAN MUSIC, Box 8374, Station A, Greenville SC 29604. (803)271-1104. President: Rick Sandidge. Music publisher, record company and record producer. BMI. Publishes 25 songs/year; publishes 3 new songwriters/year. Pays standard royalty.
How to Contact: Call first about your interest, then submit demo tape and lyric sheet or arrange personal interview. Prefers 7½ ips reel-to-reel or cassette with 4 songs on demo. SASE. Reports in 1 month.
Music: Bluegrass, blues, C&W, folk, gospel, jazz, progressive, R&B, rock, soul and top 40/pop.

ADVENTURE MUSIC CO., 1201 16th Ave. S., Nashville TN 37212. (615)320-7287. Affiliate: Touchdown Music (BMI). President/Owner: Chuck Chellman. Music publisher and record producer. ASCAP. Publishes 50 songs/year; publishes 20 new songwriters/year. Pays standard royalties.
How to Contact: Submit demo tape and lyric sheet. Prefers 7½ ips reel-to-reel or cassette with 1-4 songs on demo. SASE. Reports in 3 weeks.
Music: C&W; easy listening; rock; and soul.

ALEXIS, Box 532, Malibu CA 90265. (213)858-7282. Affiliates: Marvelle (BMI), Lou-Lee (BMI) and D.R. Music (ASCAP). President: Lee Magid. Music publisher, record company, and record and video producer. ASCAP. Publishes 100 songs/year; publishes 4 new songwriters/year. Pays standard royalty.
How to Contact: Submit by mail demo tape and lyric sheet. Prefers cassette with 3-6 songs on demo. "Try to make demo as clear as possible—guitar or piano should be sufficient. A full rhythm and vocal demo is always better." SASE. Reports in 3 weeks.
Music: Bluegrass; blues; children's; choral; church/religious; classical; C&W; disco; easy listening; gospel; jazz; MOR; progressive; R&B; rock; soul; and top 40/pop. Recently published "An Old Tin Cup" (by Max Rich), recorded by Lorne Green/RCA Records; "A Dog Named Joe" (by Rags Waldorf), recorded by Waldorf/LMI Records; and "Blues for the Weepers" (by Max Rich and Lee Magid), recorded by Lou Rawls/Capitol Records.

AL-KRIS MUSIC, Box 4185, Youngstown OH 44515. (216)793-7295. Professional Manager: Richard Hahn. Music publisher, record company and record producer. BMI. Publishes 8 songs/year; publishes 4 new songwriters/year. Pays standard royalty.
How to Contact: Submit demo tape and lyric sheet. Prefers cassette with 3-5 songs on demo. SASE. Reports in 3 weeks.
Music: Children's, C&W, folk, gospel, MOR and top 40/pop. Recently published "Here Come the Browns" (by Richard Hahn), recorded by Kardiak Kids/Keynote Records (MOR); "Teach Me Lovely Lady" (by Hahn), recorded by Jim Stack/Peppermint Records (C&W); and "Help Me I'm Falling" (by Hahn), recorded by Kirsti Manna/Genevieve Records.
Tips: "Submission package must be neat and the demo tape must be of decent quality."

ALMO/IRVING/RONDOR, 1358 N. Labrea Ave., Hollywood CA 90028. (213)469-2411. Contact: Professional Manager. Music publisher. BMI and ASCAP.
How to Contact: Submit demo tape. Prefers cassette or 7½ ips reel-to-reel with 1-4 songs on demo. SASE. Reports in 2 months.
Music: Top 40/pop, rock, R&B, soul and C&W.

ALTERNATIVE DIRECTION MUSIC PUBLISHERS, Box 3278, Station D, Ottawa, Ontario, Canada K1P 6H8. (613)820-6066. Affiliates: AD Music Publishers (CAPAC). President: David Stein. Music publisher. Estab. 1980. PROCAN. Pays standard royalty.
How to Contact: Submit demo tape and lyric sheet. Prefers cassette with 1-4 songs on demo. "Material must apply to current trends in music." SASE. Reports in 1 month.
Music: Jazz (fusion), R&B, rock (e.g., Jefferson Starship, Toto, Poco), soul, top 40/pop, country/pop (e.g., Eddie Rabitt, Dolly Parton).

AMALGAMATED TULIP CORP., 117 W. Rockland Rd., Libertyville IL 60048. (312)362-4060. Affiliate: Much More Music (BMI). Director of Publishing and Administration: Mary Chris. Music publisher and record company. BMI. Pays standard royalties.
How to Contact: Submit demo tape. Prefers cassette with 2-5 songs on demo. SASE. Reports in 1-3 months.
Music: Progressive country; easy listening; and MOR.

AMERICAN BROADCASTING MUSIC, INC., 4151 Prospect Ave., Los Angeles CA 90027. (213)663-3311, ext. 1389 or 1557. Affiliate: ABC/Dunhill Music, Inc. (BMI). Director: Georgett Studnicka. Music publisher. ASCAP. Member NMPA. Publishes 30 songs/year; publishes 6 new songwriters/year. Pays standard royalty. Sometimes hires staff writers for TV themes.
How to Contact: Submit demo tape and lyric sheet or arrange interview to play demo tape. Prefers cassette with 2-4 songs on demo. SASE. Reports in 3 weeks.
Music: C&W; easy listening; jazz; MOR; and top 40/pop. "Our copyrights number over 1,000 at this time, but consist mainly of TV themes." Recently published "Circles," "What Would They Say," "Learn To Say Goodbye" and "Leave Yesterday Behind" (all by the Carpenters).

AMIRON MUSIC, 20531 Plummer St., Chatsworth CA 91311. (213)998-0443. Affiliate: Aztec Productions. Manager: A. Sullivan. Music publisher, record company, record producer and manager. ASCAP. Publishes 10 songs/year; publishes 2 new songwriters/year. Pays standard royalty.
How to Contact: Submit demo tape and lyric sheet. Prefers 7½ ips reel-to-reel or cassette with any number songs on demo. SASE. Reports in 3 weeks.
Music: C&W, easy listening, MOR, progressive, R&B, rock and top 40/pop. Recently published "Better Run" (by G. Bonar), recorded by Newstreet/Dorn Records (rock); and "Look In My Eyes" (by P. Newstreet), recorded by 7 artists and released in Australia.

ANDRADE PUBLISHING COMPANY, Drawer 520, Stafford TX 77477. Manager: Daniel Andrade. Music publisher. BMI. Member NSAI. Publishes 24 new songwriters/year. Pays standard royalty.
How to Contact: Write first about your interest. Prefers cassette with 2-5 songs and lead sheet. "Include return postage." SASE. Reports in 2 months.
Music: Church/religious, C&W and top 40/pop. Recently published "Cheaters Never Win" (by Daniel Andrade), recorded by Daniel Andrade/New England Records (top 40/pop, country); "Hank Williams Is Singing Again," recorded by "Hank the Drifter"/Cattle Records (C&W); "A Lonely Stranger," recorded by "Hank the Drifter"/RCA Records (C&W); and "Hank Williams Ghost," recorded by "Hank the Drifter"/New England Records (C&W).

ANDUSTIN MUSIC, Box 238, Woodstock NY 12498. (914)679-6069. Affiliates: Graph (ASCAP) and Small Fortune (BMI). Contact: Professional Manager. Music publisher and record producer. ASCAP. Publishes 20 songs/year; publishes 2 new songwriters/year. Pays standard royalty.
How to Contact: Submit demo tape and lyric sheet. Prefers cassette with 1-3 songs on demo. SASE. Reports in 3 weeks.
Music: Rock; and top 40/pop. Recently published "Rock And Roll Love Song" (by Tim Moore), recorded by the Bay City Rollers (rock); "Second Avenue" (by Tim Moore), recorded by Art Garfunkel (rock); and "Steal Away" (by Robbie Dupuis), recorded by Robbie Dupree/Oozle Music Records (rock).

ANNIE OVER MUSIC, Box 23333, Nashville TN 37202. Affiliates: Tessies Tunes (BMI) and Bobby's Beat Music (SESAC). General Manager: Bobby Fischer. Music publisher. ASCAP. Pays standard royalties.
How to Contact: Submit demo tape and lyric sheet. Prefers 7½ ips reel-to-reel or cassette. Will return material "if time permits." SASE. Reports as soon as possible.
Music: C&W (modern) and MOR. Recently published "What in Her World Did I Do" (by Bobby Fischer and Don Wayne), recorded by Eddy Arnold/RCA Records (modern C&W); "The Great Chicago Fire" (by Bobby Fischer and Dave Kirby), recorded by Faron Young/MCA Records (modern C&W); "Temporarily Yours" (by Bobby Fischer), recorded by Jeanne Pruett/IBC Records (country); "Partners in Rhyme" (by Bobby Fischer), recorded by Moe Brandy and Joe Stampley/Columbia Records (country); and "One of a Kind" (by Bobby Fischer), recorded by Moe Bandy/Columbia Records (country).

ANODE MUSIC, Box 11967, Houston TX 77016. (713)987-2273. President: Freddie Kober. Music publisher, record company and record producer. BMI. Publishes 10 songs/year; publishes 2 new songwriters/year. Pays standard royalty.
How to Contact: Submit demo tape and lyric sheet. Prefers cassette with 1-3 songs on demo. SASE. Reports in 2 weeks.
Music: Gospel and soul. Recently published "That Means So Much to Me" (by Freddie Kober), recorded by Mel Starr/Freko Records (love ballad); "My Baby Can" (by Freddie Kober), recorded by Mel Starr/Freko Records (disco); and "Shake the Funk Out of It" (by Freddie Kober), recorded by Contage'us (disco).
Tips: "Songs should have good lyrics and melody; if fast, a strong bass line."

ANTISIA MUSIC, INC., 1650 Broadway, Suite 1001, New York NY 10019. (212)489-7555. General Manager: Kirk Fancher. Music publisher. ASCAP. Publishes 20 songs/year. Pays standard royalty.
How to Contact: Submit demo tape and lyric sheet. Prefers cassette with 2-4 songs on demo. "Play it straight on and just submit basics on demo—voice, piano, bass, drums." SASE.
Music: Dance-oriented, jazz, MOR, progressive and top 40/pop. Recently published "Mr. Magic" (by MacDonald and Salter), recorded by Roberta Flack and Grover Washington, Jr; and "Just the Two of Us" (by MacDonald, Salter and Withers), recorded by Grover Washington, Jr (adult contemporary).

APACHE'S RHYTHM, Box 14671, Memphis TN 38114. (901)278-7937 or 345-4409. Affiliate: Leswor (BMI). A&R: Errol Thomas. Music publisher. ASCAP. Publishes 25 songs/year; 7 new songwriters/year. Pays standard royalty. Hires staff writers; pays $200/week plus royalty.
How to Contact: Submit demo tape and lyric sheet or arrange personal interview to play demo tape. Prefers 7½ ips reel-to-reel with 4-6 songs on demo. SASE. Reports in 2 weeks.
Music: C&W; easy listening; MOR; R&B; rock; soul; and top 40/pop. Recently published "I Don't Live There Anymore" (by Chuck Bell and Paul Zaleski), recorded by Chuck Bell/Sun Records (C&W); "Everybody Cried," recorded by Rufus Thomas/XL Records (R&B); and "Crazy Days" (by Chuck Bell), recorded by Chuck Bell/Sun Records (C&W).

THE MIKE APPEL ORGANIZATION, 75 E. 55th St., New York NY 10022. (212)759-1610. Affiliates: Laurel Canyon Music, Ltd. (ASCAP) and Summerset Songs (BMI). Director of Operations: Robert L. Martin. Music publisher, record producer and personal manager. BMI. ASCAP. Member NMPA. Publishes 50 songs/year; publishes 2 new songwriters/year. Hires staffwriters; pays negotiable salary as advance against royalties. Pays standard royalty. Call first about your interest, arrange personal interview or submit demo tape and lyric sheet. Prefers cassette with 1-3 songs on demo. SASE. Reports in 2 weeks.
Music: C&W, MOR, progressive, rock (all forms) and top 40/pop. Recently published "For You" (by B. Springsteen), recorded by Manfred Mann/Warner Brothers Records (pop/rock); "City Boy" (By P. Floyd/M. Appel), recorded by Jeff Conaway/Columbia Records (pop/rock); and "Growing Up" (by B. Springsteen), recorded by Any Trouble/Stiff Records (pop/rock).
Tips: "Songs should have strong titles and intelligent, artistic lyrics. Mediocrity will not do! Today's record business demands excellence from all involved."

APPLE-GLASS MUSIC, Box 168, Madison WI 53701. (608)251-2000. Professional Manager: Daniel W. Miller. Music publisher. BMI. Publishes 10-25 songs/year. Pays standard royalty.
How to Contact: Submit demo tape and lyric sheet. Prefers 7½ ips reel-to-reel or cassette with 1-3 songs on demo. "We suggest songwriter's name, address and song titles be typed on labels affixed to tape reel (or cassette) and box for identification." SASE. Reports in 1 month "except during especially busy periods when additional review time of up to 30 days may be necessary."
Music: Bluegrass; children's; C&W; easy listening; ethnic (including polka, native American Indian, ballads); folk; gospel; MOR; R&B; rock; soul; and top 40/pop.

APRIL/BLACKWOOD MUSIC, 1801 Century Park W., 8th Floor, Century CA 90067. (213)556-4700. Professional Managers: Carol Cassano, Martin Kitcat and Donna Young. Music publisher. Pays standard royalties.
How to Contact: Submit demo tape and lead or lyric sheet. Prefers cassette with 1-3 songs on demo. SASE. Reports in 1 month.
Music: Blues; C&W; disco; easy listening; folk; jazz; MOR; progressive; R&B; rock; soul; and top 40/pop.

APRIL/BLACKWOOD MUSIC, 31 Music Sq. W, Nashville TN 37203. (615)329-2374. Manager: Charlie Monk. BMI. ASCAP. Member NMPA. Music Publisher. Does not accept unsolicited material.

ARCADE MUSIC CO., Arzee Recording Co., 3010 N. Front St., Philadelphia PA 19133. (215)426-5682. Affiliates: Valleybrook (ASCAP), Rex Zario Music (BMI), Wilson and Zario (BMI) and Seabreeze Music (BMI). President: Rex Zario. General Manager: Dave Wilson. Music publisher, booking agency and record company. ASCAP. Publishes 100-150 songs/year. Pays standard royalty.
How to Contact: Submit demo tape and lead or lyric sheet. Prefers 7½ or 15 ips reel-to-reel or cassette with 5-10 songs on demo. SASE. Reports in 1 month.
Music: Bluegrass; C&W; easy listening; folk; gospel; rock 'n roll (fifties style) and top 40/pop. Recently published "Why Do I Cry Over You" (by DeKnight and Keefer), recorded by Bill Haley/Arzee Records (C&W); "Hand Clap For Jesus" (by Rodney Harris), recorded by Gospel Blenders/Arzee Records (gospel); and "I Couldn't See the Tears" (by Miller and Marcin), recorded by Dee Dee Marcin/Arzee Records (C&W).

ARGONAUT MUSIC, Box 1800, Nashville TN 37202. Box 7300, Tulsa OK 74105. President: Eric R. Hilding. Publishing company affiliated with Hilding America, Inc. Works with songwriters and songwriter-artists on contract. Pays royalty.
How to Contact: Query or submit demo tape with lyric or lead sheet. Prefers cassette with maximum 3 songs on demo. *Must* include SASE. Reports in 3 weeks to 6 months.
Music: Top 40 pop crossover, easy listening, MOR, gospel/contemporary Christian, soul, and C&W. "We only want songs with positive lyric content and strong titles and choruses."

ARISTA/CAREERS PUBLISHING, 6 W. 57th St., New York NY 10019. (212)489-7400. Affiliates: Careers (BMI), Chinnichap (BMI) and BRM/Riva (ASCAP). East Coast Professional Manager: Steve Sussmann. Music publisher. ASCAP. Member NMPA. Pays standard royalty. Sometimes secures songwriters on salary basis.
How to Contact: Submit demo tape and lyric sheet. Prefers 7½ ips reel-to-reel or cassette with maximum 2 songs on demo. SASE. Reports as soon as possible.

Music: C&W (crossover potential); easy listening; folk (crossover potential); MOR; progressive; R&B; rock; soul and top 40/pop. Recently published "All Out of Love," (by G. Russell), recorded by Air Supply/Arista Records (pop/AC); "Someone that I Used to Love," (by G. Goffin and M. Masser), recorded by Natalie Cole/Capitol Records (AC); and "Papillon," (G. Diamond), recorded by Chaka Khan/Warner Brothers Records (R&B).
Tips: "Write great songs that could be done in more than one genre. Our standards are very tough for unknown writers to meet."

ARISTA-INTERWORLD, 8304 Beverly Blvd., Los Angeles CA 90048. (213)852-0771. Affiliates: World Song Publishing Inc (ASCAP) and Six Continents Music Publishing Inc (BMI). Contact: Tom Sturgis. Music publisher. BMI and ASCAP. Member NMPA. Hires staff writers. Pays per individual contracts.
How to Contact: Submit demo tape and *neat* lyric and lead sheets. Prefers cassette with 3 songs on demo. SASE. Reports in 1 month, "depending on backlog of submissions."
Tips: "All material is listened to, so if it's a hit!. . . ."

ART TREFF PUBLISHING, 846 7th Ave., New York NY 10019. President: Arthur Trefferson. Music publisher, record company and record producer. BMI. Publishes 30-100 songs/year; publishes 8 new songwriters/year.
How to Contact: Submit demo tape and lyric sheet. Prefers cassette with your best songs on demo. SASE. Reports in 2 months.
Music: Children's and reggae.

ASILOMAR/DREENA MUSIC, 43 W. 61st St., New York NY 10023. (212)757-8805. Creative Manager: Ron Beigel. Music publisher. Estab. 1979. ASCAP. Member NMPA. Publishes 100 songs/year; publishes 15 new songwriters/year. Pays standard royalty.
How to Contact: Submit demo tape and "always include lead or lyric sheet." Prefers cassette with 1-3 songs on demo. SASE. Reports in 1 month.
Music: C&W; easy listening; R&B; rock; and top 40/pop. Recently published "Goodbye Sweet Virginia" (by B. Minasian and B. Rich) and "Reins of Love" (by D. McCarthy and D. Miller), recorded by Rodney Leigh and The New West (country rock).
Tips: "Make sure the demo is clear and clean; include a rhythm track along with vocals."

AT THE GATE PUBLISHING CO., Box 1155, Postal Station Q, Toronto, Ontario, Canada M4T 2P4. Contact: Larry J.S. Yates. Music publisher and record company. Estab. 1980. PROCAN. Publishes 4 songs/year; publishes 1 new songwriter/year. Pays standard royalty.
How to Contact: Prefers cassette with 1-5 songs on demo. Does not accept unsolicited material. SAE and International Reply Coupons. Reports "as convenient."
Music: Top 40/pop. Recently published "At the Gate," "Lady Orange in the Evening" and "Those Who Dare" (by L.J.S. Yates), recorded by Yates/Start Records (acoustic pop).

ATLAS PUBLISHING GROUP, Box 50, Goodlettsville TN 37072. Affiliates: Black Eagle Publishing (ASCAP), Brian Scott's Music Factory (ASCAP), Allegheny Mountain Music (SESAC) and Lufaye Publishing (BMI). Professional Manager: Dick Shuey. Music publisher. BMI. Publishes 12-25 songs/year; publishes 5-10 new songwriters/year.
How to Contact: Submit demo tape and lead sheet. Prefers reel-to-reel or cassette with 1-3 songs on demo. SASE. Reports in 1 month.
Music: C&W. Recently published "This Ole Boy Ain't Gonna' Walk Your Line No More," recorded by Ernie Ashworth (C&W); "Karen Faye," "Hey, Little Woman" and "Please Save A Place for Me in Your Heart," recorded by Little Roy Wiggins (C&W); and "Country Music Crazy," recorded by Paula Wayne (C&W).

ATTIC PUBLISHING GROUP, 98 Queen St. E., Suite 3, Toronto, Ontario, Canada M5C 1S6. (416)862-0352. Affiliates: Pondwater Music (CAPAC), Abovewater Music (PROCAN), Big Bay Music (PROCAN), Downchild Music (CAPAC) and Triumphsongs (CAPAC). President: Al Mair. Music publisher and record company. Publishes 50 songs/year; publishes 15 new songwriters/year. "We publish recording artists only—no exclusive songwriters." Pays standard royalty.
How to Contact: Call first about your interest, then submit demo tape and lyric sheet. Prefers cassette with 1-4 songs on demo. SAE and International Reply Coupons. Reports in 3 weeks.
Music: Blues, MOR, rock and top 40/pop. Recently published "The Homecoming" (by Hagood Hardy), recorded by H. Hardy/Attic Records (pop instrumental); and "Shot Gun Blues" and "Almost" (by Donny Walsh), recorded by The Blues Brothers/WEA Records (blues).

ATV MUSIC CORP., 6255 Sunset Blvd., Hollywood CA 90028. (213)462-6933. Affiliates: Maklen Music (BMI), Welbeck Music (ASCAP), and Comet Music (ASCAP). Music publisher. BMI. Member NMTA, CCC, and Harry Fox Agency. Publishes hundreds of songs/year; publishes 4 new songwriters/year. Hires staff writers. Pays standard royalty.
How to Contact: Write or call first about your interest. Prefers cassette with 4 songs on demo. Refuses unsolicited material. SASE. Reports in 1 month.
Music: Bluegrass, blues, children's, church/religious, C&W, dance-oriented, easy listening, folk, gospel, jazz, MOR, progressive, R&B, rock, soul and top 40/pop. Recently published "Hit Me With Your Best Shot" (by Eddie Schwartz), recorded by Pat Benatar (rock); "He's So Shy" (by Cynthia Weil and Tom Snow), recorded by Pointer Sisters (R&B); and "Just Once" (by Barry Mann and Cynthia Weil), recorded by Quincy Jones (R&B).
Tips: "Know what's charting. ATV is looking for songs that can be placed with people that are currently charting. Have had success with ballads. Lyrics must be good."

ATV MUSIC CORP., 888 7th Ave., New York NY 10019. (212)977-5680. General Professional Manager: Marv Goodman. Music publisher.
How to Contact: Submit demo tape and lyric sheet. Prefers cassette with 2-3 songs on demo. SASE. Reports in 3 weeks.
Music: Rock and top 40/pop. Recently published "Hit Me With Your Best Shot" (by Eddie Schwartz), recorded by Pat Benatar/Chrysalis Records (rock).

ATV MUSIC CORP., 1217 16th Ave. S., Nashville TN 37212. (615)327-2753. Affiliates: Welbeck Music (ASCAP) and MacLen Music (BMI). Vice President and General Manager: Gerry Teifer. Professional Manager: Byron Hill. Contact J. Wilde for appointment. Music publisher. BMI. Member CMA, NARAS and NMPA. Pays standard royalties.
How to Contact: Arrange personal interview to play tapes. Prefers 7½ ips reel-to-reel with 1-3 songs on demo. SASE. Reports as soon as possible.
Music: Bluegrass; C&W; disco; easy listening; gospel; MOR; R&B; rock; soul; and top 40/pop. Recently published "Bombed Boozed & Busted" (by Knutson/Sun), recorded by Joe Sun/ Ovation Records (country); "Pickin' Up Strangers" (by Hill), recorded by Johnny Lee/Asylum Records (country); "He's So Shy" (by Weil/Snow), recorded by the Pointer Sisters/Planet Records (top 40/pop); "Hit Me With Your Best Shot" (by Schwartz), recorded by Pat Benatar/ Chrysalis Records (rock); "I'm Just an Old Chunk of Coal" (by Billy Joe Shaver), recorded by John Anderson/Warner Brothers Records (country); "A Little in Love" (by Alan Tarney), recorded by Cliff Richard/EMI Records (pop/rock); and "Living in a Fantasy" (by A. Tarney), recorded by Leo Sayer/Warner Brothers Records (pop/rock).
Tips: "Be extremely selective. Submit material with hit single potential."

ATV MUSIC PUBLISHING OF CANADA LIMITED, 180 Bloor St. West, Suite 1400, Toronto, Ontario, Canada M5S 2V6. (416)967-3375. Affiliates: MacLen Music of Canada (PROCAN), Welbeck Music of Canada (CAPAC) and Comet Music of Canada (CAPAC). Professional Manager: Val Azzoli. Music publisher and record producer. PROCAN. Member CMPA and CIRPA. Publishes 50 songs/year. Pays standard royalty.
How to Contact: Submit demo tape and lyric sheet. Prefers cassette with 3 songs on demo. SAE and International Reply Coupons. Reports in 1 month.
Music: Progressive, R&B, rock, soul and top 40/pop. Recently published "Hit Me with Your Best Shot" (by E. Schwartz), recorded by Pat Benatar/Chrysalis Records (rock); "He's So Shy" (by T. Snow and C. Weil), recorded by the Pointer Sisters/Planet Records (top 40/pop); and "We Don't Talk Anymore" (by A. Tarney), recorded by Cliff Richard/Capitol-EMI Records (top 40/pop).

AUDIBLE MUSIC PUBLISHING CO., 1802 Ocean Pkwy., Suite 2A, Brooklyn NY 11223. President: Cosmo Ohms. Music publisher, record producer and record company. Estab. 1979. ASCAP. Publishes 3 songs/year. Pays standard royalty.
How to Contact: Write first about your interest. Prefers cassette with 1-3 songs on demo. SASE. Reports in 1 month.
Music: Rock (new wave, future-oriented); and top 40/pop.

AUDIO ARTS PUBLISHING, 5617 Melrose Ave., Hollywood CA 90038. (213)461-3507. Affiliate: Madelon (BMI). Contact: Madelon Baker. Music publisher and record company. ASCAP. Member AIMP and NMPA. Pays standard royalty.
How to Contact: Submit demo tape and lyric sheet. Prefers cassette with 1-4 songs on demo. SASE. Reports in 1 week.
Music: Country, gospel, soul and top 40/pop.

AUTOGRAPH MUSIC, 601 E. Blacklidge Dr., Tucson AZ 85705. (602)882-9016. Professional Manager: Erin Brooks. Music publisher. BMI. Publishes 20 songs/year; publishes 4 new songwriters/year. Pays standard royalty.
How to Contact: Submit demo tape and lyric sheet. Prefers cassette with 1-3 songs on demo. Returns unsolicited material only with SASE. Reports in 3 weeks.
Music: C&W; and top 40/pop. Recently published "Time" (by E. Forrest), recorded by Two Horse/BIRC Records (Latin rock); "Road To Ruin" and "I Can Still Remember" (by D. Stitt), recorded by Rick Skinner/Bug Records (C&W); "I Live On Heartaches" (by D. Stitt), recorded by Kenny Durell/Custom Records (C&W); "Road to Ruin" and "I Can Still Remember" (by D. Stitt), recorded by Eddie Golden/BIRC Records (C&W); and "Josie's Her Name" (by D. Stitt), recorded by D. Stitt/BIRC Records (C&W).
Tips: "Suggest artists you think might record each song."

B.A.S. MUSIC PUBLISHING, 5925 Kirby Dr., Suite 226, Houston TX 77005. (713)522-2713. Affiliate: Tuff Enuff (BMI). Owner: Shelton Bissell. Music publisher, recording studio, booking agency, arranger and record producer. ASCAP. Pays standard royalty.
How to Contact: Submit demo tape and lead or lyric sheet. Prefers 7½ ips reel-to-reel or cassette with 1-4 songs on demo. "We prefer a rhythm section and vocal, but will listen to piano-vocal or guitar-vocal. Do not send material by any method requiring signature as it just slows our response." SASE. Reports in 3 weeks.
Music: C&W. Interested only in professionals (ASCAP or BMI members). "We are especially looking for hard country honkytonk, beer drinking songs and are currently reviewing material for Isaac Payton Sweat (Paid Records), Mike Compton (RDS Records), and Kathy Gilley."
Tips: "I am not in the business of 'plugging' songs. We only publish songs when we are able to use them in a production."

B.C. ENTERPRISES OF MEMPHIS, INC., 726 E. McLemore Ave., Memphis TN 38106. (901)947-2553. Affiliates: Colca Music (BMI), Insight Music (BMI), and Epitome Music (BMI). Administrative Assistant: Nat Engleberg. Music publisher, record company and record producer. BMI. Publishes 15 songs/year; publishes 1 new songwriter/year. Pays standard royalty.
How to Contact: Write first about your interest. Prefers cassette with 1-3 songs on demo. SASE. Reports in 1 week.
Music: Blues, black gospel, R&B and soul. Recently published "Selfrising Flour" (by Byron and Brandon Catron), recorded by Ironing Board Sam (blues).

BABY HUEY MUSIC, 234 East Morton Ave., Nashville TN 37211. (615)834-3481. Affiliate: Krimson Hues Music (BMI). Professional Manager: Mark Stephan Hughes. Music publisher. Estab. 1980. ASCAP. Member NSA and IMU. Publishes 40 songs/year; publishes 20 new songwriters/year. Pays standard royalty.
How to Contact: Submit demo tape and lyric sheet. Prefers 7½ ips reel-to-reel or cassette with 3 songs on demo. SASE. Reports in 3 weeks.
Music: Church/religious, C&W, gospel, MOR, R&B, rock (country, hard) and top 40/pop. Recently published "Everything's Not Enough" (by Rolle, Michelli, Sharp and Hughes), recorded by Frankie Sanchez/Charta Records (MOR); and "Lady Like You" (by Ray and Hughes), recorded by Bill Schleuter/LaJon Records (ballad).
Tips: "We are looking for catchy hit singles with good strong hooks and tight lyrics."

BACKYARD MUSIC, 1625 Woods Dr., Los Angeles CA 90063. (213)656-8490. Affiliate: Frontlawn Music (BMI). President: Ken Mansfield. Music publisher and record producer. BMI and ASCAP. Publishes varied amount of songs/year. Pays standard royalty.
How to Contact: Submit demo tape and lyric sheet. Prefers cassette. SASE. Reporting time varies.
Music: C&W, easy listening, folk, MOR, progressive, rock and top 40/pop.

BAINBRIDGE MUSIC CO., 73 Marion St., Seattle WA 98104. (206)625-9992. Affiliates: Burdette Music (BMI) and Marinwood Music (ASCAP). Director of Publishing: Bill Angle. Music publisher; associated with First American Records, Inc. BMI. Publishes 20-30 songs/year; publishes 4-6 new songwriters/year.
How to Contact: Submit demo tape and lyric sheet. Prefers cassette with 2-6 songs on demo. SASE. Reports in 2 months.
Music: Dance, rock and top 40/pop.

BAL & BAL MUSIC PUBLISHING CO., Box 369, LaCanada CA 91011. (213)790-1242. President: Adrian Bal. Music publisher, record company and record producer. ASCAP. Member AGAC. Publishes 1-4 songs/year; publishes 1 new songwriter/year. Pays standard royalty.

How to Contact: Submit demo tape and lyric sheet. Prefers cassette with 3 songs on demo. SASE. Reports in 1 month.
Music: Blues, church/religious, C&W, easy listening, jazz, MOR, R&B, rock, soul and top 40/pop. Recently published "Los Angeles" (by Rich Martin), recorded by Bob Ryer/Bal Records (ballad); "Song of the Pasadena Rose Parade" (by Jack Heinderich), recorded by Bob Ryer/Bal Records (swing).

BAND OF ANGELS, INC., 1420 K St. NW, Suite 400, Washington DC 20005. (202)347-1420. Affiliate: Heaven's Gate Music (ASCAP). Director of Publishing: Yolanda McFarlane. Music publisher and record company. Estab. 1979. BMI. Member NMPA and BMA. Publishes 10-16 songs/year; publishes 3 new songwriters/year. Pays standard royalty.
How to Contact: Submit demo tape and lyric sheet. Prefers cassette with 3-6 songs on demo. "Include name, address and telephone number *on tape.*" Reports in 2 weeks.
Music: Dance-oriented, R&B, soul and top 40/pop. Recently published "Remote Control" and "I Want It" (by N. Mann, B. Beard and C. Fortune), recorded by The Reddings/B.I.D. Records (R&B).

BARADAT MUSIC, 1310 E. Kern, Tulare CA 93274. (209)686-2533. Affiliate: Famosonda Music (BMI). President: Raymond Baradat. Music publisher and record company. BMI. Publishes 4 songs/year; publishes 1 new songwriter/year. Pays standard royalty.
How to Contact: Submit demo tape and lyric sheet. Prefers 7½ ips reel-to-reel or cassette with 1-4 songs on demo. SASE. Reports in 1 month.
Music: Recently published "The Power of Love" (by Mike Placincia), recorded by Justus/Charade Records (rock/country); "Living For The Land" (by Charles Yokum), recorded by Justus/Charade Records (rock); and "Nothing At All" (by Chuck Wing), recorded by Wing Brothers/Tadarab Records (country).

BARLENMIR HOUSE MUSIC, INC., 413 City Island Ave., New York NY 10064. President: Barry L. Mirenburg. Creative Director: Leonard Steffan. Music publisher, record company and book publisher. Publishes 10 songs/year. BMI. Pays negotiable royalties.
How to Contact: SASE. Reports in 1 month.
Music: Creative.

BARUTH MUSIC, 8033 Sunset Blvd., Suite 101, Hollywood CA 90046. (213)843-8988. Branch office: 12501 Madison Ave., Cleveland OH 44107. (216)521-1222. Professional Manager: Jain Baruth. Music publisher, record company, record producer, management firm and promoter. ASCAP. Pays standard royalty.
How to Contact: Submit demo tape and lead sheet. Prefers cassette with 2-3 songs on demo. SASE. Reports in 4 weeks.
Music: Folk; progressive; R&B; rock; and top 40/pop. Recently published "Soothe Me" (by David Baruth), recorded by Quartz/Music Adventures Records (rock); "Jack the Ripper" (by Joe Uherc), recorded by Strychnine/Music Adventures Records (rock); and "This Time to the End" (by Eddie Pecchio), recorded by Great Lakes Band/Music Adventures Records (pop).

THE BEAU-JIM AGENCY, INC., 10201 Harwin, Suite 2206, Houston TX 77036. (713)771-6256. President: James E. "Buddy" Hooper. Music publisher, record company, booking agency and management firm. ASCAP. Publishes 10 songs/year. Pays standard royalty.
How to Contact: Arrange personal interview or submit demo tape and lead sheet. Prefers cassette with 1-5 songs on demo. SASE. Reports in 3 weeks.
Music: Blues; C&W; easy listening; MOR; rock (no hard rock); and top 40/pop. Recently published "Life," recorded by Barry Kayle; "She's My Lover," recorded by Jimmy Hooper (C&W); "Merry Christmas from Lisa Marie" (by Chris Kingsley), recorded by Jana Sampson (Christmas song); and "Christmas on Our Mind" (by C. Kingsley), recorded by J. Sampson and Randall Parr (Christmas song).

BEE SHARP PUBLISHING, Box 400, Station R, Toronto, Ontario, Canada M4G 4C3. (416)421-3601. Affiliate: See Flat Publishing (CAPAC). Vice President: Jeff Smith. Music publisher and record producer. Estab. 1980. PROCAN. Pays standard royalty.
How to Contact: Submit demo tape and lyric sheet. Prefers cassette with 2-6 songs on demo. SAE and International Reply Coupons. Reports in 3 weeks.
Music: Children's, country, easy listening, jazz, MOR, rock and top 40/pop. Recently published "Sea Swept" (by Jeff Smith), recorded by Jaylus (MOR/disco).

BEECHWOOD, 6255 Sunset Blvd., Hollywood CA 90028. (213)469-8371. Affiliates: Screen Gems (BMI) and Cole Gems (ASCAP). Music publisher. BMI and ASCAP. Member NMPA. Publishes several songs/year. Hires staff writers.
How to Contact: Call first about your interest. Prefers cassette and lyric/lead sheet. Refuses unsolicited material. SASE. Reports in 1 month.
Music: MOR, rock and top 40/pop.

BEECHWOOD MUSIC, 1207 16th Ave. S., Nashville TN 37212. (615)320-7700. Music publisher. BMI. Pays standard royalty.
How to Contact: Write first about your interest. Prefers 7½ ips reel-to-reel or cassette with 3 songs on demo. SASE. Reports in 1 month.
Music: C&W, easy listening, MOR, rock and top 40/pop.

BEECHWOOD MUSIC CORP., 1370 Avenue of the Americas, New York NY 10019. (212)489-6740. Contact: Professional Manager. Music publisher and record company (Capitol and EMI Records). BMI. Hires staff writers.
How to Contact: Call first about your interest to see if they are accepting material, then submit demo tape and lyric sheet. Prefers reel-to-reel or cassette with 4 songs on demo. "Write *unsolicited material* on package if you have not called first." Reports in 2 months.
Music: MOR, R&B, rock and top 40/pop.

BELWIN-MILLS PUBLISHING CORP., 1776 Broadway, New York NY 10019. (212)245-1100. Affiliates: Multimood (BMI) and Mills Music (ASCAP). Professional Manager: Robin Feather. Member NMPA. Publishes 150 songs/year; publishes 15 new songwriters/year. Pays standard royalty.
How to Contact: Submit demo tape and lyric sheet. Prefers 7½ ips reel-to-reel or cassette with 1-3 songs on demo. SASE.
Music: C&W; easy listening; MOR; progressive; R&B; rock; and top 40/pop. Recently published "Shakin All Over" (by Heath), recorded by Robin Lane and The Chartbusters/MCA Records; and "Sleigh Ride" (by Parish and Mills), recorded by Meco Monardo on the *Star Wars Christmas Album*/RSO Records.

QUINT BENEDETTI MUSIC, Box 2388, Toluca Lake CA 91602. (213)985-8284. Affiliates: AnnBen Music (BMI) and Mi-Da-Mark Music (ASCAP). Contact: Quint Benedetti. Music publisher, record producer and artist manager. Estab. 1979. Pays standard royalty.
How to Contact: Submit demo tape and lyric sheet. Prefers cassette with 2-6 songs on demo. SASE. Reports in 1 month "or sooner."
Music: Children's; musical comedy; and C&W. Recently published *Topsy or Sorry About That Harriett* (musical comedy score).

BENT OAK MUSIC, Rt. 2, 246 Oakborough Dr., O'Fallon MO 63366. (314)625-3485. General Manager: Thomas J. McBride. Music publisher, record company and record producer. Estab. 1980. BMI. Publishes 25-50 songs/year; publishes 10 new songwriters/year. Pays standard royalty.
How to Contact: Submit demo tape and lyric sheet. Prefers cassette or phonograph record with 1-5 songs on demo. "Only BMI writers should submit." SASE. Reports in 1 month.
Music: Bluegrass, C&W and folk. Recently published "One Love Wiser" and "Wounded Lady" (by Darrel Crossen and Red Parson); and "Car Plant Blues" (by Glen Wagster), all recorded by Glen Wagster/Bent Oak Records (C&W).

HAL BERNARD ENTERPRISES, INC., Box 6507, 2181 Victory Pkwy., Cincinnati OH 45206. (513)861-1500. Affiliates: Sunnyslope Music (ASCAP), Bumpershoot Music (BMI), Apple Butter Music (ASCAP), Rong Music (ASCAP), Teakbird Music (ASCAP), Emily's Music (ASCAP), Shangrila (ASCAP) and Smorgaschord Music (ASCAP). President: Stan Hertzman. Music publisher, record company and management firm. Pays negotiable royalty.
How to Contact: Submit demo tape and lyric sheet. Prefers 7½ ips reel-to-reel stereo or cassette with 3-6 songs on demo. Prefers leadered tapes with an index. SASE. Reports in 1 month.
Music: Rock; R&B; and top 40/pop. Recently published "Your Song Is Mine" (by Fetters, Nyswonger and Toth), recorded by Mighty High/MCA Records (rock); "Eastern Avenue River Railway Blues" (by Mike Reid), recorded by Jerry Jeff Walker/Elektra Records (pop/country); "Like A Falling Star" (by C. Fletcher), recorded by Blaze/Epic Records (rock); "Slave" (by Arduser, Close, Arduser), recorded by Darts/Reckless Records (rock), and "Icy Blue" (by C. Fletcher), recorded by Charlie Fletcher/Buddah/Arista Records.
Tips: "Cast your demos. If you as the songwriter can't sing it—don't. Get someone who can present your song properly, use a straight rhythm track and keep it as naked as possible. If you think it still

needs somthing else, have a string arranger, etc. help you, but still keep the *voice up* and the *lyrics clear*."

JOHN BERNARD MUSIC, 303 W. 42nd St., New York NY 10036. (212)284-1575. Vice President of Publishing: A. Baly. Music publisher. BMI. Publishes 12 songs/year. Pays standard royalty.
How to Contact: Submit by mail demo tape and lyric sheet. Prefers cassette with 2-4 songs on demo. SASE. Reports in 1 month.
Music: Disco; easy listening; and gospel. Recently published "Get Down Anne," and "Explanation," (by T. Brown), recorded by John T. Brown (disco).

BETH-ANN MUSIC CO., 615 Baldwin Lane, Carrcroft, Wilmington DE 19803. (302)762-2410. President: Albert G. Teoli. Music publisher. ASCAP. Publishes 3 songs/year; published 2 new songwriters in 1979. Pays standard royalties.
How to Contact: Submit demo tape and lyric sheet. Prefers 7½ ips reel-to-reel or cassette with 3 songs on demo. SASE. Reports in 3 weeks.
Music: C&W; easy listening; folk; gospel; rock (country); and top 40/pop. Recently published "Time" and "It's So Nice to Dream," recorded by Mary Mulligan (gospel/easy listening); and "Paesano Mio," recorded by Clem West (novelty).
Tips: "Listen to the market—don't send songs that don't sound as acceptable as those you hear on your radio."

BETTY LOU MUSIC, 1967 Goldsmith Lane, Apt. B-6, Louisville KY 40218. (502)454-3593. Affiliates: Treva Music (BMI) and Valmon Music (ASCAP). Contact: Wayne Henderson. Music publisher, record producer and record company. Estab. 1979. BMI. Publishes 2-4 songs/year; publishes 2-4 new songwriters/year. Pays standard royalty.
How to Contact: Submit demo tape and lyric sheet. Prefers cassette with 4 songs on demo. SASE. Reports in 30-45 days.
Music: Blues (country); C&W; and MOR. Recently published "(You're) Everything I've Ever Wanted" (by Roberta Kimrough), recorded by Dave O'Connor/Cambridge Records (country); "Big Jody" (by C.H. Springer), recorded by Dave O'Connor/Cambridge Records (country/MOR); and "Sweet Music in My Mind" (by Roberta Kimbrough), recorded by Wayne Green/Telestar Records (country/MOR).
Tips: "If the songwriter has songs that he/she thinks suit certain artists, we would try to have the artist, his manager or producer listen to the songs. We are looking for *commercial* material."

BEVERLY HILLS MUSIC PUBLISHING, Box 1659, Beverly Hills CA 90213. (213)957-1756. President/Administrator: Lawrence Herbst. Music publisher and record company. BMI. Pays standard royalty.
How to Contact: Submit demo tape and lyric sheet. Prefers 7½ or 15 ips reel-to-reel or cassette with 6 songs on demo. SASE. Reports in 1 month.
Music: Bluegrass; blues; church/religious; C&W; disco; easy listening; folk; jazz; MOR; progressive; R&B; rock; soul; and top 40/pop.

JOHNNY BIENSTOCK MUSIC, 1619 Broadway, New York NY 10019. Professional Manager: Robert Bienstock. Currently overstocked with material. Member NMPA.

BIG HEART MUSIC, 9454 Wilshire Blvd., Suite 309, Beverly Hills CA 90212. (213)273-7020. Affiliate: Wooden Bear Music (ASCAP). Managing Director: Randy Bash. Music publisher. BMI. Member NMPA.
How to Contact: Submit demo tape and lead or lyric sheet. Prefers 7½ ips reel-to-reel or cassette with 3-5 songs on demo. SASE. Reports in 2 weeks.
Music: C&W; MOR; soul; and top 40/pop.

BIG MIKE MUSIC, Big Mike Productions, 408 W. 115th St., Suite 2-W, New York NY 10025. (212)222-8715. Manager: Bill Downs. Music publisher. BMI. Publishes 10 songs/year. Pays standard royalty.
How to Contact: Submit demo tape and lead sheet. Prefers cassette with 2-3 songs on demo. "Must have clean lead sheet and good demo with instrumental background. We will not accept tapes with vocal only." Does not return unsolicited material. Reports in 4 weeks.
Music: R&B, rock, soul. Recently published "Love Should Be A Crime" (by Tommie Munddy); "Don't Let Him Move In" (by Joellyn Cooperman); and "Stand-by Lover" (by Brad Smiley), all recorded by Dolly Gilmore/Whitehorse Records.
Tips: "Keep trying even after refusals. Most of the time a producer is looking for a song for now without a thought of the future."

BIG SHOE MUSIC PUBLISHING CO., 1011 Fountain Rd., Jacksonville FL 32205. (904)781-4311. President: Bruce Beard. Vice President: Jeff Jenkins. Secretary: Beverly Williams. Music publisher and record company. BMI. Pays standard royalty. "We work with artists on a standard 50-50 contract. Give us 6-12 months to place a song. If it cannot be placed within the contracted time limit, the songwriter regains all his rights to the song."
How to Contact: Submit demo tape and lyric sheet. Prefers cassette with 1-4 songs on demo. SASE. Reports in 3 weeks.
Music: C&W; contemporary gospel; novelty; and rock. Currently working with "Manhattan Moonbeam" (by Jack Rodney) and "Damn the J.E.A." (by J.J. Hunter).
Tips: "We prefer *polished* well-recorded demos."

BIG STATE MUSIC, Texas Sound, Inc., 1311 Candlelight Ave., Dallas TX 75116. Affiliate: Pineapple Music (ASCAP). President: Paul Ketter. Music publisher and record company. BMI. Publishes 20 songs/year. Pays standard royalties.
How to Contact: Submit demo tape and lead sheet. Prefers 7½ ips reel-to-reel with 3-6 songs on demo. SASE. Reports in 3 weeks.
Music: C&W; and MOR (country). Recently published "Theodore," recorded by Dave Gregory (Christmas); "Only a Woman" (by Dianne Baumgartner), "Bar After Bar (by F. Fileccia and F. Raffa) and "Mountain Boy" (by Bunnie Mills), all recorded by B. Mills/Sagittar Records (C&W); "Adam's Rib," recorded by Debbie Dierks (C&W); and "Honky Tonkin Woman" (Buddy Howard), recorded by Buddy Howard/Sagittar Records (C&W).

BILLETDOUX MUSIC PUBLISHING, 1 E. Scott St., Suite 408, Chicago IL 60610. (312)266-0040. Executive Producer: Clifford Rubin. Music publisher. Estab. 1978. BMI. Publishes 10 songs/year; publishes 3-4 new songwriters/year. Pays standard royalty.
How to Contact: Submit demo tape and lyric sheet. Prefers cassette. "We only review copywritten material; all other will be returned." SASE. Reports in 1 month.
Music: Blues; children's; choral; C&W; disco; easy listening; gospel; jazz; MOR; progressive; R&B; rock; soul; and top 40/pop. Recently published "Flash Gordon," "Love" and "Mermaid" (by Cliff Rubin), recorded by Randy De Troit/Grandville Records; "The Night It Rained in Tupelo," recorded by Wade Travis/LK Records (C&W); "I've Got Wings" (by M. Hill), recorded by Power Band/Grandville Records (black pop); and "Power Funk" and "Every Nite" (by M. Hill/C. Hill/J. Gardner), recorded by Power Band/Grandville Records, (funk/R&B).

BIMUSIXS PUBLICATIONS, 6358 Mazarin St., Montreal, Quebec, Canada H4E 2X3. (514)767-2767. Professional Manager: Gianni Primiani. Music publisher and record producer. Estab. 1980. BMI. Publishes 52 songs/year. Pays standard royalty.
How to Contact: Write or call first about your interest, arrange personal interview or submit demo tape and lyric sheets. Prefers cassette with 1-8 songs on demo. SAE and International Reply Coupon. Reports in 1 month.
Music: Bluegrass, blues, children's, choral, church/religious, classical, C&W, dance-oriented, easy listening, folk, gospel, jazz, MOR, progressive, Spanish, R&B, rock (all forms), soul, top 40/pop, jingles, and film and video music.
Tips: "One way to increase a songwriter's chance of getting a song published, is to submit a copy of a *master* recording and production of the song or songs on video."

BIRD SEED MUSIC, 1946 N. Hudson Ave., Chicago IL 60614. (312)787-6060. President: Robin McBride. Music publisher, record company and record producer. Estab. 1980. BMI. Publishes 10 songs/year; publishes 3 new songwriters/year. Pays standard royalty less 15% administration fee.
How to Contact: Submit demo tape and lyric sheet. Prefers cassette with 1-3 songs on demo. "Always looking for songs for singles or fresh pop-directed ideas. Not looking for 'heavy' concept LP material." SASE. Reports in 1 month.
Music: Rock, dance-oriented, jazz & jazz fusion, progressive soul, new wave and top 40/pop.
Tips: "Radio remains the industry's prime exposure medium, yet unique and fresh material is vital to the music business' sustenance. Fit into that pocket and professionals will break their necks to expose your material."

BLENDINGWELL MUSIC, 488 Madison Ave., New York NY 10022. (212)752-3033. Affiliate: Sister John Music (BMI). Vice President/General Manager: Bob Esposito. Music publisher and record producer. ASCAP. Member CMA and NMPA. Publishes 50 songs/year; publishes 25 new songwriters/year.
How to Contact: Submit demo tape and lyric sheet. Prefers 7½ ips reel-to-reel or cassette with 3 songs maximum on demo tape. SASE. Reports in 3 weeks.

Music: Dance-oriented rock; easy listening; R&B; rock; and top 40/pop. Recently published "Heavy On Sunshine" (by Den Henson), recorded by Spinners/Atlantic Records (pop/R&B); "Naughty" (by Mugrage and Fleischer), recorded by Chaka Kahn/Warner Brothers Records (R&B); and "When You Get Around to It" (by Thomas/Tillis), recorded by Gloria Gaynor/ Polydor Records (pop/R&B).
Tips: "The writer should bear in mind, all producers are seeking *single-oriented songs* for their artists—not album cuts. Therefore send only those songs with strong hooks and good lyrics and which you feel can fit into *top 40* MOR, C&W, rock and pop categories."

BLUE ISLAND PUBLISHING, 1446 N. Martel, Unit 3, Los Angeles CA 90046. (213)851-3161. Affiliates: Bob Fleming Music (BMI) and Dahlhouse Publishing (ASCAP). General Manager: Bob Gilbert. Music publisher, record company and record producer. Estab. 1980. ASCAP. Publishes 50 songs/year. Pays standard royalty.
How to Contact: Submit demo tape and lyric sheet. Prefers cassette with 3-6 songs on demo. "Submit only your best single-oriented songs to fit top 40 format. Easy to understand songs with strong hooks and good lyrics make it." SASE. Reports in 3 weeks.
Music: C&W, MOR, rock and top 40/pop.

BLUE MACE MUSIC, Box 62263, Virginia Beach VA 23462. (804)340-3366. President: Alex Spencer. Music publisher and record company. BMI. Pays standard royalty.
How to Contact: Submit demo tape and lyric sheet or arrange personal interview. Prefers 7½ ips reel-to-reel or cassette with 1-3 songs on demo. SASE. Reports in 2 weeks.
Music: Top 40/pop; rock; and MOR.

BLUE RIVER MUSIC, INC., 1741 N. Ivar, Suite 210, Hollywood CA 90028. (213)463-7661. Affiliate: Sheriton (ASCAP). President: Harry Bluestone. Music publisher and record company. BMI. Publishes 5 songs/year. Pays standard royalty.
How to Contact: Submit demo tape and lyric sheet. Prefers cassette with 1-4 songs on demo "unless style varies. Then submit enough songs to show your versatility." SASE. Reports in 1 week.
Music: Bluegrass; blues; classical; C&W; easy listening; gospel; jazz; MOR; R&B; rock; and top 40/pop.

BO GAL MUSIC, Box 6687, Wheeling WV 26003. (614)758-5812. Affiliate: Green Up Music (BMI). President: Bob Gallion. Music publisher and record company. BMI. Pays standard royalties.
How to Contact: Submit demo tape. Prefers reel-to-reel tape. SASE. Reports in 1 month.
Music: Bluegrass; blues; church/religious; C&W; folk; gospel; MOR; and top 40/pop. Recently published "The Next Time" (by Don Sniffin), recorded by Patti Powell/Arby Records (MOR); and "Looks Like You're Going Anyway" (by Sniffin), recorded by Powell/Arby Records (MOR).

BOURNE MUSIC, 1212 Avenue of the Americas, New York NY 10036. (212)575-1800. Office Manager: Al Tuckman. Affiliate: Murbo Music (BMI). Music publisher (estab. 1928) and record producer (estab. 1980). ASCAP. Member NMPA. Publishes 10 songs/year. Pays standard royalty.
How to Contact: Submit demo tape and lyric sheet. Prefers 7½ ips reel-to-reel or cassette with 1-2 songs on demo. SASE. Reports in 6 weeks.
Music: Published "Black Magic Woman" (by Peter Green), recorded by Santana; "Unforgettable" (by Irving Gordon), recorded by Englebert Humperdinck/CBS Records and "All of Me" (by G. Marks and S. Simons), recorded by Willie Nelson/CBS Records. Uses all types.

BOXCAR MUSIC, 13615 Pinerock, Houston TX 77079. (713) 465-6199. Manager: Peter Breaz. Assistant Manager: Paul Eakin. Music publisher, record company and record producer. Estab. 1978. BMI. Publishes 45 songs/year. Pays standard royalties.
How to Contact: Query, arrange personal interview, submit demo tape, or submit demo tape and lyric or lead sheet. Prefers 7½ ips reel-to-reel or cassette with 4-8 songs on demo. "Will also accept 45s and LPs or EPs." Also include biography and photo. SASE. Reports in 1 month.
Music: Bluegrass; C&W; easy listening; folk; MOR; progressive; rock; and top 40/pop. Recently published "If I Stay Away" (by P. Breaz), recorded by Marcia Breaz (country/pop); "Truck Stop Annie" (by P. Breaz), recorded Hickory/Country Kitchen Records (country); "Maggie" (by Bob Oldreive), recorded by Hickory/Country Kitchen Records (rock); and "I Just Want to Sing" (by P. Breaz), recorded by Marcia Glist/Country Kitchen Records (country/MOR).

BOXER MUSIC, Box 120501, Nashville TN 37212. Affiliates: Fruit Music (BMI) and KoKo Music (ASCAP). President: Curtis Allen. Music publisher. BMI. "We do not accept or review unsolicited material in any form."

TOMMY BOYCE & MELVIN POWERS MUSIC ENTERPRISES, 12015 Sherman Rd., North Hollywood CA 91605. (213)875-1711. President: Melvin Powers. Music publisher and record company. ASCAP.
How to Contact: Submit demo tape and lyric sheet. Prefers cassette with 3 songs on demo. SASE. Reports in 1 month.
Music: C&W and MOR. Recently published "Willie Burgundy" (by Tommy Boyce and Melvin Powers), recorded by Teresa Brewer (MOR); "Mr. Songwriter" (by Tommy Boyce and Melvin Powers), recorded by Sunday Sharpe (C&W); and "Who Wants a Slightly Used Woman?" (by Tommy Boyce and Melvin Powers), recorded by Connie Cato (C&W).
Tips: "Before you send your songs to a publisher, have a *professional* (musician, singer) listen to them. Get their professional critique. New songwriters waste a lot of time and money which they should be using on courses in song and lyric writing and workshops. Then test your songs against those on the radio. Do they measure up? I'd recommend collaboraton as the best source of instant feedback and critique."

BRANCH INTERNATIONAL MUSIC, Box 31819, Dallas TX 75231. (214)690-8875. Owner: Pat McKool. A&R Director: Mike Anthony. Music publisher. BMI. Publishes 20 songs/year. Pays standard maximum royalty.
How to Contact: Submit demo tape and lead or lyric sheet. Prefers 7½ ips reel-to-reel with 1-4 songs on demo. SASE. Reports in 1 month.
Music: C&W and gospel. Recently published "Tough Act To Follow" (by V. Stovall and B. Palmer), recorded by Billy Parker/SCR Records (C&W); "You're a Woman" (by Dugg Collins), recorded by DeWayne Bowman/Yatahey Records (C&W); and "The Closest Thing to You" (by J. Hudson), recorded by DeWayne Bowman/Yatahey Records.

BRAVE NEW MUSIC, 6253 Hollywood Blvd., Suite 1116, Hollywood CA 90028. (213)466-3534. President: Daniel Friedman. Music publisher. Estab. 1980. BMI. Publishes 15 songs/year; publishes 6 new songwriters/year. Pays standard royalty.
How to Contact: Write first about your interest. Prefers cassette with 1-6 songs on demo. "Good tape quality is greatly appreciated." SASE. Reports in 1 month.
Music: Choral, country, dance-oriented, easy listening, rock and top 40/pop. "Right now we mostly do choral sheet music, we are, however, always looking for good pop, rock and country songs."

BRIARPATCH MUSIC/DEB DAVE MUSIC, INC., 1216 16th Ave. S., Nashville TN 37203. (615)320-7227. Manager: Keni Wehrman. Music publisher. BMI. Publishes 150 songs/year. Pays standard royalties.
How to Contact: "Before submitting material, please inquire by mail." Prefers cassette with 2 songs on demo. SASE. Reports in 1 month.
Music: Recently published "Drivin' My Life Away" and "I Love a Rainy Night" (by Even Stevens, Eddie Rabbitt and David Malloy), recorded by Eddie Rabbitt.

BROADMAN PRESS, 127 9th Ave. N., Nashville TN 37234. (615)251-2500. Music Editor: Mark Blankenship. Music publisher. SESAC. Publishes 200 songs/year.
How to Contact: Submit demo tape and lead sheet. Prefers reel-to-reel or cassette with 1-10 songs on demo. SASE. Reports in 6 weeks.
Music: Choral; church/religious; and gospel. "We publish all forms of sacred music including solo/choral for all ages, and instrumental for handbell, organ, piano, recorder and orchestra."

BROOKLYN COUNTRY MUSIC, Suite 1705, 150 E. 39th St., New York NY 10016. (212)889-3754. A&R Director: Zhaba Jay. Music publisher, record producer, record company and management company. ASCAP. Publishes 100 songs/year; publishes 3 new songwriters/year. Pays standard royalty.
How to Contact: Submit demo tape and lyric sheet. Prefers 7½ ips reel-to-reel or cassette with 2-5 songs on demo. "Do not send rating cards. We will *not* answer enclosed post cards rating material, singer, etc. and will contact writer only if interested." Does not return unsolicited material.
Music: Blues; country rock (uptown & downtown styles); and R&B. Recently published "Two People on the Wrong Side of the Door" (by V. Jay and D. Roberts), recorded by Valerie Jay/Brooklyn Country Records (country); "Outside the Law" (by V. Jay and D. Roberts), recorded by Valerie Jay and Danny Roberts/Musicland Express U.S.A. Records (country rock); and "Evil Mama" (by Keith Fredericks), recorded by Danny Roberts/Musicland Express U.S.A. Records (country rock).

BROOKS BROTHERS PUBLISHERS, 311 Margo Lane, Nashville TN 37211. (615)834-4124. Manager: Jake Brooks. Music publisher. Estab. 1978. BMI. Publishes 12 songs/year; publishes 2 new songwriters/year. Pays standard royalty.
How to Contact: Submit vocal/guitar/piano demo tape and lyric sheet. Prefers 7½ ips reel-to-reel with 1-3 songs on demo. "Print clearly." SASE. Reports in 2 weeks.
Music: C&W (western, western country, country). Recently published "Paint Me Back Home in Wyoming" and "Ain't Had Time to Go Home" (by Jake Brooks), recorded by Chris LeDoux/ American Cowboy Songs (western country); "I Can't See the Rainbow For the Rain" (by Brooks), recorded by Clay Mac/Goldust Records (country pop); "In My Lady's Eyes" and "Moonshine Dreamer" (by David Ruthstrom), recorded by David Ruthstrom/Goldust Records (country/pop).

BROWN MOON MUSIC, Box 19274, Houston TX 77024. Manager: Rusty Holster. Music publisher. ASCAP. Publishes 20 songs/year. Pays standard royalty.
How to Contact: Submit demo tape and lyric sheet. Prefers 7½ ips reel-to-reel or cassette with 3-6 songs on demo. Include photos and biographical material. Does not return unsolicited material. Reports in 2 months.
Music: C&W ("cross-over potential only—no hardcore"); rock; and top 40/pop. "We are interested in commercial, well-structured songs. Send only if you are convinced you have a classic." Recently published "Louisiana" (by Rusty Holster), recorded by Southern Cross/Border Records (rock); and "Hot as a Pistol" (by Rusty Holster), recorded by Rusty Holster/794 Records (rock).

ALBERT E. BRUMLEY & SONS, Powell MO 65730. (417)435-2225. Affiliate: Hartford Music (SESAC). Contact: Bob Brumley. Music publisher and booking agency. SESAC. Publishes 25-50 songs/year; publishes 5-10 new songwriters/year. Pays standard royalties.
How to Contact: Submit demo tape and lead sheet. Prefers cassette with 3-4 songs on demo. SASE. Reports in 3 weeks.
Music: Choral; church/religious; C&W; and gospel.

BRUT MUSIC PUBLISHING, 1345 Ave. of the Americas, New York NY 10019. (212)581-3114. General Manager: Stan Krell. Music publisher. ASCAP. Pays standard royalty.
How to Contact: Submit demo tape and lyric sheet. Prefers cassette. SASE. Reports as soon as possible.
Music: Easy listening; MOR; rock and top 40/pop. Recently published "Now That We're In Love" (by Sammy Cahn and George Barrie), recorded by Steve Lawrence; and "Rome Is A Song" (by Cahn and Barrie), recorded by Jimmy Rosselli.

BUCKHORN MUSIC PUBLISHING CO., INC., Box 120547, Nashville TN 37212. (615)327-4590. Affiliate: Meredith Music (ASCAP). Music publisher. Professional Manager: Neil Patton Rogers. BMI. ASCAP. Member NMPA. Does not accept unsolicited material.

BUG MUSIC GROUP, Bug Music Group, 6777 Hollywood Blvd., 9th Floor, Los Angeles CA 90028. (213)466-4352. Affiliates: Bug Music (BMI) and Bug Juice Music (ASCAP). Vice President: Fred Bourgoise. BMI.
How to Contact: Submit demo tape and lyric sheet. Prefers cassette. SASE. Reports "as soon as possible."
Music: R&B and top 40/pop. Recently published "The Way We Make a Broken Heart," (by John Hiatt), recorded by Ry Cooder/Warner Brothers Records; "Dreamer" (by Moon Martin), recorded by the Association/Elektra Records; "Marie, Marie" (by Dave Alvin-Blasters), recorded by Shakin' Stevens; "Power of Love" (by T-Bone Burnett), recorded by Arlo Guthrie/Warner Brothers Records; "We Don't Get Along" (by Kathy Valentine), recorded by Phil Seymour/ Boardwalk Records; "My Baby Thinks He's a Train" (by LeRoy Preston), recorded by Rosanne Cash/Columbia Records; "Driving Wheel" (by T-Bone Burnett and Billy Swan), recorded by Robert Gordon/RCA Records; "Don't Blow Your Life Away" (by Bill Pitcock), recorded by Phil Seymour/Boardwalk Records; and "Nightclubbing" (by Iggy Pop), recorded by Grace Jones.

BURIED TREASURE MUSIC, 524 Doral Country Dr., Nashville TN 37221. Affiliate: Captain Kidd Music (BMI). Executive Producer: Scott Turner. Music publisher and record producer. ASCAP. Publishes 50-100 songs/year; publishes 2-10 new songwriters/year. Pays standard royalty.
How to Contact: Submit demo tape and lead sheet. Prefers cassette with 1-4 songs on demo. SASE. Reports in 2 weeks.
Music: C&W; easy listening; folk; MOR; progressive (country); rock; and top 40/pop. Recently published "The Catman" and "I Just Met a Memory" (by Turner, Gordon and Lampert), recorded by Robert Gordon/RCA Records (contemporary); "Comin' In the Back Door," recorded

by Baja Marimba Band (Europe); "Mexican Drummer Man," recorded by Tiajuana Brass (Europe); "Jerry," recorded by Slim Whitman (United Kingdom); and "Just Friends" (by M. Humphries), recorded by Tommy Sands (MOR).

BURNING ROPE, 415 Congress St., Austin TX 78701. (512)477-7100. Contact: Leon Eagleson, Charles Tullos. Music publisher, record producer and record company. BMI. Publishes 10 songs/year. Pays standard royalty.
How to Contact: Write or call first about your interest, then submit demo tape and lyric sheet. Prefers cassette with 2-12 songs on demo. SASE. Reports in 2 weeks.
Music: Blues; gospel; jazz; R&B; rock; soul; and top 40/pop. Recently published "I Love You Girl" and "Pay Day" (by James Shelby), recorded by James Shelby/Swoon Records (blues); and "Hi Mom" (by Mike Murphy), recorded by Mike Murphy/NL/Babe Records (disco).

BUSCH COUNTRY PUBLISHING, 1002 W. Busch Blvd., Tampa FL 33612. (813)935-6289. Affiliate: Rhythm and Rhyme (BMI). Contact: Randall Bethencourt. Music publisher and record company. SESAC. Publishes 5 songs/year; publishes 2 new songwriters/year. Pays standard royalty.
How to Contact: Submit demo tape and lyric sheet. Prefers reel-to-reel or cassette with 3-5 songs on demo. SASE. Reports in 6 weeks.
Music: C&W.

BUSH/LEHRMAN PRODUCTIONS, 119 W. 57th St., New York NY 10019. Professional Managers: Ted Lehrman, Libby Bush. Music publisher and record producer. ASCAP.
How to Contact: Submit demo tape and lyric sheet. Prefers 7½ ips reel-to-reel or cassette with 2-4 songs on demo. Reports in 6 weeks. "Please enclose self-addressed stamped envelope."
Music: MOR; rock; R&B; dance; C&W; and adult contemporary.

BUTTERMILK SKY ASSOCIATES, 515 Madison Ave., New York NY 10022. (212)759-2275. President: Murray Deutch. Professional Manager: Stu Cantor. Music publisher. BMI and ASCAP. Member NMPA. Publishes 100 songs/year; publishes 20 new songwriters/year. Pays standard royalties.
How to Contact: Arrange personal interview or submit demo tape and lyric sheet. Prefers cassette with 4 songs maximum on demo. Does not return unsolicited material. Reports in 3 months. "Include SASE with solicited submissions."
Music: Rock n' roll, dance, MOR, R&B, and top 40/pop. Recently published "Tryin' to Get to You" (by McCoy/Singleton), recorded by Phil Seymour/Boardwalk Records and "I've Had It," recorded by Louise Goffin/Electra-Asylum Records.

B-W MUSIC, The WelDee Music Co., Box 561, Wooster OH 44691. Affiliates: LaShaRuDa Music (BMI) and Spangle Music (BMI). General Manager: Quentin W. Welty. Music publisher. BMI. Published 12 songs in 1978. Pays standard royalty.
How to Contact: Submit demo tape. Prefers 7½ ips reel-to-reel with 1-5 songs on demo. "Mono or full-track only." SASE. Reports in 2 weeks.
Music: Bluegrass; C&W; folk; and gospel. Recently published "Take Your Shoes Off Moses," recorded by the Lewis Family (C&W); "Multiply the Heartaches," recorded by G. Jones and M. Montgomery (C&W); and "Unkind Words," recorded by Kathy Dee (pop/C&W).

CABRIOLET MUSIC, Box 7422, Shreveport LA 71107. Contact: Don Logan. Music publisher. BMI. Pays standard royalty.
How to Contact: Submit demo tape. Prefers 7½ ips reel-to-reel with 2-4 songs on demo. SASE. Reports as soon as possible.
Music: C&W; disco; gospel; soul; and spiritual. Recently published "That's Alright," recorded by Zion Jubilees (spiritual); "Do You Believe in Disco?", recorded by Sam Benson (disco); and "Hide Behind the Mountain," recorded by Mt. Pleasant Choir (gospel).

CACTUS MUSIC AND GIDGET PUBLISHING, 5 Aldom Circle, West Caldwell NJ 07006. (201)226-0035. Contact: Jim Hall or Gidget Starr. Music publisher, record company and record producer. ASCAP. Publishes 5 new songwriters/year. Pays standard royalty.
How to Contact: Write or call first about your interest or submit demo tape and lyric sheet. Prefers 7½ ips reel-to-reel or cassette with 5 songs minimum on demo. Does not return unsolicited material. Reports in 2 weeks.
Music: Bluegrass, blues, C&W and gospel. Recently published "House of Glass," "Old Foggy Town," and "Gone, Gone, Gone."

CAMBRIA PUBLISHING, Box 2163, Rancho Palos Verdes CA 90274. (213)541-1114. Director of Publishing: Lance Bowling. Music publisher and record company. Estab. 1979. ASCAP. Publishes 7 songs/year; publishes 2 new songwriters/year. Pays standard royalty.
How to Contact: Write first about your interest. Prefers 7½ ips reel-to-reel or cassette. SASE. Reports in 1 month.
Music: Classical and jazz (classical). Recently published "3 Dances by Madeleine Dring" and "Valse Francaise" (by M. Dring), recorded by Leigh Kaplan/Cambria Records (classical piano music); and "3 Pieces for Flute and Piano" (by M. Dring), recorded by L. Kaplan and Louise Ditullio/Cambria Records (classical).

CAMERICA MUSIC, 489 5th Ave., New York NY 10017. (212)682-8400. Affiliate: Camex Music (BMI). Professional Manager: Arty Simon. Music publisher and production firm. ASCAP. Publishes 50 songs/year; publishes 20 new songwriters/year. Pays standard royalty.
How to Contact: Submit demo tape and lyric sheet. Prefers 7½ ips reel-to-reel or cassette with 1-10 songs on demo. "Songs should have great hooks, interesting chord changes, classic melodies and conversational lyrics." SASE. Reports in 2 weeks.
Music: C&W, dance-oriented, easy listening, folk, jazz, MOR, R&B, rock, soul and top 40/pop. Recently published "Wish We Were Heroes" (by Austin Gravelding), recorded by Kenny Dale/Capitol Records (country/pop); "It Hurts Too Much" (by Eric Carmen), recorded by Robert Gordon/RCA Records (rock); and "Change of Heart" (by Eric Carmen), recorded by Donna Fargo/Warner Brothers Records (pop rock).

THE CAMERON ORGANISATION, INC., 320 S. Waiola Ave., LaGrange IL 60525. (312)352-2026. Affiliates: Monona Music (BMI), Watertoons Music (BMI), Hoochie Coochie Music (BMI), Skafish Music (BMI) and Rathsino Publishing (BMI). President/Manager: Scott A. Cameron. Music publisher. BMI. Pays standard royalty.
How to Contact: Submit demo tape and lead sheet. Prefers 7½ ips reel-to-reel or cassette with 1-3 songs on demo. SASE. Reports in 1 month.
Music: Blues; progressive; rock; soul; and top 40/pop. Recently published "Champagne and Reefer" and "The Blues Had a Baby and They Called It Rock and Roll," recorded by Muddy Waters/Watertoons Records; "What Happened to My Blues?," recorded by Willie Dixon; "Earthquake and Hurricane" (by Willie Dixon), recorded by Tina Turner; "Cruising Down Hwy 99," recorded by Might Joe Young (theme for United Artists Motion Picture "Thief"/Monona Music Co. Records); and "Obsessions of You" and "Maybe One Time," recorded by Skafish.

CANAL PUBLISHING, INC., 6325 Guilforo Ave. #4, Indianapolis IN 46220. (317)255-3116. Vice President: Terry Barnes. Music publisher. BMI. Publishes 50-100 songs/year; publishes 5-10 new songwriters/year. Usually pays standard royalty.
How to Contact: Submit demo tape and lyric sheet. Prefers cassette with 1-4 songs on demo. SASE. Reports in 1 month.
Music: Country, easy listening, MOR, rock and top 40/pop. Recently published "Dancin' Shoes" (by Carl Storie), recorded by Nigel Olsen, the Faith Band and Michael Clark (ballad); and "You're My Weakness" (by John Cascella), recorded by the Faith Band (top 40/pop).

CANDLESTICK PUBLISHING CO., 582 Armour Circle NE, Atlanta GA 30324. (404)875-2555. Affiliate: Dream Merchant Music (BMI). Partners: Larry King, R.B. Hudmon, Gwen Kesler. Music publisher. BMI. Pays standard royalty.
How to Contact: Submit demo tape and lead sheet. Prefers cassette with 1-6 songs on demo. SASE. Reports in 1 month.
Music: Rock; soul; and top 40/pop. Recently published "How Can I Be a Witness?", "If You Don't Cheat on Me" and "Holdin' On," recorded by R.B. Hudmon (soul).

CAN'T STOP MUSIC, Can't Stop Productions, Inc., 65 E. 55th St., Suite 302, New York NY 10022. (212)751-6177. Affiliate: Stop Light Music (ASCAP). President: Maximilian Dahan-Lavelle. National/International Relations Manager: Roberta Crownover. Music publisher and production company. BMI. Publishes 30 songs/year; publishes 2 new songwriters/year. Pays 30-50% royalty.
How to Contact: Submit demo tape. Cassette only. SASE. Reports in 8 weeks.
Music: Disco; easy listening; rock; soul; and top 40/pop. Recently published "Ready for the 80's" (by J. Morali, H. Belolo, P. Hurtt and B. Whitehead), recorded by the Village People (dance/rock).
Tips: "We prefer no more than 3 titles on each submission."

CAPAQUARIUS PUBLISHING & ARTIST MGT., INC., 750 Kappock St., Riverdale NY 10463. (212)369-8690. Affiliate: Yanita Music (BMI). President: P.J. Watts. Music publisher and man-

agement firm. ASCAP. Publishes 3 songs/year; publishes 1 new songwriter/year.
How to Contact: Submit demo tape and lead sheet. Prefers 7½ ips reel-to-reel with 3-5 songs on demo. Prefers leader between selections. SASE. Reports in 3 weeks.
Music: C&W, disco; gospel (rock); and soul. Recently published "Ain't it Time?" (Queen Yahna and Arthur Manning) and "Goin' Downtown to See Jesus" (by Queen Yahna, John Simmons and Sylvia Blanchcomb), recorded by Queen Yahna/P&P Records.

CAROLINA COWBOY MUSIC, Box 1077, Cleveland TN 37311. (615)479-1415. "We are not accepting outside material at this time."

CARRELL PUBLISHING CO., Box 311, Rt. 19, Wexford PA 15090. (412)935-1330. Contact: C.W. Abbott. Music publisher, record producer, record company and record distributor. Estab. 1979. BMI. Pays standard royalty.
How to Contact: Write first about your interest, then submit demo tape and lyric sheet. Prefers cassette. SASE. Reports in 1 month.
Music: Bluegrass; blues; and folk (traditional, Irish).

CARWIN PUBLISHING CO., Carwin Country Records, 13357 Lorain Ave., Cleveland OH 44111. (216)476-2695. Affiliate: Carl French Music (ASCAP). President: Carl French. Music publisher and record company. BMI. Publishes 10 songs/year.
How to Contact: Arrange personal interview or submit demo tape and lead sheet. Prefers 7½ ips reel-to-reel with 2-10 songs on demo. SASE. Reports in 2 weeks.
Music: Bluegrass; C&W; and gospel. Recently published "In the Arms of Any Stranger" (by Terry Goffee), "My Shoes Are Not That Hard to Fill" (by C. French and R. Wilhoit) and "The Touch of Gold" (by C. French and J. Campbell), all recorded by Rodger Wilhoit/Carwin Country Records (C&W).

DON CASALE MUSIC, INC., 377 Plainfield St., Westbury NY 11590. (516)333-7898. President: Don Casale. Music publisher and record company. BMI. Publishes 12 songs/year; publishes 10 new songwriters/year. Pays standard royalty.
How to Contact: Arrange personal interview or submit demo tape and lead or lyric sheet. Reel-to-reel or cassette OK. SASE. Reports in 2 weeks.
Music: C&W (catchy stories); disco; MOR (must have mass appeal); rock (soft rock); R&B; soul (ballads or uptempo); top 40/pop (strong melodies only); and "gimmick songs." Recently published "Keep on Dancin'," recorded by Herb "King" Josey/Rap-City Records (R&B/disco/funk); "I Can't Go On" (by Dino Ascari); "Don't Ever Ever Stop the Love" (by Fred Messinetti); "Fun" (by Frank Jackson and Maureen Reid), recorded by Bliss/Rap City Records; and "Take Me Now" (by Patti Gianini and Andreas Strigos).

CASTALIA MUSIC, Box 11516, Milwaukee WI 53211. President: Jim Spencer. Music publisher, record company and record producer. BMI. Publishes about 36 songs/year; publishes 10 new songwriters/year. Pays standard royalty. Write first about your interest or submit demo tape and lyric sheet. Prefers cassette with 1-6 songs on demo. SASE. Reports in 1 month.
Music: All types. Recently published "The Blues Are Out to Get Me" (by Jim Spencer and Hager), recorded by Jim Spencer/Armada Records (R&B); "Wrap Myself Up in Your Love" (by Spencer and Tossing), recorded by Spencer/Armada Records (R&B); and "Almost in Your Arms Again" (by Jim Spencer, Hager and Riley), recorded by Dan Riley/Armada (country).

CATALPA PUBLISHING CO., 2609 NW 36th St., Oklahoma City OK 73112. (405)942-0462. Professional Manager: Bobby Boyd. Music publisher, record company and record producer. BMI. Publishes 100 songs/year; publishes 6 new songwriters/year. Pays standard royalty.
How to Contact: Write first about your interest, then submit demo tape and lyric sheet. Prefers 7½ ips reel-to-reel with 3-12 songs on demo. Does not return unsolicited material. Reports in 2 weeks.
Music: C&W, R&B, rock, soul and top 40/pop.

CEDARWOOD PUBLISHING CO., INC., 39 Music Square E., Nashville TN 37203. (615)255-6535. Affiliates: Denny Music (ASCAP), Cajun Music (BMI), Driftwood Music (BMI) and Stonewall Music (BMI). President: J. William Denny. Music publisher. BMI. Member NMPA. Publishes 200 songs/year. Pays standard royalties.
How to Contact: Submit demo tape and lead sheet. Prefers 7½ ips reel-to-reel with 1-3 songs on demo. SASE. Reports in 1 month.
Music: C&W; gospel; MOR; progressive; and top 40/pop.

CETRA MUSIC, 5828 S. University Ave., Chicago IL 60637. (312)493-9781. President: Morton A. Kaplan. Music publisher. BMI. Pays standard royalties.

How to Contact: Submit lead sheet. Does not return unsolicited material. Reports in 2 weeks.
Music: Blues; church/religious; C&W; disco; folk; gospel; jazz; MOR; R&B; soul; and top 40/pop.

CHAPIE MUSIC, Chapman Recording Studios, 228 W. 5th St., Kansas City MO 64105. (816)842-6854. Owner: Chuck Chapman. Music publisher and record company. BMI. Pays standard royalty.
How to Contact: Submit demo tape. Prefers cassette with 3 songs minimum on tape. SASE. Reports in 1 month.
Music: Bluegrass; choral; church/religious; classical; C&W; disco; easy listening; folk; gospel; jazz; MOR; progressive; rock; soul; and top 40/pop. Recently published "L.A. Star" (by Farley Compton), recorded by F. Compton/Independent Records (rock); "Rainbow City" (by Bob Reeder), recorded by B. Reeder/Magic Sea Records (folk/rock); and "Granny Go Go" (by E.K. Bruhn), recorded by Kopperfield/Chapman Records (country/disco).

CHAPPELL MUSIC CANADA LIMITED, 14 Birch Ave., Toronto, Ontario, Canada M4V 1C9. (416)922-2159. Affiliate: Canadiana Music (PROCAN). President: J. Renewych. Music publisher. CAPAC. Member CMPA. Publishes 30 songs/year; publishes 6 new songwriters/year. Hires staff writers. Pays standard royalty.
How to Contact: Submit demo tape and lyric sheet. Prefers 7½ ips reel-to-reel or cassette with 1-4 songs on demo. "Demos of rock material should have rhythm tracks; piano and vocal sufficient on ballads." SAE and International Reply Coupons. Reports in 3 weeks.
Music: Easy listening, MOR, rock and top 40/pop.

CHAPPELL MUSIC CO., 11 Music Circle S., Nashville TN 37203. Affiliates: Unichappell (BMI), Trichappell (SESAC), Intersong Music (ASCAP) and Rightsong Music. ASCAP. Member NMPA. "We only review material recommended to us by music industry personnel."

CHAR BARB MUSIC, Rt. 1, Box 120F, Swoope VA 24479. (703)885-3309. President: Barbara Flowers. Music publisher, record company and recording studio. Estab. 1978. BMI. Pays standard royalty.
How to Contact: Call first about your interest. Prefers 7½ ips reel-to-reel, cassette or 8-track cartridge. SASE. Reports immediately.
Music: Bluegrass; C&W; gospel; MOR; and country rock. Recently published "The Way It's Meant To Be" (by Jerry Campbell), recorded by Jerry Campbell/Flowers Records (C&W); "The Upward Way" (by Shirley Cook), recorded by The Upward Way/Flowers Records (gospel); and "Lost Your Love Forever" (by Robert C. Call), recorded by Robert C. Call/Flowers Records (C&W).

CHASCOT MUSIC PUBLISHING, Box 3161, Atlanta GA 30302. President: Charles E. Scott. Music publisher, record company and record producer. BMI. Publishes 25 songs/year. Pays standard royalties.
How to Contact: Submit demo tape and lead sheet. Prefers cassette. SASE. Reports in 3 weeks.
Music: Blues; disco; gospel; R&B; soul; and top 40/pop. Recently published "Do It Again," by John Weber (blues); "Come On, Try It," by Bobby Lewis (R&B); and "Pay My Bills," by Janet Steinberg (pop).

CHASER FOR THE BLUES MUSIC, Box 5896, Station A, Toronto, Ontario, Canada M5W 1P3. (416)537-8749. Affiliate: Ben Kerr Music (PROCAN). President: Ben Kerr. Music publisher and record company. PROCAN. Publishes 8-12 songs/year. Pays standard royalty.
How to Contact: Write first about your interest. Prefers 7½ ips reel-to-reel or cassette with 4 songs maximum on demo. "Write and tell me about yourself." SAE and International Reply Coupons. Reports in 1 month.
Music: C&W, folk and MOR. Recently published "The Boston Marathon," "Nancy & Gayle," "Honky-Tonk-Ville" and "Distilled Water" (by Ben Kerr), recorded by Running Ben Kerr/Runathon Records (country); and "Fire on One End (A Fool on the Other)," and "Joanne My Joanne" (by B. Kerr), recorded by R.B. Kerr/Emphysema Records (country/MOR).

CHATTAHOOCHEE RECORDS, 16030 Ventura Blvd., Encino CA 91436. (213)788-6864. Contact: John or Chris Yardum. Record company. BMI. Pays standard royalty.
How to Contact: Submit demo tape and lyric sheet. Prefers cassette with 1-6 songs on demo. SASE. Reports in 2 weeks.
Music: Rock and top 40/pop.

CHEAVORIA MUSIC CO., 1219 Kerlin Ave., Brewton AL 36426. (205)867-2228. Songwriter: Roy Edwards. Producer: Mike Tracy. Music publisher, record producer and management firm. BMI. Publishes 15 songs/year; publishes 10 new songwriters/year. Pays standard royalties.
How to Contact: Query or submit demo tape and lead sheet. Prefers cassette with 2-5 songs on demo. SASE. Reports in 3 weeks.
Music: C&W; disco; easy listening; MOR; progressive; R&B; soul; and top 40/pop. Recently published "I've Changed to Your Kind of Life," "Empty Promises" and "Never Let Me Go" (by Ruby Wilson), recorded by Bobbie Roberson/Bolivia Records (C&W).

CHERRY LANE MUSIC PUBLISHING CO., INC., 50 Holly Hill Lane, Greenwich CT 06830. (203)661-0707; (212)824-7711. (New York Tie-line). Affiliated and/or administered companies: Windstar Music (ASCAP), Accabonac Music (ASCAP), Jolly Rogers Publishing (ASCAP), M-3 Music (ASCAP), Cappy Music (ASCAP), Cherry Wood Music (ASCAP), Hemlane Music (ASCAP), Cherry River Music (BMI), Windsea Music (BMI), Milton Okun Publishing (BMI), Mar-Ken Music (BMI), Chicken Key Music (BMI), Third Son Music (ASCAP), Birdwing Music (ASCAP), Rainy Now Music (ASCAP), Sparrow Song (BMI), World Artist Music Co., Inc., (BMI), Group 7 Music (BMI), Cherry Blossom Music Co. (SESAC), and His Eye Music (SESAC). Music publisher. ASCAP. Member NMPA. Pays standard royalties.
How to Contact: "We do not accept unsolicited material."

CHINABERRY MUSIC PUBLISHING CO., 2000 Madison Ave., Memphis TN 38104. (901)761-9234. Affiliate: Pecan Grove Music Publishing Co., Inc. (ASCAP). President: Jud Phillips Jr. Music publisher. Estab. 1979. BMI. Pays standard royalty.
How to Contact: Submit demo tape and lyric sheet. Prefers cassette with 1-10 songs on demo. SASE. Reports in 2 weeks.
Music: Blues; C&W; disco; easy listening; MOR; progressive; R&B; rock; soul; and top 40/pop.
Tips: "Attempt to cast the song for a particular artist, although this is not necessary or mandatory."

CHINNICHAP PUBLISHING CO., 8919 Sunset Blvd., Los Angeles CA 90069. (213)657-8585. Affiliate: Land of Dream. Director of Artistic Development: Dick Tompkins. Music publisher and record company (Dreamland Recording Co.). BMI and ASCAP. Publishes 50 songs/year. Pays standard royalty.
How to Contact: Submit demo tape and lyric sheet. Prefers cassette with 3 songs on demo. SASE: "specify that you want material returned." Reports in several months.
Music: Rock, top 40/pop and adult contemporary. Recently published "New World Romance," recorded by Spider/Dreamland Records (top 40).

CHINWAH SONGS/BIRTHRIGHT MUSIC, 3101 S. Western Ave., Los Angeles CA 90018. (213)258-8011. Affiliate: House of Talley (BMI). General Manager: Leroy C. Lovett. Music publisher and record producer. ASCAP, BMI and SESAC. Publishes 30-40 songs/year; publishes 10 new songwriters/year. Pays standard royalty.
How to Contact: Write first about your interest, then submit demo tape and lyric sheet. Prefers cassette with 3-5 songs on demo. SASE. Reports in 3 weeks.
Music: Choral, church/inspirational, gospel and Spanish.

CHIP 'N' DALE MUSIC PUBLISHERS, INC., 2125 8th Ave., South, Nashville TN 37204. (615)363-6002. Affiliates: Door Knob Music (BMI) and Lodestar Music (SESAC). President: Gene Kennedy. Vice President: Karen Jeglum. Music publisher, record company and record producer. ASCAP. Member NSAI, CMA and ACM. Publishes 200 songs/year; publishes 100 new songwriters/year. Pays standard royalty.
How to Contact: Submit demo tape and lyric sheet (include SASE) or arrange personal interview. Prefers 7½ ips reel-to-reel or cassette with 1-4 songs on demo. SASE. Reports in 6 weeks.
Music: C&W and MOR. Recently published "I Want To See Me In Your Eyes" (by Frank Stanton/Arthur Kent), recorded by Karen Jeglum and Gene Kennedy/Door Knob Records (modern country); "It's Only a Matter of Time" (by Bobby Young and Bob McCracken), recorded by Douglas/Door Knob Records (modern country); and "Why Don't You Go to Dallas" (by Buddy Landon and Janis Landon), recorded by Peggy Sue/Door Knob Records (country).

CHRIS MUSIC PUBLISHING, Box 268, Manistique MI 49854. Affiliate: Saralee Music (BMI). President: Reg B. Christensen. Music publisher and record company. BMI. Publishes 50 songs/year; publishes 15-20 new songwriters/year. Pays standard royalty.
How to Contact: Query, then submit demo tape and lead sheet. Prefers cassette with 2-5 songs on

demo. "No fancy, big band demo necessary; just one instrument with a clean, clear voice. Also, we prefer copyrighted material. Send registration number. If not registered with Copyright office, let us know what you've done to protect your material." SASE. Reports in 1 month.

Music: Bluegrass; C&W; gospel; MOR; rock (acid & hard); and soul. Recently co-published "Diamonds and Pearls," recorded by the Paradons/K-Tel Records (R&B); "Heart, You Fool," recorded by Louie Moore (C&W); and "Ask Me No Questions," recorded by Bill Woods (C&W).

Tips: "The writer should indicate if he has a certain singer in mind. We publishers have info on up and coming recording sessions of most well known recording artists (and pay big money to get this info)."

CHROMEWOOD MUSIC, Box 2388, Prescott AZ 86302. (602)445-5801. Affiliates: Hollydale Music (ASCAP) and Winteroak Music (ASCAP). Publishing Division President: Gaye Ellen Foreman. Music publisher. BMI. Publishes 30 songs/year; publishes 8 new songwriters/year. Pays standard royalty.

How to Contact: Submit demo tape and lyric sheet. Prefers cassette with 3-5 songs on demo. SASE. Reports in 3 weeks.

Music: C&W, easy listening and rock (country). Recently published "Out on the Road Again" (by M.D. Morgan), recorded by M.D. Morgan/Big Wheels Records (country); "Truckin' Woman" (by J. Pannell), recorded by J. Pannell/Big Wheels Records (country); and "Straw Hats and Stetsons" (by M.D. Morgan), recorded by Michael Hollister Morgan/Quarter Moon Records (country).

CHRYSALIS MUSIC CORP., 115 E. 57th St., New York NY 10022. (212)935-8754. Affiliates: Red Admiral (BMI), Rare Bird (ASCAP) and Moth (BMI). Music publisher and record company. ASCAP. "We are absolutely not accepting unsolicited material at this time. All unsolicited material will be returned."

CHRYSALIS MUSIC GROUP, 9255 Sunset Blvd., Los Angeles CA 90069. (213)550-0171. Professional Manager: Steve Moir. Music publisher. BMI and ASCAP. Member NMPA. Publishes several songs/year. Pays per individual contracts. Hires staff writers.

How to Contact: Call first about your interest; submit demo tape and lyric sheet. Prefers cassette with 3 songs on demo; include lead sheet. SASE. Reports in 1 month "depending on backlog of material."

Music: MOR, R&B, rock, and top 40/pop. "Open to most fields of music." Recently published "Living in a Fantasy," recorded by Leo Sayer (pop rock); and music recorded by Blondie and by Pat Benatar.

THE CHU YEKO MUSICAL FOUNDATION, Box 1314, Englewood Cliffs NJ 07632. (201)224-5811. Messages: (201)567-5524. Affiliates: Broadway/Hollywood International Music Publishers. Producer: Doris Chu Yeko. Music publisher, record company and record producer. Estab. 1979. ASCAP. Publishes 25 songs/year; publishes 2-7 new songwriters/year. Pays negotiable royalty (up to 10% of profits).

How to Contact: Submit demo tape and lyric sheet. Prefers cassette with any number songs on demo. SASE. Reports in 1 month.

Music: All types. "Complete musicals preferred." Recently published *Christy*, recorded by original cast/Original Cast Records; *The Great American Backstage Musical*/AEI Records; *Ka-Boom!*, by The Chu Yeko Musical Foundation; and *Five After Eight*, by original cast (all musicals).

Tips: Complete musicals, and top 40/pop songs. "Co-publishers welcome."

CHUCK WAGON, Box 330, Lennoxville, Quebec, Canada J1M 1Z5. (819)569-3431 or (819)569-9533. Affiliate: Hunter Publishing (CAPAC). President: Jerry Robitaille. Record company. BMI, ASCAP, CAPAC, PROCAN. Pays standard royalty.

How to Contact: Submit demo tape and lyric sheet. Prefers cassette. Does not return unsolicited material.

Music: C&W, easy listening and MOR.

CIANO PUBLISHING, Box 263, Hasbrouck Heights NJ 07604. (201)288-8935. President: Ron Luciano. Music publisher, record company and record producer. BMI. Publishes 12 songs/year. Pays standard royalty.

How to Contact: Query, submit demo tape and lead sheet or submit acetate disc and lead sheet. Prefers 7½ ips reel-to-reel, cassette or acetate with 2-6 songs on demo. SASE. Reports in 1 month.

Music: Disco; easy listening; MOR; R&B; rock; soul; top 40/pop. Recently published "Lucky" (by T. Galloway), recorded by Lucifer/Legz Records (rock n roll); "Fly Away" (by Philip Mitchell and Barron and Susan Sillars), recorded by Lucifer/Tiara Records (folk); and "Love's a Crazy Game" (by Joseph M. Leo and Paul Cannarella), recorded by Lucifer (top 40/disco).

CLAB MUSIC, Box 267, Perry Point MD 21902. Producer: Clifton Lewis. Music publisher, record company and record producer. BMI. Publishes 2 songs/year; publishes 1 new songwriter/year. Pays standard royalties.
How to Contact: Query or submit demo tape. Prefers 7½ ips reel-to-reel or cassette with 2-4 songs on demo. SASE. Reports in 1 month.
Music: C&W. Recently published "Starlight Lady" (by Ron Simon), recorded by Ron Simon/Bay Records (country); "Losin Man" (by Buddy Taylor), recorded by Chavis Brothers/Bay Records (country); and "I Love That Woman (Like the Devil Loves Sin)" (by Paul Huffman), recorded by Michael Hayes/Bay Records (country).

CLARK MUSIC PUBLISHING, Clark Musical Productions, Box 299, Watseka IL 60970. President: Dr. Paul E. Clark. Music publisher, booking agency and record company. BMI. Publishes 10-20 songs/year. Pays standard royalties.
How to Contact: Submit demo tape and lead sheet. Prefers cassette with 3-8 songs on demo. SASE. Reports in 1-2 months.
Music: Choral; church/religious; C&W; easy listening; gospel; MOR; rock (soft); and top 40/pop. Recently published "Spring Was But a Child," recorded by Mike Peterson (C&W); "Country Livin'," recorded by Cindy Lee (C&W); and "Jesus, Dear Jesus," recorded by the Gospelaires (religious).

BRUCE COHN MUSIC, Box 878, Sonoma CA 95476. (707)938-4060. Affiliates: Flat Lizard Music (ASCAP), Maybe Music (ASCAP), Quark Music (BMI), Skunkster Publishing (ASCAP), Snug Music (BMI), Noodle Tunes (BMI), Pants Down Music (BMI), Spikes Music (BMI), Soquel Songs (ASCAP), Tauripin Tunes (ASCAP), Windecor Music (BMI) and R.P. Winkelman Tunes (ASCAP). Manager/Owner: Bruce Cohn. Music publisher and management firm. Publishes 10-20 songs/year.
How to Contact: Query. SASE.
Music: C&W; MOR; rock; soul; and top 40/pop. Recently published "It Keeps You Running" and "Taking it to the Streets" recorded by the Doobie Brothers (pop).

COLLBECK PUBLISHING CO., 4817 Karchmer, Corpus Christi TX 78415. (512)854-7376. President: Gary Beck. Music publisher, record producer, record company and recording company. BMI. Publishes 10-100 songs/year.
How to Contact: Submit demo tape and lyric sheet. Prefers cassette with "as many songs as possible" on demo tape. SASE. Reports in 3 weeks.
Music: All types. Recently recorded "I Never Could Dance In Boots" (by Barbara Young), recorded by Jada (MOR); "Never Been Alone" (by Jada Vaughan), recorded by Jada (top 40); and "Haven't Heard A Good Love Song" (by Jada), recorded by Jada (country).

COMBINE MUSIC GROUP, 35 Music Sq. E, Nashville TN 37203. (615)255-0624. Music publisher. Affiliates: Southern Nights (ASCAP), Brothers Three (BMI), Silversoul Music (BMI), Sweet Baby (BMI), Tennessee Swamp Fox (ASCAP), Vintage Music (BMI), Youngun Publishing Co. (BMI), First Generation (BMI), Larry Gatlin (BMI), Music City Music, Inc. (ASCAP), Resaca Music (BMI), Rising Sun (BMI), Sherman Oaks Music (BMI) and Dropkick Music (BMI). ASCAP. Member NMPA, NMA, NARAS and CMA. Publishes 75 songs/year; publishes 2 new songwriters/year. "We are not currently accepting outside material."
Music: C&W, easy listening, gospel, MOR and top 40/pop. Recently published "Some Love Songs Never Die" (by Alice Keister, J. MacRae and B. Morrison), recorded by B.J. Thomas (MOR/country); "I Ought to Feel Guilty" (by B. Zerface, J. Zerface and B. Morrison), recorded by Jeannie Pruitt (country); and "Somethin' on the Radio" (by Pat McManus), recorded by Jackie Ward (MOR/country).

COMMERCIAL STUDIOS, INC., 412 Holly Dr. SE, Atlanta GA 30354. (404)361-7931. Affiliate: Seasun Experience (ASCAP). President: Howard Wright. Music publisher and production consultant. BMI.
How to Contact: Submit demo tape and lead sheet. Prefers 7½ ips reel-to-reel or cassette with 2-3 songs on demo. SASE. Reports in 1 month.
Music: Children's; disco; easy listening; jazz; rock; soul; top 40/pop.

COMMODORES ENTERTAINMENT PUBLISHING CORP., 39 W. 55th St., New York NY 10019. (212)246-0385. Contact: Professional Manager. Music publisher and record producer. ASCAP.
How to Contact: Write first about your interest, then submit demo tape and lyric sheet. Prefers cassette with 1-4 songs on demo. SASE. Reports in 1 month.
Music: All types.
Tips: "Protect your music! Always follow up after you submit!"

CONNEL PUBLISHING, 130 Pilgrim Dr., San Antonio TX 78213. (512)344-5033. Affiliate: J.C.E. Publishing Company (ASCAP). Owner: Jerry Connell. Record company, music publisher, record producer and booking agency. BMI. Publishes 75 songs/year; publishes 50 new songwriters/year. Pays standard royalties.
How to Contact: Query, submit demo tape, submit acetate disc, or submit lead sheet. Prefers 7½ or 15 ips reel-to-reel or cassette with 1 song on demo. Does not return unsolicited material. Reports in 2 weeks.
Music: Bluegrass; church/religious; C&W; disco; easy listening; folk; gospel; jazz; MOR; R&B; rock; and top 40/pop. Recently published "Heaven" (by Joe Brown), recorded by Joe Brown/ Cherokee Records (C&W); "Streets of San Antonio" (by Mike Lord), recorded by Mike Lord/ Cherokee Records (C&W); and "Hundred Dollar Boots" (by Ronnie Mason), recorded by Ronnie Mason/Cherokee Records (C&W).

CONTEMPORARY MUSIC, Box 2628, Los Angeles CA 90028. Affiliate: Composers Music (ASCAP). Contact: Audition Dept. Music publisher, record company and record producer. BMI. Publishes 1 new songwriter/year. Pays standard royalty.
How to Contact: Submit demo tape and lyric sheet. Prefers cassette with 1-4 songs on demo. SASE. Reports as soon as possible.
Music: Jazz (fusion), R&B, soul and top 40/pop. Recently published "Blues Before Lunch" and "Blues After Lunch" (by Tete Montoliu), recorded by T. Montoliu/Contemporary Records; and "Valse Triste" (by Art Pepper), recorded by A. Pepper/Contemporary Records (all jazz).

CONYPOL MUSIC, INC., 2595 Carrell Ln., Willow Grove PA 19090. (215)443-0935. President: Sal Barbieri. Music publisher, record company and record producer. Estab. 1980. BMI. Publishes 25 songs/year; publishes 3 new songwriters/year. Pays standard royalty.
How to Contact: Submit demo tape and lyric sheet. Prefers cassette with 1-4 songs on demo. "Use a straight rhythm track. Keep the voice up and lyrics clear." SASE. Reports in 1 month.
Music: C&W, dance-oriented, easy listening, MOR, soft rock, soul and top 40/pop. Recently published "Feeling Good" (by Sal Barbieri), recorded by S. Barbieri/BSO Records (dance rock); "Let's Get Funky" (by S. Barbieri), recorded by S. Barbieri/BSO Records (dance R&B); and "One More Try" (by S. Barbieri), recorded by S. Barbieri/BSO Records (top 40/pop).

COPYRIGHT SERVICE BUREAU LTD., 221 W. 57 St., New York NY 10019. (212)582-5030. Vice President of Administration: Ms. Jeri R. Spencer. Music publisher. BMI, ASCAP and SESAC.
How to Contact: Submit demo tape and lyric sheet. Prefers cassette with 5 songs on demo. "Include a note in your submission and follow up with a letter." Does not return unsolicited material. Reports in 6 weeks.
Music: All types.

CORE MUSIC PUBLISHING, c/o Oak Manor, Box 1000, Oak Ridges, Ontario, Canada L0G 1P0. (416)773-4371. Affiliates: Mark-Cain Music (CAPAC) and Brandy Music (BMI). Chairman: Ray Danniels. A&R Director: Pegi Cecconi. Music publisher with affiliated management, record and production companies. CAPAC. Member CMPA and CMRRA. Publishes 20-30 songs/year; publishes 1 new songwriter/year. Pays standard royalty.
How to Contact: Submit demo tape with bio material. Cassettes *only* with maximum of 3 songs on demo. SAE and International Reply Coupons. Reports in 6 weeks. Does not accept unsolicited material.
Music: Progressive, rock and top 40/pop. Recently published "Limelight" and "Moving Pictures" recorded by Rush (rock); "City Bred" (by Segarini), recorded by Segarini/Anthem Records (country rock); and "Hold On" (by Ian Thomas), recorded by Ian Thomas/Anthem Records (pop).

COTILLION MUSIC, INC., 75 Rockefeller Plaza, New York NY 10019. (212)484-8208. Affiliate: Walden Music, Inc. (ASCAP). Vice-President and General Manager: Linda Wortman. Professional Manager: Barry S. Offitzer. Music publisher. Member NMPA.

How to Contact: Does not return unsolicited material.
Music: Contemporary.

COUNTRY CLASSICS MUSIC PUBLISHING CO., 105 Burk Dr., Oklahoma City OK 73115. (405)677-6448. Affiliates: Sunny Lane Music. (ASCAP), Compo Music Publishing (BMI), and Devaney Music Publishing (BMI). General Manager: Sonny Lane. Music publisher, record company and record producer. BMI. Pays standard royalties.
How to Contact: Submit demo tape. Prefers cassette with 2-6 songs on demo. SASE. Reports in 3 weeks.
Music: Church/religious, C&W, easy listening, gospel; MOR and top 40/pop. Recently published "Forever and One Day" (by Yvonne Devaney), recorded by Hank Snow/RCA Records (country); "Teardrop Number One" (by Yvonne Devaney), recorded by Wanda Jackson/Myrrh Records (country); "Some Call Him Jesus" (by Devaney), recorded by Wanda Jackson/Myrrh Records (gospel); and "Wine From My Table" (by Devaney), recorded by Devaney/Compo Records.

COUNTRY LEGS MUSIC, 1577 Redwood Dr., Harvey LA 70058. (504)367-8501. Affiliate: Golden Sunburst Music (BMI). Manager: George Leger. Music publisher, record company, record producer, record distributor and promoter. ASCAP. Member CMA. Publishes 15-20 songs/year; publishes 1 new songwriter/year. Pays standard royalty.
How to Contact: Submit demo tape and lyric and lead sheet. Prefers 7½ ips reel-to-reel or cassette with 3-5 songs on demo. SASE. Reports in 1 month.
Music: C&W, gospel, progressive country and R&B. Recently published "A Snowman for Christmas" (by George Leger), recorded by G. Leger/Sunset Records (country/Christmas).

COUNTRY STAR MUSIC, 439 Wiley Ave., Franklin PA 16323. (814)432-4633. Affiliates: Kelly Music Publications (BMI) and Process Music Publications (BMI). President: Norman Kelly. Music publisher and record company. ASCAP. Publishes 20-25 songs/year; publishes 15 new songwriters/year. Pays standard royalty.
How to Contact: Submit demo tape and lyric sheet. Prefers 7½ ips reel-to-reel or cassette with 1-4 songs on demo. SASE. Reports in 2 weeks.
Music: Bluegrass, C&W, easy listening, folk, gospel, MOR and top 40/pop. Recently published "Hand Him Down to Me" (by Grady Daugherty), recorded by Junie Lou/Starship Records (country); "My Blue Velvet Lady" (by N. Runkles/V. Brown), recorded by Virge Brown/Country Star Records (MOR); and "Everybody Needs A Teddy Bear" (by Royce, Lynch and Durso), recorded by Debbie Sue/Country Star Records (country).
Tips: "Send only your best songs—ones you feel are equal to or better than current hits."

COURT OF KINGS MUSIC, 1300 Division St., Suite 103, Nashville TN 37203. (615)244-7116. Affiliate: Faron Young Music (ASCAP). Music publisher and booking agency. BMI. President: Billy Deaton. Manager of Material: Dave Hall.
How to Contact: Submit demo tape and lyric sheet. Prefers 7½ ips reel-to-reel with 2-4 songs on demo. "Do not send only copy of song or material." SASE. Reports in 3 weeks.
Music: Bluegrass; church/religious; C&W and MOR.

COUSINS MUSIC, 211 Birchwood Ave., Upper Nyack NY 10960. (914)358-0861. Affiliate: Neems (ASCAP). President: Lou Cicchetti. Music publisher and record producer. BMI. Publishes 5-10 songs/year; publishes 6 new songwriters/year. Pays standard royalty.
How to Contact: Submit demo tape and lyric sheet. Prefers 7½ or 15 ips reel-to-reel or cassette with any number of songs on demo. SASE. Reports in 2 weeks.
Music: C&W and rock. Recently published "Barbara-Ann" (by F. Fassert), recorded by the Regents, Jan & Dean, the Beach Boys, etc. (rock); and "Your Honor" (by J.O. Daniel), recorded by Koko/West Side Records (country).
Tips: "Most artists are writing their own material and most labels will not entertain new ideas or material from new writers. You must somehow get label attention. We do this with a good professional demo produced by us and circulated among the few creative producers and A&R people still seeking new talent."

COVERED BRIDGE MUSIC, 615 Durrett Dr., Nashville TN 37211. (615)833-1457. Affiliates: Town Square (SESAC) and Iron Skillet (ASCAP). General Manager: Bill Wence. Music publisher. BMI.
How to Contact: Submit demo tape and lyric sheet. Prefers 7½ ips reel-to-reel with maximum 2 songs on demo. SASE. Reports in 2 weeks. "Send us your best song. Use a quality, clear tape. Don't bother sending 10 or 15 songs on one tape."
Music: C&W, easy listening, MOR and progressive. Recently published "Marriage on the Rocks"

(by Carl Struck), recorded by Carl Struck/Rustic Records (country); "Quicksand" and "I Wanna Do It Again" (by Bill Wence), recorded by Bill Wence (country).

CRAZY CAJUN MUSIC, INC., 5626 Brock St., Houston TX 77023. (713)926-4431. Affiliate: Swamp (ASCAP). Contact: Huey P. Meaux. Music publisher, record producer and record company. BMI. Pays standard royalty.
How to Contact: Write first about your interest, then submit demo tape and lyric sheet or arrange personal interview to play demo tape. Prefers cassette with 1-4 songs on demo. SASE. Reports in 1 month.
Music: Blues, C&W crossover, disco, easy listening, folk, gospel, MOR, progressive, R&B, rock, soul and top 40/pop. Recently published "The Rains Came" recorded by Freddie Fender/ABC Records (country pop).

CREAM PUBLISHING GROUP, 8025 Melrose Ave., Los Angeles CA 90046. (213)655-0944. Affiliates: East Memphis Music Corp. (BMI), Butter Music (BMI), Deerwood Music (BMI), Birdees Music (ASCAP), Churn Music (ASCAP), JEC Publishing (BMI), and FI Music (ASCAP). Professional Manager/Staff Song Writer: Marty Sadler. Music publisher. BMI and ASCAP. Member NMPA. Publishes 150 songs/year; publishes 50 new songwriters/year. Pays standard royalty. Sometimes secures songwriters on salary basis. Catalogs 4,000 songs/year.
How to Contact: Submit demo tape and lyric sheet. Prefers cassette with maximum 4 songs on demo. "Include lyrics and as much information as possible and songs that could be done by more than 2 artists." SASE. Reports in 1 week.
Music: Bluegrass, blues, church/religious, C&W, disco, easy listening, folk, gospel, jazz, MOR, progressive, R&B, rock (hard and soft) and top 40/pop. Recently published "Knock on Wood" (by Eddie Floyd), recorded by Amy Steward/Arista Records (disco); "Soul Man" (by Hayes & Porter), recorded by Blues Brothers/Atlantic Records (R&B); "I Just Can't Stand Up From Falling Down" by (Homer Banks), recorded by Elvis Costello (rock); "Who's Making Love" (by H. Banks, C. Davis and R. Jackson), recorded by Blues Bros./Atlantic Records (R&B); "I Can't Turn You Loose" (by Otis Redding), recorded by Aretha Franklin/Arista Records (R&B); and "Take Me to the River" (by Al Green), recorded by Mabon Hodges/Capitol Records (country rock).

CREATIVE CORPS, 6607 W. Sunset, Suite E, Hollywood CA 90028. (213)462-6164. Affiliates: Driving Music (ASCAP) and Visual Songs (BMI). President: Kurt Hunter. Music publisher and record producer. BMI and ASCAP. Publishes 20 songs/year. Pays standard royalty.
How to Contact: Call or write first about your interest or submit demo tape and lyric sheet. Prefers cassette with 1-5 songs on demo tape. SASE. Reports in 4 months.
Music: C&W (with cross-over potential), R&B, rock, soul and top 40/pop. Recently published "Come and Love Me" (by N. Mezey), recorded by Dandy/Warner Curb Records (country); "Dancin' Wheels" (by N. Mezey, R. Pollack and L. Keen), recorded on Columbia House Records (disco); and "N.O.L.A." (by J. Selk and A. Del Zoppo), recorded by Chuck Francour/EMI Records (rock).
Tips: "Songs must be creative with strong hook-chorus."

CRIMSON DYNASTY, Crimson Dynasty Record Corp., Box 271, Jenkintown PA 19046. President: Stan Peahota. Music publisher, record company and recording studio. ASCAP. Publishes 18-20 songs/year; publishes 4 new songwriters/year. Offers cash advance against royalty. Sometimes hires staff writers.
How to Contact: Submit demo tape and lead sheet. Include photo and resume. Prefers 7½ ips reel-to-reel, cassette, 8-track cartridge or disc. SASE. Reports in 3 weeks.
Music: Blues; C&W; easy listening and novelty.
Tips: "All submissions will be reviewed. We are looking for songs that Muhammad Ali, Frank Sinatra or the Beatles would sing if they were to listen to them. That is the style we want."

CRITERION MUSIC CORP., 6124 Selma Ave., Hollywood CA 90028. Affiliates: Granite Music (ASCAP) and Atlantic Music (BMI). Contact: Professional Manager. Music publisher. ASCAP. Member NMPA, AIMP and CMA. Publishes 75 songs/year; publishes 10 new songwriters/year. Pays standard royalty.
How to Contact: Submit demo tape and lead sheet. Prefers cassette with 1-2 songs on demo. SASE. Reports in 3 weeks.
Music: MOR, progressive, rock, soul, country and top 40/pop. Recently published "My Old Pals," (by Richard Stekol), recorded by Kim Carnes/EMI Records (pop/top 40); "Seven Year Ache," (by Rosanne Cash), recorded by Rosanne Cash/Columbia Records (country/top 40); "Ain't No Money," (by Rodney Crowell), recorded by Rodney Crowell/Warner Brothers Records (top 40);

and "When the Feelin' Comes Around," (by Rick Cunha), recorded by Jennifer Warnes/Arista Records (top 40).

Tips: "Limit tape to 1 or 2 of your best songs that you feel can be placed with artists who do outside songs."

CRITIQUE MUSIC PUBLISHING CO., 100 Main St., Reading MA 01867. Affiliates: Carlwood Music (SESAC), Skys the Limit Music (SESAC) and Solid Smash Music (ASCAP). Contact: Professional Manager. Music publisher, record producer and promotion firm. BMI. Publishes 50 songs/year. Pays standard royalties.
How to Contact: Submit demo tape and lead or lyric sheet. Prefers cassette with 1-3 songs on demo. SASE. Reports in 3 weeks.
Music: C&W, disco, easy listening, MOR, rock and top 40/pop. Recently published "This Is Love" and "Draw the Line" (by R. Pinette), recorded by R. Pinette/Oak Mercury Records (top 40/pop); "Where Is the Woman" (by C. Harding), recorded by C. Harding/RSO Records (top 40/pop).

THE EDDIE CROOK COMPANY, Box 213, Hendersonville TN 37075. (615)822-1360. Affiliates: Chestnut Mound Music (BMI) and Pleasant View Music (ASCAP). Contact: Eddie Crook. Music publisher, record company and record producer. BMI and ASCAP. Publishes 10 songs/year; publishes 10 new songwriters/year. Pays standard royalty.
How to Contact: Submit demo tape and lyric sheet or arrange personal interview. Prefers cassette with 1-3 songs on demo. Does not return unsolicited material. Reports in 1 month.
Music: Gospel. Recently published "Someone Prayed For Me" (by Jerry Murphy), recorded by Happy Goodmans/Word Records; "The Anchor" (by Kyla Rowland), recorded by The Kingsmen/Heartwarming Records; and "He Wrote My Name" (by O.S. Davis), recorded by The Hemphills/Heartwarming Records (all gospel).

CUTA RUG MUSIC, Box 174, Seeley CA 92273. A&R Director: Jimmie Doyle. Music publisher. BMI. Pays standard royalty.
How to Contact: Submit demo tape and lead sheet with personal resume and photo. "Interview will be requested if material is accepted." Specializing in female writers and material. "We have contacts nationally with artists and producers. SASE. Reports in 2 weeks.
Music: C&W, country rock, blues, folk, gospel and bluegrass. Recently published "One More Night with You," recorded by Jimmie Doyle.

V&M CUTLER MUSIC CO., Box 43, Chatsworth CA 91311. (213)886-7746. Manager: Max Cutler. Music publisher. ASCAP. Publishes 7 songs/year; publishes 2 new songwriters/year. Pays standard royalty.
How to Contact: Write first about your interest. Prefers cassette and lead and lyric sheet with 3-5 songs on demo. "Keep voice up and lyrics clear." SASE. Reports in 3 weeks.
Music: Blues, easy listening, MOR, R&B and top 40/pop. Recently published "In Harmony" (by Max Cutler and Victoria-Diane Cutler), recorded by Victoria-Diane Cutler (MOR); and "Only Music" and "Heart of Gold" (by Max Cutler and Victoria-Diane Cutler), recorded by Victoria-Diane Cutler (top 40/pop).

DALSTAR PUBLISHING, 7812 5th St. SW, Calgary, Alberta, Canada T2V 1B9. (403)253-6892. Affiliate: Wild Rose Publishing. Manager: Dave Stark. Music publisher and general recording studio. Estab. 1980. BMI, CAPAC and PROCAN. Member AES. Pays standard royalty.
How to Contact: Submit demo tape and lyric sheet. Prefers cassette with 2-5 songs on demo. Include brief resume. "Make sure lyric and melody lines are clear on the tape." SAE and International Reply Coupons. Reports in 1 month.
Music: Blues, C&W, dance-oriented, easy listening, folk, jazz, MOR, R&B, rock (soft and country), soul, top 40/pop and synthesizer.

DANA PUBLISHING CO., 824 83rd St., Miami Beach FL 33141. (305)865-8960. President: Walter Dana. Music publisher, record company and record producer. BMI. Pays standard royalty.
How to Contact: Write first about your interest. Prefers 7½ or 15 ips reel-to-reel or cassette. SASE.
Music: Classical and Polish.

DANBORO PUBLISHING CO., Box 2199, Vancouver, British Columbia, Canada V6B 3V7. (604)688-1820. Affiliate: Synchron Publishing (CAPAC). President: John Rodney. Music publisher and record company. BMI. Publishes 25-35 songs/year. Pays standard royalties.

How to Contact: Submit demo tape. Prefers 7½ ips reel-to-reel with 2-6 songs on demo. "Be selective. Send only the best songs. Identify tapes fully." SAE and International Reply Coupons. Reports in 1 month.
Music: C&W, easy listening, MOR, rock and top 40/pop. Recently published "Do It," recorded by Jud Paynter (top 40); "I'm a Yo-Yo," recorded by K Country (C&W); and "Confronto," recorded by Frederico.

JOHN DANIELS PUBLISHING CO., (formerly John Harvey Publishing Co.), Box 245, Encinal TX 78019. President: John Daniels. Music publisher and record producer. BMI. Publishes 12 songs/year; publishes 2 new songwriters/year. Pays standard royalty.
How to Contact: Submit demo tape and lyric sheet. Prefers cassette with 2-6 songs on demo. Include brief resume. Does not return unsolicited material. Reports in 1 month.
Music: Children's, easy listening, folk and Latin. Recently published "Had I Known" (by Oran Medellin), recorded by Oran Medellin/JEH Records (easy listening); and "Another Time" (by John Harvey), recorded by Johnny Gonzalez/CBS Records (country).

DANTE MUSIC, INC., 311 W. 57th St., New York NY 10019. (212)765-8200. Affiliates: Da Doo Ron Ron Music, Inc. (ASCAP). Vice President/A&R: Geoff Howe. Music publisher and record producer. BMI and ASCAP. Publishes 3 new songwriters/year. Hires staff writers; pays advance and weekly salary.
How to Contact: Submit demo tape and lyric sheet. Prefers cassette with 1-4 songs on demo. SASE. Reports in 1 month.
Music: Easy listening, MOR, R&B, rock (soft and hard) and top 40/pop. Recently published "Just a Little Love" (by J. Jolis, K. Disimone and B. Martin), recorded by The Dells/20th Century Fox Records (R&B ballad).

IKE DARBY PUBLISHING, 255 Dauphin St., Mobile AL 36602. (205)432-9113. Contact: Ike Darby. Music publisher, record company and record producer. Estab. 1979. BMI. Publishes 20 new songs/year; publishes 5 new songwriters/year. Pays standard royalty.
How to Contact: Write first about your interest, then submit demo tape and lyric sheet or arrange personal interview. Prefers cassette with 2-4 songs on demo. "Songs should have strong lyrics and tell a story." SASE. Reports in 1 month.
Music: Blues, gospel, R&B and soul. Recently published "Blues In My Bedroom" (by Ike Darby), recorded by Lynn White/Ala-Miss Records (slow blues); "I Got Some News For You" (by Ike Darby), recorded by Lynn White/Darby Records (slow blues); "I Don't Wanna See Your Face" (by Ike Darby), recorded by Lynn White/Darby Records (slow blues); and "Star Fire Lady" (by Tony Warren), recorded by Young Generation/Ala-Miss Records (ballad).
Tips: "Songwriters should always write about life and the things that go on in life between man and woman or best friends."

DAVIKE MUSIC CO., Box 8842, Los Angeles CA 90008. (213)292-5138. Contact: Isaiah Jones. Music publisher. ASCAP. Publishes 5 songs/year; publishes 1 new songwriter/year. Pays standard royalty.
How to Contact: Query first, submit demo tape and lyric sheet or arrange personal interview to play demo tape. Prefers 7½ ips reel-to-reel or cassette. SASE. Reports in 1 month.
Music: Blues; choral; church/religious; disco; easy listening; folk; gospel; MOR; R&B; soul; and top 40/pop. Recently published "Abundant Life" (by Isaiah Jones and J. Hailey), recorded by Mighty Clouds of Joy/Epic Records (gospel); and "Keep Me in Your Care" and "God Has Smiled on Me" (by I. Jones), recorded by James Cleveland/Savoy Records (gospel).

DAWN TREADER MUSIC, 2223 Strawberry, Pasadena TX 77502. (713)472-5563. Affiliates: Shepherd's Fold Music (BMI), Straightway Music (ASCAP) and Dawn Treader Music (SESAC). President: Darrell A. Harris. Music publisher. Publishes 100 songs/year. Pays standard royalty.
How to Contact: Submit demo tape and lyric sheet. Prefers 7½ ips reel-to-reel and cassette with 3 songs maximum on demo. "We would like as much background information as possible on the writer and his or her musical activities." SASE. Reports in 1 month.
Music: Contemporary gospel; and top 40/pop. "We are looking for well-constructed songs with a solid Christian lyrical content." Recently published "Why Should the Father Bother?" (by Bob Hartman), recorded by Petra/Star Song Records (contemporary gospel); "Jubilee" (by Fletch Wiley), recorded by Fletch Wiley/Star Song Records (gospel jazz); and "When I Think of You" (by James Williams), recorded by Leif Garrett/Scotti Brothers Records (top 40).

DEB DAVE MUSIC, Box 2154, Nashville TN 37214. (615)320-7227. Manager: Keni Wehrman. Music publisher. BMI. Pays standard royalty.

How to Contact: Write first about your interest. Prefers 7½ ips reel-to-reel with 2 songs on demo. SASE. Reports in 1 month.
Music: Country, easy listening, MOR, rock and top 40/pop.

DELIGHTFUL MUSIC LTD., 1733 Broadway, New York NY 10019. (212)757-6770. Affiliate: Double F Music (ASCAP). Vice-President: Martin Feig. Music publisher and record company. BMI. Hires staff writers. Pays standard royalty.
How to Contact: Submit demo tape and lyric sheet. Prefers cassette as demo. SASE. Reports in 2 months.
Music: R&B and top 40/pop. Recently published "Celebration" (by George Brown), recorded by Kool & The Gang (R&B/pop).

LOU DeLISE PRODUCTIONS, 1230 Mermaid Ln., Philadelphia PA 19118. (215)248-1683. Music Director: Lou DeLise. General Manager: John Tschorn. Music publisher and record producer. BMI. Publishes 12 songs/year. Pays standard royalty.
How to Contact: Submit demo tape and lyric sheet. Prefers cassette with 1-3 songs on demo. SASE. Reports in 1 month.
Music: C&W; dance; MOR; rock; R&B; and top 40/pop. Recently recorded "Figures Can't Calculate" (by William DeVaughn).

DENTURE WHISTLE MUSIC, 2 E. Oak St., Chicago IL 60611. (312)951-0246. Affiliate: Substantial Publishing (ASCAP). Contact: Donn Marier. Music publisher and record producer. BMI. Member NMPA and NARAS. Publishes 20-30 songs/year; publishes 3 new songwriters/year. Pays standard royalty.
How to Contact: Submit demo tape and lyric sheet. Prefers 7½ reel-to-reel or cassette with 3-6 songs on demo. SASE. Reports in 3 weeks.
Music: Children's, classical (special arrangements), C&W, jazz, MOR, progressive, R&B (soul), rock and top 40/pop. Recently published "Lady, Lady, Lady" (by Marier & Marier), recorded by Boogie Man Orchestra/Boogie Man Records (instrumental dance tune); "I Like You" and "You're So Cool" (by D.J. Marier), recorded by Citizen/Ovation Records (rock pop).
Tips: "Songs should be easy to listen to and in best possible form. Include name of artist you think material is best suited for."

DERBY MUSIC, Las Vegas Recording Studio, 3977 Vegas Valley Dr., Las Vegas NV 89121. (702)457-4365. President: Hank Castro. Affiliates: Ru-Dot-To Music (BMI), She-La-La Music (SESAC) and Hankeychip Music (ASCAP). Music publisher and recording studio. (She-La-La Music/SESAC). Publishes 10-20 songs/year; publishes 4-5 new songwriters/year.
Music: Bluegrass; blues; C&W; easy listening; gospel; jazz; MOR; progressive; R&B; rock; soul; and top 40/pop. Recently published "Right in the Middle of Forever" (by Ron Fuller), recorded on ECR Records (country disco).

DEUEL-HART PUBLISHING, 441 S. Beverly Dr., #6, Beverly Hills CA 90212. (213)855-0525. Affiliate: Angelstream Music (ASCAP). Professional Manager: Kent Washburn. Music publisher, record company and record producer. BMI. Publishes 50 songs/year; publishes 2 new songwriters/year. Hires staff writers; pays $200-500/month advance against royalties. Pays standard royalty.
How to Contact: Submit demo tape and lyric sheet. Prefers cassette with 3-5 songs on demo. SASE. Reports in 1 month.
Music: Children's, church/religious, C&W, gospel, MOR, R&B, rock and top 40/pop. Recently published "Jesus Revive Me" (by Randy Matthews), recorded by R. Matthews (rock/gospel); "Sonlight Fell on Me" (by Alan Moore), recorded by Albrecht, Roley and Moore (MOR/gospel); and "Resurrection" (by Terry Lupton), recorded by Paul D. Davis (rock/gospel).

DIAMOND IN THE ROUGH MUSIC, 1440 Kearny St. NE, Washington DC 20017. (202)635-0464. Vice President A&R: Rodney Brown. Music publisher, record company and record producer. BMI. Publishes 50 songs/year. Pays standard royalties.
How to Contact: Submit demo tape. Prefers 7½ ips reel-to-reel or cassette with 2-4 songs on demo. SASE. Reports in 1 month.
Music: Disco; R&B; and soul. Recently published "You've Got What It Takes" (by Rodney Brown), recorded by Bobby Thurston (disco).

DIAMONDBACK MUSIC, 10 Waterville St., San Francisco CA 94124. Administrator: Joseph Buchwald. Music publisher. BMI. Pays standard royalty.

How to Contact: Submit demo tape and lead sheet. Prefers cassette with 3-6 songs on demo. SASE. Reports "as soon as possible."
Music: Rock; ballads; blues; jazz; and country. Recently published "Miracles" (by Balen); "Count on Me" (by Barish); and "Runaway" (by Dewey), all recorded by Balen/RCA Records.

DIGBY GAP MUSIC, 398 Coorington St., Barrie, Ontario, Canada. (705)728-1105. Affiliate: Sandy Beach Music (CAPAC). President: Brent Williams. Music publisher. PROCAN.
How to Contact: Submit demo tape and lyric sheet. Prefers cassette with 2-6 songs on demo. SAE and International Reply Coupons. Reports in 2 weeks.
Music: C&W, dance-oriented, MOR and top 40/pop.

B.L. DIXON PUBLISHING, 7212 S. Wabash Ave., Chicago IL 60619. (312)783-3186. A&R Director: B.L. Dixon. Music publisher and record company. BMI. Pays standard royalty.
How to Contact: Submit demo tape or submit demo tape and lead and lyric sheet. Prefers 7½ ips reel-to-reel with 2-3 songs on demo. SASE. Reports in 2 weeks.
Music: Blues; disco; easy listening; MOR; rock; soul; and top 40/pop.

HUGH DIXON MUSIC, INC., 292 Lorraine Dr., Montreal/Baie d'Urfe, Quebec, Canada H9X 2R1. (514)457-5959. Affiliates: Dicap Music (CAPAC) and Dipro Music (PROCAN). President: Hugh D. Dixon. Executive Assistant: C.M.A. van Ogtrop. Music publisher, record company and recording studio. Pays standard royalty.
How to Contact: Submit demo tape and lyric sheet. Prefers cassette with 2-5 songs on demo. SAE and International Reply Coupons. Acknowledgement upon receipt. Reports in 1 month.
Music: "Inspirational, uplifting, introspective, cosmic, gospel, spiritual, philosophical, metaphysical lyrics that can be marketed in a country/soft rock or avant-garde/futuristic format." Also producers/distributors of spoken word and meditation environment recordings.

DO SOL PUBLISHING, Box 2262, Dorval, Quebec, Canada H9S 5J4. (514)631-9384. Professional Manager: Robert Salagan. Music publisher and cassette producer. PROCAN. Publishes 40 songs/year; publishes 10 new songwriters/year. Pays standard royalty.
How to Contact: Submit demo tape and lyric sheet. Prefers 7½ ips reel-to-reel with 3-7 songs on demo. "Make purpose of communication clear and fog-free." SAE and International Reply Coupons. Reports in 1 month.
Music: C&W, easy listening, folk, MOR and top 40/pop. Recently published "Hey Lord!" (by Richards and Tyler), recorded by Bonny Richards/A&M Records (MOR); "One Day" (by A. DeSouza), recorded by Alan Jones/George Records (top 40/pop); and "Come Forth" (by J. Clement), recorded by Please/George Records (folk).

DOBRO PUBLISHING CO., Rt. 1, Box 49, Utica NY 13502. (315)724-0895. Manager: Floyd Ketchum. Music publisher, record company and record producer. BMI. Publishes 5 songs/year; publishes 3 new songwriters/year. Pays standard royalty.
How to Contact: Submit demo tape and lyric sheet. Prefers 7½ and 3¼ ips reel-to-reel, 8-track or cassette with songs on demo. SASE. Reports in 1 month.
Music: Bluegrass, children's, church/religious, C&W and gospel. Recently published "Sing Me a Song of the Cowboy," recorded by Marlo and Slim (western); "The Girl of the Pines Waltz," recorded by The Country Brothers (waltz); and "Lets Come Back to the Bible" (gospel).

DOC DICK ENTERPRISES, 16 E. Broad St., Mt. Vernon NY 10552. (914)668-4488. President: Richard Rashbaum. Music publisher and management firm. BMI. Publishes 5 songs/year. Pays standard royalties.
How to Contact: Query, submit demo tape, submit demo tape and lead sheet, submit acetate disc, or submit acetate disc and lead sheet. Prefers cassette with 1-4 songs on demo. SASE. Reports in 2 weeks.
Music: Disco; R&B; soul; and top 40/pop. Recently published "In the Pocket," "Sweet Love," "Fancy Dancer" and "Pick Me Up" (by Joe LaFragola); "Everybody Get Off" and "Romance at a Disco" (by Ken Simmons and Robert Stasiak); and "Music Moves Me" (by Simmons), all recorded by Daybreak/Prelude Records.

DON-DEL MUSIC/DON-DE MUSIC, 15041 Wabash Ave., S. Holland IL 60473. (312)339-0307. President: Donald De Lucia. Music publisher, record producer and record company. BMI and ASCAP. Pays standard royalty.
How to Contact: Submit demo tape and lyric sheet. Prefers 7½ ips reel-to-reel with 4-6 songs on demo. SASE. Reports in 1 week.
Music: C&W; rock; and top 40/pop.

DONNA MARIE MUSIC, c/o American Creative Entertainment Ltd., 1616 Pacific Ave., Suite 817, Atlantic City NJ 08401. (609)348-1809. Vice Presidents: Danny Luciano and Tony Angelo. Music publisher, record company and record producer. ASCAP. Publishes 6 songs/year; publishes 3 new songwriters/year. Pays standard royalty.
How to Contact: Submit demo tape and lyric sheet. Prefers 7½ reel-to-reel or cassette with 4-8 songs on demo. "No 8-tracks." SASE. Reports in 6 weeks.
Music: MOR, R&B, rock, soul and top 40/pop.

DONNA MUSIC PUBLISHING CO., Box 113, Woburn MA 01801. (617)933-1474. General Manager: Frank Paul. Music publisher, record company, record producer, management firm and booking agency. BMI. Publishes 50-75 songs/year. Pays standard royalties.
How to Contact: Submit demo tape and lead sheet. Prefers cassette with 3-6 songs on demo. "We will listen to tapes but will not return material. If we believe a song has potential, we will contact the songwriter." Reports in 1 month.
Music: C&W; easy listening; gospel; MOR; R&B; rock; soul; and top 40/pop. Recently published "Happy Happy Birthday Baby," recorded by Mango Sylvia and Gilbert Lopez/Casa Grande Records (R&B).

DOOMS MUSIC PUBLISHING CO., Box 2072, Waynesboro VA 22980. (703)942-0106. Owners: John Major, Margie Major. Music publisher and record company. BMI. Pays on royalty basis.
How to Contact: Submit demo tape. Prefers cassette. SASE. Reports in 3 weeks.
Music: Bluegrass; C&W; easy listening; gospel; and MOR. Recently published "So Good to be Loved" (by James Melvin), recorded by J. Melvin (country).

DOOR KNOB MUSIC PUBLISHING, INC., 2125 8th Ave. S., Nashville TN 37204. (615)383-6002. Affiliates: Chip 'N' Dale Music Publishers, Inc (ASCAP); and Lodestar Music (SESAC). President: Gene Kennedy. Vice President: Karen Jeglum. Music publisher, record company and record producer. BMI. Member NSAI, CMA and ACM. Publishes 200 songs/year; publishes 100 new songwriters/year. Pays standard royalty.
How to Contact: Submit demo tape and lyric sheet or arrange personal interview. Prefers 7½ ips reel-to-reel or cassette with 1-4 songs on demo. SASE. Reports in 6 weeks.
Music: C&W and MOR. Recently published "River of Love" (by Maxine Kelton/Elaine Vinson), recorded by Ernie Ashworth and Judy Sider/O'Brien Records (modern country); "When a Woman Cries" (by Betty Duke and Sammy Lyons), recorded by David Rogers/Republic Records (modern country); and "If I Could Set My Love to Music" (by Dave Hall), recorded by Jerry Wallace/Door Knob Records (modern country).

BUSTER DOSS MUSIC, Box 312, Estill Springs TN 37330. (615)649-2158. Affiliates: Little Mike Music (SESAC) and Barbara Ann Music (ASCAP). President: Buster Doss. Vice President: Bo Doss. Music publisher, record producer, record company and booking agency. BMI. Publishes 200 songs/year; publishes 10 new songwriters/year. Pays standard royalty.
How to Contact: Submit demo tape and lyric sheet or arrange personal interview to play demo tape. Prefers cassette with 2-4 songs on demo tape. SASE. Reports in 1 week.
Music: Bluegrass, church/religious, C&W, easy listening, folk, gospel, MOR, progressive, and rock. Recently published "Hanging onto a Lie" (by Larry Franklin), recorded by Cooder Browne/Lonestar Records; "Texas," recorded by Rusty Adams/Stardust Records; "I'm Not Wanted Any More" (by Larry Butler), recorded by Larry Butler/Stardust Records; "Lying Again," recorded by Jack and Randy/Stardust Records; "Love Stories Tonite," recorded by Billy Walker/Tall Texan Records.

DOVETAIL PUBLISHING CO., Box 2802, Corpus Christi TX 78403. Contact: John Davis. Record company, music publisher, record producer, management firm and booking agency. BMI. Publishes 3-5 songs/year; publishes 1-5 new songwriters/year. Pays standard royalties.
How To Contact: Submit demo tape. Prefers 7½ ips reel-to-reel or cassette with 2-5 songs on demo. Does not return unsolicited material. Reports in 2 weeks.
Music: Recently published "Old Red Rose" and "Cheatin' Street" (by Jay Vest and P. Stewart), recorded by Vest/Ram Records; and El Capitan (by J. Davis), recorded by the Gary Davis Band/Ram Records.

DRAGON FLY MUSIC, 219 Meriden Rd., Waterbury CT 06705. (203)754-3674. Owner: Ralph Calabrese. Music publisher and record producer. BMI. Publishes 4 songs/year; publishes 2 new songwriters/year. Pays standard royalties.

How to Contact: Submit demo tape or demo tape and lead sheet. Prefers 7½ ips reel-to-reel with 3-6 songs on demo. SASE. Reports in 1 month.
Music: Disco; rock; soul; and top 40/pop. Recently published "Don't Want to Live Without You," "My Baby's Gone" and "Bad, Bad Girl" (by R. Calabrese), recorded on ABC Records; and "Going Nowhere Fast" (by R. Calabrese), recorded on London Records (top 40/pop).

DRAGON INTERNATIONAL MUSIC, Box 8263, Haledon NJ 07508. (201)942-6810. President: Samuel Cummings. Music publisher, record producer and record company. BMI. Publishes 4 songs/year; 5 new songwriters/year.
How to Contact: Query. Prefers 7½ ips reel-to-reel or cassette with 3-5 songs on demo. SASE. Reports in 1 month.
Music: Reggae and soul. Recently published "Being a Woman" (by Sam Cummings and Rudolph Richards), recorded by Yolanda Brown/April Records (disco); "Disco Fever" (by Clive Waugh and S. Cummings), recorded by Rhonda Durand/April Records (disco); and "Best Time of My Life" (by Paul Davidson), recorded by Davidson/April Records (easy listening).

DUANE MUSIC, INC., 382 Clarence Ave., Sunnydale CA 94086. (408)739-6133. Affiliate: Morhits Publishing (BMI). President: Garrie Thompson. Music publisher. BMI. Publishes 16 songs/year; publishes 4 new songwriters/year. Pays standard royalty.
How to Contact: Submit demo tape and lead sheet. Prefers 7½ ips reel-to-reel or cassette with 1-4 songs on demo. SASE. Reports in 1 month.
Music: Blues; C&W; disco; easy listening; rock; soul; and top 40/pop. Recently published "Little Girl," recorded by Ban (rock); "Warm Tender Love," recorded by Percy Sledge (soul); and "My Adorable One," recorded by Joe Simon (blues).

E.L.J. RECORD CO., 1344 Waldron, St. Louis MO 63130. (314)803-3605. President: Eddie Johnson. Vice President: William Johnson. Music publisher and record company. BMI. Publishes 8-10 songs/year. Pays 5-10% royalty.
How to Contact: Submit demo tape or submit demo tape and lead sheet. Prefers 7½ ips reel-to-reel or cassette with 4 songs on demo. SASE. Reports in 2 weeks.
Music: Blues; easy listening; soul; and top 40/pop. Recently published "Take Me Back Baby," recorded by Joe Buckner (blues); "Who Am I?" and "You Got Me," recorded by Tab Smith (top 40/pop); and "Rocks in Your Pillow" and "When the Light of the Candle" (by Bill Shank), recorded by Bobby Scott (R&B).

E&M PUBLISHING CO., 2674 Steele, Memphis TN 38127. (901)357-0064. Music Director: Patti Frith. Music publisher, record company and record producer. BMI. Publishes 10 songs/year. Pays standard royalties.
How to Contact: Submit demo tape. Prefers 7½ ips reel-to-reel or cassette with 4 songs on demo. "Be sure the words are clear. Don't try to make a master, just a good clean tape." Reports in 2 weeks.
Music: Blues; church/religious; C&W; easy listening; progressive; and R&B. Recently published "It's a Little More like Heaven" (by Hoyt Johnson and Jim Atkins), recorded by Hank Lockin/Sun Records (country); "Queen of New Orleans" (by Danny Williams), recorded by Williams/Zone Records (country); and "Baby You Don't Know Me Anymore" (by J. Pullman), recorded by Pullman/Zone Records (country).

EARLY BIRD MUSIC, Waltner Enterprises, 14702 Canterbury, Tustin CA 92680. (714)731-2981. Owner/President: Steve Waltner. Music publisher and record company. BMI. Publishes 10 songs/year. Pays standard royalty.
How to Contact: Submit demo tape and lead sheet. Prefers 7½ ips reel-to-reel or cassette with 2-4 songs on demo. SASE. Reports in 3 weeks.
Music: C&W; easy listening; MOR; and top 40/pop.

EARTH AND SKY MUSIC PUBLISHING, INC., Box 4157, Winter Park FL 32793. President: Ernest Hatton. Music publisher. BMI. Publishes about 100 songs/year; publishes 15 new songwriters/year. Pays standard royalty.
How to Contact: Write first about your interest or submit demo tape and lyric sheet. Prefers 7½ reel-to-reel with 1-3 songs on demo. "We're looking for a very good demo recording with proof of copyright and lead sheet." SASE. Reports in 1 month.
Music: Bluegrass, church/religious, C&W, easy listening, jazz, MOR, progressive, R&B, rock and top 40/pop. Recently published "Seasons" (by Hatton/Hurley), recorded by Sandy Contella/EMI Records (easy listening); "Reflections" (by Hatton/Hurley), recorded by Jim Carling/Earth and Sky Records (easy listening); and "Blue Eyes" (by Kubik/Gaworecki), recorded by Trans Atlantique/Earth and Sky Records (mellow rock).

EARTHSCREAM MUSIC PUBLISHING CO., 2036 Pasket, Suite A, Houston TX 77092. (713)688-8067. Contact: Jeff Johnson. Music publisher, record company and record producer. BMI. Publishes 15-25 songs/year. Pays standard royalties.
How to Contact: Submit demo tape and lyric sheet. Prefers cassette with 2-5 songs on demo. SASE. Reports in 1 month.
Music: Blues; rock; and top 40/pop. Recently published "Teardrops Are Falling" (by Sammy Van Ness III), recorded by Van Ness (country); "Maybe Tonight" (by Watson & Sabo), recorded by Haskell Watson (rock); "It Grows on Trees" (by Scottfree-Wheels), recorded by The Rakes (new-wave); "After the Dances" (by Fridkin-Sheik), recorded by Paula Fridkin (country/pop); "I'm So Glad I Found You" (by Pete Reed), recorded by Reed (pop); "Happy Feet" (by Nicosia-Pennington), recorded by Dragon Lady (disco); "Leavin' for L.A." (by Pennington-Wells), recorded by Tempest (rock); and "Let's Get Drunk & Be Someone Tonight" (by Pennington-Wells), recorded by Issac Payton Sweat (country).

EASTEX MUSIC, 8537 Sunset Blvd., #2, Los Angeles CA 90069. (213)657-8852. Owner: Travis Lehman. Music publisher and record producer. Pays standard royalty.
How to Contact: Submit demo tape. Prefers cassette. SASE. Reports in 3 weeks.
Music: C&W and rock 'n' roll.

EDEN MUSIC CORP., Box 325, Englewood NJ 07631. Contact: Clyde Otis. Music publisher, record company and record producer. BMI and ASCAP. Member AGAC, NMPA and The Harry Fox Agency. Publishes 50+ songs/year; publishes 5 new songwriters/year. Pays standard royalties.
How to Contact: Submit demo tape and lead sheet. Wants cassette with 1-2 songs on demo. SASE. Reports in 1 month. SASE.
Music: Blues; C&W; disco; R&B; rock; soul; and top 40/pop. "We demand the highest quality material." Recently published "What's A Matter Baby (Is It Hurtin' You?)," recorded by Ellen Foley/Columbia Records (R&R); "A Lovers Question," recorded by Jacky Ward/Mercury Records (pop/R&B); "Endlessly," recorded by Eddie Money/Columbia Records (pop/R&B); and "I'm Comin' Home to You," Arista Records (R&B).

DON EDGAR MUSIC, 2312 Jasper, Fort Worth TX 76106. (817)626-3448. Contact: Don or Darrell Edgar. Music publisher and sheet music jobber and retailer. BMI. Publishes 2-5 songs/year; publishes 1 new songwriter/year. Pays standard royalty. Sometimes employs songwriters on salary basis "for professional arrangement of accepted works for publication. Payment is made per song depending upon complexity and length. Professional arrangers are always needed for a variety of music."
How to Contact: Submit demo tape, lyric sheet and "legible" lead sheet if possible. Prefers cassette or 45 record with 1-4 songs on demo. "Submit no more than 4 compositions without further invitation." Reports "no later than 5 weeks with personal reply. Nothing is returned without SASE."
Music: Protestant church/religious; country; easy listening; gospel (especially quartet); progressive; R&B (Spanish OK); and top 40/pop. Recently recorded "Think of Him" (by Esther Hendrick), recorded by Chuck Wagon Gang/Columbia Records (gospel); "Without the Lord" (by John D. Montroy), recorded by Tinsley Trio/Triangle Records (religious); and "Fill Up My Glass" (by Jim Hulsey), recorded by Jim Hulsey/Chevell Records (country).

EDITEURS ASSOCIES, 2364 Sherbrooke St. E., Montreal, Quebec, Canada H2K 1E6. (514)526-2831. Affiliates: Crisch Music (PROCAN/SDE) and Notre Musique (CAPAC). Professional Manager: Andree Badeaux-Gosselin. Music publisher and record company. Estab. 1979. Publishes 100-150 songs/year; publishes 4 new songwriters/year. Pays standard royalty.
How to Contact: Submit demo tape and lyric sheet. Prefers 7½ ips reel-to-reel or cassette with 3-7 songs on demo. SAE and International Reply Coupons. Reports in 3 weeks.
Music: Easy listening, MOR (ballads), rock (country) and top 40/pop. Recently published "Tés Plus Une Star" (by C. Marzano), recorded by Claude Michel/Quatre Saisons Records (top 40/pop); "L'Amour Et Les Fleurs" (by B. Blanc), recorded by Bernard Blanc/Quatre Saisons Records (top 40/pop); and "Le Seducteur" (by S. Badeaux), recorded by Richard Guilbert/Fleur Records (MOR ballad).

EDITIONS NAHEJ, 5514 Isabella, Montreal, Quebec, Canada H3X 1R6. (514)487-0859. Affiliate: Editions Vallor (CAPAC). President: Jehan V. Valiquet. Music Publisher and record company. PROCAN. Publishes 25 songs/year; publishes 10 new songwriters/year. Pays standard royalty.
How to Contact: Submit demo tape and lyric sheet. Prefers cassette with 3 songs minimum on

demo. SAE and International Reply Coupons.
Music: Children's (French), MOR and top 40/pop.

EDUCATOR RECORDS INC., Box 490, Wayne PA 19087. Music Director/A&R: Bart Arntz. Music publisher, record company and management firm. BMI. Offers $25 advance on royalties.
How to Contact: Submit demo tape. Prefers 7½ ips reel-to-reel or cassette with 1-4 songs on demo. SASE. Reports in 3 weeks.
Music: Disco; soul; top 40/pop; and "strong instrumentals of all types."

EL CHICANO MUSIC, 20531 Plummer St., Chatsworth CA 91311. (213)998-0443. A&R Director: A. Sullivan. Music publisher, booking agency and record company. ASCAP.
How to Contact: Submit demo tape and lead sheet. Prefers 7½ ips reel-to-reel. SASE. Reports in 3 weeks.
Music: Bluegrass; blues; C&W; disco; easy listening; jazz; MOR; progressive; rock; soul; and top 40/pop. Recently published "Dancing Mama" (disco); "Just Cruisin' " (MOR); and "Ron Con-Con" (Latin rock).

EMANDELL TUNES, 10220 Glade Ave., Chatsworth CA 91311. (213)341-2264. Affiliates: Bal-Gard Music (SESAC), Ben-Lee Music (BMI), Jepacla Music (SESAC), Together We Stand (BMI), Clevetown Music (SESAC) and Jam Bull Music (BMI). President & Administrator: Leroy C. Lovett Jr. Music Publisher and record producer. Publishes 20 songs/year; publishes 3 new songwriters/year. Pays standard royalties.
How to Contact: Submit demo cassette and lead sheet (lyric sheet OK). Prefers cassette with 4-7 songs. Submit information about the group and the songwriter. SASE. Reports in 3 weeks.
Music: Religious; easy listening; and gospel. Recently published "The Comforter" and "Wonderful" (by Edwin Hawkins), recorded by the Edwin Hawkins Singers/Birthright Records (top 40/pop, gospel); "Taylor Made" (by Steve Hunt), recorded by Bobby Humphreys/Columbia Records (jazz); "I Love You" (by Ricky Womack), recorded by James Cleveland/Savoy Records (pop/gospel). "Somebody Somewhere Needs Prayer" (by Willie Neal Johnson), recorded by Gospel Key Notes/Nashboro Records (gospel); "Lord Please Hear My Plea" (by Jim Sim and Paul Smith), recorded by Together/Cread Records (gospel); and "Take a Moment in the Morning" (1980 American Song Festival winner by Corrine Porter), recorded by Faye Hill Knight/California Gold Records.

ENGLISH MOUNTAIN PUBLISHING CO., 332 N. Brinker Ave., Columbus OH 43204. (614)279-5251. Script Manager: Jetta Brown. Music publisher, record company, record producer, management firm and booking agency. BMI. Pays standard royalties.
How to Contact: Query, arrange personal interview, submit demo, submit demo tape and lead sheet, submit lead sheet, or arrange in-person audition. Prefers 7½ or 15 ips reel-to-reel or cassette. Does not return unsolicited material.
Music: Bluegrass; blues; church/religious; C&W; folk; gospel; MOR; and top 40/pop. Recently published "Way Back in West Virginia" and "Each Side of the River" (by Kae and Walt Cochran), recorded by W. Cochran/Holly Records (C&W); and "I Already Know" (by M. Cordle and W. Cochran), recorded by Cochran/Holly Records (C&W).

ENTERTAINMENT CO. MUSIC GROUP, 40 W. 57th St., New York NY 10019. (212)265-2600. Music publisher and record producer.
How to Contact: Submit demo tape and lyric sheet. Prefers cassette with maximum 1 song on demo. Does not return unsolicited material. Reports in 1-3 months.
Music: C&W; MOR; R&B; top 40/pop and new wave.

EUROPEAN AMERICAN MUSIC DISTRIBUTORS CORP., 195 Allwood Rd., Clifton NJ 07012. (201)777-2680. Affiliates: EAMC (ASCAP) and Helicon (BMI). Editor-in-Chief: Clifford Richter. Music publisher.
How to Contact: Write first about your interest. Prefers 7½ ips reel-to-reel or cassette. "Tape should be of high quality, well produced and well recorded." SASE.
Music: Choral, church/religious and classical. "We are strictly a classical music publisher, and are only interested in serious contemporary music, choral music (secular and sacred arrangements and original works), and collections that are useful to educators."

EVANSONGS, c/o E.S.P. Management, 1790 Broadway, New York NY 10019. (212)765-8450. Music publisher. ASCAP.
How to Contact: Call first about your interest. Prefers cassette as demo. SASE. Reports as soon as possible.
Music: Rock.

EXISTENTIAL MUSIC, Box 176, 118 5th St. SW, Taylorsville NC 28681. (704)632-4735. President: Harry Deal. Music publisher, record producer, record company and recording studio. BMI. Publishes 50 songs/year. Pays standard royalty.
How to Contact: Submit demo tape and lyric sheet or arrange personal interview to play demo tape. Prefers cassette with 2-3 songs on demo. SASE. Reports in 3-4 weeks.
Music: C&W; dance; folk; MOR; R&B; rock; soul; and top 40/pop. Recently published "I Still Love You" Atlantic Records and "Uh Huh" TK Records, recorded by Harry Deal and the Galaxies.

FAIRCHILD MUSIC PUBLISHING, 14300 Buena St., SP-191, Garden Grove CA 92643. (714)554-0851. Contact: Jerry Wood. Music publisher. BMI. Publishes 6-10 songs/year. Pays standard royalty.
How to Contact: Submit demo tape and lyric sheet. Prefers 7½ ips reel-to-reel or cassette with 1-4 songs on demo. SASE. Reports in 2 weeks.
Music: C&W; easy listening; and MOR. Recently published "Many Are the Colors" and "I Won't Be There" (by Roy Dee), recorded by Roy Dee/Tribal Records (country); "99 Years" (by Ron Hayden), recorded by Ron Hayden/Tribal Records (country); "Mine Is Yours to Share" and "Put Back the Pieces of My Heart" (by Wanda Davis), recorded by Wanda Davis/Tribal Records (country); and "Genuine Gold Plated Boy Scout Knife" and "Fairy Tales and Roses" (by Jeanne Taylor), recorded by Jeanne Taylor/Tribal Records (country).

FAME PUBLISHING CO., INC., Box 2527, Muscle Shoals AL 35660. Affiliate: Rick Hall Music (ASCAP). Publishing Manager: Tommy Brasfield. Music publisher, record company and record producer. BMI. Publishes 40-50 songs/year. Pays standard royalty.
How to Contact: Submit demo tape. Prefers cassette with 1-3 songs on demo. "Please include legible lyrics." SASE. Reports in 6 weeks. "No phone calls."
Music: R&B; top 40/pop and country. Recently published "There's No Gettin' Over Me" recorded by Jeanne French/CBS Records (top 40) and (by Brasfield and Aldridge).

FESTIVE MUSIC, 15394 Warwick Blvd., Newport News VA 23602. (804)877-6877. Contact: W.H. Smith. Music publisher, record company, record producer and nostalgia (1950's-60's). BMI. Member Songwriters Guild. Publishes 2 songs/year. Pays standard royalty.
How to Contact: Write first about your interest or submit demo tape and lyric sheet. Prefers 7½ or 3¾ reel-to-reel or cassette with 4-8 songs on demo. SASE. Reports in 3 weeks.
Music: R&B, light rock and oldies ('50's). Recently published "Epitaph of Tomorrow" (by W. Smith), recorded by Fire Over Gibralter/Kim Records (rock); and "Fly Me to Nashville" (by W. Smith), recorded by L. Mack/GWS Records (C&W).

FIESTA CITY PUBLISHERS, Box 5861, Santa Barbara CA 93108. (805)969-2891. President: Frank E. Cooke.
How to Contact: Query first. Prefers cassette and lead sheet with 1-3 songs on demo. SASE.
Music: C&W, easy listening, MOR and gospel.

FIRELIGHT PUBLISHING, 12824 Lorne St., North Hollywood CA 91605. (213)764-3980. Professional Manager: Doug Thiele. Music publisher. Estab. 1980. ASCAP. Member California Copyright Conference and Academy of Country Music. Publishes 5 new songs/year; publishes 2 new songwriters/year. "We split publishing (75% to writer)."
How to Contact: Write first about your interest. Prefers cassette with 1 song maximum on demo. SASE. Reports in 3 weeks.
Music: C&W, MOR, R&B, rock (any) and top 40/pop. Recently published "Almost in Love" (by Parks and Thiele), recorded by Dolly Parton/RCA Records (ballad); "Dancin' Like Lovers" (by Herbstritt and Thiele), recorded by Mary Macgregor/RSO Records (ballad); and "Sailing Ship Majestic" (by Thiele), recorded by Mike Asquino/Red Cloud Records (country pop).
Tips: "Songs should have positive themes, highly memorable hooks and substantive but conversational lyrics. I'm after simple ideas, straight forwardly expressed and universally applicable. If your song moves listeners to tears and they remember the title easily, I want to hear it."

BOBBY FISCHER MUSIC, 50 Music Sq. W., Suite 902, Nashville TN 37203. (615)329-2278. Affiliates: Nashcal Music (BMI), Bobby's Beat (SESAC). Contact: General Manager. Music publisher, record company, record producer and promotion. Estab. 1979. ASCAP. Member CMA, NSAI and FICAP. Publishes 50 songs/year; publishes 2 new songwriters/year. Pays standard royalty.
How to Contact: Submit demo tape and lyric sheet. Prefers cassette with 2-3 songs on demo. "We review material as time permits and return (with SASE *if* time permits." Reports as soon as possible.

Music: C&W. Recently published "Temporarily Yours" (by Bobby Fischer), recorded by Jeanne Pruett; "A Little Ground in Texas" (by B. Fischer), recorded by The Capitals; and "Partners in Rhyme" (by B. Fischer), recorded by Moe Bandy and Joe Stampley (all country).

FLIN-FLON MUSIC, 102 Veteran's Ave., Mullen NE 69152. (308)546-2294. General Manager: L.E. Walker. Music publisher. BMI. Pays standard royalty.
How to Contact: Submit demo tape and lyric sheet. Prefers 7½ ips reel-to-reel with 1-3 songs on demo. SASE. Reports in 1 month.
Music: Bluegrass; disco; folk; R&B; C&W; contemporary; gospel; and soft rock. Recently published "Nine Twenty Train" (by Randy Robinson), recorded by WDLJ/Flin-Flon Records (MOR); "All Thru the Night" (by Jeanie Snyder), recorded by WDLJ/Flin-Flon Records (country); and "Hello Ba-bay" (by Earl Walker), recorded by Group/Varsity Records (jazz).

FOCAL POINT MUSIC PUBLISHERS, 922 McArthur Blvd., Warner Robins GA 31093. (912)923-6533. Affiliate: House of Melton (ASCAP). Owner/Manager: Ray Melton. Music publisher and record company. BMI. Publishes 20-25 songs/year; publishes 10-12 new songwriters/year. Pays standard royalty.
How to Contact: Submit demo tape and lead sheet. Prefers 7½ ips reel-to-reel or cassette with 2-4 songs on demo. SASE. Reports in 1 month.
Music: Bluegrass; children's; church/religious; C&W; easy listening; folk; gospel; and top 40/pop. Recently published "My Woman's Love," recorded by Hal and Charlie, Ray Aborgast and Billy Starr (C&W/top 40/pop).

FOLKSTONE MUSIC PUBLISHING CO., Box 638, Franklin WV 26807 (304)358-2504. President: I. Lynn Beckman. Music publisher. Gospel emphasis. BMI. Submit only after advance permission; no unsolicited material accepted. Prefers previously published or recorded writers and artists.

FOR MY LADY MUSIC, Box 1317, New Liskeard, Ontario Canada P0J 1P0. Music publisher, record company, record producer, management firm and public relations firm. Member PRO-CAN, CARAS. Publishes 2-3 songs/year; publishes 1-2 new songwriters/year. Pays by standard royalty of 50%.
How To Contact: Query or submit demo tape and lead sheet. Prefers 7½ or 15 ips reel-to-reel or cassette with "whatever the tape will hold with leader and separation." Would also like to "have the songs clearly titled and related to the lead sheets." SASE. Reports in 2 weeks.
Music: Easy listening; gospel; MOR; rock; and top 40/pop. Recently published "No More Reruns," "Rock and Roll Queen" and "A Sweet Dream" (all by Peter D'Amico), all recorded by Tribe/Big Harold's (rock). "No Joy This Morning," "Natural Morning," recorded by Sandra D'Aoust (Black Bear Records); "Young Girls," "Softly She Smiles," (by Peter D'Amico, Black Bear Records).

FORREST HILLS MUSIC, INC., 25 Music Square E., Nashville TN 37203. Affiliates: Ash Valley Music (ASCAP) and Roadrunner Music (BMI). Music publisher. BMI. Member NMPA. Publishes 20-22 songs/year; publishes 1-2 new songwriters/year. Pays standard minimum royalty.
How to Contact: Submit demo tape. Prefers reel-to-reel. SASE. Reports in 4 weeks.
Music: C&W; easy listening; MOR; and top 40/pop. Recently published "Alabama Rose," (by B.R. Reynolds, D. Bretts, and G. Stewart), recorded by Joe Sun/Ovation (country); "Hollywood," (by G. Stewart—W. Carson), recorded by Alabama/RCA (country); and "It's True," (by C. Anderson, M.B. Anderson, and G. Stewart), recorded by Terri Gibbs/MCA (country).

FOUR MOONS MUSIC PUBLISHING GROUP, 279 E. 44th St., Penthouse E, New York NY 10017. (212)288-2447. Affiliate: Plibby Music (BMI). Professional Manager: Sharon Swanson. Music publisher. ASCAP. Member NMPA, AGAC, NARAS and Music Publishers Forum. Publishes 8-10 songs/year; publishes 3 new songwriters/year. Pays standard royalty "and we give the AGAC contract."
How to Contact: Submit demo tape and lyric sheet. Prefers cassette with 1-2 songs on demo. Accepts "only singles—no album cuts." SASE. Reports in 3 weeks.
Music: MOR, soul and top 40/pop. Recently published "Stay the Night" (by Maxie Green), recorded by Jane Olivor (MOR); "Whip" (by Eric Matthew), recorded by Eddie Kendricks (R&B); and "Only Love" (by Marc Gabriele), recorded by KC and The Sunshine Band (rock).
Tips: "Listen to the radio and send something that will be played 6 months to a year from now, not something that sounds like songs that have already happened."

FOURTH HOUSE MUSIC PUBLISHING CO., 1417 S. Robertson Blvd., Suite 6, Los Angeles CA 90035. (213)854-1089 or (213)858-0993. Affiliates: Otis Music (BMI), Joel Webster Music (BMI), Mavid Music (ASCAP) and Golden Taylim Music (BMI). Chief of Production: Lim Taylor. Director: Deloras Anderson. Music publisher and production company. BMI. Publishes 25 songs/year. Hires staff writers.
How to Contact: Submit demo tape and lead sheet. Prefers 7½ ips reel-to-reel or cassette with 3-6 songs on demo. SASE. Reports in 1 month.
Music: Blues; dance; soul; and top 40/pop. Recently published "Heavenly Music" (by Bob Bradstreet) and "A Peace That We Could Never Before Enjoy" (by Mable John and Joel Webster), recorded by Ray Charles/Atlantic Records.

FOXY LADY MUSIC, Multi-Media Enterprises, 184 King St. W., Kitcuener, Ontario, Canada. Affiliate: Foxy Mama Music (PROCAN). Director: William Moran. Music publisher, record company and management firm. Estab. 1970. CAPAC. Pays 25-50% royalty. Buys some material outright; pays $300-1,000/song. Sometimes secures songwriters on salary basis: "preferably a singer or musician useful for making demos."
How to Contact: Submit demo tape and lead sheet. Include bio. Prefers cassette with 1-12 songs on demo. "Put titles in order. Include names of collaborators, if any, and tell whether or not you want the song published or sold outright." SAE and International Reply Coupons. Reports in 2 weeks.
Music: Blues; disco; easy listening; jazz; rock (country); soul; and top 40/pop. Recently published "Where Did the Good Times Go?", recorded by Jeff Adams (easy listening); "I Love to Sing," recorded by Terry Logan (jazz); and "It Happened One Night," recorded by Jeff and Jackie (top 40).

FRASCO MUSIC PUBLISHING, 1208 Eastview St., Jackson MS 39203. (601)969-3717. Manager: Chris Walker. Music publisher and record producer. Estab. 1979. BMI. Member NARAS. Publishes 20 songs/year; publishes 2 new songwriters/year. Pays standard royalty.
How to Contact: Submit demo tape and lyric sheet. Prefers 7½ ips reel-to-reel or cassette with 3-6 songs on demo. SASE. Reports in 1 month.
Music: Dance-oriented, gospel, R&B, rock, soul and top 40/pop. Recently published "Feelin' Free" (by Carson Whitsett and Norma Jordan), recorded by Norma Jordan/Ciaco Records, Italy; "Misty Morning Water" (by Carson Whitsett and Norma Jordan), recorded by Norma Jordan/Ciaco Records (pop); and "We Belong to the Night" (by Steve Acker), recorded by Ella Thorpe/Fonit-Cetra Records, Italy (rock).

FRIENDLY FINLEY MUSIC, 103 Westview Ave., Valparaiso FL 32580. (904)678-7211. Affiliate: Shelly Singleton Music (BMI). Owner: Finley Duncan. President: Bruce Duncan. Music publisher, record company and record producer. BMI. Published 20 songs in 1980; plans 25 in 1981. Pays standard royalties.
How to Contact: Query, arrange personal interview, or submit demo tape and lead sheet. Prefers cassette or 7½ ips reel-to-reel tape with 3-5 songs on demo. "Send what you consider your best, and at least one of what you consider your worst." SASE. Reports in 1 week.
Music: C&W; disco; easy listening; MOR; R&B; rock; soul; and top 40/pop. Recently published "Alabama" and "Feel like a Steel" (by Colwell), recorded by Bert Colwell/Country Artists Records (C&W).

FRIENDSHIP STORE MUSIC, Box M 777, Gary IN 46401. Artists Director: Joseph Cohen. Music publisher. BMI. Pays standard royalties.
How to Contact: Submit demo tape. Prefers 7½ ips reel with 1-3 songs on demo. "All songs must be copyrighted before being submitted." SASE. Reports in 2 weeks.
Music: Top 40/pop and MOR.

FUNK BOX MUSIC, 880 NE 71st St., Miami FL 33138. (305)759-1405. Affiliate: Oliva Music (SESAC). President: Carlos Oliva. Music publisher, record company and record producer. Estab. 1979. BMI. Member NARM. Publishes 70 songs/year; publishes 10 new songwriters/year. Pays standard royalty.
How to Contact: Submit demo tape and lyric sheet. Prefers cassette with any number songs on demo. SASE. Reports in 2 weeks.
Music: Dance-oriented, Spanish and rock. Recently published "Pa-Pun" (by O. Valdes), recorded by Group Alma/Alhambra Records (salsa/rock); "Se Que Pretendes" (by M. Palacio), recorded by Judge's Nephews/Common Cause Records (ballad); and "Rock Swing" (by R. Parodi), recorded by Group Babe/Common Cause Records (rock).
Tips: "Songs should have a strong hook, simple melody and sense-making lyrics."

FUNKY ACRES MUSIC CO., 145 W. 55th St, New York NY 10019, (212)245-7179; 927 United Pacific Bldg., Seattle WA 98104, (206)625-9548. Affiliates: Thea Music (BMI) and Hip Notic Music (BMI). Contact: Warren Baker or Peter Gorin (New York), Robert Krinsky (Seattle). Music publisher. Estab. 1979. ASCAP. Published 5 new songwriters in 1979. Pays standard royalty.
How to Contact: Submit demo tape, lyric sheet, and lead sheet if available, or arrange personal interview to play demo tape. Prefers cassette with 5 songs maximum on demo. SASE. Reports in 2-4 weeks.
Music: C&W; disco; MOR; R&B; rock; soul; and top 40/pop. "Our first releases have been in European markets in disco, MOR and top 40/rock."
Tips: "Suggest artists for whom you think your songs are appropriate. We rely on personal contacts to get songs directly to the artist."

FYDAQ MUSIC, 240 E. Radcliffe Dr., Claremont CA 91711. (714)624-0677. Affiliates: Jubilation Music (BMI), and Cetacean (ASCAP). President: Gary Buckley. Music publisher and production company. BMI. Member Academy of Country Music, Country Music Association, Gospel Music Association, National Academy of Recording Arts & Sciences, Audio Engineering. Publishes 30-40 songs/year.
How to Contact: Submit demo tape and lead or lyric sheet. Prefers 7½ ips reel-to-reel or cassette with 1-4 songs on demo. SASE. Reports in 3 weeks.
Music: C&W; easy listening; gospel; MOR; progressive; rock (country); soul; and top 40/pop. Recently published "You're Smiling Again" recorded by Rick Buche/Paradise Records (pop); "My Only Love" recorded by Dusk/Fubar Records (top 40); "Grandpas Song" recorded by Jerry Roark (gospel); "How Many Times" recorded by Finley Duke (gospel); "Working Man's Prayer" recorded by Jody Barry/Majega Records (gospel); "Better Get Right" recorded by Crownsmen/Manna Records (gospel); "Is It Right," "Touch Me Now," "It's All Right" and "What You Doin' to Me" recorded by Borderline/Majega Records (rock/top 40); and "She Comes to Me Softly"/ "Without You" recorded by Borderline/Quikstar Records (top 40/pop).

G.G. MUSIC, INC., 405 Park Ave., New York NY 10022. (212)355-3309. Affiliate: Wazuri Music (BMI). President: Linwood Simon. Music publisher and record producer. ASCAP. SESAC. Publishes 50 songs/year; publishes 5 new songwriters/year. Pays standard royalty.
How to Contact: Submit demo tape and lyric sheet. Prefers 7½ ips reel-to-reel or cassette with 1-6 songs on demo. SASE. Reports in 1 month.
Music: Blues, dance-oriented, easy listening, jazz, MOR, Spanish, R&B, rock, soul and top 40/pop. Recently published "I Love You Cause," "Fingers In the Fire," "I Can Stand the Pain" and "Chasin' Me Into Somebody Else's Arms" (by G.G.), recorded by G.G./Polygram Records.
Tips: "The writer should understand that he must recognize all the elements needed to make a hit record: strong lyrics, good hook and an overall progressive and commercial sound the buying public can relate to. Love songs are 90% of records sold."

G.J. MUSIC CO., Box 4171, Princeton FL 33032. Owner: Morton Glosser. Music publisher. BMI. Pays standard royalty.
How to Contact: Submit demo tape and lead sheet. "Include lyric sheet with chords." Prefers 7½ ips reel-to-reel or mono cassette. SASE. Reports "depending on placement possibilities."
Music: C&W; easy listening; MOR; pop; soft rock; and contemporary adult. "No teeny bopper, punk rock, etc."

AL GALLICO MUSIC CORP., 9255 Sunset Blvd., Suite 507, Los Angeles CA 90069. (213)274-0165. Affiliates: Algee (BMI), Altam (BMI) and Easy Listening (ASCAP). Air Assistant: Kevin Magowan. Music publisher. BMI. Member NMPA. Pays standard royalty. Hires staff writers.
How to Contact: Submit demo tape and lead sheet. Prefers 7½ ips reel-to-reel with 1-3 songs on demo. SASE. Reports in 2 weeks.
Music: C&W; easy listening; and top 40/pop. "We're very strong in contemporary country and crossover material." Recently published "Brass in Pocket" (by Chrissie Hynde), recorded by The Pretenders/SIRE Records (top 40/pop/rock); "Who's Cheatin Who" (by Jerry Hayes), recorded by Charlie McClain/Epic Records (country); and "I've Been Waiting for You All of My Life" (by Mark Sherrill and Linda Kimball), recorded by Paul Anka/RCA Records (MOR/country).
Tips: "Be aware of the acts we work with and study their style. Study what is playing on radio and come up with good ideas and titles; vivid, sincere, relationship-oriented lyrics; melodic, catchy melodies; good structure and contemporary chords and feel. The song is again the main ingredient and country is now the MOR (easy listening) of the 80's—we need fresh ideas and approaches to the man-woman relationship in the world today."

AL GALLICO MUSIC CORP., 120 E. 56th St., New York NY 10022. (212)355-5980. Contact: Professional Manager.
How to Contact: Submit demo tape and lyric sheet. Prefers cassette. SASE. "We do not accept registered mail." Reports in 1 month.
Music: C&W, MOR, R&B, rock and top 40/pop.

AL GALLICO MUSIC CORP., 50 Music Sq. W., #503, Nashville TN 37203. (615)327-2773. Manager: Josh Whitmore. Music publisher. BMI and ASCAP. Pays standard royalty.
How to Contact: Submit demo tape and lyric sheet or arrange to leave tape at office for our staff to listen to. Prefers cassette with 3 songs on demo. SASE. Reports in 3 weeks.
Music: Country. Recently published "Whispers" (by Mark Sherrill and Lacy Dalton), recorded by Lacy J. Dalton (country); "You're My Kind of Woman" (by Mark Sherrill and Linda Kimbell), recorded by Jacky Ward (country); and "Lady In the Blue Mercedes" (by Danny Dorst and Gary Gentry), recorded by Johnny Duncan (country).
Tips: "Be prepared to leave tapes at our office."

GAMELON MUSIC, Box 525, Station P, Toronto, Ontario, Canada M5S 2T1. Manager: Michael Klenier. Music publisher and record producer. PROCAN. Publishes 12 songs/year.
How to Contact: Submit demo tape and lyric sheet. Prefers 7½ ips reel-to-reel with 5-15 songs on demo. Does not return unsolicited material. Reports in 1 month.
Music: Blues, classical, folk, jazz, progressive and R&B. Recently published "Islands," "Riding the Bull," and "This Kind of Living" (by Michael Klenier), recorded by M. Klenier (jazz).

GARRETT MUSIC INTERPRISES, 6255 Sunset Blvd., Suite 1019, Hollywood CA 90028. (213)467-2181. Publisher: Randy Cate. Music publisher and production company. BMI. ASCAP. Member NMPA. Pays standard royalty. Sometimes secures songwriters on salary basis.
How to Contact: Submit demo tape and lyric sheet. Prefers 7½ ips reel-to-reel or cassette with maximum 3 songs on demo. "Affix phone number and name on everything." SASE. Reports in 1 month.
Music: C&W; easy listening; MOR and top 40/pop. Recently published "I Just Fell in Love Again" (by Dorff, Skierov, Lloyd and Herbstritt), recorded by Ann Murray/Capitol Records (MOR); "Fire in the Morning" (by Dorff, Herbstritt ·and Harju), recorded by Melissa Manchester/Arista Records (MOR/top 40); and "Every Which Way But Loose" (by Dorff, Brown, Garrett), recorded by Eddie Rabbitt/Electra Records (MOR/country/top 40).
Tips: Especially interested in "story songs, picture words and simple but old themes said in new ways."

GEAR PUBLISHING CO., 567 Purdy, Birmingham MI 48009. (313)642-0910. Music publisher and record company.

GENTILLY MUSIC, Box 536, Crookston MN 56716. (218)281-6450. Contact: Gary Emerson. Music publisher and record company. BMI. Member CMA. Publishes 12 songs/year. Pays standard royalty.
How to Contact: Submit demo tape and lyric sheet. Prefers cassette with 2-5 songs on demo. SASE. Reports in 1 month.
Music: Bluegrass, C&W and gospel. Recently published "Just Across the Way," "City Lights" and "Albuquergue Lady" (by Steve Lockman), recorded by S. Lockman/Glade Records (country).

GIL MUSIC CORPORATION, 1650 Broadway, New York NY 10019. (212)245-0110. Professional Manager: Amy Javors. Affiliates: SongFest Music Corp. (ASCAP), George Pincus & Son Music Corp. (ASCAP). Music publisher. BMI. Publishes about 12 songs/year. Pays standard royalty.
How to Contact: Submit demo tape and lyric or lead sheet. Prefers 7½ ips reel-to-reel or cassette with 1-3 songs on demo. "Keep on sending in material." SASE. Reports in 2 weeks.
Music: C&W; MOR and rock.

GOD'S WORLD, 27335 Penn St., Inkster MI 48141. (313)562-8975. Affiliates: Manfield Music (BMI), Stephen Enoch Johnson Music (ASCAP). President: Elder Otis G. Johnson. Music publisher, record company and record producer. SESAC. Member American Mechanical Rights Association, GMA, BMA, NARAS. Publishes 100 songs/year; publishes 5 new songwriters/year. Pays standard royalty.
How to Contact: Write first about your interest, submit demo tape and lyric sheet; call about your interest and arrange personal interview to play demo tape. Prefers 7½ ips reel-to-reel or cassette with 3 songs on demo. SASE. Reports in 1 month.

Songwriter's Market Close-up

"Unless a writer is sitting in my office singing to me, the demo must say it all," says Randy Cate director of publishing for Snuff Garrett Enterprises in Los Angeles. "The theme, hook, melody, whatever makes the song work, must come through at the first listen. The demo should show the song, and let the listener judge its potential."

Cate started with Snuff Garrett (the music/movie mogul responsible for *Every Which Way But Loose, Smokey and the Bandit II,* and *Bronco Billy* among others) in 1975 one day a week and has been with him since, working in publishing administration, writing and "doing whatever needs to be done around the office. I've spent time in Nashville, too, and studied music in college, but nothing prepared me (for the music business) like working everyday in an office."

His office experience also makes him advise songwriters to "keep in mind this is a business and that one should approach it as such. What you sing in the front room on Sunday may not be what will sell to the public on Monday. Be creative without being trite, paint pictures, and make it accessible to me as a listener. At the start of a demo, I try to keep an open mind to the idea of the song, and how it could possibly be developed if it isn't what I'm looking for. But many tapes I listen to have little or nothing to say and go nowhere!"

He says the decision to make your demo at home or go to the studio "depends on the song, and how much you as the writer feel it needs to show your idea clearly. I've received piano/vocal or guitar/vocal

Randy Cate

demos that are incredible. Country demos lean toward being kept simple while some pop demos need more. Consider Foreigner's 'Hot Blooded'. I can't see that as a guitar/vocal demo. When you add the vocal performance, guitar licks, and story, it works, but I don't think many people would hear it if it were presented as just an acoustic guitar/vocal demo."

"The biggest mistake beginning songwriters make," says Cate, "is being overly sensitive to criticism. A writer must believe in his work, but he must also be open to other ideas and input that might enhance a song's credibility. Publishers *do* have ideas about what they want. Beginning writers should listen to everyone, but only use what they think can help them."

Music: Church/religious, C&W, easy listening, gospel and jazz. Recently published "Use Me Lord" (by Craigt Erquhara), recorded by Sonlight/Aspro Records; "Believe in Me" (by Reynard Brown and Birchett Shan), recorded by Saved/God's World Records; "Faith in the Power of God" (by Dorothy W. Butler), recorded by The National Conventions of Choirs/Savoy Records (all gospel); "Secret Love" and "Love All" (by Sandy Hall), recorded by George Johnson (easy listening).

GOLD CLEF MUSIC PUBLISHING CO., Box 43, Chester PA 19016. President/Owner: Alexander Czarenko. Music publisher and record company. BMI.
How to Contact: Submit acetate disc and lead sheet. SASE. Reports in 1 month.
Music: Blues; C&W; disco; easy listening; MOR; R&B; and top 40/pop. Recently published

"Valentine," "Gerome" and "I Look At You" (all by F.C. Bond), all recorded by Dirk Durham (ballads)

GOLD STREET, INC., Box 124, Kirbyville TX 75956. (713)423-5516. President: James L. Gibson. Music publisher and record company. BMI. Publishes 20 songs/year; publishes 2 new songwriters/year. Negotiates payment.
How to Contact: Submit demo tape and lyric sheet. Prefers 7½ ips reel-to-reel or 1-4 songs on demo. "Send us your demos using either a rhythm track or a complete arrangement with strings, etc. We like to hear your ideas on tape, though we may not necessarily use them as you hear them." SASE. Reports in 1 month.
Music: All types including children's, church/religious and gospel.

GOLDCREST PUBLISHING, INC., 10th and Parker, Berkeley CA 94710. (415)549-2500. Associate Director A&R: Hank Cosby. Music publisher and record company.
How to Contact: Submit demo tape. Prefers 7½ ips reel-to-reel or cassette. SASE. Reports in 3 weeks.
Music: Disco; easy listening; jazz; MOR; progressive; R&B; soul; and top 40/pop.

GOLDEN DAWN MUSIC, 26177 Kinyon Dr., Taylor MI 48180. (313)292-5281. President: Peggy La Sorda. Music publisher and record company. BMI. Publishes 10 songs/year; publishes 1 new songwriter/year. Pays standard royalty.
How to Contact: Write first, then submit demo tape and lyric sheet. Prefers 7½ ips reel-to-reel or cassette with 1-4 songs on demo. SASE. Reports in 3 weeks.
Music: C&W, dance-oriented, easy listening, folk, gospel, MOR and top 40/pop.

GOLDEN GUITAR, 1824 Laney Dr., Longview TX 75601. (214)758-4063. Affiliate: Enterprize Music (BMI). Contact: Jerry Haymes. Music publisher and record company. BMI. Publishes 4-5 songs/year; publishes 1 new songwriter/year.
How to Contact: Submit demo tape and lyric sheet. Prefers reel-to-reel or cassettes. SASE. Reports "As soon as possible."
Music: Bluegrass, C&W, folk, gospel and MOR.

GOLDEN GUITAR MUSIC, Box 40602, Tucson AZ 85717. President: Jeff Johnson. Music publisher. BMI. Publishes 10 songs/year. Pays standard royalty.
How to Contact: Submit demo tape and lyric sheet. Prefers 7½ or 15 ips reel-to-reel and cassette with 2-6 songs on demo. SASE. Reports in 1 month.
Music: Bluegrass, church/religious, C&W, gospel and light rock. Recently published "Willy's Boy" (by Jeff Johnson), recorded by Brenda D./Half Moon Records (country); "Wearing a Smile of a Clown" (by Jerry Haymes), recorded by Brenda D./Umpire Records (country); and "What's This World Coming To?" (by J. Johnson), recorded by Jeff Johnson/Dewl Records (country/religious).
Tips: "Make an effort to submit a good quality demo—not necessarily complicated but clear and clean."

GOOSEPIMPLE MUSIC, 7 Colonial Ave., Myerstown PA 17067. (717)866-5067. Contact: Al Shade. Music publisher, record producer and record company. BMI. Pays standard royalty.
How to Contact: Submit demo tape and lyric sheet. Prefers 7½ ips reel-to-reel or cassette with 2-4 songs on demo. SASE. Reports in 1 month.
Music: Children's; C&W; and gospel. Recently published "Three Mile Island," "The Legendary Blue Eyed Six," and "Okies from Muskogee Never Die."

GOPAM ENTERPRISES, INC., 11 Riverside Dr., #13C-W, New York NY 10023. (212)724-6120. Affiliates: Upam Music (BMI), Zawinul Music (BMI), Taggie Music (BMI), Jodax Music Co. (BMI), Semenya Music (BMI), Margenia Music (BMI), Turbine Music (BMI), Appleberry Music (BMI), Kae-Lyn Music (BMI), Jillean Music (BMI), Jowat Music (BMI), John Oscar Music, Inc. (ASCAP), Bi-Circle (BMI), Tri-Circle (ASCAP), Dillard Music and Pril Music (BMI). Managing Director: Laurie Goldstein. Music publisher. BMI. Member NMPA. Pays standard royalties.
How to Contact: Query or submit demo tape and lead or lyric sheet. Prefers cassette with 1-3 songs. "Primarily interested in jazz and jazz related compositions." SASE. Reports as soon as possible.
Music: Blues; easy listening; jazz; R&B; soul; and pop.

GORDON MUSIC CO., INC., 12111 Strathern St. #108, Hollywood CA 91605. (213)768-7597. Affiliates include Marlen (ASCAP), JesBy (ASCAP), Tor (ASCAP), Dave (ASCAP), Bernie (AS-

CAP) and Sunshine (BMI). President: Jeff Gordon. Music publisher. ASCAP. Publishes 12 songs/
year; publishes 3 new songwriters/year. Pays standard royalty.
How to Contact: Call first about your interest and arrange personal interview to play demo.
Prefers cassette with 5-12 songs on demo. Does not return unsolicited material. Reports in 1 week.
Music: Children's, choral, church/religious, C&W, jazz, rock and top 40/pop. Recently published
"Radio Waves" (by Mockler and Lloyd), recorded by Failsafe/ZZYZX Records (rock); "Jump
Bop" and "Monica" (by Mockler and Lloyd), recorded by Failsafe/ZZYZX Records (pop).

GOSPEL CLEF, Box 90, Rugby Station, Brooklyn NY 11203. (212)773-5910. President: John R.
Lockley. Music publisher. BMI. Pays standard royalty.
How to Contact: Write first about your interest. Prefers cassette with 2 songs on demo. "All songs
submitted to our company should have a positive and direct reverence for God, Jesus, and the
spirit of the Lord, etc." SASE. Reports in 1 month.
Music: Church/religious and spiritual. Recently published "My God Is Able" (by Elder J.R.
Lockley, Jr), recorded by Glorytones/Gospel Records, Inc. (spiritual); "You've Got a Friend
When He Is Jesus" (by Ann Moncrief), recorded by Elder J.R. Lockley/Gospel Records, Inc.
(spiritual); and "Nothing but the Name of Jesus" (by Elder J.R. Lockley, Jr), recorded by The
Lockley Family/Gospel Records, Inc. (spiritual).

GOSPEL SENDERS MUSIC PUBLISHING CO., Box 55943, Houston TX 77055.
(713)686-1749. Affiliate: Redeemer Music Publishing (SESAC). President: Gary R. Smith. Music
publisher, record company, record producer, management firm and booking agency. BMI.
Publishes 10 songs/year. Pays standard royalties.
How to Contact: Arrange personal interview. Prefers reel-to-reel or cassette with 3-10 songs on
demo. SASE. Reports in 1 month.
Music: Church/religious; and gospel. Recently published "The Comforter" and "Song in the
Night" (both by Clay Howell), and "Holiday Inn" (by G. Smith), all recorded by Gary R.
Smith/Redeemer Records (contemporary/gospel).

GRAMAVISION MUSIC, Box 2772 Grand Central Station, New York NY 10012. Affiliate:
Desert Rose (BMI). President: Jonathan Rose. Music publisher, record producer and record
company. Estab. 1979. BMI. Publishes 30 songs/year. Pays standard royalty.
How to Contact: Submit demo tape and lyric sheet. Prefers 7½ ips reel-to-reel or cassette with 1-4
songs on demo. "Don't worry about production; just make sure the changes, inflections and lyrics
are clear." SASE. "Songs must be professional and commercial."
Music: Classical; jazz; progressive; R&B; rock (no hard, heavy, metal); and top 40/pop. Recently
published *Soundtrack to The Europeans* by Richard Robbins (classical); and "Love for Sandy" by
Frederick Rose (MOR).
Tips: "The song should tell its story or feeling clearly without irrelevant detail or foggy concept."

GRAND ARTISTS MUSIC, 8325 SW 132 St., Miami FL 331056. (305)238-1088. President: Paul
Stevens. Music publisher, record company and record producer. BMI. Publishes 20-30 songs/
year; publishes 2 new songwriters/year. Pays standard royalty.
How to Contact: Submit demo tape and lyric sheet. Prefers cassette with 1-5 songs on demo. SASE.
Reports in 1 month.
Music: C&W, dance-oriented, easy listening, MOR, Spanish, rock and top 40/pop.

THE GRAND PASHA PUBLISHER, 5615 Melrose Ave., Hollywood CA 90038. (213)466-3507.
Affiliates: Sasha Songs, Unlimited (BMI), The Proffer Music Co. (ASCAP). Professional Man-
ager: Coral Browning. Music publisher, record company and record producer. Publishes 100
songs/year; publishes 4 new songwriters/year. Pays standard royalty.
How to Contact: Call first about your interest. Prefers cassette with 2-4 songs on demo. SASE.
Reports in 3 weeks.
Music: MOR, rock and top 40/pop. Recently published "Daybreak" (by Spencer Proffer and
David Pomeranz), recorded by Bette Midler/Atlantic Records (top 40/pop); "Children of the
Sun" (by Billy Thorpe and S. Proffer), recorded by B. Thorpe (rock); and "Imagination's Child"
(by Allan Clunke and S. Proffer), recorded by Clunke/Electra Records (rock).

GRAVENHURST MUSIC, 105 Park Lane, Beaver Falls PA 15010; 1469 3rd Ave., New Brighton
PA 15066. (412)843-2431, (412)847-0111. Promotion Director: Roz Miller. President: Jerry Reed.
Music publisher and record company. BMI. Publishes 30-50 songs/year. Pays standard royalty.
How to Contact: Submit demo tape and lead and lyric sheets. Prefers 7½ ips reel-to-reel or cassette
with 1-3 songs on demo. SASE. Reports in 3 weeks.

Music: Blues; C&W; disco; easy listening; MOR; rock; and soul. Recently published "Dancin' Man," recorded by Q (pop); and "Alone," recorded by the JBC Band (soul).

GRAWICK MUSIC, Box 90639, Nashville TN 37209. (615)297-4174. Affiliates: Mester (BMI) and James Hendrix (ASCAP). President: James Hendrix. Music publisher and record company. BMI. Publishes 20 songs/year; publishes 6 new songwriters/year. Pays standard royalty.
How to Contact: Submit demo tape and lyric sheet. Prefers cassette with 3-4 songs on demo. SASE. Reports in 1 month.
Music: Church/religious, gospel, R&B and top 40/pop. Recently published "Love, Sweet Love" (by Bettye Shelton), recorded by B. Shelton/Carrie Records; "The Jam" (by Dicky Marable), recorded by Spice/Carrie Records (R&B); and "Who Knows" (by J. Hendrix), recorded by Cornell Blakely and produced by Berry Gordy, Jr. (R&B).

GRENOBLE SONGS, Box 222, Groveport OH 43125. Affiliate: Edanmoor Songs (ASCAP). General Manager: Ed Graham. Music publisher and record company. BMI. Publishes 10-15 songs/year. Pays standard royalty.
How to Contact: Submit demo tape and lyric sheet. Prefers 7½ ips reel-to-reel or cassette with 1-3 songs on demo. "Tape should be titled and have leader tape on each song." SASE. Reports in 2-8 weeks.
Music: C&W; gospel (including choral); and pop. Recently published "Bless Them All," "For the Truth and the Right" and "Johnny Marchin'," recorded by Barry Sadler (patriotic).
Tips: "If the songwriter has self-published sheet music of his songs on which he owns the copyright, and which are in salable, printed form, Grenoble Songs will act as 'sole selling agent' for these songs, on a contract basis. Write to us and submit copies of the songs."

GROOVESONIC MUSIC, Box 3013, Davenport IA 52808. (319)324-2133. Affiliates: Sugarvine Music (BMI), Lovelight Music (BMI), GrooveTune Music, and Grove II Music (ASCAP). Manager: Gary Unger. Music publisher. BMI. Member AGAC, CMA, NMPA and SRS. Publishes 12 or more songs/year; publishes 2 new songwriters/year. Pays standard royalty.
How to Contact: Submit demo tape and lyric sheet. Prefers 7½ ips reel-to-reel or cassette with 2-10 songs on demo. SASE. Reports in 3 months.
Music: Church/religious, C&W, dance-oriented, easy listening, hard rock, progressive, rock and top 40/pop. Recently published "Girl" (by Gary Under and Don Allcex), recorded by Lambkin (country rock); "Goodnight Angel" (by Gary Unger), recorded by Lambin (top 40 format); and "Oh! Misery" (by G. Unger), recorded by Chris Sandfur.

GROOVESVILLE MUSIC, 15855 Wyoming, Detroit MI 48238. Affiliates: Conquistador (ASCAP) and Double Sharp (ASCAP). Director: Brian Spears. Operations Manager: Dave Boyer. Music publisher, record company and record producer. BMI. Member NMPA. Publishes 100 songs/year. Pays standard royalties.
How to Contact: Query, submit demo tape, submit demo tape and lyric sheet, submit acetate disc or submit acetate disc and lyric sheet. Prefers 7½ ips reel-to-reel or cassette with 1-2 songs on demo. SASE. Reports in 3 weeks.
Music: Disco; easy listening; MOR; progressive; R&B; rock; soul; and top 40/pop. Recently published "Disco Lady" (by Don Davis, Al Vance and Harvey Scales), recorded by Johnny Taylor (pop); "You Don't Have to be a Star" (by James Dean and John Glover), recorded by Marilyn McCoo and Billie Davis (pop); "Break My Heart" (by David Garner), recorded by David Ruffin (pop); "Soft Lights, Sweet Music" (by Marilyn McLeod), recorded by Enchantment (pop); and "You're the Best Thing in My life" (by Jakki Milligan and Deborah Dennard), recorded by the Dramatics.

GROSVENOR HOUSE MUSIC, Box 1563, Hollywood CA 90028. Affiliate: Star Tunes Music (BMI). President: Art Benson. Music publisher and record company. ASCAP. Publishes 100 songs/year. Pays standard royalty.
How to Contact: Submit demo tape and lead sheet. Prefers reel-to-reel or cassette with 1-3 songs on demo. SASE. Reports in 1 month.
Music: Bluegrass; blues; church/religious; C&W; easy listening; folk; jazz; MOR; soul; top 40/pop; and big band. Recently published "The Thrill Is Gone," recorded by B.B. King (R&B); and "I'll Sing the Blues" and "Another Leaf Falls," recorded by Tommy Cooper (pop/C&W).

FRANK GUBALA MUSIC, Hillside Rd., Cumberland RI 02864. (401)333-6097. Contact: Frank Gubala. Music publisher and booking agency.
How to Contact: Submit demo tape or submit demo tape and lead sheet. Prefers 7½ ips reel-to-reel or cassette. Does not return unsolicited material. Reports in 1 month.
Music: Blues; disco; easy listening; MOR; and top 40/pop.

GULE RECORD, 7046 Hollywood Blvd., Hollywood CA 90028. (213)462-0502. Vice President: Harry Gordon. Music publisher, record company and record producer.
How to Contact: Submit demo tape or submit acetate disc. Prefers 7½ ips reel-to-reel tape with 2 songs on demo. SASE.
Music C&W; gospel; R&B; rock; soul; and top 40/pop.

HALNAT MUSIC PUBLISHING CO., Box 37156, Cincinnati OH 45222. (513)531-7605. Affiliate: Saul Avenue Publishing (BMI). President: Saul Halper. Music publisher. (ASCAP). Member NMPA. Publishes 6 songs/year; publishes 3 new songwriters/year. Pays standard royalty.
How to Contact: Submit demo tape and lyric sheet. Prefers cassette with 2-4 songs on demo. SASE. Reports in 2 weeks.
Music: Bluegrass; blues; C&W; gospel; R&B; and soul. Recently published "Kansas City," recorded by the Beatles (rock); "Ain't Never Seen So Much Rain Before," recorded by Christine Kittrell (soul); and "Meet Me at the Station" (by R. Davis, J. Railey and G. Redd), recorded by Freddy King (rock).

HAMMAN PUBLISHING, INC., Rt. 1, Box 195A, Dean Rd., Maitland FL 32751. (305)677-0611. President: Glenn Hamman. Music publisher, record company and record producer. BMI. Publishes 35 songs/year; publishes 10 new songwriters/year. Pays standard royalty.
How to Contact: Submit demo tape and lyric sheet or arrange personal interview. Prefers cassette with 2-5 songs on demo. "Please make sure all works are copyrighted before sending." SASE. Reports in 1 month.
Music: Church/religious, C&W, easy listening, gospel, jazz, MOR and R&B. Recently published "Love Letter" (by Harry D. Cup), recorded by Harry D. Cup, Silver/Pelican Records (religious); "Sick American" (by Harry D. Cup), recorded by Harry D. Cup, Silver/Pelican Records (country/MOR); and "Pink and Powder Blue" (by John Walden), recorded by John Walden, Silver/Pelican Records (country).

HAPPY DAY MUSIC CO., Box 602, Kennett MO 63857. Affiliate: Lincoln Road Music (BMI). President: Joe Keene. BMI. Pays standard royalty.
How to Contact: Submit demo tape and lead sheet. Prefers reel-to-reel or cassette. SASE. Reports in 2 weeks.
Music: Gospel and religious. Recently published "I'm Going Up," recorded by the Inspirations (gospel); and "Glory Bound," recorded by the Lewis Family (gospel).

HAPPY VALLEY MUSIC, 186 Willow Ave. Somerville MA 02144. (617)354-0700. Contact: Ken Irwin. Music publisher. BMI. Publishes over 100 songs/year; publishes 90 new songwriters/year. Pays standard royalty; 75% royalty if recorded on Rounder Records.
How to Contact: Submit demo tape and lyric sheet. Prefers cassette with 4-12 songs on demo. SASE. Reports in 1 month.
Music: Bluegrass; blues; children's; C&W; folk; R&B; and rock. Recently published "I Will Be Kind" (by Johnny Shines), recorded by J. Shines (blues).

HARRICK MUSIC, INC., Box 1780, Hialeah FL 33011. Manager: Sherry Smith. Music publisher and record company. BMI. Pays standard royalty.
How to Contact: Submit demo tape or submit demo tape and lead sheet. Prefers 7½ ips reel-to-reel or cassette with 1-3 songs on demo. SASE. Tapes should be addressed to "Attn: Preliminary Screening Committee." Lyrics unaccompanied by music are not accepted for review.
Music: Disco; progressive; rock; soul; and top 40/pop. Recently published "Shake Your Booty," "I'm Your Boogie Man," "Keep It Comin' Love" and "Please Don't Go," recorded by K.C. and the Sunshine Band (top 40/pop/soul); and "Dance across the Floor" and "Spank" recorded by Jimmy "Bo" Horne (top 40/pop/soul); and "Thoughts" and "Love's So Cruel," recorded by Leif Garrett.

HARRISON MUSIC CORP., 6381 Hollywood Blvd., Hollywood CA 90028. (213)466-3834. Affiliates: Beethoven Music (ASCAP) and Lathe Music (BMI). Professional Manager: Tad Maloney. Music publisher. ASCAP. Member NMPA, California Copyright Conference and Music Publishers Forum. Publishes 9 songs/year; publishes 5 new songwriters/year. Pays standard royalty.
How to Contact: Arrange personal interview to play demo tape. Prefers 7½ ips reel-to-reel or cassette with 3-5 songs on demo. Does not accept or return unsolicited material. Reports in 1 week.
Music: Blues; children's; church/religious; classical; easy listening; gospel; jazz; MOR; R&B; rock (country and pop); and top 40/pop. "Our requirements are a good tune and lyric that is well-constructed, with no slang or vogue words. We look ahead many years in order to properly work a song, and have found that something articulate works better in the long run." Published

"Don't Get Around Much Anymore" (by Bob Russell and Duke Ellington), recorded by Willie Nelson/CBS Records (standard); "Why Oh You" (by Jeff Spirit and Jay Gruska), recorded by Marilyn Scott/Atco Records (disco); and "Hang On" (by Jeff Spirit and Jay Gruska), recorded by 3 Dog Night/ABC Records (rock).

HATTRESS MUSIC PUBLISHING, 17544 Sorrento, Detroit MI 48235. (313)342-6884. President: Will Hatcher. Music publisher and record company. BMI. Publishes 18-20 songs/year.
How to Contact: Submit demo tape and lead sheet. Prefers 7½ ips reel-to-reel with 2-4 songs on demo. SASE. Reports in 2 weeks.
Music: Disco; gospel; soul; and top 40/pop. Recently published "Who Am I?", recorded by William Hatcher (R&B); "Let's Stick Together," recorded by Beverly and Duane (pop); "One, One, Two, Two, Boogie Woogie Avenue" (by Rickie Ross and Will Hatcher), recorded by the Spinners/Atlantic Records; and "Take a Ride" (by W. Hatcher, D. Williams and B. Williams), recorded by Beverly & Duane/Ariola Records.

HAVE A HEART MUSIC, Heart Records & Tapes of Canada Ltd., Box 3713, Station B, Calgary, Alberta, Canada T2M 4M4. (403)230-3545. Affiliate: Lovin' Heart Songs (CAPAC). President: Ron Mahonin. Music publisher, record producer, record company and management firm. Estab. 1979. Member CAPAC, PRO CANADA, and CMRRA. Publishes 20 songs/year; publishes 10 new songwriters/year. Pays standard royalty.
How to Contact: Submit demo tape and lead sheet. Prefers 7½ ips reel-to-reel or cassette with 1-4 songs on demo. "Be selective, songs submitted must be commercial. They should tell a story the public can relate to. Make sure the vocals are up front." SASE or post office voucher or $1 for U.S. Residents. Reports in 1 month.
Music: C&W; easy listening; MOR; progressive; rock; and top 40/pop. Recently published "Fire of Love" (by James Lee Hitchner), recorded by James Lee Hitchner/Heart Records (country/MOR crossover); "Thin Ice" (by Stephen & Jean Singer) (co-published with Famous Music), recorded by Doug Watt/Heart Records (top 40); and "Falling in Love (For All The Right Reasons)" (by Dick Donahue & Sam Harris), recorded by Sherry Kennedy/Heart Records (MOR).
Tips: "We want high quality demos, maximum of (4) songs per submission; we're looking for HITS—not just nice album cuts (we have lots of those); enclose lyric sheets."

HAYSTACK PUBLISHING COMPANY, Box 1528, Shreveport LA 71165. (318)742-7803. Affiliate: Hayseed Publishing Company (BMI). President: David Kent. Music published, record producer and record company. ASCAP. Publishes 25 songs/year; published 2 new songwriters in 1979 who were "contract artists with the Louisiana Hayride." Pays standard royalty.
How to Contact: Write first about your interest. Prefers cassette with 2-3 songs on demo. SASE. Reports in 3 weeks.
Music: C&W; gospel; and MOR. Recently published "Here He Comes" and "Goin' Fishin' " (by Micki Tuhrman), recorded by M. Fuhrman on Canaan Records (gospel); and "Don't You Think It's Time" (by Lee Marres), recorded by L. Marres/La Hayride Records (country).

HEAVY JAMIN' MUSIC, Box 4740, Nashville TN 37216. (615)859-0355. Affiliate: Aletha Jane (ASCAP). Manager: Susan Neal. Music publisher, record company and record producer. ASCAP. Publishes 10 songs/year; publishes 10-20 new songwriters/year. Pays standard royalties.
How to Contact: Submit demo tape and lyric sheet. Prefers 7½ ips reel-to-reel with 2-6 songs on demo. SASE. Reports in 3 weeks.
Music: Bluegrass; blues; C&W; disco; easy listening; folk; gospel; jazz; MOR; R&B; rock; soul; and top 40/pop. Recently published "Up and Down" (by Allan Mann), recorded by Allan Mann/Curtiss Records (rock); "Running Back" (by Allan Mann), recorded by Allan Mann/Curtiss Records (ballad); and "Punxsy" (by T. Russell), recorded by Rhythm Rockers/Tenock Records (instrumental); "Home Again" and "Faded Memories" (by L. Byerly), recorded by Linda Lynde (country).

HELPING HAND MUSIC, 9229 58th Ave., Edmonton, Alberta, Canada T6E 0B7. (403)436-0665. Director A&R: R. Harlan Smith. Music publisher, record company, record producer and management firm. PROCAN. Publishes 70 songs/year. Pays standard royalties.
How to Contact: Arrange personal interview, submit demo tape, or submit demo tape and lead sheet. Prefers 7½ ips reel-to-reel or cassette with 5-8 songs on demo. Would also like "a written statement verifying that publishing is available internationally on the material submitted." Does not return unsolicited material. Reports in 1 month.
Music: C&W; easy listening; MOR; rock; and top 40/pop. Recently published "Please Play It Softly," recorded by Joyce Smith/Royalty Records (country); "After the Fire Goes Out" (by S.

Mitchell), recorded by R. Harlan Smith/Royalty Records (country); "Fiddle & a Bow" (by L. Gustafson), recorded by Larry Gustafson/Royalty Records (country); "Crazy Heart" (by L. Vinson), recorded by Laura Vinson & Red Wyng/Royalty Records (country/pop); and "Real Contender" (by H. Vickers), recorded by Gary Fjellgaard/Royalty Records (country/pop).

JAMES HENDRIX ENTERPRISES, Box 90639, Nashville TN 37209. (615)297-4174. Affiliate: Grawick Music (BMI). President: James Hendrix. Music publisher, record producer and record company. BMI. Publishes 12 songs/year. Pays standard royalty.
How to Contact: Submit demo tape and lyric sheet. Prefers cassette with 3 songs minimum on demo. "Send cassette copy of tape from professionally produced master tape. If accepted, I will send standard songwriter's contract and recording contract." SASE. Reports in 3 weeks.
Music: Choral; gospel; R&B; and soul. Recently published "You've Got to Help Me" (by James Hendrix), recorded by Clifford Binns (pop re-release); "Come Holy Spirit" (by Madeline Green), recorded by M. Green (soul/gospel); and "I Know the Lord Will Make a Way" (by Kenneth Morris), recorded by Rev. W.L. Richardson.

THE HERALD ASSOCIATION, INC., Box 218, Wellman Heights, Johnsonville SC 29555. (303)386-2600. Affiliates: Silhouette Music (SESAC), Bridge Music (BMI), Heraldie Music (AS-CAP) and Huffman Publishing (BMI). Director: Ern Lewis. Music publisher, record company and record producer. Member GMA. Publishes 20-30 songs/year; publishes 6-8 new songwriters/year. Pays standard royalty.
How to Contact: Submit demo tape and lyric sheet. Prefers cassette with 4-6 songs on demo. SASE. Reports in 2 months.
Music: Church/religious and gospel. Recently publishes "Streets of Gold" (by Delores Taylor), recorded by Delores Taylor/Herald Records (gospel); "Worth Calvary" (by Delores Taylor), recorded by Alliance Trio/Herald Records (gospel); "He Led Me Out" (by Roger Horne), recorded by Singing Echoes/Mark Fine Records (gospel); "I'm Going On for Jesus" (by Rick Wilhelm), recorded by Doug Oldham/Impact Records (contemporary gospel); and "Beautiful Saviour" (by Huffman/Brown), recorded by The Speers/Hearwarming Records (gospel).

THE HIT MACHINE MUSIC CO., subsidiary of Diversified Management Group, Box 20692, San Diego CA 92120. (714)277-3141. President: Marty Kuritz. Music publisher and record company. BMI. Publishes 10-20 songs/year. Pays standard royalty.
How to Contact: Submit demo tape and lead sheet. Prefers cassette with 3 songs on demo. SASE. Reports in 1 month.
Music: MOR; rock (soft); soul; and top 40/pop. Recently published "I've Got Everthing I Need" and "I Wasn't Born Yesterday," recorded by Quiet Fire.

HITSBURGH MUSIC CO., Box 195, 157 Ford Ave., Gallatin TN 37066. (615)452-1479. Affiliate: 7th Day Music (BMI). President/General Manager: Harold Gilbert. Music publisher. BMI. Publishes 25 songs/year. Pays standard royalties.
How to Contact: Submit demo tape and lead sheet. Prefers cassette with 2-4 songs on demo. Does not return unsolicited material. Reports in 3 weeks.
Music: C&W and MOR. Recently published "Blue Tears," recorded by Hal Gilbert (MOR); "(You Know) I Really Love You," recorded by the Fox Sex (MOR); "I've Made Up My Mind," recorded by the Paramount Four (MOR); and "Step by Step" (by Hal Gilbert), recorded by the Poodles (MOR).

JERRY HOOKS Sr, 254 E. 29th St., Los Angeles CA 90011. (213)746-6499. Affiliate: Duffy Hooks III (ASCAP). Contact: Jerry Hooks Sr. Music publisher, record producer, record company and record manufacturer. ASCAP. Published 52 songs/year. Pays standard royalty. Sometimes employs songwriters on salary basis "to write songs for our other artists for different labels."
How to Contact: Submit demo tape and lyric sheet. Prefers 8-track cassette with 3-6 songs on demo. "Print all information clearly." SASE. Reports in 1-2 weeks.
Music: Blues; C&W; disco; gospel; jazz; R&B; soul; and top 40/pop. Recently published "Woman Is the Glory of a Man," by Model "T" Slim (blues); "13 Highway," by Little Boyd (blues); "I Won't Have to Cry," by Johnny Grayon and the Master Keys (gospel); "Nonsupport That What the Judge Says," by Ironing Board/Atlantic Records.

HOOSIER HILLS PUBLISHING, 1309 Celesta Way, Sellersburg IN 47172. (812)246-2959. Contact: Buddy Powell. Music publisher, record company and record producer. BMI. Publishes 10 songs/year; publishes 10 new songwriters/year. Pays standard royalty.
How to Contact: Submit demo tape and lyric sheet. Prefers 7½ ips reel-to-reel or cassette with 2-4 SASE. Reports in 2 weeks.
Music: Bluegrass, C&W and gospel.

HOT GOLD MUSIC PUBLISHING CO., Box 25654, Richmond VA 23260. (804)288-3939. President: Joseph J. Carter Jr. Music publisher, booking agency and record company. BMI. Publishes 20 songs/year; publishes 2 new songwriters/year. Pays standard royalty.
How to Contact: Submit demo tape. Prefers cassette with 1-3 songs on demo. SASE. Reports in 60 days.
Music: Rock; soul; and top 40/pop. Recently published "How Long Will I Be a Fool" (by Willis L. Barnet), recorded by the Waller Family/Dynamic Artists Records (pop/soul); "Get Up Everybody" (by Ronnie R. Cokes), recorded by Starfire/Dynamic Artists Records (funk/soul); and "Without You Tonight" (by Joseph J. Carter, Jr.), recorded by Waller Family/Dynamic Artists Records (pop/soul).

HOT WAX MUSIC PUBLISHING COMPANY, Box 299, Albert St., St. Jacobs, Ontario, Canada N0B 2N0. (519)664-3311. Affiliate: St. Jacobs Music Publishing Company (PROCAN). A&R Director: Mr. Jim Evans. Record company and music publisher. CAPAC. Member CRIA. Publishes 30 songs/year; publishes 25 new songwriters/year. Pays standard royalty.
How to Contact: Submit demo tape and lyric sheet. Prefers cassette with 3-5 songs on demo. "Send only your best material with lyrics and melody clearly discernable." SAE and International Reply Coupons. Reports in 1 month.
Music: C&W, dance-oriented, easy listening, gospel, MOR, R&B, rock (all kinds) and top 40/pop. Recently published "Me and Darlene" (by Rick Curtis), recorded by R. Curtis/Freedom Records (rock); "The Runner" (by Jim Evans), recorded by Official Theme (rock); and "Right Time for a Love Song" (by Wayne Diebold), recorded by Wayne Diebold/Circle M Records (country).

HOUSE OF DIAMONDS MUSIC, Box 449, Cleburne TX 76031. (817)641-3029. Contact: Jan Diamond. Music publisher. BMI, CMA.
How to Contact: Submit demo tape and lyric sheet. Prefers cassette.
Music: C&W; folk; gospel; MOR; progressive; country rock; and top 40/pop.

HOUSE OF GOLD MUSIC, INC., Box 120967, Aklen Station, Nashville TN 37216. (615)383-4667. Affiliates: Bobby Goldsboro Music, Inc. (ASCAP); and Hungry Mountain Music, Inc. (BMI). BMI. Member NMPA.
How to Contact: Submit demo tape and lyric sheet. Prefer cassette with 2-4 songs on demo. SASE.

HUNTLEY STREET PUBLISHING, 100 Huntley St., Toronto, Ontario, Canada M4X 2L1. (416)961-8001. Manager: Bruce W. Stacey. Music publisher. Estab. 1981. PROCAN. Publishes 30 songs/year. Pays standard royalty.
How to Contact: Write first about your interest. Prefers cassette with 2-3 songs on demo. SAE and International Reply Coupons. Reports in 1 month.
Music: Children's, contemporary church/religious and gospel.

I.A.M. MUSIC, 17422 Murphy Ave., Irvine CA 92719. (714)751-2015. Marketing Associate: Paul Leighton. Music publisher, record company and record producer. ASCAP. Member NARAS, GMA. Publishes 75-100 songs/year; publishes 10 new songwriters/year. Pays standard royalty.
How to Contact: Submit demo tape and lyric sheet. Prefers cassette with 3 or more songs on demo. SASE. Reports in 2 months.
Music: All types.

INSTANT REPLAY MUSIC CO., Box 353, Marina CA 93933. General Manager of Publishing: Robert Waldrup II. Vice President/A&R: Michael Edward Waldrup. Music publisher. ASCAP. Publishes 35-50 songs/year; publishes 3-5 new songwriters/year. Pays standard royalty.
How to Contact: Submit demo tape and lead sheet. Prefers reel-to-reel with 2-4 songs on demo. "Use piano and vocal; or bass drums, piano and vocal. Guitar can also be used." SASE. Reports in 3 weeks.
Music: Disco; jazz; and soul. Recently published "Are You Alone" (by B. Waldrup); "Your Kind of Guy" recorded by Scotty Wright; and "Trade" recorded by The Seville Band.
Tips: "Keep demos simple."

INSURANCE MUSIC PUBLISHING, 11616 S. Lafayette, Chicago IL 60628. (312)264-2166. President: Bill Tyson. Music publisher. BMI. Publishes 20 songs/year. Pays standard royalty.
How to Contact: Submit demo tape and lyric sheet. Prefers cassette with 2-4 songs on demo. Does not return unsolicited material. Reports in 3 weeks.
Music: Blues; Black church/religious/gospel; and R&B.

INSANITY'S MUSIC, 24548 Pierce, Southfield MI 48075. (313)559-7630. President: Bruce Lorfel. Music publisher and booking agency. BMI.

How to Contact: Submit demo tape. Prefers cassette with 1-4 songs on demo. SASE. Reports in 1 month.
Music: C&W; easy listening; MOR; rock; and top/40 pop.

INTERPLANETARY MUSIC, 7901 S. La Salle St., Chicago IL 60620. (312)224-0396. President: James R. Hall III. Vice President: Henry Jackson. Music publisher, booking agency and record company. BMI. Pays standard maximum royalty.
How to Contact: Submit demo tape or arrange personal interview. Prefers cassette. SASE. Reports in 3 weeks.
Music: Disco; soul; and top 40/pop. Recently published "Girl, Why Do You Want to Take My Heart?", recorded by Magical Connection (pop); and "You Blew My Mind This Time," recorded by Joe Martin (soul/pop/easy listening).

IRON BLOSSOM MUSIC GROUP, 50 Music Square W., Suite 902, United Artist Tower, Nashville TN 37203. (615)329-0714. Affiliates: Coral Blossom Music (BMI) and Orange Blossom Music (SESAC). Professional Manager: Stan Cornelius. Music publisher, record company and record producer. Estab. 1978. ASCAP. Pays standard royalities.
How to Contact: Query or arrange personal interview. Prefers cassette with 3-4 songs on demo. SASE. Will return material "if time allows." Reports as soon as possible.
Music: "Mainly modern country, but we're capable of any type if we hear what we think is a hit. We just think music." Recently published "Cheaper Crude or No More Food" (by Brent Burns), recorded by Bobby Butler/Universal Records; "Back To Back" (by Johnny McBee and Joanne Pruett), recorded by Joanne Pruett (country); and "Please Sing Satin Sheets" (by J. Pruett), recorded by Pruett (country).

IRVING/ALMO MUSIC OF CANADA, LTD., 939 Warden Ave., Toronto, Ontario, Canada. (416)752-7191. Administrator: Brian Chater. Music publisher. BMI. Member NMPA. Publishes 50-75 songs/year; publishes 3 new songwriters/year. Pays standard royalty.
How to Contact: Submit demo tape or submit demo tape and lead sheet. Prefers cassette with 3-6 songs on demo. SAE and International Reply Coupons. Reports in 3 weeks.
Music: Easy listening; folk; MOR; progressive; rock; and top 40/pop. Recently published "Sign of the Gypsy Queen" (by Lorence Hud), recorded by April Wine/Capital (rock); "Hold Me Once" (by Bryan Adams), recorded by Florence Warner/Mercury (ballad); and "I Can't Live without Your Love" (by Craig Ruhnke), recorded by Craig Ruhnke/A&M (pop).
Tips: "Listen to the radio and follow the general trend but add something new to establish a new direction."

JACKPOT MUSIC, 133 Walton Ferry, Hendersonville TN 37075. (615)824-2820. Affiliates: Eager Beaver Music and His Word Music. President: Clyde Beavers. Music publisher, record producer, record company and studio. BMI, ASCAP and SESAC. Pays standard royalty.
How to Contact: Call first about your interest, then submit demo tape and lyric sheet. Prefers 7½ ips reel-to-reel or cassette with 1-3 songs on demo. SASE. Reports as soon as possible.
Music: Bluegrass; children's; church/religious; C&W; folk; and gospel.

THOMAS JACKSON PUBLISHING, (formerly Isonode Publishing), Rainbow Recording Studios, 2322 S. 64th Ave., Omaha NE 68106. (402)554-0123. Manager: Thomas Jackson/Nils Anders Erickson. Music publisher and record company. BMI. Publishes 2-3 songs/year. Pays standard royalty. Sometimes hires songwriters on salary basis: "e.g., commercial writers who produce jingles, soundtracks and audiovisual shows."
How to Contact: Arrange personal interview or submit demo tape and lead sheet. Prefers cassette with 1-6 songs on demo. "Please, only professionally done demos." SASE. Reports in 1 month.
Music: Church/religious; C&W; easy listening; rock (soft or country); top 40/pop; and jingles/commercials.

JACLYN MUSIC, 126 Millwood Dr. L-467, Nashville TN 37217. (615)255-2289. President: Jack Lynch. Music publisher and record company. BMI. Affiliate: Nashville Music Sales. Publishes 12 songs/year. Pays standard royalty.
How to Contact: Query, then submit demo tape and lyric sheet. Prefers 7½ or 15 ips reel-to-reel or cassette with 1-12 songs on demo. SASE. Reports in 1 week.
Music: Bluegrass; church/religious; C&W; and gospel. Recently published "Mastertones" (by Les Hall), recorded by L. Hall/Jalyn Records (bluegrass); "In Memory of Carter Stanley" by Jack Lynch (bluegrass); "Bonnie & Clyde's Hop" (by Jack Lynch), recorded by Ralph Stanley/Jalyn Records (bluegrass).

JAMES BOY PUBLISHING CO., Box 128, Worcester PA 19490. (215)424-0800. President: Mr. J. James. Music publisher. BMI. Pays standard royalty.
How to Contact: Submit demo tape and lyric sheet. Prefers cassette with any number songs on demo. Reports in 1 month.
Music: C&W, dance-oriented, easy listening, folk, gospel, MOR, R&B and soul.

DICK JAMES MUSIC, INC., 119 W. 57th St., Suite 400, New York NY 10019. (212)581-3420. Nashville Office: 318 Chesterfield Ave., Nashville TN 37212. (615)292-3240. Affiliates: Cookaway Music (ASCAP), Dejamus Music (ASCAP), Maribus Music (BMI), Daramus Music (ASCAP) and Yamaha. General Manager: Arthur Braun. Professional Manager, Nashville: Bob Campbell. Music publisher. BMI. Member NMPA. Publishes 20,000 songs/year: publishes 25 new songwriters/year.
How to Contact: Submit demo tape and lead sheet. Prefers cassette with 1-3 songs on demo. SASE. Reports "as soon as possible."
Music: C&W; easy listening; MOR; rock (country and hard); soul; R&B; and top 40/pop. Recently published "We Said Good-by" (by Roger Greenaway and Geoff Stephens), recorded by Crystal Gayle (C&W); and "Heartbreaker," recorded by Pat Benatar.

JANELL MUSIC PUBLISHING/TIKI ENTERPRISES, INC., 792 E. Julian St., San Jose CA 95112. (408)286-9840 or (408)286-9845. Affiliates: Janell (BMI) and Tooter Scooter Music (BMI). President: Gradie O'Neal. Secretary: Jeannine Osborn. Music publisher and record company. BMI. Publishes 75 songs/year. Pays standard royalty.
How to Contact: Submit demo tape with lead or lyric sheet. Prefers 7½ ips reel-to-reel or cassette with 4 songs on demo. SASE. Reports in 2 weeks.
Music: C&W; easy listening; gospel; MOR; rock (soft or hard); soul; and top 40/pop. Recently published "Sweet Misery" (by Cal and Joyce Hyden), recorded by Michele Metz/Pretty Girl Records (pop); "Why Should I Worry" (by Cal and Joyce Hyden), recorded by Michele Metz/Pretty Girl Records (pop); "I Cried a Song" (by George Pickard), recorded by George Pickard/Rowena Records (country); "Too Much Horse Power," recorded by Joe Richie/Rowena Records (country); and "How Do You Get Rid Of a Hippie," recorded by Joe Richie/Rowena Records (country).

JANUS MUSIC, 519 Downie St. R, Stratford, Ontario, Canada N5A 1Y3. (519)273-2127. Contact: Tom Waschkowski. Music publisher, record company, record producer and studio. Estab. 1980. CAPAC. Publishes 20 songs/year; publishes 8 new songwriters/year. Pays standard royalty.
How to Contact: Submit demo tape and lyric sheet. Prefers cassette with 2-4 songs on demo. "Send some information on your background and ambitions." SAE and International Reply Coupons. Reports in 6-8 weeks.
Music: Children's, church/religious, country, rock (commercial), and top 40/pop. Recently published "Ain't It Funny" (by Jim Haggerty), recorded by Jim Haggerty/Maxim Records (MOR); "Magic Wind" (by Larry Dickenson), recorded by Plastic Rangers/Maxim Records (rock); and "Money Man" (by T. Waschkowski), recorded by 'Cookin'/Maxim Records (rock).

JANVIER MUSIC, INC., CP 357 St. Bruno, Quebec, Canada J3V 5G8. Director: Rancourt Rehjan. Music publisher, record producer and management firm. BMI. Publishes 50 songs/year. Pays standard royalties.
How to Contact: Query, arrange personal interview, submit demo tape, submit demo tape and lead sheet, submit acetate disc, submit acetate disc and lead sheet, or submit videocassette. Prefers 7½ ips reel-to-reel or cassette with 2-10 songs on demo. Does not return unsolicited material. Reports in 1 month.
Music: Easy listening; folk; MOR; rock; soul; and top 40/pop. Recently published "Craving," recorded by D. Lavoiz/Sefel Records in Canada, Ariola Records in Europe (MOR); "G. Entremont," by D. Deschene/Pro Culture Records (MOR); "Amarelina," by Nazare Pereira/Trafic Records (MOR); "Cross Road," by Sugar Blue/Trafic Records (blues); and "Jeteuerai," by Bernard Swell/WEA Records (rock).

JASPURR MUSIC, Box 1404, Studio City CA 91604. (213)669-1404. Affiliate: Bug Music Group (BMI). President: John Condon. Music publisher. BMI. Publishes 5 songs/year; publishes 2 new songwriters/year. Pays standard royalty.
How to Contact: Write first about your interest, submit demo tape and lyric sheet. Prefers cassette with 3-25 songs on demo. SASE. Reports in 1 month.
Music: Blues, C&W, dance-oriented, progressive, R&B, rock and top 40/pop.

JAY-ME MUSIC, Box 343, Dundas, Ontario, Canada L9H 6M1. Manager: James Taylor. Music publisher, record company and recording studio. Estab. 1980. PROCAN. Member Canadian Musical Reproduction Rights Agency, Ltd. Publishes 8 songs/year; publishes 7 new songwriters/year. Pays standard royalty.
How to Contact: Submit demo tape and lyric sheet. Prefers cassette with 1-4 songs on demo. SAE and International Reply Coupons. Reports in 1 month.
Music: Easy listening, folk, MOR, rock (all types) and top 40/pop. Recently published "Can't You Hear Me" (by Jaime), recorded by Dundas/SWP Records (country rock); "Got It in the Bag" and "I'm Not Going Anywhere" (by MacRae, Waugh and Rose), recorded by the Innocent/SWP Records (new wave).
Tips: "Our special interest is Canadian talent, although we will listen to everything submitted."

JAYMORE MUSIC, Box 100, 6260 Meyer St., Brighton MI 48116. (313)227-1997. President: John Morris. Music publisher and record company. BMI. Publishes 50 songs/year. Pays standard royalty.
How to Contact: Query. Prefers cassette with 2-20 songs on demo. SASE. Reports in 2 weeks.
Music: Bluegrass; C&W; folk; and gospel. Recently published "I've Just Seen the Rock of Ages" (by Johnny Preston), recorded by Larry Sparks/O.H. Records (sacred).

JERJOY MUSIC, Box 3615, Peoria IL 61604. (309)673-5755. Professional Manager: Jerry Hanlon. Music publisher. Estab. 1980. BMI. Publishes 4 songs/year; publishes 3 new songwriters/year. Pays standard royalty.
How to Contact: Submit demo tape and lyric sheet. Prefers cassette with 4-8 songs on demo. SASE. Reports in 2 weeks.
Music: C&W. Recently published "Love Has Gone Away" (by D. Moody), recorded by Jerry Hanlon (country ballad); "Hey, Little Dan" (by A. Simmons), recorded by Jerry Hanlon (country); and "Scarlet Woman" (by J. Hanlon and J. Schneider), recorded by Jerry Hanlon (country).

JIBARO MUSIC CO., INC., Box 424, Mount Clemens MI 48043. (313)791-2678. President/Professional Manager: Jim Roach. General Manager: Ann Roach. Music publisher and production company. BMI. Pays standard royalty.
How to Contact: Submit demo tape and lead sheet. Prefers cassette with 1-4 songs on demo. SASE. Reports in 2 weeks.
Music: Disco; jazz; MOR; and soul. Recently published "Casanova Brown," recorded by Gloria Gaynor (disco/soul); "Thank God You're My Lady," recorded by the Dells (ballad); "I Dig Your Music," recorded by the Dramatics (disco/soul); "You're My Super Hero" and "Super Heros Theme" (both by Jim Roach), both recorded by Everlife/CRC Records (pop).

JLT CHRISTIAN AGAPE MUSIC CO., 104 8th St., Salem NJ 08079. (609)935-1908. Owner: John L. Tussey Jr. Music publisher. ASCAP. Pays standard royalty.
How to Contact: Query. Prefers cassette and lead sheet with 1-3 songs on demo. SASE. Reports in 1 month.
Music: Church/religious and gospel.

JMR ENTERPRISES, 1014 16th Ave. S., Nashville TN 37212. (615)244-1630. Affiliates: Kelly & Lloyd Music (ASCAP), Mick Lloyd Music (SESAC), Street Song Music (ASCAP) and Jerrimick Music (BMI). Professional Manager: Robin Eichel. Music publisher, record producer and record company. ASCAP. Member CMA, NSAI and NARAS. Publishes 150 songs/year; publishes 20 new songwriters/year. Pays standard royalty.
How to Contact: Submit demo tape and lyric sheet. Prefers cassette with 1-3 songs on demo. SASE. Reports in 1 week.
Music: C&W; easy listening; gospel; MOR; progressive; church/religious; R&B; rock; and top 40/pop. Recently published "Take Your Time in Leavin' " (by Jerri Kelly), recorded by Loretta Lynn/MCA Records (C&W); "Fallin' for You" (by Kardyn Freeman), recorded by Jerry Kelly/Little Giant Records (C&W/MOR); "For a Slow Dance with You" (by Mick Lloyd), recorded by Dave Rowland & Sugar/Elektra Records (C&W/MOR); and "Fool by Your Side" (by Bobby Cox), recorded by Dave Rowland & Sugar/Electra Records (C&W/MOR).

JOBETE MUSIC CO., INC., 6255 Sunset Blvd., Hollywood CA 90028. (213)468-3400. Affiliate: Stone Diamond Music. (BMI). Executive Vice President: Robert Gordy. Vice President/General Manager: Jay Lowy. Music publisher. ASCAP. Member NMPA. Publishes 1,500 songs/year. Hires staff writers.
How to Contact: Submit demo tape and lyric sheet. Prefers 7½ or 15 ips reel-to-reel or cassette with 1-3 songs on demo. SASE. Reports in 1 month.

Music: Blues; C&W; disco; easy listening; gospel; jazz; MOR; progressive; R&B; rock; soul; and top 40/pop. Recently published "Three Times a Lady" and "Still," recorded by The Commodores; "Ooh, Baby, Baby," recorded by Linda Ronstadt; and "You Are the Sunshine of My Life," recorded by Stevie Wonder.

JOBETE MUSIC CO., INC., 157 W. 57th St., New York NY 10019. (212)581-7420. Affiliate: Stone Diamond Music. (BMI). Contact: Director of East Coast Professional Activities. Music publisher. ASCAP. Member NMPA. Pays standard royalty.
How to Contact: Submit demo tape and lyric sheet. Prefers 7½ or 15 ips reel-to-reel or cassette with 1-3 songs on demo. SASE. Reports in 1 month.
Music: Blues; R&B; rock; and top 40/pop. Recently published "Cruising" (by Smokey Robinson), recorded by S. Robinson (pop).

LITTLE RICHIE JOHNSON MUSIC, 913 S. Main St., Belen NM 87002. (505)864-7441. Manager: Joey Lee. Music publisher, record company and record producer. BMI. Publishes 25 songs/year; publishes 15-20 new songwriters/year. Pays standard royalty.
How to Contact: Submit demo tape and lyric sheet. Prefers 7½ ips reel-to-reel or cassette with 6-8 songs on demo. SASE. Reports in 2 weeks.
Music: C&W, gospel and Spanish. Recently published "Let It Be" (by Nadine Moore), recorded by Carol Roman/LRJ Records (C&W); "I Just Want to Be Free" (by Carol Roman), recorded by Carol Roman/LRJ Records (C&W); and "Sweet Freedom" (by Nadine Moore), recorded by Carol Roman/LRJ Records (C&W).

JOMEWA MUSIC, 135 E. 65th St., New York NY 10021. Contact: Mel Small. Music publisher. Publishes 6 songs/year. Uses AGAC-approved contract.
How to Contact: Submit demo tape and lead sheet. Prefers reel-to-reel or cassette with 1-4 songs on demo. SASE. Reports in 2 weeks.
Music: Easy listening; folk; MOR; and top 40/pop.

JON MUSIC, Box 233, 329 N. Main St., Church Point LA 70525. (318)684-2176. Owner: Lee Lavergne. Music publisher and record company. BMI. Pays standard royalty.
How to Contact: Submit demo tape. Prefers 7½ ips reel-to-reel or cassette with 2-6 songs on demo. SASE. Reports in 2 weeks.
Music: C&W; rock; and soul. Recently published "My Home Town" (by Ron Johnson), recorded by Charles Mann/Lanor Records (country); and "Something to Do" (by Paul Marx), recorded by P. Marx/Lanor Records (country).

JONAN MUSIC, 342 Westminster Ave., Elizabeth NJ 07208. Office Manager: Helen Gottesmann. Music publisher. ASCAP. Publishes 60 songs/year.
Music: Only publishes material of artists recording on Savoy Records. Recently published "Welcome to My World" (by N. Williams), recorded by Jonathan Greer Singers/Label Records (gospel); "Because of You Lord" (by J.C. White), recorded by Institutional Radio Choir/Savoy Records (gospel); and "Just a Little Love" (by J.C. White), recorded by J.C. White Singers/Savoy Records (gospel).

JOURNEYMAN MUSIC, 135-46 Grand Central Pkwy, Kew Gardens NY 11435. (212)847-6377. Manager: Ernest Petito. Music publisher and arranger. BMI, AGAC. Publishes 5 songs/year. Pays standard royalty.
How to Contact: Submit demo tape and lyric sheet. Prefers cassette with 2-5 songs on demo. "Submit *only* copyrighted material. Affix copyright symbol, author's name, date (year) on *everything*." SASE. Reports in 3 weeks.
Tips: "Give me a song, on cassette, clearly recorded; explain in a brief note the type of song you think it is and what bands, artist or market you think would be best suited to the song. Be sure that eveything is properly registered at the U.S. Copyright Office; observe professional consistency in melody and metrics; avoid lyric cliches or 'throw-away/toss-off' lines; give each rhyme careful thought; establish a mood, imagining each song as a staged dramatic piece.."

KACK KLICK, INC., Mirror Records, Inc., 645 Titus Ave., Rochester NY 14617. (716)544-3500. Vice President: Armand Schaubroeck. Manager: Kim Simons. Music publisher and record company. BMI.
How to Contact: Submit demo tape. Prefers 7½ ips reel-to-reel. Include photo. SASE. Reports in 2 months.
Music: MOR; progressive; rock; top 40/pop; and new wave.

KAMAKAZI MUSIC CORPORATION, 314 W. 71st St., New York NY 10023. (212)595-4330. Professional Manager: Miles J. Lourie. Music publisher. BMI. Pays standard royalty.
How to Contact: Submit demo tape and lyric sheet. Prefers cassette with 2-3 songs on demo. SASE. Reports in 4-6 weeks.
Music: Progressive; R&B; rock; and top 40/pop.

BOB KARCY MUSIC, 437 W. 16th St., New York NY 10011. (212)989-1989. President: Bob Karcy. Vice President: Jack Arel. Music publisher, record producer and management firm. ASCAP and BMI.
How to Contact: Query or submit demo tape and lead sheet. "No interviews without prior appointment." Prefers cassette with 1-6 songs on demo. SASE. Reports in 3 weeks.
Music: Dance; easy listening; MOR; rock ("all types except hard, acid or punk rock"); and top 40/pop. Recently published "Melody Lady," recorded by Sunshine (top 40); "Rockola-Rockola," recorded by Anne Murphy (top 40); and "More Than Happy," recorded by Sellout (top 40).

KARLA MUSIC PUBLISHING, 11042 Aqua Vista St., North Hollywood CA 91602. President: James Argiro. Music publisher. ASCAP. Publishes 20 songs/year; publishes 20 new songwriters/year. Pays standard royalty.
How to Contact: Submit demo tape and lead sheet or submit lead sheet. Prefers cassette with 1-6 songs on demo. SASE. Reports in 1 month.
Music: Easy listening; jazz; MOR; progressive; soul; and top 40/pop.

KAT FAMILY MUSIC PUBLISHING, 5775 Peachtree Dunwoody Rd. NE, B-130, Atlanta GA 30342. (404)252-6600. President: Joel A. Katz. Vice President/General Manager: Steve Weaver. Music publisher. Estab. 1979. BMI. Publishes 30-50 songs/year. Pays standard royalty.
How to Contact: Submit demo tape and lyric sheet. Prefers cassette with 2-4 songs on demo. SASE. Reports in 1 month.
Music: Rock; pop; country; MOR; R&B; and contemporary gospel.

KECA MUSIC, INC., 9440 Santa Monica Blvd. #704, Beverly Hills CA 90210. (213)278-3156. General Manager: Noreen Rae Cowan. Music Publisher and manager. ASCAP. Publishes 50 songs/year. Pays standard royalty.
How to Contact: Write first about your interest. Prefers cassette with 4-10 songs on demo. SASE. Reports in 3 weeks.
Music: C&W; easy listening; MOR; country rock; soul; top 40/pop.

JOE KEENE MUSIC CO., Box 602, Kennett MO 63857. Affiliates: Lincoln Road Music (BMI) and Cone Music (BMI). President: Joe Keene. Music publisher. BMI. Pays standard royalty.
How to Contact: Submit demo tape and lead sheet. Prefers reel-to-reel or cassette. SASE. Reports in 2 weeks.
Music: C&W; rock; and easy listening. Recently published "Will the Taste of Love Be as Sweet (in the Morning)" and "So Tired of Being Your Fool" (both by Joe Keene), both recorded by J. Keene/KSS Records (country).

KELLY & LLOYD MUSIC, 1014 16th Ave. S, Nashville TN 37212. (615)244-1630. Affiliates: Mick Lloyd Music (SESAC) and Jerri Music (BMI), part of JMR Enterprises. President: Mick Lloyd. Music publisher, record producer and record company. ASCAP. Publishes 150 songs/year; publishes 12 new songwriters/year. Pays standard royalty.
How to Contact: Pays standard royalty. Prefers cassette with 1-4 songs on demo. SASE. Reports in 1 week. "Submit a clear tape and lyrics."
Music: "I'm as Much of a Woman" (by Jerri Kelly), recorded by DeDe Church/Little Giant Records (country); "Fool By Your Side" (by Bobby Cox), recorded by Dave Rowland & Sugar/Elektra; "Take a Chance on Love" (by Bryon Gallimore), recorded by Dave Rowland & Sugar/Elektra; "Life on the Road" (by Micic Lloyd), recorded by Dave Rowland & Sugar/Elektra Records (country); and "Take Your Time in Leavin" (by Jerri Kelly), recorded by Loretta Lynn/MCA.

GENE KENNEDY ENTERPRISES, INC., 2125 8th Ave. S., Nashville TN 37204. (615)383-6002. Affiliates: Chip 'n Dale (ASCAP), Door Knob Music (BMI), Lodestar (SESAC), Bekson (BMI) and Kenwall (ASCAP). President: Gene Kennedy. Vice President: Karen Jeglum. Music publisher.
How to Contact: Query or arrange personal interview. Prefers 7½ ips reel-to-reel with 1-5 songs on demo. "We do not accept cassettes. We prefer that you make contact by phone or mail prior to submitting material. Tape should be accompanied by lyrics." SASE. Reports in 5 weeks.
Music: Bluegrass; C&W; gospel; MOR; and top 40/pop.

KICKING MULE PUBLISHING/DESK DRAWER PUBLISHING, Box 158, Alderpoint CA 95411. Manager: Ed Denson. Music publisher and record company. BMI. Member NAIRD. Publishes 300 songs/year; publishes 20 new songwriters/year. Pays standard royalties.
How to Contact: Write first about your interest. Prefers cassette with 1-3 songs on demo. Does not return unsolicited material. Reports "as soon as possible."
Music: Bluegrass (flatpicking); blues (fingerpicking); and folk (guitar/banjo only). "We publish only material released on our albums. Since we record virtuoso guitar and banjo players, virtually the only way to get a tune published with us is to be such a player, or to have such a player record your song. We don't publish many 'songs' per se, our entire catalog is devoted 95% to instrumentals and 5% to songs with lyrics. As publishers we are not in the market for new songs. This listing is more of a hope that people will not waste their time and ours sending us blue-sky demos of material that does not relate to our very specialized business." Recently published "The Sweeper" (by George Gritzbach), recorded by Gritzbach/KM Records (folk); "Thunder On The Run" (by Stefan Grossman), recorded by Gritzbach/KM Records (guitar instrumental); and "Pokerface Smile" (by Robert Force), recorded by Force & D'Ossche (country).

KILKENNY, 5825 N. 96th St., Milwaukee WI 53225. (414)462-5590. President: Tim Brophy. Vice President: Bob Ambos. Music publisher. Estab. 1979. BMI. Publishes 40 songs/year. Pays standard royalty.
How to Contact: Submit demo tape and lyric sheet. Prefers cassette with 2-8 songs on demo. Does not return unsolicited material. Reports in 3 weeks.
Music: C&W; dance; easy listening; MOR; progressive; R&B; rock; soul; and top 40/pop. Recently published "Lily" (by Dan Riley and Barry Kaya), recorded by Dan Riley/Armada Records (C&W); "Wrap Myself Up" (by Jim Spencer), recorded by Jim Spencer/Armada Records (disco); and "Fear of Failing" (by John Gladstone), recorded by Pacifica Orchestra (pop).

KIMBERLY RENE MUSIC, 18 W. 7th St., Cincinnati OH 45202 (513)421-5256. Affiliate: Lindsay-Cole Music (ASCAP). President: Carl Edmondson. Music publisher, record producer and record company. Estab. 1980. BMI. Pays standard royalty.
How to Contact: Prefers 7½ ips reel-to-reel or cassette with 1-5 songs on demo and typed lyrics. SASE. Reports in 3 weeks.
Music: Bluegrass; C&W; disco; easy listening; MOR; progressive; R&B; rock; soul and top 40/pop.

KING AND MOORE MUSIC, Box 10273, Chicago IL 60610. (312)944-1125. Vice President of Publishing: Ralph J. Moore. Music publisher, record company and record producer. Estab. 1979. BMI. Publishes 1 new songwriter/year. Pays standard royalty.
How to Contact: Submit demo tape and lyric sheet. Prefers 7½ ips reel-to-reel or cassette with 2-4 songs on demo. "Writer should show versility in writing style. Do not just send ballads." SASE. Reports in 3 weeks.
Music: Blues, easy listening, gospel, jazz, R&B, rock, soul, top 40/pop and adult contemporary.

JIMMY KISH MUSIC PUBLISHING, Box 140316, Nashville TN 37214. (615)889-6675. Music publisher and record company. BMI.
How to Contact: Submit demo tape and lead sheet. Prefers 7½ ips reel-to-reel or cassette. SASE. Reports in 2 weeks.
Music: C&W and gospel. Recently released "I Dare to Dream" (by Jimmy Kish and Les Peterson); "That's What Makes a Heartache" (by Kish and Peterson); and "Nite Plane to Nashville" (by Kish and Red River Dave), all recorded by Jimmy Kish/Kess Records (C&W).

KITCHEN TABLE MUSIC, Box 861, Edmonton, Alberta, Canada T5J 2L8. (403)477-6844. Affiliates: Gimbleco West Music/PROCAN; Stony Plain Music/CAPAC, and Eyeball Wine Music/CAPAC. Managing Director: Holger Petersen. Music publisher, record company and record producer. PROCAN. Member CIRPA and CARAS. Publishes 50 songs/year; publishes 5 new songwriters/year. Pays standard royalty.
How to Contact: Submit demo tape and lyric sheet. Prefers cassette with 1-4 songs on demo. SAE and International Reply Coupons. Reports in 3 weeks.
Music: Bluegrass, children's, folk, MOR, progressive, rock and top 40/pop. Recently published "Misty Mountain" (by Ferron), recorded by Ferron/Stony Plain Records (folk); "Running Start" (by Larry Pink), recorded by Crowcuss/Stony Plain Records (rock); and "The Matromonial Blues" (by Paul Hann), recorded by Paul Hann/Stony Plain Records (folk).

KRPCO MUSIC, 4926 W. Gunnison, Chicago IL 60630. (312)545-0861. President: Ray Peck. Music publisher, record company, record producer and record distributor. BMI, ASCAP.

Publishes 12-16 songs/year; publishes 5 new songwriters/year. Pays standard royalty.
How to Contact: Submit demo tape and lyric sheet. Prefers cassette with 4-6 songs on demo. SASE. Reports in 1 month.
Music: All types. Recently published "I Have Always Loved You" (by Paul Mahalek), recorded by Mahalek/Newbary Records (rock); "Country Music" (by Gary Cross), recorded by G. Cross/Homestead Records (country); and "Jeffery" (by Rich Rags), recorded by R. Rags/Kiderian Records (new wave).

LA LOU MUSIC, 711 Stevenson St., Lafayette LA 70501. (318)234-5577. President: Carol J. Rachou, Sr. Music publisher, record company (La Louisianne), record producer, recording studio and distributing company. BMI. Publishes 50-60 songs/year. Pays standard royalty.
How to Contact: Submit demo tape and lyric sheet. Prefers 7½ ips reel-to-reel or cassette with 1-6 songs on demo. "If possible, we would like variations of each song (tempos, styles, keys, etc.)." SASE.
Music: "We are primarily interested in Cajun French songs." Also bluegrass, blues, church/religious, C&W, folk, gospel, jazz, MOR, progressive, R&B, rock, top 40/pop, comedy and French comedy. Published "Lache Pas La Patate" (by C.J. Trahan), recorded by Jimmy C. Newman/La Louisianne Records (Canjun/French); "When the Saints Go Marching In" (in Cajun French and English by Jimmy C. Newman/La Louisianne Records); and "Sweet Cajun Love Song" (by Eddy Raven), recorded by Eddy Raven/La Louisianne Records (Cajun French/English).

LACKEY PUBLISHING CO., Box 269, Caddo OK 74729. (405)367-2798. President: Robert F. Lackey. Music publisher and record producer. BMI. Publishes 12-14 songs/year; publishes 6-8 new songwriters/year. Pays standard royalties.
How to Contact: Submit demo tape. Prefers 7½ ips reel-to-reel tape with 1-10 songs on demo. SASE. Reports in 2 weeks.
Music: Bluegrass; blues; church/religious; C&W; easy listening; folk; gospel; MOR; progressive; R&B; and top 40/pop. Recently published "Red River Rose" (by Mike Hall), recorded by Mike Hall/Uptown Records (country); "Mississippi River Take Me Home" (by Frank Lackey), recorded by Frank Lackey/Uptown Records (MOR); and "Going to Louisiana" (by Mike Hall), recorded by Mike Hall/Uptown Records (MOR).
Tips: "Have accompaniment of 3 or more musicians."

LADD MUSIC CO., 401 Wintermantle Ave., Scranton PA 18505. (717)343-6718. President: Phil Ladd. Music publisher, record company and record producer. BMI. Publishes 4 songs/year. Pays standard royalties.
How to Contact: Query or submit demo tape and lead sheet. Prefers cassette with minimum 2 songs on demo. SASE. Reports in 3 weeks.
Music: Children's; C&W; easy listening; R&B; rock; and top 40/pop. Recently published "Piano Nelly," (by Bobby Poe), recorded by Bobby Brant/Whiterock (rock); and "Miss Lucy" (by Poe), recorded by Big Al Downing/Whiterock (rock).

LAKE COUNTRY MUSIC, Box 88, Decatur TX 76234. (817)627-2128. President: Danny Wood. Music publisher, record company and record producer. BMI. Publishes 15 songs/year; publishes 2 new songwriters/year. Pays standard royalty.
How to Contact: Write first about your interest. Prefers 7½ ips reel-to-reel with 1-4 songs on demo. Does not return unsolicited material. Reports in 1 month.
Music: Bluegrass and C&W. Recently published "Day Dreams" (by Larry Quinten), recorded by L. Quinten/Lake Country Records; "Trusting Love" (by Ronnie Mac), recorded by R. Mac/Lake Country Records; and "It's Not That Easy" (by L. Quinten), recorded by Larry Wampler/Lake Country Records (all C&W).

LANCE JAY MUSIC, Box 368, Selmer TN 38375. (901)645-5423. Vice President: Carol Morris. Music publisher. ASCAP. Affiliate: Carol Faye Music. BMI. Works with songwriters on contract.
How to Contact: Submit demo tape and lead sheet. Prefers 7½ ips reel-to-reel or cassette with 2-4 songs on demo. SASE. Reports in 1 month.
Music: Bluegrass; C&W; and gospel. Recently published "Black Lung," "Fire In the Sky," and "Born In Debt."

LANDERS ROBERTS MUSIC, 9255 Sunset Blvd., Suite 915, Los Angeles CA 90069. (213)550-8819. Affiliate: Landers/Roberts Songs (BMI). Co-presidents: Hal Landers, Bobby Roberts. Vice-President: Jay Landers. General Manager: Barry Jay Josephson. Music publisher, record producer and management firm. ASCAP. Member OCMP. Publishes 30 songs/year; publishes 2-3 new songwriters/year. Pays standard royalty.

How to Contact: Query, arrange personal interview, or submit demo tape and lyric sheet. Prefers cassette with 1-3 songs on demo. SASE. Reports within 3 weeks.
Music: Easy listening; MOR; rock; and top 40/pop. Recently published "When I Need You" (by Albert Hammond and Carol Bayer Sager), recorded by Leo Sayer (MOR/pop); "It Never Rains in Southern California" (by Hammond and Mike Hazelwood), recorded by Hammond (MOR/pop); "The Air That I Breathe" (by Hammond), recorded by the Hollies (MOR/pop), and "99 Miles From LA" (by Albert Hammond/Hal David), recorded by Johnny Mathis.

CRISTY LANE MUSIC, L S Record Co., 120 Hickory St., Madison TN 37115. (615)868-7171. Affiliates: Cindy Lee Music (SESAC) and Kevin Lee Music (BMI). Publishing Director: Harold Hodges. Music publisher and record company. ASCAP. Publishes 25-40 songs/year; publishes 2-6 new songwriters/year. Pays standard royalty. Screens "all types of music for publishing for in-house artists and others." Prime interest in modern country.
How to Contact: Submit demo tape and lyric sheet or arrange personal interview. Prefers 7½ ips reel-to-reel or cassette with 3 songs maximum on demo. SASE "with sufficient return postage.". Reports in 1 month.
Music: C&W (modern); easy listening; MOR; rock (soft); and top 40/pop. Recently published "Sweet Sexy Eyes" (by Bob Jenkins), recorded by Cristy Lane/Liberty Records (country); "A Mile from Nowhere" (by Miller/Greene), recorded by Miller-Green/L.S.Records (pop/country); and "Love to Love You" (by David Heavener), recorded by Cristy Lane/Liberty Records (country).

STUART LANIS MUSIC, INC., 1273½ N. Crescent Hts. Blvd., Los Angeles CA 90046. (213)550-4500. Affiliate: Peter Piper Publishing (ASCAP). A&R: Stuart Lanis. Music publisher, record producer and record company. BMI. Publishes 15-20 songs/year. Pays standard royalty.
How to Contact: Submit demo tape and lyric sheet. Prefers cassette with 3-6 songs on demo. SASE. Reports in 3 weeks.
Music: Children's; church/religious; classical; easy listening; gospel; MOR; and top 40/pop.

LAPELLE MUSIC PUBLISHING, 1310 Centre St. S., Calgary, Alberta, Canada T2G 2E2. (403)269-7270. Contact: Bruce Thompson. Music publisher. PROCAN. Publishes 10-20 songs/year.
How to Contact: Submit demo tape and lead sheet. Prefers reel-to-reel or cassette. SASE.
Music: C&W and gospel (contemporary and "Jesus" music). Recently published "Gently Through" (by Lamar Boschman), recorded by Lamar Boschman/Praise Records (gospel); "It's Up To You" (by Paul Wylie), recorded by Stan Swindbn/Circa Records (gospel); "I Have Seen the Rain" (by B. Thompson), recorded by B. Thompson/London Records (C&W); "The Legacy" and "Angel Wings" recorded by Don Worden/Circa Records; and "Never Love a Sailor" recorded by Jann Richards/Circa Records.

LARDON MUSIC, Box 200, River Grove IL 60171. General Manager: Larry Nestor. Music publisher. BMI. Publishes 8-10 songs/year. Pays standard royalty.
How to Contact: Submit demo tape and lead sheet. Prefers 7½ ips reel-to-reel or cassette with a maximum of 3 songs on demo. SASE. Reports in 2 weeks.
Music: Children's (educational material as used on *Sesame Street* and *Captain Kangaroo*); country; and pop. Recently published "I Can't Sleep You Off," "Love Me Or Trade Me," and "Whiskey River" (by Larry Nestor), recorded by Johnny Cooper (country and pop).

LATE MUSIC CO., #3 Westminster, London Sq., Clifton Park NY 12144. (518)371-5659. President: Vincent E. Meyer, Jr. Vice President: James Lategano. A&R Director: Chuck Winans. Music publisher. BMI. Publishes 5 new songwriters/year. Pays standard royalty.
How to Contact: Submit demo tape and lyric sheet. Prefers 7½ ips reel-to-reel with 2-7 songs on demo. Reports in 1 month, if interested.
Music: Bluegrass, easy listening, folk, and top 40/pop. Recently published "Travelin' Shoes," recorded by Winans and Brown (folk); and "Maybe," recorded by Frank Mastrone and Al Nelson (pop).

LAUGHING BIRD SONGS PUBLISHING CO., Box 813, Valinda CA 91744. (213)964-1112. President: Angelo Roman, Jr. Music publisher and management consultant. ASCAP. Pays standard royalty.
How to Contact: Submit demo tape and lyric sheet. Prefers cassette with 1-5 songs on demo. SASE. Reports in 1 month.
Music: Blues, easy listening, jazz, MOR, progressive, rock and top 40/pop.

ROB LEE MUSIC, Box 1385, Merchantville NJ 08109. (609)663-4540. Affiliates: Pyramid Music (BMI) and Rock Island Music (ASCAP). Vice President: Bob Francis. Music publisher, record company, record producer, management firm and booking agency. BMI. Publishes 12-20 songs/year; publishes at least 6 new songwriters/year. Pays standard royalties.
How to Contact: Query or submit demo tape and lead sheet. Prefers 7½ ips reel-to-reel or cassette with 2-12 songs on demo. SASE. Reports in 1 month.
Music: C&W; disco; easy listening; jazz; MOR; rock; soul; and top 40/pop. Recently published "I Love You Because" (by Guy Hardin), recorded by Larry Seth (pop).

LILLENAS PUBLISHING CO., Box 527, Kansas City MO 64141. (816)931-1900. Affiliates: Beacon Hill Music (SESAC) and Faith Music (SESAC). Director: Ken Bible. Music Editor: Lyndell Leatherman. Music publisher and record producer. SESAC. Pays standard royalty.
How to Contact: Submit lead sheet. "A demo tape is helpful, but not necessary." Prefers cassette with 1-5 songs on demo. SASE. Reports in 2-8 weeks.
Music: Church/religious and gospel. Publishes primarily choral music, approximately 12 book/recordings per year, plus apprroximately 30 anthems. Also publishes some music for children, vocal solos, vocal ensembles and instruments.

LINEAGE PUBLISHING CO., Box 211, East Prairie MO 63845. (314)649-2211. Professional Manager: Tommy Loomas. Music publisher, record producer and record company. BMI. Pays standard royalty.
How to Contact: Query before submitting demo tape and lyric sheet. Prefers 7½ ips reel-to-reel or cassette with 2-4 songs on demo. SASE. Reports in 1 month.
Music: C&W; easy listening; MOR; country rock; and top 40/pop. Recently published "Country Boy" (by Alden Lambert), recorded by Lambert/Capstan Records (country); "Dawn" (by Hank Waring), recorded by Waring/Jalyn Records (country); and "Best of All" (by Tommy Loomas), recorded by Mary Nichols/Onie Records (MOR).

LISAS THEME MUSIC, 333 31st St. N., Suite 20, St. Petersburg FL 33713. (813)896-5151. Affiliate: 1st Dynasty Records, Inc. (BMI). President: Mike Douglas. Arranger/Conductor: Jerry Cobb. Music publisher, record company and record producer. Estab. 1980. Publishes 50 songs/year; publishes 53 new songwriters/year. Pays negotiable royalty.
How to Contact: Submit demo tape and lyric sheet. Prefers cassette with 1-4 songs on demo. "Use clean tapes." SASE. Reports "as soon as possible."
Music: Blues, C&W, easy listening, gospel, MOR, R&B, rock (all types), soul and top 40/pop. Recently published "J.R. Ewing/President" (by Sally Thompson), recorded by Rich Lovette/1st Dynasty Records, Inc. (country); "Doll House" (by Rita Hopkins), recorded by June Page/1st Dynasty Records, Inc. (country pop); and "Second Time Around" (by S. Thompson), recorded by June Page/1st Dynasty Records, Inc. (country).

LITTLE JOE MUSIC CO., 604 Broad St., Johnstown PA 15906. (814)539-8117. Owner: Al Page. Music publisher. BMI. Publishes 5 songs/year.
How to Contact: Submit demo tape and lead sheet. Prefers 3¾ ips reel-to-reel with 2-4 songs on demo. SASE. Reports in 2 weeks.
Music: Bluegrass; church/religious; C&W; disco; folk; and polkas. Recently published *Catholic Church Choir* (Roman Catholic music); *Orthodox Greek Catholic Choir* (religious); and *Organ* (instrumental).

LITTLE OTIS MUSIC, 101 Westchester Ave., Port Chester NY 10573. (914)939-1066. General manager: Judy Novy. Music publisher and record producer. BMI. Publishes 15-25 songs/year; publishes 2 new songwriters/year. Pays standard royalties.
How to Contact: Submit demo tape. Prefers cassette with 1-5 songs on demo. SASE. Reports in 1 month.
Music: MOR; R&B; rock; soul; and top 40/pop. Recently published "Play It the Fair Way" (by T. Masi, soul/R&B), "Rainmaker" (by G. Siano, soul/R&B) and "Let the Music Stone You" (by G. Siano, rock), all recorded by Johnny Sundance.

LODESTAR MUSIC, (Division of Gene Kennedy Enterprises, Inc.), 2125 8th Ave., S., Nashville TN 37204. (615)383-6002. Affiliates: Chip 'N' Dale Music Publishers, Inc. (ASCAP) and Door Knob Music Publishing, Inc. (BMI). President: Gene Kennedy. Vice President: Karen Jeglum. Music publisher, record company and record producer. SESAC. Member NSAI, CMA and ACM. Publishes 20 songs/year; publishes 10 new songwriters/year. Pays standard royalty.
How to Contact: Submit demo tape and lyric sheet or arrange personal interview. Prefers 7½ ips reel-to-reel or cassette with 1-4 songs. SASE. Reports in 6 weeks.

Music: C&W and MOR. Recently published "You're Still the One (Who Makes My Life Complete)" (by James Britt/Ervan James/Bobby Young), recorded by Douglas/Door Knob Records (MOR).

LONE LAKE SONGS, INC., Box 126, 93 N. Central Ave., Elmsford NY 10523. President: Ron Carpenter. Music publisher. ASCAP. Publishes 100 songs/year; published 76 new songwriters in 1979. Hires staff writers: "must be established musicians and be able to arrange and to write material for certain occasions, such as commercials."
How to Contact: Submit demo tape, submit demo tape and lead sheet, or submit lead sheet. Prefers 7½ ips reel-to-reel or cassette with 1-10 songs on demo. "Do not send original copies." SASE. Reports in 1 month.
Music: Bluegrass; C&W; disco; easy listening; folk; gospel; MOR; rock (mellow); soul; and top 40/pop. Recently published "Now and Then" (by R. Carpenter), recorded by various artists around the world/RCA/CBS/WB Records(pop); "So the Rain Is Falling" (by L. Boyd), recorded by Donna Stark (C&W); "The Next 100 Years" (by G. Cook—D. Stark), recorded by Donna Stark (C&W).

LORENZ INDUSTRIES, 501 E. 3rd St., Dayton OH 45401. Affiliates: Lorenz Publishing and Sunshine Productions (publishes monthly sacred music periodicals for youth and adult choirs as well as piano and organ periodicals); Sacred Music Press (publishes, in octavo form "a more stylized type of sacred music for church and school choirs"); Heritage Music Press (publishes choral, instrumental, and keyboard music for educational use); Triune/Triangle Cantus (Trigon); and Walton Music ("presents the more sophisticated publications with the assistance of Norman Luboff"). Music Editor: Lani Smith. Music publisher. BMI, ASCAP and SESAC. Member NMPA, MPA and CMPA. Publishes 500 songs/year; publishes 20 new songwriters/year. Pays standard royalty; 10% of retail selling price of sheet music.
How to Contact: Submit demo tape and lead sheet or submit lead sheet only. Prefers cassette. SASE. Reports in 1 month.

LORIJOY MUSIC, INC., 39 W. 55th St., New York NY 10019. (212)586-3350. Affiliates: Ace Deuce Trey Music (BMI) and Lucky Star Music (BMI). A&R Director: Nate Adams Jr. Music publisher. BMI. Publishes 10 songs/year. Pays standard royalties.
How to Contact: Submit demo tape or submit demo tape and lead sheet. Prefers 7½ or 15 ips reel-to-reel or cassette with minimum 2 songs on demo. SASE. Reports in 2 weeks.
Music: R&B; soul; and top 40/pop. Recently published "Peaceful" (by A.O. Johnson), recorded by Al Johnson/Marina Records (pop).

LOS ANGELES INTERNATIONAL MUSIC, Box 209, 102 Burbank Dr. B, Toledo OH 43695. President: Florence Lloyd. Music publisher. Estab. 1980. ASCAP. Member NMPA. Publishes 30 songs/year; publishes 8 new songwriters/year. Hires staff writers; pays negotiable salary "depending on expectations and music of songwriter." Pays standard royalty.
How to Contact: Submit demo tape and lyric sheet. Prefers 7½ ips reel-to-reel, cassette or demo records with 3-6 songs on demo. "Send only best songs with as much attention to music as to lyrics. Include lead sheets and/or arrangements. Sound and creativity are very important." Does not return unsolicited material. Reports in 3 weeks.
Music: Recently published "This Ole Heart" (by Cynthia Jones and Arron Tolbert), recorded by Backlash/Walking Tall Records; "Fair Game" (by Jimmy Lloyd Jr/Terry Snodgrass), recorded by Raymond Alexander/Fast Flight Records; "Give Me Some Credit" (by Carl Smith), recorded by La Que/Future Shock Records; "Who's Backstabbing Who?" (by Gregory Austin), recorded by La Que; and "Love Projection" (by Robert Slack), recorded by Unique Pleasure.
Tips: "Have a good knowledge of music and what type sound is making hit recordings. We prefer songwriters who are dedicated to the belief that songs are saleable in today's market."

LOVE STREET PUBLISHING, Box 2501, Des Moines IA 50315. (515)285-6564. President/Owner: Art Smart Stenstrom. Music publisher, booking agency and record company (Fanfare Records). BMI. Publishes 1-3 songs/year. Pays standard royalties. Interested only in regional groups in Iowa area for one-night engagements. Submit demo tape. Does not return unsolicited material.

LOWERY MUSIC CO., INC., 3051 Clairmont Rd. NE, Atlanta GA 30329. (404)325-0832. Affiliates: Brother Bill's Music (ASCAP), Low-Sal Inc. (BMI) and Low-Twi Inc. (BMI). Member CMA, NARAS and NMPA. Contact: Professional Director. Music publisher and record producer. BMI. Member NMPA. Publishes 20-30 songs/year; publishes 10 new songwriters/year. Pays standard royalties.

How to Contact: Submit demo tape and lyric sheet. Prefers cassette with 1-4 songs on demo. SASE. Reports in 2 weeks.
Music: Top 40; R&R; and C&W.

LUCKY'S KUM BA YA PUBLISHING, Box 6, Brohman MI 49312. (616)689-1586. Contact: Ross "Lucky" Fulton. Music publisher. ASCAP. Publishes 20 songs/year. Pays standard royalty.
How to Contact: "Not accepting outside material at present." Prefers cassette with 2 songs maximum on demo. SASE. Reports in 1 month.
Music: Bluegrass; C&W; gospel; R&B; rock; and top 40/pop. Recently published "Tomorrow Never Comes" (gospel); "Gooski's Riders" (country/rock); and "Living Is Giving" (country), all written and recorded by Ross Fulton.
Tips: "Have patience, be persistent and rework songs to make the best possible."

HAROLD LUICK & ASSOCIATES MUSIC PUBLISHER, Box B, Carlisle IA 50047. (515)989-3679. President: Harold L. Luick. Music publisher, record company, record producer and music industry consultant. Estab. 1980. BMI. Publishes 20-25 songs/year; publishes 10 new songwriters/year. Pays standard royalty.
How to Contact: Write or call first about your interest, arrange personal interview or submit demo tape and lyric sheet. Prefers cassette with 3-5 songs on demo. SASE. Reports in 3 weeks.
Music: Bluegrass, C&W, dance-oriented, easy listening, gospel, MOR, R&B, country rock-a-billy and top 40/pop. Recently published "For a Little While" (by T. Neil Smith), recorded by Blue Sky Band/Studio 2000 Records (country); "Pop Corn Song" (by Kenny Hofer), recorded by Kenny Hofer/4 Leaf Records (dance-oriented); and "Yankee Duke" (by Darrell C. Thomas), recorded by D.C. Thomas/DTC Records (country).
Tips: "Know the difference between a *tune* and a *song*. Submit only songs. Make decent 'dubs.' It is not a matter of *luck*, but a matter of being prepared when *luck* comes along. If you are unlucky then you have been unprepared. Submit only your *best* works."

JIM McCOY MUSIC/ALEAR MUSIC, Box 574, Sounds of Winchester, Winchester VA 22601. (703)667-9379. Affiliate: New Edition Publishing. Owner: Jim McCoy. Music publisher, record company, record producer and management firm. BMI. Publishes 50 songs/year; publishes 30 new songwriters/year. Pays standard royalties.
How to Contact: Submit demo tape and lead sheet. Prefers 7½ ips reel-to-reel or cassette with 5-10 songs on demo. SASE. Reports in 1 month.
Music: Bluegrass; church/religious; C&W; folk; gospel; progressive; and rock. Recently published "I've Gotta' Get Next to You" (by Bryan Fox), recorded by Fox and all songs on the following LPs: *Mr. Blue Grass—Here's to You*, by the Carroll County Ramblers; *Alvin Kesner Sings* by Alvin Kesner; *Great Gospel Talk Songs* by Jim McCoy; and *Earl Howard Sings His Heart Out*, by Earl Howard.

MACHARMONY MUSIC, 400 W. 43rd St., Suite 5C, New York NY 10036. Director: Walter Herman. Music publisher. Estab. 1979. ASCAP. Publishes 6 songs/year; publishes 3 new songwriters/year. Pays standard royalty.
How to Contact: Submit demo tape and lyric sheet. Prefers cassette with 1-3 songs on demo. SASE. Reports in 1 month.
Music: Rock (pop, hard and soft).

MAD EAGLE MUSIC, Box 8621, Anaheim CA 92802. (714)636-1208. President: Alice Maenza. Music publisher. Estab. 1980. BMI. Member BMI and Southern California Songwriters Guild. Pays standard royalty.
How to Contact: Submit demo tape and lyric sheet. Prefers cassette with 2-10 songs on demo. SASE. "We ask that all material be protected before mailing."
Music: Blues, C&W, easy listening, gospel, MOR, novelty, punk, R&B, rock and top 40. Recently published "Things I Should've Said," recorded by Eddie Dare/Love Records.
Tips: "We are a new company building a catalog. *All* of our writers are new and unknown. We are interested in all writers that show potential. Demo tapes must have lyrics clearly audible. The song should be interesting enough to grab the listener after he's heard a couple of lines. Long intros are a waste of time for a publisher. Good quality tape is a must."

MADRID MUSIC CO., Box 504, Bonita CA 92002. (714)421-0865. Affiliate: Sweet 'n Low Music (BMI). President: Virginia Anderson. Music publisher. ASCAP. Publishes 4 songs/year. Pays standard royalty.
How to Contact: Query or submit demo tape and lead sheet. Prefers 7½ ips reel-to-reel or cassette with 1-3 songs on demo. SASE. Reports in 1 month.

Music: C&W; easy listening; MOR; top 40/pop. Recently published "Run, Baby, Run" (by Virginia Anderson), recorded by Candy/TAO Records (country pop); and "I'm Just a Kiss Away" (by V. Anderson), recorded by Ron White/TAO Records (country/pop).

MAINLY MUSIC, INC., Box 120591, Nashville TN 37212. (615)269-4410. Affiliates: Herford Music (ASCAP), Perfect Union Music (ASCAP), Slimbull Music (BMI) and Together Music (SESAC). President: Gary Musick. Music publisher. ASCAP. Pays standard royalty.
How to Contact: Arrange personal interview or submit demo tape and lead sheet. Prefers cassette with 3 songs on demo. SASE. Reports in 3 weeks.
Music: Pop; C&W; gospel; and MOR. Recently published "The King Is Gone" and "I Love You," recorded by Ronnie McDowell (country/MOR).

MAINROADS PUBLISHING, 100 Huntley St., Toronto, Ontario, Canada M4Y 2L1. (416)961-8001. Manager: Bruce W. Stacey. Music publisher and record company. CAPAC. Publishes 75 songs/year; publishes 1 new songwriter/year. Pays standard royalty.
How to Contact: Submit demo tape and lyric sheet or write about your interest. Prefers cassette with 3-5 songs on demo. SAE and International Reply Coupons. Reports in 1 month.
Music: Children's, choral, church/religious and gospel.

MALACO, INC., Box 9287, Jackson MS 39206. (601)982-4522. Producer: James Griffin. President: Tommy Couch. Producers: Tommy Couch, Wolf Stephenson and James Griffin. Vice President: Wolf Stephenson. Music publisher, record producer and record company. BMI. Publishes 60 songs/year. Pays standard royalty.
How to Contact: Submit demo tape and lyric sheet. Prefers cassette with 1-5 songs on demo. SASE. Reports in 1 month.
Music: Blues; disco; easy listening; gospel; MOR; R&B; rock; soul; and top 40/pop. Recently published "Groove Me" (by King Floyd), recorded by the Blues Brothers.

MANDINA MUSIC, 6255 Sunset Blvd., #723, Hollywood CA 90028. (213)468-6933. Affiliate: Rocksmith Music (ASCAP). Vice President: Steve Stone. Music publisher and record company. BMI. Publishes 50 songs/year; publishes 10 new songwriters/year. Pays standard royalty.
How to Contact: Submit demo tape and lyric sheet. Prefers cassette with 1-10 songs on demo. SASE. Reports in 2 weeks.
Music: Bluegrass, children's, church/religious, C&W, easy listening, gospel, MOR, progressive, R&B, rock, soul and top 40/pop. Recently published "Texas Woman" and "Colorado Country Morning" (by Pat Boone), recorded by P. Boone/Warner Brothers Records (C&W); and "It Ain't Over Yet" (by Eddy Arnold), recorded by E. Arnold/RCA Records (C&W).

MANFIELD MUSIC, Holy Spirit Records, 27335 Penn St., Inkster MI 48141. (313)862-8220 or 562-8975. President: Elder Otis G. Johnson. Music Director: Ted Thomas. Music publisher, record producer and record company. BMI. Publishes 50 songs/year; publishes 5 new songwriters/year. Pays standard royalty.
How to Contact: Query or submit demo tape and lyric sheet. Prefers 3¾ or 7½ ips reel-to-reel or cassette with 3 songs minimum on tape. Include phone number. SASE. Reports in 1 month.
Music: Church/religious and gospel. Recently published "Prepare to Meet Him" (by Kenneth Wilson), recorded by Reverend James Cleveland/Savoy Records (gospel); "Receive the Power" (by Otis G. Johnson), recorded by Johnson/Holy Spirit Records (gospel); "Only Lord Jesus" (by Dorothy Butler), recorded by the Goodwill Youth Ensemble of Detroit/Holy Spirit Records; and "Patient Spirit" and "Thank You Lord" (by Michael Swangigan), recorded by Messias Temple Choir/Praise Records.

MANHOLE MUSIC, 11602-75 Ave., Edmonton, Alberta, Canada. (403)436-3096. Chief: Frank Phillet. Music publisher and record company. PROCAN. Publishes 20 songs/year. Pays standard royalty.
How to Contact: Submit demo tape and lyric sheet. Prefers 7½ ips reel-to-reel or cassette with 3-5 songs on demo. SAE and International Reply Coupons. Reports in 2 weeks.
Music: Easy listening, MOR and top 40/pop. Recently published "Baby Pictures" (by Phillet/MacIven), recorded by Chris Neilsen/Royalty Records (country); "Carry On" (by Phillet/MacIven), recorded by James Last/Polydor Records (MOR); and "Tunete Souviens Pas De Mai" (by Phillet/MacIven), recorded by Magic Music/1st International Records (French MOR).

MANNA MUSIC, INC., 2111 Kenmere Ave., Burbank CA 91504. Affiliates: Gaviota Music (BMI), Hollyville Music (SESAC) and Nashwood Music (ASCAP). President: Hal Spencer. Music publisher and record company. ASCAP. Member NMPA. Hires staff writers.

How to Contact: Submit demo tape or submit demo tape and lead sheet. Prefers cassette with 1-5 songs on demo. Does not return unsolicited material. Reports in 2 weeks.
Music: Choral; church/religious; and gospel. Recently published "How Great Thou Art," recorded by Elvis Presley (religious); "Sweet, Sweet Spirit," recorded by Pat Boone (religious); and "His Name Is Wonderful," recorded by Norma Zimmer (religious).

MARIELLE MUSIC CO., Box 11012, Chicago IL 60611. (312)266-9616. Music publisher and record producer. BMI. Pays standard royalty.
How to Contact: Submit demo tape and lyric sheet. Prefers cassette with any number songs on demo. Does not return unsolicited material. Reports in 3 months.
Music: C&W, easy listening, jazz, MOR, R&B, rock, soul and top 40/pop.

MARIELLE MUSIC CORP., Box 842, Radio City, New York NY 10019. Affiliates: Moo Moo Music (BMI) and Moorpark Music (ASCAP). President: Don Seat. Vice President: Darlene Gorzela. Music publisher. BMI. Member AFM, AGVA, AFRA and SAG. Publishes 200 songs/year. Pays standard royalties.
How to Contact: Submit demo tape. Prefers cassette. "Be sure melody and lyrics are clear." SASE. Reports in 3 months.
Music: Bluegrass; blues; church/religious; classical; C&W; disco; easy listening; folk; gospel; jazz; MOR; progressive; rock; soul; and top 40/pop. Recently published "Halfway to Heaven," by Conway Twitty/MGM Records (country music); "She Loves Me" (by Conway Twitty), recorded by Waylon Jennings/RCA Records (country); and "It's Only Make Believe" (by Conway Twitty and Jack Nance), recorded by Glen Campbell/Capitol Records (MOR).

EDWARD B. MARKS MUSIC CORPORATION, 1790 Broadway, New York NY 10019. (212)247-7277. Contact: Professional Manager. Music publisher. Member NMPA. BMI. Pays standard royalty.
How to Contact: Submit demo tape and lyric sheet. Prefers 7½ ips reel-to-reel or cassette with 1-3 songs on demo. SASE. Reports in 2 weeks.
Music: Bluegrass; blues; C&W; MOR; progressive; R&B; rock; soul; and top 40/pop.

MARMIK MUSIC, INC., 135 E. Muller Rd., East Peoria IL 61611. (309)699-7204. President: Martin Mitchell. Music publisher and record company. BMI. Publishes over 100 songs/year. Pays standard royalties.
How to Contact: Query, submit demo tape, or submit demo tape and lead sheet. Prefers reel-to-reel tape or cassette with 2-10 songs on demo. "With first submission include an affidavit of ownership of the material." SASE. Reports in 2 weeks.
Music: Blues; children's; choral; church/religious; C&W; easy listening; gospel; and MOR. Recently published "Don't Say Who" (novelty) and "The Old-Fashioned Waltz" (ballad), (by Betty Parsons), recorded by B. Parsons/Ripon Records; and "Here I Go" (by Joe Hutton), recorded by Marty McMichie/Ripon Records (country ballad).

MARSAINT MUSIC, INC., 3809 Clematis Ave., New Orleans LA 70122. (504)949-8386. A&R Director: Debra Campbell. Music publisher. BMI. Pays standard royalty.
How to Contact: Submit demo tape and lyric sheet. Prefers cassette with 3-5 songs on demo. SASE. Reports in 1 month.
Music: Blues, gospel, jazz, R&B and soul. Recently published "Released" (by Allen R. Toussaint), recorded by Patti Labelle/CBS Records (soul); "Southern Nights" (by A.R. Toussaint), recorded by Glen Campbell (country); and songs recorded by Ramsey Lewis/CBS Records (progressive jazz); and Eric Gale/CBS Records (progressive jazz).

MASTER'S COLLECTION PUBLISHING & T.M.C. PUBLISHING, Box 189, Station W, Toronto, Ontario Canada M6M 4Z2. (416)746-1991. President: Paul J. Young. Music publisher and record company. PROCAN, CAPAC. Publishes 20-30 songs/year; publishes 6 new songwriters/year. Pays standard royalty.
How to Contact: Write first about your interest. Prefers cassette with 3-6 songs on demo. Does not return unsolicited material. Reports in 1 month.
Music: Church/religious and gospel. Recently published *Gene & Marty*, recorded by Gene MacLellan/Masters Collection Records (country gospel); *Livin' in the Love*, recorded by Mark Moore/Master's Collection Records (folk gospel); and *Ask Me Why*, recorded by Pat Pepper/Master's Collection Records (folk gospel).

MCA MUSIC, MCA, Inc., 100 Universal City Plaza, Universal City CA 91608. (213)508-3166. Affiliates: Leeds Music (ASCAP), Duchess Music (BMI) and Champion Music (BMI). Music

publisher. ASCAP. Member NMPA. Publishes 3 songs/year; publishes 3 new songwriters/year. Pays standard royalties. Publishes 20 new songwriters/year. Hires staff writers.
How to Contact: Submit demo tape and lead sheet or demo tape and lyric sheet. Prefers cassette with 1-3 songs on demo. SASE. Reports in 1 month.
Music: Blues; easy listening; jazz; MOR; R&B; rock; soul; country and top 40/pop. Recently published "Love Insurance," recorded by Front Page (disco).

MCA MUSIC, MCA, Inc., 445 Park Ave., New York NY 10022. Affiliates: Leeds Music (ASCAP), Duchess Music (BMI) and Champion Music (BMI). Contact: Mike Millius. Music publisher. ASCAP. Publishes 3 songs/year; publishes 3 new songwriters/year. Pays standard royalties.
How to Contact: Write about your interest, then submit demo tape and lead sheet or demo tape and lyric sheet. Prefers cassette with 1-3 songs on demo. SASE. Reports in 2 months (on solicited material). "Company policy does not permit acceptance of unsolicited material."
Music: Blues; disco; easy listening; jazz; MOR; R&B; rock; soul; and top 40/pop.

MCA MUSIC, MCA, Inc., 1106 17th Ave. S., Nashville TN 37212. Affiliates: Leeds Music (ASCAP), Duchess Music (BMI) and Champion Music (BMI). Contact: Professional Department. ASCAP and BMI. Member NMPA, NARAS, CMA, GMA, NMA and NSA. Pays standard royalties.
How to Contact: Submit demo tape and lead sheet or demo tape and lyric sheet. Prefers 7½ ips reel-to-reel or cassette with 1-3 songs on demo. SASE. Reports in 6 weeks.
Music: "All forms of commercial contemporary music." Recently published "Take It Easy" (by D. McClinton), recorded by Crystal Gayle/CBS Records (country/pop); "Can I See You Tonight" (by D. Allen and R. Vanhoy), recorded by Tanya Tucker/MCA Records (country); "Love Knows We Tried" (by J. Crutchfield, R. Burke and K. Chater), recorded by Tanya Tucker/MCA Records (country); and Nobody's Fool (by D. Allen, R. Vanhoy and D. Cook), recorded by Deborah Allen/Capitol Records (country).

MEADOW-MORGEN PUBLISHING, LTD., Box G., 145 Station G., Calgary, Alberta, Canada T3A 2G1. (403)288-6500. President: Rick Morgenstern. Music publisher and record company. CAPAC. Publishes 4 new songwriters/year. Pays standard royalty.
How to Contact: Write or call first about your interest. Prefers 7½ ips reel-to-reel or cassette with 2-5 songs on demo. SAE and International Reply Coupons. Reports in 3 weeks to 1 month.
Music: Bluegrass, C&W, easy listening, and rock (country).
Tips: "Keep lyrics clear and simple. Tell a complete story in less than 3 minutes."

MEDIA INTERSTELLAR MUSIC, Box 20346, Chicago IL 60620. (312)476-2553. Professional Manager: V. Beleska. Music publisher. BMI. Publishes 20-40 songs/year. Also "joint ownership plans, where a songwriter becomes co-publisher. Expenses and profits are shared. We *don't* charge the songwriter for our services as publisher. We cannot consider any material without a written query first describing yourself and your songs."
How to Contact: "Inquire first, describing yourself and songs available." Prefers 7½ ips reel-to-reel, cassette or disc with 1-5 songs on demo. SASE. Reports in 2-8 weeks.
Music: Avant-garde; C&W; disco; easy listening; MOR; progressive; rock; soul; and top 40/pop. Recently published "All for You," and "The Show Never Ends," recorded by Christopher (MOR/rock); and "Tricentennial 2076," recorded by Vyto B (avant-garde).

MELLYRIC MUSIC CO., Box 1077, Cleveland TN 37311. (615)479-1415. President: Donald B. Gibson. Music publisher. ASCAP. Member CMA and NSAI. "We are not accepting outside material at this time."

MELSTEP MUSIC, Rt. 1, Box 213, Rogersville AL 35652. (205)247-3983. President: Syble C. Richardson. Music publisher and recording studio. BMI and ASCAP. Publishes 6 songs/year; published 2 new songwriters in 1979. Pays standard royalties.
How to Contact: Submit demo tape. Prefers 7½ or 3¾ ips reel-to-reel or cassette with 1-4 songs on demo. SASE. Reports in 1 month.
Music: Bluegrass; blues; C&W; gospel; MOR; R&B; rock; soul; and top 40/pop. Recently published "The Narrow Road," "Another Mountain" and "I Want to Thank You Lord" (all by Dorothy Pardon), all recorded by Pardon Trio/Woodrich Records (gospel).

MEMNON, LTD., 1619 Broadway, New York NY 10019. Affiliates: Tithonus Music, Ltd. (BMI) and Hipolit Music (ASCAP). President: Krzysztof Z. Purzycki. Music publisher. ASCAP. Publishes 39 songs/year.

How to Contact: Submit demo tape and lead sheet. Prefers 7½ ips reel-to-reel with 3-7 songs on demo. "All songs submitted on reel-to-reel must have leader at the beginning and between musical compositions. Write songs adaptable for both male and female artists; keep demos simple, and *not* over produced, but presentable." Reports in 1 month.
Music: Choral; classical; easy listening; MOR; top 40/pop; and ethnic/foreign language songs. Recently published "Walk In Peace United" (by A.L. Riley and K.Z. Purzycki), recorded by Bobbie Roberson/Bolivia Records (country/pop); and "We Can Make It Together" (by R. Miles and L. Baxter), recorded by Gene Huddleston/Puzzle Records (country).

MERCANTILE MUSIC, Box 2271, Palm Springs CA 92263. (714)320-4848. Affiliate: Blueford Music (ASCAP). President: Kent Fox. Music publisher and record producer. Publishes 12 new songwriters/year. Pays standard royalties.
How to Contact: Submit demo tape and lyric sheet. Prefers cassette with 3-12 songs on demo. SASE. Reports in 1 month.
Music: C&W; easy listening; rock; MOR; and top 40/pop. Recently published "Midnight in the Morning," "Garage Sale" and "Married to the Girl I Love."

METRONOME MUSIC PUBLISHING CO. OF PENNSYLVANIA, INC., Collins & Willard Sts., Philadelphia PA 19134. President: Albert Schwab. Music publisher. ASCAP. Publishes 5 songs/year; publishes 5 new songwriters/year.
How to Contact: Submit demo tape and lead sheet. Prefers 7½ ips reel-to-reel with 3-6 songs on demo. SASE. Reports in 1 month.
Music: Easy listening and jazz. Recently published "Hang Around," by Albert Schwab (easy listening).

MICHAVIN MUSIC, 1260 N. "F." St., Pensacola FL 32501. Owner/Manager: Vincent L. Smith III. Music publisher, record producer and music arranging service.
How to Contact: Query. Prefers cassette.
Music: Disco; jazz; R&B; soul; and top 40/pop.

MID AMERICA MUSIC, (a division of Ozark Opry Records, Inc.), Box 242, Osage Beach MO 65065. (314)348-3383. Affiliate: Tall Corn Publishing (BMI). General Manager: Lee Mace. Music publisher. ASCAP. Publishes 25 songs/year. Pays standard royalty.
How to Contact: Arrange personal interview or submit demo tape and lead sheet. Prefers 7½ ips reel-to-reel or cassette with 1-3 songs on demo. "Tape should be of good quality, and the voice should be louder than the music." SASE. Reports in 3 weeks.
Music: Bluegrass; children's; church/religious; C&W; disco; easy listening; gospel; MOR; and rock. Recently published "Never Asking for More," (by Rod Johnson), recorded by Graham Fee/Fee-Line Records (MOR); "Losing the Blues" (by Steve and Juli Ann Whiting), recorded by Steve Whiting/KRC Records (MOR); and "Iowa a Place to Grow" (by Steve Whiting), recorded by S. Whiting/KRC Records (MOR).

MIDEB MUSIC, 45-50 38th St., Long Island City, NY 11101. (212)786-7667. Affiliate: Twin Music (BMI). President: Sam Weiss. Vice President: Daniel Glass. Music publisher and record company. ASCAP. Publishes 20 songs/year. Hires staff writers.
How to Contact: Query. Prefers 7½ ips reel-to-reel or cassette with 1-3 songs on demo. SASE. Reports in 2 weeks.
Music: Blues; disco; easy listening; MOR; progressive; R&B; rock; soul; and top 40/pop. Recently published "Keep on Dancin' " (by Eric Matthew and Gary Turnier), recorded by Gary's Gang (pop); "Ain't That Enough for You" (by John Davis), recorded by John Davis and the Monster Orchestra (disco); "Don't Stop," recorded by K.I.D.; "Let's Do It," recorded by Conversion; "Love Either Grows or Goes," recorded by Scandal; and "Just How Sweet Is Your Love," recorded by Rhyze.

MIETUS COPYRIGHT MANAGEMENT, 527 Madison Ave., Suite 317, New York NY 10022. (212)371-7950. "We administer for 70 clients and listen (screen) material for them." President: Leonard Mietus.
How to Contact: Submit demo tape and lyric sheet. Prefers cassette with 2 songs on demo. SASE. Reports in 3 weeks to 1 month.
Music: Bluegrass, blues, choral, C&W, dance-oriented, easy listening, folk, gospel, jazz, MOR, progressive, Spanish, R&B, rock, soul and top 40/pop.

MIGHTY MUSIC, Box 27160, Phoenix AZ 85061. (602)276-7116. President: Mike Lenaburg. Professional Manager: Eric Lenaburg. Music publisher, record company and record producer. BMI. Pays standard royalties.

How to Contact: Query, submit demo tape, submit demo tape and lead sheet, submit acetate disc, submit acetate disc and lead sheet. Prefers cassette or 8-track tape. SASE. Reports in 1 month.
Music: Blues; disco; gospel; and R&B. Recently published "Lord Woke Me Up This Morning" (by Lee Kingdon), recorded by Willie Parker and the Sensational Souls/B&B Records (gospel); "Function Underground" (by M. Jennell and S. James), recorded by We the People/Darlene Records (disco); and "Don't Take My Money If You Won't Give Me Your Honey" (by M. Lenaburg), recorded by Oklahoma Zeke/Bluestown Records (blues).

THE MIGHTY THREE MUSIC GROUP, 309 S. Broad St., Philadelphia PA 19107. (215)546-3510. Affiliates: Assorted Music (BMI), Bell Boy Music (BMI), Downstairs Music (BMI), Razor Sharp Music (BMI), Rose Tree Music (ASCAP) and World War Three Music (BMI). President: Earl Shelton. Vice President of Publishing Administration: Constance Heigler. Administrative Assistant: Diane Stroman. Administrative Assistant, Foreign: Diana Coleman. Contact: Professional Manager: William Lacy. Music publisher. BMI and ASCAP. Member NMPA. Publishes 100 songs/year; publishes 6 new songwriters/year. Pays standard royalty. Sometimes offers advance: "If a writer is signed to us exclusively, we offer him writer advances recoupable against writer royalties after songs have been recorded and released."
How to Contact: Submit demo tape and lyric sheet. Prefers cassette with 1-3 songs on demo. "Must provide large SASE for return." Reports in 8 weeks."
Music: C&W; disco; easy listening; folk; gospel; jazz; MOR; progressive; rock (hard, country); soul; and top 40/pop. Recently published "Ain't No Stoppin' Us Now," (by McFadden, Whitehead and Cohen), recorded by McFadden & Whitehead/Philadelphia International Records (MOR/R&B/pop); "Livin' It Up (Friday Night)" (by Bell and James), recorded on A&M Records (pop); "You Gonna Make Me Love Somebody Else," recorded by The Jones Girls/Philadelphia International Records (R&B); "Strategy" (by Gene McFadden, John Whitehead, and Jerry Cohen), recorded by Archie Bell & The Drells/Philadelphia International Records (R&B); "Girl, Don't Let It Get You Down" (by Kenneth Gamble and Leon Huff), recorded by The O'Jays/Philadelphia International Records (R&B); and "Love T.K.O." (by C. Womack), recorded by Teddy Pendergrass/Philadelphia International Records; and "Together" (by K. Gamble/L. Huff), recorded by Tierra/Boardwalk Records.

MIGHTY TWINNS MUSIC, 9134 S. Indiana Ave., Chicago IL 60619. (312)264-5452. Professional Manager: Ronald Scott. Music publisher. BMI. Member NMPA. Publishes 35-40 songs/year; publishes 5-10 new songwriters/year. Pays standard royalty.
How to Contact: Write or call first about your interest, submit demo tape and lyric sheet or arrange personal interview to play demo tape. Prefers 7½ ips reel-to-reel or cassette and lead sheet with 2-4 songs on demo. SASE. Reports in 2-3 weeks.
Music: Disco; easy listening; MOR; R&B; liquid rock; soul; and top 40/pop. Recently published "Be Nice to Me" (by Ronald Scott), recorded by Danny Johnson/First American Records (ballande); "Do Yourself a Favor" (by Ronald Scott), recorded by Beautiful Zion Chorus/First American Records (gospel); and "Love Is You" (by Peggy Hines), recorded by Barbara Acklin.

BRIAN MILLAN MUSIC CORP., 3475 St. Urbain St., Suite 1212, Montreal, Quebec, H2X 2N4 Canada. President: Brian Millan. Music publisher and record producer. ASCAP. Publishes 30-40 songs/year.
How to Contact: Submit demo tape and lead sheet. Prefers cassette only with 1-4 songs on demo. SAE and International Reply Coupons. Reports in 2 weeks.
Music: C&W, disco, easy listening, MOR, rock, and soul. Recently published Maria Helaine, Ralph Bendix on Electrola, & "Till Then Arivedercci" on Redifussion—England with Vincent Chiarelli & Shirley Spilmon.

MILLER SOUL-KRAFT MUSIC, 347 Litchfield Ave., Babylon NY 11702. (516)661-9842. Publisher: William H. Miller. Music publisher and record producer. BMI.
How to Contact: Submit demo tape and lead sheet. Prefers cassette with 4 songs minimum on tape. SASE. Reports in 1 month.
Music: Blues; C&W; disco; rock; soul; and top 40/pop. Recently published "I'm Going to Get You," recorded by Allan Turner (pop); and "I Still Love You, Uh! Huh!" recorded by Maxine Miller (disco).

MIMIC MUSIC, Box 201, Smyrna GA 30080. (404)432-2454. Affiliates: Skip Sack Music (BMI) and Stepping Stone (BMI). Manager: Tom Hodges. Music publisher, record producer, record company and management company. BMI. Publishes 20 songs/year. Pays standard royalty.
How to Contact: Submit demo tape and lyric sheet. Prefers cassette with 3-10 songs on demo. SASE. Reports in 2 weeks.

Music: Bluegrass; blues; church/religious; C&W; easy listening; gospel; MOR; R&B; rock; soul; and top 40/pop. Recently published "Please Tell Her to Wait" (by Norman Skipper), recorded on Capitol Records (country); "Good Ole Country Music" (by Helen Humphries), recorded on British Overseas Records (country); and "Take Away the Roses" (by Burke-Bailey), recorded on British Overseas Records (country).

MINNA LOUSHE MUSIC, Box 1175, Victoria, British Columbia, Canada V8W 2T6. (604)652-0226. President: J. Gothe. Music publisher. PROCAN. Member MCA. Pays standard royalty.
How to Contact: Write first about your interest. Prefers reel-to-reel or cassette as demo. SAE and International Reply Coupons. Reports in 2 weeks.
Music: Jazz.

MIRACLE-JOY PUBLICATIONS, 425 Park St., Suite 9, Hackensack NJ 07601. (201)488-5211. President: Johnny Miracle. Vice President: Aileen Joy. Music publisher and record company. BMI.
How to Contact: Submit demo tape or submit demo tape and lead sheet. Prefers 7½ ips reel-to-reel or cassette with 2-6 songs on demo. SASE. Reports in 2 weeks.
Music: Children's; church/religious; C&W; easy listening; folk; and gospel. Recently published "Pizzaman," recorded by Tiny (novelty); "Memories I Hold of You," recorded by Sam Starr (C&W); and "The Ashes Are Still Warm," recorded by Al and Carrol (C&W).

MR. MORT MUSIC, 44 Music Square E., Nashville TN 37203. (615)255-2175. Affiliate: Jason Dee Music (BMI). President: Charles Fields. Music publisher, record company and record producer. ASCAP. Publishes 50 songs/year; published 6 new songwriters in 1979. Pays standard royalties.
How to Contact: Submit demo tape and lead sheet. Prefers 7½ ips reel-to-reel or cassette with 1-4 songs on demo. SASE. Reports in 2 weeks.
Music: Blues; C&W; easy listening; MOR; and top 40/pop. Recently published "Temperatures Risin' " (by Bobby G. Rice and C. Fields), recorded by Bobby G. Rice; and "Sunshine Girl" (by C. Fields), recorded by Jess Garron.

IVAN MOGULL MUSIC CORP., 625 Madison Ave., New York NY 10022. (212)355-5636. President: Ivan Mogull. Music publisher. ASCAP, BMI and SESAC. Member NMPA. Publishes 10-30 songs/year. Pays standard royalty.
How to Contact: Submit demo tape and lyric sheet. Prefers 7½ ips reel-to-reel or cassette. SASE. Reports in 2 weeks.
Music: Rock; and top 40/pop. Publisher of "The Winner Takes It All" and all other Abba hits.

MONKEY MUSIC, INC., A Monkey Business Company, Box 288, Nashville TN 37221. (615)646-3335. Affiliates: Ape's Hit Music (BMI), Deaf Monkey Music (ASCAP), Director of Publishing/A&R: Neil Signer. Music publisher. Publishes 50-100 songs/year; publishes 5-10 new songwriters/year. Pays standard royalty.
How to Contact: Submit demo tape and lyric sheet. Prefers 7½ ips reel-to-reel or cassette with 3-5 songs on demo. "Lyric and/or lead sheet must be submitted with tape along with SASE. Do not submit lyric and/or lead sheet only." Reports in 1 month.
Music: C&W; easy listening; MOR; progressive; hard rock and country rock; and top 40/pop. Recently published "Arizona Sunshine, California Rain" (by Taylor/Cunningham), recorded by Debby Lamden/Strawberry Records (country/pop); "Don't Believe It" (by Blake/Bagley), recorded by Deena Javor/Whitehorse Records (country/pop); and "Oh No! Not Another Goodbye" (by Brown/Newman), recorded by Toni Joleen/Cherry Records (country).

MONTINA MUSIC, Box 702, Snowdon Station, Montreal, Quebec, Canada H3X 3X8. General Manager: David P. Leonard. Music publisher, record company, record producer, and college of recording arts and sciences. BMI. Member MIEA. Pays standard royalty.
How to Contact: Submit demo tape and lyric sheet. Prefers cassette. Does not return unsolicited material. Reports in 1 month.
Music: Bluegrass, blues, C&W, dance-oriented, easy listening, folk, gospel, jazz, MOR, progressive, R&B, rock, soul and top 40/pop.

MONTREAL ROSE PUBLISHING LTD., 201 Perry, Morin Heights, Quebec, Canada J0R 1H0. (514)226-2419. Affiliate: Kazam Music (PROCAN). Managing Director: Y. Brandeis. Music publisher, record producer and recording studio. CAPAC and SACEM. Publishes 15 songs/year; publishes 5 new songwriters/year. Pays standard royalty.

How to Contact: Submit demo tape and lyric sheet. Prefers cassette with 5-10 songs on demo. Does not return unsolicited material. Reports in 2 weeks.
Music: Rock (of all types), soul and top 40/pop. Recently published "Backstreet Girl" and "Money Talks Loud," recorded by Leyden Zar/A&M Records (pop rock); "Complainte pour ste. Catherine." recorded by McGarrigle/Tartatcheff Records.

MONTROY MUSIC CO., 7210 Roos, Houston TX 77074. (713)774-3075 or 774-0075. Contact: Dr. John D. Montroy. Music publisher. BMI. Publishes 3 songs/year. Pays standard royalty.
How to Contact: Write first about your interest. Prefers cassette with 1-5 songs on demo. "No unsolicited material reviewed. Songwriter must write and ask permission first." SASE. Reports in 2 weeks.
Music: Church/religious; easy listening; gospel; and MOR.

MOON JUNE MUSIC, 5821 SE Powell Blvd., Portland OR 97206. President: Bob Stoutenburg. Music publisher.
How to Contact: Submit demo tape. Prefers 7½ ips reel-to-reel or cassette with 2-10 songs on demo. SASE. Reports in 1 month.

MOOSE ELBOW MUSIC, 5352 Park Ave., Suite 59, Montreal, Quebec, Canada H2V 4G8. (514)276-6371. President: Steven Tracey. Music publisher and record producer. PROCAN. Publishes 10 songs/year; publishes 2 new songwriters/year. Pays standard royalty.
How to Contact: Submit demo tape and lyric sheet. Prefers cassette with 1-7 songs on demo. "No productions are necessary for us to hear your songs. *Simplicity* is the key; try not to confuse the musical idea by filler music. A song must fit like a glove." SAE and International Reply Coupons. Reports in 3 weeks.
Music: C&W, dance-oriented, easy listening, MOR and top 40/pop. Recently published "Au Bout" (by Jean Francis William and Serge Laporte), recorded by Plastic Bertrand/Vogue Records (Europe) and Attic Records (Canada); "Honey" (by Gerry Stober), recorded by Gerry Stober/Studio A Records (MOR/top 40); and "Without Your Love" (by Gerry Stober and Mark Blumenthal), recorded by Gerry Stober/Studio A Records.

THE MORGAN MUSIC GROUP, Box 2388, Prescott AZ 86302. (602)445-5801. Affiliates: Holydale (ASCAP), Winteroak (ASCAP) and Chromewood (BMI). President/Publishing: Faye Ellen Foreman. Music publisher, record company and record producer. Estab. 1979. BMI, ASCAP. Publishes 50-75 songs/year; publishes 15 new songwriters/year. Pays standard royalty; $25-250 advance given against royalties.
How to Contact: Submit demo tape and lyric sheet. Prefers cassette with 3 songs on demo. SASE. Reports in 1 month.
Music: C&W, rock (country) and top 40/pop (country). Recently published "Run She Will" (by Greer and Morgan), recorded by Garry Greer/Big Wheels Records; "Out on the Road Again" (by M.D. Morgan), recorded by M.D. Morgan/Big Wheels Records; and "CB Blues" (by George Rawls), recorded by G. Rawls/Big Wheels Records (all C&W).

MORNING MUSIC, LTD., 1343 Matheson Blvd. W., Mississauga, Ontario, Canada L4W 1R1. Affiliate: Skinners Pond Music (PRO). General Manager: Mark Altman. Music publisher. CAPAC. Pays standard royalty.
How to Contact: Submit demo tape and lead sheet. Prefers reel-to-reel or cassette. SAE and International Reply Coupons. Reports in 2 weeks.
Music: "We seek all formats." Recently published "Don't Down Me Now," recorded by Ernie Smith (Regga); and "I Believe In You," recorded by Donna & Leroy.

MORNING MUSIC (USA), INC., Box 120478, Nashville TN 37212. (416)625-2676. Affiliates: Bathurst Music (BMI); American Rainbird Music (ASCAP); and Shanachie Music (ASCAP). President: Jury Krytiuk. General Manager: Mark Altman. Music publisher and record company. Member NMPA. ASCAP. Publishes 100 songs/year; publishes 30 new songwriters/year. Pays standard royalty.
How to Contact: Submit demo tape and lead sheet. Prefers 7½ ips reel-to-reel or cassette with 1-4 songs on demo. SASE. Reports in 1 month.
Music: Bluegrass; blues; children's; choral; church/religious; classical; C&W; disco; easy listening; folk; gospel; jazz; MOR; progressive; rock; soul; and top 40/pop. Recently published "One More Time," recorded by Crystal Gayle (C&W); "Country Hall of Fame," recorded by Hank Locklin (C&W); and "Flying South," recorded by Chet Atkins and Jerry Reed (instrumental).
Tips: "Send only your best songs—not *everything* you've written."

MORRIS MUSIC, INC., 6255 Sunset Blvd., Suite 1904, Hollywood CA 90028. (213)463-5102. Affiliate: Sashay Music (ASCAP). President: Steve Morris. Music publisher. BMI. Publishes 20 songs/year. Pays standard royalty.
How to Contact: Arrange personal interview, submit demo tape or submit demo tape and lead sheet. Prefers cassette with 1-3 songs on demo. SASE. Reports in 2 weeks.
Music: New music; progressive; rock; soul; and top 40/pop. Recently published "Sandy Beaches" (by John Jarvis & Delbert McClinton), recorded by Steve Cropper (rock); "Thief In the Night" (by Stephen Bishop), recorded by Stephen Bishop (pop); "I'm Not Ready Yet" (by Tom T. Hall), recorded by George Jones (C&W); and "I Can't Turn My Heart Away" (by John Jarvis) recorded by Art Garfunkel (pop ballad).

MORROW RIVER MUSIC CO., 1 N. Waukegan Rd., Lake Bluff IL 60044. (312)295-2253. Music Director: Bob Deshon. Music publisher and record company. ASCAP. Publishes 25 songs/year; publishes 10 new songwriters/year. Pays standard royalty.
How to Contact: Submit demo tape and lyric sheet. Prefers cassette with 2-4 songs on demo. SASE. Reports in 1 week.
Music: Bluegrass, C&W, gospel and Spanish. Recently published "Cryin' All Night Long" (by Doc Willson), recorded by D. Willson/W-W Records; "Morrow River Blues" (by Luther Watson), recorded by Morrow River Gang/W-W Records; and "Michigan Again" (by Danny Castle), recorded by Rusty Leonard/W-W Records (all country).

MOUNTAIN RAILROAD RECORDS INC., 3602 Atwood Ave., Madison WI 53714. (608)241-2001. Music publisher, record producer and record company. ASCAP. Publishes 20 songs/year. Pays standard royalty.
How to Contact: Submit demo tape and lyric sheet. Prefers cassette with 1-3 songs on demo. SASE. Reports in 1 month.
Music: Children's, C&W, folk, progressive, rock, and top 40/pop. Recently published "Good News" (rock), "Shooting Star" (rock ballad), and "Misery" (rock) by and recorded by Betsy Kaske.

MUSEDCO, Box 5916, Richardson TX 75080. (214)783-9925. Contact: Dick A. Shuff. Music publisher. Member SRS. Estab. 1979. Publishes 8-10 songs/year; publishes 1-2 new songwriters/year. Pays standard royalties.
How to Contact: Query by phone or letter (giving background). "Do not submit until query is answered." Submit demo tape and lyric sheet. Prefers cassette with 2-3 songs on demo. SASE. Reports in 1 month.
Music: Children's; choral; church/religious; C&W; folk; gospel; MOR; and top 40/pop. Recently published "Prop Up Your Brother" (by Baker, Shuff and Fargason), recorded by Gary Lanier/Hisong Records (gospel); and "Light the Light" (by Fargason), recorded by Gary Lanier/Hisong Records (gospel).
Tips: Send 2-3 of your best songs after query. Check them and rework them until they are musically good. Check lyrics against demo. Send tape of highest quality so you will have the best recording possible and send copy of a clear, legible lead sheet.

MUSIC CRAFTSHOP, Box 22325, Nashville TN 37202. Affiliates: Hit Kit Music (BMI) and Phono Music (SESAC). Manager: Jerry Duncan. Music publisher. ASCAP. Publishes 300 songs/year; publishes 150 new songwriters/year. Pays standard royalties.
How to Contact: Query, submit demo tape or submit demo tape and lead sheet. Prefers 7½ ips reel-to-reel with 1-5 songs on demo. SASE. Reports in 1 week.
Music: C&W; and MOR. Recently published "Fell into Love," recorded by Foxfire (country).

MUSIC DESIGNERS, 241 White Pond Rd., Hudson MA 01749. (617)562-6111. Affiliates: Mutiny Music and EMI Music. President: Jeff Gilman. Music publisher, record company and production company. BMI. Pays standard royalties.
How to Contact: Submit demo tape and lead sheet. Prefers 7½ ips reel-to-reel or cassette with 1-6 songs on demo. SASE. Reports in 3 weeks.
Music: Children's; C&W; disco; folk; MOR; progressive; rock; soul; and top 40/pop. Recently released "Man Enough," recorded by No Slack (pop/R&B); "Why Don't We Love Each Other?", recorded by the Ellis Hall Group (pop/R&B); and "Breaker 1-9," recorded by the Back Bay Rhythm Section (disco).

MUSIC FOR PERCUSSION, INC., 170 NE 33rd St., Fort Lauderdale FL 33334. (305)563-1844. Affiliate: Plymouth Music (ASCAP). Contact: Bernard Fisher, Fran Taber. Music publisher. BMI.

How to Contact: Submit demo tape and lead sheet. Prefers 7½ ips reel-to-reel. "Be sure that the tapes submitted are carefully labeled with title, name and address of composer." SASE. Reports in 1 month.
Music: "We are interested primarily in choral music."

MUSIC PUBLISHERS OF HAWAII, Box 25141, Honolulu HI 96825. Associate Producer: Frank Feary. Music publisher, record producer and record company. BMI. Publishes 12 songs/year. Pays standard royalty; "other options negotiable with songwriter."
How to Contact: Submit demo tape and lyric sheet. Prefers cassette with 3-6 songs on demo. SASE. Reports in 2 weeks.
Music: Disco; fusion jazz; and MOR. Recently published "Unspoken Love" (by Bonnie Gearheart and Brian Robertshaw), recorded by Music Magic/GMT Records (easy listening); "Beautiful Day" (by Alvin Okami), recorded by Paul Flynn/GMT Records (pop); and "Ray Alan" (by Al Puscua), recorded by Music Magic/GMT Records (MOR).
Tips: "A complete biography of the songwriter and a little background of the songs on the demo tape will enhance the songwriter's chance of getting a song published by our company."

MUSIC PUBLISHING CORP., 815-18th Ave. S., Nashville TN 37203. (615)327-0518. Affiliates: Singletree Music and East Memphis Music. Manager: Dave Burgers. Music publisher. BMI and ASCAP. Pays standard royalty.
How to Contact: Write first about your interest. Prefers cassette with 3 songs on demo. SASE.
Music: Country, MOR, rock and top 40/pop. Recently published "Power of Positive Drinking," recorded by Mickey Gilley/CBS Records (country); "Girls Get Prettier at Closing Time," recorded by Mickey Gilley/CBS Records (country); and "Dock of the Bay," recorded by Ottis Redding (soul/pop/MOR).
Tips: "Write before submitting tape."

MUSIC PUBLISHING CORPORATION, (formerly Cream Publishing Group), 8025 Melrose Ave., Los Angeles CA 90046. (213)655-0944. Affiliates: Singletree Music Company (BMI), Doubletree Music (SESAC), Harken Music (BMI), Lariat Music (ASCAP), Latigo Music (AS-CAP), Sage & Sand Music (SESAC), Rawhide Music Company (BMI), Barnwood Music (BMI), and Joiner Music (ASCAP). Professional Manager/Staff Song Writer: Marty Sadler. Music publisher. BMI. ASCAP. Member NMPA. Publishes 150 songs/year; publishes 50 new songwriters/year. Pays standard royalty. Sometimes secures songwriters on salary basis. Catalogs 4,000 songs/year.
How to Contact: Submit demo tape and lyric sheet. Prefers cassette with maximum 4 songs on demo. "Include lyrics and as much information as possible and songs that could be done by more than 2 artists." SASE. Reports in 1 week.
Music: Bluegrass, blues, church/religious, C&W, disco, easy listening, folk, gospel, jazz, MOR, progressive, R&B, rock (hard and soft) and top 40/pop. Recently published "Knock on Wood" (by Eddie Floyd), recorded by Amy Steward/Arista Records (disco); "Soul Man" (by Hayes & Porter), recorded by Blues Brothers/Atlantic Records (R&B); "I Just Can't Stand Up from Falling Down" by (Homer Banks), recorded by Elvis Costello (rock); "Who's Making Love" (by H. Banks), recorded by Blues Brothers/Atlantic Records (R&B); "Take Me to the River," recorded by All Green and Mabon Hodges/Capitol Records (country rock); and "I Can't Turn You Loose" (by Otis Redding), recorded by Aretha Franklin/Arista Records (R&B).

MUSIC RESOURCES INTERNATIONAL CORP., 110 W 34 St., Suite 806, New York NY 10001. (212)947-2066. President: Andy Hussakowsky. A&R Director: Gene O'Brien. Music publisher and record producer. Pays standard royalties.
How to Contact: Arrange personal interview or submit demo tape and lead sheet. Prefers cassette with 1-10 songs on demo. SASE. Reports in 1 month.
Music: Dance; rock; top 40/pop; and R&B. Recently published: "More, More, More," and "New York You Got Me Dancing," and "What's Your Name, What's Your Number," by Andrea True Connection/Buddah Records; "Jack in the Box," by David Morris/Buddah Records; "No, No, My Friend," by Devoshunn; and "Hot Shut," by Karen Young/West End Records.
Tips: "MRI has negotiated leases with Buddah, Polydor, Polygram, Casablanca, AVI and other major labels."

MUSICPRINT CORPORATION, Box 767, New York NY 10101. President: R. O'Brien. Chairman: Eugene Frank. Music publisher, record producer and management firm. Publishes 30 songs/year. Pays standard royalties.
How to Contact: Submit demo tape and lead sheet. Prefers cassette with 3-6 songs on demo. Does not return unsolicited material. Reports in 1 month.

Music: Bluegrass; choral; church/religious; classical; C&W; easy listening; folk; gospel; jazz; MOR; R&B; and rock. "Most of our music is for use in educational area."

MUSICWAYS, INC., 9033 Wilshire Blvd., Beverly Hills CA 90211. (213)278-8118. Affiliate: Filmways Music Publishing, Inc. (ASCAP). Professional Manager: Gay Jones. Music publisher. BMI. Member NMPA, BMA, California Copyright Conference, SRS, Music Publishers Forum, CMA, NARAS, NARM, NSAI. Publishes 100 songs/year; publishes 25 new songwriters/year. Pays standard royalty.
How to Contact: Submit demo tape and lyric sheet. Prefers cassette with 1-3 songs on demo. SASE. Reports in 1 month.
Music: R&B, pop/rock and top 40/pop.
Tips: "Submit professional demos—not just guitar/vocal or piano/vocals."

MUSTEVIC SOUND INC., 193-18 120th Ave., New York NY 11412. (212)527-1586. President: Brenda Taylor. Music publisher, record producer and record company. BMI. Publishes 7-9 songs/year; publishes 3-4 new songwriters/year. Pays standard royalty.
How to Contact: Write first about your interest. Prefers cassette with 3 songs maximum on demo. SASE. Reports in 1 month.
Music: Jazz. Recently published "Empty Streets" (by Brandon Ross), recorded by New Life/Mustevic Records (jazz rock); "Nova" (by S. Reid), recorded by Steve Reid/Mustevic Records (jazz instrumental); and "Rose Is" (by L. Walker), recorded by Les Walker/Mustevic Records (jazz instrumental).

MUZACAN PUBLISHING CO., 44844 Michigan Ave., Canton MI 48188. Affiliate: Noah's Ark (ASCAP). President: Bruce Young. Music publisher and booking agency. BMI. Pays 50-75% royalty.
How to Contact: Submit demo tape and lead sheet. Prefers cassette with 4 songs minimum on tape. SASE. Reports in 2 weeks.
Music: Rock (hard, acid or middle—"no country") and top 40/pop.

MY SON'S PUBLISHING, Box 2194, Memphis TN 38101. President: B.J. Cole. Vice President: Michal M. Cole. Music publisher, booking agency and record company. BMI.
How to Contact: Submit demo tape. Prefers 7½ ips reel-to-reel or cassette. SASE. Reports in 1 month.
Music: Blues; church/religious; gospel; and soul. Recently published "Yesterday," recorded by Lula Collins (gospel); "Here Larry," recorded by Larry Davis (blues); and "Days," recorded by the Gospel Song Birds (gospel).

MYKO MUSIC, 8924 E. Calle Norlo, Tucson AZ 85710. (602)885-5931. President: James M. Gasper. Music publisher, record company and record producer. Estab. 1981. BMI. Publishes 6 songs/year. Pays standard royalty.
How to Contact: Write first about your interest. Prefers reel-to-reel or cassette with 3-5 songs on demo. SASE. Reports in 1 month.
Music: Easy listening, R&B, rock, top 40/pop and pop rock. Recently published "Siren's Song," "Keep on Tryin," and "Paradise Island," (by Gasper and Dukes), recorded by Gasper and Dukes/Ariana Records (pop rock).
Tips: "Listen to the radio—*commercial* is not a dirty word. No matter what the trend, love songs and dance songs will always dominate the industry."

NASETAN PUBLISHING, Box 1485, Lake Charles LA 70602. (318)439-8839. Affiliate: TEK Publishing (BMI). Administrator: Jody Mallory. Music publisher. BMI. Publishes 50 songs/year. Pays standard royalty.
How to Contact: Submit demo tape and lyric sheet or arrange personal interview to play demo tape. Prefers cassette with 10 songs maximum. SASE. Reports in 1 month.
Music: Blues; C&W; folk; MOR; rock; and top 40/pop. Recently recorded "When I Hear Love Knocking" (by W. Wilridge), recorded by Jimmy House/Goldband Records (country rock); "Cajuns Are Tough" (by Johnny Janot), recorded by Johnny Janot/Jador Records; "Sugar Bee" (by Eddie Shuler), recorded by Jimmy Newman/Plantation Records; and "Sitting in the Bar" (by B. McCarty), recorded by Basil McCarty/Jador Records (country).
Tips: "Novelty songs are our specialty (and the hardest to write correctly), so if an aspiring writer wants to show off his/her artistic ability, just submit a novelty song."

NEVER ENDING MUSIC, Box 58, Glendora NJ 08029. (609)939-0034. Affiliates: Hot Pot Music (BMI) and Record Room Music (ASCAP). General Manager: Eddie Jay Harris. Music publisher and record company. BMI.

Songwriter's Market Close-up

Rupert Holmes' long-awaited success came with the song "Escape (The Pina Colada Song)" which has sold over three million copies world-wide. "That was the fifth complete lyric I had written to the track. I had written four others and hated them all. Then on the last recording day I finally wrote 'Escape.' "

It's the appreciation of his craft that drives Holmes to achieve perfection. It also makes him critical of any who view songwriting as anything other than what he calls "a noble profession. I hate flabby songwriting. People have a right to like or dislike my work but they certainly have to acknowledge that I *work* at my work. There are a lot of people who say they are songwriters but who are only guitarists. Nobody says 'I always wanted to be a surgeon so I'll stop by the hospital and do a little brain surgery today.' It's the same with people who think they can be a songwriter because they hum and play a guitar. It's a craft and most of the time you have to learn by the apprentice system."

Years in the business have given Holmes definite opinions on the demo. "There's a very important trick to demos. I know this not only as a songwriter but as a producer. You must create a demo about which you assume a fraudulent sense of humility. A demo should be as close to a master recording as you can make it *without* sounding like a polished recording. People in the record business get frightened when they hear a final record; it means they have to make an on-the-spot judgment. However, if you make it really good but leave a few flaws and preface it by saying it is obviously just a demo they will be able to say to themselves how good it will sound when it's a master. Give them the chance to be the geniuses."

He also has a number philosophy about demos. "Always make at least three demos. I

Rupert Holmes

have found when I try to sell one song or two songs I can never do it. But if I present three they find one that is the least offensive."

What has been his greatest thrill as a songwriter? "It's an incredible feeling to have written 'Escape' that almost everyone knows. It's like a universal passport . . . sort of my version of the American Express card—and I don't leave home without it."

He advises songwriters: "Either be a performer or find someone who can perform your work. You need an exponent, someone to say, 'here's a song by. . . .' and to sing it. I am a singer-songwriter because no one else would sing my songs, so I had to."

And he adds, "Half the time I was sure I wouldn't make it—the other half of the time I was positive I wouldn't make it. I want songwriters who feel the same to know that where they are, I have been, and they shouldn't give up hope. If you love it and need it (songwriting) you continue to hang in."

How to Contact: Write about your interest, then submit demo tape and lyric sheet. SASE (on solicited material only). Refuses unsolicited submissions.

NEWPORT BEACH MUSIC, 17422 Murphy Ave., Irvine CA 92714. (714)751-2015. Marketing Associate: Paul Leighton. Music publisher, record company and record producer. ASCAP and

BMI. Member NARAS, CMA. Publishes 75-100 songs/year; publishes 10 new songwriters/year. Pays standard royalty.
How to Contact: Submit demo tape and lyric sheet. Prefers cassette with 3 or more songs on demo. SASE. Reports in 2 months.
Music: All types.

NEWWRITERS MUSIC, 20 Music Square W., Suite 200, Nashville TN 37203. (615)244-1025. Affiliate: Timestar Music (ASCAP). National Promotion Director: Chuck Dixon. Music publisher, record company and record producer. BMI. Publishes 200 songs/year; publishes 17 new songwriters/year. Pays standard royalty.
How to Contact: Write first about your interest or submit demo tape and lyric sheet. Prefers 7½ ips reel-to-reel or cassette with 1-4 songs on demo. "Use clean tape!" SASE. Reports in 1 week.
Music: C&W and MOR. Recently published "Rev. Sam Whiskey" (by Steve Jones), recorded by S. Jones/Stargem Records (C&W); "Country Fever" (by Frankie Rich and A.W. Hodge), recorded by F. Rich/Stargem Records (C&W); and "Carolyn" (by Larry Hawkins), recorded by L. Hawkins/Stargem Records (MOR).

NICK-O-VAL MUSIC, 332 West 71 St., New York NY 10023. (212)873-2179. Associate Director: Ms. Tee Alston. Music publisher and record producer. ASCAP.
How to Contact: Submit demo tape and lyric sheet. Prefers cassette with 2 songs on demo. SASE. Reporting time depends on schedule.
Music: R&B.
Tips: "This is the publishing company of Nick Ashford and Valerie Simpson. The material you submit has to compete with their songs—it must be great!"

JOSEPH NICOLETTI MUSIC, Box 2818, Newport Beach CA 92663. (714)497-3758. President: Joseph Nicoletti. Vice President: Cheryl Lee Gammon. Music publisher, record company and record producer. ASCAP. Publishes 20-25 songs/year.
How to Contact: Submit demo tape and lead sheet. Send "good quality" cassette only with 1-3 songs on demo. SASE. Reports in 2 months.
Music: Disco; easy listening; MOR; rock; soul; and top 40/pop. Recently published "Love Has Come to Stay" (by Joseph Nicoletti), recorded by Joseph Nicoletti/California International Record and Video Works Inc. (easy listening); "I Am Free" (by Cheryl Gammon and Nicoletti), recorded by Joseph Nicoletti/California International Record and Video Works Inc. (disco/rock); and "Gypsy" (by Nicoletti), recorded by David Oliver/Mercury Records (disco).

NILKAM MUSIC/KIMSHA MUSIC, 5305 Church Ave., Brooklyn NY 11203. (212)498-7111. Owner: William R. Kamorra. Music publisher, record company and record producer. BMI. Publishes 7-10 songs/year. Pays standard royalties.
How to Contact: Query, submit demo tape and lead sheet, or submit acetate disc and lead sheet. Prefers 7½ ips reel-to-reel or cassette with 3-6 songs on demo. SASE. Reports in 2 weeks.
Music: Disco; MOR; R&B; rock; soul; and top 40/pop. Recently published "Making Love," recorded by Sammy Gordon (disco); "Love Bug," recorded by U. Robert (disco); and "Unity," recorded by Future 2,000 (disco).

NISE PRODUCTIONS INC., 413 Cooper St., Suite 101, Camden NJ 08102. (215)276-0100. Affiliate: Logo III Records. President: Michael Nise. Music publisher, record company, recording studio and production company. BMI. Publishes 10-20 songs/year. Pays standard royalty.
How to Contact: Submit demo tape. Prefers cassette with 3 songs on demo. SASE. Reports in 1 month.
Music: Children's; church/religious; C&W; dance-oriented; easy listening; folk; gospel; jazz; R&B; rock; soul; and top 40/pop. Recently published "Slow Motion Breakup" (by Sal Anthony), (R&B/pop); and "Cassablanca" (by C. Marzo, R. Marzo, and R. Nastri), recorded by William Sackett (big band).

NORTHERN COMFORT MUSIC, 10 Erica Ave., Toronto, Ontario, Canada M3H 3H2. (416)923-5717. Affiliate: Sacro-Iliac Music (PROCAN). President: J. Allan Vogel. Music publisher and record producer. CAPAC. Member LMPA. Publishes 8-10 songs/year. Pays standard royalty.
How to Contact: Submit demo tape and lyric sheet. Prefers 7½ ips reel-to-reel or cassette with 3-5 songs on demo. SAE and International Reply Coupons. Reports in 3 weeks.
Music: Jazz, MOR, progressive, R&B, rock, soul and top 40/pop.
Tips: "Be honest. Write contemporary hit material."

NORTHERN GOODY TWO-TUNES LTD., 354 Youville St., Suite 16, Montreal, Quebec, Canada H2Y 2C3. (514)845-7460. Vice President: Phyllis Goodwyn. Music publisher and record producer. Estab. 1981. CAPAC. Publishes 15 songs/year. Pays standard royalty.
How to Contact: Submit demo tape and lyric sheet. Prefers cassette with 2-6 songs on demo. SAE and International Reply Coupons. Reports in 2 weeks.
Music: Rock and top 40/pop. Recently published "Just Between You & Me" (by Myles Goodwyn), recorded by April Wine (ballad); "Roller" (by Myles Goodwyn), recorded by April Wine (rock); and "Say Hello" (by Myles Goodwyn), recorded by April Wine (rock/pop).

NOTABLE MUSIC CO. INC., 161 W. 54th, New York NY 10019. (212)757-9547. Affiliate: Portable Music Co. Inc. (BMI). General Manager: Eric Colodne. Music publisher. ASCAP. Member NMPA. Publishes 50-75 songs/year. Pays standard royalty.
How to Contact: Call first about your interest. Prefers 7½ ips reel-to-reel or cassette with 3-5 songs on demo. SASE. Reports in 1 month.
Music: Disco; easy listening; jazz; MOR; R&B; soul; and top 40/pop. Recently published "If My Friends Could See Me Now" (by Cy Coleman and Dorothy Fields), recorded by Linda Clifford/ Warner Records (slow disco); "Colors of My Life" (by Cy Coleman and Mike Stewart), recorded by Perry Como/RCA Records (MOR); "Let Me Be Your Fantasy" (by Neil Sheppard and Mitch Farber), recorded by Love Symphony Orchestra (disco/top 40); and "Never" (by C. Coleman, B. Comden and A. Green), recorded by Buddar and The Body Shop (disco/soul).

NU-GEN PUBLISHING CO., Box 2199, Vancouver, British Columbia, Canada V6B 3V7. (604)688-1820. Affiliate: Pyros Publishing (CAPAC). President: John Rodney. Music publisher and record company. PROCAN. Publishes 20-30 songs/year. Pays standard royalties.
How to Contact: Submit demo tape. Prefers 7½ ips reel-to-reel with 2-6 songs on demo. SAE and International Reply Coupons. Reports in 1 month.
Music: Classical; C&W; jazz; MOR; and top 40/pop. Recently published "Mister, Go Softly," recorded by Linda Marlene (C&W); and "Maranatha," recorded by Marek Norman (top 40).

NYAMM NEOWD MUSIC, INC., 136 E. Market St., #730, Indianapolis IN 46204. (317)634-3954. Counsel: Clarence Bolden Jr. Music publisher. BMI. Pays standard royalties. current roster. Pays standard royalties.
Music: Blues; disco; easy listening; gospel; jazz; MOR; progressive; R&B; soul; and top 40/pop. Published in 1978 "Don't Get Me Rowdy" (by Griffin and Ferrill); "Especially for You" (by C. Bush) ; and "Maybe My Baby" (by Bush), all recorded by Chi/Sound Records (R&B).
Tips: "Send a good tape which contains, if more than one song, about 1½ minutes of each song for review. If desires, company will request complete song."

O.A.S. MUSIC GROUP, 805 18th Ave. S., Nashville TN 37203. Affiliates: Arian Publications (ASCAP), Onhisown (BMI) and Shadowfax Music (BMI). Co-Directors: Dane Bryant, Steve Singleton. Music publisher. Member NMPA. Pays standard royalty.
How to Contact: Arrange personal interview for any Monday, or submit demo tape and lyric sheet. Prefers 7½ ips reel-to-reel with 3-4 songs on demo. SASE. Reports in 3 months.
Music: Bluegrass; blues; C&W; disco; easy listening; MOR; progressive; rock; soul; and top 40/pop. Recently published "Don't Believe My Heart Can Stand Another You," recorded by Tanya Tucker (C&W); "I Cheated on a Good Woman's Love," recorded by Billy "Crash" Craddock (C&W); "Atlanta's Burning Down," recorded by Dickie Betts (Southern rock); and "Could I Have This Dance," recorded by Ann Murray.

O. A. S. MUSIC PUBLISHING, 3140 E. Shadowlawn Ave., Atlanta GA 30305. (404)231-9888. Affiliate: Andgold Music (BMI). Catalog Administrator: Kathy Heiser. Music Publisher. ASCAP. Pays standard royalty.
How to Contact: Submit demo tape and lyric sheet. Prefers cassette with 1-3 songs on demo. "We like strong repetitive hooks." SASE. Reports as soon as possible.
Music: C&W, easy listening, MOR, R&B, rock, soul and top 40/pop. Recently published "My Car Won't Start," (by Wilks and Cornish), recorded by Wilks and Cornish/Centalic Records (novelty); "Now That I Know," (by J. Graham/J. Gates), recorded by J. Graham/O.A.S. Records (R&B); and "Sha La La La," (by J. Graham/J. Gates), recorded by J. Graham/O.A.S. Records (R&B).

OAK SPRINGS MUSIC, Rt. 5, Box 382, Yakima WA 98903. (509)966-1193. President: Hiram White. Music publisher. Publishes 15 songs/year; publishes 3 new songwriters/year. Pays standard royalty.
How to Contact: Submit demo tape and lead sheet. Prefers cassette with 1-4 songs on demo. "Keep it simple (voice and guitar), with no promo material." SASE. Reports in 1 month.

Music: Bluegrass; blues; C&W; disco; folk; MOR; progressive; and rock. Recently published "Yard Sale," recorded by Larry Merrit/Tell International Records (C&W); "La Rochelle," recorded by Larry Merrit/Tell International Records (C&W); and "Mr. Pruitt's Apple Farm," by Mike Wolters/Tell International Records (C&W).

OAKRIDGE MUSIC RECORDING SERVICE, 2001 Elton Rd., Haltom City TX 76117. (817)838-8001. President: Homer Lee Sewell. Music publisher and record company. BMI. Publishes 5 songs/year. Charges for some services: "If the writer is under contract to me, I don't charge for demos, etc. Otherwise, I do charge."
How to Contact: Query by mail. Prefers 7½ ips reel-to-reel or cassette with 3 songs on demo. "Send parcel post and mark the box 'Don't X-ray'." SASE. Reports in 1 month.
Music: Bluegrass; church/religious; C&W; and gospel. Recently published "Tribute to Bill Mack" (by Jessie Lightning), recorded by Jessie Lightning; "13 Steps" (by Charlie Sewall); "Ambush/If You Really Want Me To, I'll Go" (by Don Hudson); and *Praise He the Lord* (by Robert Swift).

MARY FRANCES ODLE RECORDING & PUBLISHING CO., Box 4335, Pasadena TX 77502. (713)477-9432. President: Mary Frances Odle. Music publisher, booking agency and record company. BMI. Publishes 8-10 songs/year. Pays standard royalties.
How to Contact: Submit demo tape or submit demo tape and lead sheet. Prefers 7½ ips reel-to-reel or cassette with 5 songs minimum on tape. SASE. Reports in 2 weeks.
Music: Blues; church/religious; C&W; easy listening; gospel; MOR; rock; and soul. Recently published "Women, Clothes, Cars and Whiskey" and "Hello Lonely, Lonely World" (by John Butterworth), recorded by John Butterworth (C&W); and "Looking Back Over Life," "Big, Big Mama," and "Cry, Cry on My Shoulder," written by Jerry Deyo (C&W).

OLD BOSTON PUBLISHING, 180 Pond St., Cohasset MA 02025. (617)383-9494. Writer Relations: Claire Babcock. Music publisher, record company and record producer. BMI. Publishes 10 songs/year; publishes 2 new songwriters/year. Pays standard royalty.
How to Contact: Call first about your interest. Prefers 7½ ips reel-to-reel or cassette with 1-3 songs on demo. Does not return unsolicited material.
Music: Recently published "Scollay Square" (by Tik Tinory), recorded on Old Boston Records (dixie/nostalgia); and "Music Man-Jo" (by Don Watson), recorded on Old Boston Records (folk rock).

ON THE WING MUSIC PUBLISHING CO., 937 Felix Ave., Windsor, Ontario, Canada N9C 3L2. (519)255-7067. President: Jim Thomson II. Music publisher, record company and record producer. Estab. 1979. PROCAN. Publishes 12-20 songs/year; publishes 1 new songwriter/year. Pays standard royalty.
How to Contact: Write or call first about your interest; arrange personal interview to play demo tape or submit demo tape and lyric sheet. Prefers cassette with 4 songs minimum on demo. "If you are submitting more than 1 style, submit at least 2, preferably 3, songs in each style. I want to know something about the songwriters and artists with whom I work. Send a short bio; include membership in professional organizations, outside interests and things about which you have strong convictions—abortion, religion, social issues, world hunger, etc. Lyrical depth, without sexual suggestiveness and obscenity are a definite plus." SAE and International Reply Coupons. Reports in 2 weeks.
Music: Bluegrass, blues, children's, church/religious, classical, C&W, easy listening, folk, gospel, jazz, MOR, progressive, Spanish, R&B, rock (all types), soul and top 40/pop. Recently published "I've Got Jesus" (by Jim Thomson II), recorded by Preflyte/Skylight Records (gospel); "Lonely One" (by J. Thomson II), recorded by Preflyte/Skylight Records (easy listening); and "Showdown" (by J. Thomson II), recorded by Preflyte/Skylight Records (country rock).

ONE FOR THE ROAD MUSIC CO., 3317 Ledgewood Dr., Los Angeles CA 90068. Contact: Alan Brackett. Music publisher and record producer. BMI. Pays standard royalties.
How to Contact: Submit demo tape. Prefers cassette with 1-4 songs on demo. "The words must be clear; if not, include a lyric sheet." SASE. Reports in 1 month.
Music: C&W; MOR; rock; soul; and top 40/pop. Recently published "I Really Want You Here Tonight" (by A. Brackett), recorded by Randy Meisner/E-A Records (R&B/MOR/ballad); and "Lonesome Cowgirl," (by A. Brackett and J. Merrill), recorded by Randy Meisner/E-A Records (C&W/jazz).

ONEIDA MUSIC PUBLISHING CO., 760 Blandina St., Utica NY 13501. (315)735-6187. President: Stanley Markowski. Music publisher. BMI. Publishes 20 songs/year; publishes 6 new songwriters/year. Pays standard royalty.

How to Contact: Submit demo tape and lyric sheet. Prefers reel-to-reel or cassette with "no limit" of songs on demo. SASE. Reports in 1 month.
Music: All types. Recently published "I Believe In America" (by Tiny Tim), recorded by Kama/Tiny Tim Records; "Baby I'm Possessed by You" (by Dawn Bouck), recorded by Standy/D. Bouck Records; and "Today or Tonight" (by Jim Cittadino), recorded by Standy/ARRC Records (all pop).

ONE-THREE-NINE MUSIC LTD., Box 1528, Shreveport LA 71165. (318)742-7803. Affiliate: Hayseed Publishing Company (BMI). President: David Kent. Music publisher, record producer and record company. ASCAP. Publishes 20 songs/year. Pays standard royalty.
How to Contact: Write first about your interest. Prefers cassette with 2-3 songs on demo. SASE. Reports in 3 weeks.
Music: Gospel. Recently published "Look Again" and "God Is Missing a Child," (by Micki Fuhrman), recorded by Micki Fuhrman/Dayspring Records (gospel).

ORCHID PUBLISHING, Bouquet-Orchid Enterprises, Box 4220, Shreveport LA 71104. (318)686-7362. President: Bill Bohannon. Music publisher and record company. BMI. Publishes 10-12 songs/year.
How to Contact: Submit demo tape and lead sheet. Prefers 7½ ips reel-to-reel or cassette with 3-5 songs on demo. SASE. Reports in 1 month.
Music: Church/religious (country gospel); C&W ("Dolly Parton/Linda Ronstadt type material"); and top 40/pop ("John Denver/Bee Gees type material"). Recently published "Lie to Me" (by L. Bearden and B. Bohannon) and "One More Trip" (by B. White and Bohannon), recorded by Bohannon (C&W).

RAY OVERHOLT MUSIC, 112 S. 26th St., Battle Creek MI 49015. (616)963-0554. A&R Director: Mildred Overholt. Manager: Ray Overholt. Music publisher. BMI. Publishes 25 songs/year; publishes 10 new songwriters/year. Pays 10-25% royalty. "We also use the standard songwriter's contract at the going rate."
How to Contact: Submit demo tape and lead sheet. Prefers cassette with 1-3 songs on demo. SASE. Reports in 3 weeks.
Music: Church/religious and gospel. Recently published "Tell My Daddy" (by R. Overholt), recorded by Becky Overholt/Artists Records (ballad hymn); "Another Day's Gone By" (by R. Overholt), recorded by Dodson Family/Crusade Records (country gospel); and "Lord, How Long" (by R. Overholt), recorded by Cathedrals/Word Records (country gospel).
Tips: "We desire songs with a country gospel touch—songs that tell a story, with a Biblical message, or theme."

LEE MACES OZARK OPRY MUSIC PUBLISHING, Box 242, Osage Beach MO 65065. (314)348-2702. Affiliates: Tall Corn Publishing (BMI) and Mid America Music Publishing (ASCAP). General Manager: Lee Mace. Music publisher, record company and record producer. Publishes 12 songs/year. Pays standard royalties.
How to Contact: Arrange personal interview or submit demo tape and lead sheet. Prefers 7½ ips reel-to-reel or cassette with 2-4 songs on demo. SASE. Reports in 2 weeks.
Music: Bluegrass; blues; church/religious; C&W; gospel; and R&B. Recently published "Younger Than Tomorrow" (by M. Sexton), recorded by Mark Sexton (pop/country); "I Can't Sell My Self" (by D. Thomas), recorded by Darrel Thomas (country); "Farrahs Faucet" (by Jack Selover), recorded by Lorance Aubrey (country); "Waylon Sing To Mama" (by D. Thomas), recorded D. Thomas/Ozark Opry Records (country); and "Don't Say No to Me Tonight" (by Don and Dick Addrisi), recorded by M. Sexton/Sun De Mar Records (pop/country).

PACKAGE GOOD MUSIC, 1145 Green St., Manville NJ 08835. Contact: Marc Zydiack. Music publisher. BMI.
How to Contact: Submit demo tape. Prefers cassette with 3 songs minimum on tape. SASE. Reports in 1 month.
Music: Easy listening; folk (progressive); MOR; progressive; rock; and top 40/pop. Recently published "There's No Place like You" (country rock); "Frosty the Dopeman" (progressive folk); "Nymphomaniac Blues," recorded by Marc Zydiak; and "Let's Start a Punk Rock Band," recorded by Professor Marx (punk rock).

PALAMAR MUSIC PUBLISHERS, 726 Carlson Dr., Orlando FL 32804. (305)644-3853. Affiliate: MuStaff Music Publishers (BMI). President: Will Campbell. Music publisher and record company. BMI. Publishes 4-20 songs/year; publishes 2-5 new songwriters/year. Pays standard royalty.

How to Contact: Submit demo tape and lead sheet. Prefers 7½ ips reel-to-reel with 3-6 songs on demo. SASE. Reports in 1 week.
Music: Bluegrass; church/religious; C&W; gospel; and MOR. Recently published "Dust" (by E.D. Linebarger), recorded by Big Dan Starr/Decade Records (gospel); "Third Finger Left Hand" (by E.D. Linebarger), recorded by Big Dan Starr/Decade Records (popular); and "I've Come Here to Do Some Drinking" (by W. Campbell), recorded by Will Campbell/Decade Records (country).
Tips: "Submit songs that are cleverly written with punch. I also like simple demos that are clearly recorded."

PEER-SOUTHERN ORGANIZATION, 6777 Hollywood Blvd., Hollywood CA 90028. (213)469-1667. Affiliates: Charles K. Harris Music Publishing (ASCAP), La Salle Music (ASCAP), Melody Lane (BMI), Panther Music (ASCAP), Peer International (BMI), Pera Music (BMI), RFD Music (ASCAP) and Southern Music (ASCAP). Professional Manager: Roy Kohn. Music publisher and production company. Member NMPA. Pays standard royalty; 5¢/sheet on sheet music.
How to Contact: Unsolicited tapes not accepted.
Music: C&W; disco; easy listening; MOR; rock; and top 40/pop.

PEER-SOUTHERN ORGANIZATION, 1740 Broadway, New York NY 10019. (212)265-3910. Affiliates: Peer International Corporation (BMI) and Southern Music (ASCAP). President: Monique I. Peer. Sr. Vice President: Ralph Peer II. Vice President: Mario Conti. Creative Director: Marti Sharron. Professional Manager: Roy Kohn. Main office. Music publisher. Member NMPA. Publishes 500 songs/year. Pays standard royalty.
How to Contact: Submit demo tape and lyric sheet. Prefers cassette with 1-5 songs on demo. SASE. Reports in 1 month.
Music: Bluegrass; choral; classical; C&W; disco; easy listening; MOR; progressive; R&B; rock; soul; and top 40/pop. Published "Blue Moon of Kentucky," recorded by Earl Scruggs Review, (pop/country).

PEER-SOUTHERN ORGANIZATION, 7 Music Circle N., Nashville TN 37203. (615)244-6200. Affiliates: Charles K. Harris Music (ASCAP), La Salle Music (ASCAP), Melody Lane (BMI), Panther Music (ASCAP), Peer International (BMI), Pera Music (BMI), RFD Music (ASCAP) and Southern Music (ASCAP). Director of Nashville Operations: Merlin Littlefield. Member NMPA. Pays standard royalty.
How to Contact: Query or submit demo tape and lead sheet. Prefers 7½ ips reel-to-reel or cassette with 1-4 songs on demo. SASE. Reports in 1 month.
Music: C&W; contemporary gospel; MOR; R&B; rock; and top 40/pop. Recently published "Georgia On My Mind" (by H. Carmichael), recorded by Willie Nelson; "Since I Don't Have You" (by J. Staton), recorded by Art Garfunkle (top 40); "Last Blue Yodel" (by J. Rodgers), recorded by Ernest Tubb; "Miss the Mississippi and You," recorded by Crystal Gayle; "Music Is My Way of Life," recorded by Patti LaBelle; and "Maybe I'll Cry Over You" (by E. Britt), recorded by Arthur Blanch.

PEER-SOUTHERN ORGANIZATION, 180 Bloor St. W., Suite 300, Toronto, Ontario, Canada N56 2V6. Managing Director: Matthew Heft. Music publisher. PROCAN and CAPAC.
How to Contact: Submit demo tape. Prefers cassette with 1-3 songs on demo. SAE and International Reply Coupons. Reports in 1 month.
Music: Bluegrass; blues; children's; choral; church/religious; classical; C&W; disco; easy listening; folk; gospel; jazz; MOR; progressive; rock; soul; and top 40/pop.

PENNY PINCHER PUBLISHING, INC., Box 387, Oakwood VA 24631. (703)935-4312. Affiliate: Loose Jaw Productions. President: R.J. Fuller. Music publisher and record producer. BMI. ASCAP. SESAC. Member of "most all" professional organizations. Publishes 50 songs/year; publishes 35 new songwriters/year. Pays standard royalty.
How to Contact: Submit demo tape and lyric sheet. Prefers reel-to-reel or cassette with 2-5 songs on demo. "We would like a biography." SASE. Reports in 1 month.
Music: Bluegrass, blues, C&W, folk, gospel, MOR, R&B, rock and top 40/pop. Recently published "Angel In Disguise" (by R.J. Fuller), recorded by various artists (country); "I've Got a Feeling" (by Goosby and Plante), recorded by various artists (rock); "Your Song" (by R.J. Fuller),

recorded by R.J. Fuller (MOR); and "I Could Fall for You" (by R.J. Fuller), recorded by Ken Jordan (country).
Tips: "Study the charts, get good hooks and turn arounds, use effective and not childish rhyme, be patient giving publisher all the time he wants, use return envelope, write, write and write—practice makes perfect!"

PERLA MUSIC, 20 Martha St., Woodcliff Lake NJ 07675. (201)391-2486. President: Gene A. Perla. Music publisher, record producer and record company. ASCAP. Publishes 12 songs/year; publishes 2 new songwriters/year. Pays standard royalty.
How to Contact: Call first about your interest. Prefers cassette. SASE.
Music: All types, especially jazz. Recently published "Aunt Remus" (by Gene Perla), recorded by Stone Alliance/PM Records (rock/funk/jazz); "Uncle Jemima" (by Don Alias), recorded by Stone Alliance/PM Records (rock/funk/jazz); and "Trampoline" (by Gene Perla), recorded by Stone Alliance/PM Records (pop/rock).

DON PERRY ENTERPRISES, 270 Hunters Point Dr., Thousand Oaks CA 91360. (805)497-4738. Affiliate: Invador Music Co. (BMI), Susaper Music, (ASCAP). Director of Music Publishing: Don Perry. Music publisher and record producer. BMI. ASCAP. Publishes 50 TV and film scores/year; publishes 4-5 new songwriters/year. Pays standard royalty.
How to Contact: Prefers demo tape and lyric sheet to be submitted by mail but personal interviews can be arranged to play demo tape. SASE. Reports in 1 month.
Music: Bluegrass; blues; children's; C&W; disco; easy listening; MOR; progressive; R&B; country rock; soul and top 40/pop. Recently produced "Theme of Grisly Adams" (by Tom Pace), recorded by Tom Pace/Capitol Records (MOR) and Doug Kershaw LP *Instant Hero*.

PET-MAC PUBLISHING, Damon Productions, Ltd., 6844 76th Ave., Edmonton, Alberta, Canada T6B 0A8. Affiliate: 3PM Music (CAPAC). President: Garry McDonall. Music publisher and record company. BMI. Publishes 25 songs/year; publishes 3-4 new songwriters/year. Pays standard royalty.
How to Contact: Submit demo tape. Prefers 7½ ips reel-to-reel with 3-10 songs on demo. SAE and International Reply Coupons. Reports in 1 month.
Music: C&W; disco; jazz; MOR; rock (country or commercial); and top 40/pop. Recently published "Leaving For Maui" (by Tim Feehan and Doug Buck), recorded by Footloose/Mustard Records (ballad top 40); "The Rodeo Song" (by Gaye Delorme), recorded by Showdown/Damon Records (C&W); and "Time Is Right" (by Tim Feehan), recorded by Footloose/Mustard Records (top 40).

PHILIPPOPOLIS MUSIC, 12027 Califa St., North Hollywood CA 91607. President: Milcho Leviev. Music publisher. BMI. Publishes 5-10 songs/year. Pays standard royalties.
How to Contact: Query. Prefers cassette with 1-3 songs on demo. SASE. Reports in 1 month.
Music: Jazz and classical. Recently published "Sad, a Little Bit" (by Milcho Leviev), recorded by Milcho Leviev/Mole Records (jazz); "Soup of the Day" (by Milcho Leviev), recorded by Milcho Leviev/Atlas Records (jazz); and "I.B. Fugue" (by Milcho Leviev), recorded by Milcho Leviev/Atlas Records (classical).

PHONETONES, 400 Essex St., Salem MA 01970. (617)744-7678. Logistics Co-Ordinator: J. George Perry. Music publisher and record company. Estab. 1981. ASCAP. Publishes 3 new songwriters/year. Pays standard royalty.
How to Contact: Submit demo tape and lyric sheet. Prefers cassette with 2-4 songs on demo. SASE. Reports in 1 month.
Music: Dance-oriented, R&B, rock, pop and new wave. Recently published "We Run Ourselves," (by Mare Mchugh), recorded by Tweeds/Eat Records (rock); "And Many Many More," (by Erik Lindgren), recorded by Original Artists/Eat Records (DOR); and "The Press Conference," (by Rose and Egendorf), recorded by Newshounds/Ragun Records (novelty).

PI GEM MUSIC, INC./CHESS MUSIC, INC., Box 40204, Nashville TN 37204. (615)320-7800. Professional manager: Dave Conrad. Music publisher. BMI. Member NMPA. Pays standard royalties.
How to Contact: Submit demo tape and lead and typed lyric sheet. Prefers 7½ ips reel-to-reel or cassette with 1-2 songs on demo. SASE. Reports in 1 month.
Music: C&W; easy listening; MOR; progressive; R&B; rock; soul; and top 40/pop. Recently published "Years," recorded by Barbara Mandrell; "My Heart," recorded by Ronnie Milsap; "Drifter," recorded by Sylvia and "Your Memory," recorded by Steve Wariner.

PICK-A-HIT MUSIC, 812 19th Ave. S., Nashville TN 37203. (615)327-3553. Contact: Dale Morris. Music publisher and booking agency. BMI. Pays standard royalties.
How to Contact: Submit demo tape and lead sheet. Prefers 7½ ips reel-to-reel with 3-5 songs on demo. SASE. Reports in 2 weeks.
Music: C&W. Recently published "Broken Down in Tiny Pieces" (by John Adrian), recorded by Billy "Crash" Craddock (C&W ballad).

PINE ISLAND MUSIC, Box 630175, Miami FL 33163. (305)472-7757. Affiliates: Lantana Music (BMI) and Twister Music (ASCAP). President: Jack P. Bluestein. Music publisher, record company and record producer. BMI. Publishes 10-12 songs/year; publishes 2 new songwriters/year. Pays standard royalty.
How to Contact: Submit demo tape and lyric sheet. Prefers reel-to-reel or cassette with 2-6 songs on demo. SASE. Reports in 1 month.
Music: C&W, gospel, MOR, R&B, rock and top 40/pop.

PINEAPPLE MUSIC PUBLISHING CO., 1311 Candlelight Ave., Dallas TX 75116. (214)298-9576. Affiliate: Big State Music Pub. Co. (BMI). President: Paul Ketter. Music publisher, record producer and record company. ASCAP. Publishes 20-30 songs/year. Pays standard royalty.
How to Contact: Submit demo tape and lyric sheet. Prefers 7½ ips reel-to-reel with 1-8 songs on demo. SASE. Reports in 3 weeks.
Music: C&W; folk; country MOR; and progressive country. Recently published "Bar after Bar" (by F. Feliccia and F. Raffa), recorded by Bunnie Mills/Sagittar Records (honky tonk country); "Only a Woman" (by D. Baumgartner), recorded by Bunnie Mills/Sagittar (C&W/ballad); and "Theodore" (by D. Gregory and G. Puls), recorded by Dave Gregory/Sagittar (children's Christmas).

THE PLEIADES MUSIC GROUP, The Barn, N. Ferrisburg VT 05473. (802)425-2111. Affiliates: Pleiades Music (BMI), Other Music (ASCAP), Grimes Creek (ASCAP) and On Strike Music (BMI). President: William H. Schubart. Music publisher. BMI and ASCAP. Publishes 60 songs/year. Pays standard royalty.
How to Contact: Submit demo tape and lyric sheet. Accepts cassettes only, with 3-5 songs on demo. SASE. Reports in 1 month.
Music: All types. Recently published "Up Is a Nice Place to Be" (by R. Sorrels), recorded by Bonnie Koloc/CBS Records (jazz); "Green Rolling Hills of West Virginia" (by U. Phillips), recorded by Emmy Lou Harris/WEA Records (country folk); and "Ballad of a Wanted Man" (by M. McCaslin), recorded by David Bromberg/Fantasy Records (folk).

POCKET-MONEY MUSIC, Box 29342, Dallas TX 75229. (214)243-2933. Music publisher, record company and record producer. BMI. Publishes 15-20 songs/year; publishes 3 new songwriters/year. Pays standard royalty.
How to Contact: Write first about your interest. Prefers cassette with maximum 1 song on demo. SASE. Reports in 3 weeks.
Music: Blues, C&W, dance-oriented, easy listening, gospel, MOR, new wave, R&B, rock, soul and top 40/pop. Recently published "Victim of Your Empty Heart" (by Steve Leach), recorded by The Magics/Smudge Records (pop/new wave); "I'll Be Back" (by Ralph Hollis), recorded by R. Hollis/Comstock Records (C&W); and "Love Tempo" (by Led Hopkins), recorded by Love Company/SRO Records (soul).
Tips: "We are currently publishing only material related to our record labels or production company. We do not shop songs to other artists at this time."

POLKA TOWNE MUSIC, 211 Post Ave., Westbury NY 11590. President: Teresa Zapolska. Music publisher, record company, record producer and booking agency. BMI. "We review all music once a month."
How to Contact: Submit demo tape and lead sheet. Prefers cassette with 1-3 songs on demo. SASE. Reports in 1 month.
Music: Polkas and waltzes.

POMMARD, Box 53, Nashville TN 37221. (615)646-9761. Contact: Dick Kent Withers. Music publisher and record producer. BMI, Nashville Songwriters, Country Music Ass., Nashville Music Assc., Screen Actors Guild. Publishes 5 songs/year; publishes 1 new songwriter/year. Pays standard royalty.
How to Contact: Submit demo tape and lyric sheet. Prefers cassette. Does not return unsolicited material.
Music: All types. Recently published "Rose Colored Glasses" (by John Conlee and Baber),

recorded by John Conlee; "Back Side of 30" (by John Conlee), recorded by John Conlee; and "Hold On" (by Dick Kent and John Conlee), recorded by Joe Stampley.

POSITIVE PRODUCTIONS, Box 1405, Highland Park NJ 08904. (201)463-8845. President: J. Vincenzo. Music publisher and record producer. BMI. Publishes 5 songs/year. Payment negotiable.
How to Contact: Submit demo tape and lyric sheet. Prefers 7½ ips reel-to-reel with 2-4 songs on demo. SASE. Reports in 1 month.
Music: Children's; easy listening; folk; and MOR. Recently published "Carrie's Airplane" and "Rainin' in the Morning," recorded by Chaves and James (MOR).

POWER-PLAY PUBLISHING, 1900 Elm Hill Pike, Nashville TN 37210. (615)889-8000. Vice President: Tommy Hill. Music publisher and record company. BMI. Pays standard royalties.
How to Contact: Arrange personal interview. Prefers 7½ ips reel-to-reel with 2 songs on demo. SASE. Reports in 1 month.
Music: Bluegrass; blues; C&W; disco; easy listening; folk; gospel; R&B; rock; soul; and top 40/pop. Recently published "Honey Hungry" (by Charlie Craig), recorded by Mike Lunsford/ Gusto Records (country); "Days of Me and You" (by Craig), recorded by Red Sovine/Gusto Records (country); and "Stealin' Feelin' " (by James Coleman), recorded by Red Sovine/Gusto Records (country).

POWHATAN MUSIC PUBLISHING, Box 993, Salem VA 24153. (703)387-0208. Affiliate: Double Jack Publishing (BMI). President: Jack Mullins. Music publisher and record company. BMI. Publishes 42 songs/year; publishes 4 new songwriters/year. Pays standard royalty and "if established, more").
How to Contact: Submit demo tape and lyric sheet. Prefers 7½ ips reel-to-reel with 2-4 songs on demo. SASE. Reports in 1 month ("no review").
Music: Bluegrass, C&W, R&B and top 40/pop.

PRESCRIPTION CO., 70 Murray Ave., Port Washington NY 11050. (516)767-1929. President: David F. Gasman. Music publisher, record company and record producer. BMI. Pays standard royalty.
How to Contact: Call or write first about your interest, then submit demo tape and lyric sheet. Prefers cassette with any number songs on demo. Does not return unsolicited material. Reports in 1 month.
Music: Bluegrass, blues, children's, C&W, dance-oriented, easy listening, folk, jazz, MOR, progressive, R&B, rock, soul and top 40/pop. Recently published "You Came In, " "Rock 'n' Roll Blues"(pop) and "Seasons" (country) (by D.F. Gasman), recorded by Medicine Mike/ Prescription Records.
Tips: "Songs should be good and written to last. Forget fads—we want songs that'll sound as good in 10 years as they do today. Organization, communication, and exploration of form is as essential as message (and sincerity matters, too)."

PRITCHETT PUBLICATIONS, 38630 Sage Tree St., Palmdale CA 93550. Manager: L.R. Pritchett. Music publisher and record company. BMI.
How to Contact: Submit lead sheet; "If we're interested, then a demo tape will be requested." SASE. Reports in 1 month.
Music: Gospel; MOR; soul; and top 40/pop. Recently published "Another Dawn," recorded by Charles Vickers (MOR); "Johnny Blue," recorded by Niki Stevens (folk/ballad); and "If I Can Help Somebody," recorded by Charles Vickers (gospel).

PRITCHETT PUBLICATIONS, 171 Pine Haven, Daytona Beach FL 32014. (904)252-4849. Affiliates: Alison Music (ASCAP). President: Leroy Pritchett. Music publisher and record producer. BMI. Members NSG. Publishes 30 songs/year; publishes 5 new songwriters/year. Pays standard royalty.
How to Contact: Submit demo tape and lyric sheet. Prefers 7½ ips reel-to-reel or cassette with 1-12 songs on demo. SASE. Reports in 1 month.
Music: Blues; church/religious; classical; C&W; disco; easy listening; folk; gospel; jazz; progressive; R&B; rock; soul; and top 40/pop. Recently published "Another Dawn" (by Pritchett), recorded by Charles Vickers/Accent Records (gospel); "Mister Jones" (by Herbert Woods and Joseph Pennpacker), recorded by Vickers/Neon Records (pop); "An April Fool" and "I'm Lonely" (by Jim Kelly), recorded by Vickers/Pyramid Records (pop); "For Your Love I'll Do Most Anything" (by Charles Vickers), recorded by Vickers/Pyramid Records (pop) and "Swamp Angel" (by Magnusson, Hoffman, Vickers), recorded by Vickers/Pyramid Records (rock); and "Do Me Good" by (Pirkins), recorded by Vickers/King Records (rock).

PROPHECY PUBLISHING, INC., Box 4945, Austin TX 78765. (512)452-9412. Affiliate: Black Coffee Music (BMI). President: T. White. Music publisher. ASCAP. Member NMPA. Publishes 200-300songs/year. Pays standard royalties, less expenses; "expenses such as tape duplicating, photocopying and long distance phone calls are recouped from the writer's earnings."
How to Contact: Submit demo tape and lyric sheet. Prefers cassette with 1-3 songs on demo. Does not return unsolicited material. "No reply can be expected, unless we're interested in the material."
Music: Bluegrass; blues; classical; C&W; disco; easy listening; folk; gospel; jazz; MOR; progressive; rock; soul; and top 40/pop. Recently published "Don't It Make You Wanna Dance?" recorded by Bonnie Raitt in soundtrack to *Urban Cowboy* (country disco); "Hondo's Song," recorded by Willie Nelson and Steve Fromholz (C&W); "Molly," recorded by Blue Steel (rock); and "Deep in the West," recorded by the Shake Russell-Dana Cooper Band (pop).

PUBLICARE MUSIC, LTD., Nashville Sound, Inc., 9717 Jensen, Houston TX 77093. (713)695-3648. Director of Copyright Affairs: Jim D. Johnson. Affiliate: Pubit Music (BMI). Music publisher, record company and production company. ASCAP. Member NMPA. Pays 50-75% royalty. Publishes 10-20 songs/year. Hires staff writers: determined by individual situation.
How to Contact: Submit demo tape and lead sheet. Prefers cassette with 2-4 songs on demo. SASE. Reports in 3 weeks.
Music: C&W; disco; MOR; progressive; rock; and top 40/pop. Prefers songs that have market crossover potential. Recently published "This Could Go On Forever" (by Lynn Jones), recorded by Sindy Heightman (pop); "Would You Care to Dance" (by Lenny Kerly), recorded by Jim Collins/Cherry Records (disco); "Louisiana" (by Elton Bussiner), recorded by Jimmy Neuman/Plantation Records (C&W).; and "Walkin Through the Fire" (by Lynn Jones), recorded by The Charlie Daniels Band.

GERALD W. PURCELL ASSOCIATES, 964 Second Ave., New York NY 10022. (212)421-2670, 2674, 2675 and 2676. President: Gerald Purcell. Music publisher. Pays standard royalty.
How to Contact: Submit demo tape and lyric sheet. Prefers cassette. SASE. Reports as soon as possible.
Music: Uses all types except rock.

QUALITY MUSIC PUBLISHING, LTD., 380 Birchmount Rd., Scarborough, Ontario, Canada M1K 1M7. (416)698-5511. Affiliates: Shediac Music (CAPAC), Broadland Music (PROCAN), Eskimo/Nuna Music (CAPAC), Rycha Music (PROCAN), Old Shanty Music (CAPAC) and Sons Celestes Music (CAPAC). General Manager: Madine Langlois. Music publisher and record company. PROCAN. Publishes 200 songs/year; publishes 10 new songwriters/year. Pays standard royalty.
How to Contact: Submit demo tape and lead sheet. Prefers 7½ ips reel-to-reel or cassette with 2-5 songs on demo. SAE and International Reply Coupons. Reports in 1 month.
Music: C&W; disco; gospel; MOR; progressive; rock (country or hard); and top 40/pop. Recently published "Harmonium," recorded by Harmonium (top 40/pop); "Try It Out" (by Gino Soccio), recorded by Gino Soccio/RFC/Atlantic Records; and "Set Me Free" (by Gino Soccio), recorded by Karen Silver/RFC Records (disco/pop).

QUINONES MUSIC CO., 1344 Waldron, St. Louis MO 63130. President: Eddie Johnson. Music publisher. BMI. Publishes 6-8 songs/year; publishes 2-3 new songwriters/year. Pays standard royalty.
How to Contact: Submit demo tape and lyric sheet. Prefers cassette with 3 songs on demo. SASE. Reports in 2 weeks.
Music: Blues; church/religious; gospel; R&B; soul; and top 40/pop.

RAC RACOUILLAT MUSIC ENTERPRISES, 7934 Mission Center Ct., Suite B, San Diego CA 92108. (714)296-9641. Affiliate: Mal & Rac Music Enterprises (ASCAP). President: Robert "Rac" Racouillat. Music publisher, record company and record producer. BMI. Member Songwriters Organizations National Group, Songwriters of San Diego Association. Publishes 30-50 songs/year; publishes 14 new songwriters/year. Pays standard royalty.
How to Contact: Submit demo tape and typed lyric sheet. Prefers cassette with 3-5 songs on demo. SASE. Reports in 2 weeks.
Music: C&W, dance-oriented, easy listening (A/C), MOR (A/C), new wave, R&B, rock (soft) and top 40/pop. Recently published "Bike Hustle" (by Robert "Rac" Racouillat), recorded by Bebe and Donnie Singer (pop/dance-oriented); "Kiss Your Past Good-by" (by Peter Richardson), recorded by Gary Hanley (country/pop); "That's a Lot of Lovin' for $1.69" (by P. Richardson),

recorded by Joe Trucks (country/pop); and "You're My Kind of People" (by Robert "Rac" Racouillat), recorded by Frank Joseph.

RADMUS PUBLISHING, INC., 15 E. 48th St., New York NY 10017. (212)838-8660. Affiliates: Musrad Publishing, Inc. (BMI), Celta Publishing, Inc. (ASCAP) and Flying Bear Publishing, Inc. (ASCAP). Vice President/General Manager: Martin Feely. Music publisher and record producer. ASCAP. Publishes 100-200 songs/year; published 3 new songwriters in 1979. Pays standard royalty.
How to Contact: Submit demo tape and lyric sheet or arrange personal interview to play demo tape. Prefers 7½ or 15 ips reel-to-reel with 3-5 songs on demo. SASE. Reports in 3 weeks.
Music: C&W; disco; easy listening; folk; fusion jazz; MOR; progressive; R&B; new wave rock; soul; and top 40/pop. Recently published "Saturday Night," recorded by Herman Brood/Ariola Records (new wave rock); "Souvenirs," recorded by Voyage/TK Records (disco); "Eres Tu," recorded by Mocedades (MOR); and "Born to Be Alive," recorded by Patrick Hernandez/ Columbia Records (pop disco).

RAINDANCE MUSIC, 430 3rd Ave N., Suite 20, Nashville TN 37201. (615)244-7116. Music publisher. BMI. Publishes 60 songs/year; publishes 3 new songwriters/year. Pays standard royalty.
How to Contact: Submit demo tape and lyric sheet. Prefers 7½ ips reel-to-reel or cassette with maximum 5 songs on demo. SASE. Reports in 2 weeks.
Music: Blues; C&W; easy listening; MOR; rock; soul and top 40/pop. Recently published "The Bedroom" (by Russ Allison and Ron Muir), recorded by Jim Ed Brown and Helen Cornelius/ RCA Records (country pop); "I Am the Dreamer" (by Allison, Cody and Hall), recorded by Conway Twitty/MCA Records Country; and "Dreamin' Won't Take Me That Far" (by R. Allison and Don Miller), recorded by Foxfire/Elektra Records.

RAVEN MUSIC, 4107 Woodland Park N., Seattle WA 98103. (206)632-0887. President: Ron Ellis. Music publisher. BMI. Publishes 12-15 songs/year. Pays standard royalty.
How to Contact: Write first about your interest. Prefers cassette with 2-6 songs on demo. SASE. Reports in 2 weeks.
Music: Children's (educational and worship); church/religious (worship and liturgical); and easy listening (Christian message-oriented or very positive). Recently published "There's a Time There's a Moment," "With All My Heart," "Life Is You," "Gentle Rains," "Songs For Our Children" and "Starlight" (by Ellis & Lynch) recorded for Raven Music (liturgical/worship).
Tips: "Our field is contemporary Christian and music for worship and praise. Songs must be generally singable by large groups, for worship in the hymn tradition but with contemporary style (strong melodic lines with scripture-based lyrics)."

RCS PUBLISHING CO., 5220 Essen Lane, Baton Rouge LA 70808. (504)766-3233. Affiliates: Layback Music (BMI) and Implusivo (ASCAP). General Manager: John Fred. Music publisher, record company and record producer. ASCAP. Publishes 15 songs/year; published 5 new songwriters in 1979. Pays standard royalty.
How to Contact: Submit demo tape and lead sheet. Prefers 7½ ips reel-to-reel or cassette with 1-10 songs on demo. SASE. Reports in 1 month.
Music: C&W; MOR; R&B; rock; soul; and top 40/pop. Recently published "So Hot" and "What's Your Name" (by Greg Wright), recorded by Wright; "Suddenly Single" and "Don't Take It Out on the Dog" (by Butch Hornsby), recorded by Hornsby (country/rock); "Hey, Hey Bunny" (by John Fred and the Playboys), recorded by Paula and John Fred (top 40); and "Safe with Me," (by I. Thomas), recorded by Irma Thomas (top 40/pop).

JACK REDICK MUSIC, Rt. 1, Box 85, Georgetown SC 29440. (803)546-7139. Affiliate: Wagon Wheel Records (BMI). Manager: Jack Redick. Music publisher and record company. BMI. Pays standard royalty.
How to Contact: Submit demo tape and lyric sheet. Prefers 7½ ips reel-to-reel or cassette with 1-6 songs on demo. SASE.
Music: Country and gospel. Recently published "Please Mr. D.J." (by Jack Redick), recorded by Williamson Brothers/Gold Star Records (country); "Pushin' Out One and Pullin' Two Back" (by J. Redick), recorded by Ray Jones/Ho, Ho, Ho-Kus Records (country); and "This Man Named Jesus"/"Jesus Is More Precious Than Gold" (by J. Redick), recorded by The Gospel Echo/ Wagonwheel Records.
Tips: "Keep pitchin' fresh, original songs and remember the better your songs sound, the better your chances. Keep demos clear with voice and lyrics in front and just simple rhythm track in background. Try for strong "hooks" in your songs."

RE'GENERATION, INC., Box 40772, Nashville TN 37204. (615)256-2242. Affiliates: Chenaniah Music (SESAC), Re'Generation Publications (ASCAP) and Spring Hill Publishing Group (BMI). Catalog Administrator: Eric Wyse. Music publisher, record company and record producer. Member NMPA, NARAS and GMA. Publishes 50-75 songs/year; publishes 1 new songwriter/year. Pays standard royalty.
How to Contact: Call first about your interest. Prefers cassette with 2-5 songs on demo. SASE. Reports in 1 month.
Music: Children's, choral, church/religious, easy listening, gospel and MOR. Recently published "Take a Walk on the Water," (by D. Johnson), recorded by The Re'Generation/New Dawn Records (gospel); "The Shepherd Just Smiled," (by D. Johnson), recorded by The Re'Generation/ Forever Records (gospel); and "You're the Master" (by Larry Mayfield), recorded by the Re'Generation/New Dawn Records (gospel).
Tips: "We are looking for good MOR/gospel that will work well in performance."

REN MAUR MUSIC CORP., 663 5th Ave., New York NY 10022. (212)757-3638. Affiliate: R.R. Music (ASCAP). President: Rena L. Feeney. Music publisher and record company. BMI. Member AGAC and NARAS. Publishes 6-8 songs/year. Pays 4-8% royalty.
How to Contact: Submit demo tape and lead sheet. Prefers cassette with 2-4 songs on demo. SASE. Reports in 1 month.
Music: R&B; rock; soul; and top 40/pop. Recently published "I Love Your Beat" and "Dance It Off" (by Billy Nichols), recorded by Rena/Factory Beat Records (dance) and "Rhythm Rap Rock" (by Billy Nichols), recorded by Count Coolout/Boss Records (RAP).

RHYTHM VALLEY MUSIC, 1304 Blewett St., Graham TX 76046. President: Orville Clarida. Music publisher. ASCAP. Pays standard royalty.
How to Contact: Submit demo tape and lead sheet. Prefers reel-to-reel with 1-3 songs on demo. SASE. Reports in 3 weeks.
Music: C&W and gospel. Recently published "The Smile on Your Face" and "Divided," both recorded by Orville Clarida/K-Ark Records (C&W).

RHYTHMS PRODUCTIONS, Whitney Bldg., Box 34485, Los Angeles CA 90034. Affiliate: Tom Thumb Music (ASCAP). President: Ruth White. Music publisher and record company. ASCAP. Publishes 3-4 LPs/year. Pays negotiable royalty.
How to Contact: Submit lead sheet with letter outlining background in educational children's music. Prefers cassette. SASE. Reports in 1 month.
Music: "We're only interested in children's songs for the education market. Our materials are sold primarily in schools, so artists/writers with a teaching background would be most likely to understand our requirements." Recently published "Musical Math" and "Musical Reading," (by D. White and R. White), recorded by Gris and Sotello/Tom Thumb Records (children's educational); and "Action Songs (by J. Mandel), recorded by Mandel/Tom Thumb Records (children's educational).

RMS TRIAD PUBLISHING, 30125 John R., Madison Heights MI 48071. (313)585-8887. Contact: Bob Szajner. Music publisher, record company and record producer. ASCAP. Member NARAS, NAIRD, AFM, RIAA, NMPA, BMA and NAJE. Publishes 27 songs/year; publishes 3 new songwriters/year. Pays standard royalty.
How to Contact: Write first about your interest. Prefers cassette with 1-3 songs on demo. SASE. Reports in 3 weeks.
Music: Jazz. Recently published "September Sunday," "Flying Horace," "Meeting Competition," "What's the Matter," "Extra Light," and "Reminiscence" (all by Bob Szajner), recorded by Triad/RMS Records (mainstream jazz).

CHARLIE ROACH MUSIC, 125 Taylor St., Jackson TN 38301. (901)427-7714. Owner: Charlie Roach. Music publisher and record company. BMI. Publishes 6-12 songs/year. Pays standard royalties.
How to Contact: Query or submit demo tape. Prefers 7½ ips reel-to-reel or cassette with 4-10 songs on demo. "We only want to hear work that is copyrighted." SASE. Reports in 1 month.
Music: Bluegrass; blues; church/religious; C&W; gospel; R&B; rock; soul; and Hawaiian. Recently published "Three Way Boogie" (by Charlie Roach), recorded by Westwood/White Label (country); "I'm Loving You Baby" (by Bobby Hardin), recorded by Westwood/White Label (country/rock); and "Getting Better" (by Bobby Hardin), recorded by Westwood/White Label (country).
Tips: "We also want to lease rock and R&B that was recorded between 1950 and 1979 for overseas distribution. This includes the master tapes—the finished product. Tapes should be 7½ or 15 ips. We want a very strong song—still looking for a bestseller."

FREDDIE ROBERTS MUSIC, Box 99, Rougemont NC 27572. (919)477-4077. Manager: Freddie Roberts. Music publisher, record producer and booking agency. BMI. Publishes 15-20 songs/year. Pays standard royalties.
How to Contact: Query, submit demo tape, submit demo tape and lead sheet, submit acetate disc, or submit acetate disc and lead sheet. Prefers 7½ ips reel-to-reel or cassette with 1-8 songs on demo. SASE. Reports in 2 weeks.
Music: Bluegrass; blues; C&W; disco; folk; gospel; MOR; R&B; rock; soul; and top 40/pop. Recently published "Tomorow I Won't Even Know Your Name" (by Freddie Roberts), recorded by David Laws (C&W); "That Man Is Soon Coming" (by Rodney Hutchins), recorded by Rodney K. Hutchins/Bull City Records (gospel); and "Don't Do It" (by Brenda Owens), recorded by Brenda Owens/Mil-Mar Records (southern rock).

ROBJEN MUSIC INC., Box 378, Nashville TN 37221. (615)646-4917. President: Jean Marris. Music publisher. Estab. 1979. BMI. Publishes 75 songs/year; publishes 3 new songwriters/year. Pays standard royalty.
How to Contact: Submit demo tape and lyric sheet. Prefers 7½ ips reel-to-reel or cassette with 3 songs on demo. "For every song sent in also send in typed lyric sheet." Does not return unsolicited material. Reports in 1 month.
Music: C&W, gospel, MOR, progressive, rock and top 40/pop. Recently published "I Believed in You" (by R. Wiegert), recorded by Cathy Bemis/Abacus Records (pop); "Loves a Circle" (by R. Wiegert, Bob Stills and P. Paczesny), recorded by Cathy Bemis/Abacus Records (MOR/country); and "It Must Be Love" (by R. Wiegert), recorded by Jeannie Martin/Abacus Records (MOR/pop).
Tips: "Study the market and be professional when sending in songs."

ROCKET PUBLISHING, 1416 N. Kings Rd., Los Angeles CA 90069. Affiliates: British Rocket Music Publishing (ASCAP), Jodrell Music (ASCAP) and Rocket Songs (BMI). Music publisher.
How to Contact: Submit demo tape and lyric sheet. Prefers 7½ ips reel-to-reel or cassette with 1-5 songs on demo. "Please include lyric or lead sheets, your name, address, phone number, and SASE." Does not return unsolicited material. Reports in 1 month.
Music: Disco; R&B; and rock. Recently published "Victim of Love" (by Pete Bellote, Sylvester Levay and Jerry Rix), recorded by Elton John; "Slow Down," (by John Miles), recorded by John Miles (top 40/disco); "How You Gonna See Me Now," (by Bernie Taupin and Alice Cooper), recorded by Alice Cooper (top 40/MOR); and "Part Time Love" (by E. John and Gary Osborne), recorded by Elton John.

ROCKFORD MUSIC CO., (division of Mighty Sounds and Filmworks Inc.), 150 West End Ave., Suite 6-D, New York NY 10023. (212)873-5968. Affiliate: Stateside Music (BMI). Manager: Louise A. Chielli. Music publisher and record company. BMI.
How to Contact: Submit finished master tape and lead sheet. Prefers cassette or disc with 2 songs on demo. SASE. Reports in 2 weeks.
Music: Dance and top 40/pop. Recently published *I Sing You* (by Michael Greer), recorded by Danny Darrow/Mighty Records (country Pop); "Carnival Nights" (by Vincent C. DeLucia and Raymond Squillacote), recorded by Danny Darrow/Mighty Records (country); and "For My Tommorrow" (by Steven Schoenbarg and Micahel Greer), recorded by Danny Darrow/Mighty Records (MOR).

ROCKMORE MUSIC, 1733 Carmona Ave., Los Angeles CA 90019. (213)933-6521. Music publisher and record company. BMI. Publishes 6 songs/year.
How to Contact: Submit demo tape and lyric sheet. Prefers 7½ ips reel-to-reel with 4 songs maximum on demo. SASE. Reports in 1 month.
Music: Blues; dance; gospel; R&B; soul; and top 40/pop. Recently published "One Tank of Gas" (by Willie H. Rocquemore and Bob Starr), recorded by Bob Starr/Rockin' Records; "This Energy Crisis Is Killing Me" (by Bob Starr), recorded by Bob Starr and his All-Star Band/Rockin' Records; "Soul Caravan" (by Willie H. Rocquemore), recorded by Bob Starr and his All-Star Band/Rockin' Records; and "Lonely Teals" (by Jimmy Holliday), recorded by Little Roberta/Rockin' Records.

ROCKY BELL MUSIC, Box 3247, Shawnee KS 66203. (913)631-6060. Affiliates: White Cat Music (ASCAP); Comstock Records; and Mutual Mgmt. Assoc. Professional Manager: Frank Fara. Producer/Arranger: Patty Yeats Parker. Music publisher, record company, record producer and management firm. BMI. Publishes 30-40 songs/year. Pays standard royalties.
How to Contact: Arrange personal interview or submit demo tape. Cassette only with 1-5 songs on demo. SASE. Reports in 2 weeks.

Music: C&W. Recently released "Stick to the Scriptures" (by Randy Hall), recorded by Randy Hall/Comstock (contemporary gospel); "Sad Time of the Night" (by Eric Bach and Andrew Wolf), Comstock (pop/country); "Heartache Remover" (by Ken Wesley), recorded by Ray Lansbery/Comstock (country); "Jesus, Lord of My Life" (by Wayne Graber), recorded by Wayne & Petra (MOR/gospel); "Before the colors Fade" (by Lindy Hearne), recorded by Kathy Tato/Comstock (pop/C&W).

ROCKY'S RAGDOLL PUBLISHING, Box 13781, 205A Television Circle, Savannah GA 31406. (912)927-1761. President: David M. Evans. Music Publisher. BMI. Publishes 12 songs/year. Pays standard royalty.
How to Contact: Submit demo tape and lyric sheet. Prefers 7½ ips reel-to-reel with 1-5 songs on demo. SASE. Reports in 3 weeks.
Music: C&W; rock (new wave, country); and top 40/pop. Recently published "That's the Way the World Works" (by Curtis Walker), recorded by Walker/Bet Records (disco); "Try, Try, Try" (by George Tuttle), recorded by Country Wild/Miles Records (country); and "All the Tea in China" (by Chuck Cook and Carolyn Cook), recorded by Chuck Cook/Lorelei Records (country).

ROHM MUSIC, 10 George St., Box 57, Wallingford CT 06492. (203)265-0010. Affiliate: Linesider Productions (BMI). A&R Director: Doug Snyder. Vice President: Rudolf Szlaui. Music publisher, record label and management firm. BMI. Publishes 35-50 songs/year.
How to Contact: Submit demo tape. Prefers cassette with 1-4 songs on demo. SASE. Reports in 1 month."
Music: Rock and top 40/pop. Recently published "Rescue" (by R. Orsi and K. Gronback) and "Pound For Pound" (by M. Curry and P.J. Ossola), recorded by the Scratch Band/TNA Records (pop); and "Torn In Half" (by Van Duren), recorded by Van Duren/Trod Nossel Artists Records (pop).

ROLLING DICE MUSIC PUBLISHING, Box 794, Hollywood CA 90028. (213)208-2728. Affiliates: Wall Music Publishing (BMI) and Surething Music (ASCAP). Professional Manager: Barbara Clabby. Music publisher and record producer. Publishes 25 songs/year; publishes 3 new songwriters/year. Pays standard royalty.
How to Contact: Submit demo tape and lyric sheet. Prefers cassette with 1-3 songs on demo. SASE. Reports in 1 month.
Music: Broadway, C&W, MOR, R&B, rock (all types), soul and top 40/pop. Recently published "I Want to Dance All Night" (by W. Breamer), recorded by Karen Reade/Jet Records (rock); "You Are Love" (by F. Parris), recorded by Black Satin/Kirsher Records (R&B); and "The Entertainer" (by F. Parris), recorded by Black Satin/Buddah Records (R&B).
Tips: "Songs should be commercial and oriented to the singles charts."

ROMONA MUSIC (GLORIA BLACK), 702 S. 15th, Newark NJ 07103. (202)691-8181. Professional Manager: Gloria Black. Music publisher. ASCAP. Publishes 30 songs/year. Pays standard royalty.
How to Contact: Submit demo tape and lyric sheet. Prefers cassette with 2 songs minimum on demo. SASE. Reports in 2 weeks.
Music: Blues; church/religious; C&W; dance; easy listening; gospel; jazz; MOR; R&B; rock; soul; and top 40/pop. Recently published "Double Dealing Dude" (by Gloria Black), recorded by G. Black/Jody Records (disco); "Do the Hammer" (by Eddie Hailey), recorded by E. Hailey/Jody Records (disco); and "Hustle Bustle" (by Mike Gaskin), recorded by Abracadabra/Jody Records (disco).

ROOTS MUSIC, Box 111, Sea Bright NJ 07760. President: Robert Bowden. Vice President: Jean Schweitzer. Music publisher. BMI. Publishes 1 songs/year. Pays standard royalty.
How to Contact: Submit demo tape and lyric sheet. Prefers cassette with any number songs on demo. "I only want inspired songs written by talented writers." SASE. Reports in 1 month.
Music: Church/religious, classical, C&W, folk, MOR, progressive, rock (soft, mellow), and top 40/pop.

ROUND SOUND MUSIC, 1918 Wise Dr., Dothan AL 36303. (205)794-9067. President: Jerry Wise. Music publisher. BMI. Publishes 10-20 songs/year. Pays standard royalty.
How to Contact: Write first about your interest, then submit demo tape and lyric sheet. Prefers 7½ ips reel-to-reel or cassette with 1-6 songs on demo. SASE. Reports in 1 month.
Music: C&W; easy listening; MOR; rock; soul; and top 40/pop. Recently published "Nashville Didn't Want Me" (by S. Clayton and D. Gilmore), recorded by Johnny Welden/Raven Records (country); "Tavern for the Lonely" (by F. Taylor and J. Miller), recorded by Johnny Welden/

Raven Records (country); and "How to Say Good-Bye" (by J. Broun), recorded by Norman Andrews/Raven Records (country rock).

ROWILCO, Box 8135, Chicago IL 60680. (312)224-5612. Professional Manager: R.C. Hillsman. Music publisher. BMI. Publishes 8-20 songs/year.
How to Contact: Arrange personal interview or submit demo tape and lyric sheet. Prefers 7½ or 15 ips quarter-inch reel-to-reel with 4-6 songs on demo. Submissions should be sent via registered mail. SASE. Reports in 3 weeks.
Music: Blues; church/religious; C&W; disco; easy listening; gospel; jazz; MOR; rock; and top 40/pop.

ROYAL FLAIR PUBLISHING, 106 Navajo, Council Bluffs IA 51501. (712)366-1136. Music publisher and record producer. BMI. Publishes 12-14 songs/year; publishes 3-4 new songwriters/year. Pays standard royalties.
How to Contact: Query. Prefers cassette with 2-6 songs on demo. SASE. Reports in 1 month.
Music: Old time country. Recently published "Time after Time" (by Bob Everhart), recorded by Bob Everhart (country); "A Toast to Rosie" (by Ruth Bingaman), recorded by Bob Everhart (honky tonk); and "Pahokee Sugar Cane Blues" (by Bob Everhart), recorded by Bob Everhart (country rock).

ROYAL K MUSIC, 6 Melrose Dr., Livingston NJ 07039. (201)533-0448. Affiliate: Musuque de Soleil (ASCAP). President Marc Katz. Music publisher, record producer and management firm. Estab. 1980. ASCAP. Publishes 35 songs/year; publishes 7 new songwriters/year. Pays standard royalty.
How to Contact: Submit demo tape and lyric sheet. Prefers cassette with 1-5 songs on demo. Include resume. SASE. Reports in 3 weeks.
Music: Bluegrass, church/religious, C&W, dance-oriented, gospel, MOR, R&B, rock, soul and top 40/pop. Recently published "She's Only Fourteen" (by Frank Diaz), recorded by Chakras (rock); "Dance" (by Charles Stewart), recorded by Good News (dance-oriented); and "Steppin" (by C. Stewart), recorded by Good News (gospel).

ROYAL STAR PUBLISHING CO., Box 1037, Des Plaines IL 60018. (312)824-6531. President: Joseph Starr. Vice- President: Mary Starr. Record company, music publisher and management firm. BMI, CMA, CMF of Colorado. Publishes 25-30 songs/year; publishes 10 new songwriters/year. Pays standard royalties.
How to Contact: Query, submit demo tape, or submit demo tape and lead sheet. Prefers 7½ ips reel-to-reel or cassette with 1-3 songs on demo. SASE. Reports in 1 month.
Music: Bluegrass; church/religious; C&W; easy listening; gospel; MOR; R&B; rock; and top 40/pop. Recently published "Quiet Hours" and "She's Sleeping in Somebody Else's Arms" (by Bobby Goodwin), recorded by Bobby Goodwin/Starr Records, Inc. (C&W); "A Cryin' Melody" (by Luther Robinson), recorded by Abe Chenault/Starr Records Inc. (C&W); "Get Out of My Life" (by Bobby Goodwin), recorded by Bobby Goodwin/Starr Records, Inc. (MOR); and "Graveyard of Broken Hearts" and "My Hard Workin' Woman" (both by Mary Starr), both recorded by Abe Chenault/Starr Records (C&W).

RSO MUSIC PUBLISHING GROUP, (Robert Stigwood Organization) 1775 Broadway, NY 10019. Vice President: Eileen Rothschild. Music publisher. BMI and ASCAP. Member NMPA.
How to Contact: Submit demo tape. Prefers cassette. SASE.
Music: Top 40/pop; rock; soul; R&B; progressive; easy listening; and folk.

RUBICON MUSIC, 8319 Lankershim Blvd., North Hollywood CA 91605. (213)875-1775. Affiliate: Dunamis Music (ASCAP). Vice President/Music Publishing: Teri Prio. Profession Manager: Dan Howell. Music publisher. Members NMPA, ASCAP, BMI. Publishes 50 songs/year; published 10 new songwriters in 1979. Pays standard royalty.
How to Contact: Submit demo tape and lyric sheet. Cassette with maximum 3 songs on demo. SASE. Reports in 1 month.
Music: Choral; church/religious; C&W; disco; easy listening; folk; gospel; jazz; MOR; progressive; R&B; rock; soul and top 40/pop. Recently published "Holding onto Yesterday" (by David Pack and Joe Puerta), recorded by Ambrosia/20th Century Fox Records (pop); "How Much I Feel" and "The Biggest Part of Me" (by David Pack), recorded by Ambrosia/Warner Bros. Records (pop); "Sometimes Alleluia," (by Chuck Girard), recorded by Chuck Girard/Good News Records (contemporary gospel); "You're the Only Woman," (by David Pack), recorded by Ambrosia/Warner Bros. Records (pop).

FRANK RUSSELL MUSIC, Division of Frank Russell Music & Records Group, Inc., 170 Linwood Ave., Paterson NJ 07502. (201)595-7557. President: Frank Russell. Music publisher. ASCAP. Publishes 40-50 songs/year.
How To Contact: Submit demo tape and lead sheet. Prefers cassette only with 1-3 songs on demo. "State clearly the reason for submission. Professional lead sheets and cover letter must accompany any and all material submitted. They should be packaged in clean new boxes or envelopes." SASE. Reports in 2 weeks.
Music: All types. Recently published "Let Me Count the Ways" (by F. Russell), recorded by Harvest/FRO Records (MOR ballad); and "One Day" (by F. Galardi), recorded by Harvest/FRO Records (disco).

RUSTIC RECORDS, 38 Music Square, Suite 114, Nashville TN 37203. (615)254-0892. President: Jack Stillwell. Executive Vice President: Marilyn Smith. Publishes 7-10 songs/year; publishes 2-3 new songwriters/year. Pays standard royalty.
How to Contact: Submit demo tape and lyric or lead sheet. Prefers 7½ ips reel-to-reel or cassette with 2-4 songs on demo. SASE. Reports in 3 weeks.
Music: C&W and MOR. Recently published "Hug Your Shadow," recorded by Bambi; "Quicksand," "Breakaway" and "I Wanna Do It Again" (by Bill Wence), recorded by Wence; "Have You Hugged Your Kid Today" (by Jack Schneider), recorded by Jack Stillwell; "We'll Make Music," (by Jack Stillwell and Cindy Campbell) recorded by Jack Stillwell; and "Marriage on the Rocks" (by Carl Struck), recorded by Carl Struck.

RUSTRON MUSIC PUBLISHERS, 200 Westmoreland Ave., White Plains NY 10606. (914)946-1689. Director: Rusty Gordon. Professional Manager: Ron Caruso. Music publisher. BMI, AGAC, AFTRA, Harry Fox Organization. Publishes 10-25 songs/year; publishes 6-10 new songwriters/year. Pays standard royalties; uses AGAC contract.
How to Contact: Arrange personal interview or submit demo tape and lead or lyric sheet. Prefers cassette or 7½ ips reel-to-reel. "Put leader between all songs and at the beginning and end of the tape. Use a tape box. Label it." SASE. Reports in 1 month.
Music: C&W (contemporary or story songs); disco; easy listening; folk (folk-rock); MOR; rock (pop or soft); and top 40/pop (originals only). Recently published "Look into My Eyes" (by Gordon and Caruso), recorded by Lois Britten/Rustron Records (pop ballad); "Hotter than Lightning" (by Gordon and Caruso), recorded by Christian Camilo/Rustron Records (salsa disco), "City Song" (by Gordon and Caruso), recorded by Christian Camilo/Rustron Records and Alhambra International (salsa disco); and "Where Love Can Go" (by Gordon and Caruso), recorded by Dianne Mower and Jasmise/Rustron Records (pop/jazz).
Tips: "Write strong hooks, unpredictable melodies and interesting chord changes. We want unusual or interesting concepts, commercially marketable for today's sound."

S.M.C.L. PRODUCTIONS, INC., 450 E. Beaumont Ave., St. Bruno, Quebec, Canada J3V 2R3. (514)653-7838. Affiliates: A.Q.E.M. Ltee (CAPAC), Bag Enrg. (CAPAC), C.F. Music (CAPAC), Big Bazaar Music (CAPAC), Sunrise Music (CAPAC), Stage One Music (CAPAC), L.M.S. Ltee (CAPAC), ITT Music (CAPAC), Machine Music (CAPAC), and Dynamite Music (CAPAC). President: Christian Lefort. Music publisher and record company. CAPAC. Publishes 100 songs/year.
How to Contact: Submit demo tape and lead sheet. Prefers 7½ ips reel-to-reel with 4-12 songs on demo. SAE and International Reply Coupons. Reports in 1 month.
Music: Dance; easy listening; MOR; and top 40/pop. Recently published "Put Your Feet to the Beat," recorded by the Ritchie Family/Able Records (disco); and "Take a Chance," recorded by Queen Samantha/Able Records (disco).

S & R MUSIC PUBLISHING CO., 39 Belmont, Rancho Mirage CA 92270. (714)346-0075. President: Scott Seely. Affiliates: Meteor Music (BMI) and Boomerang Music (BMI). Member AIMP and NMPA. ASCAP. Publishes 30 songs/year; publishes 20 new songwriters/year. Pays standard royalty.
How to Contact: Submit demo tape and lyric sheet. Prefers 7½ ips reel-to-reel or cassette with 1-4 songs on demo. SASE. Reports in 2 weeks.
Music: "We are mostly interested in lyrics or melodies for instrumentals." Recently published "A Touch of Love" (by Buddy Merrill), recorded by Buddy Merrill (MOR); "My Easy Side" (by Kirby Hamilton), recorded by Kirby Hamilton (jazz); and "Never Look Back" (by Robin Miller), recorded by Robin Miller (POP).

ST. CECILIA MUSIC, 1414 Summitridge Dr., Beverly Hills CA 90210. (213)858-5913. Publisher: Larry Weir. Music publisher. BMI. Publishes 20 songs/year; publishes 3 new songwriters/year. Pays standard royalty.

How to Contact: Write first about your interest, then submit demo tape and lyric sheet. Prefers cassette with 3 songs on demo. Does not return unsolicited material. Reports in 3 weeks.
Music: Jazz, MOR, progressive, R&B, rock, soul and top 40/pop. Recently published "Gotta Love Somebody" and "Being without You," recorded on Parallel Records.

SASHA SONGS, UNLTD. & THE GRAND PASHA PUBLISHER, Division of The Pasha Music Org., Inc., 5615 Melrose, Hollywood CA 90038. (213)466-3507. Affiliate: April/Blackwood, Inc. President: Spencer D. Proffer. Executive Director/Administrator: Ann Sumner-Davis. Send material to Coral Browning, assistant to the president. Music publisher, record producer and management company. BMI. Publishes 35 songs/year. Pays standard royalty.
How to Contact: Write first about your interest. Prefers cassette with 4-6 songs on demo. SASE. Reports in 3 weeks.
Music: MOR; progressive; and rock. Recently published "Goddess of the Night" (by Billy Thorpe and Spencer Proffer), recorded by Billy Thorpe/Polydor Records (progressive rock); "Daybreak" (by Spencer Proffer and David Pomeranz), recorded by Bette Midler/Atlantic Records and Cheryl Lynn/CBS Records (pop/MOR); and "Imagination's Child" (by Allan Clarke and S. Proffer), recorded by A. Clarke/Elektra Records (MOR).

SATCHITANANDA PUBLISHING, Box 2315, Springfield IL 62705. General Manager: Dave Hoffman. Music publisher. BMI. Publishes 40 songs/year; publishes 8 new songwriters/year. Pays standard royalty.
How to Contact: Submit demo tape and lyric sheet. Prefers cassette with 3-5 songs on demo. SASE. Reports in 1 month.
Music: Jazz; progressive; rock; and top 40/pop. "We are not bound by categories or types of music, and would consider any form of music if we felt that we could work it." Recently published "Crazy Women" (by Boe Perry), recorded by The Aferton Project/Aferton Records (pop); "This Cold Cold World" (by Dave Hoffman and Frank Houston), recorded by Art Carey/Aferton (R&B); and "Together" (by Flint Wilson and Satchitananda), recorded by Satchitanada/Aferton (progressive jazz-rock).
Tips: "Write what you feel. Sincerity is the heart of a good song."

SATSONG MUSIC, Box 720636, Atlanta GA 30328. (404)393-4640. Contact: Steven Kaye. Music publisher. ASCAP. Publishes 25 songs/year. Pays standard royalty.
How to Contact: Submit demo tape and lyric sheet. Prefers cassette with 1-4 songs on demo. Does not return unsolicited material. Reports in 2 weeks.
Music: Rock 'n' roll (hard to medium). Recently published "Movin' On" and "Illusion" (by J. Seay, B. Borden, J. Murdock, G. Murdock); "Rock 'n' roll 2 Nite" (by M. Keck, G. Moore, G. Borden, J. Murdock, G. Murdock, J. Seay), all recorded on Atlantic Records.
Tips: "No long intro or ending, vamps or solo—just basic melodies, verse and chorus."

SAVGOS MUSIC, INC., 342 Westminster Ave., Elizabeth NJ 07208. Affiliate: Jonan Music (ASCAP). Office Manager: Helen Gottesmann. Music publisher. ASCAP. Publishes 150 songs/year; publishes 50 new songwriters/year. Pays standard royalty—50% of mechanical.
Music: Publishes only material of artists recording on Savoy Records. Recently published "Forgive Them" (by A. Coleman and S. Lee), recorded by James Cleveland & Voices of Cornerstone/Savoy Records (gospel); "He Chose Me" (by J. Cleveland), recorded by O'Neal Twins/Savoy Records (gospel); "Call Him Up" (by R. Grundy and H. Netter), recorded by Pentecostal Community Choir/Savoy Records (gospel); "Jesus Dropped the Charges" (by R. White), recorded by Gospel Music Workshop of America Mass Choir/Savoy Records (gospel); "I'll Keep Holding On" (by M. Summers), recorded by Myrna Summers/Savoy records (gospel); and "Believe" (by J.C. White), recorded by Institutional Radio Choir/Savoy Records (gospel).

SCARLET STALLION MUSIC, Box 902, Provo UT 84601. (801)225-4674. Contact: Professional Manager. Personal management and concert promotion company. BMI. Publishes 30 songs/year. Pays standard royalty.
How to Contact: Submit demo tape and lyric sheet. Prefers 15 ips reel-to-reel or cassette with 4-6 songs on demo. SASE. Reports in 3 weeks.
Music: C&W (crossover to pop); folk; MOR; rock; and top 40/pop. Recently published "Tonight" (by Tom Ivers), recorded by Tyrant (rock/pop); "Arizona Highways" (by Bill Tuddenham), recorded by Dave Boshard (country/pop); and "How Long Has It Been" (by Dave Boshard), recorded by Dave Boshard (pop/MOR).

GUS SCHWARTZ MUSIC, Box 206, Kaleden, British Columbia, Canada V0H 1K0. (604)497-8424. General Manager: Dennis Thievin. Music publisher and record producer. PRO-

CAN. Member CMRRA. Publishes 10-15 songs/year; publishes 3 new songwriters/year. Pays standard royalty.
How to Contact: Submit demo tape only. Prefers cassette or 7½ ips reel-to-reel with 1-3 songs on demo. "Don't send long letters of apology or explanation. Songs should have clear, concise, lyrics and simple melodies with 'hooks.' Write with current top 40 always in mind." SAE and International Reply Coupons. Reports in 1 month.
Music: Top 40/pop. Recently published "I Won't Be Waiting" (by Sandi D. and D. Thievin), recorded by Sandi D./Brothers Records; and "Lovin' the Night Away" (by B. Northup and L. Christensen), recorded by Cristie Northup/Grandpa Louie Records (top 40/pop)

SCREEN GEMS/EMI MUSIC, INC., 1370 Avenue of the Americas, New York NY 10019. (212)489-6740. Affiliate: Colgems (ASCAP). Contact: Professional Manager. Music publisher and record company (Capitol and EMI). BMI. Hires staff writers.
How to Contact: Call first about your interest to see if they are accepting material, then submit demo tape and lyric sheet. Prefers reel-to-reel or cassette with 4 songs on demo. "Write *unsolicited material* on package if you have not called first." SASE. Reports in 6-8 weeks.
Music: MOR, R&B, rock and top 40/pop.

SCREEN GEMS-COLGEMS-EMI MUSIC INC., 1207 16th Ave. S, Nashville TN 37212. Affiliates: Colgems (ASCAP) and EMI Music. General Manager: Charlie Feldman. BMI. Member NMPA. "We do not actively solicit outside material."
Music: C&W and top/40 pop.

SCULLY MUSIC CO., The Sunshine Group, 800 South 4th St., Philadelphia PA 19147. (215)755-7000. Affiliate: Orange Bear Music (BMI). Assistant to President: Lisa Sable. Music publisher and record production company. Member AGAC. Publishes 40 songs/year; publishes 20 songwriters/year. ASCAP. Pays standard royalties.
How to Contact: Submit demo tape and lead sheet or disc and lyric sheet. Prefers 7½ ips or cassette with 1-4 songs on demo. SASE. Reports in 1 month.
Music: Folk; MOR; Top 40; pop; rock; and R&B. Recently published "Hot Shot," (by Andy Kahn and Walter Kahn), recorded by Karen Young/Westend Records (disco) and "While We Still Have Time," (by Ted Wortham and Cynthia Biggs), recorded by Cindy and Roy/Casablanca Records (R&B).

SEA THREE MUSIC, 1310 Tulane, Houston TX 77008. (713)864-0705. President: Charles Bickley. Music publisher, record company, record producer, studio engineer and musician. BMI. Member MSMA and AFoM. Publishes 50 songs/year; publishes 5 new songwriters/year. Pays standard royalty.
How to Contact: Call first about your interest, arrange personal interview or submit demo tape and lyric sheet. Prefers 7½ ips reel-to-reel or cassette with 1-4 songs on demo. SASE. "Sometimes" does not return unsolicited material. Reports in 1 month.
Music: Bluegrass, blues, choral, church/religious, C&W, dance-oriented, easy listening, folk, gospel, jazz, MOR, progressive, Spanish, R&B, rock, soul and top 40/pop. Recently published "Baby Ride Easy" (by Richard Dobson), recorded by Carlene Carter/Warner Brothers Records (country rock); and "Winter Time Love" (by John Bell), recorded by J. Bell/Buttermilk Records, London Records, and Decca Records-Europe (MOR).
Tips: "Write good hooks, aim at a particular artist's style and make a good demo."

SEGAL & GOLDMAN, INC., 9348 Santa Monica Blvd, 2nd Fl, Beverly Hills CA 90210. (213)278-9200. Contact: Manager/Publishing Department. Music publisher. BMI. ASCAP.
How to Contact: Send demo tape and lyric or lead sheet. Prefers cassette with titles, name, address and phone number. SASE. Reports as soon as possible. "Don't write a saga (too many words)."
Music: All types.

SELLERS MUSIC, INC., 1350 Avenue of the Americas, 12th Floor, New York NY 10019. (212)687-4800. Administrator: Mimi Ryder. Music publisher. BMI.
How to Contact: Submit demo tape and lyric sheet. Prefers cassette with 1-4 songs
Music: Top 40/pop.

SEPTEMBER MUSIC CORP., 250 W. 57th St., New York NY 10019. (212)581-1338. Affiliate: Galahad Music, Inc. President: Stanley Mills. Music publisher. BMI and ASCAP. Member NMPA. Pays standard royalty.
How to Contact: Submit demo tape and lyric sheet. Prefers 7½ ips reel-to-reel or cassette with 3 songs maximum on demo. SASE. Reports in 1 month.

Music: All types. "Good choruses and lyrics are most important. The song must be different, idea-wise, and tell a complete story." Recently published "Darlin" (by O. Blandamer), recorded by Tom Jones/Polygram Records (country/pop); "Two Minus One" (by A. Byron/P. Evans), recorded by Micki Fuhrman/MCA Records (country); and "Baby Grand" (by C. Wilkins and H. Spiro), recorded by Rita Remington/Plantation Records (country).

SEVEN HILLS PUBLISHING AND RECORDING CO., INC., 905 N. Main St., Evansville IN 47711. (812)423-1861. President: Ed Krietemeyer. Music publisher, record company and record producer. BMI. Publishes 6 songs/year. Pays standard royalty.
How to Contact: Write first about your interest. Prefers cassette with 1 song maximum on demo. SASE. Reports in 1 month.
Music: Bluegrass, blues, C&W, easy listening, folk, gospel and R&B.

SEVEN SONGS, 12403 Ventura Court, Studio City CA 91604. (213)877-0535. Affiliates: Sa-Vette (BMI), Me-Benish (ASCAP) and Ba-Dake (BMI). Vice President: Paul Politi. Music publisher, record producer and record company. BMI. Publishes 300 songs/year; publishes 50 new songwriters/year. Pays standard royalty. Hires staff writers.
How to Contact: Submit demo cassette, lead sheet and lyric sheet. SASE. Reports immediately if interested.
Music: C&W; dance; easy listening; jazz; MOR; progressive; R&B; rock; soul; and top 40/pop. Recently published "Love Makin' Music" (by Ragavoy and Schroeder), recorded by Barry White; "Let Her Dance" (by Bobby Fuller), recorded by Robin Seymour; and "Any Fool Could See" (by Paul Politi and Barry White), recorded by Wayne Newton.

SEVENTH NOTE MUSIC, Box 400843, Dallas TX 75240. (214)690-8165. Labels include Thanks Records. President: Michael Stanglin. Music publisher and record company. Publishes 20 songs/year. Pays standard royalty.
How to Contact: Submit demo tape. Prefers 7½ ips reel-to-reel or cassette with 1-3 songs on demo. SASE. Reports in 3 weeks.
Music: C&W; disco; easy listening; and top 40/pop. "The World Keeps on Spinning" (by Ron Price), recorded by Glen Campbell/Capitol Records (country/pop); and "I Hate Disco Music" (by Rick Ramirez), recorded by Ramirez/Thanks Records (country).

SEVENTH RAY PUBLISHING, Box 3771, Hollywood CA 90020. (213)467-0611. Affiliate: Hermosa Publishing (BMI). Producer: Alan Ames. Music publisher, record company and record producer. ASCAP. Member AMPAS, ATVAS, ITVA. Publishes 50+ songs/year; publishes 4 new songwriters/year. Pays standard royalty.
How to Contact: Submit demo tape and lyric sheet. Prefers cassette with 3-8 songs on demo. SASE. Reports in 1 month.
Music: Blues, reggae, easy listening, jazz, MOR, progressive, R&B, rock, soul and top 40/pop. Recently published "Abundance" (by Fantuzzi), recorded by Fantuzzi/Seventh Ray Records (R&B); "Edisa" (by Stephen Fiske), recorded by S. Fiske/Seventh Ray Records (folk-jazz); and "Nobody but You" (by Gay Martin), recorded by G. Martin/Seventh Ray Records (reggae).

SEYAH MUSIC, Master Audio, Inc., 1228 Spring St. NW, Atlanta GA 30309. (404)873-6425. Affiliates: Paydirt Music (ASCAP) and Lyresong Music (BMI). President: Babs Richardson. Music publisher and recording studio. BMI. Publishes 20 songs/year; publishes 1-2 new songwriters/year. Pays standard royalty.
How to Contact: Submit demo tape. Prefers cassette with 2-3 songs on demo. SASE. Reports in 1 month.
Music: C&W; disco; gospel; R&B; soul; and top 40/pop. Recently published *Great News*, (by Troy Ramey), recorded by Troy Ramey and the Soul Searchers/Nashboro Records (black gospel); "Try Jesus," recorded by Troy Ramey (gospel); and "Tea Cups and Doilies," (by Mac Frampton), recorded by Mac Frampton/Triumvirate Records (Broadway show type).

SHAWNEE PRESS, INC., Delaware Water Gap PA 18327. (717)476-0550. Affiliates: Harold Flammer, Inc. (ASCAP), Glory Sound, Templeton Music (ASCAP), Malcolm Music (BMI) and Choral Press (SESAC). Director of Publications: Lewis M. Kirby Jr. Music publisher and record company. ASCAP. Member NMPA. Publishes 150 songs/year.
How to Contact: Submit demo tape and lead sheet or submit lead sheet. Prefers cassette. SASE. Reports in 2 months.
Music: Children's; choral; church/religious; classical; easy listening; folk; gospel; MOR; and top 40/pop. "Shawnee Press is primarily a publisher of choral and instrumental music for educational or religious use." Published "Black and White" (by Robinson and Arkin), recorded by Three Dog

Night/ABC-Dunhill Records (top 40); "This Is My Country" (by Raye and Jacobs), recorded by Anita Bryant/Columbia Records (patriotic); "Let Me Call You Sweetheart" (by Whitson and Friedman), recorded by Mitch Miller/Columbia Records (easy listening/pop); and "If I Had My Way" (by Kendis and Klein), recorded by the Mills Brothers/Brunswick Records (pop).
Tips: "Send material for review suitable for use in schools or churches or for publication/recording for gospel market."

SHELTON ASSOCIATES, 2250 Bryn Mawr Ave., Philadelphia PA 19131. (215)477-7122. A&R Director: Leo Gayton. Adminstrator: Richard Jackson. Music publisher. BMI. Publishes 10-18 songs/year; publishes 12 new songwriters/year. Pays standard royalty.
How to Contact: Submit demo tape. Prefers 7½ ips reel-to-reel or cassette with 3-5 songs on demo. SASE. Reports in 2 weeks.
Music: Dance; easy listening; MOR; progressive; R&B; rock; soul; and top 40/pop. Recently published "Craving" (by G. Harris), recorded by Giles Crawford (pop); "Do the Funk" (by C. Bevdree), recorded by Galaxy (R&B); and "Ain't This Love?" (by R. Covington), recorded by Dream Merchants (R&B).

SHERLYN PUBLISHING CO., 65 E. 55th St., 602, New York NY 10022. (212)752-0160. Affiliates: Kimlyn Music (ASCAP) and Lindseyanne Music (BMI). Music publisher and record company. BMI. Member NMPA. Pays standard royalties. Hires staff writers.
How to Contact: Query or submit demo tape and lyric sheet. Prefers cassette with 1-3 songs on demo. SASE. Reports in 2 weeks.
Music: C&W; disco; R&B; rock; soul; and top 40/pop.

SHOW BIZ MUSIC GROUP, 110 21st Ave. S., Nashville TN 37203. Affiliates: Song Biz Music (BMI), Monster Music (ASCAP) and Lucky Pen Music (ASCAP). General manager: J.R. Dunlap. Music publisher. Pays standard royalties.
How to Contact: Query or submit demo tape and lead sheet. Prefers 7½ ips reel-to-reel or cassette with 1-2 songs on demo. SASE. Reports "as soon as possible.".
Music: C&W; disco; easy listening; folk; gospel; MOR; and top 40/pop. Recently published "Morning" and "That Time of the Night" (by Bill Graham), recorded by Jim Ed Brown/RCA Records (pop/C&W); and "Word Games" (by Graham) recorded by Billy Walker/RCA Records (country).

SIDEWALK SAILOR MUSIC, Box 423, Station F, Toronto, Ontario, Canada M4Y 2L8. Affiliates: Etheric Polyphony (CAPAC), Scales of My Head Music (PROCAN), Cumulonimbus Music (PROCAN). Professional Manager: Allen Shechtman. Music publisher and record producer. CAPAC. Publishes 5-10 songs/year; publishes 2 new songwriters/year. "We recoup any costs from publisher's income, then split publisher's side of income on a 25-75 percent basis with songwriter (25 percent)."
How to Contact: Submit demo tape and lyric sheet. Prefers 7½-15 ips or cassette with 3 songs on demo. "Check your songs before you send them to anyone. Make sure they are your best efforts and have been reworked to make them as accessible as possible." SAE and International Reply Coupons. Reports in 1 month.
Music: Bluegrass, folk and progressive. Recently published "Wanted Man" (by Ian Kemp), recorded by Ian Kemp (outlaw); "Supernatural One" and "Vision Quest" (by Graeme Card), recorded by G. Card/Change/MCA Records (progressive/AOR).

SILHOUETTE MUSIC, Box 218, Wellman Heights, Johnsonville SC 29555. (803)386-2600. Affiliates: Bridge Music (BMI) and Heraldic Music (ASCAP). Director: Erv Lewis. Music publisher and record company. SESAC. Member GMA. Publishes 12 songs/year; publishes 3 new songwriters/year. Publishes 15-40 songs/year.
How to Contact: Submit demo tape and lyric sheet. Prefers cassette with 3-6 songs on demo. "Record the tape on one side only, as we use mono equipment on playback." SASE. Reports in 2 months.
Music: Church/religious and gospel. Recently published "He Is" (by Jerry Arhelger), recorded by Jerry Arhelger/Herald Records (gospel); "Jesus Can" (by Erv Lewis), recorded by Sydna Taylor/Herald Records (gospel); and "Hold On Children" (by Erv Lewis), recorded by Judith Friday/Herald Records (gospel).

SILICON MUSIC PUBLISHING CO., 222 Tulane St., Garland TX 75043. President: Gene Summers. Vice President: Deanna L. Summers. Music publisher. BMI. Publishes 10-20 songs/year. Pays standard royalties.

How to Contact: Submit demo tape. Prefers cassette with 1-2 songs on demo. Does not return unsolicited material.

Music: C&W; MOR; and rock. Recently published "A Place Called Friendlyville" and "Dungeon of Jealously" (by Bill Kelly and Bill Ashley), recorded by Bill Kelly/Domino Records; "Tomorrow Will Never Be" (by Al Struble), recorded by the Struble Brothers Band/Domino Records (rock); "Cloudy Day," recorded by Gene Summers (MOR); "Texas Rock 'n' Roll" LP, recorded by Gene Summers/Big Beat Records/France ('50s rock); "Gene Summers Early Rocking Recordings"/Collector Records/Holland ('50s rock); and "The Ballad of Moon Dog Mayne," recorded by Ricky Ringside/Front Row Records (country).

Tips: "We are very interested in '50s rock and rockabilly *original masters* for release through overseas affiliates. If you are the owner of any '50s masters, contact us first! We have releases in Holland, Switzerland, England, Belgium, France, Sweden, Norway and Australia."

SILVER BLUE MUSIC, LTD., 220 Central Park S., New York NY 10019. Affiliate: Oceans Blue Music (ASCAP). President: Joel Diamond. Music publisher and record producer. BMI.
How to Contact: Submit demo tape and lead sheet. Prefers cassette with 3-4 songs on demo. SASE. Reports in 3 weeks "only if we are interested in the material."
Music: Top 40/pop and AC. Recently published "After the Lovin' " and "This Moment in Time" (by Richie Adams and Alan Bernstein), recorded by Englebert Humperdink (AC and top 40/pop); and "Let's Just Stay Home Tonight" (by Lottie Golden and Richard Scher), recorded by Helen Reddy.

SING ME MUSIC, INC., 501 Chesterfield Ave., Nashville TN 37212. (615)297-0024. Affiliates: Crooked Creek (BMI) and Kiss Me Music (SESAC). President: Jean S. Zimmerman. Professional Manager: Mary Louise Smith. Music publisher. ASCAP. Published 35 songs/year; publishes 20 songwriters/year. Pays standard royalties.
How to Contact: Submit demo tape, arrange personal interview, or submit demo tape and lead sheet. Prefers cassette with 1-4 songs on demo. SASE. Reports as time permits.
Music: Bluegrass; blues; church/religious; C&W; disco; easy listening; folk; gospel; MOR; rock (hard or C&W); soul; and top 40/pop. Recently published "Lord, How Long Has This Been Going On" (by Billy Lee Morris), recorded by Amarillo (C&W); "Needing You" (by Michael L. Davis), recorded by Marty Montez/Sing Me Records (MOR); and "Mechanical Bull" (by Daniel Anthony), recorded by Alan Tripp/AT Records (country).

SINGING RIVER PUBLISHING CO., INC., 205 Acacia St., Biloxi MS 39530. (601)436-3927. Affiliate: Axent Publishing (ASCAP). President: Marion Carpenter. Music publisher, record company and record producer. BMI. Pays standard royalties.
How to Contact: Query or submit demo tape. Prefers 7½ ips reel-to-reel or cassette with 1-4 songs on demo. SASE. Reports in 1 month.
Music: Bluegrass; blues; C&W; easy listening; folk; MOR; and top 40/pop. Recently published "World of Make Believe" (by Carpenter, Maddox and Smith), recorded by Bill Anderson/MCA Records and Johnny Bragg/Decca Records (country); "Searching" (by Maddox), recorded by Kitty Wells/Decca Records and Melba Montgomery (country); and "Rocking Little Angel" (by J. Rodgers), recorded by Ray Smith/Capitol Records (country).

SHELBY SINGLETON MUSIC INC., 3106 Belmont Blvd., Nashville TN 37212. (615)385-1960. Affiliates: Prize (ASCAP), Green Isle (ASCAP) and Green Owl (BMI). Professional Manager: Sidney Singleton. Music publisher and record company. BMI. Member NMPA. Publishes 200 songs/year; publishes 10 new songwriters/year. Pays standard royalties.
How to Contact: Submit demo tape and lyric sheet. Prefers cassette. SASE. Reports "as soon as possible.".
Music: C&W; easy listening; easy rock; and top 40/pop. Recently published "Before the Next Teardrop Falls" recorded by Freddy Fender (country); "Texas Tea" recorded by Orion (country); and "Such A Night" recorded by Elvis (rock).

SIVATT MUSIC PUBLISHING CO., Box 7172, Greenville SC 29610. (803)269-3961. President: Jesse B. Evatte. Music publisher and record company. BMI. Publishes 20 songs/year.
How to Contact: Submit demo tape and lead sheet. Prefers cassette with 2-6 songs on demo. SASE. Reports in 1 month.
Music: Bluegrass; church/religious; C&W; easy listening; folk; and gospel. Recently published "L-O-V-E" (by Johnny Halloway), recorded by the Gospel Jubilee (gospel); and "His Bride" (by David Abbott), recorded by Abbott/Mark Five Records (gospel).

SKINNY ZACH MUSIC, 6430 Sunset Blvd., Suite 1104, Hollywood CA 90028. (213)461-2988. Affiliates: Steelchest Music (ASCAP), AL/MC (BMI), Wedge Inc. (BMI), and Country Line (ASCAP). Manager: Zachary Glickman. Music publisher. ASCAP.
How to Contact: Submit demo tape and lyric sheet. Prefers cassette.
Music: Easy listening, gospel, MOR, R&B, rock, soul and top 40/pop.

SLIPPERY MUSIC, Box O, El Cerrito CA 94530. (415)527-6242. President: Tom Diamant. Music publisher. Estab. 1979. BMI. Pays standard royalty.
How to Contact: Submit demo tape and lyric sheet. Prefers cassette with 4-10 songs on demo. Reports in 1 month.
Music: Bluegrass, blues, children's, classical, C&W, dance-oriented, folk, jazz and R&B. Recently published "Flicking My Pick" and "Jethro's Tune" (by Jethro Burns and Ken Edison), recorded by J. Burns/Kaleidoscope Records (jazz).

EARLE SMITH MUSIC, Box 2101, Salinas CA 93902. (408)449-1706 Affiliate: Centra-Cal Music (ASCAP). President: Earle F. Smith. Music publisher. BMI. Publishes 4 songs/year. Pays standard royalties.
How to Contact: Submit demo tape and lead sheet. Prefers 7½ reel-to-reel or cassette with 1-4 on demo. SASE. Reports in 3 weeks.
Music: C&W; MOR; soul; rock and top 40/pop. Recently published "No One but You" (by Donald Pendergrass/Debbie Lowe); "If I Only Knew" (by Donald Pendergrass); and "I'm Just a Fool" (by William Layton), recorded by Johnice. Also producer for the group "City Magic" with lead guitarist, Ronnie Parker; bass, Dennis Murphy; drums, Joey Wedlake; Keyboards, Don Pendergrass; vocal, Debbie Lowe.

MACK SMITH MUSIC, 814 W. Claiborne St., Box 672, Greenwood MS 38930. (601)453-3302. Owner: Mack Allen Smith. Music publisher and record company. BMI. Pays standard royalties.
How to Contact: Submit demo tape and lead or lyric sheet. Prefers cassette with 1-5 songs on demo. SASE. Reports in 1 month.
Music: C&W; rock; and top 40/pop. Recently published "If I Could Get One More Hit" (by Mack Allen Smith), recorded by James O'Gwynn/Plantation Records (country); and "Angel Face Body Full of Sin" and "Who the Heck is Bob Wills?" (by Smith), recorded by Mack Allen Smith/Ace Records (country).

SNAPFINGER MUSIC, Box 35158, Decatur GA 30035. Affiliate: Hand Clappin' Music (AS-CAP). Owner: Don Bryant. Music publisher. BMI. Pays standard royalties.
How to Contact: Submit demo tape and typed lyric sheet. Prefers 7½ ips reel-to-reel or cassette with 1-4 songs on demo. "Please use leader tape before first song and between each song on reel-to-reel." SASE. Reports in 1 month.
Music: Country; easy listening; gospel; MOR; rock; and top 40/pop.

SNOOPY MUSIC, Graveline Enterprises, Inc., 1975 NE 149th St., North Miami FL 33181. (305)940-6999. President: Dave Graveline. Executive Vice President: Jim Rudd. Music publisher, record company, record producer and recording studio. BMI. Publishes 4-6 songs/year; publishes 3 new songwriters/year.
How to Contact: Submit demo tape and lead sheet. Prefers 7½ or 15 ips reel-to-reel. SASE. Reports in 2 weeks.
Music: Blues; C&W; dance; easy listening; Latin (with English translation); MOR; progressive; rock; soul; new wave and top 40/pop. Recently published "Scorpio Rising," recorded by Bob Needelman; "Love on a One Way Street," recorded by Toni Bishop; and "I Often Think of You" and "Please Stay with Me," recorded by Wesley and Deborah Bulla.

SNOWBERRY MUSIC, 1659 Bayview Ave., Suite 102, Toronto, Ontario, Canada M4G 3C1. (416)485-1157. Affiliate: Maple Creek Music (PROCAN). Vice President: Brian Ayres. Music publisher. CAPAC. Pays standard royalty.
How to Contact: Submit demo tape or arrange personal interview. Prefers cassette with 2-6 songs on demo; include lyrics. SAE and International Reply Coupons. Reports in 3 weeks.
Music: C&W; disco; easy listening; MOR; rock; and top 40/pop.

SOLA GRATIA MUSIC, (Division of Bee Jay Booking Agency & Recording Studios, Inc.), 5000 Eggleston Ave., Orlando FL 32810. (305)293-1781. Affiliate: Schabraf (BMI). President: Eric T. Schabacker. Music pubisher. Estab. 1978. SESAC. Publishes 20-30 songs/year. Pays standard royalty; varies for sheet music.
How to Contact: Query by mail, then submit demo tape and lyric sheet. Prefers 7½ ips reel-to-reel

or cassette with 2-4 songs on demo. Artist should enclose photos, biographies; writer needs only include background material. SASE. Reports in 2-4 weeks.

Music: Contemporary Christian "in the rock/pop genre." Recently published "In His Arms" (by Billy Hires), recorded by Chalice/Starsong Records (contemporary Christian); "Looking Back" (by Bob Strickland), recorded by Chalice/Starsong Records (contemporary Christian); and "I Just Want To Be With Him" (by Wally Joiner), recorded by Chalice/Starsong Records (contemporary Christian).

SONE SONGS, 10101 Woodlake Dr., Cockeysville MD 21030. General Manager: George Brigman. Music publisher. BMI. Publishes 10-20 songs/year; publishes 1-2 new songwriters/year. Pays standard royalty.

How to Contact: Submit demo tape and lyric sheet. Prefers 7½ ips reel-to-reel with 1-6 songs on demo. SASE. Reports in 3 weeks.

Music: Blues; C&W; disco; easy listening; folk; gospel; jazz; MOR; progressive; R&B; rock; soul; and top 40/pop. Recently published "Nashville" and "Lovin' You" (by Brigman and Amos), recorded by J. Butterworth/Equinox Records (country); and "My Cherie," "Blowin' Smoke" and "Drifting" (by Brigman), recorded by Split/Solid Records (rock; jazz).

SONG FARM MUSIC UNLIMITED, Box 24561, Nashville TN 37202. (615)242-1037. Vice President: Tom Pallardy. Music publisher and record producer. BMI. Publishes 20 songs/year; publishes 3-5 new songwriters/year. Pays standard royalty.

How to Contact: Submit demo tape and lyric sheet. Prefers cassette with 1-3 songs on demo. SASE. Reports in 1 month.

Music: C&W; easy listening; gospel; MOR; R&B; country rock; soul; and top 40/pop. Recently published "After Every Goodbye" (by Tom and Jo Pallardy), recorded by Lisa Ward/Whitehorse Records (positive/uptempo); "Champagne from a Paper Cup" (by Tom Pallardy and Sharon Tricamo), recorded by Bobby Allen/Barracuda Records (country rock); "Lonely Street" (by Ken Keene and Tom Pallardy), recorded by Frankie Ford/Briarmeade Records (MOR ballad); "You Bring Out the Best in Me" (by Tom Pallardy), recorded by Julie Lynn/Condor Records (ballad); and "I'm Proud of What I Am" (by Yvonne Robison and Dennis Turner), recorded by Frankie Ford/Briarmeade Records (country ballad).

Tips: "Material should be submitted neatly and professionally with as good quality demo as possible. Songs need not be elaborately produced (voice and guitar/piano are fine) but they should be clear. Songs must be well constructed, lyrically tight, good strong hook, interesting melody, easily remembered; i.e., commercial!"

SONG TAILORS MUSIC CO., Box 2631, Muscle Shoals AL 35660. (205)381-1455. Affiliate: I've Got the Music (ASCAP). General Manager: Kevin Lamb. Music publisher. BMI. Publishes 100 songs/year. Pays standard royalty.

How to Contact: Submit demo tape and lead sheet. Prefers 7½ or 15 ips reel-to-reel or cassette with 1-10 songs on demo. SASE. Reports "as soon as possible."

Music: Blues; C&W; dance; easy listening; folk; jazz; MOR; progressive; rock; soul; and top 40/pop. Recently published "Get It Up" (by Byrne and Brasfield), recorded by Ronnie Milsap/RCA Records (pop); "Slippen Up Slippin Around" (by Wyrick and Woodford), recorded by Christy Lane/United Artist Records (country); "Here Comes the Hurt Again" (by Johnson), recorded by Manhattan/CBS Records (R&B); "Old Flame" (by Lowery and McAnally), recorded by Alabama Band; "Hold Me Like You Never Had Me" (by Byrne and Brasfield), recorded by Randy Parton; "It's My Job" (by McAnally), recorded by Jimmy Buffet; and "That Didn't Hurt Too Bad" (by Byne and Brasfield), recorded by Dr. Hook.

SONGLINE MUSIC, 1909 Clemson Dr., Richardson TX 75081. (214)235-4653. Contact: Eddie Fargason. Music publisher and record producer. BMI. Member GMA. Produces 6 songs/year; publishes 4 new songwriters/year. Pays standard royalty.

How to Contact: Submit demo tape and lyric sheet. Prefers 7½ ips reel-to-reel or cassette with 1-3 songs on demo. SASE. Reports in 1 month.

Music: C&W (pop), gospel, MOR, progressive, R&B and top 40/pop. Recently published "Prop Up Your Brother (On The Leaning Side)," (by Baker/Shuff/Fargason), recorded by Gary Lanier/Hisong Records (gospel); and "Light the Light," (by Fargason), recorded by Gary Lanier/Hisong Records (gospel).

Tips: "Send only those songs you feel are your most commercial. We are very interested in *positive pop* material."

SONGS OF THE SOUTHLAND, Box 120536, Nashville TN 37212. (615)320-5151. Affiliate: Short Rose (ASCAP). Managing Partner: James J. Petrie. Music publisher. BMI. Publishes 10

songs/year; publishes 5 new songwriters/year. Pays standard royalty.
How to Contact: Submit demo tape and lyric sheet. Prefers cassette with 3-4 songs on demo. SASE.
Reports in 2 weeks.
Music: C&W, easy listening and top 40/pop. Recently published "Heart to Heart" (by D. Gillon),
recorded by Roy Clark/MCA Records; "Go Through the Motions" (by D. Gillon), recorded by
The Cates/Ovation Records; and "Holding Me" (by D. Gillon), recorded by Micki Furhman/
MCA Records.
Tips: "There is no place for marginal material."

SONLIFE MUSIC, (division of Paul John Music Productions, Inc.), Box 552, Woodland Hills CA
91365. (213)703-6707. Administrative Director: Cheryl Wilks. Music publisher, record company
and record producer. ASCAP. Member GMA. Publishes 55 songs/year; publishes 5 new
songwriters/year. Pays standard royalty.
How to Contact: Submit demo tape and lyric sheet. Prefers cassette with 1-4 songs on demo. "Lead
sheets should include chord symbols, lyrics and melody." SASE. Reports in 3 weeks.
Music: Children's, choral, church/religious, easy listening, gospel, jazz, MOR, R&B, soul and top
40/pop. Recently published "You Took My Heart by Surprise" (by Paul Johnson), recorded by
Debby Boone/Warner Brothers Records (ballad); "Praise You Just The Same" (by Ron Harris
and Sharalee Lucas), recorded by Evie Tornquist/Word Records (MOR-inspirational); and "Give
Me More Love in My Heart" (by Howard McCrary and Larnelle Harris), recorded by L. Harris/
Benson Records (R&B-gospel); "Wedding Song," (by Gary Hallqurst), recorded by Kathie Lee
Johnson (traditional).
Tips: "Send a courteous letter, good quality demo and legible lead sheet. Gospel titles currently
follow adult contemporary and top 40 styles."

SORO PUBLISHING, 1322 Inwood Rd., Dallas TX 75247. (214)638-7712. President: Bob Cline.
Music publisher. SESAC. Publishes 4 songs/year. Pays standard royalty.
How to Contact: Submit demo tape and lyric sheet. Prefers cassette with 2-6 songs on demo. SASE.
Reports in 2 weeks.
Music: Contemporary church/religious; and gospel. Recently published "Hallelujah Maranatha"
(by Kirk Dearman), recorded by Kenneth Copeland/KCP Records (contemporary gospel);
"Prison Song" (by Kirk Dearman), recorded by Lu Lu Roman/Rainbow Sound Records (country
gospel); "He Paid a Debt" (by Gary McSpadden), recorded by Kenneth Copeland/KCP Records
(gospel); and "At the Name of Jesus" (by Steve Starfield), recorded by John Hall/J. Hall Records
(gospel).

SOUTHERN CRESCENT PUBLISHING, 121 N. 4th St., Easton PA 18042. (215)258-5990.
Branch located at #5J, 320 W. 30th St., New York NY 10000. (212)564-3246. Affiliate: Ripsaw
Record Co. President: James H. Kirkhuff Jr. (Easton). Vice President: Jonathan Strong (New
York). Music publisher. Estab. 1979. BMI. Publishes 5-10 songs/years. Pays standard royalty.
How to Contact: Submit demo tape and lyric sheet. Prefers cassette. SASE.
Music: Bluegrass; C&W; rockabilly. Recently published "Feelin' Right Tonight" (by Tex Rubino-
witz), recorded by Tex Rubinowitz/Ripsaw Records (rockabilly); and "Knock-Kneed Nellie" (by
W.C. Hancock Jr.), recorded by Billy Hancock/Ripsaw Records (rockabilly).

SOUTHERN WRITERS GROUP USA, Box 40764, Nashville TN 37204. Office Manager: Buzz
Cason. Music publisher. BMI. Pays standard royalties.
How to Contact: "We are not soliciting outside material at this time, and we ask that songwriters
not contact us until further notice." Does not return unsolicited material.
Music: Blues; C&W; dance; easy listening; folk; jazz; MOR; progressive; R&B; rock; soul; and
top 40/pop. Recently published "Bluer than Blue" (by Randy Goodrum), recorded by Michael
Johnson/EMI (MOR); and "She Believes in Me" (by Steve Gibb), recorded by Kenny Rogers/
UA Records (country).

SPECIAL RIDER, Box 860, New York NY 10276. Affiliates: Dwarf Music (ASCAP), Big Sky
Music(ASCAP), Ram's Horn Music (ASCAP), Narrowgate Music (BMI) and Four Aces
Music(ASCAP). Professional Manager: Jeff Rosen. Music publisher. (ASCAP). Pays standard
royalty.
How to Contact: Submit demo tape and lyric sheet. Prefers cassette with 1-4 songs on demo. SASE.
Reports in 3 weeks.
Music: C&W; MOR; progressive; rock; soul; and top 40/pop. Recently published "Solid Rock"
(by Bob Dylan), recorded by Bob Dylan/CBS Records (rock); "Poor Boy" (by Willie Nile),
recorded by Willie Nile/Arista Records (rock); and "Are You Gonna Be the One" (by Mark
Johnson), recorded by Robert Gordon/RCA Records (rockabilly).

BRUCE W. STACEY PUBLISHING, 780 Bough Beeches Blvd., Unit 13, Missisauga, Ontario, Canada M4Y 2L1. (416)625-8445 or (416)961-8001. President: Bruce W. Stacey. Music publisher and record company. Estab. 1979. BMI. Member CIRPA, PROCAN, GMA. Publishes 30 songs/year. Pays standard royalty.
How to Contact: Write first about your interest. Prefers cassette with 3-5 songs on demo. SAE and International Reply Coupons. Reports in 1 month.
Music: Contemporary church/religious, gospel.

TERRY STAFFORD MUSIC, Box 6546, Burbank CA 91510. President: Terry Stafford. Music publisher. BMI. Publishes 25 songs/year. Pays standard royalties.
How to Contact: Submit demo tape or submit demo tape and lead sheet. Prefers cassette with 3-5 songs on demo. SASE. Reports in 1 month.
Music: C&W and top 40/pop. Recently published "Amarillo by Morning," "Bad to Love Her," "Texas Moon Palace," and "Darlin' Think it Over," recorded by Terry Stafford (C&W).

STALLMAN RECORDS, INC., 1697 Broadway, New York NY 10019. (212)582-6928. Assistants to President: Julio Fernandez and Gene King. Music publisher. BMI. Publishes 80-100 songs/year. Payment according to AGAC contract.
How to Contact: Submit demo tape and lyric sheet. Prefers cassette with 1-3 songs on demo. SASE. Reports in 1 month or sooner.
Music: C&W; disco; jazz; MOR; R&B; rock; soul; and top 40/pop. "Single-oriented music only." Recently published "Everybody's Got the Right to Love" (by Lou Stallman), recorded by the Supremes (soul).

STARFOX PUBLISHING, Box 13584, Atlanta GA 30324. (404)872-6000. President: Alexander Janoulis. Vice President, Creative: Oliver Cooper. General Manager: Hamilton Underwood. Music publisher. BMI. Publishes 30 songs/year. Pays 25-50% royalty. Does not charge for services.
How to Contact: Submit demo tape and lyric sheet. Prefers reel-to-reel or cassette with 2-3 songs on demo. Does not return unsolicited material. Reports "as soon as possible."
Music: Blues; C&W; disco; MOR; progressive; rock; and top 40/pop. Recently published "Hold On" (by Scott Markshausen), "R&R Radio" (by O.P. Cooper) and "Disco Rock" (by O.P. Cooper), recorded by Starfoxx/Hottrax Records (rock).

STARTIME MUSIC, Box 643, LaQuinta CA 92253. (714)564-4823. Affiliate: Yo Yo Music (BMI). President: Fred Rice. Music publisher, record company. Publishes 2-12 songs/year; publishes 3 new songwriters/year. Pays standard royalty.
How to Contact: Submit demo tape and lead sheet. Prefers cassette with 1-2 songs on demo. SASE, solicited material only. Reports in 6 weeks.
Music: Country; rock; top 40/pop; and novelty. Recently published "Olivia" (by Robert Carter), recorded by Carter/Startime Records (rock); "Stay with Me" (by Bill Bogart), recorded by Carter/Startime Records (uptempo rock); and "Awhile" (by Robert Carter), recorded by Carter/Startime Records (novelty rock).

STEADY ARM MUSIC, Box 13222, Gainesville FL 32604. (904)378-8156. General Manager: Charles V. Steadham Jr. Professional Manager: Allen R. McCollum. Music publisher. BMI. Pays standard royalty.
How to Contact: Query or submit demo tape. Prefers cassette with 2-5 songs on demo. Does not return unsolicited material. Reports "as soon as possible.".
Music: Bluegrass; C&W; dance; folk; MOR; rock (country); soul; top 40/pop; R&B; and comedy. Recently released "Micah" and "Enoch Ludford" (by Don Dunaway), recorded by Don Dunaway/Milltop Records (folk); "Kennesaw Line" (by Dunaway) recorded by Gamble Rogers/Mountain Railroad Records (folk); and "The Honeydipper" and "The Skylake Campfire Girls" (by Gamble Rogers), recorded by Rogers/Mountain Railroad Records (folk).
Tips: Submit 1-3 commercially viable songs on cassette accompanied by lyric sheets.

STONE DIAMOND MUSIC CORP, 6255 Sunset Blvd., Hollywood CA 90028. (213)468-3400. Vice President/General Manager: Jay Lowy. Music publisher. Works with songwriters on contract.
How to Contact: Submit demo tape and lead or lyric sheet. Prefers 7½ or 15 ips reel-to-reel or cassette with 3 songs on demo. SASE. Reports in 1 month.
Music: Blues; children's; C&W; dance; easy listening; gospel; jazz; MOR; progressive; R&B; rock; soul; and top 40/pop.

STONE POST MUSIC, Box 954, Emporia KS 66801. (316)343-2727. President: Richard Bisterfeldt. Vice President/Manager: Jacki Bisterfeldt. Disco Coordinator: Jann Joy. Music publisher

Songwriter's Market Close-up

Songwriter-recording artist Lola Jean Dillon is pictured here with co-writer and singing partner L.E. White (right) and legend Roy Acuff after their performance at the Grand Ole Opry. The honor of singing on the Opry stage is a reward of Nashville songwriting success Dillon appreciates—others are being known as the "female Hank Williams" and as the writer of some of Loretta Lynn's biggest hits.

Success in Nashville is, in Dillon's words, "ninety-eight percent luck, one percent talent, and then one percent more luck." She's not saying songwriters don't need talent, it's just that many gifted songwriters never are published because they don't get the right breaks or because they just are not persistent long enough.

"I was lucky, I guess." But a few connections didn't hurt. A friend took three of her songs to Harlan Howard, Wilderness Publishing. He liked what he heard and signed her to a publishing contract. It was then that a new singer in town, Dolly Parton, recorded one of her songs, "I've Lived My Life (and I'm Only Eighteen)." Dillon was only sixteen.

The credit Dillon gives Howard makes a strong argument for the benefits a songwriter can reap from a good publisher. "Harlan taught me things it would have taken years to learn myself." Within two years she had a hit record on the charts: "Rock Me Back to Little Rock," recorded by Jan Howard.

Although she had become part of the recognized Nashville group of writers by 1975, one dream still eluded her—to write for her favorite singer, Loretta Lynn. "One day I picked up the phone," she said, "and called Coal Miner's Music. I asked how I could get a song to Loretta Lynn. The person told me to hold the phone and next thing I knew Loretta was on tellin' me to bring my songs over." After that day Lola wrote and Loretta recorded.

While writing for Loretta, Lola met and

Lola Jean Dillon

began to co-write and record with White, manager and writer for Conway Twitty's Twitty Bird Music. Together they have become a successful duet on Epic Records.

Dillon's songs are unique, perceptive statements about the depths of human emotion, particularly heartbreak. She attributes her own personality to her ability to write a song that touches so many, especially women. "I have a lot of friends, but basically I'm a loner. I think a lot and anytime I get a good idea I just seem to turn it into a sad song—it's the way I am."

Dillon says her demos depend on whom the song is for. "If I have a demo for a particular artist, I will try to arrange it in their style. A lot of times it's not the words that make a song country, or MOR, or pop—it's the arrangement. And the competition is so fierce the least you should try to get by with is a four-track demo with two or three instruments on it."

The exception to her rule is Loretta Lynn. "In the case of Loretta," she says, "I just have to sing and play the guitar and she hears what the song can be."

and record company. BMI. Publishes 10-15 songs/year; publishes 2 new songwriters/year. Pays negotiable royalty.
How to Contact: Submit demo tape and lyric sheet. Prefers cassette with 2-3 songs on demo. SASE. Reports in 3 weeks.
Music: Progressive (country); rock (progressive or hard); and top 40/pop. Recently published "Who Am I to Blame" (by D. Krause), recorded by Fyre/SPR (pop country), and "Sneak Away" (by D. Krause), recorded by Fyre/Tejas Records (pop country).

STONE ROW MUSIC CO., 2022 Vardon, Flossmoor IL 60422. President: Joanne Swanson. Music publisher. BMI. Publishes 3 songs/year. Pays standard royalties.
Music: Classical (new music scores); jazz; rock (soft); top 40/pop; and electronic. Recently published "Morning Flower," by James Cooper and "One is the Human Spirit," by Dale J. Wilson.

STRAIGHT FACE MUSIC, (division of Straight Face, Inc.), Box 324, Newark DE 19711. (302)368-1211. Affiliate: White Clay Music (BMI). Contact: Professional Manager. Music publisher, record company, record producer and management firm. Estab. 1979. ASCAP. Publishes 15 songs/year; publishes 5 new songwriters/year. Pays standard royalty.
How to Contact: "We mainly publish songs of the bands we manage." Prefers cassette with 2-4 songs on demo. SASE. Reports in 3 weeks.
Music: Dance-oriented, jazz (traditional), progressive, rock and new wave. Recently published "Good One Buddy" and "Isadoro Duncan" (by C. Scott Birnoz), recorded by the Sin City Band/WCP Records (contemporary country); "Get Out" (by Stephen D. Hobson), recorded by the Sin City Band/WCP Records (new wave); and "Son of Sam" (by David Bennett), recorded by Voltages/WCP Records (new wave).

JEB STUART MUSIC CO., Box 6032, Station B, Miami FL 33123. (305)547-1424. President: Jeb Stuart. Music publisher, record producer and management firm. BMI.
How to Contact: Query or submit demo tape and lead sheet. Prefers cassette or disc with 2-4 songs on demo. SASE. Reports in 1 month.
Music: Blues; church/religious; C&W; disco; gospel; jazz; rock; soul; and top 40/pop. Recently published "Can't Count the Days" and "Hung Up on Your Love," recorded by Jeb Stuart (pop/R&B).

STUCKEY PUBLISHING CO., Suite 309, 50 Music Square W., Nashville Tn 37203. (615)327-0222. Affiliates: Monkhouse Music (BMI), Greene Pastures Music (BMI), 2 Plus 2 Music (ASCAP) and Sandrose Music (ASCAP). Manager: Ann M. Stuckey. Music publisher. BMI. Member NMPA. Published 6 new songwriters in 1979. Pays standard royalty.
How to Contact: Submit demo tape and lyric sheet. Prefers 7½ ips reel-to-reel or cassette with 1-3 songs on demo. SASE. Reports in 1 month.
Music: C&W. Published "Sun Comin' Up" (by Nat Stuckey), recorded by Nat Stuckey/MCA Records (C&W); "Sweet Thang" (by Stuckey), recorded by Stuckey and Paula (C&W); and "Pop a Top" (by Stuckey), recorded by Jim Ed Brown/RCA Records (C&W).

SUGAR N' SOUL MUSIC, INC., 109-23 71st Rd., Forest Hills NY 11375. (212)268-8060. Affiliate: Sugar Free Music (BMI). Professional Manager: Mark Sameth. Music publisher. ASCAP. Pays standard royalties.
How to Contact: Submit demo tape and lyric or lead sheet. Prefers 7½ ips reel-to-reel or cassette with 1-5 songs on demo. Prefers leader between selections. SASE. Reports in 2 weeks.
Music: C&W; disco; easy listening; folk; MOR; rock (country/pop); soul (R&B/funk); and top 40/pop (ballads). "Write for a listing of recent and current recordings."

SULZER MUSIC, Dave Wilson Productions, 4842 Rorer St., Philadelphia PA 19120. (215)329-1115. Affiliates: Arzee Music (ASCAP), Asterisk Music (BMI), Rollercoaster Records (ASCAP), Rex Zario Music (BMI), Seabreeze Music (BMI), Wilson/Zario Publishers (BMI), Jack Howard Publishers (BMI), and Arcade Music (ASCAP). President: Dave Wilson. Vice President: Claire Mac. Publishes 100-150 songs/year; publishes 10 new songwriters/year. BMI. Pays standard royalties.
How to Contact: Submit demo tape or submit demo tape and lead sheet. Prefers 7½ or 15 ips reel-to-reel cassette with 6-10 songs on demo. SASE. Reports in 1 month.
Music: C&W; easy listening; folk; top 40/pop; and pop country. Recently published "Ooh Ah" (by Mike Bennett), recorded by Diane Lynn/Clymax Records (disco); "Blue Ranger" (by Jack Howard and Tom Gindhart), recorded by Hank Snow/RCA Records (C&W); and "I Gotta Go" (by Al Rex), recorded by Al Rex/Rollercoaster Records (rockabilly).

SU-MA PUBLISHING CO., INC., Box 1125, Shreveport LA 71163. (318)222-0195. Publishing Manager: Ms. Donnis Lewis. Music publisher. BMI. Publishes 75 songs/year. Pays standard royalties.
How to Contact: Submit demo tape or submit demo tape and lead sheet. Prefers 7½ ips reel-to-reel, cassette or 8-track cartridge. SASE. Reports in 1 month.
Music: C&W; gospel; and soul. Recently published "I'm Just Another Soldier," recorded by Five Blind Boys from Mississippi (gospel; Grammy nominee).
Tips: "All songs must contain both lyrics and melody."

SUMMERDUCK PUBLISHING COMPANY, 1216 Granby St., Norfolk VA 23510. (804)625-0534. President: Don Burlage. Music publisher, record producer, record company and international music licensing organization. BMI. Publishes 10 songs/year. Pays standard royalty.
How to Contact: Submit demo tape and lyric sheet. Prefers 2 songs minimum on demo. SASE. Reports in 3 weeks.
Music: Bluegrass; blues; C&W; disco; easy listening; rock jazz; MOR; progressive; R&B; new wave rock; and top 40/pop. Recently published "Don't Disguise" and "Sweet Forgetfulness," by D Burlage; and "Home Grown," by B. Parker.

SUN-BEAR CORPORATION, 1650 Broadway, New York NY 10019. (212)765-4495. Affiliates: EMI, Watnabe, Shinko, Siegel, Castle, Peer-Southern, Pascal and ATV. A&R Directors: Ezra Cook, Steve Loeb. Music publisher and record producer. Pays standard royalty.
How to Contact: Write first about your interest, then submit demo tape and lyric sheet or arrange personal interview to play demo tape. Prefers 7½ ips reel-to-reel with 1-3 songs on demo. Does not return unsolicited material. Reports in 1 month.
Music: C&W; easy listening; MOR; rock; soul; and top 40/pop. Recently published "Rock City" and "Warrior" (by Guy Speranza and Mark Reale), recorded by Riot/Eurodisc Ariola Records (rock); "It's a Shame" (by D. Sumrall), recorded by Sumrall/Pie Records; "One Step Away" (by J. Gordon), recorded by Spinners/Atlantic Records; and "By Your Side" (by S. Loeb and B. Arnell), recorded by Ben Vereen/Buddah Records.

SUNBURY/DUNBAR MUSIC CANADA, LTD., 101 Duncan Mill Rd., Suite 305, Don Mills, Ontario, Canada M3B 1Z3. (416)449-4346. Affiliate: Dunbar Music Canada, Ltd. (PROCAN). President: Jack Feeney. Music publisher. CAPAC. Member CMPA and CARAS. Publishes 75 songs/year; publishes 5 new songwriters/year. Pays standard royalty.
How to Contact: Submit demo tape and lyric sheet. Prefers cassette with 3-5 songs on demo. SAE and International Reply Coupon. Reports in 1 month.
Music: Recently sub-published "9 to 5" (by Dolly Parton), recorded by Dolly Parton/RCA Records (top 40/pop/country); "Breaking and Entering" (by Sally Coker and James Ross), recorded by Carroll Baker/RCA Records (country/pop); and published "Crying Again Tonight" (by Ray Roper), recorded by Stonebolt/RCA Records (rock/pop).
Tips: "Have songs with good quality, commercial viability and suitability to artists with whom we have dealings."

SUNSHINE COUNTRY ENTERPRISES, INC., Box 31351, Dallas TX 75231. (214)690-8875. Producer: "The General." A&R: Mike Anthony. Music publisher and record company. BMI.
How to Contact: Submit demo tape and lead sheet. Prefers 7½ ips reel-to-reel with 1-4 songs on demo. SASE. Reports in 1 month.
Music: C&W and gospel. Recently published "Spin My Heart Around Again," recorded by DeWayne Bowman (C&W); "Pride Was the First to Go," recorded by DeWayne Bowman (C&W); "Sixth of June," recorded by Dick Hammonds (C&W); and "Let a Fool Take a Bow," recorded by Dick Hammonds (C&W).

SURE-FIRE MUSIC CO., INC., 60 Music Square W., Nashville TN 37203. (615)244-1401. Contact: Leslie Wilburn. Music publisher. BMI. Pays standard royalties.
How to Contact: Submit demo tape and lyric sheet. Accepts 7½ ips reel-to-reel only. SASE. Reports "as soon as possible.".
Music: Bluegrass; C&W; MOR; and folk. Published "Statue of a Fool" (by Jan Crutchfield), recorded by Jack Greene/MCA Records; "Coal Miner's Daughter" (by Loretta Lynn), recorded by Loretta Lynn/MCA Records; and "Someone Before Me" (by Bob Hicks), recorded by the Wilburn Brothers/MCA Records.

SWEET POLLY MUSIC, Box 521, Newberry SC 29108. (803)276-0639. Studio Manager: Polly Davis. Producer: Hayne Davis. Music publisher and record producer. BMI. Publishes 20-30 songs/year.

How to Contact: Submit demo tape and lyric sheet. Prefers 7½ ips reel-to-reel or cassette with 4-8 songs on demo. "Include brief bio, list experience, credit etc. Express a desire to actively work on helping to produce/promote material. We are looking for professional writer/co-producers especially." SASE. Reports in 2 weeks.
Music: C&W (contemporary); easy listening; MOR; rock; and top 40/pop. Recently published "Rainy Days" (by Hayne Davis), recorded by Raw Material (country rock); "Down To the Lovin'" and "Back in 1956," (by Hayne Davis), recorded by Sugar & Spice (bubblegum/disco).

SWEET SINGER MUSIC, The Mathes Company, Box 22653, Nashville TN 37202. Affiliate: Star of David (SESAC). President: Dave Mathes. BMI. Member CMA, GMA, NMPA, NARAS and AFM. Publishes 30-100 songs/year; publishes 6-20 new songwriters/year. Pays standard royalty.
How to Contact: Submit demo tape and lyric sheet. Prefers 7½ ips reel-to-reel with 3-5 songs on demo. "Enclose $1 to help defray postage and handling.
Music: Bluegrass; blues; C&W; disco; easy listening; gospel; MOR; progressive rock (country); soul; top 40/pop and instrumental. Recently published "Simple Love Song" (by Pelleteri, Mathes, Bass), recorded by DeAnna/Rising Star Records (MOR); "Hot Dog, I'm American" (by B. Anton), recorded by The Capitals/NRS Records (country); and "Touch Me" (by Lori Lee Woods), recorded by Lori Lee Woods/Legs Records (country).

SWEET SWAMP MUSIC, The Gables, Halcott Rd., Fleischmanns NY 12430. (914)254-4565. President/General Manager: Barry Drake. Music publisher, booking agency, record company and management firm. BMI. Publishes 25 songs/year. Pays standard royalties.
How to Contact: Submit demo tape and lead sheet. Prefers cassette with 3-5 songs on demo. SASE. Reports in 1 month.
Music: Bluegrass; blues; C&W; easy listening; folk; MOR; progressive; rock (hard or country) and top 40/pop. Recently published "Fallen Star," "Blues For Hobo Joe" and "Beg, Steal or Borrow" (by Barry Drake), recorded by B. Drake/Datskill Mountain Records.

SWEET TOOTH MUSIC PUBLISHING, 2716 Springlake Ct., Irving TX 75060. (214)259-4032. General Manager: Kenny Wayne Hagler. Music publisher, record company, record producer, recording artist and traveling musician. BMI.
How to Contact: Submit demo tape and lyric sheet. Prefers 7½ ips reel-to-reel or cassette with 3-4 songs on demo. SASE. Reports in 1 month.
Music: Blues, C&W, MOR, R&B, rock, soul and top 40/pop. Recently published "Baby Come On Home" (by K.W. Hagler), recorded by Kenny Wayne/Amazing Records (R&B); "I Wanna' Go Home (And Play with Them Babies)" (by James Gatlin), recorded by Kenny Wayne/Amazing Records (blues); and "Texarkana Baby" (by J. Gatlin), recorded by Kenny Wayne/Amazing Records (rock-a-billy).
Tips: "Send a quality demo that will stand up with any song on the national charts!"

SWING & TEMPO MUSIC PUBLISHING INC., 1995 Broadway, New York NY 10023 (212)787-1222. Vice President: Bill Titone. Music publisher and record producer. BMI. Publishes 50 songs/year. Pays standard royalty.
How to Contact: Submit demo tape and lyric sheet. Prefers 7½ ips reel-to-reel with 2-4 songs on demo. SASE. Reports in 1 month.
Music: Jazz; and R&B.

SWING BEE MUSIC, 1130 Colfax, Evanston IL 60201. (312)328-5593. Producer: Susan Neumann. Music publisher, record producer and record company. BMI. Publishes 12 songs/year; publishes 4 new songwriters/year. Pays standard royalty.
How to Contact: Query. Prefers cassette as demos. SASE. Reports in 1 month.
Music: Jazz. Recently published "Bambu'" (by Sal Nistico), recorded by Bee Hive Jazz (jazz).

T.P. MUSIC PUBLISHING, North Country Faire Recording Co., 314 Clemow Ave., Ottawa, Ontario, Canada K1S 2B8. (613)234-6992. President: T. Peter Hern. Music publisher and record company. CAPAC. Publishes 10-30 songs/year. Pays standard royalty.
How to Contact: Submit demo tape, arrange personal interview, or submit demo tape and lead sheet. Prefers 7½ ips quarter-track stereo reel-to-reel or cassette with 3-6 songs on demo. SAE and

International Reply Coupons. Reports in 2 weeks.
Music: AOR; MOR; easy listening; top 40/pop (progressive pop); and songs and film scores for feature length films and documentaries.
Tips: "We will act as a Canadian representative for an artist/singer/songwriter, and test and develop a market cooperatively."

TAKOMA MUSIC, 9255 Sunset Blvd., Los Angeles CA 90069. (213)550-0171. Affiliate: Take Home Music (ASCAP). General Manager: Jon Monday. Music publisher and record company. BMI. Publishes 50 songs/year. Pays standard royalty.
How to Contact: Submit demo tape and lyric sheet. Prefers cassette with 3-4 songs on demo. SASE. Reports in 1 month.
Music: Bluegrass; blues; classical; folk; jazz; progressive; R&B; and rock.

TAL MUSIC, INC., 16147 Littlefield, Detroit MI 48238. (313)863-9510. President: Edith Talley. Vice President A&R: Harold McKinney. Music publisher and record company. BMI. Publishes 8 songs/year; publishes 8 new songwriters/year. Pays standard royalty.
How to Contact: Submit demo tape, arrange personal interview, submit demo tape and lead sheet or submit lead sheet. Prefers 7½ ips reel-to-reel or cassette. SASE. Reports "as soon as possible.".
Music: Choral; church/religious; C&W; dance; easy listening; gospel; jazz; rock; soul; and top 40/pop. Recently published "Boogie Tonight," recorded by Perfect Touch/Morning Glory Records; and "Sweet Sweet Thing," recorded by J. Star/D.T. Records.

TANTALIZING TUNES/ATOMIC TUNES, 474 Atchison St., Pasadena CA 91104. (213)794-8758. Affiliate: Atomic Tunes (ASCAP). General Manager: Ben Brooks. Music publisher and record producer. BMI. Publishes 5 songs/year; publishes 4 new songwriters/year. Pays standard royalty.
How to Contact: Write or call first about your interest, arrange personal interview or submit demo tape and lyric sheet. Prefers cassette with 1-3 songs on demo. SASE. Reports in 2 weeks.
Music: C&W, MOR, R&B and rock. Recently published "Song for the Captain" (by Hansell and Parker), recorded by Roger Whittaker/RCA Records (MOR).
Tips: "The song has to communicate to and interest masses of people. It must be easily identifiable."

TAYLOR & WATTS MUSIC, INC., 1010 17th Ave. S., Nashville TN 37212. (615)327-4656. Affiliate: Tay-son Music, Inc. (ASCAP). President: Carmol Taylor. Music publisher. Estab. 1979. Member BMI, ASCAP, NSA. Publishes 35-40 songs/year; published 10 new songwriters in 1979. Pays standard royalty.
How to Contact: Submit demo tape and lyric sheet. Prefers 7½ ips reel-to-reel or cassette with 1-4 songs on demo. SASE. Reports in 2 weeks.
Music: C&W and MOR. Recently released "1959" (by Gary Gentry), recorded by John Anderson/Warner Bros. Records; "Drinkin' & Driving (by Gary Gentry), recorded by Johnny Paycheck/Epic Records (country); "Fell into Love" (by Russ Allison and Don Miller), recorded by Foxfire/NSD Records (country); "Another Way to Say I Love You" (by R. Allison and D. Miller), recorded by Randy Barlow/Republic Records (country); "Strip It Down, Let It Brown" (by Monroe Fields), recorded by Billy Crash Craddock/Capitol (C&W); and "You're the Perfect Reason" (by Buck Moore), recorded by David Huston/Country Int. (C&W).

JOE TAYLOR MUSIC, 2401 12th Ave. S., Nashville TN 37204. (615)385-0035. Affiliate: Taylor House of Music (BMI) and Ming Music (SESAC). President: Joe Taylor. Music publisher. ASCAP. Pays standard royalty.
How to Contact: Write or call about your interest, then submit demo tape and lyric sheet or arrange personal interview to play demo tape. Prefers 7½ ips reel-to-reel or cassette with 4-7 songs on demo. SASE. Reports in 2 weeks.
Music: Bluegrass; blues; C&W; dance; easy listening; MOR; R&B; and top 40/pop. Recently published "Your Love Has Been Here & Gone" (by Jerry Wall), recorded by Vic Horne (country).

10 OF DIAMONDS MUSIC, 5934 Buffalo Ave., #105, Van Nuys CA 91401. (213)997-8819. Producer: Jason Schwartz. Music publisher, record producer and record company. BMI. Publishes 18-40 songs/year; publishes 5 new songwriters/year.
How to Contact: Write first about your interest. Prefers cassette with 1-3 songs on demo. SASE. Reports in 1 month.
Music: Sophisticated country; easy listening; MOR; light rock; and top 40. Recently published "Lady from Beverly Hills" (by Jason), recorded by Jason/Survivor Records (country rock); "Words Spoken Softly by You" (by Greta Warren and Jason), recorded by Greta Warren/

Survivor Records (country); and "Climbing Out" (by Apostle), recorded by Apostle Survivor Records (rock).

THIRD HOUSE MUSIC PUBLISHING, Suite 919, Lenox Tower, Atlanta GA 30326. (404)261-0465. Affiliate: Starshower Publishing (ASCAP). Creative Consultant: John Persico. Music publisher, management and artist development company. Estab. 1979. BMI. Publishes 2-10 songs/year; publishes 4 new songwriters/year. Pays standard royalty.
How to Contact: Call first about your interest. Prefers cassette with 3-5 songs on demo. SASE. Reports in 1 month.
Music: Dance; easy listening; jazz; MOR; progressive; rock; soul; and top 40/pop. Recently published "What Goes Around" (by Leonard McDonald), recorded by Perfect Touch/Celebrity Records (R&B ballad).

THIRD STORY MUSIC, INC., 6430 Sunset Blvd., Suite 1500, Los Angeles CA 90028. (213)463-1151. President: M. Cohen. Music publisher. BMI. Member AIMP. Publishes 100 songs/year; publishes 3 new songwriters/year. Pays standard royalty.
How to Contact: Submit demo tape and lyric sheet. Prefers cassette with 1-3 songs on demo. Does not return unsolicited material. Report in 2 weeks.
Music: Disco; R&B; rock; and top 40/pop. Recently published "Everybody's Talkin'," recorded by Fred Neil/Elektra Records; and "Hey Joe" and "Ol' 55," recorded by Tom Waits/Elektra Records.
Tips: "Send simple demos; nothing elaborate."

HAROLD THOMAS MUSIC, 203 Culver Ave., Charleston SC 29407. (803)766-2500. Assistant Manager: Mike Thomas. Music publisher, record producer, record company and management company. BMI. Publishes 10 songs/year. Pays standard royalty.
How to Contact: Submit demo tape and lyric sheet. Accepts cassette only, 3 songs minimum. "Presentation should include photo and biography. We prefer tapes with more than 1 instrument, but we'll listen to anything," SASE. Reports in 3 weeks.
Music: Dance; rock; and soul. Recently published "This Precious Moment" (by Mary Kelly), recorded by Tams/Sounds South Records (soul/ballad); "Mr. DJ" (by Jimmy Tigner), recorded by Little Eric/Sounds South Records (soul); and "Plain, Simple But Sweet" (by Jenona Wade), recorded by the Drifters/Sounds South Records (soul/ballad).

THREE KINGS MUSIC, Box 22088, Nashville TN 37202. President: Robby Roberson. Vice President: Jean Roberson. Music publisher. BMI. Publishes 300 songs/year; publishes 10 new songwriters/year. Pays standard royalties.
How to Contact: Submit demo tape or "call for interview. We accept interviews when we have time available." Prefers cassette. SASE. Reports in 6 weeks.
Music: Church/religious; C&W; easy listening; gospel; and MOR. Recently published *It Is Good*, recorded by Keith Breddevold/Three Kings Records; "The Dream Is Over" (by David Faircloth)/Nugget Records; and "Heaven to a Honky Tonk" (by J. Helms), recorded by The Metheny Brothers/Nugget Records (country).
Tips: "Find out how publishing is done and what the publisher is. An education in songwriter/publishing is helpful."

3300 PUBLISHING, 3300 Warner Blvd., Burbank CA 91510. (213)846-9090. Affiliate: Sonheath Publishing (ASCAP). Contact: Linda Underhill. Music publisher and record company. BMI.
How to Contact: Submit demo tape. Prefers 7½ ips reel-to-reel or cassette. "Please include any information you feel is beneficial to the presentation of the material." SASE. Reports in 8 weeks.
Music: Bluegrass; blues; children's; choral; church/religious; C&W; dance; easy listening; folk; gospel; jazz; MOR; progressive; R&B; rock; soul; and top 40/pop.

TOM TOM PUBLISHING CO., Box 566, Massena NY 13662. (315)769-2448. Affiliate: Bop Talk Music (ASCAP). Vice President: Thomas Gramuglia. Music publisher and record company. Pays standard royalty.
How to Contact: Submit demo tape. Prefers 7½ ips reel-to-reel with 1-12 songs on demo. SASE. Reports in 1 month.
Music: Jazz and Folk.

TOMPAUL MUSIC CO., 628 South St., Mount Airy NC 27030. (919)786-2865. Owner: Paul E. Johnson. Music publisher and record company. BMI. Publishes 50 songs/year; publishes 20 new songwriters/year. Pays standard royalties.

How to Contact: Submit demo tape and lead sheet. Prefers 7½ ips reel-to-reel with 3-5 songs on demo. SASE. Reports in 1 month.
Music: Bluegrass; church/religious; C&W; easy listening; folk; gospel; MOR; rock (country); soul; and top 40/pop. Recently published "I Surrender Dear" (by Bobby L. Atkins), recorded by Chet Atkins/R.C.A. Records (pop instrumental); and "Fire on the Mountain" and "End of a Dream", (by Paul E. Johnson), recorded by Blue Ridge Mountain Boys/Stark Records (Bluegrass)

TOPSAIL MUSIC, 71 Boylston St., Brookline MA 02147. (617)739-2010. Affiliate: Mutiny Music. International subpublisher: EMI Music. President: Fred Berk. Music publisher, recording company and production company. BMI. Pays standard royalties.
How to Contact: Submit demo tape or lead sheet. Prefers reel-to-reel or cassette with 1-6 songs on demo. SASE. Reports in 3 weeks.
Music: Children's; C&W; disco; folk; MOR; progressive; rock; soul; and top 40/pop. Recently published "Man Enough," recorded by No Slack (pop/R&B); "Why Don't We Love Each Other?", recorded by the Ellis Hall Group (pop/R&B); and "Breaker 1-9," recorded by the Back Bay Rhythm Section (disco).

TRAITORS MUSIC, Box 966, La Mirada CA 90637. President: Ray Arnold. Music publisher. BMI. Pays on royalty basis.
How to Contact: Submit demo tape or submit lead sheet. Prefers reel-to-reel or cassette. Reports in 1 month.
Music: C&W and rock. Recently published "Meet Me on the Other Side of Town," recorded by Joe Gibson (C&W).

TRANSATLANTIC MUSIC, Box 1998, Beverly Hills CA 90213. (213)763-9637. President: Fred de Rafols. Music publisher. BMI. Publishes 30-50 songs/year. Payment negotiable.
How to Contact: Submit demo tape and lead sheet. Prefers cassette with 2 songs on demo. SASE. Reports in 3 weeks.
Music: Rock, new wave, top 40/pop, punk and international. Recently published "Next" and "Love You No More," recorded by J.D. Drews/MCA Records; and "Where's My Refund?" by The Nobodys.

TRANSCONTINENTAL MUSIC PUBLICATIONS, 838 5th Ave., New York NY 10021. (212)249-0100 ext. 351. Editor/Director: Ms. Judith Tischler. Music publisher. ASCAP. Member NMPA. Publishes 20 songs/year; publishes 2 new songwriters/year. Pays standard royalty.
How to Contact: Call first about performance medium and subject. Prefers cassette as demo. SASE. "Reporting time is unknown at this time, as we have a huge backlog of material."
Music: Choral, synagogue/religious (Hebrew-English sacred-Secular). Recently published "La-kol Zman (To Everything there is a Season)" (by Ben Steinberg); "Los Siete Hijos De Hanna (Ladino)" (by Richard Neumann); and "Psalm 23" (by Isaacson Michael).
Tips: "Sacred songs for women's voices are particularly in demand. Anything applicable to the Reform Jewish worship service or appeal to interest in Israel."

TREE PUBLISHING CO., INC., 8 Music Square W., Nashville TN 37203. (615)327-3162. Affiliates: Cross Keys Publishing (ASCAP), Twittybird Music Publishing (BMI), Uncanny Music (ASCAP), Warhawk Music (BMI), Tree/Harlan Howard Songs (BMI), Kentree Music (BMI) and Stairway Music (BMI). President and Chief Officer: Buddy Killen. Professional Manager/Song plugger: Dan Wilson. Song pluggers: Terry Choate, Tom Long and David Womack. Music publisher. Member NMPA.
How to Contact: Submit demo tape. Prefers 7½ ips reel-to-reel with 1-5 songs on demo. "Voice and guitar or piano accompaniment is sufficient. There is no need to have full orchestra or band on track. We just need to hear the words and melody clearly." SASE. Reports in 10-12 weeks. "We will not return material unless proper postage is on return envelope."
Music: Country; MOR; rock (hard or country); soul; and top 40/pop.

TRIPOLI MUSIC, Box 24665, Chicago IL 60625. (312)883-8667. Contact: Ed Kammer. Music publisher and record company. Estab. 1979. BMI. Publishes 30 songs/year; publishes 6 new songwriters/year. Pays standard royalty.
How to Contact: Sumbit demo tape and lyric sheet. Prefers 7½ ips reel-to-reel or cassette with any number of songs on demo. Does not return unsolicited material. Reports in 6 weeks.
Music: Dance-oriented, easy listening, R&B, rock (hard and pop) and top 40/pop. Recently published "Speed Racer" (by Mike Klehr), recorded by FreeWheelin'/Force Records (pop rock); "Out of Control" (by Brian Sarna), recorded by FreeWheelin'/Force Records (pop rock); "Beg Borrow & Steal" (by Ed Kammer), recorded by FreeWheelin'/Force Records (top 40); "Annie"

(by George Michael), recorded by George Michael/Force Records (top 40); and "Got a Lotta Love" (by Dave Kury), recorded by FreeWheelin'/Force Records (pop rock).

TRI-STATE MUSIC PUBLISHING COMPANY, 300 Court St., Box 121, Soda Springs ID 83276. (208)547-3715. President: Ronald Watts. Music publisher, record producer and record company. BMI. Publishes 6 songs/year. Pays standard royalty.
How to Contact: Submit demo tape and lyric sheet. Prefers cassette with 2-6 songs on demo. Does not return unsolicited material. Reports in 3 weeks.
Music: C&W; easy listening; and rock. Recently published "You'll Feel Better When I Hold You in My Arms" (by Rocky Watson), recorded by Rocky Watson and Country Gold/Jenero Record Co. (country/western); and "I Believe in You" (by Eugene Sibbett), recorded by Eugene Sibbett/Jenero Record Co. (easy listening).

TRIUNE MUSIC, INC., 824 19th Ave., S., Nashville TN 37203. (615)329-1429. Affiliates: Timespann Music (BMI) and Nova Press (SESAC). Administrative Assistant: Lisa Keeling. Music publisher and record company. ASCAP. Publishes 75-125 songs/year; publishes 11 new songwriters/year. Pays negotiable royalty.
How to Contact: Submit demo tape and lyric sheet. Prefers cassette with 2-4 songs on demo. Does not return unsolicited material. Reports in 3 months.
Music: Children's, choral, church/religious, classical and gospel.

TROLL MUSIC, 1201 16th Ave. S., Nashville TN 37212. (615)255-0345. Contact: Jeff Rosenberg. Music publisher. BMI.
How to Contact: Submit demo tape and lyric sheet. Prefers 7½ ips reel-to-reel or cassette with 1-4 songs on demo. SASE. Reports in 1 month.
Music: Bluegrass; C&W; jazz; MOR; progressive; R&B; rock; soul and top 40/pop.

TRUSTY PUBLICATIONS, Rt. 1, Box 100, Nebo KY 42441. (502)249-3194. President: Elsie Childers. Music publisher and record company. BMI. Member CMA and NSAI. Publishes 10-12 songs/year; publishes 2 new songwriters/year. Pays standard royalties.
How to Contact: Submit demo tape and lead sheet. Prefers 7½ ips reel-to-reel or cassette with 2-4 songs on demo. SASE. Reports in 1 month.
Music: Blues; church/religious; C&W; disco; easy listening; folk; gospel; MOR; soul; and top 40/pop. Recently published "There's a Prayer" (by Elsie Childer), recorded by The New Apostles (contemporary gospel); "That Can Change Your Life" and "Baby, Shine On!" (by Don Cottrell, White and Jenkins), recorded by Tracy White and Hartstreet (rock); and "One More Mile" (by Noah Williams), recorded by Noah Williams (contemporary gospel).

TUBE PRODUCTIONS, 66 Welleslay St. E, Toronto, Ontario, Canada M4Y 1G2. (416)961-4115. Affiliate: Cosmic Music. Manager: Robert Connolly. Music publisher and record company. CAPAC. Publishes 30 songs/year; publishes 15 new songwriters/year. Pays standard royalty.
How to Contact: Submit demo tape and lyric sheet. Prefers cassette with 3-12 songs on demo. Does not return unsolicited material. Reports in 1 month.
Music: Hard rock. Recently published "Time after Time" (by Ralph Santer), recorded by Rick Santers Band/Attic Records; "Break the Ice" and "High Times" (by Frank Soda), recorded by F. Soda/Quality Records (all rock).

TUMAC MUSIC PUBLISHING, Rt. 1, Box 143, Senola GA 30276. (404)599-6935. Affiliate: Shandy Guff (BMI). Professional Manager: Phil McDaniel. General Manager: Joe McTamney. Music publisher, record producer and record company. ASCAP. Publishes 6 songs/year. Pays standard royalty.
How to Contact: Submit demo tape and lyric sheet. Prefers cassette with 1-3 songs on demo. SASE. Reports in 3 weeks.
Music: Blues; C&W; dance; easy listening; jazz (country); MOR; rock (adult/country); top 40/pop; and R&B. Recently published "Pride" (by McDaniel and McTamney), recorded by Don Buckley/Sing Me Records (C&W); "A Spinner of Rainbows" (by Sheehy and McTamney), recorded by Roni Stoneman/Spin Check Records (MOR); and "Why Couldn't I Just Love You" (by Beneteau and McTamney), recorded by Kim Jacobsen/Jukebox Records (MOR).

TWC MUSIC, TWC Entertainment Corp., Box 2021, New York NY 10001. (212)691-4565. Affiliate: Saddle Song Music (BMI). Manager: Walter Balderson. Music publisher and record company. SESAC. Pays standard royalties.
How to Contact: Submit demo tape and lead sheet. Prefers 7½ ips reel-to-reel with 1-5 songs on demo. Does not return unsolicited material. Reports in 2 weeks.

Music: C&W; folk; and gospel. Recently published "Mother and Dog," "You're Right" and "Nature of a Man," recorded by Tommy Blue (C&W).

20TH CENTURY FOX MUSIC PUBLISHING, 8544 Sunset Blvd. Los Angeles CA 90069. (213)657-8210. Affiliates: Fox Fanfare Music (BMI); Bregman, Vocco and Conn (ASCAP); Chatham Music (ASCAP); Lombardo Music (ASCAP); Supreme Music (ASCAP); and Vernan Music (ASCAP). President: Herb Eiseman. Vice President, Creative Activities: Ron Vance. Manager, Catalog Promotion: Steve Nelson. Music publisher and record company. ASCAP. Member NMPA. Publishes 100-150 songs/year; publishes 3-12 new songwriters/year. Sometimes secures songwriters on recoupable advance basis. Payment negotiable.
How to Contact: Arrange personal interview. Prefers 7½ ips reel-to-reel or cassette with 1-5 songs on demo. SASE. Reports in 3 weeks.
Music: Country pop; easy listening; MOR; progressive; R&B; rock; soul; and top 40/pop. Recently published "Evergreen" (by Paul Williams), recorded by Barbra Streisand; "The Wiz," recorded by Diana Ross; "Star Wars," recorded by John Williams and the London Symphony; "Rhinestone Cowboy" (by Larry Weiss), recorded by Glen Campbell (top 40/country/easy listening); and "Near You" (by Kermit Goell and Francis Craig), recorded by George Jones and Tammy Wynette/Columbia Records (pop/country).

TWIN LIONS MUSIC PUBLISHING, 2024 S. Cooper St., Arlington TX 76010. Manager: Bill Stansell. Music publisher and record company. BMI. Member ACM. Publishes 2 songs/year; publishes 2 new songwriters/year. Pays standard royalties.
How to Contact: Query. Prefers cassette with 1 song on demo. SASE. Reports in 1 month.
Music: Children's; C&W; gospel; and novelty. Recently published "Box Car Wheels" and "Sad Thoughts and Pretty Women," by Bill Stansell/Stan Records.

TYMER MUSIC, Box 1669, Carlsbad CA 92008. (714)729-8406. Contact: Denny Tymer. Music publisher. BMI. Publishes 5-10 songs/year. Pays standard royalty. "We honor the AGAC contract."
How to Contact: Submit demo tape and lead sheet. Prefers 7½ ips reel-to-reel or cassette with 1-3 songs on demo. "Use leader between songs." SASE. Reports in 3 weeks.
Music: C&W; easy listening; MOR; and top 40/pop. Recently published "Blanket of Love," "We're Living in Harmony" and "Alone" (by Denny Tymer), recorded by Tymer/Wilwin Records (easy listening/country).

TYNER MUSIC, 38 Music Square E. #115, Nashville TN 37203. (615)244-4224. Affiliate: Longshot Music (SESAC) and Timberjack Music (BMI). Vice President: Dallas Laird. Music publisher. ASCAP. Publishes 75-100 songs/year; published 7 new songwriters in 1979. Pays standard royalty. Hires staff writers; pays $75-300/week.
How to Contact: Submit demo tape and lyric sheet. Prefers 7½ ips reel-to-reel or cassette with 4-7 songs on demo. "No registered mail accepted." SASE. Reports in 1 month.
Music: C&W; easy listening; MOR; and top 40/pop.

TYRANTOSAURUS SOUNDS, Box 902, Provo UT 84601. (801)225-4674. Professional Manager. Music publisher, personal management and concert promotion company. BMI. Publishes 30 songs/year. Pays standard royalty.
How to Contact: Submit demo tape and lyric sheet. Prefers 15 ips reel-to-reel or cassette with 4-6 songs on demo. SASE. Reports in 3 weeks.
Music: C&W; folk; MOR; rock; and top 40/pop. Recently published "Tonight" (by Tom Ivers), recorded by Tyrant (rock/pop); "Arizona Highways" (by Bill Tuddenham), recorded by Dave Boshard (country/pop); and "How Long Has It Been" (by Dave Boshard), recorded by Dave Boshard (pop/MOR).

ULTRA SOUNDS UNLIMITED, Box 3501, Flint MI 48502. Production Chief: M.D. Ruffin. Music publisher. BMI. Publishes 3-4 songs/year. Pays standard royalty.
How to Contact: Write first about your interest, then sumbit demo tape and lyric sheet. Prefers 7½ ips reel-to-reel or cassette with 1 song on demo. Does not return unsolicited material. Reports in 2 weeks.
Music: Blues, jazz, progressive, R&B, rock, soul and top 40/pop. Recently published "Feel Right" (by Roger McClendon), Renaissance Records (soul).

UNICORN PUBLISHING COMPANY, Box 1414, Vicksburg MS 39180. (601)638-5622. Affiliate: Legend Entertainment Services (ASCAP). Publisher/producer: Robert Garner. Music publisher, record company, record producer, and manager and booking agent. Estab. 1980. ASCAP.

Member AFM. Publishes 6-12 songs/year; publishes 3 new songwriters/year. Pays negotiable royalty.
How to Contact: Write or call first about your interest, then submit demo tape and lyric sheet. Prefers 7½ ips reel-to-reel or cassette with 2-4 songs on demo. SASE. Reports in 2 weeks.
Music: Bluegrass, church/religious, C&W, folk, gospel and MOR. Recently published "Phantom of the Trace" (by Karen Preston), recorded by Reunion/Legend Records (folk/country); "I Don't Think I'll Be Home Tonight" (by R. Garner), recorded by South Fork/Legend Records (country); and "Sing Your Love Songs to Me" (by K. Preston and others), recorded by K. Preston/Legend Records (country/MOR).

UNITED ARTISTS MUSIC, 6753 Hollywood Blvd., Los Angeles CA 90028. (213)469-3600. Affiliate: Unart Music (BMI). Professional Director: Danny Strick. Professional Manager: Loretta Munoz. ASCAP. Member NMPA, California Copyright Conference. Publishes 10 songs/year; publishes 2-3 new songwriters/year. Pays standard royalty.
How to Contact: Submit demo tape and lyric sheet. Prefers cassette.SASE. Reports in 1 month.
Music: C&W; dance; easy listening; folk; jazz; MOR; R&B; rock; soul; and top 40/pop. Recently published "Wasn't That A Party" (by Tom Paxton), recorded by the Rovers/Epic Records (novelty); and "Hearts on Fire" (by Eric Kaz/Randy Meisner), recorded by Randy Meisner/Epic Records (rock).
Tips: "We will listen to simple vocal/instrumental demos, as long as they are clear and the lyric can be heard. Do not submit just sheet music. A song has to be right for the marketplace—listen to the radio, and be aware of which type of artists cut outside songs."

UNITED ARTISTS MUSIC, 1013 16th Ave. S., Nashville TN 37212. (615)327-4594. Manager: Buzz Arledge. BMI, ASCAP and SESAC. Pays standard royalty.
How to Contact: "Bring your tape into our office and leave it." Prefers cassette with 3 songs on demo. SASE. Reports in 1 week.
Music: C&W, easy listening, MOR and top 40/pop. Recently published "Don't It Make by Brown Eyes Blue" (by Richard Leigh), recorded by Crystal Gayle/CBS Records (country/pop); "Goin' Thru the Motions" (by Allen Chapman and Shawna Harrington), a 1980 American Song Festival Grand Prize Winner; and "It's All I Can Do" (by Leigh and Jordon), recorded by Anne Murray/Capital Records.
Tips: "We accept material only when brought in person and left for us to listen to."

UNITED ARTISTS MUSIC PUBLISHING, 729 7th Ave., New York NY 10019. (212)575-3000. Assistant Professional Manager: Ramona Kipnis. Affiliate: Unart Music (BMI). Music publisher. ASCAP. Member NMPA. Publishes 50 songs/year; publishes 6 new songwriters/year. Pays standard royalty.
How to Contact: Write or call about your interest, then submit demo tape and lyric sheets. Prefers 7½ ips reel-to-reel or cassette with 3 songs maximum on demo. SASE. Reports in 6 weeks (on solicited material only). "Unsolicited material will be returned unopened."
Music: Top 40/pop; rock and roll; rock; R&B; and ballads. Recently published "Teacher, Teacher" (by K. Pickett/E. Phillips), recorded by Rockpile—Seconds of Pleasure/Columbia (rock 'n' roll); *Zanadu—Soundtrack* (by Jeff Lynne), recorded by E.L.O./MCA (rock); and Theme from *New York, New York* (by Kander & Ebb), recorded by Frank Sinatra/Reprise (standard).

UNIVERSAL STARS MUSIC, Rt. 3, Box 5B, Leesville LA 71446. Affiliate: Headliner Music. National Representative: Sherree Stephens. Music publisher. BMI. Publishes 12-24 songs/year; publishes 1 new songwriter/year. Pays standard royalty.
How to Contact: Submit demo tape and lyric sheet. Prefers cassette with 1-6 songs on demo. Does not return unsolicited material. Reports in 1 month, if interested.
Music: Bluegrass; church/religious; C&W; folk; gospel; and top 40/pop. Recently published *Jesus Came All the Way*, recorded by Sherrie Scott (religious LP); *Oh, Lord Save Me*, recorded by Melodie Scott (gospel LP); and *Praise Him*, recorded by J.J. & Sherrie Stephens (religious single and LP).

URSULA MUSIC, Box 300, Mt. Gretna PA 17064. Affiliates: Welz Music (ASCAP), Florentine Music (BMI) and Wynwood Music (BMI). President/Professional Manager: Joey Welz. Music publisher, record company and booking agency. BMI. Publishes 18 songs/year; publishes 2 new songwriters/year. Pays standard royalty.
How to Contact: Submit demo tape and lead sheet. Prefers cassette with 4-8 songs on demo. Does not return unsolicited material. "We hold until we need material for a session, then we search our files."
Music: C&W; dance; MOR; rock; and top 40/pop. Recently published "On My Way to Lovin'

You" (by Boykin and Welz); "I Remember Love" (by Joseph Welz), recorded on Music City Records (MOR/rock); and "We Should Be in Love" (by Doug Wray), recorded by Joseph Welz/Music City Records (MOR).

VADO MUSIC, 2226 McDonald Ave., Brooklyn NY 11213. (212)946-4405. Affiliate: Romona Music (ASCAP). Music publisher. ASCAP. Publishes 25 songs/year; publishes 10 new songwriters/year. Pays standard royalty.
How to Contact: Submit demo tape and lyric sheet. Prefers cassette with 4 songs on demo. SASE. Reports in 3 weeks.
Music: Gospel, jazz, R&B, rock and soul.

VECTOR MUSIC, 1107 18th Ave. S., Nashville TN 37212. (615)327-4161. Affiliate: Belton Music (ASCAP). Manager: Harry M. Warner. Music publisher. BMI. Member NMPA. Pays standard royalties.
How to Contact: Submit demo tape and lyric sheet. Prefers reel-to-reel tape or cassette with 1-6 songs on demo. SASE. Reports in 1 month.
Music: C&W; easy listening; MOR; and country rock. Recently published "East Bound and Down" (by Dick Feller and Jerry Reed), recorded by Jerry Reed (country/pop); and "Ragamuffin Man" (by Stewart Harris), recorded by Donna Fargo (country).

VELVET APPLE MUSIC, 811 18th Ave. S., Nashville TN 37203. (615)327-2338. Affiliate: Song Yard Music (ASCAP). General Manager: Carla Scarborough. Music publisher. BMI.
How to Contact: Call first about your interest. Prefers 7½ ips reel-to-reel with maximum 4 songs on demo. SASE. Reports in 3 weeks.
Music: All types.

VETTE MUSIC CORPORATION, (Larry Shayne Enterprises), #222 6362 Hollywood Blvd., Hollywood CA 90028. (213)462-5466. Affiliate: Nadamas Music (BMI). President: Dave Pell. Music publisher, record producer and record company. ASCAP. Member NMPA. Publishes 50 songs/year. Pays standard royalty.
How to Contact: Query by phone, then submit demo (cassette) and lyric sheet. "I will not return cassettes unless SASE is enclosed." Reports in 2 weeks.
Music: Easy listening; jazz; MOR; contemporary rock; and top 40/pop. Published "Ode To Billy Joe," "Girl Talk," "Chorus Line" (by Marvin Hamlisch) and "Charade" (by Henri Mancini).

VICKSBURG MUSIC, 1700 Openwood St., Vicksburg MS 39180. (601)638-6647. President: John Ferguson. Music publisher. BMI. Pays standard royalties.
How to Contact: Submit demo tape and lead sheet. Prefers cassette with 1-3 songs on demo. SASE. Reports in 3 weeks.
Music: Blues; dance; gospel; R&B; rock; soul; and top 40/pop. Recently published "Dance for Me" (by James Taylor), recorded by James Pane/GSP Records (soul); and "I'll Take Care of You" (by Wynd Chymes), recorded by Wynd Chymes/GSP Records (soul).

VIC-RAY PUBLISHING, Box 13222, Gainesville FL 32604. (904)378-8156. General Manager: Charles V. Steadham, Jr. Professional Manager: Allen R. McCollum. Music Publisher. Estab. 1979. ASCAP.
How to Contact: Query or submit demo tape. Prefers cassette with 2-5 songs on demo. Does not return unsolicited material. Reports "as soon as possible."
Music: Bluegrass; C&W; disco; folk; MOR; rock (country); soul; top 40/pop; R&B and comedy. Recently released "Rock 'n' Rye," "Rocky Top Bar-B-Que," "Not A Good Woman to Love," and "Whiskey 'Fore Breakfast" (by Mike Cross), recorded by Mike Cross/GHE Records (country/rock).

VOKES MUSIC PUBLISHING, Box 12, New Kensington PA 15068. (412)335-2775. President: Howard Vokes. Music publisher, record company, booking agency and promotion company. BMI.
How to Contact: Submit demo tape and lead sheet. Prefers reel-to-reel, cassette or 8-track cartridge. SASE. Reports "a few days after receiving."
Music: Bluegrass; C&W; and gospel. Recently published "Your Kisses and Lies," "Keep Cool but Don't Freeze," "Judge of Hearts," "Born without a Name," "I Was a Fool" and "Tomorrow Is My Last Day."

KENT WASHBURN PRODUCTIONS, 10622 Commerce Ave., Tujunga CA 91042. (213)855-0525. Affiliates: Monard Music (ASCAP) and Pencott Publishing (BMI). Contact: Kent

Washburn. Music publisher and record producer. Publishes 20 songs/year; publishes 3 new songwriters/year. Pays standard royalty.
How to Contact: Submit demo tape and lyric sheet. Prefers cassette with 1-5 songs on demo. SASE. Reports in 1 month.
Music: Church/religious, contemporary gospel, R&B, soul and top 40/pop. Recently published "Don't Burn No Bridges" (by Romain Anderson), recorded by Jackie Wilson/Brunswick Records (R&B); "Resurrection" (by Washburn and Lupton), recorded by Paul Davis/Spirit Records (gospel); and "You Don't Even Know My Name" (by Kelly), recorded by Free Love/EMKAY Records (R&B).

WATERHOUSE MUSIC, INC., 100 N. 7th St., Suite 415, Minneapolis MN 55403. (612)6575. Director of Operations: Gary Marx. Music publisher and record producer. BMI. Publishes 2 new songwriters/year. Pays negotiable royalty.
How to Contact: Call first about your interest, submit demo tape and lyric sheet. Prefers cassette with 3-10 songs on demo. "Include promo material and cover letter." SASE. Reports in 1 month.
Music: Blues, dance-oriented (mainstream), folk (rock), R&B, rock, soul and top 40/pop. Recently published "Up from the Alley" (by Lamont Cranston Band), recorded by Lamont Cranston Band/Waterhouse Records (rock); "My Babe" (Roy Buchanan version), recorded by Little Walter/Waterhouse Records (rock); and "Times of Our Lives" (by Rex Fowler), recorded by Aztec Two-Step/Waterhouse Records (rock/top 40 ballad).

WATONGA PUBLISHING CO., 2609 NW 36th St., Oklahoma City OK 73112. (405)942-0462. Music publisher. ASCAP. Pays standard royalty.
How to Contact: Submit demo tape and lyric sheet. Prefers 7½ ips reel-to-reel as demo.
Music: C&W, R&B, rock, soul and top 40/pop.

WEE-B MUSIC, 1300 Division, Suite 201, Nashville TN 37203. (615)256-7543. Affiliate: Muhlenberg Music (BMI). President: Cal Everhart. Music publisher. ASCAP.
How to Contact: Write or call first about your interest. Prefers 7½ ips reel-to-reel with 3-4 songs on demo. SASE. Reports in 2 weeks.
Music: Bluegrass; C&W; MOR; and progressive (country).

WEEZE MUSIC CO. & DOUBLE HEADER PRODUCTIONS, 61 Jane St., Suite 4N, New York NY 10014. (212)929-2068. Contact: Steve Scharf and Neal Teeman. Music publisher and record producer. BMI.
How to Contact: Call first about your interest and then submit demo tape and lyric sheet. Prefers 7½ ips reel-to-reel or cassette with maximum 4 songs on demo. SASE.
Music: Rock and roll, top 40/pop and adult contemporary.

WELK MUSIC GROUP, 14 Music Circle E., Nashville TN 37203. (615)256-7648. Contact: Roger Sovine. Music publisher. BMI. Pays standard royalty.
How to Contact: Write or call first about your interest. Prefers 7½ ips reel-to-reel or cassette when sending *requested* material. "We refuse unsolicited material." SASE.
Music: C&W, easy listening, MOR, progressive, rock, soul, and top 40/pop.

BOBE WES MUSIC, Box 28609, Dallas TX 75228. (214)681-1548. Affiliate: Wes Music (ASCAP). Publishes 20 songs/year. President: Bobe Wes. Music publisher. BMI. Pays standard royalty.
How to Contact: Submit demo tape. Prefers 7½ ips reel-to-reel or cassette. "State if songs have been copyrighted and if you have previously assigned songs to someone else. Include titles, readable lyrics and your full name and address. Give the same information for your cowriter(s) if you have one. State if you are a member of BMI, ASCAP or SESAC. Lead sheets are not required. Comments will follow only if interested." SASE. Reports in 3-4 weeks.
Music: Blues; C&W; disco; gospel; MOR; progressive; rock (hard or soft); soul; top 40/pop; polka; and Latin dance. Recently published "It Won't Seem like Christmas (without You)," recorded by Elvis Presley (pop/C&W).

WESJAC MUSIC, Box 743, 129 W. Main St., Lake City SC 29560. (803)394-3712. General Manager: W.R. Bragdton Jr. Music publisher and record company. BMI. Publishes 3-10 songs/year.
How to Contact: Submit demo tape azd lead sheet or submit lead sheet. Prefers 7½ or 15 ips reel-to-reel with 2 songs minimum on tape. SASE. Reports in 1 month.
Music: Church/religious and gospel. Recently published "I'm Glad I Wasn't Made by Man" and "Every Now and Then," recorded by the Gospel Songbirds (gospel); and "I Can't Stop Loving God," recorded by the Traveling Four (gospel).

WESTERN HEAD MUSIC, Box 19, Bulverde TX 78163. (512)438-2465. Affiliate: Brujo Music (BMI). Vice President: Carol Meyer. Music publisher, record company, record producer and booking agency. ASCAP. Publishes 15 songs/year; publishes 10 new songwriters/year.
How to Contact: Submit demo tape, submit demo tape and lead sheet, or submit acetate disc. Prefers 7½ ips reel-to-reel or cassette with 3-5 songs on demo. SASE. Reports in 2 weeks.
Music: Blues; C&W; jazz; progressive; and rock. Recently published "The Court of Kali Oz" (by Lucky Tomblin), recorded by Lucky Tomblin (rock).

WEYAND MUSIC PUBLISHING, 297 Rehm Rd., Depew NY 14043. (716)684-5323. Proprietor: C.D. Weyand. Music publisher. ASCAP. Member NMPA. Publishes 3-4 songs/year. Pays standard royalty.
How to Contact: Write first about your interest, then submit demo tape and lyric sheet. Prefers 7½ ips reel-to-reel or cassette with 2 songs on demo. "All material submitted must be complete and copyrighted by the person(s) making submission." SASE. Reports in 1 month.
Music: Bluegrass; blues; classical; C&W; easy listening; R&B; and top 40/pop. Recently published "Around the Bend," "Never Cry," "Words at Parting," "With You," "Why Can't You?" and "It's the Only Way" (all by Weyand), all recorded on DaCar Records; "We Care," "Song For Freedom" (songs for hostages in Iran), *The '80s Song Folio,* "A Thousand Stars," "Prelude in C Minor," "Prelude Op. 28-N. 7 (Chopin with variation by Weyand) and "Meditation" (classical), all by Weyand.

WHEEZER MUSIC, 1701 Nichols Canyon Rd., Los Angeles CA 90046. President: Howard Bloch. Music publisher. ASCAP. Publishes 25 songs/year; publishes 2 new songwriters/year. Pays standard royalties.
How to Contact: Submit demo tape and lead or lyric sheet. Prefers cassette with 1-3 songs on demo. SASE. "I hold interesting material and then contact the writer. All others with envelopes are returned."
Music: C&W; MOR; rock (country); and top 40/pop. Recently published "Come Fill Your Cup Again," recorded by Barry Richards (MOR); "Here Comes Love," recorded by New Top Notes (MOR); and "Rainbow City," recorded by Tightrope (MOR).

WHITE CLAY PRODUCTIONS, INC. Box 324, Newark DE 19711. (302)368-1211. Affiliates: White Clay Music (BMI) and Straight-Face Music (ASCAP). Contact: A&R Department. Estab. 1979. BMI. Publishes 20 songs/year; publishes 5 new songwriters/year. Pays standard royalty.
How to Contact: Submit demo tape and lyric sheet. Prefers cassette as demo. SASE. Reports in 3 weeks.
Music: Dance-oriented, jazz, progressive, R&B, rock and new wave.

WHITE WAY MUSIC CO., 65 W. 55th St., New York NY 10019. Affiliates: Sally Music (BMI) and Langley Music (BMI). President: Eddie White. Music publisher and record producer. ASCAP. Publishes 65 songs/year. Pays standard royalty.
How to Contact: Submit demo tape and lead sheet. Prefers cassette with 1-5 songs on demo. SASE. Reports in 2 weeks.
Music: Bluegrass; blues; church/religious; C&W; easy listening; folk; gospel; MOR; rock; soul; and top 40/pop. Recently published "Don't Take Pretty to the City," by Howdy Glenn/Warner Brothers Records (C&W).

SHANE WILDER MUSIC, Box 3503, Hollywood CA 90028. (213)762-1613). President: Shane Wilder. Music Publisher and record producer. BMI. Publishes 20 songs/year. Pays standard royalty.
How to Contact: Submit demo cassette and lyric sheet with 6-8 songs on demo. SASE. Reports in 2 weeks.
Music: Church/religious; C&W; disco; gospel; rock; soul; and top 40/pop. Recently published "Never Fall in Love" (country/MOR) and "Play" (country rock), (both by Mike Franklin), recorded by Franklin/NSD Records, Nashville. Just completed the Mike Franklin LP due for release in August 1981.

WILL-DU MUSIC PUB., 833 N. Orange Grove Ave., Los Angeles CA 90046. (213)653-8358. Affiliate: Deliver Music Pub. Co. (BMI). General Manager: Lou Dulfon. Music publisher and management company. BMI. Publishes 8-10 songs/year. Pays standard royalty.
How to Contact: "We have a full complement of writers."
Music: Disco; R&B; rock; rock soul; top 40/pop. Recently published *Screamin' the Blues* (by Screamin' Jay Hawkins), album recorded by Red Lightnin' Records, published in UK by Big Spliff Music; and "Monkberry Moon Delight" (by Linda and Paul McCartney), published by Deliver Music.

DON WILLIAMS MUSIC GROUP, 1888 Century Park E. #1106, Los Angeles CA 90067. (213)556-2458. Affiliates: Redstripe Music (BMI), Pacific View Music (ASCAP) and Wishbone Music (ASCAP). Music publisher and record producer. BMI and ASCAP. Publishes 40 songs/year; publishes 1 new songwriter/year. Pays standard royalty.
How to Contact: Call first about your interest, then submit demo tape and lyric sheet. Prefers cassette with 2-3 songs on demo. "List name, address and telephone number on package." SASE. Reports in 4-6 weeks.
Music: Progressive C&W; easy listening; jazz; MOR; R&B; rock; soul; and top 40/pop.

THE WILLIS MUSIC COMPANY, 7380 Industrial Rd., Florence KY 41042. (606)283-2050. Affiliates: R.L. Huntzinger, Inc. (SESAC), Delhi Publications, Inc. (SESAC), and Ralph Jusko Publications, Inc. (SESAC). President: Edward C. Cranley. Music publisher. SESAC. Publishes 125 songs/year. Pays by contract.
How to Contact: Submit demo tape and lyric or lead sheet. Prefers cassette with 1-3 songs on demo. SASE.
Music: Children's, choral, church/religious, C&W, easy listening, MOR, R&B, rock, country rock and top 40/pop.

THE KENNETH GREGORY WILSON PUBLISHING CO., 18945 Livernios Ave., Detroit MI 48221. (313)862-8221. Contact: Kenneth Wilson. Music publisher, record company and record producer. BMI. Publishes 300 songs/year; publishes 175 new songwriters/year. Pays standard royalty.
How to Contact: Submit demo tape and lyric sheet. Prefers cassette with 3-6 songs on demo. "Tape should be clear, not too many instruments." SASE. Reports in 1 month.
Music: Children's, church/religious, classical and gospel. Recently published "Save Us Lord," (by Kenneth Wilson), recorded by G.G. Temple/KGW Productions Records (religious); "Revival," (by Darryl Ford), recorded by Saved/God's Word Records (gospel); "I'll Never, Never Give Up," (by K. Wilson), recorded by Jessie Dixson/Light Records (gospel); and "Rapture," (by Kathy Hoke), recorded by Kathy Hoke/Light Records (gospel).

WIL-TOO MUSIC, Box 4563, Nashville TN 37216. (615)883-2457. President: Tom Wilkerson. Music publisher and record producer. Estab. 1979. ASCAP. Pays standard royalty.
How to Contact: Submit demo tape and lyric sheet. Prefers 7½ ips reel-to-reel with 1-4 songs on demo. SASE. Reports in 1 month.
Music: Bluegrass; church/religious; C&W; easy listening; gospel; and MOR.

WINDOW MUSIC PUBLISHING CO., INC., 809 18th Ave. S., Nashville TN 37203. (615)327-3211. Affiliates: Tomake Music (ASCAP), Speak Music (BMI), Ernest Tubb Music, Inc. (BMI) and Brushape Music (BMI). Office Manager: Rose Trimble. Music publisher. BMI. Publishes 300 songs/year. Pays standard royalty.
How to Contact: Not currently accepting outside material.
Music: C&W; easy listening; gospel; rock; and top 40/pop. Recently published "If Drinkin' Don't Kill Me (Her Memory Will)" (by Rick Beresford and Harlan Sanders), recorded by George Jones/Epic Records (C&W) and "I'll Be There," recorded by Gayle Davis/Warner Brothers Records (C&W).

WOODRICH PUBLISHING CO., Box 38, Lexington AL 35648. (205)247-3983. Affiliate: Mernee Music (ASCAP). President: Woody Richardson. Music publisher and record company. BMI. Publishes 15 songs/year; publishes 5 new songwriters/year. Pays 50% royalty.
How to Contact: Submit demo tape. Prefers 7½ ips reel-to-reel or cassette with 2-4 songs on demo. SASE. Reports in 1 month.
Music: Bluegrass; blues; choral; church/religious; C&W; easy listening; folk; gospel; jazz; MOR; progressive; rock; soul; and top 40/pop. Recently published "Colorado Lady" (by Daryl Hooie and Alan R. Cane), recorded by Daryl Hooie/Lamp Records (pop); "I Listen to the Mocking Bird Sing" (by J.W Malone), recorded by Whit Malone/Woodrich Records (country); and "Porch Swing" (by Ronnie Adams), recorded by Ronnie Adams/Woodrich (country).

WORD MUSIC, Division of Word, Inc., Box 1790, Waco TX 76703. Affiliates: The Rodeheaver (ASCAP), Dayspring (BMI) and The Norman Clayton Publishing Co. (SESAC). Music Editor: Bill Wolaver. A&R: Lanny Hall. Music publisher and record company. ASCAP.
How to Contact: Submit demo tape and lead sheet or submit acetate disc and lead sheet. Prefers 7½ ips reel-to-reel or cassette with 1-5 songs on demo. "Songs of a choral nature should be submitted to our publishing company." SASE. Reports in 10 weeks.

Music: Children's; choral; church/religious; and gospel. Songs of a commercial, solo nature should be submitted to the A&R department of our record company."

WYNWOOD MUSIC CO., INC., Box 101, Broad Run VA 22014. (703)754-7353. General Manager: Peter V. Kuykendall. Music publisher and record producer. BMI. Publishes 10-15 songs/year; publishes 3-4 new songwriters/year. Pays standard royalty.
How to Contact: Write first about your interest. Prefers cassette with 1-5 songs on demo. SASE. Reports in 1 month.
Music: Bluegrass, blues, C&W and folk. Recently published "Roses in the Snow," (by Ruth Franks), recorded by Emmylou Harris/Warner Brothers Records (bluegrass); "Got the Blues," (by Mississippi John), recorded by Doc Watson/United Artists Records (blues); and "Gone Lonesome," (by Pete Kuykendall), recorded by Bill Harrell/Leather Records (bluegrass).

YBARRA MUSIC, Box 665, Lemon Grove CA 92045. (714)462-6538. Contact: Richard Braum. Music publisher. ASCAP. Member AFM. Publishes up to 12 songs/year. Pays standard royalty.
How to Contact: Write first about your interest. Prefers cassette demo. Does not return unsolicited material. Reports in 1 month.
Music: Jazz and big band swing.

ZANE MUSIC, 1529 Walnut St., 6th Fl., Philadelphia PA 19102. (215)568-0500. President: Lloyd Zane Remick. Music publisher and record producer. Estab. 1979. BMI. Publishes 1 song/year; publishes 1 new songwriter/year. Pays standard royalty.
How to Contact: Submit demo tape and lyric sheet. Prefers cassette. SASE. Reports in 3 weeks.
Music: Blues, C&W, dance-oriented, easy listening, gospel, jazz, MOR, progressive, R&B, rock, soul and top 40/pop. Recently published "Lovin" (by Phil Hurtt), recorded by P. Hurtt/Fantasy Records (MOR/soul).

Geographic Index

Planning a trip to Los Angeles, New York or Nashville? Or do you specifically want to submit material to publishers in one or all of those cities? This geographic listing will quickly give you the names of publishers located in each. Then check the listings in the music publisher section for addresses, phone numbers and submission details.

Rubicon Music
St. Cecilia Music
Sasha Songs, Unltd. & the Grand Pasha Publisher
Screen Gems-Colgems-EMI Music Inc.
Seganl & Goldman, Inc.
Seven Songs
Seventh Ray Publishing
Skinny Zach Music
Terry Stafford Music
Stone Diamond Music Corp.
Takoma Music
10 of Diamonds Music
Third Story Music, Inc.
3300 Publishing
Transatlantic Music
20th Century Fox Music Publishing
United Artists Music
Vette Music Corporation
Wheezer Music
Shane Wilder Music
Will-Du Music Pub.
Don Williams Music Group

NASHVILLE
Acoustic Music, Inc.
Adventure Music Co.
Annie Over Music
April/Blackwood Music
ATV Music
Baby Huey Music
Beechwood Music
Boxer Music
Briarpatch Music/Deb Dave Music, Inc.
Broadman Press
Brooks Brothers Publishers
Buckhorn Music Publishing Co., Inc.
Buried Treasure Music
Cedarwood Publishing Co., Inc.
Chappell Music Co.
Chip 'N' Dale Music Publishers, Inc.
Combine Music Group
Court of Kings Music
Covered Bridge Music
Deb Dave Music
Door Knob Music Publishing, Inc.
Bobby Fischer Music
Forrest Hills Music, Inc.
Al Gallico Music Corp.
Grawick Music
Heavy Jamin' Music

James Hendrix Enterprises
Iron Blossom Music Group
Jaclyn Music
JMR Enterprises
Kelly & Lloyd Music
Gene Kennedy Enterprises, Inc.
Jimmy Kish Music Publishing
Cristy Lane Music
Lodestar Music
Mainly Music, Inc.
MCA Music, MCA, Inc.
Mr. Mort Music
Monkey Music, Inc.
Morning Music (USA), Inc.
Music Craftshop
Music Publishing Corp.
Newswriters Music
O.A.S. Music Group
Peer-Southern Organization
Pi Gem Music, Inc./Chess Music, Inc.
Pick-A-Hit Music
Pommard
Power-Play Publishing
Raindance Music
Re'generation, Inc.
RobJen Music, Inc.
Rustic Records
Show Biz Music Group
Sing Me Music, Inc.
Shelby Singleton Music Inc.
Song Farm Music Unlimited
Songs of the Southland
Southern Writers Group USA
Stuckey Publishing Co.
Sure-Fire Music Co., Inc.
Sweet Singer Music
Joe Taylor Music
Taylor & Watts Music, Inc.
Three Kings Music
Tree Publishing Co., Inc.
Triune Music, Inc.
Troll Music
Tyner Music
United Artists Music
Vector Music
Velvet Apple Music
Wee-B Music
Welk Music Group
Wil-Too Music
Window Music Publishing Co., Inc.

NEW YORK
Antisia Music, Inc.

The Mike Appel Organization
Arista/Careers Publishing
Art Treff Publishing
Asilomar/Dreena Music
ATV Music Corp.
Audible Music Publishing Co.
Barlenmir House Music, Inc.
Beechwood Music Corp.
Belwin-Mills Publishing Corp.
John Bernard Music
Johnny Bienstock Music
Big Mike Music
Blendingwell Music
Bourne Music
Brut Music Publishing
Bush/Lehrman Productions
Buttermilk Sky Associates
Camerica Music
Can't Stop Music
Chrysalis Music Corp.
Commodores Entertainment Publishing Corp.
Copyright Service Bureau Ltd.
Cotillion Music, Inc.
Dante Music, Inc.
Delightful Music, Ltd.
Entertainment Co. Music Group
Evansongs
Four Moons Music Publishing Group
Funky Acres Music Co.
G.G. Music, Inc.
Gil Music Corporation
GOPAM Enterprises, Inc.
Gospel Clef
Gramavision Music
Dick James Music, Inc.
Jobete Music Co., Inc.
Jomewa Music
Journeyman Music
Kamakazi Music Corporation
Bob Karcy Music
Lorijoy Music, Inc.
Macharmony Music Marielle Music Corp.
Edward B. Marks Music
MCA Music, MCA, Inc.
Memnon, Ltd.
Mietus Copyright Management
MIDEB Music
Ivan Mogull Music Corp.

Music Resources International Corp.
Musicprint Corp.
Mustevic Sound Inc.
Nick-O-Val Music
Nilkam Music/Kimsha Music
Notable Music Co. Inc.
Peer-Southern Organization
Gerald W. Purcell Associates

Radmus Publishing, Inc.
Ren Maur Music Corp.
Rockford Music Co.
RSO Music Publishing Group
Rustron Music Publishers
Screen Gems/EMI Music, Inc.
Sellers Music, Inc.
September Music Corp.
Sherlyn Publishing Co.
Silver Blue Music, Ltd.

Stallman Records, Inc.
Sugar n' Soul Music, Inc.
Sun-Bear Corporation
Swing & Tempo Music Publishing Inc.
TWC Music
United Artists Music Publishing
Vado Music
Weeze Music Co. & Double Header Productions
White Way Music Co.

The Quiet Types

In preparing *Songwriter's Market 1982*, we contacted all major American and Canadian music publishers at least once—and in some cases, two or three times. Most responded. Some, however, did not give us information for one of the following reasons:

● They are not actively seeking material from songwriters.

● They *will* listen to material, but believe that they receive sufficient material without listing in *Songwriter's Market*.

● They are a branch office that concentrates on marketing or other business endeavors, and leaves song selection to branches in other cities.

● They work only with songwriters recommended to them from other sources.

● They are staffed with inhouse songwriters.

● They don't have a staff large enough to handle the increased number of submissions a listing would create.

● They are concerned with copyright problems that might result if they publish a song similar to one they've reviewed and rejected.

● They have once listed with another songwriter directory and were deluged with inappropriate submissions.

Though many of the following firms will review material, we suggest that you not send demo tapes. Write a brief query letter describing your material and asking about the company's current submission policies. Always use a self-addressed, stamped envelope or post card for such queries (see sample reply form in "The Business of Songwriting" in the Appendix of this book).

ABKO Music, Inc., 1700 Broadway, New York NY 10019.

Al-Bo Music Co., 37 Odell Ave., Yonkers NY 10701.

Alpha Music Inc., 40 E. 49th St., New York NY 10017.

American Broadcasting, 1313 Avenue of the Americas, New York NY 10019.

American Composers Alliance, 170 W. 74th St., New York NY 10023.

Ariola America, Inc., 8671 Wilshire Blvd., Beverly Hills CA 90211.

April Blackwood Music, 1930 Century Park W., Suite 200, Century City CA 90067.

April Blackwood Music, 1350 Avenue of the Americas, New York NY 10019.

Arista-Careers Music, 1888 Century Park E., Los Angeles CA 90067.

Aunt Polly's Publishing Co., Box 12647, Nashville TN 37212.

Bicycle Music Co., 8756 Holloway Dr., Los Angeles CA 90069.

Buddah Music, 1790 Broadway, New York NY 10019.

Burlington Music Corp. 539 W. 25th St., New York NY 10001.

Charing Cross Music, Inc., 36 E. 61st St., New York NY 10021.

Chicago Music Publishing, c/o Greene & Reynolds, 1900 Avenue of the Stars, Suite 1424, Los Angeles CA 90067.

Martin Cohen, 6430 Sunset Blvd., Suite 1500, Los Angeles CA 90028.

Bruce Cohn Music, Box 359, Sonoma CA 95476.

Crowbeck, 9126 Sunset Blvd., Suite 1000, Los Angeles CA 90069.

Danor, 1802 Grand Ave., Nashville TN 37212.

Dawnbreaker Music Co., 216 Chatsworth Dr., San Fernando CA 91340.

Entertainment Company Music Group, 6430 Sunset Blvd., Suite 803, Los Angeles CA 90028.

Famous Music Publishing Companies, 6430 Sunset Blvd., Los Angeles CA 90028.

Famous Music Publishing Companies, 2 Music Circle S., Nashville TN 37203.

Fermata International Melodies, 6290 Sunset Blvd., Suite 916, Hollywood CA 90028.

Finchley Music Corp., c/o Arrow, Edelstein, Gross & Margolis, 1370 Avenue of the Americas, New York NY 10019.

Four Knights Music, 6000 Sunset Blvd., Hollywood CA 90028.

Fourth Floor Music, Box 135, Bearsville NY 12409.

Frebar Music Co., 5514 Kelly Rd., Brentwood TN 37027.

Gaucho Music, 161 W. 54th St., New York NY 10019.

Gold Hill Music, Inc., 5032 Lankershim Blvd., North Hollywood CA 91601.

The Goodman Group, 110 E. 59th St., New York NY 10022.

Hall of Fame Music Co., Box 921, Beverly Hills CA 90213.

House of Gold Music, Inc., Box 120967, Nashville TN 37216.

Impulsive Music, c/o Home Run Systems Corp., 14 E. 60th St., New York NY 10022.

Invador Music Co., 8961 Sunset Blvd., Los Angeles CA 90069.

Don Kirshner Music, 9000 Sunset Blvd., Los Angeles CA 90069.

Don Kirshner Music, 1370 Avenue of the Americas, New York NY 10019.

Lido, c/o Padell, Kaden, Nadell & Co., 405 Park Ave., New York NY 10022.

MPL Communications Inc., c/o Eastman & Eastman, 30 Park Pl., East Hampton NY 11937.

Muscle Shoals Sound Publ'g Co., Inc., Box 915, 1000 Alabama Ave., Sheffield AL 35660.

Riva Music, Inc., 232 E. 61st St., New York NY 10021.

Marty Robbins Enterprises, 713 18th Ave. S., Nashville TN 37203.

Shade Tree Music Inc., Box 500, Bella Vista CA 96008.

Shapiro Bernstein, 10 E. 53rd St., New York NY 10022.

Larry Shayne Music Co., 6290 Sunset Blvd., Hollywood CA 90028.

Track Music Co., 200 W. 57th St., New York NY 10019.

Warner Bros. Music, 9200 Sunset Blvd., Los Angeles CA 90069.

Warner Bros. Music, 75 Rockefeller Plaza, New York NY 10019.

Warner Bros. Music, 44 Music Square W., Nashville TN 37203.

Record Companies

Nowhere in the music business is the economic pinch being felt more severely than by record companies. They are responsible for providing facilities; securing artists, producers and musicians; and the manufacturing, distributing and promoting of a new release. This translates to thousands of dollars for each song. Adding to this financial responsibility is the Copyright Royalty Tribunal ruling (see "Copyright" in this book) almost doubling the rate a record company must pay publishers for each record sold (an increase from 2¾¢ to 4¢ to be shared between publisher and songwriter).

All these economic implications come into play when submitting material to a record company. Unlike music publishers who use a variety of songs and work for months shopping them in many places, record companies have more immediate needs. Each record company listens to new songs with specific artists and projects in mind. The exception would be an artist/songwriter or group who has written its own material. In that situation, the company listens to determine if the artist or group will have enough commercial appeal on the finished product to *sell records*.

This "bottom line" attitude of record companies makes them necessarily selective about the songs they pick to record. But this need for the "best" can work to the advantage of unknown songwriters. Even though most record companies count on publishers for songs—and many even have their own publishing branch—they don't care *where* a song comes from as long as it's what they're looking for!

The companies listed here told us exactly what they are looking for. If you have songs for an artist on a certain label or if you are a songwriter/artist seeking a recording contract, read through these listings and choose which companies you would like to work with. *Billboard*, *Cash Box* and *Record World* charts give the names of top recording artists and the labels on which they record. Additional names and addresses of record companies can be found in the *Billboard International Buyer's Guide*, though it contains no submission information.

Check the geographic index at the end of this section for the names of record companies in Los Angeles, Nashville and New York.

Names of companies we contacted but which did not give us enough information for a complete listing are also given at the end of this section, along with addresses and a synopsis of their reasons for not listing.

A&M RECORDS, INC., 1416 N. La Brea, Hollywood CA 90028. (213)469-2411. Record company. Releases 84 singles and 56 albums/year. Works with artists and songwriters on contract.
How to Contact: "Direct all material through a publisher." SASE.
Music: C&W, dance, easy listening, folk, jazz, MOR, progressive, R&B, rock, soul, and top 40/pop. Recently released *Paradise Theater*, by Styx (LP); *Breaking All the Rules*, by Peter Frampton (LP); and *East Side Story*, by Squeeze (LP).

A&M RECORDS INC., 595 Madison Ave., New York NY 10022. Labels include Horizon Records. National Director of A&R: Mark Spector. Record company.
How to Contact: Submit demo tape. Prefers reel-to-reel or cassette with 1-5 songs on demo. SASE. Reports in 1 month.
Music: Dance; jazz (crossover); progressive; R&B; rock; and top 40/pop. Recently released *Breakfast in America*, by Supertramp.

A&M RECORDS OF CANADA, LTD., 939 Warden Ave., Scarborough, Ontario, Canada M1L 4C5. (416)752-7191. A&R Coordinator: Michael Godin. Record company and music publisher

(Irving/Almo Music of Canada, Ltd.). Member CRIA. Works with artists on contract. Pays statutory rate to publishers for each record sold.
How to Contact: Submit demo tape and lyric sheet. Prefers cassette with 3-5 songs on demo. "Be aware of the time it takes to listen and respond. Be patient." SAE and International Reply Coupon. Reports in 1 month.
Music: Progressive, rock (hard) and top 40/pop. Recently released *Zenyatta Mondatta*, by Police; *Paradise Theater*, by Styx; *Wild Eyed Southern Boys*, by .38 Special (all rock LPs). Other artists include Bryan Adams, Cano, Payola$, Stanley Frank, Leyden Zar, Peter Pringle, Walter Zwol and the Rage, Fist, Shari Ulrich, and Eddie Schwartz.

ABACUS, Box 378, Nashville TN 37221. (615)646-4917. A&R Director: Robert Wiegert. Record company, record producer and music publisher (ROBJEN Music). Estab. 1980. Works with artists and songwriters on contract; musicians on salary for in-house studio work. Pays negotiable royalty to artists on contract; pays statutory rate to publishers for each record sold.
How to Contact: Write first about your interest; submit demo tape and lyric sheet. Prefers 7½ ips reel-to-reel or cassette with 3 songs on demo. SASE. Reports in 1 month.
Music: C&W, gospel, MOR, progressive, rock. "I Believed In You," by Cathy Bemis (MOR/pop single); and "Loves a Circle," by Cathy Bemis (MOR/country single). Other artists include Jeannie Martin (pop and country), High Rider (MOR/country rock band), Bob Stills (pop singer) and Greg Scott (pop singer).

AFERTON RECORDS, Box 2315, Springfield IL 62705. (217)528-7355. A&R Director: Kenneth A. White. Record company and music publisher (Satchitananda Publishing/BMI). Releases 10 singles and 8 albums/year. Works with musicians on salary; artists and songwriters on contract. Pays statutory rate to publishers for each record sold.
How to Contact: Submit demo tape and lyric sheet. Prefers cassette with 3-5 songs on demo. SASE. Reports in 1 month.
Music: Jazz; progressive; rock; and top 40/pop. "We are not locked in to these categories and would consider any form of music if it was very good and we could deal with it." Recently released *A Thought Away*, by Satchitananda (progressive jazz rock LP); *The Aferton Project*, by The Aferton Project (pop/rock LP); "Crazy Women," by Boe Perry (pop single); and "Nowhere," by Jill Kennedy (pop single).

AIC/ARTISTIC RECORDS, Box 3013, Davenport IA 52808. (319)324-2133. Manager: Gary Unger. Record company and music publisher (Groovesonic Music). Estab. 1981. Releases 3 singles and 3-7 albums/year. Works with musicians on salary for in-house studio work. Pays 10¢/single sold or 50¢/album sold to artists on contract; statutory rate to publishers for each record sold.
How to Contact: Submit demo tape and lyric sheet. Prefers 7½ ips reel-to-reel or cassette with 4-10 songs on demo. SASE. Reports in 2 months.
Music: Dance-oriented, progressive, rock 'n roll and top 40/pop. Recently released "Big Mama Johns" and "Peaceful Feeling" recorded by Judy MccLary (top 40 singles); and *10 Jewels*, by Union (top 40 LP). Other artists include Christi Farris (gospel/pop singer) and Christi Sandifur (pop/rock singer-songwriter).

ALEAR RECORDS, Box 574, Sounds of Winchester, Winchester VA 22601. (703)667-9379. Labels include Master Records, Winchester Records and Real McCoy Records. Secretary: Bertha McCoy. Record company, music publisher, record producer and recording studio. Releases 25 singles and 10 albums/year. Works with artists and songwriters on contract; musicians on salary. Pays 2% minimum royalty to artists; statutory rate to publishers for each record sold.
How to Contact: Submit demo tape and lead sheet. Prefers 7½ ips reel-to-reel or cassette with 5-10 songs on demo. SASE. Reports in 1 month.
Music: Bluegrass; church/religious; C&W; folk; gospel; progressive; and rock. Recently released "Leavin' on Your Mind" by Mel McQueen (country single); *Mr. Blue Grass*, by Carroll Country Ramblers (bluegrass LP). Other artists include Alvin Kesner, Jim McCoy, and Middleburg Harmonizers.

ALL EARS RECORDS, 7033 Sunset Blvd., #309, Hollywood CA 90028. (213)465-3990. A&R Manager: Jack Cornish. Record company, music publisher and record producer. Works with artists on contract. Pays 10% minimum royalty to artists on contract.
How to Contact: Submit demo tape and lyric sheet. Prefers cassette with 2-6 songs on demo. SASE. Reports in 1 month.
Music: Progressive, new wave and avant-garde rock. Recently released *Tenkujin*, by the Far East Family Band (LP); *Vision's Fugitives*, by Sensations Fix (LP); *The Pillory*, by Jasun Martz & The

Neoteric Orchestra (LP); and *Like a Message*, by Chronicle (LP). Other artists include The Decayes and Fumio Miyashta.

AMALGAMATED TULIP CORP., 117 W. Rockland Rd., Libertyville IL 60048. (312)362-4060. Labels include Dharma Records. Director of Publishing and Administration: Mary Chris. Record company and music publisher. Works with musicians on salary; artists and songwriters on contract. Pays royalty to artists and songwriters on contract.
How to Contact: Submit demo tape. Prefers cassette with 2-5 songs on demo. SASE. Reports in 1-3 months.
Music: Rock (progressive and easy listening) and top 40/pop. Recently released "Another Trip to Earth," by Gabriel Bondage (progressive rock single); and *Corky Siegel*, by Corky Siegel (folk LP). Other artists include Conrad Black (rock).

AMIRON MUSIC/AZTEC PRODUCTIONS, 20531 Plummer St., Chatsworth CA 91311. (213)998-0443. Labels include Dorn Records and Aztec Records. General Manager: A. Sullivan. Record company, booking agency and music publisher. Releases 2-4 singles and 1 album/year. Works with artists and songwriters on contract. Pays 10% maximum royalty to artists on contract; standard royalty to songwriters on contract.
How to Contact: Submit demo tape and lead sheet. Prefers 7½ ips reel-to-reel or cassette. SASE. Reports in 3 weeks.
Music: Bluegrass; blues; C&W; dance; easy listening; folk; gospel; jazz; MOR; rock ("no heavy metal"); and top 40/pop. Recently released "Blood from My Hand" and "It Feels Good," by Quicksand (R&B/disco singles), and "Act of Mercy," by Abraxas (top 40/pop single).
Tips: "Be sure the material has a hook; it should make people want to make love or fight."

ANAMAZE RECORDS, 1802 Ocean Pkwy., Suite 2A, Brooklyn NY 11223. (212)627-8499. President/A&R Director: Cosmo Ohms. Record company and record producer. Works with musicians on salary; artists on contract. Pays 3½% minimum royalty to artists on contract.
How to Contact: Write first about your interest. Prefers cassette with 3 songs maximum on demo. SASE. Reports in 1 month.
Music: New wave and future-oriented rock; and top 40/pop. Recently released "Rockin' On The Bowery," "Birthday Heaven" and "Who's Been Naughty" by Startoon (new wave rock single); and "Affectionate Type" and "Being Human" by Startoon (rock & roll single).

ANTHEM RECORDS OF CANADA, Oak Manor, 12261 Yonge St., Box 1000, Oak Ridges, Ontario, Canada. (416)773-4371. Managing Director: Tom Berry. Press & Publicity: Linda Emmerson. National Promotion: Perry Goldberg. Record company. Releases 5-10 singles and 4-8 albums/year. Works with artists on contract. Pays 5-16% royalty to artists on contract.
How to Contact: Submit demo tape.
Music: Top 40 and AOR. Recently released *Moving Pictures* (top 40 LP) and "Limelight," (top 40 single) by Rush/AOR Records; and *Universal Juveniles*, by Max Webster/AOR Records (top 40 LP).

CHUCK ANTHONY MUSIC, INC., Box 2000, Holbrook NY 11741. (516)472-0900. Labels include CVR Records. President: Chuck Anthony. Record company, booking agency and music publisher. Releases 4 singles and 3-6 albums/year. Works with musicians and songwriters on contract. Pays 9% royalty to artists on contract; standard royalty to songwriters on contract.
How to Contact: Submit demo tape and lead sheet. Prefers cassette with 1-6 songs on demo. Does not return unsolicited material. Reports in 1 month "if we decide to use it."
Music: Disco and top 40/pop. Recently released "Oh, Baby," by Wayne Miran and Rush Release (top 40 single); "Disco Ranger," by Tangerine (disco single); "Girl From Ipanema," by Zakariah (disco single); and "Helplessly," by Wayne Miranda and Rush Release (disco single).

ANTIQUE/CATFISH RECORDS, Box 192, Pittsburg KS 66762. (316)231-6443. Labels include Antique and Catfish Records. President: Gene Strasser. Record company and music publisher, (Country Party Music/BMI). Releases 4-10 singles and 1-5 albums/year. Works with songwriters on contract. Pays statutory rate to publishers for each record sold.
How to Contact: Submit demo tape and lead sheet. Prefers 7½ ips reel-to-reel or cassette with 2 songs on demo. SASE.
Music: Bluegrass, children's, C&W, dance, easy listening, folk, gospel, MOR, rock, soul, top 40/pop, and comedy. Recently released "Welcome Home" b/w "Rollin Uneasy" (country/pop); "Once More with Feeling," by Tony Teebo; *Songs about the West* (country LP) and "The Slave," by Gene Strasser (country single). Other artists include: Kenny Martin and Kay Wayman.

Tips: "About once every 3 months, print the titles to material on post card and send to Country Party Music to remind publisher of songs being considered."

APRIL RECORDS, Box 8263., Haledon NJ 07508. (201)942-6810. Labels include Alsaman, Arch, Kela, Afro and Cummings Records. Vice President: Gauntiett Cummings. Record company, music publisher (Dragon International Music) and record producer. Releases 3 singles and 1 album/year. Works with artists and songwriters on contract. Pays standard royalty to artists and to songwriters on contract; statutory rate to publishers for each record sold.
How to Contact: Submit demo tape and lyric sheet. Prefers 7½ ips reel-to-reel with 3-5 songs on demo. SASE. Reports in 1 month.
Music: Dance; reggae; and soul. Recently released *Africa Stands Alone*, by Culture (reggae LP); *Africa Shall Stretch Forth Her Hands* and *Small Street at Her Hands*, by the Mighty Threes (reggae LPs); and "Being A Woman", by Yolanda Brown and Rhonda Durand (disco single).

ARBY RECORDS, Box 6687, Wheeling WV 26003. (614)758-5812. President: S.P. Tarpley. Record company. Works with artists on contract. Pays 6% royalty to artists and songwriters on contract.
How to Contact: Submit demo tape. Prefers 7½ ips reel-to-reel with 2 songs minimum on tape. Does not return unsolicited material. Reports in 1 month.
Music: Bluegrass; blues; church/religious; C&W; easy listening; folk; gospel; MOR; and progressive. Recently released "Looks Like You're Going Anyway" and "The Next Time," by Patti Powell (country/MOR singles); and "Stranger on the Bridge," by George Elliott (C&W single).

ARC/COLUMBIA (AMERICAN RECORDING CO.), 2323 Corinth Ave., Los Angeles CA 90064. (213)479-8522. Professional Manager: George Guim. Record company and record producer. Works with musicians on contract. Pays by individual contract.
How to Contact: Write first about your interest and then submit demo tape and lyric sheet. Prefers cassette with maximum 5 songs on demo. "Interested in quality—not volume." SASE. Reports in 1 month.
Music: Easy listening, gospel, jazz, MOR, progressive, R&B, rock, soul and top 40/pop. Recently released *I Am*, by Earth, Wind & Fire (R&B LP); *8:30*, by Weather Report (jazz LP); and *Where Is Your Love*, by The Emotions (soul LP). Other artists include Denice Williams, Valerie Carter, D.J. Rogers, Gerard McMahon, Larry John McNally and After Bach.

ARGUS RECORD PRODUCTIONS, Box 58, Glendora NJ 08029. (609)939-0034. Labels include Argus and Record Room Records. General Manager: Eddie Jay Harris. Office Manager: Linda Holland. Record company.
How to Contact: Submit demo tape and lead sheet. Prefers 7½ ips reel-to-reel with 1-2 songs on demo. SASE. Does not return unsolicited material. Reports in 1 month.
Music: Children's; church/religious; dance; rock; and top 40/pop. Recently released "In the 80's," by Daniel Hartman (country rock single).

ARIANA RECORDS, 8924 E. Calle Norlo, Tucson AZ 85710. (602)885-5931. President: James M. Gasper. Vice President: Thomas M. Dukes. Record company, record producer and music publisher (Myko Music). Estab. 1981. Releases 2 singles and 2 albums/year. Works with artists and songwriters on contract; musicians on salary. Pays 50% royalty to artists on contract; statutory rate to publishers for each record sold.
How to Contact: Submit demo tape and lyric sheet. Prefers 7½ ips reel-to-reel or cassette with 3-5 songs on demo. SASE. Reports in 1 month.
Music: Easy listening, R&B, rock, top 40/pop and poprock. Recently released "Siren's Song," by Gasper & Dukes (pop/rock single); "Just Arrived," Gasper & Dukes (pop/rock EP); and "She's on Fire," by The Bandaid (new wave single).

ARISTA RECORDS INC., 1888 Century Park E., Suite 1510, Los Angeles CA 90067. (213)553-1777. Labels include Arista, Buddha, Ariola, GRP, Savoy, and Project 3 Records. A&R Directors: Bud Scoppa, Bob Feiden. Record company. Works with artists on contract.
How to Contact: Submit demo tape. Prefers cassette. SASE. Reports "as soon as possible."
Music: Dance; easy listening; folk; jazz; MOR; progressive; R&B; rock (primarily); soul; and top 40/pop. Recently released *Turn of a Friendly Card*, recorded by Alan Parsons, Project label (LP/singles); *Ghostriders*, recorded by Outlaws (AOR LP/singles); *Air Supply*, recorded by Air Supply (AC LP/singles); and *Magic*, recorded by Tom Browne (jazz LP/singles). Other artists include Barry Manilow, Greatful Dead, Al Stewart, Aretha Franklin, Allman Brothers, Raydio, Jennifer Warnes, Phylis Hymen, Dionne Warwick, Graham Parker, Kinks, Hiroshima, Gil Scott Heron, Average White Band, Michael Henderson, Melissa Manchester and Monty Python.

Tip: "Minimum standards should be adhered to. Demos don't have to be fancy—just understandable."

ARISTA RECORDS INC., 6 W. 57th St., New York NY 10019. Contact: Bob Feiden. Record company. Works with artists on contract.
How to Contact: Submit demo tape and lyric sheet. Prefers 7½ ips reel-to-reel or cassette with 1-4 songs on demo. SASE. Reports in 3 weeks.
Music: Blues; C&W; dance; easy listening; jazz; MOR; progressive; R&B; rock; soul; and top 40/pop. Recently released "Living Inside Myself," by Gino Vannelli; "The One That You Love," by Air Supply; and "Funland," by Bran Tshaikovsky.

ARMADA RECORDS, INC., 5825 N. 96th St., Milwaukee WI 53225. (414)462-5590. President: Tim Brophy. Vice President: Bob Ambos. Record company. Estab. 1979. Works with artists and songwriters on contract. Pays standard royalty to songwriters on contract.
How to Contact: Submit demo tape and lyric sheet. Prefers cassette with 2-8 songs on demo. Does not return unsolicited material. Reports in 3 weeks.
Music: C&W; dance; easy listening; progressive; R&B; rock; soul; and top 40/pop. Recently released "Blues Are Out To Get Me," by Jim Spencer (MOR single); "Warren Spahn," by Blackholes (POP/AOR single); and "Liley," by Dan Riley (C&W single). Other artists include the Pacific Orchestra.

ART ATTACK RECORDS, INC., 964 W. Grant Rd., Tucson AZ 85705. (602)622-8012. Contact: William Cashman. Record company, music publisher and record producer. Works with artists on contract.
How to Contact: Submit demo tape and lyric sheet. Prefers 7½ or 15 ips reel-to-reel with 3-10 songs on demo. "We are interested in the artist's performance abilities and would need to see photos and biographical materials as well as to hear the music." Does not return unsolicited material. Reports in 1 month.
Music: Jazz; progressive; R&B; rock; and top 40/pop. Recently released *I Get Peculiar*, by Street Pajama (jazz/R&B LP); *Split Orange*, by Randy Orange (rock LP); and "Maybe Yes, Maybe No," by Street Pajama (top 40/pop single). Other artists include Crown Glass and Bob Meighan.

ARTEMIS RECORDS, LTD., Box 110, Howard Beach NY 11414. (212)738-4806. President: John Giamundo. Record company and music publisher. Works with artists and songwriters on contract. Payment negotiable.
How to Contact: Submit demo tape. Prefers 7½ or 15 ips reel-to-reel, or disc. SASE.
Music: Classical; disco; easy listening; folk; jazz; MOR; progressive; rock; soul; top 40/pop; and reggae.
Tips: "Send copyrighted material only. Enclose SASE if you wish us to return your product after review. We will not necessarily comment on unsolicited material."

ARZEE RECORD CO., 3010 N. Front St., Philadelphia PA 19133. (215)426-5682. Labels include Arzee, Palace and Arcade Records. General Manager: Dave Wilson. President: Rex Zario. Record company, booking agency and music publisher. Releases 25-100 singles/year. Works artists and songwriters on contract. Pays standard royalty to artists and songwriters on contract.
How to Contact: Submit demo tape and lead sheet. Prefers 7½ ips reel-to-reel or cassette with 5-10 songs on demo. SASE. Reports in 1 month.
Music: Bluegrass; blues; C&W; folk; gospel; rock 'n' roll (fifties style); and rock (hard or country). Recently released "Why Do I Cry over You" and "Ten Gallon Stetson," by Bill Haley; and "I Could See the Tears," by Dee Dee Marcin.

ASAI RECORD CORP., Box 308, Hwy. #460, Vansant VA 24656. (703)935-2495. Branch located at Box 395, Oakwood VA 24631. Labels include ASI, ASII, ASAI, MODOC, Loose Jaw and Penny Pincher Records. Manager: T. Day. Record company, music publisher (Able Music), record producer and movie management. Member AFIRA. Releases 50 singles and 10 albums/year. Works with artists and songwriters on contract. Pays 5-25% royalty to artists on contract 3½¢ up. Pays standard royalty to songwriters on contract.
How to Contact: Submit demo tape and lyric sheet. Prefers 7½ ips reel-to-reel or cassette with 3-6 songs on demo. SASE. Reports in 2 weeks.
Music: C&W; gospel; rock; and top 40/pop. Recently released *Life's a Bitch*, by Goolsby & Plante (MOR single and LP); *The Biggest Lie*, by Ken Jordan (C&W single and LP); and *I Can't Keep My Hands off You*, by Roy John Fuller (C&W single and LP).

ASSOCIATED RECORDING COMPANIES, 2250 Bryn Mawr Ave., Philadelphia PA 19131. (215)477-7122. Labels include Pearl Harbor, Jaguar and Jenges Records (Shelton Associates/

BMI). A&R Directors: Ted Brown, Leo Gaton. Administrator: Richard Jackson. Record company and music publisher. Releases 12 albums and 7 singles/year. Works with artists and songwriters on contract. Pays 6% royalty to artists on contract; standard royalty to songwriters on contract; statutory rate to publishers for each record sold..
How to Contact: Submit demo tape. Prefers 7½ ips reel-to-reel or cassette with 3-5 songs on demo. SASE. Reports in 2 weeks.
Music: Easy listening; MOR; soul; and top 40/pop. Recently released "Craving," by Giles Crawford (pop single), and "Do the Funk," by Galaxy (R&B single). Other artists include George Guess, Looper, Satins Breed, Dream Merchants, Encounters, and Vee Vee.

ATLANTIC RECORDING CORP., 9229 Sunset Blvd., Los Angeles CA 90069. (213)278-9230. Labels include Atco and Custom Records. Works with artists on contract.
How to Contact: Submit demo tape. Prefers 7½ ips reel-to-reel or cassette with 3-5 songs on demo. SASE. Reports in 2 weeks.
Music: Blues; disco; easy listening; folk; jazz; MOR; progressive; R&B; rock; soul; and top 40/pop.

ATLANTIC RECORDS, 75 Rockefeller Plaza, New York NY 10019. Vice President/A&R Director: Jim Delehant. Needs vary; query about needs and submission policy.

ATTIC RECORDS LTD., 98 Queen St. E., Suite 3, Toronto, Ontario, Canada M5C 1S6. (416)862-0352. Labels include Attic and Basement. President: Al Mair. Record company and music publisher (Attic Publishing Group). Member CARAS, CRIA. Releases 25 singles and 30 albums/year. Works with artists and songwriters on contract. Pays statutory rate to publishers for each record sold.
How to Contact: Call first about your interest or submit demo tape and lyric sheet. Prefers cassette with 3-5 songs on demo. SAE and International Reply Coupons. Reports in 3 weeks.
Music: Blues, MOR, rock and top 40/pop. Recently released *Wasn't That a Party*, by The Rovers (pop LP and single); and *More*, by George Thorogood and The Destroyers (rock LP and single). Other artists include Triumph, Hagood Hardy, Michaele Jordana, Rockerarm, Teenage Head, Hot Tip, Plastic Bertrand, Bobby Fisher, Downchild Blues Band, Dutch Mason, Goddo, and Johnny & The G-Rays.

AUDIO FIDELITY ENTERPRISES INC., 221 W. 57th St., New York NY 10019. (212)757-7111. Labels include Audio Fidelity, Audio Rarities, Personality Series, First Component Classical, Chiaroscuro, Image, Thimble and Karate Records. President: Harold Drayson. Record company. Works with artists on contract. Pays negotiable royalty.
How to Contact: Call first about your interest, then submit demo tape and lyric sheet. Prefers cassette or record as demo. SASE. Reports in 2 weeks.
Music: Classical; dance; easy listening; jazz; MOR; progressive; rock; and top 40/pop. Recently released *Capetown Fringe*, by Dollar Brand (jazz LP); *Fats Waller's Heavenly Jive*, by Ruby Braff and Dick Hyman (jazz LP); and *Hazel Scott "Always"*, by Hazel Scott (jazz LP).

B & C MUSICAL SERVICES, 10 Harmony Dr., Belleville IL 62223. (618)234-2827. Labels include BRIC. Vice President: Chic Carron. Record company and music publisher (Dimba Music). Releases varied amount of singles and albums/year. Works with artists and songwriters on contract. Pays negotiable royalty to artists on contract; statutory rate to publishers for each record sold.
How to Contact: Write first about your interest, then submit demo tape and lyric sheet. Prefers 7½ ips or cassette with 1-6 songs on demo. "Tapes should be clear—no big productions necessary." SASE. Reports in 1 month.
Music: Bluegrass, C&W, easy listening, rock (country rock). Recently released "Words of Wisdom," by Easy Street (country single); and "Mountain of Love," by Easy Street (bluegrass single).

LEN BAILEY PRODUCTIONS, INC., 310 Madison Ave., Room 1225, New York NY 10017. President: Lenny Bailey. Record company, production company, advertising company promotions firm and music publisher (Len Bail Music/BMI). Estab. 1979. Released 1 album and 3 singles in 1981; plans 2 albums and 4 singles in 1982. Labels include Belize International Records. Pays standard royalties to artists and songwriters on contract.
How to Contact: Submit demo tape and lead sheet. Prefers cassette. Reports in 1 month.
Music: Disco; rock; soul; reggae; soca; MOR; jazz; and top 40/pop. Recently released "Do It With Me," by The Lenny Bailey Orchestra (top hit single). New Releases: "Everybody Let's Party," by The Lenny Bailey Orchestra 12" (disco single); "Mr. D.J. Don't Stop the Music"; by The Lenny Bailey Orchestra; "Belize Soca"; by The Lenny Bailey Orchestra and "The Joy of Music Will Always Be Love" by the Lenny Bailey Orchestra.

Songwriter's Market Close-up

In case you don't recognize this fellow without a spangled shirt, it's superstar Barry Manilow hard at work as Barry Manilow—super songwriter.

Dedicated hard work is what Manilow is all about. It has won him a Grammy, the AGVA Award for concert stage, a special Tony Award for Broadway, an Emmy for television and a string of multi-platinum albums.

As a songwriter, he collaborates on most of his songs, usually taking the work of his favorite lyricists into isolation. "They submit lyrics and I sit by myself at the piano, staring at the keys until I bleed. Sometimes I'll send them a melody I've written and ask them to try the lyrics."

The phone is as useful a tool as his piano. "Since I'm on the road for long periods of time a lot of it (collaborating) is done on the phone." Most of the songs on his latest album were written this way. "I knew I had a deadline so I started writing on the road. I'd get a piano wherever I was staying and work on the phone with my collaborator. In the afternoon I'd rehearse the new song with my band and then actually debut it that night to my audience. Every night something would change—the arrangement, the ending, the middle, a key change, lots of lyric changes—and sure enough, the audience would react differently to every change. It's an incredible luxury to work on a song until you know it's right and then be able to record it."

As one who has worked in publishing companies and now owns his own, he tells songwriters: "Be neat in sending your demos. The quality of the demo, of course, should be as good as you can make it, but if the presentation is neat and intelligent, there's a better chance of everybody taking it seriously. When I used to open the mail I would toss things in the garbage if they were sloppy. I may have passed up some great songs, but I doubt it! If the cassettes are

Barry Manilow

labeled, lyrics neatly typewritten and the lead sheet professionally written, your chances of getting listened to are greater."

He also has something to say about what should be on the demo. "Personally, I don't mind hearing just piano and voice. But if you're doing a demo, make it as elaborate as you can and spend as much as you can afford. A lot of people who listen aren't musicians or musically inclined—they're businessmen. The more you can put on the tape to demonstrate how you think the songs should sound, the better it is."

What is the best advice he can give a songwriter? "Don't do it for the money or the fame or applause or ego gratification. Do it because you have to do it! Any other reason just doesn't work. You do it because you have music to get out of your system. That's why I did it. That's why I still do it. It's great to have a couple of swimming pools but that's not the reason I do it—ever!"

BAL RECORDS, Box 369, La Canada CA 91011. (213)790-1242. President: Adrian Bal. Record company, record producer and music publisher (Bal & Bal Music). Releases 1 single/year. Works with artists and songwriters on contract. Pays 10% minimum royalty to artists on contract; statutory rate to publishers for each record sold.

How to Contact: Submit demo tape and lyric sheet. Prefers cassette with 3 songs on demo. SASE. Reports in 1 month.
Music: Blues, church/religious, C&W, easy listening, jazz, MOR, R&B, rock, soul and top 40/pop. Recently released "Los Angeles," by Rich Martin (ballad single); and "Song of the Pasadena Rose Parade," by Jack Heinderich (swing single).

BEARSVILLE RECORDS, Box 135, Bearsville NY 12409. (914)679-7303. Contact: Donald Schmitzerle. Record company and music publisher. Works with artists and songwriters on contract.
How to Contact: Submit demo tape and lyric sheet. Prefers cassette with maximum 2 songs on demo. SASE. Reports as soon as possible.
Music: Rock and top 40/pop. "No disco."

BEAU-JIM RECORDS, INC., 10201 Harwin Dr., Suite 2206, Houston TX 77036. (713)771-6256. President: James E. "Buddy" Hooper. Record company. Management firm, booking agency and music publisher (Beau-Jim Music, Inc./ASCAP and Beau-Di Music, Inc./BMI). Releases 2-3 singles and 1 album/year. Works with artists and songwriters on contract. Receive negotiable commissions.
How to Contact: Query or submit demo tape, bio and picture. Prefers cassette with 3-5 songs on demo. SASE. Reports in approximately 90 days.
Music: Blues; C&W; disco; jazz; MOR; and top 40/pop. Artists recording on Beau-Jim Records include Amanda Arnold, Jan & James, J.B. Carter Band and Joe Neddo.

BEE GEE RECORDS, INC., 3101 S. Western Ave., Los Angeles CA 90018. (213)258-8011. Labels include Birthright Records. General Manager: Leroy C. Lovett. Record company, record producer and music publisher (Chinwah Songs/SESAC, Birthright/ASCAP and House of Talley/BMI). Member RIAA. Releases 6 singles and 15 albums/year. Works with artists on contract. Pays statutory rate to publishers for each record sold.
How to Contact: Submit demo tape and lyric sheet. Prefers cassette with 1-4 songs on demo. SASE. Reports in 3 weeks.
Music: Children's, church/religious, gospel and Spanish. Recently released *Wonderful*, by Edwin Hawkins (gospel LP); *Behold*, by Billy Preston (gospel LP); and *Healing Love*, by King's Herald (religious LP). Other artists include Brenda Holloway, Rodena Preston, Gabriel Hardeman, Biblical Gospel Singers, Del Delker, Jim Teel, Robin Greer, and Stephen Swanson.

BEE HIVE JAZZ RECORDS, 1130 Colfax, Evanston IL 60201. (312)328-5593. Producer: Susan L. Neumann. Record company, music publisher and record producer. Works with musicians on salary; artists and songwriters on contract. Pays 50% royalty to artists on contract; standard royalty to songwriters on contract.
How to Contact: Write or call about your interest, submit demo tape and lyric sheet or arrange personal interview to play demo tape. SASE. Reports in 1 month.
Music: Jazz only. Recently released *Baritone Madness*, by Nick Brignola (jazz LP); *Fire & Filibree*, by Curtis Fuller (jazz LP); and *Neo/Nistico*, by Sal Nistico (jazz LP).

BELIEVE IN A DREAM RECORDS, INC. (B.I.D.), 1420 K St. NW, Suite 400, Washington DC 20005. (202)347-1420. Director of Publishing: Yolanda McFarlane. Record company and music publisher (Band of Angels, Inc. and Heaven's Gate Music). Estab. 1979. Member RIAA. Releases 2 singles and 2 albums/year. Works with artists and songwriters on contract. Pays negotiable royalty to artists on contract; statutory rate to publishers for each record sold.
How to Contact: Submit demo tape and lyric sheet. Prefers cassette with 3-6 songs on demo. "Include name, address and telephone number *on tape*." SASE. Reports in 2 weeks.
Music: Dance-oriented, R&B, soul and top 40/pop. Recently released "Remote Control," by The Reddings (R&B single); *The Awakening*, by The Reddings (R&B LP); and "Groovy Freaks," by the Real Thing (dance-oriented 12" single).

BENT OAK RECORDS, Rt. 2, 246 Oakborough Dr., O'Fallon MO 63366. (314)625-3485. Record company, record producer and music publisher (Bent Oak Music). Estab. 1980. Releases 20 singles and 15 albums/year. Works with artists and songwriters on contract; musicians on salary for in-house studio work.
How to Contact: Write first about your interest. Prefers cassette with 1-10 songs on demo. SASE.
Music: Bluegrass, C&W and rock. Recently released "One Love Wiser, "Car Plant Blues" and "Wounded Lady," by Glen Wagster (C&W singles).

BIG MIKE MUSIC, 408 W. 115th St., New York NY 10025. (212)222-8715. Labels include Right On! and Big Mike Records. Manager: Bill Downs. Record company and music publisher. Releases

5 singles and 3 albums/year. Works with artists and songwriters on contract. Pays standard royalty to artists and songwriters on contract.
How to Contact: Submit demo tape and lead sheet. Prefers cassette with 2-4 songs on demo. SASE. Reports in 1 month.
Music: Soul; rock; and new wave. Recently released "GG the Red Head," recorded by G.G. Turner (rock single) and *No Man like My Man*, by Dolly Gilmore (soul/pop LP). Other artists include Tommie Mundy and Baby Knockers.

BIG SHOE RECORDS, 1011 Fountain Rd., Jacksonville FL 32205. (904)781-4311 President: Bruce Beard. Vice President: Jeff Jenkins. Record company and music publisher. Works with songwriters on contract; "standard royalty of 50/50 in our contract should recordings be obtained for our writers within 6-12 months. We are also interested in hearing masters (45's and albums) in need of pressing or distribution."
How to Contact: Submit demo tape and lyric sheet. Prefers 7½ ips reel-to-reel with 1-4 songs on demo. "We prefer quality polished demos." SASE. Reports in 3 weeks.
Music: C&W; contemporary gospel; rock; novelty; and top 40/pop (new wave). Recently released "Lyin' round This Mudhole" and "Mother Goose Boogie," by Billy Thigpen (country rock single); and "Tree with No Lights," by V.J. Killin (Christmas ballad single).

BIG WHEELS/QUARTER MOON RECORDS, INC., Box 2388, Prescott AZ 86302. (602)445-5801. Contact: Michael D. Morgan. Record company, record producer and music publisher (The Morgan Music Group). Estab. 1979. Member CMA, NARAS. Works with artists and songwriters on contract. Pays 6%-"open" royalty to artists on contract; statutory rate to publishers for each record sold.
How to Contact: Submit demo tape and lyric sheet only. Prefers cassette with 3 songs on demo. SASE. Reports in 1 month.
Music: C&W, rock (country) and pop/country. Recently released *Song of the American Trucker*, by various artists (country LP and singles). Artists include Tim Schumacher, Garry Greer, Judy Pannell, George Gordon and Michael Hollister Morgan.

BIOGRAPH RECORDS, INC., Box 109, Canaan NY 12029. (518)392-3400. Labels include Biograph, Melodeon, Center and Historical Records. President: Arnold S. Caplin. Record company, music publisher and record producer. Works with musicians on salary; artists and songwriters on contract. Pays 4% minimum royalty to artists on contract; standard royalty to songwriters on contract.
How to Contact: Write or call first about your interest. Prefers 7½ ips reel-to-reel with 6 songs minimum on demo. SASE. Reports in 1 month.
Music: Bluegrass; blues; folk; and jazz. Recently released *American Dreamer*, by Oscar Brand and The Secret Band (contemporary/folk); *Tenors, Anyone?*, by Stan Getz, Wardell Gray, Zoot Sims and Paul Quinichette; and *Lullaby of Broadway* (LP). Other artists include Nick Seeger, Dan Smith, Allan Block and New Sunshine Jazz Band.

BIRC RECORDS, 601 E. Blacklidge, Tucson AZ 85705. (602)882-9016. President: Joe Bidwell. Record company and music publisher (Autograph Music/BMI). Works with musicians and songwriters on contract. Releases 10 singles and 4 albums/year. Pays standard royalties to songwriters on contract; statutory rate to publishers for each record sold.
How to Contact: Submit demo tape and lyric sheet. Prefers cassette with 1-3 songs on demo. SASE. Reports in 3 weeks.
Music: C&W; MOR rock; and top 40/pop. Recently released "On the Phone" and "As the Rain Goes" recorded by Stryker (rock single); and "Josie's Her Name" and "Off the Walls" recorded by Turn Duncan Stitt (country single). Other artists include Don Shipley, Dennis Fridkin, Erin Brooks, Kelly Sweeney, Gerry Glombecki, and Blaze.

BLACK BEAR RECORDS, Box 1317, New Liskeard Ontario Canada P0J 1P0. Manager: Rhoda Taylor. Record company, record producer and management firm (For My Lady Music/PROCAN). Member CARAS. Releases 3 albums and 2 singles/year. Works with artists and songwriters on contract. Pays standard royalties to songwriters on contract; statutory rate to publishers for each record sold.
How to Contact: Query or submit demo tape and lead sheet. Prefers 7½ or 15 ips reel-to-reel or cassette with whatever "the tape will hold with leader and separation. Please have the songs clearly titled and related to the lead sheets." SAE and International Reply Coupons. Reports in 4 weeks.
Music: Easy listening; gospel; MOR; rock; and top 40/pop. Recently released *The Pair Extrordinaire*, by the Pair (rock LP); *Solid Rock*, by the Gospel Sounds (gospel LP); *Together Again*, by the Lincolns (rock LP); *Songs of Praise*, by Ray Fillmore (gospel LP); *Tunes from the Irish Walking*

Cane Fiddle, by Cye Steel (country LP); and "Bright Eyes" b/w "Bitter Blue," by Joe Wood (single). Other artists include Peter D'Amico.
Tips: "Submit material often and geared to the market we are reaching. We need good demo tapes that can be presented to other artists or production companies."

BLACKLAND MUSIC CO, Box 7349, Tulsa OK 74105. (918)743-7500. President: James Garland. Record company and music publisher. Releases 4 singles and 2 albums/year. Works with musicians on salary; artists and songwriters on contract. Pays 5¢/record to artists on contract.
How to Contact: Submit demo tape and lead sheet. Prefers 7½ ips reel-to-reel. SASE. Reports in 1 month.
Music: Gospel; MOR; rock (country); and top 40/pop. Recently released "Blue Skies and Roses," "I Wanna Love You" and *Karon—Live* by Karon Blackwell.

EUBIE BLAKE MUSIC, 284-A Stuyvesant Ave., Brooklyn NY 11221. Labels include E.B.M. Records. President: Carl Seltzer. Record company. Works with artists on contract. Pays 5% royalty to artists on contract.
How to Contact: Submit demo tape. Prefers cassette with 2-4 songs on demo. SASE. Reports in 3 weeks.
Music: Blues; jazz; and ragtime. Recently released *John Arpin* by John Arpin (piano solo LP).

BLUE ISLAND RECORDS, 1446 N. Martel, Unit 3, Los Angeles CA 90046. (213)851-3161. Label includes BOB. Contact: Bob Gilbert. Record company, record producer and music publisher (Blue Island Publishing). Estab. 1980. Releases 5 singles/year. Works with artists and songwriters on contract. Pays 12% royalty to artists on contract; statutory rate to publishers for each record sold.
How to Contact: Submit demo tape and lyric sheet. Prefers cassette with 3-6 songs on demo. SASE. Reports in 3 weeks.
Music: C&W, MOR, rock and top 40/pop.
Tips: "I review *every* song presented. So many in this industry only listen to selected songs per tape. I listen to all songs because you never can tell who will present the next hit song."

BLUE RIVER RECORDS, 1741 N. Ivar, Suite 210, Hollywood CA 90028. (213)463-7661. Labels include Musi-Que, Musi-Que Contemporary and Solo Plus Records. President: Harry Bluestone. Pays standard royalty.
How to Contact: Submit demo tape and lyric sheet. Prefers cassette with 1-4 songs on demo. SASE. Reports in 1 week.
Music: Bluegrass; blues; classical; easy listening; gospel; jazz; MOR; R&B; rock; and top 40/pop. Recently released *Artistry in Jazz*, by Harry Bluestone (jazz LP).

BLUE SKY RECORDS, 745 5th Ave., New York NY 10022. (212)751-3400. Record company. Works with musicians on contract.
How to Contact: Prefers cassette with 3 songs maximum on demo.
Music: Blues; R&B; rock and top 40/pop.

BOOT RECORDS, LTD., 1343 Matheson Blvd. W., Mississauga, Ontario, Canada L4W 1R1. (416)625-2676. Labels include Boot, Cynda, Generation, Boot Master Concert Series and Boot International Records. General Manager: Peter Krytiuk. President: Jury Krytiuk. Record company and music publisher (Morning Music Ltd./CAPAC). Releases 50 singles and 40 albums/year. Works with musicians on contract. Pays statutory rate to publishers for each record sold. "We operate on a lease basis with the artist paying the cost of the session."
How to Contact: Submit demo tape. Prefers 7½ or 15 ips reel-to-reel or cassette with 3-6 songs on demo. "Prefers some originals and some standards." SASE. Reports in 1 week.
Music: Bluegrass; classical; C&W; dance, easy listening; folk; MOR; rock; and top 40/pop. Recently released *Miniatures for Guitar*, by Liona Boyd (classical LP); *Old Times Good Times*, by the Emeralds (easy listening LP); and *To Behold Jah*, by Ernie Smith (reggae LP).

BOUQUET RECORDS, Bouquet-Orchid Enterprises, Box 4220, Shreveport LA 71104. (318)686-7362. President: Bill Bohannon. Record company and music publisher. Releases 3-4 singles and 2 albums/year. Works with artists and songwriters on contract. Pays 5% royalty to artists on contract.
How to Contact: Submit demo tape and lead sheet. Prefers 7½ ips reel-to-reel or cassette with 3-5 songs on demo. SASE. Reports in 1 month.
Music: Church/religious (prefers country gospel); C&W (the type suitable for Loretta Lynn, Dolly Parton, Linda Ronstadt, etc.); and top 40/pop (the type suitable for John Denver, the Bee Gees, etc.).

BOYCE & POWERS MUSIC, 12015 Sherman Rd., North Hollywood CA 91605. (213)875-1711. President: Melvin Powers. Record company and music publisher. Releases 12 singles/year. Works with songwriters on contract.
How to Contact: Submit demo tape and lyric sheet. Prefers cassette or disc with 3 songs minimum on demo. SASE. Reports in 1 month.
Music: C&W and MOR. Recently released "Who Wants a Slightly Used Woman?", by Connie Cato (country single); "Mr. Songwriter," by Sunday Sharpe (country single); and "Willie Burgundy," by Teresa Brewer (MOR single).

BOYD RECORDS, 2609 NW 36th St., Oklahoma City OK 73112. (405)942-0462. President: Bobby Boyd. Record company and music publisher. Releases 12 singles and 4 albums/year. Works with artists and songwriters on contract. Payment negotiable royalty to artists on contract; statutory rate to publishers for each record sold.
How to Contact: Submit demo tape and lyric sheet. Prefers 7½ ips reel-to-reel with 3-12 songs on demo. "Do not send anything that has to be returned." Reports in 2 weeks "if we like it."
Music: C&W; R&B; soul; and top 40/pop. Recently released "Say You Love Me (One More Time)," by Dale Ward (C&W single); "There's No Way to Measure Love," by Dale Greear (C&W single); "Snap Your Fingers," by Debbie Smith (top 40 single); "One Teardrop at a Time," by Tina Camarillo (pop/C&W single); "Flip the Switch," by Cherie Greear; "Legends Never Die," by Jim Whitaker (pop single); and "We Miss You Red Souvine," by Marvin Ray (country LP and single). Other artists include Faye Haley and Bobby Barnett.

BRANCH INTERNATIONAL RECORDS, Box 31819, Dallas TX 75231. (214)690-4155. A&R: Mike Anthony. Record company. Works with artists and songwriters on contract. Pays 6-8% royalty to artists on contract; standard royalty to songwriters on contract.
How to Contact: Submit demo tape and lyric sheet. Prefers cassette with 3-5 songs on demo. SASE. Reports in approximately 1 month.
Music: C&W; and gospel. Recently released *Candy Noe*, by Candy Noe (C&W LP); *Baby, Baby* and *It Don't Take Much*, by Candy Noe (C&W on LP); and "I Love You," by Candy Noe (C&W single). Other artists include George Brazzel, Digger Wyatt and Jack Wyatt.

BREAD 'N HONEY RECORDS, Box 3391, Ventura CA 93003. (805)644-7618. Contact: Mark Craig. Record company, record producer and music publisher (Bread 'N Honey/ASCAP). Releases 5-6 albums/year. Member GMA. Pays statutory rate to publishers for each record sold.
How to Contact: Submit demo tape and lyric sheet. Prefers cassette as demo. SASE. Reports in 3 weeks.
Music: Gospel. Recently released *Hymns for Classic Guitars*, by Rick Foster (gospel LP); *More Hymns for Classic Guitars*, by R. Foster (gospel LP); and *Kathie Sullivan*, by Kathie Sullivan (gospel LP).

BRIARMEADE RECORDS, Box 110830, Nashville TN 37211. Labels include Burlap, Keeta, Keene and Sonor Records. President: Ken Keene. Vice President: Frankie Ford. Record company, music publisher (Briarmeade Music/ASCAP and Keeta Music/BMI) and record producer. Member CMA and NSAI. Releases 10 singles and 3 albums/year. Works with artists and songwriters on contract. Pays 5-7% royalty to artists on contract; standard royalty to songwriters on contract.
How to Contact: Submit demo tape and lyric sheet. Prefers 7½ ips 5" or 7" reel-to-reel or cassette with 2-5 songs on demo. "If artist or group has record LP available, it can be submitted, disregarding 5 song maximum. Artist/group should also send complete promo package with photos, biography, records/tapes and references." SASE. Reports in 1 month.
Music: Blues; children's; church/religious; C&W; disco; easy listening; gospel; MOR; R&B; country rock; soul; and top 40/pop. Recently released "Country Goose," by Johnny Pennino (sax international single); "Desperado," by Frankie Ford (pop vocal single); "Twelfth of Never," by Narvel Felts (country single). Other artists include Denny Barberio, The Briarmeade Singers, Marilyn Strothcamp, Larry Swift, Tom Pallardy, Phil EnLoe, Majik Dust and Matt Lucas.

BRUNSWICK RECORD CORPORATION, 888 7th Ave., New York NY 10019. (212)541-9860. A&R Director: Ray Daniels. Record company (Lena Music/BMI). Releases 12 singles and 8 albums/year. Works with musicians on contract.
How to Contact: Submit demo tape and lyric sheet. Prefers 7½ ips reel-to-reel or cassette with 3 songs maximum on demo. SASE. Reports in 3 weeks.
Music: Disco; R&B; rock; soul and top 40/pop. Recently released *Bounce, Rock, Skates, Roll* by Vaughn and Mason, (R&B LP); and *I Like What You're Doing to Me*, by Young and Co. (disco LP). Other artists include Elite, Persuaders, Dave Love, Pure Natural, First Love, Jerry Warren, and Masheen Company.

BSO RECORDS, INC., 2995 Carrell Ln., Willow Grove PA 19090. (215)443-0935. President: Sal Barbieri. Record company and music publisher (Conypol Music/BMI). Estab. 1980. Releases 8 singles and 10 albums/year. Works with songwriters on contract; musicians on salary for in-house studio work. Pays standard royalty to artists on contract; statutory rate to publishers for each record sold.
How to Contact: Submit demo tape and lyric sheet. Prefers 7½ ips reel-to-reel or cassette with 1-4 songs on demo. "Use a straight rhythm track; keep lyrics clear and voice up." SASE. Reports in 1 month.
Music: C&W, dance-oriented, easy listening, MOR, Progressive, R&B, soft rock, soul, top 40/pop. Recently released *Feeling Good*, by SB & the R.C. (LP and single).

BULLDOG RECORDS, (formerly Ember Records, Inc.) 50 E. 42nd St., Suite 401, New York NY 10017. (212)687-4516. Labels include Ember and Bulldog Records. Head of A&R: Howard Kruger. President: J.S. Kruger. Record company. Works with artists and songwriters on contract. Pays 5-8% royalty to artists on contract; standard royalty to songwriters on contract.
How to Contact: Submit demo tape and lead sheet. Prefers cassette with 2-6 songs on demo. SASE. Reports in 1 month.
Music: Dance; soul; and top 40/pop. Recently released "Fabulous Babe," by Kenny Williams (European pop single); and "I Don't Want to Put a Hold on You," by Berni Flint (United Kingdom pop single).
Tips: "We operate more in Europe than in the US, so allow time for material to flow overseas."

BUSCH COUNTRY RECORDS, 1002 W. Busch Blvd., Tampa FL 33612. (813)935-6289. Contact: Randall Bethencourt. Record company and music publisher (Busch Country Publishing and Rhythm and Rhyme Music). Member RIAA. Releases 3-5 singles and 1-2 albums/year. Works with songwriters on contract; musicians on salary for in-house studio work. Pays 3-10% royalty to artists on contract; statutory rate to publishers for each record sold.
How to Contact: Submit demo tape and lyric sheet. Prefers reel-to-reel or cassette with 3-5 songs on demo. SASE. Reports in 6 weeks.
Music: C&W. Artists include Randy Wade, Bobby Hess and Amanda Lynn.

BUTTERMILK RECORDS & MOBILE STUDIO, 1310 Tulane, Houston TX 77008. (713)864-0705. President: Charles Bickley. Record company, record producer and music publisher (Sea Three Music). Member MSMA and AFofM. Releases 12 singles and 10 albums/year. Works with artists and songwriters on contract; musicians on salary for in-house studio work. Pays 3% royalty to artists on contract; statutory rate to publishers for each record sold.
How to Contact: Submit demo tape and lyric sheet, call first about your interest or arrange personal interview. Prefers cassette with 1-4 songs on demo. SASE. Reports in 3 weeks.
Music: Bluegrass, blues, church/religious, C&W, dance-oriented, easy listening, folk, gospel, jazz, MOR, progressive, Spanish, R&B, rock, soul, and top 40/pop. Recently released *In Texas Last December*, by Richard Dobson (country LP); "Krayolas-Cry, Cry, Laugh, Laugh", by Krayolas (rock single); and "Baby Ride Easy", by Carlene Carter (country rock LP and single released on Warner Bothers Records). Other artists include The Disease, Kenny Bobo, Nat Atterly, Link Davis Jr., Eddie Money, Fat Cat, John Bell, and Bruce McElhenry.

CALIFORNIA INTERNATIONAL RECORDS & VIDEO WORKS, INC., Box 2818, Newport Beach CA 92663. (714)497-3758. President: Joseph Nicoletti. Vice President: Cheryl Lee Gammon. Record company, music publisher and record producer. Works with musicians on salary; artists and songwriters on contract. Pays 5% royalty to artists on contract; 2¾¢/record royalty to songwriters on contract.
How to Contact: Submit demo tape and lead sheet. Prefers cassette with 1-3 songs on demo. SASE. Reports in 1 month.
Music: Dance; easy listening; MOR; rock; soul; and top 40/pop. Recently released "Street-Wise," by Joseph Nicoletti (rock/wave single and LP) and "Now I Can Touch You," by Joseph and Cheryl (pop/country single).

CAMBRIA RECORD CO., Box 2163, Rancho Palos Verdes CA 90274. (213)541-1114. Director of Recording Operations: Earl Kaplan. Record company and music publisher (Cambria Publishing/ASCAP). Estab. 1979. Member NAIRD. Releases 3 albums/year. Works with songwriters on contract. Pays statutory rate to publishers for each record sold.
How to Contact: Write first about your interest. Prefers 7½ ips reel-to-reel or cassette. SASE. Reports in 1 month.
Music: Classical and jazz (classical). Recently released *Piano Music of Dring* and *Dring Dances*, by Leigh Kaplan (classical LPs). Other artists include Louise DiTullio.

Tips: "We are particularly interested in contemporary classical music by American composers, works by women composers, which is, in our opinion aurally coherent."

CANDY RECORDS, 2716 Springlake Ct., Irving Tx 75060. (214)259-4032. Labels include Sweet Tooth, Lil' Possum and Holli Records. General Manager: Kenny Wayne Hagler. Record company, record producer and music publisher (Sweet Tooth Music). Releases approximately 4 singles and 2 albums/year. Works with artists on contract. Pays 5% royalty to artists on contract; statutory rate to publishers for each record sold.
How to Contact: Submit demo tape and lyric sheet. Prefers 7½ ips reel-to-reel or cassette with 3-4 songs on demo. "Send only quality material." SASE. Reports in 1 month.
Music: Blues, C&W, rock, soul, top 40/pop. Recently released "Green Eyes", by Reign (country rock single); and *In Mothion*, by Kenny Wayne & The Komotions (top 40 LP). Others artists include Carter Holcomb.

CAPITOL RECORDS, 1370 Avenue of the Americas, New York NY 10019. (212)757-7470. A&R Director, East Coast: Mitchell Schoenbaum. Record company and music publisher (Screen Gems).
How to Contact: Submit demo tape and lyric sheet. Prefers cassette with 4 songs on demo. SASE. Reports in 3 weeks.
Music: All types.

CAPITOL RECORDS, INC., 1750 N. Vine St., Hollywood CA 90028. (213)462-6252. Contact: Bruce Garfly. Record company. Releases 170 singles/year. Works with artists.
How to Contact. Submit demo tape. Prefers cassettes with 4 songs on demo. "Have an agent, manager or publisher submit material for you and submit the best-quality demo you can afford." SASE.
Music: Progressive rock, rock, new wave. Recently released *The Tubes* and *Billy Squier* LPs (rock and roll albums).

CAPITOL RECORDS INC., 29 Music Sq. E, Nashville TN 37203. (615)244-7770. No A&R Department in Nashville. Los Angeles office handles all submissions.

CAPRICORN RECORDS, 561 Cotton Ave., Macon GA 31201. (912)745-8511. Contact: A&R Director. Record company. Releases 12 singles and 6 albums/year. Works with artists and songwriters on contract. Pays negotiable royalty to artists on contract; negotiable rate to publishers for each record sold.
How to Contact: Submit demo tape and lyric sheet with SASE. Prefers cassette with 1-20 songs on demo. "Unsolicited material will be returned only if accompanied by SASE." Reports in 1 month.
Music: Rock 'n' roll, R&B, and C&W.

CAPSTAN RECORD PRODUCTION, Box 211, East Prairie MO 63845. (314)649-2211. Contact: Archie Corlew. Record company, music publisher and record producer. Works with artists on contract. Pays 3-5% royalty to artists on contract.
How to Contact: Write first about your interest, then submit demo tape and lyric sheet. Prefers 7½ ips reel-to-reel or cassette with 2-4 songs on demo. SASE. Reports in 1 month.
Music: C&W; easy listening; MOR; country rock; and top 40/pop. Recently released "Dry Away the Pain," by Julia Brown (easy listening single); and "Country Boy," by Alden Lambert (country single). Other artists include Shuri Castle and the Burchettes.

CARIB RECORDS, 303 W. 42nd St., Suite 1000, Brooklyn NY 11226. (212)581-3766. A&R Vice President: A. Baly. Record company (BMI). Works with artists and songwriters on contract. Releases 3 singles and 4 albums/year. Payment is negotiable.
How to Contact: Call first about your interest, then submit demo tape and lyric sheet. Prefers cassette with 2-4 songs on demo. SASE. Reports in 3 weeks.
Music: Church/religious; classical; disco; easy listening; gospel; jazz; R&B; soul; and top 40/pop. Recently released "Get Down Annie," by John T & His Group (disco single); and "Sexy Mama," by Anthony Bridgeman (ballad single).

CAROUSEL RECORDS, INC., 1273½ N. Crescent Hts. Blvd., Los Angeles CA 90046. (213)550-4500. A&R: Stuart Lanis. Record company, music publisher and record producer. Works with musicians on contract.
How to Contact: Submit demo tape and lyric sheet. Prefers cassette with 3-6 songs on demo. SASE. Reports in 3 weeks.
Music: Children's; church/religious; classical; easy listening; gospel; MOR; and top 40/pop.

CARRIE RECORDS CO., Box 90639, 902-42nd Ave., N., Nashville TN 37209. (615)297-4174. Labels include Ricare and Lanrod Records). President: James Hendrix. Record company and music publisher (Grawick Music). Releases 8 singles and 4 albums/year. Works with songwriters on contract. Pays 2-4% royalty to artists on contract; statutory rate to publishers for each record sold.
How to Contact: Submit demo tape and lyric sheet. Prefers cassette with 3-4 songs on demo. SASE. Reports in 1 month.
Music: Church/religious, gospel, R&B, and top 40/pop. Recently released "Love Sweet Love," by Bettye Shelton (gospel single); "The Jam," by Spice (R&B single); and "Who Knows," by Cornell Blakely (R&B single). Other artists include Cornelius Grant, Ellison Family, Michael Hunter and P-Wee & The Psalmsters.

CASA GRANDE RECORDS, Box 113, Woburn MA 01801. (617)933-1474. Labels include Don-Mar Records and Strawhut Records. Manager: Frank Paul. Record company, record producer and music publisher (Donna Music Publishing Company and Antone Music Publishers). Amount of releases/year varies. Works with artists and songwriters on contract. Pays 3% minimum royalty to artists on contract.
How to Contact: Submit tape and lyric sheet. Prefers cassette with 3-6 songs on demo. SASE. Reports as soon as possible.
Music: Children's, C&W, easy listening, folk, gospel, MOR, Spanish, R&B, rock, soul and top 40/pop. Recently released *Happy Birthday Baby*, by TuneWeavers (R&B LP and single).

CASTALIA RECORDS/A MAJOR LABEL, Box 11516, Milwaukee WI 53211. Labels include Fair Wind Records and Balloon Records. President: Jim Spencer. Record company, record producer, and music publisher (Castalia Music/BMI). Releases 2 singles and 2-6 albums/year. Works with artists and songwriters on contract; musicians on salary for in-house studio work. Pays statutory rate to publishers for each record sold.
How to Contact: Submit demo tape and lyric sheet or write first about your interest. Prefers cassette with 1-6 songs on demo. SASE. Reports in 1 month.
Music: All types. *The Most Beautiful Song in the Forest*, by Jim Spencer (children's LP); *Gentle Friends*, by Eileen Carr (country/pop/MOR LP); and *Anonymous*, by Anonymous (progressive rock LP). Other artists include Carol Prosser and Pat MacDonald.

CASTLE RECORDS, Box 1385, Merchantville NJ 08109. (600)663-4540. Labels include Pyramid Records, Jade Records, Rock Island Records and Camden Soul Records. Executive Vice President: R.F. Russon. Record company, music publisher, record producer, management firm and booking agency. Releases 10 singles and 4 albums/year. Works with musicians and songwriters on contract. Pays 4-6% royalty to artists on contract; statutory royalties to songwriters on contract.
How to Contact: Query or submit demo tape and lead sheet. Prefers 7½ ips reel-to-reel or cassette with 2-12 songs on demo. SASE. Reports in 1 month.
Music: C&W; disco; easy listening; jazz; MOR; rock; soul; and top 40/pop. Recently released "Alabama Girl," by Big El (country rock single); Big El in Concert, by Big El and TCB Band (rock LP); and "I'm Not Destined to Become a Loser," by Ellingtons (disco single).

CBS RECORDS, INC., 1801 Century Park W., Los Angeles CA 90067. (213)556-4700. Labels include Columbia, EPA, Epic, Portrait and Associated Labels. Contact: A&R Department. Record company. Works with artists and songwriters on contract.
How to Contact: Submit demo tape and lead sheet. Prefers cassette with 1-3 songs on demo. SASE. Reports in 1 month.
Music: Blues; dance; easy listening; folk; jazz; MOR; progressive; R&B; rock; soul; and top 40/pop. "Our Nashville office handles C&W songs." Recently released *52nd Street*, by Billy Joel (LP); *Greatest Hits Vol. II*, by Barbra Streisand (LP); and *Greatest Hits*, by Earth, Wind and Fire (LP).
Tips: "Piano with vocal is totally sufficient. The simpler the better."

CELESTIAL RECORDS RELEASING CORP., 1560 N. La Brea, Box 1563, Hollywood CA 90028. Labels include Creative Records. President: Art Benson. General Manager/A&R Director: Dalton Priddy. Record company, music publisher, record producer and management firm. Releases 25 singles and 6 albums/year. Works with artists and songwriters on contract; musicians on salary. Pays 3-7% royalty to artists on contract; standard royalties to songwriters on contract.
How to Contact: Query or submit demo tape and lead sheet. "If singer, also submit picture of self or group." Prefers reel-to-reel or cassette with 1-3 songs on demo. SASE. Reports in 1 month.
Music: Bluegrass; blues; C&W; disco; easy listening; gospel; jazz; and MOR. Recently released

"Love Exchange," by Sonny Craver (R&B single); "I'll Sing the Blues," by Tommy Cooper (C&W single); *Country Dreaming*, by Cooper (C&W LP); and *20th Century Oz*, (movie score LP).

CENTURIAN RECORDS, INC. & ASSOCIATED LABELS, Box 5747, Cleveland OH 44101. (216)771-0501. Labels include Cleveland Unlimited, American Gramophone, Centurian and Capital City Records. Executive Administrator, Record Group: Gregory A. Beasley. Record company and record producer. Works with artists on contract. Payment negotiable.
How to Contact: Submit demo tape and lyric sheet. Prefers cassette or LP with 3 songs minimum. "Enclose press releases, photos and other pertinent information, i.e., management, agency affiliations." SASE. Reports in 1 week.
Music: Funk; dance; jazz; MOR; R&B; hard rock; soul; and top 40/pop. Recently released *Space V*, by Strange (rock LP); *Cold-Blooded*, by Iceberg (R&B LP); and *Eternity*, by Eternity (jazz LP). Other artists include Jay Harmon.
Tips: "We listen to everything submitted at weekly A&R sessions and will attend artist showcases by invitation."

CHA-CHA RECORDS, 15041 Wabash Ave., S. Holland IL 60473. (312)339-0307. Labels include Cha-Cha (rock) and Cap (C&W). President: Donald L. De Lucia. Record company, record producer, and music publisher (Don-Del Music/BMI and Don-De/ASCAP). Releases 2 singles and 2 albums/year. Works with artists on contract. Pays 3¢/record to artists on contract; statutory rate to publishers for each record sold.
How to Contact: Submit demo tape and lyric sheet. Prefers 7½ ips reel-to-reel with 4-6 songs on demo. SASE. Reports in 1 week.
Music: C&W, rock, and top 40/pop. Recently released *99 Chicks*, by Ron Haydock and the Boppers (rock LP). Other artists include Don Glasser and Lois Castello.

CHAPMAN RECORDS, 228 W. 5th St., Kansas City MO 64105. (816)842-6854. Owner: Chuck Chapman. Record company and music publisher. Releases 6-15 singles and 3-5 albums/year. Works with artists on contract. Pays negotiable royalty. Charges for some services: "We charge for recording services for music that we don't publish."
How to Contact: Submit demo tape. Prefers cassette with 3 songs minimum on tape. SASE. Reports in 1 month.
Music: Bluegrass; choral; church/religious; classical; C&W; dance; easy listening; folk; gospel; jazz; MOR; progressive; rock; soul; and top 40/pop. Recently released "Somewhere Down in Texas," by Norton Canfield (country single); *Telephone to Glory*, by Frank Frazier (gospel LP); *Western Electric*, by Pott Country Band (country LP); "Standard Question, by Phil Neal and "Horsehot and Gun Powder," by Bob Reeder..

CHARADE RECORDS, 1310 E. Kern St., Tulare CA 93274. (209)686-2533. Labels include Tadarab Records. President: Raymond A. Baradat. Record company and music publisher (Baradat Music). Releases 3 singles and 3 album/year. Works with musicians on salary; artists and songwriters on contract. Pays 4-6% royalty to artists on contract; statutory rate to publishers for each record sold.
How to Contact: Submit demo tape and lyric sheet. Prefers 7½ ips reel-to-reel or cassette with 1-4 songs on demo. SASE. Reports in 1 month.
Music: C&W; dance; jazz; rock (soft); soul; and top 40/pop. Recently released *The Very Thought of You*, by Charades (MOR single and LP); *The Power of Love*, by Justus (rock/country LP); and *Nothing at All*, by Wing Brothers (country LP). Other artists include Bob Dennison, Gene Short, and Randie Coulter.

CHARTA RECORDS, 44 Music Square E., Nashville TN 37203. (615)255-2175. Labels include Sun-Rize Records. President: Charles Fields. Record company, music publisher and record producer (Mr. Mort Music/ASCAP, Jason Dee Music/BMI). Member BMI. Releases 30 singles and 6 albums/year. Works with artists and songwriters on contract; musicians on salary. Pays 4-7% royalty to artists on contract; standard royalties to songwriters on contract.
How to Contact: Submit demo tape and lead sheet. Prefers 7½ ips reel-to-reel or cassette with 1-4 songs on demo. SASE. Reports in 2 weeks.
Music: Blues; C&W; easy listening; MOR; and top 40/pop. Recently released "Sunshine Girl," by Jess Garron (MOR single); "Nobody's Ever Gonna Love You Better," by Sam Hall (MOR single); and *Rock Me in Your Arms*, by Frankie Sanchez (MOR LP/single). Other artists include Jessey Higdon, Eddie Rivers, and Bobby Wayne Loftis.

CHRISTY RECORDS, 726 Carlson Dr., Orlando FL 32804. (305)644-3853. Labels include Decade Records and Green Leaf Records. President: Will Campbell. Record company and music publisher (Palamar Music Publishers/BMI). Releases 5 singles and 2-5 albums/year. Works with artists and songwriters on contract.

How to Contact: Submit demo tape or submit demo tape and lead sheet. Prefers 7½ ips reel-to-reel with 3-6 songs on demo. SASE. Reports in 1 week.

Music: Bluegrass; church/religious; C&W; gospel; and MOR. Recently released "Don't I Know You?", by Don Rader (country single); "Homespun Mem'ries," by Nelson Young (bluegrass single); and "I Get Lonely," by Larada Collins (MOR single).

CHRYSALIS RECORDS, INC., 9255 Sunset Blvd., Los Angeles CA 90069. (213)550-0171. A&R Manager: Thom Trumbo. Record company and music publisher. Member NARAS. Releases 10 singles and 25 albums/year. Works with musicians on salary; artists and songwriters on contract. Pays negotiable royalty to artists on contract; standard royalty to songwriters on contract.

How to Contact: Call before submitting demo tape. Prefers 7½ ips reel-to-reel or cassette with 3-4 songs on demo. Include photo and bio. SASE.

Music: Rock (general); and top 40/pop. Recently released *AutoAmerican*, by Blondie (pop LP/single); and *Crimes of Passion*, by Pat Benatar (rock LP). Other artists include Charlie Dore, Rory Gallagher, Ian Hunter, Billy Idol, Jethro Tull, Leo Kottke, Huey Lewis, Linx, The Specials, Stiff Little Fingers, Robin Trower, UFO, and Ultravox.

THE CHU YEKO MUSICAL FOUNDATION, Box 1314, Englewood Cliffs NJ 07632. (201)224-5811. Messages: (201)567-5524. Labels include The Chu Yeko Musical Foundation, Take Home Tunes! Record Co., and Broadway Baby Records. Producer: Doris Chu Yeko. (Broadway/Hollywood International Music Publishers). Estab. 1979. Releases 5-10 album/year. Works with songwriters on contract. Pays 1-10% royalty to artists on contract; statutory rate to publishers for each record sold.

How to Contact: Submit demo tape and lyric sheet. Prefers cassette with any number of songs on demo. SASE. Reports in 1 month.

Music: All types. Recently released *Ka-Boom!*, by the original cast (musical LP); and *Fly with Me*, by the original cast (musical LP).

CLAY PIGEON RECORDS, Box 20346, Chicago IL 60620. (312)476-2533. Labels include Clay Pigeon International and Patefonas Records. President: V. Beleska. A&R Director: Rudy Markus. Record company. Releases 3-5 singles and 2-5 albums/year. Works with musicians on salary; artists and songwriters on contract. "Royalties on records start at 2% of retail. All acts with us negotiate individually. Four percent is common. Royalties paid to publishers are often at 2¢ per selection, per record sold."

How to Contact: "Inquire by mail first, describing yourself and your material. We cannot consider any material without a written query." Prefers 7½ ips reel-to-reel, cassette or disc with 1-5 songs on demo. SASE. Reports in 2-8 weeks.

Music: Avant-garde; MOR; progressive; rock; and top 40/pop. Recently released "Tribe of Dolls,;; by Vyto B (modern rock single); "Band That Never Made It," by Bena Neva Mada (modern rock single); and "I'm Sure Now," by Seetz Executive (MOR ballad).

CLEAR GOSPEL RECORDS, R.1, Box 224, Sewell NJ 08080. (609)728-3880. General Manager/Producer: Ron Butko. Record company and record producer. Estab. 1979. Releases 2-10 singles and 7 albums/year. Works with artists and songwriters on contract; musicians on salary for in-house studio work. Pays standard royalty to artists on contract; statutory rate to publishers for each record sold.

How to Contact: Submit demo tape and lyric sheet. Prefers 7½ or 15 ips reel-to-reel or cassette with 1-5 songs on demo. "We are only interested in gospel, traditional or contemporary." SASE. Reports in 3 weeks.

Music: Church/religious and gospel (contemporary and traditional).

CLEARINGHOUSE RECORDS CORP., 110 W. 34th St., Suite 806, New York NY 10001. (212)265-6420. Labels include MRI Records. President: Andy Hussakowsky. Director: A&R: Gene O'Brien. Record company and music publisher. Estab. 1979. Releases 10 singles and 4-6 albums/year. Works with musicians and songwriters on contract. Pays 5% royalty to artists on contract; standard royalties to songwriters on contract. "We are interested in distribution of finished masters for US and foreign releases."

How to Contact: Arrange personal interview or submit demo tape and lead sheet. Prefers 7½ ips reel-to-reel with 1-10 songs on demo. SASE. Reports in 1 month.

Music: Dance; rock; top 40/pop; and R&B. Recently released "More, More, More," and "New York You Got Me Dancing" by Andrea True Connection; and "Sharing the Night Together," by Dr. Hook.

CLUB OF SPADE RECORDS, Box 1995, Studio City CA 91604. (213)656-0574. Owner: Harvey Appell. Record company and music publisher (Udder Publishing/BMI). Releases 6-15 albums/year. Works with musicians on salary; artists and songwriters on contract.
How to Contact: Submit demo tape, arrange personal interview, or submit demo tape and lead sheet. Prefers 15 ips reel-to-reel or cassette with 10-20 songs on demo. SASE. Reports in 3 weeks.
Music: Bluegrass; western swing; C&W; and folk. Recently released *Love Gone Cold*, by Rex Allen (country LP); *Country Guitar*, by Phil Baugh (country LP); and *String Band Swing*, by Light Crust Doughboys (country LP).

COAST TO COAST RECORDS, 425 E. 58th St., Suite 35A, New York NY 10022. (212)751-7078. A&R Director: Nancy Ruens. Record company and music publisher. Works with musicians on contract and songwriters on salary.
How to Contact: Submit demo tape and lyric sheet. Prefers cassette with 2-3 songs on demo. Does not return unsolicited material. Reports in 2 weeks.
Music: Disco; MOR and R&B. Artists include Duke Jupiter and Kelly Marie.

COLONIAL RECORDS, Box 8545, 3012 N. Main St., Houston TX 77009. (713)225-0450. Labels include Volunteer. President: Howard A. Knight Jr. Record company, music publisher and record producer. Estab. 1978. Works with musicians and songwriters on contract. Pays standard royalty for songwriters on contract.
How to Contact: Submit demo tape and lyric sheet. Prefers 7½ ips reel-to-reel with 5 songs maximum on demo. SASE. Reports in 2 weeks.
Music: Church/religious; C&W; gospel; MOR; country rock; and top 40/pop. Recently released "First Day of Never," by David Heavener (country/MOR single); "Evil, Evil Woman," by Rubel (country single); and "The Moonman," by Benjamin (pop single). Other artists include Bill Henry, Mark Alan, Kenny Post, Jimmy Nickels, Don Kelly, Linda Calhoun and John C. Calhoun.

COMMON CAUSE RECORDS, 880 NE. 71st, Miami FL 33138. (305)759-1405. Labels include Common Cause Records. President: Carlos Oliva. Record company, record producer and music publisher (Funk Box Music/BMI and Oliva Music/SESAC). Estab. 1979. Member NARM. Releases 10 singles and 10 albums/year. Works with artists on contract. Pays 10-15% royalty to artists on contract; statutory rate to publishers for each record sold.
How to Contact: Submit demo tape and lyric sheet. Prefers cassette as demo. SASE. Reports in 3 weeks.
Music: Dance-oriented, MOR, Spanish and rock. Recently recorded *Hay Carino*, by Clouds (salsa rock LP and single); "Babe", by Babe (disco single); *Hernan*, by H. Gutierrez; and *Hermanos*, by The Judge's Nephews (Spanish dance-oriented LP). Other artists include Salsa Express, Pedro Tamayo, Hernan Gutierrez & Orchestra, Charanga Sanchez and Oscar & Peter.

COMMUNICATION RECORDS, 7212 S. Wabash Ave., Chicago IL 60619. (312)783-3186. A&R Director: B.L. Dixon. Record company and music publisher. Releases 2-3 singles and 1 album/year. Works with musicians on salary and contract; songwriters on contract. Pays union scale to artists on contract.
How to Contact: Submit demo tape, or submit demo tape and lead or lyric sheet. Prefers 1-4 songs on demo.

COMPO RECORD AND PUBLISHING CO., Box 15222, Oklahoma City OK 73115. (405)677-6448. Branch office: 38 Music Square E., Suite 219, Nashville TN 37203. President: Yvonne De Vaney. General Manager: Sonny Lane. Record company and music publisher. Releases 4 singles and 1-2 albums/year. Works with artists and songwriters on contract. Pays standard royalty to artists and songwriters on contract.
How to Contact: Submit demo tape and lead sheet. Prefers cassette with 4-8 songs on demo. SASE. Reports in 3 weeks.
Music: C&W; gospel; MOR; and top 40/pop. Recently released "Wine from My Table" b/w "Tell Me a Lie" (C&W singles) and "How Many Times Jesus" b/w "Mother's Spending Christmas with Jesus This Year" (gospel), by Yvonne De Vaney; "One Teardrop Too Long," by Gary McCray (C&W single); and "Forever and One Day," by Hank Snow (RCA Victor Records).

COMSTOCK RECORDS, Box 3247, Shawnee KS 66203. (913)631-6060. Canadian distribution on Highrise & Comstock Records. Production Manager/Producer: Patty Parker. General Manager/Executive Producer: Frank Fara. Record company, music publisher (White Cat Music/ASCAP, Rocky Bell Music/BMI), record producer and management and promotions firm. Releases 12-16 singles and 1-3 albums/year. Works with artists and songwriters on contract; musicians on salary. Pays 2-5% royalty to artists on contract; standard royalties to songwriters on contract; pays 3¢ rate to publishers for each record sold.

How to Contact: Arrange personal interview or submit demo tape. Prefers cassette with 1-5 songs on demo. "Enclose stamped return envelope if cassette is to be returned." Reports in 2 weeks.

Music: C&W and contemporary gospel. Recently released *Well of Honey*, by Rick Greysun (contemporary gospel LP); "Can't We Start Over Agin," by The O'Roark Brothers (C&W single); and *Promises*, by Steve Gray & Jubilation (contemporary gospel LP/single). Other artists include Doc & Dusty Holliday, Randy Hall, Wayne & Petra, Alex Fraser, Loel Steinley, Kenny Simnitt, Kathy Tate, and Liberty.

Tips: "Most needed is up tempo pop/country. We are in short supply of Canadian writers for Canadian and US artist combination releases."

CONTEMPORARY RECORDS, INC., Box 2628, Los Angeles CA 90028. (213)466-1633. Labels include Contemporary, Good Time Jazz and Society For Forgotten Music Records. Contact: Richard Seidel. Record company and music publisher (Contemporary Music/BMI and Composers Music/ASCAP). Releases 8-10 albums/year. Works with artists on contract. Pays statutory rate to publishers for each record sold.

How to Contact: Submit demo tape and lyric sheet. Prefers cassette with 1-4 songs on demo. SASE. Reports in 1 month.

Music: Jazz; jazz fusion; R&B; soul and top 40/pop. Recently released *Something for Lester*, by Ray Brown (jazz LP); *Beyond the Rain*, by Chico Freeman (jazz LP); and *No Limit*, by Art Pepper (jazz LP). Other artists include Joe Farrell, George Cables, Tete Montoliu, Mike Garson and Joe Henderson.

COSMIC RECORDS OF CANADA, 292 Lorraine Dr., Montreal, Quebec, Canada H9X 2R1. (514)457-5959. Labels include Elevator Records, Fresh Records, Meta Records, Hexagon Records, Les Disques Pamplemousse (French) and Happinessville Records. President: Hugh Dixon. Record company (Hugh Dixon Music, Inc). Releases 10 singles and 3-5 albums/year. Works with artists and songwriters on contract. Pays 4-7% royalty to artists on contract; statutory rate to publishers for each record sold.

How to Contact: Submit demo tape and lyric sheet. Prefers cassette with 2-5 songs on demo. SAE and International Reply Coupons. Reports in 1 month.

Music: Country, gospel, dance-oriented and inspirational/cosmic. Recently released *Paradise Frame*, by Paradise Frame (futuristic/spiritual LP); "Why Do You Still Love Me?", by Advent (country/gospel single); and "Rocky Road," by Cindy Holland (country/gospel single). Other artists include Grai Laliberte, Sue Clancy, Muffet, Peep and Horner.

COUNTERPART CREATIVE STUDIOS, 3744 Applegate Ave., Cincinnati OH 45211. (513)661-8810. President: Shad O'Shea. Record company, music publisher and jingle company. Works with musicians on salary; artists and songwriter on contract. Pays 5% royalty to artists on contract.

How to Contact: Submit demo tape. Prefers 7½ ips reel-to-reel with 1-2 songs on demo. SASE. Reports in 1 week.

Music: Bluegrass; blues; children's; choral; church/religious; classical; C&W; dance; easy listening; folk; gospel; jazz; MOR; progressive; rock; soul; and top 40/pop. Recently released "Jamie," by Blaize (pop/MOR single); "Colorado Call," by Shad O'Shea (novelty/C&W single); and "Easy Lovin' You," by Jerry Don Martin (C&W/pop single).

COUNTRY ARTISTS RECORDS, 103 Westview Ave., Valparaiso FL 32580. (904)678-7211. Labels include Circle Records and Minaret Records. Owner: Finley Duncan. Record company, music publisher and record producer. Works with musicians and songwriters on contract; musicians on salary. Pays standard royalty to artists on contract: 1¢/record to songwriters for each record sold.

How to Contact: Query, arrange personal interview, or submit demo tape and lead sheet. Prefers 7½ ips reel-to-reel tape with 3-5 songs on demo. "Send what you consider your best, and at least one of what you consider your worst." SASE. Reports in 1 week.

Music: C&W; disco; easy listening; MOR; R&B; rock; soul; and top 40/pop.

COUNTRY INTERNATIONAL, 1010 17th Ave. S., Nashville TN 37212. (615)327-4656. Vice President, Promotion: Jake Payne. Record company. Works with artists and songwriters on contract; musicians on salary for in-house studio work. Pays statutory rate to publishers for each record sold.

How to Contact: Submit demo tape and lyric sheet. Prefers 7½ ips reel-to-reel or cassette with 1-4 songs on demo. SASE. Reports in 2 weeks.

Music: C&W.

COUNTRY KITCHEN RECORDS, 6316 Porterway, Houston TX 77084. (713)859-0332. A&R Coordinator: P. Breaz. Record company, music publisher and record producer (Boxcar Music/ BMI). Releases 2-4 singles and 2-6 albums/year. Works with artists and songwriters on contract. Pays 5-10% royalty to artists on contract; standard royalty to songwriters on contract.
How to Contact: Query, arrange personal interview, submit demo tape, or submit demo tape and lead sheet. Prefers 7½ ips reel-to-reel or cassette with 4-8 songs on demo. "Groups should include biography and photo; same for single artists." SASE. Reports in 2 weeks.
Music: Bluegrass; C&W; easy listening; folk; MOR; progressive; rock; and top 40/pop. Recently released "Dreamin' of You" (single) and *Truckstop Annie*, by Hickory (country crossovers); *Hands*, by Soto and Boullet; and *Just Two Hearts* by Peter and Marcia Breaz.

COUNTRY SHOWCASE RECORDS AND PUBLISHERS, 11350 Baltimore Ave., Beltsville MD 20705. Labels include Country Showcase America Records. President: Frank Gosman. Record company and music publisher. Releases 2-4 singles/year. Works with artists on contract. Pays 1½% royalty to artists on contract.
How to Contact: Submit demo tape. Prefers 7½ or 15 ips reel-to-reel or cassette with 2 songs on demo. SASE. Reports in 2 weeks.
Music: Country (popular) and top 40/pop. Recently released "Mrs. Jones," by Don Drum ("sexy country"); and "I Love You" and "Sweet Yesterdays," by the Country Cavaliers (country duo singles).

COUNTRY STAR, INC., 439 Wiley Ave., Franklin PA 16323. (814)432-4633. Labels include Country Star, Process Records and Mersey Records. Contact: Norman Kelly. Record company and music publisher (Country Star, Process and Kelly). Releases 10-15 singles and 4-6 albums/ year. Member AFM and AFTRA. Works with artists and songwriters on contract; musicians on salary for in-house studio work. Pays 6% royalty to artists on contract; statutory rate to publishers for each record sold.
How to Contact: Write first about your interest. Prefers 7½ ips reel-to-reel or cassette with 1-4 songs on demo. SASE. Reports in 2 weeks.
Music: Bluegrass; C&W; easy listening; folk; MOR; rock; and top 40/pop. Recently released "Blue Velvet Lady", by Virge Brown (MOR single); "Credit Cards", by Debbie Sue (country single); and *Monticello*, by Clyde and Marie Denny (bluegrass LP). Other artists include Bonnie Baldwin, Junie Lou, Bobby Mac and General Custer.

CREATIVE SOUND, INC., Box 607, Malibu CA 90265. Labels include Sonrise and Creative Sound Records. President: Bob Cotterell. Record company. Releases 10 albums/year. Works with musicians on contract. Payment varies.
How to Contact: Submit demo tape or submit demo tape and lead sheet. Prefers cassette or 8-track cartridge. SASE.
Music: "Contemporary Christian music. We're looking for good finished masters."

CUCA RECORD AND CASSETTE MANUFACTURING COMPANY, (formerly American Music Co.), Box 168, Madison WI 53701. (608)251-2000. Labels include American, Cuca, Jolly Dutchman, Age of Aquarius, Top Gun, Sound Power and Night Owl Records. Vice-President: Daniel W. Miller. Record company and music publisher (American Legend Music/ASCAP and Apple-Glass Music/BMI). Works with musicians and songwriters on contract. Pays 10%royalty to artists on contract; 50% royalty to songwriters on contract.
How to Contact: Submit demo tape, photo and complete information. Prefers reel-to-reel tape (but will accept cassettes) with 2-20 songs on demo. SASE. No calls, please. Reports within 6 months.
Music: "Old time" (polkas, waltzes), bluegrass; folk; and ethnic. Recently released "Hupsadyna," by Styczynski (ethnic single); *Polka 76*, by Meisner (ethnic LP); and "Muleskinner Blues," (million-seller) by the Fendermen (rock single).
Tips: "Cuca has an extensive catalog and is known as "America's leading line of ethnic and old-time music." Artists may have a superior chance of having their material released on Cuca, American or affiliated labels, if they present *studio-quality* tapes of *all original* material."

CURTISS RECORDS, Box 4740, Nashville TN 37216. (615)859-0355. President: Wade Curtiss. Record company and producer. Releases 6-20 singles and 2-5 albums in 1980. Works with artists and songwriters on contract. Pays 8¢/record royalty to artists on contract; 2½¢/record royalty to songwriters on contract.
How to Contact: Submit demo tape and lead sheet. Prefers 7½ ips reel-to-reel with 2-8 songs on demo. SASE. Reports in 3 weeks.
Music: Bluegrass; blues; C&W; disco; folk; gospel; jazz; rock; soul; and top 40/pop. Recently

released "Book of Matches," by Gary White; and "Rompin'" and "Punsky," by the Rhythm Rockers.

DA CAR RECORDING, 297 Rehm Rd., Depew NY 14043. (716)684-5323. Proprietor and Producer: C.D. Weyand. Record company and music publisher (Weyand Music Publishing). Member NMPA. Works with artists and songwriters on contract as negotiated.
How to Contact: Submit demo tape and lead sheet. Prefers 7½ ips reel-to-reel on 5-inch reel with 1-5 songs on demo. (Leader tape between songs) on cassette with 1-5 songs on demo. "Only copyrighted material will be listened to; all other will be returned." SASE. Reports in 1 month.
Music: Classical; dance; easy-listening and jazz.
Tips: "Keep vocal distinct and out front. We prefer piano accompaniment. Full band only required if this is a featured aspect of demo."

DAISY RECORDS, Box 330, Lennoxville, Quebec, Canada J1M 1Z5. (819)569-3431 or (819)569-0533. Contact: Jerry Robitaille. Record company, record producer and music publisher (Chuck Wagon/PROCAN and Hunter/CAPAC). Releases 2 singles and 2 albums/year.
How to Contact: Submit demo tape and lyric sheet. Prefers cassette. SAE and International Reply Coupons. Reports as soon as possible.
Music: C&W and easy listening.

DANCE-A-THON RECORDS, Station K, Box 13584, Atlanta GA 30324. (404)872-6000. Labels include Banned, Hotlanta, Hottrax and Spectrum Stereo Records. President: Aleck Janoulis. Vice President/A&R Director: Oliver P. Cooper. Record company and music publisher. Releases 10-12 singles and 2-4 albums/year. Works with artists and songwriters on contract. Pays "3½-5% on 90% sold" to artists on contract.
How to Contact: Submit tape and lyric sheet. Prefers 7½ ips reel-to-reel or cassette with 1-3 songs on demo. "Demo tapes should be submitted with voice and either guitar or piano accompaniment only. A master should be sent only after a letter is submitted and replied to." Does not return unsolicited material.
Music: C&W; disco; easy listening; MOR; rock (new wave and C&W); and top 40/pop. Recently released *The Square Root of Two*, by the Night Shadows (60's re-issue LP); and *Nockum Nekkid* (rock LP) and "Disco Rock" (rock single), both by Starfoxx.

DATE LINE INTERNATIONAL RECORDS, 400 W. 43rd St., Suite 5c, New York NY 10036. A&R Director: Jane A. Eaton. Record company, record producer and music publisher (MacHarmony Music/ASCAP and Tteltrab Music/BMI). Estab. 1979. Releases 1 single and 1 album/year.
How to Contact: Submit demo tape and lyric sheet. Prefers cassette with 1-3 songs on demo. SASE. Reports in 1 month; returned "only with SASE."
Music: Rock (hard and soft) and top 40/pop. Recently released *A Feeling's Coming over Me*, by Phyllis MacBryde (pop LP); and "Never Gonna Have, by Phyllis MacBryde (pop single).

DAWN PRODUCTIONS, Box 300, Mt. Gretna PA 17064. Labels include Bat, LeFevre, Canadian American Recordings, Grafitti, Music Machine, Music City, Palmer and Vermillion Records. President: Joey Welz. Record company, booking agency and music publisher. (Ursula Music/BMI and Welz Music/ASCAP).Releases 4 singles and 2 albums/year. Works with artists and songwriters on contract. "We lease the record to a major label, who is responsible for paying the royalties."
How to Contact: Submit demo tape and lead sheet. Prefers 7½ ips reel-to-reel or cassette with 6-12 songs on demo. Does not return unsolicited material. "We hold it until we need material for a session, then we search our files."
Music: C&W; dance; easy listening; folk; MOR; rock; and top 40/pop. Recently released "Hey Baby" b/w "On My Way to Lovin' You" by Joey Welz (top 40 single); "Right On to Rock and Roll" by New Wave Comets (rock single); *I Remember Love* by Joseph Welz (top 40 LP). Other artists include Jimmy Velvet, Dave Alford and The Solar System.

DE-LITE RECORDS, 1733 Broadway, New York NY 10019. (212)757-6770. President: Gabe Vigorito. Record company and music publisher (Delightful Music Ltd.). Releases 10 singles and 4-5 albums/year. Works with artists on contract.
How to Contact: Submit demo tape and lyric sheet. Prefers cassette as demo. SASE. Reports in 1-2 months.
Music: R&B and top 40/pop. Recently released *Celebrate*, by Kool & The Gang (R&B/pop LP).

DELTA SOUND RECORDS, 814 W. Claiborne St., Box 672, Greenwood MS 38930. (601)453-3302. Labels include Cindy Boo Records. Owner: Mack Allen Smith. Record company

and music publisher (Mack Smith Music/BMI). Releases 3-10 singles and 2-6 albums/year. Works with artists and songwriters on contract. Pays 3-5% royalty to artists on contract; standard royalties to songwriters on contract.
How to Contact: Submit demo tape and lead or lyric sheet. Prefers 7½ ips reel-to-reel or cassette with 1-5 songs on demo. "On reel-to-reel put leaders between songs and send typed or printed copy of lyrics." SASE. Reports in 1 month.
Music: C&W; rock; and top 40/pop. Recently released "All The Praises" (country single) and *We Gotta Rock Tonight* (country LP), by Mack Allen Smith.
Tips: "Submit songs that have strong lyrics with a good hook. I think a song should tell a story people can relate to."

DIMINSION RECORDS, Box 17087, Nashville TN 37217. (615)754-9400. A&R Producer: Ray Pennington. Record company. Estab. 1979. Works with musicians and songwriters on contract.
How to Contact: Arrange personal interview to play demo tape. Prefers 7½ ips reel-to-reel with maximum 4 songs on demo. SASE. Reports in 1 month.
Music: Primarily country, progressive and traditional. Also bluegrass; easy listening; folk; gospel; MOR; and top 40/pop. Recently released "Sweet Mother Texas" and "Dealing with the Devil," by Eddy Raven (country singles); and "Well Rounded Traveling Man," by Kenny Price (country single). Other artists include Peggy Foreman, Bluestone, Ray Price and Dave Kirby.

DJM RECORDS, 119 W. 57th St., New York NY 10019. (212)581-3420. Labels include Rage Records and Champagne Records. General Manager: Arthur Braun. Record company, record producer and music publisher (Dick James Music, Inc. and Dejamus, Inc.). Works with artists and songwriters on contract.
How to Contact: Submit demo tape and lyric sheet. Prefers cassette with 1-3 songs on demo. SASE. Reports as soon as possible.
Music: C&W, dance-oriented, easy listening, MOR, rock, soul and top 40/pop. Recently released *John Mayall*, by Road Show Blues (blues LP); and *Johnny Guitar Watson*, by Johnny Guitar Watson (R&B blues). Other artists include Grace Kennedy.

DOMINION BLUEGRASS RECORDINGS, Box 993, 211 E. 4th St., Salem VA 24153. (703)389-3190. Labels include Dominion and JRM Records. President: Rick Mullins. Vice President: Jack Mullins. Record company and music publisher (Double Jack Publishing/BMI and Powhatan Music/BMI). Releases 6 singles and 10-12 albums/year. Works with musicians on salary and contract; songwriters on contract. Pays 5% royalty to artists on contract.
How to Contact: Submit demo tape and lead sheet. Prefers 7½ ips reel-to-reel with 1-12 songs on demo. SASE. Reports in 1 month.
Music: Bluegrass. Recently released *Country Kitchen Pickin'*, by C. Wrenn (country LP/single) and *Simple Things*, by Mountain Magic Band (country LP/single).

DOMINO RECORDS, 37 Odell Ave., Yonkers NY 10701. (914)969-5673. Vice President/ General Manager: Joe Bollon. Record company. Works with artists and songwriters on contract. Pays musicians' scale to artists on contract.
How to Contact: Submit demo tape and lead sheet. Prefers cassette or 45 rpm disc with 2-4 songs on demo. SASE. Reports in 2 weeks.
Music: Dance; easy listening; and MOR. Recently released "Give My Broken Heart a Break," "Old-Fashioned Baby" and "Say You Love Me," by Elsie Tucker (easy listening/pop singles).

DOMINO RECORDS, LTD., 22 Tulane St., Garland TX 75043. Labels include Front Row Records and Domino. Owners: Gene & Dea Summers. Record company and music publisher (Silicon Music/BMI). Releases 5-12 singles and 2-8 albums/year. Works with artists and songwriters on contract. Pays 4% royalty to artists on contract; standard royalty to songwriters on contract.
How to Contact: Submit demo tape. Prefers only cassette with 1-3 songs on demo. Does not return unsolicited material. SASE. Reports in 2 months.
Music: C&W; R&B; rock (soft); top 40/pop; and '50s material. Recently released by Gene Summers *Southern Cat Rocks On* ('50s rock LP) and "Do Ya Think I'm Sexy?", by Gene & Dea Summers (C&W/MOR single); "Jimmy Carter Always Tells the Truth" (C&W novelty single); "A Beautiful Love Affair," by Joe Hardin Brown (C&W/MOR single); and *Early Rockin' Recordings*, by Gene Summers ('50's rock LP) Holland.
Tips: "If you own masters of 1950s rock & rock-a-billy, contact us first! We will work with you on percentage basis for overseas release. We have active releases in Holland, Switzerland, Australia, England, France, Sweden and Finland at the present. We need original masters. You must be able to prove ownership of tapes before we can accept and firm a deal. We're looking for little-known, obscure recordings."

DOOR KNOB RECORDS, 2125 8th Ave., S., Nashville TN 37204. (615)383-6002. Label includes Society Records. President: Gene Kennedy. Vice President: Karen Jeglum. Promotion Director: Bobby Young. Record company, record producer and music publisher (Door Knob Music, Publishers Inc., Chip 'N' Dale Music Publishers and Lodestar Music). Member CMA. Releases 25 singles and 2 albums/year. Works with artists and songwriters on contract. Pays 4-7% of 90% of records sold; statutory rate to publishers for each record sold.
How to Contact: Submit demo tape and lyric sheet or arrange personal interview. Prefers 7½ ips reel-to-reel or cassette with 1-4 songs on demo. SASE. Reports in 6 weeks.
Music: C&W and MOR. Recently released "I Want to See Me in Your Eyes," by Gene Kennedy/Karen Jeglum (MOR single); "Have Another Drink," by Douglas (country rock single); and "My Song Don't Sing the Same," by Kris Carpenter (MOR single). Other artists include Bonnie Shannon, Garry Goodnight, Jerry Wallace, Lee Sims, Garland Hackney, John France and Vonna Faye.

DORN RECORDS, 20531 Plummer St., Chatsworth CA 91311. (213)998-0443. Labels include DORN, AKO and AZTEC Records. Manager: A. Sullivan. Record company, record producer and music publisher (AMIRON Music/ASCAP). Releases 4 singles and 1 album/year. Works with songwriters on contract. Pays 5-10% royalty to artists on contract; statutory rate to publishers for each record sold.
How to Contact: Submit demo tape and lyric sheet. Prefers 7½ips reel-to-reel or cassette as demo. SASE. Reports in 3 weeks.
Music: Blues, C&W, dance-oriented, easy listening, MOR, progressive, Spanish, R&B, rock and top 40/pop. Recently released *Newstreet*, (rock LP and single); and "Better Run" (pop/rock single), by Newstreet. Other artists include Lista Brown, El Chicano, Zell Black, Zaral, AKO, Johnny Forever, One Flite Up, Debbie Rockwell, Pyramid and Monica Lewis.

DYNAMIC ARTISTS RECORDS, Box 25654, Richmond VA 23260. (804)288-3939. President: Joseph J. Carter Jr. Record company, music publisher, booking agency, management firm and production firm (Hot Gold Music Publishing Co./BMI). Works with musicians on salary: artists and songwriters on contract; statutory rate to publishers for each record sold. Pays 5% royalty to artists on contract.
How to Contact: Submit demo tape. Prefers cassette with 1-3 songs on demo. SASE. Reports in 60 days.
Music: Dance; rock; soul; and top 40/pop. Recently released *Love Moods*, by The Waller Family; and *Starfire*, by Starfire. Other artists include the Dynamic Soul Orchestra and June Webb, Poison.

DYNAMITE, 5 Aldom Circle, West Caldwell NJ 07006. (201)226-0035. Labels include Dynamite, Deadwood, Tar Heel, True Love, Cactus, Peek Records and Deadwood-Dynamite Cassette tapes. Contact Jim Hall or Gidget Starr. Record company, record producer and music publisher. Works with artists and songwriters on contract. Pays 5% royalty to artists on contract; statutory rate to publishers for each record sold.
How to Contact: Submit demo tape and lyric sheet or write first about your interest. Prefers 7½ ips reel-to-reel or cassette with 5 songs on demo. Does not return unsolicited material. Reports in 2 weeks.
Music: Bluegrass, blues, C&W, gospel and rock. Artists include Doc Hopkins and Tune Twisters.

DYNASTY RECORDS, Suite 20, 333 31st St., North, St. Petersburg FL 33713. (813)896-5151. Producer: Mike Douglas. Record company, record producer and music publisher (Lisas Theme Music/BMI). Estab. 1980. Releases 4-6 singles and 1 album/year. Works with artists and songwriters on contract; musicians on salary for in-house studio work. Pays negotiable royalty to artists on contract and to publishers for each record sold.
How To Contact: Submit demo tape and lyric sheet. Prefers cassette with 1-4 songs on demo. SASE. Reports as soon as possible.
Music: Blues, C&W, easy listening, gospel, MOR, R&B, rock (all types), soul and top 40/pop. Recently released "J.R. Ewing/President", by Rich Lovette (country comedy single); "Doll House", by Melody Wilcox (soft country single); and "Second Time Around", by M. Wilcox (country single). Other artists include Jeff Cobb, June Page, Duane Bunker, and James Clark Martin.

E.L.J. RECORD CO., 1344 Waldron, St. Louis MO 63130. President: Eddie Johnson. Record company, record producer and music publisher. Works with musicians on salary; artists and songwriters on contract. Releases 6 singles and 3 albums/year. Pays 3% minimum royalty to artists on contract; statutory rate to publisher for each record sold.

How to Contact: Submit demo tape or submit demo tape and lead sheet. Prefers 7½ ips reel-to-reel or cassette with 4 songs on demo. SASE. Reports in 2 weeks.
Music: Blues; church/religious; R&B; soul; and top 40/pop. Recently released "Rocks in Your Pillow" and "When the Light of the Candle," both by Bobby Scott (R&B singles); and "Who Am I," by Eddie Johnson (top 40 single). Other artists include Joe Buckner, LeRoy Harris, Vivian Harper and Bill Shank.

EARTH RECORDS, 455 W. Hanover St., Trenton NJ 08618. (609)989-9202. Contact: Eddie Toney. Record company and music publisher (Rashbone Music/BMI). Releases 3 singles and 1 album/year. Works with artists and songwriters on contract. Pays 3% royalty to artists on contract; statutory rate to publishers for each record sold.
How to Contact: Arrange personal interview. Prefers 7½ ips reel-to-reel with 1-2 songs on demo. SASE. Reports in 1 month.
Music: Church/religious; dance; easy listening; and progressive. Recently released "It's You Girl," by Dennis Roger and "Tell It Like It Is," by E. Lampans.

EAST COAST RECORDS INC., 6012 Lindbergh Blvd., Philadelphia PA 19142. (215)726-6049. President: Anthony J. Messina. Record company and music publisher. Works with artists and songwriters on contract. Pays 4-7% royalty to artists on contract; standard royalty to songwriters on contract.
How to Contact: Submit demo tape and lyric sheet. Prefers 7½ ips reel-to-reel or cassette with 3-12 songs on demo. SASE. Reports in 3 weeks.
Music: Classical; MOR; rock; and top 40/pop. Recently released "Remembering," by Lana Cantrell (MOR single from LP); "Drifting Away," by Uproar (rock single); and the soundtrack from the motion picture *England Made Me,* by London Philharmonic (classical LP). Other artists include Duke Williams & the Extreams.

EAT RECORDS, 400 Essex St., Salem MA 01970. (617)744-7678. Labels include Neat and Dial-Tone. A&R Director: Edsel Ferrari. Record company, record producer and music publisher (Phonetones). Estab. 1979. Member NAIRD. Releases 3 singles and 3 albums/year. Works with artists and songwriters on contract. Pays statutory rate to publishers for each record sold.
How to Contact: Submit demo tape and lyric sheet. Prefers cassette with 2-4 songs on demo. SASE. Reports in 1 month.
Music: Dance-oriented, R&B, rock, pop and new wave. Recently released *Fig 14*, by Humm Sexual Response (wave LP); *Compare and Decide*, by The Commericals (rock LP); and "The Press Conference," by The Newshounds (novelty single). Other artists include Tweeds and The Stones.

ECHO RECORDS, 824 83rd St., Miami Beach FL 03141. (305)865-8960. Record company, record producer and music publisher (Dana). Releases 2 singles and 1 album/year. Pays statutory rate to publishers for each record sold.
How to Contact: Write first about your interest. Prefers 7½ or 15 ips reel-to-reel or cassette as demo. SASE. Reports in 1 week.
Music: Classical and Polish.

ECI RECORDS INTERNATIONAL, 320 West 3rd St., Suite 1, Davenport IA 52808. (319)324-2133. Labels include Lovelight, BCA, Sonway, and Sugartree Records. Manager: Gary Unger. Record company. Estab. 1980. Releases 3 singles and 3-5 albums/year. Works with artists on contract; musicians on salary for in-house studio work. Pays 10¢/single sold and 50¢/album sold to artists on contract; statutory rate to publishers for each record sold.
How to Contact: Submit demo tape and lyric sheet. Prefers 7½ ips reel-to-reel or cassette with 4-10 songs on demo. SASE. Reports in 2 months.
Music: Church/religious, country rock, dance-oriented, easy listening, progressive, R&B, rock and top 40/pop. Recently released "Girl", by Lambkin (pop/rock single); and "Don't You Believe" b/w "Long Long Time" by Dolly Coulter (single).

ECLIPSE RECORDS, 118 5th St., Box 176, Taylorsville NC 28681. (704)632-4735. Contact: Harry Deal. Record company, music publisher and record producer. Works with artists and songwriters on contract.
How to Contact: Submit demo tape and lyric sheet. Prefers cassette with 2-3 songs on demo. SASE. Reports in 2-3 weeks.
Music: C&W; dance; folk; MOR; R&B; rock; soul; and top 40/pop.

EDUCATOR RECORDS, INC., Box 490, Wayne PA 19087. (215)423-5960. President and Musical Director: Bart Arntz. Record company and music publisher. Releases 33 singles and 14

albums/year. Works with musicians on salary; artists and songwriters on contract. Pays negotiable royalty to artists on contract; standard royalty to songwriters on contract.
How to Contact: Submit demo tape. Prefers 7½ ips reel-to-reel or cassette with 3-8 songs on demo. "Tape must be clearly audible. We are constantly seeking strong instrumentals of all types of music. We are also interested in license agreements on finished masters." SASE. Reports in 3 weeks.
Music: Children's (character songs); disco; soul; and show music of the '30s and '40s. "We are primarily a dance record company (tap, jazz and ballet). We also produce R&B material." Recently released *Jazz Moves*, by Ron Daniels (jazz dance LP).

EL CHICANO MUSIC, 20531 Plummer St., Chatsworth CA 91311. (213)998-0443. Labels include Dorn Records and Aztec Records. A&R Director: A. Sullivan. Record company, music publisher and booking agency. Releases 2-4 singles and 1 album/year. Works with artists and songwriters on contract. Payment negotiable.
How to Contact: Submit demo tape and lead sheet. Prefers 7½ ips reel-to-reel or cassette. SASE. Reports in 3 weeks.
Music: Bluegrass; blues; C&W; dance; easy listening; jazz; MOR; progressive; rock; soul; and top 40/pop. Recently released "Blood from My Hand" (R&B single) and "It Feels Good" (rock single), by Quicksand.

ELEKTRA/ASYLUM/NONESUCH RECORDS, 962 N. La Cienega Blvd., Los Angeles CA 90069. (213)655-8280. Head of A&R: Stephen Barncaro. Needs vary; query about needs and submission policy.

ELEKTRA/ASYLUM/NONESUCH RECORDS, 665 5th Ave., New York NY 10022. (212)355-7610. Contact: A&R Department. Record company.
How to Contact: Submit demo tape and lyric sheet. Prefers reel-to-reel or cassette with 1-4 songs on demo. SASE. Reports in 1 month.
Music: Classical (on Nonesuch only); dance; MOR; progressive; R&B; rock; and top 40/pop. Recently released albums by Linda Ronstadt, Cars, Eagles, Lenny White, Patrice Rushen and Shoes.

EMI AMERICA/LIBERTY RECORDS, 1370 Avenue of the Americas, New York NY 10019. (212)757-7470. East Coast A&R/Director of Talent Acquisitions: Bob Currie. Record company and music publisher (Screen Gems).
How to Contact: Submit demo tape and lyric sheet. Prefers reel-to-reel or cassette as demo. SASE. Reports in 3 weeks.
Music: All types of music except R&B.

EMI-AMERICA/UNITED ARTISTS, 6920 Sunset Blvd., Los Angeles CA 90028. (213)461-9141. A&R Manager: Gary Gersh. Record company. Estab. 1979. Releases 85 singles and 60 albums/year. Works with artists on contract.
How to Contact: Submit demo tape. Prefers 7½ ips reel-to-reel or cassette with 3-5 songs on demo. SASE. Reports in 2 weeks.
Music: Bluegrass; blues; dance; easy listening; folk; jazz; MOR; progressive; R&B; rock; soul; and top 40/pop. Recently released *This Little Girl*, by Gary V.S. Bonds (rock/R&B LP and single); *Bette Davis Eyes*, by Kim Carnes (rock/R&B LP and single); *Fast Fontaine*, by Fast Fontaine (rock/R&B LP and single). Other artists include Sheena Easton, J. Guils, Fools, Jon Hall, and Marty Balin.
Tips: "Present only the finest of songs and not so much a diversity but a direction that shows artist's capabilities."

EMI-UNITED ARTISTS RECORDS, 29 Music Sq. E, Nashville TN 37203. (615)244-7770. "We do not have an A&R Department. All material should be submitted through our Los Angeles office."

ENTERPRIZE RECORDS, 1824 Laney Dr., Longview TX 75601. (214)758-4063. Contact: Jerry Haymes. Record company and music publisher (Golden Guitar/BMI and Enterprize Music/ASCAP). Works with artists and songwriters on contract. Pays statutory rate to publishers for each record sold.
How to Contact: Submit demo tape and lyric sheet. Prefers reel-to-reel and cassettes. SASE. Reports as soon as possible.
Music: Bluegrass, C&W, gospel and MOR. Recently released "Welcome Home" and "Love Me Love My Dog", by Brenda D (MOR singles); and "Smile of a Clown", by Jerry Haymes (C&W single). Other artists include The Pages and Jeff Johnson.

ESI RECORDS, Box 472, Torrance CA 90509. (213)328-5590. Vice President: Bob Barron. Record company and record producer. Member RIAA. Releases 5 singles and 2 albums/year. Works with artists on contract. Pays 7-10% royalty to artists on contract; statutory rate to publishers for each record sold.
How to Contact: Submit demo tape and lyric sheet. Prefers cassette with 3-7 songs on demo. SASE. Reports in 2 weeks.
Music: R&B, rock and top 40/pop. Recently released *Greatest Hits England*, by Steppenwolf (rock LP).

ETS RECORD CO., Box 932. Honolulu HI 96808. Contact: A&R Department. Record company. Works with musicians on contract. Pays standard royalty to artists and songwriters on contract.
How to Contact: Write first about your interest. Prefers 7½ ips reel-to-reel with 1-2 songs on demo. SASE. Reports in 1 week.
Music: C&W; and easy listening.

FACTORY BEAT RECORDS, INC., 663 5th Ave., New York NY 10022. (212)757-3638. Labels include RER, Ren Rome and Can Scor Productions, Inc. President: Rena L. Feeney. Record compnay, record producer and music publisher (Ren-Maur Music Corp.). Member NARAS, BMI and AGAC. Releases 4 singles and 2 albums/year. Works with musicians on salary for in-house studio work. Pays 4-12% royalty to artists on contract; statutory rate to publishers for each record sold.
How to Contact: Submit demo tape and lyric sheet only. Prefers cassette as demo. SASE. Reports in 3 weeks.
Music: R&B, rock, soul and top 40/pop.

FAMOUS DOOR RECORDS, Box 92, Station A, Flushing NY 11358. (212)463-6281. Contact: Harry Lim. Record company. Member NARAS. Works with artists on contract. Pays 5% maximum royalty to artists on contract; statutory rate to publishers for each record sold.
How to Contact: Write first about your interest. Prefers cassette with 3 songs minimum on demo. SASE. Reports in 1 month.
Music: Jazz. Recently released *Boston-N.Y. Axis*, by Phil Wilson (jazz LP); *I'll Play for You*, by Bill Watrous (jazz LP); and *Swings Some Standards*, by Butch Miles (jazz LP). Other artists include Herb Steward, Danny Stiles, George Masso, and Glenn Zottola.

FANFARE RECORDS, Box 2501, Des Moines IA 50315. (515)285-6564. President: Art Smart Stenstrom. Works with artists on contract. Payment negotiable.
How to Contact: Not currently reviewing new material.
Music: Rock and top 40/pop. Recently released *Sailing On Fantasies* (top 40 LP) and "Don't Feel Bad" (top 40 single), by Silver Laughter.

FANTASY/PRESTIGE/MILESTONE/STAX RECORDS, 10th and Parker, Berkeley CA 94710. (415)549-2500. Associate A&R Director: Phil Jones. Record company. Works with artists and songwriters on contract.
How to Contact: Submit demo tape. Prefers 7½ ips reel-to-reel or cassette. SASE. Reports in 3 weeks.
Music: Disco; easy listening; jazz; MOR; progressive; R&B; soul; and top 40/pop. Recently released *2 Tons O'Fun*, by 2 Tons O'Fun (R&B LP).

FAR EAST RECORDS, 4810 SW 69th Ave., Miami FL 33155. (305)665-5701. Labels include Far East and Fusion Records. President: Rich Piccolo. Record company, record producer and music publisher (Anitya Songs). Estab. 1979. Releases 5 singles and 4-5 albums/year. Works with artists and songwriters on contract; musicians on salary for in-house studio work. Pays 4-6% royalty to artists on contract; statutory rate to publishers for each record sold.
How to Contact: Submit demo tape and lyric sheet. Prefers cassette with 3 songs on demo. SASE. Reports in 3 weeks.
Music: Jazz, MOR, progressive, R&B, rock, soul, and top 40/pop and reggae. Recently released *Rajas & Lions*, by Rajas & Lions (reggae LP and single); and *Build My World*, by RLP Group (pop-jazz LP).

FARR RECORDS, Box 1098, Somerville NJ 08876. (201)725-3850. Contact: Candace Campbell. Record company and record producer. Member RIAA. Releases 30 singles and 30 albums/year. Works with artists and songwriters on contract. Pays negotiable royalty to artists on contract; statutory rate to publishers for each record sold.

How to Contact: Submit demo tape and lyric sheet. Prefers cassette with 4 songs on demo. SASE. Reports in 2 weeks.
Music: C&W, dance-oriented, easy listening, folk, MOR, rock, soul and top 40/pop.

FIFTY STATES RECORDS, 248 Saunder's Ferry Rd., Hendersonville TN 37075. (615)822-5222. President: Donald L. Riis. Record company and independent record producer. Works with artists on contract. Pays 3-8% royalty to artists on contract.
How to Contact: Submit demo tape and lyric sheet. Prefers 7½ ips reel-to-reel or cassette with 1-6 songs on demo. SASE. Reports in 3 weeks.
Music: C&W; disco; easy listening; R&B; and top 40/pop. Recently released "You've Got to Mend This Heartache" and "If That's Not Loving You," by Ruby Falls (country/pop single); and "I'm Gonna Love You," by Ron Lowry (country/pop single). Other artists include Bobby Penn, Pam Hobbs, Michele Spitz and Doyle Holly.

FIRE LITE RECORD CO., 11344 Woodmont, Detroit MI 48227. (313)273-5828. Owner: Eugene Satterfield. Record company and music publisher. Works with musicians on salary or contract; songwriters on contract. Pays 5-10% royalty to artists and songwriters on contract.
How to Contact: Submit demo tape. Prefers reel-to-reel or cassette with 3-6 songs on demo. SASE. Reports in 1 week.
Music: Bluegrass; C&W; easy listening; and folk.

FIRST AMERICAN RECORDS, INC., 73 Marion St., Seattle WA 98104. (206)625-9992. Labels include First American, Music Is Medicine, Piccadilly, and The Great Northwest Music Company. Chairman of the Board: Jerry Dennon. Record company. Releases 6-10 singles and 25-50 albums/year. Prefers outright purchase of master tapes. Will work with artists on contract. Terms negotiable.
How to Contact: Submit demo tape with lyric sheet if applicable. Prefers 7½ ips reel-to-reel or cassette with 2-5 songs on demo. SASE. Reports in 2 months.
Music: Blues; easy listening; folk; country; jazz; MOR; progressive; top 40/pop; and rock. Recently released "She Touched Me," by Glenn Yarbrough (top 40/pop.)

FIST-O-FUNK, LTD., 293 Richard Court, Pomona NY 10970. (914)354-7157. President: Kevin Misevis. Record company, music publisher and management firm. Releases 4 singles and 1-4 albums/year. Works with songwriters on contract. Pays negotiable royalty.
How to Contact: Submit demo and lead sheet. Prefers 7½ ips reel-to-reel or cassette with 1-10 songs on demo. Does not return unsolicited material. Reports in 1 month.
Music: Blues; classical; disco; jazz; soul; and top 40/pop. Recently released "New York Strut," "Dance All over the World" and "Keep On Dancin'," by T.C. James and the Fist-O-Funk Orchestra (disco/pop singles).

FLEURETTE RECORDS/GOLD-CLEF MUSIC, Box 34, Claymont DE 19703. Record company and music publisher. Works with songwriters on contract. Pays standard royalties.
How to Contact: Submit acetate disc and lead sheet. SASE. Reports in 1 month.
Music: Blues; C&W; disco; easy listening; MOR; R&B; and top 40/pop. Recently released *In a Neo-Nostalgic Mood with the Music of Frances Bond*, by Dick Durham (MOR LP).
Tips: "Submit good commercial material on an acetate disc with a singer and piano or guitar."

FLOWERS RECORDS, Rt. 1, Box 120F, Swoope VA 24479. (703)885-3309. Contact: Charles A. Flowers. Record company, music publisher and recording studio. Works with musicians on salary; songwriters on contract. Pays standard royalties to songwriters on contract.
How to Contact: Call first about your interest. Prefers 7½ ips reel-to-reel. SASE. Reports in 1 week.
Music: Bluegrass; blues; classical; C&W; easy listening; folk; gospel; jazz; progressive; R&B; rock; and top 40/pop. Recently released "You Make Me Feel So Good," by Barbara Flowers (country single); *Upward Way*, by S. Cook (gospel LP); "Lost Your Love Forever," by R. Call (easy listening single); and "The Way It's Meant to Be," by J. Campbell (country single). Other artists include Shenandoah Valley Crusaders, Greg Everhart and Southern Hospitality.

FORCE RECORDS, Box 25664, Chicago IL 60625. (312)883-8660. Contact: Ed Kammer. Record company and music publisher (Tripoli Music/BMI). Estab. 1979. Releases 2-4 singles and 1-2 albums/year. Works with artists on contract. Pays negotiable royalty; statutory rate to publishers for each record sold.
How to Contact: Submit demo tape and lyric sheet. Prefers 7½ ips reel-to-reel or cassette with 4 songs minimum on demo. Does not return unsolicited material. Reports in 6 weeks.
Music: Dance-oriented, easy listening, rock (hard and pop) and top 40/pop. Recently released

"One Nite," by Freewheelin' (pop rock single); "Fool for a Pretty Face," by Freewheelin' (AOR single); "Annie," by George Michael (pop rock EP); and *Freewheelin'*, by Freewheelin' (AOR LP). **Tips:** "Have a viable act and be open to material suggestions. Also keep an open mind as far as producer goes."

FOREVER RECORDS, Box 40772, Nashville TN 37204. (615)256-2242. Labels include Chenaniah Records and Mustard Seed Records. Record company, record producer and music publisher (Chenaniah Music; Re'Gernation Publications and Spring Hill Publishing Group). Estab. 1979. Member NARAS. Releases 2 singles and 6 albums/year. Works with songwriters on contract. Pays statutory rate to publishers for each record sold.
How to Contact: Call first about your interest. Prefers cassette with 2-5 songs on demo. SASE. Reports in 1 month.
Music: Children's, choral, church/religious, easy listening, gospel and MOR. Recently released *Stop . . . Smell the Roses*, by The Re'Generation (MOR/gospel LP); *Christmas in Velvet/Volume II*, by The Re'Generation (Christmas LP); *Miles & Webb*, by Kevin Miles and Rick Webb (inspirational LP); and *Music of the People*, by The Larry Mayfield Orchestra and Singers (sacred choral LP). Other artist includes Neil Madsen.

415 RECORDS, Box 14563, San Francisco CA 94114. (415)641-1726; 522-9828. Director, A&R: Chris Knab. Record company and music publisher (Very Safe Music). Releases 10 singles and 4 albums/year. Works with artists on contract.
How to Contact: Submit demo tape. Prefers cassette only with 1-5 songs on demo. SASE. Pays statutory rate to publishers for each record sold.
Music: New wave rock; and new wave pop. Recently released *Extended Play* recorded by Sut (rock n roll LP); *Digital Stimulation*, by Units (new wave electronic rock LP); *It's a Condition*, by Romeo Void (new wave rock LP). Other artists include VKTMS, Jo Allen and The Shapes, Impostors, and Mutants.

FRANNE RECORDS, Box 8135, Chicago IL 60680. (312)787-8220. Labels include Superbe Records. A&R Director/Executive Producer: R.C. Hillsman. Record company, music publisher and producer. Works with artists and songwriters on contract. Pays 3½% royalty to artists and songwriters on contract.
How to Contact: Arrange personal interview or submit demo tape and lead sheet. Prefers 7½ or 15 ips quarter-inch reel-to-reel or cassette with 4-6 songs on demo. "By registered mail only." SASE. Reports in 3 weeks.
Music: Church/religious; C&W; disco; gospel; jazz; MOR; rock; and top 40/pop. Recently released "He's Love" and "You Better Get Right," by Allen Duo (gospel singles).

FRECKLE RECORDS, Pioneer Sq., Box 4005, Seattle WA 98104. (206)682-3200. Works with artists on contract. Pays statutory rate to publishers for each record sold.
How to Contact: Call first about your interest. SASE.
Music: Folk and contemporary. *Everyday*, by Reilly & Maloney (folk LP and single); *A Delicate Balance*, by Tom Dundee (folk LP); and *Alive* and *At Last*, Reilly & Maloney (folk LPs).

FREKO RECORDS, Box 11967, Houston TX 77016. (713)987-2273. President: Freddie Kober. Record company, record producer and music publisher (Anode Music/BMI). Estab. 1979. Releases 2 singles/year. Works with songwriters on contract. Pays negotiable royalty to artists on contract; statutory rate to publishers for each record sold.
How to Contact: Submit demo tape and lyric sheet. Prefers cassette with 1-3 songs on demo. SASE. Reports in 2 weeks.
Music: Gospel and soul. Recently released "Shake the Funk out of It", by Contage'us (disco single) and "That Means So Much to Me", by Mel Starr (love ballad single).

FULL SAIL RECORDS, Full Sail Productions, 71 Boylston St., Brookline MA 02147. (617)739-2010. President: Fred Berk. (Topsail Music/BMI). Releases 10 singles and 3 albums/year. Works with artists and songwriters on contract. Pays 5-7% royalty to artists on contract; standard royalties to songwriters on contract; statutory rate to publishers for each record sold.
How to Contact: Submit demo tape. Prefers 7½ ips reel-to-reel or cassette with 1-10 songs on demo. SASE. Reports in 1 month.
Music: Children's; C&W; dance; rock; soul; and top 40/pop.

GAMELON RECORDS AND TAPES, Box 525, Station P, Toronto, Ontario, Canada M5S 2T1. Manager: Michael Kleniec. Record company, record producer and music publisher; (Gamelon Music/PROCAN). Releases 5 albums/year. Works with artists and songwriters on contract;

musicians on salary for in-house studio work. Pays statutory rate to publishers for each record sold.
How to Contact: Submit demo tape and lyric sheet. Prefers 7½ ips reel-to-reel demo with 5-15 songs on demo. SAE and International Reply Coupons. Reports in 1 month.
Music: Blues, classical, folk, jazz, progressive and R&B. Artists include Michael Kleniec.

GHOST RECORDS, 1905 Pesos Place, Kalamazoo MI 49008. (616)375-2641. Labels include Ghost and Jobie Records. President: Don Jobe. Record company. Releases 5-8 singles and 1 album/year. Works with artists and songwriters on contract.
How to Contact: Submit demo tape and lead sheet. Prefers 7½ ips reel-to-reel. SASE. Reports in 1 month.
Music: Easy listening; rock; soul; top 40/pop and country/western. Recently released "(Just Like) Romeo and Juliet" (top 40 single) and "Hey Lover" (easy listening single), by Don Jobe; "Get a Little Bit Lonely," by the Ghosters (top 40 single); and "Come Cry for Me" (country-rock).

GLAD-HAMP RECORDS INC., 1995 Broadway, New York NY 10023. (212)787-1223. A&R: Charlie Mack. Record company. Works with artists and songwriters on contract. Pays 5-15% royalty to artists on contract; standard royalty to songwriters on contract.
How to Contact: Submit demo tape and lyric sheet. Prefers 7½ ips reel-to-reel or cassette with 2-4 songs on demo. SASE. Reports in 1 month.
Music: Jazz; R&B; and soul. Recently released *Lionel Hampton Big Band Live, Chameleon* and *Outrageous* by Lionel Hampton and Friends (jazz LPs); and "School Daze," by Brothers Unique (12" rap).

GLOBAL RECORD CO., Box 268, Manistique MI 49854. President: Reg B. Christensen. Record company and music publisher (Chris Music/BMI and Sara Lee Music/BMI). Works with artists and songwriters on contract. Pays 10% royalty to artists on contract.
How to Contact: Submit demo and lyric or lead sheet. Prefers cassette with 2-5 songs. "If songs are copyrighted, give number and date. If not copyrighted tell what, if anything you've done to protect them." SASE. Reports in 1 month.
Music: Bluegrass; C&W; gospel; MOR; acid and hard rock; and soul. Recently released "Michigan Again," by Tim Murphy.

GMC RECORDS & TAPES, 3012 N. Main St., Box 8545, Houston TX 77009. (713)225-0450. President: Jay Collier. Record company, music publisher (Music West of the Pecos/RMI and Mundo Earwood Music/ASCAP) and record producer. Releases 4 singles and 2 albums/year. Works with artists and songwriters on contract. Pays 5-10% (retail) royalty to artists on contract; standard royalty to songwriters on contract; statutory rate to publishers for each record sold.
How to Contact: Submit demo tape and lyric sheet. Prefers 7½ ips reel-to-reel with 1-4 songs on demo. SASE. Reports in 2 weeks.
Music: C&W. Recently released "You're in Love with the Wrong Man," "Can't Keep My Mind off of Her" (country singles) and *Blue Collar Blues* (country LP).

GOLD STREET, INC., Box 124, Kirbyville TX 75956. (713)423-5516. Labels include Gold Street and Glory Express. President: James L. Gibson. Record company and record producer (Gold Street Music). Releases 2 or more singles and 3 or more albums/year. Works with artists and songwriters on contract.
How to Contact: Submit demo tape and lyric sheet. Prefers 7½ ips reel-to-reel or cassette with 1-4 songs on demo. SASE. Reports in 1 month.
Music: Children's, church/religious, gospel. Recently released *The Story Never Grows Old*, by the Gibsons (gospel LP).

GOLDUST RECORD CO., 115 E. Idaho Ave., Las Cruces NM 88001. (505)524-1889. Owner: Emmit H. Brooks. Record company, music publisher (Enchantment Music/CBMI) and recording studio. Member CMA. Releases 8-12 singles and 6-10 albums/year. Works with musicians on salary; artists and songwriters on contract. Pays 4-6% royalty to artists on contract; standard royalty to songwriters on contract; statutory rate to publishers for each record sold.
How to Contact: Submit demo tape. Prefers 7½ ips reel-to-reel or cassette with 1-5 songs on demo. "We do not wish to review material which has been previously released." SASE. Reports in 1 month.
Music: C&W; easy listening; MOR; rock (soft or country); top 40/pop; and fiddle instrumentals. Recently released *Fiddlin' Around*, by Junior Daugherty (country instrumental LP); *Enchanted Mesa*, by Moon Pie Dance Band (country-rock LP); *The Clay Mac Band*, by Clay Mac Band (country LP); "Navajo Wrangler," by Clay Mac (country single); and "I Can't See the Rainbow for the Rain," by Dana Bivens (country single). Other artists include Hyram Posey, Wes Nivens,

David Ruthstrom, Dick Jonas, Jake Brooks, Raintree, Claudia Jones, Desperados, and Bill Lendrom.

GOSPEL RECORDS, INC., Box 90, Rugby Station, Brooklyn NY 11203. (212)773-5910. President: John R. Lockley. Record company, record producer and music publisher (Gospel Clef/BMI). Works with artists and songwriters on contract. Payment negotiable.
How to Contact: Write about your interest, then submit demo tape and lyric sheet. Prefers cassette with 1-4 songs on demo. SASE. Reports in 1 month.
Music: Church/religious and gospel. Recently released *Glorifying Jesus*, by the Lockley Family Spiritual Music Ensemble (gospel LP); and "Everytime I Feel the Spirit," by the Glorytones (spiritual single).

GRAMAVISION INC., Box 2772 Grand Central Station, New York NY 10163. (212)624-1652. President: Jonathan Rose. Record company, music publisher (Gramavision Music/BMI) and record producer. Member RIAA. Estab. 1979. Works with artists and songwriters on contract. Pays 5-8% royalty to artists on contract; standard royalty to songwriters on contract.
How to Contact: Submit demo tape and lyric sheet. Prefers 7½ or 15 ips reel-to-reel or cassette with 1-3 songs on demo. SASE.
Music: Classical; jazz; progressive; R&B; rock; and top 40/pop. "We are interested in innovative creative music, not formulas. Songs must come from the heart but also be commercial." Recently published *Solo*, by Earl Rose (easy listening LP); *Time Being*, by Ralph Simon (jazz LP); and *Oasis*, by Don Dagradi (jazz LP). Other artists include Tony Dagradi, Earl Rose, Ralph Simon and Dee Daniels.

GRAMEX RECORDS, INC./GOLDBERT, 100 Colony Square, 23rd Floor, Suite 2301, Atlanta GA 30361. (404)881-8800. President: Eric Sutoris. A&R Director: Columbia Jones. National Promotion Director: Bret Bowlin. Record company and music publisher (Camp Peachtree Music, Inc./ASCAP). Deals with artists, songwriters and producers. Produces 10 singles and 2 albums/year. Fee derived from sales royalty.
How to Contact: Submit demo tape. Cassette only. Reports in 2 weeks.
Music: Dance, soft rock and top 40/pop. Recently produced "Runaway Love" by the Balls Brothers Band and "In Love Again" by Paradise Radio (top 40 singles, Gramex Records). Other artists include Paradise Radio and The Survivors.
Tips: "We are only interested in material with top 40 hit potential. We cut nothing on unknown writers unless we have the publishing."

GRAND ARTISTS RECORDS, 8325 SW 132 St., Miami FL 33156. (305)238-1088. Label includes Grand Artists Records. President: Paul Stevens. Record company, record producer and music publisher (Grand Artists Music). Releases 2 albums/year. Works with artists and songwriters on contract. Pays statutory rate to publishers for each record sold.
How to Contact: Submit demo tape and lyric sheet. Prefers cassette with 1-6 songs on demo. SASE. Reports in 1 month.
Music: C&W, dance-oriented, easy listening, MOR, Spanish and top 40/pop.

GRANDVILLE RECORDS, 1 E. Scott St., Suite 408, Chicago IL 60610. (312)649-9644. President/Executive Producer: Clifford Rubin. Record company, music publisher (Billetdoux Music/BMI), and record producer. Releases 10 singles and 3 albums/year. Works with artists and songwriters on contract. Pays standard royalty to artists; statutory rate to publishers for each record sold.
How to Contact: Submit demo tape and typewritten lyric sheet. Prefers cassette with 1-5 songs on demo. "We only review copywritten material; all other will be returned." SASE. Reports in 1 month.
Music: Blues; children's; choral; C&W; dance; easy listening; gospel; jazz; MOR; progressive; R&B; rock; soul; punk; new wave; and top 40/pop. Recently released "Work All Day," (funk rock single) and "People Like Us," (gospel rock single) by Billy Always; "Power Funk," by Power Band (funk R&B 12"). Other artists include Patti Rain, Billy Hills and Randy DeTroit.

GULE RECORD, 7046 Hollywood Blvd., Hollywood CA 90028. (213)462-0502. Vice President: Harry Gordon. Record company, music publisher and record producer. Releases 20 singles and 10-15 albums/year.
How to Contact: Submit demo tape or submit acetate disc. Prefers 7½ ips reel-to-reel with 2 songs minimum on demo. SASE. Reports in 1 week.
Music: C&W; gospel; R&B; rock; soul; and top 40/pop.

HALPERN SOUNDS, 620 Taylor Way, #14, Belmont CA 94002. (415)592-4900. President: Steven Halpern. Record company and record producer. Releases 3 albums/year. Works with artists and songwriters on contract. Pays 1-10% royalty to artists on contract.
How to Contact: Submit demo tape and lyric sheet. Prefers cassette with 4-6 songs on demo. SASE. Reports in 3 months.
Music: C&W, easy listening and MOR. Recently released *Star Children*, by Ingo Swan and Steven Halpern (top 40 LP); *Prelude*, by Steven Halpern (relaxing LP); and *Comfort Zone*, by Halpern (soothing LP).

HAPPY DAY RECORDS, INC., 800 N. Ridgeland, Oak Park IL 60302. (312)848-3322. Vice President: Vince Ippolito. Record company, music publisher and record producer.
How to Contact: Submit demo tape and lyric sheet. Prefers 7½ ips reel-to-reel or cassette with 1-3 songs on demo. SASE.
Music: MOR; progressive; R&B; rock; soul; and top 40/pop. Recently released "Fightin' Jane," by Frank Pisani (MOR/country single).

HEART RECORDS & TAPES OF CANADA LTD., Box 3713, Station B, Calgary, Alberta, Canada T2M 4M4. (403)230-3545. President: Ron Mahonin. Member of CARAS, CIRPA and CRIA. Record company, record producer, music publisher (Have A Heart Music/PRO Canada and Lovin' Heart Songs/CAPAC) and management firm. Estab. 1979. Releases 10 singles and 2-3 albums/year. Works with musicians on salary; artists and songwriters on contract. Pays negotiable royalty to artists and songwriters on contract.
How to Contact: Submit demo tape and lyric sheet. Prefers 7½ ips reel-to-reel or cassette with 1-4 songs on demo. International Reply Coupons or $1 to handle postage. Reports in 1 month.
Music: C&W; easy listening; MOR; progressive; rock; and top 40/pop. Recently released *Fire of Love*, by James Lee Hitchner (country crossover LP); "Thin Ice," by Doug Watt (top 40 single); and "Falling in Love (for All the Right Reasons)," by Sherry Kennedy (MOR single).

THE HERALD ASSOCIATION, INC., Box 218, Wellman Heights, Johnsonville SC 29555. (803)386-2600. Labels include Herald, Klesis and Mark Five Records. Director: H. Ervin Lewis. Record company, music publisher and record producer. Member GMA. Releases 2-3 singles and 8-10 albums/year. Works with artists and songwriters on contract. "Several songwriters are under exclusive contract." Musicians on salary for in-house studio work. Pays 4-6% royalty to artists on contract; statutory rate to publishers for each record sold.
How to Contact: Submit demo tape and lyric sheet. Prefers cassette with 4-8 songs on demo. "Plainly mark outside of package with contents and identify each demo and lead sheet with name and address." SASE. Reports in 2 months.
Music: Choral; church/religious; and gospel. Recently released *God's Not Finished with Me*, by Carman (contemporary gospel LP); *Images*, by Rick Eldridge (contemporary gospel LP); and *Covenant Man*, by Lewis Moore (contemporary gospel LP).

LAWRENCE HERBST RECORDS, Box 1659, Beverly Hills CA 90213. Label includes Total Sound Records. President: Dr. Lawrence Herbst. Record company. Member RIAA. Works with artists on contract. Pays statutory rate to publishers for each record sold.
How to Contact: Submit demo tape and lyric sheet. Prefers 15 ips reel-to-reel or cassette with 1-6 songs on demo. SASE. Reports in 1 month.
Music: Bluegrass, C&W and top 40/pop.

HOLLY RECORDS, 332 N. Brinker Ave., Columbus OH 45204. (614)279-5251. Script Manager: Jetta Brown. Record company, music publisher, record producer, management firm and booking agency. Works with artists and songwriters on contract; musicians and songwriters on salary. Pays 2-33⅓% royalty to artists on contract; statutory royalties to songwriters on contract.
How to Contact: Query, arrange personal interview, submit demo tape, submit demo tape and lead sheet, submit lead sheet or arrange in-person audition. Prefers 7½ or 15 ips reel-to-reel or cassette. Does not return unsolicited material. Reports in 3 weeks.
Music: Bluegrass; blues; church/religious; C&W; folk; gospel; MOR; and top 40/pop. Recently released "Don't Lock the Door," "Sittin on Top of the World" and "Darlin' What Am I Gonna Do?," by Walt Cochran (C&W singles).

HOLY SPIRIT RECORDS, 27335 Penn St., Inkster MI 48141. (313)562-8975. Labels include Jesus Only, Ware, God's World and Aspro Records. Contact: Elder Otis, G. Johnson or Patricia Jones. Record company, music publisher (Manfield Music/BMI and God's World Music/SESAC) and record producer. Releases 5 singles and 10 albums/year. Works with artists and

songwriters on contract. Pays 5-10% royalty to artists on contract; statutory rate to publishers for each record sold.
How to Contact: Write or call first about your interest, then submit demo tape and lyric sheet. Prefers 7½ ips reel-to-reel or cassette with 3 songs on demo. SASE. Reports in 1 month.
Music: Church/religious; C&W; easy listening; gospel; and jazz. Recently released *Receive The Power*, by Otis G. Johnson (gospel LP); "Believe in me" by Saved (gospel single); "Use Me Lord" by Sonlight (gospel single); "Love's All" and "Secret Love" by George Johnson (easy listening/ Aspro Records). Other artists include Marcella Ratliff, Isaac Jenkins and George Johnson.

HOUSE OF LORDS RECORDS, LTD., 8441 Coronet Rd., Edmonton, Alberta, Canada T6E 4N7. (403)469-1361. A&R Director: Andy Krawchuck. Record company and music publisher (House of Lords Publishing). Estab. 1980. Member CIRPA. Releases 6 singles and 3 albums/year. Works with artists on contract. Pays 6-9% royalty to artists on contract; statutory rate to publishers for each record sold.
How to Contact: Submit demo tape and lyric sheet. Prefers cassette with 4-6 songs on demo. SAE and International Reply Coupons. Reports in 1 month.
Music: R&B and top 40/pop. Recently released *Jenson Interceptor*, by Jenson Interceptor (MOR/ pop); *Siren*, by Ronnie Spector (rock); and *Time Stands Still*, by Christopher Ward (top 40/pop). Other artists include The Rockies.

HUNGARIA RECORDS, INC., Box 2073, Teaneck NJ 07666. (201)343-5240. Product Manager: Sim Jackendoff. Record company and record producer. Releases 2 singles and 2-3 albums/year. Works with artists on contract. Payment negotiable.
How to Contact: Write first about your interest. Prefers cassette with 1 song on demo. SASE. Reports in 1 month.
Music: Hungarian folk music only. Recently released *HRLP 002*, by Kallo's Zoltan (Hungarian folk LP); and *HRLP 002*, by Teka Ensemble (Hungarian folk music/LP).

INTERMODAL PRODUCTIONS, LTD., Box 2199, Vancouver, British Columbia, Canada V6B 3V7. (604)688-1820. President: John Rodney. Record company and management firm. Releases 12-24 singles and 4-8 albums/year. Works with artists and songwriters on contract. Pays 4-14% royalty to artists on contract. Charges for some services: "depends on the type of contract the artist is comfortable with, and how much independence he wishes in the creative area."
How to Contact: Submit demo tape. Prefers 7½ ips reel-to-reel with 1-6 songs on demo. SAE and International Reply Coupons. Reports in 1 month.
Music: Classical; C&W; MOR; and top 40/pop. Recently released "Love Is to be a Stinging Bee," by Karmen; and "Kootenay Serenade," by Georges LaFleche.

INVENTION RECORDS, 7210 Roos, Houston TX 77074. (713)774-0075 or 774-3075. President: Dr. John D. Montroy. Record company. Works with artists and songwriters on contract. Pays 7-12% royalty to artists on contract; standard royalty to songwriters on contract.
How to Contact: Write first about your interest. Prefers cassette with 1-5 songs on demo. "No unsolicited material accepted. You must write and ask permission to send." SASE. Reports in 2 weeks.
Music: Choral; church/religious; easy listening; gospel; and MOR. Artists include Jerry Babin.

ISLAND RECORDS INC., 444 Madison Ave., New York, NY 10022. (213)469-1296. Vice-President: Ron Goldstein. Record company.
How to Contact: Query. "We are not actively looking for outside material." SASE.
Music: Dance; jazz; progressive; R&B; rock; top 40/pop; and reggae. Recently released *Charlie Dore*, by Charlie Dore (contemporary pop LP).
Tips: "The better quality demo, the better."

JALYN RECORDING COMPANY, 467 Millwood Dr. Nashville TN 37217. (615)366-6906. President: Jack Lynch. Record company, music publisher and distributor (Jaclyn Music, BMI). Releases 5 singles/year and 5 albums/year. Works with artists on contract. Pays 5-10% royalty to artists on contract; statutory rate to publishers for each record sold.
How to Contact: Write or call first about your interest. Prefers 7½ or 15 ips reel-to-reel or cassette with 1-12 songs on demo. SASE. Reports in 1 week.
Music: Bluegrass; church/religious; C&W; and gospel. Recently released "The Nashville Wildcat" and "Just One in a Crowd," recorded by Pat Osborne/Jaylyn Records; and "Think of What You've Done" and "Faded Love," recorded by Jack Lynch and the Nashville Travelers/Nashville Bluegrass Records.

JANUS RECORDS, 519 Downie St. R., Stratford, Ontario, Canada N5A 1Y3. (519)273-2127. Labels include Maxim Records. Contact: T. Waschkowski. Record company and music publisher (Janus Music (CAPAC), Carlingford Music (BMI), and Maxim Music (CAPAC). Releases 15 singles and 8 albums/year. Works with artists and songwriters on contract. Pays 10-14% royalty to artists on contract; statutory rate to publishers for each record sold.
How to Contact: Submit demo tape and lyric sheet. Prefers cassette with 2-4 songs on demo. Include resumé. SAE and International Reply Coupons. Reports in 2 months.
Music: Children's, church/religious, country, rock and top 40/pop. Recently released *Ain't It Funny*, by Jim Haggerty (country LP and single); *'Cookin'*, by 'Cookin' (rock/pop LP and single); and *Jim Rae*, by J. Rae (country single). Other artists include MacKenzie, 84, Full Steam Ahead, South Paw, B.W. Pawley, Ontario Youth Choir, Keith Gallagher and Wayne Jessop.

JAY BIRD RECORD CO., 1313 Washington, Parsons KS 67357. (316)421-1666. Manager/A&R Director: Albert H. Monday. Record company and music publisher. Releases 3-5 singles/year. Works with artists and songwriters on contract. Pays 9% royalty to artists on contract.
How to Contact: Submit demo or master tape and lead sheet. Prefers 7½ ips reel-to-reel or cassette with 2-4 songs on demo. Tapes should be in stereo. SASE. Reports in 1 month.
Music: Bluegrass; choral; C&W; and easy listening. Recently released "Reading My Heart" and "Big Time Joe."

JEANNIE HITMAKER RECORDS, 18 W. 7th St., Cincinnati OH 45202. (513)421-5256. President: Carl Edmondson. Record company, music publisher and record producer (Kimberly Rene/BMI; Lindsay Cole/ASCAP). Estab. 1980. Works with artists and songwriters on contract. Pays 5%-10% royalty to artists on contract; standard royalty to songwriters on contract; statutory rate to publishers for each record sold.
How to Contact: Prefers 7½ ips reel-to-reel or cassette wqh 1-5 songs on demo. "Typed lyrics." SASE. Reports in 3 weeks.
Music: Uses all types music. Artists include Zachariah, Jim Butler and Palace, Jack Reno and Dennis Henderson.

JENERO RECORD CO., Box 121, Soda Springs ID 83276. President: Ronald Watts. Record company and music publisher. Works with artists and songwriters on contract. Pays 2-7% royalty to artists on contract; standard royalty to songwriters on contract. Charges for some services: "If recording done for purposes of submitting to another record company."
How to Contact: Submit demo tape and lyric sheet. Prefers cassette with 2-6 songs on demo. Does not return unsolicited material. Reports in 3 weeks.
Music: C&W; easy listening; MOR; rock (soft or country); and top 40/pop. Recently released *Mem'rys* and *Yesterday and Today*, by Bill Corbett (easy listening LPs); "You'll Feel Better When I Hold You in My Arms," by Rocky Watson (C&W single); and "I Believe in You," by Eugene Sibbett (easy listening single).

JERSEY COAST AGENTS, LTD., 72 Thorne Place, Hazlet Township NJ 07734. (201)787-3891. Labels include Karass, Granfalloon, Anomaly, Stonehedge, Output and BMA Records. President: Joe McHugh. Vice President, A&R: D.W. Griffiths. Record company, booking agency, music publisher and management firm. Releases 4-6 albums/year. Works with musicians and artists on contract. Pays varying royalty percentages that are "higher than average."
How to Contact: Call or write describing material first. Prefers cassette with 3-4 songs on demo. SASE. Reports "as soon as work load permits."
Music: Bluegrass; folk; progressive and rock. Recently released *Conspiracy, Vol. III, Live*, by Southern Conspiracy; *Working Man's Banjo* and *Jersey Tomatoes*, by D.W. Griffiths; and *Late Night Garage*, by Late Night Garage.

JET RECORDS, INC., 9959 Beverly Grove Dr., Beverly Hills CA 90210. (213)553-6801. Director of A&R Creative Services: Pat Siciliano. Record company. Releases 7-11 singles and 4-11 albums/year. Works with artists on contract.
How to Contact: Prefers cassette with 3 songs maximum on demo. "Put name and address on cassette as well as envelope." SASE. Reports in 10 weeks.
Music: Progressive; rock; and top 40/pop. Recently released *Discovery* and *ELO's Greatest Hits*, both by Electric Light Orchestra (rock LPs); *Xandau* and *Blizzard of Ozz*, by Ozzie Osborne (LP). Other artists include Girl, Magnum, and Oz.
Tips: "Include lyrics, bio, photos and best songs. If you have a good lawyer, call us. We listen to everything that comes in."

JEWEL RECORD CORP., Box 1125, 728 Texas St., Shreveport LA 71163. (318)222-0673. President: Stanley J. Lewis. Executive Vice President: F.R. Lewis. National Promotions Director: Jo

Wyatt. Record company and music publisher. Publishing: Ms. Donnis Lewis.
How to Contact: Submit demo tape or submit demo tape and lead sheet. Prefers 7½ reel-to-reel, cassette or 8-track cartridge. SASE. Reports in 1 month.
Music: C&W; gospel; and soul.

JODY RECORDS, 2226 McDonald Ave., Brooklyn NY 11223. (212)946-4405. Labels include Atlas and Jody Records. A&R Director: Vincent Vallis. Record company, music publisher, (Vado Music/ASCAP) and record producer. Releases 25 singles and 10 albums/year. Works with artists and songwriters on contract. Pays 20-25% to artists on contract; statutory rate to publishers for each record sold. Charges for some services: custom master sessions or demos.
How to Contact: Submit demo tape and lyric sheet. Prefers 7½ ips reel-to-reel or cassette with 2-4 songs on demo. SASE. Reports in 2 weeks.
Music: Blues; C&W; jazz; R&B; rock; soul and top 40 pop. Recently released "Together Ain't So Bad" and "Wear a Smile," by Eddie Hailey (disco singles); and "Double Dealing Daddy," by Gloria Black (disco single).

JRM RECORDS, Box 993, Salem VA 24153. (703)387-0208. Label includes Dominion. President: Jack Mullins. Record company and music publisher (Powhatan Music and Double Jack Publishing). Releases 8 singles and 10 albums/year. Works with artists and songwriters on contract. Pays 5-15% to artists on contract; statutory rate to publishers for each record sold.
How to Contact: Submit demo tape and lyric sheet. Prefers 7½ ips reel-to-reel with 2-4 songs on demo. SASE. Reports in 1 month.
Music: Bluegrass, C&W and R&B. Recently released "Girl", by Simpson Allen (pop-country single); "Oh What a Feeling", by Robin Glass (top 40 single); and "B.T. Boogie", by Wayne Craig (top 40 single). Other artists include Jim Earnes, Shenandoah Cut Ups and Wildfire.

KALEIDOSCOPE RECORDS, Box 0, El Cerrito CA 94530. (415)527-6242. A&R Director: Tom Diamant. Record company and music publisher (Slippery Music/BMI). Releases 5 albums/year.
How to Contact: Submit demo tape and lyric sheet. Prefers cassette with 4-10 songs on demo. SASE. Reports in 1 month.
Needs: Bluegrass, blues, children's, C&W, folk, jazz and R&B. Recently released *David Grisman Quintet*, by David Grisman Quintet (jazz LP); *Safe at Anchor*, by Kate Wolf (folk-pop LP); *Acoustics*, by Tony Rice (jazz LP); and *The Tim Ware Group*, by Tim Ware (jazz LP). Other artists include Darol Anger, Tiny Moore and Jethro Burns.

KAT FAMILY RECORDS, 5775 Peachtree Dunwoody Rd., N.E., Suite B-130, Atlanta, GA 30342. (404)252-6600. President: Joel A. Katz. Vice President: Joel A. Cherry. Record company. Estab. 1980. Fee derived from sales royalty.
How to Contact: Submit demo tape and lyric sheet. Prefers cassette with 5-10 songs on demo. SASE. Reports in 1 month.
Music: Rock, top 40/pop and contemporary gospel. Recently recorded Darts (British do-wop band) Smashers, James Anderson, Marc Speer and William Bell.

K-D MUSIC CO. DIVISION OF KDP, INC., 111 Valley Rd., Wilmington DE 19804. (302)655-7488. A&R: Ed Kennedy. General Manager: Shirley Kay. Record company. Releases 3 singles and 12 albums/year. Works with musicians on salary; artists and songwriters on contract. Payment negotiable. Charges for some services: to "outside producers or publishers only."
How to Contact: Submit demo and lead sheet. Prefers acetate disc. SASE. Reports in 2 weeks.
Music: Bluegrass, blues; children's; choral; church/religious; classical; C&W; easy listening; folk; gospel; jazz; MOR; rock; and top 40/pop. Recently released *Autumn Leaves*, by Bill Andrews (rock LP).

KEN KEENE INTERNATIONAL, Box 24561, Nashville TN 37202. Labels include Briarmeade, Burlap, Keeta, Sea Cruise (UK), and Speedy records. President: Ken Keene. Vice President: Frankie Ford. Record company, booking agency, music publisher and management firm. Releases 15-25 singles and 4-10 albums/year. Works with artists and songwriters on contract. Pays 5% royalty to artists on contract.
How to Contact: Submit demo tape and lead sheet. Prefers 7½ ips reel-to-reel on 5- or 7-inch reel (no 3-inch reels) or cassette with 2-6 songs on demo. SASE. Reports in 1 month.
Music: Blues; children's; church/religious; C&W; dance; easy listening; gospel; MOR; rock (easy, hard or country); soul; top 40/pop; and "foreign language hits." Recently released *The Memphis Session*, by Billy Joe Duniven (rockabilly LP); *The Best Performance of My Life*, by

Denny Barberio (pop LP); "Foxy Man," by Billy Joe Duniven (pop single); "Halfway to Paradise," by Frankie Ford (pop single); and "Holy Roller," by Phil Enloe (country/gospel single).

KEYNOTE RECORDS, Box 4185, Youngstown OH 44515. (216)793-7295. Executive Producer: Richard M. Hahn. Record company, record producer and music publisher (Al-Kris Music/BMI). Estab. 1979. Releases 5 singles and 2 albums/year. Works with artists and songwriters on contract. Pays 3-5% royalty to artists on contract; statutory rate to publishers for each record sold.
How to Contact: Submit demo tape and lyric sheet. Prefers cassette with 3-5 songs on demo. "Must have decent quality tape and clear lead or lyric sheet." SASE. Reports in 3 weeks.
Needs: Children's, C&W, folk, gospel, MOR and top 40/pop. Recently released "Here Come the Browns", by Kardiak Kids (MOR single); "Jubilee" and "His Lovin", by Cycles (top 40 single); "Help Me I'M Falling, by Kirsti Manna (MOR ballad single). Other artists include Phil Hickman and Jim Stack.

KICKING MULE RECORDS, INC., Box 158, Alderpoint CA 95411. (707)926-5312. Labels include Sonet USA and Transatlantic USA Records. Head of A&R: Ed Denson. Record company and music publisher. Releases 20-25 albums/year. Works with artists on contract. Pays 10-16% royalty to artists on contract; standard royalties to songwriters on contract.
How to Contact: Submit demo tape. Prefers reel-to-reel or cassette with 3-5 songs on demo. SASE. Reports in 1 month.
Music: Bluegrass; blues; and folk. Recently released *Thunder on the Run*, by Stefan Grossman (guitarists); *The Act of Dulcimer*, by Force and d'Ossche (dulcimer duets); and *Avocet*, by Bert Jansch (folk songs).
Tips: "We are a label mostly for instrumentalists. The songs are brought to us by the artists but we contact the artists because of their playing, not their songs."

KIDERIAN RECORD PRODUCTS, 4926 W. Gunnison, Chicago IL 60630. (312)545-0861. Labels include Homestead, Newbary, Sonic Wave, Virgin Vinal and Trinity. President: Ray Peck. Record company, record producer and music publisher (KRPCO). Releases 25-30 singles and 5-6 albums/year. Works with artists and songwriters on contract; musicians on salary for in-house studio work. Pays statutory rate to publishers for each record sold.
How to Contact: Submit demo tape and lyric sheet. Prefers cassette with 4-6 songs on demo. Reports in 1 month.
Music: Bluegrass, blues, children's, choral, classical, C&W, dance-oriented, easy listening, folk, gospel, jazz, MOR, progressive, Spanish, R&B, rock, soul, top 40/pop and new wave. Recently released *Gary Cross Live*, by Gary Cross (C&W LP and single); *Rich Rags Syncopated Love*, by Rich Rags (new wave LP and single); *Tricky Zingers*, by Creme Soda (power pop LP and single). Other artists include Boyz (Paul), Tom Petreli, The 80's, Ray Peck, The Trouble Boys, Wall Street, Pirate and Mammoth.

KIM RECORDS, 15394 Warwick Blvd., Newport News VA 23602. (804)877-6877. A&R Director: W.H. Smith. Record company, record producer and music publisher (Festive Music/BMI). Works with artists and songwriters on contract. Pays 5-8% royalty to artists on contract; statutory rate to publishers for each record sold.
How to Contact: Submit demo tape and lyric sheet, write first about your interest. Prefers 7½ or 3¾ reel-to-reel with 4-8 songs on demo. SASE. Reports in 3 weeks.
Music: Rock and oldies. "Wild One", by Epics (rock single); "Epitaph of Tomorrow", by Fire over Gibraltar (rock single) and "Fly Me to Nashville" (C&W single). Other artists include Tommy Dee.

KING OF KINGS RECORD CO., 38603 Sage Tree St., Palmdale CA 93550. Labels include Carellen, Lord of Lords, Tropical and Car Records. A&R Director: Leroy Pritchett. Record company and music publisher. Releases 1 album/year. Pays 5-15% royalty to artists on contract; statutory rate to publishers for each record sold.
How to Contact: Submit lead sheet only. SASE. Reports in 1 month.
Music: Church/religious; C&W; gospel; jazz; rock and soul. Recently released *Another Dawn*, *Heaven Is Just over the Hill* (gospel LPs), and *Charles Vickers Does Disco*, (disco LP) by Charles Vickers.

KING-J RECORD CO., (subsidiary of Joe King Productions, Inc.), 1316 Vally St., Seattle WA 98109. (206)622-8358. Labels include New Meadows Records. Contact: Joe King. Record company and music publisher (Joe King Music/BMI). Estab. 1980. Releases 3 singles and 1 album/year. Works with musicians on salary for in-house studio work and songwriters on contract.

How to Contact: Submit demo tape and lyric sheet. Prefers cassette with 6-8 songs on demo. SASE. Reports in 2 weeks.
Music: C&W and gospel. Recently released "Old Whiskey," by Avery Family (country single); "Speachless," by Lloyd Green (country single); and "Statue of a Fool," by Albert Young Eagle (country single).

SID KLEINER MUSIC ENTERPRISES, 3701 25th Ave. SW, Naples FL 33999. Labels include Musi-Poe, Top-Star, This Is It, Token, and Country-King Records. Owner: Sid Kleiner. Record company and consulting firm to music industry. Releases 10 albums/year. Works with musicians and songwriters on contract. Charges for some services: "We may, at our option, charge *actual* production expense. We are not get-rich-quickers or rip-off artists. But we are too small to pay all of these bills!"
How to Contact: Submit demo tape and lead sheet. Prefers cassette. SASE, "otherwise materials aren't returned." Reports in 3 weeks.
Music: Bluegrass; C&W; easy listening; folk; jazz; and "banjo and guitar soloists and features." Recently released *Burd Boys on Stage* and *Chartbusters and Other Hits* (country LPs), by the Burd Boys; and *Find a Simple Life*, by Dave Kleiner (folk/rock LP). Other artists include Sid Kleiner.

L.M.I. (LEE MAGID, INC.), Box 532, Malibu CA 91356. (213)858-7282. President: Lee Magid. Record company, record producer and music publisher (Alexis Music/ASCAP, Marvelle Music/BMI, and Lou-Lee Music/BMI). Works with artists and songwriters on contract. Pays 2-5% royalty to artists on contract; standard royalty to songwriters on contract. Charges for some services: "only if my time is demanded for studio time or too much consultation."
How to Contact: Submit demo tape and lyric sheet. Prefers cassette with 4-8 songs on demo. SASE. Reports in 1 month.
Music: Blues; church/religious; C&W; dance; easy listening; folk; gospel; jazz; MOR; progressive; R&B; soul; and rock. Recently released *Bossman of the Blues*, by Big Joe Turner (blues LP); *Hear Me Now*, by Ernie Andrews (MOR/jazz/soul LP); *Della*, by Della Reese (MOR/soul LP); "Too Many Women," by Windstorm (R&B single). Other artists include Dorothy Donegan, Rickey Kelly, Kim Tolliver and Windstorm, "Rags" Waldorf Band, Lorez Alexandria and Randy Hart.

L.S. RECORDS, 120 Hickory St., Madison TN 37115. (615)868-7172. Labels include L.S. Records and U.E.C. Records. Publishing Director: Harold Hodges. Record company and music publisher. Works with artists and songwriters on contract. Pays standard royalty.
How to Contact: Submit demo tape and lyric sheet or arrange personal interview. Prefers cassette with 3 songs on demo. SASE. Reports in 1 month.
Music: C&W (modern); easy listening; MOR; rock (soft); and top 40/pop. "We are primarily looking for material for females." Released "Let Me Down Easy," "I'm Gonna Love You Anyway," and "One Day at a Time," by Cristy Lane (modern country singles).

LA LOUISIANNE RECORDS, 711 Stevenson St., Lafayette LA 70501. (318)234-5577. Labels include Tamm, Belle and Music Mart. President: (Mr.) Carol J. Rachou, Sr. Record company, record producer, recording studio and music publisher (La Lou Music/BMI). Releases 10-20 singles and 4-6 albums/year. Works with artists and songwriters on contract. "We also deal with promoters, managers, agents, etc." Pays statutory rate to publishers for each record sold.
How to Contact: Submit demo tape and lyric sheet. Prefers 7½ ips reel-to-reel or cassette with 1-6 songs on demo. "If possible, submit different musical variations of songs (tempos, styles, keys, etc.)." SASE.
Music: Primarily produces Cajun/French but also produces some bluegrass, blues, church/religious, classical, C&W, folk, gospel, jazz, MOR, progressive, R&B, rock, top 40/pop, comedy, French comedy and instrumental. Recently released *Lache Pas La Patate* (Gold record in Canada), by Jimmy C. Newman (French Cajun LP); *A Cajun Tradition Vol. 2*, by Nathan Abshire (French Cajun LP); *Cajun Fiddle*, by Rufus Thibodeaux (Cajun/country LP); *That Cajun Country Sound*, by Eddy Raven (French and English Cajun/country LP); and *Authentic French Music*, by Ambrose Thibodeaux (traditional Cajun LP). Other artists include Vin Bruce, Aldus Roger, Merlin Fontenot, L.J. Foret, Blackie Forestier, The Dusenbery Family, Alex Broussard, Bud Fletcher.

LADD MUSIC CO., 401 Wintermantle Ave., Scranton PA 18505. (717)343-6718. Labels include White Rock Records. President: Phil Ladd. Record company, music publisher and producer. Releases 12-24 singles and 1-3 albums/year. Works with artists and songwriters on contract. Payment negotiable for artists on contract; 4% royalty to songwriters on contract.

How To Contact: Submit demo tape and lead sheet. Prefers cassette with 1-6 songs on demo. SASE. Reports in 2 weeks.

Music: Blues; children's; choral; C&W; easy listening; MOR; rock; soul; and top 40/pop. Recently released "Miss Lucy," by Big Al Downing (rock single); and "Once in Awhile," by Clyde Stacy (MOR single).

LAKE COUNTRY RECORDS, Box 88, Decatur TX 76234. (817)627-2128. President: Danny Wood. Releases 5 singles/year. Works with artists and songwriters on contract. Pays 7-12% royalty to artists on contract; statutory rate to publishers for each record sold.

How to Contact: Write first about your interest. Prefers 7½ ips reel-to-reel with 1-4 songs on demo. SASE. Reports in 1 month.

Music: Bluegrass and C&W. Recently released "Trusting Love", by Ronnie Mac (C&W single); "Day Dreams", by Larry Quinten (C&W single); and "It's Not That Easy", by Larry Wampler (C&W single).

LANOR RECORDS, Box 233, 329 N. Main St., Church Point LA 70525. (318)684-2176. Labels include Lanor and Joker Records. Owner: Lee Lavergne. Record company and music publisher. Works with artists and songwriters on contract. Pays 3% royalty to artists on contract.

How to Contact: Submit demo tape. Prefers 7½ ips reel-to-reel or cassette with 2-6 songs on demo. SASE. Reports in 2 weeks.

Music: C&W, rock, and soul. Recently released "Pretty Poison" and "She's Walking," by Charles Mann (country single); and "Something to Do," by Paul Marx (country single).

LASALLE RECORDING CO., 8959 S. Oglesby Ave., Chicago IL 60617. (312)375-4276. Labels include Fay, LaSalle and Planet records. Vice President: Armond Jackson. Record company, music publisher and booking agency. Works with musicians and songwriters on contract. Pays 1%/record side royalty to artists and songwriters on contract.

How to Contact: Submit demo tape, or submit demo tape and lead sheet. Prefers 7½ ips reel-to-reel or cassette with 12 songs minimum on tape. SASE. Reports in 2 weeks.

Music: Blues; church/religious; gospel; and top 40/pop. Recently released "Midnight Shuffle," by Jump Jackson (R&B single).

LAVAL RECORDS, 1327 Cobb St., Kalamazoo MI 49007. (616)342-5328. Contact: Vic Laval. Record company, record producer and music publisher (VALCO Music/BMI). Releases 15 albums/year. Works with artists and songwriters on contract. Pays 3-5¢/single sold and 60-80¢/album sold to artists on contract; statutory rate to publishers for each record sold.

How to Contact: Submit demo tape and lyric sheet, call about your interest or arrange personal interview to play demo tape. Prefers 7½ ips reel-to-reel or cassette with 4-8 songs on demo. SASE. Reports in 2 weeks.

Music: Blues, church/religious, C&W, gospel, R&B, rock and soul. *Don't Tax Me In*, by Joe Blue (blues LP); *Stoop Down Baby*, by Chick Willis (blues LP); and *The Best of Jimmy Lynch*, by Jimmy Lynch (soul LP). Other artists include Eddie Vespa, Frisco, Linc Terry, Tommy Brown and The Terry's.

LEGEND RECORDS, Box 1414, Vicksburg MS 39180. (601)638-5622. Record company, record producer and music publisher (Unicorn Publishing). ASCAP. Releases 6-10 singles and 2-6 albums/year. Works with artists and songwriters on contract; musicians on salary for in-house studio work. Pays 5-10% royalty to artists on contract; statutory rate to publishers for each record sold.

How to Contact: Submit demo tape and lyric sheet. "Include bio, goals and photo." Prefers 7½ reel-to-reel or cassette with 2-4 songs on demo. Reports in 1 month.

Music: Bluegrass, church/religious, C&W, folk, gospel and MOR. Recently released "Phantom of the Trace", by Reunion (folk/country single); "Amazing Grace," by Reunion (gospel single); and *A Woman's Just a Woman*, by Reunion (folk/country LP). Other artists include McCalls Creek, South Fork, Katy Preston, Sherman Dillon and Carol Wade.

TY LEMLEY MUSIC, 430 Pearce Rd., Pittsburgh PA 15234. (412)341-0991. Labels include Tymena Music. General Manager: Bud Lemley. President: Ty Lemley. Record company and record producer. Works with artists and songwriters on contract; musicians on salary for in-house studio work. Pays maximum royalty to artists on contract; statutory note to publishers for each record sold.

How to Contact: Submit demo tape and lyric sheet. Prefers casette or 45 demo record. SASE. Reports in 1 month.

Music: Recently released "Happy Willowbee" (children); "Rock-a-Nova" (dance); "Rowdy" (rock); "You and Me" (pop/top 40); and "Offer Me Your Love," by Ty Lemley (MOR).

LISE RECORDS AND PUBLISHING, INC., 119 Riel Blvd., Hull, Quebec, Canada J8Y 5Y4. (819)776-0253. President: Lise Houle. Record company and music publisher (Lise Publishing, Inc.). Estab. 1979. Member ACCM. Releases 3 singles and 1 album/year. Works with artists and songwriters on contract. Pays 4-6% royalty to artists on contract; statutory rate to publishers for each record sold.
How to Contact: Submit demo tape and lyric sheet. Prefers cassette with 4-6 songs on demo. SAE and International Reply Coupons. Reports in 1 month.
Music: C&W. Recently released "Merry Xmas from Lisa Marie" and "I Saw Mommy Kissing Santa Claus," by Debra Kay (single); and *Voices of Alan Drayman*, by Alan Drayman (LP). Other artists include Nesbit and My 3 Sons, Orval Phophet and Hughie Scott.

LITTLE DAVID RECORDS, INC., 8033 Sunset Bvld., Suite 1037, Los Angeles CA 90046. (213)876-9602. President: Monte Kay. Labels include Hidden Records. Record company. Works with artists and songwriters on contract.
How to Contact: Query. SASE.
Music: Blues; dance; easy listening; folk; jazz; MOR; progressive; R&B; rock; soul; and top 40/pop. Recently released *An Evening With Two Grand Pianos*, by Hank Jones and John Lewis (jazz LP).

THE LITTLE GIANT. RECORD COMPANY, 1014 16th Ave. S., Nashville TN 37212. (615)244-4360. Labels include Street Song Records. President: Roy Sinkovich. General Manager: Mick Lloyd. Promotion Director: Robin Eichel. Record company, music publisher (JMR Enterprises), and record producer. Estab. 1979. Member CMA, FICAP, NARAS and NSAI. Releases 12 singles and 4 albums/year. Works with musicians on salary; songwriters on contract. Pays 5½-7½% royalty to artists on contract; statutory rate to publishers for each record sold.
How to Contact: Submit demo tape and lyric sheet. Prefers cassette with 1-4 songs on demo. SASE. Reports in 4 weeks.
Music: Church/religious; C&W; easy listening; gospel; MOR; progressive; R&B; rock; and top 40/pop. Recently released "You Beat Me to the Punch," by De De Upchurch (C&W single); "Fallin' For You," by Jeri Kelly (C&W/MOR single); and "Be My Lover, Be My Friend," by Kelly & Lloyd (C&W single). Other artists include Byron Gallimore, The Nashville Rhythm Section, Arleen Harden and The Stockard Band.

LITTLE GIANT RECORDS, Box 205, White Lake NY 12786. (914)583-4471. Label includes Killer Records. A&R Director: Mike Pell. Record company, record producer and music publisher (Karjan Music Publishing Co.). Releases 6 singles and 6 albums/year. Works with artists and songwriters on contract. Pays standard royalty to artists on contract; statutory rate to publishers for each record sold.
How to Contact: Submit demo tape and lyric sheet. Prefers cassette with 1-3 songs on demo. SASE. Reports in 3 weeks.
Music: C&W, easy listening, MOR, R&B, top 40/pop. Recently released *Introducing The Mighty Quinn*, by The Mighty Quinn (Irish LP); *Bobby Gold Live*, by Bobby Gold (comedy LP); and *Dick Wells Sings Dick Haymes*, by Dick Wells (MOR LP). Other artists include Mickey Barnett, Tom & Jay, Andy Terra, The Third Edition, Tony Pepe, and Jimmy Festa.

LOGO III, 413 Cooper St., Suite 101, Camden NJ 08102. (215)276-0100. President: Michael Nise. Record company, music publisher and record producer. Estab. 1979. Works with artists and songwriters on contract, musicians on salary for in-house studio work. Pays standard royalty to artists on contract; statutory rate to publishers for each record sold. Payment negotiable.
How to Contact: Submit cassette with 1-3 songs on demo. SASE. Reports in 1 month.
Music: Children's; Church/religious; C&W; dance; easy listening; folk; gospel; jazz; R&B; rock; soul; and top 40/pop. Recently released "The Mork and Mindy Theme," by Sunburst (dance single). Other artists include William Sackett and His Radio Orchestra.

LUCIFER RECORDS, INC., Box 263, 37 Woodside Ave., Hasbrouck Heights NJ 07604. (201)288-8935. President: Ron Luciano. Record company, booking agency and music publisher. Works with artists and songwriters on salary and contract.
How to Contact: Arrange personal interview. Prefers cassette with 4-8 songs on demo. SASE. Reports in 3 weeks.
Music: Dance; easy listening; MOR; rock; soul; and top 40/pop. Recently released "Lucky," and "Smoke Ya," by Legz (rock single); and "Loves a Crazy Game," by Voyage (disco/ballad single). Other artists include Diamond Jym, Charles Lamont and Lucifer.

LUNA RECORDS CO., 434 Center St., Healdsburg CA 95448. (707)433-4138. Labels include Luna, Lugar, Yuriko and Sony Records. President: Abel De Luna. Record company, booking agency and music publisher (Yema Publishing/ASCAP and Luna Publishing/BMI). Releases 30 singles and 20 albums/year. Works with artists and songwriters on contract. Pays 8% royalty to artists on contract; statutory rate.
How to Contact: Submit demo tape and lead sheet. Prefers cassette with 5-10 songs on demo. Does not return unsolicited Material. Reports in 3 weeks.
Music: Children's and Latin. Recently released "El Solitario," by Los Pasteles Verdes (Spanish 45 and LP); "Que Me Entierren Cantando," by Los Huracanes Del Norte (Spanish 45 and LP); and "Te Vas O Quedar Liorando," by La Banda Int'de Ray Camacho (Spanish 45 and LP). Other artists include Los Luceritos de Michoacan, Los Astros, Los Buhos, Tany Ponce, Grupo Santa Maria, Los Flamantes Del Norte, and Los Errantes Del Norte.

M.R.C. RECORDS, Box 2072, Waynesboro VA 22980. (703)942-0106. Labels include MRC, Lark and Echo Records. Owners: John Major, Margie F. Major. Record company, music publisher and recording studio. Releases 24 singles and 10 albums/year. Works with artists on contract; songwriters on salary and contract. Payment negotiable.
How to Contact: Submit demo tape and lyric sheet. Prefers 7½ ips reel-to-reel with 1-4 songs on demo. SASE. Reports in 2 weeks.
Music: Bluegrass; C&W; dance; easy listening; gospel; MOR; rock (country or hard); soul; and top 40/pop. Recently released "Afraid You'd Come Back," by Kenny Price (C&W single); "Deeper Water," by Brenda Kaye Perry (C&W single); and "Carlena and Jose Gomes," by Billy Walker (C&W single).
Tips: "Don't submit songs with tunes purchased from advertisements."

McKINNON PICTURES/RECORD CO., Box 691, Reading PA 19601. (215)372-7361. Labels include McKinnon, Slide, Holy Cross, Reading, Tar Heel, Movieland, Atlanna, Black Treasure and Ohiophone Records. President: Lenny McKinnon. Record company. Works with musicians on salary; artists and songwriters on contract. Pay 3-6% royalty to artists on contract; 5% maximum royalty to songwriters on contract.
How to Contact: Submit demo tape and lead sheet. Prefers cassette with 1-10 songs on demo. SASE. Reports in 1 month.
Music: Blues; C&W; easy listening; gospel; jazz; rock (soft); soul; and top 40/pop. Recently released *Lolita*, by Lolita R. Smith; "I Wish You the Best," by Janice and Lee; and "You Never Say I Love You," by Gentle Persuasion. Other artists include Perfect Touch, Ronnie and Gwenae, Robb Fritz, Cleveland Martin and Dee Shappard.

MAINROADS PRODUCTIONS, INC., 100 Huntley St., Toronto, Ontario, Canada M4Y 2L1. (416)961-8001. Manager/A&R: Bruce W. Stacey. Record company and music publisher (Mainroads Publishing/CAPAC and Bruce W. Stacey Publishing/PROCAN). Member CRPA and CMRA. Releases 5-10 albums/year. Works with artists and songwriters on contract; musicians on salary for in-house studio work. Pays statutory rate to publishers for each record sold.
How to Contact: Submit demo tape and lyric sheet or write about your interest. Prefers cassette with 3-5 songs on demo. SAE and International Reply Coupons. Reports in 1 month.
Music: Children's, choral, church/religious and gospel. Recently released *Stacey*, by The Stacey Band; *I Found a New World*, by Glen Rutledge; and *The Best of Gospel Music*, by assorted artists (all Christian contemporary LPs). Other artists include Norma Jean Mainse, The Breakthrough Band, Ginny Ambrose Bridle, Reynold Rutledge, and The 100 Huntley Street Singers.

MAJEGA RECORDS, 240 E. Radcliffe Dr., Claremont CA 91711. (714)624-0677. President: Gary K. Buckley. Record company. Works with musicians on salary; artists and songwriters on contract. Pays negotiable royalty to artists on contract; standard royalty to songwriters on contract; statutory rate to publishers for each record sold.
How to Contact: Submit demo tape or submit demo tape and lead sheet. Prefers 7½ ips reel-to-reel or cassette with 1-4 songs on demo. SASE. Reports in 3 weeks.
Music: C&W; easy listening; gospel; MOR; rock (country or pop); and top 40/pop. Recently released *To God, with Love* and *Country Love*, recorded by Jerry Roark (gospel/C&W LPs); "Songwriter," (pop single) and *Buche*, by Rick Buche (top 40 LP); "Steppin' Out," by The Gospelmen (gospel LP); "Our America," by June Wade and the Country Congregation (country/gospel single); and "Is It Right" and "Touch Me Now," by Borderline (top 40 singles).

MAJOR LABEL RECORD CO., Box 651, Worthington OH 43085. (614)846-2026. President: Richard H. Deitch. Record company and music publisher (XC Music Publishing/ASCAP). Releases 1 single/year. Works with artists and songwriters on contract. Pays negotiable royalty to

Songwriter's Market Close-up

Mick Lloyd started in the music business as a recording artist with GRT and Musicor Records. After moving to Nashville he became heavily involved in publishing and production and, along with friend and partner Roy Sinkovich, started Little Giant Records and the Music City Song Festival where he serves as festival director. Their publishing arm, JMR Enterprises, takes credit for, among other songs, Dave Rowland & Sugar's "Fool By Your Side," Loretta Lynn's "Take Your Time In Leavin'," and Jerri Kelly's "Fallin' for You."

"As a *producer*, I listen to the tune in terms of the 'sound' for my artists," says Lloyd. "Is it what they like to say? Does it compare to any of their previous records? Is it stronger than songs we already have?"

"As a *publisher*, I listen strictly on the basis of whether or not I feel we can get it cut. Is the lyric meaningful and understandable? Is the song 'commercial' in the sense of attracting widespread interest? If I feel the song is something we might be interested in, I set it aside and listen again in a few days. If I still feel the tune is 'cuttable,' we go after it!"

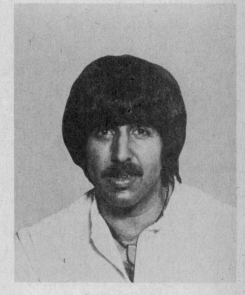

Mick Lloyd

The demo's purpose he says, is to "put across the lyric and melody line. As such, it is extremely important that it be clean and easy to hear. Too many demos concentrate on production and make the lyrics and melody line hard to follow."

The amount of production on a demo is in his opinion just that—the opinion of the person you will be submitting to. "A songwriter must take time to study his audience. Some producers only have ears for a demo which is totally produced; others really want to hear just a vocal with guitar or piano. The differences don't necessarily correspond to whether you are submitting to a publisher, producer, or record company, but rather to the individuals. After a while, it is pretty easy to figure out who wants to hear what.

"I personally prefer just a vocal with guitar or piano because we usually re-demo all the songs we publish. At most, a basic rhythm section should be utilized. It's the producer's job to produce, not the writer. And it's the publisher's job to make a professional demo after he has accepted the song."

He advises songwriters to "listen constantly because styles and 'what's hot' are always changing. In addition, concentrate on writing for a few particular artists—their albums, get a feel for the type of lyric and movement they use. Writing for a particular artist may restrict you creatively, but it has potential for achieving more immediate results. Then, once you have a few cuts, others will become more receptive to your work."

The biggest mistake beginning songwriters make is becoming discouraged. "Tunes aren't cut immediately. The nature of the business often results in tunes being cut by the very same person who rejected them earlier. The important thing is to believe in your work and keep pitching it. All it takes is for one right person to hear something you've written and like it. When that one person comes along, all past rejections become meaningless."

artists on contract; statutory rate to publishers for each record sold.
How to Contact: Submit demo tape and lyric sheet. Prefers cassette with 1-6 songs on demo. SASE. Reports in 1 month.
Music: Country, MOR, rock, and top 40/pop and new wave. Recently released "Stay", by Bob Bishop (MOR single); "You Sing Like An Angel", by Terry Foster (top 40 single); and "War Museum", by XL (rock single).

MALACO RECORDS, Box 9287, Jackson MS 39206. (601)982-4522. Labels include Chimneyville Records. Producers: Wolf Stephenson, James Griffin, Tommy Couch. Record company, music publisher and record producer. Works with artists and songwriters on contract and salary. Pays standard royalty.
How to Contact: Submit demo tape and lyric sheet. Prefers 7½ ips reel-to-reel or cassette with 1-5 songs on demo. SASE. Reports in 1 month.
Music: All types. Recently released "Talk to Me," by Dorothy Moore (R&B single); and *Groove Me,* by Fern Kinney (disco single and LP); and *Let's Do It Together,* by James Bradley (R&B single and LP). Other artists include Freedom, Jewel Bass and Natural High.

MANQUIN, Box 2388, Toluca Lake CA 91602. (213)985-8284. Labels include Quinto Records. Co-Owner: Quint Benedetti. Record company, music publisher, record producer, management firm and public relations firm. Estab. 1979. Works with artists and songwriters on contract. Pays standard royalty to artists on contract and songwriters; on contract.
How to Contact: Query or submit demo tape and lead sheet. Prefers 7½ ips reel-to-reel or cassette with 2-3 songs on demo. SASE. Reports in 1 month.
Music: Novelty and Broadway musical.

MARINA RECORDS, 39 W. 55th St., New York NY 10019. (212)586-3350. A&R Director: Nate Adams Jr. Record company and music publisher (Lori-Joy Music/BMI). Member BMA. Releases 2-8 singles and 3-12 albums/year. Works with artists and songwriters on contract. Pays standard royalties to songwriters on contract; statutory rate to publishers for each record sold.
How To Contact: Submit demo tape and lyric or lead sheet. Prefers 7½ or 15 ips reel-to-reel or cassette with 2 songs minimum on demo. SASE. Reports in 2 weeks.
Music: R&B; soul; and top 40/pop. Recently released *Peaceful,* by Al Johnson (pop LP); *Pulse,* by Pulse (soul LP); and *The Nominee,* by Lloyd Price (pop LP).
Tips: "A good song opens many doors!"

MARLO RECORD CO., Box 49, Utica NY 13502. (315)724-0895. Manager: Floyd Ketchum. Record company, record producer and music publisher (Dobro Publishing). Releases 2 singles and 1 album/year. Works with artists on contract. Pays statutory rate to publishers for each record sold.
How to Contact: Submit demo tape and lyric sheet. Prefers 3¾, 7½ ips reel-to-reel, cassette or 8-track with any number of songs on demo. SASE. Reports in 1 month.
Music: Bluegrass, children's, church/religious, C&W and gospel. Recently released *Heart of the Country Brothers,* by Marlo and Slim (country LP) and "Chewing Tobacco Rag" and "Sing Me a Song of the Cowboy," by Marlo and Slim (country singles).

MARMIK, 135 E. Muller Rd., East Peoria IL 61611. (309)699-7204. President: Martin Mitchell. Record company and music publisher. Works with musicians and songwriters. Pays negotiable royalties. Sometimes buys material from songwriters outright; payment negotiable.
How to Contact: Query, submit demo tape, or submit demo tape and lead sheet. Prefers reel-to-reel or cassette with 2-10 songs on demo. "With first submission include an affidavit of ownership of material." SASE. Reports in 2 weeks.
Music: Blues; children's; choral; church/religious; C&W; easy listening; gospel; and MOR.

MARVEL RECORDS CO., 852 Elm St., Manchester NH 03101. Labels include Banff, Marvel, Rodeo International, W&G and Melbourne Records. Executive Director: James N. Parks. Record company and music publisher (Jaspar Music Publishing Co., Ltd./BMI, Melbourne Music Publishing Co., Ltd./ASCAP). Member IRMA. Releases 8 singles and 8 albums/year. Works with musicians on salary; artists and songwriters on contract. Payment to artist negotiable; pays statutory rate to publishers for each record sold.
How to Contact: Submit lead sheet.
Tips: "All of our artists are relatively new artists from Australia, Canada and the U.K. They are released here in the U.S.A. only after strong success in their own countries."

MASTER TRAK SOUND RECORDERS, (formerly Modern Sound Studios), Miller Building, 415 N. Parkerson, Box 856, Crowley LA 70526. (318)788-0773. Owner: Jay Miller. General Man-

ager and Chief Engineer: Mårk Miller. Recording studio and record companies. Works with musicians on salary and artists on royalty basis. Pays 4% and 5% artist royalty. (No studio charges to contract artists). Studio available on an hourly basis to the public. Record labels: Master-Trak, Showtime, Kajun, Cajun Classic, Blues Unlimited, Wildwood and Par T. Works with musicians on salary; artists and songwriters on contract. Pays 4-5% royalty to artists on contract. Charges for some services: "We charge for making audition tapes of any material that we do not publish."
How to Contact: Submit demo tape and lead sheet. Prefers 7½ ips reel-to-reel. SASE. Reports in 1 month.
Music: Blues; church/religious; C&W; dance; folk; gospel; MOR; progressive; rock; and soul. Recently released "Touch Me" (progressive C&W single), *At Last* (progressive C&W LP) and "Mama Don't Care" (C&W single), by Warren Storm.

THE MASTER'S COLLECTION LIMITED, Box 189, Station W, Toronto, Ontario Canada M6M 4Z2. (416)746-1991. Labels include Little Pilgrim. President: Paul J. Young. Record company and music publisher (T.M.C. Publishing/CAPAC and Master's Collection Publishing/PROCAN). Releases 1-2 singles and 12-15 albums/year. Works with artists and songwriters on contract. Pays 4%-10% royalty to artists on contract; statutory rate to publishers for each record sold.
How to Contact: Write first about your interest. Prefers cassette with 3-6 songs on demo. Does not return unsolicited material. Reports in 1 month.
Music: Church/religious and gospel. Recently released *Gene & Marty*, by Gene MacLellan (country gospel LP); *Livin' in the Love*, by Mark Moore (folk gospel LP); and *Ask Me Why*, by Pat Pepper (folk gospel LP). Other artists include Doug Sadler, Lloyd Knight, Doug McKenzie and Bill Davidson.

MAZINGO'S, INC., Box 11181, Charlotte NC 28209. (704)375-1102. President: Ben W. McCoy. Record company. Payment negotiable.
How to Contact: Query or submit demo tape and lead sheet. Prefers cassette or 8-track cartridge with 2-8 songs on demo. SASE. Reports in 1 month.
Music: Bluegrass; blues; children's; choral; church/religious; classical; C&W; folk; gospel; jazz; polka; progressive; soul; and top 40/pop.

MCP/DAVISOUND, (formerly Mother Cleo Productions), Box 521, By-Pass 76, Newberry SC 29108. (803)276-0639. Labels include Mother Cleo, Cleo and Cub Records. Producer/Director: Hayne Davis. Studio Manager: Polly Davis. Record company, music publisher (Sweet Polly Music/BMI), recording studio, and production company producing music for films, features and commercials. MCP is a unique, small (but multifaceted) company engaged in numerous activities for the communications/entertainment industry." Releases 6 singles and 2 albums/year. Works with musicians on salary; artists and songwriters on contract. "We also work with co-producers, supplying our facility and talent for outside use for a front fee. We hire talent (vocalists, musicians and writers) of varying types, styles and capabilities at varying intervals, depending on the requirements and frequency of the work project and the individual's capabilities." Charges for some services: offers studio facilities for rental by "outside" songwriters, producers and publishers.
How to Contact: Submit demo tape and lead sheet. Prefers cassette with 2-8 songs on demo. "We are not responsible for return of tapes, lead sheets, etc. on unsolicited material. If, however, appropriate packaging and return postage is included, we make every effort to return materials and notify the sender by personal letter." SASE. Reports in 2 weeks.
Music: C&W (modern country); disco; easy listening; MOR; rock; and top 40/pop. Recently released "Sheila," by James Meadows (modern country single); "Too Far Gone," by Curt Bradford (modern country single); and *Cooks in 1 Minute*, by the J. Teal Band (rock LP).

MCA RECORDS, 27 Music Square E., Nashville TN 37203. (615)244-8944. Contact: A&R Department. Record company. Releases 60 singles and 30 albums/year. Works with artists on contract.
How to Contact: Query. Prefers 7½ reel-to-reel with 2-4 songs on demo. SASE.
Music: Recently released "Ya'll Come Back Saloon," by the Oak Ridge Boys (country single); "I Believe In You," by Don Williams (country single); "If Loving You is Wrong," by Barbara Mandrell (country single); and "Somebody's Knockin," by Terri Gibbs.

Market conditions are constantly changing! If this is 1983 or later, buy the newest edition of *Songwriter's Market* at your favorite bookstore or use the back-of-the-book order form.

MEADOW-MORGEN RECORDS, LTD., Box G 145, Station G, Calgary, Alberta, Canada T3A 2G1. (403)288-6500. President: Rick Morgenstern. Record company and music publisher (Meadow-Morgen Publishing, Ltd.). Works with artists and songwriters on contract. Pays 50% maximum royalty to artists on contract; statutory rate to publishers for each record sold.
How to Contact: Write or call first about your interest. Prefers 7½ ips reel-to-reel with 2-5 songs on demo. SAE and International Reply Coupons. Reports in 3 weeks.
Music: Bluegrass, C&W, easy listening and rock/country.

MELLOW MAN RECORDS, 184 King St. W., Kitchener, Ontario, Canada L5C 1H9. Labels include Mellow Man, Foxy Lady, Rapper and Sweet Thing Records. Director: William Moran. Record company, music publisher and management firm. Works with musicians and songwriters on salary or contract. Pays 8-10% royalty to artists on contract; standard royalty to songwriters on contract. "All studio and musician costs are an advance against sales."
How to Contact: Submit demo tape and lead sheet. Include bio and photo. Prefers cassette with 1-12 songs on demo. SAE and International Reply Coupons. Reports in 2 weeks.
Music: Blues; disco; easy listening; jazz; rock (country); soul; and top 40/pop. Recently released "Where Did the Good Times Go?", by Jeff Addams (easy listening single); "I Love to Sing," by Terry Logan (jazz single); and "It Happened One Night," by Jeff and Jackie (top 40 single).

MERCANTILE RECORDS, Box 2271, Palm Springs CA 92263. (714)320-4848. President: Kent Fox. Record company, record producer and music publisher. Works with artists on contract.
How to Contact: Submit demo tape and lyric sheet. Prefers cassette with 3-12 songs on demo. SASE. Reports in 1 month.
Music: C&W, easy listening, rock and top 40/pop.

MERRITT & NORMAN MUSIC, Rt. 5, Box 368-A, Yakima WA 98903. (509)966-6334. Labels include Tell International Records. General Manager: Hiram White. Record company, music publisher and recording studio. Works with artists and songwriters on contract. Pays standard royalty to songwriters on contract; 6¢/sheet for sheet music.
How to Contact: Submit demo tape and lead sheet. Prefers 15 ips reel-to-reel or cassette with 1 song on tape. SASE. Reports in 2 months.
Music: Bluegrass; blues; C&W; dance; folk; jazz; and rock. Recently released "I Can't Get the You Out of Me," by Barbara Jean Taylor (C&W single); and "I'm Too Shy," by Penny Stadler (C&W single).

MICHAL RECORDING ENTERPRISES, Box 2194, Memphis TN 38101. (901)774-5689. Labels include Gospel Express, Six Sisters, Del My and Bishop Records. President: Bishop J.B. Cole. Vice President: Michal Cole. Record company, music publisher and booking agency. Releases 2 singles and 5 albums/year. Works with musicians and songwriters on contract. Pays 4% royalty to artists on contract; 2½% royalty to songwriters on contract.
How to Contact: Submit demo tape. Prefers 7½ ips reel-to-reel or cassette. SASE. Reports in 2 months.
Music: Blues; church/religious; gospel; and soul. Recently released "Stronger in the City," by Shirley Jones (gospel single).

MILLENIUM RECORDS, 65 E. 55th St., New York NY 10022. (212)759-3901. President: Jimmy Ienner. Record company and music publisher. Works with musicians and songwriters on contract.
How to Contact: Submit demo tape, lyric sheets and any biographical data to Melanie Fox. Prefers cassette with 3-5 songs on demo. SASE.
Music: Rock and MOR. Artists include Tommy James, Bruce Cockburn, Franke and the Knockouts and Don McLean.

MIRROR RECORDS, INC., 645 Titus Ave., Rochester NY 14617. (716)544-3500. Labels include Mirror and House of Guitars Records. Vice President: Armand Schaubroeck. Record company and music publisher. Works with musicians on salary; artists and songwriters on contract. Pays 33% royalty to artists on contract; negotiable royalty to songwriters on contract.
How to Contact: Submit demo tape. Prefers 7½ ips reel-to-reel or cassette. Include photo with submission. SASE. Reports in 2 months.
Music: Folk; progressive; rock; and punk. Recently released *Shakin' Shakin'* and *Ice Cream Cone*, by Armand Schaubroeck (rock LPs). Other artists include Jerry Porter, Don Potter, and Click Click.

MODULATION RECORDS, 5514 Isabella St., Montreal, Quebec, Canada H3X 1R6. (514)487-0859. Telex: 055-66493. Paris: Mr. Yves Roze, Director; 60 Ave. Raymond Poincare,

Paris France 75016. 553-9750. Labels include Module 1 and Sirano (Canada). President: Jehan V. Valiquet. Record company and music publisher (Editions Nahej/PROCAN and Editions Valcor/CAPAC). Estab. 1979. Member ADISQ. Releases 15+ singles and 5+ albums/year. Works with artists on contract. Pays 10%-16% royalty to artists on contract; statutory rate to publishers for each record sold.
How to Contact: Submit demo tape and lyric sheet. Prefers cassette with 3 songs minimum on demo. SAE and International Reply Coupons. Reports in 3 weeks.
Music: Children's (French), MOR and top 40/pop. Recently released *Disco-Fizz*, by Azoto (dance-oriented LP and single); "I Dig You," by Cult Hero (new wave single); and *Ich Bin Wie Du*, by M. Rosenberg (easy German LP and single). Other artists include Hubcaps, Breton-Cyr, Tobie, African Magic Combo, Cafe Creme, J.F. Michael, Frederick Francois and Black/White and Co. (France).

MONTICANA RECORDS, Box 702, Snowdon Station, Montreal, Quebec, Canada H3X 3X8. Labels include Dynacom. General Manager: David P. Leonard. Record company, record producer, and music publisher (Montina Music/BMI). Member CARAS and MIEA. Works with artists and songwriters on contract; musicians on salary for in-house studio work. Negotiates royalty to artists on contract and publishers for each record sold.
How to Contact: Submit demo tape and lyric sheet. Prefers 7½ or 15 ips reel-to-reel or cassette. SAE and International Reply Coupons. Reports in 1 month.
Music: Blues, C&W, dance-oriented, easy listening, folk, gospel, MOR, progressive, R&B, rock, soul and top 40/pop.

MOTHER BERTHA MUSIC, INC., Box 69529, Los Angeles CA 90069. Labels include Warner-Spector, Phil Spector, Phil Spector International and Philles Records. Administrative Director: Donna Sekulidis. Record company, music publisher and production company. Works with artists and songwriters on contract. Payment negotiable. Charges for some services.
How to Contact: Submit demo tape and lead sheet. Cassette only. "A writer should only include what he feels is important." SASE. "All material must have a return self-addressed and prepaid envelope enclosed, even though there is no guarantee any material will be returned. No material will be considered without SASE." Reports "as soon as possible."
Music: Bluegrass; blues; children's; choral; church/religious; classical; C&W; dance; easy listening; folk; gospel; jazz; MOR; progressive; rock; soul; top 40/pop; and "all forms of music." Released "Da Doo Ron Ron," by Shaun Cassidy (pop single); "Then She Kissed Me," by Kiss (rock single); "Death of a Ladies' Man," by Leonard Cohen (single); and "End of the Century," by The Ramones (new wave rock & roll).

MUSIC ADVENTURES RECORDS, INC., 8033 Sunset Blvd., Suite 101, West Hollywood CA 90046 (213)650-0060. Cleveland Office: 12501 Madison Ave., Cleveland OH 44107. (216)228-8241. Labels include Ohio Records. Vice President A&R: John Baruth. Record company, music publisher, record producer, management firm and promoter. Releases 5 singles and 1-3 albums/year. Works with artists on contract. Pays 10-20% royalty to artists on contract; standard royalties to songwriters on contract.
How to Contact: Submit demo tape and lead sheet. Prefers cassette with 2-3 songs on demo. SASE. Reports within 4 weeks.
Music: Folk; progressive; R&B; rock; and top 40/pop. Recently released "With You in My Eyes," by Coyote (country rock single); "Disco Rapist," by the Other Half (rock single); "This Time to the End," by Great Lakes Band (pop rock single); "Now I'm Asking," by BBB (pop rock single); and *I'm So Positive*, by BBB (LP).

MUSIC CITY RECORDS, Box 300, Mt. Gretna PA 17064. (717)299-1600. Labels include Bat, LeFevre, Disc-go, Palmer and Canadian American Records. A&R Director: Joey Welz. President: Jimmy Velvet. Works with artists on contract. Pays 2-5% royalty.
How to Contact: Submit demo tape and lyric sheet. Prefers cassette with 4-8 songs on demo. "Interested in leasing finished masters. Have it arranged in a style—rock, pop, country, etc." Does not return unsolicited material. Holds submitted material for consideration.
Music: C&W; dance; easy listening; MOR; rock; and top 40/pop. Recently released "We Should Be in Love," by Joey Welz (pop/country single); "It's You,'" by Jimmy Velvet (pop/country single); and "Rippin' Em' Off," by the New Wave Comets (punk single). Artists include New Wave Comets (Dis-go Records); Joey Welz & Jimmy Velvet and Randy Boykin (Music City Records).

MUSICANZA CORPORATION, 2878 Bayview Ave., Wantagh NY 11793. (516)826-2735. Record company and music publisher (ASCAP). Works with artists and songwriters on contract.

How to Contact: Submit by mail lead and lyric sheet. SASE. Reports in several months.
Music: "We will only accept original children's songs; we publish them ourselves." Recently released *Dolly Dimples*, by many artists (children's LP); and *Yeaster Bunny*, by many artists (children's LP).

MUSTEVIC SOUND, INC., 193-18 120th Ave., New York NY 11412. (212)527-1586. Producer: Steve Reid. Record company, music publisher (Mustevic Sound Publishing/BMI) and record producer. Member BMA and SIRMA. Releases 2-6 albums/year. Works with artists and songwriters on contract. Pays 12-25% to artists on contract; standard royalty to songwriters on contract; statutory rate to publishers for each record sold.
How to Contact: Write first about your interest. Prefers cassette with 1-3 songs on demo. SASE. Reports in 3 weeks.
Music: Jazz. Recently released *Rhythmatism*, by Steve Reid (jazz LP); *Visions of Third Eye*, by New Life (jazz LP); and *Odyssey of the Oblong Square*, by Steve Reid (jazz LP). Other artists include Charles Tyler, Brandon Ross, David Wertman, Les Walker, Artthur Blythe, and Brandon Ross.

MYSTIC RECORDS, INC., (formerly Mystic Recording Studios), Studio Sixteen, 6277 Selma Ave., Hollywood CA 90028. (213)464-9667. Labels include Mystic, Solar, Clock and Mystic Sound Records. President: Doug Moody. Coordinator: Nancy Faith. Record company, music publisher and production firm. Also originates film and TV music and syndicated radio show. Releases 20 singles and 8-10 albums/year. Works with musicians on salary; artists and songwriters on contract. Pays "standard rates; some advances."
How to Contact: Submit demo tape or submit demo tape and lead sheet. Prefers 7½ ips reel-to-reel quarter-track, or cassette. Reports in 1 month. SAE, Att: Nancy Faith.
Music: Blues; C&W; easy listening; gospel (modern, rock or pop); MOR; rockabilly; soul; top 40/pop; and "spoken word plays (up to 1 hour)."
Tips: Mystic also releases collector item records limited editions in picture disc or shaped records.

NASHBORO RECORDS, 1011 Woodland, Nashville TN 37206. (615)227-5081. Labels include Greed, Ernie's, Kenwood, Excello, Abet, Mankind and Nasco Records. Vice President/A&R: Shannon Williams. Record company. Pays standard royalty to artists and songwriters.
How to Contact: Submit demo tape and lyric sheet. Prefers reel-to-reel demos. "Please include address and phone number." SASE. Reports in 1-2 months.
Music: Gospel. Recently released *Ain't No Stopping Us Now*, by Gospel Keynotes (gospel LP) and *There Is No Hope For This World*, by Bobby James and New Life Singers (gospel LP).

NASHVILLE INTERNATIONAL MUSIC CORP., 20 Music Square W., Nashville TN 37203. (615)373-2575. Labels include Phoenix Records, Nashville International Records and Air-Trans Records. President: Reggie M. Churchwell. General Manager, Music Group: Bob May. Record company and music publisher. Releases 10 singles and 4 albums/year. Works on "per song" basis.
How to Contact: Submit demo tape and lead sheet, attention Bob May. Prefers 7½ ips reel-to-reel with 2-6 songs on demo. SASE. Reports in 4 weeks.
Music: C&W; gospel; MOR; progressive; and top 40/pop. Recently released "The American Hamburger Way," by Howard Lips (country/rock); "I Haven't Loved There Yet," by John Wells (country/pop); "It's Hard To Be A Cowboy These Days," by Conrad Pierce (country); "Little Tear Drops" (gospel) and "I Hope We Walk the Last Mile Together (country gospel), by the Singing Holley's; and "The Legend of the Duke," by Tom Destry (country/pop).

NATIONAL FOUNDATION OF MUSIC, 1128-A Airbase Rd., Columbus MS 39701. (601)434-8510. Labels include Dove, Soultrack, Startown and N.F.M. Records. President: Allen White. Record company, music publisher, record producer and record promotion. Works with artists and songwriters on contract. Pays standard royalty.
How to Contact: Call first about your interest. Prefers 8-track cassette with 4-10 songs on demo. "Include samples of records that have already been manufactured." SASE. Reports in 2 weeks.
Music: Bluegrass; blues; church/religious; classical; C&W; dance; easy listening; gospel; jazz; MOR; R&B; soul; and top 40/pop. Recently released "Police And Preachers," by Mack Banks (country single); "Boogie Land," by Ike Strong (disco single); and "Western Union Man," by Swinging Melleraires (gospel single). Other artists include Lula Bolden and The Mighty Blasters (Startown Records); Lonnie Grah (Startown Records); The Hi-Liters (Soultrack Records); Debra Nichols (Trackdown Records); Soul, Mind and Body (Startown Records); Alex Williams (Soultrack Records); Ike Strong (Startown Records); and Carrie Wells (Startown Records).

NEW ENGLAND RECORD COMPANY, Drawer 520, Stafford TX 77477. President: Daniel Andrade. Record company, record producer and music publisher (Andrade Publishing Company/BMI). Releases 4 singles and 2 albums/year. Works with artists and songwriters on contract; musicians on salary for in-house studio work. Pays 5-10% royalty to artists on contract; negotiates rates to publishers for each record sold.
How to Contact: Submit demo tape and lyric sheet. Prefers 7½ ips reel-to-reel or cassette with 2-5 songs on demo. SASE. Reports in 2 months.
Music: Church/religious, C&W and top 40/pop. Recently released *A Lonely Stranger* and *Hank Williams is Singing Again*, by Hank The Drifter (country LP); "Hank Williams Ghost," by Hank The Drifter (country single); and "Tribute to Hank Williams," by Hank The Drifter (country cassette).

NEW WORLD RECORDS, 2309 N. 36th St., Suite 11, Milwaukee WI 53212. (414)445-4872. President: Marvell Love. Record company, music publisher (Jero Limited/BMI) and record producer. Releases 4 singles/year. Works with artists and songwriters on contract. Pays 2½- 3½% royalty to artists on contract: standard royalties to songwriters on contract.
How to Contact: Submit demo tape and lyric sheet. Prefers 7½ ips reel-to-reel or cassette with minimum 5 songs on demo. SASE. Reports in 3 weeks.
Music: Dance; soul; and top 40/pop. Recently released "Don't Break That Rule," by Marvell Love (disco single); "Jerk," by Directions (disco single); "Le-Beat," by Lo-End (disco single); and "Dance," by Brothers by Choice (disco single); and "Now I Know," by Final Chapter (ballad).

NIRVANA RECORDS, 1145 Green St., Manville NJ 08835. A&R Director: Marc Zydiak. Record company, record producer and music publisher (Package Good Music/BMI).
How to Contact: Prefers 7½ ips reel-to-reel or cassette with a minimum of 3 songs on demo. SASE. Reports in 1 month.
Music: Easy listening, folk, progressive, rock and top 40/pop. Recently released "Frosty the Dopeman," by Marc Zydiak (LP/single); "Let's Start a Punk Rock Band," by Professor Marx (single); and *No Place like You*, by Mark Zydiak (LP).

NORTH AMERICAN LITURGY RESOURCES, 10802 N. 23rd Ave., Phoenix AZ 85029. (602)864-1980. Labels include NALR and Sound of Hope. Music Editor: Henry Papale. Record company, record producer and music publisher (NALR/BMI). Releases 5-8 albums/year. Works with artists on contract; musicians on salary for in-house studio work. Pays statutory rate to publishers for each record sold.
How to Contact: Submit demo tape and lyric sheet. Prefers cassette with 5-12 songs on demo. SASE. Reports in 1 month.
Music: Children's, choral, church/religious, liturgical and Christian rock and inspirational. Recently released *Light of the World*, by Tom Kendzia (Christian rock LP); *By Name I Have Called You*, by Rev. Carey Landry (Christian LP); *The Time Has Come*, by Pat Boone (Christian LP); *On Eagle's Wings*, by Michael Joncas (Catholic LP); and *Reach For the Rainbow*, by Sheldon Cohen (choral LP). Other artists include St. Louis Jesuits; The Dameans; Tutti Camarata; Ellis and Lynch; Abraham Kaplan and Tom Conry.
Tips: "Be familiar with our recordings. Free catalogs and brochures supplied on request."

NUCLEUS RECORDS, Box 111, Sea Bright NJ 07760. President: Robert Bowden. Secretary: Jean Schweitzer. Record company and music publisher. Member AFM (US and Canada). Releases 1 single/year. Works with songwriters on contract. Pays up to 5% royalty for each record sold.
How to Contact: Submit demo tape and lyric sheet. Prefers cassette with any number songs on demo. SASE. Reports in 1 month.
Music: Church/religious, classical, C&W, folk, MOR, progressive, rock (soft, mellow), and top 40/pop. Recently released "Pressure Cooker" and "Vibrating Love," by Jean Schweitzer (pop/country single).

ODLE RECORDS, Box 4335, Pasadena TX 77502. (713)477-9432. Labels include Merry Records. President: M.F. Odle. Record company, music publisher and record producer. Releases 4-5 singles and 2 albums/year. Works with artists and songwriters on contract. Pays standard royalty to artists and songwriters on contract; statutory rate to publishers for each record sold.
How to Contact: Query, arrange personal interview, submit demo tape, submit demo tape and lead sheet, or submit lead sheet only. Prefers 7½ ips reel-to-reel or cassette with 4 songs on demo. SASE. Reports in 2 weeks.
Music: Blues; children's; church/religious; C&W; dance; easy listening; folk; gospel; jazz; MOR; R&B; rock; and soul. Recently released "The Artist" and "The Other One," by Mike Kieser and "You Passed My Way" and "Without You," by Sammy Van Ness III.

OHIO RECORDS, Box 655, Hudson OH 44236. (216)650-1330. Label includes Deco. A&R Director: Russ Delaney. Record company, record producer and personal manager. Pays standard royalty.
How to Contact: Submit demo tape and lyric sheet. Prefers cassette with 6 songs minimum on demo. Reports in one month. "Sometimes we hold material until we're ready for a session."
Music: Country. Recently released "Taste of the Blues," (country single) and *H-e-e-e-re's Ethel,* (country LP) by Ethel Delaney.
Tips: "I manage several artists who also write on the Ohio label and on occasion we do look for good commercial material. We are busy people, however, and cannot take time with someone who has no talent."

OLD HAT RECORDS, Box 946, Springtown TX 76082. (817)433-5720. Labels include T-2-Topple Records. President: James Michael Taylor. Record company, booking agency, music publisher and production company. Releases 2-8 albums/year. Works with artists and songwriters on contract.
How to Contact: Submit demo tape, arrange personal interview, submit demo tape and lead sheet. Prefers 3¾ or 7½ ips reel-to-reel or cassette with 6-12 songs on demo. SASE. Reports in 1 month.
Music: Children's; choral; C&W; folk; rock; and top 40/pop. Recently released *Feathers in the Wind,* by Snowgeese (progressive/folk LP); *Texas Rain,* by Texas Water (country/progressive LP); *First Unk,* by Bob French (folk LP); and "What To Do with the Pictures," by James M. Taylor (C&W single).

OLD HOMESTEAD RECORD CO., Box 100, Brighton MI 48116. (313)227-1997. Labels include Rutabaga, Broadway, Intermission and Old Homestead Records. President: John Morris. Record company and music publisher. Works with artists and songwriters on contract. Pays negotiable royalty to artists on contract; standard royalty to songwriters on contract.
How to Contact: Write first about your interest. Prefers cassette with 2-20 songs on demo. SASE. Reports in 2 weeks.
Music: Bluegrass; C&W; folk; and gospel. Recently released *Have I Told You Lately,* by Lulubelle & Scotty (C&W LP); *Sacred Collection,* by Molly O'Day (C&W LP); and *Wheeling,* by Charlie Moore (bluegrass LP). Other artists include The Goins Brothers and Wayne Lewis.

OMNISOUND, INC., (a subsidiary of Waring Enterprises, Inc.), Delaware Water Gap PA 18327. (717)476-0550. Manager: Yoshio Inomata. Record company. Releases 10 albums/year. Works with songwriters on contract. Pays standard royalties to songwriters on contract.
How to Contact: Submit demo tape and lead sheet, or submit lead sheet only. Prefers cassette. SASE. Reports in 2 weeks.
Music: Children's; choral; church/religious; classical; jazz; folk; gospel; MOR; and top 40/pop. "Omnisound is mainly interested in jazz, however, we also produce recordings for affiliate companies: Shawnee Press, Inc.; Harold Flammer, Inc.; and Glorysound." Recently released "Still Waters," by Harry Leahey Trio; "Solar Energy," by Bill Goodwin; Phil Woods/Lew Tabackin *In Quintet* (LP); and "Tokyo Concert," by John Coates, Jr.
Tips: "Send material for review suitable for use in schools or churches or for publication/recording for gospel market."

LEE MACE'S OZARK OPRY RECORDS, INC., Box 242, Osage Beach MO 65065. (314)348-3383. Labels include Kajac, Ven Jence, Vision, KRC and Red Rock Records. General Manager: Lee Mace. Record company, music publisher and record producer. Works with musicians on salary; artists and songwriters on contract. Pays 3-8% royalty to artists on contract; standard royalties to songwriters on contract.
How to Contact: Arrange personal interview or submit demo tape and lead sheet. Prefers 7½ ips reel-to-reel or cassette with 2-4 songs on demo. SASE. Reports in 2 weeks.
Music: Bluegrass; blues; church/religious; C&W; gospel; and R&B. Recently released "Waylon Sing to Mama," by Darrell Thomas (country single); and *Lee Mace 25 Years,* by the Ozark Opry (country LP).

P.M. RECORDS, INC., 20 Martha St., Woodcliff Lake NJ 07675. (201)391-2486. President: Gene A. Perla. Record company, music publisher (Perla Music/ASCAP) and record producer. Works with artists on contract.
How to Contact: Call first about your interest. Prefers cassette. SASE.
Music: All types, especially jazz. Recently released *A Very Rare Evening,* by Nina Simone (LP); *Music In My Heart,* by Kathryn Moses (LP); *Evol-ution, Love's Reverse,* by Sonny Greenwich (jazz LP); *Heads Up,* by Stone Alliance (fusion LP); *Bug Alley,* by Bug Alley (jazz LP). Other artists include Bernie Senensky.

PARALLEL RECORDS, 1433 Federal Ave., Los Angeles CA 90025. (213)477-3651. President: Robert Harrison. Record company, record producer, and music publisher (St. Cecilia Music/BMI). Estab. 1979. Member RIAA. Releases 3 singles and 5 albums/year. Works with artists and songwriters on contract. Pays negotiable royalty.
How to Contact: Submit demo tape and lyric sheet. Prefers cassette with 1-3 songs on demo. Reports in 3 weeks.
Music: "Any thing that is commercial." Recently released *The Weirz*, by The Weirz (pop/rock LP); *USC*, by Bernard Tarver (soul LP); and *Sharon Hendrix*, by Sharon Hendrix (top 40 LP). Other artists include Summer (rock), Bob Harrison (children's) and Danielle Brisboise.

PARASOUND, INC., 680 Beach St., San Francisco CA 94121. (415)673-4544. President: Bernie Krause. Vice President: Sid Goldstein. Record company and music publisher. Releases 1-3 singles and 1-3 albums/year. Works with artists and songwriters on contract. Payment negotiable.
How to Contact: Submit demo tape and lead sheet. Prefers 7½ ips reel-to-reel with 3-6 songs on demo. SASE. Reports in 3 weeks.
Music: MOR; rock; and top 40/pop. Recently released *Citadels* by Bernie Krause (jazz-fusion LP).

FRANK PAUL ENTERPRISES, Box 113, Woburn MA 01801. (617)933-1474. Labels include Casa Grande, Don-Mar and Strawhut Records. General Manager: Frank Paul. Record company, booking agency and music publisher. Works with artists and songwriters on contract. Pays 3% minimum royalty to artists and songwriters on contract.
How to Contact: Submit demo tape and lead sheet. Prefers cassette with 3-6 songs on demo. SASE. Reports in 1 month.
Music: Blues; children's; choral; church/religious; classical; C&W; dance; easy listening; folk; gospel; MOR; rock; soul; and top 40/pop. Recently released "Happy, Happy Birthday Baby," by the Timeweavers (R&B single); and "God Said He Would Fight My Battle," by the Fabulous Bullock Brothers (gospel single).

PCRL/DISQUES FLEUR, INC., 2364 Sherbrooke E., Montreal, Quebec, Canada H2K 1E6. (514)526-2831. Labels include Fleur, Bouquet, Sterling, Quatre Saisons, Foreign Exchange, Carats' Marguerite and Notre Maison. Professional Manager: Carole Risch. Record company, record producer, and music publisher (Crisch Music/PROCAN and Notre Musique/CAPAC). Member ADISQ. Releases 25 singles and 10 albums/year. Works with artists and songwriters on contract. Pays 4%-16% royalty to artists on contract; statutory rate to publisher for each record sold.
How to Contact: Submit demo tape and lyric sheet. Prefers 15 ips reel-to-reel or cassette with 3-7 songs on demo. SAE and International Reply Coupons. Reports in 3 weeks.
Music: Easy listening, MOR (ballads), rock and top 40/pop. Recently produced *C'est Magnifique*, by Santa Esmeralda (rock/latin American LP); *Un Coup D'amour*, by Richard Cocciante (MOR LP); and "T'es Plus Une Star," by C. Michel (top 40/pop single). Other artists include Bernard Blane, Deveze, Lili Davis, Diane Juster, Julie Arel, Alain Delorme, Evelyn John, Michel Murty, Gerard Manuel, Marie-France Paquin, Clement Ratelle and Jean-Pierre Savelli.

PEDIGREE RECORDS, 13615 Victory Blvd., Suite 216, Van Nuys CA 91401. (213)997-9100. Labels include Funnybone Records. Director A&R: Paul Armstrong. Record company, music publisher and record producer. Releases 4-5 singles and 2 albums/year. Works with artists and songwriters on contract. Pays 4-7% royalty to artists on contract; statutory royalties to songwriters on contract.
How to Contact: Submit demo tape and lyric sheet. Prefers 7½ ips reel-to-reel or cassette with 3-6 songs on demo. SASE. Reports in 3 weeks.
Music: C&W; easy listening; MOR; R&B; rock; soul; and top 40/pop.

PEER-SOUTHERN ORGANIZATION, 6922 Hollywood Blvd., Hollywood CA 90028. (213)469-1667. Labels include Spark Records. Professional Manager: Roy Kohn. Record company and music publisher. Works with artists and songwriters on contract. Pays standard royalty to artists and songwriters on contract.
Music: C&W, dance, easy listening, MOR, rock and top 40/pop. Recently released "Blue Moon of Kentucky," by Earl Scruggs (country single); *Miss the Mississippi and You*, by Crystal Gayle (country LP); and *Find My Way*, by Cameo (soul LP).
Editor's Note: "At press time it came to our attention that Peer-Southern is no longer accepting unsolicited submissions at this office."

PETCO INTERNATIONAL CORP., 88-20 Corona Ave., Elmhurst NY 11373. Record company, music publisher and record producer. Prefers 15 ips reel-to-reel. Music includes children's; and dance.

PHAROAH RECORDS, Box 143, Glastonbury CT 06025. (203)728-5639. Labels include Hardtimes Records. President: Bruce Lloyd. Vice President/A&R Director: Sue Lloyd. Record company and music publisher. Releases 1 single and 12 albums/year./Works with musicians on salary; artists and songwriters on contract. Pays 3% royalty to artists on contract; statutory rate to publishers for each record sold. Buys some masters outright.
How to Contact: Submit demo tape, lyric sheet and a "very good" full-length photo (of artist). Prefers cassette with 3-6 songs on demo. SASE. Reports in 2 weeks.
Music: Bluegrass; blues; C&W; dance; folk; and rock (soft). Recently released *St. Johns Eve*, by Paul Coyle (jazz LP); and "Dearest Daughter," by Bob Andy (rock single); and "Starting All Over Again," by David Liska (pop single).
Tips: "If a moderately good artist makes an unusually good appearance, we *can* work with them. Right now I am particularly looking for a female artist/songwriter."

PHOENIX RECORDS INC., 20 Music Square W., Nashville TN 37203. (615)373-2575. Vice President/A&R: Ken Little. Record company. Works with artists and songwriters on contract. Pays negotiable royalty to artists on contract; standard royalty to songwriters on contract.
How to Contact: Query by mail, submit demo tape and lyric sheet or arrange personal interview to play demo tape. Prefers cassette with 4-10 songs on demo. Does not return unsolicited material "unless prior contact has been made via mail or telephone." Reports in 3 weeks.
Music: C&W; MOR; R&B crossover; rock (country, pop, power pop); soul crossover; and top 40/pop. Recently released *It's Hard to be a Cowboy These Days*, by Conrad Pierce (C&W LP); "Mary Ann Taylor," by Ray Emmett (C&W single); and "Legend of the Duke," by Tom Destry (C&W single).

PLANET RECORDS, 9130 Sunset Blvd., Los Angeles CA 90069. (213)275-4710. A&R Director: Michael Arackmer. Record company. Estab. 1978.
How to Contact: Write or call first about your interest and submit demo tape and lyric sheet. Prefers cassette with maximum 4 songs on demo. Does not return unsolicited material. Reports by phone in 2 weeks.
Music: C&W; disco; easy listening; folk; gospel; jazz; MOR; progressive; R&B; rock; soul and top 40/pop. Recently released *Fire*, by The Pointer Sisters (pop LP and single); *The Cretones*, by The Cretones (rock LP); and *Sue Sadd & The Next*, by S. Sadd & The Next (rock LP). Other artists include Mark Saffan and American Noise.

PLANTATION RECORDS, 3106 Belmont Blvd., Nashville TN 37212. (615)385-1960. Labels include Sun International and SSS Records. Contact: A&R Director. Record company and music publisher. Pays standard royalties.
How to Contact: Query first, then submit demo tape. Prefers cassette. SASE. Reports as soon as possible.
Music: Bluegrass, blues, C&W, dance, easy listening, folk, gospel, jazz, MOR, progressive, R&B, rock, soul, and top 40/pop. Recently released Reborn," by Orion (country/pop LP) and "Save the Last Dance for Me," by Jerry Lee Lewis and Friend (country single). Other artists include Roy Drusky, Dave Dudley, Jimmy C. Newman, Webb and Debbie Pierce, and Leroy Van Dyke and others.
Tips: "We do not accept unsolicited material. Songwriters should not submit material to us through the mail."

PLEIADES MUSIC, The Barn, North Ferrisburg VT 05473. (802)425-2111. Labels include Philo and Fretless Records. Vice President: Bill Schubart. Record company and music publisher (The Pleiades Music Group/BMI and Other Music, Inc./ASCAP). Member NARAS, RIAA. Releases 35 albums/year. Works with artists and songwriters on contract. Pays variable royalty to artists on contract; 50% royalty to songwriters on contract; pay negotiable to publishers.
How to Contact: Submit demo tape. Must be cassette with 1-3 songs on demo. SASE. Reports in 1 month. No returns without SASE.
Music: Blues; children's; classical; C&W; folk; jazz; progressive; rock; soul; and top 40/pop. Recently released *Kilimanjaro* by Kilimanjaro (jazz LP); *Ornament of Hope*, by Do'a (new age LP); and *All Used Up*, by Utah Phillips (folk LP). Other artists include Laurie Spiegel, Hutable Christensen and Hood, Lar Duggan, Lui Collins, Dave van Ronk, Eric von Schmidt, and Jean Redpath.

POLKA TOWNE RECORDS, 211 Post Ave., Westbury NY 11590. President: Teresa Zapolska. Record company, music publisher, record producer and booking agency. Works with artists and songwriters on contract.
How to Contact: Submit demo tape. Prefers cassette with 1-3 songs on demo. SASE. "We review music once a month."
Music: Polkas and waltzes.

POLYDOR RECORDS, 810 7th Ave., New York NY 10019. (212)399-7051. A&R: Stu Fine. Record company. Works with artists on contract.
How to Contact: Submit demo tape and lead sheet. Prefers 7½ or 15 ips reel-to-reel or cassette. SASE.
Music: Rock, R&B and top 40/pop. Recently released albums by Kool and the Gang, Rush, Rainbow, Dr. Hook, Johnny Couga, and Johnny Van Zant Band.

POLYGRAM/MERCURY RECORDS, INC., 10 Music Circle S, Nashville TN 37203. (615)244-3776. Contact: A&R Department. Record company.
How to Contact: Write or call first about your interest. "Be sure to contact us before submitting material through the mail. We do not want to indicate a closed door policy but please show us the same consideration you would want." Prefers cassette with 2-3 songs on demo. SASE. Reports in 1 month "or more."
Music: C&W.

PRAISE RECORDS, 6979 Curragh Ave., Burnaby, British Columbia, Canada V5J 4V6. US Branch: 1308 Meador St., Unit C5, Bellingham WA 98225. (206)671-9562. Labels include New Born, Little People, Faith, Horizon, Tunesmith, Country Oak and Quest Records. Manager: Paul Yaroshuk. Record company, music publisher and studio (Noteworthy Publishing Co./BMI). Releases 60 singles and 24 albums/year. Works with artists and songwriters on contract. Pays 10% royalty to artists on contract; pays 2¾ in Canada rate to publishers for each record sold.
How to Contact: Submit demo tape. Prefers reel-to-reel with 12 songs on demo. SAE and International Reply Coupons. Reports in 2 weeks.
Music: Bluegrass; children's; choral; church/religious; C&W; folk; and gospel. Recently released *Rockin' Revival*, by Servant (gospel rock LP); *Till You Came In*, by Abraham & Moses (contemporary LP); and *Midnight Fire*, by Randell Waller (gospel rock LP). Other artists include Joane Cash Yates, Heir Born, Free Way and Homespun.

PRELUDE RECORDS, 200 W. 57th St., Suite 403, New York NY 10019. Director A&R: Francis Kevorkian. President: Marvin Schlachter. Record company. Releases 2-15 albums/year. Works with artists on contract.
How to Contact: Submit demo tape. Prefers 7½ ips reel-to-reel or cassette. SASE. Reports in 3 weeks.
Music: Dance; soul; "material with a strong pop crossover potential, whether dance, R&B, or dance oriented rock." Recently released *I'm Caught Up*, by Inner Life (R&B/disco LP); *France Joli*, by France Joli (pop/disco LP); and *You Got What It Takes*, by Bobby Thurston (R&B/disco LP). Other artists include Lorraine Johnson, Kumano, Musique, Passion, Saturday Night Band, U.N and Theo Vaness.

THE PRESCRIPTION CO., 70 Murray Ave., Port Washington NY 11050. (516)767-1929. President: David F. Gasman. Record company, record producer and music publisher (Prescription Co./BMI). Releases a varied amount of singles and albums/year. Works with artists and songwriters on contract. Pays statutory rate to publishers for each record sold.
How to Contact: Call or write first about your interest, then submit demo tape and lyric sheet. Prefers cassette with any number of songs on demo. Does not return unsolicited material. Reports in 1 month.
Music: Bluegrass, blues, children's, C&W, dance-oriented, easy listening, folk, jazz, MOR, progressive, R&B, rock, soul and top 40/pop. Recently released "You Came In" b/w "Seasons" (pop/country single) and "Rock 'n Roll Blues," (rock single) by Medicine Mike.

PRIME CUT RECORDS, 439 Tute Hill, Lyndonville VT 05851. (802)626-3317. President A&R: Bruce James. Record company and record producer. Releases 3-10 singles and 2 albums/year. Works with artists on contract.
How to Contact: Submit demo tape and lyric sheets. Prefers cassette with 1-5 songs on demo. "Songs should be hit material no longer than 3½ minutes each." SASE. Reports in 3 weeks.
Music: Rock AOR and top 40/pop. Recently released *Take It All*, by Fox (rock/AOR LP); "Old

Paree," by Fox (rock/AOR single); and "Heartless," by Fox (rock/ballad single). Other artists include Rockestra, Littlewing and Champlain.
Tips: "Artist should have strong desire to *make it*. Think and write hit records; songs should have two hooks in each tune, lyrics should be personal and intimate."

PYRAMID RECORDS, 26177 Kinyon Dr., Taylor MI 48180. (313)292-5281. President: Peggy La Sorda. Record company and music publisher (Golden Dawn Music/BMI). Works with songwriters on contract.
How to Contact: Submit demo tape and lead sheet. Prefers 7½ ips reel-to-reel or cassette with 4 songs on demo. SASE. Reports in 3 weeks.
Music: C&W, dance-oriented, easy listening, folk, MOR and top 40/pop.

QUADRANT RECORDS, Box 630175, Miami FL 33163. (305)472-7757. Labels include Twister and Tornado. President: Jack P. Bluestein. Record company, record producer and music publisher (Pine Island Music; Lantana Music and Twister Music). Releases 1-6 singles and 1 album/year. Works with artists and songwriters on contract. Pays negotiable royalty to artists on contract; statutory rate to publishers for each record sold.
How to Contact: Write first about your interest, then submit demo tape and lyric sheet. Prefers reel-to-reel or cassette with 1-6 songs on demo. SASE. Reports in 1 month.
Music: C&W, gospel, MOR, R&B, rock (country) and top 40/pop. Recently released "I Wake Up and It Rains," by Joe McDonald (contemporary single); and "Shed My Love," Nancy Lee (contemporary single). Other artists include Lou Garcia and Gary Oakes.

QUALITY RECORDS LIMITED, 380 Birchmount Rd., Scarborough, Ontario, Canada M1K 1M7. (416)698-5511. Domestic (owned) labels include Quality, Celebration, Birchmount and Ringside. Director of Business Affairs: Nadine A. Langlois. Record company, record producer and music publisher (Quality Music Publishing). Member CRIA, CIRPA, CMPA. Works with artists and songwriters on contract. Pays 7%-10% royalty to artists on contract; statutory rate to publishers for each record sold.
How to Contact: Submit demo tape and lyric sheet. Prefers 7½ ips reel-to-reel or cassette with 3-10 songs on demo. SAE and International Reply Coupons. Reports in 2 weeks.
Music: Dance-oriented, MOR, progressive, rock (hard metal rock and roll) and top 40/pop. Recently released *Outline*, by Gino Soccio (dance-oriented LP); and *Instructions*, by the Instructions (top 40 LP); and *Frank Soda*, by F. Soda (metal rock LP). Other artists include Ronnie Hawkins, Karen Silver and Bentwood Rocker.

QUANTUM RECORDS, LTD., 170A Baldwin St., Toronto, Ontario, Canada M5T 1L8. (416)366-6745. A&R Director: Mike Alyanak. Record company. Releases 10 singles and 8 albums/year. Works with artists and songwriters on contract; musicians on salary for in-house studio work. Pays 6-10% royalty to artists on contract; statutory rate to publishers for each record sold.
How to Contact: Submit demo tape and lyric sheet. Prefers cassette witi 2-6 songs on demo. SAE and International Reply Coupons. Reports in 3 weeks.
Music: Dance-oriented, rock (all types) and top 40/pop. Recently released *Taking Off*, by Harlow (dance-oriented LP and single); *Quick as Silver*, by Vezi (pop rock LP and single); and *Foreign Movie*, by Rex Chainbelt (new wave rock LP and single). Other artists include Keith McKie, Brandy, Billy Reed, Belinda Metz and Bob Rapson.

QUINTO RECORD PRODUCTIONS, Box 2388, Toluca Lake CA 91602. (213)985-8284. Labels include Quinto, Suzi, Fun, Top 'n' Bottom and Clovermint Records. Owner: Quint Benedetti. Record company, music publisher and demo producer. Works with songwriters on contract. Pays standard royalty.
How to Contact: Submit demo tape and lyric sheet. Prefers cassette with 2-4 songs on demo. SASE. Reports in 1 month.
Music: Children's; C&W; musical comedy; and novelty. "We are presently scouting for new musical comedy material for possible recording and stage production locally." Recently released *Chocalonia*, by original cast (rock musical LP); *The Lavender Lady*, by Agnes Moorehead (one-woman show LP); and *Topsy or Sorry about That Harriett*, by the original cast (LP). Other artists include Sheri Decartier.

RAINBOW SOUND INC., 1322 Inwood Rd., Dallas TX 75247. (214)638-7712. President: Bob Cline. Record company, music publisher, record producer and record pressing plant. Works with artists and songwriters on contract. Pays 5% royalty to artists on contract; standard royalty to songwriters on contract.

How to Contact: Submit demo tape and lyric sheet. Prefers cassette with 2-6 songs on demo. SASE. Reports in 2 weeks.
Music: Contemporary church/religious; and gospel. Recently released *Becky*, by Becky Fender (contemporary soul/gospel LP); and *Lulu Sings for Her Friends*, by Lulu Roman (country/MOR/gospel LP).

RAM RECORDS, Box 2802, Corpus Christi TX 78403. Contact: John Davis. Releases 2-3 singles and 1-2 albums/year. Works with musicians on salary; artists and songwriters on contract. Pays standard royalty to artists and songwriters on contract.
How to Contact: Submit demo tape. Prefers 7½ ips reel-to-reel or cassette with 2-5 songs on demo. Does not return unsolicited material. Reports in 2 weeks.
Music: Recently released "Cheatin' Sheet" and "One Red Rose," by Jav Yest (country artist).

RAVEN RECORDS, 1918 Wise Dr., Dothan AL 36303. (205)794-9067. Labels include Studio Four Records. President: Jerry Wise. Record company. Works with artists and songwriters on contract. Pays 2-20% royalty to artists on contract; standard royalty to songwriters on contract.
How to Contact: Write first about your interest, then submit demo tape and lyric sheet. Prefers 7½ ips reel-to-reel or cassette with 1-6 songs on demo. SASE. Reports in 1 month.
Music: C&W; easy listening; MOR; rock; soul; and top 40/pop. Recently released *Check With Your Heart*, by Norman Andrews (country rock LP and single); *She Flies*, by Norman Andrews (easy listening LP and single); and "Love Is the Power," by Clique (rock single). Other artists include Jim Broun, Ivey Brothers and Southbound Glory.

RCA RECORDS, 6363 Sunset Blvd., Los Angeles CA 90028. (213)468-4164. Head of A&R: Ed DeJoy, 1133 Avenue of the Americas, New York NY 10036. Record company. Works with artists and songwriters on contract.
How to Contact: Submit demo tape. Prefers cassette with 1-3 songs on demo. SASE. Reports in 8 weeks.
Music: Classical; dance; jazz; progressive; R&B; rock; soul; and top 40/pop.
Tips: "We're interested in a simple demo with piano and voice for songs. The same applies for artists, but get vocals out front."

RCI RECORDS/SOUND STUDIOS, INC. Box 126, 4 William St., Elmsford NY 10523. (914)592-7983. Labels include Thomas and Aster Records. A&R/Vice President: Ray Roberts. Record company, music publisher and recording studio. Releases 50-60 singles and 20-25 albums/year. Works with artists and songwriters on contract. Pays 10% royalty to artists on contract.
How to Contact: Submit demo tape and lead sheet and lyrics, or "leave tape off at office and we will contact you." Prefers 7½ ips reel-to-reel with 1-12 songs on demo. SASE. Reports in 2 weeks.
Music: Bluegrass; church/religious; C&W; dance; easy listening; folk; gospel; jazz; rock; MOR; soul; top 40/pop; Latin; polka; and R&B. Recently released "The Next 100 Years" and "I've Gone through Hell Just to Get to Heaven," by Donna Stark (C&W singles); and "Love Up and Let Me Down," by Bunnie Mills (C&W single).

RECORD COMPANY OF THE SOUTH (RCS), 5220 Essen Lane, Baton Rouge LA 70808. (504)766-3233. Vice President/General Manager: John Fred. Record company, music publisher and record producer. Works with musicians on salary; artists and songwriters on contract. Pays 3-7% royalty to artists on contract; standard royalty to songwriters on contract.
How to Contact: Submit demo tape and lyric sheet. Prefers cassette (7½ ips reel-to-reel OK) with 1-10 songs on demo. SASE. Reports in 1 month.
Music: C&W; MOR; R&B; hard and country rock; soul; and top 40/pop. Recently released "Suddenly Single," by Butch Hornsby (country single); *Don't Take It Out on the Dog*, by Butch Hornsby (country LP); and *Safe with Me*, by Irma Thomas (pop single and LP). Other artists include Luther Kent, Gregg Wright and Floyd Brown.

REDEEMER RECORD CO., Box 55943, Houston TX 77055. (713)686-1749. President: Gary R. Smith. Record company, music publisher (Gospel Senders Music/BMI and Redeemer Music/SESAC), record producer, management firm and booking agency. Releases 2-5 albums/year. Works with artists and songwriters on contract. Pays statutory rate to publishers for each record sold.
How to Contact: Arrange personal interview. Prefers reel-to-reel or cassette with 3-10 songs on demo. SASE. Reports in 1 month.
Music: Church/religious and gospel. Recently released *Comin' Home/I Found the Way*, by Gary R. Smith (contemporary gospel LP); *More About Jesus*, by Greg S. Page (contemporary gospel LP); and *Simple Praise*, by Gary R. Smith (contemporary gospel LP). Other artists include Sammy Craig, Jr. and Clay Howell.

RENAISSANCE RECORDS & FILMS, Box 3501, Flint MI 48502. Production Chief: M.D. Ruffin. Record company and record producer. Works with musicians on salary for in-house studio work; songwriters on contract. Pays statutory rate to publishers for each record sold.
How to Contact: Submit demo tape. Prefers 7½ ips or cassette with 7 songs on demo. SASE. Reports in 2 weeks.
Music: Dance-oriented, jazz, R&B, rock and soul. Recently released "Feel Right," by Roger McClendant (soul single). Other artist include Ben Jacksen.

REN-MAUR MUSIC CORP., 663 5th Ave., New York NY 10022. (212)757-3638. Labels include R&R Records and Ren Rome Records and Factory Beat Records, Inc. Producers: Billy Nichols, Rena L. Feeney, Lenny Bailey. Record company, music publisher and production company. Works with musicians and songwriters on contract. Pays 4% royalty to artists and songwriters on contract. Released 12" 1980 record album.
How to Contact: Submit demo tape and lead sheet. Prefers 7½ ips reel-to-reel with 4-8 songs on demo. SASE. Reports in 1 month.
Music: Disco; jazz; MOR; rock; soul; and top 40/pop. Recently released "High Time," by Charles Hudson (MOR single); "Love a Little Longer," by Rena Romano (top 40 single); "Do It with Me," by the Lenny Bailey Orchestra (disco single); "Everybody Let's Party," by Joe Rivers (disco single); "I Love Your Beat," by Rena (dance single) soon to be released, "Dance It Off," by Rena (dance single) on Factory Beat Records, Inc.

REVONAH RECORDS, Box 217, Ferndale NY 12734. (914)292-5965. Owner: Paul Gerry. Record company and booking agency. Releases 5-10 singles and 4-5 albums/year. Works with artists and songwriters on contract. Pays negotiable royalty.
How to Contact: Submit demo tape and lead sheet or arrange personal interview. Prefers reel-to-reel, cassette or 8-track cartridge. SASE. Reports in 1 month.
Music: Bluegrass; C&W; folk; and gospel. Recently released *Red Rector,* by Red Rector (bluegrass LP); *No Doubt about It,* by Curley Seckler (bluegrass LP); and *Bluegrass Unleashed,* b yThe Dog Run Boys (bluegrass LP). Other artists include Mac Martin, the Shenandoah Cutups, Stacy Phillips, Simon St. Pierre, Gene Elders, Fred Pike, Roger Bellow, Del McCoury, The Stuart Family, Mountain Grass, Walter Hensley, Clinton King, Jerry Oliano, and The Gospelites.

RFC RECORDS, 101 W. 55 St., New York NY 10019. (212)246-4352. Vice President/A&R: Vince Aletti. Record company. Estab. 1979. Works with artists on contract.
How to Contact: Submit demo tape and lyric sheet. Prefers cassette with 1-5 songs on tape. SASE. Reports in 3 weeks.
Music: Dance; and R&B. Recently released "Dancer," by Gino Soccio (disco single); *The Glow of Love* and *Miracles,* by Change (R&B/disco LP); and "Smack Dab In The Middle," by Janice McClain (disco single). "RFC is primarily a disco label, interested in progressive, high-energy dance music in all its forms." Other artists include Karen Silver.

RICHARDSON RECORDS, 1938 Baltimore Annapolis Blvd., Annapolis MD 21401. (301)757-3733. President: Charles A. Richardson. Record company and record producer. Works with musicians on salary; artists and songwriters on contract. Releases 5 singles and 5 albums/year. Pays 4-10% royalty to artists on contract; standard royalty to songwriters on contract; statutory rate to publishers for each record sold.
How to Contact: Write first about your interest, then submit demo tape and lyric sheet. Prefers 7½ ips reel-to-reel with 2-10 songs on demo. SASE. Reports in 3 weeks.
Music: Band music (for concert or marching bands); choral; church/religious; classical; folk; gospel; and jazz. Recently released *Handel's Messiah,* by John Talley (classical LP); *The Spirit of Christmas Brassed,* by Annapolis Brass Quintet (classical LP); and *Eternal Father,* by James Dale (choral/church LP). Other artists include Singers Madrigale, Aeolian Woodwind Quintet, Naval Academy Band, Naval Academy Glee Club, Naval Academy Drum and Bugle Corps, Maranatha Choir, Douglas Allanbrook and John Cooper.

RICHEY RECORDS, 7121 W. Vickery, Fort Worth TX 76116. (817)731-7375. Labels include Ridge Runner, Flying High, and Grass Mountain Records. President: Slim Richey. Record company and music publisher (Ridgerunner Publishing/ASCAP and Grass Mountain Publishing/ BMI). Releases 2 singles and 12 albums/year. Works with musicians on salary; artists and songwriters on contract. Pays 6% royalty to artists on contract; standard royalty to songwriters on contract.
How to Contact: Submit demo tape and lead sheet. Prefers cassette.
Music: Recently released *Texas Boogie Blues,* by Ray Sharpe (pop LP). Other artists include Tennessee Gentlemen and Alan Munde.

RICHMOND RECORDS, Short Pump Associates, Box 11292, Richmond VA 23230. (804)355-4117. President: Ken Brown. Vice President: Dennis Huber. Record company and music publisher (ASCAP). Releases 3 singles and 2 albums/year. Works with musicians on salary; artists and songwriters on contract. Pays 11% royalty to artists on contract.
How to Contact: Submit demo tape and lead sheet. Prefers cassette with 3-6 songs on demo. SASE. Reports in 2 weeks.
Music: Country rock and rock 'n roll. Recently released *Two B's Please* (LP), "Candyapple Red," and "Brite Eyes," by the Robbin Thompson Band (rock). Other artists include Good Humor Band.

RICHTOWN/GOSPEL TRUTH RECORDS, Box 7552, Richmond VA 23231. (804)226-0424. Labels include Cardinal, Richtown/Truth Gospel Records and Charity Records. Chairman of the Board: R.A. Charity Sr. Record company. Works with songwriters on contract. Payment negotiable.
How to Contact: Submit demo tape and lead sheet or arrange personal interview. "We also accept master tapes." Prefers 7½ ips reel-to-reel or cassette with 2-4 songs on demo. "Be sure material is copyrighted and sent by registered mail." SASE. Reports in 1 month; "we copy all material and return the original to the songwriter."
Music: Bluegrass; blues; children's; choral; church/religious; classical; C&W; dance; easy listening; folk; gospel; jazz; MOR; progressive; rock; soul; and top 40/pop.

RIGHT ON RECORDS, 408 W. 115th St., Suite 2W, New York NY 10025. (212)222-8715. Labels include Big Mike Records. Manager: Bill Downs. Record company and music publisher. Works with artists on contract. Pays standard royalty.
How to Contact: Submit demo tape and lead sheet. Prefers cassette with 3 songs on demo. Does not return unsolicited material.
Music: R&B; rock; soul; and new wave. "We're interested in master tapes (originals) for European releases." Recently released "The Redhead," by G.G. Turner (new wave single); and "Dance Little Children," by Ad Libs (disco/soul single). Other artists include Chris Bartley, Dolly Gilmore and Jerry Brown and the Beyond Group.

RIPSAW RECORD CO, 121 N. 4th St., Easton PA 18042. (215)258-5990. Branch located at #5J, 320 W. 30th St., New York NY 10001. (212)564-3246. President: Jim Kirk (Easton). Vice President: Jonathan Strong (NY). Record company (Southern Crescent Publishing/BMI) Releases 6 singles/year. Works with artists and songwriters on contract. Payment negotable with artists on contract; standard royalty to songwriters on contract; statutory rate to publishers for each record sold.
How to Contact: Submit demo tape and lyric sheet or "invite us to a club date to listen." Prefers cassette. SASE.
Music: Bluegrass; C&W; and rockabilly. Recently released "Feelin' Right Tonight," by Martha Hull (rock and roll single); and "Get with It," by Johnny Seaton (rockabilly single). Other artists include Billy Hancock and Tex Rubinowitz.
Tips: "Keep it rockabilly."

RMS TRIAD RECORDS, 30125 John R. St., Madison Heights MI 48071. (313)585-8887. Contact: Bob Szajner. Record company, record producer and music publisher (RMS Triad Publisher/ ASCAP). Member BMA, RIAA, NARAS and NAIRD. Releases 3 albums/year. Works withs artists on contract. Pays negotiable royalty; statutory rate to publishers for each record sold.
How to Contact: Write first about your interest. Prefers cassette with 1-3 songs on demo. SASE. Reports in 3 weeks.
Music: Jazz. Recently produced *Jazz Opus 20/40*, *Sound Ideas* and *Afterthoughts*, by Triad (mainstream jazz, RMS Records).

ROADSHOW RECORDS, 1733 Broadway, New York NY 10019. (212)765-8840. Labels include Hob and Gospel Arm Records. A&R Director: Nancy Ruens. Record company and music publisher. Works with musicians on contract and songwriters on salary.
How to Contact: Submit demo tape and lyric sheet. Prefers cassette with 2-3 songs on demo. Does not return unsolicited material. Reports in 2 weeks.
Music: Disco; MOR and R&B. Artists include Shirley Caesar, BT Express and Brass Construction.

ROBBINS RECORDS, Rt. 3, Box 277, Leesville LA 71446. Labels include Headliner Stars Records. National Representative: Sherree Scott. Record company and music publisher (Headliner Stars Music and Universal Stars Music/BMI). Releases 6 singles and 2-6 albums/year. Works with artists and songwriters on contract. Pays standard royalty to artists on contract; statutory rate to publishers for each record sold.

How to Contact: Submit demo tape and lyric sheet. Prefers cassette with 1-6 songs on demo. Does not return unsolicited material. Reports only if interested.
Music: Bluegrass; church/religious; C&W; folk; gospel; and top 40/pop. Recently released *Jesus Came All The Way*, by Sherree Scott (religious LP); *Oh, Lord Save Me*, by Melodie Scott (gospel LP); and *Praise Him,* by J.J. & Sherrie Stephens (religious single LP). Other artists include Renee Scott.

ROB-LEE MUSIC, Box 1385, Merchantville NJ 08109. (609)665-8933. Labels include Castle, TCB, Jade, Rock Island and Camden Soul Records. Vice President/A&R: Bob Francis. Record company and record producer. Member RIAA. Works with artists and songwriters on contract. Pays 4-6% royalty to artists on contract; standard royalty to songwriters on contract; pays 5¢/song or 1¢/minute to music publishers for each record sold.
How to Contact: Submit demo tape and lyric sheet. Prefers 7½ ips reel-to-reel or cassette with 2-8 songs on demo. "Include biography and photos if possible." SASE. Reports in 2 weeks.
Music: C&W (country rock); dance; jazz; progressive; rock; and top 40/pop. Recently released "I'll Never Hear the Music," by Roman (MOR single); *Live at Gatling's Saloon and Dance Hall*, by Jim Bert and The Blackfoot Country Band (C&W LP); and "Luscious," by Heavy Weather (R&B single). Other artists include the TCB Band, Mustang Sally, Don Lacy and Country Special, Loyd Lee and The Rebels, Moor Stanton, Bobby Buttons Band, Front Street Runners, Reba and the Rooters, Larry Hickman and the Red Hot Riders, Rich Gold and Mystery Train, Big El, Abbey Road and Benn Falana.

ROCKIN! RECORDS, 1733 Carmona Ave., Los Angeles CA 90019. (213)933-6521. Labels include Rockmore Records. Manager: Perry Rocquemore. A&R Director: Willie H. Rocquemore. Record company, music publisher and record producer. Works with artists and songwriters on contract. Pays standard royalty.
How to Contact: Submit demo tape and lyric sheet. Prefers 7½ ips reel-to-reel with 4 songs maximum on demo. SASE. Reports in 1 month.
Music: Country, rock, ballad and top 40/pop. Recently released "I Can't Complain," "Let's Just Fake It for Tonight," "Hello Good Times," and "Summer Lovers," all by Jennifer Joyson.

ROTA RECORDS, 5305 Church Ave., Brooklyn NY 11203. (212)498-7111. Labels include Nilkam, Cartoon and K.G. Records. President: William R. Kamorra. Record company, music publisher and record producer. Releases 3 singles and 2 albums/year. Works with artists and songwriters on contract; musicians on salary. Pays 2-5% royalty to artists on contract; standard royalties to songwriters on contract.
How to Contact: Query, submit demo tape and lead sheet, or submit acetate disc and lead sheet. Prefers 7½ ips reel-to-reel or cassette with 3-6 songs on demo. SASE. Reports in 2 weeks.
Music: Dance; MOR; R&B; rock; soul; and top 40/pop. Recently released *Unity*, by Future 2,000 (disco LP); *The Rules*, by Denis Lopsler (MOR LP); and "Answer to a Dream," by Misty (disco single).
Tips: A songwriter wishing to deal with this company "should first of all have all his music copyrighted, then send copies to us with a short letter about himself. If there is not much to write about send us a resume. We will return all the unusable material with a letter explaining why we can't use the product. Should we find something we can use, we will contact him immediately."

ROULETTE RECORDS, INC., 1790 Broadway, 18th Floor, New York NY 10019. Labels include Pyramid and A&R Records. Director: Phil Kahl.
How to contact: Submit demo tape and lyric sheet. Prefers 7½ ips reel-to-reel or cassette with 1-3 songs on demo. SASE. Reports in 1 month.
Music: Blues; choral; C&W; dance; easy listening; folk; jazz; MOR; progressive; R&B; rock; soul; and top 40/pop.

ROUNDER RECORDS CORP., 186 Willow Ave., Somerville MA 02144. (617)354-0700. Vice President: Ken Irwin. Record company. Works with artists and songwriters on contract. Pays 7% minimum royalty to artists on contract; standard royalty to songwriters on contract.
How to Contact: Submit cassette with 4-12 songs on demo. SASE. "Please don't call. We will try to provide a response within 4-6 weeks."
Music: Bluegrass; blues; children's; C&W; folk; R&B; and rock. Recently released *More George Thorogood & The Destroyers*, by George Thorogood & The Destroyers (rock/R&B LP); and *Full Moon on the Farm*, by Norman Blake (guitar LP). Other artists include John Hammond, Tony Rice, J.D. Crowe, Guy Van Duser, Artie Traum & Pat Alger, Michael Hurley, Hazel Dickens, Jerry Douglas, Mark O'Connor, Sleepy La Beef, Johnny Copeland, Steve Young, Bela Sleck, The Johnson Mountain Boys, and Butch Robins.

ROYAL T MUSIC, Box 946, Springtown, TX 76082. (817)433-5720. Labels include Old Hat and T2 Topple Records. President: James Michael Taylor. Record company, music publisher and booking agency. Works with artists and songwriters on contract.
How to Contact: Submit demo tape, submit demo tape and lead sheet. Prefers 7½ ips reel-to-reel or cassette with 6-12 songs on demo. SASE. Reports in 1 month.
Music: Children's; choral; C&W; folk; MOR; rock; top 40/pop. Recently released "Feathers in the Wind," by Snowgeese (country/rock/pop); and "First Link," by Bob French (folk/country).

ROYALTY RECORDS OF CANADA, LTD., 9229 58th Ave., Edmonton, Alberta Canada T6E 0B7. (403)436-0665. Contact: R. Harlan Smith. Record company, music publisher, record producer and management firm. Releases 12-15 singles and 4-6 albums/year. Works with songwriters on contract; musicians on scale. Pays standard royalties.
How to Contact: Arrange personal interview, submit demo tape, or submit demo tape and lead sheet. Prefers 7½ ips reel-to-reel or cassette with 5-8 songs on demo. "Also include a written statement verifying that publishing is available internationally on the material submitted." Does not return unsolicited material. Reports in 1 month.
Music: C&W; easy listening; MOR; rock; and top 40/pop.

RSO RECORDS, INC., 8335 Sunset Blvd., Los Angeles CA 90069. (213)650-1234. Labels include Dreamland Records. Contact: A&R Department. Record company. Works with artists on contract.
How to Contact: Submit demo tape; "no publishing demos." Prefers 7½ ips reel-to-reel or cassette with 2-3 songs on demo. SASE. Reports in 2 months.
Music: Easy listening; progressive; R&B; rock; soul; and top 40/pop. Recently released *After Dark*, recorded by Andy Gibb (pop LP).

RUNATHON RECORDS, Box 5896, Station A, Toronto, Ontario, Canada M5W 1P3. (416)537-8749. Labels include Walkathon Records and Emphysema Records. President: Ben Kerr. Record company and music publisher (Chaser for the Blues Music). Releases 4 singles/year. Works with artists and songwriters on contract. Pays negotiable royalty to artists on contract; statutory rate to publisher for each record sold.
How to Contact: Write first about your interest. Prefers 7½ ips reel-to-reel or cassette with 4 songs maximum on demo. SAE and International Reply Coupons. Reports in 1 month.
Music: C&W, folk and MOR. Recently released "The Boston Marathon," "Honky-Tonk-Ville," "Distilled Water," "Fire on One End (A Fool on the Other)," by Running Ben Kerr (country singles); "Nancy & Gayle," and "Joanne My Joanne," by Running Ben Kerr (country/MOR singles).

RUSTIC RECORDS, 615 Durrett Dr., Nashville TN 37211. (615)833-1457. President: Jack Stillwell. Record company. Works with musicians on salary; artists and songwriters on contract. Pays royalty to artists on contract; statutory royalty to songwriters on contract.
How to Contact: Submit demo tape with lyric or lead sheet. Prefers 7½ ips reel-to-reel with 2 songs on demo. "Use new tape." SASE. Reports in 3 weeks.
Music: C&W; easy listening; progressive and MOR. Recently released "Breakaway," "Quicksand," and "I Wanna Do It Again" by Bill Wence (country single). Other artists include Jack Stillwell, Ray Edwards and Carl Struck.

S.E.I. RECORDS, Box 18052, Minneapolis MN 55418. Labels include At The Copa Records & Tapes and Smash Records. President/Promoter: Daniel Thompson. Record company, record producer and artist management company. Estab. 1978. Works with artists and songwriters on contract.
How to Contact: Submit demo tape and lyric sheet. Prefers 3¾ or 7½ ips reel-to-reel with 5 songs maximum on tape. "We prefer artists don't call. We do not accept collect calls." SASE. Reports in 1 month.
Music: Dance; easy listening; and top 40/pop.

SAGITTAR RECORDS, 1311 Candlelight Ave., Dallas TX 75116. (214)298-9576. President: Paul Ketter. Record company, record producer and music publisher. Releases 6 singles and 1-2 albums/year. Works with musicians on salary; artists and songwriters on contract. Pays 7¢/record to artists on contract; standard royalty to songwriters on contract.
How to Contact: Submit demo tape and lyric sheet. Prefers 7½ ips reel-to-reel with 1-8 songs on demo. SASE. Reports in 3 weeks.
Music: C&W; folk; MOR (country); and progressive (country). Recently released *Only A Woman*, by Bunnie Mills (C&W).

SALSOUL RECORDS, 401 5th Ave., New York NY 10016. (212)889-7340. Executive Vice President: Ken Cayre. Record company and music publisher. Works with artists and songwriters on contract.
How to Contact: Submit demo tape and lyric sheet. Prefers 7½ ips reel-to-reel ½ track or cassette with 3 songs maximum on demo. "May or may not return unsolicited material." Reports in 3 weeks.
Music: Dance; R&B; rock; soul and top 40/pop. Recently released *Instant Funk* by Instant Funk (disco/R&B LP).

SAM PRODUCTIONS, 45 S. 38th St., Long Island City NY 11101. (212)786-7667. Vice President: Daniel S. Glass. Record company, music publisher and record producer. Works with artists on contract. Payment negotiable.
How to Contact: Call first about your interest, then submit demo tape and lyric sheet. Prefers 7½ ips reel-to-reel or cassette with 1-3 songs on demo. SASE. Reports in 2 weeks.
Music: Blues; dance; folk; MOR; progressive; R&B; rock; soul; and top 40/pop. "We are eagerly looking for artists in R&B and new rock." Recently released *Keep On Dancin'*, by Gary's Gang (disco pop LP); "Love Magic," (pop single) and *Ain't That Enough for You*, by John Davis With The Monster Orchestra (pop LP); "Let's Do It," by Convention; "Don't Stop," by K.I.D.; and "Just How Sweet Is Your Love," by Rhyze.

SANDCASTLE RECORDS, 157 W. 57th St., New York NY 10019. (212)582-6135. Labels include Tara and Coby Records. President: Mark Cosmedy. Record company. Releases 10-14 singles and 7-10 albums/year. Works with artists and songwriters on contract. Payment negotiable.
How to Contact: Submit demo tape and lead sheet. Prefers 7½ ips reel-to-reel or cassette with 2-4 songs on demo. SASE. Reports in 1 month.
Music: C&W; easy listening; folk; jazz; MOR; progressive; rock; and top 40/pop.

SAN-SUE RECORDING STUDIO, 1309 Celesta Way, Sellersburg IN 47172. (812)246-2959. Labels include Basic Records. Owner: Buddy Powell. Record company, music publisher (Hoosier Hills/BMI) and recording studio. Works with artists and songwriters on contract. Releases 7 singles and 3 albums/year. Pays 8% royalty to artists on contract; statutory rate to publishers for each record sold.
How to Contact: Submit demo tape. Prefers 7½ ips reel-to-reel or cassette with 2-4 songs on demo. "Strong vocal with piano or guitar is suitable for demo, along with lyrics." SASE. Reports in 2 weeks.
Music: Church/religious; C&W; and MOR. Recently released "Little People," by Sue Powell (MOR single); "I Missed You Again Today," by Jerry Baird (C&W single); and "Which Way You Going Billy," by Sandy Powell (country/pop single). Other artists include Camillo Phelps.

SAVOY RECORDS, Box 279, 342 Westminister Ave., Elizabeth NJ 07208. Contact: Helen Gottesmann, Milton Biggham. Record company and music publisher (Savgos Music, Inc./BMI, Jonan Music, Inc./ASCAP and Arisav Music, Inc./SESEC). Member RIAA. Releases 60 albums/year. Pays statutory rate to publishers for each record sold.
How to Contact: Query. Reports in 2 weeks.
Music: Gospel and traditional gospel. Recently released *It's A New Day*, by Rev. James Cleveland (gospel LP); *In God's Own Time*, by Triboro Mass Choir (gospel LP); and *I Don't Feel Noways Tired*, by Salem Inspirational Choir (gospel LP); and *Please Be Patient With Me*, by Albertina Walker and James Cleveland (gospel LP). Other artists include Cosmopolitan Church of Prayer Choir, Donald Vails Choraleers, Charles Fold Singers, Keith Pringle, Salem Inspirational Choir, and Pilgrim Jubilee Singers.

SCARAMOUCHE RECORDS, Drawer 1967, Warner Rubins GA 31099. (912)922-1955. Director: Robert R. Kovach. Record company and record producer. Releases 4 singles and 1 album/year. Works with artists and songwriters on contract. Pays 3-5% royalty to artists on contract; pays statutory rate to publishers for each record sold.
How to Contact: Submit demo tape and lyric sheet. Prefers 7½ ips reel-to-reel or cassette with 3-5 songs on demo. SASE. Reports in 1 month.
Music: Blues, C&W, easy listening, R&B, rock, soul and top 40/pop. Recently released "Easy on Your Feet," by Justice (dance/easy listening single). Other artists include Napoleon Starke.
Tips: "To be different makes the difference."

SCENE PRODUCTIONS, Box 1243, Beckley WV 25801. (304)252-4836. Labels include Rising Sun and Country Road Records. Executive Professional Manager Producer: Richard L. Petry. Record company, record producer and music publisher (Purple Haze Music/BMI). Member of

AFM. Works with artists and songwriters on contract. Pays 3-5% royalty to artists on contract; standard royalty to songwriters on contract; statutory rate to publishers for each record sold. Charges "initial costs, but is conditionally paid back to artist."
How to Contact: Write first about your interest, then submit demo tape and lyric sheet. Prefers 7½ ips reel-to-reel with 2-7 songs on demo. Will accept reel-to-reel or cassette. SASE. Reports in 1 month.
Music: C&W; MOR; light and commercial rock; and top 40/pop. Recently released "Gonna Find My Dream" and "Linda," by Bob McCormick (MOR singles); "Women And Music" and "City Of Love," by Stone Mountain (light rock singles); and "Love That's Torn Apart" and "Got The Urge," by Zella (rock singles). Other artists include Misle (Rising Sun Records); and Delisa Marcum (Country Road Records).

SEVEN HILLS RECORDING & PUBLISHING CO., INC., 905 N. Main St., Evansville IN 47711. (812)423-1861. President: Ed Kreitemeyer. Record company, record producer and music publisher. Releases 3 singles/year. Pays varied royalty to artists on contract; statutory rate to publishers for each record sold.
How to Contact: Write first about your interest. Prefers cassette with 1 song minimum on demo. SASE. Reports in 1 month.
Music: Bluegrass, blues, C&W, easy listening, folk, gospel and R&B.

SHILOH RECORDS, Box 368, Selmer TN 38375. (901)645-5423. President: W.R. Morris. Record company. Labels include Majesty Records. Releases 10-15 singles and 5-8 albums/year. Works with artists on contract. Payment negotiable. Charges for some services. "We charge if an artist wants record produced and we feel material is not suitable for our market."
How to Contact: Submit demo tape and lead sheet. Prefers 7½ ips reel-to-reel or cassette with 2-4 songs on demo. SASE. Reports in 1 month.
Music: C&W; gospel; and bluegrass. Recently released "Daddy's Shoes," by Guy Drake.

SILENT W. PRODUCTIONS, Box 277, Dundas, Ontario, Canada L9H 5G1. Labels include SWP Records. A&R Manager: James Taylor. Record company, record producer and music publisher (Jay-Me Music). Estab. 1980. Releases 3 singles and 2 albums/year. Works with artists and songwriters on contract. Pays negotiable royalty to artists on contract; pays statutory rate to publishers for each record sold.
How to Contact: Submit demo tape and lyric sheet. Prefers cassette with 1-4 songs on demo. "SAE and International Reply Coupons *must* be included or tape cannot be returned." Reports as soon as possible.
Music: Easy listening, folk, MOR, rock (all types) and top 40/pop. Recently released "Bloodshot in Your Eyes," by Dundas (rock single); "Got It in the Bag," by The Innocent (new wave EP); and "A Little More Time," by Tyro (rock EP). Other artists include Earl Lardcque.
Tips: "Our special interest is Canadian talent although we will listen to everything submitted."

SILVER PELICAN RECORDS, Rt. 1, Box 195A, Dean Rd., Maitland FL 32751. President: Glenn Hamman. Record company, record producer and music publisher (Hamman Publishing, Inc./BMI). Member AFM. Releases 10 singles/year. Pays 5-7% royalty to artists on contract; statutory rate to publishers for each record sold.
How to Contact: Submit demo tape and lyric sheet or arrange personal interview. Prefers cassette with 2-5 songs on demo. "Please make sure all work is copyrighted before submitting." SASE. Reports in 1 month.
Music: Church/religious, C&W, easy listening, gospel, jazz, MOR and R&B. Recently released "Love Letter," by Harry D. Cup (religious single); "Sick American," by Harry D. Cup (country/ MOR single); and "Pink and Powder Blue," by John Walden (country single).

SINGSPIRATION RECORDS, 1415 Lake Dr., Grand Rapids MI 49508. Labels include New Dawn, Milk n' Honey, Sunshine Music Mountain and Everlasting Spring Records. Director of Music Publications: Don Wyrtzen. National Music Coordinator: Randy Vader. Director of Record Dept.: Phil Brower. Record company and music publisher (ASCAP, SESAC). Member GMA, NARAS. Releases 10 artist/singles and 10-15 artist/albums/year. Works with musicians on salary; artists and songwriters on contract. Pays 5% royalty to artists on contract; statutory rate to publishers for each record sold.
How to Contact: Submit demo tape or submit demo tape and lead sheet. Prefers cassette with 3-5 songs on demo. Does not return unsolicited material. Reports in 2 months.
Music: Church/religious; Christian contemporary; gospel; MOR. Recently released *Workin' In the Final Hour*, by Wayne Watson; *Simply Love*, by Christine Wyrrzen; *Take a Walk on the Water*, by Re'Generation; and *Morning Son*, by Harvest. Other artists include Twila Paris, Bill Pearce, Robbie Hiner, Thomas Steven Smith, and Gary Rand.

SIRE RECORDS, 3 East 54 St., New York NY 10022. (212)832-0950. Assistant to the President: Michael Rosenblatt. Record company.
How to Contact: Submit demo tape and lyric sheet. Prefers cassette as demo. SASE. Reports in 1 month.
Music: Rock. Recently released *The Pretenders*, by The Pretenders (rock LP).

SIVATT MUSIC PUBLISHING CO., Box 7172, Greenville SC 29610. (803)269-3961. Labels include Pioneer, Brand-X and Accent Records. President: Jesse B. Evatte. Secretary: Sybil P. Evatte. Record company and music publisher. Publishes 4-10 singles and 11-25 albums/year. Works with artists and songwriters on contract. Pays standard royalty to artists and songwriters on contract.
How to Contact: Submit demo tape and lead sheet. Prefers cassette with 2-6 songs on demo. SASE. Reports in 1 month.
Music: Bluegrass; choral; church/religious; C&W; easy listening; folk; and gospel. Recently released *Down Home Singing*, by the Roy Knight Singers (country gospel LP); *Sincerely*, by Joyce and the Rogers Brothers (gospel LP); and *Down Home Guitar*, by Bob Dennis (instrumental gospel LP).

SKYLIGHT RECORDS, 937 Felix Ave., Windsor, Ontario, Canada N9C 3L2. (519)255-7067. Labels include JLT Records. President: Jim Thomson II. Record company, record producer and music publisher (On the Wing Music Publishing Co.). Estab. 1979. Releases 2 singles and 1 album/year. Works with songwriters on contract. Pays statutory rate to publishers for each record sold.
How to Contact: Write or call first about your interest, submit demo tape and lyric sheet or arrange personal interview. Prefers cassette with 4 songs on demo; "submit at least 2 of each style; if submitting more than 1 style, preferably 3 songs." SAE and International Reply Coupons. Reports in 2 weeks.
Music: Bluegrass, blues, children's, church/religious, classical, C&W, easy listening, folk, gospel, jazz, MOR, progressive, Spanish, R&B, rock (all types), soul and top 40 pop. Recently released *Message at 33⅓*, by Preflyte (gospel/soft rock LP); *Warning*, by Jim Thomson II (folk/rock LP); and *Out to Launch*, by Preflyte (hard rock LP). Other artists include Walterio (Spanish/classical/jazz guitarist).

THE SMILE MUSIC GROUP, 1659 Bayview Ave., Suite 102, Toronto, Ontario, Canada M4G 3C1. (416)485-1157. President: Dave Coutts. Vice President: Brian Ayres. Record company and music publisher. Releases 4 singles and 3 albums/year. Works with artists and songwriters on contract. Pays negotiable royalty to artists on contract; 50% royalty to songwriters on contract.
How to Contact: Submit demo tape or arrange personal interview. Prefers cassette with 1-6 songs on demo. SAE and International Reply Coupons. Reports in 3 weeks.
Music: Top 40/pop; C&W; dance; easy listening; MOR; progressive; and rock.

SMUDGE RECORDS, Box 29342, Dallas TX 75229. (214)243-2933. Director: Terry Rose. Record company, record producer and music publisher (Pocket-Money Music/BMI). Releases 6 singles and 4 albums/year. Works with artists and songwriters on contract; musicians on salary for in-house studio work. Pays 4-5% of 90% off suggested retail price to artists on contract; negotiated license to publishers for each record sold.
How to Contact: Write first about your interest. Prefers cassette with 1 song on demo. SASE. Reports in 3 weeks.
Music: C&W, R&B, rock (no heavy metal), soul, top 40/pop and new wave/pop. *The King Bee*, by Randy Ream (pop LP); *New Waves and Other Tonsorial Delights*, by Wally Willette and The Telecaster Cats (new wave/rockabilly LP and EP); "Bodine Brown," by Purvis Pickett (novelty single); and "Love Tempo," by Love Company (soul single). Other artists include The Magics and Love Company.

SOLID RECORDS, 10101 Woodlake Dr. Apt. M, Cockeysville MD 21030. A&R Director: George Brigman. Record company, music publisher and record producer (Sone Songs/BMI). Releases 1-2 singles and 1 album/year. Works with musicians on salary; artists and songwriters on contract. Pays 5-20% royalty to artists on contract; standard royalty to songwriters on contract.
How to Contact: Submit demo tape and lyric sheet. Prefers 7½ ips reel-to-reel with 1-6 songs on demo. SASE. Reports in 3 weeks.
Music: Blues; C&W; easy listening; jazz; progressive; hard rock and heavy metal rock. Recently released *Jungle Rot*, by George Brigman (hard rock LP); "Drifting," by Split (jazz single); "Blowin' Smoke," by Split (rock single); and "Nashville," by John Butterworth (country single). Other artists include the Mascara Snake, Russ Nixon and Buckwheat.

SONATA RECORDS, 4304 Del Monte Ave., San Diego CA 92107. (714)222-3346. President: Paul DiLella. Record company and music publisher. Member RIAA. Works with artists and songwriters on contract. Pays 5% royalty to artists on contract; 2¢/record to songwriters on contract.
How to Contact: Submit demo tape and lead sheet or submit lead sheet. Prefers 7½ ips reel-to-reel or cassette with 6-12 songs on demo. SASE. Reports in 1 month.
Music: Church/religious; classical; C&W; dance; easy listening; gospel; MOR; rock; and top 40/pop. Recently released "My Tropic Isle," by Cathy Foy (Hawaiian single). Other artists include Paul Dante.

SOUL SOUNDS UNLIMITED RECORDING CO., Box 24230, Cincinnati OH 45224. President: Alvin Don Chico Pettijohn. Record company and music publisher. Works with artists and songwriters on contract. Pays negotiable royalty to artists and songwriters on contract. Charges for some services: "We will make demo tapes for songwriters for their own use. If we feel that a writer or musician is best suited for our needs in the recording field, we will offer a recording contract."
How to Contact: Submit demo tape. Prefers 15 ips reel-to-reel, cassette or 8-track cartridge. SASE. "All tapes will become the property of Soul Sounds if return postage is not included." Reports in 3 weeks.
Music: Dance and soul. Recently released "Loving You," by the Devotions (easy listening/soul single); and "Need a Lot of Woman," by Henry R. Kyles (easy listening single).

SOUNDS OF WINCHESTER, Box 574, Winchester VA 22601. (703)667-9379. Labels include Alear, Winchester and Real McCoy Records. Owner: Jim McCoy. Contact: Bertha McCoy. Record company, music publisher and recording studio. Works with musicians on salary; artists and songwriters on contract. Pays 2% royalty to artists and songwriters on contract.
How to Contact: Submit demo tape or arrange personal interview. Prefers 7½ ips reel-to-reel with 4-12 songs on demo. Does not return unsolicited material. Reports in 1 month.
Music: Bluegrass; C&W; gospel; rock (country); and top 40/pop. Recently released "The Other Lover," by David Elliott (C&W single); "Mr. Blue Grass Here's to You," by the Carroll County Ramblers (bluegrass single); "Sweet Woman," by Larry Sutphin (C&W single); and *Leavin' On Your Mind*, Jim McCoy (c&w LP).

SOUNDS SOUTH RECORDS/WAHR RECORDS INC., 203 Culver Ave., Charleston SC 29407. (803)766-2500. Contact: Michael Thomas. Record company, music publisher, record producer and management company.
How to Contact: Submit demo tape and lyric sheet. Prefers cassette with 3 songs minimum on demo. "Cassette presentation should include biography, photo and lyric sheet. We are seeking finished masters for regional release." SASE. Reports in 3 weeks.
Music: Dance; rock; and soul. Recently released *This Precious Moment*, by Tams (soul/ballad single and LP); "Mr. DJ," by Little Eric (soul single); and "Plain, Simple But Sweet," by Drifters (soul/ballad single). Other artists include Mildred Anthony, Patsy Gallant, Strange and Billy & The Shifters (Wahr Records).

SOURCE RECORDS, 1902 5th Ave., Los Angeles CA 90018. (213)731-0693. President: Logan H. Westbrooks. Record company. Works with artists on contract.
How to Contact: Submit demo tape and lyric sheet. Prefers cassette with 1-3 songs on demo. "Make sure the tape is marked properly with a name, address and phone number." SASE. Reports in 1 month.
Music: Blues; dance; easy listening; gospel; jazz; progressive; R&B; soul; and top 40/pop. Recently released *Bustin' Loose*, by Chuck Brown & the Soul Searchers (R&B single and LP); "Reachin' Out," by Lee Moore (disco/R&B single); "Prayin'," by Harold Melvin & the Bluenotes (disco/R&B single); and "Bussle," by Opus VII (disco/R&B single). Other artists include Travis Biggs, Sharon Paige and Jeri-Q.

SPEEDWAY RECORDS, Box 4192, Huntsville AL 35802. (205)881-7976. Labels include Speedway, Fireside, New Day, Springwater and Championship Music Records. Owner: George Wells. Record company and music publisher. Releases 6 singles/year. Works with musicians on salary; artists and songwriters on contract. Payment negotiable to artists and songwriters on contract.
How to Contact: Submit demo tape and lyric sheet or arrange personal interview. Prefers 7½ ips reel-to-reel with 1-3 songs on demo. SASE. Reports in 1 month.
Music: C&W; gospel; MOR; and southern boogie. Recently released "Bear Bryant For President," by Mickey Dural/Championship Music Records (southern boogie single).

SPIRIT RECORDS, 441 S. Beverly Dr., #6, Beverly Hills CA 90212. (213)855-0525. Labels include Hartsong and Breeze Records. Executive Vice President: Kent Washburn. Record com-

pany and music publisher (Deuel-Hart Publishing/BMI, Angelstream Music/ASCAP). Estab. 1979. Member GMA and CBA. Releases 10 albums/year. Works with artists and songwriters on contract. Pays 5-8% royalty to artists on contract; statutory rate to publishers for each record sold.
How to Contact: Submit demo tape and lyric sheet. Prefers cassette with 3-5 songs on demo. SASE. Reports in 1 month.
Music: Gospel (contemporary Christian). Recently released *Randy Matthews*, by Randy Matthews (LP); *Energizin' Love*, by Paul D. Davis (LP); and *Benny Hester*, by Benny Hester (LP). Other artists include Pamela Deuel Hart, Albrecht, Role and Moore, Mike Johnson, City Limits, Annette Villbrandt and 'Ark.

STAN RECORDS, INC., 2024 S. Cooper St., Arlington TX 76010. Manager: Bill Stansell. Record company and music publisher. Releases 4-10 singles/year. Works with songwriters on contract. Pays standard royalties.
How to Contact: Query. Prefers cassette with 1 song on demo. "First request permission to submit any material." SASE. Reports in 1 month.
Music: Children's novelty; C&W; and gospel. Recently released "I Loved You Now You're Gone," "Blue Yesterdays," "Words on Paper," and "Broken Hearted Lovers," by Bill Stansell (singles).

STANDY RECORDS, INC., 760 Blandina St., Utica NY 13501. (315)735-6187. Labels include Kama Records. President: Stanley Markowski. Record company and music publisher (Oneida Music). Works with artists and songwriters on contract. Pays standard royalty to artists on contract; statutory rate to publishers for each record sold.
How to Contact: Submit demo tape and lyric sheet. Prefers 7½ ips reel-to-reel or cassette. SASE. Reports in 1 month.
Music: All types. Recently released "I Believe in America", by Tiny Tim (pop single); "Baby I'm Possessed by You," by Dawn Bouck (pop single); "We'll Build A Bungalow", by Norris The Troubador (pop single).

STAR JAZZ RECORDS, INC., 5220 SW 8th St., Fort Lauderdale FL 33317. (305)581-4310. Producer: Will Connelly. Record company. Estab. 1978. Works with musicians on salary. Payment negotiable.
How to Contact: Write first about your interest. Prefers cassette. "There are no limits on amount of material, but recommend limiting time to 15 minutes. If we like what we hear, we'll ask for more." Does not return unsolicited material. "We will return material submitted as a result of pre-inquiry." Reports in 2 weeks.
Music: Dixieland Jazz (20s-40s). Recently released *Justice Makes Love*, by Tom Justice (jazz LP); *Jazz You Like It*, by Biscayne Jazz Band (jazz LP); and *Swingin' Free*, by Sundance (jazz LP).

STAR SONG RECORDS, 2223 Strawberry, Pasadena TX 77502. (713)472-5563. Labels include Rivendell Records. President: Darrell A. Harris. Record company, music publisher, record producer and recording studio. Works with musicians on salary; artists and songwriters on contract. Pays negotiable royalty to artists on contract; standard royalties to songwriters on contract.
Music: Contemporary gospel. Recently released *Awaiting Your Reply* and *Rainbow's End*, by Resurrection Band (contemporary gospel LP); and *Washes Whiter Than*, by Petra (contemporary gospel LP). Other artists include Tom Autry, Jim Gill, Fletch Wiley, Randy Adams, Pam Mark Hall, Craig Smith, Chalice, and Jim and Jerome Cox, Steve and Annie Chapman, Scepter, Gaintkiller, David Stearman, Ark Angel, Jonathan David Brown and The Hope; and Daybreak, Damascus and Robin Surface.

STARCREST PRODUCTIONS, INC., 2516 S. Washington St., Grand Forks ND 58201. (701)772-6831. Labels include Meadowlark and Minn-Dak Records. President: George J. Hastings. Record company, management firm and booking agency. Releases 2-6 singles and 1-2 albums/year. Works with artists and songwriters on contract. Payment negotiable to artists on contract; statutory rate to publishers for each record sold.
How to Contact: Query or submit demo tape and lead sheet. Prefers 7½ ips reel-to-reel with 1-6 songs on demo. SASE. Reports in 1 month.
Music: C&W and top 40/pop. Recently released "A Good Yellow Rose," by Gene Wylos (country single); and "Holding Back Teardrops" and "Gypsy I Am," by Mary Joyce (country singles).

STARGEM RECORDS, INC., 20 Music Square West, Suite 200, Nashville TN 37203. (615)244-1025. A&R Director: Wayne Hodge. Record company, record producer and music publisher (Newwriters Music/BMI and Timestar Music/ASCAP). Member RIAA, CMA and NSAI. Releases 20-30 singles and 6-12 albums/year. Works with artists and songwriters on con-

tract; musicians on salary for in-house studio work. Pays 5-15% royalty to artists on contract; statutory rate to publishers for each record sold.
How to Contact: Write first about your interest, then submit demo tape and lyric sheet. Prefers 7½ ips reel-to-reel or cassette with 1-4 songs on demo. "Use new tape." SASE. Reports in 1 week.
Music: C&W (modern and MOR). Recently released "Rev. Sam Whiskey," by Steve Jones (C&W single); "Country Fever," by Frankie Rich (C&W single); and "Carolyn," by Larry Hawkins (MOR/C&W single). Other artists include Lee Cummins and Wade Baynes.

STARK RECORDS & TAPE CO., 628 South St., Mount Airy NC 27030. (919)786-2865. Labels include Stark, Hello, Pilot and Sugarbear. Owner: Paul E. Johnson. Record company and music publisher (Tompaul Music Company/BMI). Releases 10-20 singles and 12-15 albums/year. Works with artists and songwriters on contract. Pays 10% royalty to artists on contract; statutory rate to publishers for each record sold.
How to Contact: Submit demo tape and lead sheet. Prefers 7½ ips reel-to-reel with 3-5 songs on demo. SASE. Reports in 1 month.
Music: Bluegrass; church/religious; C&W; easy listening; folk; gospel; MOR; rock (country); and top 40/pop. Recently released *I Surrender Dear*, by Chet Atkins (instrumental LP); *Hard Ain't It Hard, Ruben's Train*, and *Riding the Waves*, by the Blue Ridge Mountain Boys (bluegrass LP). Other artists include Bruce Evans, Jim Hodges, Eddie Johnson, Paul E. Johnson and Alan Westmoreland, and Bobby L. Atkins.

STARR RECORDS, Box 1037, Des Plaines IL 60018. (312)824-6531. President: Mary L. Starr. Record company. Member CMA. Releases 3-6 singles and 1 album/year. Statutory rate to publishers for each record sold.
How to Contact: Submit demo tape and lead or lyric sheet. Prefers 7½ ips reel-to-reel or cassette with 1-3 songs on demo. SASE.
Music Recently released "My Hard Workin' Woman," and "Graveyard of Broken Hearts," by Able Chenault (C&W single); and "I Want You to Love Me Tonight," and "I'm Steppin' Out of Your Life," by Ray Jones (C&W single). Other artists include Dave Carlson and David Jones.
Tips: "Songwriters send commercial material only. Artists must have unique voice or group sound."

STARTOWN RECORDS, 1130 Airbase Rd., Columbus MS 39701. (601)434-8510. Labels include Soultrack and Dove. President: Allen White. Record company, record producer and music publisher (Dewaun Music/SESAC). Releases 4 singles and 3 albums/year. Works with artists on contract; musicians on salary for in-house studio work. Pays maximum royalty to artists on contract; statutory rate to publishers for each record sold.
How to Contact: Submit demo tape and lyric sheet. Prefers cassette with 4-8 songs on demo. SASE. Reports in 1 month.
Music: Blues, church/religious, C&W, gospel, R&B and soul. Recently released "Boogie Land," by Ike strong (disco single); "Western Union Man," by Singing Mellearies (gospel single); and "Police and Preachers," by Mack Banks (country single). Other artists include Howard Everett, Joyce Young and Chick Willis.

STASH RECORDS, INC., Box 390, Brooklyn NY 11215. (212)965-9407. Labels include Jive Records. President: Bernard Brightman. Record company and music publisher. Works with musicians on salary; artists and songwriters on contract. Payment negotiable.
How to Contact: Submit demo tape. Prefers cassette with 4 songs minimum on demo. Does not return unsolicited material. Reports in 1 month.
Music: Blues; jazz; and MOR. Recently released *Dialogue*, by Slam Stewart and Bucky Pizzarelli (jazz LP); and *Songs for New Lovers*, by Dardenelle (jazz/MOR LP).

STEADY RECORDS, 846 7th Ave., New York NY 10019. (212)772-9391. President: Arthur Trefferson. Record company, record producer and music publisher (Artreff, The Publishing Co.). Releases 30 singles and 5 albums/year. Works with artists on contract. Pays statutory rate to publisher for each record sold.
How to Contact: Submit demo tape and lyric sheet. Prefers cassette with "your best songs" on demo. SASE. Reports in 1 month.
Music: Reggae. Artists include major reggae recording stars.

STINSON RECORDS, Box 3415, Granada Hills CA 91344. (213)368-1316. President: Jack M. Kall. Record company (Starcraft/ASCAP). Releases 4 albums/year. Works with artists and songwriters on contract; statutory rate to publishers for each record sold. Pays negotiable royalty to artists on contract; statutory rate to publishers for each record sold.

How to Contact: Submit demo tape. Prefers reel-to-reel or cassette with 1-3 songs on demo. Does not return unsolicited material. Reports in 1 month.
Music: Bluegrass; folk; and jazz.

STONE PLAIN RECORDING COMPANY, LTD., Box 861, Edmonton, Alberta, Canada T5J 2L8. (403)477-6844. Label includes Mudpie Records (Children's Label). Managing Director: Holger Petersen. Record company, record producer and music publisher (Kitchen Table Music/ PROCAN and Stony Plain Music/CAPAC). Member CIRPA and CARAS. Releases 4 singles and 10 albums/year. Works with artists on contract. Pays 6-14% royalty to artists on contact; statutory rate to publishers for each record sold.
How to Contact: Submit demo tape and lyric sheet. Prefers cassette with 1-5 songs on demo. SAE and International Reply Coupons. Reports in 3 weeks.
Music: Bluegrass, blues, children's, C&W, folk, jazz, R&B, rock and top 40/pop. Recently released *Testimony*, by Ferron (folk LP); *Starting to Show*, by Crowcuss (rock LP); and *Stronger Silence*, by The Reds (rock LP).

STONE POST RECORDS/MUSIC, Box 954, Emporia KS 66801. A&R Director: J.J. Bisterfeldt. Record company and music publisher (BMI). Releases 2-4 singles and 1 album/year. Works with artists and songwriters on contract; musicians on salary for in-house studio work. Pays 25% royalty to artists on contract; statutory rate to publishers for each record sold.
How to Contact: Submit demo tape and lyric sheet. Prefers cassette with 1-2 songs on demo. SASE. Reports in 3 weeks.
Music: C&W; Progressive (country); rock (progressive/hard); and top 40/pop. Recently released "Who Am I to Blame," and "TJ's Last Ride," by Fyre (country rock singles).

STRAIGHT-FACE RECORDS, Box 324, Newark DE 19711. (302)368-1211. Record company, record producer and music publisher (Straight-Face Music/ASCAP and White Clay Music/BMI). Estab. 1979. Released 3 singles and 1 album last year. Pays statutory rate to publishers for each record sold.
How to Contact: Submit demo tape and lyric sheet. "We usually record the bands that White Clay Productions manages." Prefers cassette with 2-4 songs on demo. SASE. Reports in 3 weeks.
Music: Dance-oriented, jazz (traditional), progressive, rock and new wave. Recently released *The Sin City Band*, by The Sin City Band (contemporary county LP); "Son of Sam"/Electric Jungle," by Voltags (new wave single); "The Dummy Sons"/"Willie the Weeper," by The Kim Milliner Band (jazz traditional single); and "Rollin' Outta California" and "Tired of Talkin' Blues," by Roscoe. Other artists include Chet Bolins, Reflectors, Boni Dahl, David Power & Voltags, Favorites, The Drills, The Watson Brothers, the I.U.D.'s and the Snaps.

STRIVERS RECORDS, 303 Endicott Bldg., St. Paul MN 55101. (612)222-0922. President: Patrick W. Knight. Record company, record producer and music publisher. Releases 1 single and 1 album/year. Works with artists and songwriters on contract; musicians on salary for in-house studio work. Pays 10-20% royalty to artists on contract; statutory rate to publishers for each record sold.
How to Contact: Write first about your interest, then submit demo tape and lyric sheet. Prefers cassette with 3-5 songs on demo. SASE. Reports in 2 weeks.
Music: Blues, gospel, jazz, progressive, R&B, soul, new wave and top 40/pop. Recently released "Love Episode," by Strivers Show Band (ballad single). Other artists include Cliff Wheeler, Alexander Oneil and Bruel Henry.

STYLETONE/HOOKS RECORDS, 254 E. 29th St., Los Angeles CA 90011. (213)746-6499. Labels include Ebb-Tide, Jazz and Ground Hog Blues Records. President: Jerry Hooks. Record company, record producer and music publisher. Releases 6 singles and 4 albums/year. Works with musicians on salary; artists and songwriters on contract. Pays 3-60% royalty to artists on contract; standard royalty to songwriters on contract.
How to Contact: Submit demo tape and lyric sheet. Prefers 8-track cassette with 3-6 songs on demo. "Print information carefully." SASE. Reports in 1-2 weeks.
Music: Blues; church/religious; C&W; dance; gospel; jazz; R&B; soul; and top 40/pop. Recently released *The Master Keys In Concert* and "I Won't Have to Cry," by The Master Keys (gospel); "Somebody Voodoo Hoodoo Men," by Model 'T' Slim (blues); "13 Highway," by Little Boyd (blues); *The Jazz Meditators In Concert*, by the Jazz Meditators (jazz LP); *Give Me A Helping Hand*, by the Long Beach Southern Airs; *Stand By Me Jesus*, by the JC Brown Singers; *Who Pick Me Up*, by the Royal Dursey ensemble; and "Love Me Jesus," by the Gospel Crusaders. Other artists include Patricia White.

SUN INTERNATIONAL CORP., 3106 Belmont Blvd., Nashville TN 37212. (615)385-1960. Labels include Plantation Records and SSS International Records. Professional Manager: Sidney Singleton. Record company, record producer and music publisher (Shelby Singleton Music, Prize Music). Member RIAA and NARAS. Releases 30 singles and 25 albums/year. Works with artists and songwriters on contract. Pays 8-15% royalty to artists on contract; statutory rate to publishers for each record sold.
How to Contact: Submit demo tape and lyric sheet. Send cassette along with self-addressed envelope. Prefers cassette with 1-3 songs on demo. SASE. Reports in 1 month.
Music: C&W, easy listening, MOR, easy rock and top 40/pop. Recently releases "Rockabilly Rebel," by Orion (country LP/single); "No Aces," by Patti Page (country LP/single); and "Love on the Sly," by Rodney Lay (country-rock LP/single). Other artists include Dave Dudley, Roy Drusky, Rita Remington, Leroy Van Dyke, Webb Pierce, Chuck Bell, Jim Owen and Carl Belew.
Tips: "Present professional demo along with lyrics and explanation of career-goals. Artists should have a working band."

SUNDOWN RECORDS, Rt. 1, Box 258, Carriere MS 39426. (601)798-7099. President: Vern Pullens. Vice President: Bruce Dixon. Record company and music publisher. Releases 10 singles/year. Works with musicians on salary; artists and songwriters on contract. Pays 5% royalty to artists on contract. Charges for some services: session costs.
How to Contact: Submit demo tape and lead sheet. Prefers 7½ ips reel-to-reel with 4-12 songs on demo. SASE. Reports in 2-4 weeks.
Music: C&W; gospel; rock (country). Recently released "Goodbye, Mary," by Johnny Forster/Sundown Records (C&W).

SUN-RAY RECORDS, 1662 Wyatt Pkwy., Lexington KY 40505. (606)254-7474. Labels include Sun-Ray and Sky-Vue records. President: James T. Price. Record company and music publisher (Jimmy Price Music Publisher/BMI). Releases 9 singles/year. Works with musicians on salary; songwriters on contract; statutory rate to publishers for each record sold. Payment negotiable.
How to Contact: Submit demo tape or submit demo tape and lead sheet. Prefers 7½ ips reel-to-reel with 2-6 songs on demo. SASE. Reports in 3 weeks.
Music: Bluegrass (sacred or C&W); church/religious; C&W; and gospel. Recently released "Truck Driver's Rock," by Virgil Vickers (single); "All Them Wifes," by Harold Montgomery (single); "Flat Top Box," by Tommy Jackson (single). Other artists include James Mailicote, Chareles Hall and Kenny Wade.
Tips: "We need songs with a good story along with rhyme and meter."

SUNSET RECORDS, INC., 1577 Redwood Dr., Harvey LA 70058. (504)367-8501. Labels include Sunburst Records. President: George Leger. Record company, record producer, and music publisher (Country Legs Music/ASCAP and Golden Sunburst Music/BMI). Member CMA. Releases 5 singles/year. Works with artists and songwriters on contract. Pays 5% royalty to artists on contract.
How to Contact: Submit demo tape and lyric and lead sheet. Prefers 7½ ips reel-to-reel or cassette with 3-5 songs on demo. SASE. Reports in 1 month.
Music: C&W, gospel, progressive country and R&B. Recently released "A Snowman for Christmas," by George Leger (country/Christmas single).

SUNSHINE COUNTRY RECORDS, Box 31351, Dallas TX 75231. (214)690-8875. Labels include SCR Records. Producer: "The General." A&R Director: Mike Anthony. Record company and music publisher. Works with artists and songwriters on contract; "we also work with songwriters on royalty contract for other productions." Pays 6% royalty to artists on contract; 50% royalty to songwriters on contract.
How to Contact: Submit demo tape and lyric sheet. Prefers 7½ ips reel-to-reel with 1-4 songs on demo.SASE. Reports in 1 month.
Music: C&W and gospel. Recently released "Tough Act to Follow" and "Until the Next Time," by Billy Parker (C&W singles); and "Ain't Never Been In Love," by Shirley Townley. Other artists include Dick Hammonds, Janet Sue, Jano and Maggie.

SUNSHINE SOUND ENTERPRISES, INC., 7764 N.W. 71st St., Miami FL 33166. Contact: Preliminary Screening Committee. Manager: Sherry Smith. Record company and music publisher. Releases 10-50 singles and 5-25 albums/year. Works with artists and songwriters on contract. Pays 3% minimum royalty to artists on contract; standard royalties to songwriters on contract.
How to Contact: Submit demo tape and lead sheet. Prefers 7½ ips reel-to-reel or cassette with 1-3 songs on demo. SASE. Reports in 6-8 weeks. "No reports issued unless material is accepted or

unless we wish additional material for review."
Music: Dance; progressive; rock; soul; and top 40/pop. Recently released "Dance Across the Floor," "Spark" and "Is It In" by Jimmy "Bo" Horne (R&B/pop/disco singles).

SURVIVOR RECORDS, 5934 Buffalo Ave., #105, Van Nuys CA 91401. (213)997-8819. Contact: Jason Schwartz. Record company, record producer and music publisher (Ten of Diamonds Music/BMI and Five of Spades Music). Member RIAA. Releases 8-10 singles and 1-3 albums/year. Works with artists and songwriters on contract; musicians on salary for in-house studio work. Pays 5% minimum to artists on contract; statutory rate to publishers for each record sold.
How to Contact: Write first about your interest. Prefers cassette with 1-3 songs on demo. "Use good quality tape only—I will not play *cheap* cassettes." Reports in 3 weeks.
Music: Sophisticated C&W, easy listening, MOR, light rock and top 40/pop. Recently released "Lady from Beverly Hills," by Jason (country rock single); "Words Spoken Softly by You," Greta Warren (country single); and "Climbing Out," by Apostle (rock single). Other artists includes Silver Spoon.

SUSAN RECORDS, Box 4740, Nashville TN 37216. (615)859-0355. Labels include Denco Records. A&R Director: Russ Edwards. Record company and music publisher. Releases 2-20 singles and 1-5 albums/year. Works with artists and songwriters on contract. Pays 6¢/record to artists on contract. Buys some material outright; payment varies.
How to Contact: Submit demo tape and lead sheet. Prefers 7½ ips reel-to-reel with 1-6 songs on demo. SASE. Reports in 2 weeks.
Music: Blues; C&W; dance; easy listening; folk; gospel; jazz; MOR; rock; soul; and top 40/pop.

SWEETSONG RECORDING STUDIO, Box 2041, Parkersburg WV 26101. (304)485-0525. Labels include Mansion and Sweetsong Records. Owner: Roger Hoover. Record company and recording studio. Releases 10 singles and 10 albums/year. Works with musicians on salary; artists and songwriters on contract. Pays royalty to artists and songwriters on contract; statutory rate to publishers for each record sold. Charges for some services: freelance demo work.
How to Contact: Submit demo tape and lead sheet "preferably in person but, if not, send a demo and lead sheet that need not be returned." Prefers 7½ ips reel-to-reel with 1-12 songs on demo. Does not return unsolicited material. Reports in 2 weeks.
Music: Church/religious (contemporary and conventional); C&W (modern); easy listening ("Barbra Streisand style"); gospel (contemporary); rock; soul; and top 40/pop. "Clean lyrics only. Sweetsong Records is looking for about 35 good gospel artists to handle, record, produce and promote. We need mainly contemporary gospel but some Southern or quartet gospel. (We especially need several good female soloists, and groups.)" Recently released "Footsteps," by Steve Peters (crossover country single); *Taste the Kindness*, by Mona Fresphour (contemporary gospel LP); "Holy Roller," by Mike McGuire (contemporary gospel single); and *Going Up Yonder*, by Pam Gordon (contemporary gospel LP). Other artists include Debbie Davis (Miss West Virginia), Light and Carriers.

SWORD RECORDS, Box 8374, Station A, Greenville SC 29604. (803)271-1104. President: Rick Sandidge. Record company, record producer and music publisher (Adonika). Releases 2 singles and 3 albums/year. Works with artists and songwriters on contract. Pays 50¢ to artists for each record sold; statutory rate to publishers for each record sold.
How to Contact: Write or call first about your interest, then submit demo tape and lyric sheet. Prefers 7½ ips reel-to-reel or cassette with 4 songs on demo. SASE. Reports in 1 month.
Music: Bluegrass, blues, C&W, gospel, jazz, progressive, R&B, rock, soul, top 40/pop and church/religious. Recently released *Evening Pastoral*, by Rob Cassels; *Morning Dave*, by Bill Barnes; *Something Money*, by Barry McGee; and *Can't Buy*, by Barry McGee (Christian rock LPs). Other artists include Don DeGrote Delagation and J.D. Wilson.

TAKE HOME TUNES, Box 1314, Englewood Cliffs, NJ 07632. Labels include Broadway Baby Records. Owners: Doris Chu Yeko, Bruce Yeko. Branch office: Box 496, Georgetown CT 06829. (203)544-8288. Record company and music publisher (The Chu Yeko Musical Foundation/ASCAP). Releases 8-10 albums/year. Works with artists and songwriters on contract. Royalty payment varies for artists on contract; pays 5-10% royalty to songwriters on contract.
How to Contact: Submit demo tape. Prefers cassette. SASE. Reports in 1 month.
Music: Children's and Broadway-type show tunes. Some pop or rock. Recently released *King of Hearts*, by Millicent Martin and Don Scardino; *Bring Back Birdie*, by Donald O'Connor and Chita Rivera; and *Housewives Cantata*, by the Original cast (musical LPs).

Songwriter's Market Close-up

John Cougar is not a great one for rules. For one thing, he doesn't have the right address for a mainstream singer/songwriter. His location in Bloomington, Indiana is not even a poor relation of Hit Single City, USA.

"I'm not into the rock 'n roll lifestyle. I just stay in Bloomington, where my family and old friends are. Ian Anderson (Jethro Tull) said, 'I'm gonna go back to where I can be what I wanna be, not where people want me to be.' I think it's important that you have your roots."

So from his Indiana home, Cougar writes the words and music, foregoing some of the rules. "The less you know about songwriting, the better a songwriter you're going to be because you're not bound by rules: mathematics, or meters, or rhymes or prose. And if it's new to you and you're excited about it, then I think you create better."

Creating for Cougar means writing the words and music for hit singles like "I Need a Lover" (included on Pat Benatar's platinum album, *In the Heat of the Night*). He also wrote and released as singles "This Time" and "Ain't Even Done With the Night." But the song he's most proud of is "Taxi Dancer" (from the *John Cougar* album). "I just think it's a credible song—that's the whole thing: trying to get a moment of reality on a piece of plastic is . . . the ultimate challenge."

Cougar sometimes finds himself competing against his last hit single. That hit single would never have charted without the record company's promotion. "In my way of thinking, there are hundreds of hit songs written a year. They're all hits until they come out. . . . But if the record company doesn't do its job, they're just grooves in black plastic, noise in the air."

But first things first, namely the creative process. "I think if you want to be a

John Cougar

songwriter . . . you just have got to do it. You always have to be thinking about songs. Twenty-four hours a day I'm thinking songs—whether I'm riding in the car, or watching television. I'll be watching TV and, if a good line gets blurted, I'll write it down."

Lyrics are the thing with Cougar. He always listens and observes. "I can't imagine what kind of songs I'd write if I didn't think about it all the time. It's a 24-hour-a-day job."

P.J. Schemenaur

TAKOMA RECORDS, 9255 Sunset Blvd., Los Angeles CA 90069. (213)550-0171. General Manager: Jon Monday. Record company and music publisher. Member RIAA and NARM. Works with artists on contract.
How to Contact: Submit demo tape and lyric sheet. Prefers cassette with 3-4 songs on demo. SASE. Reports in 1 month.
Music: Blues; classical; folk; jazz; progressive; R&B; and rock. Recently released *Border Wave*, by the Fir Douglas Quintet (rock LP); *Gospel Night*, by Maria Muldaur (gospel LP); and *Crusin' For*

A Bruisin', by Mike Bloomfield (blues LP). Other artists include John Fahey, Chris Dawon and Fabulous Thunderbirds.

TAO RECORDS, Box 504, Bonita CA 92002. (714)421-0865. President: Virginia B. Anderson. Record company, music publisher (Madrid Music/ASCAP and Sweet 'N Low Music/BMI) and record producer. Works with artists and songwriters on contract. Pays 4-7½% royalty to artists on contract; standard royalty to songwriters on contract; statutory rate to publishers for each record sold.
How to Contact: Submit demo tape and lead sheet. Prefers 7½ ips reel-to-reel or cassette with 1-3 songs on demo. SASE. Reports in 1 month.
Music: C&W; easy listening; MOR; and top 40/pop. Recently released "Run, Baby, Run," by Candy (country/pop single). Other artists include Ron White.

TEENA JOY RECORDS, Box 302, Wilmington NC 28402. President: Bobby Stanley. Record company and music publisher. Works with artists and songwriters on contract. Pays standard royalty.
How to Contact: Write first about your interest. Submit demo tape and lyric sheet. Prefers cassette with 2-6 songs on demo. SASE. Reports in 1 month. "We welcome new talent."
Music: C&W and gospel. Recently released "A Special Father's Day", and "You Don't Really Want to Be Free" by Bobby Stanley (country ballad recitation singles).

TELEMARK DANCE RECORDS, 6845 Elm St., Suite 614, McLean VA 22101. Owner: Richard S. Mason. Record company. Releases 5-10 singles and 3 albums/year. Works with artists on contract. Pays 10-15% royalty to artists on contract.
How to Contact: Submit demo tape. Prefers 7½ ips reel-to-reel, cassette (1 song/side) or 8-track cartridge. SASE. Reports in 2 weeks.
Music: Dance; easy listening; and MOR. "We are interested in any good tunes that can be arranged in ballroom dance tempos, especially tunes written in ¾ time, suitable for medium tempos—30-36 measures/minute." Recently released *Come Closer to Me* and *The Nearness of You*, by Charles Barlow Orchestra (dance-instrumental LPs); and "Natasha," by Hugo Strasse Orchestra (dance-instrumental single).

TELESON-AMERICA, 333 Beacon St., Boston MA 02116. (617)353-1664. Labels include Grand Orgue, Motette-Ursina and Solist. Record company. Releases 12-20 albums/year. Works with artists on contract.
How to Contact: Write first about your interest. Prefers 7½ ips or 15 ips reel as demo. SASE. Reports in 4 months.
Music: Church/religious and classical (pipe organ). Artists include Pierre Labric, Marie-Andree Morisset-Balier, Heinz Bernhard Orlinski, Jean Langlais, Almut Rossler, Michel Morisset, Gunther Kaunzinger, Marie-Louise Jacquet-Langlais, Gaston Litaize, Hermann Harrassowitz, Johannes Ricken and Rosalinde Haas.

TELL INTERNATIONAL RECORD CO., Rt. 5, Box 368-A, Yakima WA 98903. (509)966-6334. A&R Director: Hiram White. Record company. Works with artists on contract. Pays standard royalty to artists on contract.
How to Contact: Submit demo tape and lead sheet. Prefers cassette with 1-4 songs on demo. SASE. Reports in 1 month.
Music: Bluegrass; blues; C&W; disco; folk; jazz; MOR; and rock. Recently released "Billie Joe" and "Georgia Wine," by Barbara Jean Taylor (C&W singles); and "I'm Too Shy," by Penny Stadler (C&W single).

TEROCK RECORDS, Box 4740, Nashville TN 37216. (615)859-0355. Labels include Curtiss, Susan and Denco Records. President: Wade Curtiss. Manager: S.D. Neal. Record company, record producer and music publisher. Releases 5-20 singles and 2-5 albums/year. Works with musicians on salary; artists and songwriters on contract. Pays 5-8% royalty to artists on contract; standard royalty to songwriters on contract.
How to Contact: Submit demo tape and lyric sheet. Prefers 7½ ips reel-to-reel with 2-6 songs on demo. SASE. Reports in 3 weeks.
Music: Bluegrass; blues; C&W; dance; easy listening; folk; gospel; jazz; MOR; progressive; rock; soul; and top 40/pop. Recently released "That's Why I Love You," by Dixie Dee (C&W); "Born to Bum Around," by Curt Flemons (C&W); and "Big Heavy," by the Rhythm Rockers (rock).

THANKS RECORDS, Box 400843, Dallas TX 75240. (214)690-8165. President: Michael Stanglin. Record company and music publisher.

How to Contact: Submit demo tape. Prefers 7½ ips reel-to-reel or cassette with 1-3 songs on demo. SASE. Reports in 3 weeks.
Music: C&W; dance; easy listening; and top 40/pop. Recently released "I Hate Disco Music," by Rick Ramirez; and "Hokey Pokey," and "Happy Birthday" (for skating rinks).

3 G'S INDUSTRIES, 5500 Troost, Kansas City MO 64110. (816)361-8455. Labels include N-M-I, Cory and Chris C's Records. President: Eugene Gold. Record company and music publisher. Releases 2-3 albums/year. Works with artists and songwriters on contract. Pays statutory rate to artists on contract; standard royalty to songwriters on contract; statutory rate to publishers for each record sold.
How to Contact: Arrange personal interview or submit demo tape and lead sheet. Prefers 7½ ips reel-to-reel with 6 songs minimum on tape. SASE. Reports in 1 month.
Music: R&B; dance; gospel; jazz; MOR; soul; top 40/pop. Recently released "Diamond Feather," by Bad New Band (R&B single); "Give in to the Power of Love," by The Committee (R&B single) and *Great Joy*, by the Sunshine District Chorus (gospel LP).

TK RECORDS, 65 E. 55th St., New York NY 10022. (212)752-0160. Labels include Clouds, Dash, Alston, Marlin, Inphasion, Muscle Shoals Sound, Glades and Sunshine Sound Records. Manager: Norman Rubin. Record company and music publisher. Releases 50-75 singles and 25-35 albums/year. Works with musicians on salary; artists and songwriters on contract. Pays standard royalties to songwriters on contract.
How to Contact: Query or submit demo tape and lyric sheet. Prefers cassette with 1-3 songs on demo. SASE. Reports in 2 weeks.
Music: C&W; dance; R&B; rock; soul; and top 40/pop. Recently released *Get Off*, by Foxy (R&B/disco LP); *Bobby Caldwell*, by Bobby Caldwell (R&B/pop LP); and *Voyage*, by Voyage (disco LP).

TOOL ROOM RECORDS, Box 118, Pewaukee WI 53072. (414)272-3131. Contact: Gary Lukitsch. Record company, music publisher and record producer. Works with artists on contract.
How to Contact: Call first about your interest. Prefers cassette with 1-12 songs on demo. SASE. Reports in 1 month.
Music: All types. Recently released *Woodbine Roots*, by Woodbine (contemporary country/folk LP); *Still Looking for the Cure* (rock/folk/jazz) and *Cardboard Box* (folk/country/rock), by Bill Camplin (LP).

TRADE WIND RECORDS, 5601 Odana Rd., Madison WI 53719. General Manager: Chad Dell. Record company. Works with artists and songwriters on contract. Pays negotiable royalty to artists on contract; statutory rate to publishers for each record sold.
How to Contact: Submit demo tape and lyric sheet. Prefers cassette with 3-6 songs on demo. SASE. Reports in 3 weeks.
Music: Bluegrass, C&W, rock, top 40/pop and country rock. Artists include Piper Road Spring Band (bluegrass/"hillbilly" jazz); Stone Oak (bluegrass/newgrass/western swing); and Broken Bow (country rock).

TRAVIS-LEHMAN PRODUCTIONS, 8537 Sunset Blvd., #2, Los Angeles CA 90069. (213)657-8852. Labels include Reuben Records. Contact: Travis Lehman. Record company, music publisher and management company. Works with musicians and songwriters on contract. Pays standard royalty to songwriters on contract.
How to Contact: Submit demo tape. Prefers cassette. SASE. Reports in 3 weeks.
Music: C&W and rock-n-roll.

ART TREFF PUBLISHING CO., 846 7th Ave., New York NY 10019. Labels include Steady, Phonosonic, Premier and Casset Majors Records. President: Art Trefferson. Record company and music publisher. Works with musicians on salary; artists and songwriters on contract. Pays standard royalty to songwriters on contract.
How to Contact: Submit demo tape and lead sheet. Prefers cassette. SASE. Reports in 1 month.
Music: Children's; classical; dance; folk; jazz; progressive; rock; soul; top 40/pop; and reggae. Recently released *Reggae's Greatest Hits Vols. I & II* (reggae LP).

TREND RECORDS, Box 201, Smyrna GA 30081. (404)432-2454. Labels include Trendsetter, Atlanta and Stepping Stone Records. President: Tom Hodges. Record company, music publisher, record producer and management firm. Releases 6-10 singles and 2-8 albums/year. Works with artists on contract. Pays 5-7% royalty to artists on contract: standard royalties to songwriters on contract.

How to Contact: Submit demo tape and lead sheet. Prefers cassette with 3-6 songs on demo. SASE. Reports in 3 weeks.
Music: Bluegrass; C&W; gospel; MOR; rock; and soul. Recently released *Feet*, by Jim Single (C&W single and LP), and "Sugar Daddy," by Frank Brannon (C&W single). Other artists include Jo Anne Johnson.

TRIANGLE RECORDS, INC., 824 19th Ave. S., Nashville TN 37203. Product Coordinator: Lynn Phillips. Executive Vice President: Elwyn Raymer. Record company and music publisher (Triune Music/ASCAP, Timespaun Music/BMI, Nova Press/SESAC). Releases 3-6 singles/year and 2-5 albums/year. Works with artists and songwriters on contract. Payment negotiable; statutory rate to publishers for each record sold.
How to Contact: Submit demo tape and lead sheet. Prefers 7½ ips reel-to-reel or cassette with 1-3 songs on demo. SASE. Reports in 2 months.
Music: Children's; choral; church/religious; classical; and gospel. Recently released *You're Welcome Here*, *The Way I Feel*, and *It Was His Love,* by Cynthia Clawson (sacred MOR LPs). Other artists include Bob Bailey, Ragan Courtney and Tina English.

TRUCKER MAN RECORDS, Centerline Rd., Cruz Bay, St. John VI 00830. (809)776-6814. Labels include One Number 18 Records. President: Llewellyn Adrian Sewer. Record company, music publisher, record producer, management firm and booking agency (Trucker Man Music/BMI). Releases 5-20 singles and 2-10 albums/year. Works with musicians on salary; artists and-songwriters on contract. Pays 5-10% royalty to artists on contract: standard royalties to songwriters on contract.
How to Contact: Submit demo tape and lead sheet, or submit lead sheet. Prefers cassette with 2-4 songs on demo. SASE. Reports in 3 weeks.
Music: Church/religious; dance; R&B; soul; and top 40/pop. Recently released *Ras Abijah Vs the Beast*, by Ras Abijah (reggae LP), and *The Imaginations*, by The Imaginations (calypso/reggae/Latin LP). Other artists include Star Shield, Ras Abijah, Imaginations and Eddie and the Movements.

TRUE RECORDS, 1300 Division, Suite 100, Nashville TN 37203. (615)256-7543. President: Cal Everhart. Record company. Works with musicians and songwriters on contract.
How to Contact: Write or call first about your interest. Prefers 7½ ips reel-to-reel with 3-4 songs on demo. SASE. Reports in 2 weeks.
Music: Bluegrass; C&W; MOR, progressive country and religious.

TRUSTY RECORDS, Rt. 1, Box 100, Nebo KY 42441. (502)249-3194. President: Elsie Childers. Record company and music publisher (Trusty Publications/BMI). Works with artists and song-writers on contract. Pays 2% royalty to artists on contract.
How to Contact: Submit demo tape and lead sheet. Prefers 7½ ips reel-to-reel or cassette with 2-4 songs on demo. SASE. Reports in 1 month.
Music: Blues; church/religious; C&W; dance; easy listening; folk; gospel; MOR; soul; and top 40/pop. Recently released "Look Whatcha Gone and Done," by Tracy White (rock single); "Spring In Kentucky" and "There's a Boat Leaving," by Jamie Bowles (MOR singles). Other artists include The Melvin Mud Mule Band.
Tips: "We are particularly interested now in masters for release on our label."

TUBE PRODUCTIONS, 66 Wellesley St. E., Toronto, Ontario, Canada M4Y 1G2. (416)961-4115. Manager: Robert Connolly. Record company, record producer and music publisher (Tube Productions). Releases 2 albums/year. Works with artists on contract. Pays 7% royalty to artists on contract.
How to Contact: Submit demo tape and lyric sheet. Prefers cassette with 3-12 songs on demo. Does not return unsolicited material. Reports in 1 month.
Music: Rock (hard). Recently released *In the Tube*, by Frank Soda (heavy rock LP); *Les Pucks*, by James Creasy (heavy rock LP); and *Frank Soda & The Imps*, by Frank Soda (heavy rock LP).

TVI RECORD CORP., 211 W. 56th St., Suite 8M, New York NY 10019. (212)246-6400. Vice President A&R: Karol Quinn. Record company (Listi Music/BMI and Itsil Music/ASCAP). Works with artists and songwriters on contract.
How to Contact: Submit demo tape and lyric sheet. Prefers cassette with 3-6 songs on demo. SASE. Reports in 3 weeks.
Music: Dance-oriented, R&B and top 40/pop. Recently released "Come & Get It On", by Soccer (disco LP/single); "Dancing Game", by Soccer (disco LP/single); and "You're Too Late", by Fantasy (R&B LP/single).

20TH CENTURY FOX RECORD CORPORATION, 8544 Sunset Blvd., Los Angeles CA 90069. (213)657-8210. A&R Manager: Paula Jeffries. A&R Producer: Michael Stewart. Works with musicians and songwriters on contract.
How to Contact: Submit demo tape and lyric sheet. Prefers cassette with maximum 3 songs on demo. Reports in 6-8 weeks.
Music: R&B; rock; soul and top 40/pop. Recently released *Sweet Sensations*, by Stephanie Mills (R&B/pop LP and single); *Fool In Love With You*, by James Photoglo (top 40/pop LP and single); *Any Minute Now*, by Chris Montan (top 40/pop LP and single); *Heavenly Bodies*, by the Chi-lites (R&B LP and single); and *AirRaid*, by Airraid (rock LP). Other artists include Leon Haywood, Dusty Springfield, Carl Carlton, The Staples Singers, The Dells and Shirley Brown.

UNIVERSAL-ATHENA RECORDS, Box 3615, Peoria IL 61614. (309)673-5755. A&R Director: Jerry Hanlon. Record company and music publisher (Jerjoy Music/BMI). Estab. 1980. Works with artists and songwriters on contract; musicians on salary for in-house studio work. Pays statutory rate to publishers for each record sold.
How to Contact: Submit demo tape and lyric sheet. Prefers cassette with 4-8 songs on demo. SASE. Reports in 2 weeks.
Music: C&W. Recently released *Memories*, by Jerry Hanlon (country LP). Other artists include Robby Hull.

UNLIMITED GOLD RECORDS, 12403 Ventura Court, Studio City CA 91604. (213)877-0535. Vice President: Paul Politi. Record company, music publisher and record producer. Works with musicians on salary; artists and songwriters on contract. Pays standard royalty.
How to Contact: Submit demo cassette, lead sheet and lyric sheet. SASE. Reports immediately if interested.
Music: C&W, dance, easy listening, jazz, MOR, progressive, R&B, rock/top 40, soul, and top 40/pop. Recently released "Let Her Dance," by Phil Seymour, "Masterpiece," by Leda Grace; "Any Fool Can See," by Wayne Newton, and "Louie, Louie," by Barry White.

VELVET PRODUCTIONS, 517 W. 57th St., Los Angeles CA 90037. (213)753-7893. Labels include Velvet, Kenya, Normar, and Stoop Down Records. Manager: Aaron Johnson. Record company, booking agency and promoter (BMI). Releases 2-4 singles and 1-4 albums/year. Works with artists and songwriters on contract. Pays 5% royalty to artists on contract.
How to Contact: Submit demo tape, arrange personal interview, submit demo tape and lead sheet, or submit lead sheet. Prefers cassette with 3-5 songs on demo. SASE. Reports in 2 months.
Music: Blues; gospel; rock; soul; and top 40/pop. Recently released "I Wanna Be Loved" and "How I wish," by Arlene Bell (disco singles); and "Love Stealing Ain't Worth the Feeling," by Chuck Willis (blues single).

VIDEO RECORD ALBUMS OF AMERICA, 8471 Universal Plaza, Hollywood CA 91608. (213)462-5860. Labels include VRA Records and VRA Radioplay Music. Vice President: Ken Harper. A&R Director: Lynn Mann. Record company and music publisher (Agil Publishing). Works with artists and songwriters on contract and producers with existing masters. Pays 5% royalty to artists on contract; statutory rate to publishers for each record sold.
How to Contact: Submit demo tape and lead sheet. Prefers cassette with 2-4 songs on demo. SASE. Reports in 1 month.
Music: Blues; church/religious; C&W; dance; easy listening; and top 40/pop. Recently released "I'm on Fire," by Priscilla Cory (rock/disco single); *Snowflake, Easy Lovin*, and *Country*, by Troy Cory (MOR LPs). Other artists include T.C. Stubblefield and T. Sheels.

VILLAGE RECORDS, INC., 6325 Guilford Ave., #4, Indianapolis IN 46220. (317)255-3116. Vice President/General Manager: Terry Barnes. Record company and music publisher (Canal Publishing). Member AFM. Releases 5-10 singles and 4-5 albums/year. Works with artists and songwriters on contract. Pays statutory rate to publishers for each record sold.
How to Contact: Submit demo tape and lyric sheet. Prefers cassette with 1-4 songs on demo. SASE. Reports in 1 month.
Music: Country, easy listening, MOR, rock and top 40/pop. Recently releases *Rock N Romance*, by Faith Band (top 40/pop LP); "Dancin Shoes," by Faith Band (ballad single); *Sweet Music*, by Roadmaster (rock LP); and "Wolly Bully," by Adam Smasher (rock single).

VOKES MUSIC PUBLISHING & RECORD CO., Box 12, New Kensington PA 15068. (412)335-2775. Labels include Vokes and Country Boy Records. President: Howard Vokes. Record company, booking agency and music publisher. Releases 8 singles and 5 albums/year. Works

with artists and songwriters on contract. Pays 2½-4½¢/song royalty to artists and songwriters on contract.
How to Contact: Submit demo tape and lead sheet. Prefers reel-to-reel, cassette or 8-track tapes. SASE. Reports in 2 weeks.
Music: Bluegrass; C&W; and gospel. Recently released "Old Hound Dog" and "I Love You Wherever You Are," by Tonnetta Watson, "Hey Engineer", and "Please Help Me I'm Falling," by Rita Lorraine; "Where Am I" and "Don't Ask Me," by Little Jo-Vokes; and "Liberated Woman" b/w "Soap," by Mel Anderson.

W.A.M. MUSIC CORP., LTD., 901 Kenilworth Rd., Montreal, Quebec, Canada H3R 2R5. (514)341-6721. Labels include WAM and Disques Pleiade Records. President: Leon Aronson. Record company, music publisher and record producer. Works with artists and songwriters on contract. Pays 5% minimum royalty to artists on contract; standard royalties to songwriters on contract.
How to Contact: Query or submit demo tape and lead sheet. Prefers 7½ ips reel-to-reel tape with 1-4 songs on demo. SAE and International Reply Coupons. Reports in 3 weeks.
Music: Dance; MOR; rock; and top 40/pop. Recently released "Savin' It Up," by Marty Butler (MOR single); and *Entre Nous*, by Diane Tell (pop LP). Other artists include Basic Black and Pearl, Carlyle Miller and 1945.

WALKING TALL RECORDS AND PRODUCTIONS, 8 Olympic Village, 1A, Chicago Heights IL 60411. Labels include Fast Flight Records and Future Shock Records. Chief/Record Relations: Terry Snodgrass. Record company, record producer and music publisher (Lloyd & Lloyd Music/ BMI, Los Angeles International Music/ASCAP). Estab. 1979. Member NMPA, BMA, AGAC. Works with artists and songwriters on contract; musicians on salary for in-house studio work. Pays 50% royalty to artists on contract; statutory rate to publishers for each record sold.
How to Contact: Submit demo tape and lyric sheet. Prefers 7½ ips reel-to-reel, cassette or demo-record with 3-6 songs on demo. "Send your best work—no rough demos." Does not return unsolicited material. Reports in 3 weeks.
Music: Recently released "Give Me Some Credit," by LaQue (R&B/top 40 single and LP); "Fair Game," by Raymond Alexander (top 40 single and LP); and "This Ole Heart," by Back Lash (R&B/top 40 single and LP). Other artists include Unique Pleasure.

WALKING TALL RECORDS AND PRODUCTIONS, 1621 W. Bancroft Blvd., Toledo OH 43606. Labels include Fast Flight Records and Future Shock Records. Executive Chairman: Charles H. Ruffin. Record company (Los Angeles International Music/ASCAP, Lloyd & Lloyd Music/BMI). Estab. 1979. Releases 10 singles and 5 albums/year. Works with artists and song-writers on contract; musicians on salary for in-house studio work. Pays 50% royalty to artists on contract; statutory rate to publishers for each record sold.
How to Contact: Submit demo tape and lyric sheet. Prefers 7½ ips reel-to-reel or cassette with 3 songs on demo. SASE. Reports in 3 weeks.
Music: "All recordings for our contract artists are released on one of our recording labels: Fast Flight Records, Future Shock Records or Walking Tall Records; unless otherwise designated to another record company per music producer or publisher." Other artists include Unique Pleasure, Back Lash, La Que, Anna McCance and Raymond Alexander.

WALTNER ENTERPRISES, 14702 Canterbury, Tustin CA 92680. (714)731-2981. Labels include Calico and Daisy. Owner/President: Steve Waltner. Record company and music publisher (Early Bird Music/BMI). Releases 3-4 singles/year. Works with musicians and songwriters on contract. Pays 5-10% royalty to artists on contract; standard royalty to songwriters on contract; pays statutory rate to publishers for each record sold.
How to Contact: Submit demo tape and lead sheet. Prefers 7½ ips reel-to-reel or cassette with 2-4 songs on demo. SASE. Reports in 3 weeks.
Music: C&W; easy listening; MOR; and top 40/pop. Recently released "America, Lady of the Harbor," by Tim Morgon (country/pop single); "Boogie Man," by Jason Chase (top 40 single); "I Wish," by Steve Shelby (country/pop single); and "Talkin' Pyramid Blues," by The Nile River Boys (country single).

WARNER BROTHERS RECORDS, INC., 3300 Warner Blvd., Burbank CA 91510. (213)846-9090. General Manager: Roberta Petersen. Record company. Works with artists and songwriters on contract.
How to Contact: Submit demo tape. Prefers 7½ ips reel-to-reel or cassette. SASE. Reports in 8 weeks.
Music: Bluegrass; blues; children's; choral; church/religious; C&W; disco; easy listening; folk;

gospel; jazz; MOR; progressive; R&B; rock; soul; and top 40/pop.

WARNER BROTHERS RECORDS, INC., 3 E. 54 St., New York NY 10022. (212)832-0600.
Director of A&R: Karin Berg. Record company and music publisher (Warner Brothers Music).
How to Contact: Submit demo tape and lyric sheet. Prefers reel-to-reel or cassette with 2-3 songs on demo. SASE. Reports in 3 weeks.
Music: All types.

WARNER BROTHERS RECORDS, INC., 1706 Grand, Nashville TN 37203. (615)327-4503.
Record company. "We do not take unsolicited material."

WATERHOUSE RECORDS, 100 N. 7th St., Suite 415, Minneapolis MN 55403. (612)332-6575.
Director of Operations: Gary Marx. Record company, record producer and music publisher (Waterhouse Music, Inc.). Releases 3 singles and 5 albums/year. Works with artists on contract. Pays negotiable royalty.
How to Contact: Write first about your interest, then submit demo tape and lyric sheet. Prefers cassette with 3-10 songs on demo. SASE. Reports in 1 month.
Music: Blues, dance-oriented, folk rock, R&B, rock, soul and top 40/pop. Recently released *Up from the Alley*, by Lamont Cranston Band (rock LP); *My Babe*, by Roy Buchanan (rock LP); and *Diana Hubbard Lifetimes*, by Diana Hubbard (classical pop LP). Other artists include Henny Youngman, Aztec Two-Step and Michael Bloomfield.
Tips: "We are money conscience in nature: we still give great royalty rates and promote like gangbusters, but our advances must be small and our artists must help earn their money through hard work on stage."

WAYTONE RECORD CO., 1967 Goldsmith Lane, Apt. B-6, Louisville KY 40218. (502)454-3593.
Labels include Silk Records and Cambridge Records. Contact: Wayne Henderson. Record company, music publisher, record producer and artist manager (Betty Lou Music/BMI, Valmon Music/ASCAP). Members AFM and HEW. Releases 2-3 singles/year. Works with artists and songwriters on contract. Pays 2½¢/side to artists on contract; standard royalty to songwriters on contract; statutory rate to publishers for each record sold.
Music: Country blues; C&W; and MOR. Recently released "One More Tomorrow" and "Honky Tonk Lover," by Dave O'Conner (MOR country single); and "Driftin'," by Teddy Gibbs (MOR country single).

WESLEY INTERNATIONAL RECORDS AND TAPES, 7725 Jane St., Suite 206, Concord, Ontario, Canada L4K 1B1. (416)669-5420. Label includes Long Star. A&R Director: Bill Sharpe. Record company, record producer and music publisher (Gratitude Music). Releases 8 singles and 5 albums/year. Works with artists and songwriters on contract. Pays 7-15% royalty to artists on contract; pays statutory rate to publishers for each record sold.
How to Contact: Submit demo tape and lyric sheet or arrange personal interview. Prefers cassette with 4-6 songs on demo. SAE and International Reply Coupons. Reports in 3 weeks.
Music: Children's, easy listening, R&B, rock, soul and Italian. Recently released "Rockin Girl," by Wess (rock single); "Loving You," by Gratitude (disco single); and "Let's Fall in Love Tonight," by Sandy McNeal (easy listening single). Other artists include Eddie Staxx, Clear Image, Peter Tudisco and Hell 'n' Highwater.

WESJAC RECORD ENTERPRISES, Box 743, 129 W. Main St., Lake City SC 29560. (803)394-3712. A&R Director: W.R. Bragdton Jr. Record company and music publisher. Works with musicians on salary; artists on contract. Pays 5% royalty to artists and songwriters on contract.
How to Contact: Submit demo tape and lead sheet. Prefers 7½ or 15 ips reel-to-reel with 2 songs minimum on tape. SASE. Reports in 1 month.
Music: Church/religious and gospel. Recently recorded "I'm Glad I Wasn't Made by Man" and "Every Now and Then," by the Gospel Songbirds (gospel singles); and "I Can't Stop Loving God," by the Traveling Four (gospel single).

WESTWOOD RECORDS, 125 Taylor St., Jackson TN 38301. (901)427-7714. Owner: Charlie Roach. Record company and music publisher (Charlie Roach Music/BMI). Releases 2 singles and 2 albums/year. Works with artists on contract. Pays standard royalties; statutory rate to publishers for each record sold.
How to Contact: Query or submit demo tape. Prefers 7½ ips reel-to-reel or cassette with 4-10 songs on demo. "We only want to hear work that is copyrighted." SASE. Reports in 1 month.
Music: Bluegrass; blues; church/religious; C&W; gospel; R&B; rock; and soul. Recently released *Rock of the 50's* (rock LP), *Live at Kennedy Veterans' Hospital* (country & rock LP), and *Earley*

Rock (rock LP), by different artists. Other artists include Larry Brinkley, Bobby Hardin, and Joe Richman.

Tips: "As of now I am leasing master tapes. I am looking for material and masters that were made between 1950 and 1970: rock blues, R&B, country and western with a rockabilly touch to it. But we will listen to all that has a chance of making a good seller, no matter what type of music or when it was recorded. We are also looking for a good and different sound and a strong song, as well as some new Hawaiian music suitable for recording."

WHEELSVILLE RECORDS, INC., 17544 Sorrento, Detroit MI 48235. (313)342-6884. Labels include Wheelsville and Purcal Records. President: Will Hatcher. Contact: Sharon Hatcher and Theresa Hatcher. Record company and music publisher.
How to Contact: Submit demo tape and lead sheet. Prefers 7½ ips reel-to-reel with 2-4 songs on demo. SASE. Reports in 2 weeks.
Music: Dance; gospel; soul; and top 40/pop.

WHITE ROCK RECORDS, INC., 401 Wintermantle Ave., Scranton PA 18505. (717)343-6718. President: Phil Ladd. Record company, music publisher and record producer. Releases 4-16 singles and 2-4 albums/year.
How to Contact: Query or submit demo tape and lead sheet. Prefers cassette with 2 songs minimum on demo. SASE. Reports in 3 weeks.
Music: Children's; C&W; easy listening; R&B; rock; and top 40/pop. Recently released "Drummer," by Frantic Freddy (rock single); and "Ain't Misbehavin'," by Evra Bailey (MOR single).

WILDEBEEST RECORDS, Box 311 Rt. 19, Wexford PA 15090. (412)935-1330. Contact: C.W. Abbott. Record company, music publisher, record producer and record distributor. Estab. 1979. Works with artists and songwriters on contract. Pays negotiable royalty to artists on contract; standard royalty to songwriters.
How to Contact: Submit demo tape and lyric sheet. Prefers cassette. SASE. Reports in 1 month.
Music: Bluegrass; blues; folk (traditional American and Irish). Recently released *Ghost of His Former Self*, by Devilish Merry (traditional American and Irish LP).

WILDWOOD ENTERTAINMENT, #3 Westminster, London Square, Clifton Park NY 12065. (518)371-5659. Labels include Wildwood Records. Co-Owner: Vincent Meyer II. Vice President: Erich C. Borden. Record company and music publisher (Late Music Company/BMI). Releases 6 albums/year. Works with musicians on salary; artists and songwriters on contract. Pays standard royalties.
How to Contact: Query, submit demo tape, submit demo tape and lead sheet, submit acetate disc, submit acetate disc and lead sheet or submit lead sheet. Prefers 7½ ips reel-to-reel or cassette with 2 songs minimum on demo. SASE. Reports in 3 weeks.
Music: Adult contemporary; FM rock; children's; dance; folk; jazz; progressive; rock; and top 40/pop.

MARTY WILSON PRODUCTIONS, INC., 185 West End Ave., New York NY 10023. (212)580-0255. Labels include D&M Sound and Cyma Records. Assistant to the President: Janet J. Eddy. Record company and music publisher. Works with musicians on salary for in-house work; songwriters on contract. Payment varies for artists on contract; pays standard royalty to songwriters on contract.
How to Contact: Submit demo tape and lead sheet. Prefers 7½ or 15 ips reel-to-reel or cassette with 1-3 songs on demo. SASE. Reports in 1 month.
Music: Easy listening; jazz; MOR; and top 40/pop. Recently released "Love for Sale," by the Vast Majority (single); "Boop Boop a Hustle," by Camp Galore (single); and "Help Is on the Way," by Tanden Hayes (single).

WILWIN RECORDS, Box 1669, Carlsbad CA 92008. (714)729-8406. Owner: Denny Tymer. Record company and music publisher (Tymer Music/BMI). Works with artists and songwriters on contract. Pays 5-9% royalty to artists on contract; standard royalty to songwriters on contract; pays statuatory rate to publishers for each record sold.
How to Contact: Arrange personal interview or submit demo tape and lead or lyric sheet. Prefers 7½ ips reel-to-reel or cassette with 1-3 songs on demo. "Demos should be simple and each song should not be over 3 minutes, 20 seconds long. Put leader between each song on tape." SASE. Reports in 3 weeks.
Music: C&W and top 40/pop. Recently released *It's About Tymer*, by Denny Tymer (C&W LP).
Tips: "We work with musicians according to the American Federation of Musicians (AFM) Phonographic Labor Agreement, and with vocal background singers in agreement with the Ameri-

can Federation of Television and Radio Artists (AFTRA). Listen to current country chart songs, especially the ballad type and write songs with simple, but strong lyrics that fit the trends. We are looking for original commercial country songs not only for Wilwin Records, but also for other artists and non-affiliated record labels."

WOODRICH RECORDS, Box 38, Lexington AL 35648. (205)247-3983. President: Woody Richardson. Record company and music publisher (Woodrich Publishing/BMI, Melstep Music/BMI, Mernee Music/ASCAP and Tennessee Valley Music/SESAC). Member Muscle Shoals Music Association. Releases 8-15 singles and 15-25 albums/year. Works with musicians on salary; artists and songwriters on contract. Pays 5% royalty to artists on contract; pays statutory rate to publishers for each record sold.
How to Contact: Submit demo tape. Prefers 7½ ips reel-to-reel or cassette with 2-4 songs on demo. SASE. Reports in 1 month.
Music: Bluegrass; blues; choral; church/religious; C&W; easy listening; folk; gospel; jazz; MOR; progressive; rock; soul; and top 40/pop. Recently released "Flat Land Dirt," by Whit Malone (country single); *Bluegrass Steel Guitar*, by James Kimbrough (bluegrass LP); and *R.G. Sings Gospel*, by Ronnie Green (gospel LP). Other artists include Rev. James Robinson.

WORD, INC., 4800 W. Waco Dr., Waco TX 76703. (817)772-7650. Labels include Word, Myrrh, Dayspring and Canaan Records. Assistant Director of A&R/Music Publishing: Don Cason. Vice President of A&R: Buddy Huey. Record company and music publisher. Releases 50-60 albums/year. Works with artists and songwriters on contract.
How to Contact: Submit demo tape and lyric or lead sheet. Prefers 7½ ips reel-to-reel or cassette with 2-3 songs on demo. SASE. Reports in 10-12 weeks.
Music: Children's; choral (gospel); church/religious; disco (gospel); easy listening (gospel); folk; gospel (all kinds); jazz; MOR; progressive (gospel); rock (country or hard); soul (gospel); and top 40/pop (gospel). Recently released *Priority*, recorded by the Imperials (contemporary gospel LP); and *Cloudburst*, recorded by the Mighty Clouds of Joy (soul/gospel LP).

W-W RECORDS, A Division of Weston Enterprises, Inc., 1 N. Waukegan Rd., Lake Bluff Il 60044. (312)295-1748. Labels include Jo-Jo Records. Artist & Promotions Manager: John P. Doerr. Record company, record producer and music publisher (Morrow River Music). Member CMA. Releases 20 singles and 10 albums/year. Works with artists and songwriters on contract. Pays 6-12% royalty to artists on contract; statutory rate to publishers for each record sold.
How to Contact: Submit demo tape and lyric sheet. Prefers cassette with 2-4 songs on demo. SASE. Reports in 1 week.
Music: Bluegrass and C&W. "We are looking for real country material; not interested in the New York disco trend." Recently released *There's a Star-Spangled Banner Waiving Some Where*, by Doc Willson (single and LP). Other artists include Hank Johnson, Kim Phillips, Grass Plus, Luther Watson, Uncle Harry Larry Fine, Smoky Jackson and the White Oak Mountain Boys and Morrow River Gang.

X.K.R. III RECORDS, Box 10273, Chicago IL 60610. (312)944-1125. President: Xavier King Roy III. Record company, record producer and music publisher (King and Moore Music). Estab. 1979. Releases 1 single/year. Works with artists and songwriters on contract. Pays 3-9% royalty to artists on contract; statutory rate to publishers for each record sold.
How to Contact: Submit demo tape and lyric sheet. Prefers 7½ ips reel-to-reel or cassette with 2-4 songs on demo. SASE. Reports in 3 weeks.
Music: Blues, easy listening, gospel, jazz, R&B, rock, soul, top 40/pop and adult contemporary. Recently released *It's About Time*, by Fantasie (A/C LP). Other artists include Bill Webster and Rank.

XL RECORDS, Box 14671, Memphis TN 38114. (901)774-1720. Labels include Jenny Records. A&R Director: Errol Thomas. Record company, record producer and music publisher (Beckie Music). Member NARAS. Releases 3 singles/year. Works with artists and songwriters on contract. Pays 3%-6% royalty to artists on contract; statutory rate to publisher for each record sold.
How to Contact: Submit demo tape and lyric sheet. Prefers 7½ ips reel-to-reel or cassette with 4-10 songs on demo. SASE. Reports in 2 weeks.
Music: R&B and soul. Recently released "Everybody Cried," and "I'd Love to Love You," by Rufus Thomas (R&B singles); and "Goodbye Lady," by Rayner Street Band (R&B single). Other artists include Louis Williams and the Ovations.

YATAHEY RECORDS, Box 31819, Dallas TX 75231. (214)690-8875. Owner: Pat McKool. A&R: Mike Anthony. Record company and music publisher. Works with artists and songwriters on contract. Pays 8% royalty to artists on contract.

How to Contact: Submit demo tape and lead sheet or submit demo tape and lyric sheet. Prefers 7½ ips reel-to-reel with 1-4 songs on demo. SASE. Reports in 1 month.

Music: C&W and gospel. Recently released "Always Chasing Rainbows," by Leisa Lynch (C&W single); "Lonely Lady," by George Brazzel (C&W single); "Don't Forget All the Love," by Bill Lowrey (C&W single); "Coffee Cups and Cowboy Boots," "I'd Like to Fall in Love with You" and "When You're Looking For Love," by the Brooks Brothers With Their Almost Famous Band; "Every Now and Then," by DeWayne Bowman (C&W single); "Memories of A Wasted Past," by Dick Hammonds (C&W single); and "Mail Order from Heaven," by Larry Scott (C&W single).

ZONE RECORD CO., 2674 Steele, Memphis TN 38127. (901)357-0064. Owner: Marshall E. Ellis. Record company, music publisher and record producer. Works with songwriters on contract. Pays 3¢/record royalty to artists on contract; statutory royalties to songwriters on contract.

How to Contact: Submit demo tape. Prefers 7½ ips reel-to-reel or cassette with 4 songs on demo. "Be sure the words are clear. Don't try to make a master—just a good clean tape." Reports in 2 weeks.

Music: Blues; church/religious; C&W; easy listening; progressive; and R&B. Recently released "Was It All That Bad? ," by Patti Faith (country-rock single); "Words Softly Spoken," by the Wrane Show (country single); and "Baby You Don't Love Me Anymore," by J. Pullman (country single).

Geographic Index

Date Line International
   Records
De-Lite Records
DJM Records
Domino Records
Elektra/Asylum/Nonesuch
   Records
EMI America/Liberty Rec-
   ords
Factory Beat Records, Inc.
Famous Door Records
Glad-Hamp Records Inc.
Gramavision Inc.

Island Records Inc.
Jody Records
Marina Records
Millenium Records
Mustevic Sound, Inc.
Polydor Records
Prelude Records
Ren-Maur Music Corp.
RFC Records
Right On Records
Roadshow Records
Rota Records
Roulette Records, Inc.

Salsoul Records
Sam Productions
Sandcastle Records
Sire Records
Stash Records, Inc.
Steady Records
TK Records
Art Treff Publishing Co.
TVI Record Corp.
Warner Brothers Records,
   Inc.
Marty Wilson Productions,
   Inc.

The Quiet Types

In preparing *Songwriter's Market 1982*, we contacted all major American and Canadian record companies at least once—and in some cases, two or three times. Most responded. Some, however, did not give us information for one of the following reasons:

● They are not actively seeking new artists or material from songwriters.

● They *will* listen to material, but believe that they receive sufficient material without listing in *Songwriter's Market*.

● They are a branch office that concentrates on marketing or other business endeavors, and leaves selection of artists and songs to branches in other cities.

● They work only with artists or songwriters recommended to them from other sources.

● They are staffed with inhouse songwriters.

● They don't have a staff large enough to handle the increased number of submissions a listing would create.

● They are concerned with copyright problems that might result if they record a song similar to one they've reviewed and rejected.

● They have once listed with another songwriter directory and were deluged with inappropriate submissions.

Though some of the following firms will review material, we suggest that you *not* send demo tapes. Write a brief query letter describing your material and asking about the company's current submission policies. Always use a self-addressed, stamped envelope or post card for such queries (see sample reply form in "The Business of Songwriting").

Birthright Records, 3101 S. Western Ave., Los Angeles CA 90018.

Casablanca Records & Film Works, Inc., 8255 Sunset Blvd., Los Angeles CA 90046.

CBS Records, Inc., 51 W. 52nd St., New York NY 10019.

CBS Records, Inc., 49 Music Square W., Nashville TN 37203.

Century Records, 6550 Sunset Blvd., Hollywood CA 90028.

Claridge Records, 6381 Hollywood Blvd., Suite 318, Los Angeles CA 90028.

Electra/Asylum/Nonesuch Records, 1216 17th Ave. S., Nashville TN 37212.

Hob Records, Inc., 1733 Broadway, New York NY 10019.

Island Records, Inc., 444 Madison Ave., New York NY 10022.

MCA Records, 100 Universal City Plaza, Universal City CA 91608.

MCA Records, 10 E. 53rd St., New York NY 10022.

Monitor Recordings, Inc., 156 Fifth Ave., New York NY 10010.

Monument Record Corp., 21 Music Square E., Nashville TN 37203.

Plateau Records, 200 W. 57th St., New York NY 10019.

Polydor Records, Inc., 6255 Sunset Blvd., Hollywood CA 90028.

Polydor, Inc., 21 Music Circle E., Nashville TN 37203.

Precision Records, 1500 Broadway, New York NY 10019.

RCA Records, 1133 Avenue of the Americas, New York NY 10036.

RCA Records, 806 17th Ave. S., Nashville TN 37203.

RSO Records, Inc., 1775 Broadway, New York NY 10019.

Scorpio Enterprises, Inc., 38 Music Square E., Nashville TN 37203.

Tomato Music Co., Ltd., 611 Broadway, New York NY 10012.

Vanguard Recording Society, Inc., 71 W. 23rd St., New York NY 10010.

Vee Jay International Music, 131 E. Magnolia Blvd., Burbank CA 91502.

Record Producers

The independent producer can best be described as a creative coordinator. He finds talented artists, and songs for those artists to record. He handles every aspect of the recording session and pays for all this with his own money, hoping to recoup his costs by selling the finished master to a record company.

Many record companies have, in fact, cut down or eliminated altogether their number of inhouse staff producers, and prefer to hire independent producers for specific artists. Likewise, there are top artists who only want a certain producer on their sessions.

Since independent producers are well-acquainted with the record company executives and artists with whom they deal, they can often get your material through doors that are not open to you. This is especially important if you are an artist-songwriter looking for a recording contract.

The fact that an independent producer works for himself means he can be open to a variety of material styles. And since he makes all the decisions in a project, you will usually be told right away if he does or doesn't like your songs and if he can use them in an upcoming session.

Many producers listed here are publishers and some also have management firms. This can work to your advantage in several ways. Those who are publishers will be looking for good songs, whether or not they need it for a particular artist—they can always shop it to another producer or record company. Those who are managers can easily recognize material one of their acts could use, and they will have a good deal of influence in suggesting your material to them.

Individual listings will tell you what a producer is looking for and which artists he is working with. *Billboard*, *Record World* and *Cashbox* list the producers' names on their weekly top song charts.

EUGENE ADAMS PRODUCTIONS, Box 47578, Los Angeles CA 90047. President/A&R: Eugene Adams. Record producer and management firm. Deals with artists. Produces 10-16 singles and 4-8 albums/year. Fee derived from sales royalty.
How to Contact: Query or submit demo tape and lead sheet. Prefers cassette with 4-6 songs on demo. SASE. Reports in 3 weeks.
Music: Blues; church/religious; dance; gospel; rock (hard or country); and soul. Recently produced "This Masquerade," by Mary Love (soul single, Message Records); and "All About Love," by Eugene Adams (soul single, Message Records).

ALJEAN RECORDS, 7 Colonial Ave., Myerstown PA 17067. (717)866-5067. Producer: Al Shade. Record producer and music publisher (Goosepimple Music). Deals with artists and songwriters.
How to Contact: Submit demo tape and lyric sheet. Prefers 7½ ips reel-to-reel or cassette with 2-4 songs on demo. SASE. Reports in 1 month.
Music: Children's, C&W and gospel. Recently produced "Three Mile Island," "The Ledgendary Blue-Eyed Six" and "Okies From Muskogee Never Die." Artists include Jean Romaine, Faron Shade and Al Shade.

ALLEN & MARTIN PRODUCTIONS, 9701 Taylorsville Rd., Louisville KY 40299. (502)267-9658. Chief Engineer/Producer: Bob Ernspiker. Record, music jingle and TV commercial producer. Deals with artists, songwriters and singers. Fee derived from outright fee from songwriter/artist.
How to Contact: Submit demo tape and lyric sheet. Prefers 7½ ips reel-to-reel or cassette with 3-5 songs on demo. Does not return unsolicited material. Reports in 2 weeks.
Music: Bluegrass; C&W (crossover); jazz; progressive; hard and country rock; and top 40/pop. Recently produced "Bondarz Superstarz," by Al Bondar (top 40, Starsongz Records); *Walker, Pietius & Kays*, by Walker, Pietius & Kays (jazz vocal, Bridges Records); "Remaining Faithful," by Monks of St. Meinrad (religious, Abbey Press Records). Other artists include Free Fall, Bill Owens and Quick Draw.

AMERICAN CREATIVE ENTERTAINMENT, LTD., 1616 Pacific Ave., Suite 817, Atlantic City NJ 08401. (609)348-1809. Vice Presidents: Danny Luciano and Tony Angelo. Record producer and music publisher (Donna Marie Music). Deals with artists and songwriters. Produces 2 singles and 1 album/year. Fee derived from sales royalty.
How to Contact: Submit demo tape and lyric sheet. Prefers 7½ ips reel-to-reel or cassette with 4-8 songs on demo. "No 8 track." SASE. Reports in 6 weeks.
Music: MOR, R&B, rock (all types), soul and top 40/pop. Recently produced "Ting-A-Ling Doubleplay," by Larry Bowa and Dave Cash of the Philadelphia Phillies (top 40 single, Molly Records).

APON RECORD COMPANY, INC., 44-16 Broadway, Box 3082, Steinway Station, Long Island City NY 11103. (212)721-5599. Manager: Don Zemann. Record producer and music publisher (Apon Publishing/ASCAP). Deals with artists and songwriters. Produces 20 albums/year. Fee derived from outright fee from record company.
How to Contact: Submit demo tape and lyric sheet. Prefers cassette with 2-6 songs on demo. SASE. Reports in 1 month.
Music: Classical, folk, Spanish and Slavic, polkas, and Hungarian gypsy. Recently produced *Czech Polka Festival* and *Polka Fever*, by Kunst (polka LPs, Apon Records); and *Holiday in Spain*, by Yavaloyas Orchestra (songs and dances LP, Apon Records).

THE MIKE APPEL ORGANIZATION, 75 E. 55th St., New York NY 10022. (212)759-1610. Director of Operations: Robert L. Martin. Record producer, music publisher and manager (The Mike Appel Organization). Deals with artists and songwriters. Produces 2-4 singles and 2-3 albums/year. Fee derived from sales royalty or outright fee from record company.
How to Contact: Submit demo tape and lyric sheet. Prefers cassette with 1-3 songs on demo. SASE. Reports in 2 weeks.
Music: C&W, MOR, progressive, rock (all forms) and top 40/pop. Recently produced *Back to the Midwest Night*, by Arlyn Gale (progressive rock LP, ABC Records); *Jeff Conaway*, by J. Conaway (pop/rock LP, Columbia Records); and Russell Javors, by R. Javors (rock LP, Columbia Records).

APPLE/CHIPETZ MANAGEMENT, 1808 Ludlow St., Philadelphia PA 19103. (215)567-0287. Contact: Steve Apple. Record producer and music publisher (Straight A's, Inc./ASCAP). Produces 2-4 singles and 2 albums/year. Deals with artists and songwriters. Fee derived from sales royalty.
How to Contact: Submit demo tape. Prefers cassette with 4 songs maximum on demo. SASE. Reports "as soon as possible."
Music: Rock (hard AOR) and top 40/pop. Recently produced *The A's*, by the A's (AOR LP, Arista Records).

APPROPRIATE PRODUCTIONS, 474 Atchison St., Pasadena CA 91104. (213)794-8758. Producer: Ben Brooks. Record producer and music publisher (Tantalizing Tunes/BMI and Atomic Tunes/ASCAP. Deals with artists and songwriters. Produces 2 singles/year. Fee derived from outright fee from artist/songwriter.
How to Contact: Call first about your interest or submit demo tape and lyric sheet. Prefers cassette with 1-3 songs on demo. SASE. Reports in 2 weeks.
Music: C&W, MOR, R&B, rock. Recently produced "Keep It All to Yourself" and "Starting to Show," by Oscar Scotti (new wave rock single, Appropriate Records); "Don't Worry 'bout the Night" and "Fools Don't Mind," by The Shake Shakes (rock single, Appropriate Records). Other songwriters include Dennis FitzGerald and Scott Kirby.
Tips: "Be professional and know the business and music well enough to be in the market place."

ARGONAUT MUSIC, Box 1800, Nashville TN 37202 and Box 7300, Tulsa OK 74105. (918)599-7777. President: Eric R. Hilding. Record producer and music publisher (Hilding America, Inc., Musicfile and Songfile). Interested in songwriters and songwriter artists. Royalty basis contracts.
How to Contact: Query or submit demo tape and lyric or lead sheet. Cassettes only with 1-3 songs on tape. SASE. Reports in 3 weeks to 6 months.
Music: Strong title/chorus singles material for top 40/pop (crossover); easy listening/MOR; gospel/Christian; and C&W (pop country); and soul. "We accept only *positive lyric* content songs."

ARTA PRODUCTIONS, Box 40271, Nashville TN 37204. (615)327-2417. President: Don M. Keirns. Record producer. Works with musicians and songwriters on contract.

How to Contact: Call first about your interest. Prefers 7½ ips reel-to-reel or cassette with 2-5 songs on demo. SASE. Reports in 1 month.
Music: Blues, C&W, easy listening, folk, MOR, progressive and top 40/pop.
Tips "We base selection on voice quality, writing and performance ability."

ASTRAL PRODUCTIONS, INC., (A division of the Earthraker Corp.), First National Bank Towers, Box 4527, Topeka KS 66604. (913)233-9716. Executive Vice President: Kent Raine. Record producer and talent promoters. Other corporate divisions include record companies, music publishers and a management and booking firm. Deals with artists and songwriters. Produces 8-12 singles and 4-6 albums/year. Fee derived from sales royalty.
How to Contact: Submit demo tape and lead sheet. Prefers cassette with 2-6 songs on demo. SASE. Reports in 2 weeks.
Music: Rock, country rock, C&W, dance, jazz, MOR, blues, soul, and top 40/pop.

TOM ATOM PRODUCTIONS, 1076 Queen St. W., Toronto, Ontario, Canada M6J 1H8. (416)535-3717. Producer: Tom Atom. Record producer, music publisher and record company. Deals with artists and songwriters. Fee derived from sales royalty.
How to Contact: Submit demo tape and lyric sheet. Prefers 7½ ips reel-to-reel or cassette with 1-10 songs on demo. SASE. Reports in 3 weeks.
Music: MOR, rock (heavy metal) and top 40/pop. Artists include The Sharks (wavey); Rapid Tears (heavy metal) and Winston (top 40/pop).

AZTEC PRODUCTIONS, 20531 Plummer St., Chatsworth CA 91311. (213)998-0443. General Manager: A. Sullivan. Record producer, music publisher and management firm. Deals with artists and songwriters. Produces 2-4 singles and 1-3 albums/year. Fee derived from sales royalty.
How to Contact: Submit demo tape and lead sheet. Prefers 7½ ips reel-to-reel or cassette with 6 songs maximum on demo. SASE. Reports in 2 weeks.
Music: Blues; dance; easy listening; MOR; rock; and top 40/pop. Recently produced "El Chicano" (top 40, Dorn Records); and "With You," by Abraxas (top 40, Dorn Records); and "Summer Nites," by Newstreet (rock, Dorn Records). Other artists include Julie Reina.

B.A.S. ENTERPRISES, 5925 Kirby, Suite 226, Houston TX 77005. (713)522-2713. Contact: Shelton Bissell. Record producer, arranger and conductor, booking agency and music publisher. Original company Bissell's Arranging Service. Deals with artists and songwriters. Fee derived from sales royalty.
How to Contact: Submit demo tape and lyric sheet. Prefers 7½ ips reel-to-reel or cassette with 1-4 songs on demo. "Do not send by any method requiring signature. I only review material from ASCAP or BMI writers." SASE. Reports in 3 weeks.
Music: C&W. Reviewing material for Isaac Payton Sweat (Paid Records), Mike Compton (RDS Records), and Kathy Gilley.
Tips: "Especially looking for hard country honkytonk, beer drinking songs."

B.C. ENTERPRISES OF MEMPHIS, INC., 726 E. McLemore Ave., Memphis TN 38106. (901)947-2553. Administrative Assistant: Nat Engleberg. Record producer and music publisher (Colca Music, Epitome Music and Insight Music/BMI). Deals with artists and songwriters. Produces 4 singles and 1 album/year. Fee derived from sales royalty.
How to Contact: Submit demo tape and lyric sheet. Prefers cassette with 1-3 songs on demo. SASE. Reports in 1 week.
Music: Blues, gospel, R&B and soul. Recently produced "Self-rising Flour," by Ironing Board Sam (blues single, Boss Ugly Bob Records); "Blues for My Lady," by Calvin Leavy (blues single, Boss Ugly Bob Records); and "LonLiville," by Larry Gibson group (R&B single, Boss Ugly Bob Records).

B & B PRODUCTIONS, 25 Music Square W., Nashville TN 37203. (615)242-1000. Contact: Bob McCracken. Record producer. Estab. 1980. Deals with artists, songwriters and record labels. Produces 4 single and 1 album/year. Fee derived from sales royalty or outright fee from record company.
How to Contact: Call or write first about your interest, or submit demo tape and lyric sheet or arrange personal interview. Prefers 7½ ips reel-to-reel or cassette with 1-4 songs on demo. SASE. Reports in 2 weeks.
Music: Country, MOR, rock, top 40/pop and country rock. Recently produced "You're Still the One," by Douglas (MOR single, Door Knob Records); "Have Another Drink," by Douglas (punk country single, Door Knob Records); and "It's Only a Matter of Time," by Douglas (modern country, Door Knob Records).

Tips: "New artists/writers' material must be professionally presented and as good (if not better) than his successful contemporaries. For a new artist to 'grab' the industry's ears, he or she must be unique and willing to give 100% to learning as much about each facet of the music business as possible."

B AND C PRODUCTIONS, (A Division of Remontant, Inc.), Box 400, Station R, Toronto, Ontario, Canada M4G 4C3. (416)421-3601. Vice President: Jeff Smith. Record producer and music publisher (Bee Sharp Publishing, See Flat Publishing). Estab. 1980. Deals with artists and songwriters. Produces 10 singles and 2 albums/year. Fee derived from sales royalty.
How to Contact: Write first about your interest. Prefers cassette with 2-6 songs on demo. SAE and International Reply Coupons. Reports in 3 weeks.
Music: Children's, country, easy listening, jazz, MOR, rock and top 40/pop. Recently produced "Sea Swept," by Jaylus (MOR single, MCA Records) and "Special Way," by Aura (MOR single, Change Records). Other artists include Raveons.

BAL RECORDS, Box 369, LaCanada CA 91011. (213)790-1242. President: Adriam Bal. Record producer and music publisher (Bal & Bal Music). Deals with artists and songwriters. Producers 1-4 singles/year. Fee derived from sales royalty or outright fee from artist/songwriter or record company.
How to Contact: Submit demo tape and lyric sheet. Prefers cassette with 3 songs on demo. SASE. Reports in 1 month.
Music: Blues, church/religious, C&W, easy listening, jazz, MOR, R&B, rock, soul and top 40/pop. Recently produced "Los Angeles," by Rich Martin (ballad, Bal Records); "Song of the Pasadena Rose Parade," by Jack Heindenrich (swing, Bal Records). Produces musicians in this area.

BARTISTIC MUSIC, P.O. Box 490, Wayne PA 19087. Music Director: Bart Arntz. Record producer, music publisher and management firm. Deals with songwriters and dancers. Produces 45 singles and 6 albums/year. Fee derived from sales royalty.
How to Contact: Submit demo tape. Prefers cassette with 1-4 songs on demo. SASE. Reports in 3 weeks.
Music: Dance, soul, and top 40/pop. Recently produced *Jazz Moves*, by Ron Daniels (instrumental LP, Educator Records); *Our Yiddish*, by Froni Cohen (Yiddish songs LP, Mameloshn Records); and "Tony Scott," by Tony Scott (R&B funk single, AMI Records).

BASIC RECORDS, 1309 Celesta Way, Sellersburg IN 47172. (812)246-2959. Contact: Buddy Powell. Record producer and music publisher (Hoosier Hills Publishing). Deals with artists and songwriters. Produces 15 singles and 7 albums/year. Fee derived from outright fee from artist/songwriter.
How to Contact: Submit demo tape and lyric sheet. Prefers 7½ ips reel-to-reel or cassette with 2-4 songs on demo. SASE. Reports in 2 weeks.
Music: Bluegrass, C&W and gospel.

BECKETT PRODUCTIONS-MUSCLE SHOALS SOUND STUDIOS, Box 939, Sheffield AL 35660. (205)381-2060. Assistant to Producer: Dick Cooper. Record producer, music publisher and recording studio. Muscle Shoals Sound Studios, estab. 1969; Beckett Productions, estab. 1979. Deals with artists and songwriters. Fee derived "according to individual situation."
How to Contact: Submit demo tape and lyric sheet. Prefers cassette with 1-3 songs on demo. Does not return unsolicited material. Reports "depending on work load."
Music: C&W; dance; MOR; progressive, R&B; rock; soul and top 40/pop. Recently produced "The Jealous Kind," by Delbert McClinton (blues-rock single, MSS-Capitol Records); "Break-through," by Lenny LeBlanc (pop/rock single, MSS-Capitol Records); and "Storm Windows," by John Prine (rock single, Elektra Records).
Tips: "Research artists and their style before submitting songs."

BEE HIVE JAZZ RECORDS, 1130 Colfax St., Evanston IL 60201. (312)328-5593. Producer: Susan Neumann. Record producer and music publisher. Deals with artists and songwriters. Fee derived from sales royalty.
How to Contact: Call or write first about your interest or submit demo tape and lyric sheet. Prefers cassette. SASE. Reports in 1 month.
Music: Jazz. Recently produced "Baritone Madness," by Nick Brignola, "Juicy Lucy," by Ed Salvador and "Ned Nistico," by Sal Nistico (jazz, Beehive Records).

THOM BELL PRODUCTIONS, 117 S. Main St., Seattle WA 98104. (206)682-5278. Contact: JoDee Omer. Record producer. Deals with artists. Fee derived from sales royalty or outright fee from record company.

How to Contact: "Representative contact either from record company or management. New artists with an established label deal or label deal pending only, or already established artists." Prefers 7½ ips reel-to-reel or cassette. Send resume and previous LPs or singles if released.
Music: Classical, C&W, disco, easy listening, folk, gospel, jazz, MOR, progressive, rock, soul, and top 40/pop. Recently produced material by the Spinners (Atlantic Records); the O'Jays (P.I.R. Records); and MFSB (P.I.R. Records).

ART BENSON PRODUCTIONS, 1560 N. La Brea, Hollywood CA 90028. A&R/Pop Producer: Art Benson. R&B Producer: Sonny Craver. Deals with artists and songwriters. Produces 75 singles and 48 albums/year. Fee derived from sales royalty.
How to Contact: Query or submit demo tape and lead sheet. Prefers 7½ or 15 ips reel-to-reel or cassette with 3-12 songs on demo. SASE. Reports in 1 month.
Music: Bluegrass, blues, church/religious, C&W, dance, easy listening, gospel, jazz, MOR, rock, soul, and top 40/pop. Recently produced *Energy Crisis*, by King Solomon (R&B LP, Celestial Records); *Universe Rock*, by Captain DJ (disco LP, Celestial Records); and *Country Dreaming*, by Tommy Cooper (C&W LP, Celestial Records).

BENT OAK MUSIC, Rt. 2, 246 Oakborough Dr., O'Fallon MO 63661. (314)625-3488. General Manager: Thomas J. McBride. Record producer and music publisher (Bent Oak Music). Estab. 1980. Deals with artists and songwriters. Fee derived from sales royalty or outright fee from record company.
How to Contact: Songwriters submit demo tape and lyric sheet; artists write or call first about your interest. Prefers cassette with 1-10 songs on demo. SASE. Reports in 1 month.
Music: Bluegrass, C&W, folk and rock. Artists include Glen Wagster, Kirk Parker, Music City Express and Patchwork Blue.

JACK BIELAN PRODUCTIONS, 6381 Hollywood Blvd., Suite 512, Hollywood CA 90028. Contact: Jack Bielan. Record producer and music publisher (Steamroller Music/ASCAP). Deals with artists and songwriters. Produces 4 singles and 2 albums/year. Fee derived from sales royalty or outright fee from record company.
How to Contact: Submit either demo tape or demo tape and lead sheet. Submit cassette only with 1-3 songs on demo. Lyric sheets are acceptable in place of lead sheets. Please don't send long letter of life history. A brief resume is acceptable. Put "Song Material Enclosed" on outside of envelope. Material without SASE will not be returned. Reports in 3-6 weeks.
Music: Country-pop, A/C and top 40/pop. Recently produced *Encore*, by Bobby Vinton (Tapestry Records); "Let Me Love You Goodbye," by Bobby Vinton (Tapestry Records); and "He," by Bobby Vinton. Other artist includes Jeneane Marie.
Tips: "Send samples of what you're best at. If you're a singer, show your most marketable aspects. If you're a writer, categorize your material relating to today's commercial market so that the producer has some idea of where you're at. Strong Sedaka/Kristofferson/Mac Davis-style lyrics with good repeating choruses are needed.

BIG DEAL RECORDS CO., Box 60-A, Cheneyville LA 71325. President: Launey Deal. Record producer, music publisher, booking agency and management firm. Deals with artists and songwriters. Fee derived from sales royalty or outright fee from songwriter/artist.
How to Contact: Query, arrange personal interview, submit demo tape or submit demo tape and lead sheet. Prefers 7½ ips reel-to-reel or cassette with 4-20 songs on demo. SASE. Reports in 1 week.
Music: Blues, C&W, disco, gospel, rock (hard or country), and soul. Recently produced "Somebody Have Mercy" (blues/soul single, Soul-Cat Records), and "Sometime Losers Win" (blues single, Soul-Cat Records), by Rocking Lonnie; and "No-Way," by the Reverend L. Allen (gospel single, Gospel Soul Train Records).

BIRD PRODUCTIONS/VU RECORDS, 1946 N. Hudson Ave., Chicago IL 60614. (312)787-6060. President: Robin McBride. Record producer and music publisher (Bird Seed Music). Estab. 1980. Deals with artists and songwriters. Produces 0-10 singles and 1-6 albums/year. Fee derived from sales royalty.
How to Contact: Submit demo tape and lyric sheet. Prefers cassette with 1-3 songs on demo. SASE. Reports in 1 month.
Music: dance-oriented (rock), jazz (fusion), progressive, rock (especially new wave), soul and top 40/pop. Recently produced *Live*, by Gamble Rogers (folk songs LP, Mountain Railroad Records); *Limited Edition*, by Bohemia (new wave LP, VU Records); and *Sir Douglas Quintet*, by Sir Douglas Quintet (rock TexMex LP, Takoma Records).

GLORIA BLACK PRODUCTIONS, 702 S. 15th St., Newark NJ 07013. Professional Manager: Gloria Black. Record producer. Deals with artists and songwriters. Fee derived from sales royalty.
How to Contact: Submit demo tape and lyric sheet. Prefers 7½ ips reel-to-reel or cassette with 2 songs minimum on demo tape. SASE. Reports in 2 weeks.
Music: Blues, church/religious, C&W, dance, folk, gospel, jazz, MOR, progressive, R&B, rock, soul, and top 40/pop. Recently published *Double Dealing Dude*, by Gloria Black (disco, Jody Records); *Do the Hammer*, by Eddie Hailey (disco, Jody Records); and *Hustle Bustle*, by Abracadabra (disco, Jody Records).

BLUE CHEK MUSIC, INC., Box 74, Saw Mill River Rd., Ardsley NY 10502. (914)592-3479. Contact: A&R Department. Record producer. Deals with artists. Produces 30 singles and 15 albums/year. Fee derived from sales royalty.
How to Contact: Submit demo tape and lyric sheet. Prefers 7½ ips reel-to-reel or cassette with 13 songs on demo. SASE. Reports in 1 week.
Music: Church/religious, C&W, easy listening, gospel and MOR.

BLUE ISLAND INDUSTRIES, 1446 N. Martel, Unit 3, Los Angeles CA 90046. (213)851-3161. Contact: Bob Gilbert. Record producer and music publisher (Blue Island, Rock Island and Fleming Enterprises). Estab. 1980. Deals with artists and songwriters. Produces 5 singles/year. Fee derived from sales royalty.
How to Contact: Submit demo tape and lyric sheet. Prefers cassette with 3-6 songs on demo. SASE. Reports in 3 weeks.
Music: C&W, MOR, rock and top 40/pop. "We are a new organization and our artist list is growing with new talent."
Tips: "We listen to *all* material presented. Many companies only listen to a few songs. We give everyone a fair chance to be heard. Anyone can write a hit song."

JACK P. BLUESTEIN, Box 630175, Miami FL 33163. (305)472-7757. President: Jack Bluestein. Record producer and music publisher (Twister Music, Lantana Music and Pine Island Music). Deals with artists and songwriters. Produces 1-6 singles and 1-2 albums/year. Fee derived from sales royalty.
How to Contact: Submit demo tape and lyric sheet. Prefers reel-to-reel or cassette with 2-6 songs on demo. SASE. Reports in 1 month.
Music: Blues, C&W, gospel, MOR, R&B, rock and top 40/pop.

BOUQUET-ORCHID ENTERPRISES, Box 4220, Shreveport LA 71104. (318)686-7362. President: Bill Bohannon. Record producer and music publisher (Orchid Publishing). Deals with artists and songwriters. Produces 5 singles/year. Fee derived from sales royalty.
How to Contact: Submit demo tape and lyric sheet. Prefers cassette with 3-5 songs on demo. "Include brief background information. Make lyrics clear and the demos as strong as possible." SASE. Reports in 1 month.
Music: C&W, MOR and top 40/pop. Recently produced "Gonna Be a Brighter Day," by Shan Wilson (C&W, Bouquet Records); "Cottonmouth," by Bill Bohannon (C&W, Bouquet Records); and "If You Want to Love Me," by S. Wilson (C&W, Bouquet Records). Artists include Bandoleers.

BOBBY BOYD PRODUCTIONS, 2609 NW 36th St., Oklahoma City OK 73112. (405)942-0462. Producer: Bobby Boyd. Record producer and music publisher (Watonga Publishing/ASCAP; Catalpa Publishing/BMI). Deals with artists and songwriters. Produces 10 singles/year.
How to Contact: Write first about your interest then submit demo tape and lyric sheet. Prefers 7½ ips reel-to-reel with 3-12 songs on demo. Does not return unsolicited material. Reports in 2 weeks.
Music: C&W, R&B, rock, soul and top 40/pop. Recently produced *Trucking Truth*, by Marvin Roy (country LP, Boyd Records). Artists include Dale Greear.

GEORGE BRIGMAN, 10101 Woodlake Dr., Apt. M, Baltimore MD 21030. Producer: George Brigman. Record producer. Deals with artists and songwriters. Fee derived from royalty or outright fee from record company or songwriter.
How to Contact: Submit demo tape and lyric sheet. Prefers 7½ ips reel-to-reel with 1-6 songs on demo. SASE. Reports in 3 week.
Music: Blues, C&W, dance, easy listening, folk, gospel, jazz, MOR, progressive, R&B, rock, soul, and top 40/pop. Recently published "Nashville" and "Lovin' You," by John Butterworth (country, Equinox Records); "Drifting" and "Blowing Smoke," by Split (jazz, Solid Records). Other artists include George Brigman, Russ Nixon, Bogey and Mitch Myers.

BROADWAY PRODUCTION, INC., 1307 Broadway St., Box 551, Sheffield AL 35660. (205)381-1833. President: David Johnson. Record producer. Deals with artists and songwriters. Fee derived by sales royalty.
How to Contact: Submit demo tape and lyric sheet. Prefers 7½ ips reel-to-reel or cassette with 1-3 songs on demo. SASE. Reports in 2 weeks.
Music: C&W, R&B, rock, soul, and top 40/pop. Artists include Percy Sledge and James Govan.

BROTHER LOVE PRODUCTIONS, Box 852, Beverly Hills CA 90213. (213)980-9271. Producer: Jeremy McClain. Secretary: S. Roshay. Record producer and music publisher (Pratt & McClain Music/ASCAP; Happy Days Music/BMI). Deals with artists and songwriters. Produces 5-8 singles and 1-2 albums/year. Fee derived by royalty or outright fee from record company.
How to Contact: Query with letter of introduction, arrange personal interview or submit demo tape and lead sheet. Prefers cassette with 4 songs on demo. SASE. Reports in 3 weeks.
Music: C&W, dance, easy listening, MOR, rock (commercial top 40), top 40/pop, and religious music. Recently produced "Happy Days," by Pratt and McClain (top 40, Warner Bros. Records); "What Ever Happened," by Tom Gillon (country, Brother Love Records); *Pratt & McClain*, by Pratt and McClain (top 40, ABC Records); and "Summertime in the City," by Pratt and McClain (rock). Other artists include Ocean (Warner Bros. Records, MCA Records, and Songbird Records).

RON BROWN MANAGEMENT, 319 Butler St., Pittsburgh PA 15223. (412)781-7740. Producer: Ron Brown. Record producer and music publisher (Enta Music/BMI). Produces 5-10 singles and 2 albums/year. Deals with artists and songwriters. Fee derived from sales royalty or outright fee from record company.
How to Contact: Submit demo tape or submit demo tape and lead sheet. "Submit only cassette tapes. Reel-to-reel and 8·track tapes will not be accepted." SASE. Reports in 2 weeks.
Music: Blues; dance, easy listening, MOR, progressive, rock, soul, and top 40/pop. Recently produced *Friends* and *Give Me Love*, by Shaker (top 40 LPs, Pittsburg Int. Records); and "Title Town USA," by Acappella Gold (accepella, Iron City Records). Other artists include Sha-Zam, the El-Monacs, Fun and Patchwork.

BENNIE BROWN PRODUCTIONS, 3011 Woodway Lane, Box 5702, Columbia SC 29206. (803)788-5734. Owner: Bennie Brown Jr. Deals with artists, songwriters and music publishers. Produces 12-15 singles and 4-6 albums/year. Fee derived from sales royalty.
How to Contact: Query, submit demo tape, or submit demo tape and lead sheet. Prefers cassette with 2-4 songs on demo. SASE. Reports in 3 weeks.
Music: C&W (pop country), dance, gospel, MOR, soul, and top 40/pop. Recently produced "Hold On," by Five Sing Stars (gospel, Nutone Records); "For Your Love," by Freestyle (disco, Nutone Records); and "I'll Keep On Lovin' You," by Twana Tolbert (top 40/R&B, Nutone Records).

STEVE BUCKINGHAM, Box 754, Roswell GA 30077. (404)231-4666. Producer: Steve Buckingham. Estab. 1978. Deals with artists and songwriters. Produces 2-6 singles and 2-5 albums/year. Fee derived from sales royalty and outright fee from record company.
How to Contact: Submit demo tape and lyric lead sheet. Prefers 7½ ips reel-to-reel or cassette with 1-3 songs on demo. SASE. Reporting time varies.
Music: Country (contemporary); disco; MOR; rock (any form); soul; and top 40/pop. "Any well structured commercial song." Recently produced "I Love the Nightlife" (top 40/disco/R&B) and "Body Heat" (pop) by Alicia Bridges (Polydor Records); and "Pretty Girls," by Melissa Manchester (pop, Arista Records). Other artists include Dionne Warwick and Karen Tobin (Arista Records).

BUTTERMILK RECORDS AND MOBILE STUDIOS, 1310 Tulane, Houston TX 77008. (713)864-0705. President: Charles Bickley. Record producer and music publisher (Sea Three Music/BMI). Deals with artists and songwriters. Produces 12 singles and 10 albums/year. Fee derived from sales royalty or outright fee from artist/songwriter or record company.
How to Contact: Submit demo tape and lyric sheet. Prefers 7½ ips reel-to-reel or cassette with 1-4 songs on demo. SASE. Reports in 3 weeks.
Music: Bluegrass, blues, church/religious, C&W, easy listening, folk, gospel, jazz, MOR, progressive, Spanish, R&B, rock, soul and top 40/pop. Recently produced "Cry Cry Laugh Laugh," by Krayolas (new wave single, Krayolas Records); "The Hard Way," by Richard Dobson (country single, Buttermilk Records; *Rich Girl*, by The Disease (rock LP, Buttermilk Records.

CHARLES CALELLO PRODUCTIONS, LTD., Box 2127, Beverly Hills CA 90213. (213)275-8248. President: Charles Calello. Music arranger and music publisher. Deals with artists

and songwriters. Produces 4-6 albums/year. Fee derived from royalties or outright fee from record company.
How to Contact: Submit demo tape and lead sheet. Prefers reel-to-reel or cassette with 1-5 songs on demo. SASE. Reports in 2 weeks.
Music: Pop songs. Recently produced "Forever," by Rex Smith (Columbia Records); "Connections," by Richie Havens (R&R single, Elektra Records); and *4 Seasons Live*, by 4 Seasons (pop LP, Warner Records). Arranged "Angel of the Morning," by Juice Newton (pop single, Capitol Records). Other artists include the American Standard Band (Island Records), Calello (Mid-Song International Records), Roger Voudoris and Boardwalk.

CASH WEST PRODUCTIONS, 488 Madison Ave., New York NY 10022. (212)752-3033. Vice President/General Manager: Bob Esposito. Record producer and music publisher. Deals with songwriters. Fee derived from sales royalty.
How to Contact: Submit demo tape and lyric sheet. Prefers cassette with 3 songs maximum on demo. SASE. Reports in 3 weeks.
Music: C&W; easy listening; rock; and top 40/pop.
Tips: "I am currently seeking to expand Blendingwell Music catalogues with strong ballads and uptempo songs. I'm looking for artist/writers to place with outside labels (CBS, Atlantic, Aristo, etc.)."

CASTALIA PRODUCTIONS, Box 11516, Milwaukee WI 53211. President: Jim Spencer. Record producer and music publisher (Castalia Music/BMI). Deals with artists and songwriters. Produces 2 singles and 6 albums/year.
How to Contact: Write first about your interest, submit demo tape and lyric sheet. Prefers cassette with 1-6 songs on demo. SASE. Reports in 1 month.
Music: All types. Recently produced *Gentle Friends*, by Eileen Carr (country/pop/MOR LP, A Major Label Records); *Anonymous*, by Anonymous (progressive rock LP, A Major Label Records); and *The Most Beautiful Song in the Forest*, by Jim Spencer (children's LP, Castalia Records).

CHICAGO KID PRODUCTIONS, 2228 Observatory, Los Angeles CA 90027. (213)666-0494. Contact: John Ryan. Record producer and music publisher (Cottage Grove Music). Deals with artists and songwriters. Produces 10 singles and 6 albums/year.
How to Contact: Submit demo tape and lyric sheet. Prefers cassette with 4 songs on demo. SASE. Reports in 3 weeks.
Music: Rock and top 40/pop. Other artists include Styx, Climax Blues Band, Pure Prairie League, Rare Earth, States, Doucette, Tantrum, Blackoak Arkansas and The Gap Band.

THE CHU YEKO MUSICAL FOUNDATION, Box 1314, Englewood Cliffs, NJ 07632. (201)224-5811. Messages: (201)567-5524. Producer: Doris Chu Yeko. Record producer and music publisher (The Chu Yeko Musical Foundation/ASCAP). Estab. 1979. Deals with artists and songwriters. Produces 4 albums/year. Fee derived from royalty of sales when song or artist is recorded; by outright fee from songwriter/artist; by outright fee from record company.
How to Contact: Submit demo tape and lyric sheet or "phone on Tuesday or Friday. Vacation: July and August." Prefers cassette with any number songs on demo. SASE.
Music: Children's, choral, church/religious, classical, C&W, dance-oriented, easy listening, jazz, MOR, musicals, R&B, rock and top 40/pop. Recently produced *Ka-Boom!*, by Original Cast (Broadway musical LP, The Chu Yeko Musical Foundation Records); and *Fly with Me*, by Original Cast (off-Broadway musical LP, The Chu Yeko Musical Foundation Records).
Tips: "We will co-produce records with songwriter/artist."

LOU CICCHETTI, 211 Birchwood Ave., Upper Nyack NY 10960. (914)358-0861. Contact: Lou Cicchetti. Record producer and music publisher (Cousins Music). Deals with artists and songwriters. Produces 1-2 singles/year. Fee derived from sales royalty.
How to Contact: Submit demo tape and lyric sheet. Prefers 7½ or 15 ips reel-to-reel or cassette with any number songs on demo. SASE. Reports in 3 weeks.
Music: C&W and rock. Recently produced "Your Honor," by Koko (country single, Daisy Records).
Tips: "We produce mostly demos (8-track) and try to find major labels who will sign the acts directly. But, if all else fails, we will release on our own labels."

ALEX CIMA, Box 1594, Hollywood CA 90028. (213)662-8588. Contact: Alex Cima. Record producer. Deals with artists, songwriters and producers in need of engineering or special effects. Fee derived by negotiation.

How to Contact: Not currently looking for new material.
Music: Recently produced *Cosmic Connection,* (LP, Polydor Records/Germany; Chromosome Records/USA) and *Final Alley* (LP, Chromosome Records/USA). Other productions include music for TV, films and commercials.

CLARK'S COUNTRY RECORDS, 2039 Cedarville Rd., Goshen OH 45122. (513)625-9469. Owner: Grace Clark. Record company and music publisher. Works with musicians and songwriters on contract.
How to Contact: Submit demo tape and lyric sheet. Prefers 7½ ips reel-to-reel, cassette or 8 track cartridge with 1-4 songs on demo. SASE. Reports "as soon as possible."
Music: Bluegrass; C&W; gospel; and country rock. Recently released "Little Teardrops," "I'm Not the Only Woman," "Our Man Elvis" and "Elvis is Still the King," by Linda Sue, "Love Has Died" and "Would She Do the Same to Me," by Danny Angel; and "It's All Over Now" and "What's the Matter Now," by "Pappy" Tipton.

CLAY PIGEON PRODUCTIONS, Box 20346, Chicago IL 60620. (312)476-2553. A&R Director: V. Beleska. Record producer. Deals with artists and songwriters. Produces 10-25 singles and 5-15 albums/year. Fee derived from sales royalty or outright fee from record company.
How to Contact: "We cannot consider any material without a written inquiry first, describing self and material." Prefers 7½ ips reel-to-reel or cassette with 1-5 songs on demo. SASE. Reports in 2-8 weeks.
Music: Bluegrass, blues, children's, choral, church/religious, classical, C&W, dance, easy listening, folk, gospel, jazz, MOR, progressive, rock, soul, top 40/pop, avant-garde, and punk rock. Recently produced "All for You," by Christopher (MOR single, Clay Pigeon International Records); "Disco People," by Roto Applicators (punk rock single, Broken Records); and *Tricentennial 2076*, by Vyto B (avant-garde LP, Clay Pigeon International Records).

CLEAR GOSPEL RECORDS, RR 1 Box 224, Sewell NJ 08080. (609)728-3880. Producer: Ron Butko. Record producer and music publisher (Clear Gospel Publications). Estab. 1979. Deals with artists and songwriters. Produces 2-10 singles and 7 albums/year. Fee derived from sales royalty or outright fee from artist/songwriter. "Special agreements considered."
How to Contact: Submit demo tape and lyric sheet. Prefers 7½ or 15 ips reel-to-reel or cassette with 1-5 songs on demo. "We are only interested in gospel music but it can be of a traditional or contemporary nature." SASE. Reports in 3 weeks.
Music: Church/religious and gospel.

CLOCK & MYSTIC RECORDS, 6277 Selma Ave., Hollywood CA 90028. (213)464-9667. President/A&R Director: Doug Moody. Coordinator: Nancy Faith. Record producer. Estab. 1979. Deals with artists and songwriters. Fee derived from sales royalty.
How to Contact: Submit demo tape or submit demo tape and lead sheet. Prefers 7½ ips reel-to-reel or cassette. SASE. Reports in 1 month.
Music: Blues; church/religious; rock; and soul. "No drug or sex lyrics." Recently produced "Send It On Down," by the Long Beach Southernairs (gospel, Hooks-Mystic Records); "Our Lord's Prayer," by Eddie LeJay (religious, Mystic Records); and "Non Support," by Ironing Board Sam (blues, Hooks Records).

COMMODORES ENTERTAINMENT PUBLISHING CORP., 39 W. 55th St. S., New York NY 10019. (212)246-0385. Contact: Producer. Record producer and music publisher (Commodores Entertainment Publishing Corp.). Deals with artists and songwriters.
How to Contact: Write first about your interest, submit demo tape and lyric sheet. Prefers cassette with 4 songs minimum on demo. SASE. Reports in 1 month.
Music: Bluegrass, blues, children's, choral, church/religious, C&W, dance-oriented, easy listening, folk, gospel, jazz, MOR, progressive, R&B, rock, soul and top 40/pop. Recently produced "It's Time," by Platinum Hook (R&B, Motown Records).
Tips: "Follow up after you have made your submission."

COPA COMMUNICATIONS CORP., 1208 Eastview, Jackson MS 39203. (601)969-1434. Manager: Chris Walker. Record producer and music publisher (Frasco Music/BMI). Estab. 1979. Deals with artists, songwriters and producers. Produces 10 singles and 3 albums/year. Free derived from sales royalty.
How to Contact: Submit demo tape and lyric sheet. Prefers 7½ ips reel-to-reel or cassette with 3-6 songs on demo. SASE. Reports in 1 month.
Music: MOR, rock and top 40/pop. Recently produced *I'll Pay the Price*, by Norma Jordan (pop/rock LP, Ciaco Records, Italy); *Going Back to China*, by Mis' sippi (rock LP, Ciaco Records,

Italy); and *Baby Lay Down*, by N. Jordan (pop/MOR, LP, Amadeo Records, Austria/Switzerland). Other artists include Tony Warren.

COUNTRY STAR PRODUCTIONS, 439 Wiley Ave., Franklin PA 16323. (814)432-4633. President: Norman Kelly. Record producer and music publisher (Country Star Music/ASCAP, Kelly Music/BMI and Process Music/BMI). Deals with artists and songwriters. Produces 8-10 singles and 3-5 albums/year. Fee derived from sales royalty.
How to Contact: Submit demo tape and lyric sheet. Prefers 7½ ips reel-to-reel or cassette with 2-4 songs on demo. SASE. Reports in 2 weeks.
Music: Bluegrass, C&W, easy listening, folk, gospel, MOR, rock and top 40/pop. Recently produced "Big Time Joe," by Debbie Sue (country single, Queen City Records); "Alimony Blues," by Virge Brown and Debbie Sue (country single, Joy-Bird Records); and "Jesus Makes the Difference," by Glenn Lucas Family (gospel single, Country Star Records). Other artists include Junie Lou, Denver Bill, Bobby Mac, Bonnie Baldwin, Rose Marie.

COUNTRYSIDE RECORDING, Rt. 2, Crookston MN 56716. (818)281-6450. Contact: Gary Emerson. Record producer and music publisher (Gentilly Music/BMI). Deals with artists and songwriters. Produces 8 singles and 4 albums/year. Fee derived from sales royalty.
How to Contact: Submit demo tape and lyric sheet. Prefers cassette with 2-5 songs on demo. SASE. ReDorts in 1 month.
Music: Bluegrass, C&W and gospel. Recently produced "Nothing's Gonna' Come Better," by Darcy Hagen (country single, Glade Records). Other artists include Steve Lockman.

COUSINS MUSIC, 211 Birchwood Ave., Upper Nyack NY 10960. President: Lou Cicchetti. Produces 5 singles/year. Fee derived from sales royalty.
How to Contact: Submit demo tape only. Prefers 7½ or 15 ips reel-to-reel or cassette with 2 songs minimum on demo. SASE. Reports in 2 weeks.
Music: C&W (any) and rock. Recently produced "Wall between Us," by the Earls (soul/rock, Dakar Records) and "One More Heartache," by CoCo (C&W, Daisy Records).

THE EDDIE CROOK COMPANY, Box 213, Hendersonville TN 37075. (615)822-1360. Contact: Eddie Crook. Record producer and music publisher (Pleasant View Music/ASCAP and Chestnut Mound Music/BMI). Estab. 1980. Deals with artists and songwriters. Produces 10 singles and 25 albums/year. Fee derived from sales royalty.
How to Contact: Submit demo tape and lyric sheet. Prefers cassette with 1-3 songs on demo. Does not return unsolicited material. Reports in 1 month.
Music: Gospel. Recently produced *Solid as a Rock,* by Mid-South Boys and *The Encores,* by The Encores (gospel LPs, Morningstar Records); and *Bibletones,* by Bibletones (gospel LP, Harvest Records).

CROSS-OVER ENTERPRISES, INC., 880 NE 71st St., Miami FL 33138. (305)759-1405. President: Carlos Oliva. Record producer and music publisher (Funk Box Music/BMI and Oliva Music/SESAC). Estab. 1979. Deals with artists and songwriters. Produces 10 singles and 7 albums/year. Fee derived from sales royalty.
How to Contact: Submit demo tape and lyric sheet. Prefers cassette with any number songs on demo. SASE. Reports in 2 weeks.
Music: Dance-oriented, Spanish and rock. Recently produced *Llegamos,* by Clouds and *Hermanos,* by Judge's Nephews (rock/salsa LPs, Common Cause Records); and *Salsa Express,* by Salsa Express (salsa, Common Cause Records). Regularly produces Spanish rock, Spanish love ballads and Salsa groups.

DANCER PRODUCTIONS, LTD., 1810 Calvert St. NW, Washington DC 20009. (202)234-8860. President: David Carpini. Record producer. Deals with artists and songwriters. Produces 2-3 albums/year. Fee derived from sales royalty.
How to Contact: Submit demo tape and lyric sheet. Prefers 7½ ips reel-to-reel or cassette.
Music: Recently produced "Bustin' Loose;; and "Game Seven," by Chuck Brown and the Soul Searchers (R&B/funk, MCA Records). Other artists include Wax (RCA Records) and Marie Lovellette (Ariola Records).

JOHN DANIELS PUBLISHING CO., Box 245, Encinal TX 78019. President: John Daniels. Record producer and music publisher. Deals with artists and songwriters. Produces 12 singles and 2 albums/year. Fee derived from sales royalty.
How to Contact: Submit demo tape and lead sheet. Prefers cassette with 2-6 songs on demo. "Include letter giving brief resume of artist/songwriter with submission. Also indicate what type of

plans or goals the artist/songwriter has for his songs." Does not return unsolicited material. Reports in 2 weeks.
Music: Children's, C&W, easy listening, folk, polka and Latin. Recently produced "We'll Go Our Way" and "Another Time," by Johnny Gonzalez (C&W single, CBS/Columbia Records); "Black Road," by Johnny Gonzalez (C&W single, Caytronics Records); and "Eyes of Blue" and "Patricia Waltz" by John Daniels (easy listening single, Daniels Records).

DAWN PRODUCTIONS, Cloud 40, Paradise PA 17562. President: Joey Welz. Record producer and music publisher (Ursula Music/BMI and Welz Music/ASCAP). Produces 6 singles and 3 albums/year. Deals with artists and songwriters. Fee derived from sales royalty or outright fee from record company.
How to Contact: Submit demo tape and lyric sheet. Prefers cassette with 4-8 songs on demo. Does not return unsolicited material. "We are looking for finished masters to lease. When they are leased, you are notified."
Music: C&W, dance, easy listening, MOR, rock, and top 40/pop. Recently produced "Hey Baby," b/w "On My Way to Lovin' You," Joey Welz (pop and C&W, LeCam Records); "Voices in the Sky" b/w "I Remember Love," by Joey Welz (pop/MOR, Music City records); and *Return of a Comet*, by New Wave Comets (Disco-Go Records). Other artists include Jimmy Velvet (Music City Records).

LOU DeLISE PRODUCTIONS, 1230 E. Mermaid Lane, Wyndmoor (Philadelphia) PA 19118. (215)248-1683. Owner: Lou DeLise. Managing Director: John R. Tschorn. Record producer and music publisher (Spaghettuni Music Co./ASCAP). Deals with artists, songwriters and producers. Fee derived from sales royalty, outright fee from record company, or outright fee from artist/songwriter.
How to Contact: Submit demo tape and lyric sheet. Prefers cassette with 1-3 songs on demo. SASE. Reports in 3-6 weeks.
Music: C&W (pop), dance, easy listening, MOR, rock, soul, and top 40/pop. Recently produced and or arranged *Figures Can't Calculate*, by Wm. DeVaughn (R&B/pop LP and single, TEC Records); *Ultimate*, by Ultimate (dance LP, Cassablanca Records); and "I Just Want to Love You," by Jonas (R&B/pop single, Pavillion (CBS) Records). Other artists include Rainbow, Bruce McFarland and Whitworth & Bell.

DONALD L. DELUCIA, 15041 Wabash Ave., South Holland IL 60473. (312)339-0307. President: Donald DeLucia. Record producer and music publisher (Don-Del Music/BMI and Don-De Music/ASCAP). Deals with artists. Produces 2 singles and 2 albums/year. Free derived from sales royalty.
How to Contact: Submit demo tape and lyric sheet. Prefers 7½ ips reel-to-reel with 4-6 songs on demo. SASE. Reports in 1 week.
Music: C&W, rock and top 40/pop.

STEVE DIGGS PRODUCTIONS, 22 Music Square W., Nashville TN 37203. (615)259-4024. Producers: Steve Diggs and Stan Gunselman. Record producer, music publisher and jingle production. Deals with artists and songwriters, and clients looking for musical advertising. Fee derived from sales royalty or outright fee from record company.
How to Contact: Query or submit demo tape and lead sheet. Prefers 7½ ips reel-to-reel with 2-4 songs on demo. SASE. Reports in 1 month.
Music: Bluegrass; children's; church/religious; C&W; easy listening; folk; MOR; rock; and top 40/pop.

DIRECT DISK LABS, 16 Music Circle S., Nashville TN 37203. (615)256-1680. President: Joe Overholt. General Manager: Jim Callahan. Record Producer. Deals with artists. Produces 8 albums/year. Fee derived from royalty on sales when records are shipped to wholesalers.
How to Contact: Write first about your interest. Prefers 7½ ips reel-to-reel or cassette with 1-5 songs on demo. SASE. Reports in 2 weeks.
Music: Bluegrass, jazz, progressive, R&B, rock, big bands and dixieland. Recently produced *Lenny Breau*, by L. Breau (jazz/pop LP, Direct Disk Records); *Dukes of Dixieland*, by Dukes of Dixieland (jazz LP, Direct Disk Records); and *A Cut Above*, by Dave Brubeck (jazz LP, Direct Disk Records).

JOHN DOE-LP PRODUCTIONS, 540 La Guardia Place, New York NY 10012. (212)674-3939. President/Producer: John McL. Doelp. Record producer. Estab. 1980. Deals with artists, songwriters and record companies. Produces 3 singles and 4 albums/year. Fee derived from sales royalty or outright fee from record company.

How to Contact: Submit demo tape and lyric sheet. Prefers 7½ ips reel-to-reel or cassette with 2-4 songs on demo. "Include supporting information, i.e., resume, reviews, picture, bio, etc." SASE. Reports in 2 weeks.
Music: Rock (pop, country or hard), soul, and top 40/pop and new wave. Recently produced "Figure 14," by Human Sexual Response (new rock, Passport Records); "Music For Car Radios," by Tweeds (new rock single, EAT Records); "Book of Love," by original artists (new rock single, EAT Records); and "Undecided," by Raz-mataz (swing/jazz single, Soap Records).

DOOR KNOB RECORDS, 2125 8th Ave. S., Nashville TN 37204. (615)383-6540. President: Gene Kennedy. Vice-president: Karen Jeglum. National Promotions Director: Bobby Young. Record producer and music publisher. Deals with artists and songwriters. Fee derived by sales royalty.
How to Contact: Submit demo tape and lyric sheet or call first about your interest. Prefers 7½ ips reel-to-reel or cassette with 4 songs maximum on demo. SASE. Reports in 1 month.
Music: C&W, easy listening, and MOR. Recently published "You Still Got Me," by Jerry Wallace (country/MOR, Door Knob Records); "I Want to See Me in Your Eyes," by Peggy Sue (country/MOR, Door Knob Records); and "Gently Hold Me," by Peggy Sue and Sonny Wright (country/MOR, Door Knob Records). Other artists include Sandra Kaye, Betty Martin, Taylor & Stone, Max Brown, Jimmie Simmons and Elvis Wade.

COL. BUSTER DOSS PRESENTS, Box 312, Estill Springs TN 37330. (615)649-2158. President: Col. Buster Doss. Record producer, music publisher (Buster Doss Music/BMI, Barbara Ann Music/ASCAP) and booking agency. Produces 100 singles and 20 albums/year. Deals with artists and songwriters. Fee derived from sales royalty, outright fee from record company or outright fee from songwriter.
How to Contact: Write or call first about your interest, then submit demo tape and lyric sheet. Prefers cassette with 2-3 songs on demo. SASE. Reports in 1 week.
Music: Bluegrass, church/religious, C&W, easy listening, folk, gospel, progressive, and rock. Recently produced "Beautiful Texas," by Billy Walker (Tall Texan Records); "Blue Water," by Billy Grammer (Stardust Records); "No Help Wanted," by Bill Carlisle (Stardust Records); and "Texas," by Rusty Adams (Stardust Records).
Other artists include Cooder Browne, Buck Cody, Robert Joe, Texas Cooking, Slaughter Creek, Billy Grammer, Larry Butler and Lynde Rain.

MIKE DOUGLAS & ASSOCIATES, 333 31st St., Suite 20, St. Petersburg FL 33713. (813)896-5151. President: Mike Douglas. Record producer and music publisher (Lisas Theme Music/BMI). Estab. 1980. Deals with artists and songwriters. Produces 4 singles and 1 albums/year. Fee negotiable.
How to Contact: Submit demo tape and lead sheet. Prefers cassette with 1-4 songs on demo. SASE. Reports as soon as possible.
Music: Blues, C&W, easy listening, gospel, MOR, R&B, rock (all types), soul and top 40/pop. Recently produced "J.R. Ewing/President," by Rich Lovette (country comedy single, Dynasty Records); "Doll House," by Melody Wilcox (country pop single, Dynasty Records); and "Second Time Around," by Melody Wilcox (country single, Dynasty Records). Other artists include June Page, Duane Bunker and Jerry Cobb.

DRAGON INTERNATIONAL PRODUCTIONS, Box 8263 Haledon, Haledon NJ 07508. (201)942-6810. President: Samuel Cummings. Record producer and music publisher (Dragon International Music/BMI). Deals with artists and songwriters. Produces 3 singles and 2 albums/year. Fee derived from sales royalty.
How to Contact: Submit demo tape and lyric sheet. Prefers 7½ ips reel-to-reel or cassette.
Music: Dance, MOR, reggae, rock, soul, and top 40/pop. Recently produced "Love Shine Brighter,B by Culture (reggae, April Records); and "Don't Say You Don't Love," by Mighty Throes (reggae, April Records). Other artists include Yoland Brown and Rhonda Durand (April Records).

DUANE MUSIC, INC., 382 Clarence Ave., Sunnyvale CA 94086. (408)739-6133. President: Garrie Thompson. Record producer and music publisher. Deals with artists and songwriters. Fee derived from sales royalty.
How to Contact: Submit demo tape only. Prefers 7½ ips reel-to-reel or cassette with 1-5 songs on demo. SASE. Reports in 1 month.
Music: Blues, C&W, rock, soul, and top 40/pop. Recently produced "Wichita," (C&W, Hush Records) and "Syndicate of Sound," (rock, Buddah Records).

GUS DUDGEON, The Sol, Mill Lane, Cookham, Berkshire England. (00285)20286, 20259. Managing Director: Gus Dudgeon. Record producer and music publisher. Deals with artists and Songwriters. Fee derived from sales royalty.
How to Contact: Submit demo tape and lyric sheet. Prefers cassette with 5-20 songs on demo. SASE. Reports in 3 weeks.
Music: Mainly top 40/pop; also blues; MOR; progressive (occasionally); R&B and hard rock.

EARTH AND SKY RECORDS, Box 4157, Winter Park FL 32793. Manager/Producer: William (Bill) Winborne. Record producer and music publisher (Earth and Sky Music Publishing, Inc./ BMI). Deals with artists and songwriters. Produces 5 singles and 3 albums/year. Fee derived from sales royalty per standard contract.
How to Contact: Write first about your interest, submit demo tape and lyric sheet. "Do not phone." Prefers cassette with 1-3 songs on demo. "Songwriters should send *only* copyrighted material with good lead sheets and demos." SASE. Reports in 1 month.
Music: Bluegrass, C&W, easy listening, jazz, MOR, progressive, R&B, rock and top 40/pop.

EASTEX MUSIC, 8537 Sunset Blvd., #2, Los Angeles CA 90069. (213)657-8852. Owner: Travis Lehman. Record producer and music publisher. Deals with songwriters and artists. Fee derived from sales royalty plus advance.
How to Contact: Submit demo tape. Prefers cassette. SASE. Reports in 3 weeks.
Music: Rock 'n' Roll and country.

EBB-TIDE PRODUCTIONS, Box 2544, Baton Rouge LA 70821. (504)925-2603. President: E.K. Harrison. Record producer and music publisher (Harrison Music Publishing Company, Inc./ BMI). Deals with artists and songwriters. Produces 25-30 singles and 10-15 albums/year. Fee derived from sales royalty.
How to Contact: Submit demo tape and lead sheet. Prefers cassette with 4-6 songs on demo. SASE. Reports in 2 weeks.
Music: Bluegrass, church/religious, C&W, and folk. Recently produced "Dreamland," by Pamla-Marie (country/pop single, Tiger Records); "Always," by Greg Smith (gospel/contemporary single, C.O.G.M. Records); and "Take the Sunshine," by Dan Bruce (gospel/contemporary single, C.O.G.M. Records). Other artists include Jimmy Angel and Joanie Angel.

EB-TIDE MUSIC/YOUNG COUNTRY MUSIC, Box 5412, Buena Park CA 90620. (213)864-6302. Contact: Leo J. Eiffert, Jr. Record producer. Deals with artists. Fee derived from sales royalty.
How to Contact: Call or write first about your interest, then submit demo tape and lyric sheet. Prefers 7½ ips reel-to-reel as demo. SASE. Reports in 3 weeks.
Music: C&W. Artists include Bobby Bee (country artist, K. Ark Records); Crawfish (country band); Leo J. Eiffert, Jr (country artist, Plain Country Records) and Pamela Jean (country artist).

ECHO RECORDS, 824 83rd St., Miami Beach FL 33141. (305)865-8960. Record Producer and music publisher (Dana Publishing). Deals with artists. Produces 2 singles and 1 album/year.
How to Contact: Write first about your interest. Prefers 7½ or 15 ips reel-to-reel or cassette as demo. SASE.
Music: Church/religious, classical and Polish. Recently produced "God's Children," by Don Bennett (religious single, Echo Records); "We Want God," by Regina Kujawa (religious single, Echo Records); *Chor Dana*, by Chor Dana (Polish pop LP, Echo Records); *Polish Dances*, by Walter Dana (classical LP, Echo Records); and "Come Back Lost Day," by Stas Jaworski (Polish pop single, Echo Records).

EN POINTE PRODUCTIONS, Box 1451, Beverly Hills CA 90213. (805)497-1584. President: Jeff Weber. Record producer. Deals with artists. Produces 3-7 albums/year. Fee derived from royalty of songs when song or artist is recorded; by outright fee from record company; or royalty advance from labels or private companies.
How to Contact: Write first about your interest. Prefers cassette with 2-4 songs on demo. "Record on the best tape available utilizing the best means available." SASE. Reports in 2 weeks.
Music: Bluegrass, classical, jazz, R&B, rock, soul, and top 40/pop. Recently produced *Heritage*, by Kenny Burrell (jazz, Audio Source Records); *Free Flight*, by Free Flight (jazz/classical, Audio Source Records); and *Night Plans*, by Haden Gregg/Jim Dykann (contemporary pop/rock, Night Plans Records).
Tips: "My work is primarily involved with audiophile recording techniques (i.e., direct to disc, digital and live to the two track). My recordings accentuate artistry as well as the Sham."

ENTERTAINMENT COMPANY, 40 W. 57th St., New York NY 10019. (212)265-2600. Assistant Director of A&R: Mr. Larry Osterman. Record producer and music publisher. Deals with artists and songwriters..
How to Contact: Submit demo tape and lyric sheet. Prefers cassette with 1-2 songs on demo. SASE. Reports in 1-3 months.
Music: Country/pop, MOR, R&B, crossover rock, and top 40/pop. Recently produced "It's the World Gone Crazy," by Glen Campbell (Capitol Records). Other artists include Dolly Parton, Cher, Tanya Tucker and Barbra Streisand.

GREG ERRICO PRODUCTIONS/PAPA PRODUCTIONS, 7417 Sunset, Los Angeles CA 90046. (213)874-1300. President: Greg Errico. Record producer and music publisher (Radio Active Material Publishing/ASCAP and Burlingame Music/BMI). Deals with artists and songwriters. Produces 3 singles and 2 albums/year. Fee derived from sales royalty or by outright fee from record company.
How to Contact: Submit demo tape and lyric sheet. Prefers cassette with 2-3 songs on demo. SASE. Reports in 1 month "if interested."
Music: Blues, jazz, R&B, rock, soul, and top 40/pop. Recently produced *Funkadelic Connections Disconnections*, by Funkadelic (funk, L.A.X./CBS Records) and "My Road," by Lee Oskar (pop, Electra Record).

ESQUIRE INTERNATIONAL, Box 6032, Station B, Miami FL 33123. (305)547-1424. President: Jeb Stuart. Record producer, music publisher and management firm. Deals with artists and record labels. Produces 5 singles/year. Fee derived from sales royalty or independent leasing of masters and placing songs.
How to Contact: Query, submit demo tape and lead sheet or telephone. Prefers cassette with 2-4 songs on demo, or disc. SASE. Reports in 1 month.
Music: Blues, church/religious, C&W, dance, gospel, jazz, rock, soul, and top 40/pop. Recently produced "Can't Count the Days" (R&B single, Kent Records); "Sitba" (R&B single, King Records); and "Hung Up on Your Love" (disco single, Esquire Records), all by Jeb Stuart.

FRANK EVANS PRODUCTIONS, Box 6025, Newport News VA 23606. (804)595-9000. President: Frank Evans. Deals with artists and songwriters. Produces 2-3 singles and 1-2 albums/year. Fee derived from sales royalty.
How to Contact: Submit demo tape and lead sheet. Prefers cassette with 3-5 songs on demo. "Also submit brief resume of former musical works with your name, address and age." SASE. Reports within 90 days.
Music: Choral, C&W, dance, easy listening, folk, MOR, and top 40/pop. Recently produced "Bryan's Song," by Laurie Wilson (MOR, Premiere Artist Records); "He's Gonna Cry," by Shawna Ames (MOR, New Warwick Records); and "Our Kinda Guy," by The Dickiebirds (new wave rock, Boyfriends Records). Other artists include Steve Cook, Greg Cruze and Stu Will.

FACTORY BEAT RECORDS, INC., 663 5th Ave., New York NY 10022. (212)757-3638. Record producer and music publisher (Ren-Maur Music). Produces 6 singles and 4 albums/year. Free derived from sales royalty.
How to Contact: Submit demo tape and lyric sheet only. Prefers cassette with 2-4 songs on demo. SASE. Reports in 3 weeks.
Music: R&B, rock, soul and top 40/pop. Recently produced "I Love Your Beat," by Rena (dance single, Factory Beat Records); "Dance It Off," by Rena (dance single, Factory Beat Records); and "Rhythm Rap Rock," by Count Coolout (rap single, Boss Record).

FARR RECORDS, Box 1098, Somerville NJ 08876. (201)725-3850. Contact: Candace Campbell. Record producer. Deals with artists and songwriters. Produces 30 singles and 30 albums/year. Fee derived from sales royalty.
How to Contact: Submit demo tape and lyric sheet. Prefers cassette with 4 songs minimum on demo. SASE. Reports in 2 weeks.
Music: C&W, dance-oriented, easy listening, folk, jazz, MOR, rock, soul and top 40/pop. Recently produced "Homemade Love," by Bresh (country single, Farr Records); and "Disco" and "Looking for Mr. Goodbar," by SP&G, (soul singles, Farr Records).

50/50 RECORDS, 11 E. 26th St., 21st Floor, New York NY 10010. (212)686-7706. President: Steve Martin. Vice President: Michael Goldberg. Record producer and music publisher (50/50 Music). Estab. 1979. Deals with artists, songwriters and producers. Fee derived from sales royalty.
How to Contact: Call first about your interest, submit demo tape and lyric sheet. Prefers 7½ ips reel-to-reel or cassette with 1-4 songs on demo. SASE. Reports in 3 weeks.
Music: R&B, rock, soul, top 40/pop, dance-oriented, C&W, jazz, and MOR.

FIRST AMERICAN RECORDS, INC., 73 Marion St., Seattle WA 98104. (206)625-9992. Director of Publishing, Copyright, A&R: William Angle. Record producer and music publisher (Bainbridge Music Co./BMI; Marinwood Music Co./ASCAP). Deals with artists and songwriters. Produces 20 singles and 50 albums/year. Fee derived from sales royalty.
How to Contact: Submit demo tape and lyric sheet. Prefers cassette with 2-5 songs on demo. "Either well-done voice, guitar or voice, piano for *song* demos—Masterable production for record deal." SASE. Reports in 1 month.
Music: C&W, dance-oriented (some disco), rock (soft), top 40/pop and AOR. Recently produced *Kostas*, by Kostas (pop/rock LP, First American Records); and *Glenn Yarbrough*, by G. Yarbrough (adult contemporary LP, First American Records).

FIST-O-FUNK, LTD., 293 Richard Ct., Pomona NY 10970. (914)354-7157. President: Kevin Misevis. Record producer, music publisher, management firm and record company. Deals with artists and songwriters. Produces 2-3 singles and 3 albums/year. Fee derived from sales royalty.
How to Contact: Submit demo tape and lead sheet. Prefers 7½ ips reel-to-reel with 3-10 songs on demo. SASE.
Music: C&W, dance, jazz, MOR, and top 40/pop. Recently produced "Keep on Dancin' " and "Dance All Over the World," by T.C. James (pop/disco).

FREQUENCY PRODUCTIONS, 2705 Fair Oaks Ave., Hatboro PA 19040. (215)443-0935. General Manager: Sal Barbieri. Record producer and music publisher (Conypol Music). Estab. 1980. Deals with artists and songwriters. Produces 6 singles and 2 albums/year. Fee derived from sales royalty or outright fee from record company.
How to Contact: Submit demo tape and lyric sheet. Prefers cassette with 1-4 songs on demo. SASE. Reports in 2 weeks.
Music: C&W, dance-oriented, easy listening, MOR, R&B, rock (soft and hard), soul and top 40/pop. Recently produced "Feeling Good," by Sal Barbieri (dance rock single, BSO Records); "Let's Get Funky," by S. Barbieri (dance R&B single, BSO Records); and "One More Try," by S. Barbieri (top 40/pop single, BSO Records). Other artists include The Royal Company.

FUTURA PRODUCTIONS, 300 City Island Ave., City Island NY 10464. (212)885-2380. Manager: Tony Graye. Record producer and music publisher (Futura Music). Deals with artists, songwriters and musicians. Produces 20 singles and 8 albums/year. Fee derived from sales royalty.
How to Contact: Submit demo tape and lyric sheet. Prefers cassette with 4 songs minimum on demo. SASE. Reports in 3 weeks.
Music: Jazz, MOR, progressive, R&B, soul and top 40/pop. Recently produced "Sadness and Sorrow," (composed by Ray Rivera and arranged by Tony Graye) recorded by Tony Graye (jazz single, Futura Records); "Tokyo Mama," (composed by Ray Rivera and arranged by Tony Graye) recorded by Ray Riviera (Latin jazz single, Jody Records); and *Oh Gee*, by Graye (jazz LP, Zim Records).

FUTURE 1 PRODUCTIONS, 8924 E. Calle Norlo, Tucson AZ 85710. (602)885-5931. Producers: James M. Gasper and Thomas M. Dukes. Record producer and music publisher (Myko Music/BMI). Estab. 1981. Deals with artists and songwriters. Produces 2 singles and 2 albums/year. Fee derived from sales royalty.
How to Contact: Call first about your interest, then submit demo tape and lyric sheet. Prefers 7½ ips reel-to-reel or cassette with 3-5 songs on demo. SASE. Reports in 1 month.
Music: Easy listening, R&B, rock, top 40/pop and poprock. Recently produced "Siren's Song" and "Just Arrived," by Gasper & Dukes (pop/rock EP, Ariana Records); "She's on Fire," by The BandAids (new wave/rock single, Ariana Records); and "Just an Hour a Day," by Happy Leggs (power pop, Ariana Records).

FYDAQ PRODUCTIONS, 240 E. Radcliffe Dr., Claremont CA 91711. (714)624-0677. President: Gary K. Buckley. Record producer. Deals with artists, songwriters and record companies. Produces 2-5 singles and 4-5 albums/year. Fee derived from sales royalty, outright fee from record company, or outright fee from songwriter/artist.
How to Contact: Query, submit demo tape, or submit demo tape and lead sheet. Prefers 7½ ips reel-to-reel or cassette with 1-4 songs on demo. SASE. Reports in 3 weeks.
Music: Church/religious, C&W, easy listening, folk, gospel, MOR, rock, soul, and top 40/pop. Recently produced *Buche*, by Rick Buche (top 40/MOR LP, Paradise Records); *To God, with Love*, by Jerry Roark (gospel LP, Majega Records); *Country Love*, by Jerry Roark (C&W LP, Majega Records); *Sending A Copy Home*, by Jody Barry (gospel LP, Majega Records); *Is It Right*, by Borderling (top 40/AOR single, Majega Records); and *Touch Me Now*, by Borderline (top 40/single Majega Records).

GALLANT ROBERTSON, INC., Box 477, Westmount Canada. Vice President: Ian Robertson. Record producer and music publisher. Deals with artists and songwriters. Produces 2-6 albums/ year. Fee derived from sales royalty or outright fee from record company.
How to Contact: Query, arrange personal interview or submit demo tape. Prefers 7½ ips reel-to-reel or cassette with 1-3 songs on demo. SAE and International Reply Coupons. Reports in 1 month.
Music: Dance, MOR, rock (top 40), and top 40/pop. Recently produced *Will You Give Me Your Love?* (top 40 LP, Attic Records); *Patsy* (disco/top 40, Attic Records); and *Are You Ready for Love?* (top 40 LP, EMI Records), by Patsy Gallant.

GAMELON MUSIC RECORDS AND TAPES, Box 525, Station P, Toronto, Ontario, Canada M5S 2T1. Manager: Michael Kleniec. Record producer and music publisher. Deals with artists and songwriters. Produces 1 song/year. Fee derived from sales royalty.
How to Contact: Submit demo tape and lyric sheet. Prefers 7½ ips reel-to-reel with 5-15 songs on demo. Does not return unsolicited material. Reports in 1 month.
Music: Blues, classical, folk, jazz, progressive and R&B. Recently produced *Sending* and *Live at the Sotto*, by Michael Kleniec (LP, Gamelon Records).

GEE PRODUCTIONS-DON LEONARD PRODUCTIONS, 8 Cherry Hill Court, Reisterstown MD 21136. (301)883-3816. Producer: Don Leonard. (Leonard-Gee Music/BMI). Deals with artists and songwriters. Fee derived from sales royalty. Changes fee "if hired to produce and the artist or writer wants to pay for own session. I do not charge if I see a strong potential in an artist—no fee for songs of chart possiblity."
How to Contact: Query, arrange personal interview, submit demo tape only or submit demo tape and lead sheet. Prefers cassette or 8-track cassette. SASE. Reports in 1 month.
Music: C&W, disco, easy listening, jazz, MOR, progressive, rock, soul, and top 40/pop. Recently produced "Roll Away Heartaches," by Eddie Farrel.

G-J PRODUCTIONS, INC., 2039 Antione, Houston TX 77055. (713)683-7171. President: Gene Watson. Record producer, music publisher and record company. Deals with artists and songwriters. Fee derived from sales royalty and outright fee from songwriter/artist.
How to Contact: Submit demo tape and lyric sheet. Prefers 7½ ips reel-to-reel or cassette. "If writer or artist wishes tape returned, a self-addressed postage-paid envelope must be enclosed." Reports as soon as possible.
Music: C&W; MOR; and top 40/pop. Recently produced "Between This Time and the Next Time" and "Maybe I Should Have Been Listening," by Gene Watson (MCA Records); and "Not the Real Me," by Tony Booth (C&W, Resco Records). Other artists include Lee Offman.

GOLDBAND RECORDING STUDIO, 313 Church St., Lake Charles LA 70601. (318)439-8839. Contact: Eddie Shuler. Record producer. Deals with artists and songwriters. Fee derived from sales royalty.
How to Contact: Prefers 7½ ips reel-to-reel or cassette with 1-10 songs on demo. SASE. Reports in 1 month.
Music: All types. Recently produced "Things I Used to Do," by Katie Webster (R&B, Goldband Records); "Cajun Disco," by La Salle Sisters (disco, Goldband Records); and "Ole Billy Hell," by Rickey Kelley (country, Goldband).

WALT GOLLENDER ENTERPRISES, 12 Marshall St., Suite 8Q, Irvington NJ 07111. (201)373-6050. Executive Director: Walt Gollender. Record producer, music publisher and management firm. Deals with artists, songwriters and producers. Produces 3-5 singles/year. Fee derived from sales royalty, outright fee from record company, or outright management fee from songwriter/artist.
How to Contact: Arrange personal interview or submit demo tape. Prefers 7½ ips mono reel-to-reel or cassette with 1-4 songs on demo. SASE. Reports in 2 weeks.
Music: Blues, C&W, dance, easy listening, folk, MOR, rock (pop or soft), soul, and top 40/pop.

GOLLY MUSIC, Penthouse A, 12 Marshall St., Irvington NJ 07111. (201)373-6050. President: Walt Gollender. Deals with artists, songwriters, producers, agents, publishers, backers, other managers, theatrical photographers and the industry at large. Produces 3-6 singles/year. Fee derived from sales royalty, outright royalty from record company or outright fee from songwriter/ artist.
How to Contact: Arrange personal interview. "Send or bring me demo tape. Call any evening 5-8 p.m. EST." Prefers 7½ ips reel-to-reel, cassette or dubs with a maximum of 4 songs on demo. SASE. Reports in 3 weeks.

Music: Blues, C&W, dance, easy listening, folk, MOR, rock (medium to light), soul, and top 40/pop. Recently produced "Thank You, Lord Jesus," by John Giresi (gospel, Golly Records); and "Autumn Leaves," by George Chartofillis (disco, Golly Records).

GOSPEL EXPRESS, 1899 S. 3rd, Box 2194, Memphis TN 38101. (901)774-5689. President: Bishop Cole. Deals with artists and songwriters. Produces 5-8 albums/year. Fee derived from sales royalty.
How to Contact: Submit demo tape and lead sheet. Prefers cassette. SASE. Reports in 3 weeks.
Music: Blues; church/religious; dance; and gospel. Recently produced "Phone Call From God," by The Bishop (gospel, Michal Records); "Tell Heaven," by Gospel Songbirds (gospel, Gospel Express Records); and "Save A Seat for Me," by Shirly Jones (gospel, Michal Records).

GOSPEL RECORDS, INC., Box 90, Rugby Station, Brooklyn NY 11203. (212)773-5910. President: John R. Lockley. Record producer and music publisher (Gospel Clef Music/BMI). Deals with artists, songwriters and musicians. Fee derived from sales royalty.
How to Contact: Write first about your interest. Prefers cassette with a minimum of 2 songs on demo. SASE. Reports in 1 month.
Music: Spirituals. Recently produced "Everytime I Feel the Spirit," by Glorytone (spiritual single, Gospel Records, Inc.); *Jesus* and *Glorifying Jesus*, by The Lockley Family Gospel Ensemble (spiritual LPs, Gospel Records, Inc.).

GRAMAVISION INC., Box 2772 Grand Central Station, New York NY 10017. President: Jonathan Rose. Record producer and music publisher (BMI). Estab. 1979. Deals with artists, songwriters and musicians. Fee derived from sales royalty.
How to Contact: Submit demo tape and lyric sheet. Prefers 7½ ips reel-to-reel or cassette with 1-3 songs on demo. SASE. "Please send commercial, well-thought-out material only."
Music: Jazz, progressive, R&B, rock, and top 40/pop. Recently produced *Soundtrack to 'The Europeans'* (classical, Gramavision Records) and other films. Other artists include Tony Degradi, Ralph Simon and Anthony Davis.

GRANDPA LOUIE PRODUCTIONS, INC., Box 206, Kaleden, British Columbia, Canada V0H 1K0. (604)497-8424. General Manager: Dennis Thievin. Record producer and music publisher (Gus Schwartz Music). Estab. 1979. Deals with artists and songwriters. Produces 3-6 singles and 2-3 albums/year. Fee derived from sales royalty, outright fee from artist/songwriter or record company.
How to Contact: Submit demo cassette or tape only (no lead sheet required). Prefers cassette or 7½ or 15 ips reel-to-reel with 1-3 songs on demo. SAE and International Reply Coupons. Reports in 1 month.
Music: Top 40/pop. Recently produced *Maple Leaf Hotel*, by Cristie Northup (country/pop LP, Grandpa Louie Records); *Sandi D.*, by Sandi D. (top 40/pop LP, Brothers Records); and *Hollywood Lips*, Thievin Brothers (top 40/pop LP, Brothers Records).

GRASSROOTS PROJECTS UNLIMITED, Box 4689, San Francisco CA 94101. Contact: James L. Heisterkamp. Record producer and music publisher. Fee derived from sales royalty.
How to Contact: Write first about your interest. "We are really not looking for new talent at this time. We have an in-house operations and use San Francisco talent when needed." SASE.
Music: Ragtime, songs about San Francisco.

MILES GRAYSON PRODUCTION'S, 1159 S. LaJolla Ave., Los Angeles CA 90035. (213)938-3531. Musical Director: Lerman Horton. Deals with artists and songwriters. Fee derived from sales royalty.
How to Contact: Submit demo tape and lyric sheet. Prefers cassette with 2-4 songs on demo. SASE. Reports in 2 weeks and "sometimes minutes."
Music: Dance; MOR; R&B; soul and top 40/pop. Recently produced *Filthy*, by PaPa John (Pop LP, Grunt Records); *Hartman*, by John Hartman (top 40 LP, Warner Bros. Records).

GREAT PYRAMID, LTD., 10 Waterville St., San Francisco CA 94124. Contact: Joseph Buchwald. Record producer, music publisher (Great Pyramid Music/BMI) and management firm. Deals with artists and songwriters. Produces 1-2 albums/year. Fee derived from sales royalty, outright fee from record company, or outright fee from songwriter/artist.
How to Contact: Query or submit demo tape and lead sheet. Prefers cassette with 3-6 songs on demo. Does not return unsolicited material. Reports "as soon as possible."
Music: Rock. Recently produced *Jesse Barish*, by Jesse Barish (ballad LP, RCA Records); and Marty Balin (ballad LP, EMI Records).

ABNER J. GRESHLER PRODUCTIONS, INC., 9200 Sunset Blvd., #909, Los Angeles CA 90069. (213)278-8146. President: Abner J. Greshler. Vice President: Steve Greshler. Record producer and booking agency. Deals with artists and songwriters. Produces 6-12 singles and 10-20 albums/year. Fee derived from sales royalty.
How to Contact: Query or submit demo tape and lead sheet. Prefers cassette with 2-4 songs on demo. Does not return unsolicited material. Reports in 1 month.
Music: Rock (hard or country) and soul.

GRUSIN/ROSEN PRODUCTIONS/GRP RECORDS, 330 W. 58th St., New York NY 10019. Contact: Dave Grusin, Larry Rosen, Peter Lopez. Deals with artists and songwriters. Releases 10 albums/year. Fee derived from sales royalty or outright fee from record company.
How to Contact: Query. Prefers reel-to-reel or cassette with 2-5 songs on demo. SASE.
Music: Jazz, R&B and pop. Recently released albums by Angela Bofill, Tom Browne, Dave Valentin, Bernard Wright, and Scott Jarrett.

GEORGE GUESS PRODUCTIONS, 2250 Bryn Mawr Ave., Philadelphia PA 19131. (215)477-7122. A&R Director: Ted Brown. Record producer. Deals with artists and songwriters. Produces 3-5 singles and 2-3 albums/year. Fee derived from sales royalty, outright fee from artists or record company.
How to Contact: Query with letter of introduction or submit demo tape. Prefers 7½ ips reel-to-reel or cassette with 5 songs on demo. SASE. Reports in 3 weeks.
Music: Dance, soul, and top 40/pop. Recently produced *Dreams & Nightmares*, by Dream Merchants (R&B LP, Dazz Records); "Lovin Kind of Love," by Vee Vee (rock single/Sin Records); "Roadrunner," by Satins Breed (rock, Sin Records); and "God Only Knows," by Donald Reeves (gospel, Heaven Records). Other artists include Day One and George Guess.
Tips: "If a writer, be consistent with creativity of original compositions. Stay on top of what's musically happening."

JIM HALL & GIDGET STARR PRODUCTIONS, 5 Aldom Circle, West Caldwell NJ 07006. (201)226-0035. Contact: Jim Hall or Gidget Starr. Record producer and music publisher (Cactus Music and Gidget Publishing/ASCAT). Deals with artists and songwriters. Fee derived from sales royalty.
How to Contact: Write first about your interest then submit demo tape and lyric sheet. Prefers 7½ ips reel-to-reel, cassette or 8-track tapes with 5 songs minimum on demo. Does not return unsolicited material. Reports in 3 weeks.
Music: Bluegrass, blues, church/religious, C&W, easy listening, gospel, R&B, rock and soul. Artists include Doc Hopkins, The Tune Twisters.

JOHN HALL RECORDS, INC., Box 18344, Ft. Worth TX 76118. (817)281-6605. Marketing Manager: Troy E. Bradley. Record producer. Deals with artists and songwriters. Produces 2 albuu s/year.
How to Contact: Submit demo tape and lyric sheet. Prefers cassette with 2-6 songs on demo. SASE. Reports in 1 week.
Music: Church/religious, gospel and MOR. Recently produced *The Lord Liveth* and *I Am Loved*, by John Hall (MOR LPs, John Hall Records); and *Len Mink*, by Len Mink (contemporary gospel, John Hall Records).

HALPERN SOUNDS, 620 Taylor Way, #14, Belmont CA 94002. (415)592-4900. President: Steven Halpern. Record producer. Deals with artists and songwriters. Produces 4 albums/year. Fee derived from sales royalty.
How to Contact: Query or submit demo tape and lead sheet. Prefers cassette with 2-4 songs on demo. Does not return unsolicited material. Reports in 1 month.
Music: Rock (hard or country) and soul.

R.L. HAMMEL ASSOCIATES, Rt. #4, Box 418-C, Alexandria IN 46001. (317)642-7030. Contact: Randal L. Hammel. Record Producer, music publisher (Ladnar Music/ASCAP) and consultants. Deals with artists and songwriters. Produces 2 singles and 10 albums/year. Fee derived from royalty of sales when song or artist is recorded, or negotiable fee per project.
How to Contact: Write first about your interest and send brief resume (including experience, age, goal). Prefers cassette with 3 songs maximum on demo. "Lyrics *must* accompany tapes!" SASE. Reports in 1 month maximum.
Music: Bluegrass, blues, church/religious, C&W, dance, easy listening, gospel, MOR, progressive, R&B, rock (usually country), soul, and top 40/pop. Recently produced *Singing a Love Song*, by Gary Floyd (Christian LP, Custom Records); *Word and Song*, by Judy Foskey (Christian LP,

Custom Records); *There Is a Peace* and *Reason for the Season* (instrumental Christian LPs, Custom Records). Other artists include Overeasy and Heigh-Liters.
Tips: "Though there are certain stigmas that go along with being from the Midwest, we still maintain that quality work can be done, and our good reputation with the 'biggies' in Chicago, Los Angeles, Nashville, etc. will bear us out. Only those who have a full knowledge of the sacrifice involved with this industry (or those willing to hear it) should consider contacting this office. We will shoot straight, and it is *always* explained that our observations are just that—'ours', and another company/production team/etc. might be interested."

HAM-SEM RECORDS, INC., 314 W. Sixth St., Suite 305, Los Angeles CA 90014. (213)627-0557. A&R Director: Dianna Green. Record producer (Four Buddies/ASCAP). Estab. 1980. Deals with artists and songwriters. Produces 1 single and 1 album/year. Fee derived from sales royalty or outright fee from artist/songwriter.
How to Contact: Call first about your interest. Prefers cassette with 4-10 songs on demo. Does not return unsolicited material. Reports in 1 month.
Music: Church/religious, gospel and contemporary, MOR, R&B and top 40/pop. Recently produced *Steppin' Into Now*, by Motivation (R&B LP, Ham-Sem Records); "Are You Choosing," by Gifted Four (R&B single, CSC Records); and "We're Doing It Together," by Tony Love (R&B single, Ham-Sem Records).

HAPPY DAY PRODUCTIONS, INC., 800 N. Ridgeland, Oak Park IL 60302. (312)848-3322. Vice President: Vince Ippolito. Record producer and music publisher. Deals with artists.
How to Contact: Submit demo tape and lyric sheet. Prefers 7½ ips reel-to-reel or cassette with 2-3 songs on demo. SASE.
Music: MOR, progressive, R&B, rock, soul, and top 40/pop. Recently produced "Disco Fairyland" and "Rock Me Baby," by Kitty & Haywoods (disco/R&B, Capital Records); and "Fightin' Jane," by Frank Pisani (C&W/MOR, Happy Day Records).

DR. LAWRENCE HERBST, Box 1659, Beverly Hills CA 90213. Producer: Dr. Lawrence Herbst. Record producer. Deals with artists. Fee derived from sales royalty or outright fee from record company.
How to Contact: Submit demo tape and lyric sheet. Prefers 15 ips reel-to-reel or cassette with 1-2 songs on demo. SASE. Reports in 1 week.
Music: All types.

JOHN HILL MUSIC, INC., 116 E. 37th St., New York NY 10016. (212)683-2273. President: John Hill. Record producer and music publisher (Salami Music/ASCAP). Estab. 1980. Deals with artists and songwriters. Produces 2-6 singles and 0-2 albums/year. Fee derived from royalty of sales when song or artist is recorded or by outright fee from record company.
How to Contact: Submit demo tape and lyric sheet. Prefers cassette with 3 songs on demo. SASE. Reports in 1 month.
Music: Dance-oriented (disco), rock (punk, new wave). Recently produced *City Kids*, by Sterling (top 40/new wave LP); *Pacific Gas & Electric*, by Pacific Gas & Electric (pop/R&B, ABC Records); and *I'm Gonna' Getcha*, by Jimmy Maeler (disco LP, Epic Records).

HOLY SPIRIT PRODUCTIONS, 27335 Penn St., Inkster MI 48141. (313)562-8975. President: Elder Otis G. Johnson. Record producer and music publisher (God's World/SESAC, Manfield Music/BMI and Holy Spirit/ASCAP). Deals with artists and songwriters. Produces 5 singles and 10 albums/year. Fee derived from sales royalty.
How to Contact: Write first about your interest, submit demo tape and lyric sheet. Prefers 7½ ips reel-to-reel or cassette with 3 songs on demo. SASE. Reports in 1 month.
Music: Church/religious, C&W, easy listening, gospel and jazz. Recently produced "Use Me Lord" and "Receive the Power," by Sonlight (gospel singles, ASPRO Records); "Believe in Me," by Saved (gospel single, God's World Records); "Secret Love" and "Love's All," by George Johnson (easy listening singles, ASPRO Records); and *Use Me Lord*, by Sonlight (gospel LP, CBS Records). Other artists include Marcello Ratliff.

HOMETOWN PRODUCTIONS, INC., 1625 Woods Dr., Los Angeles CA 90069. (213)656-8490. President: Ken Mansfield. Record producer and music publisher (Frontlawn Music/BMI and Backyard Music/ASCAP). Deals with artists and songwriters.
How to Contact: Submit demo tape and lyric sheet. Prefers cassette. SASE. Reporting time varies.
Music: C&W, easy listening, folk, MOR, progressive, rock and top 40/pop. Recently produced *Rock America*, by Nick Gilder (rock LP, Casablanca Records); *Diamond In the Rough*, by Jessi Colter (C&W LP, Capitol Records); *Greatest Hits*, by Waylong Jennings (C&W LP, RCA Records); and *Changin' All the Time*, by LaCosta (MOR LP, Capitol Records).

HOPSACK AND SILK PRODUCTIONS INC., 332 W. 71 St., New York NY 10023. (212)873-2179. Associate Director: Ms. Tee Alston. Music publisher (Nick-O-Val Music). Deals with artists and songwriters.
How to Contact: Submit demo tape and lyric sheet. Prefers cassette with 1-2 songs on demo. SASE. Reports as soon as possible.
Music: R&B.

HOT, Box 307, Eastham MA 02642. (617)255-6980 or (212)582-8800. Contact: John M. Hill. Record producer. Deals with artists and songwriters. Fee derived from sales royalty.
How to Contact: Submit demo tape and lyric sheet. Prefers cassette with maximum 5 songs on demo. SASE. Reports in 1 month.
Music: Hard and new wave rock; top 40/pop.

HUDDLESTON'S RECORDING STUDIO, 11819 Lippitt Ave., Dallas TX 75218. (214)328-9056. Owner/Engineer: Gene Huddleston. Engineer: Paul Hill. Record producer, music publisher (Brown Boots Music/BMI) and recording studio. Deals with artists and songwriters. Produces 6 singles and 10 albums/year. Fee derived from sales royalty or outright fee from record company. Charges for some services: Recording studio facilities are available to songwriters/artists for their own use.
How to Contact: Query with bio and photo or submit demo tape and lead sheet. Prefers cassette with 3-5 songs on demo. "Submit the best quality recording on the demo that is financially possible for the writer." SASE. Reports in 1 week.
Music: C&W, easy listening, gospel (contemporary), progressive (country), rock, and top 40/pop. Recently produced *Luanne Oakes*, by Luanne Oakes (progressive country LP, Maday Records); *Beau Jesters*, by Beau Jesters (barbershop quartet LP, Puzzle Records); and *Pete Nevin*, by Pete Nevin (progressive country LP, Puzzle Records). Other artists include Tim McNeely, Terry Mardis, Ron McAda, Storm, and Red River Connection.

KURT HUNTER, 6607 W. Sunset, Suite E, Hollywood CA 90028. (213)462-6164. Contact: Kurt Hunter. Record producer and music publisher. Estab. 1979. Deals with artists and songwriters. Fee derived from sales royalty.
How to Contact: Call or write first about your interest, then submit demo tape and lyric sheet. Prefers cassette with 1-5 songs on demo. SASE. Reports in 3 months.
Music: R&B, rock, and top 40/pop.

IN ZANE PRODUCTIONS, INC., 1529 Walnut St., 6th Floor, Philadelphia PA 19102. (215)568-0500. President: Lloyd Zane Remick. Record producer and music publisher (Zane Music/BMI). Estab. 1979. Deals with artists, songwriters and producers. Produces 1 single and 1 album/year. Fee derived from sales royalty or outright fee from artist/songwriter or record company.
How to Contact: Submit demo tape and lyric sheet. Prefers cassette. SASE. Reports in 3 weeks.
Music: Blues, C&W, dance-oriented, easy listening, gospel, jazz, MOR, progressive, R&B, rock, soul and top 40/pop. Recently produced "Giving It Back" and "Lovin," by Phil Hurtt (MOR/soul, Fantasy Records). Other artists include Spaces.

THE INNOVATION ORGANIZATION, 6684 Charing St., Simi Valley CA 93063. (213)882-0177. Owner: Ron Lewis. Record producer and jingle company. Deals with artists and songwriters. Fee derived from sales royalty.
How to Contact: Submit demo tape. Prefers 7½ ips reel-to-reel or cassette with 2 songs minimum on tape. SASE. Reports in 1 month.
Music: Dance, easy listening, MOR, rock, soul, and top 40/pop. Recently produced "This Is My Home," "That's Sunshine," and "One of the Lucky One's," by Bobbe Llynne (MOR, Aware Records). Other artists include Marilyn O 'Brien.

INTER-MEDIA, 1826 Queen St., East, Toronto, Ontario, Canada M4L 1G9. (416)690-1125. Producers: Mr. Bowen and Mr. Dusome. Record producer and music publisher (Inter-Media Publishing). Deals with artists and songwriters and audio video. Produces 4 singles and 2 albums/year. Fee derived from sales royalty or outright fee from songwriter/artist or record company.
How to Contact: Write first about your interest. Prefers cassette with 3-6 songs on demo. Does not return unsolicited material. Reports in 1 month.
Music: Blues, C&W, easy listening, folk, MOR, rock and top 40/pop.

INTERNATIONAL AUTOMATED MEDIA, 17422 Murphy Ave., Irvine CA 92714. (714)751-2015. Marketing Director: Terry Sheppard. Record production and music publishing

(I.A.M. Music and Newport Beach Music). Deals with artists and songwriters. Produces 13 albums/year. Fee derived from sales royalty.
How to Contact: Submit demo tape and lyric sheet. Prefers cassette with 3 songs minimum on demo. SASE. Reports in 2 months.
Music: All types.

BRUCE JAMES COMPANY, Box 439, Lyndonville VT 05851. (802)626-3317. President: Bruce James. Record producer. Deals with artists. Produces 5 singles and 1 album/year. Fee derived from outright fee from artist/songwriter.
How to Contact: Submit demo tape and lyric sheet. Prefers cassette with 1-5 songs on demo. SASE. Reports in 3 weeks.
Music: Rock (top 40/AOR) and top 40/pop. Recently produced "Take It All" and "Old Paree," by Fox (rock singles, Prime Cut Records); and "Heartless," by Fox (ballad single, Prime Cut Records). Other artists include Rockestra, Littlewing.
Tips: "Songs should be hit material no longer than 3½ minutes and consist of verse and 2 choruses; lyrics should be personal and intimate."

JESSE JAMES PRODUCTIONS, INC., Box 128, Worcester PA 19490. (215)424-0800. President: Mr. J. James. Record producer and music publisher (James Boy Publishing Co.). Deals with artists and songwriters. Fee derived from sales royalty.
How to Contact: Submit demo tape and lyric sheet. Prefers cassette with any number songs on demo. SASE. Reports in 1 month.
Music: C&W, dance-oriented, easy listening, folk, gospel, MOR, R&B and soul.

ALEXANDER JANOULIS PRODUCTIONS (AJP), Box 13584, Atlanta GA 30324. (404)872-6000. Independent record producer. Deals with artists and songwriters. Produces 6-10 singles and 2-3 albums/year. Fee derived "depends on particular situation and circumstance. If the songwriter/artist is not signed to me, a minimum fee of $500/song or $5,000/album plus travel expenses is charged ."
How to Contact: Query or submit demo tape. Prefers cassette with 2-3 songs on demo. Does not return unsolicited material. Reports in 6 weeks.
Music: Blues, C&W, dance, jazz, MOR, progressive, rock (new wave), and top 40/pop. Recently produced "So Much" and "The Way It Used to Be," by Little Phil and the Night Shadows (top 40/pop singles, ABC Dot Records); "Another Day" and "Don't Take It Out on Me," by Starfoxx (top 40/new wave singles, Hottrax Records); and "Love Generator" and "Silver Grill Blues," by Diamond Lil (disco, Glamour & Grease Records).

JED RECORD PRODUCTION, 39 Music Square E., Nashville TN 57203. (615)255-6535. President: John E. Denny. Record producer, music publisher, management firm and production company. Deals with artists and songwriters. Fee derived from sales royalty, production, publishing and management.
How to Contact: Submit demo tape and lead sheet. Prefers 7½ ips mono reel-to-reel with 4 songs on demo. SASE. Reports in 6 weeks.
Music: Bluegrass, C&W, gospel, and MOR.

LITTLE RICHIE JOHNSON PRODUCTIONS, 913 S. Main St., Belen NM 87002. (505)864-7441. President: Little Richie Johnson. Record producer and music publisher (Little Richie Johnson Music/BMI and Little Cowboy Music/ASCAP). Deals with artists and songwriters. Produces 25 singles and 6 albums/year. Fee derived from outright fee from songwriter/artist or record company.
How to Contact: Call first about your interest. Prefers 7½ ips reel-to-reel with 4-8 songs on demo. SASE. Reports in 2 weeks.
Music: C&W, gospel and Spanish. Recently produced *Always Late*, by Lennie Bowman (C&W LP, Snapp Records); *I Don't Want to Cry*, by Carol Roman (C&W LP, LRJ Records); and *Helpless*, by Ronnie Smith (C&W LP, Little Ritchie Records).

PAUL JOHNSON PRODUCTIONS, Box 552, Woodland Hills CA 91365. (213)703-6707. Production Assistant: Cheryl Wilks. Record producer and music publisher (Sonlife Music [ASCAP]). Deals with artists and songwriters. Produces 5 singles and 10 albums/year. Fee derived from sales royalty or outright fee from artist/songwriter or record company.
How to Contact: Submit demo tape and lyric sheet. Prefers cassette with 1-4 songs on demo. SASE. Reports in 3 weeks.
Music: Children's, choral, church/religious, easy listening, gospel, jazz, MOR, R&B, rock, soul and top 40/pop. Recently produced "You Took My Heart by Surprise," by Debby Boone (pop

ballad single, Warner/Curb Records); "Double Shot of My Baby's Love," by Rick Dees (rock 'n' roll single, Mushroom Records); and "Heavenly," by Billy Preston (gospel single, Myrrh Records).

K.G.W. PRODUCTIONS, INC., 18945 Livernios Ave., Detroit MI 48221. (313)491-7031. Producer: Kenneth Wilson. Record producer and music publisher (The Kenneth Gregory Wilson Publishing Company/BMI). Produces 3 singles and 6 albums/year. Fee derived from sales royalty.
How to Contact: Submit demo tape and lyric sheet. Prefers cassette with 3-5 songs on demo. SASE. Reports in 1 month.
Music: Church/religious, classical and gospel. Recently produced *Behold the Man*, by Greater (gospel LP, Praise Records); *Prepare to Meet Him*, by Grace Temple (classical LP, Praise Records); *Save Us Lord*, by Mighty Voices of Lighting (gospel LP, Praise Records); and "Revival," by G.G.T. Glee Club Choir (gospel single, Praise Records). Other artists include Celestial Voices Choir and Saved.

BOB KARCY PRODUCTIONS, 437 W. 16th St., New York NY 10011. (212)989-1989. President: Bob Karcy. Vice President: Jack Arel. Record producer, music publisher and management firm. Works with artists, songwriters, publishers and record companies. Produces 11-30 singles and 3-8 albums/year. Fee derived from "negotiable package."
How to Contact: Query or submit demo tape and lead sheet. "No interview without prior appointment." Prefers cassette with 1-6 songs on demo. SASE. Reports in 3 weeks.
Music: Dance, easy listening, MOR, rock (all except hard, acid and punk), and top 40/pop. Recently produced "Melody Lady," by Sunshine (top 40 single, Carrere Records); "Spimbi Theme," by Julie Jacobs (top 40/disco single, Phillips Records); and "Magician," by Royal Flush (top 40 single, A&B Records).

KASH-NEW STAR-JEL, 133 Walton Ferry Rd., Hendersonville TN 37075. (615)824-2820. President: Clyde Beavers. Record producer, music publisher and studio. Deals with artists and songwriters. Fee derived from sales royalty.
How to Contact: Call or write first about your interest, then submit demo tape and lyric sheet. Prefers 7½ ips reel-to-reel or cassette with 1-3 songs on demo. SASE.
Music: Bluegrass; children's; choral; church/religious; C&W; easy listening; folk; and gospel.

KAT FAMILY PRODUCTIONS, 5775 Peachtree Dunwoody Rd., NE, Suite B-130, Atlanta GA 30342. (404)252-660. President: Joel A. Katz. Vice President: Joel A. Cherry. Record producer and music publisher (Kat Family Music Company/BMI). Estab. 1979. Fee derived by sales royalty.
How to Contact: Submit demo tape and lyric sheet. Prefers cassette with 5-10 songs on demo. SASE. Reports in 1 month.
Music: Rock, top 40/pop and contemporary gospel. Recently produced *Teddy Baker and Friends*, by Teddy Baker (rock LP, Casablanca Records); *Darryl Kutz*, by Darryl Kutz (rock LP, Mercury Records); and *Billy Joe Royal*, by Billy Joe Royal (soft rock LP, Mercury Records). Other artists include Darts, Smashers and James Anderson.

RICK KEEFER PRODUCTIONS, Box 30186, Honolulu HI 96820. Manager: Donna-Alexa Keefer. Record producer and music publisher (Punaluu Publishing/ASCAP). Deals with artists and songwriters. Produces 15 singles and 10 albums/year. Fee derived from sales royalty, outright fee from record company or outright fee from songwriter/artist, "depending on the particulars of the project."
How to Contact: Query or submit demo tape. Prefers cassette only. SASE. Reports in 1 month.
Music: Rock, top 40/pop and R&B. Recently produced *Out of the Dark*, by Hawaii (light rock, Epic Records); *Marvin Gaye*, Marvin Gaye (R&B, Motown Records); and *Sonya*, by Sonya (rock, RCA Records). Other artists include Heart, Teazer, TKO and "new" artists.

GENE KENNEDY ENTERPRISES, INC., 2125 8th Ave., S., Nashville TN 37204. (615)383-6002. President: Gene Kennedy. Vice President: Karen Jeglum. National Promotion Director for Door Knob Records: Bobby Young. Record producer and music publisher (Chip 'N' Dale Music Publishers, Inc./ASCAP, Door Knob Music Publishing, Inc./BMI and Lodestar Music/SESAC). Deals with artists and songwriters. Produces 40-50 singles and 3-5 albums/year. Fee derived from outright fee from songwriter/artist or record company.
How to Contact: Call or write first about your interest, submit demo tape and lyric sheet or arrange for personal interview. Prefers 7½ ips reel-to-reel or cassette with up to 4 songs on demo. SASE. Reports in 6 weeks.
Music: C&W, easy listening and MOR. Recently produced "Get Me High off This Low," by Gary Goodnight (country single, Door Knob Records); "Set My Love to Music," by Jerry Wallace

Songwriter's Market Close-up

Gene Kennedy of Gene Kennedy Enterprises has gone full circle in the Nashville music scene. For six years he was a recording artist traveling with his own group. Then he entered the administrative end of the music business, promoting superstars like Conway Twitty, Loretta Lynn, Crystal Gayle, Bill Anderson and Jack Greene.

His creative ability was later put to work producing three "top 20" records for Jerry Wallace and fourteen chart records for Peggy Sue. In 1976 he started his own record company, Door Knob Records, and has produced forty-three chart records on that label. Now, once again he is a recording artist, cutting records with singer Karen Jeglum.

"Trends do not affect hit songs," says Kennedy. "I look for songs with meaningful lyrics and simple, easy-to-remember melodies. They should have a beginning, a happening and an ending."

He cites Hank Williams as a perfect example of good songwriting. "I think he was one of the best country or pop writers of our time."

The demo, he says, should have "a good clean sound whether it is one instrument and vocal or ten instruments. I prefer a decent voice and acoustic guitar or piano only demo. I'm interested in hearing words

Gene Kennedy

and melody—not a produced master. However, a lot of artists can't hear a raw piece of material and visualize what can be done with it. So, the better the demo, the better your chances are . . . but the cost should not be more than $60 per song."

The biggest mistake he believes songwriters make is not being critical enough of their songs. "Analyze them," he says. "Listen closely and see if they say something to you."

(modern country single, Door Knob Records); and "I Want to See Me in Your Eyes," by Gene Kennedy/Karen Jeglum (modern country single, Door Knob Records). Other artists include Boonie Shannon, Peggy Sue, Max Brown, Lee Sims, John France, Vonna Faye, Ernie Ashworth and Judy Sider.
Tips: "We are looking for hit songs and good talent."

BEN KERR ASSOCIATES, Box 5896, Station A, Toronto, Ontario, Canada M5W 1P3. (416)537-8749. President: Ben Kerr. Record producer and music publisher (Chaser for the Blues Music). Deals with artists and songwriters. Produces 4 singles/year. Fee negotiable.
How to Contact: "Write first and tell me about yourself." Prefers 7½ ips reel-to-reel or cassette with maximum 4 songs on demo. SAE and International Reply Coupons. Reports in 1 month.
Music: C&W, easy listening, folk and MOR. Recently produced "Distilled Water," "Honky-Tonk-Ville," "The Boston Marathon," "Nancy & Gayle," by Running Ben Kerr (country, Runathon Records); and "Fire on One End (A Fool on the Other)," and "Joanne My Joanne," by Running Ben Kerr (country/MOR, Emphysema Records).

KEYNOTE PRODUCTIONS, Box 4185, Youngstown OH 44515. (216)793-7295. Executive Producer: Richard Hahn. Record producer and music publisher (Al-Kris Music/BMI). Deals with artists and songwriters. Produces 5 singles and 2 albums/year. Fee derived from sales royalty or outright fee from songwriter/artist.

How to Contact: Submit demo tape and *neat* lyric sheet. Prefers cassette with 3-5 songs on demo. SASE. Reports in 3 weeks.

Music: C&W, gospel, MOR and top 40/pop. Recently produced "Here Come the Browns," by Kardiak Kids (MOR single, Keynote Records); "Help Me I'm Falling," by Kirsti Manna (MOR single, Genuine Records); and "Teach Me Lovely Lady," by Jim Stack (C&W single, Peppermint Records). Other artists include Phil Hickman.

Tips: "The artist or writer should be willing to compromise on creative decisions by the producer to achieve the best possible product."

KIDERIAN RECORDS PRODUCTIONS, 4926 W. Gunnison, Chicago IL 60630. (312)545-0861. President: Raymond Peck. Record producer. Deals with artists and songwriters. Fee derived from sales royalty and outright fee from record company.

How to Contact: Submit demo tape and lyric sheet. Prefers cassette with 4-6 songs on demo. SASE. Reports in 1 month.

Music: Blues, C&W, dance, MOR, new wave, power pop, R&B, hard rock, soul, and top 40/pop. Recently produced "Hoochie Goochie," by Curly (R&B, Newbary Records); "Lisa," by Paul (rock, Newbary Records); "Summer," by Blaze (MOR, Kiderian Records); "Television," The 80's (new wave, Sonic Wave Records); and "Since There's a Chance," by Lucy Mahalek (MOR, Chrysann Records). Other artists include Boyz and Mammoth.

KING AND MOORE PRODUCTIONS, INC., Box 10273, Chicago IL 60610. (312)944-1125. Vice President Marketing/A&R: Ernest L. Miller. Record producer and music publisher (King and Moore Music). Estab. 1979. Deals with artists and songwriters. Produces 1 single and 4 albums/year. Fee derived from sales royalty, or outright fee from songwriter/artist or record company.

How to Contact: Submit demo tape and lyric sheet. Prefers 7½ ips reel-to-reel or cassette with 2-4 songs on demo. SASE. Reports in 3 weeks.

Music: Blues, easy listening, gospel, jazz, R&B, rock, soul and top 40/pop. Recently produced *It's About Time*, by Fantasie (A/C LP, X.K.R III Records).

KING HENRY PRODUCTION, 1855 Fairview Ave., Easton PA 18042. (215)258-4461. President: Henry Casella. Record producer and music publisher (King Henry Music/BMI). Deals with artists and songwriters. Produces 2-4 singles and 2-3 albums/year. Fee derived from sales royalty or outright fee from songwriter/artist.

How to Contact: Submit demo tape and lead sheet. Prefers cassette with 2-4 songs on demo. SASE. Reports in 1 month.

Music: Bluegrass, C&W, dance, easy listening, MOR, and top 40/pop. Recently produced "The Girl in a Swing," by King Henry (MOR, KHP Records); "Allegheny Girl," by Kathy Fleuck (MOR, Swayze Records); and "Making It Our Way," by The American Show Band (MOR country, KHP Records).

Tips: "A good song can stand on its own merits—not on an elaborate production. A good song should be creative and easily remembered."

FREDDIE KOBER PRODUCTIONS, Box 11967, Houston TX 77016. (713)987-2273. President: Freddie Kober. Record producer and music publisher (Anode Music/BMI). Deals with songwriters. Produces 2 singles/year. Fee derived from sales royalty.

How to Contact: Submit demo tape and lyric sheet. Prefers cassette with 1-3 songs on demo. SASE. Reports in 2 weeks.

Music: Gospel and soul. Recently produced "That Means So Much to Me," by Mel Starr (love ballad single, Freko Records); "Shake the Funk Out of It," by Contago'us (disco single, Freko Records); and "My Baby Can," by M. Starr (disco single, Freko Records).

JOHN KOENIG, INC., Box 2628, Los Angeles CA 90028. Contact: Audition Department. Record producer and music publisher (Contemporary Music/BMI and Composers Music/ASCAP). Deals with artists and songwriters. Produces 8-12 albums/year. Fee derived from sales royalty.

How to Contact: Submit demo tape and lyric sheet. Prefers cassette with 1-4 songs on demo. SASE. "We receive many requests and can't guarantee an audition date."

Music: Jazz (fusion), R&B, soul and top 40/pop. Recently produced *Rain Forest*, by Jay Hoggard (jazz fusion LP, Contemporary Records); *Mistral*, by Freddie Hubbard (jazz fusion LP, Toshiba Records); and *Cables' Vision*, by George Cables (jazz fusion LP, Contemporary Records). Other artists include Chico Freeman, Peter Erskine.

Tips: "Try not to be too self indulgent. Except for a few extraordinary cases, material is of greater interest if it is not *too* personal and does have general appeal."

ROBERT R. KOVACH, Drawer 1967, Warner Robins GA 31099. (912)922-1955. Producer: Robert R. Kovach. Record producer. Deals with artists and songwriters. Produces 2 singles/year. Fee derived from sales royalty, or outright fee from songwriter/artist or record company.
How to Contact: Submit demo tape and lyric sheet. Prefers 7½ ips reel-to-reel or cassette with 3-5 songs on demo. SASE. Reports in 1 month.
Music: C&W, easy listening, R&B, rock, soul and top 40/pop. Recently produced "Easy on Your Feet," by Justice (easy listening, Sacramouche Records). Other artists include Justice with Theresa Queen of the Drums and Napoleon Starke.

KROPOTKIN MUSIC, Box 130, Huntington NY 11743. (516)261-1162. Contact: "Honest" Tom. Record producer. Deals with artists and songwriters. Produces 5 albums/year. Fee "varies in each case."
How to Contact: Write first about your interest. Prefers cassette with 1-4 songs on demo. SASE. Reports in 3 weeks.
Music: Bluegrass, blues, C&W, folk, R&B. Recently produced "Live in New York," by Mississippi Fred McDowell (blues, Blue Labor Records); "Blue Dobro," by Honest Tom Pomposello (blues, Dobro Records); and "Muscle Guys," by Barbie Shortell (C&W, Cream Puff Records).

L.A. TRAX, INC., 8033 Sunset Blvd., Suite #1010, Los Angeles CA 90046. (213)852-1980. Contact: Joe Klein. Record producer (H.S. Music Co./ASCAP). Produces 2 singles and 1 album/year. Deals with artists and songwriters. Fee derived from sales royalty.
How to Contact: Call first about your interest. Prefers cassette with 2-6 songs on demo. Does not return unsolicited work. Reports in 2 weeks.
Music: MOR, rock, and top 40/pop. Recently produced *Sunset Bombers*, by Sunset Bombers (new wave, Ariola Records); "No One's Ever Seen This Side of Me," by Patty Weaver (MOR, RE/SE Records); and "Another Island," by Arthur Wayne (pop, Casablanca Records). Other artists include Dwight Twilley.

LAKE COUNTRY MUSIC, Box 88, Decatur TX 76234. (817)627-2128. President: Danny Wood. Record producer and music publisher (Lake Country Music). Deals with artists and songwriters. Produces 5 singles/year. Fee derived from sales royalty.
How to Contact: Write first about your interest. Prefers 7½ ips reel-to-reel with 1-4 songs on demo. Does not return unsolicited material. Reports in 1 month.
Music: Bluegrass and C&W. Artists include Larry Quinten, Lake Country Five.

LAS VEGAS RECORDING STUDIO, INC., Terry Richards Productions, 3977 Vegas Valley Dr., Las Vegas NV 89121. (702)457-4365. Vice President: Hank Castro. President/Producer: Terry Richards. Record producer, music publisher, management firm and record company. Deals with artists and songwriters. Fee derived from sales royalty, outright fee from record company, or outright fee from songwriter/artist. "We do not charge songwriters for their demos, but we do ask for publishing if we place the material."
How to Contact: Arrange personal interview, submit demo tape or submit demo tape and lead sheet. Include lyric sheet. Prefers reel-to-reel or cassette. SASE. Reports as soon as possible.
Music: Bluegrass, blues, church/religious, C&W, disco, easy listening, folk, gospel, jazz, MOR, progressive, rock, soul, top 40/pop, and instrumental. Recently produced Ronnie Fuller for ECR Records; Joy Britton/ECR Records; JoAnna Neal/ECR Records; and Terry Richards/ECR Records.

LEGEND ENTERTAINMENT SERVICES, Box 1414, Vicksburg MS 39180. (601)638-5622. President: Robert Garner. Record producer and music publisher (Unicorn Publishing Co.), manager and booking agent. Deals with artists and songwriters. Produces 6-10 singles and 2-6 albums/year. Fee derived from sales royalty.
How to Contact: Write first about your interest. "Include bio, goals and photo." Prefers 7½ reel-to-reel or cassette with 2-4 songs on demo. SASE. Reports in 1 month.
Music: Bluegrass, church/religious, C&W, folk, gospel and MOR. Recently produced "Orange Blossom Special," by McCall's Creek (bluegrass, Legend Records); "Phantom of the Trace," by Reunion (folk, Legend Records); and "Woman's Just A Woman," by Karen Preston (C&W, Legend Records). Other artists include Sherman Dillon and others.

PAUL LEKA PRODUCTION, 1122 Main St., Bridgeport CT 06604. (203)366-9160. President/Producer: Paul Leka. Record producer. Deals with artists. Fee derived from sales royalty.
How to Contact: Submit demo tape and lyric sheet. Prefers cassette with maximum 3 songs on demo. SASE. Reports in 1 month.
Music: Dance, gospel, MOR, R&B, hard rock, soul, and top 40/pop. Recently produced *Lori*

Lieberman, by Lori Lieberman (top 40/MOR, Millennium Records); and "Hearts on Fire," by Randle Chowning (country rock/top 40, A&M Records). Other artists include Angela Clemmons, Michael Brown, and Janice Dempsey (Epic Records).

LEMON SQUARE PRODUCTIONS, Box 31819, Dallas TX 75231. (214)690-8874. Producer: The General. Record producer. Deals with artists and songwriters. Fee derived from sales royalty.
How to Contact: Query or arrange personal interview. Prefers 7½ ips reel-to-reel with 2-4 songs on demo. Include lyric or lead sheet. SASE. Reports in 1 month.
Music: Church/religious, C&W, and gospel. Recently produced "Coffee Cups & Cowboys," by the Brooks Brothers (with their almost famous band); "I'd LIke to Fall in Love With You," "When Your'e Looking For Love" and "Every Now & Then," by DeWayne Bowman (C&W, Yatahey Records); "Memories of a Wasted Past," by Dick Hammonds (C&W, Yatahey Records); "Barstool Cowboy," by George Freeman (C&W, Yatahey Records) and "Ain't Never Been in Love," by Shirley Townley (C&W, Yatahey Records).

LEONARD PRODUCTIONS, INC., 2241 Valwood Pkwy., Dallas TX 75234. (214)241-0254. Record producer and music publisher. Deals with artists and songwriters. Fee derived by sales royalty.
How to Contact: Write first about your interest. Prefers cassette. SASE. Reports in 2 weeks.
Music: C&W, and top 40/pop.

ERV LEWIS, Box 218, Wellman Heights, Johnsonville SC 29555. (803)386-2600. President: Erv Lewis. Record producer and music publisher (Herald Association, Inc.). Deals with artists and songwriters. Produces 3-4 singles and 8-10 albums/year. Fee derived from sales royalty or outright fee from songwriter/artist or record company.
How to Contact: Submit demo tape and lyric sheet. Prefers cassette with 4-6 songs on demo. SASE. Reports in 2 months.
Music: Children's, choral, church/religious and gospel. Recently produced It's Not Too Late, by Judith Friday (gospel LP, Herald Records); *Only Jesus*, by Donna Stephenson (gospel LP, Herald Records); and *Covenant Man*, by Lewis Moore (contemporary gospel LP, Klesis Records).
Tips: "I am interested in all good religious material. Please send only material that is well-written and reflects a study of the current market."

MIKE LEWIS/STUART WIENER ENTERPRISES, LTD., 806 Oaklawn Ave., Cranston RI 02920. (401)944-9008. President: Mike Lewis. Vice President: Stuart Wiener. Record producer, music publisher and management firm. Deals with artists and songwriters. Produced 4 singles and 3 albums in 1978; plans 5 singles and 4 albums in 1979, 6 singles and 6 albums in 1980. Fee derived from sales royalty.
How to Contact: Submit demo tape and lead sheet. Prefers 7½ ips quarter-track reel-to-reel with 1-8 songs on tape. SASE. Reports in 3 weeks.
Music: Easy listening, folk, MOR, progressive, rock, soul, and top 40/pop. Recently produced *A Painting*, by Neal Fox (MOR LP, RCA Records); *Rhythm*, by Rhythm (R&B LP, RCA Records); and *Ken Lyon and Tombstone*, by Ken Lyon and Tombstone (progressive LP, Columbia Records).

LIFESINGER PRODUCTIONS, Box 23333, Nashville TN 37202. (615)329-2278. President: Bobby Fischer. Record producer and music publisher (Bobby Fischer Music/ASCAP). Estab. 1979. Deals with artists and songwriters. Produces 20 singles and 4 albums/year. Fee derived from incoming royalties.
How to Contact: Submit demo tape and lyric sheet. Prefers cassette with 2-3 songs on demo. SASE. Reports "when possible."
Music: C&W. Recently produced "Cheater's Last Chance," by Larry Riley (country single, F&L Records); "Let the Little Bird Fly," by Dottsy (country single, Tanglewood Records); and "The Man on Page 602," by Zoot Fenster (country single, Antique Records). Other artists include Chris Blake, Ronnie Joe Friend, Roy Lee Jarrett.

LITTLE GIANT ENTERPRISES, Box 205, White Lake NY 12786. (914)583-4471. President: Mickey Barnett. Record producer and music publisher (Karjan Music/SESAC). Deals with artists and songwriters. Produces 6 singles and 10 albums/year. Fee derived from sales royalty.
How to Contact: Submit demo tape and lyric sheet. Prefers cassette with 3 songs maximum on demo. SASE. Reports in 3 weeks.
Music: C&W and MOR. Recently produced "Free as the Wind," by Dan Quinn (C&W single, Killer Records); "Almost Alive," by Tom and Jay (Little Rock single, Killer Records); and "Dick Wells Sings Dick Haymes," by Dick Wells (MOR LP, Little Giant Records); and "Doing It Again," by The Mighty Quinn/Killer Records. Other artists include The Third Edition, Mickey Barnett, Bobby Gold.

LLOYD AND LLOYD MUSIC, Box 209, 102 Burbank Dr. A, Toledo OH 43695. (419)535-1624. President: Jimmy Lloyd Jr. Record producer and music publisher. Estab. 1979. Deals with artists and songwriters. Produces 20 singles and 3 albums/year. Fee derived from sales royalty.
How to Contact: Submit demo tape and lyric sheet. Prefers 7½ ips reel-to-reel, cassette or demo record with 2-3 songs on demo. SASE. Reports in 2 weeks.
Music: R&B and top 40/pop. Recently produced *My Love*, by La Que (top 40 single and LP, Future Shock Records); *This Ole Heart*, by Back Lash (top 40 single and LP, Walking Tall Records); *Love Projection*, by Unique Pleasure (R&B single and LP, label pending); and *Stay Darling Stay*, by Raymond Alexander (top 40 single and LP, Fast Flight Records). Other artists include Anna McCance most other artists for Walking Tall Records and Productions.

MICK LLOYD PRODUCTIONS, 1014 16th Ave., S., Nashville TN 37212. (615)244-1630. President: Mick Lloyd. Director of Publishing: Robin Eichel. Record producer, music publisher (Kelly & Lloyd/ASCAP, Jerri Mick/BMI and Mick Lloyd/SESAC) and record company. Deals with artists and songwriters. Fee derived from sales royalty.
How to Contact: Call first about your interest. Prefers ½-track reel-to-reel or cassette with 1 song on demo. SASE. Reports in 3 weeks.
Music: C&W, easy listening, folk, gospel, MOR, progressive, and top 40/pop. Recently produced *Nostalgia*, by the Nashville Rhythm Section (C&W/MOR LP, Carrousel Records/RCA Records, Canada); *Mick Lloyd*, by Mick Lloyd (C&W/MOR LP, Carrousel Records/RCA Records, Canada); *De De!*, by De De Upchurch (C&W/MOR LP, Intercord Records, German); and "Fallin' for You," by Jerri Kelly. Other artists include Arleen Harden, The Stockard Band and Byron Gallimore.

LOVELIGHT PRODUCTIONS, Box 3013, Davenport IA 52808. (319)324-2133. Producer/Arranger: Gary Unger. Record producer. Deals with artists and songwriters. Produces 3 singles and 7 albums/year. Fee derived from outright fee from artist/songwriter or record company.
How to Contact: Submit demo tape and lyric sheet. Prefers 7½ ips reel-to-reel or cassette with 2-10 songs on demo. SASE. Reports in 2 months.
Music: Church/religious and country rock. Recently produced "Girl," by Lambkin (country rock, ECI, Lovelight, BCA, Sonway Records International, Aic, Artistic, Groove Sound, and Sundin Groove II and Vira Reindo). Co-producer with Sundi Industries, Inc. of "Goodnight Jackie," by Gary Unger.
Tips: "We will co-produce sessions."

LOWER MAINLAND TECHNOLOGICAL ARTS SOCIETY, Box 4672, Vancouver, British Columbia, Canada V6B 4A1. (604)430-4224. President: Klaus Kasburg. Record producer. Deals with artists and songwriters. Fee derived from sales royalty or outright fee from songwriter/artist or record company.
How to Contact: Submit demo tape and lyric sheet. Prefers 7½ ips reel-to-reel or cassette as demo. Does not return unsolicited material. Reports in 2 weeks.
Music: Classical, C&W, easy listening, jazz, MOR, progressive, rock, top 40/pop and electronic.

HAROLD LUICK & ASSOCIATES, 110 Garfield St., Box B, Carlisle IA 50047. (515)989-3679. Record producer and music publisher. Deals with artists and songwriters. Produces 30 singles and 12 albums/year. Fee derived from sales royalty, outright fee from artist/songwriter or record company, and from retainer fees.
How to Contact: Call or write first about your interest then submit demo tape and lyric sheet. Prefers cassette with songs on demo. 3-5 songs on demo. SASE. Reports in 3 weeks.
Music: Bluegrass, C&W, dance-oriented, easy listening, gospel, MOR, R&B, rock and top 40/pop. Recently produced *Brand of a Country Man*, by Darrell C. Thomas (country LP, Ozark Opry Records); "House of Memories," by Bob Schirmer (country single, RDS Records); "What You Do to Me," by Linda Cooper (pop single, LC Records); and *Proud to be a Mother*, by June Murphy (country LP, Jay/Bee Records). Other artists include Ray Faubus, Kenny Hofer Orchestra.
Tips: "Producers are becoming more and more independent (this means not having to rely on a big record company) and they can be more creative. This means they have use for more song material than ever before. Keep writing commercial material that has possibilities, let the producer work the 'probabilities.' Don't 'hype' a producer about your song. This is one of the biggest turnoffs that amateurs use."

AL McKAY, 6430 Sunset Blvd., Suite 1104, Hollywood CA 90028. (213)461-2988. Manager: Zachary Glickman. Record producer. Deals with artists and songwriters.
How to Contact: Submit demo tape and lyric sheet. Prefers cassette. SASE. Reports in 1 month.
Music: Church/religious, dance-oriented, easy listening, gospel, R&B, soul and top 40/pop. Re-

cently produced "Cloudburst," by the Mighty Clouds of Joy (single, Myrrh Records); "Out of the Woods," by Ren Woods (single, ARC Records); and "Boogie Wonderland," by Earth Wind and Fire (single, ARC Records).

LEE MAGID PRODUCTIONS, Box 532, Malibu CA 90265. (213)858-7282. President: Lee Magid. Record producer and music publisher (Alexis Music, Inc./ASCAP, Marvelle Music Co./BMI). Deals with artists, songwriters and producers. Produces 12 singles and 6 albums/year. Fee derived from sales royalty and "advance fee against royalties"; sometimes pays a flat outright sum.
How to Contact: Write first about your interest giving address and phone number; include SASE. Submit demo tape and lyric sheet. Prefers cassette with 3-6 songs on demo. SASE. Reports "as soon as we can after listening."
Music: Bluegrass, blues, church/religious, C&W, easy listening, folk, gospel, jazz, MOR, progressive, R&B, rock (soft), soul, instrumental and top 40/pop. Recently produced "Too Many Women," by Windstorm (R&B single, LMI Records); *From the Heart*, by Ernie Andrews (jazz R&B LP, Discovery Records); and *Rags Waldorf Live*, by R. Waldorf (rock & roll R&B, Judgement Records).
Tips: "The visual effect is just as important as the audio. An act should have theatrical as well as musical ability."

MAINLINE PRODUCTIONS, Box 902, Provo UT 84601. (801)225-4674. President: Richard D. Rees. Record producer, music publisher, concert promoter and personal management company. Deals with artists and songwriters. Fee derived from sales royalty and outright fee from record company.
How to Contact: Submit demo tape and lyric sheet; include photo. Prefers 15 ips reel-to-reel or cassette with 4-6 songs on demo. SASE. Reports in 3 weeks.
Music: C&W (crossover to pop), folk, MOR, progressive, rock, and top 40/pop. Recently produced *Dave Boshard*, by Dave Boshard, (country cross-over LP, ML Records); *Slyder*, by Slyder (hard rock LP, ML Records); and *Tyrant*, by Tyrant (hard rock LP, Mainline Records). Other artists include Rick Jackson and Moon Dog.

MAINROADS PRODUCTIONS, INC., 100 Huntley St., Toronto, Ontario, Canada M4Y 2L1. (416)961-8001. Manager: Bruce W. Stacey. Record producer, music publisher (Mainroads Publishing/CAPAC, Bruce W. Stacey Publishing/PRO). Deals with artists and songwriters. Produces 3 singles and 6 albums/year. Fee derived from sales royalty.
How to Contact: Write first about your interest. Prefers cassette with 3 songs on demo. SASE. Reports in 1 month.
Music: Children's, choral, church/religious and gospel. Recently produced *Only The Children Know*, by Stacey (contemporary gospel LP, Mainroads Records); *Love Line*, by Ginny Ambrose Bridle (contemporary gospel LP, Mainroads Records); and *I Found A New World*, by Glen Rutledge (MOR gospel LP, Mainroads Records). Other artists include Reynold Rutledge, Norma Jean Mainse, Circle Square Children, and 100 Huntley Street Regular Artists.

MAN QUIN, Box 2388, Toluca Lake CA 91602. (213)985-8284. Contact: Quint Benedetti or Mannie Rodriquez. Deals with artists, songwriters and writers of musical comedy. Fee derived from sales royalty.
How to Contact: Submit demo tape and lyric sheet. Prefers cassette with 2-6 songs on demo. SASE. Reports in 1 month.
Music: Broadway, children's, C&W, novelty, and musical comedy. Recently produced *Topsy or Sorry About That Harriett*, by the original cast (musical comedy LP, Quinto Records); and *Lavendar Lady*, by Agnes Moorehead and the original cast (musical comedy LP, Crissy Records).

MARIER MUSIC, 2 E. Oak St., Chicago IL 60611. (312)951-0246. Contact: Donn Marier. Record producer and music publisher (Denture Whistle Music/BMI) and Substantial Music/ASCAP). Deals with artists and songwriters. Produces 6-10 singles and 2-4 albums/year. Fee derived from sales royalty or outright fee from record company.
How to Contact: Write or call first about your interest, submit demo tape and lyric sheet. Prefers 7½ ips reel-to-reel or cassette with 3-6 songs on demo. SASE. Reports in 3 weeks.
Music: Children's, classical, C&W, jazz, MOR, progressive, R&B, rock, soul a, d top 40/pop. Recently produced "Sex & Society" and "I Like You," by Citizen (rock single, Ovation Records); and "Cha-Cha Charming," by The Burnt Flesh Singers (rock/new wave single, Wekeepno Records).

MARLO RECORD CO., Rt. 1, Box 49, Utica NY 13502. (315)724-0895. Manager: Floyd Ketchum. Record producer and music publisher (Dobro Publishing). Deals with artists. Produces 2 albums/year. Fee derived for sales royalty.

How to Contact: Submit demo tape and lyric sheet. Prefers 7½ or 3½ ips reel-to-reel, cassette or 8-track with any number of songs on demo. "You may telephone or write 3 weeks after I receive the tapes." SASE. Reports in 1 month.
Music: Bluegrass, children's, church/religious, C&W, gospel and Irish ballads. Recently produced *Country Brothers,* by the Country Brothers (country/gospel, Music City Records) and "Marlo the Dobro Man," by Slim Pikins (comedy song about Tex Ritter, Marlo Records).

MARULLO PRODUCTIONS, 1121 Market St.; Galveston TX 77550. President: A.W. Marullo Sr. Vice President: A.W. Marullo Jr. Record producer and music publisher. Deals with artists, songwriters and master owners. Produces 4-7 singles/year. Fee derived from sales royalty.
How to Contact: Submit demo tape. Prefers 7½ ips reel-to-reel, cassette or demo dub with 12 songs maximum on demo. SASE. Reports in 1 month.
Music: C&W; dance; rock; soul; and top 40/pop.
Tips: "You record it, we will lease it. Consultations and negotiations to place your masters with the major record companies and the music publishers."

MASTER AUDIO, INC., 1227 Spring St. NW, Atlanta GA 30309. (404)875-1440. President: Bob Richardson. Record producer and music publisher. Deals with artists and songwriters. Fee derived from sales royalty.
How to Contact: Arrange personal interview or submit demo tape and lead sheet. Prefers cassette with 2-5 songs on demo. SASE. Reports in 1 month.
Music: Dance, easy listening, gospel (traditional or contemporary), MOR, rock, and top 40/pop. Recently produced *Troy Ramey & Soul Searchers,* by Troy Ramey and the Soul Searchers (gospel LP, Nashboro Records); and *Ivory Roads,* by Mac Frampton (MOR/easy listening LP, Triumvirate Records).

MASTERSOURCE PRODUCTIONS, 440 N. Mayfield, Chicago IL 60644. (312)921-1446. Executive Producer: Charles Thomas. Music producer. Assists artists and songwriters. Produces 8-12 albums/year. Fee is negotiable. "We desire long-term artist relationships."
How to Contact: Query or submit demo tape and lyric or lead sheet. Prefers cassette with 1-5 songs on demo. Does not return unsolicited material. Reports in 2 weeks.
Music: POP, rock, country, jazz and Christian rock. Recently produced "Phasin' In," by Maurice Natale (commercial Jazz, Angelaco Records); "Constant Companion," by Promise (Christian Rock, Benson Records); "This Might Be the Night," by Steve Padgett (POP Rock, MSP Records). Other artists include Relayer and Ronnii Tog.

MASTERVIEW MUSIC PUBLISHING CORP., Ridge Rd. and Butler Lane, Perkasie PA 18944. (215)257-9616. General Manager: Thomas Fausto. President: John Wolf. Record producer, music publisher (Masterview Music/BMI), record company and management firm. Deals with artists and songwriters. Produces 12 singles and 3-4 albums/year. Fee derived from sales royalty.
How to Contact: Arrange personal interview or submit demo tape and lead sheet. Prefers 7½ or 15 ips reel-to-reel with 2-6 songs on demo. SASE. Reports in 2 weeks.
Music: Disco, folk, gospel, and rock. Recently produced "Up North to Bluegrass," by Country Boys (bluegrass); "I Am Happen," by El Botteon (Rheta Records) and "Footprints," by Charles Newman (religious single, Masterview Records). Other artists include Sugarcane.

MAX PROMOTIONS, Box 7386, Beaumont TX 77706. (713)866-6726. Contact: R.F. Bianco. Record producer. Deals with artists and songwriters. Produces 2 singles and 1 album/year. Fee derived from sales royalty.
How to Contact: Submit demo tape and lyric sheet. Prefers cassette with 3 songs minimum on demo. SASE. Reports in 1 month.
Music: C&W (traditional) and gospel (traditional). Recently produced "Tainted Rose" and "I Hear Music," by Mary Nell (country singles, Max Records); and *Standing By,* by Darwin Hawkins (gospel LP, Max Records). Other artists include Patsy Marshall, Jim Busby and Tim Meehan.

MBA PRODUCTIONS, 8914 Georgian Dr., Austin TX 78753. (512)836-3201. General Manager: Shirley Montgomery. Record Producer and music publisher. Deals with artists and songwriters. Fee derived from sales royalty.
How to Contact: Submit demo tape and lyric sheet. Prefers 7½ ips reel-to-reel with 1-3 songs on demo. SASE. Reports in 2 weeks.
Music: All types. Recently produced "The Shootist," by Eli Worden (C&W, Darva Records); "Country Girl," by Nona Stacey (C&W, Darva Records); and "Times Are Changing," by Steve Douglas (C&W, Darva Records). Other artists include Bill Henderson (C&W), Sue Creech (C&W), Wilson Family (gospel), Tommy Hodges (C&W) and Grassfire (bluegrass).

MCP/DAVISOUND, (formerly Mother Cleo Productions/Davisound), Bypass 76/Sunset, Box 521, Newberry SC 29108. (803)276-0639. Studio Manager: Polly Davis. Producer/Director: Hayne Davis. Record producer, music publisher and production company. Deals with artists and songwriters. Produces 5-6 singles and 2-3 albums/year. Fee derived from sales royalty, outright fee from record company, or outright fee from songwriter/artist. Charges for some services: "In special cases, where the songwriter/artist is simply booking our studio facilities, there is a charge. Also, if an artist/writer wishes us to produce him with himself as co-producer, we share profits on a 50/50 basis but at the same time, expenses of production are also shared 50/50."
How to Contact: Submit demo tape. Prefers 7½ ips reel-to-reel or cassette with 4-8 songs on demo. SASE. Reports in 2 weeks.
Music: C&W (contemporary), dance, easy listening, MOR, rock (all), and top 40/pop (all). Recently produced "Sheila," by James Meadows (C&W/rock single, Mother Cleo Records); "Too Far Gone," by Curt Bradford (C&W/rock single, Mother Cleo Records); and "Brainwasher," by J. Teal Band (rock single, Mother Cleo Records). Other artists include Raw Material and Sugar & Spice.

MERCANTILE PRODUCTIONS, Box 2271, Palm Springs CA 92263. (714)320-4848. President: Kent Fox. Record producer and music publisher (Mercantile Music/BMI and Blueford Music/ASCAP). Deals with artists and songwriters. Fee derived from sales royalty.
How to Contact: Submit demo tape and lyric sheet. Prefers cassette with 3-5 songs on demo. SASE. Reports in 1 month.
Music: C&W, easy listening and top 40/pop. Recently produced "The 8 They Left Behind," "Wild Women & Rum," and "Little White Lies."

MIGHTY "T" PRODUCTIONS, 441 S. Beverly Dr., #6, Beverly Hills CA 90212. (213)855-0525. Contact: Kent Washburn. Record producer and music publisher (Deuet-Hart Publishing/BMI and Angelstream Music/ASCAP). Estab. 1980. Deals with artists and songwriters. Produces 3 singles and 3 albums/year. Fee derived from sales royalty.
How to Contact: Submit demo tape and lyric sheet. Prefers cassette with 3-5 songs on demo. SASE. Reports in 1 month.
Music: Gospel, R&B, rock and soul. Recently produced *Jill & Deborah*, by Jill and Deborah (gospel LP, NDCB Records); *Generations*, by Nicholas (black gospel LP, Spirit Records); and *Free Love*, by Free Love (R&B LP, Emkay Records).

JAY MILLER PRODUCTIONS, 413 N. Parkerson Ave., Crowley LA 70526. (318)783-1601. Owner: Jay Miller. Manager: Mark Miller. Record producer and music publisher. Deals with artists and songwriters. Produced 11 albums and 23 singles in 1980. Fee derived from sales royalty.
How to Contact: Arrange personal interview or submit demo tape. Prefers 7½ ips reel-to-reel or cassette for audition. SASE. Reports in 1 month.
Music: Blues, C&W, Cajun, disco, folk, gospel, MOR, rock, top 40/pop, and comedy. Recently produced "Buckwheat Zydeco," "Take It Easy Baby," by Buckwheat; "Phil Menard and the Louisiana Travelers," "Fernest and The Thunders," "Hadly Castile Avec Son Violon Cajun," and "Sincerely," by Warren Storm.
Tips: "Inquires are invited."

MILLS AND MILLS MUSIC, 3364 Sasquehanna Rd, Dresher PA 19025. (215)643-2563. Vice President: Sheila Adkins. Record producer and music publisher. Deals with artists and songwriters. Produces 12 singles and 6 albums/year. Fee derived from sales royalty but "we are willing to negotiate."
How to Contact: Query, arrange personal interview, or submit demo tape and lead sheet. Prefers cassette. "Mail tapes certified mail, with return receipt, so you can be sure that we receive the material." SASE. Will return unsolicited material "if requested." Reports in 1 week.
Music: Blues; C&W; dance; easy listening; gospel; jazz; MOR; progressive; rock; soul; and top 40/pop. Recently produced *All the Way Live*, by Kalyan (reggae LP, RCA Records).

MIMOSA RECORDS PRODUCTIONS, 9315 Carmichael Dr., La Mesa CA 92041. (714)464-0910. Producer: Stephen C. LaVere. Record producer and music publisher. Deals with artists. Fee derived from sales royalty.
How to Contact: Query or submit demo tape and lead sheet. Prefers 7½ ips reel-to-reel. SASE. Reports in 1 month.
Music: Blues; folk; gospel; jazz; and rock. Recently produced "Goin' Away Baby," by Joe Hill Louis (blues single, Mimosa Records); *It's Too Bad*, by Joe Willie Wilkins (blues LP, Adamo Records); and "Rock a Little Baby," by Harmonica Frank (rock 'n roll single, Mimosa Records). Other artists include San Diego Blues & Black Music Heritage Festival, and Jack Teagarden (Mimosa Records).

MONSTER PRODUCTIONS, INC., 1919 Cobden Rd., Philadelphia PA 19118. (215)887-8371. President: John Davis. Record producer and music publisher. Estab. 1978. Deals with artists and songwriters. Fee derived from sales royalty.
How to Contact: Submit demo tape and lead sheet. Prefers cassette with 1-3 songs on demo. Does not return unsolicited material. Reports in 1 month.
Music: R&B; rock (new wave); soul; and top 40/pop. Recently produced "Love Magic," by Monster Orchestra (rock/disco, SAM/CBS Records); "Gimme Something Real," by Wardell Piper (R&B, Midsong Records); and "Back in My Life," by Joey Travolta (top 40, Midsong Records). Other artists include Ruth Waters, Collins & Collins, Jet Brown and Charo.

MONTICANA RECORDS, Box 702, Snowdon Station, Montreal, Quebec, Canada H3X 3X8. (514)342-5200. General Manager: David P. Leonard. Record producer and music publisher (Montina Music). Deals with artists and songwriters. Fee derived from sales royalty.
How to Contact: Submit demo tape and lyric sheet. Prefers 7½ or 15 ips reel-to-reel or cassette with 1 song minimum on demo. "We're looking for quality—not quantity." Reports "as soon as possible."
Music: Bluegrass, blues, classical, C&W, dance-oriented, easy listening, gospel, MOR, progressive, R&B, rock, soul and top 40/pop.
Tips: "Obtain as much writing and recording experience as possible. Study at one of the few dozen excellent music business/recording arts and sciences schools around the US and Canada."

THE MORGAN MUSIC GROUP, Box 2388, Prescott AZ 86302. (602)445-5801. Contact: Michael D. Morgan. Record producer and music publisher (The Morgan Music Group). Estab. 1979. Deals with artists, songwriters and labels. Production fees derived from "an advance against royalties up front from either the artist or record company."
How to Contact: Submit demo tape and lyric sheet only. Prefers cassette with 3 songs on demo. "Include cover letter with past experience, photo, bio and future expectations." SASE. Reports in 1 month.
Music: C&W, jazz, rock (country) and top 40/pop (country). Recently produced *Song of the American Trucker*, by various artists (country LP and singles, Big Wheels Records); *Straw Hats and Stetsons*, by Michael Hollister Morgan (country LP, Quarter Moon Records); and *Medicine Man*, by Scott Jenkins Group (jazz, Quarter Moon Records). Other artists include Garry Greer.
Tips: "We are interested in working with artists who have a lifelong commitment to the music industry—meaning, no matter what, they will continue in the business."

JOEL W. MOSS, 11940 Woodbridge St., Studio City CA 91604. Producer/Engineer: Joel W. Moss. Record producer, music publisher, engineer, audio and video production consultant. Deals with artists and songwriters. Produces 5 singles and 5-6 albums/year. Fee derived from sales royalty or outright fee from record company.
How to Contact: Query, arrange personal interview, or submit demo tape and lead sheet. Prefers cassette with 1-4 songs on demo. "Name and address on tape box." SASE. Reports in 3 weeks.
Music: Blues (R&B), children's, classical (for application with video or animation), C&W, dance, easy listening, folk, gospel (R&B), jazz, MOR, progressive, rock, soul, and top 40/pop. Recent work: *Billy T.* (pop LP, MCA Records); "Johnny Nash" (R&B/disco single, Columbia/Epic Records); "That's Why Hollywood Loves Me," by Geno Washington (disco single, DJM Records); "L.A. Light" and "Good Timin'," by the Beach Boys (rock single, CBS Records); and "Here Comes the Night," (by the Beach Boys (disco single, CBS Records). Other artists include Bobby Hatfield and Jones (Pocket Records) and Stone Country (Amherst Records), Curt Becher; Gilberto Gil (Wea Records); Joao Gilberto (Wea Records); Lou Rawls (Epic Records); Ivan Lins (EMI Records); Alvaro Davilla and David Palmer.

MUSCADINE PRODUCTIONS, INC., 297 Bass Rd., Macon GA 31210. President: Paul Hornsby. Record producer and music publisher. Deals with artists and songwriters. Produces 4-5 albums/year. Fee derived from "advance and royalty from sales."
How to Contact: Submit demo tape and lead sheet. Prefers cassette. SASE. Reports in 1 month.
Music: Rock (hard or country); and top 40/pop. Recently produced *Volunteer Jam*, by Charlie Daniels, Willie Nelson and others (Epic Records); *Good Brothers* (RCA Records); *Cooder Browne*, by Cooder Browne (Lone Star Records); *Two Guns* (Capricorn); and *Missouri* (Polydor).

MUSIC RESOURCES INTERNATIONAL CORP., 110 W 34 St. Suite 806, New York NY 10001. (212)947-2066. President: Andy Hussakowsky. Director: A&R: Gene O'Brien. Record production company and music publisher (MRI Music). Pays standard royalties to songwriters on contract.
How to Contact: Arrange personal interview or submit demo tape and lead sheet. Prefers cassette with 1-10 songs on demo. SASE. Reports in 1 month.

Music: Dance; rock; top 40/pop; and R&B. Past hits include: "More, More, More," and "New York You Got Me Dancing," and "What's Your Name, What's Your Number," by Andrea True Connection/Buddah Records; "Jack in the Box," by David Morris/Buddah Records; "No, No, My Friend," by Devoshunn; and "Hot Shot," by Karen Young/West End Records.
Tips: "MRI has negotiated leases with Buddah, Polydor, Polygram, Casblanca, AVI and other major lables."

MUSIVERSE, 10 Music Circle S., Nashville TN 37203. (615)242-5544. Administrative Assistant: Sarah Sherrill. Executive record producer and president of production company: Charles Fach. Production company. Estab. 1979. Deals with "self-contained artist/songwriters. Contract is determined by Polygram, Inc., the parent company of Musiverse."
How to Contact: Submit demo tape. Prefers cassette with 3-10 songs on demo. SASE. Reports usually in 1 month.
Music: C&W, R&B, pop, and soul. Recently produced *As One*, by BarKays (R&B/soul, Mercury Records); *Touch*, by ConFunkShun (R&B/soul, Mercury Records); *Good Black Is Hard To Crack*, by Esther Phillips (R&B/soul, Mercury Records). Other artists include L.A Boppers, George Burns and David Oliver.
Tips: "We look for acts that have some performing experience or possibly some songs previously recorded."

MUSTEVIC SOUND RECORDS, 193-18 125th Ave., St. Albans NY 11412. (212)527-1586. Director: Steve Reid. Record producer, music publisher and jazz record label. Deals with artists. Fee derived by sales royalty.
How to Contact: Write first about your interest. Prefers cassette with 1-4 songs on demo.
Music: Jazz only. Recently produced Visions of the 3rd Eye, by the New Life Trio (jazz vocal, Mustevic Sound Records); and *Odyssey of the Oblong Square*, by Steve Reid (jazz, Mustevic Sound Records). Other artists include Charles Tyler, Master Brotherhood and New Life Orchestra.

NASHVILLE INTERNATIONAL CORPORATION, 20 Music Square W., Nashville TN 37203. (615)373-2575. President: Reggie M. Churchwell. Vice President: Ken Little. General Manager, Music Group: Neil Singor. Record producer and music publisher. Labels include, Pinto Records, Phoenix Records, Nashville International Records. Deals with artists and songwriters. Fee derived by sales royalty and outright fee from record company.
How to Contact: Write first about your interest, then submit demo tape and lyric sheet. Prefers cassette with 1-4 songs on demo. Does not return unsolicited material "unless prior contact has been made."
Music: C&W, MOR, R&B (crossover), rock (country, pop, power pop), soul (crossover), and top 40/pop. Recently produced "In the Name of Love," by Gloria Goldsmith (top 40/pop, Pinto Records); "In and Out of Love," by Joyce Everson (top 40/pop/country, Pinto Records); and "Sunday Meetin'," by Spoon River Band (pop/country, Dharma Records). Other artists include Rebbie Jackson and The Stamps.

NEW HORIZON RECORDS, 3398 Nahatan Way, Las Vegas NV 89109. (702)732-2576. President: M. Corda. Record producer and music publisher. Deals with artists and songwriters. Fee derived by sales royalty.
How to Contact: Submit demo tape and lyric sheet. Prefers cassette with 1-3 songs. Does not return unsolicited material.
Music: Blues, C&W, easy listening, and MOR. Recently produced Mickey Rooney and Jonathan Swift (MOR, New Horizon Records).

THE NEXT CITY CORP., 2162 Broadway, New York NY 10024. (212)787-1900. Vice President, A&R: Ric Browde. Record producer, music publisher and management firm. Deals with artists and songwriters. Produces 5-8 singles and 4-5 albums/year. Fee derived from sales royalty.
How to Contact: Submit demo tape. Prefers cassette. SASE. Reports in 2 weeks.
Music: Progressive, rock, new wave and pop.

NISE PRODUCTIONS, INC., 413 Cooper St., Suite 101, Camden NJ 08102. (215)276-0100. President: Michael Nise. Record producer and music publisher. Deals with artists and songwriters. Produces 10 singles and 10 albums/year. Fee derived from sales royalty.
How to Contact: Submit demo tape and lyric sheet. Prefers cassette with 1-3 songs on demo. SASE. Reports in 1 month.
Music: Children's, church/religious, C&W, dance-oriented, easy listening, folk, gospel, jazz, R&B, rock, soul and top 40/pop.

NMI RECORDS, 5500 Troost, Kansas City MO 64110. (816)361-8455. President: Eugene Gold. Record producer and music publisher (Eugene Gold Music/BMI). Deals with artists and songwriters. Produces 6 singles and 3 albums/year. Fee derived from sales royalty.
How to Contact: Call first about your interest. Prefers cassette with 4-6 songs on demo. SASE. Reports in 1 month.
Music: Church/religious, gospel, jazz, R&B and soul. Recently produced "Diamond Feather," by Bad New Band (R&B single, NMI Records); and "Glad That You Could be Here," by Dawa Ward (gospel single, 3 G's Records).

NORTH AMERICAN LITURGY RESOURCES, 10802 N. 23rd Ave., Phoenix AZ 85029. (602)864-1980. Record Producer: Paul Quinlan. Music Editor: Henry Papale. Record producer and music publisher. Deals with artists and songwriters and arrangers/conductors. Produces 10 albums/year. Fee derived from sales royalty.
How to Contact: Submit demo tape and lyric sheet. Prefers cassette with 5-12 songs on demo. SASE. Reports in 1 month.
Music: Children's, choral, church/religious, liturgical and christian rock and inspirational. Recently produced "Light of the World," by Tom Kendzia (Christian rock single, NALR Records); "By Name I Have Called You," by Rev. Carey Landry (Christian single, NALR Records); "The Time Has Come," by Pat Boone, (Christian single, NALR Records); and "Reach for the Rainbow," by Sheldon Cohen, (choral single, NALR Records). Other artists include The Dameans and Micahel Joncas.
Tips: "Be familiar with our recordings. Free catalogs and brochures are supplied on request."

NORTHERN COMFORT PRODUCTIONS, 10 Erica Ave., Toronto, Ontario, Canada M3H 3H2. (416)923-5717. President: J. Allan Vogel. Record producer and music publisher (Northern Comfort Music/CAPAC and Sacro-Iliac Music/PROCAN). Deals with artists and songwriters. Produces 8 singles and 4 albums/year. Fee derived from sales royalty.
How to Contact: Submit demo tape and lyric sheet. Prefers 7½ ips reel-to-reel or cassette with 3-5 songs on demo. SAE and International Reply Coupons. Reports in 3 weeks.
Music: Jazz, MOR, progressive, R&B, rock, soul, and top 40/pop. Recently produced "Never Gonna Leave You," by David Kosab (folk-rock, Northern Comfort Records); "Rockit Trip," by King Rockit (new wave, Attic Records); "Burned Again," by Jill Vogel (top 40).

O.T.L. PRODUCTIONS, 74 Main St., Suite 5, Maynard MA 01754. (617)897-8459. Chief Producer: David Butler. Deals with artists, songwriters, publishers and managers. Produces 4-5 singles and 2-3 albums/year. Fee determined by outright fee from record company and royalty when song/artist is recorded.
How to Contact: Arrange personal interview after submitting demo tape only. "Personal contact necessary to serious consideration. Audition live if possible." Prefers 7½ ips reel-to-reel or cassette with 3-6 song on tape. SASE. Reports in 1 month.
Music: (Disco/funk), folk, jazz, MOR, progressive, rock (country/classical), and soul. Recently produced "Gang War," by Prince Charles & the C.B. Band (funk, Pavillion Records); "All I'm Waiting For," by Anne English (pop, O.T.L. Record); and "Future Winds," by Ictus (fusion jazz, Airborne Records). Other artists include Maurice Starr and Midnite Traveler.
Tips: "Submit material that shows an awareness of the marketplace!"

OZARK OPRY RECORDS INC., Box 242, Osage Beach MO 65065. (314)348-3383. A&R/Producer: Jim Phinney. Record, jingle and commercial producer. Deals with artists and songwriters. Fee derived by sales royalty.
How to Contact: Submit demo tape and lyric sheet. Prefers 7½ ips reel-to-reel or cassette with 1-3 songs on demo. "Please include cover letter, explaining general information about material." SASE. Reports in 2-4 weeks.
Music: Bluegrass, blues, children's, church/religious, C&W, dance, easy listening, gospel, jazz, MOR, progressive, R&B, rock, soul, and top 40/pop. Recently produced "Waylon, Sing to Mama," by Darrell Thomas (country, Ozark Opry Records); "Untanglin' My Mind," by Larry Heaberlin (country, Hoedown U.S.A. Records); and "Don't Say No to Me Tonight," by Mark Sexton (pop/country, Son De Mar Records). Other artists include Robbie Wittkowski.

PANIO BROTHERS LABEL, Box 99, Montmartre, Saskatchewan, Canada, S0G 3M0. Executive Director: John Panio, Jr. Record producer. Deals with artists and songwriters. Produces 1 album/year. Fee derived from sales royalty.
How to Contact: Submit demo tape and lyric sheet or write first about your interest. Prefers 7¾ ips reel-to-reel with any number of songs on demo. SASE. Reports in 1 month.
Music: C&W, dance-oriented, easy listening and Ukrainian. Recently produced "Celebrate Sas-

katchewan," by Panio Brothers (dance music, PB Records); and "Dance Music," by Panio Brothers (dance music, PB Records).

PARASOUND, INC., 680 Beach St., Suite 414, San Francisco CA 94109. (415)673-4544. President: Bernie Krause. Vice President: Sid Goldstein. Record producer and music publisher. Deals with artists and songwriters. Produces 1-4 singles/year. Fee derived from sales royalty.
How to Contact: Submit demo tape and lead sheet. Prefers cassette with 3-6 songs on demo. SASE. Reports in 3 weeks.
Music: Folk; MOR; rock; and top 40/pop.

THE PASHA MUSIC ORG., INC., 5615 Melrose Ave., Hollywood CA 90038. (213)466-3507. Executive Director/Administrator: Ann Sumner-Davis. Record producer, music publisher and personal artist manager. Deals with artists and songwriters. Fee derived by sales royalty.
How to Contact: Write first about your interest. Prefers cassette with 3-6 songs on demo. SASE. Reports in 3 weeks.
Music: Progressive, and rock. Recently produced "21st Century Man," by Billy Thorpe (progressive rock, Elektra Records); "Excuse Me," by Devin Payne (rock, Casablanca Records); "I Surrender," by Arlan Day (Metronome Records); and "Straight," by Rod Taylor (rock, Metronome Records).

PCRL, 2364 Sherbrooke East, Montreal, Quebec, Canada H2K 1E6. (514)526-2831. Contact: Carole Risch. Record producer and music publisher (Editeurs Associes). Deals with artists. Produces 15-20 singles and 5-10 albums/year. Fee derived from sales royalty.
How to Contact: Submit demo tape and lyric sheet. Prefers 7½ ips reel-to-reel or cassette with 3-5 songs on demo. SAE and International Reply Coupons. Reports in 3 weeks.
Music: Easy listening, MOR and top 40/pop.

DAVE PELL PRODUCTIONS, Suite 224, 6362 Hollywood Blvd., Hollywood CA 90028. (213)462-5466. President: Dave Pell. Record producer and music publisher (Vestone Music/ASCAP; NADAMAS/BMI). Produces 12 singles and 20 albums/year. Estab. 1979. Deals with artists and songwriters. Fee derived by sales royalty.
How to Contact: Call first about your interest. Prefers cassette. SASE. Reports in 2 weeks.
Music: Easy listening, jazz, MOR, rock, and top 40/pop. Produced "It Must Be Him," by Vikki Carr (United Artist Records); "This Is My Life," by Shirley Bassey (United Artist Records); and "What the World Needs Now Is Love," by Tom Clay (Mowest Records). Other artists include Joe Williams & Dave Pell's Prez Conference.(jazz)

PENUMBRA PRODUCTIONS LTD., c/o Electric Lady Studios, 52 W. 8th St., New York NY 10011. (212)677-4700. Producer: Howie Leder. Record producer, music publisher and recording studio. Estab. 1978. Deals with artists and songwriters. Fee derived from sales royalty, outright fee from record company and outright fee from songwriter/artist.
How to Contact: Submit demo tape and lyric sheet, or write or call first about your interest. Prefers cassette with 3-10 songs on demo. SASE. Reports in 1 month.
Music: Blues, classical, folk, jazz, MOR, progressive, R&B, rock, soul, and top 40/pop.

POSITIVE PRODUCTIONS, Box 1405, Highland Park NJ 08904. Contact: J. Vincenzo. Record producer and music publisher. Deals with songwriters. Payment negotiable.
How to Contact: Submit demo tape and lyric sheet. Prefers 7½ ips reel-to-reel with 2-4 songs on demo. SASE. Reports in 1 month.
Music: Children's, easy listening, folk, and MOR. Artists include Wooden Soldier (Ganza Records).

THE PRESCRIPTION CO., 70 Murray Ave., Port Washington NY 10050. (516)767-1929. President: David F. Gasman. Record producer, record company, and music publisher (Prescription Co./BMI). Deals with artists and songwriters. Fee derived from sales royalty or outright fee from record company.
How to Contact: Write or call first about your interest then submit demo tape or acetate disk and lyric sheet. Prefers cassette with any number songs on demo. Does not return unsolicited material. Reports in 1 month.
Music: Bluegrass, blues, children's, C&W, dance-oriented, easy listening, jazz, MOR, progressive, R&B, rock, soul and top 40/pop. Recently produced "You Came In" and "Rock 'n' Roll Blues," by Medicine Mike (pop singles, Prescription Records); and *Just What the Doctor Ordered*, by Medicine Mike (LP, Prescription Records).
Tips: "We want quality—fads mean nothing to us."

PREWITT ROSE PRODUCTIONS, Box 29342. Dallas TX 75229. (214)243-2933. Director: Terry Rose. Record producer and music publisher (Pocket-Money Music). Deals with artists. Produces 15-20 singles and 10 albums/year. Fee derived from sales royalty.
How to Contact: Write first about your interest. Prefers cassette with 2 songs maximum on demo. SASE. Reports in 3 weeks.
Music: Blues, C&W, dance-oriented, easy listening, gospel, MOR, new wave, R&B, rock, soul and top 40/pop. Recently produced *Working Country*, by Ralph Hollis (C&W LP, Sunbelt Records; *Coast To Coast*, by Dixie Echoes (gospel LP, Supreme Records); and *The Minerals*, by The Minerals (rock LP, Heat Wave Records). Other artists include The Magics, Wally Willette, Purvis Pickett, Marcel Grantello.

PRITCHETT PUBLICATION, 38603 Sage Tree St., Palmdale CA 93550. (805)947-4657. Branch located at 171 Pine Haven Dr., Daytona Beach FL 32014. (904)252-4849. President: Leroy Pritchett (Florida). A&R Director: Charles Vickers (California). Record producer and music publisher (BMI). Deals with artists and songwriters. Fee derived by sales royalty.
How to Contact: Submit only lead sheet first. SASE. Reports in 1 month.
Music: Blues, church/religious, C&W, dance, easy listening, folk, gospel, R&B, rock, soul, and top 40/pop. Recently produced *Another Dawn*, by Charles Vickers (gospel, LP); *Heaven Is Just Over the Hill*, by Charles Vickers (gospel, LP); *Charles Vickers Does Disco*(disco, LP); *Disco Pop for the 80's*, by Charles Vickers (Pop-disco, LP).

PRODIGY PRODUCTIONS LTD./BURNT OUT MUSIC, 2005 S. 16th Ave., Broadview IL 60153. (312)865-0923. President: Donald Burnside. Record producer and music publisher (Burnt Out Music/BMI). Deals with artists and songwriters. Produces 2 singles and 2 albums/year. Fee derived from sales royalty.
How to Contact: Write first about your interest. Prefers cassette with 4-6 songs on demo. SASE. Reports in 3 weeks.
Music: Dance, R&B, soul, and top 40/pop. Recently produced "Sir Jam Alot," by Capt. Sky (R&B Single, WMOT Records); *Concerned Party # 1*, by Capt. Sky (R&B LP, WMOT Records); "Don't Say Goodnight," by First Love (dance single, Brunswick Records). Other artists include Yvonne Gage.

QUADRAPHONIC TALENT, INC., Box 630175. Miami FL 33163. (305)472-7757. President: Jack P. Bluestein. Record producer and music publisher. Deals with artists and songwriters. Produces 5 singles/year. Fee derived from sales royalty.
How to Contact: Query, submit demo tape (artist), submit demo tape and lead sheet (songwriter). Prefers 7½ ips reel-to-reel with 1-4 songs on demo. SASE. Reports in 1 month.
Music: Blues, C&W, easy listening, folk, gospel, jazz, MOR, rock, soul, and top 40/pop. Recently produced "Three Things" and "A Miracle in You," by Ray Marquis (C&W singles, Twister Records); and "Red Velvet Clown" and "Love Day," by Dottie Leonard (pop singles, AMG Records)."

QUINTO RECORDS, Box 2388, Toluca Lake CA 91602. (213)985-8284. Producer: Quint Benedetti. Produces 1-2 singles and 2 albums/year. Deals with artists and songwriters. Fee derived from sales royalty.
How to Contact: Submit demo tape and lead sheet. Prefers cassette with 2-4 songs on demo. SASE. Reports in 1 month.
Music: C&W, MOR, and novelty-Broadway. Recently produced "Rock & Roll Heaven" and "A Dim Cafe," by Leti (MOR/C&W, Quinto Records).

CAROL J. RACHOU, SR., 711 Stevenson St., Lafayette LA 70501. (318)234-5577. President: Carol J. Rachou, Sr. Record producer and music publisher, (La Lou Music/BMI), record company, recording studio and distributing company. Deals with artists and songwriters, musicians, promoters, agents and managers. Produces 10-20 singles and 6-8 albums/year. Receives negotiable royalty.
How to Contact: Submit demo tape and lyric sheet. Prefers 7½ ips reel-to-reel or cassette with 1-6 songs on demo. SASE.
Music: Produces primarily Cajun/French; also some bluegrass, blues, church/religious, classical, comedy C&W, folk, gospel, jazz, MOR, progressive, R&B, rock and top 40/pop. Recently produced "Lache Pas La Patate," (Gold Record in Canada) and "The Saints (in French)," by Jimmy C. Newman (Cajun singles, La Louisianne Records); *That Cajun Country Sound*, by Eddy Raven (Cajun English LP, La Louisianne Records); and "Cajun Fiddle," by Rufus Thibodeaux (Cajun/instrumental, La Louisianne Records). Other artists include Ambrose Thibodeaux, Merlin Fontenot, Nathan Abshire, L.J. Foret, Blackie Forestier, The Dusenbery Family, Vin Bruce, Doc Guidry, Aldus Roger, Bud Fletcher, Alex Broussand and others.

RADMUS PRODUCTIONS, INC., 15 E. 48th St., Room 603, New York NY 10017. (212)838-8660. General Manager: Martin Feely. Record producer and music publisher (Radmus Publishing, Inc./ASCAP). Deals with artists and songwriters. Produces 5-10 singles and 2-3 albums/year. Fee derived by sales royalty.
How to Contact: Submit demo tape and lyric sheet. Prefers 7½ or 15 ips reel-to-reel or cassette with 2-5 songs on demo. SASE. Reports in 3 weeks "or longer depending on work load."
Music: C&W, dance, easy listening, folk, jazz (fusion), MOR, progressive, R&B, new wave rock, soul, and top 40/pop. Recently produced "First Time" and "One Good Reason," by M. Lewis (country singles, Door Knob Records); "Guilty with an Explanation," by M. Lewis (country single, Warner/Curb Records); *In the Crowd*, by VOG (rock LP, CBS Records).

RAINBOW RECORDING STUDIOS, 2322 S. 64th Ave., Omaha NE 68132. (402)554-0123. Producer: Lars Erickson. Record producer and music publisher (Thomas Jackson Publishing/BMI). Deals with artists, songwriters in production of "commercial jingles." Produces 12 12 singles and 2 albums/year. Fee derived from outright fee from client, record company or songwriter/artist.
How to Contact: Query or submit demo tape and lyric sheet. Prefers 7½ ips reel-to-reel or cassette with 4 songs maximum on demo. SASE. Reports in 1 month.
Music: Any style acceptable. Recently produced "We Can Be" b/w "Don't Fade Away," by Tommy Jackson (MOR, Jacksongs Records); "I Live For You," by John Fischer (MOR, Jacksongs Records). Other arists include The Group, Beebe Runyon & the Furniture and Skuddur.

H&G RANDALL, INC., 29 Elaine Rd., Milford CT 06460. (203)878-7383. A&R/Producer: Bill Bloxsom. Record producer and music publisher. Deals with artists and songwriters. Produces 8 singles and 2 albums/year. Fee derived from sales royalty.
How to Contact: Submit demo tape and lyric sheet. Prefers 7½ or 3¾ ips reel-to-reel, 8-track or cassette with 1 song on demo. "Most of our material is written by Eva Bonn, De Dona Bonn and Nancy Cyril discovered through our previous listing in *Songwriter's Market*." SASE. Reports in 3 weeks.
Music: Dance-oriented, easy listening, MOR, R&B, rock and top 40/pop. Recently produced "De Dona Bonn," and "Life Shuffled the Cards," by Bill and Kenny Bloxsom (MOR and country singles, Randall Records); and "Why Is Your Love Haunting Me?" by Sam Turiano (top 40, Randall Records).

RANDALL PRODUCTIONS, E. Scott St., Suite 408, Chicago IL 60610. (312)649-9644. Executive Producer: Clifford Rubin. Independent production/musical services company. Works with artists and songwriters on contract. Pays standard royalty.
How to Contact: Submit demo tape and typewritten lyric sheet. Prefers cassette with 1-5 songs on demo. "We only listen to copyrighted material; all other will be returned." SASE. Reports in 1 month.
Music: Blues, children's, choral, C&W, dance, easy listening, gospel, jazz, MOR, progressive, R&B, rock, soul, punk, new wave, and top 40/pop. Recently produced "I've Got Wings," by Power Band (funk/R&B); "Power Funk," by Power Band (funk/R&B); and "Work All Day" and "Some Kind Love," by Billy Always (funk/rock). Other artists include Wade Travis, Randy DeTroit, Brian Lordson, and Billy Hills.

R&R RECORDS, INC., 663 5th Ave., New York NY 10022. (212)757-3638. Producer/President: Rena L. Feeney. Producers: Billy Nichols, Lenny Bailey. Record production and music publishing. Deals with artists, songwriters and producers. Produces 8-12 singles and 4-6 albums/year. Fee derived from sales royalty.
How to Contact: Submit demo tape. Prefers 7½ ips reel-to-reel with 4-8 songs on demo. SASE. Reports in 1 month.
Music: Dance, easy listening, MOR, rock, soul, and top 40/pop. Recently produced "I Love Your Beat" and "Dance It Off," by Rena (disco/jazz, Factory Beat Records); and "High Time," by Charles T. Hudson (MOR, RER/Ren Rome Records).

RMS TRIAD PRODUCTIONS, 30125 John R., Madison Heights MI 48071. (313)585-8887. Contact: Bob Szajner. Record producer, record company, and music publisher (RMS Triad Publishing). Deals with artists. Produces 3 albums/year. Fee derived from outright fee from artist/songwriter or record company for services.
How to Contact: Write first about your interest. Prefers cassette with 1-3 songs on demo. SASE. Reports in 3 weeks.
Music: Jazz. Recently produced *Jazz Opus 20/40, Sound Ideas* and *Afterthoughts,* by Triad (mainstream jazz, RMS Records).

ANGELO ROMAN ENTERPRISES, Box 813, Valinda CA 91744. (213)464-1112. Producer: Angelo Roman. Record producer and music publisher (Laughing Bird Songs). Deals with artists and songwriters. Fee derived from outright fee from songwriter/artist or record company.
How to Contact: Submit demo tape and lyric sheet. Prefers cassette with 1-5 songs on demo. Include bio and photos. SASE. Reports in 1 month.
Music: Blues, C&W, easy listening, jazz, MOR, progressive, rock, soul and top 40/pop. Recently produced rock/top 40 and MOR/ballad singles by Tony Garcia and Kelly Canell.

ROOTS OF AMERICAN MUSIC, Box 155, Huntington NY 11743. (516)368-1016. President: Tom Pomposello. Vice President: Rob Witter. Record producer. Concerned with the cultural, artistic and educational aspects of traditional and contemporary American music. Deals with artists and songwriters.
How to Contact: Write first about your interest. Prefers cassette with 1-4 songs on demo; lyric and lead sheet if possible. SASE. Reports in 3 weeks.
Music: Blues, folk and ethnic. Recently produced "Blue Dobro," by Honest Tom Pomposello (for Original Music Institute, California).
Tips: "We are currently introducing American music programs into the New York school system, with an eye towards national developments. We are interested in hearing from artists and song-writers who deal within traditional and contemporary folk/blues stylings, for possible inclusion in future programs."

ROSE HILL PRODUCTIONS, 3929 New Seneca Tpk., Marcellus NY 13108. (315)673-1117. A&R: Vincent Taft. Record producer and music publisher (Katch Nazar Music/ASCAP). Deals with artists and songwriters. Fee derived from sales royalty and outright fee from songwriter/ artist.
How to Contact: Submit demo tape and lyric sheet. Prefers cassette with 3 songs maximum on demo. SASE. Reports in 2 weeks.
Music: Jazz, MOR, progressive, R&B, rock, soul, and top 40/pop. Recently produced *Time*, by Taksim (jazz); "Too Much," by Foxy (pop, Sunday Records); and "Rock & Roll Shoes," by Dan Eaton (rock, Star City Records).
Tips: "Songs should have a beginning, middle and end; melodic and strong, real lyrics. They should be concise; every note should count. Less is more."

ROSEMARY MELODY LINE CO., 633 Almond St., Vineland NJ 08360. (609)696-0943. Producer: Dennis Link. Record producer and recording studios. Deals with artists and songwriters. Produces 5 singles and 5 albums/year. Fee derived from outright fee from artist/songwriter.
How to Contact: Write first about your interest. Prefers cassette with 3-5 songs on demo. SASE. Reports in 2 weeks.
Music: Bluegrass, church/religious, gospel, rock and top 40/pop. Recently produced *Wings of Love*, by Juan and Jenny Avila and Smoked County Jam (folk/bluegrass LP, Goodworks Records); *Eternal Light*, by Eugene Palow (gospel LP, RML Records); and *Getting Our Feet Wet*, by Northwind (pop LP, RML Records). Other artists include Luther McDonald.

SY ROSENBERG ORGANIZATION, 1201 16th Ave. S., Nashville TN 37212. (615)329-0404. President: Sy Rosenberg. Record producer and music publisher (Troll Music/BMI, Baghdad Music/ASCAP). Produces 3 singles and 1 album/year. Fee derived from sales royalty and outright fee from record company.
How to Contact: Submit demo tape and lyric sheet. Prefers 7½ ips reel-to-reel or cassette with 1-5 songs on demo. SASE. Reports in 1 month.
Music: Bluegrass, C&W, jazz, MOR, progressive, R&B, rock, soul and top 40/pop. Recently produced "I Sold All of Tom T.'s Songs Last Night," by Gary Gentry (country, Elektra/Club). Other artists include Doug Clements, Jebry Lee Baily, the Le Garde Twins and David E. Lee.
Tips: "Be professional; have all materials ready and on hand. Keep abreast of current music trends, avoid cliches in writing."

BRIAN ROSS PRODUCTIONS, 7120 Sunset Blvd., Los Angeles CA 90046. (213)851-2500. A&R Producer: Brian Ross. Record producer and music publisher. Deals with artists and songwriters. Fee derived from sales royalty.
How to Contact: Submit demo tape and lyric sheet. Prefers cassette with 1-4 songs on demo. "Be professional. Pick your 2-4 best songs, enclose SASE, and label clearly." Reports in 1 week, "24 hours if good."
Music: MOR, rock, top 40/pop, and new wave (pop-oriented). Recently produced El Chicano (Latin/top 40, MCA Records); Music Machine (new wave, Warner Bros. Records); Johnny Sciarrino (disco drum, Original Sound Records); and Robert Jason (MOR, Polygram Records).

ROYAL K PRODUCTIONS, 6 Melrose Dr., Livingston NJ 07039. (201)533-0448. President: Marc Katz. Record producer and music publisher (Royal K Music). Estab. 1979. Deals with artists, songwriters and producers. Produces 14 singles and 3 albums/year. Fee derived from sales royalty or outright fee from record company.
How to Contact: Write first about your interest then submit demo tape and lyric sheet. Prefers cassette with 1-5 songs on demo. "Include resume and pertinent background information." SASE. Reports in 3 weeks.
Music: Bluegrass, C&W, dance-oriented, gospel, MOR, R&B, rock, soul and top 40/pop. Recently produced "She's Only Fourteen," by Frank Dias and Karl Pacilla (rock single, Venture Records); *Steppin'*, by Charles Stewart (rock/gospel LP, Musique de Soleil Records); and "Dance," by C. Stewart (dance-oriented single, Musique de Soleil Records). Other artists include Chakrae, Williams Brothers, and Frozen Image.
Tips: "Artist or group should be professional, solid musically and have potentially commercial songs."

M.D. RUFFIN PRODUCTIONS, Box 3501, Flint MI 48502. Production Chief: M.D. Ruffin. Record producer and music publisher (Ultra Sounds Unlimited). Deals with artists and songwriters. Receives negotiable commission.
How to Contact: Write first about your interest, then submit demo tape and lyric sheet. Prefers 7½ ips reel-to-reel or cassette with 1 song on demo. SASE. Reports in 2 weeks.
Music: Dance-oriented, easy listening, jazz, progressive, R&B, rock, soul and top 40/pop.

RUSTRON MUSIC PRODUCTIONS, 200 Westmoreland Ave., White Plains NY 10606, main office. (914)946-1689. Executive Director: Rusty Gordon. Director A&R: Ron Caruso. Independent record producers and music publishers (Rustron Music Publisher/BMI). Deals with artists and songwriters. Produces 3-4 albums and 3-8 singles/year. Fee derived from sales royalty and outright fee from record company.
How to Contact: Query, arrange personal interview or submit demo tape and lead/lyric sheet. Include promotional material and photos. Prefers 7½ ips reel-to-reel, "with leader tape between all songs and at beginning and end of tape" or cassette with 3-6 songs on demo. "Interviews are held in the evenings Monday through Thursday from 7-10 p.m. We specialize in singer/songwriter package for promotion and publishing. We will also review songs from non-performing writers." SASE. Reports in 1 month.
Music: R&B, country (popular and progressive), disco (salsa, popular, swing), easy listening, folk (rock and folk/country), MOR, rock (country/rock and rock & roll), and pop (standards). Recently produced *Lois Britten Project*, by Lois Britten (pop/rock/disco LP/Rustron Records); "Sign Painter," *Everything She Touches*, and "Llguste, Llguste," and "El Amor" (45 RPM, For International Hispanic Release) by Christian Camilo and the Tingalayo Rhythm Band (salsa/disco/American pop LP, FM Records); and "Amor Mio," by Christian Camilo Veda and the Tingalayo Rhythm Band (Spanish ballad single, FM Records); "Live Caberet Album," by Richard 'Caberet' Collins; and "Where Love Can Go," by Dianne Mover & Jasmine.
Tips: "Write commercially marketable songs with strong hooks. We want professional stage presence levels, good vocal continuity and excellent musician ship."

SAGITTAR RECORDS, 1311 Candlelight Ave., Dallas TX 75116. (214)298-9576. President: Paul Ketter. Record producer, record company and music publisher. Deals with artists and songwriters. Fee derived from sales royalty.
How to Contact: Submit demo tape and lead sheet. Prefers 7½ ips reel-to-reel with 3-12 songs on demo. SASE. Reports in 1 month.
Music: C&W, folk, MOR (country), and progressive (country). Recently produced "Diamonds Only Shine," "Bar After Bar," and "Only a Woman," by Bunnie Mills (C&W singles, Sagittar Records).

STEVEN C. SARGEANT, 31632 2nd Ave., South Laguna Beach CA 92677. Producer: Steven C. Sargeant. Record producer. Deals with artists and songwriters. Fee derived from sales royalty.
How to Contact: Query or submit demo tape. Prefers 7½ ips reel-to-reel or cassette with 3-5 songs on demo. SASE. Reports in 3 weeks.
Music: Folk, jazz, rock (country or hard), and top 40/pop.

STEVE SCHARF, Double Header Productions, 61 Jane St., New York NY 10014. (212)929-2068. Contact: Steve Scharf or Neal Teeman. Record producer, music publisher (Weeze Music Co./BMI) and independent record producer. Produces 8 singles and 2 albums/year. Deals with artists and songwriters. Fee derived from sales royalty and outright fee from songwriter/artist and record company. Production fees charged for demos and records.

How to Contact: Call first about your interest. Submit demo tape and lyric sheet. Prefers 7½ ips reel-to-reel or cassette with maximum 4 songs - n demo. SASE.
Music: Rock, top 40/pop and adult contemporary. Recently produced "Real Tears"/"Sweet Candlelight," by Peter Myers Band (pop rock, Deli Platters/MCA); *Declaration of Independents*, by Robin Lane and the Charrbusters (new wave rock, Ambitious Records).

JASON SCHWARTZ, 5934 Buffalo Ave., Suite 105, Van Nuys CA 91401. (213)997-8819. Contact: Jason Schwartz. Record producer and music publisher (Ten of Diamonds Music/BMI and Five of Spades Music). Deals with artists and songwriters. Produces 8-10 singles and 1-3 albums/year. Fee derived from sales royalty.
How to Contact: Write first about your interest. Prefers cassette with 1-2 songs on demo. SASE. Reports in 3 weeks.
Music: Sophisticated C&W, easy listening, MOR, light rock and top 40/pop. Recently produced "Lady from Beverly Hills," by Jason (country rock single, Survivor Records); "Words Spoken Softly by You," by Greta Warren (country single, Survivor Records); and "Climbing Out," by Apostle (rock single, Survivor Records).

SEA CRUISE PRODUCTIONS, Box 110830, Nashville TN 37211. President: Ken Keene. Vice President: Frankie Ford. Record producer and music publisher. Deals with artists and songwriters. Fee derived by sales royalty.
How to Contact: Submit demo tape and lyric sheet. Prefers 7½ ips reel-to-reel (no smaller than 5" reel) or cassette with 2-4 songs on demo. SASE. Reports in 1 month.
Music: Blues, children's, church/religious, C&W, dance, easy listening, gospel, MOR, R&B, country rock, soul, and top 40/pop. Recently produced "Halfway to Paradise," by Frankie Ford (top 40 ballad, Briarmeade Records); "Foxy Man," by Billy Joe Duniven (country rock, Burlap Records); and *Saxy Country Soul*, by Johnny Pennino (instrumental country rock, Burlap Records). Other artists include Denny Barberio, the Briarmeade Singers, Tom Pallardy, Larry Swift and Marilyn Strothcamp (Briarmeade Records); and Majik Dust and Phil Enloe (Burlap Records).

SEA SAINT RECORDING STUDIO, INC., 3809 Clematis Ave., New Orleans LA 70122. (504)949-8386. Contact: Debra Campbell. Record producer (Marsaint Music, Inc./BMI). Deals with artists. Produces 10 singles and 6 albums/year. Fee derived from sales royalty or outright fee from record company.
How to Contact: Submit demo tape and lyric sheet. Prefers cassette with 3-5 songs on demo. SASE. Reports in 1 month.
Music: Blues, gospel, jazz, R&B, rock and soul. Recently produced *Touch of Silk*, by Eric Gale (jazz LP, Columbia Records); *Routes*, by Ramsey Lewis (jazz LP, Columbia Records); and *Released*, by Pat Labelle (soul LP, Epic Records). Other artists include Allen Toussaint, Lee Dorsey, Earl King and Einie K. Doe.

SEVEN HILLS RECORDING & PUBLISHING CO., INC., 905 N. Main St., Evansville IN 47711. (812)423-1861. President: Ed Krietemeyer. Record producer and music publisher. Deals with artists and songwriters. Produces 3 singles/year. Fee derived from sales royalty.
How to Contact: Write first about your interest. Prefers cassette with 1 songs minimum on demo. SASE. Reports in 1 month.
Music: Bluegrass, blues, C&W, easy listening, folk, gospel and R&B.

7TH RAY RECORDS, Box 3771, Hollywood CA 90028. (213)467-0611. President: Alan Ames. Associate Producer: R.A. "Bumps" Blackwell. Record producer and music publisher (Seventh Ray Publishing). Deals with artists and songwriters. Produces 3-5 singles and 5 albums/year.
How to Contact: Submit demo tape and lyric sheet. Prefers cassette with 3-8 songs on demo. SASE. Reports in 1 month.
Music: Blues, easy listening, jazz, progressive, R&B, rock and top 40/pop. Recently produced "Full Moon Light," by Sky Salanyth (progressive folk single, 7th Ray Records); "Seeds of Peace," by Stephen Fiske (R&B/easy listening single, 7th Ray Records); "Nobody But You," by Gay Martin (top 40 single, 7th Ray Records); and "Sugar Cane Rides Again," by Sugar Cane Harris (R&B/jazz single, 7th Ray Records). Other artists include Fantuzzi and Mainland Dancer.

SHALYNN PRODUCTIONS, Box 34131, Dallas TX 75234. (214)242-6152. General Manager: Steve Jarett. Promotion Manager: Rick Jackson. President: Stephen Kedlarchuk. Record producer, music publisher and management firm (Chartreuse Music/BMI). Produces 2 singles/year. Fee derived from royalty.
How to Contact: Query, arrange personal interview, or submit demo tape and lead sheet. Prefers

cassette with 2-4 songs on demo. SASE. Reports in 2 weeks.
Music: Bluegrass, church/religious, C&W, dance, easy listening, gospel, MOR, progressive, rock, soul, and top 40/pop. Recently produced "Sunlight in Her Hair" and "Flower Song," by Shalynn (top 40/pop singles, Ice Records); "Dime a Dozen Man" and "Trouble in the Last Frontier," by Watkins and Lamb (country/rock/top 40 singles, Ice Records); "Autumn Roads" and "Morning Moon," by Ted Patton (soft rock/top 40).
Tips: "One must send the words with his or her song. The tape must be clean sounding. You only send trash to a waste basket. *Be professional.*"

SHEKERE PRODUCTIONS, Box 26034, Richmond VA 23260. (804)355-3586. President: Plunky Nkabinde. Record producer and music publisher (Shekere Music/BMI). Produces 3 singles and 6 albums/year. Deals with artists and songwriters. Fee derived by outright fee from record company or outright fee from songwriter/artist.
How to Contact: Submit demo tape and lyric sheet. Prefers cassette with 2-5 songs on demo. SASE. Reports in 3 weeks.
Music: Blues, dance, jazz, progressive, R&B, and soul. Recently produced *Make a Change*, by Oneness of Juju (jazz funk reggae, Blackfire Records); "SABI," by O. Asante (African disco, Atampan Records); and *Larry Bland and the Volunteer Choir*, by Larry Bland and the Volunteer Choir (gospel).
Tips: "Have good material, experience, contacts and be willing to work. It would be extremely helpful if you have an orientation towards African music, jazz or reggae."

SHOWCASE OF STARS, 310 Franklin St., Boston MA 02110; 77 Summer St., Suite 805, Boston MA 02110 (617)396-0751. Director: Marv Cutler. Record producer, music publisher (Maric Music/ASCAP), management firm and talent agent. Deals with artists and songwriters. Produces 25+ singles and 25+ albums/year. Fee derived from sales royalty.
How to Contact: Query or submit demo tape and lead sheet. Prefers 7½ ips reel-to-reel or cassette with 2-6 songs on demo. Does not return unsolicited material. Reports in 1 month.
Music: Blues; children's; C&W; easy listening; jazz; MOR; progressive; rock (light); soul; and top 40/pop. Recently produced "Marv's Melody," by Al Vega Trio (Latin single, Marc Records); "Hurricane Rock," by Hurricane Marty Hunter (rock single, Marc Records); and "Songs of the Pack," by The New Rat Pack (top 40 rock single, Marc Records). Other artists include the Garrison Band, John Costanzo, Rita-Lora and Scott Cutler.

THE SHUKAT CO., LTD., 211 W. 56th St., New York NY 10019. (212)582-7614. Contact: Scott Shukat, Larry Weiss. Record producer, music publisher and management firm. Deals with artists, songwriters and producers. Produces 1 album/year. Fee derived from sales royalty.
How to Contact: Submit demo tape and lead sheet. Prefers reel-to-reel or cassette with 3-15 songs on demo. SASE.
Music: Folk; rock; and top 40/pop.

SILENT W. PRODUCTIONS, Box 277, Dundas, Ontario, Canada L9H 5G1. Contact: James Taylor. Record producer and music publisher (Jay-me Music) and recording studio. Estab. 1980. Deals with artists and songwriters. Fee derived from sales royalty.
How to Contact: Submit demo tape and lyric sheet. Prefers cassette with 1-4 songs on demo. SAE and International Reply Coupons. Reports as soon as possible.
Music: C&W, folk, MOR, rock (all types) and top 40/pop. Recently produced *Tyro*, by Tyro (rock LP, SWP Records). Other artists include Dundas, and The Innocent.
Tips: "Our specialty is supporting Canadian talent, although we listen to all tapes received."

SILVER BLUE PRODUCTIONS, 220 Central Park S., New York NY 10019. (212)586-3535. Contact: Producer. Record producer and music publisher. Deals with artists and songwriters. Fee derived by sales royalty.
How to Contact: Submit demo tape and lyric sheet. Prefers cassette with 1-3 songs on demo. SASE.
Music: C&W, dance, easy listening, MOR, R&B, rock, soul, and top 40/pop. Recently produced "After the Lovin'," by Engelbert Humperdinck. (top 40, Epic Records); "You're All I Need to Get By," by Gloria Gaynor (R&B, Polydor Records); and *Joel Diamond Experience*, by Joel Diamond Experience (disco/top 40, Casablanca Records); and Helen Reddy album.

SILVER BULLET PRODUCTIONS/TRULY FINE RECORDS, Box 423, Station F, Toronto, Ontario, Canada M4Y 2L8. Professional Manager: Allen Shechtman. Record producer and music publisher (Sidewalk Sailor Music/CAPAC, Scales of My Head Music/PROCAN, Etheric Polyphony/CAPAC, Cumulonimbus Music/PROCAN. Deals with artists, songwriters, labels, producers and publishers. Fee derived from sales royalty or by outright fee from record company.

How to Contact: Write first about your interest. Prefers 7½ or 15 ips reel-to-reel or cassette with 3 songs minimum on demo. Does not return unsolicited material. Reports in 1 month.
Music: Recently produced *Dorothea's Dream*, by Graeme Card (concept LP, Change Records/ MCA Records); "Supernatural One," by G. Card (AOR/MOR single, Change Records/MCA Records); *Graeme Card*, by G. Card (LP, Truly Fine Records); and *Saskatoon*, by Humphrey and Dumptrucks, (Bluegrass LP, United Artists Records).

SKYS THE LIMIT PRODUCTIONS, INC., 100 Main St., Reading MA 01867. (617)944-0423. President: Carl Strube. Record producer, music publisher, management firm and promoter. Deals with artists and songwriters. Fee derived by sales royalty.
How to Contact: Submit demo tape and lyric sheet. Prefers 7½ ips reel-to-reel or cassette with 1-3 songs on demo. SASE. Reports in 1 month.
Music: C&W, MOR, R&B, rock, soul, and top 40/pop. Recently published "This Is Love" and "Draw the Line," by Oak (top 40/Mercury Records); and "Where Is the Woman," by Chip Harding (top 40/RSO Records). Other artists include Blend (MCA Records).

SOUL SET PRODUCTIONS, 1218 Hollister Ave., San Francisco CA 94124. Record producer and music publisher (Bay-Tone Music/BMI). Deals with artists and songwriters. Fee derived from sales royalty.
How to Contact: Submit demo tape and lyric sheet. Prefers reel-to-reel or cassette as demo. SASE. Reports as soon as possible.
Music: Blues, MOR. Artists include Frisco.

SOUND COLUMN PRODUCTIONS/SCP RECORDS, 46 E. Herbert Ave., Salt Lake City, UT 84111. (801)355-5327. Producers: Ron Simpson or Clive Romney. Record producer and music publishers (Ronarre Publications/ASCAP, Mountain Green/BMI). Produces 4 singles and 6 albums/year. Deals with artists and songwriters. Fee derived from sales royalty or outright fee from record company or artist.
How to Contact: Submit demo tape and lyric sheet. Prefers cassette with 3 songs maximum on demo. SASE. Reports in 1 month.
Music: Children's, church/religious, C&W, dance, easy listening, gospel, MOR, R&B, rock, soul and top 40/pop. Recently produced "Don't Stop the Music," by Sunshade 'n Rain (adult contemporary, SCP Records); "Turn Me Around," by Rich Push (country, SCP Records); "I Have a Song for You," by Janeen Brady (children's, Brite Records).

SOUNDS OF COUNTRY, 1210 Palm St., Abilene TX 79602. (915)677-1508. Contact: Angel or Denny Young. Record producer, music publisher and booking agency. Deals with artists and songwriters. Fee derived by sales royalty.
How to Contact: Submit demo tape and lyric sheet. Prefers cassette with 1-6 songs on demo. SASE. Reports in 2 weeks.
Music: C&W. Recently produced "Lovin' Mornin'," by Angel Young (country, Rally Records); "Better Than Before," by Skip Dowers (country, Rally Records); and "Tangled World," by Tom Druley (country, Rally Records).

SOUNDS OF WINCHESTER, Box 574, Winchester VA 22601. (703)667-9379. Owner: Jim McCoy. Record producer and music publisher. Deals with artists and songwriters. Produces 10-15 singles and 8-10 albums/year. Fee derived from sales royalty.
How to Contact: Submit demo tape and lead sheet. Prefers 7½ ips reel-to-reel with 4-10 songs on demo. SASE. Reports in 1 month.
Music: Bluegrass, C&W, gospel, MOR, and rock.

SQUILLIT PRODUCTIONS, INC., Box 98, Forest Hills NY 11375. (212)265-1292. President: K.Z. Purzycki. Record producer and music publisher (Memnon, Ltd./ASCAP, Tithonus Music, Ltd./BMI). Deals with artists and songwriters. Produces 3 singles and 1 album/year. Fee derived from royalty or outright fee from record company.
How to Contact: "We are open to review new artists; you must include a demo tape, photo and bio." Prefers cassette with 3-5 songs on demo, "leader between songs, if on reel." SASE. Reports in 1 month.
Music: C&W and top 40/pop. Recently produced "You Are Queen of My Heart," by Happy End (top 40/pop, Memnon Records); "Was Young Love Born to Die," by Bobbie Roberson (C&W, Bolivia Records); and *Swing with the King*, by King Edward and his Orchestra (polka LP, Polamart Records). Other artists include Krystof.

STAIRCASE PROMOTION, Box 211, East Prairie MO 63845. (314)649-2211. Manager: Tommy Loomas. Record producer and music publisher. Deals with artists and songwriters.
How to Contact: Write first about your interest or submit demo tape and lyric sheet. Prefers 7½ ips reel-to-reel or cassette with 2-4 songs on demo. SASE. Reports in 1 month.
Music: C&W, easy listening, MOR, country rock, and top 40/pop. Recently produced "Best of All," by Mary Nichols (easy listening, Onie Records); "Stay Baby Stay," by Shuri Castle (country rock, Capstan Records); and "Country Boy," by Alden Lambert (C&W, Capstan Records).

STARGEM RECORD PRODUCTIONS, 20 Music Square W., Suite 200, Nashville TN 37203. (615)244-1025. President/A&R Director: Wayne Hodge. Record producer and music publisher (Newwriters Music/BMI and Timestar Music/ASCAP). Deals with artists and songwriters. Produces 20-30 singles and 5-10 albums/year. Fee derived from sales royalty or outright fee from record company.
How to Contact: Call first about your interest then submit demo tape and lyric sheet. Prefers 7½ ips reel-to-reel or cassette with 1-4 songs on demo. SASE. Reports in 1 week.
Music: C&W and MOR. Recently produced "Rev. Sam Whiskey," by Steve Jones (C&W single, Stargem Records); "Country Fever," by Frankie Rich (C&W single, Stargem Records); and "Carolyn," by Larry Hawkins (MOR single, Stargem Records). Other artists include Lee Cummins, Wade Baynes, "Oliver," "Lee and Ruby."

STARTOWN ENTERPRISES, 1037 E. Parkway S., Memphis TN 38104. (901)725-7019. President: Allen White. Record producer (Dewaun Music/SESAC). Deals with artists, songwriters and producers. Produces 5 singles and 2 albums/year. Fee derived from sales royalty.
How to Contact: Submit demo tape and lyric sheet. Prefers cassette with 4-8 songs on demo. SASE. Reports in 1 month.
Music: Blues, church/religious, C&W, gospel, R&B, rock, soul and top 40/pop. Artists include Ike Strong, Mack Banks, Joyce Young, Chick Willis.

PAUL STEVENS ASSOCIATES, INC., 8325 SW 132 St., Miami FL 33156. President: Paul Stevens. Record producer and music publisher (Grand Artists Music). Deals with artists and songwriters. Produces 3 albums/year. Fee derived from sales royalty.
How to Contact: Submit demo tape and lyric sheet. "Please, no calls." Prefers cassette with 1-5 songs on demo. SASE. Reports in 1 month.
Music: C&W, easy listening, MOR, Spanish and rock. Recently produced "Soy," by Chirino (MOR/Spanish, Ariola Records) and "Music Maker," by Chirino (MOR, CBS Records). Other artis includes Facundo Cabral.

A. STEWART PRODUCTIONS, 22146 Lanark St., Canoga Park CA 91304. (213)704-0629. President: Art Stewart. Record producer and music publisher (Famosonda Music/BMI). Deals with artists and songwriters. Produces 4 singles and 2 albums/year. Fee determined by sales royalty.
How to Contact: Submit demo tape and lyric sheet. Prefers 7½ ips reel-to-reel or cassette with 1-4 songs on demo. SASE. Reports in 1 month.
Music: Soul. Recently produced "Eboni Band," by Eboni Band (Afro/American, Eboni Records); *Cherry*, by Platypus (soul, Casablanca Records); "Same Old Story," by Sai Whatt (soul, Stache Records). Other artists include Charades, Randie Coulter and Eboni Band.

STEVE STONE, INC., 6255 Sunset, #723, Hollywood CA 90028. (213)462-6933. President: Steve Stone. Record producer and music publisher (Mandina Music and Rocksmith Music). Deals with artists and songwriters. Fee derived from sales royalty or outright fee from artist/songwriter or record company.
How to Contact: Submit demo tape and lyric sheet. Prefers cassette with 1-10 songs on demo. SASE. Reports in 2 weeks.
Music: Bluegrass, choral, church/religious, C&W, easy listening, gospel, MOR, progressive, R&B, rock, soul and top 40/pop. Recently produced "Pyramid Song," by J.C. Cunningham (novelty single, Scotti Brothers Records); and *Suzanne Klee*, by S. Klee (pop LP, Capitol Records).

STONY PLAIN RECORDING CO., LTD., Box 861, Edmonton, Alberta, Canada T5J 2L8. (403)477-6844. Managing Director: Holger Petersen. Record producer and music publisher (Kitchen Table Music/Procan, Gimbleco West Music/PROCAN and Eyeball Wine Music/CAPAC). Deals with artists and songwriters. Produces 4-6 singles and 4-6 albums/year. Fee derived by outright fee from record compnay.
How to Contact: Call or write first about your interest. Prefers cassette with 1-4 songs on demo. SAE and International Reply Coupons. Reports in 3 weeks.

Music: Bluegrass, children's, folk, MOR, progressive, rock and top 40/pop. Recently produced "Testimony," by Ferron (folk, Stony Plain Records); "High Test," by Paul Hann (folk, Stony Plain Records); and "Starting to Show," by Crowcuss (rock, Stony Plain records).

STP PRODUCTIONS, INC., Box 9628, Atlanta GA 30319. (404)349-3848. Producer: Bob Langford. Record producer and music publisher. Deals with artists and songwriters. Fee derived from sales royalty.
How to Contact: Submit demo tape and lyric sheet. Prefers 7½ or 15 ips reel-to-reel or cassette with 1-6 songs on demo. SASE. Reports in 1 month.
Music: Blues, C&W, dance, easy listening, folk, MOR, progressive, R&B, rock, soul, and top 40/pop. Recently produced "Lost" and "Running Out," by the Desparate Angels (rock, December Records); and "Concrete Jungle," by Joe South (MOR). Other artists include Larry Bowie and Movers.

STRAIGHT FACE MUSIC, Box 324, Newark DE 19711. (302)368-1211. Contact: Producer. Record producer and music publisher (Straight-Face/ASCAP and White Clay/BMI). Estab. 1979. Deals with artists and songwriters. Produced 3 singles and 1 albums/year.
How to Contact: Write first about your interest. Prefers cassette with 2-4 songs on demo. SASE. Reports in 3 weeks.
Music: Dance-oriented, jazz (traditional), progressive, rock and new wave. Artists include Steve Roberts.

STRIVERS PRODUCTIONS, Box 3804, Loring Station, Minneapolis MN 55403. (612)374-9192. (612)827-4021. President: Patrick W. Knight. Record producer. Deals with artists and songwriters. Produces 2 singles and 1 album/year.
How to Contact: Call or write first about your interest then submit demo tape and lyric sheet. Prefers 7½ ips reel-to-reel or cassette with 3-5 songs on demo. SASE. Reports in 2 weeks.
Music: Blues, gospel, jazz, new wave, progressive, soul and top 40/pop. Recently produced "Love Episode," by Patrick W. Knight (ballad single, Strivers Records); and "Open Your Mind," by Walter Riley (ballad single, Atlantic Records).

STYLETONE/HOOKS RECORD CO., 254 E. 29th St. #7, Los Angeles CA 90011. (213)746-6499. Contact: Jerry Hook Sr. Record producer, music publisher (ASCAP) and record company. Deals with artists, songwriters, producers and arrangers. Produces 6 singles and 2 albums/year. Fee derived from sales royalty.
How to Contact: Submit demo tape and lyric sheet. Prefers 8-track cassette with 3-6 songs on demo. SASE. Reports in 1-2 weeks.
Music: Blues, C&W, dance, gospel, jazz, R&B, soul, and top 40/pop. Recently produced "Woman Is Glory of a Man," by Model "T" Slim (blues, Styletone Records); "13 Highway," by Little Boyd (blues, Styletone Records); and "I Won't Have to Cry," by Johnny Grayson and the Master Keys (gospel, Hooks Records). Other artists include Patricia White and Royal Dorsey.

SUMAC MUSIC, 1697 Broadway, New York NY 10019. (212)246-0575. President: Susan McCusker. Record producer and music publisher. Produces 10-15 singles and 8-10 albums/year. Deals with artists and songwriters. Fee derived from sales royalty.
How to Contact: Submit demo tape and lead sheet. Prefers 7½ ips reel-to-reel with 2-5 songs on demo. Does not return unsolicited material. Reports in 1 month.
Music: Dance; soul; and top 40/pop.

SUNBURST MUSIC PRODUCTIONS, 26949 Chagrin Blvd., Suite 209, Beachwood OH 44122. Executive Producer: Jim Quinn. Associate Producer: Otto F. Neuber. Record producer, music publisher (Solarium Music/ASCAP) and management firm. Deals with artists and songwriters. Produces 3 singles and 1 album/year. Fee derived from outright fee from record company.
How to Contact: Submit demo tape. Prefers 7½ ips reel-to-reel or cassette with 1-3 songs on demo. SASE. Reports in 3 weeks.
Music: MOR and top 40/pop. Recently produced Love Affair, L.A., and "Mama Sez" by Love Affair (rock/top 40, Radio/Atlantic Records); and "Go For The Money," by Charlie Weiner (White Light Records). Other artists include Nasty Habits.

SUNSET RECORDS, INC., 1577 Redwood Dr., Harvey LA 70058. (504)367-8501. President: George Leger. Record producer and music publisher (Country Legs Music/ASCAP and Golden Sunburst Music/BMI). Deals with artists and songwriters. Produces 5 singles/year. Fee derived by outright fee from record company.
How to Contact: Submit demo tape and lyric and lead sheet. Prefers 7½ ips reel-to-reel or cassette

(if very clear) with 3-5 songs on demo. SASE. Reports in 1 month.
Music: C&W, gospel, progressive country and R&B. Recently produced "Son Don't Walk Down My Road" and "A Snowman for Christmas," by George Leger (country/Christmas single, Sunset Records); and "Broken Homes," by Sonny Tears (country single, Sunset Records).

SURVIVOR PRODUCTIONS, 5934 Buffalo Ave., Van Nuys CA 91401. (213)997-8819. Producer: Jason Schwartz. Record producer and music publisher (Ten of Diamonds/BMI and Five of Spades Music. Deals with artists and songwriters. Produces 8-10 singles and 1-3 albums/year. Fee derived from sales royalty.
How to Contact: Submit demo tape and lyric sheet. If artist, include pictures and biography. Prefers 7½ ips reel-to-reel or cassette with 1-3 songs on demo. SASE. Reports in 1 month.
Music: Dance; MOR; R&B; rock; and soul. Recently produced "Love Is What You Make It," by Jason and David Zimjans (rock, Survivor Records); "A Little Chance, If Any," by Jason & James Drennen (rock/disco, Survivor Records); "Troubles I Have Found," by Jay Wolfe (country rock, Survivor Records); "Mama, You Promised," by Greta Warren (rock, Survivor Records); "Carry On," by Apostle (gospel, Survivor Records). Other artists include Wonder Tron, Marion Ramsey and the Diamonds.

SWEETSONG PRODUCTIONS, Box 2041, Parkersburg WV, 26101. (304)489-2911. Contact: Roger Hoover. Record producer. Deals with artists and songwriters. Produces 10 singles and 10 albums/year. Fee derived from outright fee from songwriter/artist.
How to Contact: Submit demo tape and lyric sheet. Prefers cassette with 1-5 songs that doesn't have to be returned. SASE. Reporting time varies.
Music: Contemporary gospel only. Recently produced *Miracle*, by Debbie Davis (contemporary gospel LP, Sweetsong Records); *Growing Stronger*, by Pam Gordon (contemporary gospel LP, Sweetsong Records); *Taste The Kindness*, by Mona Freshour (contemporary gospel LP, Sweetsong Records); *Come Do The Same*, by Light (contemporary gospel LP, Sweetsong Records); and "Holy Roller," by Mike McGuire (contemporary gospel single, Sweetsong Records). Other artists include Light, Mona Freshour, Mike McGuire.

SWORD & SHIELD RECORDS, Box 211, Arlington TX 76010. (817)572-1414. Contact: Calvin Wills. Record producer. Deals with artists. Produces 12 singles and 150 albums/year. Fee derived from outright fee from artist/songwriter.
How to Contact: Call first about your interest. Prefers cassette with 2-6 songs on demo. Does not return unsolicited material. Reports in 1 month.
Music: Church/religious and gospel. Recently produced "Here We Are," by Janie White; "Consider the Lillies," by Diana Farr; and "He Was There All the Time," by Harmony Boys (gospel singles, S&S Records).

SWORD RECORDS, Box 8374, Greenville SC 24604. (803)271-1104. President: Rick Sandidge. Record producer and music publisher (Adonikan Music/BMI). Deals with artists and songwriters. Produces 4 singles and 4 albums/year. Fee derived from sales royalty.
How to Contact: Submit demo tape and lyric sheet. Prefers 7½ ips reel-to-reel or cassette with 4 songs on demo. SASE. Reports in 1 month.
Music: Bluegrass, blues, C&W, folk, gospel, jazz, progressive, R&B, rock, soul and top 40/pop. Recently published *Evening Pastoral*, by Rob Cassels (contemporary gospel LP, Sword Records); *Morning Dove*, by Bill Barnes (contemporary gospel LP, Sword Records); and *I'm Strangely Attracted to You*, by Susan Atkins (country LP, Direct Records).

TAKE HOME TUNES! RECORD CO., Box 1314, Englewood Cliffs NJ 07632. (201)224-5811. Messages: (201)567-5524. Producer: Doris Chu Yeko. Record producer and music publisher (The Chu Yeko Musical Foundation and Broadway/Hollywood International Music). Deals with artists and songwriters. Produces 8 albums/year. Fee derived from sales royalty.
How to Contact: Call first about your interest then submit demo tape and lyric sheet. Prefers cassette with any number songs on demo. SASE. Reports in 1 month.
Music: Children's, classical, C&W, easy listening, jazz, MOR, musicals, R&B and top 40/pop. Recently produced *King of Hearts*, by Millicent Martin and Don Scardino and *Lovesong*, by the original cast musical LPs, Original Cast Records); *Ka-Boom!* and *Fly With Me*, by the original cast (musical LPs, Chu Yeko Musical Foundation Records); and *Christy (Playboy of the Western World)*, by the original cast (musical LP, Original Cast Records).
Tips: "We're interested in the 'top 10' pop types of songs; original cast musicals that had a production somewhere; and R&B songs; sung by new singers, groups, etc."

TALENT SOURCE INTERNATIONAL, 11 S. LaSalle #930, Chicago IL 60603. (312)327-0900. Music Coordinator: Ira M. Fields. Music publisher and management firm. Estab. 1978. Deals with

artists and songwriters. Fee derived from sales royalty.
How to Contact: Call first about your interest. Prefers cassette with 2-6 songs on demo. Will return material in SASE only if requested. Reports in 3 weeks or "the time it takes to present artist with material."
Music: Easy listening, MOR, progressive, R&B, rock, soul, and top 40/pop. Recently produced Ada Dyer (Columbia Records).
Tips: "We look for songs for artists we manage."

TEROCK RECORDS, Box 4740, Nashville TN 37216. (615)859-0355. President: Wade Curtiss. Record producer and music publisher. Deals with artists and songwriters. Fee derived from sales royalty.
How to Contact: Submit demo tape and lyric sheet. Prefers 7½ ips reel-to-reel with 2-6 songs on demo. SASE. Reports in 3 weeks.
Music: Bluegrass, blues, C&W, dance, easy listening, folk, gospel, progressive, R&B, hard rock, soul, and top 40/pop.

311 PRODUCTIONS, INC., 311 W. 57th St., New York NY 10019. (212)765-8200. President: Ron Dante. Vice President, A&R: Geoff Howe. Record producer and music publisher (Dante Music, Inc.). Deals with artists and songwriters. Produces 3 singles and 2-3 albums/year. Fee derived from sales royalty.
How to Contact: Submit demo tape and lyric sheet. Prefers cassette with 4 songs maximum on demo. SASE. Reports in 1 month.
Music: MOR, R&B, rock (soft and hard) and top 40/pop. Recently produced *Barry*, by Barry Manilow (top 40/pop LP, Arista Records); *Jolis and Simone*, by Jolis and Simone (top 40/R&B/pop LP, Columbia Records); and *Ron Dante*, by R. Dante (top 40/pop LP, Handshake Records).

THUNDER, 6362 Hollywood, Suite 219, Los Angeles CA 90028. (213)465-3202. President: Damon Alberti. Record producer. Deals with artists and songwriters. Produces 10 singles and 1 albums/year. Fee derived from sales royalty.
How to Contact: Call or write first about your interest then submit demo and lyric sheet. Prefers cassette with 2 songs on demo. SASE. Reports in 1 week.
Music: Rock and top 40/pop. Recently produced "Road Fever," by The Skull; and "Half My Way," by Rick Field (rock singles, Thunder Records).
Tips: "Visual is more important than ever. Think international!"

TIGER RECORDS, C.I.T.S. Records, Box 2544, Baton Rouge LA 70821. (504)925-2603. Producer/A&R Director: "Ebb-Tide." Director: E.K. Harrison. Record producer, music publisher (Cryin' in the Streets Music Publishers/ASCAP) and record company. Deals with artists, songwriters and composers. Publishes 15-26 singles and 5-10 albums/year. Fee derived from sales royalty.
How to Contact: Submit demo tape and lead sheet. Prefers cassette with 4-6 songs on demo. SASE. Reports in 2 weeks.
Music: Folk, MOR, rock (pop), and top 40/pop. Recently produced "No Need for a Black-Man to Cry," by George Perkins (soul single, Cryin' In The Streets Records); "Too Much Luvin at Home," by Larry Hobbs (soul single, Pure Black Soul Records); and *The Mighty Chevelle Hits*, by the Mighty Chevelles (LP, Cryin' In The Streets Records).

RICK TINORY PRODUCTIONS, 180 Pond St., Cohasset MA 02025. (617)383-9494. Artist Relations: Claire Babcock. Record producer and music publisher (Old Boston Publishing). Deals with artists. Produces 20 singles and 15 albums/year. Fee derived from standard publishing royalties.
How to Contact: Call first about your interest. Prefers cassette with 1-3 songs on demo. Does not return unsolicited material.
Music: Recently produced *Scollay Square*, by Rik Tinory (dixie/nostalgia LP, Old Boston Records); *Live on Boston Common*, by Pope John Paul II (religious LP, Old Boston Records); and *Martha's Vineyard*, by R. Tinory (folk rock LP, Old Boston Records).
Tips: "We are looking for master recordings with strong material ready for release."

TRIBAL RECORDS, Box 6495, Buena Park CA 90620. (714)554-0851. Contact: Jerry Wood. Record producer. Deals with artists and songwriters. Fee derived from sales royalty or outright fee from record company.
How to Contact: Submit demo tape and lyric sheet. Prefers 7½ ips reel-to-reel or cassette with 3 songs on demo. SASE. Reports in 2 weeks.
Music: C&W; easy listening; and MOR. Recently produced "Many Are the Colors," by Roy Dee

(country, Tribal Records); "99 Years," by Ron Hayden (country, Tribal Records); and "Gold Plated Boy Scout Knife," by Jeanne Taylor (country, Tribal Records).

TUMAC MUSIC, 2097 Vistadale Ct., Tucker GA 30084. (404)938-1210. Professional Manager: Phil McDaniel. Record company, music publisher and record producer. Produces 3 singles/year. Works with artists and songwriters on contract. Pays 3% minimum to artists on contract; standard royalty to songwriters.
How to Contact: Submit demo tape and lyric sheet. Prefers cassette with 1-3 songs on demo. SASE. Reports in 3 weeks.
Music: Blues, C&W, easy listening, country jazz, MOR, R&B, country and soft rock, and top 40/pop. Recently released "Pride," by Don Buckley (crossover/country/pop single).

SCOTT TURNER PRODUCTIONS, 524 Doral Country Dr., Nashville TN 37221. Executive Producer: Scott Turner. Record producer and music publisher. Deals with artists and songwriters. Fee derived from sales royalty or outright fee from record company. "It depends on whether or not I am producing a major act for a major label, or if I place a custom session with a label."
How to Contact: Submit demo tape and lead sheet. Prefers cassette with 1-4 songs on demo. SASE. Reports in 2 weeks.
Music: C&W, easy listening, folk, MOR, progressive, rock, and top 40/pop. Recently produced "All My Best," by Slim Whitman (country, Liberty U.A. Records) and "Early Tymes," by Nilsson (rock, C.B.S. Records). Other artists include Jimmy Clanton, Del Reeves, and Sonny Throckmorton.
Tips: "Do your homework, study the pros and pay your dues."

SCOTT TUTT MUSIC, Box 121213, Nashville TN 37212. (615)329-0856. Contact: Scott Tutt. Record producer and music publisher (Buzzherb Music/BMI and Good Token Music/ASCAP). Deals with artists and songwriters. Produces 5 singles and 2 albums/year. Fee derived from sales royalty or outright fee from artists/songwriter or record company, depending on situation.
How to Contact: Submit demo tape and lyric sheet. Prefers 7½ ips reel-to-reel or cassette with 1-3 songs on demo. SASE. Reports as soon as possible.
Music: C&W, easy listening, folk, MOR, progressive, R&B, rock, top 40/pop and new wave. Recently produced "I Wanna Be with You Tonight," by Alabama (country single, GRT Records); "Sexy Ole Lady," by Pat Garret (country single, Golddust Records); and *This Is It, by Hopper (new wave LP, Golddust Records)*.

TWO STAR PRODUCTIONS, 15 King George's DR., Toronto, Ontario, Canada M6M 2H1. (416)656-1566. Producer: Bob Johnston. Record producer. Deals with artists and songwriters. Produces 3-5 singles and 1 album/year. Fee derived from outright fee from songwriter/artist.
How to Contact: Call or write first about your interest. Prefers cassette with 2-6 songs on demo. SAE and International Reply Coupons. Reports in 2 weeks.
Music: C&W, easy listening, MOR, rock (country rock) and crossover. Recently produced "Easy Feeling Loving You," by Mary Bailey (country single, RCA Records); "Homeward Bound to the Country," by Brett McNaul (country single, Twin Star Records); and "Living in a Love Song," by Charlie Shannon (crossover single, Twin Star Records).

TYMENA MUSIC (TY LEMLEY MUSIC), 430 Pearce Rd., Baldwin Township, Pittsburgh PA 15234. (412)341-0991. General Manager: Bud Lemley. President: Ty Lemley. Vice President: Tolmena Lemley. Record producer. Deals with artists and songwriters. Fee derived from sales royalty.
How to Contact: Submit demo tape and lyric sheet. Prefers 45 demo record (7½ or 15 ips reel-to-reel or cassette OK). SASE. Reports in 1 month.
Music: C&W, easy listening MOR, and top 40/pop. Recently produced "Offer Me Your Love" and "Me and You" (top 40/pop); and "Happy Willowbee," (children's); "Rowdy," (rock); and "Rock-A-Nova" (rock, dance) all by Ty Lemley (Tymena Records).

TONY VALOR PRODUCTIONS, INC., 211 W. 56th St., Suite 8, New York NY 10019. (212)246-6449. A&R Director: Karol Quinn. Deals with artists and songwriters.
How to Contact: Submit demo tape and lyric sheet. Prefers cassette with 3-6 songs on demo. SASE. Reports in 3 weeks.
Music: Dance-oriented, R&B and top 40/pop. Recently produced "You're Too Late," by Fantasy (R&B single, CBS/Pavillion Records); "Come & Get It On," by Soccer (disco single, Salsoul Records); and "Love Has Come My Way," by Tony Valor Sounds Orchestra (disco, Paula Records).

Songwriter's Market Close-up

Songwriter-producer-singer Jeff Barry remembers his first attempt at songwriting—a cowboy-inspired tune written under New Jersey skies when he was only seven. Fifteen years later he penned the hit single "Tell Laura I Love Her" and started a string of hits not only in the popular music field, but also for motion pictures and TV. In addition to writing, he has produced such greats as Steve Lawrence, Neil Diamond, Dusty Springfield, Connie Francis and John Travolta—among others.

Although Barry has written and produced songs that span 21 years, the one song he's most satisfied with is a recent one, "I Honestly Love You." "Lyrically, it says something that isn't common. The basic thought is one of expressing love, yet it is the situation under which the song lyrically takes place that is different—when someone says to someone else, 'I just want you to know, I really love you and I have no ulterior motives in telling you that.'"

The song was written with Peter Allen in collaboration—the work method he prefers. "I think that two people working together end up with the sum being greater than the parts. With two you get elements like showing off, and inspiration and feedback which are not present when you're writing by yourself. And when there's someone right there in the room not letting you get away with stuff, you probably end up with a better song."

And better songs—better opportunities—are what Barry strives for. His most challenging singular achievement to date, he feels, is *The Idolmaker*. "I had a lot to do with the film in general. It was all day, every day for a year, so that has to stand out."

Writing for films and TV (Barry also wrote theme music for *One Day at a Time* and *The Jeffersons*, among others) has its limitations. "The music has to work watching the screen. You see whatever it is, truly, in the sense of the score. And if it's a good score, you never hear it; it becomes part of the scenery, the emotion of the scene."

Emotions are what fuel a songwriter's

Jeff Barry

material, says Barry. "You've got to make (the song) sexy or funny, a great danceable piece, or say something that makes people think, or relate to you. Make them cry."

But don't blow your budget in the process, Barry goes on to say. "I don't think (beginning songwriters) should spend much money at all (on demos) because they probably can't afford to do it with every song they write. If it's a good song, performing it with one voice and piano, or voice and guitar, or voice and bang it on your knees should be enough. I consider the song is to the record as a stone is to the ring it's set in. The finer the stone, usually the simpler the setting. If you take a great song, and over-produce, put all kinds of little stones all around it, you end up with a gaudy cocktail ring; you lose the beauty of the stone, which is the real value."

With your simple demo in hand, says Barry, you're ready to approach a publisher, "an active publisher who knows the A&R man, knows the producer, knows the artist, knows when they're recording, knows their home phone numbers. Let him or his company get the songs to where they should be."

P.J. Schemenaur

VENTURE PRODUCTIONS, (formerly Camillo/Barker Enterprises), 121 Meadowbrook Dr., Somerville NJ 08876. (201)359-5110. Producers: Tony Camillo, Cecile Barker. Record producer, music publisher and production company. Deals with artists and songwriters. Produces 21-25 singles and 5-8 albums/year. Fee derived from sales royalty or outright fee from record company.
How to Contact: Query or submit demo tape and lead sheet. "Send as complete a package as possible." Prefers cassette with 2-5 songs on demo. SASE. Reports in "1 month or longer depending on schedule."
Music: Dance, soul, MOR, top 40/pop, "excellent material only." Recently produced *Let's Burn*, by Clarence Carter; "Without You" and *Don't Make Me Eat*, by Pendullum; "Body Bait," by Symba (disco); and "Once a Night," by Charlie English (single from the movie, *Hopscotch*).

CHARLES VICKERS MUSIC ASSOCIATION, 171 Pine Haven, Daytona Beach FL 32014. (904)252-4849. President/Producer: Dr. Charles H. Vickers D.M. Record producer and music publisher (Pritchett Publication/BMI and Alison Music/ASCAP). Deals with artists and songwriters. Produces 90 singles and 4 albums/year. Fee derived from sales royalty.
How to Contact: Write first about your interest. Prefers 7½ ips reel-to-reel or cassette with 1-6 songs on demo. SASE. Reports in 1 week.
Music: Bluegrass, blues, church/religious, classical, C&W, easy listening, gospel, jazz, MOR, progressive, reggae (pop), R&B, rock, soul and top 40/pop. Recently produced *Charle Vickers Does Disco*, by C. Vickers (disco LP, Tropical Records); *Charles Vickers*, by C. Vickers (country/pop/disco LP, Tropical Records); *Disco Pop of the 80's*, by C. Vickers (ballad/rock LP, Tropical Records); and *Another Dawn*, by C. Vickers (gospel LP, Accent Records and King of Kings Records).

KENT WASHBURN, 10622 Commerce Ave., Tujunga CA 91042. Owner: Kent Washburn. Record producer and music publisher. Deals with artists and songwriters. Produces 5-6 singles and 2-3 albums/year. Fee derived from sales royalty or outright fee from record company.
How to Contact: Query or submit demo tape and lead sheet. Prefers 7½ ips reel-to-reel or cassette with 1-4 songs on demo. SASE. Reports in 1 month.
Music: Dance; easy listening; jazz; MOR; soul; and top 40/pop. Recently produced *Frenzy* and *Steppin' Out*, by High Inergy (R&B/pop LPs, Motown Records); "Lovin' Fever," by High Inergy (R&B/pop single, Motown Records); and "Always Christmas," by Pamela Hart (Christmas/pop, Hartsong Records). Other artists include Paul Davis (Hartsong Records), and Nicholas.

WATERMELON PRODUCTIONS, Box 530, Cooper Station, New York NY 10003. President/Producer: Paul Wade. Record producer and music publisher (Hot Fudge Music/ASCAP). Deals with artists and songwriters. Produces 5 singles and 2 albums/year. Fee derived from sales royalty.
How to Contact: Query or submit lead sheet. Prefers cassette with 2-3 songs on demo. "Send lead sheet. We'll ask for a tape if we want one. However, if tape is sent with SASE, we'll return it. We are interested in music with no lyrics also." SASE. Reports in 2 weeks.
Music: Children's, disco, easy listening, MOR, rock, soul, and top 40/pop. Recently produced "Ingrid Russell," by Ingrid Russell (funky rock, Balloon Records); "Jim Moses," by Jim Moses (mellow music, Rubber Records); and "Here I Am," by Ellie Frye (rock 'n roll, Rubber Records).

THE WAXWORKS RECORDING STUDIO, Box 299, Albert St., St. Jacobs, Ontario, Canada N0B 2N0. (519)664-3311 or 3332. Producer: Mr. Jim Evans. Record producer and music publisher (Hot Wax Publishing and St. Jacobs Music Publishing. Deals with artists and songwriters. Produces 15 singles and 6 albums/year. Fee negotiable.
How to Contact: Submit demo tape and lyric sheet. Prefers cassette with 3-5 songs on demo. "Send only the best material in the best form possible. Express the compositions in the best form of production available and be sure lyrics and melody are easily discernable." SAE and International Reply Coupons. Reports in 1 month.
Music: C&W, dance-oriented, easy listening, gospel, MOR, R&B, rock (all kinds) and top 40/pop. Recently produced "Rick Curtis," by Rick Curtis (rock, Freedom Records); "1st Concession," by Wayne Diebold (country, Circle M Records); and "John Saucier," by John Saucier (rock, Waxworks Records).

WEIRZ WORLD PRODUCTIONS, 1414 Summitridge Dr., Beverly Hills CA 90210. (213)858-5913. Producers: Larry Weir, Tom Weir, Robert Harrison. Record producer and music publisher (St. Cecilia Music/BMI). Estab. 1980. Deals with artists and songwriters. Produces 5 singles and 5 albums/year. Fee derived from sales royalty.
How to Contact: Write first about your interest then submit demo tape and lyric sheet. Prefers cassette with 1-3 songs on demo. Does not return unsolicited material. Reports in 3 weeks.
Music: C&W, easy listening, jazz, MOR, progressive, rock and soul. Recently produced *The*

Weirz, by The Weirz (pop/rock LP, Parallel Records); *USC*, by Bernard Tarver (soul LP, Parallel Records); and *Muffy Hendrix*, by M. Hendrix (top 40 LP, Parallel Records).

Tips: "We like to work with self-contained artists or ones with great vocal abilities looking for material."

WHITEWAY PRODUCTIONS, INC., 65 W. 55th St., New York NY 10019. President: Eddie White. Record, play, film and concert producer. Deals with artists and actors. Fee derived from sales royalty.

How to Contact: Query, arrange personal interview or submit demo tape. "We advertise or send out calls when we are doing a show." SASE. Reports in 1 week.

Music: Musical shows. Recently produced *Birmingham Rag* and *Dixieland Blues*, by Sunny Gale.

SHANE WILDER PRODUCTIONS, Box 3503, Hollywood CA 90028. (213)467-1958 or 467-1959. President: Shane Wilder. Record producer and music publisher. Deals with artists and songwriters. Produces 25-30 singles and 10-15 albums/year. Fee derived from sales royalty; plus production fee.

How to Contact: Submit demo tape and lyric sheet. Prefers cassette with 6-8 songs on demo. SASE. Reports in 2 weeks.

Music: C&W, easy listening, MOR, rock, and top 40/pop. Recently produced "Part Time Love," by Crystal Blue (disco); and "Old Liars, Umpires and a Woman Who Knows," by Mike Franklin (country, N.S.D. Records). Other artists include Priscilla Emerson and Laurie Loman (MCA recording artist).

WILDWOOD ENTERTAINMENT, 223 Broadway, Rensselaer NY 12144. (518)273-7660. President: Vincent Meyer, Jr. Vice President: Erich Borden. A&R Director: Chuck Winans. Record producer and music publisher (Late Music/BMI). Deals with artists and songwriters. Fee derived from sales royalty.

How to Contact: Submit demo tape and lyric sheet. Prefers cassette with 3-7 songs on demo. SASE. Reports in 1 month.

Music: Bluegrass, children's, easy listening, folk, jazz, rock and top 40/pop. Recently produced "Travelin' Shoes," by Chuck Winans and Geoff Brown; and "Maybe This Is It," by Frank Mastrone and Al Nelson. Other artists include Jill Hughes.

DON WILLIAMS MUSIC GROUP, 1888 Century Park E., Suite 1106, Los Angeles CA 90067. (213)556-2458. Record producer and music publisher. Deals with artists and songwriters. Fee derived from sales royalty.

How to Contact: Submit demo tape and lyric sheet or call first about your interest. Prefers 3-5 songs on demo. List name, address and telephone number on package. SASE. Reports in 4-6 weeks.

Music: All types. Recently produced "I'm On Fire," by Dwight Twilley (top 40/pop, Shelter Records); "I'd Have To Be Crazy," by Steven Fromholz (progressive/country, Capitol Records); and "Second In Your Life," by Del Shannon (top 40/pop, RSO Records).

WIL-TOO MUSIC, 2405 Pennington Bend Rd., Nashville TN 37214. (615)883-2457. President: Tom Wilkerson. Record producer and music publisher. Estab. 1979. Deals with artists and songwriters. Fee derived from sales royalty or outright fee from record company.

How to Contact: Submit demo tape and lyric sheet. Prefers 7½ ips reel-to-reel with 1-4 songs on demo. SASE. Reports in 1 month.

Music: Bluegrass; church/religious; C&W; easy listening; gospel; and MOR. Artists include Susan Coffey and Mike Palmer.

WITHOUT FAIL PRODUCTIONS, 1806 N. Normandie Ave., Los Angeles CA 90027. (213)669-1404. Producers: E.J. Emmons and Troy Mathisen. Deals with artists and songwriters. Produces 4-8 singles (45's) and 4-6 albums/year. Fees derived from sales royalty and/or outright fee from record company.

How to Contact: Write first about your interest then submit demo tape and lyric sheet. Prefers cassette with 3-25 songs on demo. SASE. Reports within 2 weeks.

Music: Progressive, rock, soul, new wave, funk and top 40/pop. Recently produced "Janitor" and "Gidget Goes to Hell", by Suburban Lawns (new wave singles, Suburban Industrial Records); "Fire," by Smokey (rock single, S&M Records); and *Welcome to Our Party*, by Rare Gems (funk LP, Trek Records).

WMOT RECORDS, 1128 Spruce St., Philadelphia PA 19107. (215)985-0633. Vice President: Nick Martinelli. Record producer and music publisher (WMOT Music/BMI). Deals with artists and

songwriters. Produces 80 singles and 10 albums/year. Fee derived from sales royalty.
How to Contact: Submit demo tape and lyric sheet. Prefers cassette. SASE. Reports in 2 weeks.
Music: R&B, soul and top 40/pop. Artists include Barbra Mason and Frankie Smith. Recently produced "Double Dutch Bus," by Frankie Smith (R&B single, WMOT Records); "Sunrise," by Slick (R&B, WMOT Records); and *A Piece of My Life*, by Barbara Mason (R&B, WMOT Records). Other artists include Blue Magic and Fat Larry's Band.

PAUL ZALESKI, Box 34032, Bartlett TN 38134. (901)388-4185. Contact: Paul Zaleski. Record producer and music publisher (Apache's Rhythm). Deals with artists and songwriters. Produces 4 singles and 3 albums/year. Fee derived from sales royalty or outright fee from record company.
How to Contact: Submit demo tape and lyric sheet. Prefers 7½ ips reel-to-reel or cassette with 4-10 songs on demo. SASE. Reports in 2 weeks.
Music: C&W, easy listening, MOR, R&B, soul and top 40/pop. Recently produced "Everybody Cried," by Rufus Thomas (R&B single, XL Records); and "I Don't Live There Anymore," by Chuck Bell (country single, Sun Records); and "Tell Me Why," by Mark O'Leary (pop single, Joker Records). Other artists include Rayner Street Band.

DAN ZAM PRODUCTIONS, 183 Thompson St., New York NY 10012. (212)982-1374. President: Dan Zam. Record producer. Deals with artists and songwriters. Fee derived from sales royalty or outright fee from songwriter/artist.
How to Contact: Submit demo tape or submit demo tape and lead sheet. Prefers 7½ or 15 ips reel-to-reel (no Dolby) with 3 songs minimum on tape. SASE. Reports in 3 weeks.
Music: New music, avante-pop and rock.

Z'S PRODUCTIONS, 904 Rayner, Box 14671, Memphis TN 38114. (901)774-1721. President: Paul Zaleski. Record producer and music publisher (Apache's Rhythm/ASCAP). Deals with artists and record companies. Produces 4 singles and 2 albums/year. Fee derived from sales royalty or outright fee from record company.
How to Contact: Submit demo tape and lyric sheet. Prefers cassette with 4-6 songs on demo. SASE. Reports in 2 weeks.
Music: Easy listening, MOR, R&B, hard and soft rock, soul (stax-type), and top 40/pop. Recently produced "Everybody Cried," by Rufus Thomas (R&B, XL Records); "I Don't Live There Anymore" and "Crazy Days," by Chuck Bell (C&W, Sun Records); "Tell Me Why," by Mark O'Leary (pop, Joker Records). Other artists include Masqueraders.

Ad Agencies

Songwriters with desire and ability to write jingles, songs and background music for commercials need look no farther than their home town for good markets in the advertising field. New York, Chicago and other large commercial centers have, of course, the greatest concentration of major advertising agencies. But, wherever there are car dealerships, grocery stores and other retail businesses, there are agencies to provide individualized advertising campaigns for TV and radio. Many top agencies also have branches in cities across the country.

Ad agencies know the value of using local talent—not only songwriters, but vocalists, musicians and studio facilities. Taking advantage of local talent means more physical control over the production of a commercial, and less expense for agency clients—an edge that's a definite advantage in the competitive field of advertising.

Advertising agencies work closely with clients on broadcast campaigns. Through consultation and input from their creative staff, agencies then establish a "feel" they believe commercials should project for a client's product. What an agency is looking for from the songwriter then, are jingles and music to stimulate the consumer to identify with a product and hum the commercial in his head while paying the cashier.

Ad agencies, unlike record companies or music publishers, work on assignment as their clients' needs arise. So, when listening to a demo, they are not looking for a finished product, but for an indication of your versatility—what you can do if and when you are given the chance. Are you able to establish a mood? Are your lyrics strong and catchy? Do you have a "hook?" How skillfully composed are your melodies? Are you able to establish—with maybe as little as ten lyrics and a background melody—a "feel" that might suit one of their client's products?

The agencies listed here tell exactly what type of clients they serve—many are willing to send you a specific list of their clients—and how songwriters should submit examples of their work. Understand, though, that most ad agencies, if they like what you present them, will want to keep your demo on file to refer to for possible future assignment. Many will return your tape at your request, however, if you have enclosed a SASE.

For more about the business of writing jingles and music for commercials, see "Advertising Agencies" in the "Business" section at the back of this book. To learn more about the craft of jingle writing, read *Music to Sell By: The Craft of Jingle Writing*, by Antonia Teixerira, Jr. (Berklee Press Publications, 1265 Boylston St., Boston MA 02215).

Check the Yellow Pages for names and addresses of agencies in your area. Additional names and addresses of agencies along with specific clients of each company may be obtained from *The Standard Directory of Advertising Agencies* (National Register Publishing Company).

ADELANTE ADVERTISING, INC., 588 5th Ave., New York NY 10036. (212)869-1470. Vice President: David Krieger. Advertising agency. Serves soft goods, entertainment, wine, financial, and other consumer products clients. Uses jingles and background music in commercials, demonstration and sales films, and audiovisuals. Commissions 6-10 songwriters and 6-10 lyricists/year. Pays $25-3,000/job. "Speculative demos to be determined." Buys all rights.
How to Contact: Submit demo tape of previously aired work. Prefers 7½ ips reel-to-reel or cassette with 3-15 songs on tape. SASE, but prefers to keep material on file. Reports in 2 weeks or as need arises.
Music: "We are an ethnic advertising agency. Our needs are to fulfill the music needs of the black and Spanish communities to enforce sales via radio and TV. We use R&B, jazz, disco, salsa, merenque, etc."

ADVERTISING & MARKETING, INC., 1 LeFleur's Square, Box 873, Jackson MS 39205. (601)981-8881. Associate Creative Director: Tom Dupree. Advertising agency. Serves financial, service and package goods clients. Uses services of songwriters and lyricists for industrial films and AV shows. "The lyricist gets campaign theme, sample copy for print, and our creative rationale plus any suggested lines we might have. It is then his job to turn our ideas into a song." Commissions plus 10-15 pieces/year. Pays $1,000-15,000/job. Prefers to buy all rights, but will negotiate for top quality work.
How to Contact: Submit demo tape of previously aired work or tape demonstrating jingle/ composition skills. Prefers 7½ ips reel-to-reel with 5-15 songs on demo. "Where possible, identify cost of production for each piece of music on reel." SASE, but prefers to keep material on file. "As a project comes up that we think is up his alley, we call a songwriter and ask him to spec a piano demo. (In some cases, we pay for spec work, but rarely to someone we haven't worked with before.)"
Music: Both long-term corporate jingles and short-term music for single campaigns. Adamantly opposed to re-treads. "We look for songwriters who can demonstrate a variety of styles and musical configurations—country and western alone will not get it. The good song impresses us, not necessarily the good production."
Tips: "Avoid condescension; we may be in Jackson, Mississippi, but we know what's good and what isn't. We have used major national sources in the past, and will in the future."

AITKIN-KYNETTE CO., Bourse Bldg., Philadelphia PA 19106. Vice President/Creative Department: Ed Bates. Advertising agency. Serves industrial, some consumer clients. Uses music houses for jingles and background music in commercials. Commissions 4 pieces/year. Pays creative fee asked by music houses.
How to Contact: Submit by mail demonstration tape of previously aired work. "If songwriter has no previous work bought by ad agency, it's OK to submit samples of work." Prefers 7½ ips reel-to-reel. Will return with SASE if requested, but prefers to keep on file.
Music: All types.

ALPINE ADVERTISING, INC., 2244 Grand Ave., Box 30895, Billings MT 59107. (406)652-1630. President: James F. Preste. Advertising agency. Serves financial, automotive and food clients. Uses jingles. Commissions 20 pieces/year. Pays $650-3,500/job. Buys all rights.
How to Contact: Submit demo tape of previously aired work. Prefers 7½ ips reel-to-reel with 5-12 songs on demo. Does not return unsolicited material. Reports in 1 month.

AMERICAN FILMWORLD COMPANY, (formerly American Media, Inc.), division of Intervision Communications Corp., 11069 Ophir Dr., Los Angeles CA 90024. President/Media & Music Director: Chip Miller. Motion picture and TV development agency. Serves film and entertainment industry. Uses jingles, background music for commercials and films. Commissions 10 pieces/ year. Pays $60 minimum/hour. Buys all rights.
How to Contact: Query with resume, submit demo tape of previously aired work or submit tape demonstrating jingle/composition skills. Prefers cassette with 3-6 songs on demo. "Send lyric sheets, when applicable." SASE, but prefers to keep material on file. Reports in 3 weeks.
Music: Needs jingles ("catchy, good solid lyrics; contemporary, folk- or rock-oriented, with hooks"); and film and commercial scoring (dramatic or lightly orchestrated arrangements). Avoid "overproduction, pretentiousness and slickness."
Tips: "Compose with a market in mind not limited to your own artistic liking."

AMVID COMMUNICATION SERVICES, INC., 2100 Sepulveda Blvd., Manhattan Beach CA 90266. (213)545-6691. Contact: Production Manager or Producer. Uses services of music houses for background music. Pays by the job.
How to Contact: Query with resume of credits or submit demo tape of previously aired work. Prefers 7½ ips reel-to-reel or cassette. SASE. Reports in 10 days.
Music: Background music written to convey specific moods.

ARNOLD & CO., 1111 Park Square Bldg., Boston MA 02116. (617)357-1900. Contact: Steve Cosmopulos. Advertising agency. Serves all types of clients, including those in fast food, banking and computers. Uses music houses and individual songwriters for jingles and background music in commercials. Commissions 8 pieces/year. Pays per job. Rights vary with project.
How to Contact: Submit by mail demonstration tape of previously aired work or send representative with tape. Prefers cassette lasting no more than 10-15 minutes. SASE; prefers to file tape.
Music: All types.

AYER/PRITIKIN & GIBBONS, 27 Maiden Lane, San Francisco CA 94108. Creative Director/ Vice President: Dick Fenderson. Advertising agency. Serves bank, restaurant, consumer and industrial clients. Uses jingles and background music for commercials. Commissions 6 pieces/ year. Pays $200 minimum/job. Buys all rights.
How to Contact: Submit demo tape of previously aired work. Prefers 7½ ips reel-to-reel with 5-12 songs on demo. Does not return unsolicited material. Reports in 1 month.

BALLARD CANNON, INC., 506 2nd W., Box 9787, Seattle WA 98119. (206)284-8800. Vice President/Creative Services: Dick Rosenwald. Advertising agency. Serves financial, retail, travel, entertainment/food and insurance clients. Uses jingles and background music for commercials. Commissions 3 pieces/year. Pays $1,000 minimum/job. Rights purchased vary.
How to Contact: Query with resume of credits or submit demo tape of previously aired work. Prefers 7½ ips reel-to-reel with 4-12 songs on demo. "Include a brief description of involvement in each project, total costs, objectives and use of material." SASE. Reports in 1 month.
Tips: "Do not try to prepackage jingles. You must approach each one individually to solve specific communication/image needs."

BATTEN, BARTON, DURSTINE & OSBORN, INC., 1640 Northwestern Bank Bldg., Minneapolis MN 55402. (612)338-8401. Producer: Rosemary Januschka. Advertising agency. Serves food and stockbroker clients. Clients include 3-M, Honeywell and Cargill. Uses individual songwriters and music houses for jingles and background music in commerials. Commissions about 5 pieces/ year. Pays creative fee and production fee. Buys all rights.
How to Contact: Submit by mail demonstration tape of previously aired work (if no previously aired work, samples OK). SASE; prefers to keep tape on file.
Music: Music varies. Can be country oriented; sophisticated; tricky jingles; or polished compositions. Agency sometimes does their own lyrics.

BATZ-HODGSON-NEUWOEHNER, INC., VFW Bldg., 406 W. 34th St., Kansas City MO 64111. Creative Director: Jim Sheiner. Advertising agency. Uses jingles and background music in commercials. Commissions 1 piece/year. Payment arranged through AFTRA. Rights purchased vary.
How to Contact: Submit demo tape of previously aired work. Prefers 7½ ips reel-to-reel with 7-8 songs on demo. SASE. Reports in 1 week.

BB&W ADVERTISING, 1106 State St., Boise ID 83702. (208)343-2572. Creative Director/ Producer: Jack Ewing. Advertising agency. Serves corporate, industrial, retail and financial clients. Uses services of songwriters and lyricists for jingles. Commissions 1-2 songwriters and 1-2 lyricist/year for jingles and background music in commercials. Pays $100-4,500/job. Buys all rights.
How to Contact: Submit demo tape of previously aired work. Prefers 7½ ips reel-to-reel with 5-25 songs on demo. SASE, but prefers to keep material on file. "We keep demo tapes on file, and contact songwriters when there is a need for their services."
Tips: "Submit resume and references, list of clients for whom preformed, and basic working rates; submit samples of material on 7½ ips reel."

BBDO, 410 N. Michigan Ave., Chicago IL 60611. Producer: Vickie Paradise. (312)337-7860. Ad Agency. Serves food clients. Uses music houses for jingles. Commissions 75 pieces/year. Pays fair price for demonstration; asks what creative fee is wanted. Buys all rights.
How to Contact: Arrange personal interview or submit demonstration tape of previous work; or submit demo tape showing jingles/composition skills. Prefers 7½ ips reel-to-reel; wants to hear instrumental first. Returns material if requested with SASE; prefers to keep tape on file.
Music: Likes melodies such as in the Juicy Fruit gum commercial. Once a melody is achieved, does own variations.

BBDO WEST, 10960 Wilshire Blvd., Los Angeles CA 90024. (213)479-3979. Creative Director: Bob Kuperman. Advertising agency. Uses jingles and background music for commercials. Pays by the job.
How to Contact: Submit demo tape of previously aired work. Prefers 7½ ips reel-to-reel. SASE.

BEAR ADVERTISING, 1424 N. Highland Ave., Los Angeles CA 90028. (213)466-6464. Vice President: Bruce Bear. Serves sporting goods, fast food and industrial clients. Uses jingles and background music in commercials. Pays by the job.
How to Contact: Submit demo tape of previously aired work. Prefers cassette. SASE. Reports "as soon as possible."
Music: Needs vary.

BELL OF THE CAPE ADVERTISING, Box 23, East Dennis MA 02641. (617)385-2334. Vice President: Robert G. Fish. Advertising agency. Serves amusement, financial, insurance, light industry, cable TV, furniture and restaurant clients. Uses jingles and background music for commercials. Commissions 3 pieces/year. Pays $300 minimum/job. "We purchase only when the client accepts." Buys all rights.
How to Contact: Submit demo tape of previously aired work or of jingles/compositions for a specific client. Prefers 7½ ips reel-to-reel with 5-15 songs on demo. SASE, but prefers to keep material on file. Reports in 2 weeks.
Music: "We work with jingles and one-shot or full series music backgrounds. Persons willing to work on spec are most valuable to us. We deal with a medium market and most clients prefer specs. Closings are better following such specs."

BERGER, STONE & RATNER, INC., 666 5th Ave., New York NY 10019. President: Joseph Stone. Advertising agency. Serves automobile, bank, jewelry, optical, corporate financial and institutional clients. Uses jingles and background music for commercials. Commissions 10 pieces/year. Pays $1,000-4,000/job. "We mainly buy orchestration and production of commercials we write." Buys all rights.
How to Contact: Query with resume. Prefers reel-to-reel or cassette, or videotape or 16mm film. Does not return unsolicited material. "Never reports, unless interested in the material."
Tips: "Realize that jingles are advertising; they must fill marketing needs within marketing plans. Learn what makes advertising work, and write that kind of material into the jingle."

DOYLE DANE BERNBACH ADVERTISING LTD., 2 Bloor St. W, Toronto, Ontario Canada M4W 1G4. (416)925-8911. Contact: Russ Jarvis. Ad agency. Serves all types of clients. Uses services of songwriters for jingles and background music in commercials. Commissions 1-10 pieces/year. Pays by union scale. Usually buys all rights.
How to Contact: Submit any type demo tape of previously aired work. Prefers maximum 10 minutes on demo. SAE and International Reply Coupon, but prefers to keep material on file. Responds as need arises.
Music: All types.

BERNSTEIN, REIN & BOASBERG, 800 W. 47th St., Kansas City MO 64112. (816)756-0640. Creative Director: Jeff Bremser. Advertising agency. Uses services of songwriters for jingles and background music in commercials. Commissions 10-20 pieces/year from 3-5 songwriters. Pays $15,000 maximum/job. "We buy complete production, not just songs."
How to Contact: Submit demo tape of previously aired work. Prefers reel-to-reel with 5 songs minimum on tape. SASE. "We keep tapes on file; we do not report."
Music: "All styles for use as jingles and commercial scores."

BLAIR ADVERTISING, INC., subsidiary of BBDO International, 96 College Ave., Rochester NY 14607. (716)473-0440. Copy Chief: John R. Brown. Advertising agency. Serves financial, industrial and consumer clients. Uses jingles, background music for commercials and music for sales meeting presentations. Commissions 10 pieces/year. Pays $1,000-10,000/job. Buys all rights.
How to Contact: Query. Prefers 7½ ips reel-to-reel with 5-20 songs on demo. Does not return unsolicited material.
Music: "We need every type. Often lyrics will be supplied. We're seriously interested in hearing from good production sources. We have at hand some of the world's best working for us, but we're always ready to listen to fresh, new ideas."

JOHN BORDEN ADVERTISING AGENCY, 5841 73rd Ave. N., #102, Brooklyn Park MN 55429. (612)566-4515. Account Executive: John Borden. Serves recruitment, industrial, financial, medical, insurance and food manufacturing clients. Uses services of songwriters and lyricists for jingles and background music. Commissions 1-3 songwriters and 1-3 lyricists/year. Pays $200-2,000/job. Rights purchased vary.
How to Contact: Submit demo tape of previously aired work. Prefers cassette. Does not return unsolicited material. SASE, but prefers to keep material on file. Reports in 1 month.
Tips: "Our specialty is recruitment advertising (beginning clericals, data processing personnel, nurses, electronic technicians, engineers and bank personnel)."

BOZELL & JACOBS, 400 Colony Square, Suite 1833, Atlanta GA 30361. (404)892-2221. Contact: Ken Haas. Advertising agency. Serves consumer, packaged goods, financial and banking clients. Uses services of independent songwriters and lyricists. "I never use 'jingles.' I use music. And there *is* a difference." Uses music houses for "musical beds and full sings depending upon the concept." Commissions 4-5 songwriters and 3-4 lyricists/year.

How to Contact: Representative should call and set up appointment to play reel. If no reel is available, don't bother. Prefers 7½ ips reel-to-reel "or whatever." SASE, but prefers to keep material on file. Responds if and when the need arises.
Music: Type of music needed depends upon project.
Tips: "Just be great at what you do. Act like mensch."

BOZELL & JACOBS INTERNATIONAL, INC., 2440 Embarcadero Way, Palo Alto CA 94303. (415)856-9000. Broadcast Supervisor: Susan C. Smith. Advertising agency. Serves consumer, industrial, vineyard, realty and computer system clients. Uses primarily music houses, some individual songwriters for jingles, background music in commercials and audiovisual shows for sales meetings. Commissions 4 jingles and 4 pieces for audiovisual shows per year. Negotiates price when union is not involved. Buys all rights.
How to Contact: Send reel or information. Prefers ¼" reel-to-reel. Tape should have variety of music. Does not return material; keeps tape on file.
Music: All types.

BOZELL & JACOBS INTERNATIONAL, INC., 444 N. Michigan, Chicago IL 60611. (312)644-9800. Broadcast Production Manager: Gail Duyckinck. Advertising agency. Serves utility, cosmetic and real estate clients. Uses individual songwriters and music houses for jingles and background music in commercials. Commissions 10 pieces/year. Pays $2,400 minimum/job. Buys all rights.
How to Contact: Submit by mail demonstration tape of previously aired work (if no previously aired work, samples OK). Prefers 7½ ips reel-to-reel. Tape should be about 3 minutes in length. SASE; prefers to keep tape on file.

BOZELL & JACOBS/PACIFIC, 10850 Wilshire Blvd., Los Angeles CA 90024. (213)879-1800. Creative Director: Robert Feinberg. Advertising agency. Serves financial, food and realty clients. Uses individual songwriters for jingles and background music in commercials. Pays according to client's budget. Buys all rights.
How to Contact: Submit by mail demonstration tape of previously aired work (if no previously aired work, samples OK). Prefers reel-to-reel. Wants a representative amount of songs. If songwriter has 10 award winning commercials, wants to hear them all. If has only 1 that has been sold, wants to hear that one and then some other work, too. SASE; prefers to keep tape on file.
Music: All types.

BOZELL & JACOBS/PR, 1200 Smith, Suite 2000, 2 Allen Center, Houston TX 77002. (713)651-3114. Creative Director: Ron Spataro. Ad agency. Serves industrial, packaged goods, service and banking clients. Uses music houses for jingles, background music in commercials, TV, slide shows and audiovisual presentations. Commissions 12-15 packages/year. Pays $500-1,000 for working demo. Buys all rights, then pays talent residuals and musician residuals.
How to Contact: Submit demonstration tape of previous work or demo tape showing jingle/composition skills. Prefers 7½ ips reel-to-reel. Tapes should be a maximum of 6 minutes. SASE; prefers to keep tape on file.

BROOKS, JOHNSON, ZAUSMER ADVERTISING, Suite 240, Milam Bldg., San Antonio TX 78205. (512)227-3454. Contact: Rick Neff or Bruce Robinett. Advertising agency. Uses music houses for jingles and background music in commercials. Commissions 7-10 songwriters/year. Payment based on bids. Buys all rights.
How to Contact: Submit demo tape of previously aired work or "call to see if we have work coming up you want to bid on." Prefers any type tape, although "it's easier to file cassettes" with 7-10 songs on demo. SASE but prefers to file submissions. Responds as need arises.
Music: Uses all types according to client's needs.
Tips: "Submit demo of work done for others."

BRUCE-GREEN ADVERTISING, LTD., #3 Felton Place, Box 549, Bloomington IL 61701. (309)827-8081. Media Supervisor: Gina Ready. Advertising agency. Serves consumer, industrial and agricultural clients. Uses services of songwriters for background music. Commissions 2 songwriters and 1 lyricist/year. Pays $100 minimum/job. Buys all rights.
How to Contact: Query with resume or submit demo tape showing jingle/composition skills. Prefers cassette. SASE, but prefers to keep material on file. Reports in 1 week.

SAL BUTERA ASSOCIATES ADVERTISING, 1824 Whipple Ave. NW, Canton OH 44708. Broadcast Services Supervisor/President: Sal Butera. Advertising agency. Serves consumer clients. Uses jingles and background music for commercials. Commissions 5 pieces/year. Pays on a per-bid basis. Buys all rights or one-time rights.

How to Contact: Query with resume of credits, submit demo tape of previously aired work or submit demo tape showing jingle/composition skills. Prefers 7½ ips reel-to-reel with 6-12 songs on demo. Does not return unsolicited material. Reports in 1 month.

HAROLD CABOT & CO. INC., 10 High St., Boston MA 02110. (617)426-7600. Contact: Debbie Long. Advertising agency. Serves 90% consumer, 10% industrial clients. Uses jingles and background music in commercials. Commissions many pieces/year. Payment negotiable. Usually buys one-time rights.

How to Contact: Submit demo tape of previously aired work. SASE. Prefers to file demos but this is not necessary.

Music: All types.

CALLAHAN & DAY, INC., Wellington Square, Pittsburgh PA 15235. (412)372-4700. Advertising agency. Serves financial, consumer product and industrial clients. Uses jingles and background music in commercials. Commissions 12-30 pieces/year. Payment negotiable. Buys all rights.

How to Contact: Submit demo tape of previously aired work. Prefers 7½ ips reel-to-reel.

CHIAT/DAY ADVERTISING, 517 S. Olive, Los Angeles CA 90013. (213)622-7454. Vice President/Creative Director: Lee Clow. Creative Secretary: Diana Barton. Serves stereo equipment, home loan, life insurance, food, beverage and hotel clients. Uses background music in commercials. Commissions 1 piece annually. Pays by the job.

How to Contact: Submit demo tape of previously aired work. Prefers 7½ ips reel-to-reel. SASE. Reports "as soon as possible."

COAST TO COAST ADVERTISING, INC., 1500 N. Dale Mabry, Box 22601, Tampa FL 33622. (813)871-4731. Vice President: Charles R. Bisbee Jr. Advertising agency. Serves retail clients. Uses jingles. Commissions 3 pieces/year. Pays on a per-job basis. Buys all rights.

How to Contact: Query with resume of credits, submit demo tape of previously aired work or submit demo tape showing jingle/composition skills. Prefers reel-to-reel or cassette. SASE. Reports "immediately if material is solicited. If it's unsolicited, I may not report back."

COLLE & McVOY ADVERTISING, INC., 6900 E. Belleview Ave., Englewood CO 80111. Broadcast/Production Director: James R. Withers. Advertising agency. Uses services of production companies for jingles and background music. Commissions 5-10 pieces/year. Pays $300-3,000/job. Buys all rights.

How to Contact: Query with resume or submit demo tape of previously aired work. Prefers 7½ ips reel-to-reel with 3-12 songs on demo. SASE, but prefers to keep material on file. Reports by phone when need arises.

Music: "Big sound, mostly donuts. Some 'full sing' and contemporary."

Tips: "You should be willing to offer free or inexpensive 'spec' cuts to demo the concept; if not, forget it."

COMMUNICATIONS TEAM, INC., 3848 Sheffield Dr., Huntingdon Valley PA 19006. (215)947-2400. President: Charles Tucker. Advertising agency. Serves real estate, graphics, casino, perfume, insurance, automobile, paint and varnish manufacturer and hospital clients. Uses services of songwriters for jingles and background music. Commissions 3 songwriters and 1-2 lyricists/year. Pays $500-50,000/job. Buys all rights.

How to Contact: Query with resume of credits or submit demo tape of previously aired work. Prefers cassette with 4-6 songs on demo. SASE, but prefers to keep material on file. Reports when the need arises.

Music: "We need jingles for our accounts, many of whom are real estate oriented, selling entire communities."

CONAHAY & LYON, INC., 380 Madison Ave., New York NY 10017. (212)599-6400. Advertising agency. Serves all types of clients. Uses music houses for jingles and background music in commercials. Commissions 12 pieces/year. "Rights purchased depend on media used."

How to Contact: Submit demo tape of previously aired work. "We discourage unsolicited demos on any accounts we now have because of possible legal problems. Will accept demos of work done elsewhere or music slanted toward general topic such as airlines." Prefers 7½ ips reel-to-reel or cassette 5-6 minutes long.

Music Classical to rock "depending on needs."

CONRADI, JOHNSON AND ASSOCIATES, INC., 7777 Bonhomme, Suite 1010, St. Louis MO 63105. Media Director: Donna Vorhies. Producer: Richard Ohms. Account Services: Kay Jones.

Advertising agency, public relations firm and marketing firm. Serves financial, automotive, fast food, industrial, restaurant and hotel clients. Uses jingles and background music for commercials. Payment negotiable. Buys all rights.
How to Contact: Submit resume of credits or submit demo tape showing jingle/composition skills. Prefers cassette with 4-5 songs on demo. SASE. Reports in 1 month.

COONS, SHOTWELL & ASSOCIATES, 1614 W. Riverside Ave., Spokane WA 99201. Advertising agency and public relations firm. Account Executive: Debra Lockhert. Serves industrial, retail, media, financial, public utility, and automotive clients. Uses production houses for jingles and background music for commercials. Commissions 4-8 pieces/year. Pays $1,500-5,000/job. Buys all rights.
How to Contact: Submit demo tape of previously aired work or submit demo tape showing jingle/composition skills. Prefers 7½ ips reel-to-reel with 7-15 songs on demo. "The cost of submitted productions would be helpful." Does not return unsolicited material. Reports "immediately, if we have a need."
Tips: "We're not interested in hearing from songwriters *per se*. We usually deal with music houses that are in the business of selling music for radio and TV commercials."

THE CRAMER-KRASSELT CO., 733 N. Van Buren, Milwaukee WI 53202. (414)276-3500. Serves consumer, financial and service accounts. Uses services of songwriters and music production companies for jingles and background music in commercials. Commissions 2-3 songwriters/year. Pays $1,800-3,000 per job. Usually buys all rights.
How to Contact: Send sample reel with cover letter; everyone in the firm who would be a potential purchaser is made aware of it. Prefers 7½ ips reel-to-reel. Prefers to keep material on file. Responds as needed.

CREATIVE HOUSE ADVERTISING, INC., 24370 Northwestern Hwy., Suite 300, Southfield MI 48075. (313)353-3344. Vice President/Creative Director: Robert G. Washburn. Advertising agency and graphics studio. Serves commercial, retail, consumer, industrial and financial clients. Uses services of songwriters and lyricists for jingles and background music for radio and TV commercials. Commissions 1 songwriter and 1 lyricist/year for 2 pieces/year. Pays $40-60/hour depending on job involvement. Buys all rights.
How to Contact: Query with resume of credits, submit tape demo showing jingle/composition skills. Prefers 7½ ips reel-to-reel with 6-12 songs on demo. SASE, but would prefer to keep material on file. Reports in 1 month, if requested.
Music: "The type of music we need depends on clients. The range is multi, from contemporary to disco to rock to MOR and traditional."

CRESWELL, MUNSELL, SCHUBERT & ZIRBEL, INC., Box 2879, Cedar Rapids IA 52406. (319)393-0200. Executive Producer: Terry Taylor. Serves primarily agricultural clients. Uses individual songwriters and music houses for jingles and background music in commercials. Commissions 10 pieces/year. Pays union rate. Buys rights on talent residuals.
How to Contact: Submit demo tape of previously aired work. Prefers 7½ or 15 ips reel-to-reel with 7-8 songs maximum on demo. SASE; prefers to keep tape on file.
Music: All types. Likes to hear a good range of music material. Will listen to anything from "simple pickin' and singin' to the Mormon Tabernacle Choir" type music.

JOHN CROWE ADVERTISING AGENCY, 1104 S. 2nd St., Springfield IL 62704. (217)528-1076. President: John F. Crowe. Advertising agency. Clients include industrial, financial, commercial, aviation, retail, state and federal agencies. Uses jingles and background music in commercials. Commissions 3-6 pieces/year. Pays $500-3,000/job. Buys all rights.
How to Contact: Submit demo tape of previously aired work. Prefers cassette with 2-4 songs on demo. Does not return unsolicited material. Reports in 1 month.

CUMMINGS/McPHERSON/JONES & PORTER, INC., 510 N. Church St., Suite 204, Rockford IL 61103. (815)962-0615. President: W.W. Jones. Advertising agency. Serves industrial clients. Uses background music in commercials.
How to Contact: Submit demo tape showing jingle/composition skills. Prefers 7½ ips reel-to-reel or cassette. SASE. Reports in 1 week.

DAILEY & ASSOCIATES, 574 Pacific, San Francisco CA 94133. (415)981-2250. Contact: Heidi Weissman. Ad agency. Serves many travel clients. Uses music houses and individual songwriters for jingles and background music in commercials. Commissions 4-5 pieces/year. Pays per project. Buys all rights.

How to Contact: Call for appointment to play tape. Seldom has time for these appointments, but will listen when time is available. Do *not* send tape through the mail; will not listen to it. Prefers 7½ ips reel-to-reel; not more than 5 minutes.
Music: All types.

D'ARCY-MacMANUS & MASIUS, INC., Gateway Tower, 1 Memorial Dr., St. Louis MO 63102. (314)342-8600. Sr. Vice President/Director of Creative Services: Carl Klinghammer. Ad agency. Serves all types of clients. Uses staff for music, but occasionally uses outside material. Uses jingles and background music for commercials. Commissions 30 pieces/year.
How to Contact: Submit demonstration tape of previously aired work. Will listen to music done for someone else, but will "*absolutely not* listen to anything done specifically for one of our clients."
Music: All types.

DE MARTINI ASSOCIATES, 414 4th Ave., Haddon Heights NJ 08035. President: Alfred De Martini. Ad agency. Serves industrial, consumer and food clients. Uses jingles and background music for commercials and educational filmstrips. Commissions 12-15 pieces/year. Pays $100-400/job. Buys all rights.
How to Contact: Query with resume of credits or submit demo tape showing jingle/composition skills. "Include typewritten or printed lyric sheet." Prefers cassette with 5-10 songs on demo. SASE. Reports in 2 months.
Music: Background music for filmstrips and audiovisual purposes, and jingles. "Synthesizer music welcome."

DKG ADVERTISING, INC., 1271 Avenue of the Americas, New York NY 10020. (212)489-7300. Producers: Frank DiSalvo, Mindy Gerber and Ron Weber. Ad agency. Uses jingles and background music for commercials. Pays $2,000-5,500/job. Buys all rights.
How to Contact: Submit demo tape of previously aired work, submit demo tape of jingle/compositions for a particular client or submit demo tape showing jingle/composition skills. Prefers 7½ ips reel-to-reel with 1-12 song son demo. Does not return unsolicited material. Material kept on file for future reference.
Music: Background and underscore for TV commercials.
Tip: "Being too aggressive will turn people off. Show consistent good work, with a successful track record."

W.B. DONER & CO., 2305 N. Charles, Baltimore MD 21218. (301)338-1600. Contact: Creative Director, Business Manager or Broadcast Producer. Ad agency. Serves consumer product clients. Uses music production houses for jingles and background music in commercials, and films for sales meetings. Commissions 12 pieces/year. Pays creative fee and union rates. Rights negotiable.
How to Contact: Call for appointment to play tape. Prefers 7½ ips reel-to-reel; 5 minutes maximum. Prefers to keep tape on file.
Music: Uses wide range of music.

DUNSKY ADVERTISING, LTD., 1640 Albert St., Regina, Saskatchewan, Canada S4P 2S6. Manager: Jean Johnson. Ad agency and public relations firm. Serves governmental, business and consumer clients. Uses jingles and background music in commercials. Commissions 8 pieces/year. Pays $3,000-7,000/job. Buys all rights.
How to Contact: Submit demo tape of previously aired work. Prefers cassette with 6-10 songs on demo. "We would like cost of songs submitted and information on the demo breakdown." Does not return unsolicited material.
Music: "Our needs vary. We usually need songs describing special government programs with room for copy or dialogue or testimonials. Usually full instrumental, intro, extro and donut; varying donut lengths. We are looking for warmth, originality, and suitability to client and program."

EASTMAN ADVERTISING AGENCY, 6842 Van Nuys Blvd., Suite 601, Van Nuys CA 91405. (213)787-3120. Account Executive: Frank Hovore. Ad agency. Serves savings and loan clients. Uses jingles and background music for commercials. Commissions 1 piece/year. Pays $1,800 maximum/job. Buys all rights.
How to Contact: Query, submit demo tape of previously aired work or submit demo tape showing jingle/composition skills. Prefers cassette. SASE. Reports in 2 weeks.
Music: "Big beat or country rock orchestration acceptable for presentation, but we prefer upbeat full orchestral arrangements. No rock." Agency sets slogan line or theme for campaign. "Vocals open and close music beds for announcer/copy inserts."
Tips: Target audience is 35-55, "so find out as much as possible about the needs of our prospects."

EHRLICH-MANES & ASSOCIATES, 4901 Fairmont Ave., Bethesda MD 20014. (301)657-1800. Contact: Creative Director. Ad agency. Serves industrial, financial, multi-chain retail and national associations clients. Uses jingles and background music for commercials. Commissions 5-10 pieces/year. Pays $1,000-6,000/job. Rights purchased vary.
How to Contact: Query with resume, submit demo tape of previously aired work or submit demo tape showing jingle/composition skills. Prefers 7½ ips reel-to-reel with 5-25 songs on demo. Does not return unsolicited material. "Submissions kept on file. We will contact with specific jobs in mind."
Music: "Musical identity packages for both radio and TV use. Style and instrumentation will vary depending upon the client and use."
Tips: "Be accurate with all estimates. Don't miss deadlines, and do sensational work."

EVANS & BARTHOLOMEW, INC., 1430 Larimer Square, Suite 309, Denver CO 80202. (303)534-2343. Ad agency. Serves consumer, public service and financial clients. Uses music houses for jingles and background music in commercials. Commissions 4 pieces/year. Pays $2,500 minimum/job. Rights negotiable.
How to Contact: Submit demonstration tape of previously aired work. Prefers 7½ ips reel-to-reel. Does not return tape; prefers to keep on file.
Music: All types.

DAVID W. EVANS/ATLANTIC, INC., 550 Pharr Rd. NE, Atlanta GA 30305. (404)261 7000. Creative Director: Michael Jones-Kelley. Ad agency. Serves primarily industrial and consumer clients. Uses songwriters and music houses for jingles and background music in commercials. Commissions 2 pieces/year. Pays per hour, job or royalty.
How to Contact: Submit demonstration tape of previously aired work. SASE, but prefers to keep tape on file.
Music: All types.

EXCLAMATION POINT ADVERTISING, 411 Stapleton Bldg., Billings MT 59101. (406)245-6341. Media Director: Bernie Nelson. President: Janet Cox. Ad agency. Serves financial, real estate, retail clothing and lumber clients. Uses jingles. Pays on a per-job basis. Buys all rights.
How to Contact: Submit demo tape of previously aired work or submit demo tape showing jingle/composition skills. Prefers reel-to-reel or cassette. SASE. Reports in 1 month.
Music: 30-second jingles.

FAHLGREEN & FERRISS, INC., Box 2128, 136 N. Summit, Toledo OH 43603. (419)241-5201. Contact: John Otto. Ad agency. Serves industrial and financial clients. Uses 90% music houses and 10% individual songwriters for jingles and background music in commercials. Commissions 1-5 pieces/year. Pays according to client's budget. Prefers to buy all rights, but negotiable.
How to Contact: Submit demonstration tape of previously aired work. Prefers 7½ ips reel-to-reel or cassette with 5-12 "of your best pieces" on demo.
Music: Uses some music for banking client on TV and radio.

FINKBEINER/WILCOX & ASSOCIATES, Box 36, 21045 Enterprise Ave., Brookfield WI 53005. Contact: Terry Finkbeiner. Advertising agency. Serves 60% industrial, 30% consumer clients, the balance is direct mail and P-O-P. Uses services of songwriters and music houses for jingles. Commissions 3-4 songwriters/year. Pays $500-10,000/yob.
How to Contact: Submit by mail demonstration tape of previously aired work. Prefers 7½ ips reel-to-reel with 5-6 songs on demo. SASE, but prefers to keep material on file.

FIRST MARKETING GROUP, 7922 State Line, Prairie Village KS 66208. President: John Strecker. Administrative Assistant: M.E. Moore. Advertising agency and public relations firm. Serves financial, hotel, convention and electronics clients. Uses jingles and background music in commercials. Commissions 1-4 pieces/year. Pays on a per-job basis. Buys one-time rights.
How to Contact: Query. Prefers 7½ ips reel-to-reel with 3 songs minimum on demo. "Through the mail only; no calls or personal appearances." SASE. Reports in 1 month.
Music: MOR.

ALEX T. FRANZ, INC., 35 E. Wacker Dr., Chicago IL 60601. (312)782-9090. Vice President/Creative Director: J.N. Wilson. Ad agency. Serves consumer package goods, industrial and bank clients. Uses jingles and background music for commercials. Commissions 2-3 pieces/year. Pays $200-5,000/job. Buys one-time rights.
How to Contact: Phone first, then submit demo tape of previously aired work.

F. WILLIAM FREE & CO., 400 Park Ave., New York NY 10022. (212)754-9696. Contact: Fonda Dicker. Ad agency. Serves all types of consumer clients. Uses music houses, songwriters and lyricists for jingles and background music in commercials. Commissions 15 songwriters and 15 lyricists for 15 pieces/year. Pays per job. Buys all rights.
How to Contact: Query. Prefers 7½ ips reel-to-reel; 5 minutes maximum. SASE, but prefers to keep material on file.
Music: Music depends on job.

FREEDMAN, INC., 118 William Howard Taft Rd., Cincinnati OH 45219. (513)861-4000. Contact: Broadcast Manager. Ad agency. Clients include retail, financial and some industrial companies. Uses jingles and background music in commercials. Commissions 2 pieces/year. Pays $150 minimum/job. Prefers to buy all or area rights.
How to Contact: Submit demo tape of previously aired work or submit demo tape showing jingle/composition skills. Prefers 7½ ips reel-to-reel with "as many songs as possible" on tape. "We may be contacted by phone, by mail or in person." SASE. Reports "as soon as possible."
Music: Uses jingles/songs for radio and television.
Tips: "Be careful of pitching an agency client direct. Granted, many agencies may be afraid to suggest something, but some have a very good reason for saying yes or no to the efforts of the composer, so don't mess up chances for a sale some time in the future. Get *all* charges on paper out front. No surprises."

FREMERMAN-MALCY SPIZAK ROSENFELD, INC., (formerly Fremerman-Malcy), 106 W. 14th St., Kansas City MO·64105. Ad agency. Chairman: Marvin Fremerman. Serves consumer, financial and public service clients. Uses jingles and background music in commercials. Commissions 5-7 pieces/year. Pays $500-3,800/job. Buys all rights.
How to Contact: Submit demo tape of previously aired work. Prefers 7½ ips reel-to-reel with 8-10 songs on demo. Does not return unsolicited material; keeps material on file.

FROZEN MUSIC, INC., 1169 Howard St., San Francisco CA 94103. (415)626-0501. Production Director: Don Goldberg. Media consultants. Serves entertainment, industrial and recreational clients. Uses jingles and background music for commercials and theme songs. Commissions 4-5 pieces/year. Pays $100 minimum/job. Buys all rights.
How to Contact: Query with resume, submit demo tape of previously aired work or submit demo tape showing jingle/composition skills for particular client. "Have commercial experience! No beginners." Prefers cassette with 5-15 songs on demo. "Send only high quality tapes, edited for time and content. No splices. We prefer examples which have been used in productions, with a list of credits." SASE. Reports in 4 weeks.
Music: "Hard/soft rock, jazz, MOR and country rock. Assignments are commercials mostly for the radio market, with some TV and independent movie scoring."

GALLAGHER GROUP, INC., 477 Madison Ave., New York NY 10022. (212)751-6700. President: James Gallagher. Executive Vice President: Nate Rind. Creative Director: Bill Murtha. Ad agency. Serves automotive, entertainment and other clients. Uses jingles and background music in commercials. Commissions 5-6 pieces/year. Pays $500-2,000/job. Buys all rights.
How to Contact: Query with resume of credits. Prefers 7½ ips reel-to-reel.

GARNER & ASSOCIATES, INC., 5950 Fairview Rd., 2 Fairview Plaza, Charlotte NC 28210. (704)554-1454. Contact: Dennis Deal or Bill Bryant. Advertising agency. Serves a wide range of clients; client list available on request. Uses services of songwriters for jingles. Pays by the job. Buys all rights.
How to Contact: Arrange personal interview or submit demo tape of previous work. Prefers 7½ ips reel-to-reel with enough songs to showcase best work. SASE.
Music: All types.

GEER, DuBOIS, INC., 1 Dag Hammarskjold Plaza, New York NY 10017. Contact: Ethel Rubinstein. Ad agency. Serves all types of clients including financial, industrial, fashion and packaged goods. Uses music houses for jingles and background music for commercials. Buys original and stock pieces. Commissions 5-6 pieces/year. Buys all rights.
How to Contact: Submit demonstration tape of previously aired work. Prefers 7½ ips reel-to-reel. SASE, but prefers to keep tape on file.
Music: All types.

GILLHAM ADVERTISING, 15 E. 1st S., 5th Floor, Desert Plaza, Salt Lake City UT 84111. (801)328-0281. Producers: Katherine Gygi. Ad agency. Serves financial, real estate, fast food,

tourist and automobile dealer clients. Uses services of songwriters and local production companies for jingles and background music in commercials and for radio. Commissions 2-4 songwriters and 1 lyricist/year. Payment negotiable. Buys all rights.
How to Contact: Submit demo tape of previously aired work. Prefers 7½ ips reel-to-reel with 6-12 songs on demo. Does not return unsolicited material. "We like to know who is available to do what for what price, but please don't call and bug us twice a month. We're happy to meet people and review their work, but we don't like hard sell. An occasional (semiannual) contact is enough. If we really like the demo and a need arises we investigate for bids."
Music: "Financial and automotive jingles are our primary market."
Tips: "Keep us up-to-date on your work with occasional demo tapes and inquiries about our needs. You might also send us demos when you know it's a product we're heavy in. We may be looking for economical, quick turnaround on jingles for seasonal use—updated *new* sounds."

GOLDEN QUILL, Drawer 444, Executive Plaza, Nokomis FL 33555. (813)488-9999. Ad agency and public relations firm. Serves various commercial clients. Commissions over 100 pieces/year. Pays a flat fee and/or royalty. Rights purchased vary.
How to Contact: Query. Prefers cassette. "Suggestions sent by letter are given first and full consideration." SASE. Reports in 2 weeks.

GOODWIN, DANNENBAUM, LITMAN & WINGFIELD, INC., 7676 Woodway, Houston TX 77063. (713)977-7676. Creative Director: Cliff Gillock. Ad agency. Serves multi-market, retail, financial, real estate and food products clients. Uses services of songwriters and production companies for jingles, background music for commercials and audiovisual presentations. Commissions 10-15 songwriters/year. Pays $2,500-5,000/job. Buys commercial use rights.
How to Contact: Submit demo tape of previously aired work and price structure. Prefers 7½ ips reel-to-reel with 10-20 songs on demo. SASE, but prefers to keep material on file. Responds as need arises.
Music: "We want music that enhances the selling message or image building efforts for our clients. Send proof of performance on tape, showing how you helped solve a marketing problem with your music. Include costs."
Tips: "We use lyricists to supply marketing info, idea of style and theme line where applicable."

GREY ADVERTISING, 1000 Midwest Plaza E., Minneapolis MN 55402. (612)341-2701. Creative Supervisors: Lon Cross and Judy Kirk. Copy Supervisor: Lon Cross. Serves retail department store, bookseller, jeweller, bedding, television, media, business machine, airline and hairstylist clients. Uses songwriters and music houses for jingles and background music in commercials. Commissions 5 pieces/year.
How to Contact: Submit demonstration tape of previous work or submit demonstration tape showing jingle/composition skills. Prefers 7½ ips reel-to-reel with 5-10 songs on demo. SASE; prefers to keep tape on file.
Music: All types.

GRIFFITH & SOMERS ADVERTISING AGENCY, LTD., 1615 Douglas, Suite 2, Sioux City IA 51105. (712)277-3343. President: Margaret Holtze. Ad agency. Uses jingles. Commissions 4 pieces/year. Pays $700-5,000/job.
How to Contact: Submit demo tape of previously aired work. Prefers reel-to-reel or cassette with 3-5 songs on demo. SASE. Reporting time varies.
Music: 30- to 60-second jingles.

GROUP TWO ADVERTISING, 2002 Ludlow St., Philadelphia PA 19103. (215)561-2200. Creative Director: Marian V. Marchese. Ad agency. Serves industrial, entertainment, financial, real estate, hotel/motel and retail clients. Uses jingles. Commissions 1 songwriter/year. Pays $1,000-4,000/job. Buys one-time rights.
How to Contact: Submit demo tape of previously aired work. Prefers 7½ ips reel-to-reel with 5 songs minimum on demo. SASE. "We prefer to keep material on file for future reference. We'll contact the person when a job comes up. A price list (no matter how general) is also helpful for us to keep on file."
Music: "Due to the variety of clients we handle, with various budgets, assignments can be of any nature."

CLAUDE HARRISON AND CO., 7 Mountain Ave. SE, Box 2780, Roanoke VA 24001. (703)344-5591. President: Claude Harrison. Ad agency and public relations firm. Serves consumer, industrial and financial clients. Uses services of songwriters for jingles and background music for commercials. "Our copy staff usually writes needed lyrics." Commissions 4-5

songwriters/year. Pays $1,000-6,000/job, "depending on the client's budget. Fee must include scratch track, which must be approved by the client." Buys all rights.
How to Contact: Query, submit demo tape of previously aired work or submit demo tape of jingles/compositions for specific client. Prefers reel-to-reel. SASE, but prefers to keep material on file. Reports when need arises; "depends on decision by client."

HEPWORTH ADVERTISING CO., 3403 McKinney Ave., Dallas TX 75204. (214)526-7785. President: S.W. Hepworth. Ad agency. Serves financial, industrial and food clients. Uses jingles. Pays on per-job basis. Buys all rights.
How to Contact: Query by phone or submit demo tape of previously aired work. Prefers cassette. SASE. Reports in 1 week.

HERMAN ASSOCIATES, 488 Madison Ave., New York NY 10022. Contact: Creative Director. Ad agency. Serves industrial, travel, insurance, fashion, electronics, and photographic clients. Uses background music for commercials and audiovisual presentations. "To date, we have never purchased original music." Pays $250 minimum/job. Buys one-time rights.
How to Contact: Query with resume of credits. Prefers cassette with 3-6 songs on demo. SASE. Reports in 3 weeks.
Music: Possible assignments related to travel, photography or fashion: "primarily speculative generic music is also of interest. Music influenced by foreign destinations might be needed."
Tips: "Don't over-orchestrate. The simpler, the better. Plan pieces that are adaptable to audiovisuals, not simply commercials."

HOOD, HOPE & ASSOCIATES, 6440 S. Lewis, Tulsa OK 74136. (918)749-4454. Senior Vice President/Creative Director: J.B. Bowers. Ad agency and public relations firm. Serves industrial, entertainment and financial clients. Uses jingles, background music in commercials and original tracks for sales films. Commissions 3-4 pieces/year. Pays by the job. Buys all rights.
How to Contact: Submit demo tape of previously aired work. Prefers 7½ ips reel-to-reel. SASE.

E.T. HOWARD CO., 6 E. 43rd St., New York NY 10017. (212)832-2000. Vice President/Creative Director: Nino Banome. Ad agency. Serves consumer goods clients. Uses jingles and background music in commercials. Commissions 10 pieces/year. Pays on per-job basis. Buys broadcast or sales meeting use rights.
How to Contact: Query by phone or submit demo tape of previously aired work. Prefers 7½ ips reel-to-reel. SASE. Reports "in a few days."

INGALLS ASSOCIATION, INC., 857 Boylston St., Boston MA 02116. (617)261-8900. Contact: Producer. Ad agency. Serves industrial, financial and retail clients. Commissions 10-15 pieces/year. Pays $7,500 maximum/creative job.
How to Contact: Submit demo tape of previously aired work, then call. Prefers 7½ ips reel-to-reel with 5-12 songs on demo. SASE.
Music: Needs commercial jingles in all styles.
Tip: "Put together a demo which reflects an ability to write a variety of types of commercial music."

JOHN PAUL ITTA, INC., 680 5th Ave., New York NY 10019. Administrative Assistant: Marci Maxey. Ad agency. Serves package goods clients. Uses jingles and background music for commericals. Commissions 15 pieces/year. Payment negotiable. Rights purchased vary.
How to Contact: Submit demo tape of previously aired work. Prefers 7½ ips reel-to-reel. Does not return unsolicited material.

JONATHAN ADVERTISING, INC., 866 3rd Ave., New York NY 10013. President: Jonathan Gubin. Ad agency. Serves consumer products clients. Uses services of songwriters for background music for commercials. Commissions 2 lyricists/year. Pays by the job.
How to Contact: Submit demo tape showing jingle/composition skills. Prefers cassette. Prefers to keep material on file. Responds when the need arises.
Tips: "Keep in touch."

KENYON & ECKHARDT, INC., 10 S. Riverside Plaza, Chicago IL 60606. (312)346-4020. Contact: Scott Seltzer. Ad agency. Serves automotive and packaged good clients. Uses music houses for jingles and background music. Commissions 12 pieces/year. Pays on per job basis. Buys all rights.
How to Contact: Submit demonstration tape of previously aired work. Prefers 7½ ips reel-to-reel; tape should be 5 minutes or less. Keeps tapes on file for reference.
Music: All types.

KETCHUM, MACLEOD & GROVE, 4 Gateway Center, Pittsburgh PA 15222. (412)456-3700. Contact: Creative Director. Ad agency. Serves consumer and business clients. Uses jingles and background music for commercials. Commissions 15-20 pieces/year. Pays $250-1,200 minimum/job. Buys all rights.
How to Contact: Query with resume of credits or submit demo showing jingle/composition skills. Prefers 7½ ips reel-to-reel with 7-15 songs on demo. Does not return unsolicited material. "Material is kept on file in our creative department."
Music: "We use a wide range of styles with memorable melodies and excellent production. Assignments are generally original, specific and with excellent lyrics supplied as a direction."

DENNIS KING KIZER, (formerly Kizer & Kizer Advertising), Box 14267, Oklahoma City OK 73113. (405)478-3343. President/Creative Director: Dennis Kizer. Ad agency and production service. Serves fast food, food service and financial clients. Uses jingles. Commissions 5 pieces/year. Pays $500-5,000/job. Buys all rights or one-time rights.
How to Contact: Query with resume of credits or submit demo tape of previously aired work. Prefers 7½ ips reel-to-reel. SASE. Reports in 2 weeks.
Tips: "Don't be too persistent. We'll yell when we're ready."

LA GRAVE KLIPFEL ADVERTISING, INC., 1707 High St., Des Moines IA 50309. (515)283-2297. President: Ron Klipfel. Advertising agency. Serves wide range of clients including financial, industrial and retail; client list available on request. Uses services of songwriters for jingles. Pays by the job. Rights negotiable.
How to Contact: "Telephone first then follow up with mailed information." Prefers reel-to-reel or cassette with any number songs on demo. SASE.
Music: Primarily interested in jingles.

LANE & HUFF ADVERTISING, 707 Broadway, Suite 1200, San Diego CA 92101. (714)234-5101. Executive Vice President: Robert V. Maywood. Traffic Manager: Peggy Toth. Ad agency. Serves financial clients. Uses services of songwriters for jingles and background music in commercials. Commissions 4 songwriters and 4 lyricists/year. Pays $2,500-30,000/job. Buys all rights.
How to Contact: Submit demo tape of previously aired work. Prefers reel-to-reel with 8 pieces on demo. Prefers to keep material on file. Reports in 1 month.
Music: Full lyric jingles.
Tips: "Include only your best work, even if it is only a few selections."

LD&A ADVERTISING CORP., 717 Main St., Batavia IL 60510. (312)879-2000. President: Leo Denz. Ad agency, public relations firm and audiovisual company. Serves consumer and industrial clients. Uses jingles and background music for commercials and audiovisual shows. Payment depends on use. Buys one-time rights or all rights.
How to Contact: Query with resume of credits or submit demo tape of previously aired work. Prefers cassettes. "Don't mix 'types' on a single cassette; for example, don't put jingles on the same tape as background music." SASE. "We'll keep material on file for client review. We like to let our clients have a hand in choosing talent for their commercials and films. Usually we select 3 and let them make the final choice."
Music: "Jingles: We will furnish the points to cover and their relative importance. Background: We will furnish the edited film with a description sheet of what the music is to accomplish."

AL PAUL LEFTON CO., 71 Vanderbilt Ave., New York NY 10017. (212)689-7470. Director of Broadcast: Joe Africano. Ad agency. Clients include financial, industrial and consumer products clients. Uses jingles and background music for commercials. Commissions 15 pieces/year. Buys all rights.
How to Contact: Submit demo tape of previously aired work. Prefers 7½ ips reel-to-reel with 5 songs minimum on demo. SASE. Reports in 3 weeks.

S.R. LEON COMPANY, INC., 515 Madison Ave., New York NY 10022. (212)752-8200. Contact: Myron Linder. Ad agency. Serves industrial, drug, automotive and dairy product clients. Uses jingles and background music for commercials. Commissions vary. Rights purchased are limited to use of music for commercials.
How to Contact: Submit demo tape of previously aired work. Prefers 7½ ips reel-to-reel with no length restrictions on demo.
Music: Uses all types.

LONDON & ASSOCIATES, 6666 N. Western Ave., Chicago IL 60645. Creative Director: Kaye Britt. Advertising agency. Serves retail, consumer products and trade clients. Uses services of songwriters for jingles and background music in commercials. Commissions 3-6 songwriters/year. Pays $500-3,000/finished job and by "straight buy out." Buys all rights.

How to Contact: Submit demo tape of previously aired work. Prefers 7½ ips reel-to-reel with 6-12 songs on demo. SASE, but prefers to keep material on file. Reports in 2 weeks.

Music: "We need highly identifiable music/jingles. The type depends on clients. Be willing to work on small budget for spec tape."

Tips: "Be willing to work on spec basis—small budget for spec."

LONG, HAYMES & CARR, INC., 2006 S. Hawthorne Rd., Box 5627, Ardmore Station, Winston-Salem NC 27103. (919)765-3630. Vice President/Creative Director: Bill Kent. Ad agency. Clients cover "broad spectrum: food, hosiery, banking, industrial." Uses jingles and background music in commercials and films. Commissions 10-15 pieces/year. Pays on a per-job basis. Buys all rights.

How to Contact: Query with resume of credits. Prefers 7½ ips reel-to-reel. SASE. Reports "as soon as possible."

Music: "Primarily jingles for TV: usually for 30-second spots."

LORD, SULLIVAN & YODER, INC., 196 S. Main St., Marion OH 43302. (614)387-8500. Producer: Neil Pynchon. Ad agency. Serves industrial and consumer clients. Uses jingles and background music for commercials. Commissions 6-10 pieces/year. Pays $3,500-15,000/job. Buys all rights.

How to Contact: Query with resume of credits, submit demo tape of previously aired work or submit demo tape of jingles/compositions for particular client. Prefers 7½ reel-to-reel with 6-12 songs on demo. SASE. Reports in 2 weeks.

Music: Jingles.

Tips: "Submit fresh, non-jingly ideas. Show an understanding of what commercial music should do. Stress strong enunciation in lyrics. Remember that music can't exist for itself alone, but has to help sell something, and sometimes creative genius—but never musicianship—has to be sacrificed for the sake of the message."

McCANN-ERICKSON/LOUISVILLE OFFICE, (formerly Zimmer-McClaskey), 1469 S. 4th St., Louisville KY 40208. (502)636-0441. Creative Administrator: Emery Lewis. Ad agency. Serves packaged goods, industrial, service, race track, etc. clients. Uses jingles and background music in commercials. Commissions about 12 pieces broadcast music/year. Buys rights on "13 week or yearly cycles according to AFM codes, etc."

McCANN-ERICKSON WORLDWIDE, Briar Hollow Bldg., 520 S. Post Oak Rd., Houston TX 77056. (713)965-0303. Contact: Pat Devine. Ad agency. Serves all types of clients. Uses services of songwriters for jingles and background music in commercials. Commissions 10 songwriters/year. Pays production cost and registrated creative fee. Arrangement fee and creative fee depend on size of client and size of market. If song is for a big market, a big fee is paid; if for a small market, a small fee is paid. Buys all rights.

How to Contact: Submit demonstration tape of previously aired work. Does not like to deal with agents. Prefers 7½ ips reel-to-reel. There is no minimum or maximum length for tapes. Tapes may be of a variety of work or a specialization. Very open on tape content; agency does own lyrics. SASE; prefers to file tapes. Responds by phone when need arises.

Music: All types.

AL MAESCHER ADVERTISING, INC., 25 S. Bemiston, Clayton MO 63105. (314)727-6981. President: Al Maescher. Ad agency. Serves industrial, retail and financial clients. Uses services of songwriters for jingles. Pays on a per-job basis. Buys one-time rights, for exclusive use in service area.

How to Contact: Submit demo tape of previously aired work. Prefers 7½ ips reel-to-reel or cassette. SASE, but prefers to keep material on file. Responds as need arises.

MAISH ADVERTISING, 280 N. Main, Marion OH 43302. (614)382-1191. Contact: Creative Director. Ad agency. Serves industrial, financial and home building products clients. Uses jingles. Commissions 4-6 pieces/year. Payment negotiable for complete packages, including production. Buys all rights.

How to Contact: Submit demo tape of previously aired work. Prefers 7½ ips reel-to-reel.

MARS ADVERTISING CO., 18470 W. Ten Mile, Southfield MI 48075. (313)559-0300. Creative Director: Michael Reese III. Advertising agency. Serves supermarket and retail clients. Uses services of songwriters for jingles and background music in commercials. Commissions 5-6 songwriters/year for 10-12 pieces/year. Pays $2,000-3,000/job. Buys all rights.

How to Contact: Arrange personal interview or submit demo tape of previously aired work. Prefers cassette with 10-25 songs on demo. SASE, but prefers to keep material on file. Reports in 3 weeks.
Music: "We're constantly looking for retail jingles that have simple 'nursery rhythm' melodies. Also, we're looking for catchy lyrics that 'turn on the listener' to the supermarket. We're not looking for sophisticated pieces of music."

THE MARSCHALK COMPANY, 1345 Avenue of the Americas, New York NY 10019. (212)974-7700. Contact: Head of Broadcast. Ad agency. Serves all types clients. Uses jingles and background music for commercials. Commissions about 30 pieces/year. Pays by the job. Buys all rights.
How to Contact: Submit demo tape of previously aired work. Prefers ¼ ips reel-to-reel demo "5-6 minutes long. Best to use bits and pieces rather than entire songs on tape." Does not return unsolicited material.
Music: Uses all types.

MELDRUM & CAMPBELL ADVERTISING, 1717 E. 9th St., Suite 2121, Cleveland OH 44114. (216)696-3456. Director, Radio/TV: Charles E. Ford Jr. Ad agency. Serves financial, utilities, direct response, car dealers, and industrial clients. Uses services of commercial music production companies for jingles, background music and film/program scores. "We use lyricists for re-writing agency-submitted lyric suggestions." Commissions 2 songwriters and 2 lyricists/year. Pays $500-4,000/job. Buys all rights for regional or local use only.
How to contact: Submit demo tape of previously aired work or submit demo tape showing jingle/composition skills. Prefers 7½ ips reel-to-reel with 5-15 songs on demo. SASE. Reports in 2 weeks.
Music: "Includes program themes, commercial instrumental underscoring, song stories. Primarily MOR sound; some country and contemporary."
Tips: "Work through a music production company" to increase your chance of working with this agency.

METCALFE-COOK & SMITH, INC., 4701 Trousdale Dr., Nashville TN 37220. (615)834-6323. Contact: Betty Cook Sanders. Serves industrial and entertainment clients. Uses jingles and background music in commercials. Commissions 2 pieces/year. Payment depends on pre-determined budget.
How to Contact: Query first by mail. Prefers 7½ ips reel-to-reel with 3 songs minimum on demo. SASE. Reports in 2 weeks.

METROPLEX MARKETING, INC., (formerly Allan Keyne Associates, Inc. Advertising), 3999 Main St., Philadelphia PA 19127. Creative Director: Allan Keyne. Ad agency. Serves retail and consumer clients. Uses jingles. Commissions 12 pieces/year. Pays $500 minimum/job. Buys all rights.
How to Contact: Query with resume of credits. Submit demonstration tape of previously aired work. Prefers cassette with 8 songs minimum on demo. SASE. Reports in 2 weeks.

MINTZ & HOKE, INC., 10 Tower Lane, Avon CT 06001. Contact: Broadcast Manager. Ad agency and public relations firm. Serves industrial retail, financial, telephone company and entertainment clients. Uses jingles. Commissions 4 pieces/year. Payment depends on client's budget. Buys all rights.
How to Contact: Submit demo tape of previously aired work or submit demo tape showing jingle/compositions for a particular client. Prefers 7½ ips reel-to-reel with 5-10 songs on demo. "Tape submitted should show a wide variety of styles." Does not return unsolicited material. "We want to keep tapes on file so that when a jingle comes up, we can refer to tapes to find someone who has the style we need."
Music: "We give writers the type of feeling that we want, the slogan and, possibly, all the lyrics."
Tips: "We'll call when and if we have something."

MITHOFF ADVERTISING, INC., 4105 Rio Bravo, El Paso TX 79902. Producer Radio/TV: DeDe Sons. Advertising agency. Serves financial, supermarket and rifle equipment clients. Uses jingles, background music in commercials and soundtracks. Commissions 5-10 pieces/year. Pays $2,000-5,000/job. Buys regional rights or all rights.
How to Contact: Prefers 7½ ips reel-to-reel with 5-15 songs on demo. SASE. Reports in 2 weeks.
Music: "We need development of musical concepts. We usually provide the lyrics."

MOHAWK ADVERTISING CO., 149 4th St. SW, Mason City IA 50401. (515)423-1354. Vice President/Production Manager: Jim Clark. Ad agency. Serves financial and industrial clients,

agricultural industries, fast food restaurants and insurance companies. Uses jingles and background music in commercials. Commissions 4-10 pieces/year. Payment negotiable; supply fee estimate. Prefers to buy one-time rights.
How to Contact: Submit demo tape of previously aired work or submit demo tape showing jingles/compositions for a particular client. Prefers 7½ ips reel-to-reel or cassette with 5-10 songs on demo. Material kept on file for reference.

MOSS ADVERTISING, 633 3rd Ave., New York NY 10017. (212)687-7377. Contact: Michael Carreri. Ad agency. Serves all type of clients including utility and restaurant. Uses jingles and background music in commercials. Commissions about 10 pieces/year. Pays by the job; "negotiates if work particularly desired." Usually buys all rights.
How to Contact: Arrange personal interview with M. Carreri and/or submit demo tape of previously aired work. Prefers 10-15 minute cassette which can be kept on file. SASE.
Music: Uses all types.

MZB INC., (formerly Ruben-Montgomery & Associates, Inc.), 1812 N. Meridian St., Indianapolis IN 46202. (317)924-6271. Contact: Creative Director. Ad agency. Uses jingles. Commissions 10-15 pieces/year. Pays $500-1,000/year for demo only. Package payment for final versions needed from demo. Buys all rights.
How to Contact: Submit demo tape showing jingle/composition skills. Prefers 7½ ips reel-to-reel with 10-15 songs on demo. SASE. Reports "as needed."
Music: Needs vary.

NEALE ADVERTISING ASSOCIATES, 7060 Hollywood Blvd., Suite 1204, Los Angeles CA 90028. (213)464-4184. President: Ted Neale. Ad agency. Serves financial, manufacturing, mail order and retail clients. Uses jingles and background music in commercials. Pays on a per-job basis. Buys all rights.
How to Contact: Query. Submit demo tape of previously aired work. Prefers 7½ ips reel-to-reel or cassette. SASE. Reports "as soon as possible."
Music: Needs vary.

NOWAK/BARLOW/JOHNSON ADVERTISING, 117 Highbridge St., Fayetteville NY 13066. (315)637-9895. Broadcast Production Director: Ed Gabriel. Ad agency. Serves retail, industrial and financial clients. Uses jingles. Commissions 5 pieces/year. Buys all rights.
How to Contact: Query with resume of credits or submit demo tape of previously aired work. Prefers 7½ ips reel-to-reel or cassette with 3 songs minimum on demo. SASE. Reports in 1 month.

OGILVY & MATHER, INC., 120 Green St., San Francisco CA 94111. (415)981-0950. Production/Broadcasting Department: Carol Lee Kelliher. Ad Agency. Serves financial, entertainment, outdoor apparel and consumer product clients. Uses individual songwriters and music houses for jingles and background music in commercials. Commissions 20 pieces/year. Pays per job. Buys all rights.
How to Contact: Submit demonstration tape of previously aired work. Prefers 7½ ips reel-to-reel. Returns material if requested with SASE; prefers to keep tape on file.
Music: Usually sophisticated.

OGILVY & MATHER INC., 2 E. 48th St., New York NY 10017. (212)688-6100. Music Producer: Faith Norwick. Ad agency. Serves all types client. Uses jingles and background music for commercials. Commissions about 50 new pieces/year. Pays by the job. "A nationally used jingle pays $5,000-10,000."
How to Contact: Send demo tape of previously aired work or demo tape showing jingle/composition skills to F. Norwick. Do not include unsolicited jingles relating to their clients because of possible legal implications. Prefers 7½ ips reel-to-reel with "bits of songs, 2 minutes is enough. 10 pieces on a jingle demo is sufficient." Likes to file tapes for later review. SASE.
Music: Uses all types.

OGILVY & MATHER (CANADA) LTD., 1401 McGill College Ave., Montreal, Quebec, Canada H3A 1Z4. (514)849-3601. Contact: Micheline LaRoche. Ad agency. Primarily uses jingles. Commissions 30-40 pieces/year. Buys all rights.
How to Contact: Arrange personal interview to play demo. Prefers 7½ ips reel-to-reel demo.
Music: Uses all types depending on client's needs.

THE PATTON AGENCY, 407 W. Osborn, Phoenix AZ 85013. (602)241-0600. Director, Client Services: Tim Loy. Ad agency and public relations firm. Serves retail, auto, financial and dairy clients. Uses services of songwriters for jingles, background music in commercials and presenta-tions. Occasionally uses lyricists for presentations and AV shows. Commissions 4-5 songwriters and 2 lyricists/year. Pays on a per-job basis or by "applicable charges from house/writer." Buys all rights.

How to Contact: Submit demo tape of previously aired work. Prefers cassette with 5-10 songs on demo. SASE, but prefers to keep material on file. Responds when "writer can solve a problem for us."

Tips: "Do not send samples of any work in which the lyrics are not totally clear and understand-able. From a strong original concept a truly great jingle writer can propose all sorts of new re-scores and re-sings of the original melody, a la McDonald's. No client likes to abandon a good campaign, but, unfortunately, they tire of it before the market as a whole."

PEARSON, CLARKE & SAWYER ADVERTISING & PUBLIC RELATIONS, 5640 S. Florida Ave., Box 5400, Lakeland FL 33803. (813)646-5071. Copywriters: Carolyn Black, Jim Ising. Ad-vertising agency and public relations firm. Serves industrial, financial, fast food, shelter and packaged goods clients. Uses services of songwriters for jingles and music for audiovisual presenta-tions. Commissions 1-3 songwriters/year. Pays $500-10,000/job. Prefers to buy all rights.

How to Contact: Submit demo tape of previously aired work. SASE, but prefers to keep material on file. Reports by phone or mail as need arises.

Tips: "Be willing to work with us on a spec basis; if the client buys, we buy."

PHELPS ADVERTISING, (formerly Allvine Advertising Associates), Suite 505, Security Na-tional Bank Bldg., Kansas City KS 66101. (913)281-0222. President: Jon Phelps. Advertising agency. Primarily serves financial clients. Uses jingles and background music in commercials. Commissions 3-5 pieces/year. Pays $1,000-7,000/job. Buys all rights.

How to Contact: Submit demo tape of previously aired work. Prefers cassette with 5 songs minimum on tape. "Include statement of what the songwriter is available to do, whether he needs outside lyrics, etc. Material is kept on file." SASE. Reports in 2 weeks.

PRINGLE DIXON PRINGLE, 3340 Peachtree Rd. NE, Atlanta GA 30326. (404)261-9542. Cre-ative Director: Mike Hutchinson. Advertising agency. Serves fashion, financial, fast food and industrial clients; client list available on request. Uses services of songwriters for jingles and beckground music. Pays by the job. Rights vary, depending on job.

How to Contact: Submit tape of previous work. Prefers 7½ ips reel-to-reel. SASE.

Music: All types.

PRO/CREATIVES, 25 W. Burda Place, Spring Valley NY 10977. President: David Rapp. Adver-tising and promotion agency. Serves consumer products and services, sports and miscellaneous clients. Uses background music in TV and radio commercials. Payment negotiable.

How to Contact: Query with resume of credits. SASE.

ROGERS, WEISS, COLE & WEBER, INC., 2029 Century Park E., Suite 920, Los Angeles CA 90067. (213)879-7979. Ad Agency. Serves consumer clients. Uses individual songwriters for jingles and background music in commercials. Pays per job.

How to Contact: Arrange personal interview or submit demonstration tape of previously aired work. Prefers 7½ ips reel-to-reel. SASE.

ALBERT JAY ROSENTHAL & CO., 400 N. Michigan Ave., Chicago IL 606ll. (312)337-8070. Executive Art Director: Bill Daniel. Ad agency. Serves fashion, consumer foods, kitchen utensils, automotive repair and cosmetics clients. Uses jingles, background music for commercials and sales films. Commissions 15-20 pieces/year. Pays by the job. Buys all rights.

How to Contact: Submit demo tape of previously aired work. Prefers 7½ ips reel-to-reel demo 3-5 minutes long. Prefers to file tapes. SASE.

Music: Uses all types; currently has needs for modern and jazzy renditions.

CHUCK RUHR ADVERTISING, INC., 10709 Wayzata, Box 9373. Minneapolis MN 55440. (612)546-4323. Contact: Art Director. Advertising agency. Serves consumer and industrial clients; client list available on request. Uses services of songwriters for jingles and background music. Initial fee negotiated, after that pays union scales. Pays residuals for subsequent use of material.

How to Contact: Submit demo tape of previous work. Prefers 7½ ips reel-to-reel.

SCHINDLER & HOWARD ADVERTISING, INC., Suite 118, 7710 Reading Rd., Cincinnati OH 45237. Contact: Creative Director. Ad agency and public relations firm. Serves "60% industrial, with the balance including financial and consumer goods" clients. Uses jingles and background

music in commercials. Commissions 2 pieces/year. Pays $350-1,500/job. Buys all rights.
How to Contact: Query, submit demo tape of previously aired work or submit demo tape showing jingle/composition skills. Prefers 7½ ips reel-to-reel with 3-7 songs on demo. "Anything but cold calls will be considered. Hype or too much hard sell turns us off. The work can speak for itself." SASE. Reports in 3 weeks.
Music: "Our most recent jobs using music were a 21-minute 16mm and a 10-minute 16mm motion picture on house construction and materials handling respectively. No lyrics, but music arranged to accentuate action. In next 12 months we anticipate 2 additional films. The remainder of jobs in the past 18 months have been 30-second VTR TV spots and 60-second radio spots, all for local airing."
Tips: "If possible, have an idea of our client list, make proposals, even though of a sketchy and speculative nature, for specific accounts. We are not looking for 'free' ideas, but appreciate creative/thoughtful salesmanship. In the demo reel, show how you can work for different client categories, audiences and needs. We prefer to work with composer/songwriter from the beginning. In most instances, we would write the lyrics, or at least inspire them."

ROBERT D. SCHOENBROD, INC., 919 N. Michigan Ave., Chicago IL 60611. (312)944-4774. Vice President: Jerry R. Germaine. Ad agency. Serves all types of clients. Uses jingles and background music in commercials and trade shows. Payment negotiable; "usually music writers have their own schedules." Buys all rights.
How to Contact: Query, submit demo tape of previously aired work or submit demo tape showing jingle/composition skills. Prefers 7½ ips reel-to-reel or cassette. "Do not submit unsolicited material."

SHAILER DAVIDOFF ROGERS, INC., Heritage Square, Fairfield CT 06430. (203)255-3425. Broadcast Manager: Barbara Boyd. Advertising agency. Serves consumer and financial clients. Uses jingles and background music for commercials. Commissions 6-8 pieces/year. Pays $400-4,500/job. Rights purchased vary.
How to Contact: Submit demo tape of previously aired work. Prefers 7½ ips reel-to-reel with 4 songs on demo. Does not return unsolicited material.

SILTON/TURNER ADVERTISING, 320 Statler Office Bldg., Boston MA 02116. (617)542-9460. President: Ramon H. Silton. Administrative Assistant: Philip Mathews. Ad agency and public relations firm. Serves consumer, industrial and financial clients. Uses jingles and background music in commercials. Pays $500-5,000/job. Rights purchased vary.
How to Contact: Query with resume of credits or submit demo tape of previously aired work. Prefers cassette with 3 songs minimum on demo. SASE. Reports in 3 weeks.

SIMONS ADVERTISING & ASSOCIATES, 29429 Southfield Rd., Southfield MI 48076. Creative Director: Bill Keller. Advertising agency. Serves retail clients. Uses jingles and background music for commercials. Pays $750 minimum/job. Buys all rights.
How to Contact: Query with resume or submit demo tape of previously aired work. Prefers 7½ ips reel-to-reel.

SOUND IDEAS, 224 Bellevue Ave., Haddonfield NJ 08033. Owner: Frank Knight. Advertising agency. Serves advertiser clients. Uses jingles and background music in commercials. Commissions numerous pieces/year. Pays union fees plus $1,000 for jingles. Rights purchased vary.
How to Contact: Submit demo tape of previously aired work. Prefers 7½ ips reel-to-reel or cassette. Does not return unsolicited material.
Music: Commercial lead-ins, TV tracks and jingles.

EDGAR S. SPIZEL ADVERTISING, INC., 1782 Pacific Ave., San Francisco CA 94109. (415)474-5735. President: Edgar S. Spizel. Advertising agency, public relations firm and TV/radio production firm. Serves consumer clients "from jeans to symphony orchestras, from new products to political." Uses background music in commercials. Pays $1,500 minimum/job. Buys all rights.
How to Contact: Query. Prefers cassette with 3-5 songs on demo. SASE. Reports in 3 weeks.

STAUCH-VETROMILE-GILMORE, INC., 55 S. Brow St., East Providence RI 02914. (401)438-0614. Creative/Copy Director: Kathy Silvestri. Advertising, marketing and public relations firm. Serves industrial, amusement, financial, retail and consumer clients. Uses services of songwriters and sound production companies for jingles and background music in commercials. Payment negotiable. Rights purchased negotiable.
How to Contact: Query with resume, or submit demo tape of previously aired work. Prefers reel-to-reel or cassette with 1-10 songs on demo. SASE, but prefers to keep material on file.

Reports in 2-3 weeks or "in most cases, following a decision to use a particular sound(s) for a client. Material is returned to songwriters if agency is provided with SASE and the songwriter requests return of material."

STEVENS, INC., 809 Commerce Bldg., Grand Rapids MI 49502. (616)459-8175. Creative Director: Burl Robins. Advertising agency. Uses jingles and background music for commercials. Commissions 1-3 pieces/year. Pays $2,000 minimum/job. Buys all rights.
How to Contact: Submit demo tape of previously aired work. Prefers 7½ ips reel-to-reel with 5 songs on demo. SASE. Reports in 3 weeks.

STOLZ ADVERTISING CO., 7701 Forsyth, St. Louis MO 63105. (314)863-0005. Contact: John Smith. Advertising agency. Serves consumer product clients. Will provide names of clients on request but has no formal list prepared. Uses services of songwriters for background music in commercials. Pays by the job. Rights purchased varies.
How to Contact: Submit demo tape of previous work. Prefers ¼" reel-to-reel or cassette with enough songs to showcase songwriter's best work. SASE, but prefers to keep on file.
Music: Needs vary.

STONE & ADLER, INC., 150 N. Wacker Dr., Chicago IL 60606. (312)346-6100. Ad Agency. Serves industrial, entertainment and financial clients. Uses music houses for background music in commercials. Commissions 3-4 pieces/year. Pays according to budget. Usually buys one-time rights.
How to Contact: Submit demonstration tape of previously aired work. Prefers cassette. Returns material if requested with SASE; prefers to keep tape on file.
Music: All types.

SULLIVAN & BRUGNATELLI, 300 E. 42nd St., New York NY 10017. (212)986-4200. Contact: John Benetos. Ad agency. Serves beverage, food, medicinal and cosmetic clients. Uses music houses and songwriters for jingles. Commissions many pieces/year. Usually buys all rights.
How to Contact: Arrange personal interview to play tape. Prefers ¼" reel-to-reel; 15 minutes maximum. SASE, but prefers to keep tape on file.
Music: All types.

THOMAS ADVERTISING, Box 17015, Los Angeles CA 90017. (213)651-5991. President: Thomas Waller. Media Buyer: Linda Ward. Ad agency. Serves entertainment and publishing clients. Uses jingles, background music for commercials and movie scores. Commissions 50 pieces/year. Pays $125 minimum/job or 1-2% royalty. Buys all rights.
How to Contact: Submit demo tape showing jingle/composition skills. Prefers cassette with minimum 3 songs on demo. SASE. Reports "as soon as possible."
Music: C&W and MOR.

J. WALTER THOMPSON CO., 2828 Tower Place, 3340 Peachtree Rd. NE, Atlanta GA 30326. (404)266-2828. Creative Director/Vice President: Michael Lollis. Ad Agency. Serves financial, automotive, sporting goods and pest control clients. Uses music houses for jingles and background music in commercials.
How to Contact: Submit demo tape of previously aired work or demo tape showing jingles/composition skills. Prefers 7½ ips reel-to-reel with 6 songs maximum. Returns material if requested with SASE; prefers to keep tape on file.
Music: Types vary with needs and campaign. Sometimes wants music plus lyrics, and sometimes needs just music for lyrics written inhouse.

J. WALTER THOMPSON CO., 17000 Executive Plaza, Dearborn MI 48126. (313)336-6900. Contact: Bob Lyon, executive art director or Jerry Apoian. Ad Agency. Serves industrial, recreational, banking, media clients and major car companies. Uses music houses and individual songwriters for jingles (often writes own lyrics) and background music in commercials. Commissions 30-40 pieces/year. Pays union rates. "If music is written for specific needs of client, buys all rights."
How to Contact: Call first about demo tape. Prefers 7½ ips reel-to-reel. Use best works. SASE.
Music: All types.

JERRE R. TODD & ASSOCIATES, 1800 CNB Bldg., Fort Worth TX 76102. Ad agency and public relations firm. Serves financial, oil and gas, and automobile dealership clients. Uses jingles. Commissions 5-6 pieces/year. Pays $1,000-15,000/job. Buys all rights.
How to Contact: Submit demo tape of previously aired work. Prefers 7½ ips reel-to-reel or cassette. Does not return unsolicited material. "We might hold for future use."

Music: "Needs jingles for financial, car dealers and other clients with assortment of full-sing and donuts in both 30- and 60-second lengths."

CALDWELL VAN RIPER, 1314 N. Meridian, Indianapolis IN 46202. (317)632-6501. Executive Creative Director: Deborah Karnowsky. Ad agency and public relations firm. Serves industrial, financial and consumer/trade clients. Uses jingles and background music for commercials. Commissions 25 pieces/year. Buys all rights.
How to Contact: Submit demo tape of previously aired work or submit demo tape showing jingle/composition skills. Prefers 7½ ips reel-to-reel. SASE. Reports "as soon as possible."

VANDECAR, DEPORTE & JOHNSON, 255 Lark St., Albany NY 12210. (518)463-2153. Production Director: Marc W. Johnson. Ad agency. Serves financial, automotive, consumer and other clients. Uses services of lyricists and music houses for jingles, background music in commercials and filmtracks. Commissions 15 pieces/year. Pays on a per-job basis. Rights purchased vary.
How to Contact: Submit demo tape showing jingle/composition skills. Prefers 7½ ips reel-to-reel with 3 songs minimum on demo. SASE, but prefers to keep material on file "but will dub off and send back if specified." Responds by phone when need arises.
Music: Jingle work, music tracks, demo work, chart writing, conceptualization and assistance on assignments.

VANGUARD ASSOCIATES, INC., 15 S. 9th St., Minneapolis MN 55402. (612)338-5386. Creative Director: Ira Frank. Advertising agency. Serves consumer product clients; client list available on request. Uses services of songwriters "mostly for the arranging of jingles; some background music for commercials." Pays creative fee on project basis plus more, depending on number of musicians, singers, etc. Buys all rights.
How to Contact: Submit demo tape of previous work. Prefers 7½ ips reel-to-reel with enough songs to display best work. SASE, but prefers to keep material on file.
Music: All types but "we do a lot of radio work aimed at the black market so that black sound is important with us."

STERN WALTERS/EARLE LUDGIN, INC., 150 E. Huron St., Chicago IL 60611. (312)642-4990. Broadcast Production Supervisor: Ann Johnston. Ad Agency. Serves consumer clients. Uses services of songwriters for jingles and background music in commercials. Commissions 10 songwriters/year. Pays $500 minimum/job.
How to Contact: Arrange personal interview or submit demonstration tape. Prefers 7½ ips reel-to-reel. SASE, but prefers to keep material on file. "We respond when we need information, when songwriters ask for something or when we want their services."

WARWICK, WELSH & MILLER, 375 Park Ave., New York NY 10022. (212)751-4700. Broadcast Manager: Lou Kohuth. Ad agency. Serves consumer products clients. Uses jingles and background music for commercials. Commissions 50 pieces/year. Pays $250-7,500/job. Buys all rights.
How to Contact: Submit demo tape of previously aired work. Prefers 7½ ips reel-to-reel tape, 5-7 minutes long. Does not return unsolicited material.

TUCKER WAYNE & CO., 230 Peachtree St. NW, Suite 2700, Atlanta GA 30303. (404)522-2383. Contact: Mr. McNulty or Markay Wiley. Serves financial, industrial, software, textile, food and tobacco clients. Uses services of songwriters and lyricists for jingles and background music in commercials. Commissions 5-50 pieces/year. Pays by the job. Buys all rights.
How to Contact: Call for appointment to listen to demo. Prefers 7½ ips reel-to-reel; tape should be no longer than 7-8 minutes. Prefers to keep tape on file.
Music: All types.

WEBER, COHN & RILEY, 444 N. Michigan Ave., Chicago IL 60611. Contact: Creative Director. Ad agency. Serves real estate, financial and food clients. Uses jingles and background music for commercials. Commissions 3-5 pieces/year. Pays $1,000 minimum/job. Rights purchased vary.
How to Contact: Submit demo tape of previously aired work. Prefers 7½ ips reel-to-reel with 3-8 spots on tape. "We listen to and keep a file of all submissions, but generally do not reply unless we have a specific job in mind."
Music: "We expect highly original, tight arrangements that contribute to the overall concept of the commercial. We do not work with songwriters who have little or no previous experience scoring and recording commercials."
Tips: "Don't aim too high to start. Establish credentials and get experience on small local work, then go after bigger accounts. Don't oversell when making contacts or claim the ability to produce any kind of 'sound.' Producers only believe what they hear on sample reels."

WEBSTER & HARRIS ADVERTISING AGENCY, 1313 Broadway, Suite 1, Lubbock TX 79401. (806)747-2588. Contact: Account Executive. Ad agency and public relations firm. Serves financial, industrial, automobile and agricultural clients. Uses jingles and background music for commercials. Commissions 5 pieces/year. Pays $1,200-2,000 maximum/job. Buys all rights.
How to Contact: Submit demo tape of previously aired work or demo tape showing jingle/composition skills. Prefers 7½ ips reel-to-reel with 1-10 songs on demo. SASE. Reports in 1 week.
Music: "We need all types of music—C&W, top 40, etc. Before any songwriter fould begin working for us, they'd have to know the client inside out, the problems involved and what type of background music/jingles would fit the products. To gain this, they would have to work closely with us and the client."

WILCOX/MYSTROM ADVERTISING, INC., Box 80252, Fairbanks AK 99708. (907)479-4401. President: Brenda Wilcox. Ad agency. Serves retail and industrial clients. Uses jingles. Commissions 5 pieces/year. Pays $600-2,000/job. Buys all Alaskan rights, with option to obtain rights for the other 49 states.
How to Contact: Query, submit demo tape of previously aired work, submit demo tape of jingles/compositions for particular client or submit demo tape showing jingle/composition skills. Prefers cassette with 5 songs minimum on demo. SASE. Reports in 2 weeks.
Music: "Preferably jingles for small clients with low budgets. They should be catchy, and not too upbeat."

WILDRICK & MILLER, INC., 1 Rockefeller Plaza, New York NY 10020. (212)977-8080. President: Donald Wildrick. Vice President: Roy Gorski. Advertising agency. Serves industrial clients. Uses background music in commercials. "We have just begun to buy music." Pays on a per-job basis. Buys all rights.
How to Contact: Query. "We do not accept unsolicited material and we neither evaluate it nor or return it."

WILK & BRICHTA ADVERTISING, 875 N. Michigan, John Hancock Center., Chicago IL 60611. (312)280-2836. Director of Broadcast Production: Mr. Clair Callahan. Uses services of songwriters for jingles, background music in commercials and longer films/filmstrips. Commissions 3-4 pieces/year. Pays per job. Buys all rights.
How to Contact: Query by mail or phone, then submit by mail demonstration tape of previous work with cover letter. Will also review video cassettes and 16mm film but *call* before submitting. Prefers ¼" audio reel-to-reel. SASE.
Music: All types.

WOMACK/CLAYPOOLE/GRIFFIN, 2997 LBJ Business Park, Dallas TX 75234. (214)620-0300. Art Director: Matthew Gleason. Advertising agency. Serves petroleum, aviation, financial, insurance and retail clients. Uses servies of songwriters for jingles and background music in commercials. Pays by the job. Buys all rights.
How to Contact: Submit demo tape of previous work. Prefers reel-to-reel. SASE, but prefers to keep on file.
Music: Radio spots and TV background.

ED YARDANG & ASSOCIATES, 1 Romana Plaza, San Antonio TX 78205. (512)227-8141. Assistant Producer: Katie A. Keller. Advertising agency. Uses services of songwriters for jingles. Sometimes uses services of lyricists. Commissions 10-15 pieces/year. Payment varies with job. Buys all rights.
How to Contact: Query with resume of credits or submit demo tape of previously aired work. Prefers 7½ ips reel-to-reel or cassette with 2-10 songs on demo. Does not return unsolicited material. Reports in 3 weeks. "If we don't like the material, it is unlikely that we'll report back."
Music: Jingles and instrumentals. "We're especially interested in Latin and Hispanic ethnic style. We like jingles with a lot of liveliness and memorability."
Tips: "We like lyricists and songwriters who are willing to work very closely with us and are sensitive to our needs."

YECK & YECK ADVERTISING, Box 225, Dayton OH 45406. (513)294-4000. Ad agency. Serves retail, industrial and financial clients. Uses jingles and background music in commercials and for audiovisual productions. Commissions 3-5 pieces/year. Pays $800-4,000/job. Buys all rights.
How to Contact: Submit demo tape of previously aired work. Prefers cassette or 7½ ips reel-to-reel with 6-8 songs on demo. Does not return unsolicited material.
Music: "Types vary. We provide a guideline sheet that specifies the types of products wanted. Don't try to sell us a stock track or rewrite to some other hot jingle in another market."

YOUNG & RUBICAM WEST/LOS ANGELES, 3435 Wilshire Blvd., Los Angeles CA 90010. (213)736-7400. Contact: Selwyn Touber or Kitt Zeldman. Ad agency. Serves financial, food, beverage, and various product clients. Uses individual songwriters for jingles and background music in commercials. Commissions 30-35 pieces/year. Pays by royalty and creative service. Buys all rights.

How to Contact: Submit demo tape of previously aired work or demo tape showing variation of composition skills. Prefers cassette with 9 songs on demo. Returns material if requested with SASE; prefers to keep tape on file.

Music: All types.

Audiovisual Firms

There are many opportunities for the songwriter in the audiovisual field: film-strips, multimedia kits, educational films, feature films for entertainment, videotape. The advent of video discs, video cassettes and cable television has broadened the market even more.

Schools, government, business and industry, advertising agencies, libraries, publishers and organizations use audiovisuals to teach, inform or sell. Other audiovisual presentations are meant primarily to entertain and are geared with the mass audience in mind: documentary films; network, syndicated and local television; and feature-length movies.

Many companies have their own inhouse production unit specializing in the type of audiovisual presentations pertinent to the company's product or interests. Independent producers, on the other hand, much like a record producer, shop for all the parts needed for a particular job assignment.

Where music is concerned, both corporate and independent producers may look to the stock libraries of music houses for background scores. But as the demand for high-quality original work has increased, so has the opportunity for a songwriter with the technical knowledge and ability to compose for audiovisual presentations.

Visuals will of course be the producer's main concern. Music is used in the background to maintain interest, set mood and complement the visual. Unless you've written the score for a major motion picture where songs can top popular music charts and even win an Academy Award, your reward will only be payment for your work and a sense of achievement in knowing you helped create an excellent *total* package.

Companies listed in this section are open to the fresh material of top-notch songwriters. The key to submitting is to demonstrate your versatility in writing specialized background music. Listings for specific companies will tell you what facet of the audiovisual field and what type of clients they serve.

Additional names of audiovisual firms can be found in the *Audiovisual Market Place* (R.R. Bowker) and *Audio-Visual Communications* magazine (United Business Publications, Inc.).

ADS INC., 1823 Silas Deane Hwy, Rocky Hill CT 06067. (203)529-2581. President: J.J. Wall. Audiovisual firm. Clients include publishers, business and industry. Uses services of music houses for background music for sound filmstrips; lyricists for writing lyrics. Commission 100+ pieces and 3 lyricists/year. Pays $50 minimum/job. Buys all rights.
How to Contact: Arrange personal interview. Prefers cassette with 1 song on demo. SASE. Prefers to keep material on file. Reports as needed for projects.

ALLISON PRODUCTIONS, INC., The 1833 Kalakaua Bldg., Suite 404, Honolulu HI 96815. (808)955-1000. President: Lee Allison. Clients include advertising agencies in Hawaii and Asia, and businesses. Uses services of music houses, songwriters and stock music libraries for background music in commercials and films. Commissions 50-100 pieces/year. Pays $50-2,500/job. Buys one-time rights.
How to Contact: Submit demo tape of previously aired work, or submit demo tape of compositions for particular client. "If we are interested, we will contact you for a personal or phone interview." Prefers 7½ ips reel-to-reel or cassette with 6-15 songs on demo. Does not return unsolicited material. Reports "only if we are interested in the material or talent submitted."

AMERICAN MIND PRODUCTIONS/POP INTERNATIONAL CORPORATION, 253 Closter Dock Rd., Box 105, Closter NJ 07624. (201)767-8030. Producers: Augie Borghese, Arnold De Pasquale and Peter DeCaro. Motion picture production company. Clients include "political campaigns, commercial spots, business and industry concerns as a production service; feature films

and documentaries as producers." Uses services of music houses and songwriters for "mood purposes only on documentary films. However, American Mind does conceptualize major theatrical and/or album musical projects." Commissions about 3-5 commercial and 25 soundtrack pieces for entertainment specials and 25 lyricists/year. Pays $500-1,250/job; 10%-49%/royalty. Buys all rights and one-time rights.
How to Contact: Submit demo tape of previously aired work. Prefers cassette with 2-4 songs on demo. SASE. Reports in 3 weeks.
Music: Uses "mood music for documentaries, occasionally jingles for spots or promotional films or theme music/songs for dramatic projects (the latter by assignment only from producers or agencies). Some material is strictly mood, as in documentary work; some is informative as in promotional; some is motivating as in commercial; some is entertaining as in theatrical/TV."
Tips: "Develop a reputation, if not a recognized, successful 'pro,' with credits, then develop a reputation as very consistent and co-operative."

ARZTCO PICTURES, INC., 15 E. 61st St., New York NY 10021. (212)753-1050. President/ Producer: Tony Arzt. Clients include industry, government and advertising agencies. Uses services of music houses and songwriters for film scores. Commissions 20-50 pieces/year. Pays $150-6,000/job, or $25-750 royalty. Buys all rights or one-time rights.
How to Contact: Submit demo tape of previously aired work or submit demo tape of composition skills. Prefers 7½ ips reel-to-reel or cassette with 6-12 songs on demo. SASE. Reports "immediately, if appropriate for a job on hand."
Music: "We generally prefer small group sound—no large orchestras with too much brass and strings. Good beat and melody are important."

AUDIOVISUAL RESULTS, 334 E. 31st St., Kansas City MO 64108. (816)931-4103. Contact: Carl James. Clients include industrial firms. Uses services of songwriters for thematic scores in films and filmstrips. Payment negotiable. Buys all rights.
How to Contact: Query with demo tape of previously aired work. Prefers reel-to-reel or cassette. Keeps tapes on file.
Music: Broad range of musical styles for industrial, sales training and promotional shows.

CLIFF AYERS ENTERPRISES, 62 Music Square W., Nashville TN 37203. (615)327-4538. President: Cliff Ayers. Audiovisual firm, music publisher and record company. Uses services of songwriters and lyricists for music and lyrics for commercials. Commissions 200 pieces/year. Pays 50% minimum royalty.
How to Contact: Submit demonstration tape of previous work or tape demonstrating composition skills. Prefers cassette with 3 songs on demo. SASE. Reports in 2 weeks. Free book catalog.
Music: C&W, pop, R&B, rock and roll.

BACHNER PRODUCTIONS, INC., 45 W. 45th St., New York NY 10036. (212)354-8760. President: A. Bachner. Motion picture production company. Clients include users of TV film and videotape commercials and industrial and sales training films. Uses services of music houses and songwriters for commercial jingles and background music for TV and inhouse use. "Assignments are for music only or music and lyrics for commercials. Background music is scored to film." Commissions 6-10 pieces/year. Pays $750-5,000/job. Buys all rights or one-time rights.
How to Contact: Query with resume of credits. Prefers 7½ or 15 ips reel-to-reel. Does not return unsolicited material. Reports in 1 month.
Tips: "Be able to supply complete package."

BELLE STREET PRODUCTIONS, INC., 3620 Bell St., Kansas City MO 64111. (816)753-4376. Producer: Bill Foard. Chief Engineer: Larry Johnson. Clients include business and promotional firms. Uses services of songwriters for music in radio and TV commercials. Payment negotiable. Rights purchased vary.
How to Contact: Submit demo tape of previously aired work. Prefers 7½ ips reel-to-reel or cassette with 4-5 songs on demo. SASE. Reports in 1 week.

ROBERT BERNING-FILM PRODUCTIONS, INC., 327 Dauphine St., New Orleans LA 70112. (504)581-2996. Sales Director: Robert Berning. Motion picture production company. Clients include advertising agencies, industrial firms and corporations. Uses services of music houses and songwriters for background music, TV and radio commercials, international sales films, and safety/training films. Commissions 10 composers and 4 lyricists/year. Pays on a per-job basis. Buys all rights or one-time rights.
How to Contact: Submit demo tape of previous work or query with resume of credits. Prefers 7½ ips reel-to-reel with 4 songs minimum on tape. SASE. Reports in 1 month.

Music: Jingles and movie scores with a wide range of subjects.
Tips: "Submit examples of past work and accept the financial terms."

BILL BRITTAIN ASSOCIATES, 130 Lakeside Park, Hendersonville TN 37075. (615)824-1593. President: William D. Brittain. Audiovisual firm and jingle producer. Clients include schools, publishers, business, industry, radio and TV. Uses services of songwriters for background music for sound filmstrips, musical scores in films, original songs for themes, music scoring and jingles for commercials. Pays outright purchase/job. Buys all rights.
How to Contact: Query with resume of credits, then submit demonstration tape of previous work. Prefers cassette with 2-5 songs on demo. Does not return unsolicited material. Catalog $2.50.
Music: Uses musical scoring for audiovisual training tapes. Submit tape and resume for our files.

CINETUDES FILM PRODUCTIONS, 293 West 4th St., New York City NY 10014. (212)966-4600. Producer: Gale Goldberg. Motion picture production company. Clients include television. Uses services of songwriters for musical scores in films; lyricists for writing lyrics for themes and other music. Commissions 3-4 pieces/year. Buys all rights.
How to contact: Submit tape demonstrating composition skills. Prefers reel-to-reel with 2-4 songs on demo. "Recommendations are helpful." SASE. Reports in 2 weeks.
Music: Film music.

CLARUS MUSIC, LTD., 340 Bellevue Ave., Yonkers NY 10703. (914)375-0864. President: Selma Fass. Contact: New Product Department. Music publisher and record company (educational). Clients include educational and retail markets. Uses services of songwriters and lyricists for musical plays (script and songs) for the educational market. Commissions 2-3 composers and 2-3 lyricists/year. Pays standard royalties. Buys all rights.
How to Contact: Query with resume of credits or submit demo tape of previously aired work or submit demo tape showing flexibility of composition skills. Prefers 7½ ips reel-to-reel or cassette with 3-20 songs on the tape. SASE. Reports in 3 weeks. Free book catalog.
Music: Various kinds of music.
Tips: "Submit material for consideration; no assignments until we've communicated and an agreement is made between our company and the writer(s)."

COCONUT GROVE PRODUCTIONS, 3100 Carlisle, #107, Dallas TX 75204. (214)748-2755. Producer: Tim Pugliese. Clients include business firms. Uses services of music houses for background music and TV/radio commercials. Commissions 3-4 pieces/year. Pays $500-2,500/job. Buys all rights.
How to Contact: Submit demo tape of previously aired work with cover letter explaining prices. Prefers 7½ ips reel-to-reel with 5-10 songs on demo. Does not return unsolicited material. Reports "only if we are going to use the person."
Music: Needs "anything from full instrumentals to synthesized music."

THE CREATIVE ESTABLISHMENT, 50 E. 42nd St., New York NY 10017. (212)682-0840. Executive Producer: Ted Schulman. Audiovisual firm and motion picture production company. Clients include business and industry. Uses services of music houses, songwriters for scores in films, themes for business meetings; lyricists for writing lyrics for themes. Commissions 10-15 pieces/year. Pays by the job. Buys all rights and one-time rights.
How to Contact: Query with resume of credit; submit demonstration tape of previous work or tape demonstrating composition skills. Prefers 7½ ips reel-to-reel with 5-10 songs on demo. "All material is kept on file."

CULPEPPER'S CINEMATICIANS, LTD., (formerly Marvin Plus, Inc.), 1145 S. Barry Ave., #212, West Los Angeles CA 90049 or MPI, c/o Sgt. Culpepper's, 1800 N. Highland Ave., Suite 707, Hollywood CA 90028. Producer/Director: Larry Randall Vincent, DGA. Audiovisual firm, motion picture production company, and player piano roll sales (label "BIG-W"). Clients include corporations, government and advertising agencies. Uses services of songwriters and music houses for musical scores in films cutting new player piano rolls for sale of BIG-W label this fall. Commissions 3 pieces/year. Pays $100 for piano rolls and 15% royalty, $110 minimum/minute for films. Buys all rights ("world wide").
How to Contact: Submit demo tape of previously aired work. Prefers 7½ ips reel-to-reel with 5 songs on demo. Does not return unsolicited material. Replies "only if the writer calls. There will be a "kit" printed for pianists and available at no charge this fall, which will fully explain the BIG-W label and how to prepare player piano pieces for our manufacturers."
Music: "Besides our film producing department, BIG-W music rolls will begin cutting new and original tunes this fall. We want to build a very large selection."

Tips: "Our firm is a 'boutique'—one producer/director shop. We freelance out most of our production work, including music, occasionally. Write a letter expressing a desire to compose roll music and mail a 5 inch large hub ¼ inch tape (7½ ips) of piano style."

D4 FILMS STUDIOS, INC., 109 Highland Ave., Needham Heights MA 02194. (617)444-0226. President: Stephen Dephoure. Clients include educational, industrial and medical firms, and governmental agencies. Uses services of music houses and songwriters for background music. **How to Contact:** Submit resume of credits. Prefers cassette. Reports in 10 days.

CHARLES ELMS PRODUCTIONS, INC., 163 Highland Ave., North Tarrytown NY 10591. (914)631-7474. Producer/General Manager: Charles D. Elms. Clients include business and industry. Uses services of music houses for background or opening, bridges, closing for film strips, and scores for films. Pays on a per-job basis. Buys one-time rights. **How to Contact:** Query with resume of credits. "Do not send material until requested." Reports after client has indicated preference. **Music:** "I do not like singing commercials—I use music for mood. Other than opening, closing and bridges the level should be kept so low that you do not realize it is there. I do not produce 'screaming Meemies' commercials!"

ENTERTAINMENT PRODUCTIONS, INC., Box 554, Malibu CA 90265. (213)456-3143. Motion picture production company. President: Edward Coe. Clients include distributors/exhibitors. Uses services of music houses and songwriters for background and theme music for films. Commissions/year vary. Pays scale/job. Rights purchased vary. **How to Contact:** Query with resume of credits. Prefers reel-to-reel. Demo should show flexibility of composition skills. "Demo records/tapes sent at own risk—returned if SASE included." Reports in 1 month. **Tips:** "Have resume on file."

EPIGRAM MUSIC, Box 9498, Rochester NY 14604. Contact: Michael Fishbein. Scoring service and marketing agent. Clients include publishers, film companies and performers. Uses services of songwriters for film-background and educational music. Pays by the job. Buys all rights. **How to Contact:** Submit demonstration tape of previous work or tape demonstrating composition skills. Prefers cassette with 3-8 songs on demo. SASE. Reports in 3 weeks.

EQUINOX FILMS, 50 Kearney Rd., Needham MA 02194. Vice President, Music Services: Daniel A. Radler. Marketing Director: Lisa J. Podoloff. Clients include local and federal government, schools, and business and industrial firms. Uses services of music houses and songwriters for film scores and commercials. Pays $25 minimum/job. Buys all rights. **How to Contact:** Submit resume of credits and demo tape of previously aired work or submit demo tape showing flexibility of composition skills. Prefers 7½ ips reel-to-reel with 3-5 songs on demo. SASE. Reports in 1 week. Free catalog.

MARTIN EZRA & ASSOCIATES, 48 Garrett Rd., Upper Darby PA 19082. (215)352-9595 or 9596. Producer: Martin Ezra. Audiovisual firm and motion picture production company. Clients include business, industry and education. Uses services of music houses, songwriters and stock music for background music for sound filmstrips, musical scores in films, and original songs for themes; uses lyricists for movie themes. Commissions 5-6 compositions/year and 1-2 lyricists/year. Pays $100-2,000/job. Buys all rights or one-time rights. **How to Contact:** Submit demonstration tape of previous work. "We do not return tapes." Prefers cassette with 1-20 songs on demo. Does not return unsolicited material. Reports in 3 weeks. **Music:** Uses music for film and audiovisual productions.

F.E.L. PUBLICATIONS, LTD., 1925 Pontius Ave., Los Angeles CA 90025. (213)478-053. Treasurer: James D. Boyd. Clients include the religious folk liturgical market. Uses services of songwriters. Commissions 20-50 pieces/year. Pays 4-7% royalty. Buys all rights. **How to Contact:** Submit demo tape of compositions for particular client. Prefers cassette with 10-15 songs on demo. SASE. Free catalog. **Music:** Religious folk hymns and songs.

THE FILM WORKS, (a division of Patterson & Hall), 1250 Folsom St., San Francisco CA 94103. Vice President: Thomas F. Hall. Uses services of songwriters for films, audiovisual shows and occasional live shows. Commissions 2 pieces/year. Pays on a per job basis. Buys all rights, unless otherwise specified.

How to Contact: Submit demo tape of previously aired work. Prefers 7½ ips reel-to-reel or cassette with optional number of songs on demo. SASE.
Music: "Very tight TV spots, 6-10 minute sales films, to a 20-25 minute industrial film."

FOURNIER FILMCOM, INC., Outer Winthrop Rd., Hallowell ME 04347. President: Paul J. Fournier. Clients include federal and state government agencies, business and industry, medical associations, television networks and promotional agencies. Uses services of music houses and songwriters for thematic backgrounds for films, multimedia audiovisual programs and filmstrips. Commissions 5-10 pieces/year. Pays $50 minimum/job. Buys one-time rights.
How to Contact: Query, submit demo tape of previously aired work or submit demo tape showing flexibility of composition skills. Prefers 7½ ips reel-to-reel or cassette with 1-5 songs on demo. SASE. Reports in 3 weeks.
Music: Needs outdoor themes: scenic; pastoral; environmental; outdoor sports action (skiing, whitewater canoeing); light industrial (lab work, electronic); and heavy industrial (power plant construction).

JOHN N. GEKAS FILM PRODUCTIONS, 5610 Westheimer, Suite 548, Houston TX 77056. (713)748-2978. President: John Gekas. Clients include business and industrial firms; "we also consult for other producers and our inhouse industrial audiovisual departments." Uses services of songwriters and lab libraries for film scores and background music. Pays on a per-job basis: $1-250/film reel; or a negotiable fee for original scores. Buys all rights or one-time rights.
How to Contact: Query with resume of credits or submit demo tape of previously aired work. Prefers 7½ ips reel-to-reel or cassette with 3-6 songs on demo. SASE. Reports in 4 weeks.
Music: Needs "custom music appropriate to basic industrial and business film scripts" and "original film scores, as needed. Contact us to determine our needs and check in periodically."

INDIANER MULTI-MEDIA, 16201 SW 95th Ave., Box 550, Miami FL 33157. (305)235-6132. Vice President Systems: David Gravel. President: Paul Indianer. Uses services of music houses and songwriters for background music scored to action. Commissions 40 pieces/year. Pays $50/finished minute. Buys all rights or one-time rights.
How to Contact: Query with resume of credits or submit demo tape showing flexibility of composition skills. Prefers 7½ ips reel-to-reel with 5 songs minimum on tape. SASE. Reports in 3 weeks.

INTERNATIONAL MOTION PICTURES, LTD., Box 3201, Erie PA 16512. Contact: Producer. Motion picture production company. Uses services of songwriters and lyricists for musical scores in films and original songs for themes. Pays by the job. Buys all rights.
How to Contact: Query with resume of credits.
Music: Music for feature films.

JACOBY/STORM PRODUCTIONS, INC., 101 Post Rd. E., Westport CT 06880. Vice President: Doris Storm. Clients include schools, publishers, business and industrial firms. Uses services of music houses and songwriters for film scores, background music and an occasional theme song. Commissions 2-3 pieces/year. Payment negotiable. Buys all rights or one-time rights.
How to Contact: Query with resume of credits or submit demo tape of previously aired work. Prefers 7½ or 15 ips reel-to-reel. SASE. Reports in 2 weeks. "Don't send any material without querying first."
Music: Needs songs and background music for films geared to elementary or high school students; also suitable for industrial and documentary films.

KEN-DEL PRODUCTIONS, INC., 111 Valley Rd., Wilmington DE 19804. (302)655-7488. A&R Director: Shirley Kay. General Manager: Ed Kennedy. Clients include publishers, schools and industrial firms. Uses services of songwriters for film scores and title music. Pays on a per-job basis. Buys all rights.
How to Contact: Submit demo of previously aired work. Prefers acetate discs, but will accept tapes. SASE; "however, we prefer to keep tapes on file for possible future use." Reports in 2 weeks.

KEY PRODUCTIONS, INC., Box 2684, Gravois Station, St. Louis MO 63116. President: John E. Schroeder. Audiovisual firm. Clients include churches, colleges, church schools, industry and festivals. Uses services of songwriters for stage and educational TV musical dramas, background music for filmstrips, some speculative collaboration for submission to publishers, and regional theatrical productions. Commissions "10 pieces/year, but selects up to 50 songs." Pays $50 minimum/job or by 10% minimum royalty. Buys one-time rights or all rights.
How to Contact: Query with resume of credits or submit demo tape showing flexibility of composi-

tion skills. "Suggest prior fee scales." Prefers cassette with 3-8 songs on demo. SASE. Reports in 1 month.
Music: "We almost always use religious material; some contemporary Biblical opera; and some gospel; a few pop; blues; folk-rock; and occasionally soul."

KIMBO EDUCATIONAL-UNLIMITED SOUND ARTS, INC., 10-16 N. 3rd Ave., Box 477, Long Branch NJ 07740. (201)229-4949. Producers: James Kimble or Amy Laufer. Audiovisual firm and manufacturer of educational material: records, cassettes and teacher manuals or guides. Clients include schools and stores selling teachers' supplies. Uses services of music houses, songwriters, and educators for original songs for special education, early childhood, music classes, physical education and pre-school children; lyricists for lyrics to describe children's activities centering on development of motor skills, language, fitness or related educational skills. Commissions 12-15 pieces and 12-15 lyricists/year. Pays by the job or 2½¢ royalty. Buys all rights.
How to Contact: Submit demonstration tape of previous work, tape demonstrating composition skills, manuscript showing music scoring skills or lead sheet with lyrics. Prefers 7½ or 15 ips reel-to-reel or cassette with 1-12 songs on demo. "Upon receipt of a demo tape and/or written material, each property is previewed by our production staff. The same chances exist for any individual if the material is of high quality and we feel it meets the educational goals we are seeking." Reports in 1 month. Free book catalog.
Music: "Contemporary sounds with limited instrumentation so as not to appear too sophisticated nor distracting for the young or special populations. Lyrics should be noncomplex and repetitive."

SID KLEINER MUSIC ENTERPRISES, 3701 25th Ave. SW, Naples FL 33999. (813)455-2693 or 455-2696. Managing Director: Sid Kleiner. Audiovisual firm. Clients include the music industry. Uses services of music houses, songwriters, and inhouse writers for background music; lyricists for special material. Pays $25 minimum/job. Buys all rights.
How to Contact: Query with resume of credits or submit demo tape of previously aired work. Prefers cassette with 1-4 songs on demo. SASE. Reports in 3-5 weeks.
Music: "We generally need soft background music, with some special lyrics to fit a particular project. We also assign country, pop mystical and metaphysical."

KOESTER AUDIO-VISUAL PRESENTATIONS, Box 336, Far Hills NJ 07931. (201)766-2143. President: Ralph Koester. Clients include industrial and sales firms, schools and museums. Uses services of music houses and songwriters for opening, closing and background music for slide shows and films. Pays by license fee or contract. Buys all rights or nonexclusive one-time rights.
How to Contact: Contact by phone, query with resume of credits, submit demo tape of previously aired compositions, submit demo tape of compositions for particular client or submit demo tape showing flexibility of comosition skills. Prefers 7½ ips reel-to-reel or cassette with 3-10 songs on demo. Does not return unsolicited material. Reports in 3 weeks. "Leave demo tape, and we will call when the need arises."
Music: "We need openings, closings and backgrounds in both modern and classical moods. Usually, we use no vocals."

LAVIDGE & ASSOCIATES, INC., 409 Bearden Park Circle, Knoxville TN 37919. (615)584-6121. Account Executive: R. Lyle Lavidge. "Full-service advertising agency with complete in-house film production facility." Uses services of music houses for jingles, musical commercials and audiovisual/film scores. Pays $1,000 minimum/job. Buys all rights or one-time rights, "depending on the client, market, etc."
How to Contact: Arrange personal interview or submit demo tape of previously aired work. Prefers 7½ ips reel-to-reel or cassette with 4-12 songs on demo. SASE. Doesn't report unless interested.

W.V. LEVINE ASSOCIATES, INC., 31 E. 28th St., New York NY 10016. (212)683-7177. President: W. Levine. Clients include industrial firms. Uses services of New York City based songwriters for live industrial presentations at sales meetings, conferences and trade shows. Commissions 12 pieces of music and 12 lyricists/year. Pays $250-1,500/job. Buys all or one-time rights.
How to Contact: Query with resume of credits. "We deal only with New York City-based talent." Prefers 7½ ips reel-to-reel or cassette with 4-6 songs on demo. SASE. Reports in 3 weeks.

JACK LIEB PRODUCTIONS, 200 E. Ontario, Chicago IL 60611. (312)943-1440. Contact: Susan Schrier. President: W.H. Lieb. Clients include governmental agencies and industrial firms. Uses services of music houses and songwriters for background music and public service announcements. Pays on a per-job basis. Buys all rights.
How to Contact: Query with resume of credits, submit demo tape of previously aired composi-

Songwriter's Market Close-up

"I was in the music business for quite a long time and the irony is my commercial success came through a movie." Michael Gore is referring to his two Academy Awards—best song and best score—for "Fame."

"I've been influenced by a great variety of music. I grew up in New York with pop music at a very early age (as Lesley Gore's younger brother). There was also the Broadway theater in growing up. There was rhythm and blues and Aretha Franklin and all the records coming out of New York in the middle sixties. And there were the Beatles. Then I studied classical music (Yale University) and spent a great deal of time in Europe where I concentrated on classical music exclusively for about six years."

But he doesn't necessarily think everyone needs an extensive educational background in music. "There are certain people who benefit from on-the-job professional training, meaning simply being out there and 'doing it.' I liked the academic environment and benefitted greatly from it. But it does occur that you can't follow all the rules. My theory is that it's nice to know them—and then break them."

On the subject of demos, Gore says, "Simple is often stronger. I send the simplest demo possible. People have various philosophies about it, but as one who's also a producer, when I receive material from somebody, I don't want to hear production ideas already in the song. I like to hear a song unembellished and then try to impose those production ideas myself."

Although a skilled musician, composer, arranger and producer, he most always collaborates. "I prefer working with lyricists. I think that collaboration is great in terms of the various ideas that can come out of it."

Today he thinks there are probably more advantages than disadvantages for aspiring songwriters. "The market is far more diversified than it was ten or fifteen years ago. In the eighties anything that is good or 'has it' can go. I think that allows for

Michael Gore

many more musical openings in terms of styles. You can submit a song and, if it's a good song, it might end up being recorded by a country and R&B and even rock artist."

The big mistake he believes songwriters make is writing for trends. "You could always be a foot behind trends out there already." He warns songwriters to work toward excellence rather than commercial success. "Commercial success is so random in terms of whether one person or one million will like your song and buy it—it's always an unknown. The best you can do is to write what you do the best and what pleases you the most."

What pleases him for the future? "What I'd like to do is keep moving between different fields. I have a great desire to write a Broadway musical and I will do another movie, possibly a classical score. But I will always write songs for the commercial market because I enjoy that. If there is one thing that keeps me going it is the fact I can work hard on something and see people enjoying my music. That in itself is the most incredible reward possible!"

tions, or submit demo tape showing flexibility of comosition skills. Prefers 7½ ips reel-to-reel. Does not return unsolicited material.

LIGHTHOUSE PRODUCTIONS, 2345 Symmes St., Cincinnati OH 45206. (513)721-9900-303. Operations Manager: Mark Ackley. Audiovisual firm. Clients include coporations. Uses services of songwriters and music libraries for background music for audiovisual shows for sales meetings, training seminars, meetings, entertainment, etc. Commissions 5-15 pieces/year. Pays by the job. Payment depends on budget and contract agreements. Buys all rights and one-time rights.
How to Contact: Submit demonstration tape of previous work. Prefers cassette with 5-10 songs on demo. SASE. Reports in 1 month.

HARLEY McDANIEL FILMPRODUCTION, INC., 4444 W. Capitol Dr., Milwaukee WI 53216. President: John R. McDaniel. Clients include colleges, national associations, TV stations and advertising agencies. Uses services of music houses and songwriters for film scores and background music. Commissions 10 original scores/year; 40-60 needle drops/year. Pays $1,500-12,000/job. Buys all rights.
How to Contact: Query with resume of credits or submit demo tape of previously aired work. Prefers 7½ ips reel-to-reel with 5-15 songs on demo. SASE. Reports in 3 weeks.
Music: "We need bright and catchy music. Much of our music is used for TV promos. For longer films, we guide the music writing, but we rely on the writer's judgment."
Tips: "Make music easy to edit to different lengths."

MAGNETIC STUDIOS, Lindy Productions, Inc., 4784 N. High St., Columbus OH 43214. Studio Administrator: Diana White. Clients include advertising agencies, industrial/consumer manufacturers, and educational publishers. Uses songwriters and music libraries for radio/TV commercial jingles; and background music for slide, filmstrip, motion picture and multi-image presentations. Commissions 5-10 pieces/year. Pays $150 minimum/job. Buys all rights.
How to Contact: Query with resume of credits or submit demo tape of previously aired work. "*No telephone queries.*" Prefers 7½ ips reel-to-reel with 3-10 songs on demo. Does not return unsolicited material. Reports "at our discretion."

MAJOR MEDIA, INC., 747 Lake Cook Rd., Deerfield IL 60015. (312)498-4610. President: Jay Steinberg. Audiovisual firm. Clients include educational and industrial firms. Uses services of music houses, songwriters and lyricists for filmstrips, slides, audio tapes, live show and packaged audiovisual moduial productions. Commissions 3-4 pieces and 2 lyricists/year. Payment negotiable. Buys all rights.
How to Contact: Submit tape demonstrating composition skills; prefers 7½ ips reel-to-reel. SASE. Reports in 3 months.
Music: Industrial show themes.

ED MARZOLA & ASSOCIATES, 839 N. Highland Ave., Hollywood CA 90038. (213)469-1961. Technical Manager: Manny Gozdzinski. Executive Vice President: Marta Ruibal. President: Ed Marzola. Motion picture production company. Clients include business/industry, schools, TV stations and theaters. Uses services of music houses and songwriters for background music and scoring. Commissions 3 pieces/year. Pays negotiable royalty. Buys all rights or one-time rights.
How to Contact: Query with resume of credits or submit demo tape of previously aired work. Prefers 7½ ips reel-to-reel or cassette with 3-10 songs on demo. SASE. Reports in 1 week. Free book catalog.
Music: Uses "background for industrial films, music for educational films, and TV promos. Lot's of children's songs."
Tips: "We are not heavy users; most of the time we try to pull music from libraries, stock, etc. But sometimes we do use a good songwriter, provided we have a budget for it."

MAXFILMS, 2525 Hyperion Ave., Los Angeles CA 90027. (213)662-3285. Vice President, Production: Sid Glenar. Production Assistant: Y. Shinn. Audiovisual firm and motion picture production company. Clients include corporations, nonprofit organizations and schools. Also produces films for theatrical and television release. Uses services of songwriters "for background on a theatrical or television film. Occasionally, an original score will be contracted for use in a corporate or educational film." Commissions 8-10 pieces/year. Pays $500-10,000/job. Buys all rights.
How to Contact: Submit demo tape of previously aired work, submit demo tape of composition for particular client or submit demo tape showing flexibility of composition skills. Prefers 7½ ips reel-to-reel or cassette with 1-6 songs on demo. "Tapes submitted should have some background as to the type of picture or presentation the music was scored for." SASE. Reports in 3 weeks.

Music: "Complete scoring, or a title song or intro to a film or audiovisual presentation. State complete capabilities in terms of composing, arranging and performing with some indication of the type of music that you handle best."

MEDIA MANAGEMENT CORP., 1500 Broadway, New York NY 10036. (212)398-1880. Creative Director: Rus Wolgast. Audiovisual firm. Estab. 1979. Clients include schools, publishers, business and industry; "majority are corporate, business, or industrial in nature." Uses services of music houses and songwriters for background music for audiovisual presentations and multi-image shows. Pays by the job. Buys all rights.
How to Contact: Query with resume of credits; arrange personal interview; submit demonstration tape of previous work or tape demonstrating composition skills. Prefers 7½ or 15 ips reel-to-reel or cassette with 3 songs on demo. SASE. Reports in 1 month. Free book catalog.
Music: "Type of music will depend on the use—mostly contemporary, uptempo or dynamic sounds."

FORNEY MILLER FILM ASSOCIATES, 5 Timber Fare, Spring House PA 19477. (215)643-4167. Owner: Forney Miller. Clients include institutions, industrial and business firms. Uses services of songwriters and composers for film scores and background music. Pays $200 minimum "for open/close music." Buys all rights or one-time rights.
How to Contact: Submit demo tape of previously aired work. Prefers cassette. SASE. Reports "as soon as possible."
Music: Uses background music for business, promotional and documentary films.

WARREN MILLER PRODUCTIONS, 505 Pier Ave., Hermosa Beach CA 90254. (213)376-2494. Production: Robert Knop. Clients include industrial, sports film, resort and airline firms. Uses services of music houses for background music in films. Commissions 1 piece/year. Pays $2,000 minimum/job; $25/needle drop. Buys one-time rights.
How to Contact: Submit demo tape of previously aired work. Prefers cassette with 1-10 songs on demo, or disc. SASE. Reports in 3 weeks.
Music: Needs action, outdoors, symphonic, soft rock, "energy music that is light and youthful."
Tips: "It is important to be in this area to score a film. The musician must work closely with the editor. Be adept at scoring several instruments. Instrumentals will be better for us than vocals."

ARTHUR MILLS ASSOCIATES, INC., (formerly Nodus Productions), 47 W. 68th, New York NY 10023. (212)787-1066. President: Arthur Mills. Clients include TV networks, advertising agencies, film companies and industrial firms. Uses services of music houses and songwriters for film scores, and original material for performers and TV specials. Pays "participation in profits." Rights purchased vary.
How to Contact: Query with resume of credits, submit demo tape of previously aired work, submit demo tape of compositions for particular client or submit demo tape showing flexibility of composition skills. Prefers cassette with 4-6 songs on demo. SASE. Reports in 1 month.
Music: "Anything from classical music to rock. We especially need music that can be adapted to film scores, and material for cabaret and nightclub performers. We also need songs for TV movies and specials, the legitimate theater, and industrial shows (live and film)."

MONUMENTAL FILMS & RECORDINGS, 2160 Rockrose Ave., Baltimore MD 21211. (301)462-1550. President: John A'Hern. Audiovisual firm and motion picture production company. Clients include business and industry. Uses services of music houses for background music for sound filmstrips and musical scores in films; lyricists for writing lyrics for themes and other music and translations. Commissions 10 pieces and 10 lyricists/year. Pays by the job. Buys all rights.
How to Contact: Arrange personal interview, submit demonstration tape of previous work or tape demonstrating composition skills. Prefes reel-to-reel or cassette with 5-10 songs on demo. SASE. Reports in 2 weeks. Free book catalog.
Music: Musical background for documentary films.

JACK MORTON PRODUCTIONS, 830 3rd Ave., New York NY 10012. Vice President, Production: Paul Kielar. Clients include business and industry. Uses songwriters for musical scores for live dramatizations, sound filmstrips, films, etc. Commissions 500 pieces/year. Pays $1,500-7,500/job. Buys one-time rights.
How to Contact: Query with resume of credits, arrange personal interview, submit demo tape of previously aired work or submit demo tape showing flexibility of composition skills. Prefers cassette with 3-6 songs on demo. Reports in 3 weeks.
Music: "Pop, rock, disco—the music being played today."

MOYNIHAN ASSOCIATES, 1717 S. 12th St., Milwaukee WI 53204. (414)645-8200. Producer/ Director: Diane Wittenberg. Clients include schools, non-profit organizations, businesses and industrial firms. Uses services of music houses and songwriters for film title and background music. Commissions 1-2 pieces/film. Buys all rights.
How to Contact: Submit demo tape showing flexibility of composition skills. Prefers 7½ ips reel-to-reel with 5-7 songs on demo. SASE. Reports in 3 weeks. Free catalog with SASE.
Music: Needs "bold, exciting music for industrial films. Light, easygoing background and credit music. Use music as an extension of the film visuals."

MULTI-MEDIA INC., (formerly Multi-Media Productions, Inc.), 7348 S. Alton Way, Englewood CO 80112. (303)741-4600. Media Supervisor: Robert J. Taylor. Audiovisual firm and jingle production house. Clients include business, industry, state and federal government, and schools. Uses music houses and composers/arrangers for background music for sound filmstrips, musical scores in films, original songs for themes, scoring and radio/TV jingles. Commissions 3 composers/year. Pays $100-1,000/job. Buys all rights and one-time rights.
How to Contact: Query with resume of credits, arrange personal interview or submit demo tape showing flexibility of composition skills. Prefers 7½ reel-to-reel or cassette with 3 songs on demo. SASE. Reports in 1 week.
Music: "Radio/TV commercial cuts, station and product sound logos, media backgrounds, arrangements."
Tips: "Be available and be easy to talk to."

MULTI-MEDIA WORKS, 6061 W. 3rd St., Los Angeles CA 90036. (213)939-1185. President: Art GaNung. Sound Engineer: Phil Singer. Clients include business and industry. Uses services of music house for background, theme music and lyrics. Commissions 4 pieces/year. Pays $150-500/job. Buys all rights or one-time rights.
How to Contact: Submit demo tape of previous work. Prefers 7½ ips reel-to-reel with 3-5 songs on the tape. SASE. Reports in 1 month.
Music: Background and theme music and lyrics for sales and marketing presentations.

LARRY NICHOLSON PRODUCTIONS, 2100 Stark, Kansas City MO 64126. President: Larry Nicholson. Clients include government, industrial and educational firms. Uses services of music houses and songwriters for background music, themes and jingles. Commissions 6-12 pieces/year. Pays on a per-hour, per-job or royalty basis. Buys one-time rights or all rights. Complete in-house sound recording studio.
How to Contact: Submit demo tape of previously aired work. Prefers reel-to-reel or cassette with 6-10 songs on demo. SASE. Prefers not to return material, but will if requested. Reports in 2 weeks.
Music: "Frequently looking for 'stingers,' 6- to 20-second pieces for bridges, transitions, openers and closers."

OCEAN REALM VIDEO PRODUCTIONS, 3514 S. Dixie Hwy., Miami FL 33133. President/ Producer: Richard Stewart. Video picture production company. Estab. 1979. Clients include ABC, "Good Morning America," and Home Box Office. Uses services of music houses for background music for TV series. Commissions 3 pieces/year. Pays $250 minimum/job. Buys all rights and one-time rights.
How to Contact: Submit demonstration tape of previous work. Prefers cassette for demo. SASE. Reports in 2 weeks. Free book catalog.
Music: Ocean-related.

ORIGIN, INC., 4466 Lacrede, St. Louis MO 631-8. (314)533-0010. Creative Director: George Johnson. Audiovisual firm, scoring service and music contractor. Clients include business, industry, government, agricultural conglomerates and hospitals. Uses services of songwriters and lyricists for music for conventions, industrial shows, films, video, etc. Payment negotiable. Rights purchased as requested by client.
How to Contact: Query with resume of credits; submit demonstration tape of previous work or tape demonstrating composition skills or manuscript showing music scoring skills. Prefers cassette with any number of songs on demo. SASE. Reports in 2 weeks.
Music: Depends on client's needs.
Tips: "Try to write lots of comedy songs and find words and ideas that make sense and rhyme with cat chow, soybeans and carburetor."

PADDOCK PRODUCTIONS, INC., 9101 Barton, Shawnee Mission KS 66214. (913)492-9850. Sound Engineer: Fred Paddock. President: Chuck Paddock. Clients include industrial and educational firms. Uses services of music houses and songwriters for filmstrips, films, commercials and

jingles. Commissions 50 pieces/year. Pays on a per-job basis. Buys one-time rights or all rights.
How to Contact: Submit demo tape showing flexibility of composition skills. Prefers 7½ ips
reel-to-reel with 5 songs minimum on demo. SASE. Reports "as soon as possible."

VERNE PERSHING, 1417 N. Vista, Hollywood CA 90046. (415)346-7825. Produces documentary, commercial and industrial films. Uses services of songwriters and musicians. Commissions 5
pieces/year. Pays $50-1,500/job. Rights purchased vary.
How to Contact: Submit demo tape of previously aired work. Prefers cassette with 5 songs on
demo. SASE. Reports in 2 weeks.

GERARD PICK, PRODUCER, AUDIO/VISUAL MEDIA, Box 3032, Santa Monica CA 90403.
(213)459-5596. Producer/Owner: Gerard Pick. Clients include business and industrial firms. Uses
services of songwriters for background music, and "sometimes front and end titles." Pays $500
minimum/job. Buys all rights.
How to Contact: Query with resume of credits. Prefers cassette. SASE. Reports "immediately,
after submission has been discussed."
Music: One-instrument or electronic accompaniment.

HENRY PORTIN MOTION PICTURES, 709 Jones Bldg., Seattle WA 98101. (206)682-7863.
Producer: Henry Portin. Motion picture production company. Clients include industrial, airline
and touring firms. Uses services of songwriters for original songs for themes and scoring. Commis-
sions 2 pieces and 1 lyricist/year. Pays $500 minimum/job. Buys all rights.
How to Contact: Query with resume of credits. Prefers cassette with 2-4 songs on demo. SASE.
Reports in 1 month. Free book catalog.
Music: Background music for documentaries.

PREMIER FILM AND RECORDING CORP., 3033 Locust St., St. Louis MO 63103.
(314)531-3555. President: Wilson Dalzell. Secretary/Treasurer: Grace Dalzell. Audiovisual firm
and motion picture production company. Uses services of songwriters for original background
music and lyrics to reinforce scripts. Commissions 6-10 pieces and 5-10 lyricists/year. Pays $100 to
"whatever maximum the contribution of music is to the production" per job. Buys all rights and
"occasionally a one-time right with composer retaining title."
How to Contact: Query with resume of credits. Prefers 7½ or 15 ips reel-to-reel or cassette with any
number of songs on demo. SASE. Reports "as soon as possible."
Tips: "Be sure a resume is direct, to the point and includes an honest review of past efforts."

JOHN M. PRICE FILMS, INC., Box 81, Radnor PA 19087. President: John M. Price. Clients
include business, government and ad agencies. Uses music houses for occasional background
music and musical scores for films. Pays $100-500/job. Buys one-time rights.
How to Contact: "Mail description of work, and we will file information for future reference."
Prefers 7½ ips reel-to-reel tape "but none until requested."

PROTESTANT RADIO & TV CENTER, INC., 1727 Clifton Rd. NE, Atlanta GA 30329.
(404)634-3324. Chief Engineer: Jim Hicks. Clients include denominational projects, local
churches, schools and colleges (educational needs), and social campaigns. Uses services of songwriters for film scores, commercials and radio programs. Payment negotiable. Rights purchased
vary.
How to Contact: Query or submit demo tape of previously aired work. Prefers 7½ or 15 ips
reel-to-reel or cassette with 2-8 songs on demo. Does not return unsolicited material. Reports in 1
month.
Music: Themes for radio, TV, film and audiovisual productions.

RAINY DAY PRODUCTIONS, INC., 16283 10th NE, Seattle WA 98155. (206)364-0682. Contact:
Michael Wacker. Clients include industrial, advertising and public relations agencies, and inde-
pendent producers. Uses services of songwriters and music libraries for commercials and films.
Pays $100-1,000/job. Buys all rights or one-time rights.
How to Contact: Query with resume of credits, submit demo tape of previously aired work or
submit demo tape showing flexibility of composition skills. Prefers 7½ or 15 ips reel-to-reel or
cassette with 4-8 songs on demo. "We like to keep copies of demos for future reference." SASE.
Reports "as soon as possible."

RAMIC PRODUCTIONS, INC., Box 7530, 4910 Birch St., Newport Beach CA 92660.
(714)833-2444. Executive Vice President: Evan Aiken. Motion picture production company. Clients include schools, business and industry. Uses services of music houses for musical scores in

films and original songs for themes; lyricists for writing lyrics for themes. Commissions 6 pieces/year. Pays $2,400 minimum/job. Buys all rights.
How to Contact: Query with resume of credits. Prefers cassette as demo. SASE. Reports in 3 weeks.

RICHTER McBRIDE PRODUCTIONS, INC., 330 W. 42nd St., New York NY 10036. President: Robert Richter. Motion picture production company. Clients include public and commercial TV, government agencies and nonprofit organizations. Uses services of music houses, songwriters and composers/arrangers for film scores and background music. Commissions 2 pieces/year. Pays on a per-job basis. Buys all rights or one-time rights.
How to Contact: Submit demo and resume of previously aired work. Prefers cassette with 2-5 songs on demo. SASE. "Also, put name, return address and phone number on the tape itself." Reporting time varies "according to our business rush."
Music: "We have varying needs—sometimes we need a musical score to which we cut the film; at other times, we need music for already edited film."

SEVEN OAKS PRODUCTIONS, 8811 Colesville Rd., Silver Spring MD 20910. (301)587-0030. Production Manager: Marcia Marlow. Production Chief: M.A. Marlow. Audiovisual firm and motion picture production company. Clients include blue chip companies, government agencies and foreign film producers. Uses services of music houses and songwriters for film scores and background music; lyricists to help develop musical narratives or theme and title songs for features and educational films. "Often a ballad can create mood and tone better than an all-knowing narrator." Commissions 10-30 composers and 2-6 lyricists/year. Payment negotiable. Buys all rights or one-time rights.
How to Contact: Query with resume of credits or submit demo tape showing flexibility of composition skills. "If possible, submit a film with soundtrack so we can judge if the score fits the film's mood." Prefers 7½ ips reel-to-reel or cassette tape with 3 songs minimum to 1 hour long maximum, or 16mm film. SASE. "We prefer to keep tapes on file to select potential composers for our projects." Reporting time varies "with the demands of the project."
Music: Needs scores and theme songs for "family-type feature films and educational, documentary productions. Our production people rely heavily upon music to raise audience interest and make even the most pedantic subjects interesting. We are interested in working with male and female composers and arrangers on future children's feature projects."

SMF PRODUCTIONS, 41 Union Square W., New York NY 10003. (212)675-3298. President: Shel Freund. Estab. 1979. Clients include advertising agencies and advertisers. Uses services of songwriters for records, jingles and film scores. Pays "depending on assignment. Outside songwriters use AGAC guide." Buys all rights.
How to Contact: Submit demo tape of previously aired work. Prefers 7½ ips reel-to-reel with 1-5 songs on demo. "Mail with reel-to-reel leadered and lyric or lead sheets—copyrighted material only." SASE. Reports in 1 month.
Music: "Hit songs in all idioms (disco, country, etc.)."

PHOEBE T. SNOW PRODUCTIONS, INC., 240 Madison Ave., New York NY 10016. (212)679-8756. Creative Director: Pennie E. Wilfong. Audiovisual firm. Clients include business and industry. Uses services of songwriters and lyricists for original music and songs for business shows. Commissions 10 pieces and 5-10 lyricists/year. Pays by the job. Buys all rights.
How to Contact: Query with resume of credits, then arrange personal interview. SASE. Reports in 1 month.
Music: Needs theme music for business shows.

THE SOUND SERVICE, 860 Second St., San Francisco CA 94107. (415)433-3674. Staff Composer: Stephen Shapiro. Music/sound effects library. Clients include business and TV. Uses the services of staff writers for commercials and audiovisual shows. Buys all rights.
How to Contact: Submit demonstration tape of previous work. Prefers 7½ or 15 ips reel-to-reel with 3-8 songs on demo. SASE. Reports "as soon as possible, depending on work load."
Music: "Our needs are too various to describe in detail."

SOUND STUDIOS, 230 N. Michigan Ave., Chicago IL 60601. (312)236-4814. Vice President/General Manager: Dan Tynus. Audiovisual firm, full-service studio, record manufacturer and cassette duplication service. Clients include AV producers, advertising agencies, record producers and educational audiovisual producers. Payment "based on producer's budget and songwriter's needs." Rights purchased "determined by tape of finished product."
How to Contact: Query with resume of credits, then arrange personal interview or submit demonstration tape of previous work or tape demonstrating composition skills or manuscript showing

Songwriter's Market Close-up

"I'm an actress predominately," says Grammy-winner Amanda McBroom. "I started songwriting about six years ago during periods of long unemployment. I've always loved music and always sang, so writing just seemed a natural extension."

She was trying to write a rock and roll song when she wrote "The Rose." "I was sitting at the piano trying to write a Bob Seger hit and that's what came out. It's one of the fastest songs I ever wrote. It took about 45 minutes and I never had to change a thing in it."

But having it published was not fast or easy. "I sent it around to a lot of artists and if I even got a response the most they would say was: 'It's an interesting song but it's not commercial.'" It might never have been a success had it not been for a movie called *The Rose*. The producer Paul Rothchild and star Bette Midler liked the song and included it in the musical score.

McBroom agrees with the analysis of "The Rose" as a song which is not *commercial*. "It's just a three chord hymn. It doesn't have a bridge; it doesn't have a hook; it doesn't have a chorus. It has nothing that should make it a commercial song."

But the public decided differently. "I am pleased that people have responded to the song the way they have," says McBroom. "It obviously means a great deal to them—that's what pleases me most."

McBroom taught herself to play the guitar and studied piano as a child, but the bulk of her musical background comes from performing in musicals. She recommends songwriters learn to play at least one instrument. "And they should take music theory, which I am in the process of doing now so I can learn more than four basic chords. There are some geniuses running around who have never studied music at all, but you have to have some basic knowledge if you are going to write. You also need some basic knowledge of the language so you can write lyrics."

On the demo she says, "a single piano/

Amanda McBroom

vocal will suffice—but it can't be amateurish because it may not get listened to. About half my demos are piano/vocal. For the other half I take a rhythm section into an inexpensive studio and do a quality two-track."

It's tough having songs published, but knowing where to go can make it easier. "I had the good fortune to have a manager who helped me considerably in getting my songs to people. It really helps if you can find someone within the industry. The best way to get songs to people is through a publishing company. It's their business and if they like you and believe your tunes are commercial, they can certainly open many more doors than you can."

She finds herself always ending up with ballads no matter what she sets out to write, but advises songwriters "learn how to write up-tempo tunes. Everybody's starving for them. You can't fill an entire album with ballads."

music scoring skills. Prefers cassette with "not more than 5 minutes total time" of songs on demo. SASE.

SOUNDCEPT, Box 68, Silver Spring MD 20907. (202)269-6144. Executive Director: Tom Colvin. Audiovisual firm. Clients include nonprofit social agencies, hospitals, colleges, and government agencies. Uses services of songwriters and music libraries for original songs thematically related to script for slide shows and multi-image presentations. Commissions 3 pieces and 3 lyricists/year. Pays $100-500/job. Buys all rights or one-time rights.
How to Contact: Query with resume of credits or submit demonstration tape of previous work. Prefers 7½ reel-to-reel (half-track stereo) or cassette with 2-8 songs on demo. "Resume and demo tape should appear professional. Messy, poorly presented submissions seldom receive a fair hearing. We prefer working with people located between Virginia and New York." SASE. Reports in 1 month.
Music: Folk, folk rock, soft rock. "We usually need strong human interest lyrics on themes relating to social policy and human development."
Tips: "Produce an attention-getting 'highly produced' demo tape."

SPACE PRODUCTIONS, 451 West End Ave., New York NY 10024. (212)986-0857. Producer: J. Alexander. Motion picture production company. Clients include broadcast, commercial and corporate clients. Uses music houses and songwriters for music for sound filmstrips, musical scores in films, original songs for themes, and music scoring, etc. Commissions 6-10 pieces/year. Pays $250-5,000/job depending on assignment. Rights purchased depend on assignment.
How to Contact: Query with resume of credits, submit demonstration tape of previous work or submit tape demonstrating composition skills. Prefers 7½ ips reel-to-reel, cassette or video (if scored to picture) with a representative sampling of songwriter's work. Include a resume. SASE. Reports in 2-8 weeks.
Music: Commercial and theme music for commercial and industrial features.

STAGE 3 SOUND PRODUCTIONS, 12 E. 39th St., Kansas City MO 64111. (816)531-3375. President: Don Warnock. Clients include business and advertising agencies. Uses services of songwriters for background music in productions. Pays AFTRA scale. Buys all rights.
How to Contact: Query. Prefers 7½ ips reel-to-reel. SASE. Reports "as soon as possible."

CARTER STEVENS STUDIOS, INC., 269 W. 25th St., New York NY 10001. President: Carter Stevens. Produces theatrical feature films and business documentaries. Uses services of music houses and songwriters for film scores. Commissions 40-60 pieces/year. Pays $250-1,000/job. Buys all rights or one-time rights.
How to Contact: Submit demo tape of previous work or query with resume of credits. "Do not call our office." Prefers cassette with 2-8 songs on demo. SASE. Returns material if totally unusable; "we keep everything for future reference if we feel the writer has any potential. Send a sample of as many styles and moods of music as possible."
Tips: "There is a 3- to 6-month lag time on our projects, as we are working at least one to two films ahead at all times."

E.J. STEWART, INC., 525 Mildred Ave., Primos PA 19018. (215)626-6500. Creative Director: David Lindquester. Audiovisual firm and video tape production company. Clients include broadcasting companies, cable TV, advertising agencies, schools, business, industry, government and the medical profession. Uses services of music houses and songwriters for background music for commercials and programs. Commissions 50 pieces and 5 lyricists/year. Payment negotiable by the job. Buys all rights.
How to Contact: Query with resume of credits or submit demonstration tape of previous work. Prefers reel-to-reel or cassette with any number of songs on demo. SASE. Reports "when needed."

TELECINE SERVICES & PRODUCTION LTD., 11 Ely Place, Dublin 2, Ireland. (01)763188. Director: Anabella Jackson. Audiovisual firm and video productions. Clients include advertising and commercial business. Uses services of music houses for original songs for TV commercials and audiovisual programs. Commissions 15 pieces and 8 lyricists/year. Pays $750 minimum/job. Buys all rights or rights within one country.
How to Contact: Query with resume of credits or submit tape demonstrating composition skills. Prefers 15 ips reel-to-reel or cassette with 3-10 songs on demo. SASE. Reports in 1 month.
Music: Scoring for TV commercials.

TELESOUND, INC., Box 1900, San Francisco CA 94101. Manager, Creative Division: Karl H. Sjodahl. Audiovisual firm and production company. Serves TV stations, production companies

and commercial clients. Uses services of songwriters for commercial scores and identification jingles. Commissions 30 pieces/year. Pays $500 minimum/job or 5% minimum royalty. Purchases all rights or rights purchased vary with job.
How to Contact: Submit demo tape of previously aired work or submit demo tape showing flexibility of composition skills. Prefers 7½ ips reel-to-reel or cassette with 2-10 songs on demo. "Show as much variety as possible. We are particularly interested in material that will work visually."
Music: Specific commercial songs.

TOTAL CONCEPTS, 424 Valley Rd., Warrington PA 18976. (215)343-2020. Executive Producer: Hal Fine. Audiovisual firm and motion picture production company. Clients include business, industry and advertising agencies. Uses services of music houses for musical scores in film, TV commercials, background music, etc. Commissions 3-4 pieces/year. Pays by the job. Rights vary, depending on job.
How to Contact: Submit demonstration tape of previous work or tape demonstrating composition skills. Prefers 7½ ips reel-to-reel as demo. SASE. Reports in 3 weeks. Free book catalog.

TULSA STUDIOS, 6314 E. 13th St., Tulsa OK 74112. (918)836-8164. Business Manager: Syble Crouch. General Manager: Tom Claiborne. Scoring service, motion picture production company and music/sound effects library. Clients include schools, producers, industry, business and advertising agencies. Uses services of songwriters, lyricists and inhouse writers to provide ideas or concepts; lyricists to provide ideas, concept, or musical content. Commissions 20 pieces and 5 lyricists/year. Pays $100-800/job, or 50% royalty. Buys all rights or one-time rights.
How to Contact: Query with resume of credits and submit demo tape of previously aired work or submit demo tape showing flexibility of composition skills. Prefers 7½ or 15 ips reel-to-reel or cassette with 3-6 songs on demo. SASE. Reports in 10 days.
Music: Needs vary with client's desires. "We have our own staff for music scores, which we use most of the time. Therefore, very few writers are selected without showing unusual capabilities."

US GOVERNMENT, National Park Service, Division of Audiovisual Arts, Harpers Ferry Center, Harpers Ferry WV 25425. Chief Branch of Audio Production: Blair Hubbard. Clients include national parks, recreational areas and historic sites. Uses services of music houses and songwriters for thematic and background music for films and sound-slide and multimedia programs. Commissions 50 pieces/year. Pays $200-4,000/hour for film; or $25-500/job for stock music. Buys all rights.
How to Contact: Query with resume of credits, submit demo tape of previously aired work or submit demo tape showing flexibility of composition skills. Prefers 7½ or 15 ips reel-to-reel with 3-10 songs on demo. Does not return unsolicited material. "We maintain a permanent file." Reports "when we have specific needs." Free book catalog.
Music: "Needs vary; usually background for a film or a sound-slide program for a national park, recreational or historic area."

UNIVERSAL IMAGES, 6321 Blue Ridge Blvd., Kansas City MO 64133. (816)358-6166. Vice President: Ralph Papin. Clients include theater, TV and business firms. Uses services of music houses and songwriters for background music in films. Commissions 15-20 pieces/year. Pays on a per-job basis. Buys all rights.
How to Contact: Submit demo tape of previously aired work. Prefers 7½ ips reel-to-reel with 5-6 songs on demo. SASE. Reports as soon as possible.

VIDEO ONE, INC., 1216 N. Blackwelder Ave., Oklahoma City OK 73106. (405)524-2111. President: Robert M. Howard. Clients include business, industry, institutions and advertising agencies. Uses services of music houses, songwriters and stock libraries for video training productions, background, transitions and open/close. Commissions 5-10 pieces/year. Pays $100 minimum/job. Buys all rights.
How to Contact: Query or submit demo tape of previously aired work. Prefers 7½ ips reel-to-reel or cassette with 3-10 songs on demo. SASE. Reports in 3 weeks.

NORM VIRAG PRODUCTIONS, 3415 N. East St., Lansing MI 48906. (518)374-8193. President: Norman J. Virag. Clients include government, industry, advertising agencies and independent producers. Uses services of songwriters for background music in films, filmstrips and slide programs. Commissions 6 pieces/year. Pays $200-1,000/job. Buys all rights.
How to Contact: Query with resume of credits or submit demo tape of previously aired work or submit demo tape showing flexibility of composition skills. Prefers 7½ ips full-track reel-to-reel with 6-12 songs on demo. SASE. Reports in 1 week. Free catalog.

DORIAN WALKER PRODUCTIONS, 2000 P St. NW, Suite 608, Washington DC 20036. (202)452-1776. Producer: John Simmons. Clients include corporations and government agencies. Uses services of music houses and songwriters for animated gorporation logos and film scores. Commissions 4 pieces/year. Pays $100-250/finished screen minute. Rights purchased vary.
How to Contact: Query with resume of credits, submit demo tape of previously aired work or submit demo tape showing flexibility of composition skills. Prefers 7½ ips reel-to-reel or cassette with 3-5 instrumental pieces on tape. SASE. Reports in 1 month.
Music: "We're looking for tasteful use of 3-4 instruments; we have a heavy accent on instrumentals. Our composer needs to be loose and flexible, ready to execute a musical idea coming from the producer. In addition, he must be able to convey a variety of moods from the same musical theme. It helps to have a wide repertoire of clear and simple musical effects."

WING PRODUCTIONS, 1600 Broadway, New York NY 10019. (212)265-5179. President: Jon Wing Lum. Clients include NBC and the New York State Education Department. Uses services of songwriters for film scores. Commissions 35 pieces/year. Pays $500 minimum/job. Buys all rights.
How to Contact: Submit demo tape of previously aired work or submit demo tape showing flexibility of composition skills. Prefers 7½ or 15 ips reel-to-reel or cassette with 5 songs on demo. SASE. Reporting time "depends on need." Free book catalog.
Music: Needs all types of music.

Managers & Booking Agents

This is the first appearance of managers and booking agents in our "Markets" section. Previously they were listed in "Services and Opportunities" as a reference particularly for songwriters who are also performers.

However, when we asked this year how many reviewed new material for their acts, nearly all replied that they did. The manager is, then, more than only a confidant who guides, decides, pushes and promotes talent. He is the person, many times closest to the artist, to whom you can submit your songs. This is especially important if you are trying to get your songs to one particular act. Those who do review material will say so in their listing.

Both managers and agents can deal with solo artists, groups or songwriters. Some will specialize in promotion or booking one category, such as groups, while others will work with all three types. Make sure you submit to a manager or agent who handles your type of act or music. If a company works only in a specific region, the listing will tell you that. Otherwise, assume the company will deal with acts from across the country.

If you're a songwriter/performer the most important consideration is finding a manager who unfailingly believes in your ability and your future. Your manager advises you in the selection of material, your stage performance, your publicity campaign, and your industry dealings. He's also your representative. His job is to get people to listen to you, to promote you as a first-class artist or songwriter. Your job is to prove him right; you must believe in yourself as much as the manager or booking agent does.

Talent, originality, credits, dedication, self-confidence and professionalism are things that will attract a manager to you. Your press kit should contain a high-quality, interesting, professional 8x10 publicity photo; a three- to four-paragraph biographical data sheet; a list of songs (both commercial and original material) performed; a list of engagement credits; a current itinerary; any relevant press clippings; and a live, unedited cassette tape of an actual performance. Your submission package to managers and booking agencies will resemble your material for record companies and producers. In each case, you are auditioning. You want to include your best material, the most exciting part of your act.

If you are a songwriter submitting songs to managers for their artists, notice the names of acts they represent and the types of music they need for those particular artists. Managers of the nationally-known artists and groups are located mostly in Los Angeles, New York or Nashville and approaching them is often more difficult. But you need go no farther than your town, or a short radius thereof, to find talent needing songs. Managers of local acts will have more to say in the choice of material than those located in music centers where the producer often makes the final decision about which songs an artist should record. Locally, it could be the manager who not only chooses songs, but picks the producer, studio and musicians as well.

Local acts work hard to make a reputation for themselves in hope of going on to stardom. Today's big acts were in most cases yesterday's local entertainers, maybe even playing dances and weddings during their high school years. It certainly doesn't hurt to become a favorite songwriter of a talented local entertainer. If the artist goes on to bigger things, it could be you'll go with him.

Additional names of personal managers and artists can be found in the *Billboard International Talent Directory* (Billboard Publications, Inc., 9000 Sunset Blvd., Los Angeles CA 90069).

THE ACT FACTORY, A Division of Myriad Productions, 1314 N. Hayworth Ave., Suite 402, Los Angeles CA 90046. (213)851-1400. President/Executive Producer: Ed Harris. Management film and production company, providing performing arts services to professional artists, groups and industrial show productions. "We work with performers, management companies and record companies in producing live stage acts and in recording production in studio and location situations." Payment varies per assignment or show/record.
How to Contact: Submit demo tape and lead sheet. "No telephone inquiries!" Prefers 7½ ips reel-to-reel or cassette with 1-4 songs on demo. "We keep extensive files of submitted material for the artists we work with and refer to them for live stage acts as well as recording dates. Should an artist pick a song on file, we then contact the songwriter/publishing company to arrange royalties for the songwriter. We do not return submitted material for this reason."
Music: Blues, C&W, easy listening, folk, jazz, MOR, progressive, Spanish, R&B, rock (hard, country, folk, etc.), soul and top 40/pop. Works primarily with all of performing artists and groups as well as "classifications," corporate clientele in writing and producing industrial shows (live industrial theater and multimedia A/V productions). "We are constantly looking for new musical material for our varied clientel in all areas of music."

ACTION TICKET AGENCY AND PROMOTIONS, 2609 NW 36th St., Oklahoma City OK 73112. (405)942-0462. Manager: Bobby Boyd. Management and booking agency and promotions firm. Represents individual artists from anywhere; currently handles 4 acts. Receives 25% minimum commission. Reviews material for acts.
How to Contact: Query by mail, then submit demo tape only. Prefers 7½ ips reel-to-reel with 3-12 songs on demo. Does not return unsolicited material. Reports in 2 weeks.
Music: C&W, R&B, rock and top 40/pop. Current acts include Dale Greear, Faye Haley and Bobby Barnett; all country acts.

AJAYE ENTERTAINMENT CORP., Box 6568, 2181 Victory Pkwy., Cincinnati OH 45206. (513)221-2626. Artist Relations: Suzy Evans. Booking agency. Represents artists and groups; currently represents 33 acts. Receives 10-20% commission.
How to Contact: Submit demo tape and write or call to explain the purpose of submission. Prefers 7½ ips reel-to-reel or cassette with 3-6 songs on demo. SASE. Reports in 1 week.
Music: Progressive; rock; soul and top 40/pop. Current acts include Bell Jar, Relay, The Raisins, Hyroller, The Young Invaders, Spike, Buster Brown, The Sharks, Jani & The Boulevards, Highwind, Swan. All rock groups.

ALIVE ENTERPRISES, 8600 Melrose Ave., Los Angeles CA 90069. (213)659-7001. Director of Business Affairs: Bob Emmer. Management agency. Represents artists, groups and songwriters; currently represents 7 acts. Receives 20% minimum commission.
How to Contact: Query or submit demo tape and lead sheet. Prefers cassette with 2-4 songs on demo. SASE. Reports in 3-5 weeks.
Music: Rock (all types); soul and top 40/pop. Works with "major record company signed artists." Current acts include Alice Cooper (rock); Teddy Pendergrass (R&B); and Blondie (top 40/AOR).

ALL STAR TALENT AGENCY, Box 82, Greenbrier TN 37073. (615)643-4192. Owner/Agent: Joyce Brown. Booking agency. Represents professional individuals, groups and songwriters; currently handles 12 acts. Receives 15% commission.
How to Contact: Submit demo tape and lead sheet. Prefers reel-to-reel or cassette with 1-4 songs on demo. SASE. Reports as soon as possible.
Music: Bluegrass; C&W; gospel; MOR; rock (country); and top 40/pop. Works primarily with dance bands, club acts and concerts. Current acts include Bill Carlisle and the Carlisles (C&W group); Ronnie Dove (MOR/C&W artist); Randy Parton (pop artist); Charlie McCoy (instrumentalist); and Del Wood (Grand Ole Opry star).

ALLIED BOOKING CO., 2250 3rd Ave., San Diego CA 92101. (714)234-8767. Associate: Jim Deacy. Booking agency. Deals with individuals in California and Arizona. Receives 10-20% commission.
How-to-Contact: Query or submit demo tape. Prefers cassette with 5-10 songs on demo. SASE. Reports in 2 weeks.
Music: MOR and top 40/pop. Works primarily with dance bands. "We book all types of musical groups, and many different ones throughout the year."

AMERICAN CREATIVE ENTERTAINMENT LTD., Professional Arts Bldg., 1616 Pacific Ave., Suite 817, Atlantic City NJ 08401. (609)348-1809. Producers: Danny Luciano and Tony Angelo. Booking agency and record producer. Represents artists, groups and songwriters from anywhere.

Receives 10-25% commission. Reviews material for acts.
How to Contact: Submit demo tape and lead sheet. Prefers 7½ ips reel-to-reel or cassette with 4-8 songs on demo. "No 8-tracks." "Include picture and promotion package if self-contained performing artist.' SASE. Reports in 6 weeks.
Music: C&W, MOR, R&B, soft country rock and top 40/pop. Works primarily with dance bands, bar bands, show groups and recording artists. Current acts include Fannelli Sisters and Terry Lee (vocalists).

AMERICANA CORPORATION, Box 47, Woodland Hills CA 91365. (213)347-2976. President: Steve Stebbins. Management and booking agency. Represents artists and groups; currently represents 15 artists. Receives 10-15% commission. Reviews material for acts.
How to Contact: Submit demo tape only. Reviews material for country acts only. Prefers cassette tape with 4-5 songs on demo. SASE. Reports in 3 weeks.
Music: C&W. Works with dance and bar bands and single artists. Current acts include Johnny & Jonie Mosby (country); Current acts include Johnny & Jonie Mashy, Red Simpson, Ray Sanders, Jersey Lily Band (all country).
Tips: "We consider country music only."

AMUSEMENT ENTERPRISES, (formerly American Amusement) 610 White St., Houston TX 77007. (713)864-6561. Manager/President: Bill Siros. Management firm and booking agency. Represents individuals and groups; currently handles 4 acts. Receives 10-20% commission.
How to Contact: Query or submit demo tape. Prefers cassette with 3-6 songs on demo. SASE. Reports in 2 weeks.
Music: C&W; disco; MOR; rock; and top 40/pop. Works primarily with rock, variety and C&W bands. Current acts include Mundo Earwood (C&W); Harts (variety); Actor (rock); and Neve (disco).

AMUSEX CORP., Box 902, Menlo Park CA 94025. (415)324-1444. Artists Managers: David Elder. Management firm and booking agency. Represents artists, groups and songwriters; currently handles 10 acts. Negotiates commission. Reviews material for acts.
How to Contact: Submit demo tape and lead sheet. Prefers cassette or video-VHS format with 2-8 songs on demo. Prefers top 40/pop oriented music. Reports in 3 weeks.
Music: Disco; rock (all); and top 40/pop. Current acts include Santa Esmeralda (disco); Jimmy Goings (disco); and Gotcha (pop/rock); and Duncan Sisters (R&B/pop/disco).

ANDERSON AGENCY, INC., 290 California Dr., Burlingame CA 94010. (415)342-8500. President: Don Anderson. Management and booking agency. Represents artists and groups. Represents artists from anywhere; currently handles 25 acts. Receives 15-25% commission. Reviews material for acts.
How to Contact: Submit demo tape and lead sheet. Prefers cassette with 3-5 songs on demo. SASE. Reports in 1 month.
Music: Bluegrass, C&W, gospel, MOR, soul and top 40/pop. Works primarily with small hotel combos to name artists. Current acts include Cynthia Black (MOR); Brothers Owens (soul); Infinity (gospel) and Glenn Yarbrough (MOR).

ANGEL PRESENTATIONS, 13010 W. 30th Dr., Golden CO 80401. (303)278-8367. President: Ellen Walsh. Booking agency. Represents artists and groups, "mostly local artists, but we are looking nationally for new groups"; currently handles 20 acts. Receives 15% minimum commission.
How to Contact: Query by mail or phone; then submit demo tape and pictures and songlists. Prefers cassette as demo. SASE. Reports in 3 weeks.
Music: Works primarily with bar bands.
Tips: "We book national acts and bar bands. Acts should have a handle on the current music scene and know what area they want to target."

ARMAGEDDON TALENT ASSOCIATES, 1604 W. Juneway Terrace, Chicago IL 60626. (312)465-3373. Co-owners: Gail Smith and Fred Tieken. Management agency and recording studio. Represents groups; currently represents 4 groups. Receives 10-20% commission. Reviews material for acts.
How to Contact: Submit demo tape only. Prefers cassette with 2-6 songs on demo. SASE. Reports in 1 month.
Music: Rock (hard or new wave). Works with original rock and new wave bands. Current acts include Gary Jones (new wave); Kevin Lee and Heartbeat (rock).

ARMSTRONG & DONALDSON MANAGEMENT, INC., 2 East Read St., Suite 209, Baltimore MD 21202. (301)727-2220. President: Rod Armstrong. Represents artists, groups and songwriters; currently handles 4 acts. Receives 15-25% commission. Reviews material for acts.
How to Contact: Submit demo tape and lyric sheet. Prefers 7½ ips reel-to-reel or cassette with 2-4 songs on demo. SASE. Reports in 3 weeks.
Music: Disco; progressive; soul; and top 40/pop. Current acts include Walter Jackson, the Softones, First Class, Pamoja Experience, Skip Mahoaney, Flight International and Parris.

ARTISTS'/HELLER AGENCY, (formerly Jerry Heller Agency), 6430 Sunset, Suite 1516, Los Angeles CA 90028. (213)462-1100. President: Jerry Heller. Booking agency. Represents artists, groups, songwriters and producers from anywhere; currently handles 25 acts. Reviews material for acts.
How to Contact: Arrange personal interview, submit demo tape. Prefers cassette with 4 songs on demo. SASE. Reports in 4 weeks.
Music: Bluegrass, blues, C&W, dance-oriented, easy listening, folk, jazz, MOR, progressive, R&B, rock, soul and top 40/pop. Works primarily with "major international concert attractions. But we don't limit ourselves to 'stars'—we also represent many local acts." Current acts include Rose Royce, Joan Armatrading, 20/20, and John Mayall.

WILLIAM ASHWOOD ORGANIZATION, 230 Park Ave., New York NY 10169. (212)682-5400. Contact: Artist Relations or Producer Relations. Management agency, publishing/production records and film. Represents artists, groups, songwriters and record producers; currently represents 5 acts and various recording producers. Reviews material for acts and foreign label deals..
How to Contact: Submit demo tape only or demo tape and lyric sheet. Prefers cassette with 3-5 songs on demo. SASE. Reports in 3 weeks. Feel free to resubmit new songs over and over again.
Music: Blues; children's; R&B; rock; and top 40/pop. Works with bands and songwriters of "unique individuality." Current acts include Star Spangled Washboard (musical comedy band); The Ants (blues); Lee Geneis; Jeremiah Samuels; Richard Renzicoff; and Judy Dozier.

AUGUST ARTISTS MANAGEMENT, 584 8th Ave., Suite 303, New York NY 10018. (212)869-3885. President/General Manager: Camille Barbone. Management agency and rehearsal/recording studio. Represents artists, groups and songwriters from anywhere; currently handles 3 acts. Receives 20% commission. Reviews material for acts.
How to Contact: Submit demo tape and lead sheet. Prefers cassette with 3-5 songs on demo. SASE. Reports in 3 weeks.
Music: C&W, easy listening, MOR, R&B, hard rock and top 40/pop. Works primarily with recording artists. Current acts include Apache (pop and heavy rock); Amy Malcolm (pop/MOR) and Madonna.

CLIFF AYERS PRODUCTIONS, 62 Music Square West, Nashville TN 37203. (615)327-4538. Vice President: Connie Wright. Management firm, booking agency, record production and distribution company, publisher. "We publish *Music City Entertainer* newspaper." Represents artists, groups and songwriters; currently represents 79 acts. 15-20% minimum commission. Reviews material for acts.
How to Contact: Submit demo tape and lead or lyric sheet. Prefers cassette with a maximum of 2 songs on demo. SASE. Reports in 1 week.
Music: Church/religious; C&W; disco; gospel; MOR; soft rock; and top 40/pop. Current acts include Ernie Ashworth (C&W, Grand Old Opry star); Vicki Knight (rock); and Teddy Burns (rock-French).
Tips: "Submit material as soon as you have it."

AZTEC PRODUCTIONS, 20531 Plummer St., Chatsworth CA 91311. (213)998-0443. General Manager: A. Sullivan. Management firm and booking agency. Represents individuals, groups and songwriters; currently handles 7 acts. Receives 10-25% commission.
How to Contact: Submit demo tape and lead sheet. Prefers 7½ ips reel-to-reel or cassette. SASE. Reports in 3 weeks.
Music: Blues; C&W; disco; MOR; rock; soul; and top 40/pop. Works primarily with club bands, show groups and concert groups. Current acts include El Chicano (Latin/rock); Abraxas (MOR); Storm (show group); Tribe (soul/R&B); New Street, Kelly Lynn, Ako, Zaral and Debbie Rockwell.

B. A. S. ENTERPRISES, 5925 Kirby Dr., Suite 226, Houston TX 77005. (713)522-2713. Contact: Shelton Bissell. Booking agency and music publisher. Represents artists and groups from anywhere "as far as booking is concerned. I only sign songs when I know I can use them in a

production. We don't plug songs to other companies, etc;" currently handles 100 acts. Receives AFM commission. Pays standard royalty to songwriters. Reviews material for acts.
How to Contact: Submit demo tape and lyric sheet. Prefers cassette with 1-4 songs on demo. "We will refuse any package requiring a signature for delivery. Send by regular mail." "Material sent without SASE will be destroyed." Reports in 3 weeks, or ASAP.
Music: C&W. Works primarily with C&W artists. Current acts include Isaac Payton Sweat, Mike Compton, J.C. & The Moonshine Band and Kathy Gilley; all C&W acts.
Tips: "I'm only interested in professional songwriters (ASCAP or BMI members)."

BAND AID ENTERTAINMENT, INC., Box 3673, Baton Rouge LA 70821. (504)387-5709. President: Vicki Leger. Booking agency. Represents Southern groups; currently handles 10 acts. Receives 15-20% commission.
How to Contact: Query; prefers phone call. SASE. Reports in 2 weeks.
Music: Gospel and top 40/pop. Current acts include Billy Pendleton and Earth (rock group); Papa Joe & Riverboat (dance/show); and Featherstone (dance/show).

BAUER-HALL ENTERPRISES, 138 Frog Hollow Rd., Churchville PA 18966. (215)357-5189. Contact: William B. Hall III. Booking agency. Represents individuals and groups; currently handles 10 acts. Receives 10-15% commission. Reviews material for acts, depending on engagement.
How to Contact: Query ("include photos, promo material, and record or tape") or submit demo tape and lyric sheet. Prefers cassette with 2-3 songs on demo. "Letter of inquiry preferred as initial contact." Does not return unsolicited material. Reports in 1 month.
Music: Circus; ethnic; and polka. Works primarily with "unusual or novelty attractions in musical line, preferably those that appeal to family groups." Current acts include Coco's Musical Comix (all clown band); Philadelphia Mummers' String Bands (string bands); Ruth Daye (novelty xylophonist); Fred Wayne (circus bandmaster); Joseph Kaye (one-man band); Loki Ontai (Hawaiian revue); Jos. Dallas-Dan Conn (Show-Circus Band); Bobby Burnett (harmonica virtuoso-comedian-encee); Steel Band; Greater Pottstown Concert Band; Organ Grinder & Monkey; and Bill (Boom-Boom) Browning (circus bandmaster).

BEACON INTERNATIONAL ARTISTS, (A division of Beacon International Entertainment Corporation), Box 1746, Miami FL 33176. (305)255-4911. Regional Manager: R.W. Augstroze. Management agency and record producer and promoter. Estab. 1979. Represents artists, groups and songwriters from worldwide. Receives 15-25% commission. Reviews material for acts.
How to Contact: Query by mail then submit demo tape and lead sheet. Prefers cassette with 2-5 songs on demo. SASE. Reports in 2-3 weeks.
Music: Choral, church/religious, classical, gospel, jazz, MOR, progressive, rock (all), soul and top 40/pop. Works primarily with classical singers, rock groups and classical/religious choirs. Current acts include Silvia Erdmanis (classical soprano); Equinox (rock group); and Surface (rock/jazz group).
Tips: "Submit no information without the inclusion of a tape. Material should be original—no top 40 impersonators. Be professional and tell it straight—no hype."

BEAVERWOOD TALENT AGENCY & RECORDING STUDIO, 133 Walton Ferry Rd., Hendersonville TN 37075. (615)824-2820. Owner/Manager: Clyde Beavers. Management firm, booking agency, music publisher and record company. Represents individuals, groups and songwriters; currently handles 15 acts. Receives 15% commission.
How to Contact: Query, arrange personal interview, submit demo tape, or submit demo tape and lead sheet. Prefers 7½ or 15 ips reel-to-reel or cassette with 1-5 songs on demo. SASE. Reports as soon as possible.
Music: Bluegrass; blues; children's; choral; church/religious; classical; C&W; disco; folk; gospel; jazz; MOR; opera; polka; progressive; rock; soul; and top 40/pop. Works primarily with variety, C&W, gospel and top 40 acts. Current acts include Nick Nixon (C&W artist); Lois Johnson (C&W artist); and the Telestials (gospel group).

THE BELKIN MADURI ORGANIZATION, 28001 Chagrin Blvd., Suite 205, Cleveland OH 44122. (216)464-5990. Contact: Chris Maduri or Jim Fox, A&R Department. Management firm and production company. Represents artists, groups and songwriters; currently handles 5 acts. Reviews material for acts.
How to Contact: Query or submit demo tape and lyric sheet. Prefers 7½ or 15 ips reel-to-reel or cassette with 2-4 songs on demo. "Send a tape and follow up with a phone call." SASE. Please call back for report.
Music: Dance-oriented, rock (hard); soul; and top 40/pop. Works with commercial pop, R&B

artists/songwriters. "Would like to pursue disco acts much more aggressively. We are involved in crossover acts. Current acts include The Michael Stanley Band (rock/pop/top 40); Donnie Iris (rock/pop); Canter & Chanel (R&B); and LaFlavour (top 40/soul/disco).

J. BIRD BOOKING AGENCY, Box 1015, Lake Helen FL 32744. (904)228-3131. Contact: John Bird. Booking agency. Represents artists and groups from anywhere; currently handles 70 acts. Receives 15% commission.
How to Contact: Arrange personal interview, then submit demo tape and lead sheet. Prefers cassette with 3-4 songs on demo. "Initial interview is usually by phone; after demo material is received we usually ask person to contact us again in 1 week-10 days." Does not return unsolicited material.
Music: Bluegrass, C&W, dance-oriented, country rock and top 40/pop. "Most of our demand is for dance bands since we generally work with high schools and universities." Current acts include Nantucket (group); James Durst (songsmith); and Gina Crute & Tasty (top 40 group).

BLADE AGENCY, Box 12239, Gainesville FL 32604. (904)372-8158, (904)377-8158. General Manager: Charles V. Steadham Jr. Management firm and booking agency. Represents professional individuals and groups; currently handles 36 acts. Receives 15-20% commission. Reviews material from acts.
How to Contact: Query or submit demo tape, publicity materials and itinerary. Prefers cassette with 2-5 songs on demo. Does not return unsolicited material. Reports as soon as possible on solicited material.
Music: Bluegrass, blues, C&W, dance-oriented, easy listening, folk, MOR, rock (country), soul and top 40/pop. Current acts include Gamble Rogers (C&W/folk artist); Peyton Brothers (contemporary bluegrass group); Tom Parks (comedian); Rambo Street (top 40/pop group); Mike Cross (country/folk artist); Johnny Shines (blues); Mike Reid (MOR/pop); and Louise Dimiceli (MOR/pop).

RICK BLOOM'S OFFICES, 6338 Jackie Ave., Woodland Hills CA 91367. (213)883-7160. Agent/Owner: Rick Bloom. Represents individuals and groups in the jazz and contemporary field. Currently handles 7 acts. Receives minimum 15% commission. Reviews material for acts.
How to Contact: Submit demo tape and lyric sheet. Prefers 7½ ips reel-to-reel or cassette with 3-6 songs on demo. SASE. Reports in 3 weeks.
Music: Jazz, MOR, progressive, R&B, rock (new wave) and comedy. Works only with self-contained performers. Current acts include The Busboys (songwriters/rock group); Klaus Doldinger (songwriter/jazz artist, Atlantic Records); Roland Vazquez (songwriter/jazz instrumentalist); Franklyn Asaye (comedian); and Roach & The Whiteboys (rock).

BLUEGRASS MUSIC PROMOTIONS, 732 Brandon Ave. SW, Roanoke VA 24015. (703)342-4765 after 6 pm. Booking agent: Bill Sykes. Booking agency. Represents artists, groups and songwriters from anywhere; currently handles 10 acts. Receives 10-15% commission. Reviews material for acts.
How to Contact: Submit demo tape and lead sheet. Prefers cassette or 8-track tape with 6-10 songs on demo. SASE. Reports in 3 weeks.
Music: Bluegrass, church/religious, C&W, folk and gospel. Works primarily with bluegrass bands. Current acts include the New Grass Revue; L.W. Lambert/Blue River Boys; and Clinton King/Virginia Mountaineers (bluegrass recording artists).

BOUQUET-ORCHID ENTERPRISES, Box 4220, Shreveport LA 71104. (318)686-7362. President: Bill Bohannon. Management firm. Represents individuals and groups; currently handles 2 acts. Receives 15% minimum commission. Reviews material for acts.
How to Contact: Submit demo tape and lyric sheet. Prefers 7½ ips reel-to-reel or cassette with 2-5 songs on demo. Include brief resume. SASE. Reports in 1 month.
Music: C&W; rock (country); and top 40/pop. Works primarily with solo artists and small combos. Current acts include Shan Wilson (C&W singer/songwriter); and the Bandoleers (top 40/pop group).

BOBBY BOYD, 2609 NW 36th St., Oklahoma City OK 73112. (405)942-0462. President: Bobby Boyd. Management agency. Represents artists and songwriters. Receives minimum 25% commission.
How to Contact: Submit demo tape and lead sheet. Prefers 7½ ips reel-to-reel with 5-6 songs on demo. "Send tapes that do not have to be returned." Does not return unsolicited material. Reports in 2 weeks.
Music: C&W; rock; soul; and top 40/pop. Current acts include Jim Whitaker (single); Dale Greear (single); and Belinda Eaves (single).

BUG MUSIC GROUP, 6777 Hollywood Blvd., 9th Floor, Hollywood CA 90028. Vice President: Fred Bourgoise. Music publisher. Represents songwriters from anywhere; currently publishes and administers over 200 writers, publishers and artists.
How to Contact: Submit demo tape only. Prefers cassette with 2 songs on demo. SASE. Reports as soon as possible.
Music: All types, including C&W, easy listening, R&B, rock (all), soul and top 40/pop.

BOB BURTON/MIRAMAR MANAGEMENT, Bob Burton Management, 1248 Devon Ave., Los Angeles CA 90024. (313)276-8684. Owner: Bob Burton. Management agency. Represents individuals, groups and songwriters; currently handles 1 act. Receives 15-30% commission.
How to Contact: Query. Prefers cassette with 1-3 songs on the tape. SASE. Reports in 1 month.
Music: Jazz and rock (melodic). Works with concert acts. Currently represents Connie Mims (singer/songwriter).

C.F.A., Seabird Recording Studio, 415 N. Ridgewood Ave., Edgewater FL 32032. (904)427-2480. President: Dick Conti. Management firm and booking agency. Represents groups and songwriters from the South, the Midwest and the Southeast; currently handles 15 acts "and a multitude of songwriters." Receives 10-33⅓% commission. Reviews material for acts.
How to Contact: Query or submit demo tape and lyric sheet. Prefers 7½ ips reel-to-reel or cassette. SASE. Reports in 1 month.
Music: Bluegrass, blues, children's, choral, church/religious, C&W, disco, folk, gospel, MOR, rock and soul. Works primarily with large "Mike Curb Congregation" type groups, rock groups (black and white); and commercial/jingle writers and arrangers. Current acts include the Conti Family (group); Gino Conti, Angela Conti, and Frank Richards Big Band.

C M E PRODUCTIONS, Box 1606, Chico CA 95927. General Manager: Cliff Mickelson. Booking agency and publishing company. Represents artists, musical groups and songwriters from anywhere; currently handles 7 acts. Receives 10-15% commission. Reviews material for acts.
How to Contact: Query by mail, submit demo tape and lyric sheet. Prefers cassette with 1-3 songs on demo. Artists or songwriters include bio information. "Strictly professional submissions please." SASE. Reports in 3 weeks.
Music: C&W, dance-oriented, MOR, rock (soft) and top 40/pop. Works primarily with dance and recording commercial oriented bands. Current acts include Gun Shy (country rock/MOR); Montezumas Revenge (country); and the Bends (new wave).

THE CAMERON ORGANISATION, INC., 320 S. Waiola Ave., La Grange IL 60525. (312)352-2026. President/General Manager: Scott A. Cameron. Management firm. Represents individuals, and songwriters; currently handles 4 acts.
How to Contact: Submit demo tape and lead sheet. Prefers 7½ ips reel-to-reel or cassette with 1-3 songs on demo, or acetates. SASE. Reports in 1 month.
Music: Blues; progressive; rock; soul; and top 40/pop. Current acts include Muddy Waters and Willie Dixon (blues); Mighty Joe Young (blues/rock); and Skafish (rock) ·

CAMPUS SERVICES, INC., 172 Main St., Spencer MA 01562. (617)753-1318. President: Patrick George. Booking agency and management firm. Deals with artists in the Boston-Washington D.C. area, also Great Britain and Bermuda. Represents groups and songwriters; currently handles 25 acts. Receives 10-30% commission. "We also serve as career development and marketing consultants at $50/hour or will travel to artists area for $250 per day plus expenses."
How to Contact: Query by mail. Prefers cassette with 2-4 songs on demo. SASE. Reports in 3 weeks if favorable response.
Music: Top 40/pop. Works with dance bands, bar bands and pop concert acts. Looking for pop material. Current acts include Dakota (rock group/Columbia Records).

CAPITOL BOOKING SERVICE, INC., 13826 Beaver Rd., New Springfield OH 44443. (216)549-2155. Musical Dept.: David Musselman, Gary Wilms. Booking agency. Represents show groups; currently handles 11 acts. Receives 15-20% commission. Reviews material for acts.
How to Contact: Query. Prefers cassette with 3 songs minimum on tape. "We would like references. We also have video equipment, and if artist has videotape, we would like to see this." SASE. Reports "as soon as possible."
Music: Church/religious, C&W, dance-oriented, easy listening, folk, gospel, MOR and top 40/pop. Works primarily with "self-contained musical groups that play all-around music for mixed audiences." Current acts include Life (show group); and Sunshine Express (show group).

CAPITOL STAR ARTIST ENTERPRISES, INC., 1159 Jay St., Rochester, NY 14611. (716)328-5565. President: Don Redanz. Management and booking agency. Represents artists, groups, songwriters and clowns from anywhere; currently handles 7 acts. Receives 10-20% commission. Reviews material for acts.
How to Contact: Query by mail, then submit demo tape and lead sheet. Prefers 7½ ips reel-to-reel with 4-5 songs on demo. SASE. Reports in 3 weeks.
Music: Bluegrass, church/religious, C&W, easy listening, gospel, jazz, rock and country rock. Works primarily with show bands, vocalists, dance bands and bar bands. Current acts include Don Bailes and Tony Starr, Gladys Smith, and Country Outlaws (C&W acts).

CARMAN PRODUCTIONS, INC., 15456 Cabrito Rd., Van Nuys CA 91406. President: Tom Skeeter. Manager: W. Trowbridge. Management firm. Represents individuals and groups; currently handles 8 acts. Receives 15-20% commission. Reviews material for acts.
How to Contact: Query or submit demo tape and lead sheet. Prefers cassette with 1-6 songs on demo. SASE. Reports in 1 month. Reviews material for acts.
Music: C&W, MOR, R&B, rock and top 40/pop. Works primarily with recording artists. Current acts include Rick Springfield (rock/MOR); Les Emmerson (rock/MOR); Lorence Hud (rock/C&W); and Jeff Silverman (rock/jazz).

CAROLINA ATTRACTIONS, INC., 203 Culver Ave., Charleston SC 29407. (803)766-2500. President: Harold Thomas. Vice President, A&R: Michael Thomas. Management firm. Represents only nationally known individuals, groups and songwriters; currently handles 3 acts. Receives 10-25% commission. Reviews material for acts.
How to Contact: Submit demo tape. Cassette only. "Send cover letter with tape and any additional promo material (pictures, news releases, etc.) available. Bio if possible." SASE. Reports in 3 weeks.
Music: R&B, beach and top 40/pop. Works primarily with artists for show and dance groups and concerts. Current acts include the Tams (show/concert group); Cornelius Brothers and Sister Rose (show/concert group); and the Original Drifters (show/concert group).

CORINNE CARPENTER COMMUNICATIONS, 549 Roscoe, Chicago IL 60657. (312)248-1478. President: Corinne Carpenter. Management agency and public relations firm. Represents artists, groups and songwriters; currently handles 4 acts. Receives 20% commission. Reviews material for acts.
How to Contact: "I prefer that the initial package include a tape and lead sheets (if the individual's a writer), plus photos, bio material and resume giving specifics." Prefers cassette with 3-5 songs on demo. SASE. Reports in 1 month.
Music: Bluegrass, blues, C&W, dance-oriented, easy listening, jazz (pop, "no avant garde"), MOR, R&B, soul and top 40/pop. "I am primarily interested in hearing from stong lyricists, as well as composers." Current acts include Edward Zelnis (tenor/pianist/composer/arranger); Judy Mangione (MOR); Cara Spicer and Wyld Oats (pop country).
Tips: "I expect both composers and lyricists to work through me, not simply expect me to serve as an initial contact person. I am interested in on-going relationships, not one-shot efforts."

CHECK PRODUCTIONS, INC., 936 Moyer Rd., Newport News VA 23602. (804)877-0762. President: Wilson Harrell. Management firm and booking agency. Works with local individuals and groups; currently handles 10 acts. Receives 10-15% commission. Reviews material for acts.
How to Contact: Query or submit demo tape. Prefers cassette with 5-10 songs on demo. "Submit song list, resume and 8x10 glossy." SASE. Reports in 1 month.
Music: Bluegrass, dance-oriented, disco, folk, MOR, rock (country rock), soul and top 40/pop. Works primarily with dance bands for lounges and private parties. Current acts include Harvest (top 40/disco group); Taboo (top 40/rock 'n' roll group); and The Nerve (top 40/new wave rock).

CLARK MUSICAL PRODUCTIONS, Box 299, Watseka IL 60970. President: Dr. Paul E. Clark. Management firm, booking agency and music publisher. Deals with artists in the Midwest and South. Represents individuals, groups and songwriters; currently handles 6 acts. Receives 10-20% commission.
How to Contact: Query or submit demo tape and lead sheet. Prefers cassette with 1-3 songs on demo. Does not return unsolicited material. Reports in 1 month on solicited material.
Music: Church/religious, C&W, gospel, rock (soft) and top 40/pop. Works primarily with acts for concerts, dances and club dates. Current acts include Mark Peterson (C&W solo artist); and Basic Basses (country and rock vocal quartet); and Pat Gould (top 40/pop solo artist).

CLOCKWORK MANAGEMENT, Box 1600, Haverhill MA 01830. (617)374-4792. President: Bill Macek. Management firm and booking agency. Deals with artists throughout New England.

Represents groups and songwriters; currently handles 6 acts. Receives 10-15% commission. Reviews material for acts.
How to Contact: Query or submit demo tape only. Include "interesting facts about yourself in a cover letter." Prefers cassette with 3-12 songs on demo. "Also submit promotion and cover letter with tape." Does not return unsolicited material unless accompanied with a SASE. Reports in 2 weeks.
Music: MOR; rock (all types); and top 40/pop. Current acts include Renegade (FM/AM rocker); Sahara (5-piece top 40/rocker group); USA (5-piece FM rocker); and Bogash (4-piece FM rocker).

COME ALIVE ARTIST MANAGEMENT, Box 86, Medford NJ 08055. (609)654-8440. Assistant Director: Greg Menza. Management and booking agency and concert and festival producers. Represents artists, groups, songwriters, speakers and DJ's exclusively; represents local groups; booking for selected artists from throughout the country; currently handles 12 acts. Receives 10-20% commission. Reviews material for acts.
How to Contact: Query by mail. Prefers cassette with 3-6 songs on demo. "Because of our festival schedule March and June are bad months to contact us." SASE. Reports in at least one month.
Music: Gospel and rock (contemporary Christian). Works primarily with contemporary Christian rock artists. Current acts include Christian Stephens (duo), Harry Thomas, Rick & Shelley Poole, Gary & Linda Sclafani (contemporary Christian); and Servant (contemporary Christian rock group).

BURT COMPTON AGENCY, Box 160373, Miami FL 33116. (305)238-7312. Contact: Burt Compton. Booking agency. Represents groups; currently handles 36 acts. Receives 10-20% commission. Reviews material for acts.
How to Contact: Query by mail, then submit demo tape. Prefers cassette with 3-6 songs on demo. "Include complete repertoire on cassette, 8x10 photo and resume." Does not return unsolicited material. Reports in 1 month.
Music: Progressive and rock (hard). Works primarily with dance bands/bar bands. Current acts include Heroes (dance band); Fantasy (recording/concert group); and Wildlife (recording/concert group).
Tips: "Have your promotional materials professionally packaged. We don't like having to decipher handwritten resumes with misspelled words and incomplete sentences."

CONCERT IDEAS, Box 669, Woodstock NY 12498. (914)679-6069 or 679-2458. President: Harris Goldberg. Vice President: Tom Astens. Management and book agency. Represents artists, groups and songwriters; currently handles 4 acts. Receives 10-20% commission. Reviews material for acts.
How to Contact: Query by mail, then submit demo tape and lead sheet. Prefers cassette with 2-4 songs on demo. SASE. Reports in 3 weeks.
Music: Easy listening, rock and top 40/pop. Works primarily with singer/songwriter. Current acts include Artie Traum/Pat Alger (singer, songwriter); Tim Moore (singer/songwriter); Robert Dupree ("We co-publish his writing through Oozle Music"); and Skywire (group).

CONTINENTAL ENTERTAINMENT ASSOCIATES, 680 Craig, Suite 4, St. Louis MO 63141. Attention: Stephanie Vermilyea. Management and booking agency and promotion firm. Represents artists, groups and speciality acts (hypnotists, mimes, etc.). Currently works with "numerous" acts. "We have no standard commission, generally we take our commission on what we can make for the group/band, etc. . . . (i.e., if there is a minimum payment for a performance, we charge a minimum commission)." Reviews material for acts.
How to Contact: Submit demo tape and lead sheet. Prefers cassette with 1-3 songs on demo. "Absolutely no 8-tracks." Also include photos, description of the style written or performed by musicians/songwriters, names and phone numbers of all person in the group, and the mailing address of the band leader. SASE. Reports in 2 weeks "if the information is something we feel has some market value."
Music: Blues, dance-oriented, jazz, progressive, R&B, rock (commercial), top 40/pop, MOR and new wave. Works primarily with bar bands, wedding bands, some new wave, club bands, bands with original material as well as copy music, and bands that play all copy material for the top 40/pop listeners.
Tips: "Make sure information is *legible* and original (if performer is doing copy material, be sure a song list is included)."

COUNTERPOINT/CONCERTS, INC., 211 West 56 St., New York NY 10019 (212)246-6400. Director: Peter Mallon. Management firm. Represents individuals and groups; currently handles 8 acts. Receives 10-25% commission. Reviews material for acts.

How to Contact: Query or submit demo tape. Prefers 7½ ips reel-to-reel or cassette. SASE. Reports in 1 month.
Music: Blues, dance-oriented, jazz, MOR, R&B and top 40/pop. Works primarily with dance bands, commercial jazz and pop. Current acts include Lee Castle-Jimmy Dorsey Orchestra (jazz); Marty Napoleon-Louis Armstrong Alumni All Stars Band (jazz); Jersey Pops Jazz Symphony (jazz); Johnny Hartman (jazz/pop singer); Don Cornell (pop singer); Fantasy (R&B-dance group); Janice Harper (pop singer); and Henny Youngman (comic).

CRASH PRODUCTIONS, Box 40, Bangor ME 04401. (207)794-6686. Manager: Jim Moreau. Booking agency. Represents individuals and groups; currently handles 5 acts. Receives 10-25% commission.
How to Contact: Query. Prefers cassette with 4-8 songs on demo. Include resume and photos. "We prefer to hear groups at an actual performance." SASE. Reports in 2 weeks.
Music: Bluegrass, C&W, dance-oriented, easy listening, 50s & 60s, folk, MOR, rock (country) and top 40/pop. Works primarily with bar bands and festivals. Current acts include Woody Woodman Combo (easy listening/dance-oriented); Susan Oliver & Cindy Bond (folk); and Band of Gold (50s & 60s).

CREATIVE CORPS, 6607 W Sunset Blvd., Suite E, Hollywood CA 90028. President: Kurt Hunter. Management firm and music publisher. Represents songwriters and top 40 bands; currently handles 10 acts. Receives 10-20% commission. Reviews material for acts.
How to Contact: Submit demo tape and lyric sheet. Prefers cassette with 1-5 songs on demo. SASE. Reports in 3 months.
Music: Country, R&B, and top 40/pop. Works primarily with original songwriters. Current acts include Denny Martin (songwriter); Norman Mezey (songwriter); Tom Barger (songwriter); and the Double Shuffle Band.

CREATIVE MINDS, INC., 1560 N. La Brea, Hollywood CA 90028. President: Art Benson. Management firm. Represents individuals, groups and songwriters; currently handles 5 acts. Receives 25% commission and "cash or a percentage of salary for promotion and publicity."
How to Contact: Arrange personal interview or submit demo tape. Prefers reel-to-reel or cassette. SASE. Reports in 1 month.
Music: Bluegrass; blues; children's; choral; church/religious; classical; C&W; disco; folk; gospel; jazz; MOR; opera; polka; progressive; rock; soul; and top 40/pop. Current acts include Tommy Cooper (pop/MOR); King Solomon (R&B); and Al Jarvis (piano).

CROSBY MUSIC AGENCY, 7730 Herschel Ave., La Jolla CA 92037. (714)276-7381. Agent: Suzanne Morris. Booking agency. Deals with regional artists only. Represents artists and groups; currently handles 80+ acts. Receives 10-20% commission.
How to Contact: Submit demo tape, photo and song list. Prefers cassette with 5-10 songs on demo. SASE. Reports in 2 weeks.
Music: Jazz; rock (hard rock and country rock); and top 40/pop. Works with wide variety of performers; show bands, dance bands, bar bands, duos and single acts. Current acts include Burrito Bros., (C&W); Bob Crosby Orchestra (jazz); and Freddie Martin Orchestra (big band).
Tips: "Send a complete promotional package including a good photo, complete song list, and clear demo tape."

CULTURAL ENCOUNTERS, INC., 606 Ridge Ave., Kennett Square PA 19348. (215)444-1157. Secretary/Treasurer: Marc Pevar. Management agency and audiovisual production company. Represents artists and groups; currently handles 10 acts. Receives 15-20% commission. Reviews material for acts.
How to Contact: Submit demo tape. Prefers 7½ ips reel-to-reel, cassette or LP with 5-10 songs on demo. SASE. Reports in 2 weeks.
Music: Bluegrass, blues, folk and gospel. "We work with artists and bands which reflect an ethnic heritage through their music." Current acts include Kevin Roth (singer/songwriter—folk/pop); Rev. Tommy Brown (singer/songwriter—gospel with choir); and Abdu Raschid Yahya (composer/arranger—jazz with 16-piece band).

G. DAVID H. ENTERPRISES/G.D.H. RECORDS, Box 634, Sugarland TX 77478. (713)980-1839. Director/artist development: Micheal K. Hollis. Management firm and music publisher. Represents artists, groups, songwriters and playwrights. "We are promoting the new and exciting sound of Houston and the third coast." Receives 10-20% commission. Reviews material for acts.
How to Contact: Submit demo tape and lead sheet. Prefers cassette but "will accept a 7½

ips reel-to-reel" with 1-5 songs on demo. "Include a resume telling your background, published titles and publishers, affiliations with professional organizations and giving an overview of your talent." SASE. Reports in 6 weeks.
Music: Church/religious, C&W, folk, funk, gospel, jazz (fusion), MOR, raggae, rock (new wave and country) and soul. Works primarily with "solo vocalists and self contained jazz fusion, C&W, new wave and funk acts." Current acts include Carl (Sweets) Pogue and Co. (jazz fusion/sax lead with vocals); Wayne Monget and Rezoo (contemporary rock fusion show band); David Harris (crossover rock/jazz vocalist); and Macian Cobb (pop/rock/C&W vocalist; female).

DAWG MUSIC, INC., C.M. MANAGEMENT, Box 2999, San Rafael CA 94912. (415)457-5474. Associates: Craig Miller and Isabel Miller. Management agency and music publisher. Represents artists, groups, songwriters and record producers; currently handles 7 acts. Receives 10-20% commission. Reviews material for acts.
How to Contact: Query by mail, then submit demo tape and lead sheet. Prefers cassette with 3-5 songs on demo. "Artists/songwriters should present a suitable representation by mail; if they can't represent their material to us, we can't represent it to anyone else." SASE "if accompanied with $2.50 return postage charge." Reports in 2 weeks.
Music: Jazz, MOR, progressive and accoustical. Works primarily with virtuoso musicians. Current acts include David Grisman Quintet (jazz crossover accoustic); Mark O'Connor (soloist); and Darol Anger (violinist).

DAWN TALENT, Box 48597, Niles IL 60648. (312)228-0969. Contact: Tiffany Dawn or Francyne Dale. Management agency and tour co-ordinators. Estab. 1979. Represents groups, tribute, theatrical and all female bands; currently handles 7 acts. Receives 10-15% commission. Reviews material for acts.
How to Contact: Query by mail or phone, then submit demo tape. "Include promo kit consisting of photos and biography (background, references)." Prefers cassette with 2-10 songs on demo. SASE. Reports in 1 week.
Music: Rock and all female bands of any nature. "We prefer hard rock bands incorporating a show or special effects, tribute bands, all female bands and unusual rock bands." Current acts include Impulse (rock band with laser lights and fire show); Joker (hard rock); Manhole (all female band); and Stud (rock band with fire magic effects).
Tips: "We accept only bands willing to travel nationally and internationally; must have some gimmick or effect to make them unusual, separating them from the others. Miminum 4 pieces. We look for outstanding vocals and consider a good attitude as necessary as the talent."
Tips: "Bands must have it all together; talent, image, visual show and rapport with each other and the audience. They must also be willing to take and understand criticism."

DE SANTO ENTERPRISES, Box 4796, Nashville TN 37216. President: Duane De Santo. Management firm and booking agency. Represents individuals and groups; currently handles 5 acts. Receives 10-15% commission. Reviews material for acts.
How to Contact: Submit demo tape and lyric sheet. Prefers 7½ ips reel-to-reel with 2-6 songs on demo. SASE. Reports in 3 weeks.

JOE DEANGELIS MANAGEMENT, 79 Kingsland Ave., Brooklyn NY 11211. (212)389-2511. President: Joe DeAngelis. Management agency. Represents artists, groups and songwriters; currently handles 10 acts. Receives 10-15% commission. Reviews material for acts.
How to Contact: Query by mail. Prefers cassette with 10 songs on demo. SASE. Reports in 2 weeks.
Music: Blues, C&W, R&B, soul and top 40/pop. Works primarily with female groups and single artists. Current acts include Devonnes (lounge group; Hill Twins (lounge group); and Pat Core (solo artist) and Traci Core (dancer-model).
Tips: "Have great tunes and good lyrics."

CONNIE DENAVE MANAGEMENT, 300 E. 74th St., New York NY 10021. (212)737-4805. President: Connie DeNave. Management agency. Represents artists, groups and songwriters; currently handles 4 acts. Receives 20% commission. Reviews material for acts.
How to Contact: Submit demo tape and lyric sheet. Prefers cassette with 3-6 songs on demo. SASE. Reports in 3 weeks.
Music: Disco; MOR; progressive; rock (all kinds); soul; and top 40/pop. Works with artists for concerts and recording. Current acts include Rhetta Hughes (pop/top 40/disco/R&B); Linda Webb (contemp./country/folk); and Julie Gold (pop/top40).

DAVID DIAMOND MANAGEMENT, 5446 Topeka Dr., Tarzana CA 91356. (213)960-2395. Contact: David Diamond. Management agency. Represents artists, groups and songwriters; cur-

rently handles 1 act. Receives 15-25% commission. Reviews material for acts.
How to Contact: Query by mail. Prefers cassette with 3-5 songs on demo. SASE. Reports as soon as possible.
Music: C&W, jazz, MOR, progressive, rock (jazz-rock). Works primarily with soloists and groups, "from bars to world tours, records, etc." Current acts include Bryan Diamond (bar singer); Lee Ritenour (jazz soloist); and Friendship (jazz group).

DIAMONDACK MUSIC CO., 10 Waterville, San Francisco CA 94124. Administrator: Joseph Burchwald. Management firm and publishing company. Represents artists, groups and songwriters; currently handles 15 clients. Receives 10-25% minimum commission. Reviews material for acts.
How to Contact: Submit demo tape and lyric sheet. Prefers cassette with 3 songs minimum on demo. SASE. Reports ASAP.
Music: MOR and ballads. Works primarily with vocalists and rock shows. Current clients include Marty Balin, Jesse Barish and Ric Knowles.

DIVERSIFIED MANAGEMENT AGENCY, 17650 W. Twelve Mile Rd., Southfield MI 48076. (313)559-2600. Mid-West Agent: Trip Brown. Booking agency. Represents individuals and groups; currently handles 25 acts. Receives 15-20% commission.
How to Contact: Submit "promo pack including song list, demo tape and photo of act." Prefers cassette with 3-6 songs on demo. Does not return unsolicited material. Reports in 2 weeks "if interested."
Music: Rock (hard or top 40 rock). Works primarily with concert acts. Current acts include Ted Nugent, Nazareth, The Romantics, Blackfoot and Krokus.

DMR ENTERPRISES AGENCY, Suite 316, Wilson Bldg., Syracuse NY 13202. (315)471-0868. Owner: David M. Rezak. Booking agency. Represents individuals and groups; currently handles 50 acts. Receives 10-15% commission.
How to Contact: Submit demo tape and press kit. Prefers cassette with 1-4 songs on demo. SASE.
Music: Rock; blues; progressive; top 40/pop; and country rock. Works primarily with bar and concert bands. Current acts include The Alligators (pop/rock); 805 (progressive rock); New York Flyers (rock); Alecstar, (rock); Pictures (rock); Mr. Edd . . . of course (comedy-rock).

DR. COOL PRODUCTIONS, Flagler Station, Box 011321, Miami FL 33101. (305)374-9717. President: Dr. Cool. Talent management firm and booking agency. Represents artists and groups; currently handles 50 acts. Receives 10-15% commission. Reviews material for acts.
How to Contact: Arrange personal interview. Prefers cassette with 3-4 songs on demo. Reports in 3 weeks.
Music: Blues; disco; folk; gospel; and soul. Works with soul, blues, gospel bands and vocalists. Current acts include Sandra Cool and her Coolettes (soul); Charles 'King Kong' Butler (comic); Blues Boy Fleming (blues) and Baby King (blues); Dr. Cool and his New Breed Blues Band (blues); Dr. Cool and his Famous Sapphires (soul); Moe Bee Ready (soul); Miss Sexy Way (soul); Brown Sugar (soul); Joanne Murray (soul); Guitar Red (blues); Dr. Cool-World's Greatest Rag Popping Champion (art); and Billy Miranda and his Royal Sheiks Band (blues).

COL. BUSTER DOSS PRESENTS, Box 927, Manchaca Station, Austin TX 78652. President: Buster Doss. Management firm and booking agency. Represents groups; currently handles 20 acts. Receives 15-50% commission, or $100/hour consultant's fee.
How to Contact: Arrange personal interview or submit demo tape. Prefers 7½ ips reel-to-reel with 3-6 songs on demo. SASE. Reports in 2 weeks.
Music: Bluegrass, blues, church/religious, C&W, dance-oriented, folk, gospel, jazz, MOR, progressive, R&B, rock, soul and top 40/pop. Works primarily with show bands, vocalists and dance bands. Current acts include Cooder Browne, (C&W artist); Jess Demaine, (C&W artist); and Sherry Bee and Summit Ridge (C&W group). Billy Walker and Billy Grammer (Grand Ole Opry); and The Golden Wizard.

MIKE DOUGLAS & ASSOCIATES, 333 31st St. North, Suite 20, St. Petersburg FL 33713. (813)896-5151. President: Mike Douglas. Management and booking agency, record producer, artist and record promotion firm. Estab. 1979. Represents artists, groups, songwriters in Southeaster US and Canada; currently handles 25 acts. Receives 20% minimum commission. Reviews material for acts.
How to Contact: Submit "clean" demo tape and "readable" lead sheet. Prefers cassette with 1-4 songs on demo. "Demo should be straight ahead-no instrumental breaks or repeats. Artists should include photos, biography, news clips and cassette of repertoire." SASE. Reports as soon as possible.

Music: Blues, C&W, easy listening, gospel, MOR, R&B, rock and soul (of all types) and top 40/pop. Works primarily with singles, vocal trios, vocal groups (4 or more), and bands (4-7 members). Current acts include Jeff Cobb (Las Vegas MOR vocal act); and Melody Wilcox (Las Vegas country vocal act).

THE BOB DOYLE AGENCY, Box 1199, State College PA 16801. (814)238-5478, 237-3746 or 234-1647. President: Bob Doyle. Booking agency. Deals with artists in Pennsylvania and neighboring states. Represents groups and singles; currently handles 50 acts. Receives 15-25% commission.
How to Contact: Submit demo tape, lead sheet and promo photograph. Prefers cassette with 3-5 songs on demo. Does not return unsolicited material. Reports in 1 week. "I prefer a phone call first to see if this agency can work with the group. Then we like to have the promo and tape. We need to know if the group can work the markets we are involved with."
Music: Bluegrass; folk (American & ethnic); rock; and C&W. Works college markets and some clubs. Current acts include Whetstone Run (traditional bluegrass); Jim Corr & Friends (Irish); the Adams Brothers Band (traditional bluegrass); and The Allegheny String Band (old-time and square-dance).

TIM DRAKE PRESENTS, Box 602, Woodcliff Lake NJ 07675. (201)666-5553. Vice President: Paul Dreifuss. Booking agency and middle agency for clubs and college concert promotions. Represents artists, groups and songwriters; currently handles 5 acts. Receives 10-20% commission. "If we are the manager and also act as booking agent the commission will be 20%." Reviews material for acts.
How to Contact: "Please submit a well recorded demo. If artist is well known, telephone call will do. If unknown, submit tape, biography, press clippings, etc." Prefers cassette with 3-5 songs on demo. SASE. Reports in 2 weeks.
Music: Rock (all types) and top 40/pop. Works primarily with touring rock acts, solo acoustic artists, jazz, jazz fusion artists and groups. Current acts include Melanie (folk/rock singer-songwriter with back up band); Billy Falcon's Burning Rose (rock act, MCA Records); Michael Ross (folk/rock singer-songwriter); and Blotto (rock act, Blotto Records).
Tips: "Take the time to carefully prepare your submitted tape. Try to make your presentation as professional as possible."

BARRY DRAKE/JON IMS AGENCY, The Gables, Halcott Rd., Fleischmanns NY 12430. (914)254-4565. Contact: Barry Drake, Patricia Padla. Management firm and booking agency. Represents individuals, groups and songwriters; currently handles 2 acts. Receives 10-20% commission. Reviews material for acts.
How to Contact: Query or submit demo tape and lyric sheet. Prefers cassette with 1-3 songs on demo. SASE. Reports in 1 month. Reviews material for acts.
Music: Bluegrass; blues; C&W; folk; MOR; progressive; rock; and top 40/pop. Works primarily with solo singer/songwriters. Current acts include Barry Drake, Jon Ims and Jim Ritchey.

THE DREAMSPUN MANAGEMENT AND PUBLICITY GROUP, 11 Riverside Dr., New York NY 10023. (212)581-1810. Directors: Nina Cranton, Lydia Lilli and Davina Wells. Management agency and publicity firm. Estab. 1980. Represents artists and groups from anywhere; currently handles 2 acts. Receives 15% minimum commission.
How to Contact: Query by mail or phone, then submit demo tape. Prefers cassette with 3 songs on demo. SASE. Reports in 2 weeks.
Music: Easy listening, jazz, MOR, R&B, rock and top 40/pop. Works primarily with 4-5 piece bar bands. Current acts include The C.I.'s and Split Second (rock bands).

DYNAMIC TALENT AGENCY, Box 13584, Atlanta GA 30324. (404)872-6000. Vice President, Promotions: Ari Poulos. President: Alex Janoulis. Booking Agency. Represents individuals and groups; currently handles 6 acts. Receives 10-15% commission.
How to Contact: Submit demo tape. Prefers cassette with 2-3 songs on demo. "Send photos and bio." Reports as soon as possible.
Music: Blues; jazz; rock (new wave). Works with top 40 bands. Current acts include The Wayne Chaffin Group (top 40/pop); Starfoxx (top 40/rock); and The Night Shadows (new wave); Diamond Lil (female impersonator) and WJNA (top 40/new wave).

E. A. T. MUSIC, N. Brewster Rd., Newfield NJ 08344. (609)697-0850. President: Ernie Trionfo. Management and booking agency and referral service. Estab. 1979. Represents artists, groups and songwriters; currently handles 8 acts. Receives 5-15% commission. Reviews material for acts.
How to Contact: Query by mail or phone, then submit demo tape. Prefers cassette with 1-5 songs

on demo. "Include resume. If we can't use it we'll send it to other associates who might." SASE. Reports in 3 weeks.

Music: Bluegrass, blues, C&W, dance-oriented, easy listening, folk, gospel, jazz, MOR, progressive, R&B, rock (all forms) and top 40/pop. Works primarily with songwriters, original bands, lounge acts and dance bands. Current acts include The Ford (original rock band); Fred Lambert (singer/songwriter); and Glory Road (acoustic trio).

EAGLE PRODUCTIONS, Box 1274, Merchantville NJ 08109. (609)663-8910. Contact: Rob Russen or Jim Creech. Management and booking agency. Estab. 1980. Represents artists and groups; currently handles 12 acts. Receives 10-20% commission. Reviews material for acts.
How to Contact: Query by mail, then submit demo tape and lead sheet. Prefers 7½ ips reel-to-reel or cassette with 2-6 songs on demo. SASE. Reports in 1 week.
Music: C&W, easy listening, jazz, MOR, R&B, rock, soul and top 40/pop. Works primarily with funk-fusion; 10-piece horn bands; Vegas-style show acts; and C&W bands. Current acts include Heavy Weather (funk-fusion); Front Street Runners (new wave); and TCB Revue (Vegas revue).

EAST COAST ENTERTAINMENT, 1901 N. Hamilton St., Box 11283, Richmond VA 23230. (804)355-2178. Agent: Lee Moore. Manager: Dennis Huber. Management and booking agency. Represents groups; currently handles 50 acts. Receives 10-20% commission. Reviews material for acts.
How to Contact: Query by mail, then submit demo tape and lead sheet. Prefers cassette with 3-10 songs on demo. "Include photo and resume." Does not return unsolicited material. Reports in 1 month.
Music: Dance-oriented, MOR, R&B, rock (contemporary/hard/pop) and top 40/pop. Works primarily with dance bands, bar bands and concert bands. Current acts include Robbin Thompson Band (MOR); and Steve Bassetts Virginia Breeze (dance-oriented/R&B).

EBB-TIDE BOOKING AGENCY, Box 2544, Baton Rouge LA 70821. (504)925-2603. Director: E.K. Harrison. Booking agency. Represents professional individuals and groups; currently handles 50 acts. Receives 20-50% commission. Reviews material for acts.
How to Contact: Query or submit demo tape along with photographs and biographical information. Prefers cassette tape. SASE. Reports in 1 month.
Music: Bluegrass, blues, children's, church/religious, C&W, dance-oriented, easy listening, gospel, jazz, MOR, R&B, rock (hard or punk), soul and top 40/pop. Works primarily with "commercial/selling acts and talents. They have to be good and commercial for today's market." Current acts include George Perkins and Band (soul/pop); Pamla-Marie (country pop rock) and Larry Hobbs (soul).

STEVE ELLIS AGENCY, LTD., 250 W. 57th St., Suite 330, New York NY 10019. (212)757-5800. President: Steve Ellis. Vice President: Nanci Linke. Agent: Dan Brennan. Booking agency. Represents individuals and groups; currently handles 11 acts. Receives 10% commission.
How to Contact: Query. Prefers cassette with 3-5 songs on demo. Does not return unsolicited material. Reports in 3 weeks.
Music: Works with one night concert groups (vocalists w/band). Current acts include Chic (disco/pop group); Jerry Butler (soul); Cameo (disco/funk group); Mass Production (soul/MOR); Slave (disco/funk); and Mtume (songwriters/producers).

RICHARD LEE EMLER ENTERPRISES, 8601 Wilshire Boulevard, Suite #1000, Beverly Hills CA 90211. (213)659-3932. Owner: Richard Lee Emler. Management firm. Represents professional artists and songwriters; currently handles 12 acts. Receives 10-20% commission.
How to Contact: Query. Prefers cassette. SASE. Reports in 1 week.
Music: C&W; disco; folk; MOR; rock; soul; top 40/pop; and music for films and TV. Current acts include Peter Matz, Henry Mollicone, Tim Simon, Fred Werner and Lalo Schifrin (composers/arrangers/conductors); Susan Keller and Dennis Shippy (lyricists); Susan Keller and Trisha Noble (vocalists) and Joe Bennett, Susan Keller, Trisha Noble, Cassandra Peterson, Dick Sargent and Byron Webster (actors/actresses).

BOB ENGLAR THEATRICAL AGENCY, 2466 Wildon Dr., York PA 17403. (717)741-2844. President: Bob Englar. Booking agency. Represents individuals and groups. Receives 10-15% commission.
How to Contact: Query or submit demo tape. Prefers 8-track cartridge with 5-10 songs on demo, or disc. Include photo. SASE. Reports in 3 weeks.
Music: Bluegrass; blues; children's; choral; church/religious; classical; C&W; disco; folk; gospel; jazz; polka; rock (light); soul; and top 40/pop. Works primarily with string quartets and dance bands.

ENTERTAINERS MANAGEMENT & BOOKING AGENCY, Box 11306, Charlotte NC 28220. (704)364-1433. President: Bernard Bailey. Management firm, booking agency and placement firm for "yet undiscovered talent." Deals with acts in Southeast region, unless group is a national recording act. Represents groups and songwriters; currently handles 8 acts. Receives 10-20% commission. Reviews material for acts.
How to Contact: Query, arrange personal interview, submit demo tape only, or if the group is established submit a complete promo package. Prefers 7½ ips reel-to-reel or cassette with 2-3 songs on demo. SASE. Reports in 3 weeks.
Music: Disco, gospel, jazz, R&B, rock, soul, steel drum variety and top 40/pop. Works with artists for nightclubs, colleges, major concerts, dances (high school). Current acts include Force (disco, R&B); Continental Divide (top 40/pop); Charlotte Chorale (gospel); and Trinidad Symphonette (steel drum variety).

ENTERTAINMENT SERVICES CONCEPT, Box 2501, Des Moines IA 50315. (515)285-6564. President: Art Smart Stenstrom. Management firm, booking agency, record company and music publisher. Represents groups and songwriters; currently handles 2 acts and books 10-20 acts. "We generally deal only with regional attractions primarily Iowa groups. Receives 7½-20% commission.
How to Contact: Submit all promotional materials available, with song list and demo tape. Prefers cassette tape. "On a demo tape of a live performance, any number of songs. Telephoning prior to sending materials will ensure that materials get attention." SASE. Reports in 2 weeks.
Music: Rock (only material that is recognizable), MOR, and top 40/pop (commercial or nostalgia shows). Works primarily with "regional attractions that work club, small concert, college, high school and ballroom gigs." Current acts include Colt .45 (original country-rock/top 40); Spencer (top 40/rock); and Hard Times (country rock/top 40).

THE EXCALIBUR GROUP, Rt. 3, Sweeney Hollow, Franklin TN 37064. (615)794-5712. General Manager: Jeff Engle. Management agency, booking agency, and music publisher. Represents artists, musical groups and songwriters from anywhere; currently handles 10 acts. "There is no standard commission: the agency end charges 10% flat; the management end charges 15% flat." Reviews material for acts.
How to Contact: Submit demo tape and lead sheet. Prefers cassette with 1-4 songs on demo. SASE. Reports in 1 month.
Music: MOR, progressive rock, rock, and top 40/pop. Current acts include Gene Cotton (pop/rock singer-songwriter); Oliver (pop/rock singer-songwriter); Dianne Darling (pop/rock singer-songwriter); and American Ace (rock 'n roll band).
Tips: "We are not currently looking to sign new artists, but we are looking for good songs."

FANTASMA PRODUCTIONS, INC., 1675 Palm Beach Lakes Bldg., Suite 902, West Palm Beach FL 33401. (305)686-6397. Director of Booking: Gary Propper. President: Jon Stoll. Management firm, booking agency and promotion agency. Represents groups; currently handles 4 acts. Receives 10-20% commission. Reviews material for acts.
How to Contact: Query or submit demo tape. Prefers 7½ ips reel-to-reel or cassette with 3-5 songs on demo. Include bio and photo. SASE. Reports in 1 month.
Music: Bluegrass, C&W, easy listening, folk, jazz, MOR and rock (all). Works primarily with concert attractions. Current acts include Night and Day (country/folk); Sugar (rock); and Dixie Desperados (rock).

FRED T. FENCHEL ENTERTAINMENT AGENCY, 2104 S. Jefferson Ave., Mason City IA 50401. General Manager: Fred T. Fenchel. Booking agency. Represents professional individuals and groups; currently handles 15 acts. Receives 15-20% commission.
How to Contact: Query. Prefers cassette. SASE. Reports in 3 weeks.
Music: C&W; rock; and top 40/pop. Current acts include Southern Kumfort (top 40 group); Cruise (top 40 group with "speciality features"); and Pearl (top 40 group).

FISHER & ASSOCIATES ENTERTAINMENT, INC., Box 240802, Charlotte NC 28224. (704)525-9220. Agent: Ed Duncan. Booking agency. Represents musical groups in the Southeastern states including NC, SC, VA, GA, TN, AL, MS and FL; currently handles 60 groups. Receives 15-20% commission. Reviews material for acts.
How to Contact: Submit demo tape, include resume, bio, references and publicity photos. Prefers cassette with 6-10 songs on demo. SASE. Reports in 1 month.
Music: Dance-oriented, R&B, rock (commerical and danceable), soul, top 40/pop and variety groups. Works primarily with club and lounge groups (4 to 8 pieces), bar bands, and dance groups suitable for the young adult market (ages 16-40). Current acts include Sugarcreek (top 40/rock); Stratus (top 40/rock); Janice (top 40/pop/gospel); and The Mighty Majors (top 40/R&B/soul).

JOE FONTANA ASSOCIATES, 161 W. 54th St., New York NY 10019. (212)247-3043. President: Joe Fontana. Management firm. Represents artists, groups and songwriters; currently handles 5 acts. Reviews material for acts.
How to Contact: Query by mail, submit demo tape and lead sheet. Prefers cassette with 4-8 songs on demo. Does not return unsolicited material.
Music: Gospel, jazz and soul. Current acts include Lonnie Liston Smith (jazz); Ahmad Samal (jazz); and Chuck Brown (soul).

4-K PRODUCTIONS, Box 557, Knoxville IA 50138. (515)842-3723. Contact: Larry Heaberlin. Management firm and booking agency. Represents artists, groups and songwriters in Iowa, Minnesota and Nebraska; currently handles 14 acts. Receives 15-20% commission. Reviews material for acts.
How to Contact: Query by mail. Prefers cassette with 4 songs on demo. SASE. Reports in 1 month.
Music: C&W, gospel and top 40/pop. Works primarily with dance bands. Current acts include Sharry Hanna (country vocalist); Dave Belleganti (country instrumentalist); and Larry Heaberlin (country artist).

JOAN FRANK PRODUCTIONS, Suite 101, 9550 Forest Lane, Dallas TX 75243. (214)343-8737. Manager: R.D. Leonard. Booking agency. Represents individuals and groups; current handles 12 acts. Receives 15% minimum commission.
How to Contact: Query. Prefers cassette tapes. SASE. Reports in 2 weeks.
Music: C&W, dance-oriented and easy listening. Works primarily with dance bands, show bands, combos and singles. Current acts include the Gary Lee Orchestra (big band); The Nat "King" Cohen Combo (combo); and Chuck Pangburn & His Men of the West (C&W group).

THE FRANKLYN AGENCY, 1010 Hammond St., #312, Los Angeles CA 90069. (213)272-6080. President: Audrey P. Franklyn. Management agency and public relations firm. Represents artists and musical groups, and businesses; currently handles 7 acts. Receives 5-15% commission. Reviews material for acts.
How to Contact: Query by mail, arrange personal interview or submit demo tape and lead sheet. Prefers cassette or video cassette. SASE. Reports in 1 month.
Music: Blues, easy listening, gospel, jazz, MOR, progressive, R&B, rock and top 40/pop. Works primarily with rock bands and single soloist singers. Current acts include Talisman Band (jazz/rock); Merrell Frankhauser (soft rock); and Marilyn Johnson (pop singer).

FREDDIE CEE ATTRACTIONS, 370 Market St., Box 333, Lemoyne PA 17043. (717)761-0821. Owner: Fred Clousher. Booking agency. Represents groups and comedy and novelty acts in Pennsylvania, Maryland, Virginia, West Virginia, New York, New Jersey and Ohio; currently handles approximately 75 acts. Receives 15-20% commission.
How to Contact: Query or submit demo tape. Include "photos, list of credits, etc." Prefers 7½ ips reel-to-reel, cassette or 8-track cartridge with 5-10 songs on demo. Does not return unsolicited material. Reports in 3 weeks.
Music: Bluegrass, C&W, dance-oriented, gospel, polka, top 40/pop and Hawaiian. Works primarily with "commercial, commercial/rock, country and novelty show groups. Most dates are one-nighters." Current acts include the Hawaiian Revue '81 (show and dance act); Showdown (country/rock); Sound Foundation (variety dance group); Frankie Dee Show (C&W and '50s); and Harmonica Rascals (vaudeville).
Tips: "We obtain employment for marketable groups and performers. Those desiring to use our services, should submit complete promo material (demo tape, photos, credits, etc.)"

FROST & FROST ENTERTAINMENT, 3985 W. Taft Dr., Spokane WA 99208. (509)325-1777. Owner/Agent: Dick Frost. Booking agency. Represents individuals and groups; currently handles 10-15 acts. Receives 10-15% commission. Reviews material for acts.
How to Contact: Query or submit demo tape and lyric sheet. Prefers cassette with 5 songs on tape. Include information on past appearances, as well as list of references. SASE. Reports in 2 weeks.
Music: C&W, dance-oriented, easy listening, MOR, rock (country and 50s) and top 40/pop. Works primarily with dance bands, show bands and individual artists. Currently some acts include Tex Williams (western act); Kay Austin (C&W/MOR act); Big Tiny Little, Kenny O & Rhinestone, Stagecoach West, and High Country (show and/or dance).

GAIL AND RICE PRODUCTIONS, 11845 Mayfield, Livonia MI 48150. (313)427-9300. Account Representative: Chris Nordman. Booking agency. Represents individuals and groups; currently handles 25 acts. Receives 10-20% commission.
How to Contact: Submit demo tape and lead sheet. Prefers cassette with 3-6 songs on demo. Does

not return unsolicited material. Reports in 3 weeks.
Music: Bluegrass, children's, C&W, dance-oriented, jazz and top 40/pop. Works primarily with "self-contained groups (1-8 people), show and dance music, listening groups, and individual name or semi-name attractions." Current acts include 21st Century Steel Drum Band (show group); the Dazzlers (vocal/dance act); and Glenn Haywood (comedian/ventriloquist).

MICK GAMBILL ENTERPRISES, INC., 1617 N. El Centro, Suite 12, Hollywood CA 90028. (213)466-9777. President: Mick Gambill. Management firm and booking agency. Represents West Coast groups; currently handles 30 acts. Receives 15-20% commission. Reviews material for acts.
How to Contact: Submit demo tape. Prefers cassette with 3-6 songs on demo. SASE. Reports in 2 weeks.
Music: Dance-oriented, rock and top 40/pop. Works primarily with top 40 groups. Current acts include Whizz Kidds (rock); Frontseat (top 40/pop); Light (top 40); Motion (rock); and Kelly Hansen & Jinx (rock).

GENERAL TALENT/GENERAL MANAGEMENT ASSOCIATES, 4110 Monroeville Blvd., Monroeville PA 15146. (412)373-3860. Contact: Richard Foreman. Management firm and bo; k-ing agency. Represents artists, groups and songwriters. Receives 15-35% commission. Reviews material for acts.
How to Contact: Query by mail, submit demo tape and lead sheet. Prefers cassette with 2-4 songs on demo. SASE. Reports in 1 month.
Music: C&W, dance-oriented, easy listening, MOR, progressive, rock and top 40/pop. Works primarily with concert and nightclub bands. Current acts include Risque; Mixz; and Joe Scott.

ZACH GLICKMAN, 6430 Sunset Blvd., Hollywood CA 90028. (213)461-2988. President: Zach Glickman. Management agency. Represents artists, groups and songwriters.
How to Contact: Submit demo tape and lead sheet. Prefers reel-to-reel tape. SASE. Reports in 1 month.
Music: Church/religious; dance; gospel; rock; soul; and top 40/pop. Current acts include Dion (rock); and Mighty Clouds of Joy (gospel).

PETER GOLDEN & ASSOC./CROSSLIGHT MANAGEMENT, LTD., 1592 Crossroads of the World, Hollywood CA 90028. (213)462-6156. Contact: Bill Siddons. Management firm. Represents artists, songwriters, and producers/engineers; currently handles 6 acts. Receives negotiable commission. Reviews material for acts.
How to Contact: Query by mail, then submit demo tape. Prefers cassette with 2-4 songs on demo. Does not return unsolicited material. Reports in 2 months.
Music: Blues, R&B, rock (country), and top 40/pop. Current acts include Jackson Browne, Poco; and Jesse Colin Young.

GOLDMAN-DELL MUSIC PRODUCTIONS, 421 W. 87th St., Box 8680, Kansas City MO 64114. (816)333-8701. Owner: Irv Goldman. Management firm and booking agency. Represents individuals, groups and songwriters; currently handles over 30 acts. Receives "minimum commission set by the union." Reviews material for acts. Also contract producer of shows with local or national acts. Reviews material for acts. Operates Deggis Music Co. (BMI) with (ASCAP) co-publishing available.
How to Contact: Arrange personal interview, submit demo tape and lead sheet or contact by phone. Bandleaders or acts send cassette tape and photo. Prefers reel-to-reel or cassette with 2 songs minimum on tape. "Allow 4-6 weeks for reply on songs submitted for publishing/recording. Material returned only if SASE is included. Tapes must be labeled to identify same!"
Music: Bluegrass, blues, C&W, dance-oriented, easy listening, gospel, jazz, Latin/chicano, MOR, R&B, rock, and top 40/pop. Works primarily with variety and dance bands but accepts all types. Current acts include Classmen (show band); Jesse Rose Band (country variety); Harbour (easy rock, top 40); Whitewater (boys & girls, together!); and Brothers Heritage (show-dance-stage band). Also handles some National, Nashville and TV performers, musical or not. To other qualified agents and managers or producers: "I am your man in Kansas City." Also provides direction for Bruce Gordon ("Frank Nitti") character on *The Untouchables* for musical and non-musical sketches or plays, plus TV commercials and other acts. Can produce original music for any commercial situation.
Tips: "Songwriters: Identify (label) all tapes send to us. Artists: Be outstanding, have wardrobe and good stage presence."

DAVID GOLIATH AGENCY, 1272 Lynn Terrace, Highland Park IL 60035. (312)266-0040. Director: Cynthia Winston. Management and booking agency. Represents artists and musical groups; currently handles 5 acts. Receives 10-20% commission.

How to Contact: Query by mail; submit demo tape only. Prefers cassette with 3-6 songs on demo. "Good promo material or at least the desire or ability to gather and process this information is most important." Does not return unsolicited material. Reports in 1 month.

Music: C&W, MOR, R&B, rock, soul and top 40/pop. Works primarily with dance bands/show groups/bar bands. Current acts include The Power Band (funk/R&B); Billy Always (funk/rock/gospel/pop/top 40); and Pilot (hard rock).

WALT GOLLENDER ENTERPRISES, 12 Marshall St., Suite 8Q, Irvington NJ 07111. (201)373-6050. Executive Director: Walt Gollender. Management firm. Represents artists and songwriters. Receives sales royalty, outright fee from record company or outright fee from songwriter/artist.

How to Contact: Submit demo tape and lyric sheet, or arrange personal interview. Prefers 7½ ips reel-to-reel (mono mix) or cassette with a maximum of 4 songs on demo. "Call any evening 5-8 p.m. EST." SASE. Reports in 1 month.

Music: Blues; C&W; dance; easy listening; folk; MOR; rock (light); soul; and top 40/pop. Works primarily with rock groups, vocalists, small combos, songwriters and C&W vocalists. Current acts include Dan and Bob (folk/pop duo); Mary Lee Martin (C&W vocalist); Chuck Ehrmann (C&W); Tina Sanderson (rock/disco); Ben Wiggins (soul/disco); Sparkle, (soul/disco); Hipnotics (soul); and a gospel act.

GOOD KARMA PRODUCTIONS, INC, 4218 Main St., Kansas City MO 64111. (816)531-3857. Co-Owner: Paul Peterson. Management agency. Deals with Midwest artists only. Represents artists and groups; currently handles 4 acts. Receives maximum 20% commission. Reviews material for acts.

How to Contact: Submit demo tape and lyric sheet. Prefers cassette with 2-4 songs on demo. SASE. Reports in 2-3 weeks.

Music: Rock (hard and country); and top 40/pop. Works with rock and country rock bands, concert and recording artists only and songwriters. Current acts include the Ozark Mountain Daredevils (country-rock recording artists); the Randle Chowning Band (rock recording group); and The Clocks (modern rock).

GOOD MUSIC MANAGEMENT, INC., Box 4087, Missoula MT 59806. President: Doug Brown. Booking agency. Represents artists and groups; currently handles 10 acts. Receives 15-20% commission.

How to Contact: Submit demo tape and press kit only. "Send all information possible; no phone calls please." Prefers cassette with a minimum of 5 songs on demo. Also send references on live performance. SASE. Reports in 3 weeks.

Music: C&W; rock; top 40/pop; and country rock. Current acts Montana (bluegrass/country/rock); Michael Murphey (pop/country); The Dillman Band (rock); and John Bayley (reggae).

BILL GRAHAM MANAGEMENT, 201 11th St., San Francisco CA 94103. (415)864-0815. Creative Development: Mick Brigden. Management firm. Represents artists and groups; currently handles 5 acts. Reviews material for acts.

How to Contact: Submit demo tape and lead sheet. Prefers cassette. SASE. Reports as soon as possible.

Music: Progressive, R&B, rock and top 40/pop. Works primarily with rock 'n' roll bands. Current acts include Santana; Eddie Money; and Van Morrison.

JOE GRAYDON & ASSOCIATES, Box 1, Toluca Lake CA 91602. (213)769-2424. President: Joe Graydon. Management firm. Represents artists, groups, songwriters and package shows for tours; currently handles 12 acts. Receives 10-15% commission.

How to Contact: Submit demo tape and lyric sheet. Prefers cassette tape with 3-10 songs on demo. SASE. Reports in 1 week.

Music: Bluegra.s; C&W; dance; MOR; soul; and primarily top 40/pop. Works with show groups that play Nevada lounges and individual singers, male and female. Current acts include Helen Forrest (singer); The Boos Brothers (show group); Connie Haines, (singer); January Jones, (:singer); The Pied Pipers (vocal group); The Big Band Festival of the Fabulous Forties (23 people); and Concert Attraction.

GREAT PLAINS ASSOCIATES, INC., Box 634, Southern Hills Shopping Center, Lawrence KS 66044. (913)841-4444. Contact: Scott Winters, Mark Swanson, Stuart Doores or Greg Mackender. Booking agency. Represents groups in Midwest; currently handles 30 acts. Receives 10-20% commission. Reviews material for acts.

How to Contact: Submit demo tape. Prefers cassette with 3-5 songs on demo. SASE.

Music: C&W, R&B, rock and soul. Works primarily with dance bands "for college mini-concerts to bar band dances." Current acts include Limousine (rock); The Glory Boys (new soul); and Denver Locke (country swing).
Tips: "We are constantly looking for and expect our artists to have a *definite* idea of what they want and where they are going."

GREAT PYRAMID MUSIC, Box 1340, Pacifica CA 94044. Administrator: Josep Buchwald. Management firm. Represents artists, groups and songwriters; currently handles 12 acts. Receives 10-25% commission. Reviews material for acts.
How to Contact: Query by mail, submit demo tape and lead sheet. Prefers cassette with 3-5 songs on demo. SASE. Reports as soon as possible.
Music: MOR and ballads. Works primarily with vocalists, songwriters and groups. Current acts include Marty Balin, Jesse Barish and Ric Knowles (solos).
Tips: "Don't pressure."

THE MALCOLM GREENWOOD AGENCY, Box 72303, Atlanta GA 30339. (404)433-1979. Personal Manager: Malcolm Greenwood. Management firm and booking agency. Represents individuals and groups; currently handles 4 acts. Receives negotiable commission. Reviews material for acts.
How to Contact: Query by phone. Prefers cassette with 1-4 songs on demo. SASE. Reports in 2 weeks.
Music: Gospel (contemporary Christian). Works with contemporary Christian solo artists and groups. Current acts include Pat Terry (artist and songwriter/contemporary Christian act, New Pax Records); Chalice (songwriters/contemporary Christian group, Starsong Records); and Tim Sheppard (artist and songwriter/contemporary Christian act, Greentree Records); and The Wall Brothers (artist and songwriters and contemporary Christian group, Greentree Records).

THE GROUP, INC., 1957 Kilburn Dr., Atlanta GA 30324. (404)872-6000. General Manager: Hamilton Underwood. Vice President: Robert Biser. Management agency. Represents individuals and groups. Receives 15-25% commission..
How to Contact: Submit demo tape only. Prefers cassette with 2-3 songs on demo. Include photo and bio. Doesn't return unsolicited material. Reports as soon as possible.
Music: Blues; jazz; progressive; rock; and top 40/pop. Works with total package groups (artists and songwriters). Current acts Starfoxx (group/rock, Hottrax Records); and Little Phil (artist-songwriter/rock, ABC/Dot Records).

BOB HALE TALENT/JESTER SOUND, 423 Kuhlman Dr., Billings MT 59101. (406)245-2174. President: Bob Hale. Management firm, booking agency, record label, music publisher and recording studio. Represents artists, groups and songwriters; currently handles 30 acts. Receives 15% (booking) to 20% (management). Pays standard royalty to songwriters; negotiable royalty to artists on recording contract. Reviews material for acts.
How to Contact: Submit demo tape. Prefers 7½ ips reel-to-reel or cassette with 5 songs maximum on demo. "Demo should emphasize vocal with minimum amount of production." SASE. Reports in 2 weeks.
Music: Bluegrass, C&W, dance-oriented, easy listening, MOR and top 40/pop. Works primarily with C&W, bluegrass and top 40/pop. Current acts include Prairie Fire (C&W show group); Lost Highway Band (rock/country rock group); Linda Jordan (country/country rock artist); and The Horse Brothers (country/top 40 artists).

JERRY HALE PRODUCTIONS, Box 5054, ELRB, Parker AZ 85344. (602)669-9274. President: Gerald M. Hale. Management firm and promoter. Represents artists, groups and songwriters; currently handles 6 acts. Receives 15% commission. Reviews material for acts.
How to Contact: Submit demo tape and lead sheet. Prefers cassette with 1 song on demo. Does not return unsolicited material. Reports in 1 month.
Music: Church/religious, C&W, easy listening, MOR, rock (soft) and top 40/pop. Works primarily with dance, show and bar bands and individual artists. Current acts include Ron Shaw (C&W).

FOREST HAMILTON PERSONAL MANAGEMENT, 9022 Norma Pl., Los Angeles CA 90069. Manager: Forest Hamilton. Assistant Manager: Phil Casey. Management firm. Represents individuals and groups; currently handles 8 acts. Receives negotiable commission. Reviews material for acts.
How to Contact: Submit demo tape and lead sheet. Prefers cassette with 2-4 songs on demo. Does not return unsolicited material. Reports in 1 month.

Music: Jazz, MOR, R&B, soul and top 40/pop. Works primarily with vocalists. Current acts include Ronnie Laws (artist-songwriter/jazz); David Oliver (artist-songwriter/contemporary); the Dramatics (songwriters/R&B/pop); Side Effect (songwriters/R&B/jazz/pop); Eloise Laws (artist/pop/jazz); A Taste of Honey (artist/songwriters); L.A. Boppers (songwriters/artist); Ren Woods (artist); and Elecktra/Asylum/Nonesuch.

THE JACK HAMPTON AGENCY, 226 S. Beverly Dr., Beverly Hills CA 90212. (213)274-6075. Artists' Manager/Agent: Donovan Moore. Management firm and booking agency. Represents artists, groups, songwriters, recording artists, entertainers and lecturers. Receives 10-20% commission. Percentage 50% if from acts as producer.
How To Contact: Arrange personal interview if in Los Angeles area. Prefers cassette with 3-5 songs to be mailed with resume, song list and photo to agency with proper amount of postage affixed. SASE. Reports in 2 weeks.
Music: Bluegrass, blues, children's, classical, C&W, disco, folk, jazz, MOR, progressive, rock (original, MOR, hard, soft), soul, top 40/pop and diverse instrumental and vocal acts. Works with dance and bar bands and original groups looking for recording contracts. Current acts include Buddy de Franco (jazz); Tilman Thomas (rock, original); Paul Cypress (classical guitarist); Rocket 88 (rock, clubs/original); Pacific Flyer (top 40/pop); and Paul Gann (lecturer).

GEOFFREY HANSEN ENTERPRISES, LTD., Box 63, Orinda CA 94563. (415)937-6469. Artist Relations: Marvin Farkelstein. Management agency. Represents artists, groups and songwriters; currently handles 10 acts. Receives 10-25% commission. Also paid on a contract (or double/contract) basis. Reviews material for acts.
How to Contact: Submit demo tape and lead sheet. Prefers cassette. SASE. Reports in 1 month or longer.
Music: Blues, C&W, MOR, rock (and country rock), top 40/pop, and comedy/novelty tunes. Works with top 40 and C&W artists. Current acts include Garmon Hines (C&W); Aabci (studio band); and Bert Friel (Hawaiian).
Tips: "Send letter—if it is interesting and there is possible talent . . . "

HARMONY ARTISTS, INC., 8833 Sunset Blvd., Suite 200, Los Angeles CA 90069. (213)659-9644. President: Michael Dixon. Booking agency. Represents groups; currently handles 100 acts. Receives 15% commission. Reviews material for acts.
How To Contact: Submit demo tape and lyric sheet and photo. Prefers cassette with 3-5 songs on demo. Reports in 2 weeks.
Music: Easy listening, MOR, progressive, rock and top 40/pop. Current acts include Auracle, Ohio Players and Nick Gilder.
Tips: "Persistence is important."

GEORGE HARNESS ASSOCIATES, 27 N. Lake Rd., Springfield IL 62707. (217)529-8550. President: George Harness. Management firm and booking agency. Represents artists and groups; currently handles 10 acts. Reviews material for acts.
How to Contact: Submit demo tape and lead sheet. Prefers cassette with 4-6 songs on demo. Does not return unsolicited material. Reports in 2 weeks.
Music: C&W, dance-oriented, easy listening, jazz, MOR and top 40/pop. Current acts include Linda Baily; Fuller Brothers; and Alex Glover (show, dance, variety acts).

HARVEST AGENCY, 317 Taft Ave., West Paterson NJ 07424. (201)278-3735. Manager: Frank Galardi. Represents artists and groups in New York and New Jersey area only; currently handles 4 acts. Receives 10-15% commission. Reviews material for acts.
How to Contact: Query by mail, submit demo tape and lead sheet. Prefers cassette with 3-6 songs on demo. SASE. Reports in 2 weeks.
Music: Church/religious and gospel—"must be in the gospel style." Works primarily with gospel groups and solo artists. Current acts include Cindy Zaforanio; Ronny G.; and Sojurnors.

GLENN HENRY ENTERTAINMENT AGENCY, 55 S. LaCumbre Rd., Suite 9, Santa Barbara CA 93105. (805)687-1131. Contact: Glenn Henry. Booking agency. Represents individuals and groups; currently handles 16 acts. Receives 10-15% commission. Reviews material for acts.
How to Contact: Query or arrange personal interview. Prefers 8-track cartridge with 3-6 songs on demo. Artist may submit 8x10 promo pictures and/or credits. SASE. Reporting time varies.
Music: C&W (modern), MOR, rock and top 40/pop. Works with lounge and hotel bands (all top 40/MOR) with female vocalist if possible and/or modern country dance groups. At present, needs pop rock band with female vocalist. Current acts include Waterfall (dance/lounge); Sizzle (dance/lounge); and Double or Nothin' (modern country).

HITCH-A-RIDE MUSIC, Box 201, Cincinnati OH 45201. Manager: J.H. Reno. Management firm. Represents professional individuals, groups and songwriters; currently handles 6 acts. Receives negotiable commission. Reviews material for acts.
How to Contact: Query or submit demo tape and lyric sheet. Prefers 7½ ips reel-to-reel or cassette with 1-5 songs on demo. SASE. Reports in 1 month.
Music: Bluegrass; C&W; and MOR. Current acts include Pam Hanna and Jack Reno (C&W vocalists).

GLENN HOLLAND MANAGEMENT, 2368 Stanley Hills Dr., Los Angeles CA 90046. (213)656-6834. President: Glenn Holland. Management agency. Represents local artists, musical groups and songwriters. Reviews material for acts.
How to Contact: Query by mail, then submit demo tape only. Prefers cassette with 1-4 songs on demo. Does not return unsolicited material. Reports in 3 weeks.
Music: C&W, easy listening, MOR, R&B, Rock (any type), soul and top 40/pop. Works primarily with recording artists with overall commercial potential.

GEORGE B. HUNT & ASSOCIATES, 8350 Santa Monica Blvd., Los Angeles CA 90069. (213)654-6600. Owner: George B. Hunt. Management firm and booking agency. Represents professional individuals and groups. Receives 10-15% commission.
How to Contact: Query. SASE. Reports in 1 month.
Music: Current acts include Sunshine 'n' Rain (folk group); Dirk Arthur (magician); René & His Continental Artists (marionettes); Lainie Kazan (international recording artist); Barbara McNair (vocalist); Torill (European and USA pop recording artist); George West (comedy and music); Jesse Lopen (pop, Latin and C&W); Jon Gary (MOR & C&W concert/club performer); and Jon & Sondra Steele (the "My Happiness" duo). "In addition to the above, we book all types of acts for fairs, conventions, banquets, etc."

ICR INTERNATIONAL CELEBRITY REGISTER, INC., (Music Division), First National Bank Towers, Box 4527, Topeka KS 66604. (913)233-9716. Executive Vice President in charge of entertainment: Kent Raine. Management firm and booking agency, a division of the Earthraker Corporation. Represents artists, groups and songwriters; currently handles 8 acts. Receives 10-25% commission.
How to Contact: Query or submit demo tape and lead sheet. Photos and short biography helpful. Prefers 7½ ips reel-to-reel or cassette with 2-6 songs on demo. SASE. Reports in 2 weeks.
Music: Blues; C&W; dance; jazz; MOR; rock (and country rock); soul; and top 40/pop. Works with artists for concert attractions and recording groups. "We're always on the lookout for a promising young songwriter or artist; however, don't expect any miracles in this business."

IF PRODUCTIONS, INC., 15 Glenby Lane, Brookville NY 11545. (516)626-9504. 22240 Schoenborn St., Canoga Park CA 91304. (213)883-4865. New York: Producer/Staff writer: Tom Ingegno. Los Angeles: Producer/Staff writer: Mike Frenchik. Management agency and production company. Represents individuals, groups and songwriters; currently handles 4 acts. Receives 15-20% commission. Reviews material for acts.
How to Contact: Query or submit demo tape and lyric sheet. Prefers cassette with 3-5 songs on demo. SASE. Reports in 3 weeks.
Music: MOR, progressive, rock and top 40/pop. Works primarily with recording acts and solo performers. Current acts include Thrills (rock act); Tony Monaco (songwriter/recording artist); Dave Fullerton (songwriter/recording artist); Pat O'Brien (songwriter/recording artist).

INNOVATIVE ARTISTS MANAGEMENT, 172 Main St., Spencer MA 01562. (617)885-6912. A&R Director: Patrick George. Management firm. Represents artists, groups and songwriters; currently handles 5 acts. Receives 10-40% commission. Reviews material for acts.
How to Contact: Submit demo tape. Prefers cassette with 1-5 songs on demo. SASE. Reports in 1 month.
Music: MOR, rock and top 40/pop. Works primarily with bar bands, vocalists and recording artists. Current acts include Kim Page (vocalist); Numbers (recording artists); and Fate (bar band). Tips: Artists "must be able to take direction!"

INTERMOUNTAIN CONCERTS, Box 942, Rapid City SD 57709. (605)342-7696. Contact: Ron Kohn. Management firm and concert production agency. Deals with artists from the upper-Midwest region. Represents artists and groups; currently handles 12 acts. Negotiates management fees. Reviews material for acts.
How to Contact: Query or submit demo tape and lyric sheet. Prefers cassette with 3-5 songs on demo. SASE. Reports in 2 weeks.
Music: Rock.

J & J PRODUCTION AGENCY, Box 476, Benham TX 75418. (214)583-7112. Manager: R.J. Vandygriff. Booking agency. Represents artists and groups; currently handles 7 acts. Receives 10-20% commission. Reviews material for acts.
How to Contact: Query by mail, then submit demo tape. Prefers 7½ ips reel-to-reel or cassette with 3-6 songs on demo. Does not return unsolicited material. Reports in 1 month.
Music: C&W and R&B. Works primarily with bar bands and show groups. Current acts include Robert Joe (country); Showdown (progressive); and Shades of Country (country).

JACKSON ARTISTS CORP., 7251 Lowell Dr., Suite 200, Shawnee Mission KS 66204. Management firm, booking agency and music publisher. Represents individuals and songwriters; currently handles 40 acts. Receives 15% minimum commission from individual artists and groups; 10% from songwriters. Reviews material for acts.
How to Contact: Query, arrange personal interview, submit demo tape and lead sheet or phone. Prefers cassette with 2-4 songs on demo. "Mark names of tunes on cassettes. May send up to 4 tapes. We do most of our business by phone." Will return material if requested. SASE. Reporting time varies.
Music: Bluegrass; blues; C&W; disco; MOR; progressive; rock (soft); soul; and top 40/pop. Works primarily with dance and show bands. Current acts include Stumpwater (C&W/pop, Brass Records); and "Ragtime Bob" Dancer (ASCAP songwriter/entertainer, Universal Records).
Tips: "Although it's not necessary, we prefer lead sheets with the tapes—send 2 or 3 that you are proud of. Also note what 'name' artist you'd like to see do the song."

BRUCE JAMES COMPANY, Box 439, Lyndonville VT 05851. (802)626-3317. President: Bruce James. Management firm. Estab. 1979. Represents artists, groups and songwriters in New England area; currently handles 8 acts. Receives 20% commission. Reviews material for acts.
How to Contact: Submit demo tape and lyric sheet. Prefers cassette with 1-5 songs on demo. "Songs should be hit single material under 4 minutes long each. Melodies should be catchy, tunes should have chorus, bridge, verse. Lyrics should be very personal and intimate." SASE. Reports in 3 weeks.
Music: Rock (hard/top 40) and top 40/pop. Works primarily with rock artists with strong desire to make it. Current acts include FOX (rock/top 40); Rockestra (rock/layered vocals/hard rock); and Littlewing (fresh, new rock).

BOB KNIGHT AGENCY, 185 Clinton Ave., Staten Island NY 10301. (212)448-8420. General Manager: Bob Knight. Management firm, booking agency and music publisher. Represents artists, groups and songwriters; currently handles 10 acts. Receives 10-25% commission. Reviews material for acts.
How to Contact: Submit demo cassette tape and lead sheet. "Phone calls accepted 6-9 p.m." Prefers cassette with 3-10 songs on demo. SASE. Reports in 1 month.
Music: C&W, easy listening, MOR, R&B, soul and top 40/pop. Works primarily with lounge and show groups, high energy dance and show groups. Current acts include The Elegants (oldie show); Grease Lightning (grease show); and Creations (high energy dance).

KRAGEN & COMPANY, 8 Cadman Plaza W., Brooklyn NY 11201. (212)858-2544. Contact: Lynne Volkman. Management firm. Represents artists, groups and songwriters; currently handles 8 acts. Receives 15-20% commission. Reviews material for acts.
How to Contact: Submit demo tape and lead sheet. Prefers cassette with 1-4 songs on demo. Does not return unsolicited material. Reports as soon as possible.
Music: C&W, dance-oriented, easy listening, folk, MOR, R&B, rock and top 40/pop. Works exclusively with recording and concert artists. Current acts include Kenny Rogers; Tom Chapin; Bill Medley; Harry Chapin; and Gallagher..

CHUCK KRONZEK MANAGEMENT, P.O. Box 8120, Pittsburgh PA 15217. (412)422-7052. President: C.M. Kronzek. Management firm and booking agency. Represents individuals and groups; currently handles 25 acts. Receives 10-35% commission: "partnerships with acts, hourly billing." Reviews material for acts.
How to Contact: Query or submit demo tape and lyric sheet. "Include bio, photo, availability, other affiliations and prices. Submit the promo by mail." Prefers cassette with 3-7 songs on demo. Does not return unsolicited material. Reports in 3 weeks.
Music: Bluegrass, C&W, MOR and rock (including country). Most of our acts travel full time. We are strong with country rock and motel lounge bands. Most of our acts are exclusive." Current acts include Duster (country rock); Daybreak (lounge/top 40); and Pearl (jazz).

L & R PRODUCTIONS, Doc Dick Enterprises, 16 E. Broad St., Mt. Vernon NY 10552. (914)668-4488. President: Richard Rashbaum. Management firm and music publisher. Represents artists, groups and songwriters; currently handles 10 acts. Receives 10-20% commission. Reviews material for acts.
How to Contact: Submit demo tape and lead sheet. Prefers 7½ ips reel-to-reel or cassette with 1-4 songs on demo. SASE. Reports in 2 weeks.
Music: Blues, dance-oriented, disco, easy listening, MOR, R&B, rock, soul and top 40/pop. Works primarily with dance bands, lounge acts, recording artists and groups, and songwriters. Current acts include Daybreak (dance band/recorded act); MTV (dance band); and "(10)" (songwriters).

JOSEPH LAKE AND ASSOCIATES, 4105 Morning Star Dr., Salt Lake City UT 84117. (801)278-3587. President: Joe Lake. Public relations and promotion agency. Represents individuals, groups, and songwriters; currently handles 4 acts. Receives 10-15% commission. Reviews material for acts.
How To Contact: Query, arrange personal interview, submit demo tape and lyric sheet or send press material (photos, write-ups, etc.) Prefers cassette with 2-4 songs on demo. SASE. Reports in 3 weeks. "Please send only your very best and only 2-4 songs."
Music: Church/religious; disco; rock (country rock); and top 40/pop. Works with concert groups with full back-up band/some dance bands/songwriters. Current acts include SunShade 'n' Rain (concert group, SCP Records); G.C. Inc. (recording and concert group and night club singers and dancers); Day, Light & Dawn (a female trio); and Rick Coats (concert performer/songwriter).

LAKE FRONT TALENT AGENCY, Box 2395, Sandusky OH 44870. (419)626-4987. Owner/Manager: Larry Myers. Management firm and record company. Represents individuals, groups and songwriters from Ohio, Pennsylvania, West Virginia, Michigan and "possibly" other areas; currently handles 10 acts. Receives 15% commission. Reviews material for acts.
How to Contact: Query by mail or phone. Prefers 7½ ips reel-to-reel or cassette with 3-5 songs on demo. SASE. Reports in 1 month.
Music: C&W, easy listening, MOR, rock (top 40) and top 40/pop. Works primarily with dance bands, bar bands and good show bands. Current acts include Llynn Stevens (country rock); West Fall (rock); and Anna Jane Allen Family Show (C&W/rock/polka/standard).

LANDSLIDE MANAGEMENT, 119 West 57th St., New York NY 10019. Principals: Ted Lehrman, Ruth Landers, Libby Bush. Management Firm. Represents actors, singers and songwriters. Receives 15% commission. Reviews material for acts.
How to Contact: Submit demo tape and lead sheet. SASE. "Include picture and resume."
Music: C&W, easy listening, MOR, R&B, rock, soul and top 40/pop. Current acts include Audrey Landers, Judy Landers, Elvera Roussel, Jack Parrish, and Robert Bendall.

THE CHARLES LANT AGENCY, Box 1085, Cornwall, Ontario, Canada K6H 5V2. (613)938-1532. Contact: Charles W. B. Lant. Booking agency. Represents individuals and groups. Receives 10-20% commission.
How to Contact: Query or phone. Prefers cassette with 3-10 songs on demo. SAE and International Reply Coupons. Reports as soon as possible.
Music: C&W and big bands. Works primarily with dance bands. Current acts include The Stardusters Orchestra (17-piece band), and the Gilles Godard Show (C&W).

STAN LAWRENCE PRODUCTIONS, 191 Presidential Blvd., Bala Cynwyd PA 19004. (215)664-4873. President: Stan Lawrence. Management agency. Represents individuals and groups on the East coast; currently handles 3 acts. Reviews material for acts.
How to Contact: Query or arrange personal interview. Prefers cassette with 3 songs on demo. SASE. Reports in 1 month.
Music: Disco and top 40/pop. Current acts include Bill Collins (male/vocal/R&B); Tonnee Collins (female vocal/R&B); Tony Branco and Innervisions (jazz group/pop); and Collins & Collins (R&B vocal duo, A&M Records).

GARY LAZAR MANAGEMENT, 3222 Belinda Dr., Sterling Heights MI 48077. (313)977-0645. Contact: Robin Gaines. Management firm, booking agency and music publisher. Represents artist, groups and songwriters; currently handles 15 acts. Receives 10-20% commission. Reviews material for acts.
How to Contact: Submit demo tape and lead sheet. Prefers cassette with 3 songs maximum on demo. Does not return unsolicited material. Reports in 1 month.
Music: Rock (hard) and top 40/pop. Works primarily with recording artists, club bands and songwriters. Current acts include The Rockets (rock band/recording artists, RSO Records); The Buzztones (rock band); and Don Wellman (songwriter/lyricist).

LE SUEUR MANAGEMENT, 803 1st Ave., Athens AL 35611. (205)233-2462. General Manager: Mike Lessor. Management firm, publishing company and promotion agency. Represents individuals; currently handles 12 acts. Receives 15-30% commission. Reviews material for acts.
How to Contact: Submit demo tape and lead sheet. Prefers 7½ ips reel-to-reel or cassette with 3-5 songs on demo. SASE. Reports in 1 month.
Music: C&W, gospel, R&B, rock, soul and top 40/pop. Works primarily with "singers and musicians who write. We look for entertainment values. We don't do much folk type things." Current acts include Darlene Hill (R&B/pop); and Ravven (rock).

BUDDY LEE ATTRACTIONS, INC., 38 Music Square E., Suite 300, Nashville TN 37203. (615)244-4336. Artists and Groups Contact: Tony Conway. Songwriters Contact: Nancy Dunn. Management firm and booking agency. Represents individuals and groups; currently handles 60 acts. "Principally, we deal with established name acts who have recording contracts with major labels." Receives 10-15% commission. Reviews material for acts.
How to Contact: Submit demo tape and lead sheet. Prefers 7½ ips reel-to-reel with 4 songs minimum on tape. Does not return unsolicited material. Reports as soon as possible on solicited material.
Music: Bluegrass, C&W, MOR, rock, soul and top 40/pop. Works primarily with concert attractions. Current acts include Danny Davis and the Nashville Brass (C&W/MOR instrumental); Johnny Paycheck (C&W); Willie Nelson and Family; John Conlee (C&W/pop); Freddy Fender (C&W); Mitch Ryder (pop/rock); and Joe Cocker (pop/rock).

ED LEFFLER MANAGEMENT, 9229 Sunset Blvd., Suite 625, Los Angeles CA 90069. (213)550-8802. President: Ed Leffler. Management firm.
How to contact: Query by mail.
Music: Current acts include Sweet and Sammy Hagar.
Tips: "We are looking for established, self-contained artists with a track record."

LEGEND ENTERTAINMENT SERVICES, Box 1414, Vicksburg MS 39180. (601)638-5622. President: Robert Garner. Management firm, booking agency and recording company. Represents artists, groups and songwriters in Vicksburg; currently handles 12 acts. Receives 10-15% commission. Reviews material for acts.
How to Contact: Query by mail. Prefers 7½ ips reel-to-reel or cassette with 2-4 songs on demo. "Include bio, goals, and photo." SASE. Reports in 1 month.
bands, bar bands, solo acts and lounge acts. Current acts include Reunion (bluegrass); Jackson (C&W); Carol Wade (folk soloist).
Tips: "We are looking for artists who don't try to imitate existing stars, who have developed their own style."

JOHN LEVY ENTERPRISES, INC., 181 S. Sycamore Ave., Suite 101, Los Angeles CA 90036. (213)934-0255. President: John Levy. Management agency. Represents individuals and songwriters; currently handles 3 acts. Receives 10-20% commission.
How to Contact: Submit demo tape only or demo tape and lead sheet. Prefers 7½ ips or cassette with 1-5 songs on demo. SASE. Reports in 2 weeks.
Music: Jazz, soul, and top 40/pop. Current acts include Nancy Wilson (singer); and Joe Williams (singer).

LEW LINET MANAGEMENT, 7225 Hollywood Blvd., Hollywood CA 90046. (213)876-4071. President: Lew Linet. Management agency and independent record producer. Represents artists, groups and songwriters; currently handles 1 act. Receives 20% commission. Reviews material for acts.
How To Contact: Submit demo tape and lyric sheet. Prefers cassette with 3 songs on demo. Include lyrics sheet. SASE. Reports in 1 month.
Music: Folk; rock (country or soft); and top 40/pop. Works with recording artists. Current acts include Noel Butler & Cherokee (country rock).

LINGERING MUSIC, INC., 2 Bay St., Thomaston ME 04861. (207)354-8928. President: Chuck Kruger. Management firm and booking agency. Estab. 1979. Represents artists, groups and songwriters in the Northeast; currently handles 3 acts. Receives 10-15% commission. Reviews material for acts.
How to Contact: Query by mail, submit demo tape. Prefers 7½ ips reel-to-reel or cassette with 2-5 songs on demo. "Brief biography okay, but let material speak for itself." SASE. Reports in 1 month.
Music: C&W, dance-oriented, easy listening, folk, gospel, jazz, MOR, progressive, R&B, rock,

soul and top 40/pop, calypso and reggae. Works primarily with soloists, trios and dance bands. Current acts include Chuck Kruger (singer/songwriter); The Fabulous Prizes (club trio); and Cruzan Confuzion Band (dance and college concert band).

LOCONTO PRODUCTIONS, 7766 NW 44th St., Sunrise FL 33321. (305)741-7766 or (305)940-2626 (Miami). President: Frank X. Loconto. Management firm and booking agency. Estab. 1980. Represents artists and groups; currently handles 3 acts. Receives 10-25% commission. Reviews material for acts.
How to Contact: Submit demo tape. Prefers 7½ ips reel-to-reel or cassette with 2-6 songs on demo. "We are looking primarily for C&W artists and songs with strong hooks and crossover potential." SASE. Reports in 1 month.
Music: Bluegrass, C&W, folk, gospel and MOR. Works primarily with country vocalists, country bands, MOR vocalists and bluegrass artists.

LOGSDON ASSOCIATES, Box 137, New Providence PA 17560. (717)284-2063. President: Paul K. Logsdon. Management firm and booking agency. Represents artists, groups, songwriters and a sound company. Represents local artists who also tour nationally; currently handles 5 acts. Receives 15-20% commission. Reviews material for acts.
How to Contact: Query by mail, submit demo tape and lead sheet. Prefers cassette with 1-4 songs on demo. SASE. Reporting time varies—"usually 3 weeks."
Music: Gospel rock, contemporary Christian music with pop, rock, or jazz-rock feel. Works primarily with Christian rock artists; groups with a mellow to progressive rock style (ala Steely Dan), able to play the college circuit, 'Jesus Festivals,' conventions and related outlets. Current acts include Glad (5 man band; jazz/pop/rock blend); Lilly Green (mellow contemporary soloist); and Daybreak (6 man band; pop/rock).
Tips: "Material must have Christian appeal (not 'churchy,' but morality conscious) and be inspirational or uplifting in attitude. The best example of what we are looking for is 'Bezond A Star,' by Glad on Myrrh Records (Word, Inc., MSB-6634)."

RON LUCIANO MUSIC CO., Box 263, Hasbrouck Heights NJ 07604. (201)288-8935. President: Ron Luciano. Management firm and booking agency. Represents artists, group and recording/speciality acts; currently handles 7-8 acts. Receives 10-20% commission. Reviews material for artists.
How To Contact: Query or submit picture and biography. Prefers 7½ ips reel-to-reel or cassette with 4-8 songs on demo. "Can also approach by sending a copy of their record release." SASE. Reports in 2-6 weeks.
Music: Disco; MOR; rock; soul; and top 40/pop. Works with 4- 5- piece,self-contained groups "that play in Holiday Inn, Sheratons, etc. We also book a lot of oldie groups like the Belmonts and Flamingos." Current acts include Voyage (top 40/disco); Legz (rock 'n' roll); and Charles Lamont.

RICHARD LUTZ ENTERTAINMENT AGENCY, 5625 0 St., Lincoln NE 68510. (402)483-2241. General Manager: Cherie Hanfelt. Management firm and booking agency. Represents individuals and groups; currently handles 220 acts. Receives 15% minimum commission.
How to Contact: Query by phone or submit demo tape and lead sheet. Prefers cassette with 5-10 songs on demo. SASE. Reports in 1 week.
Music: C&W, dance oriented, MOR and top 40/pop. Works primarily with show and dance bands. Current acts include Cottonwood (C&W/pop); Charlie Bandy & Fourcast (C&W); and Autumn (top 40/pop).

McMEEN TALENT AGENCY, Rt. 3, Hillsboro Rd., Franklin TN 37064. (615)794-8582. President: John McMeen. Booking agency. Represents individuals and groups; currently handles 7 acts. Receives 15-20% commission. Reviews material for acts.
How to Contact: Submit deMo tape and lyric sheet. Prefers 7½ ips reel-to-reel or cassette with 2-6 songs on demo. SASE. Reports in 1 month.
Music: C&W and progressive (country). Works primarily with show bands and vocalists. Current acts include Jeanne Pruett, The Capitals, Ronnie Robins, B.J. Thomas, Ray Price, Freddie Weller and Tommy Jennings.

McWING MANAGEMENT, INC., Charlotte NC 28205. (704)372-9563. President: Mike Wingate. Vice President: Mick McClelland. Management firm and booking agency. Represents artists and groups; currently handles 100 acts. Receives 15-20% commission. Reviews material for acts.
How to Contact: Query by mail. Prefers cassette with 3-10 songs on demo. SASE. Reports in 2 weeks.

Music: Bluegrass, blues, C&W, jazz, rock and top 40/pop. Works primarily with C&W, country rock and hard rock bar bands, dance bands and groups. Current acts include Plum Hollow Band (progressive/bluegrass/country rock); Ronnie Reno (pop/country); and Billy Joe Crowe and Trottin Sally (country).

MAD MAN MANAGEMENT, Box 54, Man's Field TX 76063. (817)477-2897. President: James Michael Taylor. Management firm, booking agency, publisher and recording company. Represents individuals, groups and songwriters; currently handles 3 acts. Reviews material for acts.
How to Contact: Query, arrange personal interview, submit demo tape or submit demo tape and lead sheet. "Include bio, goals and photo." Prefers 7½ ips reel-to-reel or cassette with 1-12 songs on demo. SASE. Reports in 1 month.
Music: C&W; folk; and MOR. Current acts include TxH2O (Texas Water); Rick Babb (country single); and James Michael Taylor (singer/songwriter).

LEE MAGID, INC., Box 532, Malibu CA 90265. (213)858-7282. President: Lee Magid. Management firm and music publisher. Represents artists, groups, songwriters and comics, etc.; currently handles 10 acts. Receives 20-25% commission. Reviews material for acts.
How to Contact: Submit demo tape. Prefers cassette with 3-4 songs on demo. SASE. Reports in 3 weeks—"sometimes longer."
Music: Blues, C&W, gospel, jazz, R&B, rock and soul. Works primarily with self-contained and solo singers and instrumental jazz groups. Current acts include Lorez Alexandria (jazz vocalist); Ernie Andrews (pop/jazz vocalist); Rags Waldorf (rock/jazz vocalist and keyboard); and Big Joe Turner (blues).

MANAGEMENT VII, 1811 NE 53rd St., Fort Lauderdale FL 33308. (305)776-1004. President: Ramona Beri. Management agency. Represents artists and groups; currently represents 4 acts. Negotiates commission.
How to Contact: Arrange personal interview. Prefers 7½ ips reel-to-reel and cassette tape. SASE. Reports ASAP.
Music: C&W, disco (soft), MOR, rock and top 40/pop.

MARSAINT MUSIC, INC., 3809 Clematis Ave., New Orleans LA 70122. Management firm and publishing company. Represents artists, groups and songwriters; currently handles 10 acts. Receives 15-25% commission.
How To Contact: Submit demo tape only or demo tape and lead sheet. Prefers cassette with 1-5 songs on demo. SASE. Reports in 1 month.
Music: Blues; C&W; dance; folk; gospel; progressive; rock; soul; top 40/pop. Current acts include Allen Toussaint (R&B, progressive jazz); and Lee Dorsey (R&B, pop).

MARSH PRODUCTIONS, INC., 1704 West Lake St., Minneapolis MN 55408. (612)827-6141. President: Marshall Edelstein. Management firm, booking agency and promotion company. Represents artists and groups; currently handles 44 exclusive acts and 25 songwriters. Receives 15-20% commission. Reviews materials for acts.
How To Contact: Query, arrange personal interview, submit demo tape or submit demo tape and lead sheet. Prefers 7½ ips reel-to-reel or cassette with 3-6 songs on demo. SASE. Reports in 2-4 weeks.
Music: R&B, rock (all types), soul and top 40/pop. "We have eight fulltime agents who have all been in the rock industry; that's our specialty." Works with dance, bar and concert bands. Current acts include Fairchild Flight (hard rock); Gypsy (MOR); London (rock); and Dare Force (rock).

MASADA MUSIC, INC., 888 8th Ave., New York NY 10019. (212)757-1953. Vice President: Gene Heimlich. Management firm and production house. Deals with artists in East Coast region only. Represents artists, groups and songwriters; currently handles 3 acts. Receives 15% commission. Reviews material for acts.
How To Contact: Query or arrange personal interview. Prefers 7½ ips reel-to-reel with 2-5 songs on demo. SASE. Reports in 3 weeks.
Music: Blues; dance-oriented, easy listening, folk, jazz, MOR, progressive, R&B and soul. Works with singer-songwriters and self contained bands. Current acts include Diane Snow (contemporary); Tucker Smallwood (jazz); and Arlen Polk (contemporary country/blues/pop).

MASCARA SNAKE PRODUCTIONS (MSP), 1478 Crafton Blvd., Pittsburgh PA 15205. (412)921-1319. President: Bob Bishop. Management firm and production company. Represents artists, groups, songwriters, and producers; currently handles 15 acts. Receives 5-20% commission. Reviews material for acts.

How to Contact: Submit demo tape. Prefers cassette with 2-5 songs on demo. SASE. Reports in 3 weeks.
Music: Bluegrass, blues, C&W and rock (hard and soft). Works primarily with concert rock, C&W. Current acts include The Adams/Michaels Band (concert rock); Highway Ghost (country rock); and Gallery (concert rock).

MASTERSTAR MUSIC AND MPM PRODUCTIONS, Box 727, Sunnymead CA 92388. (714)653-3328. President: Daniel Porter. Management agency, booking agency and full services. Represents artists, musical groups and songwriters. "We prefer artists interested in management to be in Southern California; songwriters can be from anywhere." Currently handles 4 acts. "Commission on each contact is different." Reviews material for acts.
How to Contact: Query by mail. Prefers cassette with 1-5 songs on demo. SASE. Reports in 3 weeks.
Music: Blues, children's, church/religious, folk (rock), R&B, rock (soft) and top 40/pop. Works primarily with solo acts and combos for Class A clubs. Current act includes Susan Gift (adult comtemporary soloist with band).

MAXCY TALENT AGENCY, 50 Music Square W., Suite 102, Nashville TN 37203. (615)329-9671. President: Lee Maxcy. Management firm and booking agency. Estab. 1979. Represents groups in local area only; currently handles 12-15 acts. Receives 10-20% commission. Reviews material for acts.
How to Contact: Submit demo tape. Prefers 7½ ips reel-to-reel or cassette with 2-4 songs on demo. SASE. Reports in 2 weeks.
Music: R&B, soul and top 40/pop. Works primarily with club bands, college and high school groups. Current acts include Black Widow (7-piece black horn group); Jimmy Church (7-piece black horn group); and Contraband (9-piece horn group).
Tips: "We are looking for material for a high energetic 7-piece 3-horn black act, cross-over top 40/R&B."

MEADOWLARK VENTURES, Box 7218, Missoula MT 59807. (406)728-2180. President: Chris Roberts. Management firm and booking agency. Represents artists and groups in the western states; currently handles 85 acts. Receives 10-20% commission. Reviews material for acts.
How to Contact: Query by mail. Prefers cassette with 3-6 songs on demo. SASE. Reports in 3 weeks.
Music: Blues, C&W, jazz, MOR, R&B, rock (country, hard) and top 40/pop. Works primarily with dance and bar bands. Current acts include Dogwater (country rock); Seattle Rhythm Band (Latin jazz rock/reggae); and Stewball (folk).

JOHN MEDLAND PRODUCTIONS, 334 Dufferin St., Toronto, Ontario, Canada. (416)536-4882. President: John Medland. Represent local artists and musical groups; currently handles 2 acts. Receives 10-15% commission. Reviews material for acts.
How to Contact: Submit demo tape only. Prefers cassette with 1-5 songs on demo. SAE and International Reply Coupons. Reports in 1 month.
Music: Rock, top 40/pop and 50s R&R. Works primarily with full time traveling bands (bars, high schools, etc.). Current acts include Jeannie & The Rubies (50s R&R); Paul Saunders (jazzy club act); and Arthur Decco (power pop).

MEMNON TALENT CORP., Box 98, Forest Hills NY 11375. Contact: Krzysztof Z. Purzycki. Management agency. Represents artists and songwriters from anywhere; currently handles 5 acts. Receives 10-25% commission. Reviews material for acts.
How to Contact: Query by mail, then submit demo tape and lead sheet. Prefers cassette with 3-5 songs on demo. SASE. Reports in 1 month.
Music: Choral, classical, C&w, easy listening, jazz, MOR and top 40/pop. Works primarily with self-contained bands; individual artists must have their own back-up group. Current acts include Bobbie Roberson (C&W); Lee Conway (C&W); and Happy End (top 40/pop group).
Tips: "Be familiar with music in the field. Material should be commercial as well as artistic."

MERCANTILE PRODUCTIONS, Box 2271, Palm Springs CA 92263. (714)320-4848. President: Kent Fox. Management firm and booking agency. Represents artists, groups and songwriters; currently handles 2 acts. Receives 10-25% commission. Reviews material for acts.
How to Contact: Submit demo tape. Prefers cassette with 3-12 songs on demo. SASE. Reports in 1 month.
Music: C&W, easy listening, MOR and top 40/pop. Works primarily with bar bands.

MINIMUM MUSIC/JOSEPH CASEY MANAGEMENT, 739 Astor Station, Boston MA 02123. (617)545-6293. Contact: Joseph Casey. Management (US and International) booking for clubs, promoters, schools; video production and brokerage firm. Represents artists, groups and songwriters; currently handles 4 acts. Receives 15% commission; "All arrangements are particular to each artist's career needs." Reviews material for acts.
How to Contact: Submit demo tape. Prefers cassette with 2-6 songs on demo. SASE. Reports in 1 month.
Music: Dance-oriented (rock) and new wave. Works primarily with rock and new wave writers, and performers for touring and management/artist development. Current acts include The Neighborhoods (3-piece original rock band and recording group); Boys Life (young, 4-piece original rock band and recording group); and Willie Alexander (songwriter).

MONTCLAIR RECORDS, 13755 Bayliss Rd., Los Angeles CA 90049. A&R Director: L.Z. Dough. Management firm. Represents artists, groups and songwriters; currently handles 12 acts. Reviews material for acts.
How to Contact: Query by mail. Prefers cassette demo tape. Does not return unsolicited material. Reports in 1 week.
Music: Easy listening, R&B, rock, soul and top 40/pop.

RON MOSS MANAGEMENT, 11257 Blix St., North Hollywood CA 91602. (213)508-9865. Manager: Ron Moss. Management firm and jazz record label. Represents artists, groups and United Kingdom Record Company; currently handles 3 acts. Receives 15-20% commission. Reviews material for acts.
How to Contact: Query by mail, submit demo tape. Prefers 7½ ips reel-to-reel or cassette with 3-5 songs on demo "or 1 hit single. Include address and telephone number on cassettes." SASE. Reports in 3 weeks.
Music: Easy listening, jazz, MOR, progressive, rock (hard) and top 40/pop. Works primarily with pop and jazz fusion groups and crossover artists. Current acts include Korgis (top 40/pop); Walkie Talkies (top 40/pop); Al Vizzutti and Bunny Brunel Band (jazz); and Daniel Webster (rock)..

MOTOBOY MOTIONS, 1145 E. Hortter St., Philadelphia PA 19150. (215)424-3394. President: Alan Moss. Management firm, booking agency and promotor. Represents artists and groups. Receives 10-20% commission. "Most business commands the standard industry rates." Reviews material for acts.
How to Contact: Query by mail, arrange personal interview. "Include bio material." Prefers cassette with 2 songs minimum on demo. SASE. Reports in 3 weeks.
Music: Bluegrass, blues, C&W, dance-oriented, easy listening, folk, jazz, MOR, new wave, progressive, R&B, rock and top 40/pop. Works primarily with bar, club, and dance bands. Current acts include Chronicles (hard rock/new wave); Robin Rhythm (top 40 rock-cover and original); and Rob Sukol (single act-sometimes with backup group).

MR. I. MOUSE, LTD., 7876 Woodrow Wilson Dr., Los Angeles CA 90046. (213)650-5930. President: Ira Bracker. Management firm. Represents artists, groups and songwriters; currently handles 5 acts. Receives 20% commission. Reviews material for acts.
How to Contact: Submit demo tape or phone about your interest. Prefers 7½ or 15 ips half- or quarter-track reel-to-reel or cassette with any number songs on demo. SASE. Reports in 1 week.
Music: MOR and top 40/pop. Works primarily with contemporary chart attractions. Current acts include Curves (pop); Leroy Gamez (pop); Gene Clark; Savoy Brown (rock); and Mzzouri Foxx (pop).

MOUSEVILLE NOSTALGIA, 5218 Almont St., Los Angeles CA 90032. (213)223-2860. President: Mr. Perez. Management firm, recording firm. "We sponsor, refer and represent only specialized oldies-but-goodies acts for rock 'n roll revue concert specials and other areas of live entertainment." Estab. 1978. Represents artists, groups, songwriters, "exclusively 1950s/early 60s oldies-but-goodies nostalgia, rock-a-billy and surf performers; and instrumental and instrumental surf sounds from the 50s and early 60s." Receives 20-25% commission, also negotiable union contracts. Reviews material for acts.
How to Contact: Query, submit demo tape only or demo tape and lead sheet or promo kit, etc., with any current single or album. Prefers cassette with 6-12 songs on demo. "Studios, A&Rs, recording labels, agents, managers and producers are invited to call, write or wire direct anytime." SASE. Reports in 1 week.
Music: Deep blues; R&B; children's; C&W (plus 1950s rock-a-billy rock); folk (and folk-rock); MOR; polka; rock (all 1950s through 1960s varied styles and sounds, oldies but goodies vintage); soul; top 40/pop; Hawaiian; Polynesian; Latin; mid 60s British Mersey and Liverpool R&R

sounds; surf; instrumentals; pop; standards; doo-wop; ballads; novelty tunes; cinema—cartoon soundtracks; and commercials/jingles.

MPL ASSOCIATES, LTD., Box 2108, Pheonix AZ 85001. President: Louis P. Goldstein. Management firm. Represents artists and songwriters; currently handles 2 acts. Commission negotiable. Reviews material for acts.
How to Contact: Submit demo tape and lead sheet. Prefers cassette with 1-5 songs on demo. "Be sure that any tapes submitted have clear vocals and be sure to include a lead sheet for each song . . . and a current picture if possible." SASE. Reports within 2 weeks to 1 month.
Music: C&W, easy listening, MOR and top 40/pop. Works primarily with songwriters and songwriting performers. Current acts include Jack Wright and Keira Hayes (songwriting performers).

ALEXANDER MURPHY, 508 Penn Square Bldg., Filbert & Juniper Sts., Philadelphia PA 19107. (215)567-2050. Contact: Alexander Murphy. Management firm and entertainment attorney. Represents artists, groups, songwriters end record company. Receives 15-20% commission. Reviews material for acts.
How to Contact: Query by mail, submit demo tape and lyric sheet. Prefers cassette with 1-3 songs on demo. "Include background information and reviews, if any." SASE. Reports in 1 month.
Music: Easy listening, Jazz, MOR, progressive, rock (country and mainstream) and top 40/pop. Works with singer/songwriters and original material bands only. Current acts include John Flynn (singer/songwriter); Reverie (jazz group); B.B. Jackson Band (country/R&B/rock group); Bad Sneakers (pop); and Johnny Neel Band (southern rock).

THE MUSIC MANAGEMENT COMPANY, 2729 Lake City Way, Burnaby, British Columbia, Canada V5A 2Z6. (604)420-3404. President: Donald W. Marsh. Management agency. Represents artists in Western Canada and the US; currently handles 4 acts. Receives 10-25% commission. Reviews material for acts.
Music: Submit demo tape and lead sheet. Prefers 7½ ips reel-to-reel or cassette with 3-6 songs on demo. "Most of our clients are female. Songs should suit female artists. We desire strong single material. Keep demos clean. Clear, clean recording. Lyric sheet with lead sheet." SAE and International Reply Coupons. Reports in 1 month.
Music: C&W, MOR and top 40/pop. Works primarily with "star" potential artists (mostly female) and "class' concert and show lounge class artists. "All should be recording artists or have recording potential." Current acts include Lynne Donovan (soft rock artists with 3-6 piece band); Vicki Roe (country artist); and Wanda Mundy (country/blues artist).
Tips: "Unless writer has established hits, music should be available for publishing. This company is also established in music publishing and record production. Any songs we accept will most likely be recorded. Our quality standards are high but all tapes will be listened to carefully. American and Candian writers welcomed."

MUSKRAT PRODUCTIONS, INC., 44 N. Central Ave., Elmsford NY 10523. (914)592-3144. Contact: Linda Simpson. Represents individuals and groups; currently represents 11 acts. Deals with artists in the New York City area. Reviews material for acts.
How to Contact: Query. Prefers cassette with 3 songs minimum on tape. SASE. Reports "only if interested."
Music: "We specialize in old-time jazz and banjo music and shows." Works primarily with dixieland, banjo/sing-along groups to play parties, dances, shows and conventions. Current acts include Smith Street Society Jazz Band (dixieland jazz); Your Father's Mustache (banjo sing-along); and Harry Hepcat and the Boogie Woogie Band ('50s rock revival).

MUTUAL MANAGEMENT ASSOCIATES/COMSTOCK RECORDS, Box 3247, Shawnee KS 66203. (913)631-6060. General Manager: Frank Fara. Management agency, music publisher, record producer and promotion firm. Represents artists, musical groups and songwriters primarily from Canada and the US; currently handles 30 acts. Receives 10-15% commission. Reviews material for acts.
How to Contact: Check by phone for specific needs, then arrange personal interview or submit demo tape only. Prefers cassette with 1-5 songs on demo. "After phone call, submit bio, tape, photo, etc." SASE. Reports in 2 weeks.
Music: C&W, gospel and pop. Works primarily with 2-6 member self-contained groups for concert or club appearances primarily in support of artists' record releases in the U.S. and Canada. Current acts include The O'Roark Brothers (country show/dance act-high energy); Doc & Dusty Holliday (country/pop Duo); Steve Gray & Jubilation (contemporary gospel); and Kathy Tate/Kenny Sumnit Group (pop/country).

NIGHTSTREAM MUSIC, 634 Washington Rd., Pittsburgh PA 15228. (412)561-7111. General Manager: Sam Balistreri. Management firm and music publisher. Represents artists, groups and songwriters; currently handles 7 acts. Receives 10-20% commission. Reviews material for acts.
How to Contact: Query by mail, submit demo tape and lead sheet. Prefers cassette with 1-5 songs on demo. SASE. Reports in 1 month.
Music: Blues, C&W, dance-oriented, MOR, progressive, R&B, rock and top 40/pop. Works primarily with lounge groups and singers. Current acts include Nightstream (lounge band); Tom Balistreri (singer-lounge and concert); Estamira (rock band); Graystone (R&B act); and Gary Gallagher (songwriter).

NOVA ENTERTAINMENT, INC., Box 521173, Miami FL 33152. (305)551-1866. President: Thomas Chelko. Estab. 1980. Represents musical groups from anywhere; currently handles 2 acts. Receives 5-15% commission. Reviews material for acts.
How to Contact: Query by mail. Prefers cassette with 3-6 songs on demo. SASE. Reports in 2 weeks.
Music: C&W, dance-oriented, easy listening, MOR, rock (mellow) and top 40/pop. Works primarily with nightclub dance bands. Current acts include KB (country); and Feather (top 40).

NORTHEAST PRODUCTIONS, LTD., Box 555, Bristol VT 05443. (802)453-2411. President: Steven C. Wyer. Management firm and production company. Represents artists, groups and songwriters; currently handles 5 acts. Receives 10-20% commission. Reviews material for acts.
How to Contact: Query by mail, then submit demo tape. Prefers cassette with 3-5 songs on demo. "Include bio material." Does not return unsolicited material. Reports in 1 month.
Music: Church/religious, folk, gospel, R&B and top 40/pop. Works primarily with contemporary Christian music, soloists or bands. Current acts include Steve Camp (pop gospel); Howard McCrery (R&B/soul); and Janet Sweetland (gospel/folk).

NORTH-SOUTH ARTSCOPE, 1914 White Plains Rd., Chapel Hill NC 27514. (919)929-5508. Personal Representative: Mary Nordstrom. Personal representative of performing artists and attractions. Represents artists, groups, conductors and music directors; currently handles 8 acts. Receives 10-20% commission. "We charge an annual career development fee for artists or ensembles with concert fees below $2,500."
How to Contact: Query by mail, arrange personal interview. Prefers cassette with 2-4 songs on demo. Does not return unsolicited material. Reports in 1 month "or more."
Music: Classical and contemporary. Works primarily with chamber music ensembles, classical music soloists and special attractions featuring classical music. Current acts include Boaz Sharon (piano soloist/recitalist); Christopher Berg (classical guitar soloist/recitalist); and the Guillaume Piano Duo (concert/recital).
Tips: "If you already have a publisher who needs outstanding musicians to record promotional material we are interested in mutual benefits at moderate performance fees for recording purposes."

ONSTAGE MANAGEMENT, INC., 3227 River Dr., Columbia SC 29201. (803)765-0087. Agent: Key Thrasher. Booking agency. Deals with regional individuals in North and South Carolina and Georgia. Represents artists and groups; currently handles 4 acts. Receives 10-15% commission.
How to Contact: Query. Prefers cassette with 3-6 songs on demo. SASE. Reports in 2 weeks.
Music: Bluegrass; folk; jazz (progressive); rock (country); and top 40/pop. Works primarily with acoustic artists, club bands, country rock and rock groups. Current acts include Corbett/Urquia (light rock); Rob Crosby (country rock group); Victor Jory (top 40/rock and roll); and Backbone (rock & roll).

OPERATION MUSIC ENTERPRISES, 233 W. Woodland Ave., Ottumwa IA 52501. (515)682-8283. President: Nada C. Jones. Management and booking agency. Represents artists and groups; currently handles 6 acts. Receives 10% minimum commission. Reviews material for acts.
How to Contact: Submit demo tape and lead sheet. Prefers cassette as demo. "Lyrics should be clear; melodies simple." SASE. Reports in 1 month.
Music: C&W, blues, gospel and R&B. Works primarily with show groups. Current acts include Reesa Kay Jones (country show); John Richards (country/easy listening show); and Badlands (country show/dance).

ORANGE BLOSSOM PRODUCTIONS, 380 Lexington Ave., Suite 1119, New York NY 10017. (212)687-9000. President: Douglas Tuchman. Booking agency and production company. Represents groups; currently handles 6 acts. Receives 15% commission. Reviews material for acts.

How to Contact: Submit demo tape of performance recorded "live." Prefers 7½ ips reel-to-reel or cassette with 4-8 songs on demo. "Make package as complete as possible." SASE. Reports in 2 weeks.

Music: Bluegrass and C&W. Works primarily with touring bluegrass bands. Current acts include Bill Harrell and The Virginians (bluegrass band); Fly By Night String Band (traditional country music); John Herald Band (bluegrass); and The Seldom Scene (bluegrass band).

ORGANIC MANAGEMENT, 745 5th Ave., New York NY 10022. (212)751-3400. Contact: A&R Director. Management and record company.

How to Contact: Submit demo tape and lyric sheet. Prefers cassette with 1-3 songs on demo. SASE. Reports in 1 month "or more."

Music: Blues; R&B; rock; and top 40/pop.

ORPHEUS ENTERTAINMENT, Box 213, Vauxhall NJ 07088. (201)677-1090. Contact: A&R Department. Management and booking agency and production company. Represents artists, groups and songwriters; currently handles 15 acts. Receives 10-20% commission. Reviews material for acts.

How to Contact: Query by mail, then submit demo tape and lead sheet. Prefers cassette with 2-6 songs on demo. Does not return unsolicited material. Reports in 1 month.

Music: Jazz, MOR, progressive, R&B, rock, soul, top 40/pop and fusion. Works primarily with national and regional recording and concert artists. Current acts include Teruo Nakamura and The Rising Sun Band (fusion/progressive rock); Jimmy Ponder (guitar jazz); and Michal Urbaniak and UBX (fusion/jazz).

P. D. Q. DIRECTIONS, INC., 1474 N. Kings Rd., Los Angeles CA 90048. (213)656-4870. President: Leo Leichter. Management agency and production company. Represents artists and musical groups from anywhere; currently handles 5 acts. Receives 15-25% commission. Reviews material for acts (cassettes and videos only).

How to Contact: Submit demo tape and lead sheet. Prefers cassette with 4-6 songs on demo. Does not return unsolicited material. Reports in 1 month.

Music: C&W, rock (country), top 40/pop and MOR. Current acts include Johnny Guitar Watson (R&B); Herman Brood (rock); and Society of Seven (MOR).

Tips: "Artists should be earning at least $100,000/year and have strong work experience and professional stage presence."

RANDALL PARR ORGANIZATION, LTD., 411 E. Crosstimbers, Houston TX 77022. (713)691-6151. Director of Promotions: Randall Parr. Booking agency. Represents artists and groups; currently handles 10 acts. Receives 10-25% commission. Reviews material for acts.

How to Contact: Query by mail. Prefers cassette with 3-7 songs on demo. SASE. Reports in 1 month.

Music: C&W, dance-oriented, easy listening, jazz, MOR, R&B, rock (new wave and hard), soul and top 40/pop. Works primarily with national dance/show groups and artists. Current acts include Scott St. John & Nightwatch (show band); All Carte; Axxis (jazz/pop); and Boyer Twins (country).

PATHFINDER MANAGEMENT, INC., Box 30166, Memphis TN 38130. (901)324-5385. Executive Secretary: Naomi McGowan. Management firm. Represents individuals, groups and songwriters. Administers Abe and Goldwax Records. Receives 15-20% commission. Reviews material for arts.

How to Contact: Submit demo tape and lead sheet. Prefers 7½ ips reel-to-reel or cassette with 1-4 songs on demo. SASE. Reports in 1 month.

Music: Blues; church/religious; gospel; rock; soul; and top 40/pop. Works primarily with dance bands. Current acts include Sugar Bush (5-piece rock band) and Shawn Von Bull (male vocalist).

HARRY PEEBLES AGENCY, Box 1324, Kansas City KS 66117. (913)596-1220. Owner: Harry Peebles. Booking agency. Represents individuals and groups; currently handles 3 acts. Receives 15% minimum commission.

How to Contact: Submit demo tape with photos and bio. Prefers cassette or 8-track cartridge with 3 songs minimum on tape. SASE. Reports in 6 months.

Music: C&W. Works primarily with show bands for fairs and celebrations. Current acts include Sherwin Linton (C&W); The Castle Family (MOR); and The Ark Valley Boys (country).

PELICAN PRODUCTIONS, Room 10, 3700 East Ave., Rochester NY 14618. President: Peter Morticelli. Management firm and booking agency. Represents artists and groups from upstate

New York; currently handles 2 acts. Receives 15-25% commission. Reviews material for acts.
How to Contact: Query or submit demo tape. Prefers cassette with 3-6 songs on demo. SASE.
Reports in 1 month.
Music: Rock (all kinds) and top 40/pop. Works with "any type of act as long as the songwriting
ability is very strong." Currently represents Duke Jupiter (original rock artist) and The Rods
(heavy metal trio).

PERFECTION LIGHT PRODUCTIONS, Box 690, San Francisco CA 94101. (415)626-0655.
Vice President: Gregory DiGiovine. Management agency and production company. Represents
artists, groups and producers in Northern California; currently handles 4 acts. Receives negotiable
commission. Reviews material for acts.
How to Contact: Query by mail, then submit demo tape and lyric sheet. Prefers cassette with 1-4
songs on demo. Does not return unsolicited material.
Music: Dance-oriented, R&B, rock, soul and top 40/pop. Works primarily with R&B/pop solo
artists and groups. Current acts include Narada Michael Walden, Wanda Walden and Uncle
Rainbow & Visions (R&B/pop).

RITA CARTER PERRY, Box 12241, Jacksonville FL 32209. (904)642-0530. President: Rita Carter
Perry. Management firm and booking agency. Deals with artists in Southeastern region only.
Represents artists, groups and songwriters; currently handles 6 acts. Receives 10-20% commission.
How to Contact: Query or submit demo tape and lead sheet. Prefers 7½ ips reel-to-reel with 3-10
songs on demo. SASE. Reports in 1 month.
Music: Blues; church/religious; dance; gospel; jazz; MOR; rock; soul; and top 40/pop. Works
with horn sections, jazz and disco bands, soul, rock and pop self contained units and single artists.
Current acts include The Terry Perry Horns; The Jazz Keynotes (jazz); Sun City Jazz Band
(jazz/rock); Kenobe (soul/rock); Nathaniel Huff (gospel); and KUDU (pop/soul/rock).

THE JOE PHILLIPS ORGANIZATION, Box 5981, Greenville SC 29607. President: Joe Phillips.
Management and booking agency and record producer. Represents artists, groups and song-
writers; currently handles 3 acts. Receives negotiable commission. Reviews material for acts.
How to Contact: Query by mail, then submit demo tape and lead sheet. Prefers cassette with any
number of songs on demo. SASE. Reports in 1 month.
Music: Classical, easy listening and MOR. Current acts include Joe Phillips (MOR soloist); N.
Phillips (songwriter); and M. Spade (songwriter).

PINNACLE PRODUCTIONS, INC., Box 40662, Nashville TN 37204. Contact: Tommy Overstreet. Management agency, music publisher and record producer. Represents artists, musical
groups and songwriters from anywhere; currently handles 7 acts. Receives 10-15% commission.
Reviews material for acts.
How to Contact: Query by mail, arrange personal interview or submit demo tape or demo tape and
lead sheet. Prefers 7½ ips reel-to-reel or cassette with 1-5 songs on demo. "It's best to write and
submit tape; we will arrange future appointment if we're interested." Does not return unsolicited
material. Reports in 2 weeks.
Music: C&W, MOR, rock and top 40/pop. "I work with mainly show groups and individuals who
are working fulltime as performers but also want to record. They *must* be professionals, and willing
to listen." Current acts include Tommy Overstreet (singer/songwriter); Darrell Dodson (singer/
songwriter); and Susan St. Marie (singer).

PIZAZZ PRODUCTIONS, 35 Hambly Ave., Toronto, Ontario, Canada M4E 2R5 (416)699-3359.
Manager: Craig Nicholson. Management agency. Represents musical groups and songwriters
from anywhere; currently handles 10 acts. Receives 12-25% commission. Reviews material for acts.
How to Contact: Submit demo tape only. Prefers cassette with 2-4 songs on demo. SAE and
International Reply Coupons. Reports in 1 month.
Music: MOR and top 40/pop. Works primarily with adult-oriented pop/top 40 show groups with
recording contracts with independent labels and producers. Current acts include Crackers (original rock); Spring Fever (top 40/pop group with vocal harmony); Mama Coco (top 40/pop group
with vocal harmony); and The Cases (power pop).

PLAIN GREAT ENTERTAINMENT CORPORATION, 6525 Sunset Blvd., Suite 8, Hollywood
CA 90028. (213)469-3936. Executive Vice President/General Manager: Ron Henry. Management
agency and music publisher. Estab. 1980. Represents artists, musical groups and songwriters in
Southern California; currently handles 9 acts. Receives 15-20% commission. Reviews material for
acts.
How to Contact: Submit demo tape only. Prefers cassette with 2-6 songs on demo. SASE. Reports
in 3 weeks.

Music: C&W, easy listening, jazz, MOR, progressive, rock and top 40/pop. Works primarily with vertically creative artists who compose their own material." Current acts include Moon Martin (pop/rock); Susie Allanson (pop/country/NC); Billy Cioffi (rock/pop); and Scott Richardson (pop/rock).

JERRY PLANTZ PRODUCTIONS, 1703 Wyandotte, Kansas City MO 64108. (816)471-1501. Agent: Jerry Plantz. Sub-Agents: Rex Calhoun, Cheryl Reimal. Management firm and booking agency. Represents individuals, groups and songwriters from Missouri, Kansas, Iowa and Nebraska; currently handles 50 acts. Receives 10-20% commission.
How to Contact: Query by phone or submit demo tape and lyric sheet. Include complete press kit. Prefers cassette with 10-15 songs on demo. SASE. Reports in 1 month.
Music: Bluegrass, blues, children's, classical, C&W, dance-oriented, folk, jazz, MOR, progressive, rock, soul and top 40/pop. Works primarily with dance bands. Current acts include Danny Byrd (C&W); Morganna (Baseball's Kissing Bandit); and Jimmy Dixon (illusionist).

PREFERRED ARTIST MANAGEMENT, INC., 9701 Taylorsville Rd., Louisville KY 40299. (502)267-5466. Vice President: Dan Green. Secretary: David H. Snowden. Management agency. Deals with artists in eastern United States and Midwest states. Represents artists and groups; currently handles 6 acts. Receives 10-25% commission. Reviews material for acts.
How to Contact: Query or submit demo tape and lead sheet. Prefers cassette with 3-5 songs on demo. SASE. Reports in 2 weeks.
Music: Dance, rock (funk, medium) and top 40/pop. Works with bar artists ranging from bar bands to both single and group concert acts. Current acts include Free Fall (rock/show act); New Horizon (country/blue grass); Ambush (original artists) and Peaches (MOR/original).

PRO TALENT CONSULTANTS, Box 29543, Atlanta GA 30359. (404)424-1684. Coordinator/Product Manager: John Eckert/Glenn Elliott. Management agency and public relations firm. Represents artists, groups and songwriters; currently handles 7 acts. Receives 15-20% commission. Reviews material for acts.
How to Contact: Submit demo tape. Prefers cassette with 4-6 songs on demo. SASE. Reports in 2 weeks.
Music: C&W, folk, jazz, MOR, rock (top 40/country) and top 40/pop. Works primarily with bar bands, novelty/comedy acts and top 40 club bands. Current acts include Glenn Elliott Band (rock group); Tristan (vocal group); and Simeaul (artist/songwriter).

PROCESS TALENT MANAGEMENT, 439 Wiley Ave., Franklin PA 16323, (814)432-4633. Contact: Norman Kelly. Management agency. Represents artists and groups; currently handles 20 acts. Receives 10-15% commission. Reviews material for acts.
How to Contact: Query. Prefers 7½ ips reel-to-reel, cassette or 8-track cartridge with 2-6 songs on demo. SASE. Reports in 2 weeks.
Music: Bluegrass; blues; C&W; dance; folk; gospel; jazz; MOR; polka; progressive; rock; soul; and top 40/pop. Works with C&W artists (70%), gospel (10%) and pop/rock etc. (20%). Current acts include Junie Lou (C&W); Debbie Sue (C&W); Glen Lucas Family (gospel); Bonnie Baldwin (C&W); Virge Brown (C&W) and Tessa Carol (soul and jazz).

PROS FROM DOVER, Box 1211, Beverly Hills CA 90213. Vice President, Operations: Donovan Moore. Management agency. Represents artists, groups and songwriters in Beverly Hills; currently handles 4 acts. Receives 10-20% commission. Reviews material for acts.
How to Contact: Submit demo tape and lead sheet. Prefers cassette with 2-4 songs on demo. SASE. Reports in 3 weeks.
Music: Gospel. Current acts include TIL (country); Solid State and The Redeemed (gospel).

ROBERT RAYMOND MANAGEMENT, 15312 Longbow Dr., Sherman Oaks CA 91403. (213)995-8999. Contact: Robert Raymond. Management agency. Represents artists, groups and songwriters; currently handles 7 acts. Receives 15% minimum commission. Reviews material for acts.
How to Contact: Query by mail, then submit demo tape and lead sheet. Prefers cassette with 3-7 songs on demo. SASE. Reports in 3 weeks.
Music: Rock (all types)and top 40/pop. Works primarily with recording artists. Current acts include Night, Boatz and Marty Kristian (rock).

THE RECORD COMPANY OF THE SOUTH (RCS), 5220 Essen Ln, Baton Rouge LA 70898. (504)766-3233. Vice President/General Manager: John Fred. Management agency, music publisher and record company. Represents artists, groups and songwriters; currently handles 5 acts.

Receives 20-25% commission. Reviews material for acts.
How to Contact: Submit demo tape and lyric sheet. Prefers cassette with 2-6 songs on demo. SASE. Reports in 6 weeks.
Music: C&W, R&B, rock, soul and top 40/pop. Works primarily with artists, bands and songwriters. Current acts include Irma Thomas (top 40/pop and R&B); Luther Kent (top 40/pop and R&B); Butch Hornsby (country); and Floyd Brown (pop/country).

REDBEARD PRESENTS PRODUCTIONS, LTD., 1061 E. Flamingo Rd., Box 19114, Las Vegas NV 89119. (702)739-6494. President: Robert Leonard. Management firm, booking agency, production company and music publisher. Represents individuals, groups and songwriters; currently handles 12 acts. Receives 10-15% commission. Reviews material for acts.
How to Contact: Query or submit demo tape and lyric sheet. Prefers cassette with 4-12 songs on demo. "It is most helpful if the artist or group can arrange for me to see them work." SASE. Reports in 3 weeks.
Music: Blues; dance; jazz; MOR; progressive; rock (soft or country); soul; and top 40/pop. Works primarily with jazz "names"; Latin show and dance bands; rock 'n roll show groups; and Las Vegas show groups. Current acts include Karen Nelson (RCA-Finland Records and Chameleon Records); Marlena Shaw (Columbia Blue Note Records); Timi Yuro (United Artists and Mercury Records); Odia Coates (RCA Victor Records); and Doris Troy (Brunswick Records).
Tips: "Group should be costumed, choreographed, double instruments, and contain plenty of group vocals for Nevada and Atlantic City work."

REDWOOD PROMOTIONS, 2 Hawkes Ave., Ossining NY 10562. (914)762-2867. Contact: Red Brigham or Marianne Burguiere. Booking agency and promotions firm. Represents artists from the US. Receives 10-15% commission. Reviews material for acts.
How to Contact: Query by mail. Prefers 7½ ips reel-to-reel or cassette with 3-6 songs on demo. SASE.
Music: Bluegrass and C&W. "We are primarily a promotional company. We do some booking of acts locally and nationally but they are usually booked to work on our own shows. Red Brigham (country artist) is the only act we represent."

REED SOUND RECORDS, INC., 120 Mikel Dr., Summerville SC 29483. (803)873-3324. Contact: Haden Reed. Management agency. Represents artists; currently handles 3 acts. Receives 2-4% commission. Reviews material for acts.
How to Contact: Query by mail. Prefers cassette with 1-3 songs on demo. SASE. Reports in 1 month.
Music: C&W, easy listening and gospel. Current acts include Becky Knowles and The Country Blues; Haden Reed (songwriter/country); Vocalettes (gospel); and Country Blues (show band).

MICHAEL REGENSTREIF MANAGEMENT, 200 Kensington, Suite 510, Westmount, Quebec, Canada H3Z 2G7. (514)935-5066. President: Mike Regenstreif. Management agency and booking agency. Represents artists, musical groups and songwriters from anywhere; currently handles 5 acts. Receives 15-20% commission. Reviews material for acts.
How to Contact: Submit demo tape and lead sheet. Prefers cassette with 4-10 songs on demo. SAE and International Reply Coupons. Reports in 1 month.
Music: Bluegrass, blues, children's, C&W, easy listening, folk, jazz, MOR, rock (light) and top 40/pop. Works primarily with acoustic-oriented singer/songwriters and concert artists. Current acts include Priscilla Herdman (contemporary folk/pop interpreter); Mason Oaring and Jeanie Stahl (singer/songwriters); and Martin Grosswendt (blues singer).
Tips: "We tend towards recording artists straddling the folk and adult pop markets. Artists must offer something unique and interesting that differentiates them from anyone else."

GEORGE RICHEY MANAGEMENT CO., 6 Music Circle N., Nashville TN 37203. (615)254-9605. Manager: John Paule. Managment agency. Estab. 1980. Represents local musical groups; currently handles 2 acts. Receives 15-25% commission. Reviews material for acts.
How to Contact: Query by mail, then submit demo tape only. Prefers 7½ ips reel-to-reel or cassette with 2-4 songs on demo. SASE. Reports in 3 weeks to 1 month.
Music: C&W, MOR and rock (country). Works primarily with club bands. Current acts include Tammy Wynette (country); Wightstreets (country); and Skin Deep (rock).

RNJ PRODUCTIONS, INC., 11514 Calvert St., North Hollywood CA 91606. President: Rein Neggo Jr. Vice President: Roger Montesano. Management firm. Represents professional individuals and groups; currently handles 6 acts. Receives 15-20% commission.
How to Contact: Submit demo tape and lead sheet. Prefers 7½ ips reel-to-reel or cassette with 1-3

songs on demo. SASE. "Material is reviewed monthly."
Music: Folk; MOR; and top 40/pop. Works primarily with artists for concerts and tours. Current acts include Glenn Yarbrough (pop/folk artist with 9-piece back-up band); the Limeliters (folk group); and Mike Settle (singer/songwriter).

ROCK HARD, INC., 13010 W. 30th Dr., Golden CO 80401. (303)278-8367. Contact: Barry Higgins or Mike Walsh. Management agency and production company. Represents artists, groups and songwriters; currently handles 8 acts. Receives 20% minimum commission. Reviews material for acts.
How to Contact: Query by mail, then arrange personal interview or submit demo tape. Prefers cassette as demo. SASE. Reports in 1 month.
Music: All types. Works primarily with original rock groups and country acts. Current acts include Attack! (rock 'n' roll); Chriss Voss (rock); Capa City (rock); and The Paul Wayne Band (country).

RODANCA MUSIC, 3627 Park Ave., Memphis TN 38111. (901)454-0300. Music publisher. Represents songwriters from anywhere; currently handles 40 acts. Receives standard royalty. Reviews material for acts.
How to Contact: Submit demo tape and lead sheet. Prefers 7½ ips reel-to-reel or cassette with 4 songs on demo. Does not return unsolicited material. Reports in 2 weeks.
Music: Gospel and R&B.

JEFFREY ROSS MUSIC, Box 5943, Portland OR 97208. (503)281-8322. Contact: Jeffrey Ross or Jan Charkow. Management agency. Represents artists, groups and songwriters; currently handles 3 acts. Receives 15% minimum commission. Reviews material for acts.
How to Contact: Submit demo tape. Prefers cassette with 4-6 songs on demo. SASE. Reports in 3 weeks.
Music: Jazz, progressive, R&B, soul and top 40/pop. Works primarily with touring bands with members that write their own music. Current acts include Jeff Lorber Fusion (jazz/R&B fusion); Jeff Lorber (songwriter); Kenny Gorelick (writer/multi-reedist); and Danny Wilson (writer/bassist).
Tips: "It is important to set your goals based on what you do best. If you write well in a certain idiom, concentrate and develop what you do best before trying other directions. A strong intention to be successful in this business is fueled by acquired knowledge of how the music business operates."

RAY ROYAL AGENCY, One Fairway Plaza, Suite 311, Huntingdon Valley PA 19006. (215)947-7743. Represents artists, musical groups and songwriters from anywhere; currently handles 17 acts. Receives 15-20% commission. Reviews material for acts.
How to Contact: Query by mail, then submit demo tape and lyric sheet. Prefers 7½ ips reel-to-reel or cassette with 1-5 songs on demo. SASE. Reports in 1 month.
Music: Bluegrass, C&W, dance-oriented, folk, gospel, MOR, progressive, rock (hard and country), and top 40/pop. Works primarily with solo performers and bar bands. Current acts include John Gill (soloist, singer, guitarist); Master Jam (club band); and Mister Quick (country rock).

ROYAL T MUSIC, Box 946, Springtown TX 76082. (817)433-5720. President: James Michael Taylor. Management and booking agency and music publisher. Represents local artists, groups and songwriters, but "considers material from anyone, anywhere;" currently handles 3 acts. Receives 10-15% commission. Reviews material for acts.
How to Contact: Query by mail, then submit demo tape and lyric sheet. Prefers cassette with any number of songs on demo. "Include photo and statement of goals.". SASE. Reports in 1 month.
Music: Bluegrass, blues, choral, C&W, folk, MOR, progressive, Spanish, R&B, rock (any), soul (any) and top 40/pop. Works primarily with bar and folk bands for colleges; rock and pop bands that can do concert work. Current acts include TxH2o (Texas water) (country/pop trio); James Michael Taylor (contemporary folk single); and Honey Lake (pop/rock band).

DICK RUBIN, LTD., 60 W. 57th St., New York NY 10019. (212)541-6576. President: B. Richard Rubin. Management firm. Represents individuals and groups; currently handles 2 acts. Receives 10-15% commission.
How to Contact: Query. SASE. Reports in 1 month.
Music: Bluegrass; C&W; and progressive. Works primarily with show groups. Current acts include the Mission Mountain Wood Band.

RUNAWAY ENTERPRISES, 225 Central Park West, #702A, New York NY 1024. (212)580-1747. President: Nina Marson. Management and booking agency. Estab. 1980. Represents artists, groups and songwriters; currently handles 3 acts. Receives 10-20% commission. Reviews material for acts.

How to Contact: Query by mail. Prefers cassette with 3-5 songs on demo. SASE.

Music: C&W, dance-oriented, easy listening, progressive, rock, top 40/pop and unique. "We are mostly interested in mainstream." Works primarily with contemporary rock and roll bands. Current acts include Chris Spedding (rock and roll singer/songwriter, guitar player and producer); David Van Tieghem (solo drummer/percussionist); and Busta Jones (rock and roll/funk/singer/songwriter/bass player).

RUSTRON MUSIC PRODUCTIONS, 200 Westmoreland Ave., White Plains NY 10606. (914)946-1689. Artists' Consultant: Rusty Gordon. Composition Management: Ron Caruso. Management firm, booking agency, music publisher and record producer. Represents individuals, groups and songwriters; currently handles 8 acts. Receives 10-25% commission for management and/or booking only. Reviews material for acts.

How to Contact: Query, arrange personal interview, or submit in person or by mail demo tape and lead sheet. Prefers 7½ ips reel-to-reel or cassette with 3-6 songs on demo. SASE. Reports in 1 month.

Music: Blues (country & rock), C&W (rock, blues, progressive), easy listening (ballads), folk/rock (contemporary/topical), MOR (pop style), rock (folk/pop), top 40/pop and salsa/disco. Current acts include Gordon and Caruso (songwriter/producers); Rick McDonald (folk/rock singer/songwriter); Lois Britten (disco/rock/pop/singer/songwriter); Christian Camilo and the Tingalayo Rhythm Band (salsa-disco/pop); Dianne Mower and Jasmine (modern jazz instrumental and vocal); Orfen Annie Band (country blues/rock); Ellis Hooks Band (country rock/blues); and Casse Culver and the Belle Starr Band (progressive country).

S.R.O. PRODUCTIONS, INC., c/o Oak Manor, 12261 Yonge St., Box 1000, Oak Ridges, Ontario, Canada L0G 1P0. (416)881-3212. Chairman: Ray Danniels. A&R Director: Michael Tilka. Represents individuals, groups and songwriters; currently handles 7 acts. Receives commission based on individually negotiated contracts. Reviews material for acts.

How to Contact: Solicited demo tapes only and lyric sheet with bio material. Prefers cassette with 3 songs on demo. SAE and International Reply Coupons. Reports in 8 weeks.

Music: Progressive; rock; and top 40/pop. Works primarily with rock concert acts. Current acts include Rush; Max Webster (rock act); Ian Thomas; B.B. Gabor (new wave cabaret); *Segarini* (pop/wave); and *Zero-One* (pop/wave).

SAGITTARIAN ARTISTS INTERNATIONAL, 970 Aztec Dr., Muskegon MI 49444. (616)733-2329. Coordinator/Director: G. Loren Ruhl. Management firm. Represents individuals and songwriters; currently handles 6 acts. Receives 15-25% commission.

How to Contact: Query or submit demo tape and lead sheet. Prefers cassette with 2-4 songs on demo, or record. SASE. Reports in 1 month.

Music: Top 40/pop. Works primarily with dance bands and bar bands. Current acts include Ricky Briton (pop vocalist); Les Basilio (vocalist); and Tobie Columbus (pop vocalist).

PETE SALERNO ENTERPRISES, 317 Temple Place, Westfield NJ 07090. President: Pete Salerno. Management firm and booking agency. Represents professional individuals, groups and songwriters; currently handles 45 acts. Receives 15-25% commission.

How to Contact: Query, then submit demo tape and lead sheet.

WILLIAM SEIP MANAGEMENT, INC., Box 413, Waterloo, Ontario, Canada N2J 4A9. (519)885-6570. President: William Seip. Managment agency. Represents musical groups from the Ontario region (at present); currently handles 6 groups. Receives 10-25% commission.

How to Contact: Query by mail or phone, then arrange personal interview. Prefers cassette with 1-10 songs on demo. SAE and International reply Coupons. Reporting time varies.

Music: C&W, easy listening, MOR, progressive, rock (commercial, heavy), and top 40/pop. Works primarily with bar bands and concert acts. Current acts include Helix (heavy rock 'n roll); Tracy Kane (commercial rock 'n roll); and Mike Biker & Kickstands (50's and 60's group).

SELECT ARTISTS ASSOCIATES, 7300 E. Camelback Rd., Scottsdale AZ 85251. (602)994-0471. President: Charles T. Johnston. Booking agency. Represents groups; currently handles 45 acts. Receives 15% minimum commission. Reviews material for acts.

How to Contact: Query or submit demo tape and lead sheet. Prefers cassette with 3 songs minimum on tape. SASE. Reports in 1 month.

Music: C&W, dance-oriented, easy listening, jazz, progressive, R&B, rock, soul and top 40/pop. Works primarily with show/dance groups. Current acts include Gringo; Quantrell; Phoenix Express; Mirage; and Enrico Bros. (top 40/contemporary acts).

SHORT PUMP ASSOCIATES, Box 11292, Richmond VA 23230. (804)355-4117. President: Ken Brown. Vice President: Dennis Huber. Management and production agency. Deals with artists in the Virginia, North Carolina, Washington D.C. and Maryland region. Represents artists, groups and songwriters; currently handles 3 acts. Receives 10-20% commission. Reviews material for acts.
How to Contact: Submit demo tape and lyric sheet. Prefers cassette or 7½ ips reel-to-reel with 1-5 songs on demo. "Biographies and itineraries are helpful." SASE. Reports in 2 weeks.
Music: Rock (country rock and hard rock); and top 40/pop. Works with concert acts, dance bands (usually 4-8 piece w/horns), concert, rock and country rock artists. Current acts include The Robbin Thompson Band (rock); Good Humor Band (rock); and Andrew Lewis Band (soul).

SHOWCASE ATTRACTIONS, Box 6687, Wheeling WV 26003. (614)758-5812. President: R.H. Gallion. Management firm and booking agency. Represents individuals, groups and songwriters; currently handles 44 acts. Receives 15% minimum commission.
How to Contact: Query or submit demo tape. Prefers 7½ ips reel-to-reel with 2 songs minimum on demo. Does not return unsolicited material. Reports in 1 month.
Music: Bluegrass; C&W; folk; gospel; MOR; and top 40/pop. Works primarily with C&W and gospel artists and groups. Current acts include Bob Gallion (C&W); Patti Powell (C&W); and The Younger Brothers Band.

SIDARTHA ENTERPRISES, LTD., 1504 E. Grandriver Ave., Suite 101, East Lansing MI 48823. (517)351-6780. President: Thomas R. Brunner. Management firm and booking agency. Represents artists and groups. Receives 15-25% commission. Reviews material for acts.
How to Contact: "Always make phone contact first." Submit demo tape and lyric sheet. Prefers cassette tape with at least 4 songs on demo. SASE. Reports in 1 month.

BRAD SIMON ORGANIZATION, 176 E. 77th St., New York NY 10021. (212)988-4962. President: Brad Simon. Represents individual artists, record producers, musical groups and songwriters; currently handles 7 acts. Receives 20% commission.
How to Contact: Arrange personal interview by mail or phone after submission of demo cassette. Prefers cassette with 3 songs minimum on demo. SASE. Reports in 3 weeks.
Music: C&W/pop, jazz, MOR, progressive, rock (all types) and top 40/pop. Works with artists, groups and songwriters in contemporary rock, pop, jazz with strong commercial appeal and crossover potential, vocal and instrumental artists with strong performing skills. Current acts include Robert Grace (rock); Robert Ore & Fan the Flame (pop/rock); and Robin Greenstein (pop/rock).

SKYBLUE MANAGEMENT AGENCY, 2323 E. Newberry Blvd., 3rd Floor, Milwaukee WI 53211. (414)963-9315. President: Marc M. Dulberger. Management firm, booking agency and advertising agency. Represents individuals, groups and songwriters; currently handles 3 acts. Receives 5-20% commission. Reviews material for acts.
How to Contact: Query or submit demo tape and lyric sheet. Prefers cassette with 3 songs on demo. Artist may submit video cassette. SASE. Reports in 1 month.
Music: Jazz (salsa progressive), MOR, progressive, rock and top 40/pop. Current acts include Howard Epstein (rock songwriter); Marty Jupp (songwriter); and Rage (rock group).

JON SMALL MANAGEMENT, 166 E. 61st St., New York NY 10021. (212)888-0144. Contact: Jon Small. Management agency. Represents artists; currently handles 3 acts. Receives 20-25% commission. Reviews material for acts.
How to Contact: Submit demo tape. Prefers cassette with 3-5 songs on demo. SASE. Reports in 3 weeks.
Music: All types. Works primarily with rock singers/songwriters (hard, new wave, progressive and mainline). Current acts include D.L. Byron (rock singer/songwriter); and the Kenny Brothers (rock singers/songwriters).

JAMES R. SMITH/HANK WILLIAMS, JR., Box 790, Cullman AL 35055. (205)734-8656. Manager: James R. Smith. Management firm and booking agency. Represents individuals and songwriters; currently handles 4 acts. Receives negotiable commission.
How to Contact: Query or submit demo tape and lead sheet. Prefers 7½ ips reel-to-reel or cassette with 1-3 songs on demo. Does not return unsolicited material.
Music: C&W, rock (country), and top 40/pop. Works primarily with vocal acts. Current acts include Hank Williams Jr. and the Bama Band (group); Merle Kilgore (singer); and Nate Harvell (singer).

SOLID SOUL PRODUCTIONS, 3282 E. 119th St., Cleveland OH 44120. (216)231-0772, 752-1904. Executive Vice President: Anthony Luke. Concert consultant and promotion. Represents individuals and groups; currently handles 3 acts. Receives 10-20% commission. Reviews material for acts.
How to Contact: Send letter of introduction. Prefers cassette with 6-12 songs on demo. SASE. Reports in 1 month.
Music: Blues, jazz, Spanish, R&B, rock and soul.

SONGSHOP RECORDING COMPANY, 126 W. 22nd St., New York NY 10011. (212)691-2707. Studio Manager: Jean Petrucelli. Management and booking agency, recording studio and record production company. Represents artists, groups and songwriters; currently handles 4 acts. Receives 15-20% commission. Reviews material for acts.
How to Contact: Query by mail. Prefers cassette with 4 songs on demo. "Include all pertinent material regarding your act and your interest." SASE. Reports in 3 weeks.
Music: Dance-oriented, progressive, R&B, rock and top 40/pop. Works primarily with recording acts—"major labels as well as small independent single releases." Current acts include Tommy Mandel (rock 'n' roll); Fats Deacon and the Dumbwaiters (rock 'n' roll); The Lights (rock 'n' roll/new wave); and The Ribitones (rockapella).

SOUND III MANAGEMENT, 9046 Sunset Blvd., Los Angeles CA 90069. (213)271-7246. President: Bruce Berlow. Management firm. Represents individuals, groups and songwriters; currently handles 6 acts. Receives 20% commission. Reviews material for acts.
How to Contact: Submit demo tape and lyric sheet. Prefers 7½ ips reel-to-reel or cassette with 3-6 songs on demo. SASE. Reports in 2 weeks.
Music: Bluegrass, blues, C&W, dance oriented, progressive, R&B, rock and top 40/pop. Works primarily with solo artists or rock groups and with composers and singer/songwriters. Current acts include Bob Darcy (producer-writer).
Tips: "Concentrate on quality of songs."

SOUNDS OF COUNTRY, 1210 Palm St., Abilene TX 79602. Contact: Angel or Denny Young. Booking agency and music publisher. Represents artists, groups and songwriters; currently handles 14 acts. Receives 10-20% commission. Reviews material for acts.
How to Contact: Query by mail, then submit demo tape and lead sheet. Prefers cassette with 2-6 songs on demo. SASE. Reports in 1 month.
Music: C&W only. Works primarily with bar bands, show bands, duos, and "single artists backed by our bands or house bands. Besides looking for and reviewing songs for our own people, we screen material to be sent for review to three top country artists who are personal friends." Current acts include Out Behind the Barn (show band); Wilbur & Bliss Revue (duo); Chuck Aney (solo artist); and Skip Dowers (solo artist).

SOUTH PRODUCTIONS, LTD., Box 227, Chicago Ridge IL 60415 (312)599-9178 or 636-1253. Contact: Bud Monaco or Jerry Gamauf. Management agency and artist development firm. Represents artists and groups in the local region; currently handles 3 acts. Reviews material for acts.
How to Contact: Query by mail, then submit demo tape and lead sheet. Prefers cassette with 3-6 songs on demo. Does not return unsolicited material. Reports in 2 weeks.
Music: MOR, progressive, rock and top 40/pop. Works primarily with vocalists, solo artists with groups. Current acts include John Hunter, Rich Hazdra and Tony Wilson (rock/top 40).

SOUTH WIND ENTERTAINMENT, 2500 Forsyth Rd., Bldg. 31, Orlando FL 32807. (305)677-5300. President: Michael Orlando. Vice-President: Mark Spinicelli. Management and booking agency and production company. Represents artists and groups from the Florida region only; currently handles 3 acts. Receives 10-20% commission. Reviews material for acts.
How to Contact: Query by mail, then submit demo tape and lead sheet. Prefers cassette with 6-8 songs on demo. Does not return unsolicited material.
Music: Easy listening, MOR, R&B, rock, soul and top 40/pop. Current acts include Clockwork (top 40); Cloudburst (top 40) and Ronnie Duncan (easy listening).

SOUTHERN MANAGEMENT BOOKINGS, Box 262, Rt. 2, Landenberg PA 19350. Manager: Bob Paisley. Management firm and booking agency. Represents artists, groups and songwriters; currently handles 4 acts. Receives 10-20% commission. Reviews material for acts.
How to Contact: Submit demo tape and lyric sheet. Prefers cassette with 3 songs on demo. SASE. Reports in 3 weeks.
Music: Bluegrass and C&W. Works with bar bands, festival bands and works with artists for recording sessions. "Music should be in the traditional style." Current acts include Southern Mountain Boys (bluegrass); Country Class (C&W); and Caroll County Boys (bluegrass).

SOUTHERN TALENT INTERNATIONAL, 2925 Fallowridge, Snellville GA 30278. (404)979-0847. President: John M. Titak. Management and booking agency. Represents groups and songwriters; currently handles 76 acts. Receives 10-15% commission. Reviews material for acts.
How to Contact: Submit demo tape and lead sheet. Prefers cassette with 3 songs on demo. SASE. Reports in 1 month.
Music: Rock and top 40/pop. Works primarily with rock bands.

SPECIAL AGENTS TALENT & BOOKING, One Necco Place, Boston MA 02210. (617)426-3888. Contact: Joseph Casey or Warren Scott. Booking agency.
How to Contact: Submit demo tape. Prefers cassette with 2-6 songs on demo. SASE. Reports in 1 month.
Music: Dance-oriented (rock) and new wave. Current acts include Boys Life, Nervous Eaters, The Neighborhoods, The Atlantics, Lou Miami and the Kozmetix, Jon Butcher, Axis, The Probers, Numbers, The Dawgs, Prime Movers and Future Dads.
Tips: "We offer our artists as models for advertising agencies, film and video, and also co-ordinate their national and international tours."

STAR ARTIST MANAGEMENT INC., Box 114, Fraser MI 48026. (313)979-5115. President: Ron Geddish. Chairman: Dick Bozzi. Director of West Coast Operations: Ray Shelide. Director of Canadian Operations: Brian Courtis. House Producers: Brian Ferriman/Declan O'Doherty. Director of Public Relations: Rikki Hansen. General Counsellor: Tom Werner. West Coast Counsellor: S.D. Ashley. Management firm. Represents individuals, groups and songwriters; currently handles 10 acts. Receives 10-20% commission. House Label: Trillium Records. Reviews material for acts.
How to Contact: Submit demo tape. Prefers cassette with 3-5 songs on demo. SASE. Reports in 2 weeks.
Music: Easy listening, MOR, progressive, rock and top 40/pop. Works primarily with MOR and rock groups. Current acts include Tilt; Toby Redd (rock); Doug Kahan; Bitter Sweet Alley (rock), and Look Out (MOR).

STAR REPRESENTATION, 4026 Bobby Lane, Schiller Park IL 60176. (312)678-2755. Prj sident: James Stella. Management agency and production company. Represents artists, groups and songwriters; currently handles 9 acts. Receives 15-25% commission.
How to Contact: Arrange personal interview or submit demo tape and lead sheet. Prefers 7½ ips reel-to-reel or cassette with 2-6 songs on demo. SASE. Reports in 2-3 weeks.
Music: Children's; dance; MOR; progressive; rock (hard or melodic rock); soul; and top 40/pop. Works with bands—looking for national potential. Current acts include Steve Busa (songwriter/artist).
Tips: "We are dealing with new record labels, Vinage Records, which deals with oldies, and our gang records, which deals with all new talent and placement of new talent."

STARCREST PRODUCTIONS, INC., 2516 S. Washington St., Grand Forks ND 58201. (701)772-6831. President: George Hastings. Management firm and booking agency. Represents individuals, groups and songwriters; currently handles 4 acts. Receives 10-15% commission. Reviews material for acts.
How to Contact: Query, then submit demo tape and lyric sheet. Prefers 7½ ips reel-to-reel or cassette with 2 songs minimum on demo. SASE. Reports in 1 month.
Music: Classical; C&W; gospel; MOR; and top 40/pop. Current acts include Mary Joyce (C&W vocalist); the Pioneers (C&W group); Bob Angel (C&W songwriter); and Gene Wyles (C&W artist), all on Meadowlark Records.

STARLOFT AGENCY, INC., 2067 Broadway, Penthouse B, New York NY (212)496-8670. Vice President: Bruce Nichols. Secretary: Paul Zukoski. Booking agency. Represents artists, musical groups and songwriters; currently handles 16 acts. Receives 10-20% commission. Reviews material for acts.
How to Contact: Submit demo tape or demo tape and lead sheet. Prefers cassette with 3-6 songs on demo. SASE. Reports in 3 weeks.
Music: Bluegrass, blues, C&W, easy listening, folk, jazz, progressive, R&B and rock. Works primarily with recording artists. Current acts include Gil Scott Heron (progressive); Persuasions (rock/soul/gospel); and James Cotton (rock/blues).

STARSTRUCK PRODUCTIONS, 701 Seneca St., Buffalo NY 14210. (716)856-2984. Managers: Fred Caserta and Mike Faley. Management agency. Represents groups from Northeast Canada; currently handles 11 acts. Receives 15% minimum commission. Reviews material for acts.

How to Contact: Submit demo tape. Prefers cassette with 2-5 songs on demo. SASE. Reports in 1 month.
Music: Blues, R&B, rock (hard and country) and top 40/pop. Works primarily with bar bands "with a potential for the future, i.e., recording and touring." Current acts include the Alyn Syms Group (hard rock 'n roll); and Cock Robin (top 40/rock 'n roll).

STERLING ENTERTAINMENT AGENCY, 2726 Eden Lane, Rapid City SD 57701. (605)342-2697. Owner: Lowell Sterling. Booking agency. Represents groups; currently handles 22 acts. Receives 10% minimum commission.
How to Contact: Query. Prefers cassette. SASE. Reports in 1 week.
Music: C&W, dance-oriented and MOR. Works primarily with country Western lounge bands and dance variety lounge acts. Current acts include Brothers Plus (variety); 2 Outa 3 (C&W/variety); and the Catalinas (C&W).

TOM STINNETTE ENTERTAINMENT AGENCY, Box 06404, Portland OR 97206. (503)235-5988. President: Tom Stinnette. Office Manager: Becky Horner. Management firm and booking agency. Represents singles and groups; also handles special promotions for clubs, fairs and concerts for businesses. Currently handles 40 units booking northern Canada and Alaska. Receives 10-20% commission or percentage of gross. Reviews material for acts.
How to Contact: Submit demo tape and song list. "Please include all pertinent details of your act. Follow up with a phone call to make sure we received your material." Prefers cassette with 5-10 songs on demo. "Please make all tapes audible and refrain from sending catalogs of your material." SASE. Reports in 1 month.
Music: C&W, dance-oriented, easy listening, jazz, MOR and rock (country). Works primarily with dance lounge artists. Current acts include Front Page (top 40/MOR); 24 Karret (top 40/MOR; and Roadhouse (modern country).

SUREFIRE PRODUCTIONS, Box 1808, Asheville NC 28802. President: Ron Weathers. Management firm and booking agency. Represents artists, groups and songwriters; currently handles 25 acts. Receives 15-20% commission. Reviews material for acts.
How to Contact: Submit demo tape and lyric sheet. Prefers cassette with 6-10 songs on demo. Does not return unsolicited material. Reports in 1 month.
Music: C&W, easy listening, R&B, rock, soul and top 40/pop. Works with recording artists plus southeast regional dance and show bands. Current acts include Toby King (top 40 R&B); Little Royal (R&B); and Hollywood Bratts (top 40 rock).
Tips: "We look for good radio commercial type material leaning toward an AM radio audience."

SUTTON ARTISTS CORP., Suite 520, 11777 San Vicente, Los Angeles CA 90049. (213)826-5002. Regional Manager: H.D. McElroy. Booking agency. Represents artists and groups; currently handles 25 acts. Receives 10-20% commission.
How to Contact: Query by phone first. Submit demo tape and lyric sheet. Prefers cassette with 2-6 songs on demo. "Phone first and describe original music, then mail demo." Does not return unsolicited material. Reports in 4-6 weeks. Reviews material for acts.
Music: Bluegrass, blues, C&W, dance-oriented, folk, jazz, R&B and top 40/pop. Works with concert artists, "no nightclub locations. Only interested in jazz, hard rock, country crossover or original comedy." Current acts include Chuck Howard (C&W); Charles "Rick" Kelly (comedy/guitar); and Don Glaser (jazz/piano).

T.D.I. DIRECTION & MANAGEMENT DIVISION, 4100 W. Flagler St., Miami FL 33134. (305)446-1900. Manager: Larry Brahms. Management firm, publishing and production company. Represents artists, groups, songwriters and record producers; currently handles 6 acts. Reviews material for acts.
How to Contact: Query or submit demo tape and lyric sheet. Prefers cassette with 3-4 songs. SASE. Reports in 2 weeks.
Music: C&W, dance-oriented, R&B, soul and top 40/pop. Works with national recording acts only. Looking for additional artists. Current acts include Ritchie Family (vocal group); Celi Bee (vocalist); Hot Walker Band (country); and Ray Martinez & Friends, Amant, Passion (vocal group).

TALENT MASTER, 50 Music Sq., W., Suite 507, Nashville TN 37203. (615)320-0881. President: Steve Bess. Vice President: Charli McMillan. Booking agency. Represents artists and musical groups from Tennessee and surrounding states; currently handles 14 acts. Receives 15-20% commission. Reviews material for acts.
How to Contact: Arrange personal interview (artist/group only). Prefers cassette with 1-3 songs on

demo. Does not return unsolicited material. Reports in 2-3 weeks.
Music: C&W, dance-oriented, MOR and top 40/pop. Works primarily with dance and show, top 40 and C&W acts. Current acts include Glass Hammer (dance/top 40/C&W); John Wesley Ryles (country); and Steve Bess Show (show band/dance).

TALENTHOUSE, (formerly Jerry Lee Lewis & Co. Talenthouse), 1719 West End, Suite 1100, Nashville TN 37203. Manager: Robert Porter. Management firm and booking agency. Represents professional individuals; currently handles 2 acts. Receives 10-20% commission.
How to Contact: Submit demo tape and lead sheet. Prefers 7½ ips reel-to-reel with 1-4 songs on demo. Does not return unsolicited material. Reports as soon as possible.
Music: Bluegrass, blues, C&W, folk, gospel; rock (country) and top 40/pop. Current acts include Jerry Lee Lewis (C&W/pop vocalist); and Bill Littleton (C&W/pop vocalist).

DON TAYLOR ARTIST MANAGEMENT/TAMMI RECORDS, LTD., 9400 S. Dadeland Blvd., Suite 220, Miami FL 33156. (305)665-2552. President: Don Taylor. Management agency. Represents artists, groups and songwriters; currently handles 8 acts. Receives 15-20% commission. Reviews material for artists.
How to Contact: Query by mail, then submit demo tape. Prefers cassette with 3-5 songs on demo. SASE. Reports in 2 weeks.
Music: R&B, soul and reggae. Works primarily with concert performers. Current acts include Jimmy Cliff (reggae) and T-Connection (R&B).

TENTH HOUR PRODUCTIONS, 4470 Brownsville Rd., Pittsburgh PA 15236. (412)621-4734. President: Carl M. Grefenstette. Management agency. Represents artists, groups and songwriters; currently handles 10 acts. "As a management company we get heavily involved with our acts. We are therefore, limited in the number of acts we can work with. We are not a booking agency." Receives 10-20% commission. Reviews material for acts.
How to Contact: Submit demo tape and lyric sheet. Prefers cassette with 2-3 songs on demo. SASE. Reports in 3 weeks.
Music: R&B, rock (top 40/country-rock/hard rock) and top 40/pop. Works with college concert bands, dance bands and bar bands. Current acts include The Flashcats ('60s soul group); The Leslie Smith Band (country-rock); Eddie & the Others (pop-rock group); The Ratriderz (heavy metal group); The Swarm (new wave group); and The Dialtones (new wave group).

STEVE THOMAS MANAGEMENT, INC., 1901 E. N. Hamilton St., Box 11283, Richmond VA 23230. (804)355-2178. President: Steve Thomas. Management agency. Represents artists and groups; currently handles 2 acts. Receives 10-15% commission. Reviews material for acts.
How to Contact: Submit demo tape and lyric sheet. Prefers cassette with 2-5 songs on demo. Does not return unsolicited material. Reports in 2 weeks.
Music: Dance; rock; soul; and top 40/pop. Works primarily with dance and concert bands. Current acts include Power Play (disco band) and Sandcastle (concert/dance band).

MIKE THOMAS MANAGEMENT, Box 70486, Charleston SC 29405. (803)554-6768. President: Mike Thomas. Management and booking agency and record company. Represents artists, groups, songwriters and lighting companies; currently handles 8 acts. Receives 10-15% commission. Reviews material for acts.
How to Contact: Query by mail, then submit demo tape. Prefers cassette with 1 song on demo. Include photo and bio. SASE. Reports in 3 weeks.
Music: Soul and top 40/pop. "We work with anyone who is serious about what they do." Current acts include The Tymes (oldies group); Natural Light Band (variety dance music band); and The Charleston Connection (R&B oriented group).
Tips: "The tapes you send need not be finished masters. We do, however, give consideration to finished material for release on our WAHR label."

TOPDRAW ARTIST MANAGEMENT, Box 2787 Station A, Champaign IL 61820. (217)398-1221. President: Jeff Ross. Vice President: Mark Ross. Management firm, production and publishing company. Represents artists, groups and songwriters; currently handles 3 groups and 8 writers. Receives 10-25% commission. Reviews material for acts.
How to Contact: Query or submit demo tape. Prefers cassette with 3-6 songs on demo. SASE. Reports in 3 weeks.
Music: R&B, rock, soul, top 40/pop and wave. Works with anything from bar bands to concert performers. Current acts include The Invaders (rock); Coal Kitchen (rock); and Mantia (pop/rock).

TOWER ROAD PRODUCTIONS, 9025 Wilshire Blvd., Beverly Hills CA 90212. (213)271-5261. Contact: Peter Bayles. Management agency. Estab. 1979. Represents local artists, groups and songwriters from the immediate region only; currently handles 3 acts. Receives 15-25% commission. Reviews material for acts.
How to Contact: Query by mail, then arrange personal interview, submit demo tape or demo tape and lead sheet. Prefers cassette with 3-5 songs on demo. SASE. Reports in 1 month.
Music: Jazz, rock, top 40/pop and new wave. Works primarily with performing bands.

TRIANGLE TALENT, INC., 9701 Taylorsville Rd., Box 99035, Louisville KY 40299. (502)267-5466. President: David H. Snowden. Booking agency. Represents artists and groups; currently handles 110 acts. Receives 10-20% commission.
How to Contact: Query or submit demo tape. Prefers cassette with 2-4 songs on demo. SASE. Reports in 2 weeks.
Music: Bluegrass; dance; rock (both heavy and funk); top 40/pop; and country. Current acts include Free Fall (rock/concert); Mid-night Star (jazz, disco/concert); Pure Pleasure (disco/top 40); Epics (show/concert); and Debi Bass (country, show/concert).

UMBRELLA ARTISTS MANAGEMENT, INC., Box 6507, 2181 Victory Pkwy., Cincinnati OH 45206. (513)861-1500. President: Stan Hertzman. Management agency. Represents artists, groups and songwriters; currently handles 4 acts. Receives 10-20% commission.
How to Contact: Submit demo tape and lyric sheet. Prefers 7½ ips reel-to-reel or cassette with 1-6 songs on demo. SASE. Reports in 1 month.
Music: Progressive; rock; and top 40/pop. Works with contemporary/progressive pop/rock artists/writers. Current acts include Charlie Fletcher (pop rock, artist-songwriter); Adrian Belew (artist/guitarist/songwriter). Credits include: Frank Zappa, David Bowie, Talking Heads, Garland Jeffrey, and Tina Wymouth. Presently working on joint album with Robert Fripp, Bill Bruford and Tony Levin.

VALEX TALENT AGENCY, 105 E. Clinton St., Ithaca NY 14850. (607)273-3931. Publishing Vice President: Rick Gravelding. Booking Vice President: Tom Brennan. Management firm, booking agency and publishing house (Flying Horse Music). Deals with artists in northeast US only. Represents artists, groups and songwriters; currently handles 25 acts. Receives 15-25% commission. Reviews material for acts.
How to Contact: Submit demo tape and lead sheet. Prefers 7½ ips reel-to-reel or cassette with 3-6 songs on demo. SASE. Reports in 1 month. "Songwriters please send material in care of Rick Gravelding, Flying Horse Music; also send cassettes or 7½ ips tapes to same."
Music: Country pop, dance-oriented, easy listening, MOR, R&B, rock, soul and top 40/pop. Works with vocalists, show, dance and bar bands. Current acts include Charlie Starr (single, guitar and vocals); Bobby Comstock (rock); Jamo (rock); Tokyo (rock/new wave); and Paul Bros. (country/Southern rock).

GARY VAN ZEELAND TALENT, INC., 1750 Freedom Rd., Little Chute WI 54140. (414)788-5222. Manager: Randy Schwoerer. Booking agency. Represents groups; Currently handles 85 acts. Receives 15% commission from road groups. Reviews material for acts.
How to Contact: Submit demo tape and lyric sheet. Prefers cassette with 8-10 songs on demo. Include photo, songlist and references. Does not return unsolicited material. Reports in 1 week.
Music: Rock (country or regular); top 40/pop; and dance. Works primarily with lounge acts, and bar and hotel bands. Current acts include Jonas, (McCoys); Gail Society (all show groups).

VOKES BOOKING AGENCY, Box 12, New Kensington PA 15068. (412)335-2775. President: Howard Vokes. Booking agency. Represents individuals, groups and songwriters; currently handles 25 acts. Receives 10-20% commission.
How to Contact: Query or submit demo tape and lead sheet. Prefers 7½ ips reel-to-reel, cassette or 8-track with 3-6 songs on demo. SASE. Reports in 2 weeks.
Music: Bluegrass; C&W; and gospel. "We work with bluegrass and hard country bands who generally play bars, hotels and clubs. However, we also book in ole-time artists as singles. We want nothing to do with hard rock or country rock." Current acts include Bluefield Boys (bluegrass); and Country Boys (C&W).

WILLIAM F. WAGNER AGENCY, 14343 Addison St., Suite 218, Sherman Oaks CA 91423. (213)501-4161. Owner: Bill Wagner. Management agency and record producer. Represents artists and groups; currently handles 5 acts. Receives 15% commission. "For recording production of artists other than my own clients I receive $100/hour, live studio time; $50/hour overdub, editing and mix-down time." Reviews material for acts.

How to Contact: Submit demo tape and lyric sheet. Prefers 7½ or 3¾ ips reel-to-reel (2- or 4-track) or cassette with 15 minutes maximum on tape. SASE. Reports in 2 weeks.
Music: Blues, choral, C&W, dance-oriented, easy listening, jazz, MOR, progressive, Spanish, R&B, rock (all kinds), soul and top 40/pop. Works with singers, songwriter-singers, instrumentalists and 2- to 19-piece groups. Current acts include Bryan Fox (composer/singer/instrumentalist); Mary Dellinger (contemporary/pop/MOR/rock vocalist); JoAnne Kurman (country/pop vocalist); Los Dominics (7-piece Mexican show group); Pete Christlieb (jazz tenor); Pat Longo Super Big Band; and Mark Vogel (contemporary/pop singer).

JIM WAGNER, INC., DBA American Management, 17530 Ventura Blvd., Suite 108, Encino CA 91316. (213)981-6500. President: Jim Wagner. Booking agency. Represents individuals and groups; currently handles 7 acts. Receives 15% commission.
How to Contact: Query. Prefers 7½ ips reel-to-reel with 1-3 songs on demo. SASE. Reports as soon as possible.
Music: C&W and progressive. Works primarily with C&W artists and groups. Current acts include Freddie Hart and the Heartbeats (C&W artist); Eddie Raven, New Christy Minstrels, Susie Allanson, Hoyt Axton, Susan Raye, Larry McNeely, Tommy Roe, Johnny Tillotson, Jim Weatherly, Donna Fargo and Lee Dresser.

NORBY WALTERS ASSOCIATES, 1650 Broadway, New York NY 10015. (212)245-3939. President: Norby Walters. Management firm and booking agency. Represents individuals and groups; currently hanBles 50 acts. Receives 10-20% commission. Reviews material for acts.
How to Contact: Submit demo tape and lyric sheet. Prefers reel-to-reel or cassette tape with 1-3 songs on demo. Does not return unsolicited material. Reports in 2 weeks.
Music: Dance; MOR; soul; and top 40/pop. Current acts include Kool and the Gang (pop/R&B group, Delite Records); Michael Henderson (R&B/pop, Artista Records); and S.O.S. Band (R&B/pop group, C.B.S. Records).

WHIMPIA MANAGEMENT, INC., 77 Milltown Rd., East Brunswick NJ 08816. (201)254-3990. President: William Franzblau. Management agency. Deals with artists in East Coast region only. Represents artists, groups and songwriters; currently handles 4 acts. Receives 12-20% commission. Reviews material for acts.
How to Contact: Arrange personal interview or submit demo tape and lyric sheet. Prefers cassette with 3-8 songs on demo. SASE. Reports in 2 weeks.
Music: Blues; dance; jazz; rock (country rock); and top 40/pop. Works with concert and bar bands. Current acts include Kinderhook (concert group); Cowtown (bar band); Cloverhill (bar band); and Beatlemania (concert group).

WHITE CLAY PRODUCTIONS, INC., Box 324, Newark DE 19711. (302)368-1211. Manager: Nicholas C. Norris. Management agency. Estab. 1979. Represents artists, groups and songwriters from the Delaware Valley area; currently handles 10 acts. Receives 15% commission. Reviews material for acts.
How to Contact: Query by mail. Prefers cassette with 2-4 songs on demo. SASE. Reports in 3 weeks.
Music: Dance-oriented, progressive, R&B, rock and new wave. Works primarily with original bands. Current acts include Sin City Band; Boni Dahl; and Reflectors.

SHANE WILDER ARTISTS MANAGEMENT, Box 3503, Hollywood CA 90028. President: Shane Wilder. Management agency. Represents artists and groups; currently handles 14 acts. Receives 15% commission. Reviews material for acts.
How to Contact: Submit demo tape and lead sheet. Prefers cassette with 4-8 songs on demo. SASE. Reports in 2 weeks.
Music: C&W, easy listening, MOR and rock (soft and country). Works primarily with recording artists. Current acts include Crystal Blue, Laurie Loman and Mike Franklin (country artists).
Tips: "Only top commercial material with strong lyric content will be considered."

LARRY WILT AND ASSOCIATES, Box 22638, Nashville TN 37202. (615)859-4457. Contact: Larry Wilt. Management agency and booking agency. Represents artists and musical groups from anywhere; currently handles 15 acts. Receives 10-20% commission.
How to Contact: Query by mail. Prefers cassette with 4-6 songs on demo. SASE. Reports in 1 month.
Music: Bluegrass and C&W. Works primarily with country singers and groups. Current acts include Lois Johnson (country); Don Silvers (country); and Little David Wilkens (country).

WINTERSWAN, Division of Great Plains Associates, Box 634, Lawrence KS 66044. (913)841-4444. Presidents: Mark Swanson, Scott Winters. Management firm. Represents groups; currently handles 1 act. Receives 10-20% commission. Reviews material for acts.
How to Contact: Submit demo tape and lyric sheet. Prefers cassette with 3-7 songs on demo. SASE. Reports in 1 week.
Music: C&W, R&B, rock (straight) and soul. Works primarily with dance/concert bands, for small college circuit and dance halls. Current acts include The Glory Boys (rock/soul); and Greg Mackender (R&B/soul/rock artist/songwriter).

PAUL WOLFE, Box 262, Abe Lincoln Station, Carteret NJ 07008. (201)541-9422. President: Paul Wolfe. Vice President: Gary Hills. Management firm, booking agency and record producer. Represents individuals, groups, songwriters and show and oldie acts from the US, Canada, Japan, England, France, Sweden, Belgium and Holland; currently handles 38 acts. "We try to locate outlets for all material we receive in our agency." Receives 10-15% commission; "the artist picks up his money directly — we receive deposits only with signed contracts." Reviews material for acts.
How to Contact: Submit demo tape and lyric sheet. Prefers 7½ ips reel-to-reel or cassette with 6-12 songs on demo. "Send material with demo, photographs and short bio on yourself to get a better idea of the sender." SASE. Reports in 1 month.
Music: C&W, dance-oriented, easy listening, MOR, progressive, rock (country) and top 40/pop. Works primarily with dance bands, show groups and singles. Current acts include The Flamingoes; The Del Satins; and The Belmonts (all oldies).
Tips: "We welcome new songwriters as well as new groups; we want to develop tomorrow's hit artist as well as our agency's future."

WOODEN LADY PRODUCTIONS, 1154 N. Western Ave., Suite 208, Los Angeles CA 90029. (213)463-7578. Contact: Albert Williams or Colleen Mickey. Management agency and music publisher (Wooden Lady Music/ASCAP). Represents artists, musical groups and songwriters from anywhere; currently handles 2 acts. Receives 10-20% commission (flat fees for demo packages, arranging and promotion). Reviews material for acts.
How to Contact: Arrange personal interview (if local); or submit demo tape or demo tape and lead sheet. "Ask for sample of our artist's recordings, which we'll send COD for postage. You decide if you have appropriate material." Prefers 7½ ips reel-to-reel or cassette with 2-4 songs on demo. SASE. Reports in 2 weeks.
Music: C&W, R&B, rock and pop. Works primarily with mainstream rock and roll and adult contemporary acts. Current acts include The Rachel Williams Band (rock/pop); Rachel Williams (singer/songwriter); Albert Williams (songwriter/producer); and Greg Curda (avant-garde composer).
Tips: "Know what you are after, have a positive attitude, but don't come on too strong, and have a professional presentation."

YBARRA MUSIC, Box 665, Lemon Grove CA 92045. (714)462-6538. Owner: D. Braun. A&R Director: R. William. Booking agency, music publisher and record company. Deals with artists from Southern California. Represents groups; currently handles 4 acts. Receives 5-20% commission.
How to Contact: Query. Prefers cassette. Does not return unsolicited material. Reports in 1 month.
Music: Blues, classical (chamber, woodwind or strings), folk and jazz (swing, dixieland, progressive or big band). Works primarily with dance-oriented dixieland, traditional jazz and swing acts. Currently represents the Dick Braun Big Band; and Dixieland Band (dance and show bands).

ZANE MANAGEMENT, INC., 1529 Walnut St., 6th Floor, Philadelphia PA 19119. (215)568-0500. President: Lloyd Zane Remick. Represents artists, songwriters and athletes; currently handles 7 acts. Receives commission.
How to Contact: Submit demo tape and lyric sheet. Prefers cassette. SASE. Reports in 3-4 weeks.
Music: Children's; dance; easy listening; folk; gospel; jazz (fusion); MOR; rock (hard and country); soul; and top 40/pop. Current acts include Instant Funk (disco/funk); Michael Pedicin, Jr. (jazz fusion), Phil Hurtt; Bunny Sigler (disco/funk); Spaces (jazz fusion); and Grover Washington, Jr. (management).

Play Producers & Publishers

Inflation continues to have its effect on theater. Rising costs force producers and directors to seek material that can be produced unpretentiously and inexpensively. Today's wise playwright keeps it simple: shows with uncomplicated sets and small casts are a must for little theaters with limited facilities and funds. Musical arrangements should likewise sound good whether played by a small group of two or three musicians or by a full orchestra.

Keeping the play versatile will also give you a shot at a wide variety of theatrical markets. Professional casts can handle complex songs and arrangements, but remember that Broadway need not be your only goal. Many local groups—dinner theaters, children's theaters, high school and college groups, and community theaters—provide outlets for musicals, and their casts appreciate less complex material.

These same groups are open to original work from local playwrights, and are excellent testing grounds for your musical. Once your play has proven itself locally, you can send reviews of the performances along with a letter asking permission to submit your musical to producers in New York and elsewhere.

Even New York-based playwrights know the value of feedback from smaller audiences before submitting their plays to a Broadway producer. Read the Close-up of Carol Hall in the "Workshop" section to learn how she used an American Guild of Authors and Composers workshop as testing ground for the songs from "Best Little Whorehouse in Texas."

For more details on the business of writing musicals, see the "Business" section at the back of this book.

ACTORS THEATRE OF LOUISVILLE, 316 W. Main, Louisville KY 40202. (502)584-1265. Literary Manager: Elizabeth King. Play producer. Produces "19 equity shows, including 8-10 new plays per year." "Actors Theatre is a resident equity professional theater operating for a 35-week season, from September to June. Subscription audience of 18,000 from extremely diverse backgrounds. Repertoire spans classics to contemporary, all genres. There are two theaters: a 640-seat thrust, and a 200-seat three-quarter arena." Payment negotiable. Submit complete ms, score and cassette tape of songs. SASE. Reports in 4-6 months.
Musicals: "Should be full-length (two or more acts) with a strong story line and a basically positive life view. Story can be either original or an adaptation; music any style. Of foremost importance is a literate book with strong characterizations and dialogue. No situation comedies or absurdist work." There are two theaters. "For the small theater, musicals should be very small: 8 actors or less, 1 or 2 pianos. For the large theater: 15 actors or less, 3- or 4-piece ensemble. We cannot produce multimedia shows. Multiple set shows are difficult for us."
Recent Productions: *Getting Out*, by Marsha Norman (woman's first day out of prison); *The Gin Game*, by D.L. Coburn (two nursing home residents confront each other while learning gin rummy); *Andronicus*, by Jon Jory and Jerry Blatt (rock music version of Shakespeare's *Titus Andronicus*); *Lone Star*, by James McLure; *Matrimonium*, by Peter Ekstrom (musical based on Shaw comedies); *Crimes of the Heart*, by Beth Henley (three sisters fight family battles in Mississippi); *Gold Dust*, by Jon Jory and Jim Wann (musical of Old West prospector trying tp hoard money and son's girl).

ALLENBERRY PLAYHOUSE, Boiling Springs PA 17007. (717)258-6120. Managing Director: Nelson Sheeley. Play producer. Produces 10 plays (2-3 musicals)/year. Pays 3-5% royalty. Query with synopsis. SASE. Reports as soon as possible.
Musicals: "Other than established material, we are looking for small cast, 4-10 characters, simply produced musicals—they should run between 2-2½ hrs in length. Take into account that we are in a conservative, religiously oriented part of the country. Four letter words are fairly taboo, but then again, it depends on the four letter word! Stay away from what middle America finds objectionable: excessive dwelling on any violation of the Ten Commandments, slurs on the country (not necessarily the government), nudity, or esoteric subject matter."
Recent Productions: *The Merry Widow*; *The Sound of Music*, and *You're a Good Man, Charlie Brown*.

AMERICAN THEATER ARTS (CONSERVATORY), ATA News Plays Program, 6240 Hollywood Blvd., Hollywood CA 90028. (213)466-2462. Play Development Director: Mary Bomba. Play producer. Produces 5+ (4 plays that are in development stages performed on what is called Dark Nights and 1 musical)/year. "There are 2 equity waver theatres at ATA plus a conservatory. They are located in Hollywood, across from Pantages Theatre, and seat about 69 people each. Since ATA is still new and developing we are also finding our audience. Shows run 6 weeks; Thursday, Friday and Saturday nights and Sunday matinee (hoping to attract senior citizens)." Royalty varies, "especially if work goes on to other houses." Submit complete manuscript, score, and tape of songs. Prefers cassette. "Tape need not be elaborate—just guitar and voice are OK." SASE. Reports in 4-6 weeks.
Musicals: "ATA is looking for musicals that have a good storyline. Topics can be about anything. We are also interested in producing plays/musicals for children. Be careful that they are not too long. This is a small theatre, so staging is limited and casts of more than 20 are almost impossible. No elaborate set changes. ATA wants to produce at least one new musical each season."
Recent Productions: *Richards Corkleg*, by Brendan Beehan (Ireland, light comedy); and *River Wind*, by John Jennings (turn of the century on the banks of Wabash).
Tips: "Stay away from writing hoping for TV production. *Write for the theatre*, if you want it produced in a theatre."

ARENA PLAYERS REPERTORY THEATRE, 296 Route 109, East Farmingdale NY 11735. (516)293-0674. Producer: Frederic De Feis. Play producer. Produces 3 plays (2 musicals)/year. Plays performed in a "professional, arena-style repertory theater playing to a broad cross-section of teenagers to senior citizens, drawn from all over Long Island as well as Manhattan." Pays royalty averaging $600-1,200. Query with synopsis. SASE. Reports in 1 month.
Musicals: "We are particularly interested in full-length intimate musicals which can be mounted with minimal orchestration and are well-suited to production in a small, arena-style theater."
Recent Productions: *Sweeney Todd, The Barber*, by Burton (a new adaptation of the original script with new musical numbers, and full new score).

ARKANSAS STATE UNIVERSITY-BEEBE CAMPUS, Box H, Beebe AR 72012. (501)882-6452. Director of Theater: L.R. Chudomelka. Play producer. Produces 6 plays (3-4 musicals)/year. Plays are performed in a "600 seat theater (proscenium) in a city of 4,000, 30 miles from metropolitan area of more than 200,000." Payment negotiable according to production expenses. Submit complete manuscript and score. SASE. Reports in 2 weeks.
Musicals: "Material should be within the ability of traditional community college with traditional and non-traditional students: simple dancing; innovative and traditional: not over-sophisticated (somewhat family oriented). Variety of music styles. Flexible cast size, props, staging, etc. We do not want extremes, unnecessary profanity or 'operatic' material."
Recent Productions: *Charles and Algernon*, by Rogers and Strouse (based on *Flowers for Algernon*); *Diamond Studs*, by Wann and Simpson (life of Jessee James); *Hello Dolly*; *Kiss Me, Kate*; and *Godspell*.
Tips: "Music should be singable and vary in style. Songs should be an intricate part of the show and not just put in for spectacle. Major roles should be balanced between 4 or 5 characters, rather than one-character shows with chorus."

ASOLO STATE THEATER, Drawer E, Sarasota FL 33578. (813)355-7115. Literary Manager. Play producer. Produces 15 plays (1 musical)/year. Plays are performed at the Asolo Theater (325-seat proscenium house) or by the Asolo Touring Theater (6-member company touring the Southeast). Pays 5% minimum royalty. Query. SASE. Reports in 3 months.
Musicals: "We want nonchorus musicals only. They should be full-length, any subject, with not over 20 in the cast. There are no restrictions on production demands; however, musicals with excessive scenic requirements may be difficult to consider. Submit finished works only."
Recent Productions: *The Tempest*, by Shakespeare; *Da*, by Hugh Leonard; *Ah, Wilderness!*, by Eugene O'Neill; *the Shadow Box*, by Michael Christofer; *History of American Film*, by Christopher Durang (affectionate look at the movies); *Merlin!*, by Jim Hoskins and John Franceschina (children's show with magic); and *Oh, Coward!*.
Tips: "Musicals are produced infrequently here due to the 'classical' basis of Asolo's repertory and inability to 'job-in' musical-theater talent."

BARTER THEATRE, STATE THEATRE OF VIRGINIA, Abingdon VA 24210. (703)628-2281. Producing Director: Rex Partington. Business Manager: Pearl Hayter. Play Producer. Produces 12 plays (2 musicals)/year. Plays performed in Barter Theatre. Pays minimum 5% royalty. SASE. Reports in 3 months.
Musicals: Full length, all styles and topics, small casts, basic instrumentation and minimal set

requirements. "Keep it small. Think in relevant and romantic subjects."
Recent Productions: *I Do! I Do!*; *Oh Coward*; and *The Apple Tree*.

QUENTIN C. BEAVER, 32 Horatio St., Yonkers NY 10710. (914)968-0488. Producer: Q.C. Beaver. Estab. 1979. Produces 6 plays (3 musicals)/year. Plays presented at Fort Salem Theatre, Salem NY—summer stock in Saratoga Springs area. Pays $50-200/performance. Query with synopsis. SASE. Reports in 1 month.
Musicals: Musicals should be "full-length, contemporary, entertaining (not heavy) and include comedy (most important) and good chorus numbers. Sets must be simple and cast should include no more than 4 principals, 10 secondary leads and 8 dancers." Does not want "historic, period, overly dramatic or absurd material."
Recent Productions: *Down River*, by Tom Hather (musical view of Huck Finn); and *The Admiral*, by Buddy Zeck (Columbus pre sail).

DAVID BLACK, 251 E. 51st St., New York NY 10022. (212)753-1188. Producer: David Black. Play producer. Produces 2 plays/year. Plays are performed on Broadway, Off-Broadway and in London. Pays 2% royalty of "gross weekly box office plus $500 average advance." Query with synopsis. SASE. Reports in 2 weeks.
Musicals: "I'm interested in all types of musicals. Playwrights should write for themselves, not me."
Recent Productions: *A Funny Thing Happened on the Way to the Forum*, by Bert Shevelove (musical comedy); and *George M!*, by Michael Stewart (musical).

CALIFORNIA STATE COLLEGE, BAKERSFIELD, DEPARTMENT OF FINE ARTS, 9001 Stockdale Hwy., Bakersfield CA 93309. (805)833-3093. Associate Professor of Theater: Peter Grego. Chairman, Fine Arts: Jerome Kleinsasser. Play producer. Produces 3 plays/year (1 musical every other year). Plays performed in the 500-seat Dore Theatre to the college community and the community at large. Pays 1% minimum royalty. Query. Does not return unsolicited material. Reports in 1 month.
Recent Productions: *Trial By Jury*, by Gilbert and Sullivan (punk/new wave treatment of operetta); and *Camelot*, by Lerner and Lowe.

WILLIAM CAREY COLLEGE DINNER THEATRE, William Carey College, Hattiesburg MS 39401. (601)582-5051, ext. 228. Managing Director: O.L. Quave. Play producer. Produces 2 plays (2 musicals)/year. "Our dinner theater operates only in summer and plays to family audiences." Payment negotiable. Submit complete manuscript and score. SASE. Reports as soon as possible.
Musicals: "Plays should be simply-staged, have small casts (8-10), and be suitable for family viewing; two hours maximum length. Score should require piano only, or piano, electric piano, and drums."
Recent Productions: *Rainbow Jones* (fantasy); *Brass* (original), by Jay Rogers and Keith Thompson (theater company facing the closing of their theater); and *Make Believe* (original), by Jay Rogers and Keith Thompson (boy meets girl).

CARROLL COLLEGE, Little Theatre, Helena MT 59625. (406)442-3450, ext. 276. Director of Theater: Jim Bartruff. Play producer. Produces 4-5 plays (1 musical)/year. "Our plays are produced in our Little Theatre for campus and community. The Little Theatre is a small proscenium house with flexible seating (90-120)." Pays $25-50/performance. Query or submit complete manuscript score and tape of songs. SASE. Reports in 2 weeks.
Musicals: "We consider all types of plays geared for small cast (15 maximum) and minimal settings (unit preferred). Scoring should be for piano and percussion." Does not want musicals based on other musicals or musicals based on non-musical material, e.g. tragedy.
Recent Productions: *Celebration*, by Tom Jones and Harvey Schmidt (love story); *Kiss Me, Kate*, by Spewack and Porter; and *Working*, by Stephen Schwartz and Studs Terkel (working people).
Tips: "Find a place, any place, to do it and get it done. There are literally thousands of little markets yearning for new and good material."

EUGENE S. CASASSA, Ashby West Rd., Fitchburg MA 01420. (617)342-6592. Producer: Eugene S. Casassa. Play producer. Produces 8 plays (1 musical)/year. Plays are produced in an arena with thrust type stage; resident company and small house (120). Pays negotiable fee. Query with synopsis. Does not return unsolicited material. Reports as soon as possible.
Musicals: "We have done a wide variety with success. We are essentially looking for low set requirements; should use piano and/or small combo. Musical should have strong story line."
Recent Productions: *Little Mary Sunshine*, by Besoyan; *Celebration*; and *Godspell*.

CIRCLE IN THE SQUARE THEATRE, 1633 Broadway, New York NY 10019. (212)581-3270. Contact: Assistant to the Literary Director. Play producer. Produces 4 plays (1 musical)/year. Query with synopsis. SASE. Reports in 3-4 months.
Musicals: "The only consideration is that this is theater-in-the-round."

COCKPIT IN COURT SUMMER THEATRE, Essex Community College, Baltimore MD 21237. (301)682-6000. Managing Director: F. Scott Black. Play producer. Produces 7 plays/year. "We operate three separate theaters on our campus. Broadway type musicals are performed in a well-equipped, beautiful theater. Cockpit, upstairs, is a cabaret theater. Classics are performed outdoors in the courtyard with stylized sets and full makeup." Pays through rental and royalty agreement with firms who control rights. Submit complete ms and score. SASE. Reports in 1 month.
Musicals: "Wholesome shows which are suitable for audiences of all ages. Musical score should be of top quality. We use a full orchestra in the pit. Large casts are OK. We like good leading and supporting roles." No material that is politically controversial, vulgar or offensive to the audience. "We prefer a cast of 20-30 for most of our summer musicals with some doubling. We use wagon sets, no turntables or revolving stages."
Recent Productions: *Kiss Me Kate*, by Cole Porter; *I Do, I Do*, by Tom Jones and Harvey Schmidt (*The Fourposter* with music); and *West Side Story*, by Leonard Bernstein (modern day *Romeo and Juliet*).

DAVID J. COGAN, 350 5th Ave., New York NY 10003. (212)563-9562. Contact: David Cogan. Play producer. Produces 1 play/year. Produces musical comedy, straight comedy, and drama in New York. Pays on a royalty basis, or buys script outright for $5,000 maximum. Query. SASE. Reports in 1 month.
Musicals: Interested only in completed projects.
Recent Productions: *A Raisin in the Sun*, by Hannesbury (drama); and *The Odd Couple*, by Neil Simon (comedy).

CONSERVATORY OF THEATRE ARTS AT WEBSTER COLLEGE, 470 E. Lockwood Ave., St. Louis MO 63119. (314)968-6929. Chairman: Peter E. Sargent. Play producer. Produces 10 plays (2-3 musicals)/year. "Our plays are performed in the Loretto Hilton Center for the Performing Arts in the 500-seat Main Stage, the 150-seat Studio Theater and also in a space and schedule called Stage 3, a 125-seat proscenium house." Pays 3% royalty or $15-200/performance "depending on the space." Query with synopsis. SASE. Reports in 1 month.
Musicals: "The Conservatory has a training program in musical theatre and, as a result, would be interested in musicals of all types and performance needs. Send a letter including a statement of production needs, scale of orchestration and such elements that would include cast size, nature of vocal skills and anything the author might consider unusual, within the normal needs of musical productions. Our audience is a midwestern one and we consider that when we choose scripts. However, we would welcome most scripts and would make that judgement upon reading the material."
Recent Productions: *Company*, by Sondheim; *Kurt Weill/From Berlin to Broadway* (a review based on Weill's music); and *Boys from Syracuse*, by Rogers and Hart.
Tips: "Make the musical for a general appeal and include the potential for some strong dance. The story must always be interesting, do not rely on heavy production values to make the play successful. A strong story with supporting music can work."

GLENN CRANE, 6260 Birdland Dr., Adrian MI 49221. (517)263-3411. Producing Director: Glenn Crane. Play producer. Produces 6-12 plays (2 musicals)/year. Pays 15-20% royalty; $200 minimum outright purchase; $50-200/performance or $1,000 for 1 year option. Submit complete ms, score and tape of songs. Prefers 7½ ips reel-to-reel or cassette. SASE. Reports in 1 month.
Musicals: "Any creative, clever, original treatment—full-length or 1-act. We are especially interested in children's musicals with large cast; adult musicals with small cast, but can give first class production to large scale musicals after laboratory production proves worth."
Recent Productions: *Without a Song*, by Young and Hurley (variety of love); *The Whistler's Christmas*, by Harbison and Ames (folk tale); and *Young Willow*, by Gastleton and Ames (Civil War romance).

THE CRICKET THEATRE, Hennepin Center for the Arts, 528 Hennepin Ave., Minneapolis MN 55403. (612)333-5241. Literary Manager: John Orlock. Play producer. Produces 14 plays (1-2 musicals)/year. Royalty negotiable; pays $500 minimum for main season. Submit complete ms and cassette tape of songs. SASE. Reports in 3-6 months.
Musicals: "We seek musical plays by American playwrights and songwriters. We do not seek

mainstream, escapist, 'huge production' musicals like *Music Man, Hello Dolly* or *1776*, but 'medium production' musicals in the 'new play tradition' of *Promenade, Subject to Fits, The Club* and *Starting Here, Starting Now.* Small orchestras only." Maximum cast size: 6.
Recent Productions: *Starting Here, Starting Now,* by Richard Maltby Jr. and David Shire (male-female encounters: a musical review).

CYPRESS COLLEGE THEATER ARTS DEPARTMENT, 9200 Valley View St., Cypress CA 90630. (714)821-6320. Theater Arts Department Chairman: Kaleta Brown. Play producer. Produces 5-6 plays (2 musicals)/year. "Our audience at Cypress College is basically a middle-class, suburban audience. We have a continuing audience that we have built up over the years. Our plays now are produced in our Campus Theater (seating capacity 623) or workshop theater (maximum seating capacity 250)." Pays $50-125/performance. Submit complete ms, score and 7½ ips reel-to-reel tape of songs. SASE. Reports in 1 month.
Musicals: "We must do large-cast shows, generally, because the shows are done as a class. Because we are on a slightly limited budget, we must look carefully at scenery requirements, costume requirements and props.
Recent Productions: *The Royal Family,* by George Kaufman and Edna Ferber; and *Man of La Mancha,* by Mitch Leigh and Joe Darion, *Pippin,* by Roger O Hirson and Stephen Schwartz. Guest artists are frequently used.
Tips: "Open show with a large group, energetic number. Intersperse dance (especially tap) throughout shows and end with a 'ripping' choral number."

DEPARTMENT OF THEATRE, MICHIGAN STATE UNIVERSITY, 149 Auditorium, East Lansing MI 48823. (517)355-6690. Director: Dr. Jon Baisch. Play producer. Produces 10-15 plays (1-2 musicals and many cabaret shows)/year. "Our audiences are students, faculty, and members of the Lansing community. We use two large performance spaces: 3,500-seat either proscenium or platform; 700-seat proscenium. We also use two small spaces: 150-seat thrust stage; 100-seat small proscenium. We stage everything from large-scale productions with orchestra and large casts to small-cast, intimate shows and cabaret entertainment." Performance rights negotiable. Query with synopsis and production specifications. SASE. Reports in 1 month.
Musicals: "We are interested in all types of original material, especially small-cast shows and revues for our small spaces."
Recent Productions: *Pippin, Jesue Christ Superstar,* and *Jacques Brel.*
Tips: "Write a good, modern show. Either write a good story or find one to adapt. The public—much of it—still wants a story."

DEPARTMENT OF THEATRE, SOUTHERN CONNECTICUT STATE COLLEGE, New Haven CT 06515. Chairman: Daniel E. Cashman. Play producer. Produces 4-6 plays (1-2 musicals)/year. Plays performed to general audiences and college students. Pays $25/performance or standard royalty. Submit cassette and/or manuscript. SASE. Reports as soon as possible—"depends on time of year."
Musicals: "We are interested in any musicals as long as they are not religious or polemical in a narrow sense." Should require small cast, props, staging, etc. Does not want "big, old-fashioned musicals."
Recently Produced: *Three Penny Opera,* by Brecht and Weil; and *The Boy Friend,* by Wilson.

DORSET THEATRE FESTIVAL, Box 221, Dorset VT 05251. Artistic Director: Jill Nassivera. Play producer. Produces 6 plays (1 musical)/year. "We perform a summer season at the Dorset Playhouse. The audience is composed partly of tourists to the southern Vermont area, partly of local year-round residents, and partly of second-home owners. Most of the audience (particularly the latter group) attend New York commercial theater frequently and are fairly sophisticated theatrically in their tastes and exposure. They are also accustomed to new scripts, as we do at least one each season." Pays $250 minimum royalty for 6-10 performances, plus transportation and room and board during rehearsal period. "Scripts should be submitted by December for consideration for the summer season."
Musicals: "We are looking for full-length musicals; topics can vary widely, but should have strong audience appeal. We will gladly consider adaptations from other genres. We are also interested in 'plays with music' as well as 'musicals;' that is, the work need not have as many songs as are usually expected of a musical. We are especially interested in works that call for a strong ensemble acting company, capable of being produced with a limited orchestra (piano alone, or piano and one or two other pieces). We require relatively small cast shows (under 12) that can be produced on a unit set. We work on a fairly small but well-equipped stage, and on a tight production budget. Large casts and big choruses are impractical. We don't want material with a very narrow audience appeal, plays with nudity or explicit sexual scenes or plays with 'slick', superficial plots."

Recent Productions: *A Penny Earned*, book by Stephen Kelsey and songs by Annie Lebeaux (Moliere's *Miser*); *Sweeney Todd*, adapted by Nassivera and Wright with music by Paul J. Ascenzo (based on 19th century melodrama); and *Nobody and Me*, by C.A. Philips (supernatural romance play with songs).

DRAMA DEPARTMENT, CLARKE COLLEGE, Dubuque IA 52001. (319)588-6384. Chairman: Karen Ryker. Play producer. Produces 4-5 plays (1 musical)/year. Plays are presented in 750-seat theater to college community and residents of Midwestern town of 65,000; one children's audience year. Submit complete manuscript and score. SASE. Reports in 3 weeks.
Musicals: "We're looking for 2-2½ hour musicals with strong raison d'etre and good score; can be unconventional. We also produce children's musicals (1-1½ hour)—same qualities. Small-cast musicals with simple staging (unit set) are preferred."
Recent Productions: *Stop the World, I Want to Get Off*, by Anthony Newley; *Cabaret*, by Joe Masteroff; and *Aesop's Falables*, by Ed Gryzcke (children's farce).

EAST WEST PLAYERS, 4424 Santa Monica Blvd., Los Angeles CA 90029. (213)660-0366. Artistic Director: Mako Iwamatsu. Administrator: Janet Mitsui. Play producer. Produces 4 plays/year. "We have produced original musical revues and some children's musicals in our theater which is a 99-seat Equity waiver house. Our actors are professional actors. We are an Asian-American theater and consequently the audience is primarily ethnic in make up." Pays 5% minimum royalty. Query with synopsis. SASE. Reports in 1 month.
Musicals: "We look for material dealing with Asian-American culture and produce adult and children's musicals in book and/or revue form. We make no limitations on the writing approach. We look for theme and above all originality. We primarily produce shows with casts under 15. The stage is not huge and has certain limitations; however, we do have a turntable at our disposal."
Recent Productions: *Godspell*, by Tebelak/Schwartz (Jesus Christ); *Happy End*, by Brecht/Weil (Salvation Army vs. Hoods); and *Pacific Overtures*, by Sondheim/Weidman (opening of Japan).

ETC. COMPANY, Michigan School of The Arts, 2111 Emmons Rd., Jackson MI 49203. (517)787-0800. Director: G.L. Blanchard. Play producer. Produces 10-11 plays (2-3 musicals)/year. Plays are produced in a new proscenium theater with thrust capabilities seating 367, or a multiform theater seating 100-200 depending on arrangement. Pays $100-200 outright purchase or by agreement. Query with synopsis. SASE. Reports in 2 weeks.
Recent Productions: *Pippin*; *Over Here!*, and *Reflections* (original).
Tips: "We lean in the direction of shows with casts in the area of 20 or under, with 'moderately sensible' staging."

FESTIVAL PLAYHOUSE, Kalamazoo College, Kalamazoo College MI 49007. (616)383-8509. Artistic Director: Clair Myers. Play producer. Productions attended by city and regional audience as well as student body. Three theaters available: 406-seat open stage; 306-seat thrust stage; and 75-seat experimental stage. Produces 3-4 plays (1 or 2 musicals)/year. Pays $50-150/performance. Query. SASE. Reports in 1 month.
Musicals: "There is no limit on type of musical except those which are operas or require either excessive scenic elements or casts in excess of 30."
Recent Productions: *Jacques Brel*; *Death of a Salesman*, by Miller; and *Tartuffe*, by Moliere; *Carousel*, by Rodgers and Hammerstein; *It's DeLovely*, by Cole Porter, Tim House and Gary Stock (original review); and *Candide*, by Bernstein.

THE FIRST ALL CHILDREN'S THEATRE, INC., 37 W. 65th St., New York NY 10023. Producer: Meridee Stein. Produces 5 plays (4 musicals)/year. "For children, ages two and up, teenagers and their families. These plays are developed with and for our special company to appeal to an audience of young theatergoers." Pays 5% maximum royalty; buys script outright for $750 maximum, or pays $15/performance. Query or submit complete ms and score; "outline is best. If we like it, then we help develop it with the author. All pieces must be created especially for our company." SASE. Reports in 8-10 weeks.
Musicals: "ACT musicals are 45-50 minutes in length and include 8-10 songs with incidental music. We do plays in all genres featuring many kinds of music, i.e., commedia dell' arte, baroque musical fairy tales, modern pop, old tales made new, and originals with challenging, meaningful messages. We do not want material unsuitable for children and their families. The music must be a very important part of the work. Harmonies, arrangements and selection of a band are all done later. Plays include 15-35 children and teenagers. Props, staging can be creative and challenging, though not unrealistic. We have as many as nine pieces in our orchestra. We seldom produce completed scripts. We prefer to develop works from an outline in a cooperative effort between writer, composer, artistic director and staff."

Songwriter's Market Close-up

"If you aim for the stars you should at least land on top of the mountain." This philosophy, passed down to Los Angeles-based Michael Ricciardi (second from the left) from his grandmother, typifies the high hopes and optimistic outlook of Ricciardi and his collaborators, Randy Ames (left) and Eddy Clement (seated at the piano). They know where they want to go and have combined their training and talents to get them there.

"We want to write new, exciting, original ideas for the musical theater. We keep writing and are constantly working on a new project. We keep writers' notebooks and scour bookstores for forgotten pearls. We keep a cassette or reel-to-reel tape recorder loaded with tape at all times, and keep our pencils sharpened and imaginations soaring. In addition, we attend countless musicals, sometimes two or three times, go to talent shows, and read magazine and newspaper articles—always looking for the spark, the idea, the genesis."

Ricciardi was the spark behind their original association. In 1979 he auditioned for the scarecrow role in a local theater company's production of *The Wizard of Oz*. He ended up not only with the role, but with the task of composing music and lyrics for 10 original songs and writing the script.

From that time on "I wanted to write musicals for the stage. But the experience taught me a lesson—I needed help. I called the various college placement services looking for an arranger." The result was his teaming with Ames and Clement, both graduate students in music at California State University.

"We became the Three Musketeers of Songwriting," says Ricciardi. "We began with what we knew, writing a sequel to *The*

Ames-Ricciardi-Clement

Wizard of Oz entitled *The Return of the Wizard of Oz*. We are writing a musical based on the book *Master Skylark* and have loads of ideas for the next four."

They haven't received national acclaim yet, but have the right attitude and formula and are well on their way. When they have a project finished and ready to submit, it is complete. "Each musical score has an overture, curtain call and incidental theme music throughout. Everything we write we score for a seventeen piece orchestra. Our scripts are complete: property lists, sound effects, character descriptions and any notes for options we feel will help."

Just recently they sat in an office at Disney Studios as the director listened to their version of *The Return to the Wizard of Oz*. "We're supposed to hear from them," says Ricciardi. "Nothing may come of it, but then again—maybe!"

Recent Productions: *Grownups*, by Vicki Blumenthal and John Forster (relationships between children and adults); *Incredible Feeling Show*, by Elizabeth Swados (a young person's self-discovery); and *Alice through the Looking Glass*, by S. Dias, M. Stein and P. Namanworth (musical version of Lewis Carroll's classic, performed in commedia style).

Tips: "Our theater stresses excellence and professionalism. Flexibility on everybody's part is the key to our success. The work we produce is extremely creative and highly original. Each production is developed and nurtured over a long period of time—sometimes as long as two years. Each show has a team of adult theater professionals who direct and supervise the entire production."

FOOLKILLER ETC., 2 W. 39th St., Kansas City MO 64111. (816)756-3754. Chairman: Bill Clause. Play producer. Produces 7-15 plays/year. Pays negotiable royalties. "Foolkiller is an excellent exposure showcase for new talent." Query with synopsis or contact by phone. SASE. Reports in 2 months.
Musicals: "We consider everything but prefer topics dealing with problems aimed at working and middle-class people — comedies and political and social commentaries. We prefer material that doesn't last more than one hour. Our stage is about 15x35; cast should be 2-15 people. We don't want to see any slick, sophisticated kinds of writing that may go over everyone's head, or anything terribly pessimistic."
Recent Productions: *Drop Hammer*, by Manny Fried (labor unions); and *Turn of the Century Vaudeville*, by Joyce Constant, Don Carlson and Carol Smith (historical vaudeville musical).
Tips: "The Foolkiller is an organization that has many facets. It is a showcase for new talent. Musicians have frequent public jam sessions and walk-on talent is encouraged. Freedom of expression is emphasized in all activities. There is a large public following and community support. All material is original."

SAMUEL FRENCH, INC., 25 W. 45th St., New York NY 10036. (212)582-4700. Editor: Lawrence R. Harbison. Play publisher (musicals only). Publishes about 70 scripts (6-8 musicals)/year. Plays used by community, stock and dinner theaters, regional repertories, and college and high school markets. Pays 10% royalty on play scripts sold, generally an advance against future royalties, and a per-performance royalty depending on various factors. "We take 10-20% agency fee. Submit only the libretto (book). If we like it, we may ask to see and/or hear music." SASE. Reports in 8 weeks minimum. If the work has been recommended for further consideration, the process may take considerably longer.
Musicals: "We publish primarily New York-produced musicals, though we do occasionally bring out a show which has not had a New York City production (1 in 1980). These are intended primarily, but not necessarily, for children's and community or dinner theaters. No religious material, or anything unstageworthy. We are particularly looking for small-cast, easy-to-produce musicals with good female roles. We are not interested in publishing big, splashy 'Broadway' musicals—unless they have been done on Broadway. Send us only the book of your musical. The music seems to be the easiest part of a musical; the book, the most difficult. Musicals succeed or fail on the basis of their book, not their music. If we like the book, we may ask to hear a tape of the score."
Recent Publications: *I Love My Wife*, by Cy Coleman and Michael Stewart (about marital infidelity in middle-class America) from Broadway; *The Grand Tour*, by Michael Stewart and Mark Bramble (musical version of play *Jacobowsky and the Colonel*) from Broadway; *Sherlock Holmes and the Curious Adventure of the Clockwork Prince*, by Cleve Haubold and James Alfred Hitt (children's play with music); and *Hot Grog*, by Jim Wann and Bland Simpson (about pirates) from off Broadway.
Tips: "Start small. Do a small-cast, easy-to-produce, inexpensive show. Then, once you have achieved a 'track record,' only then, try your 2 million dollar Broadway musical. Never, ever, imitate what you think is 'commercial'—it never *will* be. You *must* have a strong *story*. Without that, all your wonderful music is for naught."

GEORGIA COLLEGE THEATRE, Box 654, Milledgeville GA 31061. (914)453-5139. Director: John P. Blair Jr. Play producer. Produces 3-4 plays (1 musical)/year. "Plays are presented in 1,100 capacity proscenium to small-town, provincial audience whom we are trying to educate." Pays 50% royalty. Submit complete manuscript and score. SASE. Reports in 1 month.
Musicals: "We like serious topics and intents, but with color, humor and lots of life—like *Fiddler on the Roof, Threepenny Opera* and *Man of La Mancha*. We are catholic in our tastes. We cannot handle casts of more than 35 comfortably. Our space is limited with no fly or wing space to speak of. We don't want bright, happy, nonsensical pieces (*Brigadoon* is about as much like that as we intend to get.)"
Recently Produced: *Threepenny Opera, Man of La Mancha, Camelot, Brigadoon,* and *Fiddler on the Roof.*

THE GOODMAN THEATRE, 200 S. Columbus Dr., Chicago IL 60603. Artistic Director: Gregory Mosher. Play producer. Produces 6 plays (1 musical) and several special events each year. "The Goodman has a six-play Mainstage season and a varied Stage Two season. Pays on a royalty basis. Submit complete ms and cassette tape of songs. SASE. Reports in 4-8 months.
Musicals: "The Goodman seeks musicals with serious musical and literary purpose and merit; those that seek to be more than light entertainment. Except under extraordinary circumstances, cast size should not be above 12. Physical production demands should not be great. Emphasis should be on the script, music and actors, not the physical production values."

Recent Productions: *Lone Canoe*, by David Mamet, with music and lyrics by Alaric (Rokko) Jans (a serious drama with songs); and *Working*.

GREEN MOUNTAIN GUILD, White River Junction VT 05001. (802)295-7016. Managing Director: Marjorie O'Neill-Butler. Play producer. Produces 18 plays (8-10 musicals)/year. Produces plays for a summer theater audience in 4 locations in Vermont: Stowe, White River Junction, Killington and Mt. Snow. Pays $75 minimum/performance. Query with synopsis. Send script and cassette with music. SASE. Reports in 1 month.
Musicals: We are looking for musicals with "a small cast, a good story line, well-developed characters, songs and music that come naturally out of the story and music that works with piano and drums only." No frivolous material. Prefers one-set shows.
Recent Productions: *Shenandoah* (about Civil War farm family); *Carousel*, by Rodgers and Hammerstein; and *Pippin*, by Stephen Schwartz; *The Wizard of Oz*, by L. Frank Baum (traditional story); *My Fair Lady*, by Lerner & Loewe (Shaw's *Pygmalion*); *Two by Two*, by Rodgers & Charnin (Noah and the ark); and *I Do! I Do!*.

ROBERT A. HOLDER, Box 5132, University of North Alabama, Florence AL 35630. Director of Theater: Robert A. Holder. Play producer. Produces 4 plays (1-2 musicals)/year. Plays presented for college and community audiences. Pays by royalty or performance. Submit complete manuscript and score or submit complete manuscript, score, and tape of songs. SASE. Reports in 3 weeks.
Musicals: "We want primarily those with leads that can be convincingly played by college-age students. Any topic, any style, not exceeding 2 hours. We want contemporary themes primarily (*Pippin*-type would be welcomed exception) with good balance of dance and choral work; small or large orchestra and casts. Complicated set or costume plots or period plays are not desirable."
Recent Productions: *A Funny Thing Happened on My Way to the Forum*; *South Pacific* and *Music Man*.

HOLLINS COLLEGE THEATRE ARTS DEPARTMENT, Hollins College VA 24020. (703)362-6518. Chairman: Thomas Atkins. Play producer. Produces 2 plays (2 musicals every 4 years)/year. Plays are performed in Hollins College and Roanoke, Virginia communities. Payment negotiated "according to the involvement of writers in the production." Submit complete manuscript, score, and tape of songs. Prefers cassette. SASE. Reports in 1 month.
Musicals: "Hollins College has a literary festival each year. We are open to receive all types of new musical materials: one-acts, full-lengths, children's musicals, modern topics, etc. Requirements for musical accompaniment should be limited, however, for our budget only allows for hiring a
Recent Productions: *Caste*, by Mary Ellen O'Brien (Victorian romance); *The Boy Friend*, by Wilson (20s romantic comedy); *No, No, Nanette*, by Youmans (20s romantic comedy); and *Pigeons*, by Thomas Atkins (southern family comedy).

HOWARD UNIVERSITY DEPARTMENT OF DRAMA, Washington DC 20059. (202)636-7050. Chairperson: Henrie Edmonds. Play producer. Produces 1 play/year. Pays $75-100/performance. Submit complete ms and cassette of songs. SASE. Reports in 4 months.
Recent Productions: *Mushy Mouth*, by Henri Edmonds (about a speech handicapped child); *Brother, Brother Mine*, by Henri Edmonds/Kelsey Collie (comedy of errors); and *Wearing the Mask*, by Henri Edmonds (black poetry).

HUDSON GUILD THEATRE, 441 W. 26 St., New York NY 10001. (212)760-9810. Producing Director: David Kerry Heefner. Play producer. Produces 5 plays (1 musical)/year. "Plays are done at the Hudson Guild Theatre to very diverse audiences, ages 25-65." Pays $500 for a limited run. Submit complete manuscript and score. SASE. Reports in about 2 months.
Musicals: "The only limitation is that material should *not* have been performed in New York before." Maximum cast size should be 20 people.
Recent Productions: *Snapshot*, by Bernard and Kaplan; and *My Mother Was A*, by Laurents and Neuman.

IMPOSSIBLE RAGTIME THEATRE, 120 W. 28th St., New York NY 10001. (212)929-8003. Artistic Director: Ted Story. Play Producer. Produces 5 plays/year. "Writers are seldom paid—this is off-Broadway." Query with synopsis. "Enclose card for response." SASE. Reports in 3 months.
Musicals: No limitations on format or staging.

THE INNER CITY CULTURAL CENTER, 1308 S. New Hampshire Ave., Los Angeles CA 90006. (213)387-1161. Executive Director: C. Bernard Jackson. Administrative Director: Elaine Kashiki. Play producer. Produces 4-6 plays (2 musicals)/year. "The Inner City Cultural Center is a multi-ethnic, multi-cultural arts organization primarily aimed at the community in which it is located." Query with synopsis. Does not return unsolicited material. Reports in 1 month.

Recent Productions: *Crenshaw Boulevard*, by James Bronson (1940s musical); *A New Liliom*, by C.B. Jackson (adaptation of *Liliom* on which Rodgers' and Hammerstein's *Carousel* was based); *Deadwood Dick, Legend of the West*, by Warren Burdine (Black western musical satire).

INTERLOCHEN ARTS ACADEMY PLAYWRIGHT PROJECT, Interlochen MI 49643. (616)276-9221. Chairman: Anne Marie Gillis. Play producer. Produces 4 plays (1 musical)/year. "We are a unique preprofessional boarding school dedicated to sophisticated training in the fine arts. With about 400 students in five 'major' art areas: music, visual art, creative writing, dance and drama. We struggle to establish curricula allowing our students as complete a picture of work in their field as possible. Our plays are performed in Grunow Theatre (250 seats) on the campus of Interlochen Arts Academy. The audience is made up of students and faculty and some local people from Traverse City." Pays $200, travel expense, and room and board during stay on campus. Submit complete manuscript and tape of songs. Prefers cassette. SASE. Plays should be submitted by December 1 and are returned by February 1.

Musicals: "Plays should be suitable for our peformers' ages (15-19). Do not, however, be misled by this: our students are well-read, reasonably well-trained, dedicated, and many go on to professional work or continued schooling in their field. They study four hours of varied drama classes per day, of which half (a two-hour block called Acting/Production) could be given daily to our Playwright Project next April and May. Evening rehearsals of 2-3 hours may also be called as necessary."

Recent Productions: *Experimental Reader's Theatre, Landscape of the Body, The Cave Dwellers,* and *Marlowe and Friends*, an Elizabethan Pastiche in One Act, by Carroll P. Cole. Also produced *When the War Is Over*, by Schlesinger and Dansicker (Jewish children); and *The Tempest*.

JEKYLL ISLAND MUSIC THEATRE, 181 Old Plantation Rd., Jekyll Island GA 31520. (912)635-3378. Resident Manager: Ms. Leila El-Bisi. Musical play producer. Produces 1 musical/year. "Musicals are produced for either educational or entertainment purposes and often both. Audiences are conservative middle- or upper-middle-class. New musicals we produce are workshop productions that should help the creators as much as educate our students or entertain our patrons. The composer-lyricist-writer is hired for 3 months at $125-200/week, plus room." Query with synopsis. SASE. Reports whenever possible and as soon as possible.

Musicals: "We use musicals involving a relatively young cast (teenage to mid-twenties). Lengths have never been past 2½ hours. Musicals have ranged in subject matter from fantasy to an adaptation of an F. Scott Fitzgerald short story. Periods of particular interest are the gay nineties through the roaring twenties. We perform new works on a workshop basis and are more interested in the developmental phase of a new musical than anything else. We work with very limited production budgets on new works. We want the writers to hear and see their work and *change* it—*rework* it, free from final production constraints. We don't want perfect sets to obscure flaws that need to be corrected in the material. We are sensitive to language, vulgarity for its own sake is useless to us."

Recent Productions: *Soap* (soap operas), (produced in 1977, before the TV show), *Bernice Bobs Her Hair* (based on F. Scott Fitzgerald short story), by Bob McDowell, and *Pisbee Cocola,* (a musical fantasy).

Tips: "Work on your script and music for a long time anywhere and with anyone you can with no sets, costumes, lights, etc. That way you find out how good your work is. There are a lot of 'this is what the theater is really like' musicals being written—it's getting redundant and self-indulgent. Musical writers should go outside the theater and find material in the streets, the schools, history, people. Musical writers should not be afraid to draw on the techniques and styles of past musical traditions."

JEWISH COMMUNITY CENTER OF GREATER WASHINGTON, 6125 Montrose Rd., Rockville MD 20852. (301)881-0100. Director, School of Theatre: Darrell Calvin. Play producer. Produces 3-4 plays (3-4 musicals)/year. Produces plays in a 300-seat theater. Query. SASE. Reports in 1 month.

Musicals: "We produce popular and original musicals and dramas performed by teens and professional adults."

Recent Productions: *Berlin to Broadway with Kurt Weill* and *Threepenny Opera.* Upcoming: *Everyone's Gerschwin* (an original musical) and *Promenade* by Al Carmines.

JITASCA, 313 Heston Ave., Norristown PA 19403. (215)539-9284. Play producer. Produces 1 play/year. "We need a composer to set lyrics to music. *Experienced only please.*" Pays 2% minimum royalty. Query. SASE. Reports in 1 week.

Songwriter's Market Close-up

Fran Landesman has created a unique niche for herself in the music world not by fitting the mold, but by breaking it. Instead of the verse-chorus formula lyric, she writes what are really hip poems. Alec Wilder, George Shearing and Steve Allen are among the many composers who have turned her verse into recorded songs. Landesman burst on the music scene, not in Nashville, LA or New York, but in—of all places—St. Louis, with the world premiere of her musical, *The Nervous Set*.

The original cast album of that 1959 Broadway satire on the beat generation is now a collector's item and two of its songs, written with composer Tommy Wolf, have become jazz classics. The mention of either title—"Ballad of the Sad Young Men" or "Spring Can Really Hang You Up the Most"—will elicit an admiring gasp of recognition from jazz buffs familiar with interpretations by such artists as Ella Fitzgerald, Tony Bennett, Shirly Bassey and Roberta Flack. And the number of recordings and performances continues to grow.

Critics have compared the sharp edges of her wit to Cole Porter and Noel Coward; that's not surprising since those urbane lyricists, along with Larry Hart, "were my heroes," says Landesman. The works of humorist Dorothy Parker and Gilbert and Sullivan were the real role models for her sophisticated style. "I read every word they ever wrote."

A resident of London since 1964, the Manhattan-born "punk" poet has acquired an international following with the publication of three books of her wryly witty verses. In the last few years Landesman has been encouraged to take her poetry to the people, frequently performing her bittersweet chronicles of the human predicament on the BBC as well as in such diverse settings as London's National Theatre, the Edinburgh Festival and New York's Duplex.

Fran Landesman

Landesman views her twin writing and performing careers as only beginning to gain momentum. "I want to do it all . . . record an album, appear in intimate rooms and huge rock festivals, and play the Hollywood Bowl." She would like to expand her audience by collaborating with a pop recording artist/composer. "I'd love to team up with Elton John . . . I keep waiting for him to realize that I'm around."

Meanwhile, a newly discovered theatre writer, Jason McAuliffe, has woven over 40 of Landesman's verses into *Loose Connections*, a musical entertainment on its way to New York. The show's arrival should help refocus the spotlight on her offbeat lyrical talents.

Where does she get her ideas? "Most of my songs come from sitting around, talking with my friends and remembering the lines they throw out." What she aims for is truth. "Truth is what matters . . . and a sense of humor."

Sheila Davis

LYRIC THEATER OF NEW YORK, 363 E. 76th St., 8J, New York NY 10021. Artistic Director: Neal Newman. Play producer. Produces 10 plays (6 musicals)/year. Plays presented in "small off-off Broadway theater in New York; during summer in a lovely old playhouse in North

Conway, New Hampshire." Pays $25-50/performance. Query with synopsis. SASE. Reports in 3 months.

Musicals: "We consider anything that is not a typical commercial Broadway-type musical. We search for works that advance the musical theater as an artform. Strong characters, situations, and individual expression in play, lyrics and music. Full length works are preferred but one acts are occasionally done. Any topic or type, but we are always searching for a great dramatic musical. Any format is possible providing music is used in some way to tell the story. Cast size is not a problem. Due to budget limitations, however, we are unable to present works calling for many or elaborate settings and properties. Costumes are always first rate. We don't want commercial musicals (*Sugar, No, No, Nanette*), non-musicals or revues.)"

Recent Productions: *Dance on a Country Grave*, by Kelly Hamilton (works of Thomas Hardy); *Mrs. Moses*, by Bill Solly (Bible through the eyes of Moses' wife); and *Willie the Weeper*, Jerome Moross (surreal reefer nightmare).

Tips: "Don't expect Broadway for a long, long time. If it's good it will get done eventually. Strong characters and situations are better than big budgets. Also, know what market you are writing for: opera house, Broadway, summer stock, etc."

MANHATTAN THEATRE CLUB, 321 E. 73 St., New York NY 10021. (212)288-2500. Literary Manager: Jonathan Alper. Play producer. Produces 10 plays (2 musicals)/year. Plays are performed at the Manhattan Theatre Club before varied audiences. Send synopsis first *or* a letter of recommendation with the manuscript. SASE. Reports in 6 months.

Musicals: Small scale musicals—revue types are best because of theatre's limited space. *No* historical drama, verse drama or children's plays."

Recent Production: *Ain't Misbehavin.*

MEMPHIS STATE UNIVERSITY, Theatre Department, Memphis TN 38152. (901)454-2565. Director of Theatre: Dr. Prof. Russell G. Whaley. Play producer. Produces 12 plays (2-4 musicals)/year. Audience is the faculty, students and townspeople of Memphis. Pays 10-15% of gate or $20-100/performance. Query with synopsis. SASE. Reports in 1 month.

Musicals: "We are most interested in noncommercial, nonformula works. We can also handle difficult music and large cast demands. We do both extravaganza and studio type productions. No pageants, historical epics or satires on satires."

Recent Productions: *Carousel*, by Rodgers & Hammerstein; *Roar of the Greasepaint, The Smell of the Crowd*, by Bricusse and Newley.

Tips: "Write non-formular, do not duplicate, write for today's audience."

MID-PLAINS COMMUNITY COLLEGE, State Farm Rd., North Platte NE 69101. (308)532-8980. Chairman, Communication and Drama Department: Colin Taylor. Play producer. Produces 3-4 plays (1 musical)/year. Plays performed "at the college auditorium (small house and on tour to area schools." Pays $100 maximum/performance. Query with synopsis or submit complete manuscript and score. SASE. Reports in 1 month.

Musicals: Needs musicals with small cast (under 25 characters) and flexible staging. "Beginning singers need consideration. We cannot fly scenery, but use free-standing sets and projections in a 'theatre of light.' We work with a limited budget and unlimited imagination."

Recent Productions: *Joe Egg*, by Nichols (family love); *J.B.*, by MacLeish (Job story); and *Count Dracula* (parody comedy based on Stoker).

MILWAUKEE REPERTORY THEATER, 929 N. Water St., Milwaukee WI 53202. (414)273-7121. Artistic Director: John Dillon. Play producer. Produces 12 plays (1 musical)/year. "We have mainly a subscription audience." Pays negotiable royalty. Submit ms and cassette tape of songs. SASE. Reports "as soon as possible."

Musicals: "We seek small cast musicals suitable for resident theater productions. We're interested in quality material (not froth) performable in a 500-seat three-quarter round theater."

Recent Productions: *On the Road to Babylon*, by Richard Wesley, Peter Link and Brent Nicholson (urban life in New York City); *Dead Souls*, by Gogol; *Dance of Death*, by Strindberg; and *Island*, by Peter Link and Brent Nicholson (life in the Caribbean).

NASHVILLE ACADEMY THEATRE, 724 2nd Ave., South and Lindsley, Box 7066, Nashville TN 37210. (615)254-9103. Director: Michael Y. Walters. Play producer. Produces 8 plays/year. Plays are performed in a 696-seat theater for audiences ranging in age from kindergarten through high school. Pays $15-50/performance. Submit complete ms and score. SASE. Reports "after play-reading committee is through."

Musicals: "We want wholesome entertainment for various age groups, e.g. *Cinderella* for the very young, *Tom Sawyer* for teens and pre-teens and *Man of La Mancha* for high schoolers. Average

cast size is 15. We do not want to see any poorly written, sensational or pornographic materials."
Recent Productions: *1984*, by George Orwell (future); *Ten Little Indians*, by Agatha Christie (revenge); and *Really Rosie*, by Maurice Sendak (imagination).

NEGRO ENSEMBLE COMPANY, 165 W. 46th St., New York NY 10036. (212)575-5860. Artistic Director: Douglas Turner Ward. Play producer. Produces 4 plays/year. Pays by office percentage of box office take. Submit complete manuscript and score. Returns material "only if writer insists, *otherwise, play is kept on file."*
Musicals: "Submit only plays that deal with black life and the black experience."

THE NEW PLAYWRIGHT'S THEATRE OF WASHINGTON, 1742 Church St. NW, Washington DC 20036. (202)232-1122. Script Evaluations: Harry Bagdasian. Play producer. Produces 5 plays (1 musical)/year. For general audience with interest in new works. Payment individually negotiated; averages $600/work. Submit complete ms and cassette tape of music. Score is optional. SASE. Reports in 4-6 months.
Musicals: Seeks all types: revues, musical comedies and musical theater with strong story line. Does not want material that has had major, fully professional prior production." Instrumental forces should be chamber-size; no more than 12 musicians. Cast can be up to 15."
Recent Productions: *Dear Evelyn*, by Tim Grundmann (story about an advice columnist).

THE NICOLET PLAYERS, Nicolet College, Box 518. Rhinelander WI 54501. (715)369-4476. Play producer. Produces 6 plays (2 musicals)/year. "Nicolet College is a small community college of about 1,000 students, in a town of about 10,000 people." Pays $25-100/performance. Query with synopsis. SASE. Reports in 1 weeks.
Musicals: "We consider musicals that are interesting and theatrical. We have a small stage, a ¾ thrust, which is approximately 25-feet in diameter and limited backstage area. No fly space, just a ceiling 12 ft. above the stage. Keep it small and simple."
Recent Productions: *The Fantasticks*, by Schmidt and Jones; *A Funny Thing Happened on My Way to the Forum*, by Sondheim, Shevelove and Gelbert; *The Apple Tree*, by Feiffer, Bock and Harnick; and *Diamond Studs*, by Wann and Simpson.

NORTH CAROLINA CENTRAL UNIVERSITY, DEPARTMENT OF DRAMATIC ART, Box 19593, Durham NC 27707. (919)683-6242. Chairperson: Linda Kerr Norflett. Play producer. Produces 4 plays (1-2 musicals)/year. "North Carolina Central University is a traditionally black university but the theater department is racially mixed. We put great emphasis on producing new works by black playwrights as well as other minorities. Pays by royalty. Query with synopsis or submit tape of songs with or without manuscript and score. SASE. Reports in 2 weeks.
Musicals: "We are looking for plays that are non-racial by playwrights from major ethnic groups, racial with clean humanistic themes, music and dance compilations (revue styles), and experimental performance pieces. Be as creative and experimental as your talent will let you and don't underestimate the power of metaphor. Keep staging simple, props at a minimum and cast size below 20." Does not want culturally limiting material.
Recent Productions: *Don't Bother Me, I Can't Cope*, by Micki Grant (race relations); *Guys and Dolls*; and *Purlie* (race relations).

KEATH NORTH, Box 1259, Hot Springs National Park AR 71901. (501)767-2351. Producer: Keath North. Play producer. Produces 2 plays (2 musicals)/year. Plays presented to visitors to Hot Springs National Park in a 1,600-seat amphitheater. Pays 5-15% royalty. Query. SASE. Reports in 2 weeks.
Musicals: Musicals should be family-oriented.
Recent Productions: *Papa Bear—Mama Bear*, by Hopkins and Goetz (family musical).

OFF CENTER THEATRE, 436 W. 18th, New York NY 10011. (212)929-8299. Producer: Abigail Rosen. Play producer. Produces 4 plays (1-3 musicals)/year. The plays are performed "off-Broadway." Pays percentage of box office receipts after initial expenses have been recouped. Submit complete ms, score and type of songs. SASE. Reports in 1 week.
Musicals: "We're interested in any and all types of musicals but prefer a small cast."
Recent Productions: *The Last Vaudeville Show at Radio City Music Hall*, by Seidman, Rosen and Field (vaudeville); and *Just for Fun—The Music of Jerome Kern* (revue).

PERFORMANCE PUBLISHING CO., 978 N. McLean Blvd., Elgin IL 60120. (312)697-5636. Editor: Virginia Butler. Play publisher. Publishes 30-50 plays (4-6 musicals)/year. Plays are used by children's theaters, junior and senior high schools, colleges and community theatres. Pays standard royalty/performance. Submit complete ms, score and cassette tape of songs. SASE. Reports in 3 months.

Musicals: "We prefer large cast, contemporary musicals which are easy to stage and produce. We like children's musicals if the accompaniment is fairly simple. Plot your shows strongly, keep your scenery and staging simple, your musical numbers and choreography easily explained and blocked out. Originality and style are up to the author. We want innovative and tuneful shows but no X-rated material. We are very interested in the new writer and believe that, with revision and editorial help, he can achieve success in writing original musicals for the amateur market."

Recent Productions: *Disco! Disco!*, by Phillip and Marie Scott, Edward and Kathleen Darby and John and Marsha Glover (school disco contest); and *Nashville Jamboree*, by Tim Kelly and Jim and Mary Stuart (country and rock musical).

PERFORMING ARTS DEPARTMENT, Avila College, 11901 Wornall Rd., Kansas City MO 64145. (816)942-8408. Chairman, Performing Arts: Dr. William J. Louis. Play producer. Produces 8 plays (1 musical)/year. Four plays are produced in a 500-seat thrust stage theater and four in Actors Laboratory Theatre (250 seat theatre-in-the-round). To date, only well known musicals have been produced. Original shows would have to be individually contracted for. Submit through agent. SASE. Reports in 2 months.

Musicals: "We prefer shows 2 hours in length and topics for a liberal school but still a Catholic-sponsored institution. Wholesome, those with merit, family audience oriented. We prefer cast not larger than 25."

Recent Productions: *110 in the Shade*, by Jones and Schmidt (love, faith and self-confidence); and *Paint Your Wagon* (romantic comedy), and *Brigadoon* (fantasy and idealism), by Lerner and Loewe.

Tips: "Return to romantic plot of substance, like *110 in the Shade* or *Man of LaMancha* or *West Side Story*."

REPERTORY THEATRE OF ST. LOUIS, (formerly Loretto-Hilton Repertory Theatre), 130 Edgar Rd., St. Louis MO 63119. (314)962-8410. Artistic Director: Wallace Chappell. Play producer. Produces 8 plays/year. "We produce two seasons: one of five works of broad appeal, the other of three new plays or classical works of relatively narrow appeal. The former are presented in a 724-seat thrust theater for 30-odd performances; attendance runs about 90% of capacity, 80% season subscribers. Audiences are cross-sectional, with a distinct bias towards upper-income and high eduction. We could consider 'experimental' musicals for the second season, but it's not likely." Pays 4% royalty "and up on a sliding scale." Query or query with synopsis. SASE. "Plays/librettos that are obviously outside our range are returned fairly soon (say, six weeks); others are held until we start planning in February for the following fall. Setting the season generally takes us until July or August."

Musicals: "Dramatic values are paramount; intellectual and/or artistic qualities rank well ahead of entertainment. We are primarily an acting company, not a musical one. Emphasize characterization and theme. We are at our best expressing the complexity and depth of real characters in humanly significant (not necessarily real—fantasy is acceptable) situations; at our worst in inventing or pretending to three-dimensionality where the playwright's imagination has failed. We look more kindly on scores that call for relatively small orchestras. As to mise-en-scene, we regard that by and large as the designer's problem, not the playwright's. Likewise, business if not dramatically integral, is the concern of actors and directors."

Recent Productions: *Tom Jones*, by Arrick and Damashek (adaptation of Fielding's novel); *Canterbury Tales*, by Starkie, Coghill, Hall and Hankins (adaptation of Chaucer's epic); *Have I Stayed Too Long at the Fair* (a look at the St. Louis World's Fair of 1904); and *Threepenny Opera*, planned in the fall of 1981.

C.M. REYNOLDS/THE THEATRE, WINTHROP COLLEGE, 319 Kinard Building, Rock Hill SC 29733. (803)323-2171. Associate Professor: C.M. Reynolds. Play producer. Produces 4 + plays (1 musical)/year. Plays presented to general college audience. Pays $65 maximum/performance. Query with synopsis. Does not return unsolicited material. Reports in 3 weeks.

Musicals: Standard; avante garde possible. "We have a small stage and no orchestra pit." No lavish spectacles.

Recent Productions: *Godspell; Handsome Harry's Guide to Happiness* (original); and *The Fantasticks*.

ST. NICHOLAS THEATER, 2851 N. Halsted St., Chicago IL 60657. Contact: Literary Manager. Play producer. Produces 8 plays (0-2 musicals) and 3 special events/year. Submit complete ms and tape of songs. SASE. Reports in 4-6 months.

Musicals: "We are not interested in commercial musical ventures. We are interested in small cast

musicals where the music is an organic part of the piece and not an extenuation or addendum to a flimsy plot.
Recent Productions: *Funeral March for a One-Man Band,* by Ron Whyte and Mel Marvin (reawakening to the meaning of life); *The Prince, The Dwarf, and the Blacksmith's Daughter,* by Tom Mula and Les Stahl (individuals discovering their true feelings from a story by John Gardner); and *The Enchanted Cottage,* by Perry Granger and John McKinney (discovery of true beauty through love).
Tips: "Write well, have something you want to say, and look around to see who is producing work in a similar vein."

SHOWBOAT MAJESTIC, Foot of Broadway, Cincinnati OH 45202. (513)241-6550. Producing Director: F. Paul Rutledge. Play producer. Produces 10 plays (3-5 musicals)/year. Plays are produced on the Showboat Majestic, the last of the original floating theaters located on the Ohio River. Pays $75-110/performance. "Most musicals are rented through New York. We follow regular royalty rental plan from them." Query. SASE. Reports in 1 month.
Musicals: "We are seeking original songs, musical comedies no longer than two hours with an intermission, revues and small cast shows." No avant-garde or experimental scripts. Cast should be less than 10.
Recent Productions: *The Fantasticks,* by Schmidt and Jones; *Gold Dust,* by Wann; *I Do! I Do!,* by Schmidt and Jones; and *Show Me Where the Good Times Are.*
Tips: "Begin with an acknowledged good story line. Find a play in the public domain that could be turned into a musical."

MARK TAPER FORUM-CENTURY THEATRE, Group/Literary Dept., 135 N. Grand Ave., Los Angeles CA 90012. (213)972-7353. Literary Manager: Russell Vandenbroucke. Play producer. Produces 5 plays (5 musicals in 15 years)/year. Equity house with a *loyal* following—mostly through subscription; 700 seat theatre in downtown Los Angeles. Payment negotiable. Submit complete manuscript, score, and tape of songs. Prefers cassette. SASE. Reports in 1 month.
Musicals: "We cannot have elaborate sets, scene changes, etc."
Recent Productions: *Tin Types,* by Mary Kyte with Mel Marvin and Gary Pearle (turn of century America); and *Bill Bishop Goes to War,* by John Gray/Eric Peterson (famous WWI pilot).

THEATER 3, 10426 95th St., Edmonton, Alberta, Canada T5H 2C1. (403)426-6870. Artistic Director: Keith Digby. Play producer. Produces 6-9 plays/year. Plays are performed in a 250-seat theater. Payment negotiable. Query. SAE and International Reply Coupons. Reports in 1 month.
Musicals: "Ours is not basically a musical theater. Occasionally a high quality, profile musical is performed. Family orientations are preferred for the Christmas season. Small casts and back-up musicians are essential. Simple unit staging is also necessary."
Recent Productions: *Godspell,* by Stephen Schwartz and John Michael Tebelak; *Vanities,* by Jack Heifner (drama); and *A Taste of Honey,* by Shelagh Delaney (drama).

THEATRE DEPARTMENT, Centenary College, Shreveport LA 71104. (318)869-5242. Chairman: Robert R. Buseik. Play producer. Produces 6 plays (3 musicals)/year. Plays are presented in a 350-seat playhouse to college and community audiences. Submit ms and score. SASE. Reports in 1 month.
Recent Productions: *No, No Nanette; Carnival; Something's Afoot; Pippin;* and *Pajama Game.*

THEATRE FOR THE NEW CITY, 162 2nd Ave., New York NY 10003. (212)254-1109. Director: George Bartenieff. Play producer. Produces 30 plays (6 musicals)/year. Plays are performed for a mixed audience. "Some writer are commissioned; others share the box office take with actors." Submit complete manuscript with lyrics. SASE. Reports in 2 months.
Musicals: No limitations on cast size, props, staging, etc. "No children's plays with bunny rabbit feel."
Recent Productions: *The Meehans,* by Chuck Chosid.

THEATRE FOR YOUNG AMERICA, 7204 W. 80th St., Shawnee Mission KS 66208. Artistic Director: Gene Mackey. Play producer. Produces 8 plays (2-3 musicals)/year. For children, preschool to high school. Pays $10-25/performance. Query with synopsis. SASE. Reports in 1 month.
Musicals: 1-1½ hour productions with small cast oriented to children and high-school youths. "A clear, strong, compelling story is important; a well known title is very important."
Recent Productions: *Androcles and the Lion,* by Aurand Harris and Glen Mack (music); *The Tale of Peter Rabbit,* by Rita Lovett and Gene Mackey (adapted from Beatrix Potter's *Peter Rabbit*);

The Hare and the Tortoise, by Cheryl O'Brien and Gene Mackey (adapted from Aesop's fable); and *Tom Sawyer*, by Michael Dansicker and Sarah Marie Schlesinger (adapted from Mark Twain's novel).

THEATRE OF THE RIVERSIDE CHURCH, 490 Riverside Dr., New York NY 10027. (212)864-2929. Coordinating Director: David ·Manion. Play producer. Produces 6 plays/year. Plays are produced for black and Hispanic audiences in New Jersey and New York. Pays $125. Submit complete ms, score and tape of songs. Prefers cassette. SASE. Reports in 1-3 months.
Musicals: "All types are accepted, full-evening or one-act. We are very involved with Hispanic and black themes and are specifically searching for an American Indian show. We favor smaller casts (under ten) and do not want to see sexual overtness or nudity for no purpose."
Recent Productions: *Fixed*, by Robert M. Riley (a beauty parlor in Detroit in the 1930s); *Corral*, by Allan Albert (musical saga of the West); and *A Broadway Musical*, by William F. Brown, Charles Strouse and Lee Adams; *Abdul and the Night Visitors*; and *Godspell*.
Tips: All submissions should be as brief as possible and include a resume and synopsis.

13th STREET THEATRE REPERTORY CO., 50 W. 13th St., New York NY 10011. Artistic Director: Edith O'Hara. Play producer. Produces 20 plays/year. Pays 6% royalty for Off-Broadway productions; does not pay for workshop productions. Submit complete ms, score and cassette or reel-to-reel tape of songs. SASE. Reports in 1-6 months.
Musicals: "Open to anything but prefer small casts, and simple sets, costumes and technical requirements. However, we will do anything if it's good enough. We'd love to see some experimental musicals that work. The writer should keep in mind current producing costs, if he has an expectation of the show moving Off-Broadway. We are the only nonprofit theater in New York dedicated to producing original works for the American musical theater as a primary focus. We do not want musicals on a gay theme, unless they're exceptionally well-done."
Recent Productions: *Boy Meets Boy*, by B. Solly and D. Ward ('30s spoof); *Line*, by I. Horovitz (power); *Joan and the Devil*, by S. Reiter and D. Hyman (Americana satire); and *Movie Buff*, by J. Raniello and H. Taylor ('30s movies).

UNIVERSITY OF ARKANSAS AT PINE BLUFF, Dept. of Speech and Dramatic Arts, Pine Bluff AR 71603. (501)541-6731. Chairperson: Dr. E.J. Fisher. Play producer. Produces 6 plays (3 musicals)/year. "Audience is basically black, but it depends on the show." Pays $0-100/performance. Submit complete ms, score, and tape of songs. SASE. Reports as soon as possible.
Musicals: Uses one-act and full-length musicals and revues. No "choiry" scripts. Accepts "raw scripts."
Recent Productions: *Michael: A King*, by Al Boswell (about Martin Luther King); *The Clock*, by Emmanuel Robles (drama); *Simply Heavenly*; and several variety musicals.

UNIVERSITY OF MAINE AT FORT KENT, Pleasant St., Fort Kent ME 04743. (207)834-3162. Director of Performing Art: Charles Closser. Play producer. Produces 5 plays (1 musical)/year. Plays are produced in a university theater to university and community audience. Pays $300 maximum for royalty or $100 maxium/performance. Query with synopsis. SASE. Reports in 1 month.
Musicals: We are looking for musicals of 2 hours "for general audience family theater. No strong language, nudity or shows with more than six sets."
Recent Productions: *Anthing Goes*, by Cole Porter (musical comedy); *Applause*; and *I Do! I Do!*.

UNIVERSITY THEATRE, Oregon State University, Corvallis OR 97331. Coordinator, Theatre Arts: C.V. Bennett. Play producer. Produces 8 plays/year and 1 musical every 2 years. Produces plays in 2 theaters seating 80 and 426 to an audience of faculty, students and townspeople. Pays flat royalty fee of $25-150 and by performance: $25-50 for first performance and $10-35 for each additional performance. Submit complete ms and score. SASE. Reports in 2 weeks.
Recent Productions: *Stop the World*, by Bricusse and Newley; *Music Man*, by Willson; *Charlie Brown* by Gesner; and *Celebration* by Schmidt and Jones.

CEDRIC VENDYBACK, Brandon University, Brandon, Manitoba, Canada R7A 6A9. (204)728-9520. Professor: C. Vendyback. Play producer. Produces 2-6 plays/year. Rarely produces musicals. Audience is urban and rural, middle-class, faculty and students. Query with synopsis. SASE. Reports in 1 month.
Musicals: Prefers "one- to three-act; social comment, smallish cast. We also like simple props and staging. Nothing lavish."
Recent Productions: *All My Sons*, by Miller (social conscience); *The Love of Four Colonels*, by Ustinov (good vs evil); and *Getting Married*, by Shaw (social awareness).

WABASH COLLEGE THEATER, Wabash College, Crawfordsville IN 47933. (317)362-0677. Chairman/Theater Department: James Fisher. Play producer. Produces 4 plays/year. "Musicals are produced occasionally as schedule and personnel permit. Audience is small college town and the male student body of the college. We have two theaters: a 370-seat intimate proscenium with lift for stage; and a black box, seating up to 150. Looking for plays with moderate size cast with more male than female roles." Pays standard royalty. Query with synopsis or submit complete ms and score. SASE. Reports as soon as possible.
Musicals: Any type. Plays require mostly male characters with small- to medium-size orchestra and up to 25-30 in cast.
Recent Productions: *Guys and Dolls*; *Cabaret*; *Fantasticks*; *Canterbury Tales*; *The Crimson Bird*, by Strawn and Enenbach (medieval French nightingale legend); and *S.H. Ades*, by Seward (ghosts and aspiring showbiz hopeful).

WALDO ASTORIA PLAYHOUSE, 5028 Main, Kansas City MO 64112. Producer: Richard Carothers. Associate Producer: Raymond Bonnard. Play producer. Produces 12 plays (1 musical)/year. For general audience. Pays negotiable royalty. Submit complete ms. SASE. Reports in 1 month.
Musicals: Wants musical comedy. "No special format, just appeal to public taste. Three acts, 40-40-40 maximum, rated G. Do not exceed 15 in cast with minimal orchestra; we have a relatively small stage. Not interested in burlesque."
Recent Productions: *Oklahoma!*, *Cactus Flower*, and *The Latest Mrs. Adam* (comedies); *Surprise, Surprise* (based on stories of O. Henry); *The Sound of Music*, by Rodgers and Hammerstein; *Jenny*, by Don Wilde and Hayden Wayne (old age); and *Fiddler on the Roof.*
Tips: "Don't over write. Don't become too attached to any particular song. Be open minded in working with the director and producers."

WATERLOO COMMUNITY PLAYHOUSE, Box 433, Waterloo IA 50704. (319)235-0367. Managing Director: Charles Stilwill. Play producer. Produces 6-7 plays (1-2 musicals)/year. "Our audience prefers solid, wholesome entertainment, nothing risque or with strong language. We perform in Hope Martin Theatre, a 368-seat house." Pays $25-150/performance. Submit complete ms, score and tape of songs on cassette. SASE.
Musicals: "Casts may vary from as few as 6 people to 54."
Recent Productions: *Annie Get Your Gun; A Funny Thing Happened on My Way to the Forum; You're a Good Man Charlie Brown; Man of La Mancha;* and *Oklahoma!*

WESTERN COLLEGE, 900 Otay Lakes Rd., Chula Vista CA 92010. (714)421-6700. Artistic Director: W. Virchis. Play producer. Produces 7 plays (2 musicals)/year. Query with synopsis. SASE. Reports in 3 weeks.
Recent Productions: *Pippin* (a boy's coming of age); *Man of La Mancha*, by Dale Wasseman (about Don Quixote); *Plymouth Rock*, by Scott Busack (journey of the Pilgrims); and *Grease*, college national premier.

YORK COLLEGE OF PENNSYLVANIA, Country Club Rd., York PA 17405. Director of Theatre: Richard D. Farrell. Play producer. Produces 2-4 plays/year. Plays are produced in a college theater to a college and community audience. Pays royalty through publishing house. Submit complete ms, score and tape of songs. SASE. Reports in 1 month.
Recent Productions: *Man for All Seasons*, by Robert Bolt; *The Corn is Green*, by Emlyn Williams; *You're a Good Man Charlie Brown*, by Charles Schultz; *The Veldt*, by Ray Bradbury; *Sganarelle*, by Moliere; *The Bear*, by Chekhov; *The Effects of Gamma Rays on Man-in-the-Moon Marigolds*, by Paul Zindel; and *You're a Good Man, Charlie Brown*, by Clark Gesner.

Services & Opportunities

Contests and Awards

Songwriter or musician competitions can be a pleasant and sometimes lucrative endeavor. What's more, participation in contests is a good way to expose your work and your talents. Some contests are judged by music publishers and other industry officials, guaranteeing a professional hearing for your material. Contacts, and sometimes contracts, result from a good showing in a major competition.

Contests may not seem to be a good "market" in the usual sense, yet you are selling yourself and your work. Thus, marketing techniques shouldn't be forgotten. Each contest you enter, for example, should be studied so that you can slant your material to the award you seek.

Contests listed here encompass all types of music and all levels of composition expertise: some are on a level requiring a degree in music while others require only talent to write strong lyrics and melodies that touch people's hearts (hopefully the judges') and have great commercial appeal. Most of these contests are annual. Read each listing carefully and write a letter to any that interest you asking that you be put on the list to receive information about upcoming competitions.

AMERICAN SONG FESTIVAL, Box 57, Hollywood CA 90028. An international songwriting competition. Offers lyric and song competitions for amateur and professional songwriters and performers. Query for complete information and official entry form.

ASCAP FOUNDATION GRANTS TO YOUNG COMPOSERS, ASCAP Bldg., 1 Lincoln Plaza, New York NY 10023. (212)595-3050. Director of Grants: Martin Bookspan. For composers. Purpose: to provide grants to young composers to help them pursue their studies in music composition and develop their skills or talents.
Requirements: "Applicants must be citizens or permanent residents of the US who have not reached their 30th birthday by November 1. Applicants must submit professional recommendations; complete an application listing prior education, experience and background in the field of music; and submit 1-2 examples of their composition. Music of any style or category will be considered. Submissions must be original works and not previously published or winners of previous competitions or grants." Deadline: November 1. Send for application; samples required. "Submit copies only. Score reproductions and/or manuscripts may be submitted on regular music paper or reproduced by an accepted reproduction process. Tapes will be accepted also. Tapes must be on 5- or 7-inch reels, 7½ ips, head out."
Awards, Grants: ASCAP Foundation awards grants of $500-2,500. Length: 1 year. Applications judged by screening-panel of musical authorities.

BMI AWARDS TO STUDENT COMPOSERS, 320 W. 57th St., New York NY 10019. (212)586-2000. Director: James J. Roy Jr. For composers of "serious concert music." Annual.

Songwriter's Market Close-up

When "Music, Sex, and Cookies" placed first as the amateur open winner in a recent American Song Festival Competition, it was literally a landslide victory for Cincinnati songwriter George Uetz. The toe-tapping, tongue-in-cheek tune about three things Uetz holds dear netted him enough money to rescue him from a natural disaster—a landslide on top of his new home—and introduced him to the world of professional songwriting.

Uetz is not a songwriter by profession, but a biology professor at the University of Cincinnati. When his song took first place in the ASF, however, music publishers were suddenly offering incredible contracts with promises of glittering riches and early retirement, and the professor had to take a crash course in the *business* of songwriting: the copyrights and con men and contracts with carefully-concealed clauses that plague beginning and professional songwriters alike.

"It's good advice to get a lawyer who specializes in entertainment law before you sign any contracts with music publishers," Uetz recommends. "Too often you hear of people who sign their songs away forever. You've got to be careful."

Uetz has been writing and performing his songs locally for several years. But since winning the Festival, he's become more serious about his songwriting. "It was a real boost for me—gave me incentive to get my songs to publishers."

He advises amateur songwriters to beware the praises of friends and relatives. "Show your songs to as many impartial people as you can. The more people you *don't* know who like your song, the better indication the song is good."

Competitions and contests are good means for amateur songwriters to receive

George Uetz

impartial criticism of their material, Uetz believes. But be careful, he warns, of contest rules that mislead the songwriter into thinking a "simple voice and piano" demonstration tape is sufficient. "What publishers consider a simple demo and what amateur songwriters consider a simple demo are often very different things," Uetz contends. "The better the quality of your demo, the better chance you have of it being heard."

Uetz speaks highly of the American Song Festival. "It's been a highlight for me, and given me a nice credential in the music world." He laughs, "I'm still singing the same songs, but now people look at them in a different light."

It cost George Uetz $23 to enter the American Song Festival. In totaling the results in terms of money, contracts, contacts, and future songwriting success, he says it's obviously the best $23 he's ever spent.

Colleen Cannon

Estab. 1951. Purpose: "to pick outstanding young (25 or under) composers and make cash awards for furthering their musical education."

Requirements: Applicants must not have reached their 26th birthday by Dec. 31 of the year preceding the Feb. 15th contest deadline. "Serious concert music is preferred to popular songs, but all music is considered. All geographic locations of the world, but applicant must be a citizen or permanent resident of the western hemisphere enrolled in an accredited public, private or parochial secondary school, in an accredited college or conservatory of music, or engaged in private

study with recognized music teachers." Deadline: Feb. 15. One entry per student. Send for free application and rules. Rights retained. Entries returned, include SASE.
Awards: BMI Awards to Student Composers: "prizes totaling $15,000 ranging from $500 to $2,500 may be given to winning students, by check, with certificate of honor." Contest judged by "outstanding composers, music publishers and musicologists."

COMPOSERS GUILD, 2333 Olympus Dr., Salt Lake City UT 84117. (801)278-1745. President: Sharon Nielson. For songwriters and composers. "We are a nonprofit organization working to help the composer/songwriter. Each year we sponsor classes, workshops, seminars, a composition contest, and a performance at the University of Utah."
Requirements: "Annual membership of $15 entitles entry to contest. Cassette demo and lead sheet required for all *popular* entries only. No other restrictions." Deadline: August 31. Send for application.
Awards, Grants: $2,000 distributed among 8 categories: keyboard, popular, choral, vocal solo, jazz, humorous and instrumental. The best-of-the-show (can be from any music category) is awarded $500. "Detailed critique is given to every contest entry. Applicants judged by professional, usually head of university music department or firmly established producer of performed music."
Tips: "Sloppy manuscripts will not be accepted by Composers Guild."

CONCERT ARTISTS GUILD COMPETITION, 154 W. 57th St., Studio 136, New York NY 10019. (212)757-8344. Contact: Auditions Chairperson. For musicians, soloists and ensembles. "CAG was founded to help young professionals of exceptional talent win recognition through a nationwide competition. Six to ten winners are chosen."
Requirements: "Applicants must be under 32 years of age, or 35 years old for vocalists." Deadline: January 15, 1982. Send for application. Samples required; prefers 7½ ips reel-to-reel of "good quality."
Awards, Grants: Concert Artists Guild Award: $1,000. Includes "debut in Carnegie Recital Hall, preview concert, major press coverage and all concert expenses are paid." Applications judged by panel screening tapes, "then three rounds of live auditions. Judging is based on programming, tone, intonation, technique, interpretation and musicality."
Tips: "Pay special attention to programming. Musicians need to choose pieces that will show off their talent."

INTERNATIONAL ORIGINAL CONCERT, 3-24-22, Shimo Meguro, Meguro-ku, Tokyo, 153, Japan. Sponsored by Yamaha Music Foundation. "This concert is an attempt at creating a 'musical renaissance,' a return to the roots where musical expression communicates one's emotions directly. It is also an attempt to promote all varieties of music which have universal appeal by encouraging, in whatever ways we can, those who wish to perform their own compositions."
Requirements: Entries must be an original but not yet published or performed compositions in which rhythm, melody and harmony are included for instrumental performance. Each composer must participate significantly in the performance of his composition by either playing an instrument or conducting. Write for more information and entry form.

MUSIC CITY SONG FESTIVAL, Box 17999, 1014 16th Ave. S., Nashville TN 37217. (800)251-1790. Festival Directors: Roy Sinkovich, Mick Lloyd. Country, easy listening, pop/R&B songwriting and performance competitions for amateurs and professionals. Deadline: November. Write or call for complete information.
Awards: Separate awards in country, easy listening, and pop/R&B categories will be given for songwriting, lyric writing and vocal performance. Prizes for a single award range from $50-5,000 with over $40,000 in cash and recording prizes to be awarded. Contest judged by persons active in the industry (disc jockies, publishers and record company executives). LP's of winning entries are produced and released by The Little Giant Record Company.

NEW YORK SONGWRITING CONTEST, 40 W. 57th St., New York 10019. (212)757-8833. Project Director of AGAC and Chairman of Contest: Jonathan Holtzman. Presented annually by AGAC and the New York Music Task Force. Different sponsor each year; the 1981 competition was sponsored by Chappell Music. Deadline: June. Free to residents of New York City area. Send for application and more information after March.
Awards: First prize, $250 plus AGAC contract with sponsoring publisher; second prize, $150; third prize, $100. The ten finalists appear at New York's Bottom Line.

RICHARD RODGERS PRODUCTION AWARD, American Academy and Institute of Arts and Letters, 633 W. 155th St., New York NY 10032. (212)368-5900. Assistant to the Executive Director: Lydia Kaim. "This award subsidizes a production in New York City by a nonprofit theater group or professional school of a musical play by composers and writers who are not already established in this field."

Requirements: Applicants must be citizens or permanent residents of US. Only one submission per group/writer. Work must be of significant length, but may consist of a group of smaller, related pieces. Deadline: November 1. SASE for application form and instructions.

Awards: Production award of $60,000 to be used within the year the award is granted.

THE UNIVERSITY OF MICHIGAN PROFESSIONAL THEATRE PROGRAM, The Michigan League, 227 S. Ingalls, Ann Arbor MI 48109. (313)763-5213. General Manager: Jean B. Galan. Musical theater contest. Estab. 1977. Gives 1 or more major award each year.

Awards: $2,000 maximum for an original full-length musical. Submit 3 manuscripts and cassettes of songs. Does not return unsolicited material. Reports in May of each year. Deadline: end of January.

WORLD POPULAR SONG FESTIVAL, Yamaha Music Foundation, 3-24-22, Shimo Meguro, Meguro-ku, Tokyo, 153, Japan. Contact: Festival Committee.

Requirements: Entry must be an original song, which has never been published or performed in public. Send for deadlines and application.

Awards: Prizes to winners of song and performance awards range from donated gifts to $10,000.

Organizations and Clubs

A major benefit of membership in a club or professional organization is access to specialized information and publications. Organizations often serve as information clearinghouses, forums for idea exchange among members, and sources of market information. Some organizations also sponsor workshops, conferences and seminars; some make grants to songwriters; some sponsor contests.

The problem is there are not nearly enough local songwriter clubs. If there is one in your town you can learn about it from other songwriters or musicians. If there is none in your town, why not start one? The Songwriters Organizations National Group (SONG), the recently formed national alliance of independent songwriting organizations, will forward information on starting a songwriting group in your town. Contact Billy James, SONG, 6772 Hollywood Blvd., Hollywood CA 90028.

Since success as a songwriter depends on national acceptance, it's very important that you consider joining at least one national organization or club. Association with professional groups sometimes helps build your professional image. Their newsletters will keep you informed of happenings and trends in the industry that affect you as a songwriter. Annual (sometimes more frequent) get-togethers for seminars, workshops, awards dinners, etc. are informative and inspiring and give you a chance to meet songwriters from across the US and foreign countries as well. What's more, an organization can serve as a liaison between you and some of the people you deal with, and can sometimes act as your representative in certain kinds of disputes.

To choose the national organization(s) of most benefit to you, read each listing carefully, noticing the membership description and programs offered. Each lists its services, activities and requirements for membership. For more information, write to the individual organizations that interest you.

THE ACADEMY OF COUNTRY MUSIC, Box 508, 1777 N. Vine St., Suite 200, Hollywood CA 90028. (213)462-2351. Executive Secretary: Fran Boyd. For "professional persons connected with the country music industry. We have a separate membership for fans. For professional membership the person must be affiliated with the country music industry in some manner." Offers newsletter and showcases. "Purpose is to promote country music."

AMERICAN COUNCIL FOR THE ARTS, 570 7th Ave., New York NY 10018. (212)354-6655. Contact: Membership Dept. "We are the leading private national nonprofit organization that serves all the arts." Members are state, regional and community arts agencies, arts centers, performing arts organizations, museums, libraries, parks and recreation departments, professional arts managers and artists and individuals interested in supporting the arts. Services include advocacy for the arts at the federal level; arts management training conferences and seminars; *American Arts Magazine*, a bimonthly national magazine of news and information for policy-makers in the arts; *ACA Update*, a monthly up-to-the-minute news bulletin; resource books for artists and the arts; a research library of 15,000 books and documents; and reference and information services.

AMERICAN FEDERATION OF MUSICIANS, 1500 Broadway, New York NY 10036. (212)869-1330. Membership available to all qualified musicians and vocalists in the United States and Canada. "The American Federation of Musicians of the United States and Canada is the largest entertainment union in the world and exists solely for the advancement of live music and the benefit of its 300,000 members. In addition of enhancing employment opportunities for members the AFM aids members in negotiating contracts; enforces employers' observance of working conditions and wage scales; arbitrates members' claims at no cost to members; protects musicians from unfavorable legislation at the federal, state and local levels; negotiates pension, welfare and retirement benefits; offers instrument insurance to members; and keeps membership informed of happenings in the business through its publication *International Musician*. Members also receive numerous benefits provided by each local." Initiation fees vary; a small percentage of work dues are contributed by members and local dues average $24/year. Write for further information or contact AFM Local nearest you.

THE AMERICAN GUILD OF AUTHORS & COMPOSERS, 6430 Sunset Blvd., Suite 1113, Hollywood CA 90028. (213)462-1108. Regional Director: Leslie Lates. Serves songwriters. Members are pre-professional and professional songwriters, composers, lyricists, melodists, film and TV scorers, etc. No eligibility requirements other than the "desire to be a songwriter." Applications accepted year-round. Offers instruction, lectures, newsletter and workshops. "AGAC is a protective and advisory agency for songwriters."

AMERICAN GUILD OF AUTHORS & COMPOSERS (AGAC), 40 W. 57th St., New York NY 10019. (212)757-8833. West Coast: 6430 Sunset Blvd., Hollywood CA 90028. (213)462-1108. Founded as the Songwriter's Protective Association with present name adopted in 1958. Executive Director: Lewis M. Bachman. Projects Director: Jonathan Holtzman. West Coast Regional Director: Leslie Lates. "A full member must be a published songwriter. An associate member is any unpublished songwriter with a desire to learn more about the business and craft of songwriting. The third class of membership comprises estates of deceased writers. The AGAC contract is conceded to be the best available in the industry, having the greatest number of built-in protections for the songwriter. The guild's Royalty Collection Plan makes certain that prompt and accurate payments are made to writers. The ongoing Audit Program makes periodic checks of publishers' books. For the self-publisher, the Catalogue Administration Plan (CAP) relieves a writer of the paperwork of publishing for a fee lower than the prevailing industry rates. The Copyright Renewal Service informs members a year in advance of a song's renewal date. Other services include workshops in New York and Los Angeles, free ASKAPRO rap sessions with industry pros (see Workshops), critique sessions, collaborator service and bimonthly newsletter. In addition AGAC reviews your songwriter contract on request (AGAC or otherwise); fights to strengthen songwriters' rights and to' increase writers' royalties by supporting legislation which directly affects your copyright; offers a group medical and life insurance plan; issues news bulletins with essential information for songwriters; provides a songwriter collaboration service for younger writers; financially evaluates catalogs of copyrights in connection with possible sale and estate planning; operates an estates administration service; and maintains a nonprofit educational foundation (The AGAC Foundation)."

AMERICAN GUILD OF MUSIC, Box 3, Downers Grove IL 60515. (312)968-0173. Executive Secretary: Elmer Herrick. For musicians and students. Members are music studio operators, teachers, students all interested in teaching and performing. Offers competitions, instruction, lectures, newsletter, performance opportunities and workshops. "Purpose is to improve teaching methods, promote interest in string instruments, accordion, etc."

AMERICAN MECHANICAL RIGHTS ASSOCIATION, 250 W. 57th St., New York NY 10107. (212)246-4077. Executive Director: Mrs. R.W.~Miller. Members include songwriters and music publishers from the US, Canada and 18 European countries. Applicants must have released a record, or have a record released in the US. Purpose is to collect mechanical, synchronization, and background royalties.

AMERICAN MUSIC CENTER, INC., 250 W. 54th St., Room 300, New York NY 10019. (212)247-3121. Executive Director: Margaret Jory. For musicians and composers. Members are "composers of American music, as well as critics, publishers and performers." Offers newsletter, workshops, library of classical music and reference services. Purpose is "to increase knowledge about and interest in performances of serious American contemporary music. Members receive AMC *Newsletter* quarterly, discounts on other AML publications and invitation to annual members party."

AMERICAN MUSIC CONFERENCE, 1000 Skokie Blvd., Wilmette IL 60091. (312)251-1600. President: Gene Wenner. Director of Special Services: Jan Whitlock. National nonprofit association for anyone interested in the future of music. Membership includes companies and associations from all parts of the music industry, from musical instrument manufacturers and music publishers to suppliers. Offers competitions, publications and music promotional materials. "Purpose is to educate the public in the benefits of lifetime participation in music; to foster interest in

---

Market conditions are constantly changing! If this is 1983 or later, buy the newest edition of *Songwriter's Market* at your favorite bookstore or use the back-of-the-book order form.

the extension of music education in the schools; to increase appreciation of the value of music in the home, the church and the community; and to give recognition to distinguished service, personal effort, and leadership in the development of musical activities."

AMERICAN SOCIETY OF COMPOSERS, AUTHORS AND PUBLISHERS, 1 Lincoln Plaza, New York NY 10023. (212)595-3050. Director of Membership: Paul S. Adler. Membership Department Staff: Tyrone Jenkins, Joan Robb, Lisa Schmidt. Members are songwriters, composers and music publishers. Applicants must "have at least one song copyrighted for associate membership; have at least one song published, commercially recorded, or performed in media licensed by the Society for full membership." Purpose: "ASCAP is a nonprofit, membership-owned, performing rights licensing organization that licenses its members' nondramatic musical compositions for public performance and distributes the fees collected from such licensing to its members based on a scientific random sample survey of performances." Primary value is "as a clearinghouse, giving users a practical and economical bulk licensing system and its members a vehicle through which the many thousands of users can be licensed and the members paid royalties for the use of their material.".
Tips: "The Society sponsors a series of writers' workshops in Los Angeles, Nashville and New York; open to members and nonmembers. Grants to composers available to members and nonmembers. Contact the public relations or membership departments of the New York office or the following branch offices: 6430 Sunset Blvd., Los Angeles 90028; 2 Music Square W., Nashville 37203; 60 Old Compton St., London, W1, England."

AMERICAN SOCIETY OF MUSIC ARRANGERS, Box 11, Hollywood CA 90028. President: Eddy Lawrence Manson. Secretary: Fred Woessner. "In conjunction with American Federation of Musicians responsible for determining and protecting the rights and income of orchestrators." Full members are qualified arrangers, orchestrators and composers. Associate members are anyone in the music profession (playing musicians, students, songwriters, etc.). Offers newsletter. "Considered to be bellweather organization in field of arranging and orchestrating. Conducts workshops for composition and performance of works of members as well as instrumental clinics."

ARIZONA SONGWRITERS ASSOCIATION, Box 678, Phoenix AZ 85001. (602)537-2746. Membership Director: Jo Ann Cluff. Serves songwriters and musicians. "Our members are ages 14-73. Most are both lyricists and composers; some are lyricists only. Many are artist/songwriters. Members should have a real interest in music and be willing to contribute talent and time to some of our special events. Neither, however is mandatory." Applications accepted year-round. Offers competitions, instruction, lectures, library (limited), newsletter, performance opportunities and workshops (monthly); and two 6-8 week showcases (spring and fall) that include performer/songwriter competitions. "Our purpose is educational: to teach all phases of songwriting."

ATLANTA SONGWRITERS ASSOCIATION, Box 1306, Marietta GA 30060. (404)262-0486. President: Don Bryant. Secretary: Pat Sullivan. For songwriters and performing artists of all ages. "Our only requirement is that the member be interested in songwriting." Offers competitions, instruction, library, newsletter, performance opportunities, social outings and workshops. "Our purpose is to help members become better songwriters and get their songs cut."

BLACK MUSIC ASSOCIATION, 1500 Locust St., Philadelphia PA 19102. (215)545-8600. President: LeBaron Taylor. Executive Director: Glenda Gracia. Membership: Hope Glomer. For songwriters, musicians and anyone interested in music, entertainment, and arts industries. Members are individuals, companies and organizations involved in the music industry. Offers lectures, library, newsletter, performance opportunities, workshops, job opportunities, discounts, industry contact resource center, seminars and an annual conference. "Purpose is the dedication to the advancement, enrichment, encouragement and recognition of black music."

BROADCAST MUSIC, INC., 320 W. 57th St., New York NY 10019. (212)586-2000; 6255 Sunset Blvd, Suite 1527, Hollywood CA 90028; and 10 Music Square E., Nashville TN 37203. President: Edward M. Cramer. Senior Vice President: Theodora Zavin. Vice President, California: Ron Anton. Vice President, Nashville: Francis Preston. Performance rights organization. "Applicants must have written a musical composition, alone or in collaboration with other writers, which is commercially published, recorded or otherwise likely to be performed. Purpose: BMI licenses the nondramatic performing rights of musical compositions to users of music which include radio and TV stations, hotels, night clubs, universities, colleges and the many other places in the US where music is publicly performed."

CANADIAN ACADEMY OF RECORDING ARTS & SCIENCES (CARAS), 89 Bloor St. E., Toronto, Ontario, Canada M4W 1A9. (416)922-5029. National Co-ordinator: Daisy C. Falle. Serves songwriters and musicians. Membership is open to all employees (including support staff) in: broadcasting, record companies and producers, personal managers, recording artists, recording engineers, arrangers, composers, music publishers, album designers, promoters, talent and booking agents, record retailers, rack jobbers, distributors, recording studios and other music industry related professions (on approval). Applicants must be affiliated with the recording industry. Applications accepted year-round. Offers newsletter, performance opportunities, social outings, workshops, and annual Juno Awards show. "CARAS strives to foster the development of the Canadian music and recording industries and to contribute toward higher artistic standards." Fees: $25/year.

CANADIAN RECORDING INDUSTRY ASSOCIATION, 89 Bloor St. E., Toronto, Ontario, Canada M4W 1A9. (416)967-7272. President: Brian Robertson. Serves record companies. Membership open to record company executives, independent record producers and recording studios (engineers and producers). Applications accepted year-round. Offers performance opportunities, social outings and workshops. "CRIA is the 'voice' of the recording industry in Canada. Its 50 members represent over 98% of the sound recordings manufactured and sold in this country. The association represents the industry on many levels including communication with government, international liaison with music and recording industry organizations around the world, the control of record and tape piracy and other legal matters, the direction of industry marketing programs such as the certification of gold and platinum records and the production of the National Chart of best selling recordings." Fees: $100/year.

THE CANADIAN SINGER SONGWRITERS SHOWCASE, 2-262 Flora St., Ottawa, Ontario, Canada K1R 5R9. Director: Quincy Patterson. Estab. 1980. Serves songwriters. Applications accepted year-round. Offers performance opportunities, critique of work and career counseling. A nonprofit service organization for singer/songwriters.

CENTRAL OPERA SERVICE, Metropolitan Opera, Lincoln Center, New York NY 10023. (212)957-9871. Membership Secretary: Jeanne Kemp. Administrative Director: Maria F. Rich. For musicians, librettists, opera producers and performers and composers. Members are individuals and companies involved with or interested in opera/musical theater (producers, performers, supporters, patrons, educators, students, composers, librettists, conductors and directors) all age groups; nationally in the US and Canada and abroad. Offers information on competitions, newsletter and national and regional conferences of professionals. "The Central Opera Service (COS) is the national information agency on all aspects of opera."

COLUMBUS SONGWRITERS ASSOCIATION, 3312 Petzinger Rd., Columbus OH 43227. (614)239-0280. President: Rich Kimmle. Executive Director: Deborah E. Greenawalt. Public Relations: Don Franklin Perry. Executive Secretary: Shirlee Wickham. Production Director: Michael Kimmle. Executive Director of Video: Joseph Bruno. Financial Director: Bruce Walloce. For songwriters and musicians. Fee: $25/year. Offers competitions, field trips, instruction, newsletter, performance opportunities, social outings, consultation workshops; and access to collaborators, computers, songwriters library, mini four-track studio and video equipment. Purpose is to guide and educate songwriters. Holds monthly showcases.

COMPOSERS, ARRANGERS AND SONGWRITERS OF KANSAS, 117 W. 8th St., Hays KS 67601. (913)625-9634. Administrator: Mark Meckel. Estab. 1980. Serves songwriters, musicians, arrangers and lyricists. Membership open to "anyone desiring information on the business of songwriting, copyrights or marketing—from professional musicians to housewives." No eligibility requirements other than "a desire for a career in the music industry." Applications accepted year-round. Offers competitions, library, newsletter, personal consultations and demo tape discounts. "Our purpose is to educate members about the business end of the music industry. Our newsletter profiles markets and offers technical articles." Fees: $15/year.
Tips: "We are working toward area song contests in conjunction with local radio stations and also have a *homegrown* album project in the works."

CONNECTICUT SONGWRITERS ASSOCIATION, 226 Great Neck Rd., Waterford CT 06385. (203)447-3665. President: Don Donegan. Estab. 1979. Serves songwriters and musicians. "Our membership consists of over 100 songwriters (published and non-published), musicians and some full-time performers. Ages range from 20-70 (average age 31). No eligibility requirements. Applications accepted year-round. Offers instruction, lectures, library, newsletter, performance opportunities, social outings, workshops, discounts, awards, and song tape library. Purpose is to "educate, encourage and promote songwriters." Fees: $30/year; $15/after July 1.

COUNTRY MUSIC ASSOCATION, INC., Box 22299, Nashville TN 37202. (615)244-2840. Membership Director: Rob Parrish. Membership falls within following categories: advertising agency; artist manager/agent; artist/musician; composer; disc jockey; international; publication; publisher; radio/TV; record company; record merchandiser; talent buyer/promoter; and affiliated. Members must earn a portion of their income from the country music industry. Offers newsletter, lists of industry contacts, special discounted insurance policies and AVIS discount cards. Purpose is to promote country music.

COUNTRY MUSIC FOUNDATION OF COLORADO, Box 19435, Denver CO 80219. (303)936-7762. President: Gladys Hart. Serves songwriters and musicians, promoters, publishers and record companies to assist them in learning the proper method of presenting new material to the publisher. "The membership roster comes from the country music industry in general with special interest in the annual Colorado Country Music Festival." Offers lectures, newsletter, performance opportunities and an annual convention. Purpose is "to promote country music in all facets of the industry. The association provides new artists with information on the basic fundamentals essential for career advancement. Songwriters Day will be scheduled to include songwriter/publisher meeting. The evening show will be dedicated to the presentation of new material by bands and artists."

FLORIDA COUNTRY MUSIC FOUNDATION & HALL OF FAME, 2409 Winona Ave., Indian Oaks, Leesburg FL 32748. (904)787-1051. Administrator: 'Mama' Jo Hunt. For songwriters, musicians and anyone who likes country music. "Members are people in music and anyone who would like to join our group." Offers instruction, newsletter, performance opportunities, social outings and workshops. Purpose is to help new artists put on shows where they can be heard and have records sent to radio programs. New artists can send 25 pictures or more and 50 singles or albums for promotion purposes. "Individual memberships are $15/year; organization memberships are $100/year."

GOSPEL MUSIC ASSOCIATION, 38 Music Square W., Nashville TN 37203. (615)242-0303. Executive Director: Don Butler. For songwriters, broadcasters, musicians, merchandisers, promoters, performance licensing agencies, church staff musicians, talent agencies, record companies and publishers. Offers lectures, newsletter, workshops and awards programs.

HARLEM TALENT ASSOCIATES, INC., 1 W. 125th St., Suite 219, New York NY 10027. (212)289-8300. Executive Director: Brenda Murphy. Estab. 1979. Serves songwriters, musicians and "all music business people." Ages range from 17-60. The areas of interest for most members are songwriting, publishing, production, recording, and promotion, etc. Offers instruction, lectures, library, performance opportunities and workshops. "Our purpose is to inform and educate members about career opportunities in the music business, give free legal advice and bring professionals and aspiring professionals together." Recently sponsored the Harlem Talent Associates Recording Industry Career Series (23 weeks) and the Music Industry Legal Clinic (15 weeks).

INTERNATIONAL FAN CLUB ORGANIZATION, Box 177, Wild Horse CO 80862. (303)962-3543. Co-Presidents: Loudilla Johnson, Loretta Johnson and Kay Johnson. For songwriters, musicians and performers and their fan club presidents. Members are fan club presidents and/or artists/songwriters etc. Applicants must be involved in the field of country music. An artist must have a fan club—"we assist them in setting up the fan club although we do not personally manage each individual operation for them." Offers competitions, instruction, newsletter, performance opportunities, social outings, workshops, business meetings, overseas tours and showcases. Purpose is to promote/publicize country music in an effort to spread good will, understanding and enjoyment of it around the world. "We hold an annual overseas showcase (London), plus dinner/ show/business meetings/showcases in Nashville, annually in conjunction with Fan Fair. We believe fan clubs are a vital part of any entertainer's life."

THE LOS ANGELES SONGWRITERS SHOWCASE, (formerly The Alternative Chorus Songwriters Showcase), 6772 Hollywood Blvd., Hollywood CA 90028. (213)462-1382. Co-Directors: Len H. Chandler Jr., John Braheny. Executive Assistants: Tim Horrigan and Carl Byron. The Los Angeles Songwriters Showcase, a nonprofit service organization for songwriters, auditions more than 150 songwriters/month, both live and by tape. Less than 6% of the songs auditioned are presented in a showcase, making it a focus for record industry people looking for new songs and writer/artists. 5-7 professional and amateur writers are showcased each week. "Writers must participate in the performances of their own material. This unique service is free and is sponsored by Broadcast Music, Inc. (BMI). LASS also provides counseling, conducts lectures and interviews top music industry professionals at the showcase. A new feature has been added called 'Cassette

Roulette', live publisher song evaluation hosted by BMI at the Wednesday night Showcase at the West L.A. Music Store, 7001 Hollywood Blvd. in Hollywood." Also produces an annual Songwriter Expo every June. "In February 1981 a membership organization was formed offering, in addition to general membership, 'Professional' and 'Showcase Alumni' categories, the latter two offering a unique 'Priority Referral' service by which ASCAP, BMI and SESAC members and those who have been showcased (or been chosen but unable to showcase) are given stickers to attach to tapes sent to publishers. This notifies publishers that the tapes have been pre-screened by LASS."

MEMPHIS SONGWRITERS ASSOCIATION, Box 63075, 800 Madison, Memphis TN 63075. President: Juanita Tullos. Correspondence Secretary: Frances Ferloni. For songwriters, musicians and artists; "we have people from all walks of life, including amateur and professional songwriters, publishing company executives and recording company people." Offers competitions, lectures, newsletter, performance opportunities, social outings and contact lists and guides. Purpose is to "assist the songwriter in contact information and to guide and direct the songwriter in the basic steps of songwriting." Fees: $12/year.
Tips: "We have an annual competition in which we have awards for the best original songs members have written. We solicit tapes for this once a year and 12 songs are chosen from this screening to be presented before a panel of judges."

MISSOURI SONGWRITERS ASSOCIATION, INC., 3711 Andora Pl., St. Louis MO 63125. (314)894-3354. President: John G. Nolan, Jr. Estab. 1979. Serves songwriters and musicians. "We have members ranging from ages 14 through 87, which includes professionals, amateurs, and people who write songs just for the enjoyment it provides." No eligibility requirements. Applications accepted year-round. Offers competitions, field trips, instruction, lectures, library, newsletter, performance opportunities, social outings, workshops, seminars, showcases, collaborator referral and musician referral. "The main purpose of our nonprofit organization is to educate our members with respect to the business and the artistic sides of the craft of songwriting. Songwriters gain support from their fellow members when they join the MSA, and the organization provides 'strength in numbers' when approaching music industry professionals, along with (of course) the promotional and educational benefits we offer." Fees: $15/year.

MUSCLE SHOALS MUSIC ASSOCIATION, Box 2009, Muscle Shoals AL 35660. (205)381-1442. Executive Director: F.E. "Buddy" Draper. For songwriters, musicians, engineers, artists, producers, studio owners and "others interested in music and recording." Members are "from all over the world. Age limits run from 14 to 82 years old. We have over 400 active members with our board of directors meeting monthly. There are no limitations on membership if applications are approved by the board of directors." Offers competitions, newsletter, performance opportunities, social outings, workshops and seminars. "We have an annual songwriter's showcase for songwriters who belong to the association. We have a monthly songwriter's workshop, and our newsletter is quarterly." Purpose is to "assist our membership in obtaining employment; hold workshops; present at least four concerts yearly using our own members; and to hold an annual seminar with top record executives and independent producers giving lectures and serving on panels. We have proven instructors at the workshops who have a minimum of 10 songs published and who have written at least 3 chart tunes." Fee: $25/year. "Our year runs from January 1 to December 31. Applications are accepted any time but we do not prorate dues, that is, $25 is due regardless of the date joined."

MUSIC LIBRARY ASSOCIATION, INC., 2017 Walnut St., Philadelphia PA 19103. (215)569-3948. Administrative Secretary: John A. Shiffert, Jr. Serves musicians, music librarians and musicologists. "Our membership is international, and our members range in age from college students to retired musicians and music librarians. They all have an interest in the classification and cataloging of music materials (musical scores, books about music, etc.) The only eligibility requirements are for student members (who receive a discounted membership rate). They must prove that they are enrolled in an institution of higher learning." Applications accepted year-round. Offers annual meeting, and a subscription to quarterly journal, *NOTES*. "We are a service organization, and keep our members informed of the latest developments in the field of library science. We also review music materials and books for our members, and supply them with various information concerning the latest publications affecting the music world."

MUSICIANS CONTACT SERVICE, 6605 Sunset Blvd., Hollywood CA 90028. (213)467-2191. For songwriters, musicians, agents, managers, production companies, record labels and recording studios. Average age of members is 25 (any age acceptable); any and all styles of music are acceptable. Offers performance opportunities. "We are a placement/referral service for musical performance where groups can reach musicians and vice versa. We have hundreds of resumes of composers and lyricists seeking one another—a way for them to find each other for collaboration."

NASHVILLE SONGWRITERS ASSOCIATION, INTERNATIONAL, 25 Music Square W., Nashville TN 37203. (615)254-8903. Executive Director: Maggie Cavender. For songwriters. Applicants may apply for 1 of 2 memberships; "active membership is having had at least one song published with an affiliate of BMI, ASCAP or SESAC. An associate membership is for the yet-to-be-published writer and others interested in the songwriter." Offers newsletter, counseling, seminars, symposium, workshop, showcases and awards. "Purpose is to gain recognition for the songwriter, to serve any purpose toward this recognition, and to pursue this on a worldwide basis."

NATIONAL ACADEMY OF POPULAR MUSIC, 1 Times Square, New York NY 10036. (212)221-1252. Executive Director: Abe Olman. President: Sammy Cahn. Curator: Oscar Brand. Manager/Archivist: Frankie MacCormick. Serves songwriters, musicians, school groups and other visitors to the Songwriters' Hall of Fame Museum. Members are songwriters and those interested in songwriting. Offers library, research on songs and songwriters, special exhibits honoring songwriters, and newsletter. Purpose: To honor and recognize the creators of American popular songs, to call attention to the important role of popular music in American life and history, and to maintain a library and archive of music and music-related material. Membership year: July 1-June 30.

NATIONAL MUSIC COUNCIL, 250 W. 54th St., New York NY 10019. (212)265-8132. Executive Secretary: Doris O'Connell. "The council is an umbrella organization chartered by Congress composed of representatives of over 60 music associations of national scope and activity. Its purpose is to provide a forum for the free discussion of our country's national music affairs and problems; coordinate action and provide for the interchange of information among its members; and to speak with one voice for music whenever an authoritative expression of opinion is desirable." Offers the *Bulletin*, a semi-annual magazine, $5/year. Full membership meetings are held in January and June of each year.

NATIONAL MUSIC PUBLISHERS' ASSOCIATION, INC., 110 E. 59th St., New York NY 10022. (212)751-1930. President: Leonard Feist. Trade Association for popular music publishers. Offers newsletter, workshops, special reports and information.

NEW ORLEANS JAZZ CLUB OF CALIFORNIA, Box 1225, Kerrville TX 78028. (512)896-2285. President: Bill Bacin. For songwriters, musicians and jazz fans. Members support the preservation and development of jazz music and musicians, primarily the traditional and mainstream styles. Offers instruction, library, newsletter, performance opportunities and referral services.

THE NEW ORLEANS SONGWRITERS ASSOCIATION, INC., 2643 DeSoto St., New Orleans LA 70119. (504)949-9400. President: Bud Tower. Estab. 1980. Serves songwriters. Membership consists of lyricists, composers, arrangers, songwriters and musicians ages 16-65—"professional as well as hobbyists." Applications accepted year-round. Offers lectures, library, newsletter, performance opportunities and workshops. "Our purpose is to educate members in the creative aspects of songwriting and the promotion of their material; and to offer opportunities locally to showcase their material." Fees: $25/year.

PACIFIC NORTHWEST SONGWRITERS ASSOCIATION, Box 98324, Seattle WA 98188. (206)824-1568. "We are a nonprofit association, dedicated to serving the songwriters of the Pacific Northwest. Our focus is on professional songwriting for today's commercial markets. We offer monthly workshops, newsletters and a music directory. Membership: $15/year.

PENNSYLVANIA ASSOCIATION OF SONGWRITERS, COMPOSERS & LYRICISTS (PASCAL), 244 N. 9th St., Allentown PA 18102. (215)821-7778. Director of Membership: Sherry Zboyousky. Estab. 1979. Serves songwriters. Members are songwriters, composers, lyricists, producers, radio personalities, recording technicians, musicians, publishers, lawyers, performers, businessmen, promoters, advertising people and lovers of music. Applications accepted year-round. Offers competitions, field trips, instruction, lectures, library, newsletter, performance opportunities, social outings workshops, copyright information, discounts, musicians referral service, collaboration service, etc. "The primary purpose of PASCAL is to educate members in the art of songwriting; provide business knowledge of the music industry; and provide an easier, faster, cheaper and more efficient way to conquer the problems facing songwriters, composers and lyricists today."

Songwriter's Market Close-up

"I'm a very goal-oriented person," says Randy Goodrum. Goodrum is an entertainer, producer (Dottie West), and songwriter ("Bluer Than Blue," "You Needed Me," and "What are We Doin' in Love"). "Every day I just try to realize my potential." That philosophy explains why one so busy would take time to accept the presidency of the Nashville Songwriters Association International.

"One of my goals as president is to make other professional writers understand the organization can help not only amateurs but professionals as well. We don't promise songwriters hits, but we help. We assist them when they come to town; provide workshops and critique sessions; work on songwriting legislation; and supply information on studios where they can demo songs inexpensively and places to buy discount equipment, etc."

Goodrum realizes that songwriters need all the help they can get. "This is not a 9-5 job where you get a paycheck every week. It's a lot like wildcatting for oil. You're writing a song and throwing it out (into the business world) just like a guy taking a pick and shovel and saying he thinks oil is right here. If you don't strike something, you're out of luck."

Although now a multi-award winning songwriter, Goodrum knows what it is to be out of luck. One of his biggest hits, "You Needed Me," was a song that was not commercial enough to suit any music business people until it was finally cut by Anne Murray. "It didn't have a chorus. They wanted the old stand-up-and-sing-along type thing. I tried putting it in but it just didn't work. There's a humbleness about certain songs that needs to be maintained. Each song should dictate that. Practically every song I had that became a hit has a different structure to it. You must keep in mind the mood you're going for and use choruses and verses simply as tools for maintaining the idea or mood."

Goodrum received excellent musical

Randy Goodrum

training as a piano major at Hendrix College and he believes there are certain basic things a songwriter must know. "The main thing songwriters need to understand is a scale and how the various chords sound so they can use them as tools. Study piano or guitar. A lot of people are lyricists, I think, simply because they can't play an instrument."

The biggest mistake songwriters make, according to Goodrum, is wanting to go too far too fast. "They can play a few chords so they write three songs and want to have all three on the charts next week. What they need is to develop, develop, develop. We all have room for improvement—always."

His best piece of advice to songwriters is to enjoy the craft. "I'm in it for the enjoyment. When someone calls me and says 'your song's going to be number one this week,' it's still not the same satisfaction as I get from bringing the song into existence. If you can just savor songwriting as an enjoyable experience then it will never be a drag. And having your song become a hit is just a cherry on the top."

PERFORMING RIGHTS ORGANIZATION OF CANADA LIMITED, 41 Valleybrook Dr., Don Mills, Ontario, Canada M3B 2S6. (416)445-8700. Writer/Publisher: Charlie Gall. Publicity Manager: Nancy Gyokeres. For Canadian songwriters and publishers. Offers competitions, magazine, workshops, advice and direction. Purpose is to collect performance royalties and distribute them to songwriters and publishers.

RADIO & TV REGISTRY, 850 7th Ave., New York NY 10019. (212)582-8800. Manager: Joyce LaTassa. Serves songwriters, musicians and announcers. Members are professional freelance musicians and songwriters. "Most jingles and record dates produced in New York City come through our office." Applicants must be recommended by two members and an opening must be available. Applications accepted year-round. "We provide a telephone answering service geared to the needs of the music industry. We take 'work calls' for our members and relay messages to them."
Tips: "Most music contractors in New York City find it convenient to call us to leave a work call for musicians or songwriters."

RASCAL SONGWRITERS, Box 8267, Rochester NY 14617. (716)266-0679. President: Jerry Englerth. Estab. 1979. Serves songwriters, musicians and vocalists. "Our members are people from all works of life—truck drivers to Xerox and Kodak executives. Ages range from 17-67 and musical interests vary from country/western to bluegrass, Broadway, MOR, jazz and classical. We have professional and non-professional musicians, vocalists and songwriters. Membership is open to anyone who feels they can derive some benefit from what we offer. Everyone is treated equally and encouraged to perform and participate to the best of their ability." Applications accepted year-round. Offers competitions, lectures, library, newsletter, performance opportunities, social outings and workshops. "Musicians and vocalists donate their time and talent for recording studio sessions which benefits songwriters. Our purpose is to promote original song material and opportunities for songwriters and assist each other in developing various songwriting talents. We are a nonprofit organization designed to educate, encourage, protect and promote songwriters, and are a member of the Arts for Greater Rochester."

SACRAMENTO SONGWRITERS SHOWCASE, 2791 24th St., Sacramento CA 95818. (916)739-0773. Director: Martin Cohen. "Through our workshop series we educate songwriters in their craft and inform them about the legal and business aspects of songwriting: copyright, marketing songs, publishing, etc. Workshop speakers have been Doug Thiele (SRS); John Braheny (LA Songwriter's Showcase); the BALA Bay Area Lawyers for the Arts; representatives of local recording studios, etc. Our media showcase in co-production with local TV and radio features local talent. The resource library offers information on all aspects of the songwriting network of publications, organizations, etc."
Tips: "Crayon, a local group, was discovered by the Showcase and songwriter Phil Sillas has signed with Jimmy Webb's publishing company. Many others have benefitted by getting local gigs, media attention and radio play."

SAN GABRIEL VALLEY MUSIC ASSOCIATION, Box 396, West Covina CA 91790. (213)332-2504. President: Angelo Roman. Estab. 1980. Serves songwriters, musicians, lyricists and composers. Members are mostly songwriters and performers who want to learn more about the music industry. No eligibility requirements. Applications accepted year-round. Offers lectures, newsletter, performance opportunities and workshops.

SANTA BARBARA SONGWRITERS' ASSOCIATION, c/o Creative Music Associates, 3 West Carrillo, Suite 8, Santa Barbara, CA 93108. (805)962-2493. President: Edwin Bowman. Estab. 1980. "SBSA is dedicated to the promotion and development of the art of songwriting. Membership is open to anyone wishing to support these objectives." Membership is $10/year. SBSA sponsors the monthly showcase, workshops, clinics, meetings with representatives of publishing/recording companies and a monthly newsletter. "We offer discounts at local music outlets and recording studios, collaboration facilitation, loads of fellow-songwriter feedback, and encouragement and an occasional hot meal!"

SESAC, INC., 10 Columbus Circle, New York NY 10019. (212)586-3450; 11 Music Circle S., Nashville TN 37203; 9000 Sunset Blvd., Los Angeles CA 90069. Vice President of Affiliation: Vincent Candilora, New York. Membership Director, Los Angeles: Kathy Cooney. Director of Country Music: Dianne Petty, Nashville. Director of Gospel Music: Jim Black, Nashville. Send membership applications to New York, Nashville, or Los Angeles for all types of music. For writers and publishers who have their works performed by radio, television, nightclubs, cable TV, etc. in all types of music. "Prospective affiliates are requested to present a demo tape of their works which is reviewed by our Screening Committee." Purpose of organization is to collect and distribute performance royalties to all active affiliates. Send membership applications to New York or Los Angeles for all types of music; contact Nashville office for country or gospel music.

SONGWRITERS RESOURCES AND SERVICES, 6772 Hollywood Blvd., Hollywood CA 90028. (213)463-7178. Collective staff includes Kathy Gronau, Billy James, Bruce Kaplan, Pat Luboff and Doug Thiele. A nonprofit organization dedicated to the protection and education of songwriters. Membership is $30/year. Offers song protection service, Helen King Festival of New Music, forums, music business orientation workshops, bimonthly newsletter. Some services restricted to members and include workshops on lyric writing, harmony and composition, songwriting, song evaluation, performance and others as the need and interest develop; counseling, hotline, library, *Open Ears* (bimonthly listing of publishers and producers, type of material they're looking for, and how and whom to present it to), collaborator's and artist's directories, lead sheet service and a group legal plan. "We answer any of our members' music-related questions; as the nation's largest organization exclusively for songwriters, we speak on their behalf."

SOUTH BAY SONGWRITERS ASSOCIATION, Box 50443, Palo Alto CA 94303. (415)327-8296. Director: Patricia Silversher. Estab. 1980. Serves songwriters and musicians. "Our members are lyricists and composers from ages 16-70 who have backgrounds that vary considerably. There are several professional songwriters along with those people who are at the earliest stages of writing. We also have several businesses in the community that have joined SBSA to further advance the strength of the music community." No eligibility requirements. Applications accepted year-round. Offers competitions, instruction, lectures, library, newsletter, performance opportunities, social outings and workshops. "Our purpose is to teach the songwriter as much about the craft of songwriting and the business of music as is needed to survive."

THEATRE COMMUNICATIONS GROUP, INC., 355 Lexington Ave., New York NY 10017. (212)697-5230. Serves composers, lyricists, librettists for the theater. "TCG has a constituency of 180 nonprofit professional theaters for which it is the national service organization. It provides services in casting, personnel, management, as well as numerous publications and literary services to innumerable organizations and individuals." Services are available to all theater artists. "We are the national service organization for nonprofit professional theater and work to provide a wide range of information services. Publications are at the heart of our primary concern: communications. Our new monthly newsletter, *Artsearch*, provides employment information for theater artists, managers and technicians. Literary Services publishes the yearly *Information for Playwrights*, a guide for those who write and compose for the theater and also operates Plays in Process, a script distribution services for works performed at TCG constituent theaters. Writers of musicals may benefit from this program if their works receive full production at a TCG constituent theater and have not been otherwise published."

TUCSON SONGWRITERS ASSOCIATION, 620 N. 6th Ave., Tucson AZ 85705. (602)624-8276. Treasurer: Earl Wettstein. Serves songwriters and musicians. Members are primarily lyricists, ages 21-65. No eligibility requirements. Offers library, newsletter, performance opportunities and workshops. "Our purpose is to teach the craft of writing music and lyrics."

VOLUNTEER LAWYERS FOR THE ARTS, 36 W. 44th St., Suite 1110, New York NY 10036. (212)575-1150. Administrator: Katharine Rowe. For songwriters, musicians and all performing, visual, literary and fine arts and artists. Members are lawyers and artists, 20 years and older interested in art and law. Offers free legal assistance and representation to artists and arts organizations who are unable to afford private counsel. "We provide a growing library of manuals and guides to art and the volunteer lawyers. In addition, there are affiliates nationwide who handle local arts organizations and artists and their problems in their immediate areas." Fees: $25/year. Members receive the quarterly journal *Art and the Law* and discounts for other manuals and publications. Subscriptions to *Art and the Law* to non-members: $18/year. Offers instruction, lectures, library, workshops and publications and guides suited to particular problems.

WEST ROCKIES WRITERS CLUB, 2841 Teller Ave., Sp 10, Grand Junction CO 81501. (303)245-6448. Past President/Founder: Eva Carter. Meets monthly. Open to all beginning and professional writers. "We have speakers, informative programs and contests and publish a newsletter 9 times/year. Our membership includes writers in all fields, versifiers and published songwriters."

Publications of Interest

This section is divided into two groups. The first lists magazines that inform songwriters about songwriting and the music industry in general. These periodicals contain articles on songwriters, publishers, record company executives, how-to pieces and trends in the industry.

Before investing in a subscription, read what each editor says about his magazine. Some are of great interest to musicians as well as songwriters while others are aimed at only songwriters or a particular type of music (e.g. country, rock).

Many of these magazines can be purchased at newsstands. This gives you a chance to look first, then decide which benefit you as a songwriter or songwriter/musician. If you can't find a certain publication on the newsstand, write the publisher for more information.

Books are the second part of the section and answer many questions about the actual process of writing songs, along with detailed information on different aspects of the industry (contracts, copyright, etc). Some may be available at your local library or bookstores. If not, write the publisher whose name is listed with each book.

Periodicals

BILLBOARD, (The International Music/Record/Tape Newsweekly), Billboard Publications, Inc., 9000 Sunset Blvd., 12th Floor, Los Angeles CA 90069. (213)273-7040. Vice President of Circulation: Ann Haire. Promotion Director: Elvira Lopez. Weekly magazine; 108 pages. "*Billboard* documents the most recent developments in the music business, every week." Includes record charts, industry information, and "the thousands of weekly events" that tell what is happening in the music business.

THE CANADIAN COMPOSER/LE COMPOSITEUR CANADIEN, Creative Arts Company for Composers, Authors, and Publishers Association of Canada, 1240 Bay St., Suite 401, Toronto, Ontario, Canada M5R 2A7. Subscription Dept. Editor: Richard Flohil. Published 10 times/year; 48 pages. "*The Canadian Composer* is a bilingual magazine for the members of CAPAC. Its articles are about members of the organization."

CASHBOX MAGAZINE, Cashbox Publishing Co., Inc., 6363 Sunset Blvd., Suite 930, Hollywood CA 90028. (213)464-8241. Circulation Manager: Theresa Tortosa. Subscription address: 1775 Broadway, New York NY 10019. Weekly magazine; 75 pages. "*Cashbox* is an international music trade weekly. We provide record charts, news and information on executives, companies and artists that are making news, as well as an all-inclusive radio section. We also provide features for new and developing artists."

CODA, THE JAZZ MAGAZINE, Coda Publications, Box 87, Station J, Toronto, Ontario, Canada M4J 4X8. (416)368-3149. Business Manager: Dan Allen. Bimonthly magazine; 36 pages. "We cover interviews, reviews and news on jazz and blues music of interest to those who are into the artistic and creative—as opposed to the commercial—aspects of the music. We have become the most respected jazz periodical in English and have worldwide circulation to individuals and institutions."

COUNTRY SONG ROUNDUP, Charlton Publications, Inc., Charlton Bldg., Derby CT 06418. Contains lyrics to currently popular country songs and interviews with country artists, songwriters and disc jockeys. Monthly magazine.

DOWN BEAT, 222 S. Adams St., Chicago IL 60606. (312)346-7811. Editor: Charles Carman. Published monthly; 72 pages. For amateur and professional musicians with published interviews, record reviews, industry news, profiles, music workshops together with a pro shop section.

GUITAR AND LUTE MAGAZINE, Galliard Press, Ltd., 1229 Waimanu St., Honolulu HI 96814. Editor: Henry Adams. Quarterly magazine; 56 pages. "We cover the classic guitar, lute, and related plucked instruments. It has a varied format which is international in scope, including interviews and articles on the major performers, pedagogues, composers, and instrument builders in this field of music from around the world. Eash issue also contains news items on master classes, competitions, music festivals, etc., along with record, book and music reviews. We also include lute tablature and premiere publications of music as a regular feature."

HIT PARADER, Charlton Publications, Inc., Charlton Bldg., Derby CT 06418. Bimonthly magazine. Contains lyrics to top 40, rock, country and soul songs. Articles on rock music personalities, information about trends in the music industry and rock music in particular.

KEYBOARD WORLD, Keyboard World, Inc., Box 4399, Downey CA 90241. Contact: Circulation Dept. Publisher: Bill Worrall. Monthly magazine; 48 pages. "*Keyboard World* is of interest to the keyboard hobbyist. Its editorial matter deals with instruction, personality interviews, new products, organ sheet music and record reviews."

LEAD SHEET, 6772 Hollywood Blvd., Hollywood CA 90028. (213)462-1382. Editor: Tim Horrigan. Publisher: The Los Angeles Songwriters Showcase. Annual magazine; 18 pages. "*Lead Sheet* is a resource guide for songwriters. Articles on the art, craft, and business of songwriting include information about demos, protection, collaboration, contracts, the 'trades' and publishers. There are also listings of agencies and organizations songwriters should know about; classes and workshops geared to the songwriter; and periodicals and magazines of interest to songwriters. It is particularly of help to those in (or coming to) the LA area." $3 donation.

MUSIC CITY ENTERTAINER, 62 Music Square W., Nashville TN 37203. (615)327-4538. Contact: Advertising and Subscription Dept. Promotional Director: Connie L. Wright. Monthly tabloid; 24 pages. "Our paper is published to inform the public and music industry of new artists—top stars—and of all people involved in the music industry. We have stories and a record chart which appears on the back page which always includes records and songs by new artists, giving the artists a chance to be read nationally."

MUSIC CITY NEWS, Box 22975, 1302 Division St., Nashville TN 37202. Monthly country music publication focusing on the Nashville music scene; 40 pages. Circulation: 100,000. Host of the Music City News Cover Awards and the Top Country Hits of the Year Awards for songwriters, both nationwide television programs. Also publishes articles on Nashville songwriters. One songwriters special issue each year.

THE MUSIC CONNECTION, 6640 Sunset Blvd., Suite 201, Hollywood CA 90028. (213)462-5772. Contact: Subscription Dept. Biweekly magazine; 40 pages. "*The Music Connection* is a local musicians' trade magazine. Departments include a gig guide connecting musicians with agents, producers, publishers and club owners; a free classified section; music personal ads; and articles on songwriting, publishing and the music business."

MUSIC MAKERS, The Sunday School Board of the Southern Baptist Convention, 127 9th Ave. N., Nashville TN 37234. (615)251-2000. Contact: Church Music Dept. Music Editor: Terry Kirkland. Quarterly magazine; 36 pages. Publishes "music for use by 1st, 2nd and 3rd graders in choir at church. Includes spiritual concept and musical concept songs, plus simple rounds and partner songs."

NATIONAL MUSIC COUNCIL BULLETIN, 250 W. 54th St., New York NY 10019. (212)265-8132. Contact: Subscription Dept. Semiannual magazine; 40-44 pages. Reports activities of national music organizations, international music news, contests and competitons, government action in the field of music and music education.

SHEET MUSIC MAGAZINE, 223 Katonah Ave., Katonah NY 10536. For amateur and professional musicians, primarily piano and organ. "We feature articles on piano technique, rhythm workshops and composers' workshops, as well as interviews with successful songwriters."

SONGWRITER MAGAZINE, Len Latimer Organization, Inc., Box 3510, 6430 Sunset, Suite 908, Hollywood CA 90028. (213)464-7664. Contact: Subscription Dept. Editor-in-Chief: Len Latimer. Editor: Rich Wiseman. Monthly magazine; 64-96 pages. "A trade/craft magazine for professional and amateur songwriters with emphasis on MOR/pop, country and rock songwriting. Interviews with top songwriters and music business executives, how-to features and industry news."

TRUSTY TIPS FROM THE COLONEL, Trusty International, Rt. 1, Box 100, Nebo KY 42441. (502)249-3194. President: Elsie Childers. Monthly 1-page newsletter. "Producers and artists who need material contact us and we fill an 8½x11 sheet full of names and addresses of people needing songs for recording sessions or shows. Subscribers to our sheet have been placing their songs regularly through tips from our tip sheet. Sample copy for SASE and 25¢."

Books

ARRANGING POPULAR MUSIC, edited by Genichi Hawakami. 657 pages. Price: $25. Direct orders to Mike Honda, Foundation Liason, Music Education Division of Yamaha International Corp., 6600 Orangethorpe Ave., Buena Park CA 90620.

BRINGING IT TO NASHVILLE, by Michael J. Kosser. The inside information on what it's like to make it as a songwriter in Nashville. Available through the Nashville Songwriter's Association, 25 Music Square W., Nashville TN 37203.

IF THEY ASK YOU, YOU CAN WRITE A SONG, by Al Kasha & Joel Hirschhorn. The A-Zs of how to write songs from two Academy Award-winning songwriters. Published by Simon and Schuster, Inc., 1230 Avenue of the Americas, New York NY 10020.

HOW I WRITE SONGS (WHY YOU CAN), by Tom T. Hall. Tom T. uses his own experiences as a songwriter to demonstrate how you can write songs too. Available through the Nashville Songwriter's Association, 25 Music Square W., Nashville TN 37203.

HOW TO BE A SUCCESSFUL SONGWRITER, by Kent McNeel and Mark Luther. Mac Davis, Paul Williams, Henry Mancini and twenty other successful songwriters tell you how they do it. Published by St. Martin's Press, 175 5th Ave., New York NY 10010.

MAKING IT WITH MUSIC, by Kenny Rogers and Len Epand. Practical information on forming a group and making it succeed: equipment, recording, touring, songwriting and taking care of your money. Published by Harper & Row, 10 E. 53rd St., New York NY 10022.

MORE ABOUT THIS BUSINESS OF MUSIC, by Sidney Shemel and M. William Krasilovsky. A practical guide to five additional areas of the music industry not treated in *This Business of Music*: serious music, background music and transcriptions, tape and tape cartridges, production and sale of printed music, and live performances. Published by Billboard Publications, Inc., 1 Astor Plaza, New York NY 10036.

THE MUSIC BUSINESS: CAREER OPPORTUNITIES AND SELF-DEFENSE, by Dick Weissman. Covers all facets of the music industry: how record companies operate, the functions of agents and personal managers, the field of commercials, the roles of the performing and the studio musician, music publishing, contracts, record production, unions, radio, using your college education, and careers in music. Published by Crown Publishers, Inc., 1 Park Ave., New York NY 10016.

MUSIC TO SELL BY: THE CRAFT OF JINGLE WRITING, by Antonio Teixeira, Jr. A valuable, easy to read, how-to book on the preparation of jingles and compositions for radio and TV commercials. Published by Berklee Press Publications, 1265 Boylston St., Boston MA 02215.

THE PLATINUM RAINBOW (How to Succeed in the Music Business Without Selling Your Soul). *"The Platinum Rainbow*, a new book by Grammy Award-winning record producer Bob Monaco and nationally syndicated music columnist James Riodan, gives you an inside look at the recording industry and tells you how to think realistically in a business based on fantasy; how to promote yourself, how to get a manager, producer or agent; how to get free recording time, how to make a deal, how to recognize and record a hit song, how to be a session musician, how to kick your brother out of the band, how to put together the six key elements a record company looks for. There are quotes from some of the biggest names in pop music and a complete analysis of: *The Song, The Studio; The Stage; Demo Or Master; Cutting A Record; Hooks And Arrangements; The Producer; The Engineer; The Budget; The Basic Track; Vocals; Overdubs; The Mix; The 24 Track Monster; Things You Can Hear But Can't See; The Deal; The Creative Businessman; The Music Attorney; The Manager, Agent, Promoter; The Artist As Vendor; Leverage, Clout And The Ladder; Getting A Job With A Record Company; Gigs; The Golden Rell To Reel And The Platinum Turntable; Staying Happy; Waiting To Be Discovered And Nine Other Popular Myths About The Music Business.* Also included is a completed directory of record companies, producers, managers, publishers, agents, studios, engineering schools, concert promoters, all the names, addresses and phone numbers of who to contact." Published by Swordsman Press, 15445 Ventura Blvd., Suite 10, Box 5973, Sherman Oaks CA 91413.

SO YOU WANT TO BE IN MUSIC!, by Jesse Burt and Bob Ferguson. An inside look at songwriting and the music industry by two Nashville professionals. Available through the Nashville Songwriter's Association, 25 Music Square W., Nashville TN 37203.

THE SONGWRITER'S HANDBOOK, by Harvey Rachlin. Starts with the basic components of a song and covers the entire spectrum of the profession—from the conception of an idea for a song to getting it recorded. Published by Funk & Wagnalls, 10 E. 53rd St., New York NY 10022.

THE SONGWRITERS' SUCCESS MANUAL, by Lee Pincus. Answers to many questions including do-it-yourself publishing, how much a songwriter can earn, and four ways songwriters lose money. Published by Music Press, Box 1229, Grand Central Station, New York NY 10017.

THIS BUSINESS OF MUSIC, by Sidney Shemel and M. William Krasilovsky. Edited by Paul Ackerman. A practical guide to the music industry for publishers, songwriters, record companies, producers, artists and agents. Published by Billboard Publications, Inc., 1 Astor Plaza, New York NY 10036.

Workshops

As this section's Close-up of Carol Hall points out, workshops are a valuable source of tips, instruction, evaluation and constructive criticism. The workshops listed here offer all these things to you and other songwriters who are, just like you, trying to become better at their craft.

Location is a major factor in choosing a workshop. It's ideal if you live in New York or Los Angeles where songwriting workshops abound. If you don't, however, you may want to plan a vacation around attending a workshop *and* "pitching" your songs. Some workshops are purposely planned for the summer months just so you can combine vacation time and workshop training.

Many universities offer workshops and classes (both credit and noncredit) in songwriting. Check the bulletin of one near you.

To choose a workshop wisely you must know where your weaknesses as a songwriter lie and seek a workshop with a program that can strengthen your abilities in that area. To help you make that decision, the following workshops describe programs offered, costs, available facilities, program length and average class size.

Most want you to write or call about your interest. They will then reply with brochures giving complete details of their particular programs and an application or registration form.

American Guild of Authors and Composers (AGAC) Workshops, 40 W. 57th St., New York NY 10019. (212)757-8833. Director of Special Projects: Jonathan Holtzman.
ASKAPRO: "2 hour weekly music business rap session to which all writers are welcome. It features industry professionals—publishers, writers, producers, artists—fielding questions from new songwriters." Offered year-round. 40-50/meeting. Each session lasts 2 hours. Charge: free to member, $1 to nonmembers. Phone reservation necessary.
The Craft of Lyric Writing: "10 week course designed to give thorough grounding in the elements of successful lyric writing with a special emphasis on craftsmanship. Contemporary songs will be analyzed from the standpoints of form, hooks, style, devices and emotional content. Assignments are given to write to specific forms as well as to given melodies. Work evaluated in terms of clarity, originality, singability and competitive commerciality." Offered year-round with 10-12 in each workshop. Instructor for the Craft of Lyric Writing is Sheila Davis, whose songs have been recorded by Shirley Bassey, Hank Snow, and a gold record with Ed Ames. Cost: $80 to AGAC members, $100 to nonmembers. Requirements: two typewritten lyrics; "groups are formed that are as homogeneous as possible." Send for application. Course accredited by Hunter College for graduate students in masters program.
Harmony & Theory for Songwriters: "12-week course for which the reading and writing of music is a requisite. The syllabus includes: intervals; inversions of triads; seventh chords; modulation (related and remote); common harmonic patterns (ascending and descending); substitute chords within diatonic system; bass patterns (walking bass, pedal point); and diatonic circle (root movement). Assignments will be given employing all the foregoing elements as they apply to ballads, rock and reggae." Offered year-round. 10-12 students/class. Each session lasts 2 hours. Instructor for Melodic and Harmonic Techniques is Dan Ricigliano, Chairman of the Theory Department of the Manhattan School of Music and author of *Melody and Harmony in Contemporary Songwriting*. Cost: $95 to AGAC members, $120 to nonmembers. Course accredited by the Dean of Music of Hunter College.
Introduction to Theory and Composition: "12 week course designed to give a fundamental understanding of notation and harmonic theory as they relate to composition. Syllabus covers: notes and scales and their relationship to keyboard and guitar strings and musical staff, rhythm, intervals, melodic curves, voice leading, harmonizing melodies, and writing of lead sheets. Each class will devote some time to dictation (melodic, harmonic and rhythmic) and sightsinging. Weekly exercises will be assigned and reviewed." Offered year-round. 1-12 students/class. Each session lasts 2 hours. Cost: $95 to AGAC members, $120 to nonmembers. Course accredited by Hunter College for graduate students in masters program.
The Strategy of the Hit Single: "for writers who are writing for the charts. Program encompasses

Songwriter's Market Close-up

Back in Texas Carol Hall grew up in a family dedicated to music and the theater. "I've always been surrounded by music and have no specific memory of ever doing anything except singing, dancing and writing." Today as a New York City resident her life continues to revolve around music and the theater.

As a performer she has recorded two albums of her own material for Elecktra Records and has been on the road with such varied artists as Kris Kristofferson and Sha Na Na. Her songs have been performed by Barbra Streisand, Big Bird and Johnny Cash. As a composer-lyricist for the theater she has written both words and music for *The Best Little Whorehouse in Texas*—a rarity on Broadway where few musicals have lyrics and music written by the same person—for which she received two Drama Desk Awards and a Grammy Award nomination. The project for which she would most like to be remembered is the album *Free to Be You and Me*, which also became a book, an Emmy-winning TV special and soon will be a Broadway show.

She has completed a new play, *Good Sports*, which she describes as some of the best work she's ever done. Hall emphasizes that it is very hard to get an original musical presented on Broadway today. "The only way we got *The Best Little Whorehouse in Texas* on stage was to put it on ourselves. If we had sent it around I can guarantee you nobody would have done it. We invited people to a free production at Actors' Studio. We'd done all the work—so what the audience saw was almost a completed project. That's what Universal Pictures picked up."

She stresses the advantages New York offers struggling playwrights and songwriters. "There are BMI and ASCAP workshops where writers can come and bounce their songs or librettos off listening ears which are both critical and supportive. There's the American Guild of Authors and

Carol Hall

Composers (AGAC) workshop and also ASKAPRO sessions in which people who produce the records tell you exactly what they are looking for. If I was a young writer I would take advantage of every one."

Hall did just that while she was writing the songs for *Whorehouse*. "I took the songs to an AGAC workshop long before the musical was on anyone else's mind except mine. I just wanted to see if the songs worked by themselves."

Above all, Hall tells aspiring playwrights to get their play presented somewhere before trying for Broadway. "If it has to be at your local church or high school—do it. At that point you will learn whether the play works or not. Then you can write a letter (to producers) saying this musical was presented and when you come to New York you would like to meet with them to show them the script and score." And, she says, offices in New York have people who do nothing but scout outside the city for plays. "If your play is good, someone will show up to see it—they find plays outside of New York all the time."

musicians and lyricists. Course primarily concerned with media theories about how people perceive music over the radio and consequently how to write for that medium." Offered year-round. 12-15 students/class. Each session lasts 2 hours. Instructor of Strategy of the Hit Single is songwriter Norman Dolph whose credits include recordings by Jane Olivor, KC and the Sunshine Band, Isaac Hayes, Millie Jackson, and many more. Cost: $70 to AGAC members, $85 to non-members. "Applicants must submit a cassette of some current work. The applicants are screened to keep the level high for everyone's benefit."

Song Critique: Published and ready to be published songwriters can play one song every other session at the Songwriters' Room at Uncle Lulus, 16 W. 56th St., New York City, NY. These weekly 3 hour sessions start at 8 pm every Wednesday night and writers interested in performing their songs must call the Guild (212)757-8833 on Tuesdays from 11 am-2 pm to make an appointment. All other writers are invited to attend and help provide feedback. Host of the Song Critique is Jonathan Holtzman whose credits include everything from the music to a new show starring Hume Cronyn and Jessica Tandy, to records by Coffee (Delite/Polygram), Laurie Beechman (Atlantic) and Pure Energy (Prism).

Songwriters' Seminars: On the last Tuesday of every month, the AGAC Foundation presents a panel of top music industry professionals at the Songwriters' Room in Uncle Lulus (16 W. 56th St., New York NY). Starting at 8 pm, these two hour sessions cover topics relevant to the working songwriter as well as the newcomer. Questions are answered at the end of the sessions and all writers are invited to attend. There is a $2 cover charge for non-AGAC members with a $2 drink minimum for all (limited to 40 people).

AMERICAN GUILD OF AUTHORS AND COMPOSERS (AGAC) WORKSHOPS, 6430 Sunset Blvd., Suite 1113, Hollywood CA 90028. (213)462-1108. Regional Director: Leslie Lates.
ASKAPRO: "2-hour music business rap session to which all writers are welcome held on the first and third Tuesday of each month. Features industry professionals—publishers, writers, producers, artists—fielding questions from new songwriters." Offered year-round. 40-50/meeting. Each session lasts 2 hours. Free to all in Los Angeles. Reservations necessary. Phone for more information.
Jack Segal's Songwriting Workshop: "designed to give the songwriter additional techniques to write for today's song market. Both lyrics and music will be treated in terms of contemporary content and form. Spontaneous, in-class and weekly assignments will be given. Workshop activities will include: the basics—form, content, design; tools; collaboration; the demo; the lyric and lead sheet; and the music business. Offered year-round. 12-15/class. Each session lasts 2 hours. Cost: $70 to AGAC members, $85 to nonmembers. Classes held in private home in Beverly Hills. "All applicants must submit a tape and Jack Segal will make final selection."

DICK GROVE MUSIC WORKSHOPS, 12754 Ventura Blvd., Studio City CA 91604. (213)985-0905. Administrator: Alan K. Yoshida. Offers programs for songwriters in lyric writing, composition, harmony, theory, and rhythmic dictation. "Songwriters workshop is a class that combines lecture and roundtable critique to develop a more precise approach to songwriting. Many classes have advanced levels of study." Offers programs for musicians "ranging from beginning sight-reading to advanced record mixing. All classes are taught by professional musicians. Workshops are offered for guitarists; bassists; drummers; keyboardists; vocalists; and brass, reed and string players. Other classes include record production, arranging, conducting, ear-training, improvisation, film scoring, music preparation and sight-singing." Four 10-week terms/calendar year. "Enrollment is 800/term; average class size is 15. Most classes are $60, covering five 2-hour sessions. Some classes require texts or materials that are not included in the tuition fee. Record mixing classes are $200." Complete classroom facilities. "We also offer year long, full-time programs for arrangers/composers and players. We will be offering a brand-new program beginning July, 1981, and every 6 months thereafter. The Composing and Musicianship Program (COMD) is for students wishing a primary career as songwriter and the related experience in record producing, the record industry and publishing. Students will obtain in-depth experience in all styles of song composition and concept from both the lyrical and compositional aspects." Applicants must be "interviewed prior to enrolling for placement. Certain classes require auditions." Request current catalog by mail or telephone.

NASHVILLE SONGWRITER'S ASSOCIATION WORKSHOP, 25 Music Square W., Nashville TN 37203. (615)254-8903. Executive Director: Maggie Cavender. Membership Coordinator: Dot Thornton. Meets weekly for 2½-hour educational/critique sessions. Nashville and national songwriters and publishers are frequent guest speakers. Questions relative to songwriting and the industry are answered. Free to members of the Nashville Songwriter's Association International, but out-of-town guests are welcome. Attendance: 40-60/workshop. Send for application.

THE NEW SCHOOL, 66 W. 12th St., New York NY 10011. (212)741-5600. Offers two programs in "Writing for the Musical Theater." Offered fall and winter semesters. 12-25 students/class. Meet at the Guild Rehearsal Studios in the Ansonia Hotel, Broadway and 73rd St. Contact: Registration office.

Introductory Course: Practice assignments provide members with a vocabulary and working tools; increase individual and collaborative skills; and help start or further projects for Workshop (see below). writers may enter as already existing teams, or find a collaborator in class. 12 two-hour classes. Cost $160.

Workshop: Professional weekly class tryout of projects in progress and, where far enough along, in workshop performance by professional actors and under direction. Broadway guests are occasionally invited to share their experience. Prerequisite: Preliminary course (see above), plus permission of the instructors. 12 three-hour sessions. Cost: $200.

SACRAMENTO SONGWRITERS SHOWCASE, 2791 24th St., Sacramento CA 95818. (916)739-0773. Director: Martin Cohen. Offers instruction programs, lectures, newsletter, performance opportunities, workshops and co-production with local media (TV and radio) for songwriters and musicians. Members are all ages with a major interest in music of original nature. "We are a non-profit organization working for the development and education of songwriters/composers. We are establishing a network for writers that will make them artistically competent and economically viable." Membership: $15/year. Benefits include discounts to concert and workshop series and discounts at local music stores and recording studios. Open auditions for concerts all year. "We work with peers for development and feedback. Information on marketing songs and legal protection services available to a groups and individuals." Applications accepted any time throughout the year.

SAN GABRIEL VALLEY MUSIC ASSOCIATION, Box 396, West Covina CA 91790. (213)332-2504. President: Angelo Roman, Jr. Offers lyric and song evaluation. Year-round; 10-15 students/class. Each session lasts 2-3 hours. Cost: $10. Location varies, e.g. public library, recording studios. Call or write for more information.

FRANKS SILVERA WRITERS' WORKSHOP, 317 W. 125 St., 3rd Floor, New York NY 10027. (212)662-8463. Contact: Garland Lee Thompson. "Our workshop is open to *all* writers who are prepared to participate by reading their work. Each year 70-80 plays are read. Third World and women writers are especially encouraged."

SONGWRITER SEMINARS AND WORKSHOPS, 119 W. 57th St., New York NY 10019. (212)245-2449. President: Ted Lehrman. Vice President: Libby Bush. Offers programs for songwriters: intermediate pop songwriting; advanced workshop; and at-home songwriter workshop. Year-round with cycles beginning in September, December, March and June. Approximately 12 in each songwriter workshop. Each cycle lasts 10 weeks, except for the June cycle which is an 8-week cycle. "Our programs stress the craft and business realities of *today's* pop music industry. We guide our members in the writing of the hit single song (both lyrics and music) for those recording artists who are open to outside material. We also share with them our considerable experience and expertise in the marketing of commercial pop music product. Our instructors, Ted Lehrman and Libby Bush, both members of ASCAP, have had between them more than 80 songs recorded and commercially released here and abroad. They continue to be highly active in writing and placing pop songs for publication." Cost of 10 week workshops: $145, Pop Songwriting—Preparing for the Marketplace; $150, Advanced Songwriter Seminar and Workshop—Ready for the Marketplace. Cost of at-home songwriter workshop: $12.50/lyric; $15/song. Private song and career consultation sessions: $30/hour. Top 40 single stressed. Collaboration opportunities available. No housing provided. Interviews/auditions held for songwriters and singer/songwriters to determine which workshop would be most helpful. Call for free brochure and/or set up interview.

SONGWRITING WORKSHOP AND THE BUSINESS OF MUSIC, Rustron Music Productions, 200 Westmoreland Ave., White Plains NY 10606. (914)946-1689. Course Instructor: Rusty Gordon. Offers programs for songwriters "about the music industry and how it works. Lecture material is very specific and complete, covering all areas of the subject. Includes instruction in the techniques of the craft and the mechanics needed to write commercially marketable songs. We teach from both the lyrical and musical points of view. We specify universality, concept uniqueness and mood development for clear-cut media marketing." Year-round. 10 students/class. 2½-hour evening classes meet once/week for 8 weeks. "The entire course including workbook/folder and all additional printed material is $125. We have a payment plan requiring $20 paid at the first class and $15 paid at each successive class. Group discount available. We have no boarding facilities. Classes are held at main office and at sites in NYC. Applicants must be at least 16 years old. This is a college-level course. In addition, we have a new public class with unlimited enrollment at the Rauchambeau School, Fisher Ave., White Plains, New York 10606. Write for starting dates. This course will be taught year-round. Minimal fees will be set by the school.

Correspondence course available; for specific details and general course information write or call 6 am to 11 pm, Monday through Thursday."

SRS WORKSHOPS, 6772 Hollywood Blvd., Hollywood CA 90028. (213)463-7178. Staff Members: Kathy Gronau, Billy James, Pat Luboff, Bruce Kaplan, Doug Thiele. Offers programs for songwriters: performers workshop, song evaluation workshop, lyric writing, legal and practical aspects of the music business, harmony and theory, advanced songwriting, collaborator's and artist's directory, leadsheet service, pamphlets and cassettes, Helen King Festival of New Music, showcase information, registration service, resource books, and bimonthly newsletter. Offers programs year-round. Attendance: up to 25/workshop. Length: 2-4 hours/workshop. Some workshops are available on tape. Instructors include hit writer/publisher Doug Thiele; columnists Pat and Pete Luboff; Tom Sturgis, publisher with Arista; Ruben Duarte with April Blackwood publishing and others. "Some of our workshops are free to members. Others usually are $30-50 for 8-10 week sessions. Membership is $30." Send for application. "SRS is a nonprofit membership organization dedicated to the protection and education of songwriters. We also provide an 'Open Ears' Tip Sheet telling members which publishers, producers and artists are looking for material."

Appendix

The Business of Songwriting

Being creative is not enough to assure success as a songwriter. A little business savvy is a great advantage when you approach music executives who may themselves be more business-oriented than creative.

The articles in this section give you insights into the structure and operation of the music business as well as detailed information on contracts, copyright, submitting your songs, and more.

The Structure of the Music Business

Los Angeles, New York City and Nashville claim the largest concentrations of companies involved in the music business. There are, of course, companies in cities across the country which continue to make important contributions to today's music scene. But it's the decisions made in the three music centers that determine the direction the industry takes: which songs are published, which artists are signed to recording contracts and which records are released.

No matter which city you're dealing in, the chart showing the structure of the music business (Chart 1) shows the possible routes a song can take to becoming published, recorded and released. Those routes include taking your songs to the A) artist; B) artist's manager; C) music publisher; D) independent record producer; or E) the record company.

Choosing where to submit your songs depends on many things. If you know a recording artist (A) personally and have a song you think would suit him, approach the artist first. If he likes the song he will take it to his producer and, if the producer agrees, it will be scheduled for the artist's recording session.

If you don't know an artist personally, you might try to contact the artist's personal manager (B). Check the Manager section of this book for names of personal managers. *Billboard's International Talent Directory* (Billboard Publications, Inc., 9000 Sunset Blvd., Los Angeles CA 90069) lists artists and personal managers but gives no submission information.

You can also submit your songs to the independent record producer (D), or the A&R director of a record company (E). They are always looking for songs for the artists they produce. If they and their artists think your song is a hit, it will be recorded and released.

If the artist being produced by the independent producer is already signed to a recording contract, the song will be released on that record company's label. Many times, however, the independent producer will pay for and produce a session by an

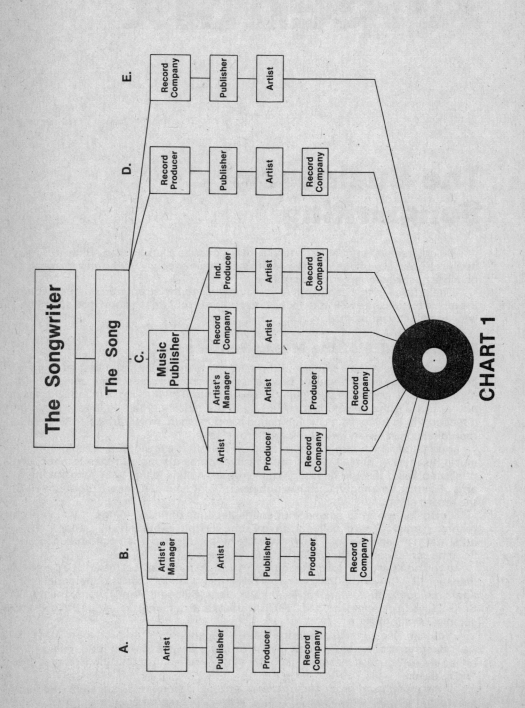

CHART 1

artist who is not yet under contract to a recording company. The producer then tries to sell the master tape of that session to the A&R directors of various recording companies. If he sells the master and negotiates a contract for the artist, the record is released on that label.

Each of the above approaches to the music industry requires that, somewhere along the line, someone either publishes your song or recommends a publisher. The advantage to those approaches is that many artists, producers, and record companies *do* have their own publishing companies. Since publishing means money if the song is successful and more money if it is recorded by other artists, a good song can have even greater appeal to artists, producers and record companies if the publishing is "open" (if the song has not yet been published).

There is much to be said, however, for taking your songs to a publisher *first*. Songs are the publisher's business. In music centers, the artists, producers and record companies look to publishers to supply them with a constant flow of new material. Competition is stiff. Even if an artist, producer or record company has a publishing company, they *will* use another publisher's song—if it's better than one in their own publishing company.

Publishers not only look for songs, but also for songwriters. Sometimes, but usually only to songwriters with credentials, they offer an exclusive writing contract that can include advances, salary, an office and work area, and a studio for demo purposes.

The publisher pitches (an industry term meaning to play your songs for artists and producers who might record them) your songs to artists, producers and A&R directors. Major publishers in music centers are regularly sent notification of who will be recording and when.

The greatest advantage, then, to approaching a music publisher first is his know-how and clout with the industry as a whole. You can concentrate on your business—writing songs—while the publisher works on getting cuts (recordings) on the songs you write. Some publishers do encourage their writers to do some pitching. That is not necessarily bad since it keeps the writer even closer to what's happening in the industry.

Any one (or a combination) of these ways of getting your song heard, published, recorded and released is the best way if it works for you. In this book are listed music publishers, record companies, record producers and managers with specifications on how to submit your material to each.

Submitting Your Songs

Here are guidelines to help when submitting material to companies listed in this book:

- Read the listing and submit exactly what a company asks for and exactly how it asks that it be submitted.
- Listen to each demo before submitting to make sure the quality is satisfactory.
- Enclose a brief, neat cover letter of introduction. Indicate the types of songs you're submitting and, if you wish, recording artists you think they might suit.
- Include typed or legibly printed lyric sheets. If requested, include a lead sheet. Place your name, address and phone number on each lead or lyric sheet.
- Label neatly each tape and tape box with your name, address, phone number and the names of songs on the tape in the sequence in which they appear.
- Keep a record of the date, the names of the songs and the company to which you are submitting.
- Include a SASE for the return of your material. Your return envelope to Canadian companies should contain International Reply Coupons.
- Wrap and tie the package neatly and write or type the address and your return address so they are clearly visible. Your package is the first impression a company has of you and your songs, so neatness is very important.
- Mail First Class. Stamp or write "First Class Mail" on the package and on the SASE you enclose. Don't send by registered mail. The recipient must interrupt his day to sign for it and many companies refuse all registered mail.

If a company is not listed in *Songwriter's Market*, or if, at the end of the Music Publisher or Record Company section, it is noted as a company that does not usually accept unsolicited material, don't submit to them without first writing and receiving a reply to a query.

The query letter should be neat (preferably typewritten), brief and pleasant. Explain the type of material you have and ask about their needs and current submission policy.

To expedite a reply, you can enclose a self-addressed stamped postcard asking the information you need to know. Your typed questions (see Sample Reply Form) should be direct and easy for the receiver to answer. Don't forget to include a line for the respondent's name and title. Also remember to place the company's name and address in the upper left-hand space on the front of the postcard so you'll know what company it was you queried. Queries, like tape submissions, should be recorded for future reference.

Sample Reply Form

I would like to hear:

( ) "Name of Song"   ( ) "Name of Song"   ( ) "Name of Song"

I prefer:

( ) reel-to-reel   ( ) cassette   ( ) either

With:

( ) lyric sheet   ( ) lead sheet   ( ) either   ( ) both

( ) I am not looking for material at this time, try me later.

( ) I am not interested.

_____

Name   Title

Submitting in Person

A trip to Los Angeles, New York or Nashville can give you an inside glimpse of the music business at work. If you've planned ahead, outlined your schedule, made appointments, and carefully prepared demos, you have only to reap the rewards of first-hand reaction to your material. Use the geographic index at the end of both the Music Publishers and Record Companies sections to contact, before you leave home, companies you'd like to visit.

Take several reel-to-reel and cassette copies and lyric sheets of each of your songs. More than one of the companies you visit may ask that you leave a copy with them. If the person who's reviewing material likes a song, he may want to play it for someone else. There's also a good chance the person you have the appointment with will have to cancel (expect that occasionally), but wants you to leave a copy of your songs and he will contact you later.

Listen attentively to what the reviewers say. When you return home, summarize their reactions to your material and look for similarities in their critiques. That information will be invaluable as you continue to submit material to the people who now know you personally.

The Money

The songwriter's money comes in the form of royalty checks. Unless your contract (see "Contracts" in this book) stipulates you will receive a salary or advance on future royalties, you shouldn't expect your first money before three to six months after the song is released.

A look at the royalties chart (Chart 2) shows that the songwriter receives:
- Mechanical royalties from the sale of records and tapes.
- Performance royalties for airplay on radio and TV, plays on jukeboxes and live performances.
- Foreign royalties from foreign sub-publishers.
- Money for sheet music, choral arrangements and folio sales.

Mechanical royalties are due the songwriter and the publisher every time a recorded copy of your song is sold and not returned. You and the publisher split a portion of that revenue (50-50 is standard). The Copyright Royalty Tribunal has set maximum royalty at 4¢/song.

The money for mechanical royalties flows from retail record shops to the record company. The record company then pays the music publisher 4¢ per record *sold*. You and the publisher split the 4¢ less reasonable publisher's expenses. Reasonable publisher's expenses means only the cost incurred for that particular song: phone calls, postage, etc.

The songwriter also shares 50-50 in any royalties the publisher receives from the sub-publisher who·collected the publishing monies generated by your songs in the foreign music market.

The publisher pays you a share of the profit from the sale of sheet music, orchestrations, choral arrangements and folio sales. You earn 3-8% for each sheet of piano music sold and about 10% of the wholesale price of orchestrations, choral arrangments and folios.

Periodically (usually every six months) the publisher sends the songwriter a check that reflects his share of the mechanical royalties, foreign sub-publishing royalties, and sheet music, orchestrations, choral arrangments and folio sales.

Performance royalties are collected from radio and television stations, night clubs and jukeboxes by the performance rights organizations (ASCAP, BMI and SESAC). A published songwriter *must* belong to the same organization to which the publisher belongs. You'll notice that many publishers listed in this book have affiliate companies belonging to a different performance rights organization. That allows the publisher to deal with writers of more than one affiliation.

Each performance rights organization has its own unique method of determining how many times your song is performed during a given period. Their primary difference is *how* they make that determination. ASCAP monitors individual radio and television stations as well as concerts and clubs where music is performed. BMI uses logs sent them from radio and TV stations. SESAC uses the charts of the trade magazines (*Billboard*, *Cashbox* and *Record World*) to determine the popularity of individual songs. ASCAP charges a membership fee. BMI and SESAC do not.

The songwriter receives a statement of performances and a royalty check from his chosen performance rights organization quarterly. The amount earned depends on how many times the organization determined the song was performed.

ASCAP, BMI and SESAC are highly professional and reputable friends of the songwriter. To look into the specific policies, procedures, benefits and requirements of each before joining, use the addresses given in our Organizations & Clubs section to write them. Also, consult the chapter on these organizations in *This Business of Music* by Sidney Shemel and M. William Kasilovski (Billboard Publications).

Record Keeping

Your record keeping should include a list of income from royalty checks as well as expenses incurred as a result of your songwriting business: cost of tapes, demo sessions, office supplies, postage, traveling expenses, dues to songwriting organiza-

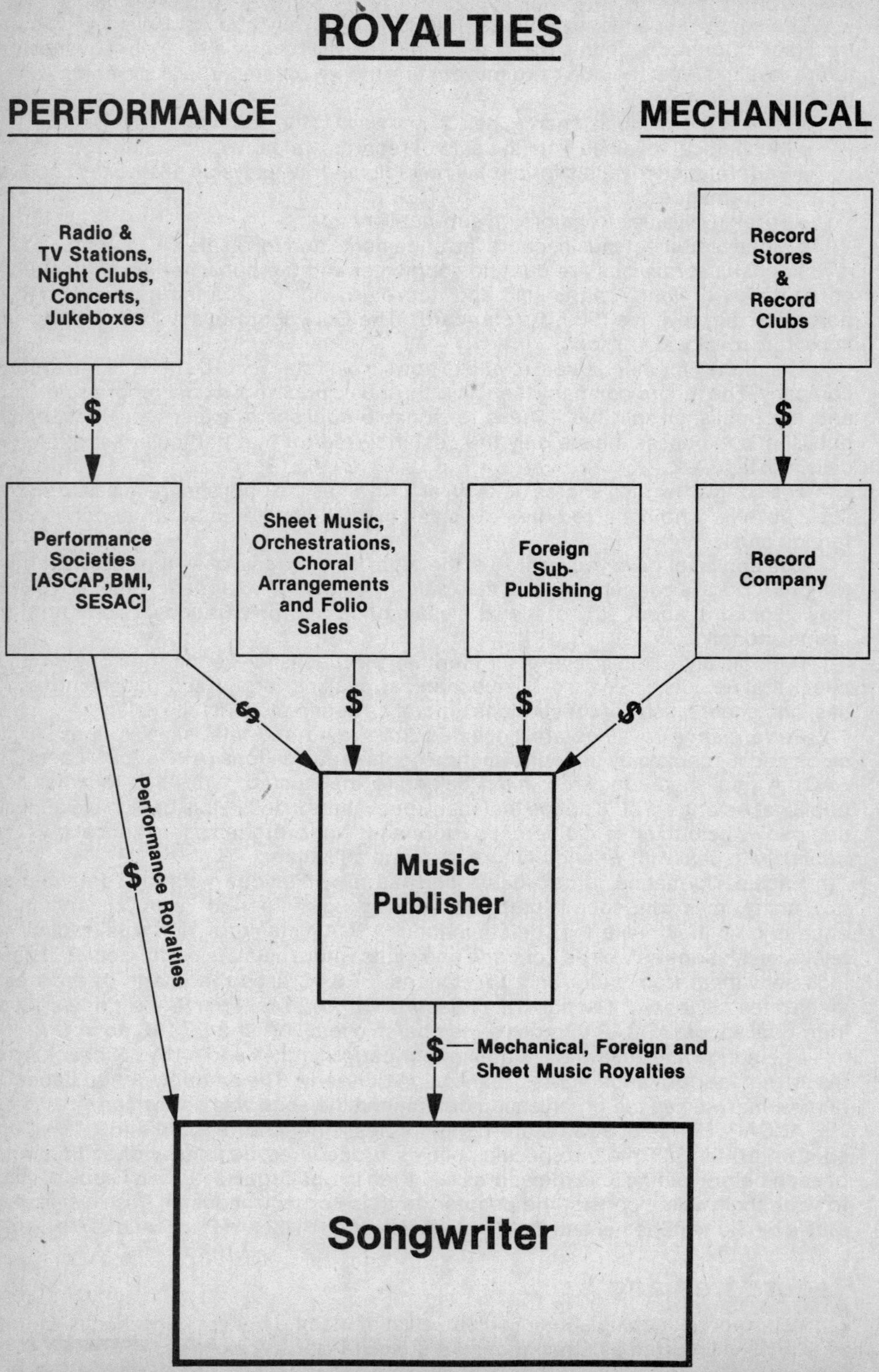

ROYALTIES

PERFORMANCE   **MECHANICAL**

Radio &
TV Stations,
Night Clubs,
Concerts,
Jukeboxes

Record
Stores
&
Record
Clubs

$

$

Performance
Societies
[ASCAP, BMI,
SESAC]

Sheet Music,
Orchestrations,
Choral
Arrangements
and Folio
Sales

Foreign
Sub-
Publishing

Record
Company

$ $ $ $

Performance Royalties

$

**Music
Publisher**

$—Mechanical, Foreign and
Sheet Music Royalties

Songwriter

CHART 2

tions, class and workshop fees, and publications of interest. It's also advisable to open a checking account exclusively for your songwriting activities, not only to make record keeping easier, but to establish your identity as a business for tax purposes.

The Rip Offs

There are those who use the music business as a means to unfairly exploit others. Here are some guidelines to help you recognize when you've come upon such a person or company:

- *Never pay* to have your songs published. A reputable company interested in your songs assumes the responsibility and cost of promoting your material. That company invests in your material because it expects a profit once the song is recorded and released.
- Never pay to have your music "reviewed." Reviewing material—free of charge—is the business of a reputable company.
- Never pay to have your lyrics or poems set to music. "Music mills"—for a price—may use the same melody for hundreds of lyrics and poems. Publishers can recognize one of these melodies as soon as it hits their tape player.
- Read *all* contracts carefully before signing and don't sign any contract you're unsure about or that you don't understand.
- Don't pay a company to pair you up with a collaborator. Better ways include advertising (or checking the ads) in magazines like *Songwriter* and contacting organizations which offer collaboration services to their members (see the Organizations and Clubs section in this book).
- Don't "sell your songs outright." It's unethical for anyone to offer you such a proposition.
- If you are being offered a "recording contract" you should not be expected to pay upfront for the session, musicians, promotion, etc. Major record companies recoup such expenses from record sales. If you *are* asked to pay expenses upfront, beware. No matter how much is promised to you verbally or in your contract, you will probably never see a return on your money. With such companies, it's a good idea to ask to speak with other artists who have signed such contracts with them before signing one yourself. And if, after weighing expenses, you think you can afford the longshot, then it's your decision. Read the stipulations of the contract carefully, however, and go over them with an attorney.
- Verify any situation about a company or individual if you have doubts: 1) contact the performance rights organization with which they are affiliated; 2) check with the Better Business Bureau in the town where they're located; 3) contact professional organizations listed in our Organization and Clubs section.

Co-Writing

A quick check of the charts in *Billboard*, *Cashbox* or *Record World* will show that collaboration is not just an alternative way of writing—it's the most popular way. Among its advantages is the instant feedback and criticism of the songs you're writing. Another plus for collaboration is the talent that each songwriter brings to the task.

Where do you find collaborators? Try the classified section of publications like *Songwriter* magazine. Check the bulletin board at your local musician's union hall. Professional organizations like Songwriter's Resources and Services (SRS) in Los Angeles, The American Guild of Authors and Composers (AGAC) in New York City and Los Angeles, and The Nashville Songwriters Association (NSA) in Nashville offer collaboration services. Check the Organizations and Clubs section for addresses.

For a discussion of collaboration agreements, see "Contracts" in this book.

Alternatives

Alternatives a songwriter might consider other than the popular music market are advertising agencies, audiovisual firms and the theater. Each is a specialized market requiring not only talent, but technical knowledge of that particular field.

The "total package" resulting from work in any of these three alternative categories will most always result from the "team" efforts of several or many people other than yourself. Working with advertising agencies and audiovisual firms means not only getting involved with the company's production staff, but many times even with their clients. Likewise, the playwright may find himself working with the musical director, production staff and technical crew as his work is being staged.

Advertising Agencies

Advertising agencies usually pay by the hour or by the job and assign work as it is needed for clients. Most agencies want all rights to jingles and music they buy from songwriters. This permits the buyer (the agency) to use the material however and as many times as it pleases without further reimbursement to the writer. Some agencies buy one-time rights, meaning that more than one use of that particular work must be renegotiated between agency and writer. The writer should obviously expect to be paid more for selling all rights to his work than just one-time rights.

The demo you send an agency should have approximately six (unless otherwise stated in a company's listing) 30- 60-second jingles. One should fade out (get progressively softer and then fade away) while the next one fades in. Unlike songs, jingles should *not* be separated by leader tape. More and more agencies are accepting cassettes for their ease in handling and filing, but check listings for individual preferences.

Audiovisual Firms

Most audiovisual firms pay by the job, but some pay by the hour, and others may negotiate a contract that includes royalty payments. You may be asked to sell all or one-time rights, depending upon the particular job and the needs of the client. Be sure to understand upfront exactly what job they expect of you (how many songs, the length of the presentation, etc.) and how much they are agreeing to pay. And, as with ad agencies, payment for all rights should be more than that for one-time rights. songs used.

Musicals

Meshing music and script into a single, unified entity is difficult, especially since musicals are often products of collaboration. Playwright and songwriter must share not only work schedules, but also a concept of the goals and direction of the product they're co-writing. Collaborate with a person with whom you can work creatively, yet efficiently.

You should work closely with at least one theater group to get a look at theater operation. Working with a local group—in any capacity—will give you a pragmatic grounding in what you can and can't do on stage.

If it's impossible for you to work on plays, watch them. Attend as many musicals (nonmusicals, too) as possible. Regional theaters and dinner theaters give plenty of opportunities to witness high-quality productions.

Write play publishers, request copies of their catalogs and order a few playscripts to study. This will give you an idea of how song lyrics relate to the entire show, how and when songs are woven into the plot, and the number of songs used.

The Theatre Communications Group publishes a list called Information for Playwrights (355 Lexington Ave., New York NY 10017). You can also get useful information by joining the American Theatre Association (ATA, 1029 Vermont Ave. NW, Washington DC 20005), which publishes various theater and membership directories; and the Dramatist's Guild (234 W. 44th St., New York NY 10036), which publishes a newsletter that covers, as do the other periodicals mentioned here, contests, producers, markets and trends.

Writers of musicals receive royalty in the form of a percent of box office receipts or a flat fee per performance. Other monies may come as royalties for sales of scripts and cast albums.

Another Profitable Outlet for Your Writing Talent

Writer's DIGEST

THE WORLD'S LEADING MAGAZINE FOR WRITERS

Would you like to:

● get up-to-the-minute reports on the writing markets?

● receive the advice of editors and professional writers about what to write and how to write it to maximize your opportunities for getting published?

● read interviews of leading authors that reveal their secrets of success?

● hear what experts have to say about writing and selling fiction, nonfiction, and poetry?

● get a $3 discount?

(See other side for your discount.)

POSTAGE WILL BE PAID BY ADDRESSEE

BUSINESS REPLY MAIL

FIRST CLASS   PERMIT NO. 17   CINCINNATI, OHIO

Writer's DIGEST

Subscriber Service Dept.
205 West Center Street
Marion, Ohio 43306

Copyright

BY DOUG THIELE

One of the first questions songwriters ask is, "How do I protect my songs?" The new copyright law which went into effect January 1, 1978, made significant changes in the law which had stood without revision since 1909. The following answers to important questions about copyright also include information on the most recent decision of the Copyright Royalty Tribunal to increase the mechanical royalties which record companies must pay publishers and songwriters.

To what rights am I entitled under copyright law?

With two significant exceptions, a song should be considered a piece of property in every sense of the word. Owning a copyright entitles you to the same rights you have with any other piece of property; you have the right to exploit the song in every possible way. It's your right to sell it, to lease it, to forbid its use without your permission, and to do all this throughout the world (some companies are now careful to make it "throughout the universe"). You even have the right to will a song to your heirs. In short, you have the exclusive right to do what you will with your song for the full length of copyright.

The two points which distinguish ownership of a song from ownership of a car or sculpture are: first, there is a limit placed on the length of time you may own your song. Second, although you have the right to decide who records your song *first*, after that anybody may record and release it *without* your permission, provided they pay you the statutory royalty rate. This is called the "right of first license."

The new copyright law, passed by Congress in 1976, went into effect January 1, 1978. What does it mean to me, the songwriter?

One of the most important things it means is that you no longer have to apply for a copyright. The new law states that there's a full copyright on your song the minute you put it down in fixed form, which means that the second you finish your tape, or even the moment you stop writing down your lyric on paper, your song is fully protected. Of course, you then need to establish yourself as the *owner* of that copyright, which is why you must register the song. It's still very important to do this.

The new law also allows you to submit your song for registration (including just your lyric) in a tape or disc or any other form of the song you have. Lead sheets are still accepted, of course.

You've been given two raises. When the law went into effect January 1, 1978, it provided that you could set any amount for mechanical royalties (your income from sale of records or tapes) the first time you issue a license to an artist, but if anyone wished to record your song afterwards, they were only required to pay 2¾¢ per song or ½¢ per minute, whichever was greater. This initial raise was ¾ over the 2¢ rate set in 1909.

The Copyright Royalty Tribunal, the regulating body for mechanical rates, spent much of 1980 and at least the first half of 1981 deciding on and implementing an

Doug Thiele *is a songwriter, publisher, journalist, lecturer and on the staff of* Songwriter's Resources and Services *in Los Angeles. His most recent credits include songs for Cristy Lane and Tycoon. He is also a contributing editor of* Songwriter *magazine and is actively involved in projects to aid and inform the songwriter (e.g. royalty increases, showcases, workshops and seminars).* .

increase in the 2¾¢ rate. After hearing testimony from record companies and their representatives and publishers and songwriters, the tribunal raised the mechanical royalty rate to 4¢, effective July 1, 1981. Both record company representatives, who generally feel the rate is too high, and publishers who feel the rate is too low, have filed objections in court to the tribunal's decision. Although it's anticipated the rate will increase to the 4¢ mark, no final decision has been reached as of this printing.

The tribunal has also ruled that between now and the next time they consider the mechanical royalty rate in 1987, it will increase proportionally with the rise in record prices, though the mechanism to accomplish this is not clearly established.

How long are songs protected?

Assuming you do things right (the penalty for not following copyright rules is loss of ownership of your song), length of copyright in this country is fifty years after your death, or fifty years after the death of the last surviving writer of the song.

Does the songwriter have any power to change the law?

Other than anyone's fundamental right to change any law, writers can make their voices heard at any of the meetings of the Copyright Royalty Tribunal. The tribunal will consider the issue of mechanical royalty rates again in 1987, and then every ten years. There's a strong move under way to urge the tribunal to meet more often than once every ten years. However, if the above-mentioned automatic rate increase proportional with the rise in record prices goes into effect, the tribunal's consideration of the mechanical royalty rate once every ten years may suffice.

When should I register my song?

You should register your song the minute you finish it so that you can prove that you were first in possession of the material. It's the person who can prove he was first in possession of the song who is considered the Proprietor (or owner) of the song.

What is the procedure for registering my song?

The standard procedure to register an unpublished song is to get form PA from the copyright office (or your local Federal Information Center) and submit it with a copy of your song and the fee of $10. You'll receive a certificate from the offices in about sixteen weeks.

You may also register unpublished songs in a group for the same fee, but it's very difficult to separate one song from the group to place with a publisher or other party without assigning *all* the songs in the group, since the group will only be given one PA number. If the work is released to the public in fixed form (records, sheet music, etc.), then it has been published, and you must follow different procedures.

In the case of published works, you may use form PA, or you may also use form SR, which will protect the song, and your arrangement of the song, against being illegally duplicated. The notice for protecting the arrangement of the song is a "p" with a circle around it.

Can I register band names or titles with the Copyright Office?

No. You must register band names with the Trademark and Patent office. Nor can you register titles or phrases of music or lyric in most cases. Remember, the copyright law is designed to protect against *copying* your work; it's not there to protect ideas.

Will someone steal my songs if I don't register them right away?

It's possible. But to ease your mind, songs aren't often stolen. First of all, most songs aren't commercially valuable . . . that's just the way it is. Of the ones that are, there's a danger, but it usually never comes from reputable publishing or recording companies. The reason is that their reputation must remain impeccable; if they rip you off, word will hit the streets, and the offending company will soon not be seeing good writers.

How does the copyright law stop someone from stealing my song?

While no one can stop someone from stealing your song, the copyright law does provide a course of action if someone *does* steal your song. The Copyright Office does not protect songs. They are a filing service which officially records possession of a song on a certain date. That's all. To be more specific, the Copyright Office doesn't have any way of actually knowing that a writer wrote a song, as curious as that sounds. But, if a question should come up about if and when you wrote a song, the Copyright Office will provide the forms you filed and the date they were registered.

What constitutes infringement, and how much of a lyric or melody can be copied before infringement occurs?

Infringement is the unauthorized use or claim to another's song or part of a song. Infringement occurs when the amount of "borrowing" from the original work sufficiently confuses the public so as to measurably inhibit the sale of the original work.

Many people believe that eight measures is the limit of what you can "borrow" for another song; nothing could be farther from the truth. For instance, even though most titles are not protectable, infringement occurs when you use a title which is so ingrained in the American consciousness so as to only be connected with one song, as in *Moon River*, or *Killing Me Softly*, and it's my feeling that if anybody used the *music* to the hook of the Bee Gees' *Stayin' Alive* (ah, ah, ah, ah, stayin' alive, stayin'), they'd be in big trouble. In fact, there's a story going on that the company who owned the rights to Handel's *Messiah* sued the owners of *Yes, We Have No Bananas* because the first four notes of the latter were identical to the first four notes of the Hallelujah Chorus. Whether it's true or not, it makes a great story, and points to the fact that there's no set length required to infringe on someone else's work. The best course of action is to borrow nothing.

What is copyright "notice"?

Copyright notice is the notice on records or tapes or sheet music that a certain work is copyrighted. The notice may be used at any point after a work has been created, since a copyright exists at the point of creation. But it's most important to include notice of copyright on fixed forms of songs which are published (records, tapes, sheet music, video discs, piano rolls, etc.) because failure to do so may cause the songs to revert to the public domain, which means no one is required to pay a fee on the song.

Check with the Copyright Office for the exact placement of the copyright notice; it will be the "c" and/or "p" with the circle around it (or the word or abbreviation "copyright") followed by the date of publication and the Proprietor of the song.

Even though sending out demo tapes doesn't constitute publishing the work because it's not available to the public, many writers like to include the notice just in case, and there's certainly no law against it.

When does the copyright law take effect and for what duration?

Copyright, under the new law, takes effect the moment a song is committed to paper or tape or any other fixed form. Before the law was changed in 1978, copyright didn't go into effect until granted.

Duration, under the new law, is life plus fifty years and depends therefore, on how long the writer lives after a work is created. You *must* remember, however, that, if your song was copyrighted *before* 1978, copyright will need to be renewed under the terms of the old copyright law.

What happens to the copyright when someone accepts my song?

It depends on whom and for what purpose. If a publisher accepts your song, he will want you to assign the copyright to him, which means even though you're the writer, the publisher becomes the Proprietor, or owner of the song. Make no mistake . . when you place a song with a publisher, you cease to own the rights to the song, unless you enter into a co-publishing agreement, or some other sort of contract.

If, on the other hand, you place a song directly with an artist who doesn't want the publishing, you need only issue the artist a Mechanical License, giving him permission to record the song, and setting the mechanical rate you must be paid for each record or tape sold. In this case, the copyright remains unchanged (except that you've used up your right of first license).

How can I learn if a song is out of copyright?

There are books which list Public Domain songs. If your library doesn't have that set of books, the Copyright Office (Register of Copyrights, Library of Congress, Washington DC 20559) will do a search for a fee ($5 at last check). You might also find out through ASCAP or BMI, the two major performing rights societies in this country. They have offices in Los Angeles, New York and Nashville.

Can I get my copyright back if I assign my songs to someone else?

Yes. The new copyright law allows you to get your copyright back no matter who has it after 35 years if the song was never actually published and 40 years if it was published. You can't waive that right, and you need only write the owner to accomplish the reversion.

You may not want the rights back, however, if the holder of the copyright is doing a good job of exploiting it. And you *can't* get the rights back without all co-writers agreeing to that move. This right isn't worth a whole lot to a short-lived top forty song, but it can mean a great deal to standards.

Other than this right, you can't legally get your song back before the full length of copyright without a reversion clause in the contract (See "Contracts").

What exactly is a work for hire?

When a writer is hired to write a song, or part of a song, for pay, this is called a work for hire. In such cases, the song produced is considered the work of the person paying the money, not the writer. If you're ever in doubt about the terms under which you're doing an assignment, clearly define the terms of your agreement with another party. If not, you may find that you've opted yourself out of the possibility of receiving royalties or even credit on your song. Staff writers for publishing companies do not usually have this problem. They are paid an advance, not a fee, against future royalties, and a contract almost always spells out the royalties a staff writer will receive. The point is, be careful in *any* "work for hire" situation.

Does copyright law determine my royalty payments?

Only in the general sense of the question. The Copyright Royalty Tribunal has established 4¢ as the statutory limit an artist must pay you back on covers (subsequent recordings) of a song. Record companies may, however, find alternate ways of dealing with the 4¢ rate when licensing their records. Since many labels don't want to pay the 4¢ for each song they record, they may only cut nine songs per album instead of the usual ten. And with no ceiling for the first recording, they may hold the line against paying the full 4¢ for first licenses, and stay at 3¢ or even less. Time and the outcome of the Copyright Royalty Tribunal's decision will tell.

Sheet music royalties, foreign royalties and performances here or abroad are issues separate from copyright.

What are alternatives to registering each song?

You may register songs in a group with the Copyright Office. You may also do anything else which will establish proof of ownership. It's admissible as evidence for your best friend to testify that you wrote a song on a certain date. But it's not very strong evidence, since your friend would obviously want to help you out. Sending a song to yourself via certified mail is no better proof: you could have opened the envelope and switched the contents. Any competent defense attorney could prove that you had motive to switch contents. Having a lead sheet notarized or leaving songs in a safe deposit box without reopening are of greater or lesser value, depending on their acceptance in court, and whether there are possible loopholes.

One alternative to a Washington registration is provided by Songwriter's Resources and Services, a non-profit, Hollywood-based corporation, for which I currently work. They accept songs in any fixed form, seal them in an envelope and lock the envelopes in their vaults, to be retrieved in case of an infringement claim. Since SRS is a disinterested third party, this idea similar to sending a letter to yourself and not opening it, does away with the problem of vested interest.

SRS doesn't claim to supplant the Washington registration. It's a technical requirement of the law, in fact, that you can't sue anybody for infringement without a certificate from Washington. But using SRS as a repository for your song can prove your possession of it on a certain date. So, while to start a lawsuit you must re-register your infringed song in Washington you could use SRS as proof of first date of ownership. And SRS registration is faster and less expensive.

Some people choose the alternative of simply not worrying about registering their songs. A few publishers even suggest *not* registering your works. They're taking a great gamble if the song in question happens to be a money-maker. Whichever system you use, *use a system* . . . protect your songs.

Where can I get more information?

Start with the Copyright Office. All the information is free.

One word about filling out the forms: it's easy and the instructions are fairly clear. Don't pay anyone vast amounts of money for help. When in doubt, the Copyright Office can answer your questions and/or send you a copy of the Copyright Law (Library of Congress, Washington DC 20559). Most publications such as *This Business of Music* (S. Shemel/W. Krasilovsky) or *The Musician's Manual* (Beverly Hills Bar Association) include information on copyright. Some publications deal solely with the topic, as does a $2 SRS pamphlet called "The New Copyright Law; It Does Affect You."

Contracts

BY DOUG THIELE

There are various types of contractual agreements you may be asked to sign as a songwriter. To help you make a wise decision when you're asked to put your name on the dotted line, here are answers to key questions about contracts.

Are songwriter contracts really standard?

Many clauses in major-company contracts are intended to accomplish the same things, but there is no really uniform publishing contract.

Beware of contracts entitled "Standard Uniform Popular Songwriters Contract." There are a few varieties on the theme. As a matter of fact, a major contract reference book used by some attorneys to draw up contracts lists a variety of single song contracts as "more favorable to publisher than writer" or "more favorable to writer than publisher."

Become familiar with the issues involved in a single song contract and you'll see that most contracts from reputable companies cover the same issues in similar ways. Those contracts will soon begin to look familiar to you. But unless you speak fluent *legalese*, let your attorney check out the contract *before* you sign it.

How many songs can one songwriting contract cover?

It depends on the contract. In most cases, a "single song contract" covers only one song. Occasionally it will cover two or three songs, but your attorney may advise you to sign a separate contract for each song.

"Catalog deals" are contracts designed to assign many songs at once, usually for a large advance, from a writer with great material and, usually, some credentials. These contracts may assign four, five or up to twenty songs at a time.

What is an exclusive songwriter contract?

Companies are always looking for a songwriter who can make them money. These companies often sign promising writers—usually with a track record—to an *exclusive* deal requiring that they write only for that company. These contracts are usually six months or one year long, with one to four yearly options (the company's) to renew the contract.

Exclusive contracts, or "staff deals" can be very dangerous. You must usually assign your entire catalog to the company, you may not write for any other company, your collaborations are usually limited in some way, and you're expected to produce commercial songs.

On the plus side, you are paid a regular sum of money (usually $125-$300/week to start) which is not a salary, but an advance against future royalties from the *cuts* (songs recorded) the company gets for you. A good staff deal can springboard your career. On the minus side, if the company you're signed to can't get your songs recorded, it can seriously damage your career, because all those great contacts you've developed will forget about you after a while. And remember that, while you're signed exclusively to a company, you can't pitch tunes to anyone else.

Why do I need a contract?

Maybe you don't, but just in case, let's look at some problems that could develop without one. Let's say you assigned a song to publisher "A" because you really like his enthusiasm and credentials. A few weeks later, he leaves to become president of another company. Without a contract, the publisher "A" might not feel obligated to pay you royalties. Or what if your publisher who is also your lifelong friend with whom you've never signed a contract lapses into a coma? What proof do you have that the company has a working relationship with you? And it doesn't take a coma to initiate problems or disputes. If your song begins to make money, you might be shocked to find that your friend's recollection of the verbal terms of your agreement isn't all that accurate.

Contracts are necessary to provide a clear answer to future disputes, whether you're dealing with an impersonal company or your best friend. In a more realistic sense, most companies won't deal with your song *without* a contract.

When can I expect to be asked to sign a contract?

Make it a practice never to sign a contract on the spot. Reputable companies will give you a reasonable amount of time to sign . . . up to a few weeks after they send the contract(s) to you. In the case where you're in a studio with Linda or Barry, and they want you to sign so they can record your song that night, call your attorney and get him over to the studio somehow, but always sign your contract in the cool objective light of reason. If you should impulsively sign a contract and have second thoughts about it, a recent Truth-In-Advertising law allows you to change your mind within three days after signing.

Occasionally a company will express interest in your song, then never send contracts to you. Unfortunately, this may mean they've lost their initial enthusiasm for your material. After a few weeks of waiting, a phone call will determine if there's been an administrative or postal error, or if you can assume the deal is off.

Do I need an attorney?

Yes, at least at first. You'll need to become intimately familiar with the issues involved in single song contracts, and you should get an entertainment attorney to review and explain your contract to you.

Don't use your uncle who is a lawyer specializing in corporate law, and whose fee may be more palatable. There are many changing issues in the entertainment business, and entertainment law is very specialized. You should have help from an expert until you know the issues by heart.

A list of lawyers (located mainly in Los Angeles, Nashville, New York or Chicago) with experience in the music industry can be found in the *Billboard International Buyer's Guide* (Billboard Publications, Inc., 9000 Sunset Blvd., Los Angeles CA 90069). If cost is a problem, free legal assistance and information is available to qualified songwriters through the Volunteer Lawyers for the Arts listed in the Organizations and Clubs section of this book.

Can I ask for changes before I sign?

Of course. It's your job to negotiate the very best deal you can possibly get. You'll be negotiating with a representative of a company which expects its people to get the best deal for them, so each contract involves give and take.

You'll see contracts which are good but may contain a clause which is simply awful. You'll see contracts which just don't fit your idea of a fair deal, and you'll see contracts which are fine, but don't offer you the kind of deal you think a very special tune deserves. You can negotiate all these cases. Your success in negotiating may even mean the difference in accepting or declining the contract.

Whatever you do, don't sign a contract below your minimum expectations just to get some action on a song. If the song is really as good as you believe, you *will* find a fair deal.

What should I look for in a publishing contract?

There is a long and very complex set of issues. Let me describe the major issues in a single song contract, but remember that your contract may be good and still address different issues than the ones I mention here. It's a fact that everything is negotiable in a contract, depending on your credentials as a songwriter, the nature and interest of the company and the strength of the song in question. But let's start at the beginning:

The purpose of a single song contract is to assign all rights you now own in the song you've written, to another person or company. Signing a contract doesn't mean the tune is published. "Published" means the song is released to the public in fixed form, such as a record or sheet music. The contract you sign will transfer your rights to another entity, establish your payment for that assignment, and establish guarantees between you and the company. Although contracts vary from company to company, a good publishing contract should:

● Name, in the beginning, the parties involved and the title of the song and will clearly state that the writer is "selling, assigning, and transferring to the publisher" all rights in the song. The contract will be specific about the scope of those rights: the publisher will take them all, for the full term of copyright and throughout the world (some contracts now read "for the universe").

● Warrant that you have declared your right to enter into the contract and that you haven't assigned rights in the song to anybody else. Signing one song exclusively to two different companies, by the way, will guarantee instant doom for the song and a possible lawsuit for you.

● Spell out your payment for assigning the rights in your song to the publisher. You may be entitled to an *advance* (a sum of money, usually $100-200, for assigning the song). This sum is not returned if the publisher doesn't get you a recording, but if he does, the amount of the advance will be deducted from your future mechanical royalties (royalties from the sale of records and tapes). You may also ask for an advance that reimburses you for your demo costs. If the song is destined for the theater or films, the advance should be much more because you normally won't see money from the sale of records or tapes unless there's a cast album.

The next payment clause should read that you will receive a *percentage* (usually 50%) of any and all sums actually received by the publisher. Some contracts say "50% of any and all *net* sums," and in this case, you'll want to know what the publisher considers "net." "Net" should mean gross receipts minus expenses with regard to your song only, such as demo costs, lead sheet work, postage and long-distance calls.

This is the major source of money you'll receive from the publisher and it's important that you understand the premise of 50%. It has become the custom for publishers to take 50% of mechanical royalties. So when a publisher uses the term "standard royalty," you can expect half of the money from the sale of records and tapes. Your 50% is deemed the *Writer's Share*, and the publisher's 50% is considered the *Publisher's Share*, or "*The Publishing.*" So if a publisher wants "*All The Publishing,*" that's considered 50% of the value of the song. If you're a writer with some credentials, or the song is an obvious hit, you may convince the publisher to give up some of his publishing money (no more than *half* of the publishing money). In this case, you may hear the term "*Split Publishing,*" which means that you'll receive your 50% of the song as the writer, and also half of the publisher's 50%, for a grand total of 75% of the royalties of the song.

I realize this is a confusing concept, but you must become familiar with the terminology. As a new writer, you probably won't be able to dip into the publisher's share, but you should always try. And if it's a choice between getting $200 in advance money or even one-fourth of the publisher's share (12½% of the royalties), *always* go for the publishing share. The money is great to have, but you may be giving away many thousands of dollars in royalties that way. In other words, always negotiate toward getting a piece of the publishing money.

The way mechanical royalties work is fairly straightforward: when an artist wants to record a song, he is issued a Mechanical License, giving him permission to do so and sets the rate at which the record company must pay back the publisher. The current rate set by the Copyright Royalty Tribunal is 4¢. This means that if a song sells a total of one million records and tapes (singles or albums), the publisher will receive $40,000 from the record company. It's this money we're talking about splitting. If the publisher takes all the publishing share, you'll each take home $20,000. Remember though, the record company only pays for records sold and not returned by the record store . . . not on promotional copies.

Your major source of income will come from the performing rights organizations (ASCAP, BMI or SESAC) if you're getting good airplay. This money is split by the organization so your contract will probably read that you're not entitled to the publisher's share of performance royalties.

The contract will also spell out your royalties for sheet music. 5¢ for each sheet of piano music sold is standard, though the publisher will receive more like 35¢ (publishing deals are *not* partnerships). Some forward-thinking writers are now asking for a percentage here as a hedge against inflation. Most contracts allow you 10% of the retail price of folios or song collections, as well as orchestrations.

You'll see that 50% figure in a few other places too; usually in the case of synchronization licenses for films and for foreign sales.

● Spell out the method and frequency of payments to you (either twice or four times a year) and should give you the right to audit the company during regular office hours at your own expense for the purpose of verifying their records. You may have the right to audit without such a clause, but it will be harder.

● Hold you responsible for damages if the company is sued by another for *anything* (remember that first clause that says you have the right to enter into the agreement in the first place?), and will reserve the right to settle any dispute in any way they deem proper. That includes settling out of court if they feel that's the best way out. The company will reserve the right to withhold your royalties in such a case, but you should have the right to post a bond to retrieve your money. The amount they withhold shouldn't exceed the amount of the suit plus reasonable attorney's fees and court costs.

The *reversion clause* is another issue you should consider: if there's nothing to the contrary in the contract, the publisher will own your song for at least 35, if not for 50, years after your death. There's no way to get your song back before that time unless you have a stipulation added which allows you to recover your song after one or, at the most, two years. A reversion clause states that if a commercial recording is not released within a year (or two) from the signing of the contract, all rights revert to the writer(s). This is also called an "option." The simpler this clause is, the better. Many publishers argue that they need a song for several years to work it properly. Others have more inventive reasons for holding on to your song, but you are signing over the song so that the publisher will produce results within a reasonable period of time. It either happens in a year or it doesn't. Most companies *will* give you a reversion clause if you ask . . . but you may have to ask.

There are other issues to be considered. Most contracts allow the publisher to assign your song to anyone else. You should ask for a clause which requires your permission for such a move. The publisher will also want permission to rewrite your song to better fit a particular recording situation, up to a complete rewrite of lyric or music (and your reduction of royalties). You should try to get first shot at any rewriting, but publishers will usually jealously guard this right, so striking the clause is usually impossible.

What are the advantages or disadvantages of being a songwriter dealing directly with a record company?

First of all, many record companies have publishing branches and, in this respect there's no difference in dealing with them as publishers. But if you're a writer/artist, signed to the company as an artist, it will usually require you to also enter into an exclusive writer contract. In this case, try for a split-publishing deal. Since most recording artists are self-contained these days, it's an advantage if you do write and sing as well.

As a writer/artist, what should I look for in a record company contract?

There are probably as many record deals as there are artists but there are a few guidelines. In a major recording contract you'll be asked to sign over your exclusive services in recording masters to a record company. For these services you'll usually receive an advance, a fee for recording, and a percentage of record sales.

The usual album deal (there are also singles deals) is one year with up to six yearly company options to renew the contract. You'll be told how many albums you'll be required to record each year. Your royalties will usually escalate as time goes by (if the company picks up your option). The company will usually force you to turn over ownership of the masters. If you're a major artist, you may get the masters after a few years beyond the contract period.

The standard deal is called an "all-in" deal, which means the company will pay royalties to the artist, producer and production company. These royalties are called "points," and correspond roughly to percentage points, but only after the record company deducts some of their costs. You might find yourself in the position of getting, let's say, eleven points of retail sales (or about double that for wholesale sales). It might be split so that the artist gets five points, and the producer and production company each get three. If you want to figure out points, assume that a point equals about one percent of 80% of the price of the album or single.

But before you start counting your money, keep in mind that the artist pays for *everything*: recording costs, tours, players, even the advance you got at the beginning of the deal (or the beginning of each album's session date). This is why almost 4 out of 5 artists on major labels in 1981 never saw any royalties from record sales; all those royalties went into paying expenses. Of course if you're an established artist, you'll be selling more records and your royalties will be higher . . . up to ten points or more.

The advance you receive may be as little as $5,000 or as much as $1,000,000 depending on your status as an artist. If $20,000 is a normal sum for a new artist on a major label, it may interest you to know that many artists are turning part or all of that advance back into tours, since it's a proven fact that tours sell records. And with the uncertainty of the economic outlook some record companies won't spring for tour money.

Again, you should have the right to audit the company, you should not be assigned to another company, and your publishing royalties should *not* go toward paying off your artist advances. That's called "cross-collateralization," and it's wrong.

Record company contracts are normally fifteen to fifty pages long. An attorney must help you not only in understanding the contract, but in negotiating the finer points with the company. Here's where an entertainment attorney really earns his money. There are many other issues which could fill this entire book. If you're about to sign a record deal, be prepared for a real lesson in the power of contracts.

What other contracts might I be asked to sign?

There are as many contracts in this business as there are situations. To touch on a few:

Collaborator's Agreements. If you're co-writing, you'll need one of these. There's no stock form, so you'll have to have one drawn up to your specifications. It's hard for some people to ask their co-writer to sign paper, but a collaborator's agreement is essential in the event that your co-writer dies or disappears. A collaborator's agreement spells out who gets what share of the royalties and should also touch on who controls the copyright in certain circumstances, as well as any other issues of importance to either writer.

Administration Deals. It's great if you're lucky enough to get to an artist who will record your song without asking you to give up some or all of your publishing money; now you're the writer and the publisher. The problem is that unless you've set up an international organization, it's going to be hard to collect your foreign royalties

2">rt

2">rt

---

or even to set up foreign business. Many major publishers will be happy to "administrate" your recorded song, and exploit it in foreign markets for a percentage of the profit. It's very little extra work for them and it can really increase your profits as well as save you a lot of hassle. There are even some companies which almost exclusively administrate songs.

You'll find that the fee varies greatly, but expect to pay anywhere from 7½% to 33% of the royalties collected to the administrating agency.

Producer/Artist Agreements. If you're a writer/artist, you may find yourself tied to a production company or a producer. The agreements between you will state that you'll allow the producer to produce a certain number of songs and shop the results with the industry for a certain number of months (6-12) exclusively.

Payment varies. It can be half of your publishing and a hefty percentage of your advance money as an artist as well as a few points on the first album. Or it can be a really great deal of his getting a small percentage of the advance and a point or two. Never pay a producer up front for his services.

Personal Management Contracts. People assume that personal managers get record deals for artists. The fact is that they're prohibited by law from doing so. These people take from 10% to 25% (20% is standard) of your earnings as an artist for advising you on your career. There's a new category of management called the "talent agency" which requires a license, and allows a personal manager to secure employment (including a record deal) for his artist. Contract length is from six months on up.

Other Contracts. If you're doing major business, you'll need a full-time business manager who will handle your money and take a small percentage of the gross (2-5%).

If you're doing a lot of concert work in established clubs, you'll need more than a handshake. Bookers will give you a contract which is union-supervised and demands 10-20% of your gross wages.

Performing Rights Agreements. Each performing rights society will require that you turn over your right of public performance on your recorded song exclusively to them. Unless you care to travel the world collecting your performances from each nightclub or radio station, let these societies perform their valuable function.

One more word about your contractual relationships in the industry: it's certainly true that companies will try to negotiate for the very best deal they can get for themselves. Due to a few unscrupulous companies and a few disgruntled writers, the industry has developed a bad reputation for trying to bilk writers. Most companies, however, are honest and willing to negotiate with a writer of a good song. Negotiate your best deal, then have your attorney ascertain that what you negotiated actually made it into the contract.

For More Information

There are many books specifically on the subject of contracts in the music business, and many more which touch on contractual matters. Here are a few of the best:
The Musician's Manual, Beverly Hills Bar Association, 606 S. Olive, Beverly Hills CA 90014.
This Business of Music, Billboard Publications, 9000 W. Sunset Blvd., Los Angeles CA 90069.
How to Have Your Hit Song Published, Songwriter Magazine, Box 3510, Los Angeles CA 90028.
Music Business Contracts in Current Use, Law Arts Press, 453 Greenwich, New York NY 10013.
Songwriter Agreements, through Songwriter's Resources and Services, 6381 Hollywood Blvd., Suite 503, Hollywood CA 90028.

Glossary

A&R director. Record company employee who deals with new artists, songs and masters coordinating the best material with a particular artist.

Acetate dub. A demonstration record that is individually cut, often referred to as a disc.

Advance. Money paid to the songwriter or recording artist before regular royalty payments begin. Sometimes called "upfront" money, advances are deducted from royalties.

AFM. American Federation of Musicians. A union for musicians and arrangers.

AFTRA. American Federation of Television and Radio Artists.

AGAC. American Guild of Authors and Composers.

AIMP. American Independent Music Publishers.

AOR. Album-oriented rock.

Arrangement. Adapting a composition for performance by other instruments, voices or performers.

ASCAP. American Society of Composers, Authors and Publishers.

A-side. Side one of a single promoted by the record company to become a hit.

Assignment. Transfer of rights to a song from writer to publisher.

Audiovisual. Presentations using audio backup for visual material.

Bed. Prerecorded music used as background material in commercials.

BMI. Broadcast Music, Inc.

Booking agent. Solicits work and schedules performances for entertainer.

b/w. Backed with.

CAPAC. Composers, Authors & Publishers of Canada Ltd.

CARAS. Canadian Academy of Recording Arts and Sciences.

Catalog. The collected songs of one writer, or all songs handled by one publisher.

Chart. The written arrangement of a song.

Charts. The weekly trade magazines' lists of the bestselling records.

CIRPA. Canadian Independent Record Producers Association.

CMRRA. Canadian Musical Reproduction Rights Association.

Collaborator. Person who works with another in a creative situation.

CMA. Country Music Association.

Copyright. Legal protection given authors and composers for an original work.

Cover record. A new version of a previously recorded song.

CRIA. Canadian Musical Reproduction Rights Association.

Crossover. A song that becomes popular in two or more music fields.

Cut. Any finished recording; a selection from an LP; or to record.

C&W. Country and western.

Demo. A rough recording, usually a tape, of a song.

Disc. A record.

Distributor. Sole marketing agent of a record in a particular area.

Donut. Jingle with singing at the beginning and end and only instrumental background in the middle.

Engineer. A specially trained individual who operates all studio recording equipment.

Evergreen. Any song that remains popular year after year.
FICAP. Federation of International Country Air Personalities.
Folio. A softcover collection of songs prepared for sale.
Harry Fox Agency. Organization that collects mechanical royalties.
Hook. A memorable "catch" phrase or melody line which is repeated in a song.
IMU. International Musicians Union.
IPS. Inches per second; a speed designation for reel-to-reel tape.
IRMA. International Record Manufacturers Association.
Jingle. Usually a short verse set to music designed as a commercial message.
LP. Designation for long-playing record synonomous with album and played at 33⅓ rpm.
Lead sheet. Written version (melody, chord symbols and lyric) of a song.
Leader. Tape at the beginning and between songs for ease in selection.
Lryic sheet. A typed copy of a song's lyrics.
Manager. Guides and advises artist in his career.
Market. A demographic division of the record-buying public.
Master. Edited and mixed tape used in the pressing of records.
MCA. Music Critics Association.
Mechanical right. The right to profit from the reproduction of a song.
Mechanical royalty. Money earned from record and tape sales.
MIEA. Music Industry Educators' Association.
Mix. To blend a multi-track recording into the desired balance of sound.
MOR. Middle of the road. A song considered "easy listening."
Ms. Manuscript.
Music publisher. A company that evaluates songs for commercial potential, finds artists to record them, finds other uses such as TV or film for the songs, collects income generated by the songs and protects copyrights from infringement.
NARAS. National Academy of Recording Arts and Sciences.
Needle-drop. Use of a prerecorded cut from a stock music house in an audiovisual soundtrack.
NSG. National Songwriters' Guild.
Performing rights. A specific right granted by US copyright law that protects a composition from being publicly performed without the owner's permission.
Performing rights organization. An organization that collects income from the public performance of songs written by its members and then proportionally distributes this income to the individual copyright holder based on the number of performances of each song.
Pitch. To attempt to sell a song by audition; the sales talk.
Playlist. List of songs, usually top 40, that a radio station will play.
Plug. A favorable mention, broadcast or performance of a song. Also means to pitch a song.
Points. Percentage paid to producers and artists for records sold.
Press. To manufacture a record from the master tape.
PROCAN. Performing Rights Organization of Canada Ltd.
Production company. Company that specializes in producing jingle packages for advertising agencies. May also refer to companies that specialize in audiovisual programs.
Professional manager. Member of a music publisher's staff who screens submitted material and tries to get the company's catalog of songs recorded.
Producer. Person who controls every aspect of recording a song.
Program director. Radio station employee who screens records and develops a playlist of songs that station will broadcast.
Public domain. Any composition with an expired, lapsed or invalid copyright.
Purchase license. Fee paid for music used from a stock music library.
Query. A letter of inquiry to a potential song buyer soliciting his interest.
R&B. Rhythm and blues.
Rate. The percentage of royalty as specified by contract.
Release. Any record issued by a record company.

Residuals. In advertising, payments to singers and musicians for subsequent use of a commercial.

Rhythm Machine. An electronic device that provides various tempos for use as background rhythm for other instruments or vocalists.

RIAA. Recording Industry Association of America.

Royalty. Percentage of money earned from the sale of records or use of a song.

SASE. Abbreviation for self-addressed stamped envelope.

Scratch track. Rough working tape demonstrating idea for a commercial.

SESAC. Performing rights organization.

Shop. To pitch songs to a number of companies or publishers.

Single. 45 rpm record.

SIRMA. Small Independent Record Manufacturers Association.

Song shark. Person who deals with songwriters deceptively for his own profit.

Soundtrack. The audio, including music and narration, of a film, videotape or audiovisual program.

Split Publishing. To divide publishing rights between two or more publishers.

Staff writer. A salaried songwriter who writes exclusively for one publishing firm.

Standard. A song popular year after year; an evergreen.

Statutory royalty rate. The minimum payment for mechanical rights guaranteed by law that a record company must pay the songwriter and his publisher for each record or tape sold.

Stiff. The first recording of a song that commercially fails.

Subpublishing. Certain rights granted by a US publisher to a foreign publisher in exchange for promoting the US catalog in his territory.

Synchronization. Technique of timing a musical soundtrack to action on film.

Synchronization rights. Right to use composition in timed-relation to action on film.

Track. Portions of a recording tape (e.g., 24-track tape) that can be individually recorded in the studio, then mixed into a finished master.

Trades. Publications that cover the music industry.

Work. To pitch or shop a song.

Index

H

Q

X, Y, Z

Other Writer's Digest Books

Market Directories
    Artist's Market, 528 pp. $13.95
    Fiction Writer's Market, 504 pp. $15.95
    Photographer's Market, 576 pp. $14.95
    Writer's Market, 936 pp. $17.95

General Writing Books
    Beginning Writer's Answer Book, 264 pp. $9.95
    How to Get Started in Writing, 180 pp. $10.95
    Law and the Writer, 240 pp. (paper) $7.95
    Make Every Word Count, 256 pp. (paper) $6.95
    Treasury of Tips for Writers, (paper), 174 pp. $6.95
    Writer's Resource Guide, 488 pp. $12.95

Magazine/News Writing
    Complete Guide to Marketing Magazine Articles, 248 pp. $9.95
    Craft of Interviewing, 244 pp. $9.95
    Magazine Writing: The Inside Angle, 256 pp. $10.95
    Magazine Writing Today, 220 pp. $9.95
    Newsthinking: The Secret of Great Newswriting, 204 pp. $11.95
    1001 Article Ideas, 270 pp. $10.95
    Stalking the Feature Story, 310 pp. $9.95
    Write on Target, 240 pp. $12.95
    Writing and Selling Non-Fiction, 317 pp. $10.95

Fiction Writing
    Creating Short Fiction, 228 pp. $11.95
    Handbook of Short Story Writing, (paper), 238 pp. $6.95
    How to Write Best-Selling Fiction, 300 pp. $13.95
    How to Write Short Stories that Sell, 212 pp. $9.95
    One Way to Write Your Novel, 138 pp. (paper) $6.95
    Secrets of Successful Fiction, 119 pp. $8.95
    Writing the Novel: From Plot to Print, 197 pp. $10.95

Category Writing Books
    Cartoonist's and Gag Writer's Handbook, (paper), 157 pp. $9.95
    Children's Picture Book: How to Write It, How to Sell It, 224 pp. $16.95
    Confession Writer's Handbook, 173 pp. $9.95
    Guide to Greeting Card Writing, 256 pp. $10.95
    Guide to Writing History, 258 pp. $9.95
    How to Write and Sell Your Personal Experiences, 226 pp. $10.95
    How to Write "How-To" Books and Articles, 192 pp. (paper) $8.95
    Mystery Writer's Handbook, 273 pp. $9.95
    The Poet and the Poem, 399 pp. $11.95
    Poet's Handbook, 224 pp. $10.95
    Sell Copy, 205 pp. $11.95
    Successful Outdoor Writing, 244 pp. $11.95
    Travel Writer's Handbook, 274 pp. $11.95
    TV Scriptwriter's Handbook, 322 pp. $11.95
    Writing and Selling Science Fiction, 191 pp. $8.95
    Writing for Children & Teenagers, 269 pp. $9.95

The Writing Business
    Complete Handbook for Freelance Writers, 391 pp. $14.95
    How to Be a Successful Housewife/Writer, 254 pp. $10.95
    How You Can Make $20,000 a Year Writing: (No Matter Where You Live), 270 pp. (paper) $6.95
    Jobs For Writers, 281 pp. $11.95
    Profitable Part-time/Full-time Freelancing, 195 pp. $10.95
    Writer's Digest Diary, 144 pp. $14.95

Photography Books
How You Can Make $25,000 a Year with Your Camera (No Matter Where You Live), 224 pp. (paper) $9.95
Sell & Re-Sell Your Photos, 323 pr. $14.95

To order directly from the publisher, include $1.25 postage and handling for 1 book and 50¢ for each additional book. Allow 30 days for delivery.

For a current catalog of books for writers or information on *Writer's Digest* magazine, *Writer's Yearbook*, Writer's Digest School correspondence courses or manuscript criticism, write to:

Writer's Digest Books, Department B
9933 Alliance Road, Cincinnati OH 45242

Prices subject to change without notice.

Use an up-to-date Market Directory!

Don't let outdated information slow your marketing effort down.

After a while, you may become positively reluctant to give up this copy of Songwriter's Market. After all, you would never discard an old friend.

But resist the urge to hold onto an old Songwriter's Market! Like your first guitar or your favorite pair of jeans, the time will come when this copy of Songwriter's Market will have to be replaced.

In fact, if you're still using this 1982 Songwriter's Market when the calendar reads 1983, you may find that your old friend has deserted you. The editors listed here may have moved or been promoted. The addresses may now be incorrect. Rates of pay have certainly changed, and even each record company's music needs are changed from last year.

You can't afford to use an out-of-date book to plan your marketing efforts. But there's an easy way for you to stay current — use the 1983 Songwriter's Market. All you have to do is complete the attached post card and return it with your payment or charge card information. Best of all, we'll send you the 1983 edition at the 1982 price — just $12.95.

The 1983 Songwriter's Market will be published in October 1982. If you order your 1983 edition before publication, we will send you 1983 edition the month of publication. Otherwise, please allow 30 days for delivery.

Make sure Songwriter's Market stays friendly to you — order the new edition as soon as it's published.

Make sure you have a current edition of Songwriter's Market

Songwriter's Market has been the song writer's bible for years. Each edition contains hundreds of changes to give you the most current information to work with. Make sure your copy is the latest edition.

This card will get you the 1983 edition... at 1982 prices! ⬇